THE CAMBRIDGE
ANCIENT HISTORY

VOLUME VI

THE CAMBRIDGE
ANCIENT HISTORY

SECOND EDITION

VOLUME VI
The Fourth Century B.C.

Edited by

D. M. LEWIS F.B.A.
Professor of Ancient History in the University of Oxford

JOHN BOARDMAN F.B.A.
Lincoln Professor of Classical Archaeology and Art in the University of Oxford

SIMON HORNBLOWER
Fellow and Tutor of Oriel College and Lecturer in Ancient History in the University of Oxford

M. OSTWALD
*William R. Kenan, Jr, Professor Emeritus of Classics, Swarthmore College
and Professor Emeritus of Classical Studies, University of Pennsylvania*

Published by the Press Syndicate of the University of Cambridge
The Pitt Building, Trumpington Street, Cambridge CB2 1RP
40 West 20th Street, New York, NY 10011-4211, USA
10 Stamford Road, Oakleigh, Victoria 3166, Australia

First published 1994

Printed in Great Britain by Woolnough Bookbinding Ltd,
Irthlingborough, Northants

A catalogue record for this book is available from the British Library

Library of Congress card no. 75-85719

ISBN 0 521 23348 8 hardback

CONTENTS

CONTENTS

NOTE ON THE BIBLIOGRAPHY

The bibliography is arranged in sections dealing with specific topics, which sometimes correspond to individual chapters but more often combine the contents of several chapters. References in the footnotes are to these sections (which are distinguished by capital letters) and within these sections each book or article has assigned to it a number which is quoted in the footnotes. In these, so as to provide a quick indication of the nature of the work referred to, the author's name and the date of publication are also included in each reference. Thus 'Finley 1979 (G 164) 100' signifies 'M. I. Finley, *Ancient Sicily*, revised edn London, 1979, p. 100', to be found in Section G of the bibliography as item 164.

MAPS

TEXT-FIGURES

PREFACE

The predecessor of this volume in the first edition was entitled 'Macedon, 401–301 B.C.'. This symbolized the understandable view that the overriding theme of the fourth century was the unification of the Greek world and its expansion into the Near East. The years before the accession of Philip II to the throne of Macedon were seen as having their main significance in illustrating the confusion from which he delivered the Greek city states. It was a view which could be held even without the overtones of the nineteenth-century unification of Germany and Italy which so often accompanied it in the scholarship of the day.

This volume covers a shorter span. The main practical reason for this has been the great expansion in our understanding of the early hellenistic period, which necessitated a more extended treatment of the late fourth century in Volume VII.1. We thus end our formal narrative with the death of Alexander.

This shortening of the period changes the balance of the volume, and accounts for the disappearance of Macedon from the title. For the first forty-odd years of our period, it was only peripheral to the main course of events. The narrative chapters are split to reflect the difference between the years of the continued struggles between the city states, ending, as Xenophon's history did, with the Battle of Mantinea in 362, and the period in which Philip and Alexander are the main guiding forces.

We find the first of these periods interesting in itself, not simply illustrative of the political and other weaknesses of the Greek city states, and hope that we have now done more justice to it. After its victory in the Peloponnesian War, the initiative lay with Sparta, which remained close to the centre of the stage, even after the battle of Leuctra revealed the progress made by Thebes, at least in warfare. Although Athens continues to dominate our source-material and was never unimportant, we have deliberately shifted the narrative focus to Sparta and Thebes and rather reduced the usual coverage of Athens. Though the political achievement of the period was ultimately unimpressive, it was nevertheless full of ideas and innovation; chapter 11 pulls together some of the threads.

xvii

Persia, which had returned to the Greek scene in 413, is an essential part of the story throughout; recent work on it has been lively and we now understand more. We compensate for the deliberately narrow geographical limits of Volume v² with a new series of surveys of non-Greek areas, inside and outside the Persian empire, parallel to those in Volume ɪv². In the chapters on Sicily, Carthage and Italy, these constitute a reminder that not all matters of importance were happening in the eastern Mediterranean. The contemporary rise of Rome has already been treated in Volume vɪɪ.2.

For the workings of life in the Greek world itself, the evidence is a great deal richer than for the fifth century. We have thus been able to do more to describe the economy and its essential agricultural base. It is seldom possible to be certain what is novel about the fourth century in these matters, and that is even more true of religion, where contributors to Volume v² admitted their dependence on later sources. That there is no separate treatment of the traditional religion in this volume is not intended as a denial of its continued importance.

Fourth-century art lives very much on its High Classical past but elements are introduced that will develop rapidly into Hellenistic baroque and it is more diverse in function. It does appear that poetry temporarily lost its capacity for innovation. Rhetoric, perhaps losing some of its freshness, except in the hands of the greatest masters, became dominant in literature, certainly to the disadvantage of the writing of history. Not all prose was thus dominated, and in the hands of Plato, Greek became a uniquely flexible tool for expressing thought. Others with less polish built up a storehouse of technical literature, reflecting important technological developments, not least in warfare.

Even without the employment of technical rhetoric, the masters of prose were also masters of the spoken word in their teaching. The formation of the great schools assured to Athens in her political decline a future as a cultural centre which was to last physically for 900 years and intellectually, particularly in the heritage of Aristotle, a great deal longer than that.

After the accession of Philip, the line of the political and military narrative becomes much clearer. Since 1927, the date of the first edition, there has been intensive work on both Philip and Alexander, though primary evidence remains sparse for both. We can at least claim a better understanding of Macedon itself, owed not least to Professor Hammond, the guiding spirit of this second edition, and a richer and more complex picture of the Macedonian invasion of Asia to compensate for the loss of the first edition's incandescent, but ultimately misleading, portrait of Alexander. We have offered in the Epilogue some thoughts on Alexander in his more general fourth-century context.

A single Volume of Plates is published to accompany this volume and Volume v². It presents a fuller account of Classical art and architecture than has been attempted in the text volumes, as well as consideration of material evidence for other aspects of classical life, trade, religion, warfare and the theatre.

Professor J. K. Davies gave inestimable help in the planning of this volume before being forced by other commitments to lay down his editorship. We are grateful to our contributors for their tolerance of our slow progress. We have to mourn the death of one contributor, Professor H. D. Westlake.

With this volume the second edition of the Greek volumes of *The Cambridge Ancient History* is completed. Its editors, past and present, wish to thank especially the Cambridge University Press editor, Pauline Hire, for her patience and calm efficiency over the years of its preparation and above all for her unwavering commitment and enthusiasm. The drawings have been prepared by Marion Cox; David Cox drew the maps; the index was compiled by Barbara Hird.

D. M. L.
J. B.
S. H.
M. O.

CHAPTER 1

SOURCES AND THEIR USES

SIMON HORNBLOWER

No guide comparable to Thucydides exists for the fourth century. This means that we have no firm framework for political and military events, and this lack is a serious obstacle to one sort of knowledge. Thucydides' mind, however, was limited as well as powerful, or perhaps we should say its limits were the price of its power; and in the fourth century certain types of history which he had treated only selectively, particularly social, economic and religious topics, can actually be better studied than was possible in the Thucydidean period. Xenophon, for instance, has glaring faults when judged as a political reporter but is a prime source for the modern historian of religion. In general, fourth-century literary sources (Xenophon, Aeneas Tacticus and others) are less preoccupied than Thucydides had been with the polar opposites, Athens and Sparta. This probably reflects the new multi-centred reality. But we should recall that Thucydides, especially in books IV and V, had allowed us peeps at the politics of Argos, Macedon, Thessaly and Boeotia. A history of the Peloponnesian War written by Xenophon might have told us more about second-class and minor city states than Thucydides did: compare the remarkable detail about the minor cities Sicyon and Phlius at Xen. *Hell.* VII.1–3. But a Xenophon with only Herodotus, not Thucydides, for a predecessor and model would have looked very different anyway.

Another important reason why history of a non-traditional sort, that is history of things other than war and politics, can be more confidently written for the fourth century, is the greater abundance of inscriptions on stone. This is especially true of places other than Athens.

For the years 403–362 there is only one surviving primary account, books II.3 to VII of Xenophon's *Hellenica*. The first two books of that work have already been briefly discussed in an earlier volume (*CAH* v² 8). With the beginning of book III Xenophon breaks away from Athenian affairs and moves to Asia Minor. Internal evidence however shows a clear break in composition somewhat earlier, at II.3.10. This finding is the result of stylometric tests done before computers made such operations routine; but it carries such overwhelming conviction that it is not likely to be overthrown.[1]

---

[1] Maclaren 1934 (B 69); Cartledge 1987 (C 284) 65.

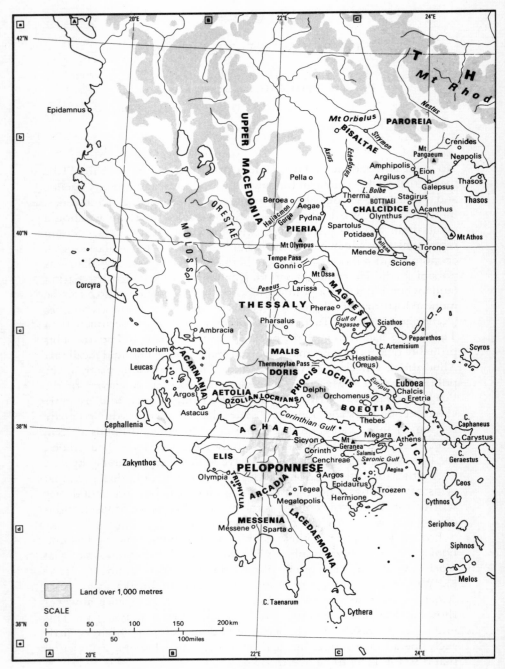

Map 1. Greece and Western Asia Minor.

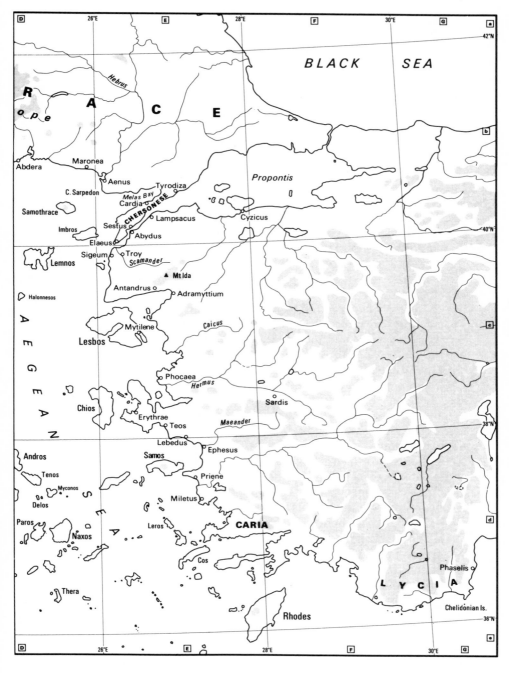

The most striking characteristic of the section beginning at II.3.11, which we may call Part Two, is its parochial concentration on Peloponnesian affairs.[2] It is true that books III and IV cover Asiatic events, but that is the exception which tests the rule because Xenophon is interested in Asia only when there is Spartan activity there. We find for instance virtually no sign in the *Hellenica* of the great revolts of the satraps in the 360s (VII.1.27 may be an exception). This Spartan viewpoint has its advantages; for instance Xenophon has a better understanding of the Spartan military and political system than did Thucydides, who had complained of the secrecy of the Spartan constitution, Thuc. V.68.2. Xenophon had good Peloponnesian contacts and eventually settled at an estate at Scyllus in the Peloponnese (*An.*v.3). He is thus able to report such a dangerous and – for the Spartan authorities – embarrassing episode as the Cinadon affair (*Hell.* III.3; see below, p. 43). This was a massive attempted revolt by the Spartan helots or state slaves in *c.*399. Xenophon also knows plenty of technical terms for Spartan institutions: the phrase 'the so-called small assembly' is mentioned at III.3.8 but nowhere else in Greek literature.[3] He knows about liberated helots, *neodamodeis* (III.1.4, compare already Thuc. VII.19.3 etc.), and about other groups halfway between full Spartiate and helot status, for instance, the *trophimoi*, boys reared with full Spartan children, and the bastard sons of Spartans, 'men not unacquainted with the good things of the Spartan way of life' (v.3.9). Above all, Xenophon understands and sympathizes with the system of 'congenial oligarchies' (in Thucydides' brief phrase, I.19), support of which enabled Sparta to keep control of the Peloponnesian League. (But Xenophon is not the only focalizer behind the comment on 'troublesome demagogues' at v.2.7, said about Mantinea.) The exponent *par excellence* of the system was Agesilaus,[4] who was one of the two Spartan kings from 400 to 362, roughly the period covered by Xenophon's Part Two. He was a powerful figure in the Greek world, and Xenophon's benefactor in his long exile from Athens. As well as giving Agesilaus generous space in the *Hellenica*, Xenophon also wrote an encomium of him after his death, the first surviving Greek essay in biography. Another minor treatise, the *Constitution of the Spartans* (*Lac. Pol.*), is in effect an institutional encomium of the Spartan way of life.[5]

It has often been held that Xenophon in the *Hellenica* is biased towards Sparta and correspondingly antipathetic to Thebes who displaced her in so many respects. 'Bias' is however a slippery term: it can mean anything from outright falsification – with which Xenophon cannot seriously be

[2] Cawkwell 1979 (B 26) 23.   [3] Andrewes 1966 (C 274) 18 n. 7.
[4] Cawkwell 1976 (C 285); Cartledge 1987 (C 284).
[5] *Agesilaus*: Momigliano 1971 (B 82) 50–1 and 1975 (B 84). *Lac. Pol.*: Cartledge 1987 (C 284) 56; *contra*, Chrimes 1948 (B 30).

charged – to the manifestation of those sympathies and contemporary preoccupations from which no historian is (or ought to be) free. Xenophon was overwhelmingly interested in Sparta, certainly, but that should not be confused with partisan bias in Sparta's favour.[6] In any case Xenophon was capable of censuring the Spartans, when they behaved irreligiously. For instance, his way of explaining the Spartan defeat at Leuctra in 371 was to treat it as divine punishment for the unjustified Spartan seizure of the Theban acropolis in 383: 'already the god was leading them on', he says at VI.4.3. The moral judgment on the seizure is made explicit at V.4.1: 'There are many instances from both Greek and barbarian history to show that the gods do not overlook impiety or irreligious behaviour.'

Anti-Theban feeling is discernible in, for instance, the sneer at Theban greed over the tithe to Apollo (III.5.5), which the Thebans claimed at Decelea at the end of the Peloponnesian War. Or there is the criticism of Theban 'medizing', that is subservience to Persia, in 367, Pelopidas being singled out (VII.1.33ff). In fact, Spartan medizing on this occasion was no less eager.

But Xenophon's omissions – of which that Spartan medizing is an example – are not a simple matter. The most conspicuous tend to be explicable in terms of his political sympathies. Thus, for instance, he fails to record the extent of Theban penetration into Thessaly after the battle of Haliartus in 395. The truth is inadvertently revealed in the list of Theban allies, including Thessalian Crannon and Pharsalus, at IV.3.3, and again at VII.1.28, dealing with 367, where he records a suggestion that some Sicilian troops should be used in Thessaly 'against the Thebans'. But for the full story of Theban ambitions in Thessaly we have to go to inscriptions or to a different literary tradition altogether (see further below, p. 10). Again, there is nothing in Xenophon about the battle of Tegyra in 375, admittedly a minor affair in itself but a Theban success which anticipated the smashing Theban defeat of Sparta at Leuctra four years later. Still on Boeotian topics, V.4.46 is the vaguest possible allusion to the reconstitution of the Boeotian Confederacy. But not all his omissions are straightforwardly explicable. At VI.3.1 it is surprising that he does not list Orchomenus among the places attacked by Thebes in the 370s, since this would have strengthened his general view of Theban bully tactics (Diod. XV.37, cf. Xen. *Hell.* VI.4.10.).

Xenophon is also very thin on the Second Athenian Naval Confederacy, whose foundation he does not record at all (Tod no. 123 = Harding

---

[6] This is stressed in what is now the best (excellent, thorough and thoughtful) recent study of the *Hellenica*, C. J. Tuplin, *The Failings of Empire: A Reading of Xenophon Hellenica 2.3.11–7.5.27, Historia Einzelschrift* 76 (Stuttgart, 1993), 163 and *passim*. Schwartz 1956 (B 103) 167 detected in Xenophon some partiality for *Athens*, but Tuplin shows that even this is not consistently true. Rather, *nobody* stays in favour with Xenophon for very long (Tuplin, *Failings of Empire*, 47).

no. 35 lines 9–11, cf. Diod. xv.29). Incidental allusions have been detected: at v.4.34 the re-gating of the Piraeus looks like a practical consequence of the new confederacy, and at vi.5.2 (cf.3.19) he speaks of 'decrees of the Athenians and their [?confederate] allies'.

Persia is another area of serious omission in Xenophon, as indeed it had been in Thucydides before his book viii. A feature of the 'Xeno-phontic' period is the series of common peaces (κοιναὶ εἰρῆναι) 'sent down' to Greece by Persia.[7] After mentioning the first King's Peace of 386 (v.1.31), which greatly strengthened Sparta in mainland Greece at the price of the abandonment of her claims in Asia, Xenophon systematically under-reports the Persian involvement in renewals of the original peace. His motive is presumably to downplay Spartan 'mediz-ing'. A clear instance is vi.2.1, the peace of 375: it is only from Philochorus (*FGrH* 328 f 151) that we learn that this peace was sent from Persia. (Cf. also above on his neglect of the revolts of the 360s.)

Xenophon's own feelings about Persia and Persians were mixed, though not illogically so – nor even unusually so for a man of his time (see below, p. 69f). He admired many Persian qualities and the in-dividuals who displayed them. But some of his writings, notably the *Agesilaus*, are undoubtedly characterized by political 'panhellenism', which means advocating that the Greeks should unite against Persia, if necessary enlisting dissident satraps. Where does the *Hellenica* stand? Panhellenism is there, but it is not virulent.[8] Panhellenism of a mild sort makes its appearance early in the *Hellenica*. Already in Part One Xenophon had written approvingly of the stand taken by the Spartan admiral Callicratidas, who was trying to get money from the Persian Cyrus but was kept waiting. Callicratidas said that the Greeks were wretched in that they had to flatter barbarians in order to get money, and that if he reached home safely he himself would do his best to reconcile Spartans and Athenians (1.6.7). There is a remarkable echo of this sentiment far on in Part Two, an implied criticism of Antalcidas by Teleutias (two prominent Spartans) for flattering anybody, whether Greeks or barbarians, for the sake of pay (v.1.17). Xenophon's speeches[9] are not, however, simple statements of his own views, any more than are those of Thucydides. For instance, it would be naive to transfer to Xenophon, the author of the *Cyropaedia*, the opinion of Jason that in Persia everybody except for one man is educated to be a slave rather than to stand up for himself; while the inclusion of Antiochus of Arcadia's

[7] For Thucydides, Andrewes 1961 (B 5); for the Common Peaces Ryder 1965 (C 67) and Bauslaugh 1991 (C 7) 182–255.
[8] Admiration for Persia: Hirsch 1985 (B 59); Tatum 1989 (B 114). Panhellenism of *Hellenica* not virulent: Tuplin, *Failings of Empire* 60, 67, 121 (Jason); cf. 104–8 (important reinterpretation of the ostensibly panhellenist speech of Callias at vi.3); 112 (Procles of Phlius).   [9] Gray 1989 (B 49).

remark, that 'the famous golden plane-tree of the Persian kings would not give shade to a grasshopper', proves only that Xenophon had a sense of humour (VI.1.12; VII.1.38). Certainly we can no longer accept the simple view of a century ago[10] that panhellenism was the key to the whole *Hellenica*; that is, that the aged Xenophon of the 350s was seeking to remove the enmity between his adoptive fatherland, Sparta, and the Athens where he was born and brought up.

In the present century the *Hellenica* has sunk in critical esteem: its author, it is said, cuts a poor figure as a historian by comparison not only with Thucydides but with the relatively recently discovered Oxyrhynchus Historian (*Hell. Oxy.*; on whom see below and *CAH* v² 8 and 482). One, not wholly satisfactory, defence is to challenge the assumption that Xenophon intended to write 'history' at all: he was an explicit *moralist*.[11] There is something in this: it explains some odd exceptions to the general characteristics noted above. So, as we noted above in connexion with Leuctra, his admiration for Sparta was not blind (see also the problematic *Lac. Pol.* XIV). But nothing much is gained by denying Xenophon the title of 'historian', a technical term not yet invented when he wrote. Another, more subjective, reply would be to stress Xenophon's great literary merits, which can be lost sight of in a positivistic preoccupation with his 'omissions' and so forth. An apt but temperate summing-up of Xenophon in the *Hellenica* is 'not a pedantically accurate writer, rather an impressionist with a singular gift for vivid description'.[12] Certainly Xenophon has great strengths as a social historian, most evident in his glimpses of life in Persian Asia Minor (see below, p. 213). And we have already noticed his account of the Cinadon affair.

Of Xenophon's other works, the *Agesilaus* and *The Constitution of the Spartans* have been mentioned already, and the *Anabasis* will be exploited in ch. 3. The *Cyropaedia* or *Education of Cyrus* is controversial. It is usually dismissed as 'completely fictitious' from the factual point of view,[13] and this is better than the other (perverse) extreme, which seeks to detect in it a source of otherwise lost Persian traditions about their own past.[14] Historians of the Persian empire continue to use material from the *Cyropaedia* without making it clear where they stand on the issue of the work's status.[15] A more interesting approach is to see in it a precursor of the treatises 'On Kingship' which we know to have been a feature of the hellenistic age.[16] It is even more rewarding, since so little 'Kingship' literature actually survives, to compare the behaviour described or recommended in the *Cyropaedia* and *Hipparchicus* (or 'Cavalry Com-

---

[10] Schwartz 1956 (B 103: originally published 1887) esp. 156, 160; but see Tuplin, *Failings of Empire*.   [11] Grayson 1975 (B 50), criticized by Tuplin, *Failings of Empire*, 15–16.
[12] Andrewes 1966 (C 274) 10–11.   [13] Murray 1986 (B 88) 198.
[14] Hirsch 1985 (B 59) ch. 4.   [15] Briant 1982 (F 10) 175ff.   [16] *CAH* VII².1, 75–81.

mander'; another Xenophontic treatise), with the actual tactics, stratagems and exercise of leadership attested for real-life generals of the later
fourth century. This has been successfully done for the literary tradition
about men like Eumenes of Cardia.[17] The latter falls just outside the
scope of the present volume, but his was surely not the first career to
demonstrate the *military* importance of Xenophon's writings.

    Technical treatises (like that of Aeneas Tacticus,[18] see below, p. 679)
abound in the fourth century, and the *Poroi* (otherwise known as
Vectigalia; *Ways and Means*; *Revenues*) of Xenophon is a monograph on a
topic in which the Greeks made little theoretical progress: economics.
To the usual verdict that the *Poroi* exemplifies without redeeming that
failure, it has been countered that Xenophon has again (cf. above on his
intentions in the *Hellenica*) been misunderstood: his aim was political, the
achievement of peace.[19] Nevertheless the *Poroi* is of particular interest for
what it says about the Laurium silver-mines, on which much archaeological and epigraphic work has been done since the Second World War.
Xenophon's suggestions here may be unrealistic; but in a valuable and
detailed book about the Laurium mines, by a practising engineer who
was Minister of Industry and Energy in the Karamanlis government of
the 1970s, Xenophon gets credit for being a 'precursor of economic co-
operation between individuals' and for 'stressing the interdependence of
the different sectors of the economy'.[20] Finally, there is Xenophon's
Oeconomicus, which is about estate management (see further ch. 12*d*
below, p. 662). As scholars begin to shift their attentions to the
countryside and away from the city, it might have been thought that this
treatise would earn their approval but no, 'he fails totally to describe the
very real problems of all farmers in Attica . . . the practical value of this
discussion is almost nil'.[21] For the student of the ancient economy, the
Oeconomicus serves merely to illustrate landed attitudes (pious, hierarchical and amateur), and thus re-defined as a work of ethics[22] it regains a
certain academic dignity. Its fate is thus not unlike some other Xenophontic treatises we have been considering. Its sections on the duties of
wives (including a denunciation of make-up) are revealing, if only about
the expectations of Athenian males at a certain social level.[23]

    We may now pass to the literary sources other than Xenophon.

    The other surviving narrative of the period to 362 is books XIV–XV of
the *Bibliotheke* or 'library' (a universal history) of Diodorus Siculus.

---

[17] J. Hornblower 1981 (B 60) 196–211; cf. *CAH* VII².1, 45–6.
[18] Whitehead 1990 (B 131), bringing out well Aeneas' *general* value for the student of the Greek
city state, cf. below p. 530.   [19] Gauthier 1976 (B 42) with Cawkwell 1979 (B 27).
[20] Conophagos 1980 (I 26) 114.
[21] Osborne 1987 (I 115) 18. A commentary by S. Pomeroy is announced.
[22] Finley 1973 (I 36) 18.   [23] e.g. Lefkowitz and Fant 1982 (I 96) no. 106.

Diodorus wrote in Roman times (late first century B.C.); for his general working methods see *CAH* v² 7. He used one main source at a time;[24] there is nothing to be said for a recent attempt to revive an old view that he interwove two sources in book XVII, which is about Alexander.[25] Book XVI is problematic as we shall see; but there is no doubt that for at least the first four decades of the century (books XIV–XV and parts of XVI) his source continued to be Ephorus, as it had been for the fifth century in books XI–XIII.[26] Diodorus found Ephorus' moralizing tendencies congenial (cf. XI.46) but he got into difficulties reorganizing Ephorus' material; one famous blunder, an apparent confusion between the peaces of 375 and 371, may be due to a misplacing by Diodorus under 375 of an introductory discussion in which Ephorus anticipated his own later narrative of 371.[27] What was said above about 'one main source' needs some, but only some, qualifying to take account of Sicily. The qualification is a double one: not only does the separate Sicilian strand of material run alongside the main Greek narrative; but it seems that for fourth-century Sicily Diodorus *was* prepared to draw on two writers rather than one. Here too the principal source was Ephorus. The other was Timaeus, from Tauromenium and so like Diodorus a Sicilian by origin; but he lived and worked from *c.*315–265 in Athens (*FGrH* 566). He is a figure of exceptional importance, the first great historian of western hellenism; we may note here that he was extensively used by Plutarch in his two fourth-century Sicilian *Lives*, those of Dion and of Timoleon.[28] Distinguishing 'Ephorean' from 'Timaean' material in Diodorus is not an easy matter.[29] The better view[30] is that Diodorus drew primarily on Ephorus and supplemented him from Timaeus; so his approach in the Sicilian sections was different, but not all that different, from that in the main Greek narrative (see further below, ch. 5, p. 121). Behind parts of both Ephorus' and Timaeus' Sicilian material may lie the more shadowy figure of Philistus (*FGrH* 556).[31] Another qualification to the 'one main source' doctrine is required by Diodorus' regular insertions from the chronographic source. This source gives dynastic and other dates. These dates work reasonably well for e.g. the Persian and Hecatomnid rulers but there are serious problems about the Macedonian and Spartan dates; and one Bosporan ruler is killed off in 349 whereas an inscription shows

---

[24] Schwartz 1903 (B 101) = 1957 (B 104) 35–97; J. Hornblower 1981 (B 60); Sacks 1990 (B 98).

[25] Hammond 1983 (B 57) with Hornblower 1984 (B 61).

[26] For the fifth century, the correspondence Diod. XI.45 ∼ *FGrH* 70 Ephorus F 191 is almost decisive on its own, despite Africa 1962 (B 2). For the fourth, see Diod. XV.5.4 and 32.1 ∼ Ephorus FF 79, 210, and the direct citation Diod. XV.60.5 = F 214.   [27] Andrewes 1985 (B 7).

[28] Westlake 1952 (G 321), Talbert 1974 (G 304). On Timaeus see Brown 1958 (B 19), done without knowledge of Jacoby's 1955 comm.; Fraser 1972 (A 21) 763–74; Momigliano 1977 (B 85) 37–66; Pearson 1987 (B 92).   [29] Meister 1967 (B 74).   [30] Jacoby Komm. IIIC (Text) 529.

[31] Zoepffel 1965 (B 133).

he was alive in 346 (Diod. XVI.52; Tod no. 167 = Harding no. 82). Some earlier views on the reliability of this source were too generous.[32]

Ephorus himself was briefly characterized in an earlier volume (*CAH* v² 7). It is essential to realize that behind Ephorus, who was the immediate source for Diodorus, lie yet other, ultimate, sources, of whom we may single out two who dealt, in part or whole, with the period 404–362. The first is the Oxyrhynchus Historian (see above p. 7). For the modern political historian of the fourth century this writer's best contribution is his account (ch.XVI Bartoletti) of the Boeotian federal constitution, an account which makes intelligible some stray hints in Thucydides.[33] But historiographically the most important thing about the Oxyrhynchus Historian is that he, who clearly represents a tradition independent of and preferable to Xenophon, seems to have been used by Diodorus/Ephorus. (For instance, Xenophon's and Diodorus' accounts of the 395 campaign of Agesilaus in Asia are irreconcilable. Xenophon has an open engagement, Diodorus an ambush, which is less glamorous and so probably right.[34] But *Hell. Oxy.* agrees with Diodorus, down to verbal correspondences e.g. εἰς πλινθίον συντάξας ∼ ∼ ἐξ]ωθὲν τοῦ πλιν[θίου, Diod. XIV.80.1 and *Hell. Oxy.* XI.3.) This means that in Diodorus we have a corrective to Xenophon on some points of detail and interpretation; though it cannot be said, as it can about Callisthenes (the next writer we shall discuss), that *Hell. Oxy.* may have offered a radically different picture of the age from that of Xenophon.

Another demonstrable source of Ephorus, to whom he seems to have turned for events after 386 when *Hell. Oxy.* ended, is a writer whose significance is greater than could be guessed from the small number (nineteen) of the surviving fragments of his *Hellenica*: he is Callisthenes of Olynthus (*FGrH* 124), the nephew of Aristotle.[35] The Christian authority Eusebius tells us explicitly that Ephorus drew on Callisthenes (*FGrH* 70 T 17); and it is probable[36] that Callisthenes lies behind some of Plutarch's *Pelopidas*, for instance the account of Theban penetration into Thessaly. Through the medium of Diodorus and Plutarch we can vaguely discern a tradition very unlike Xenophon, above all in giving proper space and significance to Thebes. For instance two fragments or quotations of Callisthenes by earlier writers (FF 11 and 18) mention Tegyra; see above for this battle, which Xenophon omitted completely. The most important piece of evidence for the general line taken by Callisthenes – much less pro-Spartan than Xenophon – is F 8. This

[32] Schwartz 1957 (B 104) 44: 'im grossen und ganzen sehr zuverlässig'; see however Hornblower 1990 (C 366) 74. Cf. below pp. 480, 495.

[33] Bruce 1967 (B 20) 157–62. The terminal date of *Hell. Oxy.* is less certain than is sometimes stated; see Hornblower 1990 (C 366) 73 n. 6.   [34] Cawkwell 1979 (B 26) appendix.

[35] Jacoby 1919 (D 200) and comm on *FGrH* 124; Schwartz 1900 (B 100) reprinted in Schwartz 1956 (B 103).   [36] Westlake 1939 (B 127).

fragment, from a commentary on the *Ethics* of Aristotle, concerns events of 370/69 and has the Spartans deliberately sending to Athens to appeal for help against the Theban invasion (see below, ch. 7 p. 191). This is very close to the line taken by Diodorus in xv.63, and this closeness confirms the general notion that Callisthenes ultimately lies behind Diodorus. But this agreed version of Callisthenes and Diodorus is very different from Xenophon's account at vi.5.33ff: in Xenophon, some Spartans merely 'happen to be present' at Athens and they put their request incidentally. Proof in such matters is not to be had, but this is very close to an 'outright falsification' (cf. above on bias). Xenophon, it seems, recoiled from depicting Spartans as clutching the begging-bowl. Ephorus had much to say about the good qualities, the *arete*, of Epaminondas, judging by Diodorus book xv; Strabo preserves an interesting analysis of the failure of the Theban hegemony (VIII.2.1–2 = Ephorus F 119): despite the personal qualities of Epaminondas, Thebes failed for want of *paideia* and *agoge*, education and discipline. These were the positive qualities associated with Athens and Sparta respectively. This judgment is usually thought to reflect the views of Ephorus' teacher Isocrates (see Isoc. v, the *Philippus*), but note the very similar view of Callisthenes' uncle Aristotle, that Thebes was successful when [and only when?] her leaders were also philosophers (*Rhetoric* 1398). In any case, there were other historians of Boeotia on whom Ephorus could have drawn. (The topic was evidently much debated. Note the interesting discussion of fourth-century Thebes and Athens at Polyb. vi.43–4.) It has even been doubted recently, but not conclusively, whether the Strabo passage is undiluted Ephorus after all.[37] On the hegemony itself, especially on its naval aspects, Diodorus provides much basic material, some of which may ultimately derive from Callisthenes.

The source of Ephorus' Persian material is a special problem. Some was no doubt based on personal knowledge: he came from Cyme in Asia Minor. But written *Persica* existed. For the expedition of the Ten Thousand at the beginning of the century (see below, ch. 3), Ephorus went to Xenophon's *Anabasis*, a decision which meant that Diodorus does after all preserve, at one remove, a Xenophontic tradition (see above for his avoidance of the *Hellenica*). For Persian, and satrapal, material thereafter other writers were available; some of these are discussed below, p. 47. A favourable re-evaluation of Dinon of Colophon (*FGrH* 690) and other authors of *Persica*[38] has disproved the facile view that all fourth-century Greek writing about Persia was trivial gossip,[39] of which there is admittedly too much in Ctesias of Cnidus (*FGrH* 688). But which of these authors lies behind Diodorus' import-

---

[37] Milns 1980 (B 78).   [38] Stevenson in Sancisi-Weerdenburg and Kuhrt 1987 (F 51) 27–35.
[39] Momigliano 1975 (A 41).

ant account of the Revolt of the Satraps (xv.90ff; see below, p. 84) is not
an answerable question on present knowledge. On the view of Diodorus
accepted above, the *immediate* source should be Ephorus; that is, it is not
to be supposed that Diodorus himself crossed over to a volume of *Persica*
for a short stretch.

A final strand in the historical tradition for the fourth century
continues from the fifth: the local historian of Attica, collectively known
as the *Atthis*, discussed in *CAH* v² 10–11. For the period under review,
the numerous relevant fragments of Philochorus (*FGrH* 328) have more
than merely chronological importance. Indeed, to say 'merely' is
churlish, when Xenophon and Diodorus provide so few reliable
signposts; in particular, the ingenious modern hypothesis that in
Philochorus ἐπὶ τούτου following an archon-name indicates the first
event of a year,[40] has been no less ingeniously exploited in the hope of
reaching a higher degree of precision on some key issues.[41] On
substantive topics we have already seen that Philochorus' evidence can
be decisive, for instance on Persian involvement in the 375 peace (see
above, p. 6). For Androtion (*FGrH* 324) see *CAH* v² 11 and 475.

Several of the lost or fragmentary writers so far mentioned were used
by Plutarch (*c.* A.D. 50–120; see *CAH* v² 9–10) in his fourth-century
Lives. Plutarch's loss of interest in Athenian figures in the fourth century
correctly reflects the changed historical and historiographical reality, but
it is very extreme: there is no Athenian biography between the *Alcibiades*
on the one hand and the *Demosthenes* and *Phocion* on the other; contrast
the six fifth-century *Lives*. (This lop-sidedness gives to the Ephorus-
based Athenian *Lives* of Cornelius Nepos, a minor writer of the first
century B.C., an occasional importance which they would not otherwise
have; he covered Thrasybulus, Conon, Iphicrates, Chabrias and Timotheus, in addition to some figures whom Plutarch *did* cover. Nepos'
occasional value is illustrated by *Timotheus* 11.2, which shows that the
peace of 375 explicitly recognized Athenian naval hegemony. This
amplifies Diod. xv.38.4. See however below p. 176.)

Instead Plutarch followed the altered historiographical fashions of the
age he was describing, by moving out to centres of power other than the
traditional Athens and Sparta (the *Agesilaus* is, apart from the *Lysander*
whose subject died in 395, the only fourth-century Spartan *Life*, though
there are clues for the social historian of classical Sparta in the hellenistic
Lives of *Agis* and *Cleomenes*).[42] Thus we have the *Artaxerxes*, unique in its
Persian principal subject; here Plutarch was indebted to Dinon, who may
also have lain behind the unique material in Nepos' *Datames*, another
Nepos *Life* to which there is no equivalent in Plutarch;[43] for the revolt of

40 Jacoby Komm. IIIB 532.   41 e.g. Cawkwell in Perlman 1973 (D 111) 147.
42 Africa 1961 (B 1).   43 Thiel 1923 (B 115); Sekunda 1988 (F 59).

Datames see below, p. 84f. On Plutarch's important Sicilian *Lives*, the *Dion* and the *Timoleon*, see briefly above, and below, ch. 13. The *Pelopidas* was not Plutarch's only Theban *Life*, but the other, the *Epaminondas*, is lost. It may survive in epitome form (Paus IX.13ff), though this is not agreed.[44]

Among the works of Plutarch has come down to us the *Lives of the Ten Orators* (*Mor.*832B–852C). This is surely not by Plutarch himself. And it should be evaluated against the healthy recent tendency to suspect such literary 'biographies' of having been faked, with the writings of the author in question serving as the base.[45] Allowing for that reservation, these lives are usable: they contain a little independent material. They are evidence of a hellenistic desire – shared by the commentators (such as Didymus) to whom we owe a number of our quotations from the *Atthis*, and perhaps also by Diodorus' chronographic source[46] – for the historical means to the understanding of the orators. Oratory is a category of evidence which becomes important only at the end of the fifth century. It is impossible, in the framework of this chapter, to discuss every aspect of fourth-century history which the evidence of the orators illustrates. The canonical 'ten' (the numerical schematism is characteristically hellenistic, cf. the Seven Wonders or the Seven Sages) were as follows: the fifth-century Antiphon, Andocides, Lysias, Isocrates, Isaeus, Aeschines, Lycurgus, Demosthenes, Hyperides, Dinarchus.

Andocides III, *On the Peace* – that is, the abortive peace negotiations of 392, see p. 106ff – is of cardinal importance for the 390s. The reason is not so much that it brings out a Persian aspect to those negotiations which Xenophon characteristically neglects, but that it reveals (see especially paras. 12–15) the early revival of Athenian imperial ambitions, public and private. The speech is also notable for its reckless mistakes about fairly recent history,[47] in which respect it is far from unique among the products of Attic oratory: we can trace back to Thucydidean speeches the 'invention' of an Athens which never existed outside the orator's head.[48] This kind of thing was bad history but good ideology.

Lysias also, in his political speeches, enables us to make good certain deficiencies in Xenophon. To identify Lysias' own political views (if any) is a slippery matter.[49] He was a *logographos* or writer of speeches for other people; see further below under Demosthenes for this notion. But there are enough damaging accusations in Lysias of involvement with the late fifth-century oligarchies, however little this kind of thing reflects

---

[44] Tuplin 1984 (B 118).   [45] Lefkowitz 1981 (B 68A).   [46] Hornblower 1984 (B 61).

[47] Meiggs 1972 (C 201) 134; Thompson 1967 (B 117); Missiou 1992 (B 79).

[48] Loraux 1986 (C 190); Nouhaud 1982 (B 89).

[49] Dover 1968 (B 35). On Lysias a commentary by S. Todd is projected; see meanwhile his *The Shape of Athenian Law* (Oxford, 1993).

the orator's own convictions, to belie Xenophon's confidence (*Hell.* II.4.43) that the amnesty after 403 was honoured in fact and in spirit.[50] This tendency is already strongly present in the long and full speech XII *Against Eratosthenes*, the only one in the 'Lysianic corpus' which was certainly written by Lysias and Lysias alone. At 65ff he drags in the political activity of Theramenes, with whom the defendant had been associated but who was by now dead. The interest of the speech – confirmed by a scrap of papyrus which closely echoes, but is not a quotation from, the relevant section of Lysias[51] – is that it is an early (403) example of the frequent and vigorous forensic use of the recent past which Xenophon would have us believe the Athenians had buried. Elsewhere (XXVI.9f) Lysias appeals to anti-oligarchic feeling as late as 382 B.C., and we often find forensic references to the democratic liberation, as at XXVIII.12 (early 380s): 'I expect the defendant will not try to justify the charges but will say that he came down from Phyle [see below, p. 36 for the significance of this], that he is a democrat and that he shared in your time of peril.' (Cf. Aeschin. 1.173 of 345 B.C.: 'you [the jury] put Socrates the sophist to death, because he was shown to have been the teacher of Critias, one of the Thirty who put down the democracy'. Nothing about strange gods or corrupting the youth. For Socrates' trial see p. 39f.)

Nobody today should be happy about accepting Lysias' political insinuations. But he remains a precious document for the events, attitudes and economic climate of Athens in the early fourth century: XXVIII (*Against Ergocles*) illustrates (like Andoc. III) the pertinacity of imperial aspirations at Athens *c.*390 B.C., but here the subject-matter is deeds not thoughts, the depredations of Thrasybulus at Halicarnassus. The speech *On the Corn Dealers* (XXII) attests financial hardship in the Corinthian War and strikingly illustrates Athens' dependence on, and vulnerability to, private suppliers even for the staples of her diet.[52] A fragment of a speech *Against Theozotides*, which came under the scholarly microscope in 1971 after a portion of the relevant proposal was discovered on stone (*SEG* XXVIII 46 = Harding no. 8), nicely attests both Athens' political desire to be generous to the men who had liberated her from the Thirty Tyrants and the plain economic difficulty of doing so. The proposal, which Lysias opposed, probably aimed to restrict the benefits payable to orphans of the 'liberators'. Other speeches illustrate a range of topics, including the social position of women (I); the liturgical

---

[50] On the amnesty see Loening 1987 (C 188).

[51] Merkelbach and Youtie 1968 (B76); Henrichs 1968 (B 58); Andrewes 1970 (B 6); Sealey 1975 (B 106); *CAH* v² 495 n. 68.

[52] Seager 1966 (C 249) and Todd 1993 (see above, n. 49) 316–22.

system (XXI; for the system see below, p. 548ff) citizenship (XXIII); and attitudes to lending and borrowing.[53]

The work of undermining the general credibility of the property lawyer Isaeus, as a presenter of fact, was done as long ago as 1904 in what remains one of the very best (and most amusing) commentaries on an ancient author.[54] But in his twelve preserved speeches Isaeus throws out incidentally much Athenian social, prosopographic and economic evidence which there is no reason to reject. He can also, with extreme care, be used as a source on his own speciality, the Athenian law of inheritance and adoption, in particular on the difficult topic of phratries (for which see *CAH* III².3, 366ff).[55]

Isocrates,[56] though included in the 'canon' of the Ten, is really a figure apart. It is true that some of his early speeches were forensic productions which were or could have been delivered in the normal way; but his most important writings were polished political tracts of a kind more familiar in the seventeenth century than today (it is not an accident that Milton's *Areopagitica* recalls the title of an essay of Isocrates – who is referred to early on, though not by name. But the conclusions, on government censorship and interference in morals, are the exact opposite.) On some issues, like the career of Timotheus, Isocrates provides facts not otherwise known (XV, the *Antidosis*); and in XIV (the historically unreliable *Plataicus* of 373)[57] and V (see below) he attests the distrust and dislike which Theban pretensions excited at particular moments. And the *Peace* (VIII) of 355, just after Athens' failure in the Social War, is an interesting and hostile analysis of the dynamics of imperialism.[58] Equally important is the evidence he provides for the general mood ('panhellenist', less than enthusiastic for radical democracy)[59] of the educated, propertied classes in fourth-century Greece. That – rather than as a topical and effective pamphlet – is how we should read the *Panegyricus* (IV) of 380, which so accurately 'predicts' the formation of the Second Athenian Confederacy a year or so later; or the attempts (of which the most interesting is the *Philippus* (V) of 346, another uncanny 'prediction') to raise a panhellenic war under the command of some leader in the

[53] Theozotides: Stroud 1971 (B 176). For Lysias I see Todd 1993 (see above, n. 49). For Lysias XXIII (early fourth-century) and citizenship see esp. para. 6, the Plataeans gather in the fresh cheese market on the last day of the month, nice corroboration of Thuc. V.32 which implies that the Plataeans remained a separate group at Athens for social purposes at least, despite the citizenship grant attested by Thuc. III.55, cf. Dem. LIX. 104. On the grant see Osborne 1981-3 (B 165) II 11–16. III/IV 36–7, and Hornblower 1991 (B 62) on Thuc. III.55, and on the speech generally Todd 1993 (see above, n. 49). For lending and borrowing note the use made of Lysias by Millett 1990 (I 107) 1–4.
[54] Wyse 1904 (B 132A), and see Todd in Cartledge *et al.* 1990 (A 15) 31.
[55] Wevers 1969 (B 130); Isaeus on phratries: Andrewes 1961 (C 90).
[56] Most recently Cawkwell in Luce 1982 (B 29) giving bibliography.
[57] Buckler 1980 (C 330).   [58] Davidson 1990 (B 33) 20–36.   [59] Finley 1986 (A 18A) 50.

public eye at the time. In that way – by organized colonization – the 'troubles' of Greece could be cured (see e.g. v 120). For these 'troubles' Isocrates himself provides some of the best evidence, which has duly been exploited; though we must allow, in some of what he says, for the hostility towards new citizens, and the 'men without a city' (i.e. mercenaries and the like), felt by the man of property.[60] But Isocrates' most lasting importance, which falls outside the scope of this chapter, is his contribution to a theory of education as vocational training, *via* practical rhetoric, for the politician. This was a consciously different recipe from that of Plato, with his insistence on the primacy of what we would call philosophy (Isocrates also claimed that word).[61] Like Plato in Sicily (p. 695), Isocrates sought to educate the monarchs of the emergent fourth-century states. His Cypriot 'orations', like the *Cyropaedia* (above), are a valuable contribution to that literature on kingly duties whose importance lay in the future: see esp. speeches ii and ix (*To Nicocles* and *Evagoras*). But we shall see in a later chapter that, historically, the *Evagoras* in particular is a travesty: ch. 8*d*, p. 316.

Most of the extant writings of the remaining five of the 'Ten' fall within the period of Philip and Alexander, to which we may now turn. But first, we should note the importance to the social and economic historian of the so-called 'private' speeches of Demosthenes. (The Demosthenic authorship of some of them is doubtful, and others are certainly *not* by him but by Apollodorus; but in this area of research that does not matter provided the speeches are authentically fourth-century – which they are.) They illustrate (e.g.) deme affairs (LVII);[62] the financing of shipping ventures, and other commercial matters including mining,[63] on all of which see further ch. 10 below; the role of women in Athens (LIX, by Apollodorus)[64]; the organization of the navy (XLVII, XLIX, L, LI); and the liturgical system generally, including the organization of festivals (XXI)[65]. Speech L (*Against Polycles*), actually by Apollodorus, demonstrates the difficulty of separating the study of political and of 'private' speeches: it is a valuable source of information on events in the north Aegean in the later 360s. This in turn (it has been suggested)[66] provides reason for discounting its value as evidence for the weaknesses of normal Athenian naval arrangements: this was an exceptionally disturbed time (see below, ch. 7, p. 203).

As to the political speeches of Demosthenes, who (with Aeschines) is the most important orator not so far considered, no account and critique

[60] Fuks 1984 (C 23) esp. 52–79; McKechnie 1989 (I 100); Davidson 1990 (B 33) 34–5 for new citizens.   [61] Jaeger 1944 (H 66) III 49.   [62] Whitehead 1986 (C 268) *passim*.
[63] Isager and Hansen 1975 (C 176). For mining see esp. Dem. XXXVII.
[64] Fisher 1976 (C 136) 128–44. For Apollodorus see now J. Trevett, *Apollodoros the Son of Pasion* (Oxford, 1992).   [65] MacDowell 1990 (B 68B).   [66] Cawkwell 1984 (C 114).

of individual speeches can be attempted here. The narrative of chs. 14 and 15, below, inevitably draws on them extensively, and the events and policies there discussed are often those which Demosthenes himself describes, urges, or criticizes:[67] he is, to a degree quite unlike Lysias and the others, part of the political history for which his writings are evidence (but see below for the risk of exaggerating that part). Instead some general points may be made.

First, there is a difficulty already alluded to under Lysias, above: a few of the earlier 'political' speeches of Demosthenes were written for somebody else, as a *logographos* or speech-writer. (For instance, xxii *Against Androtion*.) This means that the problem of sincerity (not wholly absent even where Demosthenes speaks in his own person) is specially acute.

Second, a speech like xxiii (*Against Aristocrates*), shows that it may be crude and anachronistic to speak of the 'date' and of the 'publication' of a Demosthenic speech. That speech endorses a view of Athens' northern interests which would be surprising, if not untenable, if really expressed at or after the latest date implied by events mentioned in the speech. More probably different parts were 'thought' at different times.[68] As for ancient 'publication', this was so haphazard and uncontrollable by the author that it has been suggested we should almost always avoid the word.[69]

Not only the effectiveness but the basic veracity of Demosthenes, especially in his literary masterpiece *On the Crown* (xviii), have been denied: 'historical judgment need not follow what he said of himself and his opponents'.[70] On the other hand some explanation is required for Demosthenes' increasing effectiveness after 346; it has been sought in his powerful but essentially emotive appeals to honour and tradition[71] – in fact, to the 'invented' city of ideology rather than of history. As to veracity, it has been countered – not wholly convincingly – that 'an adviser of the people who told lies repeatedly about contemporary or recent happenings, lies which could be contradicted instantly by other speakers and which would be shown up as lies very soon by the actual course of events, was not one to win the people's confidence decisively and permanently'.[72] As Demosthenes eventually did.

Finally, there is the related problem of proportion and balance. We face a risk, easier to recognize than to avoid, of writing the history of the period in terms of Demosthenes and Athens. It is comparable to the risk

[67] Schaefer 1885–7 (C 71); Pickard-Cambridge 1914 (C 222); Jaeger 1938 (C 177); Perlman 1973 (D 111); Wankel 1976 (B 122A) on Dem. xviii. [68] Hornblower 1983 (A 31) 249 and n. 16.
[69] Dover 1968 (B 35).
[70] Cawkwell 1978 (D 73) 19, quoted with approval by Finley 1985 (A 18) 19, cf. Cawkwell 1979 (B 28) 216 on Wankel 1976 (B 122A). [71] Montgomery 1983 (B 87).
[72] Griffith in Hammond and Griffith 1979 (D 50) 476.

of equating the history of the late Roman Republic with the career of
Cicero. Our evidence for Philip's reign is skewed and will remain so
unless the state of the other sources, to which we may now turn, were to
change miraculously.

It is doubtful whether any such miracle would be performed by the
discovery on papyrus of a complete text of the *Philippic Histories* of
Theopompus of Chios (*FGrH* 115). Too wayward and malicious to have
appealed to Diodorus, this account (like its author's *Hellenica*, covering
411–394) is known to us only from fragments i.e. quotations, and from
epitomated extracts, not from any of the surviving general histories
(unless it underlies Justin's occasionally useful epitome of the *Philippica*
of the first-century B.C. writer Trogus.[73] Justin himself lived in perhaps
the fourth century A.D., see below, ch. 5 n. 2.) The spicy and intelligent
Theopompus (for whom see also *CAH* v² 9) has often, perhaps unjustly,
had a bad press, both in antiquity and now.[74] His interests were broad,
taking in satraps, Zoroastrians and Etruscans; but the title of the
Philippica reflects his firm and historiographically important decision
explicitly to centre his history on the personality of the king. How he
handled that personality is a controversial question. Theopompus' claim
that Philip was a 'phenomenon such as Europe never bore' can be
interpreted (n. 74) as an ironic introduction to an account whose subject
would be depicted as conspicuous for his vices not his virtues. But the
Polybian context (VIII.11 = Theopompus F 27) suggests, not least with
its talk of *arete*, virtue, that Theopompus' account was indeed troubl-
ingly inconsistent.[75]

If Diodorus did not go to Theopompus for Philip, whom did he use?
The question is one of the hardest problems in all Diodoran study.[76]
Ephorus was available to Diodorus till 341/0, the date of the siege of
Perinthus (T 10 = Diod. XVI. 76), and Diodorus surely used him as far as he
could. But Ephorus had not treated one major episode, the Third Sacred
War of 355–346; this was finished by his son Demophilus (Ephorus T 9).
Now that the idea that there is a massive 'doublet' in Diodorus' account
has definitely been disproved,[77] we need look no further than Demophi-
lus for the origin of XVI.23–40 and 56–64. Demophilus' work was no
doubt appended, in the most literal, physical, sense, to copies of
Ephorus. This would have made Diodorus' job easy. For 340–336 B.C.
the problem is greater. Rather than postulating the early hellenistic
Diyllus (*FGrH* 73), which is like postulating 'x' because we know so

---

[73] Momigliano 1969 (B 81).
[74] Lane Fox 1986 (B 65); Connor 1967 (B 31); Shrimpton 1991 (B 109).
[75] Walbank 1957–1979 (B 122) II on Polyb. *loc. cit.*
[76] Momigliano 1975 (B 83) 707ff; Kebric 1977 (B 63).
[77] Hammond 1937 (B 55), cf. 1937–8 (B 56) and Ehrhardt 1961 (C 20).

little about him, it is better to say 'x' frankly.[78] We might even suppose that the interest in oratory shown in these chapters points not to Diyllus but to Diodorus himself – as do the frequent historical mistakes.[79]

A wariness of Theopompus' imbalance has been invoked to explain why Plutarch wrote no *Life* of Philip.[80] A *Philip* paired with the *Caesar*, followed by an *Alexander* paired with an *Augustus*, would have had its attractions. (The assassinated father, his eastern conquests a mere project, leaves the empire to be founded by the son.) But it seems that the pull of the parallelism between Caesar and Alexander was too strong;[81] in any case Augustus was the subject of a lost *Life* in a different Plutarchan series, the *Lives of the Caesars*. Besides, Augustus was on record, elsewhere in Plutarch himself, as saying rather stuffily that Alexander should have spent less time conquering places and more on administering them (*Mor.* 207C–D).

The important surviving sources for Alexander's own reign share a curious feature for which there is no single good explanation: they date from periods between 300 years and half a millennium after Alexander's own time. (But Alexander's contemporaries Demosthenes and Aeschines[82] continue to be relevant for Athenian aspects, as are Lycurgus, Hyperides and Dinarchus.)[83]

The special feature just noted creates special problems: so long a gap between the recorder and the events recorded was bound to be an obstacle, even in antiquity, not only to interpretation but to knowledge. To a large extent the study of Alexander is the study of the literary sources, and modern disagreement centres on the competence and good faith which they brought to the job of bridging the gap in time. It should be said straight away that relevant inscriptions[84] are few and that coins and archaeology do not help much.[85]

The essential narrative is the *Anabasis* of Alexander, by the second-century A.D. Romanized Greek, Arrian of Nicomedia.[86] He belonged to the intense period of literary activity ('renaissance' is too strong a word) known as the Second Sophistic. Thanks to a recent renewal of interest in this period, Arrian can be better placed in his setting as a Roman provincial governor and literary man, in an age when the educated upper classes were unusually absorbed by the culture and history of the past.[87]

---

[78] For Diyllus (*FGrH* 73) see Hammond 1983 (B 57) with Hornblower 1984 (B 61); Beloch 1912–27 (A 5) 27; Schwartz 1957 (B 104) 64–5.   [79] Hornblower 1984 (B 61).

[80] Lane Fox 1986 (B 65).   [81] Green 1978 (D 181).

[82] On Aeschines see the works at n. 67 above and on Aeschin. 1 add Dover 1978 (I 31) and N. Fisher, forthcoming commentary (Oxford).

[83] For Lycurgus see Humphreys 1985 (C 175).

[84] Tod 1948 (B 179), Heisserer 1980 (B 143).

[85] Bellinger 1963 (B 187).   [86] Stadter 1980 (B 110), Bosworth 1980 (B 14).

[87] Bowie 1974 (B 17), Vidal-Naquet 1984 (B 120).

Arrian's own aim was literary renown: see *Anab*. 1.12, where he hopes to be Homer to Alexander's Achilles, but Xenophon was another conscious model.[88] In all this he reflects the values and fashions of his time, so it is to his credit that he was not satisfied by stylistic pretensions alone but explicitly sought out those previous authorities he considered to be *truthful* (Arr. *Anab*., preface). But often Arrian either did not understand, or bother to record correctly or fully, the technical and prosopographical material which his sources gave.[89]

The chief of those authorities were Ptolemy, the first of a long line of hellenistic kings of Egypt; and Aristobulus of Cassandrea (*FGrH* 138, 139). Earlier in the present century an exaggerated, Thucydidean stature was claimed for Ptolemy's history. A reaction was inevitable, and he has been charged more recently with subtle bias (against his political rivals) and self-magnification – so 'subtle' in fact that there has been a slight counter-reaction. Aristobulus' picture of Alexander undoubtedly tended to flattery.[90] But behind both Ptolemy and Aristobulus lay the commissioned account of Callisthenes, a writer we have discussed already. Criticized in antiquity for encouraging Alexander's too exalted view of himself, he fell foul of the king on this very issue and was executed, as will be described in a later chapter (p. 825f). His *Deeds of Alexander* did not go beyond perhaps 331 but may have dropped hints about events of 330 and 329.[91]

Ptolemy and Aristobulus are often called the 'main sources' of Arrian, as opposed to the 'vulgate'. This is the modern term for the other chief literary tradition about Alexander. It was known to Arrian and is sometimes given by him, flagged in various ways such as *legetai*, 'it is said'; unfortunately Arrian is capricious and such formulae can sometimes introduce 'main source' items.[92] There is general agreement that the 'vulgate' goes back to the early hellenistic Cleitarchus of Alexandria,[93] although Arrian oddly does not cite this man directly for any 'vulgate' item. Over-confident attempts have been made to characterize Cleitarchus' history, which is the chief and probably single source (see above, p. 9) for Diodorus book XVII (see e.g. *FGrH* 137 F 11 ~ Diod. XVII. 72); also for Curtius Rufus' account.[94] It was certainly more

---

[88] Bosworth 1980 (B 14) intro. 36 (guarded).   [89] Brunt 1976–83 (B 21) 483–90, 509–17.

[90] Ptolemy: Phase 1 of modern scholarship: Strasburger 1982 (A 57) 83–147 (originally 1934); Kornemann 1935 (B 64). Phase 2 (reaction): Welles 1963 (B 124), but note protests by Fraser 1967 (D 175), Seibert 1969 (B 108); Errington 1969 (B 38). Phase 3 (counter-reaction): Roisman 1984 (B 97); Brunt 1976–83 (B 21) II 510: 'to be effective, obloquy has to be laid on more heavily'. Aristobulus: Brunt 1974 (B 20A), not refuted by Pédech 1984 (B 93). Generally on the lost historians: Schwartz 1957 (B 104); Jacoby 1956 (B 62A); Wirth 1985 (D 249); Pearson 1960 (B 90); Pédech 1984 (B 93).

[91] Parke 1985 (D 218) 63 on the problem of Callisthenes' terminus.

[92] Brunt 1976–83 (B 21) II 553.

[93] Schwartz 1957 (B 194); Jacoby 1956 (B 62A); Pearson 1960 (B 90).

[94] Goukowsky 1978–81 (B 45) with Fraser 1980–4 (B 41). See Atkinson 1980 (B 8) for Curtius Rufus.

sensational, romantic and fanciful (or rather, fanciful in more obvious ways) than the 'main sources'; but we have recently been reminded that Diodorus reduced to a single book a Cleitarchan original which ran to at least a dozen; our knowledge of that original is therefore certainly very imperfect.[95] We should also remember that all the sources, main and vulgate, must have used or at least been aware of *Callisthenes*' account until its terminal point, whenever that is taken to be.

In his *Indike* (see below, p. 838) Arrian drew on Nearchus the Cretan, (*FGrH* 133) who in modern times has been said, a little unfairly, to illustrate the Greek proverb 'All Cretans are liars.'[96]

Most of the above 'primary' sources, and some others like Chares of Mytilene (*FGrH* 125), were used by Plutarch in his long and extremely valuable *Life of Alexander*.[97]

A final surviving source is an attractive and very readable work in seventeen books, the *Geography* of Strabo (late Augustan period, that is, the very first years of the Christian era). We have already (p. 11) met Strabo as a source for the Theban hegemony: here he surely drew on Ephorus and so perhaps ultimately on Callisthenes. Strabo is also useful on fourth-century Peloponnesian topics, for instance his book VIII describes (384–385) the events surrounding the great earthquake which destroyed Achaean Helice in 373 B.C.; Strabo's source for this was the fourth-century Heraclides of Pontus.[98] There was also an Anatolian aspect to this complicated episode: the Ionian League became involved. This is a reminder that Strabo is sometimes of the utmost value to us on Asia Minor topics, cf. ch. 8*a*, p. 220 below on Cappadocia. But Strabo becomes most obviously valuable for fourth-century history when he deals with Alexander. Strabo drew on the more ethnographically minded of the Alexander-historians, especially Aristobulus, for his account of the eastern territories conquered by Alexander. Strabo also used the early hellenistic writer Megasthenes for India. Where Arrian and Strabo can be compared, as (a nice example) over their reproduction of Megasthenes' description of the capture and taming of elephants, each of the two later writers turns out to have his virtues and his weaknesses.[99] Strabo seems to précis his sources more efficiently than does Arrian, and is less prone to indulge in merely literary elaboration. On the other hand Strabo abbreviates his sources more severely, and this can result in loss not just of detail but of clarity. Behind Strabo lies the great lost work of Eratosthenes of Cyrene (third century B.C.), who addressed his conservative but original mind to the new horizons opened by Alexander's eastern acquisitions;[100] that was in his third and final book.

---

[95] Brunt 1980 (B 22).   [96] Badian 1975 (B 9); Brunt 1976–83 (B 21) II; Bosworth 1988 (B 16).
[97] Hamilton 1969 (B 54).   [98] Baladié 1980 (B 10) 145–63.
[99] Bosworth 1988 (B 15) 40–60.   [100] Fraser 1972 (A 21) 525–39.

Eratosthenes, however, neglected Italy and Sicily, no doubt because
Alexander went in the opposite direction (merely 'raiding a harem', as
his kinsman and contemporary Alexander of Epirus, who did invade
Italy, witheringly put it). Slightly, but only slightly, more interest in the
West was shown by Aristotle's pupil Theophrastus of Eresus, alleged by
Pliny to have been the first person to write about Rome (*HN*
III.57 = *FGrH* 840 F 24a).[101] A systematic treatment of the west had to
wait for Timaeus (above, p. 9); Theophrastus probably did no more than
draw on the unsystematic knowledge of western ethnography which had
been accumulated by the Aristotelian school. Theophrastus' botanical
material about the East is, by contrast, of great importance. But he, like
Eratosthenes, simply used earlier writers like Androsthenes of Thasos,
whom Alexander had sent to sail round the Arabian peninsula and who
later wrote up his experiences (*FGrH* 711). The more ambitious view
prevalent earlier in the present century, that Alexander was accompanied
by a corps of scientists who systematically transmitted information back
to Greece, and thus eventually to researchers like Theophrastus, is
implausible: Strabo II.1.6 (= *FGrH* 712 F 1) was the main specific
evidence, and is too vague. But the material which Androsthenes
bequeathed to Theophrastus and Strabo is of great interest to us, because
it featured (FF 2–5) the islands of Bahrain (Tylos) and Failaka (Icarus),
now known from inscriptions to have been the sites of Seleucid and
perhaps earlier occupation: see below, p. 843f and *SEG* XXXV 1476 and
XXXVIII 1547–8.

Finally, some categories of evidence which are relevant throughout the
period. First, comedy. The fourth century down to 321 is the age of
Middle Comedy; the last plays of Aristophanes belong to this (somewhat
artificially named) category. They are the *Ecclesiazusae*, of 392, a valuable
source for students of Athenian democracy, and the *Plutus* of 388.[102]
Direct political allusions are still found in the latter, so there is some
continuity with Old Comedy (cf. below, p. 66 for an example, the alliance
with Egypt); though there is less obscenity. Middle Comedy resembles
both Old and New in what it offers for the social historian – for instance
in the remarkable scene (*Plut.* 659ff) which gives an idea what it was like
to spend a night of 'incubation' in a Greek sanctuary. Other Middle
Comedists (e.g. Eubulus) survive only in fragments. Otherwise, the
fourth century is an age of prose.

The *Politics* of Aristotle is a work of fundamental importance for the
understanding of the Greece of the fourth century even more than of the

[101] Fraser 1972 (A 21) 763–5 and forthcoming in Hornblower (ed.) *Greek Historiography* (Oxford).
Note also the extensive use made of Theophrastus for Greek agriculture in ch. 12*d* below.
[102] Dover 1972 (B 36).

fifth (see ch. 11 below). A good up-to-date commentary is badly needed.[103] For the Aristotelian *Athenaion Politeia* or *Constitution of the Athenians* see *CAH* v² 10–11.

For the fourth century in general (we have seen that the reign of Alexander is an exception), inscriptions are a rich source of evidence for the historian.[104] They are not so numerous as in the hellenistic age, but areas like Asia Minor start to be epigraphically significant in the fourth century. As more places caught the 'epigraphic habit',[105] which Attica never lost, it becomes increasingly possible to illustrate, via inscriptions, such topics as hellenization and social and religious life.[106] And inscriptions help to correct the bias in our literary sources towards the main centres like Athens; this is a bias by which ancient historians nowadays are rightly worried.[107] But in view of the gaps in authors such as Xenophon (above), inscriptions like the so-called Charter of the Second Athenian Confederacy (Tod no. 123 = Harding no. 35) can also inform us about central political topics which the literary sources neglect or under-report. The chapters which follow draw too frequently on epigraphic evidence to make necessary more than these brief remarks, and the same is true of the evidence of coinage.[108] Documentary papyri are scarcely significant in this period: the earliest known example was discovered a few years ago. It dates from Alexander's time and is a notice in the name of Peucestas son of Macartatus (known from Arr. *Anab.* III.5.5), putting a temple out of bounds to private soldiers: Turner 1974 (F 542). Peucestas' scrap of papyrus takes us from the age covered by this volume to the hellenistic world where such evidence will be so abundant.

---

[103] Huxley 1979 (H 62). W. Newman's edn of 1887 (H 88) is useful despite its age.

[104] Tod 1948 (B 179); Harding 1985 (A 29) for translations, bibliog. and nn.

[105] Macmullen 1982 (B 70).

[106] See e.g. Fisher 1976 (C 136) for social life; Rice and Stambaugh 1979 (H 97) for religion, including deme calendars.   [107] Gehrke 1986 (C 28); Finley 1985 (A 18).

[108] Kraay 1976 (B 200).

CHAPTER 2

SPARTA AS VICTOR

D. M. LEWIS

I. THE LEADER OF GREECE

The Greek world had long been accustomed to a situation in which there had been two sources of power, Athens and Sparta. The disappearance of Athenian power left the determination of the future to Sparta. Theoretically, the future was clear. The Spartans and their allies had fought the Peloponnesian War for the freedom of Greece[1] and the day on which Lysander sailed into the Piraeus and the demolition of Athens' Long Walls began was seen as the beginning of that freedom (Xen.*Hell.* II.2.24). However, the course of the war had inevitably shaped attitudes and aspirations. The simple hope of 431 that all would be well if Athens allowed her allies autonomy had become infinitely complex. It was not only that Sparta had made commitments to Persia which substantially modified the freedom of the Greeks of Asia Minor.[2] The course of the war had produced political changes in many cities which were not easily reversible, and at Sparta itself the effect of success and growing power was to produce a taste for their continuance.[3]

Sparta had serious disqualifications for the role of a leading power, even more for that of an imperial power. Her full citizen population was not more than a few thousand and seems to have been in continuing decline.[4] By the time of the Peloponnesian War, she was already using perioecic hoplites alongside full citizens, and from 424 onwards we find increasing use of freed helots, a group rapidly institutionalized under the name of *neodamodeis* (new members of the *demos*).

The traditional training of these citizens was purely military and calculated to produce obedience and conformity rather than independence of thought and enterprise.[5] Convention had even forbidden the

---

[1] Lewis 1977 (A 33) 65–7.
[2] Lewis 1977 (A 33) 122–5 argues that by the "Treaty of Boiotios" of 408, the autonomy of the Greeks of Asia Minor was guaranteed provided they paid tribute to Persia. Tuplin 1987 (A 60) prefers the traditional view by which they were simply handed over to the King.
[3] For discussion of the ways in which the war had changed Sparta, see Cartledge 1987 (C 284) 34–54.   [4] Contrasting views in Cawkwell 1983 (C 286), Cartledge 1987 (C 284) 37–43.
[5] Finley 1973 (C 290).

employment of men of military age outside the city (Thuc. IV.132.3). Under war conditions many Spartans had in fact seen a wider world and been faced with untraditional situations. Some of them had no doubt learned how to deal with non-Spartans; others were perpetuating a stereotype, created by Pausanias the Regent in the 470s, by which a Spartan outside the restraints of his own system found himself unable to observe the conventions of others or create new ones of his own. Thucydides (1.77.6, cf. 76.1) represented an Athenian embassy at Sparta in 432 as predicting the likely failure of Sparta as an imperial power for this reason.

During the war, some Spartans had surmounted these disadvantages. Brasidas, besides being a good soldier, had won the trust of allies as well, and had created a store of goodwill on which his successors could draw (Thuc. IV.81). Lysander had won the confidence not only of Greeks but of Cyrus the Persian. His success in this had made him the principal architect of victory without winning a major fought-out battle. But the success of individuals placed new stresses on the Spartan system, which had little place for successful individuals who were not kings. Brasidas had had difficulties with the home government, when pursuing different aims from it (Thuc. IV.108.7). The return of Lysander to command after he had already had one year of office as admiral had required a legal fiction to avoid a breach of constitutional convention (Xen. *Hell.* II.1.7). Already more prominent in the Greek world than any Spartan since Pausanias, who had at least been regent, his continued employment would pose problems for which there was no precedent. At Athens, on the other hand, continued re-election to the generalship had never constituted a difficulty; experience could be built up and used.

At Sparta, in normal circumstances, continuous periods of employment were reserved for the hereditary kings. In 404 Agis had been king for twenty-three years. He had had his difficulties with public opinion, notably in 418 (see *CAH* v² 438), but he had come through them. Based at Decelea since 413, he had had a longer independent position (Thuc. VIII.5.3) than any Spartan before him. He should have learnt a lot, had made no obvious mistakes, and had made a major contribution to wearing Athens down. But he was at least in his late fifties (Xen. *Hell.* III.3.1) and might not have much more to contribute. His colleague Pausanias was just over forty.[6] He had only been king in his own right for four years, though he had been king throughout his childhood and youth during the long exile of his father Plistoanax. When he led the main Spartan and Peloponnesian army to Athens in 405 (Xen. *Hell.* II.2.7), it may have been his first time in the field. Plistoanax had not been much employed even after his return from exile, and we may guess that,

[6] Beloch 1912–27 (A 5) I.2, 178.

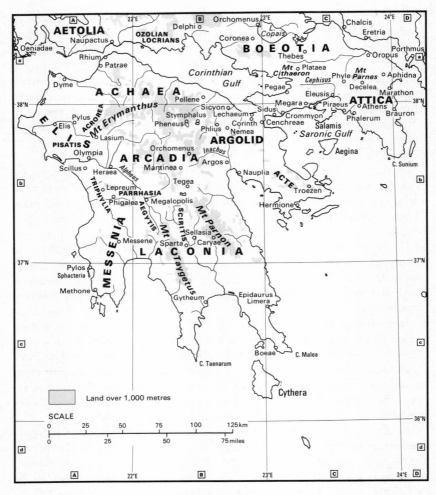

Map 2. Attica and the Peloponnese.

in so far as Spartans had had a choice of attaching themselves to one royal
house or the other (Xen. *Hell.* v.4.32), they had preferred Agis.

The importance of the kings when not actually in the field was a matter
of prestige and influence rather than of their powers.[7] The normal centre
of policy making was a smallish group. Though others may have
participated, its institutional core lay in the *gerousia*, a body of twenty-
eight men over sixty appointed for life, and the five annually elected
ephors. Taking a lead and giving executive orders rested with the

---

[7] On the institutional bases of Spartan policy, see in general Cartledge 1987 (C 284) 116–38.

ephors, but the *gerousia* was of substantial importance, not least because of its role in political trials.[8] We have little material about the composition of these bodies, except the suspicion that there were some families more likely to be elected to the *gerousia* than others and a statement (Arist. *Pol.* 1270b8–10) that ephors might be very poor. By 404 the attitudes of all will have been shaped in varying degrees by the war; how far practical experience was a necessary qualification for office or influence is unknown. What the central group could do was to send out advisers to commanders overseas or more temporary missions of inspection. Both practices are frequently found, and will have contributed to educating those at home who really took decisions.

Inside the central group, disagreements are sometimes visible. They could be finally resolved by the assembly, otherwise confined to elections, but it only had the power to accept or reject motions put to it.[9] The larger body was perhaps more likely to be moved by more general, more idealistic, considerations than the central group.[10] There have been attempts to analyse Spartan politics in terms of parties,[11] and there were surely groupings, most obviously those of 'friends' of one king or the other. They should not be thought to be always relevant; we have many occasions when policy and action are simply attributed to 'the Spartans' and we have no reason to assume that they were anything but unanimous.[12] When there were disagreements, there may have been a strong element of personalities as well as policies involved.

By 404, Sparta's involvement with the outside world had gone too far for the survival of any feeling that her activities should be confined to the Peloponnese, except perhaps in the minds of theorists who regretted a supposed past when Spartans were uncorrupted by outside influences and lived by the laws of Lycurgus.[13] The alliance with Persia had finally proved its worth, and an anti-Persian panhellenism, expressed as late as 406 by the admiral Callicratidas (Xen. *Hell.* 1.6.7) was temporarily quiescent. That it was capable of revival emerges from the reason given by the Spartans (Xen. *Hell.* 11.2.20) for not destroying Athens in 404; they would not enslave a Hellenic city which had done great good to Hellas in the greatest dangers. But for the moment the arrangements with Persia stood. Wherever else Sparta might maintain or extend her

[8] Andrewes 1966 (C 274); de Ste Croix 1972 (C 68) 132–6; Lewis 1977 (A 33) 36.

[9] Andrewes 1966 (C 274) argued against Aristotle for the importance of the assembly. de Ste Croix 1972 (C 68) 126–31 doubted it. Lewis 1977 (A 33) 36–9 adopted an intermediate position (but would no longer argue from Thuc. VI.88–93 that the assembly did have powers of amendment).

[10] Lewis 1977 (A 33) 111–12.

[11] For this period, Hamilton 1970 and 1979 (C 293–4), David 1981 (C 289) 5–42.

[12] Thompson 1973 (C 319).

[13] For the attraction which this concept had outside Sparta see Ollier 1933–45 (C 304); Tigerstedt 1965–74 (C 320); Rawson 1969 (C 310).

influence, the Greeks of Asia Minor had been in some sense abandoned.[14] The more limited watchword was autonomy,[15] promised to all
Greek states from the beginning of the war and frequently (e.g. Thuc.
IV.88.1) reaffirmed. Pericles had commented (Thuc. 1.144.2, cf.19) that
the kind of autonomy that Sparta had allowed her Peloponnesian allies
was one which suited her, and the event would show the word was
capable of considerable manipulation.

Despite her limited citizen numbers, it seemed that there would be no
immediate constraint on Sparta's ability to raise as much infantry as she
might need for her policies from her allies and from mercenaries. The
fleet which had won Aegospotami was still in being and of relatively new
construction. But mercenary troops and rowers would need financing.
For the moment, there were reserves. Lysander handed over the remains
of what he had been given by Cyrus (470 talents according to Xen. *Hell.*
11.3.8, 1,500 according to Diod. XIII.106.8).[16] Future income was another
matter. How far the traditional haphazard nature of Spartan finance[17]
had been improved under war conditions is uncertain; the allies who had
been won from Athens had made or had been expected to make their
contributions (e.g. Thuc. VIII.36.1, 44.4, 45.5), but we have as yet no sign
of regular payments and some of the richest would now be paying tribute
to Persia.

One possible weakness in the Spartan position remained. Although
no trace of concern about her large helot and subject population (see
CAH v² 430) is reported after 421 and the threat of the Messenian base
at Pylos had been removed in 410 (*CAH* v² 486), it was always possible
that trouble might recur.[18]

One point about the future had already been settled. It had already
been agreed that Athens as a city would survive in some form. What
would happen to her former subjects was less clear. The arrangements
with Persia meant that Sparta would not succeed to Athens' position on
the Asiatic mainland, but, at the time of the fall of Athens, Darius II was
dead or dying[19] and the future position of Sparta's friend Cyrus was still
uncertain. As possible compensation, Sparta as a land-power might
consider expansion of her influence on the Greek mainland to the north.

There is little trace of any Spartan thought for her traditional allies
who had fought the war with her. Those of their representatives who

---

[14] See note 2.

[15] Despite Ostwald 1982 (C 55), it is not impossible that the concept originated in the
Peloponnese.   [16] David 1979/80 (C 288).

[17] Although Lewis' attempt to downdate the random contributions of M–L no. 67 to 396 (see the
commentary there) is supported by Jeffery 1988 (B 145), a new fragment (Matthaiou and Pikoulas
1989 (B 154)) makes a date between 430 and 416 highly probable.

[18] On Sparta's internal structure, see in general Cartledge 1987 (C 284) 160–79.

[19] See p. 238.

had asked for the destruction of Athens had been overruled. Nothing was done to rebuild the shattered remains of Corinthian influence in the north west, a matter so prominent before and during the Archidamian War, and the plans for northern Greece, so far as we can see them, took no account of what Boeotians might think. What was more evident was a feeling that the opportunity had come to settle some old scores; a grudge against Elis in particular (see *CAH* v² 437) still festered.

Whatever thinking was going on elsewhere, it was for the moment Lysander who commanded the fleet and could shape policy by action.[20] Samos still held out against Sparta, maintaining her loyalty to Athens (cf. M–L no. 94) even after Athens' fall, well into the summer of 404. Eventually, she capitulated (Xen. *Hell.* II.3.6–7). The free inhabitants were allowed to leave with what they stood up in and nothing else (cf. Thuc. II.70.3),[21] and Lysander restored the city and everything in it to 'the former citizens', that is, to those expelled by successive revolutions; these would be controlled by a board of ten magistrates, presumably one of the decarchies to which we have frequent references, and a Spartan harmost, Thorax, who had been serving with the fleet for at least two years (Diod. XIV.3.5; Poralla 1913 (C 307) s.v.).[22]

Samos is not only the only place where we actually see a decarchy being appointed;[23] it gives us the most striking example of gratitude to Lysander. Other cities might set up his statue (e.g. Ephesus, Paus. VI.3.15). At Samos those whom he had restored after the bloodbaths of the preceding period not only set up his statue at Olympia (*ibid.*), but gave him honours normally reserved for the gods, an altar and the singing of a paean, and renamed the festival of Hera the Lysandreia.[24] Nothing like this had ever happened before in the Greek world, though Brasidas had been posthumously converted into the founding hero of Amphipolis (Thuc. v.11.1: *CAH* v² 430).

From Samos Lysander was summoned back to Athens, where there was turmoil.[25] The peace settlement had dictated nothing about the political future there. Although the *Athenaion Politeia* (34.3) reports that

---

[20] For Lysander, see Lotze 1964 (C 301); Andrewes 1971 (C 275); Bommelaer 1981 (C 279); Cartledge 1987 (C 284) *passim*.

[21] At some stage in the next year they were at Ephesus and Notium (Tod no. 97 = Harding no. 5, lines 8–9).

[22] For the settlement of Samos, see Shipley 1987 (C 382) 131–4, who doubts whether the entire citizen population was expelled.

[23] Nep. *Lys.* 2 is probably evidence for adding Thasos.

[24] Duris *FGrH* 76 F 26, 71, confirmed for the last detail by a statue-base (Homann-Wedeking 1965 (J 19) 440). See Habicht 1970 (A 26) 3–6; de Ste Croix 1981 (C 70) 74; Badian 1981 (D 141) 33–8 (arguing that the Samian honours were posthumous); Cartledge 1987 (C 284) 82–6.

[25] For Athens in 404/3, Hignett 1952 (C 174) is still a useful guide, though more ready to detect prejudice in Diodorus and *Ath. Pol.* than in Lysias. See also Rhodes 1981 (B 94) 415–81; Krentz 1982 (C 182); Ostwald 1986 (C 214) 460–96.

it had contained the condition that Athens should be governed by the 'ancestral constitution' (πάτριος πολιτεία), it surely only contained a phrase, conventional in Peloponnesian treaties, that the Athenians could follow their traditional constitution (πολιτεύεσθαι κατὰ τὰ πάτρια).[26] That was enough, however, to provoke dispute between traditional democrats, survivors of 411 (see *CAH* v² 474–81) who favoured a more restrictive franchise, and others, including exiles who had returned under the peace-treaty, who favoured extreme oligarchy. The democrats were fighting a losing battle. To follow an account written from their point of view (Lysias XIII), Cleophon, the most prominent demagogue of the last years of the war, had been judicially disposed of even before the peace, and a loyal group of generals and taxiarchs were already under arrest for a suspected coup.

Lysander sailed in with a hundred ships and enforced a solution, claiming that the Athenians were already in breach of the treaty through their slowness in pulling down the walls. On the proposal of Theramenes,[27] a body of thirty was appointed to draft new laws for the government of Athens (Xen. *Hell.* II.3.11, Diod. XIV.4.1).[28] That would at any rate ensure that democracy would not remain unaltered. Though the detail is not clear, the Thirty would enjoy executive power as well, and they proceeded to appoint magistrates and a council for the year 404/ 3 (Xen. *loc. cit.*, *Ath. Pol.* 35.1). What they did with the executive power has made more impression on the sources than their primary function. Having settled the matter for the moment, Lysander finally sailed home in triumph.

Lysander, therefore, in both Athens and Samos, had imposed a regime which he thought reliable; there is no difficulty in thinking of the Thirty as a larger decarchy for a larger state. These cities had finally been the core of the Athenian empire, and one might wonder whether they were thought of as needing special solutions, but they could be held to fit into an already predetermined personal plan, described in Plutarch's *Lysander*. In his first nauarchy of 407, he had formed personal followings, which were the origin of the later decarchies (4.5), and the implementation of the policy came in between Aegospotami and the fall of Athens (13.5–9), with a systematic liquidation of democracies and other consti-

---

[26] Fuks 1953 (C 138) 60–1, Rhodes 1981 (B 94) 427; against, McCoy 1975 (C 191).

[27] It is clear that Lys. XII.74–6 takes priority over Diod. XIV.3.5–7 on this point. For a compromise position by which Theramenes spoke twice, once against and once for oligarchy, see Salmon 1969 (C 247), accepted by McCoy 1975 (C 191) 142–4; Krentz 1982 (C 182) 49 n. 21; Ostwald 1986 (C 214) 476–7. It is preferable to stress the drafting character of the Thirty's appointment (see next note).

[28] Krentz 1982 (C 182) 50 and Ostwald 1986 (C 214) 477 n. 70 argue that the laws to be drafted are those by which the Thirty will govern, but the traditional interpretation that they are the laws by which the Athenians will conduct their affairs is to be preferred.

tutions and the establishment of decarchies, in all cities, whether previously hostile or not, each with a Spartan harmost. These new regimes rested not on birth and wealth, but on personal loyalty to him, and would contribute to a personal leadership of Greece.

There is here surely some later distortion of Lysander's career and ambitions, and the suggestion of a plan for personal power, exercised beyond the state, is not plausible. The end of Athenian control meant the end of many regimes, democratic or of democratic colour (cf. *CAH* v² 383–5). Unanimity among those who replaced them is not to be expected, and those factions which won the ear of the Spartan commander were likely to come out on top and to gain any protection they might think necessary to maintain themselves. Not all sources think of the system as purely Lysander's, and Diodorus (xiv.10.1) in fact attributes to the Spartans as a whole an instruction to Lysander after the war to establish harmosts and oligarchies in every city, and follows it with a statement that they now established tribute on the conquered cities, which raised more than 1,000 talents a year.[29] Although the timing and credentials of this passage present difficulties,[30] there is no real reason to suppose that any serious measure of renunciation and withdrawal was contemplated by anyone at Sparta in 404.

There may already have been thinking about an extension of Spartan influence into areas which had remained untouched by Athenian imperialism. By 395, we can see a substantial degree of control in central Greece, which, in the first phase of the Corinthian War, the Boeotians exert themselves to undo (see below, p. 101). It has been argued[31] that a strand of Spartan thinking had been looking northwards since the foundation of Heraclea Trachinia in 426 (*CAH* v² 390). The main argument for supposing that an extensive plan for northern expansion went into operation in 404 unfortunately lies in a speech set in Larissa in Thessaly and attributed in its manuscripts to the orator of the second century A.D., Herodes Atticus. The speech has been widely held to be a genuine product of the end of the fifth century and many of those who hold this view have settled for a date in the summer of 404;[32] it would

---

[29] On the detail of the 'second Spartan empire' nothing has really replaced the judicious discussion of Parke 1930 (C 305), certainly not Bockisch 1965 (C 278). On Spartan imperialism in general, see Andrewes 1978 (C 276); Cartledge 1987 (C 284) 86–98.

[30] See Andrewes 1971 (C 275) 209–10, who thinks that Diodorus has created a formal decision out of a description by Ephorus of a gradual development. That a formal tribute structure existed by 403 results from *Ath. Pol.* 39.2, where both parties to the final settlement at Athens are to pay out of their income *eis to symmachikon*. We know nothing else about the tribute; 'more than a thousand talents' seems high.

[31] Andrewes 1971 (C 275) 217–26 is fundamental for what follows. See also Funke 1980 (C 24) 39–40.

[32] Morrison 1942 (C 373) and Wade-Gery 1945 (C 388), followed by Andrewes. The older view of 400/399 (Meyer 1921 (A 38) 56–8, Beloch 1912–27 (A 5) III.2, 16–8) is preferred by Funke.

result that Sparta was at that time proposing an alliance to Larissa against Archelaus king of Macedon. The speech is surely a later rhetorical production,[33] and, whatever recondite knowledge of detail is claimed for it, it is hazardous to affirm that its occasion ever took place.[34]

Even without this support, there is evidence for Spartan activity in the north, though its beginnings cannot be dated. Whatever view we take of the Herodes speech, there was considerable disturbance in Thessaly at the time the war ended. The Athenian Critias had taken part in civil strife in Thessaly during his exile (Xen. *Hell.* II.3.36). Lycophron of Pherae, 'wishing to rule the whole of Thessaly', won a victory over Larissa and other states in September 404 (*ibid.* II.3.4). Sparta had a friendship with him at some time (*ibid.* VI.4.24), and the hardest evidence for Spartan intervention in Thessaly is that Sparta had a garrison at Pharsalus in 395 (Diod. XIV.82.5–6), which does put her on the side of Pherae against Larissa. Heraclea had had more or less continuous troubles with its neighbours and with Thessalians since its foundation (Thuc. III.93.2, V.51, VIII.3.1, Xen. *Hell.* I.2.18). This had been an interest of Agis, but the first attention we hear of after the war is a Spartan mission in 400 or 399 to deal with *stasis* there and punish its neighbours (Diod. XIV.38.4–5, Polyaen. II.21; cf. Diod. XIV.82.7). Some of these neighbours turn up in the mixed force from central Greece which Lysander was sent to bring to Haliartus in 395 (Xen. *Hell.* III.5.6; see below, p. 99). That forces are available from this area shows that there has been rather more activity around here than is actually attested, and the mission of Lysander has suggested that he might have been involved there before. Activity west and north of Boeotia will have provoked attention in Thebes; Heraclea had already caused friction between Boeotia and Sparta in 419 (Thuc. V.52.1).

II. ATHENS

By far our fullest accounts of events after the peace are, as usual, for Athens, and Athens turned into a test for Spartan policy. The accounts are full and at times contradictory. The deepest contradiction, of which we have already seen traces, is over the role of Theramenes. The most important factual clash is over the timing of the introduction of a Spartan garrison. Variation in the accounts will have started very early, when survivors of the Thirty attempted to emphasize their differences with the

---

[33] Albini 1968 (B 3); Russell 1983 (H 102) 111.

[34] Funke appeals to a consensus that, whatever the authorship, the speech contains reliable material, but there is no real corroboration for the projected Spartan attack on Macedonia. That Archelaus had recently made a successful attack on Larissa is found plausible by Hammond and Griffith 1979 (D 50) 140–1.

extremists. Lysias XII makes the process clear; the defendant has been maintaining that he had been a Theramenes man, not a Critias man.

For once, the Diodorus account (cf. pp. 9–10) seems to have no *Hellenica Oxyrhynchia* material in it; Ephorus seems to have overlaid an account taken from Xenophon with a very low-level pro-Theramenean source. Aristotle, *Athenaion Politeia*, for once has a very full account (34.3–40), perhaps taken from the Atthidographer Androtion (see *CAH* v² 11). Starting with a very dubious pro-Theramenean account, it ends with invaluable documentary detail about the final settlement and amnesty. Apart from this section, Xenophon must have the priority in all purely factual matters. Although his account was written a good deal later (see p. 1), it is surely that of an eye-witness among the Athenian cavalry. The detectable stages of his disillusion are a document in themselves.[35]

Defeat inevitably led to reassessment of the institutions under which the war had been fought. Though convinced democrats could satisfy themselves with thoughts of treachery at Aegospotami (Lys. XIV.38, cf. Xen. *Hell.* II.1.32, Dem. XIX.191), opponents of democracy, silent since 410, now had their chance. It was not only that the ultimate say in Athens' future was now in Spartan hands. Athens had been stripped of her empire and her internal make-up may well have been much changed. Though the absolute figures remain violently debated, it is clear that population losses through plague and war had been enormous, particularly among the lowest, thetic, class, and only to a small extent compensated by the enforced return of citizens from colonies and cleruchies.[36]

Our accounts of political opinion at Athens vary, not least about the attitude of Theramenes.[37] We have already dismissed the version in which he opposed the setting-up of the Thirty. It was surely he who proposed it, but it perhaps remains uncertain whether he now was prepared to remake the state through a tight oligarchy (the view of Lysias XII) or saw the opportunity of re-establishing the hoplite franchise which he had engineered briefly in 411–410 (see *CAH* v² 479–81, 484). Xenophon lets him claim in his dying speech (*Hell.* II.3.48)[38] that this had consistently been his ideal.[39]

Even Lysias XII admits some measure of compromise in the compo-

[35] Apart from a willingness to accept Xenophon material in Diodorus (cf. Krentz 1982 (c 182) 135–9), this represents a fairly orthodox view of the sources. Krentz continues (139–47) by attributing *Ath. Pol.*'s account ultimately to the *Hellenica Oxyrhynchia* rather than to an Atthidographer, and gives it priority over Xenophon. This is not a very plausible position.

[36] See, most recently, Strauss 1986 (c 259) 70–81; Hansen 1988 (c 167) 14–28.

[37] Fuks 1953 (c 139); Harding 1974 (c 169); Rhodes 1981 (b 94) 359–60.

[38] For qualifications about the authenticity of this speech, see Usher 1968 (c 264).

[39] But the claims made for his consistency by *Ath. Pol.* 28.5 are different.

sition of the Thirty,[40] but disagreement only emerged slowly. The
sources highlight Theramenes and the returned exile Critias.[41] Whereas
Theramenes' family can be traced no further back than his father
Hagnon, the Periclean general and founder of Amphipolis, Critias'
family was much older and widespread; in the same generation it
produced Plato. Talented and well versed in the sophistic movement,[42]
Critias, like Theramenes, had previous associations with Alcibiades.
Returning from exile in 404, he showed a clear-minded instinct for
personal power. It should not be thought that all those who joined in the
establishment of the Thirty were men of birth and wealth; the largest
single identifiable element is that of men who had been in trouble with
the democracy.[43]

There were some points about the present Athenian law and constitution on which the new regime in its drafting capacity could agree. Some
of the codification in progress since 410 (*CAH* v² 484–5) was deleted.[44]
Ephialtes (*CAH* v² ch. 4) had been a decisive figure in the construction
of radical democracy; his and later laws about the Areopagus were
repealed (*Ath. Pol.* 35.2), though no further steps seem to have been
taken to rehabilitate that body.[45] Solon too, it was said, had made
mistakes in complicating his laws, thereby giving the popular courts too
much say, so they were simplified (*ibid.*, cf. 9.2 and, probably, *Pol.*
1274a4–11).[46] Dislike of the operations of those courts came out more
vigorously in the prosecution and execution of so-called sycophants;
none of our sources has any sympathy for them. These measures are
Athenian responses to Athenian problems. Though we may agree that
the Thirty may have had a coherent view of the future of Athens which

[40] He says (XII.76) that ten were nominated by the 'ephors who had been established', evidently
extreme oligarchs, ten by Theramenes, ten by those present. That is not official language but what
could be alleged to be an unofficial deal. A different kind of factional difference appears in *Ath. Pol.*
34.3. Here the 'ancestral constitution' which it says was imposed by the peace treaty is interpreted by
democrats as democracy, oligarchs as oligarchy, but by the best people, headed by Theramenes, as
the ancestral constitution; since two of the other four named went into exile and only Theramenes
joined the Thirty, the kindest view which can be taken of this account is that the similarity of views
alleged of the five was not translated into similar action. For the attempt by Loeper 1896 (C 189) to
show that the Thirty represented the thirty Cleisthenic *trittyes* (*CAH* IV² 312–15), see Whitehead
1980 (C 266); Krentz 1982 (C 182) 51–4.
[41] That other views were possible emerges from the emphasis on the almost unknown Charicles
(see Ostwald 1986 (C 214) 461) in Arist. *Pol.* 1305b26.
[42] D–K 88; see Ostwald 1986 (C 214) 462–5. The striking account of the origin of religion in the
Sisyphus (*TGF* 43 F 19) surely belongs, not to him, but to Euripides; see Dihle 1977 (H 28).
[43] This is the contention of the speaker of Lysias xxv, who denies that there are natural democrats
and natural oligarchs; analysis seems to confirm it, but cannot of course disprove the presence of
political conviction. Cf. Ostwald 1986 (C 214) 460–8. Krentz 1982 (C 182) 55–6 sums up rather
differently.   [44] Fingarette 1971 (C 135).
[45] Hall 1990 (C 148) argues that the Thirty had no wish to rehabilitate the Areopagus, and assesses
the motives for the repeal differently.   [46] Lewis 1993 (C 187).

has been obscured, the evidence does not really support the recent view that they were trying to remake Attica in the Spartan image.[47]

We need have reached no further than the late summer of 404, but precise and even relative chronology is unavailable.[48] We should follow Xenophon in placing the request for a Spartan garrison before the death of Theramenes,[49] but we have no certain means of placing the exile of certain prominent figures[50] and, most important, a request to the Persian satrap Pharnabazus for the execution of Alcibiades.[51] The Spartan garrison was sent, but funds were needed to pay for it, and the execution, partly for financial reasons, of wealthy metics[52] and even prominent Athenians,[53] begins in this phase.

This violence apparently alienated Theramenes, and constitutional differences emerged when the majority of the Thirty put through a measure to reduce the citizen body to three thousand. Theramenes argued that the number was arbitrary and should be larger; how much further theoretical differences went we do not know. If Theramenes thought that he could repeat his success of 411 in curbing the extremists (see *CAH* v^2 479–81), he was wrong. Critias had enough armed support at his disposal to convince the Council and force Theramenes' execution. All outside the Three Thousand were now forced out of the city.

How much convincing the Council or indeed the wider citizen body needed, we do not know. The movement which eventually broke the regime started outside Attica and, through terror, apathy or general satisfaction, support inside Attica was extremely slow to emerge.[54]

That not all rich men saw the future of Athens in the same way as Critias is clear from the fact that it was two wealthy ex-generals,

[47] Krentz 1982 (c 182) 63–8; Whitehead 1982–83 (c 321); Ostwald 1986 (c 214) 485–7, stressing Critias' interest in Spartan ideas, the nickname 'ephors' for the extremists and the coincidence of the number thirty with that of the *gerousia*, but glossing over the important role of the totally non-Spartan council.

[48] The sources are most clearly laid out in Hignett 1952 (c 174) 384–9; Rhodes 1981 (b 94) 416–19. For the most recent attempt at a reconstruction see Krentz 1982 (c 182) 131–52.

[49] Krentz *ibid.* and Ostwald 1986 (c 214) 481–4 take the opposite view. It is not clear whether its displacement in *Ath. Pol.* is a conscious attempt to exculpate Theramenes.

[50] The exile of Thrasybulus, Alcibiades and Anytus is referred to in Theramenes' dying speech in Xen. *Hell.* II.3.42, but see n. 38.

[51] Varying accounts in Diod. xiv.11, Plut. *Alc.* 38–9. See Hatzfeld 1940 (c 173) 319–49; Robert 1980 (f 711) 257–307.

[52] The outstanding case was that of the very wealthy shield-maker Polemarchus, best known now from his prominence in Plato *Rep.* 1. The episode is described by his brother Lysias (xii.6–24), who managed to escape.

[53] Another aim, according to Plato *Ep.* vii 325a, was to force others to take part in the arrests and implicate them with the regime. Leon, against whom Socrates was sent (*ibid.*), was not a metic, but a former democratic general (Andrewes and Lewis 1957 (c 2) 179 n. 10). Niceratus, son of Nicias, was a particularly rich and important victim.

[54] So, rightly, Krentz 1982 (c 182) 83–4.

Thrasybulus of Steiria[55] and Anytus, who, with a force of only seventy, crossed the Boeotian border and seized the hill of Phyle[56] in winter 404. They had had some private support in Thebes (*Hell. Oxy.* 17.1), and indeed one of the most notable facts about the democratic revival is the wide range of support it enjoyed in other states, some of whose representatives had, less than a year before, called for the destruction of Athens.[57] This is eloquent testimony to the suspicion of Sparta that now ruled in Greece; a puppet-regime in Athens was not acceptable. The Thirty moved out with the Three Thousand and the Spartan garrison to nip disaffection in the bud, without great success. Their situation gradually deteriorated, and some of their measures of mass terrorism, notably a massacre at Eleusis,[58] belong to this period. Eventually, the exiles, now up to about a thousand in strength, managed to force their way into Piraeus. Civil war was now in full swing.

In a battle on the river Cephisus, Critias was killed. During the truce for taking up the dead, Cleocritus, herald of the Eleusinian Mysteries, appealed for reconciliation against the un-Athenian activities of the Thirty. Dissent set in in the city, and the immediate effect was the deposition of the Thirty, who were replaced by a new body of Ten.[59] These struggled to save the situation by appealing to Sparta, on the grounds that the *demos* had revolted from Sparta. They negotiated a loan of 100 talents and Lysander secured his own despatch to wipe out the Piraeus group with an allied force and the despatch of the Spartan fleet under the *nauarch*, his brother Libys. He seemed still to be able to control Spartan policy.

But it is at this point that dissension in Sparta surfaces.[60] King Pausanias, 'afraid lest Lysander might not only win reputation by achieving this, but make Athens his own', persuaded three (that is, a majority) of the ephors to let him take out a Peloponnesian League force to settle the situation. Not all allies saw his motives clearly, and the Boeotians and Corinthians, in their first open gesture of disaffection, refused to march against the Athenians on the grounds that they were in

---

[55] Confusingly, there is another prominent Thrasybulus, of Collytus, who had denounced Alcibiades' behaviour with the fleet in 407 (*CAH* v² 490); his intermittently successful career can be traced as far as 373.

[56] There was a fort there in the fourth century, but no evidence for this time. See Ober 1985 (K 49) 145–7.   [57] For the evidence see Hignett 1952 (C 174) 290–1; Funke 1980 (C 24) 47 n. 3.

[58] Xenophon (*Hell.* 11.4.8–10) describes this massacre, in which he evidently took part, with considerable distaste.

[59] The statement (*Ath. Pol.* 38.1, cf. Lys. XII.55) that they were expected to end the war is not supported by their actions; contrast Fuks 1953 (C 138). That there was later a second Ten (*Ath. Pol.* 38.3) goes, despite Walbank 1982 (B 180) 93 n. 47 and Krentz 1982 (C 182) 97, against all the contemporary evidence; see Rhodes 1981 (B 94) 459–60.

[60] The execution of Thorax, Lysander's appointee in Samos, on a charge of possessing coined money (Diod. XIV.3.5, Plut. *Lys.* 19.7), is not easy to date.

no way breaking the peace-treaty; they were clearly expecting him to maintain the puppet-state. Pausanias indeed opened operations with a show of strength against the Piraeus; they would at any rate be shown where the power of decision lay. But it rapidly became clear that the settlement of Athens had gone disastrously wrong. Nicias' family had gone to seek Pausanias' help, and a member of it claimed later (Lys. XVIII.10–12) that it had been their plight which had shown Pausanias what the Thirty had really been like. 'For it had become clear to all the Peloponnesians who had come that they were not killing the most objectionable of the citizens, but those who were most deserving of honour for their birth and wealth and other virtue.' This is a plausible claim. No Athenian had been better thought of in Sparta than Nicias, and Sparta could not afford that kind of advertisement for her new world.

The contending parties were encouraged to send to Sparta. The ephors and the assembly sent fifteen men to settle the matter on the spot with Pausanias, and they presided over the negotiation of a settlement[61] which would satisfy the men of the Piraeus while doing everything possible to allay the political and economic fears of the 'City men' who had gone along with the Thirty. There would be an amnesty for all, except for the Thirty, the Ten, the Eleven commissioners of police, and the board which had controlled the Piraeus before the exiles recovered it, and for them too if they were prepared to render account of their actions.[62] All other magistrates would render accounts before representatives of their group.[63] Even property which had been confiscated by the Thirty would stay with its new owners. Those who could not reconcile themselves with the new regime would be allowed to withdraw to a separate city state at Eleusis. In September 404 the exiles returned in procession and sacrificed to Athena on the Acropolis.

In theory, provided that Athens met her financial and military obligations to the Peloponnesian League, she would be allowed to get on with her own affairs. The settlement imposed no particular political solution. That the Piraeus faction had not been composed of straight democrats was made clear when one of them, Phormisius,[64] suggested

[61] For the settlement see Cloché 1915 (C 116); Funke 1980 (C 24) 1–26; Loening 1987 (C 188).

[62] At least one member of the Thirty, Eratosthenes, remained in Athens to argue that he had been a Theramenes man and meet the charge of murdering Polemarchus (Lys. XII); whether he won his case and survived to be later killed in an act of adultery (Lys. I) is not agreed. Rhinon, one of the Ten, was immediately elected strategos by the new regime. But a considerable amount of property was confiscated from this group and sold in 402/1 (Walbank 1982 (B 180) = *The Athenian Agora* XIX P 2). The proceeds were used to make, among other things, new processional silver hydriae for Athena (Philochorus *FGrH* 328 F 181; *IG* II² 1372 + 1402 + Woodward 1958 (B 183)).

[63] The oligarchic Treasurers of Athena made the normal transfer to their democratic successors (*IG* II² 1370 + 1371 + 1384 + (?)1503; West and Woodward 1938 (B 182) 78–83), and their accounts were published (*IG* I³ 380), so they stood their account; Lewis 1993 (B 151).

[64] One of those who was said to have supported the ancestral constitution in *Ath. Pol.* 34.3 (see note 40).

that citizenship be confined to landowners, which, we are told, would have excluded 5,000 from the citizenship (Lys. xxxiv with *hypothesis*). Though there seems to have been some Spartan support for the proposal, it was rejected. The activities of the Thirty had thoroughly discredited anything short of full democracy in Athens for over eighty years to come. But, despite the population losses, the democracy remained restrictive in its citizenship policy. The Periclean citizenship-laws, which seem to have been slightly relaxed towards the end of the war, were re-enacted,[65] and, when Thrasybulus attempted to get a citizenship grant for some of his supporters, the attempt was blocked.[66] The permanent consequence seems to have been that fourth-century Athens was a much more bourgeois and less split society than it may have been in the fifth century.[67]

The condition for this overall harmony lay in a fairly determined attempt by the returning party to reconcile themselves with those of the city who chose to remain in Athens. For this the sources, even those whose sympathy for democracy was weak (e.g. Xen. *Hell.* ii.4.33, Pl. *Ep.* vii.325b5), give them very good marks, particularly for the gesture of assuming the debts incurred by the oligarchs in fighting against them (*Ath. Pol.* 40.3, Isoc. vii.67–9, Dem. xx.11–12). Their record is of course not totally blameless. The oligarchic state at Eleusis was wiped out in 401 by a mixture of treachery and persuasion (Xen. *Hell.* ii.4.43, *Ath. Pol.* 40.4). The cavalry who had served under the Thirty in particular were subject to intense suspicion and dislike (Xen. *Hell.* iii.1.4, Lys. xxvi.10), and, despite the oath taken 'not to remember the evils' (μὴ μνησικακεῖν), the whole corpus of speeches attributed to Lysias shows that arguments about an opponent's behaviour in 404 were still being used as late as 382 (Lys. xxvi). But on the whole the record is remarkably good.

The process of law reform started in 410 was resumed.[68] The result was the establishment of a comprehensive corpus of written law, a regular procedure for amending it, and a clear distinction between the permanence of laws and the temporary nature of decrees. Other reforms are discussed in chapter 9. The most significant is perhaps the introduction of Assembly pay, to ensure the presence of a quorum in the Assembly and probably not paid to more than a quorum.[69] Its introduc-

---

[65] See Funke 1980 (c 24) 19–20 n. 9.

[66] *Ath Pol.* 40.2. The relationship of Thrasybulus' attempt to what looks like the final settlement of the matter (Tod no. 100 with new fragments = Harding no. 3) remains controversial (Krentz 1980 (c 181); Osborne 1981–83 (B 165) D6; Whitehead 1984 (c 267)).

[67] Social class is still sometimes said to be relevant to political views (*Hell. Oxy.* 6.3, Ar. *Eccl.* 192–3), but for anything like a really drastic statement of a split between rich and poor, we have to wait till the late 340s (Dem. x.35–45). See, on rich and poor, Mossé 1962 (c 208) 147–66.

[68] Harrison 1955 (c 171); Dow 1953–1959, 1960, 1961 (c 129–31); Ostwald 1986 (c 214) 509–24; Robertson 1990 (c 232); Rhodes 1991 (c 230).   [69] Rhodes 1981 (B 94) 490–2.

tion cannot be precisely dated; it had risen in two stages from one to three obols by 392.

In the first years of liberation, it was inevitably the principal liberators who were most prominent, although some City men can be traced in office. Modern scholarship no longer finds it helpful to speak of 'parties' in analysing Athenian politics. We do see personal groups and can sometimes wonder whether they differed in principle as well as on personalities, but analyses[70] have tended to lay too much stress on the line-up on one particular issue in the winter of 396/5. Even on the very few issues, whether of particular policies or about individuals, where we have information, the groupings are not always solid.[71] On the corner-stone of Athenian policy, the necessity of adhering to the Spartan alliance, there seems to have been no dissent before, in 397, the appointment of an Athenian exile, Conon, to command the Persian fleet (see below, p. 67) offered an alternative possibility. Athens fulfilled her obligations as a member of the Peloponnesian League throughout.

Two major trials about which we happen to be well informed illuminate some more general issues. The orator Andocides had been in exile since confessing his part in the mutilation of the Hermae in 415 (*CAH* v² 449). His main contact with Athenians in his exile (Andoc. II.11–12) had been with the fleet during the period when it had functioned independently of the city under Alcibiades and Thrasybulus (*CAH* v² 485–6). Taking advantage of the amnesty, he had returned to Athens and held posts of distinction appropriate to his birth and wealth before, probably in 400, his past caught up with him and he was prosecuted for impiety. Some purely personal and political issues can perhaps be dimly detected from his own defence (Andoc. I), but, in the prosecution speech which we possess (Lys. VI), religion is not a mere political weapon, but the whole breath of the accusation. This speaker at least is convinced that the evils which have defeated Athens indicate that special care is needed to make her right with the gods. Andocides, defended by the powerful Anytus, was however acquitted.

There is a strong case[72] for identifying the speaker of Lysias VI with the Meletus who, in the next year, joined Anytus in the prosecution of Socrates, accused of not believing in the city's gods (D.L. II.40). It is an almost impossible task to disentangle from later literary debate the various strands which were relevant to Socrates' trial and death.[73] Even

[70] E.g. Sealey 1956 (C 253); more elaborately, Strauss 1986 (C 259) 89–120. General good sense in Funke 1980 (C 24) 1–26.
[71] The key-word ἔστεργον in *Hell. Oxy.* 6.3 does not mean that 'the sensible and propertied people' actually liked the present situation (so Funke 1980 (C 24) 13 n. 55), but that they put up with it. [72] Dover 1968 (B 35) 78–80.
[73] A useful introduction to the problems in Guthrie 1962–81 (H 56) III 380–5. Stone 1988 (C 258) has plenty to offer, even to the professional.

if we could be sure about the charges and the way the real prosecution went about its case, we cannot know what influenced individual members of the jury. That the associations of Alcibiades and Critias with Socrates were in some way relevant seems certain, though 'corrupting the young' is not likely to have been part of the formal charge. We need not doubt that the whole trial is evidence of a deep civic unease, whether at the level of worrying about the gods' displeasure or in a feeling that Socrates was associated with an unhealthy spirit of questioning and disbelief which, in some hands, had contributed to bring Athens down. That Socrates' death, rather than his exile, was intended seems unlikely, but he himself blocked all routes of escape, in court and afterwards.

Economically, the loss of her empire and fleet transformed Athens. She still possessed the advantages of a central position, and a stray text (Andoc. 1.133–4) shows the yield of the 2 per cent import tax rising by a fifth from 402 to 401. But it could also be plausibly asserted that there was a desperate shortage of public funds (Lys. xxx.21). Individuals were no better off. The few attested figures for sizes of private fortunes show much lower figures for the fourth century than for the fifth; agricultural property will have been slow to recover from the years of neglect while Sparta had held Decelea, and any money which had been invested in land overseas (*CAH* v² 295) will have been lost. At the other end of the scale, those who had been forced to return to Athens by Lysander may well have found it hard to get started again, even in a period of reduced population. It is not surprising to find in 391 that there was a mood to go on fighting for 'the Chersonese, the colonies, the overseas possessions and debts' (Andoc. iii.15). That it was possible even to think of such things thirteen years after Athens' defeat depended almost entirely on external circumstances.

III. SPARTA, 403–395 B.C.

The situation at Athens had been taken out of Lysander's control, and Sparta had seen the dubious results of allowing a regime which was, or might become, too narrowly based. It is likely that it was now, in autumn 403, that the ephors, presumably after consultation, took the point and proclaimed that Lysander's decarchies should be abolished and that the cities should return to their ancestral constitutions (Xen. *Hell.* iii.4.2).[74] Withdrawal of Spartan control may have gone even further than that. In the next year we find (Diod. xiv.12.2) that there is no Spartan presence in

---

[74] The date argued by Andrewes 1971 (c 275) 206–16 has been generally accepted; cf. Funke 1980 (c 24) 31 n. 15. The alternative, less satisfactory, date is 397, argued by Smith 1948 (c 316) 150–3 and Hamilton 1979 (c 294) 128–9. For the sense in which the ephors' proclamation applied to Asia Minor, not strictly within their control in 403, see Lewis 1977 (A 33) 137–8.

the key point of Byzantium; the harmost left there at the end of 405 (Xen. *Hell.* II.2.2) must have been withdrawn.

This shift in Spartan policy was not put through without some tension. On his return to Sparta, Pausanias was put on trial for his conduct at Athens and, for the only time in Spartan history, we happen to have the voting (Paus. III.5.2). The twenty-eight members of the *gerousia* split evenly; the other king, Agis, voted for condemnation,[75] but all five ephors for acquittal. This is good evidence of split opinion among the elite. We should not think in terms of anything like a total fall or eclipse of Lysander, but certainly his influence was not all that it had been, and he may have judged it prudent to remove himself from the scene by taking on a diplomatic mission to Syracuse (Plut. *Lys.* 2.7, cf. p. 135).[76]

If there was a mood at this point to lessen overseas commitments, it rapidly became clear that this was inconsistent with being the great Greek power. After the withdrawal of its Spartan harmost, Byzantium soon ran into difficulties with internal *stasis* and the neighbouring Thracians, and asked for a Spartan general. The experienced Clearchus was sent, but used the opportunity to set himself up as tyrant. This was too embarrassing, and Sparta actually had to send a force to suppress him (Diod. XIV.12.2–7, very different from Xen. *Anab.* II.6.2–6). A more acceptable way of using his energies would be found shortly.

In 402[77] it was decided to do something about a long cherished design nearer home. Relations with Elis had long been bad (see *CAH* v² 437), and the major insults of 420, the exclusion of Sparta from the Olympic games and the public beating (Thuc. v.50.4) of the wealthy Lichas, had not been forgotten;[78] there had been other insults. More importantly, perhaps, Elis had been accumulating a local hegemony of the type that Sparta disliked in the Peloponnese (see *CAH* v² 104, 106). 'Autonomy' was a useful watchword here, and the Eleans were told that the Spartan authorities thought it right that they should let their perioecic cities be autonomous. Their refusal meant war, which extended into 400. At the end Elis had to agree to a large loss of territory, but the democratic

---

[75] For speculation about Agis' attitude, see Cartledge 1987 (C 284) 134–5, but he has not established that Agis had backed Pausanias' mission in the first place.

[76] See Hamilton 1979 (C 294) 96–7, but this mission is very poorly attested and not everyone believes in it; see p. 135 n. 66.

[77] The chronology of this war remains controversial; see the summary in Funke 1980 (C 24) 32 n. 16. Xenophon synchronizes its beginning with the operations of Dercyllidas in Asia, which would produce 399–397 and intolerable results for estimating the dates of Agesilaus' reign. Once we are free of that synchronism, the absence from all accounts of the Olympic games of 400 dictates 402–400, which happens to be Diodorus' date. There are substantial differences in the accounts of the war, which is discussed by Cartledge 1987 (C 284) 248–53.

[78] There is little reason to think that Lichas is still alive, as supposed by Pouilloux and Salviat 1983 (C 308) 384.

regime which had come to power there during the war was left
undisturbed (Xen. *Hell.* III.2.21–31; Diod. XIV.17.4–12, 34.1). An even
older score was settled after that war. The Messenians whom Athens had
settled at Naupactus in 456 and another group on Cephallenia were
thrown out of these homes (Diod. XIV.34.2–6); Messene, it seemed, was
once more off the map – this time for good.

There were greater events elsewhere. By the end of the Peloponnesian
War, Spartan relations with Persia had become in practice the relations
of Lysander with the King's son Cyrus. It might have been hoped in
Sparta that Cyrus would in fact succeed Darius at his death in 404, but the
succession of his elder brother Artaxerxes made Cyrus' position doubtful. He did in fact manage to hold his former position in the west under
the new reign,[79] but his relations with the satrap Tissaphernes were
difficult, not least in the Greek cities.[80] By 402, he had determined on
revolt against his brother and begun to collect troops; the displacement
of Clearchus from Byzantium provided a suitable commander for the
Greek hoplites which would be necessary. At least the opening stages of
the campaign would be easier with naval support, and he requested the
Spartans to be to him what he had been to them in their Athenian war
(Xen. *Hell.* III.1.1). The ephors accepted the obligation, lent him the use
of the fleet, and even provided troops.[81] His campaign in 401 was
ultimately unsuccessful (see below, pp. 49, 52, 64–5), and left two main
legacies. The more permanent was that the successful retreat of the Ten
Thousand left the Greeks with a conviction that Persian power was by
no means as great as it looked. The immediate point was that Sparta had
compromised itself badly with Artaxerxes. Whatever the final arrangements with Darius about Asia Minor had been (see above, p. 24 n. 2),
they were now effectively void, and Artaxerxes would conduct himself
for the next thirteen years on the basis that 'the Spartans were the most
shameless of all men' (Dinon *FGrH* 690 F 19).

The new situation took some time to sink in, and meanwhile, just after
the end of the Elean War, in early summer 400, Agis died. This provoked
an argument about the succession, which surely had political overtones,
though we lack practically all the background.[82] Agis' son Latychidas
was not of age, and his paternity was suspect; it was even suggested that
his real father was Alcibiades. The next in line was his uncle Agesilaus,
now about forty-five. His record was said to be good, but he was
congenitally lame. An old oracle was produced which warned Sparta to
beware of a lame kingship, but Lysander maintained that this referred to

[79] Lewis 1977 (A 33) 120–1 against Andrewes 1971 (C 275) 208–9.
[80] Tuplin 1987 (A 60) 142–5 discusses their position.
[81] Spartan support is glossed over by Xenophon in the *Anabasis*, but the evidence is ample (Lewis
1977 (A 33) 138 n. 14).   [82] A full discussion in Cartledge 1987 (C 284) 110–15.

a king who was illegitimate, not to one who was physically lame. Agesilaus was chosen. What motives Lysander had is unclear, but he had carried his point at the centre of affairs. Time would show how real the success would be.

Before the summer of 400 was out, the pressures of great power status reasserted themselves in an acute form. Tissaphernes had succeeded to Cyrus' position in the west, and was subduing Greek cities. A mission to Sparta asked that the leaders of all Greece should look to the freedom of the Greeks in Asia also. Compromised with Artaxerxes in any case, the Spartans agreed; the wartime alliance was at an end and the appeal seemed just. The activities of Thibron and his successor Dercyllidas are discussed in the next chapter, but one overall point must be made. It has been held that answering the appeal was motivated by imperialism, a desire to extend the Spartan empire, perhaps inspired by Lysander, once more in the ascendant, perhaps by Agesilaus, anxious for glory.[83] This is surely too simple a view. Not only were the decarchies not restored, but the story lays heavy emphasis on the nature of conduct to the allies. Thibron was recalled and charged with maltreating them. Dercyllidas was praised for his proper conduct to them, and it is hard to give any very black colour to his civilizing operations in the Chersonese (Xen. *Hell.* III.2.8–10) or his expulsion of the Chians at Atarneus (*ibid.* III.2.11).[84] It is unsafe to deny that the Spartan assembly collectively or even individually had some kind of conscience, and there was nothing to be gained now from Persia by suppressing better feelings.

At the time of the opening moves in Asia Minor,[85] Sparta had a fright at the centre, which reminds us of the roots of this contradictory society (Xen. *Hell.* III.3. 4–11). Whether it was unique or one we simply happen to hear of, we do not know. A young man called Cinadon, who, though not a full Spartiate, had been trusted with various tasks, was accused of plotting against the state. The ephors succeeded in suppressing the plot, secured a confession and executed the ringleaders. Whether there was really a serious plot or not, we remember it for the story of how Cinadon is said to have taken an associate into the agora and invited him to count the Spartiates. He got up to about forty, and was then told to regard them as enemies; all the other 4,000 there were friends. The plotters, it was reported, were not many, but they had the sympathy of helots, *neodamodeis*, *hypomeiones*, and perioeci; whenever these groups talked about Spartiates, they could not conceal that they would gladly eat them

---

[83] Judeich 1892 (F 663) 41–2; Cartledge 1987 (C 284) 191–2.

[84] A case could be made (cf. Diod. XIII.65.4) for calling these 'democrats', but that would not make them less of a nuisance to the stability of Ionia.

[85] Agesilaus had not been a year in the kingship. Whether Thibron left for Asia in autumn 400 or spring 399 is not easy to establish.

raw. With efficient and ruthless controls, as the Spartans certainly exercised, large subject populations are slow to translate their feelings into action. The Spartans were able to use *neodamodeis* in Asia in this period,[86] whether because they thought them reliable or to remove them to a safer area.

In autumn 397, the news came in of the Persian rearmament. This time it is certainly Lysander who is credited with persuading Agesilaus to offer to go to Asia with thirty Spartiates, 2,000 *neodamodeis* and 6,000 allies. His calculation was said to be that the Spartans still had naval superiority and that the performance of the Ten Thousand had shown Persian weakness by land, but he also hoped for Agesilaus' help in re-establishing his decarchies. Agesilaus presented the mission as a crusade, and went to Aulis to sacrifice, as Agamemnon had done before going to Troy, but the boeotarchs intervened (see pp. 97–8). He arrived in Asia, asking for autonomy for the Greek cities. It is by no means clear that this was only a facade, and, when all the allies assumed that it was Lysander who had the true power, he rapidly showed his alienation from him. Lysander eventually went home to meet his death outside Haliartus in 395, in the first battle of the war which was to bring Agesilaus home next year (see below, ch. 4). In Asia Agesilaus matured into the leadership which made him the most influential king in Spartan history, though one with clear limitations who did little to slow Spartan decline.

There was perhaps another solution. After Lysander died, posthumous papers were said to show that he had long been meditating a constitutional reform which would have brought him the kingship.[87] It may be doubted whether, given the nature of Spartan society, that would have done much to ensure the permanence of Spartan power. The future of true monarchies lay elsewhere.

---

[86] 1,000 with Thibron (Xen. *Hell.* III.1.4), 2,000 with Agesilaus (III.4.2).

[87] Diod. XIV.13, Plut. *Lys.* 24–6, 30. See Hamilton 1979 (C 294) 92–6 and Cartledge (C 284) 94–6, who believe Ephorus' view that Lysander did conceive such a plan in 404 or 403. That the thought occurred to him is likely; how much he actually tried to do about it, we cannot know.

CHAPTER 3

PERSIA

SIMON HORNBLOWER

I. INTRODUCTION

Problems of method and evidence make it particularly difficult to write a history of Persia in the fourth century B.C., or rather, an account of Persia which will fit satisfactorily into a general history of a century whose study has traditionally been dominated by Greek evidence, or evidence perceived as Greek.[1]

There are two main, related, difficulties. The first is the risk of 'hellenocentricity' – that is, the adoption of an unduly Greek viewpoint.[2] This fault is easier to identify than to avoid. Nor would it be right to avoid it in all areas, for instance the military: the extensive Persian use of Greek infantry soldiers means that there will always be one Greek dimension to the study of fourth-century Persia. To the general charge of hellenocentricity, the traditionalist might reply that the dominance, in the relevant modern studies, of Greek evidence is the result not of cultural bias, but of a recognition of the quantity and quality of that evidence. In the same way the existence of Thucydides' text makes it possible to talk about the Peloponnesian War in far greater depth and detail than about the eighth-century Lelantine or the third-century Chremonidean Wars, for neither of which is a text as rich as Thucydides available. This does not prove scholarly 'bias' against the eighth century, or the third. Students have tended to fasten on the Greek evidence because the Persian period seems in some respects (for instance, in the archaeological record) curiously invisible. On the other hand, it can be argued that in the relevant areas of study, which include art and iconography, the very distinction between 'Greek' and 'Persian' evidence needs to be re-assessed, and that the apparently meagre impact of Persia on the culture of the western satrapies was the result of deliberate

---

[1] On the Greek sources generally see Sancisi-Weerdenburg and Kuhrt 1987 (F 51).

[2] For warnings against the risks see esp. F 51, but also F 47, F 40 and F 52 *passim* e.g. F 40, xiv and F 52, 267; also Kuhrt 1988 (F 130) 60. But note the admission of Sancisi-Weerdenburg 1987 (F 51) 118: a history of the Achaemenid period without the Greek sources would be a 'history without backbone'. And note the surprising claim of Austin 1990 (F 2), 291 that the topic of Persian relations with the Greek tyrants has been approached too exclusively from the *Persian* side.

45

policy: the Persians deliberately tried to play down their own power.[3] Again, we shall see (below) that it may be too absolute to speak of an 'absence' of Persian historiography: Greeks in long-term employment within the Persian governmental system, and so presumably affected by Persian attitudes, may have contributed to the 'Greek' literary tradition which has come down to us.

An honest account of the sources for the Persian empire as a whole should, however, stress their poverty, relative to what survives from the Athenian or Roman empires (the hellenistic Seleucids are a better analogy). The Persepolis Fortification Tablets, though they are welcome and valuable evidence, not yet fully published or exploited,[4] are not comparable, on present showing, with the Athenian Tribute Lists of the fifth century. And in any case the tablets themselves relate to the fifth century not the fourth. Nor can a Greek, or Greco-Macedonian aspect, be excluded altogether from the study of the tablets, which survive only because they were baked hard when Alexander fired the palace. (If one of his aims was to obliterate the memory of Persia, history cheated him nicely.)

Above all, there is (after Herodotus, who was born a subject of the Persian empire and travelled inside it) no fully surviving 'inside source' to reveal the attitudes of the Persians themselves. We should however reckon with the important possibility that Persian-employed Greeks with bureaucratic expertise may have influenced the documentary form and even the content of some of Herodotus' Persian material. Nevertheless Herodotus' own understanding of, and his curiosity about, the Persians had its limits.[5] Among Greek literary sources, Xenophon's *Anabasis* comes closest to being an inside source (see below at pp. 51ff). Perhaps the nearest *Persian* approach to an imperial viewpoint is to be found in the way subject peoples are depicted on the Persian palace reliefs.[6] In some parts of the empire, notably Greek Asia Minor and to a lesser extent Judaea, the encounter with articulate subject races has left informed comment, whether admiring like Xenophon, Isaiah and Nehemiah, or mistrustful like the Athenians of the fifth century, whose tragedians seem to have invented the concept of 'barbarian' only after the Persian Wars of 490–479 – or re-invented it: the word is after all in Homer.[7] And in western Anatolia in particular, epigraphic finds have made it a well-documented district even by Greek or Roman standards (ch. 8a). Again, we know a reasonable amount about Achaemenid Egypt; but it has to be acknowledged[8] that it is not safe to generalize from

[3] Invisibility: Root in F 53, 7, cf. Hornblower 1990 (F 36) 90. Persians 'playing down power': Root in F 53, 3.   [4] Hallock in Gershevitch 1985 (F 25) ch. 11; Lewis in F 52, 1ff.
[5] Momigliano 1975 (A 41); Lewis in F 51, 79; Murray in F 51, 108ff.
[6] Walser 1966 (F 67); Seager and Tuplin 1980 (C 74) 149ff; Root 1979 (F 46); Calmeyer in F 51, 11ff.   [7] Hall 1989 (B 53); *Iliad* 11.867.   [8] Briant in F 47, 15.

the Egyptian experience (Egypt was in any case outside Persian control between *c*.404 and 343). There are after all many much darker areas, notably in the eastern satrapies. All this means that it is easier to accept in principle, than to implement in practice, the interesting suggestion[9] that we study the Persian empire in terms of the interaction between central power and local structures, rather than in terms of the priority of the one over the other ('centralism' versus 'autonomism').

The second main problem is the persistent ancient and modern tendency to disparage fourth-century Persia for its 'decadence'.[10] This problem flows from the first. If the fifth-century 'barbarian' is to some extent a Greek literary construct, so too is the decadent and effeminate fourth-century Persian: perhaps Ctesias of Cnidus, for whom see above, p. 11, was the first writer to see Persia as somehow 'feminine'.[11] To accept insights like these is not to endorse the modern view[12] that all Greek historical interest in Persia was trivial after 400: on the contrary, the Persepolis Fortification Tablets have revealed an elaborate system of rationing, and payments in kind, which was evidently well understood by Heraclides of Cyme (*FGrH* 689 F 2).[13] In Greece, he says, soldiers get money, *but their Persian counterparts get food instead*. The Oxyrhynchus Historian (p. 10) has a good discussion (*Hell. Oxy.* XIX) of the pragmatic reasons for the fitfulness of Persian subsidies to 'governors'. And reliable information about Persian affairs, transmitted by our surviving Greek sources, can plausibly be traced to the *Persica* or Persian History of Dinon of Colophon, the father of the celebrated Alexander-historian Cleitarchus.[14]

How decadent *was* fourth-century Persia? Some counts in the traditional indictment are, we may readily agree, misconceived.[15] First, inability to cope with an exceptional invader like Alexander is not proof of exceptional military or structural weakness.

Second, the extent and significance of satrapal unrest in the fourth century may have been exaggerated by our sources (see below, p. 84), and in any case some flexibility at the margins can be seen as a sign of Persian strength not weakness; see further below, p. 51. (Paul Veyne has criticized the tendency of historians to attempt to explain complex phenomena, like feudalism, by the use of facile abstract language such as 'the central power being weak and far away, each man looked for a protector close by'. He asks the question:[16] '. . ."Weak and far-off power". What power is not?')

---

[9] Briant in F 47, 3ff. [10] Sancisi-Weerdenburg in F 47, 33ff, cf. xiff; F 40, 117ff.
[11] Sancisi-Weerdenburg in F 47, 43f.
[12] Momigliano 1975 (A 41), still echoed at F 51, xiii; but see Stevenson in F 51, 27 and Lewis in F 51, 79, also Stevenson (B 111) forthcoming. [13] Lewis 1977 (A 33) ch. 1, cf. n. 4 above.
[14] Stevenson (B 111) forthcoming. [15] Hornblower 1990 (F 36) 93.
[16] P. Veyne, *Writing History* (Manchester, 1984) 111f.

Third, dependence on Greek infantry troops may simply reflect a shrewd value placed on professionalism (just as the private arrangements made by the rich fourth-century Athenian, for the discharge by others of his obligation to take to the sea in person, may be evidence of something more constructive than the lack of personal commitment for which the orators blame him).[17]

There remains a fourth count, Persia's inability to reconquer Egypt, despite huge efforts from the end of the fifth century to the 340s. Egypt mattered to Persia economically (see below, pp. 63, 344), and it remains surprising that Persian efforts at recovery were not more successful sooner.

So there were failures, which it would be reasonable to ascribe to weakness in some departments. But Persian 'decadence' in the first half of the fourth century is something of a myth. It arose, we may suspect, from an excessive ancient – and modern – interest in the personality of one man, Artaxerxes II (for whom see below; Plutarch wrote a biography of him, which was not however altogether disparaging, see especially Plut. *Artox.* 24). His alleged characteristics, or the less attractive of them, have too often been projected by modern scholars, admittedly following some cues in Plato and Xenophon, on to Persia as a whole. Thus it has been said of Artaxerxes II that 'his incapacity and subservience to the will of his mother and of his wife, Statira, caused a progressive decline and disintegration of the Empire'.[18] Tacitus knew better than to suppose that the whole first-century A.D. Roman empire shared in, or suffered as a result of, Nero's personal defects of character.

The present chapter does not claim to be a history of the fourth-century Persian empire: such a thing is desirable, but not possible in the present state of our knowledge. It is unapologetically constructed out of the often Greek evidence which we happen to have. First the Persian Kings and their dates will be given, then a sketch of satrapal powers, then a narrative account.

II. THE ACHAEMENID DYNASTY, 479–330 B.C.[19]

Xerxes I died in 465. His successor Artaxerxes I probably ended the old quarrel with Athens in 449, with a definitive Peace of Callias, which may however have been foreshadowed as early as the 460s.[20] Thereafter Athens and Persia rubbed along together in the areas where their

[17] Cawkwell 1984 (C 114).
[18] D. Wormell *OCD*[2] 1970, 126 s.v. Artaxerxes II. See already Plato *Laws* 694–8, and Xen. *Cyr.* VIII.8 (with Hirsch 1985 (B 59) 91–100 on the problems of this final chapter).
[19] For the dates, see below, pp. 234ff; for the facts, Cook 1983 (F 14) and Gershevitch 1985 (F 25).
[20] Badian 1987 (F 3), better in *From Plataea to Potidaea* (Baltimore, 1993).

influence overlapped, with only isolated moments of tension.[21] The reign of Artaxerxes ended in late 424 and after brief confusion he was succeeded by Darius II.[22]

Darius II's reign, like that of Artaxerxes I, falls outside the scope of this volume, but for Greek historians he is remarkable as the Persian King who – whatever his other failures, like the loss of Egypt – settled the Peloponnesian War in Sparta's favour in the years 407–404, so producing the Spartan supremacy with which the fourth century begins. Darius' decision to abandon the Peace of Callias was perhaps motivated by exasperation at Athenian support of the rebel satrap Amorges (*CAH* v² 465). The King's attempt to exclude the Spartans from Asia in 411, as the price of his financial support, may have had to be qualified four years later, see below, p. 65 for the "Treaty of Boiotios".

Nearly a quarter of a century after the troubles of 424, after the reign of Darius II, the throne was again contested when at the end of the fifth century Cyrus the Younger sought to dislodge the new king Artaxerxes II. Cyrus was defeated and killed at the Battle of Cunaxa.[23]

Artaxerxes II's reign (404–359) saw some loosening of control in the west; some of this may have been deliberate, see ch. 8a for the emergence of smaller, subdivided satrapies and of local dynasts with or without the satrapal title. But some was involuntary, see p. 84f below for the Satraps' Revolt. Against all this must be set the King's Peace of 386 (p. 79f), an undoubted success for Persian diplomacy, comparable to, but more lasting than, Darius' settlement of 411. It secured undisputed Persian control of Asia Minor for half a century. This Artaxerxes' reign may have been characterized by religious innovation: he is supposed to have favoured Anaitis (*FGrH* 680 Berossus F 11) and Mithras, as well as the traditional Ahura-Mazda. Certainly there is literary evidence that he introduced a statue of Anaitis (Greek Artemis) into the temple at Sardis (Clement of Alexandria *Protr.* v.65.6,[24] cf. ch. 8a, p. 230 for a new Artemis/Cybele relief). But 'religious innovation' may, as at classical Athens, just be a scholarly way of saying that there is now evidence for the cults which was not there before.

The third Artaxerxes (Ochus) acceded in 359 and re-established Persian authority in the west. But the collapse of the Satraps' Revolt through treachery meant that the worst was already over by 360, and as we shall see, the extent of the trouble may in any case have been exaggerated by our sources. Artaxerxes III straight away ordered the dismantling of satrapal mercenary armies (scholiast on Dem. IV.19); and

[21] *Ibid.*

[22] Lewis 1977 (A 33) 69ff, with Stolper 1983 (F 60) and 1985 (F 177) 116–24.

[23] Westlake 1989 (A 62) ch. 17.

[24] Bidez and Cumont 1938 (F 8) 4; Cook 1983 (F 14) ch. 14; L. Robert 1969–90 (B 172) VI 137–68; Briant 1982 (F 10) 458ff. Cf. below p. 258 (Stolper).

in the late 340s he recovered Egypt, which had been in revolt since about 404.[25] The death of this able ruler in 338 has prompted speculation[26] as to Macedon's chances later in that decade if he had lived on: they would have been less good.

King Arses, now known to have taken the title Artaxerxes IV (*SEG* XXVII 942 = M9),[27] lasted from 338 to 336. He was succeeded by Darius III Codomannus, Alexander's cowardly opponent, who despite an early personal reputation for bravery (Diod. XVII.6, against the Cadusians, for whom see p. 64) was to flee at the battles of Issus and Gaugamela and end the direct line of the Achaemenids.

III. THE NATURE OF PERSIAN RULE AND THE POWERS OF SATRAPS[28]

Persian methods, though of great interest and importance for the student of imperialism in the ancient world, have had less attention, in modern comparative works, than might have been hoped.[29] Persian imperialist aims have until recently been neglected still more comprehensively: for a long time, few of the sophisticated questions familiar from the study of Athenian or Roman imperialism were even asked. Were the Persians' aims fundamentally aggressive, or was Persia merely drawn involuntarily into Greek affairs?[30] How conscious was support of 'medizing' (i.e. pro-Persian) factions and individuals, or did Persia just respond to power-seeking overtures as and when they came her way?[31] Did Persia routinely support oligarchies?[32] There are certainly grounds for supposing so,[33] of which not the least, to confine ourselves to the fourth century, is Alexander's subsequent installation of democracies in Greek territories taken from Persia (Tod no. 192 = Harding no. 107 is the clearest instance). But if the policies of Athens, Sparta and Alexander (not to mention Republican Rome) can all be shown to have been

---

[25] Bresciani in Gershevitch 1985 (F 25) 512, 522.

[26] A. Toynbee, *Some Problems of Greek History* (Oxford, 1969) 421ff.

[27] For the date Badian 1977 (B 135); Burn in Gershevitch 1985 (F 25) 380f and n. 1 should be corrected. For 'M'-numbered inscriptions see Hornblower 1982 (F 644) 364ff.

[28] See generally Petit 1990 (F 45); Tuplin 1987 (F 65) and below pp. 251ff (Stolper).

[29] A. N. Sherwin-White 1980 (A 56), reviewing Garnsey and Whittaker 1978 (A 22) and commenting on the absence in that book of a Persia chapter.

[30] Walser in F 51, 155ff, but see Hornblower 1990 (F 36) 92. Balcer 1984 (F 5) ch. 1 has a discussion of Achaemenid imperialism but it is over-theoretical and schematic.

[31] Austin 1990 (F 2).

[32] Hornblower 1982 (F 644) ch. 5, where the fourth-century evidence for this proposition, and the exceptions to it, are discussed.

[33] For the fifth century, M–L no. 40 = Fornara no. 71 (Ionian Erythrae), has traditionally been taken to show that if you opposed democratic Athens you looked for support to Persia, but see Lewis 1984 (C 41), who shows that the situation at 'democratic' Erythrae was not straightforward, with general cautionary remarks about Athenian 'support of democracies'.

pragmatic and ideologically flexible, may not the same have been true of Persia? Some suggested answers to some of these questions will, it is hoped, emerge from the present chapter, but the first step must be an attempt to examine the concrete realities of Persian control.

We may begin by contrasting two passages in Xenophon's *Anabasis*, the first highly general, the second highly particular.

First, I.5.9: the Persian empire is strong in respect of extent of territory and number of inhabitants; but it is weak in respect of its lengthened communications and the dispersal of its forces, that is, if one can attack with speed. Second, IV.5.24: a *komarch* (village head man) in Armenia agrees to co-operate with Xenophon's troops who have billeted themselves on him, and he shows them where some wine is buried. The interesting thing about the second passage is that although the Persian satrap is said earlier in the same chapter to be only 5 km away, and although there is a mention of seventeen colts on their way from the village via the *komarch*,[34] cf. para. 34, to the Persian King as tribute (all of which shows the reality of the Persian presence), still the *komarch* is the man with whom Xenophon and his colleague Cheirisophus automatically negotiate. We should like to know more about the sequel: were there Persian reprisals against the village? Or did the *komarch* (whom Xenophon later forced to act as guide, until he ran away) find a means of saving his credit with the satrap? Or did the satrap just shrug the incident off? Whatever happened, this second passage rings absolutely true, and would be easy to parallel from the writings of travellers in outposts of any large, peasant-populated empire run on Burke's principle of 'wise and salutary neglect', from Roman to Ottoman or Tsarist Russian. We could, for example, compare Roman Thessaly in the second century A.D., the world of Apuleius' *Golden Ass*, where the administrative picture is one of self-help, organized by communities which largely ran themselves, for protection against brigandage and so forth.[35] 'The Emperor's distant existence was felt by all. But only very special circumstances would bring his forces into action.' Thus the donkey at the centre of the Roman story is requisitioned for the governor, such commandeering of transport being, for Rome as for Persia, one way – road-building was another[36] – of shortening the 'lengthened communications' which Xenophon had criticized in the first passage above; and we should remember the seventeen colts of his second passage. (Note also Diod. XVI.42.5: fodder, for horses, is collected at Phoenician Sidon by the King's satraps in the 340s.) Such demands, like those for wine and corn

[34] Briant 1982 (F 10) 416 and n. 52; cf. Strabo XI.14.9. For Achaemenid Armenia generally see Cook 1983 (F 14) 197f.

[35] Millar 1981 (A 40); cf. Robert 1937 (F 705) 94ff; Sancisi-Weerdenburg in F 52, 268.

[36] Cawkwell 1973 (B 25) 62 n. 3; Cook 1983 (F 14) 107ff.

at *An.* III.4.31, were probably the most obvious way in which at normal times the central power impinged. Otherwise, the *komarch* coped and controlled, as no doubt his grandson did in Alexander's time. (For similar latitude enjoyed in western as opposed to eastern Anatolia in the fourth century see ch. 8*a*, where more formal, epigraphic evidence is adduced, for control by Greek or hellenized local communities of such matters as citizen intake and, up to a point, taxation.)

What, though, of Xenophon's first, more general, passage? The positive half – the strength conferred by human and territorial resources – is not to be denied; though the battles of Marathon in 490 and Gaugamela in 331, and the persistent failure in Egypt, showed that numbers did not guarantee victories.[37] But the other, the negative half, of Xenophon's assessment, is more doubtful. The idea that the Persian empire was vulnerable to rapid *anabasis*, thrust up-country, from the west was a dangerous, because delusory, myth, much promoted by Isocrates (IV, *Panegyricus* esp. 145ff; V *Philippus*) and owing its origin precisely to the events of 401 B.C. and the near-success of Cyrus and his Greeks at Cunaxa. But when Alexander crossed to Asia, the Persian satraps lined the banks of the river Granicus to repel him. It was, as Arrian rightly called it (*Anab.* VII.9.7), a 'satraps' battle', mounted extempore by loyal satraps at the head of mostly local levies. We can add that the fiercest resistance to Alexander west of Iran came from places such as Halicarnassus, Tyre and Gaza, which had a long tradition of clientship to Persia, and whose rulers therefore had nothing to gain from seeing Persia overthrown. This was true throughout the fourth century, and has to be set against the revolts of the period.

What was the difference between 400 and 334? That is, why did Cyrus nearly succeed? The key was surely in the position of Cyrus himself, and in the anomalous conditions in western Asia Minor at the end of the Peloponnesian War. At that time, Tissaphernes and Cyrus had competing and simultaneous claims to the seaboard, with Tissaphernes being granted 'the cities' (i.e. their revenues, as Themistocles had been: p. 213).[38] This created inter-satrapal rivalry, and the result was political confusion in which Cyrus was able to recruit mercenaries extensively in Ionia[39] (as well as the Peloponnese and Thessaly) without attracting too much notice. Even so, he had at first to pretend to be planning a punitive campaign against the Pisidians; this was a plausible tale, cf. p. 219 for the Pisidians. (Tissaphernes, Xen. *An.* 1.2, suspected the truth when Cyrus was still at Sardis, but seems not to have been strong enough to do more than report Cyrus to the King, and this took time. The delay enabled Cyrus to leave Anatolia.) It was Cyrus' anomalous standing in 407–401,

[37] Cawkwell 1968 (F 13).   [38] Lewis 1977 (A 33) 122.
[39] Roy 1967 (K 53) 297, 300, 302, 307.

as 'satrap of Lydia, Greater Phrygia and Cappadocia, and lord of those who muster in the Plain of Castollus' (Xen. *An.* 1.9.7) which enabled him to turn Persia's first line of defence, namely the loyalty of the great west Anatolian satraps, by the simple means of being those satraps himself, rolled into one. None of that was true in 334. Nor was it true even when Agesilaus invaded Asia Minor, perhaps with the more limited objective of creating a cordon of rebel satraps (see below, p. 69): he could not secure Ionia and Caria, so, unlike Cyrus who got out of Anatolia before trouble could start, he could not – even supposing he wanted to – have gone east with an unprotected rear. He would have been bottled up in the interior. (The further question, why Alexander succeeded in this area where Agesilaus failed, is to be answered by pointing to Alexander's ability, the largely fortuitous result of technological advance in places like Sicily and Thessaly, to take fortified cities.)[40]

The loyalty of the satraps at the Granicus is striking, and important; by explaining it we shall have explained the secret of Persian success over so long a period. To a large extent the fall of the Achaemenids is to be laid at the door of Darius III personally, and is not, despite Xenophon, to be attributed to the nature of the Persian empire as a whole. There was nothing fatally wrong with the troops, or with the generals and satraps. True, Persian infantry was weak, but Persian cavalry fought bravely and well against Alexander at the Battles of Issus and Gaugamela. As for the Persian commanders, it is only the obsession of the literary sources with Alexander and his glorification which has concealed the effectiveness of the Persian counter-offensive in the Aegean in the late 330s.[41]

For Xenophon in his more theoretical writings on the Persian empire, namely the *Oeconomicus* (book IV) and the relevant parts of the *Cyropaedia*, as also by implication for Isocrates, the good behaviour of satraps was guaranteed by a set of institutional controls: a standing royal army (Isoc. IV.145), divided commands to encourage spying and delation (Xen. *Oec.* IV.11), garrisons appointed by the Great King to supervise and guard against potentially delinquent governors[42] (Xen. *Cyr.* VIII.6.1), touring inspectors with police functions (*ibid.* 16), royal scribes at satrapal courts (Hdt. III.128.3) and so on. The idea of the King's Eye (Hdt. 1.114, Aesch. *Pers.* 980, Plut. *Artox.* 12), and even the King's Ear (Xen. *Cyr.* VIII.2.11) was an attractive one to Greeks – but of the two, the oriental evidence has so far corroborated the existence only of the 'Ear', in the Aramaic form *guskaye*, 'listeners'. But even this is not certain.[43] (Cf. p. 301.)

Indeed, not much of this Greek picture gets support from the Persian

---

[40] Anderson 1970 (K 3) 140 and 1974 (B 4) 28, cf. Meyer 1909 (B 77) 7.
[41] Burn 1952 (D 164).   [42] Hornblower 1982 (F 644) 145ff.
[43] Eilers 1940 (F 18) 22f; Kraeling 1953 (F 465) 37; Cook 1983 (F 14) 143; but note Hirsch 1985 (B 59) and Sancisi-Weerdenburg in F 52, 269. On *guskaye* see the doubts of Petit 1990 (F 45) 171 n. 282.

side. For the Greeks it was natural – remembering the last tyrannies of
their own archaic age, backed up by club-bearing bodyguards; or
looking sideways to the methods of the Syracusan Dionysius I – to
associate one-man rule with close and oppressive control. Thus in
Xenophon's *Hellenica* (VI.1.12) a Thessalian speaker, Polydamas of
Pharsalus, is made to say 'in Persia everybody except for one man is
educated to be a slave rather than to stand up for himself'. (He goes on to
remark on the extremities to which the Great King was brought by
comparatively small forces, those of Cyrus and Agesilaus, a judgment
whose weakness as applied to Cyrus we have already discussed, and
which as applied to Agesilaus was plain false, or at best untested, though
no less popular a belief for that.) Greeks, then, for whom society was
polarized between the citizen hoplite and the chattel slave, tended to see
Persian subjects in the metaphorical terms of the second or servile
category – since they evidently did not belong to the first. (Cf.
Diod. IX.31.3; Hdt. 1.89.1; II.1.2.) Persian imperial diction may have
given some support to this conception: Gadates is addressed by the
Persian King as his *doulos* or slave, see the Greek inscription M–L no. 12,
a letter of Darius I; and the same Darius in the Behistun inscription calls
Gobryas his *bandaka*, Old Persian for 'servant'. But in the first of these
texts the Greek word for 'slave' may represent some form of the semitic
'ebed, which can 'mean' anything from a household man-servant to a
political subject – or an officer of the King.[44] Old Persian *bandaka* is
similarly imprecise (servant or subject? Cf. Kent 1953 (F 39)). The truth is
that oriental terms for dependent status are notoriously treacherous, and
Greek terminology is poor evidence for Persian attitudes. It is slightly
more significant that the status of Persian 'slave' was objected to in the
380s by Evagoras of Cyprus, who wanted to be '*subject* as king to king',
Diod. xv.8: Evagoras presumably knew the semitic nuances of whatever
Aramaic word meant 'slave'. But in the end the Persians were not fussy
about Evagoras' label: they conceded Evagoras' right to be subject as
king to king (*ibid.* 19.2), a concession by Orontes which was not reversed
by Artaxerxes. But the whole point of this incident is that Evagoras
wanted to be treated as a special case – or perhaps like the 'kings' of
Sidon in Phoenicia.

It is best to start, not with terminology or Greek misconceptions, but
with attested satrapal actions and areas of inaction. The relationship
which emerges is a feudal one, allowing much satrapal freedom of action,
in return for military service, and dependent ultimately not on formal
controls but on loyalty to a system of allegiance, protection, and
territorial and other kinds of gift-giving, which was foreign to Greeks of

[44] F. Brown, S. R. Driver and C. A. Briggs, *Hebrew and English Lexicon of the Old Testament* (Oxford, 1907) 713–14.

the classical age. Their ancestors of the seventh century and earlier might have understood the relationship better, if the pre-Solonian status of 'hektemorage' has been correctly interpreted in an earlier volume as in some sense voluntary and contractual: *CAH* III².3, 380. Though the word 'feudal' was there avoided, we need not be afraid of using it or 'serf' and so on either for the interpretation of Solon or of Persia:[45] the differences from medieval Europe are obvious enough, and are less important than the similarities. It is true that classical Greeks themselves like Herodotus were very 'reciprocity-minded', and Herodotus' *History* can be understood as a network of acts of requital for good or evil done by others.[46] But Herodotus, Xenophon and even Thucydides (II.97)[47] would surely not have commented on the importance of Persian gift-giving unless they had seen it as truly exceptional even by their own hospitable standards.

The actual behaviour of Persian satraps does not, as already briefly indicated, show much sign of deference to, or inhibition by, the royal controls listed by the Greek sources. (What were the royal scribes and King's Eyes doing in the unrest of the 360s?) Xenophon (above) says that garrisons, responsible only to the King, watched over the loyalty of satraps.[48] There is *some* confirmation in the sources for this: thus there are gates on the Royal Road (Hdt. v.52), and a royal garrison at the Cilician Gates (Xen. *An.* 1.4.4); again, Orontas (*ibid.* 1.6) at the royal fortress of Lydian Sardis is loyal to Artaxerxes not the rebel Cyrus. But in the great trilingual inscription found at Lycian Xanthus and published in 1974, the satrap Pixodarus himself appoints the garrison-commander of the city (*SEG* XXVII 942 = M9: 337 B.C.). Perhaps Xenophon was seduced into shaky generalization by the single instance of Lydia, which does contain a number of the classic literary mechanisms of control.[49]

More generally, the military competence of satraps was in practice unfettered, as far as routine campaigning and policing went, despite Ephorus' exaggerated statement that the 'Persian commanders, not being plenipotentiaries, refer to the King about everything' (Diod. xv.41.5). Fourth-century satraps like Orontas, Abrocomas and Tiriba-zus take minor military action without (as far as we can see) telling the King,[50] and Pharnabazus is not likely to have asked for the King's consent every time he raided Mysian brigands (Xen. *Hell.* III.1.13). The forces used were probably either mercenaries, some no doubt drawn from the garrisons (mercenaries are attested in satrapal hands as early as

---

[45] Rhodes 1981 (B 94) 94. Achaemenid feudalism: Petit 1990 (F 45) 243ff.
[46] Gould 1989 (B 46).
[47] Briant in F 51, 6; Hornblower 1991 (B 62), commentary on Thuc. II.97.
[48] Tuplin 1987 (F 66) and in F 40, 67ff.   [49] Tuplin 1987 (F 66) 234.
[50] Meyer 1901 (A 37) 72f; Hornblower 1982 (F 644) 146; Cook 1983 (F 14) 84 and ch. 16 generally.

the time of Pissouthnes in *c*.440: Thuc. 1.115);[51] or else they were *ad hoc* native or Persian levies, men like those who are said by Xenophon to muster under their *karanos* or commander[52] in the plain of Castollus (*An.* 1.1.2; 9.7, with *OGIS* 488) or 'at Thymbrara' (*Cy.* vi.2.11).[53] Such a force is glimpsed in action in the 350s, the levy from the 'territory of the Persian Tithraustes', attested in a papyrus published in 1903, covering events of the Social War between Athens and her allies (*FGrH* 105, P. Rainer, with scholiast to Dem. iv.19). And in the great set battles like Salamis and Gaugamela, satraps more often than not command troops from their own territories.[54]

All this can be used to dispose of yet another Greek myth, the Persian standing army. Such a thing is poorly attested: the famous 'Immortals' may just be a mistranslation of a word meaning feudal 'Followers'; and Darius I's 'Persian and Median army that was with me' (the Behistun inscription) dates from an untypical period of imperial convulsion.[55] (Better evidence would be the 'royal army' of 120,000 who were sent against the Cardouchi, Xen. *An.* iii.5.16, if this incident were wholly credible, see below, p. 64.) And we need not deny that satraps could ask for troops 'from the King', as Tissaphernes does in 396, and gets plenty of them, too: Xen. *Hell.* iii.4.6; 11. But why should this sort of thing not have been done in the Flavio-Antonine way, by shuffling troops around different trouble spots, according to what the strategic analysts call a 'regional deployment policy'?[56] For Persia as for Rome, difficulties of communication and transport were good arguments against having a 'single centralised reserve in the modern manner'.[57] Naval operations were certainly organized in something like the way here suggested (cf. Diod. xiv.98.3; xvi.42, both against Cyprus). Fleets were purpose-built when necessary, a lengthy business:[58] cf. p. 67 for 397 B.C. More important than the question of attestation, which could be a matter of chance, a standing army was unnecessary: the Persian system was flexible, informal – and feudal. Heraclides of Cyme speaks (*FGrH* 689 F 2) of the king's 'fellow-diners', and he connects this status with military service: as we have seen, this insight is confirmed by the Persepolis Fortification Tablets inasmuch as they are evidence of a 'rations' system. But, as in later feudal societies, the relationship was reproduced at levels

---

[51] Roy 1967 (K 53) 322f; Seibt 1977 (K 54); Lavelle 1989 (K 32).

[52] On the *karanos* Petit 1983 (F 44) and 1990 (F 45) 133ff.

[53] Thymbrara is perhaps at or near Adala/Satala, and is not the same place as Castollus 50 km ESE, *pace* Cawkwell 1979 (B 26) 405. For the better location Buresch 1898 (F 595) 184 and Robert 1962 (F 706A) 100ff. Thymbrara is not identical with Thybarna, again *pace* Cawkwell; see Buresch, already rejecting this. See too Meyer 1909 (B 77) 13 and n. 1.

[54] Hornblower 1982 (F 644) 147.

[55] Immortals: Frye in Walser 1972 (F 68) 87. *Contra*: Cook 1983 (F 14) 101 and 246 n. 1; Petit 1990 (F 45) 145 and n. 152. Behistun inscription: Andrewes 1961 (B 5) 17ff.

[56] Luttwak 1976 (A 34) 8off.   [57] *Ibid.* 84.   [58] Cawkwell 1970 (C 109) 47f.

lower than the royal: so Cyrus the Younger has his 'table-sharers' (Xen. *An.* 1.8.25), and the satrap Spithrobates at the Granicus has his own 'kinsmen', his personal 'Companion Cavalry', as it were (Diod. XVII.20.2).[59] Some of these, though hardly all, were perhaps real kinsmen, like Pharnabazus' half-brother Bagaeus, who commands a detachment of cavalry at Xen. *Hell.* III.4.14. In his obituary of Cyrus the Younger (*An.* 1.8), Xenophon praises above all the loyalty and love which he inspired; certainly the gesture with which Orontas the traitor clutches Cyrus' girdle is authentically feudal, and can be paralleled, more or less, from medieval times.[60] (In the Arab historian Tabari, the belt of the Abbasid general Afsin is grasped by his Turkish executioner.)

Another technique claimed by literary sources as a way of weakening satrapal authority was to separate civil and military responsibility (Xen. *Oec.* IV.11), or to divide the authority in some similar way. This happens to be attested for one satrapal capital, Lydian Sardis, both at the beginning of Achaemenid rule (Hdt. 1.153, not however a success) and its end (Arr. *Anab.* 1.17.7 gives Alexander's dispositions, which exactly match those of Cyrus the Great two centuries earlier). Indeed Lydian arrangements may, as we have seen, be the basis for Xenophon's generalization.

Power could be 'divided' in less formal ways: the two most famous satraps of Thucydides' day, Pharnabazus and Tissaphernes, are explicitly said to be in competition at Thuc. VIII.109, cf. 99. Again, from Xen. *Hell.* III.4.26 bad blood may be inferred between Pharnabazus and Tithraustes;[61] and Diodorus (xv.8ff) proves the same for Tiribazus and Orontes. Though these rivalries mostly stop short of being mutually destructive, that between Cyrus and Tissaphernes certainly is (Plut. *Artox.* 3.3); while 'the Persians' at Sardis (identity and status not specified), are dissatisfied with Tissaphernes' conduct even before the Battle of Sardis,[62] denounce him (Xen. *Hell.* III.4.25), just as he had denounced Cyrus, and because Cyrus' mother Parysatis feels the same way Tissaphernes is beheaded.[63] Neighbourly rivalry is one thing, but actual joint satrapies are very rare indeed. It is not clear whether the 'sons of Pharnaces' at Thuc. VIII.58.1 are joint satraps. Orontobates, a Persian, and the Hecatomnid Pixodarus share the rule in Caria (Strabo XIV.2.17), but the context of the appointment of Orontobates is not disloyalty by Pixodarus but its opposite, a return to allegiance; while the shared brother–sister satrapies of the earlier Hecatomnids in Caria (Mausolus-

[59] Sekunda in F 40, 185 follows the view here suggested.
[60] M. Bloch, *La société féodale* (Paris, 1949) 224ff. 'La formation des liens de dépendance'. For Tabari, Widengren 1969 (F 71) 27f.   [61] Lewis 1977 (A 33) 143 n. 51.
[62] Anderson 1974 (B 4) 52; Lewis 1977 (A 33) 142 n. 47; Beloch 1912–27 (A 5) III² 1.46 n. 1; Meyer 1909 (B 77) 20.   [63] Westlake 1989 (A 62) ch. 17.

+ Artemisia: *ILabraunda* 40 = M7; Idrieus + Ada: L. Robert, *Hellenica* VII.63ff = M5) are incestuous anomalies, not a central Achaemenid device for weakening, but a Hecatomnid device for strengthening, the native family's power. It was also perhaps an imitative gesture towards their endogamous Achaemenid masters, and a way of posing as legitimate in the grand Iranian manner.[64] However, it should be mentioned that it is precisely this sort of thing, particularly the unprecedented *female* satrapies of Artemisia and Ada, which has led to doubts about whether the Hecatomnids were 'really' satraps at all,[65] though they certainly use the title on Greek inscriptions (see p. 215 and n. 23).

Ephorus' generalization, about satrapal deference to the King in all things, is widely expressed, and is presumably supposed to cover diplomacy as well as warfare. Here too Greek theoretical notions, and the attested reality, diverge. The Carduchi of southern Armenia are said to make treaties with the 'satrap in the plain' (Xen. *An.* III.5.16): how typical was the satrapal independence which this implies? Modern historians speak of 'peripheral imperialism' to describe far-reaching decisions made by the man on the spot who is in no position to consult the distant home authorities.[66] Perhaps the Persian empire expanded at the edges in this way, via satrapal initiatives which the King did not authorize – but did not repudiate either. Such initiatives are not exactly evidence for disloyalty. On the other hand, Demosthenes (xv.11–12) and Xenophon's Agesilaus (*Hell.* IV.1.36, said to Pharnabazus: 'increase your own rule (*arche*) not the King's') do coolly assume that satraps will seek to profit from the King's setbacks; and Isocrates in both 380 and 346 was similarly optimistic: IV.162 and V.103, both expressing the hope that the Carian Hecatomnids will be disloyal to Persia in the Greek interest. Actually Isocrates in 346 got it conspicuously wrong: soon afterwards, Idrieus invaded rebel Cyprus on Persian authority (p. 329f). In other words, Greek literary generalizations, especially those of orators or pamphleteers, do not get us very far. We should also remember that satraps may themselves invoke Ephorus' principle as a bluff, or to win time.[67]

A notable instance of satrapal action is Mausolus' help to the enemies of Athens – island secessionists from the Second Naval Confederacy, and others – in the Social War of the 350s: since the war was brought to an end (Diod. XVI.22) by a threat of the Great King to involve himself, evidently for the first time, the implication is that Mausolus' original interference (*ibid.* 7) was not royally sanctioned. Diodorus (XV.10.2), that

---

[64] For Thuc. VIII.58.1 see Andrewes in Gomme, Andrewes and Dover 1945–81 (B 44) *ad loc.*, and Lewis 1977 (A 33) 52 n. 17. For Caria see Hornblower 1982 (F 644) 151, 167; 358ff.

[65] Petit 1988 (F 693).   [66] Richardson 1986 (A 49) 177, citing Fieldhouse 1981 (A 17) 23.

[67] Lewis 1977 (A 33) 58.

is Ephorus, implies that it was open to Artaxerxes to disapprove (and to repudiate?) Orontes' settlement with Evagoras, though he actually does neither. Inscriptions survive which record dealings between the Greek states and Persian satraps as apparently independent agents: the difficulty is that there is reason to doubt the loyalty, at the time, of some of the satraps concerned. Thus the 'Reply to the Satraps' (Tod no. 145 = Harding no. 57, cf. p. 88f), and Athens' grant of citizenship to Orontes (*IG* ii² 207a, see p. 88) may both date from periods of instability in the western provinces. Epigraphically, the best attested satrapy is Caria, and here two diplomatic documents, a proxeny decree for Cnossus in Crete standing in the names of Mausolus and Artemisia, and a treaty with Pamphylian Phaselis (*ILabraunda* 40; Bengtson, *SdA* 260 = M7 and M10) show no sign of deference to Persia. Nor are there any but question-begging grounds for dating them to the short period in the late 360s when Mausolus was in open revolt from Persia (he was loyal again by 361/0: Tod no. 138 line 17). Anyway the Phaselis text probably included the 'royal oath',[68] a formula which, though it does not exclude satrapal diplomatic initiative in the matter, surely does exclude rebellion. The Cnossus decree uses the phrase 'the land which Mausolus rules', *archei*, and this verb is audacious; although Herodotus (VII.19), Thucydides (VIII.6.1; 99) and Xenophon (*An.* 1.1.8) had all used the *noun (arche)* of satraps. (Xen. *Hell.* IV.1.36, about Pharnabazus, quoted above, is a particularly revealing use.) The problem with the Hecatomnid satraps (cf. above) is to know whether they are unusually independent, or unusually well documented. Perhaps both.

The last major area of satrapal competence, after military and diplomatic activity, is finance and taxation. That satraps were obliged to forward tribute to the King is stated by Thucydides (VIII.5, about Tissaphernes) and implied by Diodorus, who says (XV.90) that in the Satraps' Revolt half the King's revenues were cut off. Satraps certainly coined money, but the view taken in the first edition of this work (*CAH* VI¹ 21) that satraps who strike gold are aiming for the throne, has been disproved:[69] a number of places and individuals under Persian suzerainty, and not in revolt at the time, strike gold in the fourth century. Gold is 'money of necessity' – a symptom at most of emergency, which might or might not be an act of revolt.

So money and other kinds of tribute (like the horses and wheat in Armenia: above) were collected by satraps. (Even Persis itself, non-tributary according to Hdt. III.97.1, seems in fact to have paid a tribute, called *bazis*.[70] But this did not need to be forwarded far, and in any case

---

[68] Hornblower 1982 (F 644) 153.   [69] Hornblower 1982 (F 644) 179.

[70] Dandamayev *VDI* 1973, 3ff; Briant 1982 (F 10) 414 n. 43; also 501ff discussing Hdt. III.97. See also Koch 1981 (F 39A) and 1990 (F 39B) 8–40.

1. Tetradrachm of Cyzicus; Pharnabazus (413–372 B.C.). (After Kraay and Hirmer 1966 (B 201) fig. 718.)

Persis does not always seem to have had its own satrap.)[71] In the western provinces, at any rate, some of this tribute was restruck into Greek-style coins, no doubt for payment of mercenaries. (An example is a coin of Pharnabazus (Fig. 1) with his portrait on the obverse, and a warship on the reverse, possibly[72] used to pay some Greek sailor at the battle of Cnidus, for which see below, p. 73.) Of the tributes listed at Hdt. III.89ff, we have to assume[73] that some part at least was retained by the satrap for his own expenses – the payment of mercenaries, or, in the Hecatomnid case, the upkeep of a hundred-ship fleet: Xen. *Ages.* II.26ff. The Oxyrhynchus Historian (XIX) says that Tithraustes subsidized Conon with 220 talents out of the former *ousia*, property, of Tissaphernes; but the same chapter implies that satrapal resources on their own would not normally have financed a war for long, or at all. But surely not everything was forwarded to court (a long influential view, according to which Persia went in for economically disastrous hoarding of precious metal, has been challenged,[74] despite Greek evidence like *FGrH* 128 Polyclitus F 3). There is no explicit, general, ancient statement that satraps subtracted something for running expenses, though the passage from Xenophon's *Anabasis* already discussed (III.4.31) says that the wheat-flour, wine and barley had 'all been collected for the man who was satrap of the country'.[75] But the Persepolis Fortification Tablets show a complex, centrally organized ration system.

The commonsense conclusion is that the running expenses of a

[71] Dandamayev and Lukonin 1989 (F 16) 106f; Petit 1990 (F 45) does not really seem to realize that there is a problem about a satrapy of Persis.

[72] Kraay and Hirmer 1966 (B 201) 72ff and plate 718.   [73] Petit 1990 (F 45) 160.

[74] Briant 1982 (F 10) 489, Stolper 1985 (F 177) 143–6; Petit 1990 (F 45) 162, against Olmstead 1948 (F 43). But cf. Cameron 1948 (F 12) 10ff and Cook 1983 (F 14) 137, 204.

[75] Altheim and Stiehl 1963 (F 1) 137ff, 150ff.

satrapy were indeed locally derived: the satrap took what he needed before sending the rest on. But we frankly do not know how the balance was struck between central and local expenditure. This is not a kind of ignorance confined to Persia: we think we know a lot about classical Athens, but it is equally unclear how an Attic deme (village) like Rhamnous could put up an expensive temple to Nemesis out of her deme funds, attested as small, without 'some subvention' from the state (M–L no. 53 and comm.). The phrase 'taxes over which the community has control', which implies the coexistence of a partially autonomous, exemption-granting, local unit and of a fiscally sovereign higher power, first occurs approximately simultaneously in fourth-century Persian Asia Minor (ch. 8*a*, p. 226) and in fourth-century Attic deme administration: *SIG* 1094, relating to Eleusis, a text which implies a contrast with taxes paid to the city of Athens. In other words, the satrapally held communities of western Anatolia may have borrowed from Athens the fiscal concepts and terminology needed to draw the line between where the claims of the local community ended and those of the King began.

But as we have seen, not all the dues exacted by Persia were of a kind we can call financial. Persian open-handed gift-giving, *polydoria* (Xen. *Cyr.* VIII.2.7, cf. VII.1.43), conferred prestige on the giver (above, p. 55). It was also a euphemism for what could be seen as a system of expropriations and dispossessions, if viewed from the angle of those who had to move out to make room for the Persians or Persian favourites who were endowed in this way by the crown (cf. p. 213 for the position in fifth-century Ionia). Finally, it was a system of *reciprocal* obligation: a man like Tithraustes on his *chora* or estates had to lead out the militia from those estates when the empire, or his corner of it, was under threat. The link between gift-giving and military dues or service is provided[76] by the most general word for 'dues' in Achaemenid Babylonia, *nadanattu*, which is related to the Hebrew root 'to give'. And the ambiguity between 'dues' and military service is illustrated by another word for 'dues', namely *ilku*, which is connected with a semitic root meaning 'to go'.

In Babylonia, dues were forwarded to the King by the heads of the local collectives, the *hatru* (we may compare the role of the Armenian *komarch*,[77] or of the local *eklogeis* or collectors, Antiphon F 52 Blass, who collected the tribute for the Athenian empire); perhaps the dues were forwarded through intermediaries – the Babylonian satrap? It would be easy to imagine a similar system operating in the villages and *poleis* of Anatolia, with the villages serving as the chief unit of collection. Thus Alexander lays claim to the *chora*, territory, of Priene (he remits the

---

[76] Hornblower 1982 (F 644) 157, citing Cardascia 1951 (F 83) and 1958 (F 84) and Dandamayev 1967 (F 92), 1969 (F 93) and 1984 (F 95).   [77] Briant 1982 (F 10) 416 and n. 52; below p. 245f.

'contribution' of the city)[78] and tells the villages, whose inhabitants were non-Greeks and so in his eyes less entitled to consideration than the Greeks of the polis, to go on paying *phoros*, tribute, to him. Some of this tribute, as suggested above, would be used to meet local expenses; we may compare a land conveyance from hellenistic Sardis (Buckler and Robinson 1932 (F 594) no. 1) which shows that certain villages were liable for the upkeep of detachments of soldiers. This may be a legacy from Achaemenid practice (or from Macedonian? cf. *SEG* XIII 403 for a similar set-up in the hellenistic Macedon of Philip V).

The Aristotelian *Oeconomica*, probably an early hellenistic treatise describing Seleucid conditions, but with some Persian-looking features, distinguishes private, civic, satrapal and royal taxation (1345b7ff). We have seen that the distinction between satrapal and royal is blurred, partly because, although the satraps were obliged to forward revenues, they had their own expenses; and partly because the kinds of 'tribute' levied by Persia include obligations of a non-financial, or personal, kind: transport, requisitioned food, and liability to military service under the command of a satrap or Persian feudatory. It would be hard to say if these obligations were owed to the King or to the satrap. But the distinction between satrapal/royal tax on the one hand and civic on the other is clear and important. Two inscriptions, from Labraunda and Lagina respectively[79] record grants by local communities of tax-freedom from 'all but royal taxes' (Lagina), or confer tax-freedom on Dion of Cos (the Labraunda text) 'from royal or civic imposts' (*epigraphai*), but without prejudice to the royal *tele*, which must be paid (*tele* = 'dues', obviously different from *epigraphai*, though we cannot say how). The community honouring Dion is that of the Plataseis. These people will be calling themselves a polis by the year 319/18: *REA* 92 (1990) p. 61, a decree noted below p. 226 n. 93. And a text from Achaemenid Sinuri, a sanctuary in Caria, first published in 1945 (*Hell.* VII.63ff = M5), confers 'tax-freedom except for the *apomoira*'. The *apomoira* has long been known as a Ptolemaic royal tax (*OGIS* 90, *SEG* XII 550), and is now here attested as Achaemenid Persian.

The revelation of the debt owed by the Seleucids and the Ptolemies to Persian institutions is an interesting feature of these inscriptions; and its significance for Asia Minor is brought out elsewhere, p. 226. But for the purpose of understanding the powers of Persian satraps another aspect may be stressed: these documents are ratified by the satrap alone, they show no sign that the King was consulted. Nor should we suppose that Persian Kings, any more than Roman emperors,[80] were too grand to

---

[78] Bosworth 1980 (B 14) 280f, a different view from Hornblower 1982 (F 644) 163; see also S. M. Sherwin-White 1985 (B 175).

[79] Crampa 1972 (F 619) 42 and *SEG* XXVI 1229 (Lagina) = Hornblower 1982 (F 644) M8 and M12. See further below, p. 226.   [80] Millar 1977 (A 39).

concern themselves with trivialities like grants of citizenship or tax-exemption by the Carian Plataseis to Dion of Cos. After all, Darius II writes to the Jews at Egyptian Elephantine with astonishingly detailed orders about the keeping of the Feast of Unleavened Bread: 'word was sent from the King to Arsames saying: let there be a Passover for the Jewish garrison . . . drink no beer, and anything at all in which there is leaven do not eat, from the 15th day from sunset till the 21st day of Nisan' (Cowley, *AP* no. 21, with some editorial restoration). Possibly, like such imperial rescripts as Trajan's letter on the Christians (Pliny *Ep.* x.97) this was intended[81] to have general application to all the Jews of the empire. Persian Kings, like Roman emperors (see n. 80), may have tended to react rather than act, answering appeals via rescripts and so forth, rather than taking initiatives. Compare Tod no. 138 line 5 for a Carian delegation to Artaxerxes II, apparently leap-frogging the satrap; and perhaps (see n. 81) Darius' Elephantine letter is the product of another such appeal, as is Darius I's letter to Gadatas (M–L no. 12: above p. 54): evidently the sacred gardeners of Apollo have been complaining and the King sets inquiries on foot, line 5 ('I ascertain that . . .'). But if so, it was precisely this passivity which gave such latitude to their satraps. The satraps were the people with whom the locals had to deal, and in the satrapies for which we have good evidence they largely left these locals to their own devices. Alexander's liberation and restoration of auton-omy to Ionia (Arr. *Anab.* 1.17–18) was hollow.

It is tantalizing that we do not know how far Ionian and Carian conditions were typical. Take two extreme cases: though sixth-century *India* had been tributary, it seems[82] that 'there was by Alexander's time no memory of Persian dominion beyond the Indus' (but note that Ctesias F 45 speaks of Indian deference to Persia via gift-giving. Like the Romans, the Persian Kings could have regarded such gift-giving neighbours as *membra partesque imperii*, Suet. *Aug.* 48.) By contrast, Curtius (IV.7.1) speaks of the arrogance and avariciousness of Persian rule in *Egypt* (cf. Diodorus' very similar language about the Persian satraps in Phoenicia, XVI.41.2: Sidon). This is supported by the history of rebellion in, and the evidence for Persian economic exploitation of, this great satrapy, the spoils from which, it was said, paid for the building of Susa and Persepolis. Rostovtzeff said of Egypt that it was 'apart from Greece, the only powerful rival of Persia'.[83] India then, was lost because control was so loose (permissiveness taken to the point of abandonment); Egypt was lost through over-harsh treatment. Again, *Bactria* had been dissident in the fifth century (Diod. XI.71: 460s), so it is interesting to find Orontes, leader of the Satraps' Revolt a century later, described in a later

---

[81] Meyer 1912 (F 489) 96.
[82] Brunt 1976–83 (B 21) I 547, preferable to Vogelsang in F 47, 183ff. On Achaemenid India see Cook 1983 (F 14) 61f, 292; *CAH* IV² ch. 3d.   [83] Rostovtzeff 1953 (A 51) 82; below p. 344.

inscription as 'a Bactrian by race' (*OGIS* 264) – the phrase is emphatic and surely excludes the idea[84] that Orontes' family were mere settlers in Bactria. But Bactrians fought well at Gaugamela, and even afterwards Sogdia and Bactria were more trouble for Alexander to subdue than anywhere else. (We cannot be sure that Sogdia was no longer Achaemenid by the 330s.)[85]

We are back where we began: as with the satraps at the Granicus, so with the lords of Bactria: they put aside old animosity in defence of the system by which they were sustained on their fertile, irrigated meadows.[86] In any case, two centuries is a long time, and the local Bactrian aristocracy may have coexisted happily with Persian settlers at Bactrian Ai Khanum in Afghanistan (for such settlers cf. *SEG* XXVIII 1327, a hellenistic attestation of the Iranian name Oxybazos). Fraternization, intermarriage and religious syncretism were surely not confined to the western satrapies (for the position in these satrapies see p. 229). Such coexistence may have produced what has been called a 'dominant ethnoclass',[87] a powerful factor making for stability.

But in general our ignorance makes the picture at points east of Sardis very opaque. Thus we hear intermittently of serious revolts by the Cadusians near the Caspian (e.g. Diod. xv.8: 380s),[88] an old problem, and one surprisingly close to the Persian home. It is even more remarkable that the Uxian hillmen, who actually lived between Susa and Persepolis, had never been subject to Persia but allowed the King to pass through only on payment of a fee (Arr. *Anab.* III.17.1). Again, of the Carduchi in Southern Armenia, Xenophon says that 'a royal army of 120,000 had once invaded their country and not a man of them had got back, because of the terrible conditions of the ground they had to go through'. The details of this story are not completely convincing, and not only because of the implication that there was a standing army of this staggering size (above). But the casual mention of this fiasco, whatever really happened, is a good reminder that our knowledge of the Persian empire is not only poor, but too often derives from the Greek side.

IV. PERSIAN POLITICAL HISTORY: THE INVOLVEMENT WITH
THE GREEKS, 400–336 B.C. ·

The failure of Cyrus the Younger at the battle of Cunaxa in 401 reopened the issue of Persian policy towards the Greeks, because the Spartans had

---

[84] Cook 1983 (F 14) 193.
[85] Altheim and Stiehl 1963 (F 1) 163. For Sogdiana and Bactria, Cook 1983 (F 14) 192ff.
[86] Gardin and Gentelle 1976 (F 23); Gardin and Lyonnet 1978–9 (F 24); Gardin 1980 (F 22); cf. *CAH* IV² 183.
[87] Briant in F 40 137ff. But see the reservations of Sancisi-Weerdenburg in F 52, 267f.
[88] Syme 1988 (F 64).

helped Cyrus. Xenophon plays this down in the *Anabasis* but is more candid about it in the *Hellenica* (III.1.1). The Athenian Alcibiades (Thuc. VIII.46) had warned Tissaphernes more than a decade earlier that Persia should be careful whom she backed in the Peloponnesian War: the Athenians were old hands at imperialism, and Persia would not find it hard to reach an accommodation with them after the war. The accommodation Alcibiades had in mind would presumably have been on the lines of the Peace of Callias (*CAH* v² 121), which Athenian support of the rebel Amorges had shattered. Thucydides makes Alcibiades speak of 'partnership in rule (*arche*)', a phrase with a certain resonance to us, because picked up by Arrian to describe Alexander's policy of fusion with, once again, Persia, *Anab.* VII.11.9. Sparta, on the other hand (Alcibiades continues) came to the Peloponnesian War posing as a liberator (cf. Thuc. II.8). It would therefore be illogical of her to stop short of liberating the Asiatic Greeks from Persia once she had liberated the rest of the Greek world from Athens. So far Alcibiades. It is true that Sparta, by the end of Thucydides' narrative, has effectively abandoned her pretensions in Asia; but a strong case has been made[89] for thinking that the question was reopened in 407, and for speaking of a "Treaty of Boiotios" of that year (Xen. *Hell.* 1.4.2ff), by which the autonomy of the Greeks of Asia was conceded by Persia. (Boiotios was the name of the Spartan diplomat who negotiated this.) In other words, Alcibiades' prophecy was coming true well before the fifth century was out. The full vindication came after Cunaxa.

With Cyrus dead, Tissaphernes, now firmly reinstated as 'satrap of his own former possessions and those of Cyrus also' (Xen. *Hell.* III.1.3), mounted hostilities against the Ionian cities, which had supported Cyrus in his revolt. These cities promptly appealed to Sparta (*ibid.*), who told Tissaphernes not to commit any hostile acts against the cities, and in 400 B.C. sent out Thibron to enforce that requirement. How far fear of Sparta's Anatolian policy was a cause of the Corinthian War, fought against her in Greece by Athens, Thebes and Corinth, is a topic which lies outside the scope of this chapter (see ch. 4, pp. 97ff). But the 'liberator' Thibron was very unpopular with the cities in Asia friendly to Sparta, because he allowed his army to plunder them: Xen. *Hell.* III.1.8.

He had to be replaced by Dercyllidas. Whatever the rest of Greece felt about such behaviour, it certainly went down badly in Persia. Artaxerxes reacted strongly, ordering a fleet to be built. (He was evidently untroubled by scruples about the "Treaty of Boiotios", which had anyway been made with his predecessor and did not bind him, cf.

---

[89] Lewis 1977 (A 33) 124. *Contra*, Seager and Tuplin 1980 (c 74) 144 n. 36; Cartledge 1979 (c 282) 266 and 1987 (c 284) 189f; Westlake *JHS* 99 (1979) 195, review of Lewis 1977 (A 33); Tuplin in F 51, 133ff.

Hdt.VII.151.) More powerful with the Persian King than any opinion or feeling that the "Boiotios Treaty" had lapsed, was surely his simple personal loathing for the Spartans, those 'most shameless of men' (Dinon F 19 = Plut. *Artox.* 22.1), who had helped Cyrus (it is relevant to this that many ex-Cyran mercenaries had re-enlisted under Thibron).

There were moreover good reasons, both strategic and political, for Persia to be alarmed by an energetic Spartan presence in the south-east Mediterranean and west/south-west Asia Minor.

First, strategic: it is clear that Sparta, as early as Dercyllidas' expedition in 399–397, which follows that of Thibron, perceived the importance of naval supremacy in the south-east Aegean as a necessary precondition for a land offensive. This follows from the instructions given to Dercyllidas in 397 by the Spartan ephors to co-operate with Pharax, the Spartan *nauarch* (admiral) off Caria: Xen. *Hell.* III.2.12. Now Caria was not merely the seat of the private *oikos*, estate, of Tissaphernes (*ibid.*), and therefore a vulnerable and desirable target; it was the key to Persian control of Ionia, since the Maeander valley was the main thoroughfare joining southern Ionia to the Anatolian interior, and was more strategically important for this purpose even than the Royal Road, further to the north. This also helps to explain the importance of the island of Rhodes in the naval warfare of the 390s and 380s: the Hecatomnids of Caria later in the century needed Rhodes and her fleet for their own security – and took them. Demosthenes was to call Rhodes a 'fortress to overawe Caria' (xv.12). Conversely, when the boot was on the other foot, whoever controlled Rhodes could not afford the hostility of Caria over the water. Hence hellenistic Rhodes in her great period of hellenistic power and prosperity did well to spend money on fine ashlar fortifications for her possessions on the *peraia*, or Carian mainland opposite.

Second, political: most of our sources see the warfare of this period from too Greek a perspective; but Egypt had been in revolt since about 404 and its pharaoh, when appealed to by Sparta for an alliance, sent generous material help instead: equipment for a hundred triremes, and 500 measures of grain (Diod. XIV.79), which however went astray. As pointed out in an earlier volume (*CAH* III².3,39), with a reference to this very passage, the 'equipment' referred to probably included papyrus for cordage, something Greeks could always do with. A Spartan–Egyptian axis was, for Persia, a threat indeed. An Athenian–Egyptian one, such as in fact materialized (Ar. *Plut.* 179) later in the war when the political alignments shifted, was no better. So, when Diodorus implies, rightly, that one of the King's motives for imposing the peace of 386 was to have a free hand against revolted Cyprus (XIV.110), he could have added 'and against Egypt'. This was especially true since Evagoras of Cyprus was himself another ally of Egypt (Diod. xv.2.3), and like the Spartans a decade earlier got a consignment of Egyptian grain, supplies and triremes: *ibid.* 3.3.[90]

No wonder, then, that, as early as 397, the Great King, through Pharnabazus the satrap of Hellespontine Phrygia, ordered a full-scale naval armament, appointing the Athenian Conon (*CAH* v² 495) as admiral, *nauarch.* See Diod. xiv.39.2, where however a wrong date (399) is given. That 397 is the right date is certain. It follows from three pieces of evidence. First, a fragment of Philochorus (*FGrH* 328 f 144/5) mentions Conon's appointment and is dated to the Athenian archon-year 397/6. Second, Isocrates (iv.142) says that the Battle of Cnidus, which is dated by an eclipse to August 394, happened three years after the Persian rearmament. And third, in 396 Herodas the Syracusan was able to bring news to Sparta of massive Persian preparations, by now well under way: Xen. *Hell.* iii.4.1ff, cf. *CAH* iii².3,11.

Herodas' news caused a Spartan expedition to be sent to Asia, under the new king, Agesilaus. The outbreak of the Corinthian War, the stab in the back which, on Xenophon's interpretation, brought Agesilaus home again, was only a year away (395). But there is one more event which is needed before we can explain why Athens and other Greek states were prepared to tackle Sparta in mainland Greece. After all, the Battle of Cnidus, which halted the Spartan naval offensive off Caria, was in 394, but war had broken out a year earlier, in 395. How then could the enemies of Sparta feel so confident of success in 395? The answer, as so often in the late fifth and early fourth centuries, lies in an event known from the Diodoran not the Xenophontic tradition. The key event was the revolt of Rhodes from Sparta in 396 (Diod. xiv.79.6, confirmed by *Hell. Oxy.* xv: Conon said to be in charge of Rhodes in 395). This was the first really solid success against Sparta in that part of the world; hitherto the honours had been the other way, with Conon besieged by Pharax in 397 at Carian Caunus. The change of pattern between 397 and 396 is easily explained: ships take time to build and it was not until they were finished (Diod. xiv.79.5) that Conon could be relieved by the newly completed fleet. Then the Rhodians saw which way the wind was blowing, and they revolted. An Athenian general, albeit a Persian admiral in name, had now, eight years after the defeat of Athens at the Battle of Aegospotami, won a major moral and strategic victory over Sparta, foreshadowing the more concrete victory at Cnidus in 394. It adds to the piquancy that Conon was actually a fugitive from Aegospotami, having taken refuge afterwards with Evagoras of Cyprus. The appeal of the Thebans to Athens in 395 would have been ineffective, whatever the prospective attractions of empire (Xen. *Hell.* III.5.10), if it had not already been known at Athens that Rhodes' allegiance had changed and that Conon was beginning to look like a winner. It was a Rhodian, a man called Timocrates, who was sent by Pharnabazus in 396, perhaps after and because of the Rhodian revolution,[91] with Persian money to induce Athens to fight Sparta. (If Timocrates' mission belongs in 397 – the alternative chronology[92] – it would be too early for events in his home state, though not for a general Rhodian strategic perspective, to be relevant. But if as has sometimes been held[93] Timocrates made a second Athenian visit in 395, the persuasiveness of his Persian gold could after all have been enhanced, on that occasion, by arguments from recent events. Timocrates may conceivably have been an exile, but it is surprising that his origins have excited virtually no ancient or modern comment.[94] For a Rhodian honoured at Athens in 394–3 see *IG* II² 19.)

Timocrates and his gold became a famous bribery scandal, a motive for the Corinthian War which the Oxyrhynchus Historian, ch. VII, discounts, by comparison with the 'truest cause' (cf. Thuc. 1.23) of fear of Sparta. But that historian is right against Xenophon (III.5.2) to say that money was accepted at Athens. 'It is certain that the fleet which won the Battle of Cnidus was paid, however erratically, with Persian money and built in Persian-controlled harbours.'[95]

But to speak of the outcome of the Battle of Cnidus is to anticipate. We left Agesilaus departing for Asia. His place of embarkation was Aulis opposite Euboea. This was not the obvious place from the practical point of view, but was chosen for symbolic reasons: it was where Agamemnon had left for Troy, after sacrificing his daughter Iphigenia. (Sparta's propaganda had long stressed an affinity with Agamemnon and Orestes: Hdt. 1.67.8; VII.159.) Like Agamemnon, Agesilaus (Xen. *Hell.* III.4.4), made a solemn though less drastic sacrifice for his oriental invasion, or he tried to, until he was prevented by the jealous magistrates of federal Boeotia. The implication here, that Agesilaus was making a bid for Asia i.e. the Persian empire, is spelt out by Xenophon at *Ages.* 1.8. Elsewhere (*Hell.* IV.1.41, the last fling in 394), Xenophon's formulation is even more extreme and explicit: Agesilaus was 'planning to march as far as possible into the interior with the idea of detaching from the King all the nations through which he should pass'. But straight after his arrival at Ephesus, Agesilaus tried to come to terms with Tissaphernes on a footing of 'autonomy for the Greeks of Asia'. In other words, he was suggesting a return to something like the Peace of Callias, only with

---

[91] Seager 1967 (C 250) 95 n. 2.   [92] Bruce 1967 (B 20).
[93] Bruce 1967 (B 20) 60; Hamilton 1979 (C 294) 207 n. 76.
[94] Beloch 1912–27 (A 5) III² 2.216, whom Seager 1967 (C 250) follows, perhaps makes the point obliquely.   [95] Lewis 1977 (A 33) 143.

Persia and Sparta, rather than Persia and Athens, as the principals (Xen. *Hell.* III.4.5; *Ages.* 1.10 adds that the truce was to be for three months initially).

The inconsistency between the pomp and pretensions of the Aulis sacrifice and the reality of Agesilaus' diplomacy can be, and has been explained in a number of ways, not all exclusive. We can say either, that bargaining often does involve a climb-down from an impossible position. Or, that Agesilaus was really inviting a return to the "Treaty of Boiotios", cf. above, and that this would make Spartan policy, apart from the Aulis incident, consistent and intelligible over a longer period (cf. Xen. *Hell.* III.2.20 for Dercyllidas). Or, that Aulis tells us less about Agesilaus' 'panhellenist', i.e. anti-Persian, sentiments than about Xenophon's own. (This may well be true, but Xenophon surely did not invent the historical fact of the sacrifice.) Or, finally, we can say[96] that Agesilaus' aim was always different from the conquest of Asia. It was no more (and no less) than to create 'a buffer zone of rebel satraps and tribes' (cf. generally *Hell.* IV.1 for Paphlagonia and elsewhere) 'between the territory still controlled by the King and that of the Greek cities on the seaboard'. That would account for Agesilaus' invitation to Pharnabazus to secede (cf. p. 72 on *Hell.* IV.1.36), and perhaps also for Agesilaus' guest-friendship, *xenia*, with the young Mausolus of Caria, son of the Hecatomnus who was soon to be promoted satrap.[97] (See Xen. *Ages.* II.26 for this *xenia*, describing events of the 360s; but the *xenia* is there said to have existed 'beforehand' and could date from much earlier, in fact from the mid 390s.) Hecatomnus was to give the King very half-hearted and even treacherous help against Evagoras of Cyprus, whom he secretly supplied with money (Diod. xv.2). Agesilaus' visit to Asia had perhaps sowed a seed of disaffection.

Such guest-friendships, and the fellow-feeling which they presuppose between upper-class Greeks and Persians, run through the writings of Xenophon, despite his 'panhellenist' propaganda against Persia. Fellow-feeling of that kind deserves to be stressed not just as an aspect of social and cultural fusion (ch. 8*a*), but because it surely affected policy. We should, however, remember not just the obvious qualification made at Xen. *Hell.* IV.1.34 (guest-friends sometimes kill each other when their city's interests require it) but also the actual history of one such relationship: a hereditary Spartan *proxenia* (consulate) in the family of Alcibiades was made, renounced and reactivated by different generations (Thuc. v.43, vi.89). Nevertheless, if Artaxerxes' personal hatred of Sparta helps to explain his hostility to her on the political level in the 390s, the 'long-standing guest-friendship' between the Persian satrap

[96] Seager 1977 (C 315) (cf. Kelly 1978 (C 299)); Lewis 1977 (A 13) 154ff; Cartledge 1987 (C 284) 193.
[97] Herman 1987 (C 34) for guest-friendship generally, but not this one.

Ariobarzanes and the Spartan Antalcidas (Xen. *Hell.* v.1.28) helps to explain why the Great King in 387/6 accepted peace on terms nearly identical to those he had refused in 392/1 (p. 74). Political *homonoia*, harmony or fusion, between Greeks and Persians was no more Alexander's invention than was social or cultural fusion; and this is relevant to the problem (to which a final answer must be given in another chapter, p. 840) whether Alexander could have hoped for such political *homonoia*. If we recall that Artabazus (son of the Pharnabazus who is so prominent in Thucydides book VIII) spent years at the court of Philip II (Diod. XVI.52) before eventually being made Alexander's satrap of Bactria, we will find it easy to suppose that Alexander knew something of *homonoia* before he ever set out for Asia. Finally, no hatreds were permanent. Not Artaxerxes' for Sparta, as we have seen; nor even Athens' for Persia. How far Demosthenes or others looked to Persia against Macedon in the 340s and 330s is a question lying outside this chapter (though see p. 93), but one item may be cited. By the time of Artabazus' appointment to Bactria, Athens passed a decree, Tod no. 199 = Harding no. 119 of 327 B.C., which would have surprised Thucydides (less so Xenophon or any other historian of the victory at Cnidus in 394, won by the Athenian Conon with Persian forces). The decree calls Pharnabazus a 'benefactor of Athens and helper in her wars'. As a speaker in Polybius says (v.104), even the freedom to fight one's own wars looks like a luxury when you have lost it. There were worse people than Persians.

Whatever the reasons for Agesilaus' readiness to do a deal, there was no deal: Tissaphernes asked the Persian King for an army (see above, p. 56 for what this might mean), and the result was the Battle of Sardis, a Persian defeat. Xenophon on the one hand, and the alternative tradition represented by Diodorus and the Oxyrhynchus Historian on the other, give discrepant accounts of this engagement. Both Xenophon and the alternative tradition[98] have modern defenders; neither can be thrown out without qualms, but one of them must be. In Xenophon, Agesilaus marches directly from Ephesus to Sardis, and in the absence of Tissaphernes there is a cavalry battle, a straight fight with no mention of an ambush. In the alternative tradition (Diod. XIV.80; *Hell. Oxy.* XI) Agesilaus first strikes north via Mount Sipylus and thence east to Sardis, in a hollow square formation because he was being harried by Tissaphernes; he ravages the outskirts of Sardis, Xen. *Ages.* 1.33. Then he turned back to a point midway between Sardis and a place called Thybarna and ambushed Tissaphernes. (For Thybarna see p. 56 above; 'turned back' rules out a position for Thybarna in the immediate Castollus region further east.) It is in Xenophon's favour that in his

---

98 Anderson 1974 (B 4); Cawkwell 1979 (B 26) 405ff; Gray 1979 (B 47); Cartledge 1987 (C 284) 215; Hamilton 1991 (C 295) 99 n. 50.

account the achievement of his hero Agesilaus is actually less spectacular (cavalry only; Tissaphernes absent) than on the alternative account; but the ambush is decisive in favour of the alternative account (which we must therefore prefer as a whole, after eliminating blemishes like Diodorus' tenfold magnification – 600/6,000 – of the Persian losses). Like Alexander (Arr. *Anab.* III.10.2), Agesilaus could not be allowed to have 'stolen a victory', and this is why Xenophon suppresses the ambush. (Xenophon was not consistent about this, because he does sometimes report stratagems by Agesilaus involving deceit, *Hell.* III.4.11 and v.4.48.) Finally, a chronological point: Xenophon is wrong to link the Sardis defeat and Tissaphernes' downfall as cause and effect. More time than that must be allowed for the appointment of Tissaphernes' successor as satrap of Lydia, namely the 'chiliarch'[99] Tithraustes. So the dissatisfaction felt with Tissaphernes by the Persians at Sardis, and at the royal court, must have antedated his most conspicuous failure on the field (cf. above, p. 57).

This was the high point of Agesilaus' Asiatic achievement. Tithraustes' first move, after cutting off Tissaphernes' head (through the agency of Ariaeus, for whom see below, p. 78) was to offer Agesilaus something similar to the deal rejected by Tissaphernes. What Tithraustes now suggested was that the Greek cities in Asia should, first, be autonomous, but, second, they should *pay the ancient tribute*: Xen. *Hell.* III.4.25. The addition this time of the formula about 'ancient tribute' makes more explicit the aim of a return to the position in the middle of the fifth century. At that time Persia probably did not abandon her claims to the revenues of Asia, despite the Peace of Callias.[100] Agesilaus, however, said that he was not competent to accept this offer without reference to the Spartan government at home, and Tithraustes then urged him to move on to Pharnabazus' territory and ravage that instead, until orders came from Sparta.

Why did Agesilaus refuse Tithraustes' 'autonomy' offer? His doubts about what the Spartan government would swallow must, if sincere, be confined to the second clause, about tribute: earlier on, during the negotiations with Tissaphernes (III.4.5), Agesilaus had evidently felt competent, without further instructions from Sparta, to climb down from grand invasion plans to mere 'autonomy for the cities'. If this is right, Agesilaus, we may feel, was splitting hairs. Alternatively, it has been held[101] that it was Tithraustes, not Agesilaus, who was insincere, and that the satrap was practising the old politics of procrastination familiar from the last decade of the Peloponnesian War. But this will not quite do: Xenophon explicitly says that the offer came from the King,[102]

[99] Lewis 1977 (A 33) 17ff and n. 96; Cook 1983 (F 14) 143ff.   [100] Murray 1966 (F 687).
[101] Judeich 1892 (F 663) 68.   [102] Judeich 1892 (F 663) speaks only of Tithraustes.

not his mouthpiece Tithraustes. Perhaps the explanation of Agesilaus' refusal should be sought, not in the proposed treaty clauses, but in the obvious but sometimes[103] neglected demand which precedes Tithraustes' offer. 'The King *requires that you should sail home*, and that the cities ...' etc. Tissaphernes, in the earlier phase of diplomacy, had spoken as if sailing home was merely something that Agesilaus himself might wish to do. Dercyllidas, even earlier, had been invited more or less frankly to go home, III.2.20. But it is in Tithraustes' mouth that the Persian demand becomes absolute.

But Agesilaus, flushed with the victory at Sardis, did not feel like sailing home, and perhaps could not do so without authority: when orders from Sparta do arrive (para. 27) nothing is said about autonomy or the ancient tribute, but only about what is to happen to the Spartan fleet and army. So perhaps as early as this, the future of Spartan power in Asia, not the status of the Greek cities, was what exercised the Spartan government, and Agesilaus guessed as much when he declared himself unable, on his own authority, to settle things with Tithraustes.

Even after he reached Pharnabazus' country, Agesilaus' own intentions remain hard to ascertain. On the one hand, he tried to detach Pharnabazus from his allegiance, *Hell.* IV.1 – but that chapter ends with one of the strongest statements in all Xenophon of Agesilaus' intention to 'go as far east as he could' (the whole passage is quoted above, p. 68. It refers to spring 394). So it is unclear right to the end of his stay in Asia whether his thinking was genuinely panhellenist or whether Xenophon was exaggerating and Agesilaus merely intended to cut off the western satrapies.[104] Agesilaus' reluctance (endorsed by the home government) to quit Asia may have concealed personal motives as well: he had made some friendships in Asia, not just the young Mausolus but the sons of Pharnabazus and of Spithridates as well (for the latter see *Hell. Oxy.* XXI.4, but contrast Xen. *Ages.* v.4). And in Asia he had enjoyed 'conscious mastery of men and events', to borrow Syme's phrase about Julius Caesar's psychologically liberating decade in Gaul.[105] If the options in 394 were conquest of Persia or co-operation with individual Persians, Agesilaus may have been genuinely torn.

His dilemma, if there was one, was solved for him by events in Greece, namely the beginnings of the Corinthian War (recounted elsewhere in this volume) which led to his recall. Before leaving for Pharnabazus' satrapy, Agesilaus had appointed his brother-in-law Peisander to the command of the fleet.[106] In Agesilaus' absence from Asia, the eighty-five Spartan triremes engaged Pharnabazus' and Conon's fleet of 170, now

[103] E.g. by Judeich.   [104] Cawkwell 1979 (B 26) 193, cf. 1976 (C 285) 71.
[105] R. Syme, *The Roman Revolution* (Oxford, 1939) 53.
[106] Cawkwell 1976 (C 285) 67 n. 24 defends Xenophon's chronology.

ready at last; and the result of the Battle of Sardis was reversed at sea off Caria in a Spartan disaster, the Battle of Cnidus. Xenophon could not bring himself to recount it. (*Hell.* IV.8.1 is the barest mention.) Diodorus (XIV.83) records the capture of fifty Spartan triremes and 500 crew.

The Battle of Cnidus is a break in two ways, historical and historiographical. (Theopompus recognized this, when he ended his *Hellenica* at this point: Diod. XIV.84.7.)

First, historiographic. With Agesilaus back in Greece, and the Spartan fleet defeated, Xenophon's narrative in the *Hellenica* has not much more to say in detail about Asia Minor. Diodorus' Persian and satrapal material, even when it is derived from parts of Ephorus not enriched by Ephorus' own use of the Oxyrhynchus Historian, is precious, and noticeably better than his offerings for the fifth century; and Diodorus gives some satrapal dates from an independent, reasonably well-informed 'chronographic source'.[107] But Diodorus was a Sicilian, and his distribution of attention in books XIV and XV, though welcome to the modern historian of Dionysius and Sicily, has led to severe abbreviation of Ephorus' Anatolian and Persian material. (This, it should be said, is true of the whole period from 404 on.) In general, after 394 and still more after 386, we have to make progressively more use of incidental literary references, with help from inscriptions. This is a procedure which makes Persian and satrapal history seem more jerky and episodic from now on. Thus the so-called Revolt of the Satraps surely lasted several years, but is described by Diodorus (improbably but characteristically under one year, 362) in just three chapters, amounting to about the same quantity of Greek as the one long chapter which Xenophon devotes to a few months of campaigning on Corcyra in 373/2 by Mnasippus and Iphicrates (*Hell.* VI.2). It is unlikely (but see below) that Diodorus' brevity of treatment here is a reliable index of the episode's importance.

Second, historical: the events of 394 ended a wholly anomalous period of alliance between Athens and Persia. The victory at Cnidus was not the first manifestation of revived Athenian imperialism, but it was the most spectacular so far. Henceforth, Sparta and Persia had a common interest in the repression of that imperialism; in other words there was a return to the alignments of the Ionian War. Every Athenian success made it more urgent for Persia and Sparta to 'settle their diplomatic differences'.[108]

The changes did not however come about immediately or smoothly: there is an impression of jerkiness about Persian policy towards Greece from 394 to 386 which is not just the fault of the sources.

At first, Persia and Athens, or rather Pharnabazus and Conon, continue to co-operate, taking advantage of what Diodorus sweepingly

---

[107] See Hornblower 1990 (C 366) 74 and nn. [108] Lewis 1977 (A 33) 147 for this phrase.

calls Spartan loss of sea-power, XIV.84.4: their successes in winning allies
in Asia and the islands are listed in that chapter (reading 'Telos' for
'Teos').[109] As will be explained later (ch. 8a, p. 216), epigraphic evidence
(*SEG* XXVI 1282 = Harding 28A) suggests that the Persian and Athenian
promises of autonomy to Ionia (Xen. *Hell.* IV.8.1) were not after all
empty, despite the existence at this time of a 'satrap of Ionia' attested in
Tod no. 113 (= Harding no. 24) of *c*.392.[110] (An independent 'alliance'
coinage of the east Aegean and islands may also belong here.)[111] This
shrewd behaviour by Persia weakened in advance any serious effort by
Sparta to recover her standing as liberator in Asia Minor. But what really
precluded Spartan operations in the east Aegean was the voyage (Xen.
Hell. IV.8.8) of Pharnabazus and Conon to Spartan waters, where they
established a garrison and governor on the offshore island of Cythera.[112]
That must have shaken Spartan morale badly so soon after the abortive
helot rising known as the Cinadon affair (*ibid.*, III.3).[113] Throughout the
fifth century, Spartan foreign policy had fluctuated between aggression
and timidity as the threat of helot disloyalty advanced or receded; and the
puncturing of Spartan imperialism abroad, by means of helots at home,
was no secret to Pharnabazus or Conon. They were after all both
veterans of the great Peloponnesian War: each man first appeared in
history in the year (413) of Demosthenes' similarly motivated landing
opposite, precisely, Cythera (Thuc. VII.26). Some Persian sling-bullets
have been published from Anticythera, the smaller island to the south,
bearing the King's 'signature'. They are presumably a relic of this period
(*Arch. Rep. for 1974–75* p. 42).

The result was that Sparta sued for peace (392/1), sending Antalcidas
to Tiribazus (for whose status see below, p. 77f). The sources are
Andocides III *On the Peace* and Xenophon *Hell.* IV.8.[114] The terms offered
involved the complete sell-out of the Greeks in Asia (Xen. *Hell.* IV.8.14):
the islands and cities of Greece were to be autonomous, and Sparta
would not fight Persia for the Greeks in Asia. Antalcidas the Spartan
offered these terms to Tiribazus, rightly describing them as 'a peace such
as the King desired' (Xenophon). This errs only on the side of
understatement.

Diplomatically, at least between Sparta and Persia, the position which
had now been reached was exactly the same as that represented by the
King's Peace of 386. Why then did negotiations break down as they did?

---

[109] Marshall 1905 (C 200) 2 n. 4 and Robert 1969–90 (B 172) I 569ff.

[110] But see Petit 1988 (F 693) 310, who thinks Strouthas is called 'satrap of Ionia' in Tod no.
113 = Harding no. 24 merely because he is handling Ionian business at the time.

[111] Cawkwell 1956 (B 189); 1963 (B 190); Cook 1961 (B 191 = F 608).

[112] Coldstream and Huxley 1972 (C 287) 39.   [113] Cartledge 1987 (C 284) 362.

[114] Badian 1991 (F 4) argues against the usual view that Philochorus F 149 relates to the 392
attempt at peace, rather than to the King's Peace proper of 386.

Persia's position is the least logical of that of any of the principals to the affair. Tiribazus urged Artaxerxes to accept the 392 terms. These were first proposed at Sardis; Andocides omits this stage. They were then considered by the other Greek states at Sparta, a stage which Xenophon the panhellenist admirer of Sparta omits. (The order Sardis–Sparta is the likelier one; the order Sparta–Sardis would have involved Persia, inconceivably, in considering the consequences of a *Greek* decision.)[115] Tiribazus was right, but the king would not see it. So the Spartan proposals were not ratified. Why not? The answer must lie in Artaxerxes' hatred of Sparta for helping Cyrus the Younger's revolt (p. 66). Practical politics would soon require that that hatred should be given up. But for the moment Strouthas or Strouses was sent down instead of Tiribazus (Xen. *Hell.* IV.8.17, cf. Tod no. 113) to carry on the war against Sparta. Sparta sent out Thibron again to Asia Minor.

Sparta's position is simplest: combined Athenian-Persian hostility meant that she had to fight on.

Then there is Athens. It was Athens' refusal to accept the decision taken at Sparta which caused negotiations to break down at the Greek end. Why did she refuse? First, there is some evidence for anti-Persian feeling at Athens.[116] We should not make too much of this,[117] but the alliance of Athens and Persia during the years before 392 had certainly been an unusual one. A fragment of Athenian honours to Evagoras of Cyprus (*SEG* xxix 86 + Tod no. 109) may show that already in 393 the Athenians, by using extravagant language about Evagoras as a Greek benefactor of Greece, were seeking to disguise from themselves the Persian aspect of the Cnidus victory: Evagoras had given a refuge to Conon and had introduced him to Pharnabazus, and it was more congenial to stress Evagoras' role than that of Pharnabazus.

Second, there was Athens' desire (Andoc. III.12ff; 36) to get back the old 'overseas possessions . . . and debts' (i.e. money lent under the fifth-century empire by individual Athenians to individuals in the allied states, no doubt at high rates of interest: Androtion in Tod no. 152 = Harding no. 68, of perhaps the 360s, is praised for making *interest-free* loans, no doubt because this was something unusual). The details of Athens' attempts to realize this aim over the next forty years belong to Athenian history, but not exclusively. After all, Persia and her satraps had good cause for alarm at this Athenian programme of recovery, in its private as well as its public aspects (the fifth-century private possessions of rich Athenians had included land in the Persian Troad at a place called Ophryneum); and the satraps were later to capitalize on the general

[115] But see Badian 1991 (F 4) 33: agnostic.
[116] Jacoby comm. on Philochorus F 149, at 517; Lewis 1977 (A 33) 86 and n. 19. Cf. Isoc. IV.157.
[117] Finley 1985 (A 18) 80.

mistrust of Athens, a mistrust which her territorial ambitions aroused among her allies and others in the period of, and well before, the Social War of 357–355. It is also relevant to Athenian attitudes that Conon's fleet passed to Athens (Clark 1990 (B 138) 58), a boost to Athenian confidence.

One of Tiribazus' last actions before his supersession had been to imprison Conon (Xen. *Hell.* IV.8.16) who had been associated with the Sardis proposals. More vigorous and openly anti-Persian policies now prevailed at Athens. These were associated with the name of Thrasybulus; they can be described here only to the extent that they affect Persia directly. That extent is not negligible.

One immediate consequence of the breakdown of the 392 negotiations was the help (ten ships) sent by Athens, perhaps as early as 391,[118] to Evagoras of Cyprus, now in revolt from Persia: Athens' policy here had been adumbrated by the honours conferred in 393, see above. In a celebrated passage, Xenophon comments (*Hell.* IV.8.24) on the paradoxical character of Athens' actions: the King's allies were helping the King's enemy. The point of this remark is not much weakened by the possibility[119] that the ships were sent before Evagoras went into open hostility. The original ten ships were captured, but immediately afterwards, Thrasybulus was sent out with forty triremes, a more formidable force: his mission was in response to an appeal from Rhodian democrats (Xen. *Hell.* IV.8.25) after a Rhodian counter-revolution (Diod. XIV.97) supported by Sparta. Given the importance of Rhodes, which we have examined, Diodorus' remark (above) about the destruction of Spartan sea-power at Cnidus had been a little premature. Successful elsewhere in gaining or recovering allies for Athens (Thasos, Samothrace, Byzantium, Mytilene, Chios, etc.), Thrasybulus could do nothing about Rhodes; and it was the Spartan possession of the two great corn-routes, Egypt via Rhodes (cf. Dem. LVI and Thuc. VIII.35.2) and the Hellespont (below) which explain why Athens would have to agree to the King's Peace.

But from Persia's point of view the most annoying Thrasybulan successes were those which affected her own cities and *chora*, territory, on the Asiatic mainland. A speech of Lysias (XXVIII) shows Thrasybulus exacting money from Halicarnassus, an Asiatic polis. That was not quite what Persia had in mind by Pharnabazus' promises of 'autonomy' (above); and Thrasybulus was killed at Pamphylian Aspendus, a startlingly long way round the south coast of Asia Minor. He was evidently up to the same extortionate game there: Xen. *Hell.* IV.8.30. His exactions did not stop at that: from an inscription (Tod no. 114 = Harding no. 26) honouring Clazomenae, an Ionian island which could however be

[118] Cawkwell 1976 (C 112) 274.   [119] *Ibid.*

regarded as a kind of *peninsular* site (below), i.e. one in the King's ancestral Asia, we learn that Athens had levied a '5 per cent tax in the time of Thrasybulus'. Putting that together with the help to Evagoras of Cyprus, we will not be surprised to find that in the King's Peace precisely those two places[120] are singled out as exceptions to the autonomy of the islands. (Clazomenae's position, joined to the mainland by a causeway of probably hellenistic construction, and in modern times housing a quarantine station,[121] perhaps made its status ambiguous. But the ambiguity was not allowed to extend to the political sphere, hence Persia's emphatic claim to the place.) There is to be no mistake: these two places are to be *Persian* possessions. As the last of Persia's irritations, we should not forget the Athenian alliance with rebel Egypt (above).

Finally the Persians realize their true interests. Strouses or Strouthas, with his anti-Spartan mission, is superseded by Tiribazus, who thus reappears at the beginning of *Hellenica* book v. (Xenophon, as so often, merely leaves us to infer the truth, in this instance Tiribazus' reappointment.) The supersession of Strouses was surely a direct consequence of Thrasybulus' depredations at places like Halicarnassus in Caria. (Caria, like Ionia, and for similar reasons, gets separate satrapal status about now.) The reason is that Thrasybulus' oppressions surely made the Persians see that Athens must be compelled explicitly to abandon all claims to the Asiatic mainland. (In view of this, the good relations between Athens and Persia which Xenophon implies at *Hell.* iv.8.27, cannot have lasted long.)

The satrapal dispositions of this period deserve a word, because not all the appointees are territorial satraps of the normal type. The view taken here is that Tissaphernes' replacement in 395, the chiliarch Tithraustes, was briefly caretaker satrap of the normal territorial satrapy of *Lydia*. He was succeeded (we do not know exactly when) by the Autophradates whom Theopompus (*FGrH* 115 F 103) says was satrap of Lydia *c*.390, and who was still satrap of Lydia in 362, a long tenure (Diod. xv.90). During the later 390s and early 380s, however, there was, running parallel to the tenure of the ordinary Lydian satrapy, and co-ordinate with or better super-ordinate to it, a short series of non-territorial satraps with special powers in the west. Tiribazus was succeeded by Strouses, who was succeeded by Tiribazus again. Tiribazus is the 'King's general', in control of 'Ionia' (Xen. *Hell.* iv.8.12; v.1.28, unless – an old suggestion[122] – we read *choras* for *Ionias* in the latter passage, 'territory' instead of 'Ionia'). Strouses is described in Tod no. 113 (= Harding no. 24) as 'satrap of Ionia'; *not* Lydia as a modern reconstruction[123] makes

[120] Ryder 1965 (c 67).   [121] Cook 1953/4 (F 601).

[122] Krumbholz 1883 (F 670) 67; cf. Petit 1988 (F 693) 310 n. 22. Cf. Hornblower 1982 (F 644) 37 n. 11.   [123] Cawkwell 1976 (c 112) n. 19.

him. That this is an anomalous appointment, and that 'Ionia' means something particular (see ch. 8*a*, p. 216) is shown by Xenophon's description of Strouses, whom he calls Strouthas, as 'looking after the affairs of the coast' (*Hell.* IV.8.17). After the King's Peace of 386, the need for such western Anatolian appointments with special powers comes to an end, and Tiribazus' extraordinary mandate, his *maius imperium* to use an anachronistic but apt Roman expression, is exercised in *southern* Anatolia instead. He is given the 'supreme command' (Diod. XV.8.2), based apparently in Cilicia, for the war against Cyprus. (For the later position of Ionia see p. 216 below.)

The satrapal tenure of *Greater Phrygia* in the Anatolian interior is a blank to us between the beginning of the fourth century and Atizyes in 334 (Arr. *Anab.* 1.25.3). The Arsames mentioned by Polyaenus (VII.28) is undated even as to his century; and another Tithraustes attested in the 350s is surely resident not in this but in Hellespontine Phrygia on the coast, and is anyway not a satrap.[124] He is certainly not the same man as the Tithraustes who was satrap of Lydia in the 390s. Other problems are raised by Ariaeus, who helped that Tithraustes to kill Tissaphernes (above). The question is, was he a territorial satrap or just an agent of other satraps? He is usually, but wrongly, held to have been satrap of Greater Phrygia in 395. (His position in 400, to which Xen. *Hell.* IV.1.27 is just a back reference, is not relevant here.) It is true that Diodorus calls Ariaeus 'a certain satrap' at XIV.80 (where Ariaeus' name is a very plausible emendation for 'of Larissa').[125] But this cannot be pressed, especially in the light of 'a certain'; and Polyaenus (VII.16) may imply parity of esteem for Ariaeus with both Tissaphernes and Tithraustes. But in the *Hellenica Oxyrhynchia* (XIX), Ariaeus looks more like a subordinate of Tithraustes than a colleague at the territorial satrapal level: he is there bracketed with an unknown figure called Pasiphernes, both men being appointed by Tithraustes as 'generals to deal with the current situation'. Diodorus also (above) says that Tithraustes worked 'through' Ariaeus to bring about Tissaphernes' death; this may be another indication of inferiority. Further evidence of a kind is to be found in the very fragmentary thirteenth chapter of the *Hellenica Oxyrhynchia*: if Ariaeus is the name of one of the 'best of generals' there mentioned at para. 2 line

---

[124] Hornblower 1982 (F 644) 144 n. 57. (but Beloch is there misrepresented: he says that T. is satrap of Greater Phrygia). The view of Cook 1983 (F 14) 172ff that Greater Phrygia was not a satrapy at all fails because of Atizyes. On the satrapy list at Xen. *An.* VII.8.25 (which mentions an Artakames satrap of Greater Phrygia) see Cook 1983 (F 14) 82. Xen. *Cyr.* II.2.5., VIII.6.7 also has an Artakames satrap of Phrygia (whence *An.*?) which is at least evidence of a kind for the existence of the satrapy, though hardly evidence that Artakames is himself historical, *contra*, Beloch 1912–27 (A 5) III² 2.152. Note also Andrewes 1971 (C 275) 209 n. 9 and Sekunda in F 53 110ff.

[125] The emendation is by Paulmier and is clearly right; it removes the basis for Briant in F 47 16 and n. 31; F 40, 161 and n. 39. See Hornblower 1990 (F 36) 93.

35, that could support the view here taken. But the original editors were doubtful about the traces of the name. Finally, if Ariaeus was really satrap of Greater Phrygia, he was not taking his domestic duties very seriously by the time of Xen. *Hell.* IV.1.27, when we find him at Sardis, 'minding the shop' for Tithraustes against the arrivals of both Tiribazus as 'King's general' (above) and of Autophradates as satrap of Lydia in the normal way (Theopompus, above).

For the other satrapies and districts of Asia Minor see ch. 8*a*, pp. 217ff. This is a good place to make a general point. We should not think of the satrapies of Asia Minor (and this is no doubt true of other parts of the empire also) as covering the map of Anatolia completely, capable of being inked in different colours like the modern *vilayets* of Turkey. There were areas and peoples which at times it would be hard or positively wrong to attribute to any one satrap: Pisidia (p. 219), Mysia (not a satrapy itself, p. 220), parts of Cappadocia (p. 220f), Lycia (dynastic in the early fourth century, but subsumed under Hecatomnid Caria by 337, presumably with royal permission; see p. 218f); the Pamphylians (a rebellious *ethnos* or tribal people in the 360s, Diod. XV.90, and containing a city, Phaselis, which treats with Mausolus as an equal, Bengtson, *SdA* = M10). A satrap who could make his writ run in these areas might expect to get away with it, as far as the King's approval went. Finally, the case of Tralles, put in Caria at Xen. *Hell.* III.2.19 (cf. for the 340s Robert, 1936 (B 169) no. 96), but in Ionia by Diodorus (XIV.36.3) perhaps suggests that boundaries were fluid (rather than vague): these things were subject to adjustment. There were however some clear and firm frontiers, like the Oxus River which divides Sogdia and Bactria, Strabo XI.11.2. Between one Roman province and another there were customs posts, so that you knew where you were. We do not hear of this in Achaemenid Persia. None of all this means that we should be defeatist about trying to ascertain which satrap ruled what, and when. Mausolus knew what he meant when he spoke of 'the land which Mausolus rules' (Crampa 1972 (F 619) no. 40).

In *Hellespontine Phrygia*, Pharnabazus had been succeeded (Xen. *Hell.* V.1.28) by the beginning of the 380s by Ariobarzanes, who may have been a usurper satrap. Or rather, perhaps, a caretaker with official sanction. At any rate he helped to bring about the King's Peace, by helping his guest-friend Antalcidas (cf. p. 69f above) to seal off the Hellespont and its corn-route, and so threaten Athens with starvation 'as once before' (Xen. *Hell.* V.1.29. This is a more or less explicit back-reference to Aegospotami). Now that both the Hellespont and Rhodes were in hostile possession, Athens' hand was played out and she accepted the Peace on the terms given at Xen. *Hell.* V.1.28: the cities of Asia were to be the King's, including the 'islands' Cyprus and Clazomenae (inverted commas because of Clazomenae, cf. above), while the other Greek cities, great and small, with the exception of three Athenian cleruchies, were to be autonomous. If either side declined these terms, the King would make war on them by land and sea, with ships and with money.

A more detailed document[126] may have contained very specific requirements, like a stipulation that Athens pull down the gates of Piraeus, as well as more general rules about the taking back of exiles. (But the Peace did not, it seems, restrict Athenian naval activity.) More relevant for the history of Persia and Asia Minor is the likelihood (ch. 4, p. 118) that by the terms of the King's Peace the fertile mainland possessions, *peraiai*, of islands like Tenedos, Chios, Samos and Rhodes passed to Persian control in 386 as part of 'royal Asia'. This must have been a blow to the economies of these islands, and must be relevant to their absence of vigour in face of satrapal infiltration over the next decade – all except Samos, where Athens moved in instead. Chios and Mytilene perhaps tried to recover their *peraiai* in the 340s through the agency of Hermias of Atarneus, see below, p. 94. Similarly, Tenedos and Mytilene tried to recover theirs in the 330s. But they were told by the Persians, who were now in a position to give orders again as a result of the anti-Macedonian counter-offensive, to 'return to the King's Peace' (Arr. *Anab.* II.1–2). That expression is problematic, but is best interpreted as meaning that the islands should give up their *peraiai* on the Persian mainland. On any other construction the reference to the King's Peace is mystifying, because the Peace did not, as we have seen, give islands like Tenedos to Persia; the reverse is true.

How complete a divide is the King's Peace, considered as an event in western Asiatic history? For Persia, as we have noted, it meant not less but more warfare in the western satrapies. The difference now was that the fighting was against the combined forces of Cypriots and Egyptians rather than against Greeks (for the Cyprus–Egypt revolts as a 'common', i.e. shared, war against Persia see Diod. xv.4.3). Hecatomnus, the new satrap of Caria, was expected to earn his keep by subduing Cyprus (*ibid.* 2), and though he actually helped the rebel, Tiribazus and Orontes had settled Cyprus by the end of the 380s (see above, p. 57). In 385–383 Abrocomas, Tithraustes (formerly satrap of Lydia) and Pharnabazus, formerly of Hellespontine Phrygia, led an unsuccessful assault on Egypt (Isoc. IV.140, virtually the only source). The repulse of the Persians by Acoris of Egypt with the help of the Athenian Chabrias and his mercenaries shows the real as opposed to the 'mythical' (above p. 52) significance of Cyrus and his 10,000, namely the introduction of the

---

[126] Cawkwell 1973 (C 111); 1981 (C 113), *contra*, Sinclair (C 76) and Clark 1990 (B 138), specifically on the naval aspects. See also Badian 1991 (F 4) 35ff.

Greek mercenary as a decisive factor in Mediterranean warfare. It is wrong to try to minimize this.[127] To Artaxerxes' preoccupations in the 380s should be added a long-standing revolt of the Cadusians (p. 64). The crisis of this revolt is synchronized by Diodorus (xv.8) with the later phases of the Cyprus operations.

So Persia's hands were full. But it was not even true that she had seen quite the last of Spartans and Athenians on the Asiatic mainland; and this is the proof that the King's Peace was not final for them either. (The following discussion ignores famous instances of help to rebel satraps like Ariobarzanes in 366 – for which see p. 85 – although that should be remembered too.)

First, Sparta. One of the Persian admirals in the Cyprus operations, Glos, himself moved into revolt, perhaps in central Ionia (Diod. xv.9.3f, cf. xv.18). He received help from Sparta, at a date perhaps as late as 380/79.[128] This revolt fizzled out after the deaths of Glos and his son (after which 'the Asian rebellions spontaneously ended', as Diodorus says at xv.18.4, not quite correctly). But the revolt is of interest as showing that Spartan opportunism in Asia was not a thing of the past.

As for Athens, an inscription shows her general Timotheus during his Samian adventure of about 365 (p. 201) embroiled in some way with Erythrae in mainland Ionia (IG ii² 108 = Engelmann and Merkelbach 1972 (F 627) no. 7, cf. Dem. xv.9). It is tempting to associate this with a remark of Demosthenes in 341 (viii.24) about Athenian generals visiting places like Chios *and Erythrae* looking for money. The mention of Erythrae here is interesting, because Erythrae was now part of the King's Asia, having been 'handed over to the barbarian' in 386 (in the language of the new Erythrae inscription discussed at p. 216 below). Evidently, then, there were moments even after 386 when Athens, like Sparta, was prepared to interfere directly in the Persian King's Asia. And an inscription mentioning Athenian soldiers who 'fought with Chabrias at Aianteion' in the Hellespontine region (Burnett and Edmonson 1961 (C 100)) is probably evidence that Athens, in about 375, gave some help to Philiscus the 'hyparch' or subordinate of Ariobarzanes, on what for Persia was her Hellespontine Phrygian mainland.

Nor was Persia for her part wholly scrupulous about keeping her hands off the *islands*. From Demosthenes (xv.9) we learn that by 366 there was a Persian garrison on Samos, under Cyprothemis, installed by 'Tigranes the hyparch', a man otherwise unknown. The notorious Athenian cleruchy on Samos was actually (on one way of looking at the

[127] With Cartledge 1979 (C 282) 272; 1987 (C 284) 209.
[128] Ryder 1963 (C 313). Cawkwell 1976 (C 285) 70 says that it is impossible that Sparta actually helped. He does not mention Ryder. Surely there were some dealings between the Spartans and Glos.

matter) no more than a pre-emptive response to this clear provocation. As for Hecatomnid Carian encroachment in the islands to the south, that is now thought to have begun in the 360s also (F644, 134: Cos).

The King's Peace, then, created no impenetrable iron curtain for either side. Nor, we can add, was it a commercial or social curtain of any kind. Thus Phaselites are found trading as a routine matter at mid-century Athens (Dem. xxxv, *Against Lacritus*). There is also evidence for Phoenician trade with Athens and vice versa, cf. p. 335. Again, Attic epigraphy is rich in Asiatic immigrants, and statue-bases and other evidence from the most hellenized provinces, Lycia and Caria, attest an eastward diaspora of Athenian craftsmen and intellectuals to satrapal and dynastic courts in the Persian empire. Aristotle's stay at Atarneus is only the most celebrated. The effects of mercenaries on warfare is a topic discussed elsewhere in this volume (p. 678), but the social consequences, for racial and other attitudes, deserve a word here. Mercenary service was something you did not any longer need to feel ashamed of as in Alcaeus' day (the archaic period). To have served with the great mercenary commander Iphicrates is a matter of pride for the speaker of Isaeus 11.6; and in New Comedy the mercenary is by no means always portrayed as the 'braggart' of literary convention.[129] Returning mercenaries, naturally, brought with them native women; and a more complex family history – though still, surely, one with mercenary service at the back of it – is implied by Aristotle's mention (*De Gen. Anim.* 722a) of a woman from Elis whose child had an Ethiopian father.[130] All this produced the mental climate in which Menander was able to say 'the man whose natural beauty is good, though he be an Ethiopian, is nobly born' (F 612 K, cf. Agatharchides *GGM* 1 118; [Callisthenes] III.8.16). But these attitudes did not prevail overnight, or at all levels of society (just as *homonoia*, 'harmony of outlook', or guest-friendships between upper-class Persians and Greeks – whether Greek visitors like Agesilaus or Greek residents like the Demaratids, p. 213 – tell us nothing about the prejudices of ordinary Spartans or the Athenian *demos*). Thus when the soldiers of Xenophon's *Anabasis* in 400 B.C. discover that Apollonides the self-styled Boeotian has actually got pierced ears, 'just like a Lydian', he is soon sent packing: III.1.16.[131]

The year 380, when Sparta helped Glos, is given by Diodorus as the acme of her power. Henceforth, with the founding of the Second Athenian Naval Confederacy, whose first stirrings are to be dated early in 378 (p. 166), Persia's main enemy among the Greek states must have

---

[129] A. W. Gomme and F. Sandbach, *Menander Commentary* (Oxford, 1973) 25.

[130] F. M. Snowden, Jr., *Blacks in Antiquity: Ethiopians in the Greco-Roman Experience* (Cambridge, MA and London, 1970) 104 and generally.

[131] The interest of this passage was pointed out to the present writer by Mr Thomas Braun.

seemed once again to be Athens. The charter of the confederacy, though probably framed in deference to the King's Peace (Tod no. 123 = Harding no. 35, lines 13–14), menaces not just Sparta but (line 42) *anyone* who attacks a confederate state, and it is fair to assume that Persia and the satraps are here included. Certainly the earliest names on the list of members at the end of the text include islands, such as Chios and Rhodes, for whom Persian satrapal aggression was a nearer and more real threat than Sparta. This aspect of the new confederacy's origins should not be neglected as it often is (Isoc. IV.163 makes the point). In Caria, where Mausolus had succeeded his father Hecatomnus in 377, his move of capital to coastal Halicarnassus from inland Mylasa may be part of an aggressive attempt by the satrap to stem Athenian political influence. That is, to forestall, at least in his own back yard, financial exactions like those of Thrasybulus at Halicarnassus in the period before the King's Peace, or of Timotheus at Erythrae in (?) the 360s.

But Egypt was still the major Persian preoccupation, and the years 377 to 374 and 373 (an abnormally long period even by Persian standards, p. 56) were absorbed in massive preparations for an attack under Pharnabazus (Diod. xv.29;42): this time however it was Persia who made most conspicuous use of Athenian talent – under first Iphicrates then Timotheus – and of Greek mercenaries, 20,000 of them. It was the need to recruit these which provided a strong motive for Persia to effect the second 'King's Peace' of the year 375:[132] Diod. xv.38 and *FGrH* 328 Philochorus F 151. But this huge effort against Egypt also failed, and Pharnabazus gave way to Datames (below, p. 84f) as Persian commander in Egypt (372). It goes a little too far to speak[133] of an 'Atheno-Persian entente between 380 and 374'. Nevertheless the presence of the Athenian Iphicrates on the Persian side, where he had been since 379 when Chabrias was recalled at Persian insistence from helping the rebels (Diod. xv.29), needs an explanation, or more than one, if it is right to see the new Athenian confederacy as constructed with at least one eye on the Persian King and his Anatolian delegates. Can we simply write off Iphicrates as an independent operator? It is true that, given Athens' poor public finances in the period, fourth-century Athenian generals were less obviously servants of the state than their predecessors of the fifth; but their independence of action can be exaggerated, especially if we believe everything said by Athenian orators.[134] Thus stiff diplomatic notes from Persia led to the smart recall not just of Chabrias (above), but of Chares in the 350s: p. 89 below. So that explanation will not do. The truth is that Athens preferred to be non-committal, except when she was roused to counter absolutely flagrant satrapal encroachment in the east Aegean

[132] Cawkwell 1963 (c 16) 123.   [133] Cloché 1934 (c 117) 77.
[134] Pritchett 1971–91 (k 51) II 59ff.

(below); or when she gauged that the political wind was blowing very hard indeed against Persia. This non-committal attitude is clearly enunciated in Tod no. 145 = Harding no. 57, the Reply to the Satraps of (?) 362 (p. 88f). Another motive, though, for the so-called 'entente' with Persia was simply Athens' desire to get jobs and pay for her officers and men. (Chabrias' help to Philiscus and Ariobarzanes in ?375, for which see above p. 81, is not of great moment, because Ariobarzanes is not yet in revolt. But as we have noted it is interesting as showing Athens acting on the Asian mainland.)

The elevation of Datames marks the beginning of the unrest tradition-ally known as the Revolt of the Satraps.[135] The main literary sources are Nepos' *Life of Datames*[136] (which is one of the most valuable of that author's *Lives*, comparable to the *Atticus* in that it provides for once material not better reproduced elsewhere); chapters 90–3 of Diodorus book xv[137] (with more material about Artabazus in book xvi); further Ephorus-derived material in writers like Polyaenus; the Tenth Prolo-gues of Trogus; and for the Ariobarzanes affair Xenophon's *Ages.* 11.26f. But there are also several helpful inscriptions, and some informative coinage.[138] Finally, the Rainer Papyrus on the Social War, *FGrH* 105, adds to our knowledge about Artabazus.

The scale, the importance and even the historicity of the Revolt have been reasonably, but not in the end convincingly, questioned.[139] Cer-tainly, 'regional instability' of this sort does not prove Persia to have been basically weak, nor can it be proved that the revolts were planned or co-ordinated. But it is not likely that Diodorus' source Ephorus made the whole thing up, or that he was merely transmitting the panhellenist wishful thinking of his teacher Isocrates. Things are not so simple: Ephorus got his own account from some even more nearly contempor-ary authority (Dinon? Callisthenes?).

The four periods of the Revolt or revolts – that of Datames which began in the 370s, of Ariobarzanes in the mid 360s, the general insurrection in the second half of the 360s, and Artabazus' revolt in the next decade – occupy nearly twenty years. (What Diodorus records under the single year 362 can only be the climax of the third or main phase.) It is therefore not surprising that it was not until the late 350s that Persia had the energy or resources to resume the struggle for Egypt (half of the King's revenues were cut off by 362, if we may believe Diodorus).

Datames' revolt probably began soon after 372, when Timotheus replaced Iphicrates in Egypt. He can be traced via the mints of Tarsus

---

[135] Hornblower 1982 (F 644) 170–82; Weiskopf 1989 (F 69).   [136] Sekunda 1988 (F 59).
[137] Stylianou 1985 (B 112).   [138] Moysey 1989 (B 210).
[139] Against Weiskopf 1989 (F 69) see Hornblower 1990 (F 37) 363ff and R. Moysey, *Ancient History Bulletin* 5 (1991) 111–20.

and Side (whose coins he overstruck)[140] in southern Anatolia, to Sinope and Amisus in the north. He remained in north Cappadocia, though under siege by Autophradates of Lydia (who was later a rebel but was still loyal at this time) and also perhaps, as coinage suggests,[141] by the Lycian dynast Artumpara. Datames detached north Cappadocia completely from Persian control. (For the later history of Cappadocia see ch. 8a, p. 220f.) His example showed other potentially disloyal satraps what they could hope for: an independent enclave.

The second phase of insurrection begins far away, at Delphi in 368, where Philiscus of Abydus distributed money provided by Ariobarzanes, satrap of Hellespontine Phrygia, in exchange for Greek mercenaries (Xen. *Hell.* VII.1.27). This was ostensibly to help Sparta but more probably for himself in his planned revolt. It seems that the 'legitimate' satrap of Hellespontine Phrygia was Pharnabazus' son Artabazus, who had Achaemenid blood[142] through his mother Apame. Artabazus' uncle Ariobarzanes was under instructions to hand over the satrapy to his nephew, now of age (cf. Xen. *Hell.* IV.1.40, assuming that 'Pharnabazus' brother' there is Ariobarzanes).[143] But Ariobarzanes refused, and the satraps Mausolus of Caria and Autophradates of Lydia were sent against Ariobarzanes at his current base in the gulf of Adramyttium (either at Adramyttium itself, modern Edremit, or at Assus. See Xen. *Ages.* II.26 and Polyaen. VII.29.6). At this point Athens and Sparta joined in on Ariobarzanes' side, with forces commanded by Timotheus (in a campaign which was more celebrated for its operations against another Persian force, that on Samos: Dem. xv.9) and Agesilaus (Xen. *Ages.* II.26) respectively. Now Agesilaus and Mausolus are described by Xenophon as guest-friends, and this relationship is explicitly said to be older than the episode which prompted Xenophon to mention it. Perhaps (see above, p. 69) it goes back to the 390s. That may be relevant to Mausolus' odd behaviour at Assus: he and Autophradates gave money to Agesilaus and raised the siege. This, we may suppose, was part of a deal for Greek mercenaries, reminiscent of the Philiscus affair at Delphi; if so, it would show that Mausolus and Autophradates were contemplating revolt *as early as the middle of the 360s*.[144]

There are therefore reasons for linking the second and third phases of

---

[140] *Sylloge Nummorum Graecorum* Berry II nos. 1294–5.   [141] S. Atlan, *Anadolu* 3 (1958) 89ff.

[142] But Hornblower 1982 (F 644) 173 is wrong to make Pharnaces one of the Seven to whom Darius I owed his throne.

[143] Doubted by Weiskopf 1989 (F 69) and Sekunda in F 40, 180; but see Hornblower 1990 (F 37) 365.

[144] Xen. *Ages.* says that Tachos was associated with Mausolus on this occasion; for the difficulties of this (and an attempted solution) see Hornblower 1982 (F 644) 174ff, but see p. 341 below. Note R. Moysey, 'Diodorus, the Satraps, and the Decline of the Persian Empire', *Ancient History Bulletin* 5 (1991) 111–20.

the revolt, or rather for seeing the central period of disturbances as a
long-drawn-out process. This idea is supported by the mention at Diod.
xv.90, describing the third and main phase of the revolt, of rebellious
ethne (Mysians, Pamphylians, Lycians, etc.); this suggests general and
protracted upheaval.

(The issue is not straightforward. In Diodorus' account it is unclear
whether the revolt is a revolt like that of the Ionians in 500–499 B.C., that
is, a revolt of subject peoples against their Persian masters; or a revolt by
dissident satraps against the King; or both. The introductory sentence
certainly leads us to expect an account of a revolt by subject peoples –
'the coastal inhabitants of Asia revolted from the Persians' – but
Diodorus continues 'and some of the satraps and generals made war on
Artaxerxes'. This implies that the revolt was one of both subjects and
satraps. But in the narrative which follows the revolt is represented as a
series of satrapal initiatives, based on Greek mercenary support. In view
of the general quiescence of Asia Minor in the fourth century after the
King's Peace, it is hard to believe in a general rebellion, although in ch.
90 Diodorus does include the 'Greek cities in Asia' among the King's
enemies, and he emphatically lists the rebellious *ethne* at the end of the
chapter.)

The leader of the revolt was neither of the satraps just mentioned,
Mausolus and Autophradates, nor Tachos, the rebel satrap of Egypt
(prominent though he was among the rebels, Diod. xv.90.3), but
Orontes, satrap of Armenia. (This is what Trogus calls him; Diodorus
calls him satrap of *Mysia*. There are strong grounds for thinking[145] that
Diodorus' description is a mistake; or rather that there has been a
displacement in the text, and the Mysians belong in his list of rebellious
ethne and have been wrongly attached to Orontes' name.) Orontes was a
half-Bactrian, cf. *OGIS* 264 (with p. 63f above). He was also married to
the king's daughter (Xen. *An.* II.4.8 and *OGIS* 391). This suggests that
he may have had grander aims than mere territorial enlargement, in fact
that he hoped to do a Cyrus the Younger not a Datames. (But his gold
coinage, of which three examples survive, should not be counted among
the proofs that he aimed for the throne; cf. p. 59.) Artabazus, apparently
loyal for the moment (it is a feature of these revolts that satrap *a* is sent to
subdue satrap *b*, and that we next find *a* himself in revolt) was imprisoned
by Autophradates (Dem. XXIII.154). This momentarily made a clean
sweep of the western satrapies: Datames and Ariobarzanes of Hellespontine Phrygia were certainly involved, Polyaen. VIII.21.3 and Diod.
xv.90.3. The position in Greater Phrygia, in the interior, is unknown (cf.
p. 78); but the later achievement of Antigonus as Alexander's satrap at
Celaenae, where he kept open the line of Macedonian communications

[145] Hornblower 1982 (F 644) 177; another view: Osborne 1981–3 (B 165) II 1982, 65ff.

under huge pressure, shows that an obstructive satrap there would have been hard to circumvent. The way was now open for a push on the Iranian heartland.

Datames crossed the Euphrates (Polyaenus), Orontes moved on Syria (Trogus, *Prologue* x) and Tachos and Agesilaus on Phoenicia (Diod. xv.92.4). Was this a grand pincer attack? If so, Artaxerxes must have been steeling himself for another Cunaxa. But a co-ordinated rebel strategy is no more than speculation. In any case, the second Cunaxa never happened. Tachos was finished off by mutiny at the lower levels, and there was treachery at the higher: Orontes and an associate Rheomithres took the Great King's money and submitted (Diod. xv.91–2). Datames (*ibid.* 91) was killed, though his Cappadocian kingdom survived (ch. 8*a*, p. 221). Mausolus, the great opportunist (he is not mentioned for any specific action while the revolt was at its height) rapidly returned to his allegiance, in fact by 361/0 (as an inscription shows, Tod no. 138. This is a text from Carian Mylasa, and is dated by Mausolus' satrapy and the 45th year of Artaxerxes: line 17). There is no evidence, though it is often assumed, that he received Lycia as his reward for leaving the revolt.

The Greek attitude to all this is enigmatic to us, and the level of Greek involvement hard to determine. Athens' intervention on Samos was against a Persian garrison (Dem. xv.9), which justified morally the cleruchy which Athens installed there – something anyway justified technically, despite the renunciations of cleruchies in the confederacy charter (Tod no. 123 = Harding no. 35), because Samos was not a member. It was consistent with this anti-Persian stance, one might think, that Athens should help Ariobarzanes, who was now in Persian disfavour; but did Athens greatly care who held the Dascyleum satrapy? If the Ariobarzanes episode is really just a deal for mercenaries, it may be safer once again to invoke, as a motive, Athens' desire for pay for her officers and men. But that is not the whole story, because there is independent evidence for strong Athenian resentment of Persia in the early to mid-360s: a quadrilateral (Persian–Athenian–Spartan–Theban) peace conference at Susa in 367 had endorsed a Theban proposal (which never came to anything) for the disbandment of the Athenian fleet. One of the Athenian ambassadors there present threatened that Athens would now 'look for some friend other than the Great King' (Xen. *Hell.* VII.1.37). These words were not wholly idle: Ariobarzanes apart, an inscription in the Ashmolean Museum in Oxford, for which a date has been argued around 364,[146] attests an Athenian alliance with Strato, the king of Sidon in Phoenicia (Tod no. 139 = Harding no. 40). Now Phoenicia was on the direct line of any rebel thrust towards Persia

[146] Moysey 1976 (F 305).

(above), and there is an interesting wisp of evidence for collusion between Strato and King Tachos of Egypt (Hieron. *Adv. Iovinian.* 1.45). Certainly Tachos fled to Sidon in 360 (Xen. *Ages.* 11.3). Again, a (chronologically problematic) Athenian decree honouring Orontes may belong *c.* 361/0 (*IG* ii² 207a, see below). Finally, the Athenian Chabrias helped the rebel cause with mercenaries and perhaps naval help (Diod. xv.92.3, Nep. *Chabr.* 11.3, Hicks and Hill no. 122). But see above, p. 83 on Iphicrates, for the difficulties of evaluating this kind of appointment.

As for Greek relations with Mausolus, Agesilaus may have taken his money (the Susa talks were no more pleasing to Sparta than to Athens, involving as they did the recognition of Messenian independence – hence Spartan readiness to injure Persia by helping Ariobarzanes. In 362 Agesilaus perhaps just needed money). But what of Athens? The Samos cleruchy imposed by the Athenian Timotheus was not a friendly move towards a nearby satrap who may already have had designs on Samos.[147] In other words the Persian hyparch Tigranes, who garrisoned Samos, may have been working in the same direction and interest as the nearest and most powerful satrap, namely Mausolus of Caria. (He is not likely to have been working directly and openly for him, because this is a point which Demosthenes is not likely to have missed.) Athens saved Samos from Persian Hecatomnid intervention, if that was the threat; but Rhodes, Cos and Chios were to succumb (Dem. xv; v.25). What made these encroachments possible was, in large part, the distrust of Athens caused by precisely the Samos cleruchy, whatever its justification. So Mausolus was the long-term gainer, even if he was perhaps the short-term loser, from the Samos affair of 366. It is interesting in this connexion that places in the Persian empire, some of them specifically in Mausolus' sphere of influence (including islands gobbled up by Caria at one time or another), offered a refuge to Samians expelled as a result of the cleruchy.[148] In so doing, they were making an anti-Athenian gesture. There was thus a long prehistory to Persian support of the Social War rebels of the 350s (see below). Samos, where events in 366 helped to concentrate allied feeling against Athens, can be seen as a testing-ground for the open collision of Athenian and Persian interests and forces in the next decade.

Officially, though, the Greeks, in the Reply to the Satraps (Tod no. 145 = Harding no. 57 of, probably, 362/1) declined involvement on the rebel side. Athens took the lead in the matter, if we may judge from the

---

[147] Hornblower 1982 (F 644) 109 and n. 19; 135 and n. 247; note however Shipley 1987 (C 382) 137 n. 55 (but the coins are not essential to the argument. Samian proximity to Caria is reason enough to suppose that Mausolus was alarmed by Timotheus' activities).

[148] *SEG* I 352: Phaselis; *Ath. Mitt.* 87 (1972) 192 no. 2: Erythrae; *ibid.* 199 no. 4: Miletus; *ibid.* 72 (1957) 190 no. 23: Heraclea on Latmus; *ibid.* 94 no. 26 and *SIG* 312: Iasus; *Ath. Mitt ibid.* 196 no. 29: Rhodes; *SEG* I 350: Cos.

Attic dialect of the inscription, although the stone was found at Argos. Athens' own difficulties in the Aegean, which are described elsewhere in this volume (p. 203), meant that she had few resources to spare. Sparta, deprived of Messenia by Epaminondas, was also in very low water. The Great King had won.

Almost the first act of the new King Artaxerxes III, who succeeded to the throne in 359, was to order the disbandment of the mercenary armies of the coastal satraps: scholiast on Dem. IV.19. He was obeyed. The purpose and scope of this order are debatable. It surely did not (despite the word 'coastal') include satrapal *fleets*, in satrapies where they existed (cf. p. 56 for the usual Persian way of raising a navy). Thus Mausolus, whose ships number 100 at Xen. *Ages.* II.26f. (366) still has a navy in 357, Diod. XVI.7, with which he helps Chios, Rhodes and Byzantium in their war against Athens. As to the purpose of the order, the scholiast says that it was an economy measure. It is tempting to reject this curiously modern-looking explanation, in terms of 'defence-cuts', in favour of a political motive, the need to discipline the satraps after recent experiences. If *that* was the purpose, it failed badly, because the mercenaries thus disengaged eventually hired themselves out to Chares, the Athenian commander in the Social War; and when Chares ran short of funds, he engaged himself and his forces to Artabazus, now in revolt (scholiast on Dem. IV.19; Diod. XVI.22).

This revolt of Artabazus is the fourth and final phase of the Revolt of the Satraps. Chares was successful at first, ravaging the (Hellespontine) Phrygian territory of Tithraustes, a Persian (scholiast on Dem. IV.19; *FGrH* 105, the Rainer Papyrus) and winning a 'Second Marathon' in the Anatolian interior. But the Great King now took a hand: he threatened to help Athens' rebel allies unless Chares was recalled. (This may show that Mausolus' original help to Rhodes and the others was given independently, cf. p. 58.) Athens complied and Artabazus had to look for mercenaries elsewhere; in fact, from Thebes. Thebes was in bad financial trouble in the Third Sacred War (p. 741), where she had bitten off more than she could chew against the Phocians, who had the advantage of the Delphic temple treasures. So she sent 5,000 men (citizen-soldiers, perhaps, rather than mercenaries; or better, perhaps, 'citizen-mercenaries'): Diod. XVI.34.1, winter 354/3. Pammenes, the Theban commander, was briefly successful at first (*ibid.* 2), but then he quarrelled with Artabazus, who had him killed. What happened to Pammenes' mercenary force after that is strictly unknown, but an acute modern suggestion[149] has them hire themselves out to the obvious employer, the Persian King himself, poised for another attack on Egypt.

---

[149] Ehrhardt 1961 (c 20) 5off (whence also 'citizen-mercenaries' and the pay calculations). *Contra*, Buckler 1989 (D 67) 100, n. 24.

Certainly the King sent Thebes 300 Attic talents (Diod. XVI.40), which is
exactly a year's pay for 5,000 men at the rate of 1 drachma per day; and
this was surely not for the 'beautiful blue eyes'[150] of the Thebans. This
kind of side-switching anticipates the behaviour of some of the early
hellenistic armies, more concerned with their *aposkeue*, baggage (i.e.
booty)[151] than with the fate or identity of their paymaster. These
Thebans, stuck in the Persian-held interior without a leader, at least have
the excuse that there was not much else they could do. Artabazus fled to
the court of Philip of Macedon (Diod. XVI.52). This was neither the first
(cf. p. 213 for Amyntas son of Boubares) nor the last (p. 863) instance of
Macedonian co-operation with individual Persians. Young Alexander
surely took note. (Artabazus was eventually recalled to Persia at the
instance of his kinsman Mentor.)

Before we turn to Egypt again, Orontes must have a final mention. It
seems[152] that there is no epigraphic evidence for a second phase of
insurrectionist activity by him in the 350s. But a reference to him in
Demosthenes' *On the Symmories* in 354/3 (XIV.31) does look like an
allusion to a currently, if briefly, dangerous enemy of Persia. In any case,
Artabazus is evidently the main rebel of the 350s – the hero, so to speak,
of the '45 rebellion, as Orontes, a tarnished hero, had been of the '15
(both men had royal blood). The details of any post-360 activity by
Orontes elude us; his bribery by Artaxerxes II and his 'desertion of those
who trusted him' (Diod. XV.91.1) would in any case have made him, in
Browning's phrase about Wordsworth, a 'lost leader'.

The Persian attack on Egypt in 351/0, which certainly happened (it is
alluded to by Dem. XV.12 of that year), has unfortunately slipped from
Diodorus' account. It was mentioned by Ephorus: Diod. XVI.40.3 (cf.
44) has a reference to an 'earlier', but in the extant narrative non-existent,
campaign. This omission has produced a muddle: Diodorus records
under 351 a successful campaign which belongs in 344 or 343. (Dem. XIV.
31 may imply an even earlier attempt, in 354/3, cf. 'for a third time' in
Trogus *Prologue* x.) Of the details of the Persian repulse from Egypt in
351 Diodorus has ensured that nothing can be said. But it was that
Persian failure in Egypt which now stimulated, and it was the Egyptian
king who now encouraged and helped, a revolt in Phoenicia as well (we
may compare the Strato–Tachos axis of the 360s). The Phoenicians must
also have resented[153] the demands on them which Persian preparations

---

[150] Beloch 1912–27 (A 5) III² 1.483 n. 1.

[151] M. Holleaux, 'Ceux qui sont dans le bagage', *Etudes d'épigraphie et d'histoire grecques* III (Paris,
1968) 15–26; cf. Cook 1983 (F 14) 263 n. 22.

[152] Osborne 1971 (B 164) and 1973 (F 688); Weiskopf 1989 (F 69) 79; but note Moysey 1987 (B
161).   [153] Cook 1983 (F 14) 220.

against Egypt involved: Phoenicia was the main Persian base for that campaign.

Diodorus' account of this Phoenician revolt (XVI.42ff) is for a change satisfyingly full, and we get a glimpse, not afforded us in the half-century since the events of Xenophon's *Hellenica* book III, of what Persian rule was actually like. We have already noticed the fodder collected by the satraps for the war, surely typical of countless such requisitions. There is also a mention (XVI.41.5) of the 'royal paradise' (= enclosed garden or park, *pardesh*, cf. the 'keeper of the king's *pardesh*' at Nehemiah 3.8), 'where the Persian Kings took their ease'. Posidonius adds the detail that at Damascus, 80 km inland from Sidon but perhaps not far from Diodorus' 'paradise', there were vineyards which supplied Chalybonian wine for the Persian King. This was allegedly the only kind he would drink: *FGrH* 87 F 68. Readers of *Seven Pillars of Wisdom* will remember the galloping horseman who accosts Lawrence of Arabia with a bunch of yellow grapes: 'Good news: Damascus salutes you!' (p. 644).

The satraps Belesys of Syria and Mazaeus of Cilicia commanded the Persian invasion force, which assembled in Babylonia. Tennes, king (i.e. client-king) of Sidon was the leader of the rebel forces ('many triremes and a host of mercenaries'), which were strengthened by 4,000 mercenaries loaned by Egypt and commanded by Mentor of Rhodes.

A third revolt, on Cyprus, now broke out, 'in imitation of the Phoenicians' (Diod. XVI.42.5), who had themselves imitated the Egyptians. The suppression of this revolt can be dated fairly closely because Idrieus (satrap of Caria 351–344, succeeding Artemisia who ruled 353–351 after Mausolus' death in 353) and the Athenian Phocion were entrusted with its suppression by the Great King. The resources of Syria, Cilicia and Babylonia were now fully committed, and Artaxerxes must have been feeling the strain; hence this unusual pair of commanders. The chronological argument goes like this: Isocrates in the *Philippus* of 346 expressed the hope (v. 103) that Idrieus might prove disloyal to Persia. These hopes of 346 were dashed by, and therefore antedated, Idrieus' behaviour on Cyprus. But Idrieus was dead by 344. Therefore, Cyprus was crushed 346–344. Idrieus' action on this occasion proved the strength of Persia's policy in the western empire: a native Carian satrap crushes a native Cypriot king in the name of Persia. But his father Hecatomnus' help to Evagoras earlier in the century is a warning against generalization.

Meanwhile the Phoenician revolt was so seriously viewed in Persia that the King himself set out to deal with it, a rare event. (In the 390s the King had 'crossed the upper [eastern] satrapies' to deal with Evagoras of Cyprus, but he does not seem to have got there: Diod. XIV.98.4. The text should not be emended so as to make Hecatomnus of Caria rather than the King do the 'crossing', a geographical impossibility.)[154] Tennes took fright and negotiated secretly by letter with Artaxerxes, who therefore felt free to proceed against what was in reality the more important object, namely Egypt. For this purpose he needed mercenary help on an unusual scale and sent to Sparta and Athens: Diod. xvi.44. (The visit to Athens of this embassy is also recorded by Philochorus, *FGrH* 328 F 157, cf. 324 Androtion F 53.) The Spartans and Athenians replied that friendship was one thing, help another. (Note that in Athens' case this was the usual equivocation, given that Athens had had no qualms about sending Phocion to help the Persians on Cyprus, see above.) Once again it was Thebes which obliged, with 1,000 hoplites under Lacrates; there were also 3,000 Argives, and 6,000 Asiatic Greeks. This was a large total (cf. ch. 8*a*, p. 225), making 10,000 in all, a 'myriad', and perhaps a believable Diodoran 'myriad' for once: myriads are suspiciously frequent in Diodorus. To these, Mentor's 4,000 would soon be added, see below. On the other side, Nectanebo had 20,000 Greeks, not to mention some Libyans and Egyptians. Even allowing for exaggeration, this stupendous grand total of 34,000 Greek mercenaries on the two sides put together marks the climax of Greek mercenary activity in the fourth century.

Sidon meanwhile had fallen by treachery even without direct Persian assault: Tennes, after betraying Sidon, was executed by the King 'as being of no further use'. The Sidonians scuttled their navy and the population committed a mass Wagnerian suicide by fire; gold and silver in huge quantities was later discovered in the burnt rubble of their houses. (This precious metal was then sold off by Artaxerxes, Diod. xvi.42.5. He had mercenary bills to pay.) Mentor and his mercenaries, like Pammenes' army in the previous decade, joined Artaxerxes; for Mentor this was the beginning of a distinguished career in Persian service. He now became one of the three Persian field-commanders against Egypt, the others being Rhosaces, satrap of Lydia and Ionia (ch. 8*a*, p. 216) and Aristazanes (xvi.47.2 and 3). The last two co-operated with the Greek mercenary *condottieri*, Nicostratus of Argos and Lacrates of Thebes.

In Egypt, Nectanebo's Greek contingents succumbed one by one: first 5,000 of them under Cleinias of Cos, slaughtered by fellow-Greeks for whom the cause of re-establishing Persian authority in Egypt was not specially close to the heart, one would have thought. (Diod. xvi.49.3 however indicates that there was some fellow-feeling felt by Greek for

[154] C. Reid, *Phoenix* 28 (1974) 123ff at 136 n. 37; Hornblower 1982 (F 644) 37 n. 10; Petit 1988 (F 693) 311f, preferring the view of Cawkwell *ap.* Hornblower 1982 (F 644) 37 n. 10 that Autophradates is meant.

Greek.) There is, to turn to the Egyptian side, no reason to attribute anti-Persian sentiments to Cleinias of Cos[155] merely on the strength of his presence with Nectanebo; and the same goes for most of the individual Greeks known from the affair. It may be slightly more significant that Thebans and Argives were to be found on one side while Athenians fought on the other, that is the Egyptian, side. (As we may infer they did from Tod no. 199 = Harding no. 119, an *Athenian* decree acknowledging Mentor's role in saving 'the Greeks who had fought in Egypt'. In 351 Athenian and Spartan generals had certainly been used by the Egyptians, Diod. XVI.4.2.)

Thebans had a reputation going back to 480 as inveterate 'medizers' or Persian sympathizers; and though on the present occasion they may have been helping Persia in order to spite their enemy Philip of Macedon,[156] the medizing Thebans were not popular with other Greeks in general or with the Athenians in particular. The reasons for their unpopularity go beyond the events of 480, and have to do with the 'Leuctran arrogance' which Thebes had shown in the years after 371. Greek loathing of Thebes is attested by the events of 335 (below, p. 848), when the city was destroyed by Alexander with full Greek support as an act of 'piety'.

Argos too had 'medized' in the fifth century, or rather had stayed neutral in a way which was thought culpable: Hdt. VIII.73.3. (But Argos was never hated for this as Thebes was hated.)

It would therefore be tempting to think that the Athenians, by taking up arms against Thebans and Argives, were trying to be good panhellenists. Isocrates certainly called the Thebans and Argives betrayers of Greece (XII.159) for helping Persia in Egypt. But the Persian service of Iphicrates in the 370s, and Phocion's activities in the 340s, as also the prompt recalling of Chabrias in 380 and of Chares in 355 when Persia required it, show that Athens' attitude is too complex and too heavily compromised to earn the panhellenist label. In 341, if the manuscripts of Demosthenes are sound (IX.71), that orator would be urging that an Athenian delegation should be sent to the Great King asking for help against Macedon, and a little later this was actually done, Dem. XII.6.

To return to Egypt: Lacrates at Pelusium now surrendered, and so finally did the third group of Greeks, the mercenaries at Bubastis. Nectanebo, whose failure in 343 (contrast 351) Diodorus puts down to his refusal to delegate the supreme command, fled from his bunker at Memphis to Ethiopia. The date of the conquest of Egypt, the last great success of the Achaemenids (despite a brief Egyptian revolt in the 330s, p. 344f) is 343/2: the *Letter of Speusippus* speaks in spring 342 of a 'shortage of papyrus' due to Artaxerxes' reconquest of Egypt: *FGrH* 69

---

[155] Sherwin-White 1978 (C 381) 73; 549 for the correct form of the name.
[156] Cawkwell 1963 (C 106) 129.

T 1 para. 14. Pherendates, who has a good Iranian name (no native appointment here) was installed as satrap: Diod. XVI.51.3. A satrap of Egypt in the time of Darius I had been called Pherendates too; perhaps an ancestor.[157]

From Egypt, Mentor proceeded to the suppression of Hermias, the ruler of Atarneus in the Aeolid (north-western Asia Minor). This man's pocket principality is discussed elsewhere (ch. 8a, p. 220). Diodorus says (XVI.52) that he ruled many cities and strongholds, and that he had revolted from Persia. An inscription (Tod no. 165 = Harding no. 79) records a treaty between him and Erythrae, to the south. Now Erythrae, which had honoured Mausolus in the 350s (Tod no. 155), was still on good terms with the Hecatomnids as late as the time of Idrieus, who died in 344; see *SEG* XXXI 969 = Harding 28B, Erythraean honours to Idrieus. So it seems wrong to conclude that Hermias' treaty with Erythrae implies that 'Carian power is declining there' i.e. at Erythrae.[158] Erythrae could surely have honoured both men, Idrieus and Hermias, within a short space of time. (The likelihood of this is not much reduced if the honours to Idrieus were actually granted in the 350s, i.e. in his brother Mausolus' satrapal tenure. The honours to Mausolus and to Idrieus seem to have been carved on the same stone.)

From Theopompus we learn (*FGrH* 115 F 291) that Hermias possessed Assus as well as Atarneus, and that he was put in charge in some capacity (the noun is missing) of (?recovering) some territory, by Chios and Mytilene.[159] But Hermias pulled out when his mercenaries were not paid. This is normally taken to refer to interference on the islands themselves, but there is another possibility: the 'territory' could be land on the Asiatic mainland (*peraia*), which had been lost since the King's Peace (p. 80), but which the anti-Persian elements on the islands were seeking to recover. (Tenedos and Mytilene seem to have made another such attempt a few years later, pp. 80, 804.) It is in favour of this that Chios had once owned Atarneus (Hdt. 1.160.4; Xen. *Hell.* III.2.11), and if she wanted it back, to make some contact with the present ruler would be the obvious first step. If that was Hermias' game, Persian misgivings about him look even better founded. Idrieus' successor Ada, the ruler of Chios in the late 340s (because she was satrap of Caria in 344–340, a period when Caria controlled Chios) cannot have been much pleased at the intrigues between Hermias and Chios. But the main charge against Hermias was correspondence with Philip (Dem. x.32, with the scholiast on para. 10, p. 202 Dindorf edn). In 341 Mentor lured him to negotiations and sent him to Artaxerxes who tortured and executed him. Hermias did 'nothing unworthy of philosophy' (*FGrH* 124 Callisthenes F 2), that is he did not talk when tortured.

---

[157] Cook 1983 (F 14) 64.   [158] Wormell 1935 (H 124) 70.
[159] Lane Fox 1986 (B 65) 111 n. 51.

The philosophical and literary consequences of this moving affair cannot be examined here. It is however of great political interest because it is early and concrete evidence that Philip already had designs of some kind on the Persian empire. Arrian (*Anab.* II.14.2) alludes to 'friendship and alliance' between Persia and Philip. Some scholars put this in 351, as part of a Persian effort to secure a free hand against Egypt. Others put it in 344/3. Others, more plausibly perhaps, deny its historicity altogether.[160] More credible is the evidence for hostile *Macedonian* intentions: leaving the *Philippus* of Isocrates out of account, we have, first, the harbouring of Artabazus in the 350s (p. 90); second, the explicit statement of Diodorus (XVI.60) that Philip, already after the Peace of Philocrates in 346 (p. 751) hoped to be chosen as 'leader of the "Persian War"' – an item which some would like to reinforce by pointing to his mild handling of Athens in the late 340s: he wanted to break away east, not be bothered with Demosthenes and company; third, perhaps, the organization of Thrace in 342–334 into something like a 'satrapy' on a consciously Achaemenid model[161] (cf. Diod. XVI.71; XVII.62.5; Arr. *Anab.* VII.9.3); fourth, the possibility that as early as the end of the 340s, Philip was encouraging pro-Macedonian factions in the Persian-held cities and islands of the east Aegean and on the Asiatic mainland.[162] Thus there were altars to Zeus Philippios at Eresus on Lesbos (Tod no. 191 line 5) and a statue to Philip at Ephesus on the mainland: see Arr. *Anab.* 1.17. Fifth and finally, there is the Hermias episode.

There was, however, no open clash between the Persians and Macedon (and, we can add, no concrete co-operation between Persia and Athens) until Philip's sieges of Perinthus and Byzantium. In 340/39 (following Philochorus F 54 rather than Diod. XVI.75: 341) the 'coastal satraps', as Diodorus calls them, helped Perinthus against Philip. Philochorus' mention of the *royal* satraps, and Diodorus' language, preclude attempts[163] to see this as an exercise of independent satrapal initiative. The only named satrap is Arsites of Hellespontine Phrygia (Paus. 1.29.10); but what happened at Byzantium (below) may suggest that satraps as far south as Caria (which was certainly 'coastal') were involved.

In the next year, Byzantium got help from Chios, Cos and Rhodes: Diod. XVI.77, confirmed for Chios by *IG* II² 234 (cf. perhaps Tod no. 175 = Harding no. 97, Tenedos). Again, this should be seen as satrapal, Persian action, not as a manifestation of independence by the islands. All

---

[160] Cawkwell 1963 (C 106) 127ff; Bosworth 1980 (B 14) 229ff.

[161] Kienast 1973 (D 102); Griffith in Hammond and Griffith 1979 (D 50) 559. The title 'general over Thrace' is not actually attested until Alexander's time.

[162] Ehrenberg 1938 (D 170); Badian 1966 (D 137); Heisserer 1980 (B 143); Fraser review of Heisserer, *CR* 1982, 241.

[163] Beloch 1912–27 (A 5) III² 1.601; *contra*, Hornblower 1982 (F 644) 123.

three places were still under Hecatomnid control (see Dem. v.25 for the year 346). It is wrong to argue independent status for these islands from literary references to Athenian diplomacy with 'Chios and Rhodes' (see e.g. *FGrH* 115 F 164; Dem. IX.71; or the lost Rhodian and Chian orations of Hyperides). Behind 'Chios and Rhodes' stood the Carian satrap who controlled them. The better view is that places like these (Cos is another) remained under Persian garrisons until Alexander. They may, however, have briefly attempted to recover their mainland possessions from Persia in the short initial period of Macedonian liberation in the 330s, before the Persian counter-offensive: p. 80.

Philip's invasion of the Persian empire after his defeat of the Greeks at Chaeronea was planned to take place in two stages; the second, led by himself, never happened because he was assassinated. But the first did: an advance force of 10,000 crossed under Parmenion and Attalus (Polyaen. v.44.4). It has been wrongly assumed[164] that this force stayed in Asia until the arrival of Alexander, and its inclusion or non-inclusion in the total of his foot-troops is then held to explain a discrepancy between the two ancient estimates of this arm of his forces (30,000: 40,000). But even if we believe that conventional 'myriad' (see p. 92), what Polyaenus actually says is that the Macedonian force was very substantially reduced. It was mauled, Polyaenus says, by the Persian general Memnon near Magnesia (probably Magnesia on the Maeander rather than Magnesia ad Sipylum, the modern Manisa).[165] 'Many were killed, many captured.' The rump surely came home.

Alexander's invasion of Asia should thus be reckoned as, in the narrow military sense, a new beginning. But we have argued at several points in this chapter that in the social sense it was anything but that (pp. 69f, 72, 90 on political *homonoia*); and in a later chapter (8a, p. 229ff) it will be shown how far, in western Anatolia at least, cultural fusion and hellenization had already progressed under the fourth-century Achaemenid kings and their satraps.

---

[164] Brunt 1976–83 (B 21) I ixx. On Philip's Persian War see Ruzicka 1985 (D 116A).
[165] Judeich 1892 (F 663) 303 n. 1.

CHAPTER 4

THE CORINTHIAN WAR

ROBIN SEAGER

I. THE CAUSES AND OUTBREAK OF WAR

The outcome of the Peloponnesian War had left many of the victors discontented.[1] Sparta had totally disregarded the wishes and interests of her allies and had pursued a policy of aggressive expansion in the Peloponnese, central and northern Greece and the Aegean which had at times seemed directed specifically against them. Though Lysander had been a prime exponent of this policy, it had not been his alone, and his temporary eclipse in 403 had not led to any softening of Spartan attitudes.[2] Corinth had wanted to see Athens annihilated, but her desire had been thwarted and she had had no share in the spoils of victory (Xen. *Hell.* II.2.19). Moreover, Spartan intervention in Syracuse had damaged Corinthian interests there (Diod. XIV.110.2ff). Thebes had been even more displeased. She alone of Sparta's allies had ventured to claim her share of the profits, but in vain (Xen. *Hell.* III.5.5, Plut. *Lys.* 27.2), and she too had demanded to no avail that Athens be destroyed. Instead Sparta had put ominous pressure on Thebes by strengthening her own position in central Greece and Thessaly, securing control of Heraclea in about 400 (Diod. XIV.38.3f) and garrisoning Pharsalus (Diod. XIV.82).[3] Thebes had responded by making a major contribution to the overthrow of Sparta's puppet government at Athens, the Thirty, only to be somewhat disappointed by the cautious behaviour of the restored democracy, whose subservience to Sparta had led to tension between Athens and Thebes (Lys. XXX.22). Both Thebes and Corinth, with the Thebans taking the lead, had pursued a policy of military non-co-operation with Sparta. They had refused to take part in the expedition to the Piraeus, the war against Elis, and Agesilaus' expedition to Asia (Xen. *Hell.* II.4.29, III.2.25, 5.5, Diod. XIV.7.7, Paus. III.9.2ff). On this last occasion Thebes had been stirred to still greater provocation. When Agesilaus had attempted to imitate Agamemnon by sacrificing at Aulis

---

[1] Funke 1980 (C 24) 46ff.
[2] Funke 1980 (C 24) 27ff; Thompson 1973 (C 319); against: Hamilton 1979 (C 294) 25ff.
[3] Andrewes 1971 (C 275) 223ff.

before his departure, the boeotarchs had forcibly disrupted proceedings (Xen. *Hell.* III.4.3f, 5.5, Plut. *Ages.* 6.4ff, Lys. XXVII.1).

The course of events in Asia had done much to determine the degree of overt opposition to Sparta expressed in Greece. At first she had enjoyed some success on land, which had offered no encouragement to the malcontents at home. But the mounting by the Persians of a major offensive at sea, which had led to the defection of Rhodes from Sparta in summer 396 (Diod. XIV.79.6), had given them hope at a time when Lysander's recent return to prominence had sharpened their dislike of Sparta. A more practical stimulus had soon followed, for the activities of Agesilaus had inspired the Persians to foster and co-ordinate discontent in Greece in the hope that the outbreak of a war at home would force Sparta to recall her army from Asia. Of their Rhodian emissaries the first, Dorieus, had been caught and executed by the Spartans (Paus. VI.7.6), but the second, Timocrates, in autumn 396, had done his work well, finding a sympathetic hearing for his promise of Persian subsidies not only at Thebes, Corinth and Argos, but probably at Athens too (*Hell. Oxy.* VII.2ff, Plut. *Artax.* 20, Paus. III.9.8, against Xen. *Hell.* III.5.1f).[4]

For even defeated Athens, though she had dutifully provided troops for the Elean war and the expedition of Thibron (Xen. *Hell.* III.1.4, 2.25, Diod. XIV.17.7), had been aroused to provocative acts by the resurgence of Persian naval power. In 397 naval officers and equipment had been officially dispatched to Conon and an embassy had been sent to the King, which on its way home had fallen into Spartan hands and perished (*Hell. Oxy.* VII.1, Isae. XI.8). In 396 Athens had followed the lead of Thebes and Corinth and refused, albeit with copious excuses, to contribute to Agesilaus' expeditionary force (Paus. III.9.2). Yet when in winter 396/5 Demaenetus had sailed off to join Conon with one of Athens' permitted twelve ships, he had been denounced to the Spartan harmost on Aegina on the advice of Thrasybulus, Aesimus and Anytus, who judged that Athens was not yet strong enough to risk facing Sparta's wrath alone (*Hell. Oxy.* VIf).

In all this there is no reason to suppose that social, economic or ideological factors in the various cities had played any significant part.[5] Resentment of Sparta's high-handed neglect of their interests and fear of her ruthless expansionism will have been almost unanimous at Corinth and Thebes. At Athens even the unconvincing analysis offered by the *Hellenica Oxyrhynchia* does not obscure the essential fact that hostility to Sparta was by now universal. The only point at issue was whether Athens was as yet strong enough to go to war. In the preceding years the

---

[4] Seager 1967 (C 250) 95f; Lehmann 1978 (C 39).

[5] Perlman 1964 (C 56), 1968 (C 220); Seager 1967 (C 250); Lehmann 1978 (C 39); Funke 1980 (C 24) 1ff, 46ff; against: Kagan 1961 (C 35), Hamilton 1979 (C 294) 137ff.

vital division had been that between the City and the Piraeus. This was not economic: there were rich men on both sides. Nor was the constitution a live issue: by now there can have been few in the ranks of the City who nursed serious regrets for the passing of the oligarchy. Some of their number saw perhaps in the subservience of Athens to Sparta a guarantee of their own safety, but there is every reason to suppose that a large majority would have been glad to see Athens once again independent of Sparta and able to assert herself as a force in Greece.

It was the leaders of the Thebans who precipitated the conflict in Greece which Persia had tried to encourage (Xen. *Hell.* III.5.3ff, *Hell. Oxy.* XVII, Paus. III.9.9ff). Ismenias and Androcleidas were aware that the Boeotians would be afraid to attack Sparta while she seemed to be at the height of her power, while Sparta would be reluctant to incur the guilt of breaking the peace, though she would welcome the chance to humble the arrogance of Thebes if someone else initiated hostilities. Their task was therefore to contrive a situation in which Sparta would be provided with a morally plausible excuse for doing what she wanted to do, attack Thebes, so that Boeotia would then have to fight to defend herself. A long-standing squabble between Phocis and Ozolian Locris gave them their opportunity. Both parties had been in the habit of making raids in disputed territory, but in the past these quarrels had been settled by peaceful means. Now Ismenias and Androcleidas persuaded the Phocians to mount a full-scale invasion of Locris. Since the Locrians were allies of Boeotia, the Theban leaders were then able to urge the Boeotians to a counter-invasion of Phocis. On hearing of the Boeotian decision to invade, the Phocians appealed to Sparta to restrain the Thebans. Though the Spartans did not believe the Phocian story that they had been forced to invade Locris in self-defence, they were glad of the pretext to interfere and ordered the Boeotians to keep out of Phocis. This ultimatum was couched in terms which suggest that they hoped the Boeotians would refuse. The Spartan demand was angrily rejected and the Boeotian invasion of Phocis went ahead. Once again the Phocians turned to Sparta, this time for military aid, and Sparta happily agreed to protect her ally. So, with consummate skill, Ismenias and Androcleidas had achieved their objective.

The Spartan attack was planned to take place in two stages (Xen. *Hell.* III.5.6ff, Diod. XIV.81.1ff, Plut. *Lys.* 28f, Paus. III.5.3ff). First Lysander was sent to Phocis to pick up Phocian troops. He was then to make his way to Haliartus in Boeotia. The king Pausanias was to follow with the full force of Sparta's allies and join Lysander at Haliartus on a predetermined day. So Lysander marched into Boeotia from Phocis and scored an initial success by detaching Orchomenus from Thebes. Then

he headed for Haliartus. Only now, when they could unequivocally
claim to be acting in self-defence, did the Thebans turn to Athens (Xen.
Hell. III.5.7ff).[6] Their envoys played on the yearning for empire that still
smouldered in the breasts of the Athenian people (cf. Andoc. III.20ff)
and suggested that Sparta's hold on the Peloponnese itself could easily be
broken if the disaffected had a leader to turn to. This expectation was not
unreasonable – something similar had happened after the Peace of Nicias
– though in the event it proved false. In formulating their appeal they
had judged the mood of Athens well. A few months before Thrasybulus
had not been prepared to challenge Sparta alone. But now he played a
leading role in promoting the alliance, and according to Xenophon the
vote in favour was unanimous (Xen. *Hell.* III.5.16, cf. Ar. *Eccl.* 195f),
even though it was tantamount to a vote for war, for the alliance, though
defensive, was made with the Boeotians (Tod no. 101 = Harding no. 14,
Lys. XVI.13), and Lysander was already on Boeotian soil.

In the mean time Lysander had reached Haliartus (Xen. *Hell.*
III.5.17ff). But instead of waiting for Pausanias, he first tried to persuade
its people to follow the example of Orchomenus, then, when the Theban
garrison which had been hastily installed prevented this, he besieged the
city. In a Theban counter-attack Lysander was killed, and though the
Thebans suffered some losses when they pursued his men, his Phocian
troops seized the chance to slip off home. When Pausanias arrived at
Haliartus, he found himself confronted not only by the victorious
Thebans but also by an Athenian force commanded by Thrasybulus
(Xen. *Hell.* III.5.22ff, Lys. XIV.5, 14, XVI.13f, Plut. *Lys.* 29.1, Paus.
III.5.4). His position was unattractive, he lacked cavalry, and his
Peloponnesian troops were reluctant to fight. So the king decided not to
offer battle and chose instead to recover the bodies of Lysander and his
men under a truce before withdrawing under the insults of the Thebans.
At Sparta he was put on trial for his life on charges that seem to stem
from the friends of Lysander: he was accused of arriving too late at
Haliartus, of failing to fight to recover the bodies of the dead, and most
revealingly of all of allowing the *demos* of Athens to go free when he had
had it in his power. Since he wisely did not present himself for judgment,
he was condemned to death in absence and went into exile at Tegea.

II. THE WAR ON LAND, 395–394 B.C.

After Haliartus Athens and Thebes set out to strengthen themselves
(Diod. XIV.82.1ff, cf. Tod no. 102 = Harding no. 16: Athenian–Locrian
alliance). Corinth and Argos were quickly persuaded to join forces with
them: the belief with which the Theban envoys had tempted Athens, that

[6] Seager 1967 (c 250) 96ff.

the universal hatred in which she was held would make the overthrow of
Sparta an easy matter, seems to have been shared by all the major powers.
The allies established a council of war at Corinth, about the detailed
workings of which nothing is known. Their first step was to send out
embassies to detach as many cities as possible from Sparta. In regions
where Athens and Corinth had long been influential they had considerable success: according to Diodorus Euboea, Acarnania, Leucas,
Ambracia and the cities of Chalcidice all threw in their lot with the allies,
though the surviving Athenian alliance with Eretria belongs to 394/3
(Tod no. 103 = Harding no. 2). But ominously, despite the Theban
prophecy at Athens, there were no further defections from Sparta within
the Peloponnese itself.

The first operations of the alliance, probably in the autumn of 395,
were conducted in central and northern Greece, with a view to
weakening Sparta's position in the region and perhaps to hindering
Agesilaus' return should he be recalled (Diod. xiv.82.5ff). A force was
sent north in answer to an appeal from Medius of Larissa, who expelled
the Spartan garrison from Pharsalus, while the Boeotians and Argives
took Heraclea and restored the place to its Trachinian inhabitants with
an Argive garrison. Of the prisoners taken, the Spartans were killed,
while the other Peloponnesians were allowed to depart unharmed, a
decision which shows the desire to drive a wedge between Sparta and her
allies. Ismenias then detached the Aenianes and Athamanes from Sparta
and led a force recruited from these peoples into Phocis, where he won a
victory. The armies then dispersed to their various homes.

It is also probable that, immediately after Haliartus, work was begun
at Athens on the rebuilding of the Long Walls and the restoration of the
fortifications of the Piraeus.[7] Thrasybulus had stressed Athens' defence-
less condition in his reply to the Theban envoys, and though the earliest
surviving evidence for work on the walls comes from the last month of
395/4 (Tod no. 107A = Harding no. 17), there is every reason to suppose
that it began as soon as war broke out. The task was an urgent one, on
both military and psychological grounds. Not only must Athens be able
to defend herself; she was also setting out to recover her empire, of
which the walls were a potent symbol as well as the practical foundation.[8]

In winter 395/4 Sparta came to a decision which marked a further
triumph for Persian policy. Convinced that she could not face the
alliance now ranged against her and carry on a major war in Asia, and
deprived of two experienced commanders by the death of Lysander and
the exile of Pausanias, she recalled Agesilaus (Xen. *Hell.* iv.2.1ff, Diod.
xiv.83.1ff, Plut. *Ages.* 15). The king was bitterly disappointed at this

[7] Maier 1959 (B 153) 32; Perlman 1968 (C 220) 261; against: Pritchett 1971–91 (K 51) II 120, in
ignorance of the date of Cnidus, for which cf. Lys. xix.28.   [8] Seager 1967 (C 250) 112.

blow to his ambitions, but obeyed without question, though he promised to return if circumstances should permit and left a substantial force in Asia. In spring 394 he set out for home by the roads once taken by Xerxes. He was accompanied by contingents of troops from his Asiatic allies, though his own men needed the stimulus of prizes for turn-out to overcome their reluctance to fight against Greeks.

In Greece both sides were busy with preparations for the new campaign (Xen. *Hell.* IV.2.9ff). Timolaus the Corinthian urged the allies to fight in Laconia or as close to it as possible, before Sparta could assemble her full complement of allied forces. His advice was recognized as good, but the inevitable arguments over the division of command and disposition of troops caused delay, while the Spartans, led by Aristode-mus, regent for the young king Agesipolis, were already on the move after collecting men from Tegea and Mantinea. So the Spartans reached Sicyon at the same time as the allied army arrived at Nemea. As well as the forces of the four major powers, the latter included contingents from Euboea, Locris, Malis and Acarnania (Xen. *Hell.* IV.2.17). The battle of Nemea (or Corinth) took place probably in April or May 394, for inscriptions alluding to Athenian losses in the territory of Corinth in 394/3 (Tod nos. 104, 105, *IG* II² 5221 = Harding no. 19B, C and A) need not refer to it.[9] To Xenophon's partial eye it was a triumph for the organization of the Spartans over the arrogance and indiscipline of the Thebans. Though all Sparta's allies were defeated, the Spartans them-selves inflicted substantial casualties on all four of their principal opponents as their forces rashly pursued the routed Spartan allies. The eventual losses of the anti-Spartan alliance were more than double those on the Spartan side, and the allied army fled for refuge to Corinth, where at first it found the gates shut against it, though thanks to the efforts of a minority of Corinthians they were opened in time to prevent further losses. Their action was gratefully remembered at Athens (Dem. xx.52ff), but the original closing of the gates continued to rankle (Ar. *Eccl.* 199f). In general Athenian enthusiasm for the war seems to have been waning. Even before the battle men had tried to evade service, and Thrasybulus, who was again in command, was free with accusations of cowardice afterwards, while morale grew even worse at the news of Agesilaus' approach (Lys. XVI.15f).

Agesilaus had reached Amphipolis when he heard of the victory at Nemea. Much encouraged, he pressed onwards through Macedon to Thessaly, where the allies of the Boeotians did their best to delay his advance, but with little success (Xen. *Hell.* IV.3.1ff, *Ages.* II.2, Plut. *Ages.* 16). By 14 August 394 (the date is given by an eclipse) the king had crossed the borders of Boeotia and was encamped at Chaeronea (Xen.

⁹ Funke 1980 (C 24) 79ff; against: Aucello 1964 (C 4) 33ff.

Hell. IV.3.10ff, Plut. *Ages.* 17). There he received news of a different kind:
the report that Spartan naval power in the Aegean had been shattered by
the victory of Conon and Pharnabazus at Cnidus. For the sake of morale
he told his troops that Sparta had won a naval battle, then advanced into
Boeotia, where he was joined by Spartan and allied reinforcements from
the Peloponnese and contingents from Orchomenus and Phocis. The
Boeotians and their allies had gathered at Coronea, and there a battle was
fought towards the end of August (Xen. *Hell.* IV.3.15ff, *Ages.* II.6ff,
Diod. XIV.84.1f, Plut. *Ages.* 18f). Agesilaus routed the Argives, but an
initial success won by the Thebans drove him to adopt dangerous tactics
and, though he emerged victorious, he was wounded. The Thebans
refused to fight again, and so the Spartans set up a trophy. They then
disbanded their forces, and Agesilaus sailed home (Xen. *Hell.* IV.4.1).

There was to be no further major land battle between the more or less
complete forces of the two sides. Until the first Spartan invasion of the
Argolid in 391, the land war was confined to the neighbourhood of
Corinth, which served as a base for the allies, while the Spartans operated
from Sicyon. At the end of this first phase of the war none of the major
Greek powers had much cause for satisfaction. If Athens, Thebes,
Corinth and Argos had hoped to see Spartan power in the Peloponnese
crumble to nothing, that hope had been disappointed. To that extent
Sparta could claim success, but she had been forced to abandon her
enterprise in Asia, while beyond the Isthmus she had suffered setbacks in
central and northern Greece. This last point gave Thebes some comfort.
But the only power to have derived unmitigated gain from the struggles
of the Greeks was Persia.

III. THE RETURN OF CONON

After the Persian naval victory at Cnidus, Conon and Pharnabazus spent
the rest of the summer of 394 on a tour of the islands and coastal cities,
driving out Spartan harmosts but promising respect for the autonomy of
Sparta's former subjects (Xen. *Hell.* IV.8.1ff, Diod. XIV.84.3ff). This
approach was recommended to the Persian by Conon on the cynical but
practical ground that any open admission of Persia's imperial objectives
might provoke troublesome, perhaps even concerted, resistance. Conon
may also have had at the back of his mind the thought that, if the
liberated cities kept a measure of independence, it would be easier at
some time in the future to detach them from Persia and bring them once
more into a revived Athenian empire. His policy met with considerable
success, both among the islands and on the mainland. Sparta was
deprived of Cos, Nisyros and Telos, Chios expelled its Spartan garrison,
and Mytilene, Ephesus and Erythrae followed suit. Statues were erected

in Conon's honour at Erythrae, Ephesus and Samos (Tod no.
106 = Harding no. 12D, Paus. VI.3.16). Some of these cities then formed
an alliance known from its surviving coins.[10] While Pharnabazus spent
the winter trying in vain to dislodge Dercyllidas from Abydus, he sent
Conon to win over the cities of the Hellespont, to recruit mercenaries,
and to assemble as large a fleet as possible by spring 393.

At the beginning of spring the expedition set sail and made its way
through the Cyclades to Melos. A garrison was placed on Paros, which
was seized with the aid of Siphnian exiles, while the approach of the
Persians provoked an exodus from Siphnos itself (Isoc. XIX.18ff). The
Spartan garrison was driven from Cythera and replaced by one commanded by the Athenian Nicophemus. Not only could Cythera serve as a
base for raids on Laconia; it occupied a crucial position on the sea routes
round the Peloponnese and from Egypt. Pharnabazus then proceeded to
the Isthmus, where he encouraged the coalition to vigorous prosecution
of the war and, according to Diodorus, made an alliance with its
members. He then returned to Asia, leaving behind all the money he had
had with him (Xen. *Hell.* IV.8.7ff, Diod. XIV.84.4ff).

His fleet he entrusted to Conon, who promised to maintain it from the
islands (Xen. *Hell.* IV.8.9ff, Diod. XIV.85). Conon also expressed his
intention of joining in the rebuilding of the Long Walls and the
fortifications of the Piraeus. Pharnabazus accepted that by strengthening
Athens this enterprise would benefit Persia and gave the project his
blessing. Apart from the beginning of work on the walls there had
already been certain other signs of reviving Athenian ambitions: the
embassy of Phormisius and Epicrates to Persia probably belongs to the
summer of 394, as soon as the news of Cnidus reached Athens,[11] and
honours were paid to Dionysius of Syracuse early in 393 (Tod no.
108 = Harding no. 20). But when Conon came to Athens in the middle of
summer 393 his contribution to the work of rebuilding was so vital that
it is hardly surprising that he gained almost all the credit.[12] His crews
performed a large part of the labour, and Persian gold was employed in
paying for the services of others, both Athenians and from elsewhere,
including a contingent of 500 skilled men from Thebes (cf. Tod no.
107 = Harding no. 17, Diod. XIV.85.3).

Whether Conon also conducted naval operations in the Aegean is
obscure. He is unlikely to have had much time in 393, but the accusations
brought against him by Antalcidas on his mission to Tiribazus in
summer 392 suggest at least some measure of activity. The psychological
significance of Cnidus for Athenian imperialism had been great.[13] The
fact that it had been a Persian victory was conveniently forgotten and

[10] Cawkwell 1956 (B 189), 1963 (B 190).   [11] Funke 1980 (C 24) 106.
[12] Seager 1967 (C 250) 103.   [13] Seager 1967 (C 250) 99ff.

Conon was hailed at Athens as the liberator of the allies (Dem. xx.69). The implication is clear: in theory at least the unfortunate hiatus in the history of the Athenian empire brought about by Aegospotami and the peace of 404 was now at an end, and any city which had been an ally of Athens before 404 was still an ally, whether it liked it or not. It may be that Conon found it necessary to use his fleet to explain this development to bewildered and perhaps reluctant allies and persuade them to accept the situation, but no specific instance is recorded.[14] Naval intervention may not have been needed to restore Athenian control of the amphictyony at Delos, which had taken place by 393/2 (*Inscr. Délos* 97), but in any event is not ascribed to Conon.

Conon certainly financed and perhaps organized the establishment of an Athenian mercenary force at Corinth, the first commander of which was Iphicrates (Dem. iv.24, Ar. *Plut.* 173, Androt. 324 F 48 = Philoch. 328 F 150). And although the Athenians had not needed his prompting to honour first Dionysius and then Evagoras of Salamis, for his part in the victory of Cnidus (Tod no. 109, *SEG* xxix 86), it was Conon who devised the more grandiose scheme of persuading Dionysius to contract a marriage alliance with Evagoras and to give his active support to Athens against Sparta. However, all that the Athenian embassy to Syracuse achieved was to dissuade Dionysius from sending a squadron of ships he had prepared to help the Spartans (Lys. xix.19ff).

The summer of 393 also saw the renewal of naval activity in the Corinthian Gulf (Xen. *Hell.* iv.8.10f).[15] The Corinthians had used their share of Pharnabazus' money to man a fleet, of which Agathinus was placed in command. With it they gained control of the Gulf, and were at first successful against Spartan countermeasures. The Spartan *nauarch* Podanemus was killed, perhaps late in 393, perhaps not until the spring of 392, and his *epistoleus* Pollis was wounded and returned to Sparta.

In the spring of 392, after a season of campaigning in 393 in which only Corinth had suffered from the ravages of war while the lands of her allies had been cultivated without hindrance, men whom Xenophon somewhat paradoxically describes as the 'most and best' of the Corinthians decided to try to take their city out of the conflict (Xen. *Hell.* iv.4.1ff, Diod. xiv.86.1ff).[16] But their intentions became known, and the other allies, together with those Corinthian leaders who had been responsible for the original decision to go to war, set about forestalling them. Athens, Thebes and especially Argos were afraid that Corinth would return to her allegiance to Sparta, while the Corinthians involved were doubtless also concerned for their lives. The universally accepted dictum that they wished to impose a democratic constitution on Corinth rests solely, however, on a rather adventurous emendation in the text of

[14] Funke 1980 (c 24) 127ff.   [15] Funke 1980 (c 24) 83f.   [16] Funke 1980 (c 24) 84f.

Diodorus. They planned to massacre their opponents on the last day of the festival of the Eukleia, but the plot was only partially successful. Many of the older partisans of peace were cut down, but the younger men had gathered in a gymnasium, for one of their leaders, Pasimelus, had got wind of what was afoot. They occupied Acrocorinth and resisted an attempt by Argive troops to dislodge them. But omens persuaded them to abandon their position and so they withdrew from the city. Some later returned to Corinth under a guarantee of safe conduct from those who had seized power, but they found themselves unable to endure the situation they found there. For politically Corinth was being swallowed up by Argos. Argive citizenship was being forced on the Corinthians and the city was no longer even known by the name of Corinth but was called Argos. It is likely that, despite modern doubts, Xenophon is right in his consistently expressed view that this union of Corinth with Argos took place in a single stage and was completed not long after the coup of March 392.[17]

So a group led by Pasimelus and Alcimenes plotted to restore Corinthian independence of Argos, expel the perpetrators of the massacre and re-establish ordered government. Pasimelus and Alcimenes succeeded in making contact with the Spartan polemarch at Sicyon, Praxitas, and promised to admit him within the long walls which joined Corinth to her port of Lechaeum. Praxitas duly accepted the offer and set out with his own troops, the Sicyonians and the Corinthian exiles. But at first he was reluctant to enter the gates, then, when he was once inside, he did no more than fortify a position within which he could wait for assistance. One day passed without incident, but on the next a force of Argives and Corinthians and Iphicrates' mercenaries came up. The Argives first drove the Sicyonians down to the sea, but were later thrown into a panic by the Spartans and Corinthian exiles and suffered heavy losses. More seriously, the Boeotian garrison which had held Lechaeum for the allies was wiped out and the port fell into Spartan hands. But despite this success Praxitas was in no position to try to force an entry into Corinth proper. Instead he first of all breached the walls between Corinth and Lechaeum to strengthen his hold on the port, then captured and garrisoned Sidus and Crommyon and fortified Epieicea before disbanding his troops and withdrawing to Sparta.

IV. THE PEACE NEGOTIATIONS OF 392–391 B.C.

Early in the summer of 392, before Praxitas' success at Lechaeum, Sparta decided to make an attempt to detach Persia from her enemies (Xen. *Hell.* IV.8.12ff).[18] Four years before it had been the activities of Agesilaus

---

[17] Tuplin 1982 (C 387); against: Griffith 1950 (C 362) and Whitby 1984 (C 390).
[18] Aucello 1965 (C 5); Seager 1967 (C 250) 104ff; Funke 1980 (C 24) 136ff.

on land that had threatened Persian dominion in Asia Minor and Persia had moved with uncommon speed to counter the danger. But now it could be argued that the principal threat to Persian interests lay in the resurgence of Athenian naval power, even though the 4,000 men whom Agesilaus had left behind under Euxenus (Xen. *Hell.* IV.2.5) were still in Asia. Conon's position had from the first been full of ambiguities, and as Athens' ambitions grew with her confidence there was ground for suspicion that Conon was in fact betraying the King by using Persian money with the ultimate object of restoring the Athenian empire. So Antalcidas was sent out to put this point of view to the satrap Tiribazus at Sardis and to try to negotiate a peace between Sparta and the King. The Spartans hoped that, if he succeeded, Tiribazus would give them active support or at least stop financing Conon.

The news of Antalcidas' mission alarmed Sparta's enemies, and Athens took the lead in organizing countermeasures. She sent envoys to Sardis, who were accompanied by Conon, and persuaded Boeotia, Corinth and Argos to do the same. In his proposed peace between Sparta and Persia Antalcidas had suggested terms which were eventually to become the nucleus of the King's Peace: that Sparta would not challenge the King for control of the Greek cities of Asia – she was of course in no position to do so – and that the islands and the Greek cities elsewhere should be declared autonomous. This, he pointed out, would be sufficient to secure Persia against the ambitions of either Sparta or Athens. Tiribazus found the proposal attractive, but the allies were unimpressed. According to Xenophon Athens feared that she would be deprived of Lemnos, Imbros and Scyros, which were not only vital stations on the corn route from the Black Sea but important sources of supply in their own right; Thebes that she would have to restore the independence of the Boeotian cities; and Argos that she would be unable to maintain her hold over Corinth. The objection ascribed to Athens does less than justice to the scope of her ambitions, but the fears of Thebes and Argos make clear what Antalcidas may not have seen fit to stress to Tiribazus, that the terms he was proposing would not only guarantee Persia's position in Asia Minor but would also restore Spartan supremacy in the Peloponnese and central Greece. The allies' attitude must also have made it clear to Tiribazus, if he had not realized it already, that, however attractive the terms were on paper, a purely bilateral peace with Sparta could not bring the desired results unless the other Greek cities were prepared to accept its conditions. For the moment they refused to do so, and the envoys all went home. Tiribazus did not dare to commit himself openly to Sparta without instructions from the King, but he gave Antalcidas money to strengthen the Spartan naval effort and arrested Conon for acting against Persian interests, though the Athenian later escaped and made his way to Cyprus, where he died (Nep. *Con.* 5.4).[19] The satrap then set out to consult his master.

The representatives of the Greek states met again at Sparta in the winter of 392/1. It must have been Sparta who took the lead in arranging the meeting, but Tiribazus will obviously have been interested in the outcome, though he may not have sent a representative. One of the Athenian envoys was Andocides, and the speech in which he recommended acceptance of the peace to the Athenian Assembly reveals the nature of the people's ambitions.[20] In his bizarre account of fifth-century history he purported to show that peace with Sparta had never threatened the existence of democracy at Athens. But democracy and empire had flourished and fallen together, and it is plain from the detail of his arguments that what he was really trying to prove to his hearers was that peace with Sparta had always been compatible with, and had indeed fostered, the acquisition and enjoyment of empire. At the same time he issued a warning. A concession had been made: Athens was to be allowed to keep Lemnos, Imbros and Scyros. But any attempt to recover other lost ground would not be tolerated by Persia or by Athens' Greek allies. That was as close as Andocides dared to come to a mention of the fate of the Greeks of Asia. In conclusion he urged the Athenians to be patient, to rest content for the moment with possession of their walls and fleet, the foundations on which any empire must be built, and to wait for a better opportunity for further expansion, since to fight both Sparta and Persia could lead only to disaster.

Of the other allies, Boeotia was now prepared to make peace, for Sparta had made a much greater concession to Thebes than she had to Athens. Autonomy need be granted only to Orchomenus; the rest of the Boeotian confederacy was to remain intact and under Theban control (Andoc. III.13,20). But for Sparta compromise on the independence of Corinth was out of the question, and so Argos still pressed for war, for her territory had so far suffered no damage and she was eager to maintain her dominion over her neighbour (Andoc. III.41). Andocides stressed the change in the attitude of Thebes, for he knew that the opposition to peace at Athens was led by the architect of the Boeotian alliance, Thrasybulus (Andoc. III.25,28,32, Ar. *Eccl.* 202f,356).[21] The lack of success at Nemea and Coronea had driven Thrasybulus from the centre of the stage, and the excitement of Cnidus and Conon's return had kept him out of the limelight. But now Conon's arrest and the terms of the proposed peace had made it clear that Athens' imperial ambitions could no longer be pursued without offending Persia. So the way was open for Thrasybulus to reassert himself as the champion of unlimited expansion

---

[19] Barbieri 1955 (C 93) 185ff.   [20] Seager 1967 (C 250) 105ff.
[21] Seager 1967 (C 250) 107f.

in defiance not only of Sparta but of Persia too, and he intervened decisively in favour of continuing the war. The Spartan ambassadors may not even have been allowed to state their case, and the assembly voted, as Philochorus puts it (328 F 149, cf. Pl. *Menex.* 245b), not to abandon the Greeks of Asia to the King. Andocides and his colleagues were charged with neglect of duty by Callistratus and condemned to exile. The mood of disillusionment with Conon's achievement and the renewed ascendancy of Thrasybulus are both reflected in Lysias' *Epitaphios* (11.59f,63), where Cnidus is lamented as a disaster for Greece and the rebuilding of the Long Walls is ascribed, not as elsewhere to Conon, but to the men of Phyle.

V. THE WAR ON LAND, 391–388 B.C.

During the period of the diplomatic moves at Sardis and Sparta there had been no change in the nature of the war on land (Xen. *Hell.* IV.4.14ff, Diod. XIV.86.4). The allies continued to hold Corinth, the Spartans Sicyon. For the former the most important objective was the recovery of Lechaeum and the rebuilding of the walls which linked it with Corinth. This was accomplished in the winter of 392/1, probably after the failure of the negotiations at Sparta (cf. Andoc. III.18). Xenophon speaks only of the restoration of the walls by a major Athenian expedition, but Diodorus mentions a siege of Lechaeum, with Boeotians, Argives and Corinthians involved as well as Athenians, and suggests, though the text is uncertain, that the siege was successful and that Lechaeum was again garrisoned by Boeotian troops. Since the rebuilding of the walls would be pointless, even if it could be carried out, while Lechaeum itself remained in enemy hands, it is reasonable to suppose that Xenophon has taken this for granted.

However, the allied success was shortlived. The Spartans sent out Agesilaus in spring 391 (Xen. *Hell.* IV.4.19ff, *Ages.* II.17, Diod. XIV.86.4, Plut. *Ages.* 21.1). His initial and, in Xenophon's view, principal target was Argos, for her attitude had played a major part in the outcome of the conference at Sparta. But after ravaging widely in the Argolid the king turned towards Corinth by way of Tenea, and it may be that the move against Argos, though worthwhile in itself, was intended in part as a diversion, to lull the occupants of Corinth into a false sense of security and perhaps to draw off Argive forces. At all events the second phase of the operation was a brilliant success. Agesilaus recaptured the newly rebuilt long walls, while his brother Teleutias, with only twelve ships, seized the port and dockyards of Lechaeum, driving the survivors of the garrison back to Corinth. This completed the restoration of Spartan naval supremacy in the Gulf, for Teleutias' predecessor Herippidas had already dislodged Agathinus' successor Proaemus from Rhium (Xen. *Hell.* IV.8.11).

Elsewhere Iphicrates' mercenaries ranged far afield, trapping a Phliasian force in an ambush and ravaging widely in Arcadia (Xen. *Hell.* IV.4.15ff, Diod. XIV.91.3). The former exploit was counter-productive, for the Phliasians were so alarmed that, despite their fear that Sparta would restore the exiles to power, they called in the Spartans and asked them for protection, which was granted.

In 390 Agesilaus again invaded Corinthian territory (Xen. *Hell.* IV.5.1ff, *Ages.* II.18f, Diod. XIV.91.2). The main object of his expedition is again uncertain. Xenophon presents it as solely an attempt to weaken the position of those in the city by capturing or destroying the cattle which they kept on the peninsula of Piraeum and which formed one of their major sources of food. This would have been, of course, a perfectly adequate target for the Spartans. But Diodorus speaks of a would-be coup by the exiles now re-established in Lechaeum, who were actually admitted into Corinth, but were driven back with heavy losses by Iphicrates when they tried to seize the walls. If this is so, then Agesilaus' move from Piraeum towards Corinth, which in Xenophon is no more than a feint to draw off Corinthian forces from his real objective, may have been intended to support the coup, only to be forestalled by Iphicrates' prompt response. At the Isthmus Agesilaus found the Argives celebrating the Isthmia. They fled back to the city at his approach, and Agesilaus waited in the neighbourhood until the festival had been held by the Corinthian exiles (Plut. *Ages.* 21.1ff, cf. Diod. XIV.86.5). But after his departure the Argives returned and conducted their own Isthmia.

The Corinthians on Piraeum took refuge in the Heraeum, while Agesilaus captured the fort of Oenoe. The occupants of the Heraeum then surrendered to him, and those who had played any part in the massacre of 392 were handed over to the exiles. This series of Spartan successes encouraged the Boeotians to send a fresh embassy to the king to enquire about terms (Xen. *Hell.* IV.5.6ff, Diod. XIV.91.2, Plut. *Ages.* 22.1ff). Agesilaus pretended to be unaware of their existence, but then came news which completely changed the situation. Iphicrates had followed up his prevention of the attempted coup at Corinth with another, more dramatic victory. Agesilaus had left at Lechaeum all the Amyclaeans in his army so that they could return home, as was their custom, to celebrate the Hyacinthia. The polemarch at Lechaeum escorted them past Corinth with the *mora* which was stationed at the port and his Spartan cavalry. He then set out to return to Lechaeum with some 600 hoplites, apparently convinced that no force would come against him from Corinth. But Iphicrates and Callias (the commander of the Athenian hoplites in the city) seized their opportunity and led out their men, though the fighting seems to have been almost exclusively the work of Iphicrates' peltasts. The polemarch compounded his initial arrogance with a display of suicidal tactics which resulted in the loss of about 250 of his men. The survivors escaped to Lechaeum. Agesilaus made at once for the port, but when he heard that the bodies of the dead had already been recovered, he returned to Piraeum and went on with the sale of his booty. The Boeotian envoys now said nothing more about peace, but asked instead for safe conduct into Corinth to visit their troops. Agesilaus refused, but took them with him to the walls of Corinth. When his challenge to battle had not surprisingly been ignored he sent the ambassadors home by sea, installed a fresh *mora* at Lechaeum, and led the survivors of the battle home past those Arcadian cities whose fear of the mercenaries the Spartans had recently mocked and who now in their turn jeered the Spartans in their defeat.

But for all its short-term psychological effect and its place in the orators' roll of the triumphs of Athens the defeat of the *mora* was of little real importance. Spartan losses had not been great, and although Iphicrates was able to undo most of Praxitas' work, driving the Spartan garrisons out of Crommyon and Sidus and also recapturing Oenoe, the Spartans retained control of Lechaeum (Xen. *Hell.* IV.5.19). It is possible that at this point the Argives sent a large force to strengthen their hold on Corinth (Diod. XIV.92.1f, cf. Xen. *Hell.* IV.8.34), though Diodorus is almost certainly mistaken in placing the union of Corinth with Argos as late as this.[22] This increase in the Argive presence led to friction with Iphicrates, who in winter 390/89 went so far as to plan a coup of his own to seize the city for Athens. But his designs were thwarted and the Argives asked for his removal. Reluctant to offend an ally close to home when their thoughts were on naval adventure in the Aegean, the Athenians complied. In spring or summer 389 Iphicrates was replaced by Chabrias, who had recently returned from Thrace, where he had been serving with Thrasybulus. In this year or the next he too scored successes at Phlius and Mantinea and made raids into Laconia (Scholiast on Aelius Aristides *Pan.* 274f.D, Polyaen. III.11.6,15).

In 389 Agesilaus was diverted to north-west Greece. There the Achaean garrison which had occupied Calydon was under pressure from the Acarnanians, who had some help from Boeotia and Athens (Xen. *Hell.* IV.6.1ff, *Ages.* II.20, Plut. *Ages.* 22.5). So the Achaeans sent envoys to Sparta, who discreetly threatened to withdraw from the Spartan alliance unless she gave them support. Agesilaus presented the Acarnanians with an ultimatum, saying that he would ravage their land unless they renounced their alliance with Boeotia and Athens and changed

---

[22] Tuplin 1982 (C 387).

sides. They refused, and so he began to carry out his threat and also, in response to Achaean pressure, made assaults on some Acarnanian cities, though with no success. When autumn came he returned to the Peloponnese despite Achaean complaints that he should at least prevent the enemy from sowing next season's crops. The king pointed out that if the Acarnanians had a crop at stake they would be more likely to make peace in the following spring, when he promised to return. He then made his way through Aetolia (for the Aetolians hoped that he would help them to recover Naupactus) and crossed to the Spartan-held port of Rhium, for the presence of Athenian ships at Oeniadae made a crossing direct from Calydon impossible. Xenophon's sudden surprising mention of this squadron is a reminder of how scrappy our information is, even on so vital a strategic matter as control of the Corinthian Gulf, but at least it highlights the strain that was being placed on Athenian resources by this time.

Early in 388 Agesilaus kept his promise and announced a fresh expedition to Acarnania (Xen. *Hell.* iv.7.1). His prediction was at once fulfilled. Without waiting for the invasion to take place the Acarnanians made peace with the Achaeans and an alliance with Sparta. This left Sparta free to turn her attention to Argos, with the alleged objective of clearing the ground for a possible campaign against Athens or Boeotia (Xen. *Hell.* iv.7.2ff, Diod. xiv.97.5). While the Spartan army assembled at Phlius, the young king Agesipolis consulted Zeus and Apollo about the propriety of ignoring the old Argive ploy of delaying the invasion by resort to a sacred truce. Reassured by the gods that such abuse of religion had no force, he marched into Argive territory, but on his first night in the field an earthquake led his men to expect a return home. However, Agesipolis insisted that the tremor demonstrated the favour of Poseidon and went on with the campaign in an effort to outdo Agesilaus. Only after he had done considerable damage did unfavourable omens finally compel him to withdraw.

VI. THE AEGEAN, 391–386 B.C.

It was not only in Greece that Antalcidas' mission failed to bear the fruit that Sparta had hoped for. When Tiribazus reached Susa he found Artaxerxes unsympathetic to the notion of co-operation with Sparta (Xen. *Hell.* iv.8.16ff, Diod. xiv.99.1ff). Tiribazus was retained at court, and in his place the King sent down Struthas, who was more concerned with what Persia had actually suffered at the hands of Agesilaus than with the threat of a revival of Athenian imperialism and so preferred to help Athens. So the Spartans were forced to renew the war in Asia, sending out Thibron in the summer of 391. He established himself at Ephesus and soon gained control of the plain of the Maeander. But as Struthas bided his time, Thibron's raids on Persian territory grew increasingly arrogant and careless, and eventually the Persian cavalry caught him off his guard. Thibron himself was killed at the outset of Struthas' attack, and his force suffered heavy losses.

But Sparta was now offered an opportunity to recover at least some of the ground that she had lost in the Aegean as a result of her defeat at Cnidus. An embassy arrived from the oligarchic exiles on Rhodes, who had been expelled from their city in 395. The envoys suggested that Rhodes was in danger of falling completely under Athenian influence, and the Spartans were both alarmed by this prospect and eager to restore their own position on Rhodes (Xen. *Hell.* IV.8.20ff, Diod. XIV.97.3).[23] In autumn 391 they sent out Ecdicus with eight ships, to aid their friends on Rhodes; and Diphridas, to take over the survivors of Thibron's army, protect the cities which had welcomed Thibron, and raise troops to fight against Struthas. Diphridas enjoyed some success, capturing Struthas' daughter and son-in-law on their way to Sardis and exacting a substantial ransom with which to hire more men. But Ecdicus, though he contrived to detach Samos from Athens, got no further than Cnidus, where he spent the winter, for he had heard that the *demos* was in full control on Rhodes, with twice as many ships as he had himself.

Early in spring 390 Teleutias was ordered to take over from Ecdicus, with the twelve ships under his command at Lechaeum (Xen. *Hell.* IV.8.23ff, Diod. XIV.97.4). He sailed by way of Samos and Cnidus, more than doubling the size of his fleet on the voyage, for he eventually arrived at Rhodes with twenty-seven ships. On the last leg of his journey, between Cnidus and Rhodes, he captured ten Athenian ships, commanded by Philocrates, which had been on their way to Cyprus to help Evagoras of Salamis, whose policy of expansion had provoked Persian countermeasures in 391. It is striking that the Athenian rejection of peace in the previous year does not seem to have been followed by any immediate resumption of naval activity in the Aegean. The cessation of Persian subsidies after Conon's arrest may have contributed to the delay. Nor, until Sparta's attempt to intervene on Rhodes in autumn 391, was there any urgent task for an Athenian fleet to perform. But Philocrates' mission makes it clear that the spirit in which Athens had rejected the peace still prevailed, for the sending of help to Evagoras was a blatant act of provocation towards the King.

The voyage of Teleutias convinced Athens that steps must be taken to check the resurgence of Spartan power in the Aegean.[24] Thrasybulus, the principal advocate of war in 391, proposed the sending out of a fleet, and

---

[23] Seager 1967 (C 250) 108ff; Perlman 1968 (C 220); Cawkwell 1976 (C 112); Funke 1980 (C 24) 94ff.   [24] Seager 1967 (C 250) 109ff; Perlman 1968 (C 220); Funke 1980 (C 24) 152ff.

he himself was put in command of forty ships (Xen. *Hell.* IV.8.25ff, Diod. XIV.94.2ff, Lys. XXVIII.4). His expedition was conceived specifically as a counter to that of Teleutias and he had firm orders to assist the democrats on Rhodes. His precise movements are unclear, but it seems likely that he came as close to Rhodes as Halicarnassus (Lys. XXVIII.17) before deciding for the moment against intervention on the grounds that his own force was not strong enough to dislodge the exiles from their fortress, while the *demos* was in no danger of losing control of the cities. Instead he sailed up the Ionian coast towards the Hellespont, collecting money as he went from the allies of Athens. Athens was now interfering on the mainland of Asia for the first time since Cnidus. This lack of concern for Persian sensibilities is typical of Thrasybulus and the change in Athenian policy.

In the north Thrasybulus achieved considerable success. He reconciled the Thracian princes Amadocus and Seuthes and brought them into alliance with Athens (*IG* II² 21, cf. 22). He also won over Thasos, where Athenian sympathizers led by Ecphantus ejected the Spartan garrison, and probably Samothrace (Dem. XX.59, Xen. *Hell.* V.1.7). Thasos was required to pay the 5 per cent tax which had replaced the old tribute in 413, and may have been subject to judicial interference and the presence of an Athenian *archon* (*IG* II² 24). The 5 per cent tax is also recorded at Clazomenae, which Thrasybulus visited in either 390 or 389 (Tod no. 114 = Harding no. 26). At Byzantium he established a democracy and revived the 10 per cent duty, first imposed in 410, on all goods coming from the Black Sea (Dem. XX.60). He also intervened again in Asia, securing Chalcedon, though without causing offence to Pharnabazus, whose sympathies lay largely with Athens. But it is probable that complaints had been made at home about his neglect of his original mission, and during the winter a decree was passed recalling the other generals on the expedition, though Thrasybulus himself retained his command (Lys. XXVIII.5). Inspired by this warning he moved southwards in spring 389 (Xen. *Hell.* IV.8.28ff, Diod. XIV.94.3f, 99.4f). On Lesbos he found Mytilene favourable to Athens, but the other cities, obeying the canons of local rivalry, were pro-Spartan; Methymna had even retained a Spartan garrison and harmost, despite the general upheaval after Cnidus. Thrasybulus anchored off Eresus, but had the misfortune to lose twenty-three ships in a storm. Nevertheless he defeated the harmost and received the surrender of Eresus and Antissa.

He now made haste towards Rhodes with his surviving ships and others drawn from Mytilene and Chios. The motive for his hurry may have been the news that the situation on Rhodes had taken a turn for the worse: the principal city of the island had fallen to the exiles (cf. Diod. XIV.97.1f, confused and misplaced). But he still went as far afield as

Aspendus in his quest for money, and there the activities of his men provoked a night attack by the inhabitants, in which Thrasybulus himself was one of the victims. The fleet was brought to Rhodes by the trierarchs, who joined forces with the Rhodian democrats, now exiled in their turn.

Thrasybulus' campaigns demonstrate not only the determination of Athens to restore as much as possible of the fifth-century empire regardless of what this might do to relations with Persia, but also the desperate shortage of money felt by the treasury at home and commanders in the field (cf. Ar. *Eccl.* 823ff, 1006f). The speeches composed by Lysias (xxviii, xxix) for the prosecution of Ergocles, one of Thrasybulus' colleagues, and Philocrates, perhaps Ergocles' *tamias*, bear witness to the preoccupations of the people. The generals had been appointed to make Athens 'great and free', a familiar euphemism for the enjoyment of imperial power. Instead they had allegedly diverted into their own pockets money intended for the war, rendered the people's fleet ineffective, and betrayed cities which belonged to the people. Of concern about the way in which the missing funds had been acquired or the treatment meted out to the allies there is no trace.

Nor did Thrasybulus' death and the disgrace of his colleagues bring about any change in Athenian policy. Agyrrhius was at once sent out to the Hellespont to try to retain control of Thrasybulus' gains (Xen. *Hell.* IV.8.31ff, Diod. XIV.99.5). The Spartans too were well aware of the vital importance of the region and sent out Anaxibius to succeed Dercyllidas as harmost of Abydus. At first Anaxibius enjoyed some success, but the Athenians in their turn sent out Iphicrates, whose enforced withdrawal from Corinth had not damaged his credit, to protect Thrasybulus' achievement. For the remainder of 389 the two commanders limited themselves to skirmishes, but in the next year Iphicrates laid an ambush for Anaxibius, who was returning in unguarded fashion from a mission to win over Antandrus, and the Spartan harmost was killed.

Meanwhile, however, Athens had been brought under pressure nearer home.[25] The Spartan harmost on Aegina, Eteonicus, encouraged raids on the Attic countryside, and this nuisance compelled the Athenians to send out a force under Pamphilus, with naval support, to establish a base from which to blockade Aegina. Teleutias, who had returned from Rhodes, drove off the Athenian fleet, but Pamphilus succeeded in holding on to his fort. The new Spartan naval commander, Hierax, sailed to Rhodes in summer 389, but stationed his *epistoleus* Gorgopas at Aegina with twelve ships, and the Athenians were forced to mount a relief expedition to evacuate their fort. In consequence the raids on Attica

[25] Funke 1980 (C 24) 98ff.

started up again, though a fleet under Eunomus was manned to try to prevent them.

By spring 388 Athens had allied herself with another rebel against the King, Acoris of Egypt (Ar. *Plut.* 178), and Artaxerxes had at last seen enough to realize that Tiribazus had been right when he claimed that Athens would be a greater threat than Sparta. So Tiribazus was restored to his post and the pro-Athenian Pharnabazus was recalled to court, to be replaced by another friend of Antalcidas, Ariobarzanes. These changes gave Sparta new hope, and in late summer Antalcidas was appointed as *nauarch* (Xen. *Hell.* v.1.6ff). His first task was to reopen negotiations with Tiribazus and if possible to gain access to the King himself. When he reached Ephesus he placed his *epistoleus* Nicolochus in command of his ships and set off for Susa in company with Tiribazus.

On Aegina in the summer of 388 Gorgopas inflicted a defeat on Eunomus, but was in his turn defeated and killed by Chabrias, who put in at Aegina on his way to Cyprus to help Evagoras. For a time the Athenians controlled the Saronic Gulf unopposed, since Eteonicus was unable or unwilling to pay his crews, who therefore refused to man the ships. In this critical situation the Spartans turned once again to Teleutias, whose popularity with the men had been emphatically shown at the end of his previous command. He not only persuaded them to return to duty, but carried out with twelve ships a daring night raid on the Piraeus, which succeeded in its principal objectives of undermining Athenian confidence and securing sufficient booty to pay the troops.

But it was not only on Aegina that spring 387 was to prove a turning-point. Antalcidas now returned to the coast with Tiribazus, bearing a promise from Artaxerxes that if the Athenians and their allies refused to accept the peace terms to which the Spartan had persuaded the King to commit himself, Persia would come into the war on the Spartan side to enforce compliance (Xen. *Hell.* v.1.25ff). Antalcidas now emerged as an able commander as well as a skilful diplomat. By a feint he drew off the Athenian fleet from Abydus and so was able to capture a squadron of eight ships under Thrasybulus Collyteus which was attempting a rendezvous. He was soon reinforced by twenty ships from Syracuse and others from the territories of Tiribazus and Ariobarzanes. This brought his naval strength up to more than eighty ships and he was able to control the sea. Though he was not strong enough to repeat in every detail Lysander's strategy in the final phase of the Peloponnesian War, he imitated its most important element, the cutting off of supplies of corn from the Black Sea to Athens. This move was both militarily and psychologically effective. Athens' concern about the corn supply is revealed by her dealings with Satyrus of Bosporus[26] and the prosecution

[26] Tuplin 1982 (E 404).

of the *sitopolai* (Lys. XXII). She still enjoyed some support on the coast of Asia, at Clazomenae, to which she made important concessions (Tod. no. 114 = Harding no. 26), and at Erythrae, which was soon to beg her not to deliver the city into the hands of the barbarians (*SEG* XXVI 1282 = Harding no. 28A), though significantly both places were divided by faction. But she feared another disastrous defeat, while Argos was reluctant to face another Spartan invasion after that of 388. When in the autumn Tiribazus summoned to Sardis all those who wished to hear the terms sent down by the King, representatives of all the major Greek powers convened with flattering speed.

VII. THE KING'S PEACE

On this occasion Tiribazus was armed with a royal rescript, on which the King's seals could be displayed (Xen. *Hell.* v.1.30ff, Diod. XIV.110.3, XV.5.1). In it Artaxerxes proclaimed the terms which he deemed just. The cities of Asia, as well as the islands of Clazomenae and Cyprus, were to belong to Persia. The other Greek cities, both large and small, were to be left autonomous, except for Lemnos, Imbros and Scyros, which were to belong to Athens. If either side did not accept this peace, the King would make war on them with any who were willing to help him. Two features of the rescript stand out. First, the concession made in 392/1 to the Thebans was withdrawn. This will surely have been at Sparta's suggestion: the matter can have been of little interest to Persia, but it was important to Sparta, who was stronger now than she had been in 391 and will not have forgotten the Theban reaction to the defeat of the *mora* at Lechaeum. Secondly, Artaxerxes threatened the Spartans as well as the Athenians and their allies. This seems unnecessary, since the whole scheme was of Spartan devising, but the King may have wished to set himself equally above both parties, while despite the impression that Antalcidas had made on him he probably still distrusted Sparta.

The envoys reported to their various cities and then assembled at Sparta in spring 386 to swear to a peace based on Artaxerxes' rescript. The precise nature of this peace is highly controversial. It may, however, be regarded as certain that the rescript was not the peace. At the very least its provisions would have had to be recast and clauses added concerning such matters as the taking of the oaths and the publication of copies of the peace. It may also be accepted that a representative of the King took part in the oath-swearing ceremony, as documentary evidence attests (Tod. no. 118 = Harding no. 31 lines 10ff), despite claims that the nature of oriental monarchy made such participation unthinkable. What remains debatable is whether the peace contained only the two substantive clauses propounded in the rescript, or whether other clauses found in later renewals of the peace were already present in this original version. It might, for instance, have been prescribed that each city should possess its own territory (though that would have created a problem with regard to *peraiai* on the mainland of Asia, which it is reasonable to suppose were claimed by the King), that garrisons and governors were to be withdrawn, and that all forces, military and naval, were to be demobilized. But such clauses, which aimed at greater clarity and precision, may well have been the product of later experience. It would have suited the Spartans in 386 if the autonomy clause were as general as possible: autonomy was to mean what Sparta wanted it to mean in any given case.[27]

The taking of the oaths did not pass off without incident. The Thebans tried to circumvent the autonomy clause by swearing on behalf of all the Boeotians (Xen. *Hell.* v.1.32ff, Plut. *Ages.* 23.3). Agesilaus firmly rejected this subterfuge and when the envoys temporized told them to warn their people that if Thebes did not back down she would be excluded from the peace. Without waiting for a reply he then began preparing for war in the hope that the Thebans would refuse. But while he was still at Tegea mustering his troops, the envoys returned, ready now to concede the autonomy of the Boeotian cities. The Corinthians too were reluctant to dismiss their Argive garrison. Even if there were in fact a clause in the peace which guaranteed freedom from foreign garrisons, it would hardly have been rational to apply it to a case where the presence of the garrison was welcome to its hosts. But Agesilaus knew perfectly well what the autonomy clause was meant to achieve where Argos and Corinth were concerned. He declared that he would make war on both cities if the Corinthians did not dismiss the Argives or the Argives refused to leave. The Argives duly evacuated the city and Corinth recovered its independence. The authors of the coup of 392 and their supporters prudently withdrew, finding a welcome at Athens (Dem. xx.54), and the exiles returned.

The peace was then sworn and the military and naval forces of both sides were disbanded. Though Sparta had done no more than hold her own during the war, she did extremely well, as Xenophon justly observes, out of her championship of the peace and in particular of the autonomy clause, which enabled her to put an end to Theban domination of Boeotia, to terminate Argive control of Corinth, and to restore Corinth to her own alliance. There is, however, no reason to suppose that the position of *prostates* of the peace was officially assigned to Sparta by a clause of the treaty or in any other way. It was simply that the favour of Persia and her own military strength made Sparta able to interpret the

---

[27] Sinclair 1978 (c 76); against: Cawkwell 1981 (c 18). See also Badian 1991 (F 4) and Clark 1990 (B 138).

terms of the peace to her own advantage and to enforce her will on the other Greek states. Within a decade the weapon which served her so well in 386 would be turned against her. But for the moment, with her enemies humbled, Sparta was free to examine the recent conduct of her friends.

CHAPTER 5

SICILY, 413–368 B.C.

D. M. LEWIS

In the period between the Peloponnesian War and the accession of Philip of Macedon, it is perhaps the events in Sicily which carry the greatest potential interest. Although in the eastern Mediterranean the military and political battle for the Greeks of Asia Minor continues, Greek civilization there is not in cultural danger; in fact, it continues to expand despite its political subjection. In Sicily it remains unclear whether Greeks, the semitic power of Carthage or some Italian people will come out on top. Politically, Sicily offers a chance to see in operation a possible solution to the Greek political dilemma. The Athenian democracy has failed to expand political control beyond the city state, and Sparta will show that oligarchy is no more successful. In Sicily, monarchy has its chance, and operates on a larger scale than the city state. Dionysius I, with his one-man rule over a large territory, his professional army, and his technological resourcefulness, prefigures the hellenistic period with some clarity. On a different level, it is arguable that much of Plato's political experience is Sicilian experience and that understanding Sicily is a prerequisite for understanding him.[1]

That study of these matters is relatively undeveloped compared to the amount of effort put into mainland Greece in the same period is attributable to the nature of the evidence. A very few references in Xenophon and Athenian orators, three Athenian inscriptions, and the controversial letters under the name of Plato practically exhaust the fourth-century evidence for us, and then we have a long gap until the first century B.C. Even then, the once useful evidence provided by Pompeius Trogus[2] is hopelessly obscured for us by his epitomator Justin. Essentially, the story comes to us in one source, Diodorus, and he poses two problems: Firstly, his coverage is wildly uneven; the second half of the reign of Dionysius is covered in very brief references.

---

[1] Narrative and other help throughout this chapter may be sought in Stroheker 1958 (G 302), Caven 1990 (G 134). There is much useful material on relations between Sicily and Carthage in Manni *et al.* 1982–3 (G 225). For Carthaginians in Sicily see Tusa 1988 (G 312).

[2] On Trogus and Justin, see Seel 1972 (B 107); Forni and Bertinelli 1982 (B 39); Syme 1988 (B 113). On Trogus' Sicilian books, see Jacoby, *FGrH* III b (Noten), 314–15 n. 42; Forni and Bertinelli 1982 (B 39) 1334–40.

Secondly, at any rate on the surface, he presents a picture very hostile to Dionysius. There are possibilities for manipulating his evidence, but we have to have some idea of what it is we are manipulating.

On Diodorus' Sicilian narrative, there have been many opinions. Volquardsen,[3] who first established the general principle that Diodorus only used one source at a time, argued that Diodorus used Timaeus of Tauromenium (the modern Taormina) (c. 350–270 B.C.), the famous historian of the West,[4] for western matters; there are many named quotations from him in books XIII–XIV. Some major authorities[5] have followed the overwhelming evidence for supposing that Ephorus, as long as he lasted, was Diodorus' main source for mainland Greek affairs[6] and have found it improbable that he just rolled up Ephorus when he moved to the West, although they have acknowledged the clear evidence that he used Timaeus as well for books XIII and XIV. Unfortunately, the detail of this position has only been worked out in such an extravagant way[7] as to leave it amply vulnerable to successors of Volquardsen. These,[8] satisfied that Diodorus only used one source at a time and knowing that Timaeus was later than Ephorus, find no difficulty in distinguishing features in Diodorus' narrative which they can say are essentially Timaean and prove that he was Diodorus' source. Even they have some difficulty in finding much use of Timaeus in Diodorus book XV.[9]

In recent years, there has been a reaction against crudely single-source views of Diodorus, and many now allow him more independence.[10] The view has some weight in Sicilian history. It seems likely that his own addition or selection has produced an undue emphasis on his native Agyrium (e.g. XIV.95, XVI.82.4–5,83.3), and there is a fair amount, not always successfully executed, which may well be attributed to his own interests and work (XIII.34.6–35, 90.5, XIV.16.3–4, XVI.70.6). As far as his major predecessors are concerned, the most plausible view is that he tried to reinforce Ephorus with Timaeus in books XIII–XIV, but

---

[3] Volquardsen 1868 (B 121) 72–107.

[4] On Timaeus (*FGrH* 566), see Jacoby's commentary on the fragments; Manni 1957 (B 71); Brown 1958 (B 19); Sanders 1987 (G 283) 79–85; Pearson 1987 (B 92).

[5] Schwartz 1903 (B 101) 681–2 = 1957 (B 104) 62–3; Jacoby, *FGrH* III b (Text), 528–30.

[6] See *CAH* V² 7, and pp. 8–10 here.   [7] Laqueur 1937 (B 66) 1082–162 and 1958 (B 67).

[8] Meister 1967 (B 74); Pearson 1984 (B 91).

[9] A native Sicilian school (Lauritano 1956 (B 68); Manni 1957–8 and 1970 (B 72–3)) knows that Diodorus only used one source at a time, but claims that for the West it was the virtually unknown Silenos of Caleacte (*FGrH* 175); the hypothesis is not only unfruitful, but improbable. Nor is there much to be said for the view (Hammond 1938 (B 56)) that Diodorus used Theopompus for Sicilian affairs; see Westlake 1953–4 (B 128).

[10] The most careful treatment of a single stretch of Diodorus along these lines is that by J. Hornblower 1981 (B 60) 18–75. For the West, see now Sanders 1987 (G 283), too dismissive of the probable use of Ephorus.

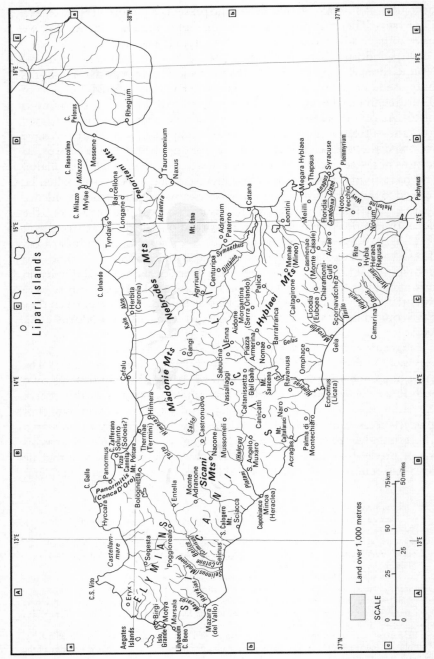

Map 3. Sicily.

Land over 1,000 metres

SCALE

0   25   50   75km
0   25   50miles

Lipari Islands

Aegates Islands
C.S. Vito
Eryx
Islo Grande
Marsala
Lilybaeum
C. Boeo
Mazara (del Vallo)
Motyà
Birgi
Mazaroès
Halykias
Selinus
Mt. Selinus (Mediani)
Cotone
S. Calogero
Sciacca
S. Angelo
Platani
Capobianco
Minoa (Heraclea)
Acragas
Caltafaraci
Palma di Montechiaro
Segesta
Poggioreale
Castellam-mare
C. Gallo
Panormus
C. Zafferano
Pizzo Canita
Solunto (Soloeis?)
Mt. Pòrcara
Conca D'Oro
Bolognetta
Entella
Monte Adranone
Nacone
Mussomeli
Muxaro
Mt. Naro
Canicatti
Ecnomus (Licata)

ELYMIANS
SICANI Mts
SICANIANS
Madonie Mts
Hyblaei Mts

Cefalu
Thermae (Termini)
Castronuovo
Himera
Himeras
Salso
Sabucina
Caltanissetta
Gibil Gabib
Mt. Saraceno
Himeras
Ravanusa
Omphace
Gela
Camarina

C. Orlando
Kale Akte
Herbita (Coronia)
Gangi
Agyrium
Centuripa
Enna
Aidone
Morgantina
Piazza Armerina (Serra Orlando)
Nomae
Palice
Barrafranca
Licodia (Euboea)
Gulfi
Scorravacche
Chiaramonti-
Acrae
Casmenae (Monte Cásale)
Menae (Mineo)
Caltagirone Mts
Symaethus
Dittàino
Nebrodes Mts

C. Milazzo
Mylae
Tyndaris
Barcellona
Longane
Milazzo
Pelorus
C. Rasocolmo
Messene
Taurominium
Naxus
Alcantara
Mt. Etna
Adranum
Paterno
Catana
Leontini
Melilli
Thapsus
Megara Hyblaea
Anapus
Floridia
Cavadonna
Diana
Noto Vecchio
Helorus Way
Syracuse
Plemmyrium
Pachynus
Rito
Hybla
Heraea (Ragusa)
Hyrminus
Irminio
Dirillo
Motyèllo
Hirminus

C. Milazzo
Peloritani Mts

37°N

38°N

16°E

15°E

14°E

13°E

37°N

A   B   C   D   E

abandoned the attempt thereafter; the result was a much reduced account of Dionysius I's last years and a strangely curtailed account of Dion.[11]

The only clear fact about the way that Ephorus and Timaeus treated western history is that Timaeus had much lower figures than Ephorus for the numbers of military forces; there is no real reason for supposing that one was more hostile to Dionysius than the other. The essential point is to try to get behind them[12] to what was perhaps the only contemporary narrative source, the history of Philistus.[13] Philistus was a contemporary and very early supporter of Dionysius, who was trusted for the first twenty years of the reign and then in exile for the rest of it. We know that he wrote most of his history in exile, but that no hostility to Dionysius was visible because he hoped to secure his recall. However, he was not thought to be a mere flatterer, but rather someone who actually believed in tyranny as a form of rule. A historian of this character will have found much to interest him in the hard world of Thucydides, and in fact it is clear that he was the most determined imitator of Thucydides in antiquity. There is no real trace of any other contemporary narrative, and it seems likely that Diodorus' account must be ultimately, though indirectly, dependent on Philistus for facts, but that its hostile elements are not due to the use of another contemporary source, but to positive deformation of those facts by an intermediary or intermediaries. It is clear enough that some bits of Philistus have come through virtually unchanged, above all, the account of the plague which hit the Carthaginian army in 396 (XIV.70.4–71), or the accounts of Dionysius' fortification (XIV.18) and his armaments (XIV.41–2), which show him in a very favourable light. There are other tracts of narrative (e.g. XIV.9) where one only needs to omit a few rude words to get an account basically favourable to Dionysius, perhaps not even that if Philistus was prepared to take a frank, Machiavellian attitude.[14] There is therefore an important sense in which Diodorus can be used if we look at his facts and leave out the colour and interpretation which now enfold them.

If we operate on these principles, it becomes, for example, more than possible that Diodorus has substantially antedated Dionysius' wish to become tyrant. Though the text assumes that this was his wish from the first, everything he is actually said to recommend during the first year,

<hr/>

[11] There is much to be said for Schwartz's view (B 101, 681–2 = B 104, 63) that the abandonment of Dion at XVI.20.6 is due to the fact that Ephorus may well have stopped in 356, but it can be partly neutralized by arguing that *FGrH* 70 F 221 shows that Ephorus described Timoleon's expedition.

[12] Sanders 1979–80 (G 282), 1981 (B 99), 1987 (G 283), and Caven 1990 (G 134) 4–5 believe that Diodorus used Philistus directly. The practical difference of adopting this approach is not great.

[13] *FGrH* 556 with commentary; Manni 1957 (B 71); Zoepffel 1965 (B 133); Pearson 1987 (B 92) 19–30; Sanders 1987 (G 283) 43–71.

[14] XIV.8 *fin.* is possibly such a case, XIV.107.4 even more likely.

406, of the resumed Carthaginian invasion can be amply paralleled on other occasions in Syracusan history when military preparedness was needed, most obviously in lines taken by Hermocrates during the Athenian invasion of 415–413. Dionysius had been an adherent of Hermocrates. Few other sequences can be dealt with as neatly, but the attempt must be made.

By Greek standards, Syracuse in 413 was a largish place. Thucydides (especially VII.58.4) repeatedly speaks as if there were a difference in scale between the cities of western Greece and those of the mainland. We have no figures for Syracusan population. Acragas was evidently the second largest city, and Diodorus (XIII.84.3) gives her 20,000 citizens in 406, 200,000 including foreigners.[15] Thuc. VI.67.2 suggests a Syracusan hoplite-force of over 5,000 and affirms a cavalry-force of more than 1,200; a relative shortage of hoplites in relation to population is suggested by Hermocrates' proposal to share out weapons (Thuc. VI.72.4; cf. Polyaen. 1.43.1). The nature of the Greek population is far from clear. Alcibiades' assertions (Thuc. VI.17.2–3) of the mixture and shifting of Sicilian populations and consequent lack of local patriotism are *ex parte* and may be exaggerated. There had been very marked shifts of population under Gelon in the interests of building up a greater Syracuse (*CAH* IV² 769–70) and more after the fall of the tyranny (*CAH* V² 154–61), and these would be sufficient to create such an opinion at Athens. The 7,000 foreign mercenaries who had been given citizenship by Gelon had long since left (Diod. XI.72.3–73, 76), and the only recent shift of which we know is the move to Syracuse of some of the upper class of Leontini in 423/2 (Thuc. V.4.2–3).[16]

Even more enigmatic is the non-Greek population. Although Nicias asserts and Thucydides endorses the view that nothing much was to be gained by encouraging class warfare at Syracuse (Thuc. VI.20.2, VII.55.2), we do hear of an abortive slave-revolt during the Athenian siege (Polyaen. 1.43.1).[17] It is tempting to associate these slaves with the Cillicyrioi who appear in the 480s, who are evidently some form of indigenous population,[18] though the name does not reappear. It is not possible from the sources to distinguish them from straight slaves or from the local Sicel population under direct Syracusan control, some of whom deserted to the Athenians (e.g. Thuc. VI.88.4).[19] These indigenous populations are rarely of political importance, but they may well have been fundamental to the social structure. We have next to no evidence, but it may be the case that agricultural work was in their hands

[15] Beloch 1886 (A 4) 281–5 doubts the second figure; see De Waele 1979 (G 156). For Himera see Asheri 1973 (G 103).   [16] Diod. XIII.18.5 suggests that they were not yet fully integrated by 413.
[17] Lewis 1977 (A 33) 28 n. 11.
[18] Hdt. VII.155, Phot. *Lex.* s.v.; Dunbabin 1948 (G 160) 111.   [19] See Vattuone 1979 (G 317).

and that the citizen of Syracuse (and indeed of other Sicilian cities) was less closely associated with the land he owned than the Athenian citizen; the mobility of Sicilian populations would be easier to understand if this were so.[20]

For Thucydides, Syracuse appears to be more or less indistinguishable from Athens, in character and in institutions (VIII.96.5, VII.55.2). The demagogue Athenagoras (VI.35.2) is described in terms very similar to those applied to Cleon (III.36.6, IV.21.3), and not much in his defence of democracy (VI.38-9) would sound strange on Athenian lips. The Syracusan *demos* can be exhibited as no less unstable than that of Athens (VI.63.2). Diodorus (XI.68.6) and Aristotle (*Pol.* 1316a33) also speak of democracy in this period. Precise constitutional pointers are few. There were fifteen *strategoi* when the Athenians arrived (VI.72.4).[21] In VI.72.5–73 the board is reduced to three (including Hermocrates); they are to have full powers (*autokratores*) and an oath is to be sworn to allow them to conduct affairs as best they can. This is in no sense a revolution. They do not take office until VI.96.3; the oath is not observed, and they are replaced by three new generals in VI.103.4. The *demos* evidently remains in ultimate control.[22]

Despite Thucydides' emphasis on democracy in the period of the Athenian siege, there is a substantial tradition that there were more radical political changes after 413. Aristotle (*Pol.* 1304a27) says that the success of the *demos* in the war against Athens resulted in a change from a moderate constitution (*politeia*) to democracy. Diodorus has much more. In a passage certainly taken from Ephorus,[23] he introduces us to a demagogue Diocles (XIII.19.4; Eurycles in Plut. *Nic.* 28.1) and moves from the debate about the fate of the Athenian captives to a short account (XIII.34.2–3) of how he later made laws for Syracuse. A longer account attached to the next year (XIII.34.6–35) describes how Diocles persuaded the citizens to change the constitution, have magistrates appointed by lot and have new laws. This account, almost certainly Diodorus' own,[24] is unusable in detail, since it surely confuses the fifth-century Diocles with an archaic law-giver.[25] All we can say is that the number of *strategoi* was

---

[20] For an attempt to see the economic relations between Syracuse and the Sicels, see Ampolo 1984 (G 99). Archaeological evidence of the classical period for the countryside of the Greek cities is sparse; for farm-sites at Camarina see *Arch. Rep. for 1981–2*, 90.

[21] It is not a necessary inference from VI.41.1 that they presided over the assembly. In Diodorus (XI.92.2, XIII.91.3) *archontes* preside.

[22] The command situation is changed by the arrival of the Spartan Gylippus and the Corinthian Pythen, but there are further changes among the Syracusan generals (VII. 46, 50.1, 70.1), not specifically noted.   [23] Barber 1935 (B 11) 164–5.

[24] It refers to King Hiero, probably too late even for Timaeus, and events of 44/3 B.C.

[25] For the archaic Diocles, see Beloch 1912–27 (A 5) I.1, 350 n. 1. There are impossible chronological features in Diodorus' account, and the laws described were in archaic language, hard to understand in the time of Timoleon.

raised again,[26] and that there are arguments for an expansion of state pay.[27]

In the West, after the defeat of the Athenian expedition, there were still mopping-up operations to be done against Athenian allies. A campaign against Catana, where there were Athenian survivors, and Messene was still going on at the time of the Carthaginian invasion (Thuc. VII.85.4, Lys. XX.24–5, Paus. VII.16, Diod. XIII.56.2).[28] Syracuse took less interest in western Sicily, where Selinus resumed her interrupted war (Thuc. VI.6.2) against Elymian Segesta (Diod. XIII.43.2–3). Segesta was conciliatory, but Selinus greedy; there would be substantial consequences.

Revenge on Athens seemed a more important matter. In late summer 412 Hermocrates led twenty Syracusan and two Selinuntine ships to help finish off Athens (Thuc. VIII.26.1).[29] Later reinforcements from the West included ten ships from Thurii under the command of the Rhodian exile Dorieus (Thuc. VIII.35).[30] The Syracusan and Thurian crews were, evidently untypically, mostly free men (Thuc. VIII.84.2). The Syracusan ships were not only effective militarily (Thuc. VIII.28.2, Xen. *Hell.* I.2.10); Hermocrates was a powerful spokesman in negotiations with Tissaphernes (Thuc. VIII.29, 45, 85). But they shared the general disaster at Cyzicus in spring 410 (*CAH* v² 483), and had to rebuild their ships at Antandrus (Xen. *Hell.* I.1.26). It was there apparently that news came from home that Hermocrates and his colleagues had been exiled (Xen. *Hell.* I.1.27, Diod. XIII.63.1). We need not place the 'Dioclean revolution' as late as this. If Syracuse had expected quick success and instead heard of the loss of the fleet after two years, dissatisfaction is not surprising. Hermocrates resisted suggestions from the officers of the fleet to ignore his dismissal, but waited for the arrival of his successors, who arrived to take over the rebuilt fleet at Miletus late in 410. Yet another five ships arrived from home in spring 409 (Xen. *Hell.* I.2.8).[31] All fought well at the battle of Ephesus in summer 409 (*CAH* v² 485); the Syracusans were given fiscal privileges, the Selinuntines, 'since their

[26] Even if we did not have the direct assertion (Pl. *Ep.* VIII.354d) that there were ten generals at the time of Dionysius' rise, it could be inferred that the groups of three generals in the Aegean (e.g. Thuc. VIII.85.3) were members of a larger board.

[27] Meyer 1921 (A 38) 59–60. The pay to citizen troops (Diod. XIII.93.2, 95.1) is obviously more than a ration allowance.

[28] See Giuffrida 1979 (G 184). Further from Syracusan influence, Thurii, where the pro-Athenian party had come to the top in 413 (Thuc. VII.33.6, 57.11), ejected 300 atticizers, including the orator Lysias, in 413–12 ([Plut]. *Mor.* 835D).

[29] The thirty-five ships of Diod. XIII.34.4 evidently include the returning sixteen Peloponnesian ships of Thuc. VIII.13.

[30] In 411, there was an unspecified number from Taras and Locri (Thuc. VIII.91.2, M–L no. 82).

[31] Their commanders were among those who had replaced Hermocrates in 414 (Thuc. VI.103.4), and may have been regarded as politically more reliable.

city had been destroyed', citizenship as well (Xen. *Hell.* 1.2.10). Shortly afterwards, they disappear from the Aegean. Other events have called them home.

All this, based on the chronology argued in *CAH* v² 503–5, allows the inference that the Carthaginian threat had not seemed important at Syracuse when five more ships were sent in early 409, but that the news of the fall of Selinus had reached the Aegean by, say, June. It follows that the preliminaries to the Carthaginian invasion described in Diod. XIII.43–4 belong to 410 and that the year of the Carthaginian invasion which destroyed Selinus and Himera was 409.[32]

It has in general been held (*CAH* iv² 775, and ch. 11e here) that the years after the battle of Himera in 480 had seen a retreat of Carthage from Mediterranean history. In Sicily, she had been penned back on her three settlements in the north-west corner, Motya, Soloeis and Panormus,[33] with friendly ties perhaps with Elymian Segesta, possibly also Selinus.[34] There was trade with Greek Sicily, best attested for Acragas, which had been exchanging the crops of its olives and perhaps its vines for the wealth of Libya. It is not easy to identify this wealth; perhaps Spanish silver was going into Acragas' substantial coinage.[35] The extensive settlements of Carthaginian traders attested for Syracuse and elsewhere in Greek Sicily in 397 (Diod. XIV.46) may only have arrived after the Carthaginian successes of 409–405, but the Greek settlers in Carthage of Diod. XIV.77.5 can have been there for some time. Politically, Carthage is quiescent; only a difficult allusion (Diod. XI.86.2)[36] attests any kind of brush. It seems that some Athenians had long had Carthage in mind (Ar. *Eq.* 1302–4, Plut. *Per.* 20.4);[37] Hermocrates in 415 suggested using Carthaginian fear of Athens to get help, evidently not thinking her a threat comparable to Athens (Thuc. VI.34.2). Nevertheless, it was not

---

[32] It is neither certain nor important that the interpolator of Xen. *Hell.* 1.1.37 dated the fall of Selinus to the Attic year 409/8. See also Meyer 1921 (A 38) 64–5, who arrived at 409 using the wrong Aegean chronology, and Beloch 1912–27 (A 5) II.2, 255–6, who used the right Aegean chronology, but arrived at 408.

[33] There is no evidence that Carthage had more than the loosest control of them before this time: Meyer 1921 (A 38) 69; Finley 1979 (G 164) 64; Whittaker 1978 (G 91); the fullest study is by Hans 1983 (G 30).

[34] Selinus had been on the Carthaginian side in 480 (Diod. XI. 21.4–5, XIII.55.1), but Gescon, exiled from Carthage after his father Hamilcar's defeat at Himera, had found a welcome there (Diod. XIII.43.5). It is doubtful how much Punic influence can be demonstrated at Selinus before 409; see *Arch. Rep. for 1976–77*, 74.

[35] Kraay 1976 (B 200) 226. Note also the Acragantine overstrike on a Carthaginian coin, Jenkins 1974 (G 201) 24–5.

[36] See *CAH* v² 159 n. 10. That Lilybaeum could be an anachronistic reference to Motya is possible (cf. Diod. V.9.2), but it would still be unclear what is going on.

[37] Treu 1954/55 (G 86) 45–9, thinks, probably rightly, that the proposition that it was an aim of the Athenian expedition in 415 was a bogey raised by Alcibiades to frighten the Spartans (Thuc. VI.90.2), but Thucydides accepted it (VI.15.2).

Syracuse but Athens which had made an attempt to get Carthaginian help in 415–413 (Thuc. VI.88.6).

Nothing had happened to suggest any Carthaginian threat to deter Syracuse from her operations in north-east Sicily and in the Aegean. Selinus, still relying on her services to Carthage in 480, had neglected her walls (Diod. XIII.55.7)[38] while pursuing an elaborate temple-building programme.[39] If Segesta had already attempted to get Carthaginian help against Selinus in 416 (Diod. XII.82.7; not in Thuc.), she had had no success. It was therefore surprising that a renewed application in 410 was more warmly received (Diod. XIII.43.4–5). The Carthaginian *gerousia*, we are told, was eager to acquire a well-placed city (not an obvious description of Segesta), but was afraid of reaction from Syracuse. The weight of emphasis is on the attitude of Hannibal, the current head of the Magonid house, grandson of the Hamilcar who had died at Himera in 480 (*CAH* IV[2] 771–5), naturally hostile to Greeks and anxious to wipe out the family disgrace. His precise position is unclear. He was at the time '*basileus* according to the laws'. What is meant by that is obscure,[40] but it is distinguished from the generalship he is now given. It is slightly clearer that the Magonids had been hereditary generals since the sixth century.[41] One nuance in his appointment, 'if there is need to make war', suggests that the *gerousia* may have hoped that war would be unnecessary. The diplomatic negotiations of 410 (Diod. XIII.43.6–7) not only produced a peace-party in Selinus (*ibid.* 59.3). They may well have been a genuine attempt to isolate Selinus and keep out Syracuse; even in 409, Hannibal beaches his ships to avoid giving the Syracusans the impression that he has designs on them (*ibid.* 59.5).[42] Though Syracuse offered Selinus some form of help (*ibid.* 44.4–5), she seems to have been as over-

---

[38] For the walls of Selinus see Di Vita 1984 (G 158) and *Arch. Rep. for 1987–88*, 145–6. For the town-plan, see Rallo 1984 (G 273); Di Vita 1984 (G 159).

[39] For temple-building at Selinus, see Berve and Gruben 1962 (J 5) 421–32; Lawrence 1983 (J 22) 151–5. There is no agreement about the implications for fifth-century Selinuntine activities from the major text M–L no. 38.

[40] That '*basileus*' means that he was one of two annual 'suffetes' (cognate with the Hebrew word for 'judge') is normally assumed (most recently by Huss 1985 (G 39) 458–66), and there is sufficient evidence to show that the latter office already existed. Picard (p. 367 here) rightly doubts the identification; it is Aristotle (*Pol.* 1272b37ff) who first asserts that Carthage had a dual kingship, noting with pleasure that, unlike the Spartan kings, they did not have to be of a given family; if his 'kingship' was also annual, he should have said so. That Greeks saw Carthaginian institutions through Greek eyes is only too likely; see Weil 1960 (B 123) 246–54; Seston 1967 (G 79). Without more evidence, we are helpless.

[41] It used to be held (e.g. by Warmington 1964 (G 90) 60–1) that they had lost the post shortly after Himera, at a time when a commission was instituted to check the generals (Justin XIX.2.5–6). Maurin 1962 (G 48), accepted by Huss 1985 (G 39) 464, argued that this did not happen until shortly after Himilco's defeat and suicide in 396 (see below, p. 144), but was unduly agnostic about the evidence that there were Magonid generals even after Himilco; see Picard, G. Ch. and C. 1970 (G 75) 125–9; however, see p. 373 here.   [42] See Hans 1983 (G 30) 53–5.

confident as she had been about Athens in 415 when she sent five more ships to the Aegean in early 409.

It seems to be a universal rule that big Carthaginian expeditions take at least a year to prepare, and all that Hannibal had available in 410 was 5,000 Libyans and 800 Campanians (*ibid.* 44.2).[43] These Campanians, ominous for the future of Sicily, are said to have been hired for Athenian use by the Chalcidians of Sicily.[44] They sufficed to keep Selinus in play, while Hannibal prepared a fleet and accumulated a much larger force of Iberians, citizens and Libyans, which appeared in 409 (*ibid.* 44.6, 54).[45] Here and later, Carthaginian forces are deployed in two sections in a most unGreek way, a front-line force and one to exploit opportunities. The siege-engines ruined the neglected walls and the shock-troops went in, after a mere nine days (*ibid.* 56.5).[46] Diodorus paints a picture of dreadful savagery, but the unfinished temples were apparently not destroyed, only looted, and surviving Selinuntines were allowed to remain in the city and farm the land, paying Carthage tribute (*ibid.* 59.3).

Whether Himera had offered help to Selinus, we do not know, but, in any case, nothing would stop Hannibal from avenging his grandfather's defeat. As he moved to the north coast, again in two groups, he was joined by the native Sicels and Sicans, 20,000 according to Diodorus, evidently eager to shake off Greek control. Greek Sicily, which had underrated Carthaginian siegecraft, was now alert to the danger. Gela and Acragas had been waiting for Syracuse. Three thousand Syracusans had arrived at Acragas by the time of Selinus' fall, and Diocles now concentrated 4,000 men in Himera. There was some inconclusive fighting, and the fleet had now arrived from the Aegean, but Diocles despaired. Professing worry that the Carthaginians might sail against an unprotected Syracuse, he decided to evacuate Himera. He moved so fast as to abandon unburied Syracusan bodies, a political mistake, but not fast enough to get his ships back to evacuate the population of Himera before it fell.[47] Hannibal executed 3,000 captives, expiating the disaster of 480, broke up his army (the Campanians were not pleased at the loss of their paymaster), and went home. He had evidently done all he had set

[43] For fuller narrative accounts of all the wars with Carthage in this chapter, see Huss 1985 (G 39), not always followed here on details of the chronology.

[44] Thucydides knows nothing of Campanians; the Etruscans and Iapygians of Thuc. VII.57.11 (cf. 33.4) are different. For Campanians in this period, see Frederiksen 1968 (G 171), especially 12–13, and 1984 (G 173) 106.

[45] Ephorus gave him 60 long ships and 1,500 transports, siege-engines, 200,000 infantry and 4,000 cavalry, Timaeus 'not many more than 100,000 men'. There are some mysterious Greeks on the Carthaginian side at Diod. XIII.58.1.

[46] See Di Vita 1984 (G 158) 76–9.

[47] Asheri 1973 (G 103). For what is claimed as archaeological evidence of destruction at Himera see *Arch. Rep. for 1987–88*, 139 (Tusa 1984–85 (G 311) 629).

out to do, in a campaign which had lasted a mere three months.[48] The
Greek cities had been totally ineffective in stopping him.

The coins of Selinus and Himera now disappear, though those of
Egesta and Eryx may continue for a short time. The coins of Panormus,
which had looked purely Greek, continue to imitate Syracuse, but get
the Punic inscription ZIZ.[49]

After leaving the fleet in late 410, Hermocrates had attached himself to
Pharnabazus (see also *CAH* v² 478). The sources (Xen. *Hell.* 1.1.31,
Diod. XIII.63) suggest that he started at once to prepare a return to Sicily,
but, on the late Aegean chronology, he and his brother Proxenus were
still in the Aegean in late 408, preparing to go on an embassy to the King
of Persia (Xen. *Hell.* 1.4.1–3).[50] This suggests that nothing happened in
Sicily in 408 and that the appearance of continuity between Diod. XIII.62
and 63 is misleading. Enough Sicilian news reached him in 408 to show
that he had a chance to carve out a place in Sicily, perhaps even in
Syracuse, now that the Dioclean regime was partly discredited.

With help from Pharnabazus, he returned to Sicily, hired 1,000
mercenaries, picked up 1,000 Himeraeans, and, after an attempt to get
back into Syracuse, established himself at Selinus. Here, he built his force
up to 6,000, ravaged the Carthaginian area, and shook the security of
Motya and Panormus; the news was heard in Syracuse, and a feeling in
his favour set in (Diod. XIII.63, continued in 75). His first step was to
collect the unburied Syracusan bones at Himera and send them back to
Syracuse to discredit Diocles; with perfect propriety, he himself waited
at the frontier. The bones were accepted and Diocles exiled, but
Hermocrates was not recalled; some Syracusans feared a tyranny. Some
time later, his friends sent for him and he was killed while trying to force
his way in. Those of his party who were not killed were exiled or given
out for dead. We have no reason at all to deny him patriotism, but he
never seems to have had more than minority support; even the upper
classes will have worried about tyranny.[51]

Greek sources totally obscure Carthaginian policy, assuming that it
had always been the intention to subdue the whole island and ignoring
the gap of two and a half years between Himera and the next Carthagi-

---

[48] The timing from the interpolator of Xen. *Hell.* 1.1.37; from Timaeus, whose army numbers he
follows?

[49] So argued by Jenkins 1971 (G 201); see Kraay 1976 (B 200) 227–8, but there has been
considerable scepticism about attributing ZIZ coins to Panormus; see Lo Cascio 1975 (G 45)
(attributing them to the *epikrateia* as a whole); Tusa Cutroni 1983 (G 314–15) and *ap.* Manni *et al.*
1982–3 (G 225) 213–36; Gandolfo 1984 (G 178). Note Jenkins 1974 (G 201) no. 36 *QRTHDST
MHNT*, apparently a Carthaginian campaigning coin of 410–390.

[50] That he fought at Aegospotami (Polyb. XII.25 k. 11) must be a mistake for Cynossema. A
discussion of the chronology of his return with slightly different conclusions: Seibert 1979 (C 75)
238–41 with 558 n. 124.   [51] See in general Westlake 1958–9 (G 322); Sordi 1981 (G 297).

nian move.[52] Doubtless, the successes of 409 had whetted some appetites and the operations of Hermocrates showed that security had not yet been attained. Hannibal was re-elected, though because of his age Himilco of the same family was associated in the command, and there was a big recruiting drive, including a new group of Campanians (Diod. XIII.80). Apparently with Syracuse in mind, the naval component was increased.[53] In fact, there was greater Syracusan energy in 406; a force of forty ships was sent as far as Eryx, without in fact impeding Hannibal's crossing. Syracuse sent embassies throughout Sicily, to Italy, from which some help came, and to Sparta, from which, unsurprisingly in 406, it did not. It appears from a desperately fragmentary text (*IG* I³ 123 = M-L no. 92) that Carthage applied to Athens and got at least a sympathetic hearing; Athens had no help to spare, but would be glad to see Syracuse further distracted.

It was universally clear that the first target would be Acragas, the most resplendent prize, at the height of her prosperity (see *CAH* IV² 776-8, V² 168-70). Although she had been neutral during the Athenian expedition, she had been the obvious base for helping Selinus in 409 and had been impressed and generous about her fate (Diod. XIII.58.3). She turned down proffered terms, and hired Dexippus, a Spartan mercenary commander, 1,500 Greek mercenaries, and the 800 Campanians whom Hannibal had upset. The Carthaginian force, split as usual, started to suffer almost immediately from a 'plague', which killed the aged Hannibal; even they thought this due punishment for attacking Theron's tomb. A Syracusan force, under Daphnaeus, with reinforcements from Italy and Messene, picking up troops from Camarina and Gela on the way, built up to 30,000 infantry and 5,000 cavalry, supported with a fleet of thirty ships. A victory over the Carthaginian reserve was however not pressed, and the troops' wish for a sortie from Acragas was ignored; four Acragantine generals were stoned, and Dexippus became less popular. The strategy was not necessarily wrong;[54] the Carthaginians became hungry and were unwilling to face a pitched battle. Command of the sea was crucial, but it was lost through casualness about convoying a supply squadron. Himilco brought his fleet round from Panormus and Motya, and won a naval battle. It was now Acragas which was hungry, and the Campanians changed sides again. The Italian allies went home, and it was agreed that Acragas could not be held, and that it would be better to retire on Gela. The evacuation was better conducted than at Himera; the Acragantines were later settled in Leontini, deserted

---

[52] Some allowance has to be made for the time needed to prepare the new expedition, but there must be a substantial gap.   [53] If the forty and fifty ships of Diod. XIII.80.6-7 are distinct.

[54] Polyaen. v.7a shows that someone thought well of Daphnaeus.

since 423. The siege had lasted eight months (Diod. XIII.91.1 (Ephorus?); seven in Xen. *Hell*. I.5.21 (Timaeus?)) and ended a little before the winter solstice of 406. Himilco wintered in Acragas, while the enormous booty was digested.

There was panic throughout Sicily: some fled to Syracuse, some even to Italy. The Acragantines arrived in Syracuse and were vocal about the faults of their own generals, and there was, we are told, criticism about Syracusan choice of leaders. The story goes that, at an assembly in Syracuse, no one was prepared to speak except Dionysius, a young man of twenty-five or·so (Cic. *Tusc*. v.20.57; cf. Ephorus *FGrH* 70 F 218), who had participated in Hermocrates' last attempt at a coup. His origins are unclear;[55] on the most plausible story, he had held minor clerical office.[56]

It was not unHermocratean that he should attack the generals, but he had learnt the need for broad support, and took a demagogic line. The generals had been bribed; other notables were oligarchs; there should be new generals who were real democrats (Diod. XIII.91. Cf. Arist. *Pol*. 1305a26; he attacked Daphnaeus and the rich). The magistrates tried to fine him, but the wealthy Philistus (the later historian) announced that he would be prepared to pay the fines all day. The *demos*, already dissatisfied with the conduct of the war, did elect a new board, including Dionysius, who however professed distrust of his colleagues and refused to sit with them. At further assemblies, he proposed and carried a motion for the return of exiles. This was appropriate to a time of national emergency, though the chief beneficiaries would be what remained of Hermocrates' party.[57]

Dionysius' refusal to sit with the other generals, if authentic, was met by giving him an independent command at Gela, held by Dexippus, now in Syracusan service. There too there was *stasis*; Dionysius supported the *demos*, and wealthy men were condemned to get funds to pay the mercenary garrison and double the pay of the Syracusans. Revolutionary Gela sent to Syracuse to sing his praises, but he did not get on with Dexippus and went home, redoubling his attack on the traitors in their midst. He claimed to have learnt from Himilco's herald that the other generals had sold out, and offered to resign rather than be the only loyal

---

[55] All sources give his father's name as Hermocrates, though making no point of it, but it was probably Hermocritus, like his son (Tod no. 133 line 20); an adopted father, Heloris, appears later.

[56] Cicero *loc. cit*. gives a vague, but favourable, account of his family and position, but all other sources, even of the fourth century (Isoc. v.65), put him pretty low. Dem. xx.161 is the earliest evidence for the clerical office; cf. Diod. XIII.96.4, XIV.66.5, Polyaen. v.2.2 (secretary to the *strategoi*).

[57] The colouring of the source claims all this as part of a plan for tyranny already made; the exiles would be glad to get their property back, murder their enemies and seize their property, and would in gratitude back him for tyrant.

general. It is hardly impossible that there had indeed been some feelers to see on what terms Carthage might be bought off.

The next section of Diodorus (XIII.94.5–96), when deprived of the source's insistence that Dionysius was already aiming at tyranny, can be rationally read as a Hermocratean programme of military reform. A proposal to dismiss the board of ten generals and replace them by Dionysius as general with full powers (*strategos autokrator*) was justified by an appeal to the model of Gelon. We do not know whether Gelon in fact ever held such a post, though this might well have been believed in 405.[58] A much more recent precedent was the proposal of Hermocrates (Thuc. VI.72.5) to replace a board of fifteen by three *strategoi autokratores*, and the implication that sole power for Dionysius was involved would be reduced if we accepted the statement of Pl. *Ep.* VIII 353a (whence probably Plut. *Dion* 3) that Hipparinus was associated with him in the *strategia* as an adviser and older man.[59] The prominence of Hipparinus in this phase is confirmed by Aristotle (*Pol.* 1306a1) who ranks him among the dissolute aristocrats who go in for tyranny themselves or as supporting others. Given the appointment of Dion and Megacles as joint *strategoi autokratores* after the fall of the tyranny in 357 (Plut. *Dion* 29.4), Diodorus' source may well be tendentiously over-simplifying.

Dionysius' first move was to double the soldiers' pay. His second was to take a force of those aged under forty to Leontini. Besides the possibility of collecting troops there (there were other refugees besides those from Acragas), it might not be unreasonable to retrain the army away from the comforts of their homes. At Leontini, we are told, he claimed a plot against him and made the classic request for a body-guard.[60] Since the request was for one of precisely 600, the standard fifth-century number for Syracusan elite forces (Diod. XI.76.2, Thuc. VI.96.3), we need see nothing sinister in this, and the subsequent selection of more than a thousand citizens, lacking in money, but bold in spirit, to be armed expensively follows Hermocrates' proposals (Thuc. VI.72.4) to increase hoplite strength. That he spoke in a friendly way to the mercenaries, changed their officers and dismissed Dexippus to Greece need hardly be due to a worry that he should give the Syracusans back their liberty; we have not had much reason to see military ability in the officers or Dexippus. A further concentration of forces from Gela and elsewhere is not unreasonable. The hardest phrase to interpret is what is intended to be the key one: after returning to Syracuse, he camped in the

---

[58] Caven 1990 (G 134) 56 thinks Dionysius' friends now invented it.

[59] The statement has been regarded as a falsification by Niese 1905 (G 244) 883 and Sanders 1979–80 (G 282) 79–80. Caven 1990 (G 134) 56 thinks there were more than two generals.

[60] Compare the slightly different account in Arist. *Pol.* 1286b35–40.

dockyard, openly proclaiming himself (or showing himself) tyrant (XIII.96.3); there may be some Gelonian nuance which escapes us. To this the Syracusans could not object, because the city was filled with mercenaries and they were frightened of the Carthaginians. Two more specific facts might be more easily interpreted as exhibiting the triumph of the Hermocratean party. Dionysius married Hermocrates' daughter and gave his sister to Hermocrates' brother-in-law. An assembly was summoned to order the execution of Daphnaeus and of Demarchus, who had been one of the generals who replaced Hermocrates in 410 (Thuc. VIII.85; Xen. *Hell.* 1.1.29). The hostile source[61] does not conceal that constitutional forms were used.

As an organizer, Dionysius may have been doing well; as a commander, he was less successful. At the beginning of summer 405, Himilco razed Acragas (Diod. XIII.108.2) and moved against Gela, which defended itself gallantly. Dionysius, getting help from Italy, came, on the lower figures quoted from Timaeus, with 30,000 infantry and 1,000 cavalry, together with fifty ships which he used in close support and with which he tried to cut off Carthaginian supplies. After twenty days, he decided on more aggressive measures, but an over-elaborate three-pronged attack failed because of the slowness of his own force in going through the middle of the city. Though the losses were hardly decisive, a council of his friends thought the place unsuitable for a pitched battle, and it was decided, for no very obvious reason, to abandon both Gela and Camarina.[62]

The troops were furious, and evidently suspected treachery. Feeling was strongest in the upper-class cavalry. A group of them rushed home, plundered Dionysius' house and so maltreated his new wife that she committed suicide (Plut. *Dion* 3.2). With 100 loyal cavalry and the 600 elite troops, Dionysius briskly followed and suppressed the revolt; what was left of the cavalry retired to Etna (Diod. XIII.113.3, emended from XIV.7.7). The main body of the army arrived next morning, but the Geloans and Camarinaeans were understandably angry with Syracuse and joined the growing settlement at Leontini.

A lacuna in our manuscripts of Diodorus now breaks the story. There was evidently further 'plague' in the Carthaginian camp (Diod. XIII.114.2), which forced Himilco to send a herald. Whatever the constraints on him, he exacted severe terms (Diod. XIII.114.1; *SdA* 210).

---

[61] There is no obvious link in the account to the relevant fragments of Philistus (*FGrH* 556 F 57–8) or Timaeus (*FGrH* 566 F 29, 105), and we have no relevant Ephorean material.

[62] If Timaeus' synchronism with Tyre is right, we are already in August; Arr. *Anab.* 11.24.6 (Beloch 1912–27 (A 5) II 2, 257 f). The topography of the siege of Gela has been studied by Adamesteanu 1956 (G 92). Caven 1990 (G 134) 59–72 attempts a full reconstruction of Dionysius' plans.

Carthage would keep her own area, and get the Elymians and Sicans too.[63] *Poleis* would be allowed at Selinus, Acragas, Himera,[64] Gela and Camarina, but they were to have no walls and must pay tribute to Carthage. Leontini, Messene and the Sicels were to be autonomous. The Syracusans were to be under Dionysius.[65] He can hardly have accepted this as a permanent solution, but must have welcomed the chance to reorganize and regroup his forces. That Himilco was induced by disastrous losses by plague to be content with his very substantial gains rather than risk further operations against Syracuse with a depleted force needs no special explanation. He had certainly brought Carthaginian power in Sicily to its highest point.

We have detected some positive aspects of Dionysius' first rise to power, but it is pointless to think of him as anything but a monarch thereafter. Some fairly drastic measures to be discussed in the next paragraph are placed by Diodorus immediately after the peace. If this timing is correct, Dionysius was already settling in for good. He was clearly very badly scared by the cavalry revolt, and an even worse mutiny broke out not long after the peace, in which he is said to have nearly despaired; there was some competition later among his friends as to who had encouraged him with the remark that 'tyranny was a good shroud'. It is not improbable that resistance will have strengthened his will to rule, and, as Pericles said in another context (Thuc. II.63), abandoning tyranny is dangerous. Formal recognition came in a sense when, after the end of the war in Greece, a Spartan and a Corinthian came to investigate the situation they had been unable to help in 406 (Diod. XIV.10, cf. 70.3), and decided to back Dionysius.[66] By 400, an orator in an Athenian court (Lys. VI.6) can casually refer to Dionysius as a *basileus*.

The text which shows Dionysius beginning to remake Syracuse as a personal structure is Diod. XIV.7. The Island (Ortygia) was divided from the rest of the city by a substantial wall and contained a fortified acropolis and the dockyards. Houses in it were confined to his friends and his mercenaries. There had already been confiscation of land at Gela, and its practice at Syracuse was implicit in the attacks on the rich and the execution of political opponents. The best Syracusan land was given to

[63] See on this clause Anello 1986 (G 101) 115–21.

[64] Himera had already been replaced by Thermae, 10 km to its west (Diod. XIII.79.8).

[65] That he was actually personally named in the treaty seems unlikely. See Freeman 1891–4 (G 174) III 579–86, with App. XXXI; Caven 1990 (G 134) 76.

[66] The story is connected with an alleged disarming of Syracusan citizens and a decision to rely on mercenaries in future; the rule does not seem to have been as absolute as that (see, e.g. Diod. XIV. 44.2). There were also contacts with Lysander, perhaps even a visit from him (Plut. *Lys.* 2.7–8, accepted by Caven 1990 (G 134) 84, but see Sansone 1981 (C 314), who, comparing the text of Plut. *Mor.* 229A, shows that the story in 2.8 refers to the ambassador named by Diodorus). See also Bommelaer 1981 (C 279) 177–9.

his friends and commanders. We later find that Dion had an estate valued by Plato at 100 talents (*Ep.* VII.347b); his father Hipparinus had been near bankruptcy in 405. It is clear that Dionysius kept a good deal for himself; when his son was negotiating his abdication in 356 (see below, p. 700), he tried to retain the revenues of the Guatas estate, a large and fertile area stretching from the sea into the interior (Plut. *Dion* 37.2). The rest of the land was given on equal terms to foreigners and citizens, but (the Gelonian model again) the concept of citizenship was widened. Diodorus here speaks of manumitted slaves whom he called *neopolitai*. It is not clear whether this refers to the Cillicyrioi (see above, p. 124). That citizenship went to mercenaries and to favoured inhabitants of conquered towns goes without saying.[67] Houses outside the Island were also distributed, presumably carefully. At the end of the tyranny, the question of land-distribution was inseparable from the question of freedom.[68]

Constitutionally, we are left very much in the dark. Assemblies continue to be referred to. It is clearly at least possible that the title of *strategos autokrator* continued to be used, and there is clear evidence for an office of admiral, which also recurs after the end of the tyranny. The most substantial evidence for official organization is lost in lacunae in the Athenian alliance with Dionysius of 368–367 (Tod no. 136 = Harding no. 52 lines 34–7). Restorations are largely conjectural,[69] and all one can really say is that, though the treaty is with Dionysius and his descendants, some aspects of Syracusan polis organization are recognized.

What Athenian texts (Tod no. 108 lines 6–7 (Harding no. 20), no. 133 lines 19–20, no. 136 line 8 (Harding no. 52)) do tell us is what title Dionysius chose to use for the outside world. Gelon and Hieron had used no title in Greece proper. Gelon had simply called himself a Syracusan in his tripod-dedication at Delphi (M–L no. 28); Hieron paired himself with the Syracusans in dedicating the spoils of Cyme at Olympia (M–L no. 29, with *BCH* 84 (1960), 721, *SEG* XXXIII 328). This was not without some arrogance. The situation of Gelon's monument set it as a pendant to the golden tripod dedicated by the Spartans and their allies for their victory over the Persians, nor was anyone expected to inquire who Hieron was. Court-poetry had a rather different picture; Pindar three times (*Ol.* II.23, *Pyth.* II.60, III.70) refers to Hieron as *basileus*, once even as *tyrannos* (*Pyth.* III.85). We are still in a period in

---

[67] Cf. e.g. the case of Dikon, the brilliant sprinter from Caulonia (Moretti 1957 (A 43) nn. 379, 388, 389), transferred to Syracuse just in time for the Olympic games of 384.

[68] See below, p. 700; Asheri 1966 (C 3) 85–93; Fuks 1968 (G 176). For Dionysius I's land policy, see Mossé 1962 (C 208) 221–2, 340–7, right to see that the citizenship grants have implications for land, but wrongly implying that all upper-class estates remained untouched.

[69] Cf. Stroheker 1958 (G 302) 239 n. 17; even the last word might be φρου]ραρχούς as well as the current τριη]ραρχούς.

which verse, at any rate, can use *basileus* and *tyrannos* as interchangeable.[70]

The model of Gelon could hardly be irrelevant to a later ruler of Syracuse, and he crops up twice in Diodorus' narrative about Dionysius. We have already seen him used as a model for the post of *strategos autokrator*, and there is a long speech made in the assembly by a disaffected Syracusan in which a whole chapter (XIV.66) compares Dionysius very unfavourably with Gelon.[71] We cannot do more than note that the model was there to be used, and may have been of wider importance than titles.[72]

Even though Dionysius could be named in an Athenian court in 400 as the only one of many *basileis* who had not been deceived by Andocides (Lys. VI.6–7) and even if, which is clearly very doubtful, Gelon and Hieron had been *basileis* in any official usage, there might well be some doubt about using the word now. In some other areas the title had more continuity,[73] but the word and its cognates are avoided for Macedonian kings in foreign relations at least until 338.[74] By and large, there seems to be a feeling in sources before Alexander that *basileus* is best reserved for someone who rules non-Greeks.[75]

The Deinomenid dedications and the Macedonian precedents show that no title at all would be necessary, but by 393, at least, one had been decided on. When the Athenian *boule* in winter 394/3 (Tod no. 108 = Harding no. 20) drafted an honorary decree for Dionysius, it named him as 'the *archon* of Sicily', [τὸν Σικ]ελίας ἄρχ[ο]ντ[α]. The title recurs in Athens in two decrees from Dionysius' last year (Tod nos. 133, 136 (= Harding no. 52)), and we cannot doubt that it was known to be acceptable to him. Curiously, and probably accidentally, it echoes a less formal phrase in a Spartan ambassador's speech to Gelon in Hdt.

<hr />

[70] Andrewes 1956 (A 1) 20–6. Later in the century, Gelon is a *tyrannos* for Herodotus (VII.156.3), though the speech at VII.161.1 has *basileus* (cf. Ferrill 1978 (C 21) 388), and Thucydides describes the last Sicilian tyrants as *tyrannoi* (1.14.2, 18.1). Diodorus' source is curiously consistent about the Deinomenids. After Gelon's victory at Himera, he summoned an assembly in arms, which he attended without arms, and gave an account of his life (XI.26.5–6). The Syracusans, so far from proceeding against him as a *tyrannos*, acclaimed him as 'benefactor, saviour and king'. Thereafter in book XI, both he and his successor-brothers, Hieron and Thrasybulus, are described as *basileis* and their rule as *basileia*.

[71] Sanders 1981 (B 99) argues improbably that Philistus wrote a bad speech to show the intellectual inadequacies of the opposition. Whoever wrote the speech, we certainly cannot be sure that its details are contemporary.

[72] Timoleon also appealed to the Gelonian precedent (Diod. XVI.79.2). There is no evidence for Agathocles, but the Syracusan royal house revived Deinomenid names in the third century.

[73] It is a shade surprising that the new fragments (Lewis and Stroud 1979 (B 152) = *SEG* XXIX 86) of the Athenian decree for Evagoras in 393 refer to him (as the fifth-century decree *IG* I³ 113 had not) as *Salaminion basileus*.

[74] Errington 1974 (D 30); Hammond and Griffith 1979 (D 50) 387–9.

[75] The nuance is clear in the Bosporan kingdom (see pp. 496–7), where Leucon and Pairisades are described in a double title as *archon* of Greek cities and *basileus* of barbarian *ethne* (Tod no. 115B (Harding no. 27c), 171).

VII.157.2. We should probably look for other origins, but they are not easy to find. Epigraphic texts take us back to the middle of the sixth century, with an *archos* of Teichioussa (*DGE* 723 (3)); it is not clear whether he is an independent ruler or an official subordinate to Miletus. Herodotus has one instance of a singular *archon* plus a genitive of place, the *archon* of Babylon at 1.192.4.[76]

It would be foolish to affirm that we have a complete knowledge of the repertoire available for Dionysius, and something better than Herodotus' satrap of Babylon may yet turn up. Both parts of his chosen title have their interest. The word *archon* is apparently totally neutral, with nothing of the unfavourable colour which might surround *tyrannos*, *basileus*, *monarchos*, or *dynastes*. If it has any colouring, it may be that of military control. *Sikelias* is a geographical term. It does not directly involve rule over individuals. It asserts a wider sphere than simply Syracuse.[77] We can see it as on the way to the monarchy of a territorial state, but in this period it is perhaps not more than vague and grand.

That anecdote made play with the tyrannical nature of Dionysius' rule is hardly surprising,[78] but there is little direct contemporary evidence which would justify us in asserting that Syracuse was a police-state. When Aristotle (*Pol.* 1312b34ff) discusses repressive methods of tyranny, it is Hieron's network of informers which constitutes the Sicilian example; for Dionysius he merely speaks of harsh taxation. It is, however, sufficiently clear that his associates found it inadvisable to cross his will.

Construction of such a personal rule could not be merely a matter of force and judicious benefaction. The two army revolts among native Syracusans early in the reign hardly encourage a very favourable view of Dionysius' capacity for leadership, but he seems to have learnt. The clear Philistan passages (Diod. xiv.18 and 41) describing his wall-building and his preparations for renewing the war against Carthage in 397 give quite a different picture, which cannot be totally distorted. Besides careful organization of the workforce and splendid prizes for achievement, there is enormous stress on his personal participation. He in person, together with his *philoi*, oversaw the work on the walls for whole days at a time, visiting every section and lending a hand to the toilers. He laid aside the heaviness (*baros*) of his office (*arche*) and showed himself as a private citizen (*idiotes*). Putting his hands to the hardest tasks, he endured the same toil as the other workers, so that great rivalry was engendered

---

[76] Thucydides is full of *archontes*, though we can seldom be sure whether he is reporting a technicality or avoiding one. The nearest he gets to using the word in this way is the *archon* that Alcibiades puts into Cos at VIII.108.2. For semi-technical uses in official Attic, note the *archon* for Pylos (ἐς Πύλον) in M–L no. 84.10, and, with a genitive, the *archontes* of the fleet in 409 (*Agora* XVII 23. 104–9).   [77] The coinage, however, (see n. 93) continues to bear the name of Syracuse.

[78] See Sanders 1987 (G 283) 21–4.

and some even added a part of the night to the day's labour; such eagerness had infected the multitude. And, when we get on to the armaments drive, the language is similar. He circulated daily among the workers, conversed with them in kindly fashion, and rewarded the most zealous with gifts and invited them to his table.

Abroad, it was not merely the speaker of Lysias VI who put him on a monarchical plane. That he had in some sense moved on to such a plane is equally implied by a diplomatic plan contemporary with Tod no. 108. One of the elements in an idea of Conon's in 393 about detaching Dionysius from his Spartan sympathies (see above, p. 105) was to arrange a marriage-alliance between him and Evagoras (Lys. XIX.19–20); in the passage needs neither title nor other identification. The mission did not persuade Dionysius to change sides from Sparta and further relations between Athens and him had to wait over twenty years until Athens moved closer to Sparta.

Dionysius surely had ideas about how a Greek quasi-monarchical figure should behave.[79] There were precedents here, as we have seen. Unfortunately a substantial and recognizable victory over barbarians continued to elude him, so there is no trace of any notable dedication at Delphi or Olympia, or any move to one,[80] until, at the end of his life (Tod no. 133), we find him writing letters at least to Athens and her allies 'about the building of the temple'. That is surely Apollo's temple at Delphi which had burnt down four years before, and the attractions to him are obvious. If he was attempting to take a lead in the rebuilding, it came to nothing.[81]

It needed less diplomatic preparation to imitate the other ways in which the Deinomenids had exhibited themselves. No Greek could be stopped from competing in the Olympic games. On one famous occasion,[82] Dionysius tried to do a thorough job. There was at least one nearer model than Hieron. Like Alcibiades in 416 (Thuc. VI.16.2, Plut.

[79] Sanders 1979–80 (G 282) 65–70 and 1987 (G 283) 2–3 tries to extract some formal theory out of the names of his daughters and fragments of his tragedies.

[80] The expensive dedications of 372 intended for Delphi and Olympia in Xen. *Hell.* VI.2.33–6 (see below, p. 150) are evidently not architectural.

[81] There is no trace of him or his successor in the extensive building-accounts, and there is only one known Syracusan contribution to the funds during the period, 30 drachmae from an unknown Eudamos in 360 (Tod no. 140 line 40 = Harding no. 60 (misprinted) = *Corpus des Inscriptions de Delphes* II 4, 1 40).

[82] In Diodorus (XIV.109), the date is 388, while Dionysius was besieging Rhegium, (though there is a partial doublet under 386, XV.7.2), and that date for the siege of Rhegium had been established before Polyb. 1.6.1–2. But, as Grote 1846–56 (A 25) X 103–4 n. 2, XI 48–9 n. 1 observed, it is much easier to date Lysias XXXIIII to 384 than to 388; in 388, Lysias, resident at Athens, can hardly have described the Spartans as 'leaders of the Greeks, not unjustly' (XXXIII.7, which need not imply that there is a war on). There is some confirmation for 384 in Paus. VI.3.11 (cf. VI.2.6), and it is easier to reconstruct Dionysius' conduct to his relations (see below) by using the date. But the uncertainty is serious.

Alc. 11–12), he sent several four-horse chariots; like him he set up elaborately decorated marquees. But there was one way in which he was unlike Hieron or Alcibiades. He would be his own poet, even before the victory. He may have been engaged in literary composition for some time.[83] The delegation, headed by his brother Thearidas, also included rhapsodes and actors to recite his verses. The crowd, at first attracted by the beautiful voices of the actors, did not like the poems or said they did not, and started wrecking the marquees. They were encouraged in this by the orator Lysias, who, perhaps conscious of his Syracusan ancestry, happened to be present and ready with a powerful speech (XXXIII), denouncing the subservience of Greeks to Dionysius 'the *tyrannos* of Sicily' and to Artaxerxes. The chariots all crashed during the race, and there was trouble on the return journey as well. According to Diodorus, the survivors blamed the quality of the verses, and Dionysius was so upset by the fiasco that he embarked on a purge of his nearest and dearest, of which more later. Some of this must be taken seriously; there was certainly a conscious propaganda enterprise. It is hard to determine in what proportions its failure was due to inefficiency, bad luck, sabotage, or a simple failure to recognize the possible unpopularity of monarchs in Hellas. He did not repeat it.[84]

The time would come to deal with Carthage, but the first task was to extend his control in eastern Sicily (Diod. XIV.14–17), in defiance of what the treaty of 405 had provided. The recovery of Etna from the dissident Syracusans presented no great problem, but his siege-techniques were not yet equal to the task of subduing the settlement at Leontini. Sicels were dealt with by a mixture of force and diplomacy; he regained control of Enna and made peace with Herbita. Use of traitors enabled him to succeed where the democracy had failed. He captured Catana and Naxus, and sold their populations; Naxian land was given to Sicels, Catana to Campanians. Leontini was now isolated and submitted. Its population was moved to Syracuse. Since its largest component must have been the refugees from Gela and Camarina, the inference must be that he found their Dorian stock more assimilable than the Ionians of Catana and Naxus.[85]

Facilitated by the Carthaginian destructions, a renewed Gelonian model was beginning to take shape in eastern Sicily. There would be a great Syracuse, and not much else in the way of Greek towns. Sicels

---

[83] If we trust the story that, after Euripides' death, he paid the heirs a talent for the poet's lyre, writing-table and desk to improve the quality of his inspiration (*TGF* 76 T 10 Snell).

[84] Belated recognition of a sort for his poetry came with his victory at the Athenian Lenaea of 368 (see below, pp. 150–1).

[85] There may be a Gelonian model here; cf. the paradox of Hdt. VII.156 (*contra*, *CAH* IV² 766). Another Dorian group, Messenians expelled from Naupactus (see p. 42), were also acceptable, at least as mercenaries (Diod. XIV. 34.3).

would be allowed a good deal of local independence, provided that, we may assume, they sustained Syracuse economically.[86] Either now or eventually, there would be a scattering of mercenary settlements, situated as much for defence as for anything else;[87] we happen to have a date, 400/399, for the foundation of Adranum (Diod. xiv.37.5, from his chronographic source). The enlarged Syracuse was given a new and splendid wall-circuit,[88] presented (see above) as a matter of national urgency.

The new settlement might yet come under threat. Syracusan exiles were gathering on the Straits, based on Rhegium and Messene. The government of Messene was prepared to back an attempt on Syracuse, but its troops thought the war a purely upper-class cause, and refused to move.[89] It is entirely plausible that Dionysius should have thought that readiness to receive exiles might be a preparation to join Carthage, as Anaxilas, in control of both sides of the Straits, had done in 480 (*CAH* iv² 763–75). Messene was bought off with a territorial concession, presumably from the territory of Catana; by 396 it is in alliance with Dionysius. Rhegium, which rejected friendly overtures, was neutralized by a marriage-alliance with her neighbour Locri. With that trouble out of the way and the new wall-circuit built, thought could be given to renewed war with Carthage. Reports that Carthage was immobilized by plague had already encouraged some Greeks to move back into the Carthaginian area, and Dionysius began to stockpile weapons. With timber brought down from Etna and imported from Italy, the fleet was to be trebled from its present strength of 110; half its crews would be citizen, the other half hired. Technical invention was encouraged;[90] lack of success at Leontini had shown Syracusan deficiencies in siegecraft, and there may have been early experiments with catapults.[91] Despite this activity, there is an emphasis on economy. Weapons would be built up before mercenaries actually came, since they would be expensive to keep hired for long. It is hardly surprising that Dionysius should be financially cautious. We have heard of no money raised except by

[86] For numismatic evidence, some surely of this period, on Sicel communities, see Jenkins 1975 (G 203).

[87] I learned much about the sites of mercenary settlement from unpublished work by P. J. Tickler. For various coinages, some later than 396, which may be associated with mercenary foundations, see Consolo Langher 1961 (G 143); Kraay 1976 (B 200) 229–30; Macaluso 1979 (G 220).

[88] It is virtually impossible to distinguish Dionysius' fortifications from the largely later constructions we now see. See Lawrence 1946 (G 210) and his general comment (1979 (K 33) 117).

[89] For events at Messene and Rhegium in this period, see Raccuia 1981 (G 271).

[90] In doublet passages (Diod. xiv.41.3, 42.2, cf. 44.7), it is claimed that quadriremes and quinqueremes were now built and the latter invented. (Ancient tradition (Arist. F 600 *ap.* Pliny *HN* vii.207; Clem. Alex. *Strom.* 1 p. 132) claimed the quadrireme for Carthage.) These types do not appear until the 320s at Athens. See Morrison and Williams 1968 (K 48) 249.

[91] These too do not appear elsewhere until much later in the century; see Marsden 1969–71 (K 45) and below, p. 683.

confiscation,[92] and it is by no means clear where the resources came from for the issues of gold pieces and silver decadrachms, clearly intended for mercenary pay, which should be associated with the period.[93]

In 397,[94] when all the equipment was ready, mobilization could start. Citizen troops were enrolled and mercenaries hired on a large scale, with active assistance from Sparta. The more genial atmosphere at home was still further promoted by great public banquets to celebrate Dionysius' double marriage, of which more later. A few days later, the assembly was summoned in due constitutional form and induced to declare war on Carthage, unless she set free the Greek cities she had enslaved. The property of Carthaginians now settled in Syracuse and their ships were seized, and hatred of the barbarians was similarly manifested in a series of Sicilian Vespers even in cities outside his control.

Carthage was unprepared, and clearly had no substantial force in Sicily. Dionysius drove straight through the Greek zone tributary to Carthage. Camarina, Gela, Acragas rose to meet him, and forces from Himera and Selinus came to join him at the Carthaginian stronghold of Motya,[95] an offshore island joined to the mainland by a causeway. It was imperative to destroy this Carthaginian forward base.[96] Here he is said to have assembled 80,000 foot, 3,000 cavalry, 200 warships and 500 supply-ships, with siege-engines. Leaving his brother Leptines to begin the siege, he himself subdued the other Carthaginian settlements. To begin with, Himilco only had ten ships to spare for a remarkably successful diversionary raid on Syracuse harbour, but he rapidly raised a hundred to relieve Motya by catching the Syracusan fleet on land. Dionysius hauled his ships across the peninsula, and the Carthaginian ships were

[92] A battery of financial expedients, not always easy to understand, is listed by [Arist.] *Oec.* II 1349a14–1350a5, 1353b20–6.

[93] Older arrangements of Syracusan coinage left little for Dionysius. For revision of the dates, see Kraay and Hirmer 1966 (B 201) 280–1, 287–9; Jenkins 1966 (G 200) 30; Kraay 1976 (B 200) 231–3. We have two denominations of gold coinage, which, at a gold–silver ratio of 15:1, would be equivalent to two and one respectively of the contemporary silver decadrachms, many signed by Euainetos, which were much copied. There was no other coinage in precious metals under Dionysius; the tetradrachm denomination of the fifth century had disappeared along with the neighbours who had shared and imitated it. This does not amount to all that much. Very rough computation from the number of decadrachm dies might suggest that they produced a total coinage of about 250 talents. The bronze coinage has not yet been fully restudied; Consolo Langher 1964 (G 144) 161–6, 293–300, has some basic material.

[94] Diodorus' date will be confirmed if we accept the identification of Pharacidas the Spartan who arrives in the second summer of the war (below, p. 143) with Pharax, the Spartan nauarch (*Hell. Oxy.* VII (II).1; he was probably still in the Aegean in spring 396 (Diod. XIV.79.4). The reader will observe how little we know about Dionysius' activities between the two Carthaginian Wars.

[95] See Whitaker 1921 (G 324); Isserlin and du Plat Taylor 1974 (G 40); for more recent work there, see *Arch. Rep. for 1987–88*, 149–50. For the siege, Diodorus is for once supplemented, by Polyaen. v.2.6; see Whitaker 1921 (G 324) 75–91; Caven 1990 (G 134) 100–6.

[96] For the importance of denying forward bases to the enemy in galley-warfare, see Guilmartin 1974 (K 21) 97–107, 217, 264.

driven off by archers and slingers on the ships and land-based catapults. Himilco had to leave Motya to its fate. After heavy fighting for some days, it fell to the siege-engines. There was much slaughter, and a good deal of booty. The new siege-engines had proved their worth, but summer was at an end, with the island not entirely conquered; Elymian Segesta and Entella still held out. A Sicel garrison was put into Motya; Leptines was left with a squadron to watch the straits, and Dionysius went home.

It would seem that, despite the booty of Motya, he was under some financial stringency, since in 396 he evidently had many fewer troops.[97] When he returned to the field, Segesta still held out. Himilco this year had raised substantial forces and, despite losing many ships to Leptines' force, landed at Panormus and recovered Eryx and Motya. Dionysius abandoned western Sicily, and gave Himilco a clear march along the north coast.

His objective was Messene (now evidently under Dionysius' control), both for the sake of its harbour and to cut off possible reinforcements from Italy, and he took it fairly easily. Most of the Sicels of east Sicily went over to him.[98] Dionysius sent for mercenaries, strengthened the fortresses of Leontini and Etna, and marched north from Syracuse to meet him. Leptines also took the fleet to sea. Though the Carthaginian fleet was superior in numbers, Himilco's plan had been to move down the east coast with army and fleet in close conjunction.[99] Although an eruption of Etna made the coast road impassable, so that he had to take the army round the west of it, his admiral Mago broke Leptines' fleet, and sailed into Catana.

The threat this posed to Syracuse was unmistakable. Dionysius retreated there, to the irritation of the Greeks thus abandoned, and sent his brother-in-law Polyxenus off to Italy and Greece to implore help to save Greek Sicily. Before long, the Carthaginian fleet was filling the Great Harbour and Himilco's army was at the gates of Syracuse, preparing to succeed where the Athenians had failed seventeen years before. That Polyxenus' mission brought thirty ships and the Spartan Pharacidas[100] seemed of no great moment.

Dionysius and Leptines were away bringing in a supply squadron when a chance battle brought the Syracusans something of a naval

[97] What proportion of the 80,000 troops of 397 (Diod. XIV.47.7) were mercenaries is not clear (the armament figures of 43.2 are no real help), but the general impression left by the conduct of the two campaigns is perhaps confirmed by the figure of 10,000 mercenaries left in service at the end of 396 (XIV.78.2).

[98] But Dionysius was confident enough in the city-slaves to recruit them for the fleet.

[99] For a discussion in a sixteenth-century context of the necessity of co-operation between galley-fleets and land forces, particularly if a siege was imminent, see Guilmartin 1974 (K 21) e.g. at 186.

[100] See n. 94.

victory.[101] This, we are told, encouraged a feeling that Dionysius was not indispensable, and Diodorus reports an assembly and a long speech[102] demanding his dismissal and his replacement, perhaps from their mother-city Corinth or from the Spartans, the leaders of Greece. Pharacidas was however unresponsive; his instructions, he said, were to help the Syracusans and Dionysius against Carthage, not to overthrow Dionysius. The mercenaries present were equally firm for Dionysius, and he stayed in control.

That the danger was dispelled was so remarkable that supernatural reasons had to be invoked for it. The Carthaginians, it was said, as they prepared their siege, had plundered the temples of Demeter and Kore and destroyed the tomb of Gelon and Demarete. It was little wonder that they first became prey to irrational fears and then to an exceptionally virulent plague.[103] Dionysius seized his chance by both land and sea, and won victories on both.

Himilco was forced into negotiation, and eventually secured a promise that at least Carthaginian citizens would be allowed to escape. The rest of the force, except for the Sicels who got home and the Iberians whom Dionysius enrolled, were enslaved. The scandal was that Dionysius had been bribed, worse, that he wanted to preserve some element of Carthaginian threat to ensure that he would remain tyrant. It might also be said that he was enhancing the Carthaginian disaster by disgracing them as well.[104] Himilco did reach home, but was very badly received and starved himself to death. The disaster and disgrace sparked a major revolt against Carthage in Libya (see below, p. 373).

Although the mercenaries had stood with Dionysius against the dissatisfaction of the citizens, they wanted their pay and had to be bought off with Leontini.[105] Further regrouping was made possible by Himilco's destruction of Messene. Here Dionysius settled Italian Greeks from Locri and her colony Medma.[106] This was a continuation of the insight of 397 (p. 141) that the Straits had to be controlled. Although a bride from Rhegium might have been preferable then, the negotiations had ended

101 Caven 1990 (G 134) 115–16 disbelieves in this battle.

102 For this speech see n. 71.

103 The plague (see Littman 1984 (G 217)) is described in great detail; evidently Philistus was trying to repeat Thucydides' achievement in the line. As usual, it is vain to speculate about its identity, though it may be worth noting that mental symptoms, the absence of which is a substantial obstacle to identifying the Athenian plague as typhus, are present here in abundance. A useful discussion of plague in these campaigns by Seibert 1982–3 (G 289).

104 For a similar arrangement made by Athenians to discredit Spartans, see *CAH* v² 411.

105 From this point until 388 or so, the chronology is very fluid for those who place no particular faith in the years under which Diodorus gives his accounts.

106 He also intended, appropriately, to include his 600 exiles from mainland Messenia who had joined him after the destruction of Naupactus in 400 (see n. 85 and Asheri 1984 (G 104) 35–6), but his Spartan allies objected to the idea and they were moved to the west to found Tyndaris, on which see Barreca 1957 (G 115).

with an alignment with Locri which lasted for fifty years.[107] When Locrians now moved into Messene, Rhegium not unnaturally felt herself encircled. While Dionysius was settling with the Sicels and making a good deal of progress with them, Rhegium stepped up its support for Dionysius' opponents, settled Naxians and Catanians at Mylae, west of Messene, and, under the Syracusan exile Heloris, laid siege to Messene itself. The attempt failed and brought with it the loss of Mylae.

War with Rhegium was now inevitable, but delayed by the continuation of the Sicel campaign against Tauromenium (Taormina), where Himilco had established a Sicel position in 396 (Diod. xiv.59.2). Diodorus' picture of a winter attack on it gives us the clearest picture we have of Dionysius personally involved in battle, scrambling up the rocks in the frost, and barely getting away with his life. The disaster did no good to outside appreciations of the strength of his position.[108]

At this point Carthage re-enters the story.[109] Mago, now in command, once again made for Messene, but was beaten off. It is legitimate to suppose that the tradition, which will want to dilate on the heroism of Rhegium, has suppressed the fact that she was effectively acting with him, and Dionysius forthwith tried a *coup de main* against her. All he succeeded in doing was make it clear that he had ambitions beyond the Straits, thus contributing a reason for the formation of the Italiote League (see below, p. 387). Mago, now reinforced, saw his best chance in continued action with the Sicels and tried a drive through central Sicily,[110] but found himself running out of supplies in rough country. Dionysius was content to let him see the error of his ways, despite the wish of his Syracusan troops to engage; they are even said to have taken themselves off home. Peace now at last followed. The terms were those of 405 (p. 135), with the exception that the Sicels were now explicitly put under Dionysius.[111] Modern scholarship is reluctant to believe that Diodorus can have got this right.[112] Could Dionysius' successes of 397 and Carthage's failure outside Syracuse in 396 have gone for nothing? It is widely assumed[113] that the position of the Greek states outside Dionysius' control must have been improved. It would be foolish to

---

[107] For Dionysius' marriage-alliance with Locri, see Musti 1977 (G 236) 92–9, arguing that the marriage gave Dionysius and still more his son by it, Dionysius II, permanent rights in Locri.

[108] Diod. xiv.88.5 says that Acragas and Messene now abandoned their alliances with Dionysius. This is plausible enough for Acragas, but not for Messene (cf. xiv.90.3), despite Caven 1990 (G 134) 127–8, 131, trying to find a place for Polyaen. v.2.18.

[109] There may be little duplication between Diod. xiv.90 and 95.

[110] Diodorus' account puts a suspicious amount of emphasis on his native city of Agyrium.

[111] Tauromenium, which Himilco had hoped would be a permanent Sicel threat to Syracuse, was abandoned and turned by Dionysius into yet another mercenary settlement. It is clear that the site was already thoroughly hellenized (*Arch. Rep. for 1987–88*, 121).

[112] Confrontation with Diod. xv.17.5 (see below, p. 149) certainly poses problems for one passage or the other.   [113] See e.g. Stroheker 1958 (G 302) 82–5.

place implicit faith in Diodorus, here or anywhere, but it is not obvious that he was wrong. On any rational assessment, the Greek cities were no longer of real importance. What was important was that Carthage had, after several attempts to invade eastern Sicily, in effect acknowledged that the task was beyond her powers.[114]

Dionysius could now turn his attention to Rhegium, and sailed, evidently fairly late in the year, with 20,000 infantry, 1,000 cavalry and 120 ships to its border with Locri (from which some help doubtless came; cf. Dion. Hal. *Ant. Rom.* xx.7.2). On his way to the Straits, he ravaged the land. The Italiotes tried to relieve Rhegium with a fleet of sixty ships from Croton, but their efforts did less to upset Dionysius' plans than a nasty storm, which cost him seven ships and sent him into Messene. He broke off the campaign for the year, but laid a more firm foundation for the future by an alliance with the Lucanians, which might divert the Italiotes.

The Lucanians duly attacked Thurii in the next year,[115] supported by a Syracusan fleet under Dionysius' brother Leptines. But Leptines, moved apparently by the heavy defeat which the Lucanians inflicted on Thurii, negotiated peace between the Italiotes and the Lucanians instead. This was totally contrary to Dionysius' plans; not unnaturally, he sacked Leptines and replaced him with his younger brother Thearidas.

Thus deprived of Lucanian help, he changed his strategy for dealing with the Italiotes. With a much smaller fleet,[116] but a larger cavalry force and ample supplies, he laid siege to Caulonia,[117] thus drawing on himself whatever the Italiotes could put in the field. The exile Heloris, based on Croton, marched to relieve the siege, with 25,000 infantry, thus outnumbering Dionysius, and 2,000 cavalry. But Dionysius had scouts out and surprised Heloris with his advance guard at dawn on the river Elleporus.[118] Heloris was killed, and the rest of the Italiotes, coming up in no sort of formation, were put to a disorderly flight. The main body, 10,000 men, spent two days on a waterless hill before surrendering unconditionally. To their surprise, Dionysius let them go without ransom, and gave generous terms to most of the cities involved, 'the finest act of his life'. Rhegium settled by handing over its fleet of seventy ships, paying 300 talents and handing over a hundred hostages. Caulonia was destroyed as a city and its territory given to Locri, but its inhabitants

---

[114] So Caven 1990 (G 134) 130–1.

[115] Diodorus has managed to miss a clear division of campaigning season here.

[116] Sufficient, however, to give Thearidas a useful victory over a squadron from Rhegium off the Lipari Islands.   [117] Presumably with unmentioned assistance from Locri.

[118] The Galliparo Caven 1990 (G 134) 137, the Stilaro Walbank 1957–79 (B 122) on Polyb. 1.6.2, following Nissen 1883–1902 (G 245) II 949. On the battle, see also Gianelli 1928 (G 180) 73–6, 108–10; De Sensi Sestito 1988 (G 155) 282–3.

were moved to Syracuse, given citizenship and freedom from taxation for five years.

Next year[119] he took similar action with Hipponium. His friends in Locri now controlled a massive territory across the toe of Italy; Rhegium was completely isolated and had lost her fleet. Pretending to be returning to Sicily, he manufactured a *casus belli* by asking her for the courtesy of the provision of a market for supplies.[120] When, after some days, they became suspicious and suspended the market, he returned their hostages and opened his siege.

The siege of Rhegium lasted eleven months,[121] and Dionysius conducted it with bitter determination, despite a serious spear-wound in the groin. The Rhegines countered everything he could put against them in the way of siege-engines, but in the extremities of famine eventually surrendered. Picking his way through piles of corpses, he found 6,000 survivors. He ransomed those who could pay a mina, and sold the rest as slaves. The general Phyton he reserved for an unparalleled flogging round the city before drowning him. Our sources attribute this violent hostility of Dionysius to the Rhegines to their having refused him a bride in 397; we may rather think of its constant willingness to serve as a refuge for Syracusan refugees and of at least one actual alignment with Carthage. Eastern Sicily, in association with Locri, now included the toe of Italy as well; Dionysius even tried to build a wall across the isthmus (Strabo VI.1.10).[122]

After this, Dionysius' dealings with southern Italy become very obscure, and yet they must have a bearing on the next item of foreign policy which Diodorus chooses to relate, a venture in the Adriatic and beyond (XV.13–14).[123] Under 385/4 B.C., we are told that Dionysius resolved to found cities in the Adriatic Sea, with the intention of controlling the *Ionios poros*, which ought to mean the crossing.[124] The alleged intention was to invade Epirus and rob the temple of Delphi; the second half of that can at any rate be discounted. With the help of Alcetas

[119] If we accept that 'in the previous year' in XIV.107.4 comes from the source and is not editorial work by Diodorus, who has made a year-break between Caulonia and Hipponium; there might be some doubt about this, since nothing is said about his wintering in Italy. Cf. n. 115.

[120] For this custom, see the partial collection of references in de Ste Croix 1972 (c 68) 399–400.

[121] It is universally held to run over 388 and 387, but this should not be founded on Diodorus' chronology (see n. 82 for doubts about the Olympic games he places during it), but rather on Polyb. 1.6.1, who is already using a synchronism, perhaps established by Timaeus, in which the siege is in progress in a year which must be 387/6; see Walbank 1957–79 (B 122) I 46–8.

[122] What actually happened to the site of Rhegium before it was refounded by Dionysius II as Phoebia (Strabo VI.1.6) is unclear, except that Dionysius had a *paradeisos* there, in which he tried to naturalize plane-trees, which did not grow well (Theophr. *Hist. Pl.* IV.5.6; Pliny *HN* XII.7 adds a house).   [123] Vial's Budé text (1977) should be used for book XV.

[124] Anello 1980 (G 100) 83 ff emphasizes the importance of the Straits.

the Molossian, in exile in Syracuse,[125] he made an alliance with the
Illyrians and sent them troops and weapons, with which they invaded
Epirus (see below, p. 428). He also assisted the Parians to found a colony
on Pharos (Hvar). Both these events are presumably meant to refer to
385/4, and, not many years earlier, he had already established a colony on
the east coast at Lissus[126] (Lesh), at the mouth of the Drin. A lacuna of
uncertain length follows, and ch. 13 returns to Syracuse. Under the next
year, 384/3, the Parians are in trouble with the barbarian inhabitants of
their island, who have called in help from Illyrians, but they are assisted
by the governor appointed by Dionysius in – where? The manuscripts
have *Lishi, Lisshi, Lissoi* and argument continues as to whether they
mean Lissus or Issa (Vis), 320 km to the northwest. It is not now held
that both passages refer to Issa, but there is still quite a strong possibility
that the second one does,[127] in which case Dionysius' direct interests
extended far beyond the Straits.[128] On the present evidence, we can
hardly speculate on his motives, and a substantial historical phenomenon
may have been lost.[129]

That new evidence can bring some unexpected light to aspects of the
story is demonstrated in the next episode, also reported under 384/3.
Dionysius, saying that he was suppressing pirates, raided the Etruscan
Pyrgi, the port of Caere, and took enormous booty, which strengthened
his financial position. We could view this as simply a piratical raid,[130] but
another dimension has been added to it by the discovery of the Pyrgi
gold tablets, which attest considerable Carthaginian influence there, at
least in the previous century (*CAH* VII².2, 256).

With the Carthaginian War which follows, all recounted under 383/2
B.C., Diodorus confessedly more or less gives up, and not much can be

---

[125] Whether this man, well known from his alliance with Athens in 375 (Tod no. 123 line
109 = Harding no. 35; cf. Xen. *Hell.* VI.2.10, [Dem.] XLIX.22), is identical with the Alcetas son of
Leptines of Syracuse honoured at Athens in 373 (*IG* II² 101) is an intractable problem; see Tod pp.
217–18.   [126] Mss *Lisson, Lison*; there can be no doubt what is intended here.

[127] Stroheker 1958 (G 302) 123–4 suggests that the foundation of Issa was recorded in the lacuna
in ch. 13. [Scymn.] 414–15 is reasonable evidence that Issa was a Syracusan foundation of some date.
However, Ditt. *SIG* 141 frequently quoted in this context, does not belong to the 380s but to the
early third century; see Woodhead 1970 (G 325) 509–11. Note also Ancona, founded by Syracusans
exiled by Dionysius (Strabo v.4.2, p. 241). See also n. 143.

[128] That it was Dionysius who first opened up the Adriatic to Greeks was a theory made
untenable by Beaumont 1936 (G 116), but his attempt (202–3) to puncture an older picture of
Dionysius' 'Adriatic Empire' and to reduce Dionysius' interests to Lissus (so also Woodhead 1970
(G 325)) was modified by Gitti 1952 (G 183), who showed that there was rather more evidence,
though even he did not think the venture lasted very long. See also Anello 1980 (G 100).

[129] Stroheker 1958 (G 302) 119–28, places the weight on a desire to solidify communications with
old Greece; Caven 1990 (G 134) 149–53 sees Dionysius attempting to build up an empire which
would match the resources of Carthage. That Illyrian piracy was as yet a problem is denied by Dell
1967 (E 64) 344–6.

[130] For the theory of Sordi 1960 (G 291) 62–72 that Dionysius was acting in concert with the
Gauls who had been attacking Rome, see *CAH* VII².2, 305–6.

got from him. It may have lasted as long as eight years.[131] Apparently, Dionysius started it by detaching cities under Carthage. Carthage sought the collaboration of the Italiote League and actually landed troops in Italy. Dionysius had to fight a war on two fronts. Of the Italian front, all that we hear of Carthaginian activity is a re-establishment of Hipponium (xv.24.1, not connected with the war narrative), and we merely have the bare fact that Dionysius captured Croton by finding a way up its acropolis and may have held it for some time (Livy xxiv.3.8, Dion. Hal. *Ant. Rom.* xx.7.3).[132] For Sicily, we cannot even place the final battles, Cabala, in which the Carthaginians lost 10,000 killed, including Mago, and 5,000 prisoners, and Cronium, perhaps somewhere on the north coast, in which Leptines was killed and the Carthaginians, giving no quarter, were supposed to have killed 14,000 Sicilians. The peace terms are again (see pp. 135, 145) described as being on the same terms as before, but, since Carthage explicitly gets Selinus and part of Acragantine territory, both of which should have technically been tributary to her since 405, there is something seriously wrong. The new element is that Dionysius agreed to pay an indemnity of 1,000 talents, which he can hardly have afforded.[133]

We hear a certain amount of Dionysius' interventions in old Greece. As we have seen (p. 139), the outbreak of the Corinthian War might have been thought to create a doubt as to whether he would act with Sparta or with Corinth, mother-city of Syracuse. Despite Athenian honours for him and an embassy in 393 (Tod no. 108 = Harding no. 20, Lys. xix 19–20), which claimed to have stopped him sending help to the Spartans, he never seems to have been seriously doubtful about backing Sparta; if he had any regard for Syracusan public opinion, he could hardly have taken the Athenian side. His first actual intervention was in 387, when his brother-in-law Polyxenus took twenty ships from Sicily and Italy to help Antalcidas in the final campaign which blockaded the Hellespont and ended the Corinthian War (p. 116) (Xen. *Hell.* v.1.26).[134] That he was a supporter of the system created by the King's Peace is taken for granted all round (Lys. xxxiii.6, Isoc. iv.126, Diod. xv.23.5). The only break in this picture comes with his support of the Illyrians (p. 148), who used it in such a way that Sparta had to help the Molossians (Diod. xv.13.3).

That nothing is heard of Syracuse when war broke out again on the mainland in 378 may be due to the Carthaginian War. Indeed, the first

---

[131] 382–374, Beloch 1912–27 (A 5) iii.2, 376–7.

[132] Since the latter passage groups the falls of Rhegium and Croton, we cannot use it with any assurance to date the capture of Croton to 378.

[133] Note Plato *Ep.* vii 332c, 333a; Dionysius barely escaped and arranged to pay tribute to the barbarians.

[134] Presumably the Italian ships came from Locri. The siege of Rhegium can hardly have been over when this fleet left.

sign of renewed contact involves a Spartan fleet in autumn 373 trying to enlist Dionysius' support for an attempt on Corcyra, on the grounds that it would be important to him that Corcyra should not be under Athenian control (Xen. *Hell.* VI.2.4; cf. Diod. XV.46.2). In 372, a Syracusan fleet of ten ships in fact appeared. They were ambushed by Iphicrates, and turned out to contain expensive dedications intended for Delphi and Olympia, presumably for the Olympic games of 372. Iphicrates, with clearance from home, sold them off, attracting a very angry letter to Athens with a complaint of sacrilege (Xen. *Hell.* VI.2.33–6, Polyaen. III.9.55, Diod. XV.47.7, XVI.57.2–4).

No other force arrived from the west until after Leuctra, but then Dionysius did something to repay his old debts to Sparta. In 369, more than twenty ships arrived with 2,000 Celts and Iberians, the first appearance of such a force in mainland Greece, with fifty cavalry and pay for five months. They made a very good impression (Xen. *Hell.* VII.1.20–2, Diod. XV.70.1), and a similar force appeared the next year. Though instructed to return within a fixed time, it played an important part in the 'Tearless Battle' (pp. 192–3; Xen. *Hell.* VII.1.28–32). The time-limit is presumably in some way connected with the renewal of war in western Sicily in this year (Diod. XV.73). It says much for Dionysius' loyalty to Sparta or his desire to assert himself on the mainland that he sent the force at all.

This desire to make himself felt in Greek affairs at this time emerges from two decrees from Athens, whose rapprochement with Sparta (p. 188) brought her back into contact with him. In summer 368 (the last prytany of the archon-year 369/8), ambassadors came from Dionysius to Athens bearing letters about the 'building of the temple', i.e. the temple of Apollo at Delphi, destroyed in 372, and about the Peace (Tod no. 133). The *boule* referred the foreign policy aspects of the letters to the *synedrion* of the confederacy, but proceeded to recommend to the Assembly purely Athenian honours for Dionysius and his sons, crowns and Athenian citizenship for their services to the 'King's Peace, which the Athenians and the Spartans and the other Greeks made'. There is other evidence that the confederacy was not happy about some of the consequences of drawing close to Sparta, and Dionysius was apparently a particularly unwelcome associate. The decree which followed (Tod no. 136 = Harding no. 52) was a purely Athenian alliance with Dionysius and his descendants, with no word of the Athenian allies.[135]

The rapprochement with Athens was crowned in the following winter when Dionysius won the tragic contest at the Lenaea with his *Ransoming*

---

[135] That this decree belongs to the spring of 367, as used to be held, is unlikely; it should be dated as close to its predecessor as we can put it, perhaps in the second prytany of 368/7 (Lewis *ap.* Develin 1989 (C 127) 255). For an Athenian embassy to Sicily about this time, cf. [Dem.] LIII.5.

of Hector. The story went that he greeted the news with such drunken jubilation as to bring on his death, and at least the time-relationship must be right. We can therefore place his death in spring 367.

From time to time, we have alluded to associates of Dionysius, and it is an essential part of the story to look at them and the inner fabric of the reign.[136] It is a question, not only of the nature of his supporters, but of the succession. Even nowadays, students of the Roman empire are allowed to turn their minds from the development of institutions to the fascinating topic of Augustus' search for an heir; the succession in monarchies is an important matter. The tensions are the same for Dionysius as they will be for Augustus: the interlocking of friends with marriages, the implicit rivalry of different family groups, the matching of the hereditary principle against competence. Augustus' two families stem from his own daughter by his first marriage and his step-sons by his second. Dionysius was more thorough. After the loss of his first wife, the daughter of Hermocrates, he married two wives simultaneously, Doris, a foreigner from Locri, and Aristomache the Syracusan, daughter of his early supporter Hipparinus and the sister of Dion.[137] He is said to have taken great precautions to conceal which marriage was consummated first; as it happens, Doris produced sons long before Aristomache.[138] But, of course, he needed friends long before his children started growing up; he had friends, brothers and a brother-in-law.[139] He lost some of the early friends very early. Hipparinus died quite soon. Heloris, his 'adopted father', as we have seen, went into irreconcilable exile, shortly after 402, and led an exiles' party in south Italy (Diod. XIV.8.5, 87.1, 103.4–104.1). The only known early supporter who was left was Philistus, not yet a historian, who for a long period commanded the fort on Ortygia and, allegedly, had Dionysius' mother as a mistress (Plut. *Dion* 11.5). But in the early part of the reign Dionysius put most reliance on his brother Leptines, who has the formal title of admiral and acts as such (Diod. XIV.48.4, 53.5, 59.7–60.4, 72.1, 102.2–3) from 397 until his dismissal in 390 (p. 146), and on his brother-in-law Polyxenus, brother of Hermocrates' wife, clearly influential and useful (Diod. XIV.62.1, 63.4, Tod no. 108 = Harding no. 20, Xen. *Hell.* V.1.26).

At one stage or another, Philistus, Leptines and Polyxenus all went

[136] Besides the general books, see Beloch 1912–27 (A 5) III.2, 102–7; Gernet 1953 (C 29); Sartori 1966 (G 288).

[137] She was presumably older than Dion, who seems to have been born about 409 (Nep. *Dio* 10.3, misread by Beloch).

[138] In Tod no. 133 (368 B.C.), only Dionysius and Hermocritus, the sons of Doris, are named. That Aristomache was long childless (Plut. *Dion* 3.6) is not literally true, since her daughters were marriageable fairly early (Beloch *loc. cit.*) 102–3, 105, but drawing the conclusion that the story of the double marriage is false).

[139] Tod no. 108 = Harding no. 20 (393 B.C.) honoured Leptines, Thearidas and Polyxenus alongside Dionysius; the text is incomplete, but it is not obvious who else will have been included.

into exile. We have no material on Polyxenus' flight in fear (Plut. *Dion* 21.7–8), but we can see clearly enough a picture in which Leptines had more obvious popularity than Dionysius and was tactless enough to settle Italian affairs without reference to him. The culmination came in 386, according to Diodorus (xv.6–7). His story is that the fiasco at Olympia reduced Dionysius to such a state of mad rage that he killed many of his friends on false charges[140] and exiled not a few, including Philistus and Leptines, who fled to Thurii, where they were well received by the Italiotes, but afterwards returned to Syracuse, when Leptines was given Dionysius' daughter. The story is improbably motivated, in that nothing seems to have happened to Thearidas who had headed the mission to Olympia. We find a better story[141] in Plutarch (*Dion* 11.6), in which Leptines offers one of his daughters to Philistus without consulting Dionysius. This reads as if it could appear that the dismissed admiral and the garrison-commander were aligning themselves to force Dionysius into a triumvirate, if not worse;[142] it is not surprising that Dionysius' reaction was swift. In this version, Philistus did not return during Dionysius' lifetime, and this is evidently correct.[143] That Leptines did return is certain,[144] but he had been replaced as admiral by the youngest brother Thearidas. Both brothers were given daughters of Dionysius to marry, and there must have been interesting tensions until Leptines was killed in battle and Thearidas died not long after. Meanwhile Dionysius' own sons were getting older, but in his last years he was again opting for tension and balance. This time it was between the two families he himself possessed. He seems to have been backing the eldest son, by the foreign wife, the later Dionysius II, but his chief adviser[145] was now Hipparinus' son Dion, his own brother-in-law and son-in-law, himself uncle of two other sons of Dionysius. Dion was not unnaturally credited with preferring his own nephews, and Dionysius eventually died, like most tyrants, to the accompaniment of rumours of a succession crisis and a doctors' plot (Timaeus *FGrH* 566 F 109, Nep. *Dion* 2.4–5, Plut. *Dion* 6.2). Chapter 13 will show how inadequately Dionysius had provided for

---

140 No names are given.

141 What is by far the earliest story (Aen. Tact. x.21–2; *c.* 350 B.C.) assumes Leptines' popularity and Dionysius' suspicion of him, and reports a ruse by which he was made to leave the city without fuss.

142 Some confirmation for the alignment comes from Philistus *FGrH* 556 F 60; Philistus wrote about the sufferings of Leptines' daughters.

143 In this version, Philistus is exiled to the Adriatic, where he wrote most of his history. For a mysterious *fossa Philistina* and attempts to relate this to Dionysius' Adriatic ventures (pp. 147–8), see Gitti (G 182 and G 183, 172–6).

144 He was represented as continuing to disagree with Dionysius (Polyaen. vi.16.1); Plut. *Mor.* 338B, Ael. *VH* xiii.45 represent a tradition in which Dionysius deliberately failed to save him from his death.

145 That Dion was admiral under Dionysius I is likely enough, but it should not be deduced from Plut. *Dion* 7.2, which is a reference back to 6.5.

the succession; on this test of successful monarchy, he must be faulted.

The main lines of his reshaping of Sicily and its extension into the toe of Italy have already been traced (pp. 140, 167). As later events would prove, there continued to be a feeling of civic solidarity in greater Syracuse, despite its changes in population. Outside Syracuse, the older cities had become unimportant, but there were now several new foundations, e.g. Tauromenium and Tyndaris, which had resulted from mercenary resettlement. Not all of these were purely Greek, and, outside the direct area of his control, we have evidence of at least one example of the way in which the events of his reign had reshaped the ethnic map. In 404 a group of Campanians for which he had no further use did not return to Italy, but went to the west and forced themselves on Elymian Entella, killing the men and marrying the women (Diod. xiv.9.9). They maintained themselves under Carthaginian control, defying attempts by Dionysius to dislodge them (Diod. xiv.48.5, 53.5, 61.5). A remarkable epigraphic discovery[146] shows them still there, perhaps in the 280s, despite many vicissitudes, retaining in part their Oscan nomenclature, but expressing themselves, at least publicly, in Greek constitutional forms and a form of *koine* Doric.

Elsewhere, at Selinus[147] and various hilltop sites,[148] above all at Monte Adranone,[149] with its Punic temples, the fourth century shows considerable evidence of increasing Punic influence. There are, however, overlaps between regions of influence. On Monte Caltafaraci 6 km east-north-east of Acragas, there seems to be a Greek fort of Dionysius' time.[150]

Since Diodorus' accounts of the Carthaginian Wars become more and more inadequate, we cannot make a full assessment of Dionysius' failure to drive Carthage out of Sicily altogether. It seems likely that his resources were always inadequate for the task. What we know of the coinage (see p. 142 n. 93) suggests that his basic method of rewarding mercenaries had to be in land-allotments. These could not always be found without alienating others,[151] and perhaps mercenaries once settled were reluctant to get involved in new enterprises.

To assess Dionysius' character through the hostility of the tradition is perhaps beyond us. On the whole, the story seems to go downhill. It is certainly the case that Diodorus' account gets thinner and thinner, but we do get a picture of growing isolation and bad temper, even without

---

[146] Nenci 1980 (B 162, summarized in *SEG* xxx 1117–23); Nenci *et al.* 1982 (B 163, summarized in *SEG* xxxii 914); Knoepfler 1987 (G 206); see also *SEG* xxxv 999 (a new text). The dossier also includes a text from a similar settlement at Nacone, even more Italian in character; cf. *SEG* xxxiv 934.   [147] Rallo 1982–83 (G 272).

[148] *Arch. Rep. for 1987–88*, 131; Anello 1986 (G 101).   [149] Fiorentini 1979 (G 165).

[150] Castellana 1984 (G 132), trying to reconstruct Dionysius' penetration in this area.

[151] Compare Dion's final dilemma (p. 703), as succinctly described by Nep. *Dio* 7.1–2.

the mass of later[152] picturesque anecdote about suspicion and precaution.
Of this there is a rich collection. He built a sort of moat around his
bedroom and raised the drawbridge before going to bed. He trusted no
one but his daughters to shave him, and, when they grew up, he took the
razors away even from them and had himself shaved with hot walnut-
shells.[153] These will serve as specimens.

How much can we really believe? Scholars, particularly perhaps
Anglo-Saxons, are prone to scepticism over stories about the corruption
of monarchs, whether by luxury or suspicion, particularly when their
public lives show some signs of cohesion and success. Alexander and
Caligula are not corrupted; they are trying logically to work out new
forms of monarchy. Stories of violent action and atrocity are discounted.
Periander of Corinth turns into a Lorenzo de Medici, despite the fact that
virtually all Periander's misconduct can be paralleled in the career of Ali
Pasha of Jannina in the early nineteenth century with a British consul
down the road sending in regular reports. In a generation which has had
the opportunity of watching the career of, say, Field Marshal Amin,
there should be no need to argue that there are at least some people
whom absolute power can corrupt absolutely, and that this sort of thing
is not incompatible with considerable military and political success can
be demonstrated quite adequately by a close examination of Stalin as he
appeared to men close to him.

Recent work on Dionysius[154] has overwhelmingly tried to trace the
hostile nature of Diodorus' account to prejudice, and discounts it
accordingly. It is true that our sources for Dionysius are very bad and
that scepticism is in order. But one important source remains to be
considered.

It is certain that Plato visited Sicily in the early 380s, though the
accounts of Dionysius' treatment of him are full of myth.[155] His
description in the *Republic* (562–71, 577–80) of how democracy changes
into tyranny and how the tyrant himself develops is familiar. Some of it,
notably the emphasis on the tyrant's sexual habits, does not seem to suit
Dionysius well, but much of it does: the impeachment of the rich as
oligarchs, the bodyguard, confiscations and redistribution, the distrust
of friends, the recruitment of mercenaries, the provoking of wars to
cover a weak position at home. Powerful voices[156] have been raised
against those who see Dionysius here, holding that the picture of the
tyrant is a generalized picture; if Plato had anyone in mind, it was

152 Not all later; see n. 141.
153 During the revision of this chapter, a hostile press reported that the President of Iraq changed
his barber frequently.
154 Stroheker 1958 (G 302), Sanders 1979/80 (G 282) and 1987 (G 283) 1–40, Caven 1990 (G 134),
varying on the sources of the prejudice.   155 See Sordi 1979 (G 294).
156 Wilamowitz 1920 (H 120) 432; Stroheker 1958 (G 302) 106.

Pisistratus of Athens. Even more of the account, however, cannot apply to Pisistratus. We may agree that Plato's tyrant is not only Dionysius, but Dionysius was surely much in Plato's mind. Even more certainly, he would inevitably be in the mind of any reader of the 370s and 360s.[157] Who, after all, was the tyrant of the age? And with the scene at Olympia (p. 140) before us, it is hard to resist the reference to the tragic poets who will go the round of other states and hire actors with fine sonorous voices to sway the inclination of the assembled crowd to tyrannies.

The most important passage is that on the tyrant as a person. The passage which describes the unparalleled degradation of the tyrant, unable to trust anyone and a prey to constant fear, is introduced in a very peculiar way. In order to see what a tyrant is really like, the judgment is needed of one who is not dazzled by the outward pomp and parade of absolute power, but whose understanding can enter into a man's heart and see what goes on within. Such a competent judge should be listened to, if he had also lived under the same roof and witnessed the tyrant's behaviour, not only in the emergencies of public life but towards intimates in his own household. 'Shall we then make believe that we ourselves are qualified to judge from having been in contact with tyrants, so that we may have someone to answer our questions?' It is hard to believe that Plato is not saying 'I have seen Dionysius and I know.'[158] The devastating passage which follows amounts, on our terms, to a judgment that tyranny had destroyed Dionysius' personality. A more explicit passage (332c) in the Seventh Letter (see below, p. 693) attributes what Plato saw as Dionysius' failure to the fact that, in his wisdom (*sophia*; the word can be bitterly ironic), he trusted nobody.

[157] So Caven 1990 (G 134) 167–8, 226.
[158] Wilamowitz 1920 (H 120) 437 n. 1 denied this, but see, e.g. Heintzeler 1927 (C 33) 77. Caven 1990 (G 134) 168–9, 226–7 argues that Plato did not meet Dionysius on his first visit to Sicily and was reporting the views of the young Dion, which fitted his own prejudices. It is hard to reconcile this with Dion's successful career at Syracuse over the next twenty years.

CHAPTER 6

THE KING'S PEACE AND THE SECOND
ATHENIAN CONFEDERACY

ROBIN SEAGER

I. THE SUPREMACY OF SPARTA

The Peace of Antalcidas had humbled Sparta's enemies and left them impotent, at least for the time being. The breaking of the Theban hold over Boeotia was followed by the refoundation of Plataea (Paus. IX.1.4), which probably took place at this time rather than after the seizure of the Cadmea, the citadel of Thebes, and it is likely that Thebes was forced into alliance with Sparta (Isoc. XIV.27, Plut. *Pel.* 4.5). This has been doubted,[1] but the absence of any allusion to the alliance at the time of the Theban negotiations with Olynthus and the trial of Ismenias is not sufficient to prove that it did not exist.

The Corinthian War was over. Now, as she had in 421 and 404, Sparta turned her attention to the conduct of her friends in the war. Her aim (Xen. *Hell.* v.2.1) was to punish those of her allies who had favoured the enemy and make such disloyalty impossible for the future. The first victims of her displeasure were the perennially restive Mantineans, who had shown their unreliability in various ways. They had evaded military service under pretext of a sacred truce, shown little enthusiasm when they had served, rejoiced at Sparta's military failures and even supplied the Argives with corn. Therefore, in 385, Sparta issued an ultimatum. Mantinea must dismantle her fortifications: compliance would be accepted as retrospective proof of loyalty. The Mantineans refused, and so an expedition was mounted. Agesilaus was reluctant to command, allegedly because of Mantinea's services to his father, so Agesipolis led the Spartan army, even though his father Pausanias had been on good terms with the leaders of the Mantinean people (Xen. *Hell.* v.2.3).

Diodorus (xv.5) condemns the Spartan action as a flagrant violation of the peace, and it is highly likely that the Mantineans made this point when they appealed to Athens for help. But the Athenians voted not to break the peace, and Mantinea was left to fight alone. This decision need of course reveal nothing about views held at Athens on the legality or morality of the Spartan attack; it merely reflects her isolation and military

---

[1] Buckler 1980 (C 330).

weakness. Sparta, on the other hand, called upon her new allies, perhaps chiefly for psychological reasons, for she can hardly have expected to need their assistance. A Theban contingent duly served on the Spartan side, in which both Pelopidas and Epaminondas were present (Plut. *Pel.* 4.4f, Paus. IX.13.1).

After ravaging the land, Agesipolis settled down to a siege. Throughout the summer the Mantineans kept up their resistance, allegedly aided by sympathizers among Sparta's allies who sent in supplies secretly by night (Polyaen. II.25). But with the onset of the rainy season the Spartans dammed the river which flowed through the city, so that it began to undermine the fortifications (Xen. *Hell.* v.2.4f, against Diod. xv.12.1, Paus. VIII.8.7). The Mantineans now offered to pull down their walls, but Sparta was no longer satisfied with this concession, insisting instead that the city of Mantinea must be abandoned and destroyed and its people dispersed into the four or five village communities into which they had been divided in ancient times (Xen. *Hell.* v.2.5ff, Ephorus 70 F 79, Diod. xv.12.1f, Strabo VIII.3.2, Paus. VIII.8.9). It is just possible, but hardly likely, that the autonomy clause of the peace was perversely cited to justify this demand. The defenders had no choice but surrender. The partisans of Argos and leaders of the people, some sixty in number, expected to be put to death, but the former king Pausanias intervened from his exile at Tegea to negotiate a safe-conduct for them. The dioecism was then carried out. At first the burden of moving provoked general discontent, but those whom the purge had left in power eventually decided that the change was a good thing. Sparta too had reason to be satisfied, for when troops were levied from the villages they served with much greater enthusiasm than they had when united under a democratic government (Xen. *Hell.* v.2.7).

Sparta's preoccupation with the conduct of her allies in the war and in particular with their willingness to supply troops was next exploited by the exiles from Phlius (Xen. *Hell.* v.2.8ff).[2] They pointed out that, while they had been in power, Phlius had provided men and welcomed Spartan armies into the city, whereas after their exile the Phliasians had refused to follow the Spartans and closed their gates against them. The charges were exaggerated, but the ephors, perhaps more impressed by their own opportunity than by the exiles' case, issued a thinly veiled threat. The exiles, they said, were friends of Sparta and their expulsion had been unjustified. Nevertheless Sparta would prefer to see them return by mutual agreement, without the use of force. The Phliasians feared treachery if Sparta sent out an army, since there were many friends and relatives of the exiles in the city, some of whom desired a change of

---

[2] Cf. Legon 1967 (C 369) not refuted by Piccirilli 1974 (C 375) or Thompson 1970 (C 385).

government. So they voted to readmit them, restore their property, and settle any disputes that might arise in open court.

It was not until 382 that affairs outside the Peloponnese again engaged Sparta's attention. Some ten years before, Amyntas of Macedon had been driven out of his country by an Illyrian invasion and had ceded some border territory, of uncertain location and extent, to Olynthus in return for help. On recovering his position the king somewhat optimistically asked for the return of this land, but Olynthus refused. Amyntas resorted to war, but the Olynthians, posing as liberators, secured the upper hand and by summer 382 had even gained control of Pella. So Amyntas appealed to Sparta (Xen. *Hell.* v.2.11ff, Diod. xiv.92.3, xv.19.2f, Dio Chrys. xxv.6). Envoys also came from Acanthus and Apollonia and were brought by the ephors before the assembly and the allies. The theme on which the Acanthian ambassador Cleigenes spoke was one to which the terms of the King's Peace were clearly relevant: the expansion of Olynthus at the expense not only of Amyntas but also of the smaller and weaker cities of Chalcidice. Olynthus had threatened to force Acanthus into membership of the Chalcidian state if she refused to lend assistance in Olynthus' wars, and while Acanthus was eager to retain her autonomy and political identity, she needed help if she were to resist the pressure which Olynthus could bring to bear.

Thus far the argument might appeal to Sparta if she wanted to establish her influence in the Thraceward region, as Diodorus insists (xv.19.3), on the respectable pretext of upholding the autonomy clause against Olynthian aggression. But the greater part of Cleigenes' speech was, if Xenophon can be trusted, directed at questions of Spartan security not only in Chalcidice but nearer home (Xen. *Hell.* v.2.15ff). Already, he warned, there were in Olynthus envoys from Athens and Thebes, and the Olynthians had voted to send missions to both cities to negotiate alliances. The combination of Athens, Thebes and Olynthus might prove a major threat to Sparta. It would therefore be irrational if, after taking steps to undo the unity of Boeotia, she were to stand by and watch the growth of a much greater power, and one which was still on the increase, for Olynthus, already holding Potidaea, would soon control all Pallene, while her friendship with the kingless Thracians would give her access to the gold of Pangaeum. It is striking that the parallel with Sparta's treatment of Thebes is presented in terms of pure power politics and not, as it might easily have been, of her credibility as champion of the King's Peace.

Cleigenes stressed the need for rapid intervention. For the moment the cities which had been compelled to join the Chalcidian state would be happy to defect if a leader came forward, but if once their new status had time to become established, they would prove much less easy to detach.

His apparent belief that Sparta was far more concerned with questions of security and military strength than with posing as the defender of the autonomy clause was vindicated by the Spartan response (Xen. *Hell.* v.2.20ff). She asked for the opinion of her allies, not on the question of whether the King's Peace had been broken, but as to what would be best for the Peloponnese and themselves. It is noteworthy that in Xenophon's opinion those who wanted to curry favour spoke for war. Nevertheless their enthusiasm knew bounds, for it was in preparing for this expedition that Sparta was forced for the first time to accept financial contributions from her allies in lieu of men.

Conscious of the need for haste, the Acanthians asked that a Spartan commander with as large a force as possible should be sent north at once while the allies were mustering. Eudamidas was duly dispatched with 2,000 men who might be considered expendable. On his arrival in the north he occupied Potidaea, which gave colour to Cleigenes' claims by coming over of its own accord, and garrisoned various towns that had not yet fallen to Olynthus. The bulk of the Peloponnesian forces was commanded by Eudamidas' brother, Phoebidas, who marched by way of Thebes.

The King's Peace had not only put an end to Theban control over Boeotia but had no doubt at least temporarily diminished the standing within the city of those like Ismenias and Androclidas who had conceived the policy that provoked the Corinthian War.[3] Leontiades and his supporters will have returned to power, paying with as good a grace as possible Sparta's price: the dissolution of the Boeotian Confederacy, the restoration of Plataea and the enforced alliance. But by 382 it seems that the opponents of Sparta had regained some of their strength. Both Ismenias and Leontiades were polemarchs in that year, and the city was in the throes of a struggle for supremacy between them (Xen. *Hell.* v.2.25ff). The opening of negotiations with Olynthus in disregard of Sparta's predictable wishes suggests that Ismenias was gaining the upper hand, and he had just achieved one important success in a matter very close to Sparta's heart: Thebes had decreed that no Theban should join the expedition to Olynthus. Leontiades saw a chance to recover his position, albeit in exchange for the total sacrifice of Theban independence. He proposed to Phoebidas that the Spartans should seize the Cadmea. This would put the city completely under Spartan domination, and if he and his friends were given power, they would ensure that Thebes provided Sparta with a host of troops. Phoebidas agreed, and Leontiades led the Spartans into the city. He arrested Ismenias in the council-chamber, but Androclidas and at least 300 of his supporters made their escape to Athens (cf. Androtion 324 F 50).

[3] Hack 1978 (C 338).

In Xenophon's version the initiative came solely from Leontiades, for purely selfish motives, while Phoebidas did no more than accept his suggestion. But there were those in Greece who believed that Agesilaus had put the idea into Phoebidas' head before he ever left Sparta (Plut. *Ages.* 23.4, 24.1), while Diodorus (xv.20.2) goes so far as to claim that all Spartan commanders had secret standing orders to seize Thebes if they got the chance. This last is probably an exaggeration. The resurgence of Ismenias and the consequent growth of Theban recalcitrance were of recent date, and Xenophon's circumstantial account of reactions at Sparta to the news of the coup makes it clear that the mass of Spartans at least was taken completely by surprise. Nor need the fact that Phoebidas appeared at Thebes at all have any sinister implications: a desire to put pressure on the Thebans to join the expedition would suffice to explain his choice of route. Yet it is not incredible that Agesilaus, who had surely supported a hard line against Olynthus,[4] and whose hatred of Thebes may have made him particularly sensitive to any manifestation of Theban independence, had suggested that Phoebidas explore the possibility of setting up a reliable puppet government.

When Leontiades came to Sparta to justify himself, he found the ephors and most of the people hostile, not, it must be admitted, because Thebes had come under Spartan control but because Phoebidas had acted with no instructions from the city (Xen. *Hell.* v.2.32ff). Agesilaus, however, showed a guarded approval, proclaiming that initiative might be tolerated if exercised for the good of the city. Leontiades was equally pragmatic. In the past, he said, Sparta had repeatedly complained of Theban hostility, but now Thebes, which had been on the brink of alliance with Olynthus, would never again be a threat to Sparta, providing that he and his adherents were maintained in power. Sparta's eventual course of action was even more cynical. Phoebidas was fined, but the garrison remained on the Cadmea, while arrangements were made to put Ismenias on trial before judges drawn from Sparta and her allies. She might have appealed to the terms of the peace and accused Ismenias of undermining her crusade in defence of the Thraceward cities against Olynthian encroachment. But in fact the charges looked back to the Corinthian War: Ismenias was said to have favoured Persia to the detriment of Greece and taken Persian money, and he and Androclidas were blamed for all the confusion in Greece. Inevitably he was condemned and executed.

The occupation of Thebes was decried throughout Greece as the most flagrant and outrageous of the violations of autonomy which Sparta had been perpetrating ever since 386 (Xen. *Hell.* v.4.1, Diod. xv.19.4, 20.2, Polyb. iv.27.4ff, Plut. *Ages.* 23.3, Justin viii.1.5). She might perhaps

---

[4] Cawkwell 1976 (C 285) 77.

have made some attempt to defend herself by pointing to Leontiades'
invitation, but the case would have been a pitiful one, and it was better to
say nothing. Indeed, Sparta's behaviour since 386 consistently reveals a
single-minded pursuit of power and military resources accompanied by
total unconcern for the dictates of the peace.[5]

In the north the Spartans and their ally Amyntas had achieved little
during the summer of 382. So, in autumn of that year, Teleutias was sent
out as harmost with a force of Spartans and allies (Xen. *Hell.* v.2.37ff,
Diod. xv.21). He received enthusiastic help from the Thebans, in part
because they knew that he was Agesilaus' brother. His first aim was to
collect as large a force as possible, and to that end he urged Amyntas,
who may have relaxed his efforts when the Spartan threat drew off the
Olynthians from Macedon, to hire mercenaries and buy the support of
neighbouring kings. He based himself at Potidaea, and before the end of
the season fought a battle before Olynthus in which only one of those
kings, Derdas, saved the Spartans from defeat. The spring of 381
brought varying fortunes (Xen. *Hell.* v.3.1ff). At the beginning of the
campaigning season Derdas defeated the Olynthians at Apollonia, but a
little later, in an action at Olynthus, Teleutias himself was killed, while
the Spartan army suffered heavy casualties and was dispersed among the
friendly cities of Spartolus, Acanthus, Apollonia and Potidaea. Reaction
at Sparta was prompt and energetic (Xen. *Hell.* v.3.8f, 18ff, Diod.
xv.21.3, 22.2, 23.2). The king Agesipolis was sent out with thirty
advisers. He too had the support of Amyntas and Derdas. At first he
enjoyed some success, ravaging the territory of Olynthus and storming
Torone, but soon he fell ill with a fever and was dead by the middle of
summer (Tod no. 120). Xenophon sees fit to remark that Agesilaus did
not rejoice at his passing (*Hell.* v.3.20), and indeed the schematic contrast
between Agesipolis the champion of autonomy and Agesilaus the
ruthless exponent of Spartan self-aggrandizement (Diod. xv.19.4) is
grossly exaggerated. To replace him yet another Spartan commander,
Polybiades, was sent out as harmost, either in autumn 381 or spring 380.

The summer of 381 also saw fresh trouble in Phlius (Xen. *Hell.*
v.3.10ff). The Phliasians had won praise from Agesipolis for the
readiness with which they had supplied him with funds for his campaign
against Olynthus, and they reckoned that with the other king so far from
home Agesilaus would not feel free to move against them. So they
plucked up courage, first to make allegedly unjust decisions in disputes
involving the exiles whose return Sparta had enforced in 384, then, when
the exiles and their supporters complained at Sparta, to fine them for
going on an embassy unauthorized by the city. The victims complained
again, playing on the old Spartan grievance: the men who were now

[5] Seager 1974 (C 73) 39ff.

denying them their rights were the same, they said, who had excluded the
Spartans from Phlius in the Corinthian War. The ephors decided on an
expedition, which pleased Agesilaus, for among the exiles were friends
he had inherited from his father and others he had made himself. On
reaching Phlius he asked that the acropolis be handed over to the
Spartans, and when this demand was refused settled down to a siege
which was to last until summer 379. The Phliasians conducted their
assemblies in full view of the besiegers, and there was even some
muttering in the Spartan ranks at undertaking an arduous campaign
against such worthy opponents just to please a few exiles. But the
number of the exiles gradually increased as their friends and relatives
slipped out of the city to join them, till Agesilaus was eventually able to
form them into a unit a thousand strong.

Not all the opponents of the exiles in Phlius were passionately hostile
to Sparta, even if they did not want to be her puppets. By 379, when the
defenders were holding out on half rations, Xenophon reckons that the
supporters of Delphion, the chief spokesman for continuing resistance,
numbered only 300 (Xen. Hell. v.3.21ff). When Phlius finally surrendered, Agesilaus arranged that the details of the settlement should be left
in his hands. Delphion prudently escaped. Agesilaus' terms, predictably
enough, showed a complete disregard for Phliasian autonomy. A
committee comprising fifty exiles and fifty men from the city was first to
put to death whomsoever it pleased, then to draw up laws for the
conduct of public affairs. To ensure that the committee carried out its
functions properly, Agesilaus left a garrison and six months' pay. There
is no sign that Sparta tried to defend her behaviour by stressing that the
purge would be carried out and the new constitution drafted by
Phliasians, not Spartans.

The same summer, 379, also saw the successful conclusion of the
Olynthian War (Xen. Hell. v.3.26f, Diod. xv.23.3). Since his arrival
Polybiades had won several victories, of which no details are known, and
had finally subjected Olynthus to a blockade so effective that its people,
faced with starvation, sent to Sparta to sue for peace. The terms, that
Olynthus should have the same friends and enemies as Sparta and follow
wherever she led, were on the one hand traditional but on the other
reflect faithfully Sparta's current concerns: military expansion and
sources of manpower. However, it is probable that she also dissolved the
Chalcidian state, perhaps in the name of autonomy, though the Olynthians continued to call themselves Chalcidians.[6]

Both Xenophon and Diodorus see this moment as the pinnacle of
Spartan power (Xen. Hell. v.3.27, Diod. xv.23.3). Since 386 her military
undertakings, at Mantinea, Thebes, Phlius and Olynthus, had all been

[6] Zahrnt 1971 (c 392) 95ff.

crowned with success. She had even risked the anger of Persia, first perhaps in 381 by thinking of helping Evagoras (Isoc. IV.135, Theopomp. 115 F 103. 10, cf. Diod. xv.8.4), then, in about 380, by concluding an alliance with the rebel commander Glos, though his assassination brought this strange adventure to an end before the pact could bear fruit for either side (Diod. xv.9.3ff, 18.1, 19.1).[7] But at the same time her ruthless dedication to imperialism and her contempt for the peace which she herself had championed while it benefited her to do so had stirred up bitter resentment not only in those cities which had felt the weight of her hand but all over Greece. As yet no city had been strong enough to offer a challenge, but events at Thebes and Athens were soon to show how precarious Sparta's apparent supremacy really was.

II. THE RESURGENCE OF ATHENS

The cautious response of Athens to the Mantinean appeal in 385 had been typical of her behaviour since 386. The King's Peace had brought an abrupt and humiliating end to that brief attempt to restore the fifth-century empire which had culminated in the expedition of Thrasybulus. Resentment was deep and, as always at Athens, there were those who thought the generals were to blame for the outcome of the war (cf. Lys. XXVIII, XXIX, Tod no. 116). Both Agyrrhius and Thrasybulus Collyteus suffered condemnation (Dem. XXIV.134f). But for the moment all that Athens could do was to try very discreetly to maintain some of the links that had been forged in the preceding decade. In 386/5 she honoured Hebryzelmis of Thrace (Tod no. 117 = Harding no. 29), successor of Amadocus, with whom Thrasybulus had concluded an alliance. A little later the Athenians granted immunity from taxation to those Thasians and Byzantines who after the King's Peace had been exiled for their Athenian sympathies and had taken refuge at Athens; they had granted similar immunity to refugees from the dioecism of Mantinea (*IG* II^2 33, Dem. xx.59f). Events at Byzantium may cast doubt on Isocrates' claim (XIV.28) that it, as well as Chios and Mytilene, remained loyal to Athens after 386, though both Lesbos and Chios might fear potential Persian encroachment, against which Sparta would be most unlikely to protect them. In the case of Chios more detail is provided by the surviving treaty made between her and Athens in 384 (Tod no. 118 = Harding no. 31). The terms once again show Athens in cautious mood, taking great care not to tread on Persian toes. The alliance is strictly defensive, and both parties insist that their action is not merely compatible with, but conducive to, the maintenance of the King's Peace. All allusions to the peace are entirely passive. There is here, in sharp contrast to the posture

[7] Ryder 1963 (C 245) 105ff; above p. 81.

of Athens in the seventies, no accusation brought against Sparta for her offences against the autonomy clause, no suggestion that Athens is setting herself up in rivalry as the new *prostates* of the peace.[8]

It is true that Isocrates in his *Panegyricus*, to be dated probably to 381, perhaps 380,[9] could preach a panhellenic crusade against Persia and claim leadership for Athens (Isoc. IV.3, 18ff). His diatribes against Spartan imperialism (78ff, 110ff), the King's Peace in general (115ff) and Spartan breaches of the autonomy clause in particular (126) might have won applause not only from Athenians but from the Greeks at large. But his unabashed defence of the fifth-century empire (100ff), with its justifications of Athenian judicial and constitutional interference and even of the hated cleruchies, was hardly likely to win support for Athenian hegemony (cf. Diod. XV.23.4), and his final appeal for the repudiation of the peace (175) fell on deaf ears. Indeed, it was probably late in 380 that, in response to a complaint from Pharnabazus, the Athenians recalled Chabrias, who had on his own initiative taken service with the rebel Acoris of Egypt (whom Athens had supported before the King's Peace), and instead sent out Iphicrates to help the Persians (Diod. XV.29.2ff).

In mainland Greece Athens' flirtation with Olynthus in 382 had come to nothing. But in the same year she had offered a haven to Androclidas and those of his supporters who had escaped Leontiades' coup. Androclidas himself had been assassinated at Athens, but Spartan pressure to surrender the rest of the exiles had been resisted (*IG* II[2] 37, Din. 1.39, Plut. *Pel.* 6.2f). In the depths of the winter of 379/8 a number of them at last matured a plot to liberate their city and secure their own return. The leading figures in the conspiracy were Pelopidas, Phillidas and Melon among those at Athens, and Charon inside Thebes (Plut. *Pel.* 7ff, *Mor.* 576ff, Xen. *Hell.* V.4.2ff). Unlike the previous generation of Theban nationalists these younger men favoured democracy and planned, if they were successful, to establish a democratic constitution at Thebes. Our sources disagree over the details of the story, but it is certain that the leaders of the exiles, after penetrating Boeotia in the guise of hunters, gained entry to the city and assassinated their principal opponents, Leontiades and Archias, even though they knew that a plot was afoot. It is even said that Archias had received a letter which revealed the conspirators' plans in full but had put it aside to be opened in the morning (Plut. *Pel.* 10.3). The assassins were now joined by two other men who were to be prominent in the years to come, Epaminondas and Gorgidas. They released those of their sympathizers who were in jail, summoned the remainder of the exiles from outside the city and made a proclamation to the Thebans. However, the people did not respond until daybreak. Then an assembly was held, at which boeotarchs were elected

---

[8] Seager 1974 (C 73) 44ff.   [9] On the date, cf. Tuplin 1983 (C 263) 179ff.

for the first time since 386. Their number is uncertain – it may even have been the full seven of later years – but they included Melon, Charon, Pelopidas and perhaps Gorgidas (Plut. *Pel.* 12f, Xen. *Hell.* v.4.8f).[10] The significance of this step is clear. Even before the Spartans had been dislodged from the Cadmea, the new leaders of Thebes were asserting her claim to rule the whole of Boeotia.

Xenophon's version of the retaking of the Cadmea is very different from that of Diodorus (*Hell.* v.4.9ff). On hearing of the coup the Spartan garrison sent to Plataea and Thespiae for aid, while the Thebans summoned help from an Athenian force under two generals, stationed on the border. Despite Athens' later repudiation of the generals, this contingent must surely have been intended to assist the exiles, and the Thebans knew where to find it. A relief force from Plataea was turned back by the Thebans, then, as soon as the Athenians had arrived, preparations were made to storm the Cadmea. The garrison surrendered, apparently at the first assault, in return for a guarantee of safe-conduct, despite which the Thebans among them were lynched as they departed, except for those who were protected by the Athenians. When the Spartans heard what had happened, they condemned the harmost to death because he had not held out until the promised reinforcements came and mounted an expedition against Thebes. Agesilaus refused the command, and so the ephors, impressed by the stories of the Theban refugees who had come to Sparta, appointed Cleombrotus.

Diodorus (xv.25.3–27.4) offers a more protracted siege, at the beginning of which the defenders of the Cadmea sent to Sparta itself for assistance and the Thebans dispatched an embassy to Athens. In response the Athenians voted to send out as large a force as they could. On the next day Demophon set out with 5,000 men, while preparations were begun for an expedition in full force, though this did not in the event prove necessary. Only after prolonged resistance in the hope that help would come from Sparta did the garrison commanders finally decide to surrender, for their allied troops were reluctant to fight on, though the Spartans were ready for a struggle to the death. By this time Cleombrotus' expedition was already on its way, and so the three senior Spartan officers were condemned on their return, two to death, the third to a heavy fine.

This account receives confirmation from several sources. Isocrates too (xiv.24) has the Theban embassy to Athens, and may well be right in suggesting that the envoys made much of the autonomy clause, though in Diodorus they base their appeal on Theban services to Athens in 404. Dinarchus (1.38f) adds the detail that it was Cephalus who proposed the decree to send out a force. Plutarch (*Pel.* 13.2) tells us that the members

[10] Buckler 1979 (C 328).

of the garrison on their way home had got no further than Megara when they met Cleombrotus and his army, and agrees that three Spartan officers were condemned. While doubts must remain, it seems likely that Xenophon's story is as severely truncated as it appears and his chronology of events at Sparta misleading, and that Diodorus' version of the length of the siege and of the nature of Athenian involvement is historical.[11] If Isocrates (XIV.29) is telling the truth, the liberators also sent an embassy to Sparta immediately after their success, offering friendship on the same terms as before, that is, a return to the Spartan alliance. However, Sparta's conditions were too harsh: she demanded the restoration of the exiles and the expulsion of the leaders of the coup, and so the Thebans withdrew. The story has often been rejected, but, although Isocrates may have overstated the objective, it is not implausible that the new rulers of Thebes should have made some attempt to mollify Sparta and counteract the propaganda of the refugees.

The Athenian forces in Thebes had returned home after the capture of the Cadmea, but a contingent of light-armed troops under Chabrias was sent to hold the road through Eleutherae against Cleombrotus.[12] But the king took a different road to Plataea, wiping out a Theban guard post on the summit of Cithaeron, then made his way to Thespiae. However, after only sixteen days in Theban territory he led his army home, leaving his men in doubt whether they were at war with Thebes or not. At Thespiae he left Sphodrias as harmost, with a third of his allied troops and money to hire mercenaries (Xen. *Hell.* v.4.15f). It is possible that the Theban embassy, despite its failure, had given rise at Sparta to hopes that a full-scale war would prove unnecessary, and such hopes may have contributed to Cleombrotus' moderation, while the king himself, in contrast to Agesilaus, may have subscribed to the view that Athens represented a greater potential danger to Sparta than did Thebes. The apparent weakening of Theban resolution, as much as fear at the strength of Cleombrotus' army (Xen. *Hell.* v.4.19), may also have been the cause of a sudden attack of cold feet at Athens, where the two generals who had lent their aid to the original coup were selected as scapegoats, put on trial and condemned (Xen. *Hell.* v.4.19, Plut. *Pel.* 14.1). Unfortunately the charge is not recorded.

But if Athens was as yet reluctant to become involved in a struggle on land between Sparta and a possibly wavering Thebes, her determination to reassert herself at sea was by now gaining momentum. It is likely that the establishment of the nucleus of the Second Athenian Confederacy belongs, as Diodorus suggests (XV.28.2ff), early in 378, before the raid of Sphodrias.[13] The first recorded members were Chios, Byzantium,

[11] Judeich 1927 (C 340) 173ff.   [12] Cawkwell 1973 (C 111) 58.
[13] Cawkwell 1973 (C 111) 47ff.

Rhodes, Mytilene and perhaps Methymna (Diod. xv.28.4, Tod nos. 121, 122 = Harding nos. 34, 37, *SEG* xxxii 50). A common council or *synedrion* was established at Athens, in which each member state was to have one vote, and the autonomy of members was guaranteed, though they accepted Athens as *hegemon*. Unlike the alliance with Chios in 384, the negotiations which brought the confederacy into being made it clear from the first that the object of the exercise was to defend freedom and autonomy against Spartan encroachment, even though some of the earliest members may have been more frightened of Persia than of Sparta. In other words Athens was now for the first time proclaiming herself as the champion of the principles laid down in the King's Peace.

It may well have been resentment and alarm at this open challenge to her supremacy that prompted Sparta to send an embassy to Athens (Xen. *Hell.* v.4.22), though the original object of the mission is not recorded. However, while the envoys were in Athens, the Spartan harmost at Thespiae, Sphodrias, made a foolhardy attempt to seize the Piraeus, which still had no gates (Xen. *Hell.* v.4.20ff, Diod. xv.29.5ff, Plut. *Pel.* 14.1, *Ages.* 24.4). He had reckoned to reach his objective before dawn, but when day came he had got no further than Thria. Nevertheless, instead of slipping off as quietly as possible, he did all he could to advertise his presence before withdrawing. The Athenians arrested the Spartan ambassadors, who insisted, probably with truth, that they and Sparta knew nothing of the scheme and promised that Sphodrias would be tried and condemned to death. Of Sphodrias' intentions there can be no doubt: his provocative behaviour shows a clear determination to bring about a breach between Sparta and Athens. It may also be regarded as certain that he had not been acting on his own initiative, but our sources disagree as to who was behind him. Xenophon blames the Thebans, who were afraid that they would have to fight Sparta alone and so bribed Sphodrias to provoke a war between Athens and Sparta. Plutarch agrees, and names Pelopidas and Gorgidas as the authors of what for him was a brilliant stratagem. Diodorus on the other hand makes Cleombrotus responsible. These suggestions are not of course mutually exclusive. The former is extremely plausible: the motive ascribed to the Thebans is rational and cogent. But it may also be true that Cleombrotus was alarmed enough at the revival of Athens to devise a wild scheme to nip it in the bud.

Despite her outrage Athens was prepared to keep the peace provided that Sparta honoured her ambassadors' promise and Sphodrias was condemned (Xen. *Hell.* v.4.24ff). Sphodrias himself expected the worst and did not present himself for trial. The friends of Cleombrotus were inclined to acquit him, which may lend support to Diodorus' accusation, but they feared the hostility of the mass of Spartans and of Agesilaus,

who believed, or affected to believe, that Sphodrias had been bribed by
the Thebans. But whatever his reasons Agesilaus eventually changed his
position, declaring that, although Sphodrias had done wrong, Sparta
had need of such soldiers. This must mean in practical terms that he had
decided Sparta was capable of fighting a war simultaneously against
Thebes and Athens, foreseeing perhaps that their alliance would prove
uneasy. So Sphodrias was acquitted.

Reaction at Athens was swift and vigorous (Xen. *Hell.* v.4.34, Diod.
xv.29.7). The Athenians decreed that Sparta had broken the peace and
prepared energetically for war. Gates were put on the Piraeus, troops
were to be levied and ships built and manned, and Timotheus, Chabrias
and Callistratus were appointed to command. An alliance was made with
the Thebans (*IG* ii² 40 = Harding no. 33; Diod. xv.28.5 is probably non-
technical and proleptic, rather than misplaced), and Thebes was admitted to membership of the confederacy.[14] It was on Thebes that Sparta for
the moment concentrated her efforts (Xen. *Hell.* v.4.35ff, Diod. xv.32f).
In summer 378 Agesilaus led an invasion and established himself at
Thespiae, on which the Thebans had already made an unsuccessful
attack (Diod. xv.27.4). This was the first campaign undertaken by Sparta
after the military regrouping of her allies into nine divisions: Arcadia
accounted for two, Elis and Achaea one each, Corinth and Megara
another, Sicyon, Phlius and the cities of Acte a sixth, while the last three
units were drawn from central Greece and the north: Acarnania, Phocis
and Locris, and Olynthus and the other allies in the Thraceward area
(Diod. xv.31.2). Agesilaus broke through the defensive works of the
Thebans and ravaged the land right up to the city, but the Thebans
would not risk a pitched battle, while the king declined to challenge
Chabrias and his mercenaries in an incident later made famous by
Chabrias' statue.[15] After fortifying Thespiae Agesilaus went home,
leaving Phoebidas as harmost. Fighting in Boeotia continued: first
Phoebidas carried out raids on Theban territory, then the Thebans made
a full-scale attack on Thespiae. It failed, but Phoebidas was killed. From
this point on the Thebans sent out repeated expeditions against Thespiae
and other neighbouring cities, while those who sympathized with the
Theban democracy gathered at Thebes. The Spartans for their part
contented themselves with sending out one *mora* under a polemarch to
reinforce the garrison at Thespiae.

The behaviour of the Thebans made it clear that they intended to
pursue the objective implied by their election of boeotarchs immediately
after the democratic coup, the recovery of Theban dominion over

---

[14] Burnett 1962 (C 99); Buckler 1971 (C 324). Clark 1990 (B 138) shows, however, that ship-
building at Athens did not cease in the 380s.

Boeotia. This put Athens in an embarrassing position. She had founded the confederacy and challenged Sparta in the name of freedom and autonomy, and the Thebans in their hour of need had been prepared to join as Thebans, not Boeotians. Both she and her allies might have doubts about a war, the successful conclusion of which would leave Thebes, freed from the threat of Spartan invasion, at liberty to destroy freedom and autonomy in Boeotia. So the need to reassure existing allies as well as to secure new ones may have contributed to the passing, in February or March 377, of the decree of Aristoteles (Tod no. 123 = Harding no. 35, Diod. xv.29.8), which set out to encourage more cities to join the confederacy by reiterating and defining in greater detail Athens' dedication to the principles of freedom and autonomy. The measure was timely, for many Greeks, whatever they thought of Sparta, must still have distrusted Athens' motives, whether or not they had read the *Panegyricus* (cf. Diod. xv.23.4).

The decree restated the confederacy's fundamental aim: to force Sparta to allow the Greeks secure possession of their territory in freedom and autonomy. This clear reference to the terms of the King's Peace may have been followed by a specific commitment to its preservation, though the lines in question were erased at a later date and their content must remain uncertain.[16] Applications for membership were invited from anyone, Greek or barbarian, mainlander or islander, who was not a subject of the King of Persia. Plainly Athens still wished to present herself as the champion of the King's Peace, not to repudiate it and so risk Persia's wrath. The conditions of membership which follow are best seen as glosses on the basic guarantee of freedom and autonomy, which had probably received no closer definition in the King's Peace itself. Each member state was to have what constitution it wished, to receive no garrison or governor, and to pay no tribute. Moreover, Athens relinquished all claims to property, public or private, in the territory of member states, and existing records of such claims were to be destroyed. Henceforth neither the Athenian state nor any Athenian citizen was to acquire a house or land in allied territory by any means whatever. Any charges that might arise from this provision were to be heard not in an Athenian court but in the allied *synedrion*.

These clauses were obviously meant to serve a double purpose: first, to remind those still inclined to be loyal to Sparta of the outrages perpetrated by her above all in the time of Lysander, secondly, and surely a more important matter in context, to renounce those abuses practised by Athens herself in the fifth century which had stirred up such resentment against her rule and inspired a stubborn reluctance to believe that she had really changed her ways. There followed a guarantee that, if any member were attacked, the forces of Athens and the rest of the alliance would come to her aid. This must have been directed chiefly at Sparta, but may also have been intended as a discreet warning to Persia. The names of all members of the alliance, present and future, were to be inscribed on the same stone which bore the decree.

It is ominous that at the same time a further decree was passed, authorizing an embassy to Thebes, 'to persuade the Thebans of whatever good it may' (Tod no. 123 = Harding no. 35 lines 72ff). It may well be that the conduct of the Thebans in Boeotia was already causing Athens concern, though she may also have been eager to secure a contribution from Thebes for the naval operations which the confederacy was soon to mount. Meanwhile she soon had grounds for satisfaction, for the decree of Aristoteles served its purpose well, allaying suspicion and creating good will towards her (Diod. xv.29.8). The first to respond were the cities of Euboea, with the exception of Hestiaea (Diod. xv.30.1); the alliance between Athens and Chalcis survives (Tod no. 124 = Harding no. 38). It is significant that Euboea had suffered much in the fifth century from both cleruchies and private Athenian property holdings.

The growth and workings of the confederacy in the years before Leuctra raise a number of questions to which no certain answer can be given. The eventual total membership is given as seventy by Diodorus (xv.30.2), seventy-five by Aeschines (ii.70). Yet the names appended to the decree of Aristoteles cannot have numbered more than fifty-eight. Therefore either the figures in the literary sources are inflated, perhaps by the inclusion of allies of Athens who were never confederacy members, or, at some unknown date and for some unknown reason, the Athenians stopped adding the names of new members to the list which was begun in 377 and kept up at least until 375, probably until 373. No compelling date or reason has ever been suggested, nor is there any state whose membership is securely attested elsewhere – though such attestation is admittedly extremely rare – whose name is not or could not have been recorded on the extant list. Thus it is probable, though not quite certain, that at some point Corcyra joined the confederacy, though her name does not appear;[17] however, it could have stood in a lacuna. It may therefore be better to reject the evidence of Diodorus and Aeschines and opt for the lower figure.[18] If this is correct, the confederacy had reached its fullest extent by 373 at the latest, and after that time no new members were added. Instead, treaties were made which bound new allies to Athens and the league without actually admitting them to membership. Attempts have been made to date the accession of various known

[17] Coleman and Bradeen 1967 (c 121); Tuplin 1984 (c 81) 544ff; *SEG* xxxii 53.
[18] Cargill 1981 (c 101)38ff; Cawkwell 1981 (c 113) 41ff.

members and to connect their adhesion with the naval expeditions undertaken by Chabrias in 377 to 375 and Timotheus in 375 and 373.[19] But not enough is known about the details of the procedure adopted in making and recording admissions for anything to be said with confidence on this subject.[20]

The promises made in the decree of Aristoteles have often been dismissed as empty, never meant to be kept and quickly broken. But at least in the years down to Leuctra, before Athens fell victim to her fatal obsessions with Amphipolis and the Chersonese, her record will bear examination.[21] No cleruchies were inflicted on confederacy members,[22] and no constitutional interference is recorded, while if garrisons were temporarily installed in allied cities, this was done in response to the needs of the military situation and with the consent of the recipients. It was easy to say (Theopomp. 115 F 98) that the *syntaxeis* paid by members of the confederacy were merely *phoros* under a different name, but extortion and misapplication of confederacy funds are again not attested before Leuctra, though it is equally clear that Athens had begun to slip back into her old ways long before the critical period of the Social War.[23]

The decree of Aristoteles says almost nothing about the composition, powers and general functioning of the *synedrion* and its relationship to the Athenian *boule* and Assembly, or about finance, apart from the repudiation of *phoros*, though the existence of a common treasury is implied (Tod no. 123 = Harding no. 35 line 46). No doubt all these matters had been dealt with in the lost decrees which actually brought the confederacy and the *synedrion* into being. We know that the *synedrion* met at Athens and that every member had one vote (Diod. xv.28.4). It would be natural to assume that every member therefore sent one *synedros*, and this may well be correct (cf. Tod nos. 153, 175 = Harding nos. 65, 97; *IG* ii² 232); the apparent indication in one inscription that Mytilene had more than one *synedros* (Tod no. 131 = Harding no. 53, cf. 126) may be due to careless drafting. How the president was chosen and for how long he served is not known; a Theban president is attested in 372 (Accame 1941 (c 87) 229ff). On one occasion the *boule* is found instructing the *synedrion* to bring a *dogma* before the Assembly, while at the same time publishing its own *probouleuma* (Tod no. 133). On another a decree of the Assembly was preceded by a *dogma* of the allies, which had been presented first to the *boule* (Tod no. 144 = Harding no. 56). It may be that both these cases offer partial descriptions of a normal procedure in which the *boule* first suggested business for the *synedrion*, then vetted the allied *dogma* before

[19] Accame 1941 (c 87) 72ff; Woodhead 1962 (c 273).
[20] Cargill 1981 (c 101) 38ff; Cawkwell 1981 (c 113) 45ff.
[21] Cargill 1981 (c 101) 134ff; Cawkwell 1981 (c 113) 50f.
[22] Cawkwell 1973 (c 110) against Davies 1969 (c 123).
[23] Cargill 1981 (c 101) 125; Cawkwell 1963 (c 16) 91ff, 1981 (c 113) 48.

passing it on to the Assembly. It might be hoped that usually there would be no controversy, that the *boule* would approve the *dogma* and simply reinforce it with its *probouleuma*. But later, in the negotiations which led up to the Peace of Philocrates, though the *synedrion* had promised in advance to ratify whatever the Assembly decided, it seems that the *boule*, influenced by Demosthenes, sent on a *probouleuma* which contradicted the *dogma* of the allies instead of endorsing it. Whether in such circumstances the allied *dogma* never reached the Assembly is unclear, but it is perhaps more likely that when there was a conflict both *dogma* and *probouleuma* were put before the people.

Whether the original constitution of the league made any provision at all for the financing of confederate operations is also uncertain. The earliest mention of *syntaxeis* refers to 373 ([Dem.] XLIX.49), but even these need not have been fixed and regular amounts, while Athenian annoyance in 375 that Thebes was not contributing to the cost of the fleet (Xen. *Hell.* VI.2.1) need imply no more than a moral obligation. It is not unlikely that until 373 Athens bore the cost of campaigning alone, and that even after that date the levying of *syntaxeis* was carried out on an irregular and *ad hoc* basis.

In spring 377 Agesilaus again marched into Boeotia and penetrated the Theban stockade, ravaging the land between Thebes and Tanagra, which was still loyal to Sparta (Xen. *Hell.* v.4.47ff, Diod. xv.34.1f). The Thebans were prepared to challenge him to battle, but Agesilaus declined and instead moved on the undefended city. However, the Thebans succeeded in turning him back, and after settling a civil disturbance at Thespiae Agesilaus returned home by way of Megara. There he fell victim to a circulatory disorder, and an emergency operation weakened him further by causing massive loss of blood. He was seriously ill until the next year and was still unfit to go on a campaign six years later. Indeed, he disappears from history till summer 371, and it is possible that during this interval his influence on Spartan policy was diminished.

Chabrias and his peltasts had again gone to the aid of the Thebans (Xen. *Hell.* v.4.54). But after Agesilaus' withdrawal from Boeotia Chabrias took command of a naval expedition which went first to Euboea to protect Athens' newly acquired allies there and attack Hestiaea, which had remained loyal to Sparta because Sparta, some three years before, had liberated it from the tyrant Neogenes, who had established himself with the support of Jason of Pherae (Diod. xv.30.2ff). Chabrias ravaged the territory of Hestiaea, fortified the hill known as its Metropolis and left a garrison there before departing for the Cyclades, where he won over various islands which had been subject to Sparta, including Peparethos and Sciathos. It was, however, the Thebans who detached Hestiaea from Sparta. They were suffering from a shortage of corn, for it was now two years since they had been able to work their land. An expedition to Pagasae to buy Thessalian corn fell into the hands of Alcetas, the Spartan commander in Hestiaea. But thanks to Alcetas' neglect of duty the Thebans escaped and, after seizing the citadel, were able to bring the city over. Henceforth Thebes was able to import corn unimpeded (Xen. *Hell.* v.4.56f).

In 376, because of the illness of Agesilaus, the annual Spartan invasion of Boeotia was entrusted to Cleombrotus (Xen. *Hell.* v.4.59). But when he found the Thebans and Athenians holding Cithaeron against him, he turned back without engaging the enemy and went home. Irritation at this fiasco, coupled with exhaustion, led the allies to complain at Sparta. They urged the Spartans to take to the sea and starve Athens into submission by a blockade, and also pointed out that an army could be shipped to Boeotia. The Spartans duly manned a fleet of sixty ships under Pollis, which controlled the waters around Aegina, Ceos and Andros and was able during the summer of 376 to interfere with the import of corn from the Black Sea to Athens (Xen. *Hell.* v.4.60f, Diod. xv.34.3–35.2). Athens could not ignore this menace. First the blockade was broken, when a large corn fleet was successfully escorted into the Piraeus, then in September Chabrias set sail with eighty-three ships to besiege Naxos and challenge the Spartan fleet to a decisive battle (Plut. *Phoc.* 6.3, Polyaen. III.11.2, 11). Pollis accepted, despite his inferior numbers, and indeed had some initial success. But eventually Chabrias got the upper hand and put the Spartans to flight, though, mindful of Arginusae, he did not pursue them but stopped to save the crews of his own disabled ships. At the end of the day the Athenians had lost eighteen ships, the Spartans twenty-four, with eight more captured (cf. *IG* ii^2 1606.78, 82). The victory of Naxos had important consequences. Not only was the threat to Athens' corn supply removed, but she also regained control of the amphictyony of Delos (Tod no. 125), which she had first recovered after Cnidus, but of which she had probably then again been deprived by the King's Peace.

Cleombrotus' failure to invade had left the Thebans free to work towards their goal of renewed domination in Boeotia (Xen. *Hell.* v.4.63). It may have been in this year that the Spartan harmost at Tanagra was killed in battle, though that need not mean that the city fell into Theban hands (Plut. *Pel.* 15.4). But Thebes' most striking success so far was to come in 375 (Plut. *Pel.* 16f, Diod. xv.37.1), when again there was no Spartan invasion. The Spartan garrison of Orchomenus had made an expedition into Locris, and so Pelopidas attacked with the Sacred Band, hoping to find the city undefended. In this he was disappointed, but on his way home he fell in with the Spartans returning from Locris at

Tegyra and inflicted a heavy defeat, to which Spartan over-confidence made an important contribution.

At sea in 375 Chabrias operated in the Thraceward area, where he saved Abdera from attack by the Triballi, who had come from beyond Mt Haemus, driven by famine, and established a garrison in the city (Diod. xv.36.4, cf. Dem. xx.77). Moving on to the Hellespont, he may even have risked intervention in Asia in defiance of the King's Peace, though the details are obscure and he may have been invited (*Hesp.* 30 (1961) 79ff). But Athens' principal naval undertaking in this year was mounted at the request of Thebes. The Thebans asked her to send a fleet round the Peloponnese, so that Sparta would be too busy protecting herself and her allies to bother with Boeotia (Xen. *Hell.* v.4.62ff). Continuing resentment at the raid of Sphodrias overcame any qualms which Athens might have felt at the growth of Theban power and Theban disregard of the King's Peace. Timotheus was sent out with sixty ships, though Athens was already suffering grave financial problems and he received only thirteen talents (Isoc. xv.109, cf. [Arist.] *Oec.* 1350a31).

Timotheus' mission was a brilliant success. He gained control of Corcyra, and by his moderate conduct – he enslaved no one, exiled no one and did not interfere with the laws – encouraged other peoples in the region to adhere to Athens, including the cities of Cephallenia, the Acarnanians, and Alcetas, king of the Molossi, and his son Neoptolemus (Diod. xv.36.5). However, apart from Alcetas and his son, only the Acarnanians and one of the Cephallenian cities, Pronnoi, are recorded as members of the confederacy, which suggests that the arrangements made in a decree of this year (Tod no. 126 = Harding no. 41), which mentions Corcyra and the Cephallenians, must somehow have fallen through.[24] Whether Jason of Pherae, a friend of Timotheus and an ally of Athens by 373, ever joined the confederacy now or later is also open to doubt.[25]

The Spartans were sufficiently alarmed to send out a counter-expedition under Nicolochus, who joined battle with Timotheus at Alyzia. He had fifty-five ships, for six from Ambracia had failed to arrive. The Athenians were victorious and set up a trophy (cf. *IG* ii² 1606.11, 24, 29, 69, 74, 86). But while Timotheus was refitting his ships, Nicolochus challenged him to a second engagement and, when the offer of battle was declined, put up a trophy in his turn. By now, however, Timotheus had secured enough ships from Corcyra to give him numerical superiority, though he was desperately short of money, for which he sent repeated requests to Athens (cf. [Arist.] *Oec.* 1351a31).

The successes of the Thebans in Boeotia inspired them to range

[24] Tuplin 1984 (c 81) 545ff.   [25] Woodhead 1957 (c 272) but cf. Cawkwell 1981 (c 113) 44.

further afield and mount an invasion of Phocis (Xen. *Hell.* VI.1.1). The Phocians appealed to Sparta, warning that they would have to surrender if no help came. Sparta took the matter very seriously and sent out Cleombrotus with four *morai* and contingents from the allies. This vigorous response frightened the Thebans off, and they withdrew from Phocis and prepared to resist an invasion. But Sparta was compelled to return a negative answer to another appeal which she received at about the same time (Xen. *Hell.* VI.1.2ff). Polydamas of Pharsalus, the Spartan *proxenos*, came to ask for Spartan assistance against the growing power of Jason of Pherae, whose designs allegedly encompassed the building of a navy larger than that of Athens and the organization of a panhellenic crusade against Persia. The Spartans would have been happy to check Jason's expansion, but on reviewing their resources they decided that worthwhile intervention was beyond them and told Polydamas to find his own salvation.

Nor did the Spartan invasion of Boeotia take place (Xen. *Hell.* VI.2.1); instead, in the summer of 375, the King's Peace was renewed.[26] In his encomium of Timotheus Isocrates gives him the credit for compelling Sparta to make peace (XV.109), and the battle of Alyzia was no doubt a relevant factor, as was Tegyra (Plut. *Ages.* 27.3). Her allies for their part resented the protracted war with Thebes (Plut. *Ages.* 26.3). But Sparta may already have begun to think of peace after her defeat at Naxos at the end of the previous summer, and she may well have been negotiating with Persia over the winter. Artaxerxes wanted mercenaries for his war in Egypt and so had good reason to assist in putting an end to the wars of the Greeks (Diod. XV.38.1). A peace conference was summoned at Sparta, and the Athenians, despite their recent naval successes, responded eagerly (Xen. *Hell.* VI.2.1f). The navy lists of this decade reveal that Athens was building almost no new ships. Two thirds of her fleet consisted of old vessels, many of which were in poor repair and badly equipped.[27] Nor are the problems experienced by Timotheus the only evidence for Athenian preoccupation with finance. A recently discovered law of 375, which unfortunately cannot be dated in relation to the peace, shows concern for the purity of Athenian silver coinage. The need for a reputable currency will have increased with the growth of the confederacy, while the financial distress of these years may have encouraged forgery.[28] By now the Athenians were exhausted physically as well as economically and were coming more and more to believe that the only people to benefit from the war were the Thebans, who were pursuing their own ends while Athens kept Sparta occupied, and did not even contribute to the cost of the fleet.

[26] Cawkwell 1963 (C 16); Buckler 1971 (C 12).
[27] Wilson 1970 (C 271); Davies 1969 (C 123) 311ff.   [28] Stroud 1974 (B 177).

The manner of the making of the peace and its terms are bedevilled by confusion in Diodorus' account between it and the peace of Sparta in 371.[29] However, Persian participation is certain (Philoch. 328 F 151). Perhaps for the first time it was specifically stated that no city was to be subject to a foreign garrison, and officials were appointed to oversee the evacuation of existing garrisons (Diod. xv.38.2). Though the Thebans had no reason to want peace, their participation is assured by Isocrates (xiv.10). The argument between Callistratus and Epaminondas which allegedly led to their exclusion (Diod. xv.38.3) belongs to 371, but it may have been at this conference that the threat of exclusion forced Thebes to abandon her claim to Oropus (Isoc. xiv.37). Whether the Thebans swore as Thebans or Boeotians is not recorded. The lack of any mention of a dispute on the point may suggest the former, but if Thebes made the concession, she did not allow it to influence her future conduct. Both Diodorus (xv.38.4) and Nepos (*Tim.* 2.2) speak of an agreement between Athens and Sparta whereby Sparta acknowledged Athenian hegemony at sea, Athens Sparta's supremacy on land. It is, however, unlikely that the peace contained a clause to this effect. The basis of the belief was probably no more than a tacit acceptance by Sparta that the continuing existence of the confederacy did not constitute an infringement of the autonomy clause.[30] This was Athens' only concrete gain from the peace, for the recognition of her claims to Amphipolis and the Chersonese by Persia and the Greeks at large belong to a later date.[31] Nevertheless the conclusion of peace was hailed with great joy at Athens and an altar was set up to Eirene, with annual sacrifices (Philoch. 328 F 151, Isoc. xv.110, Nep. *Tim.* 2.2).

III. THE RISE OF THEBES

If Diodorus is to be believed, the making of the peace led to numerous civil upheavals in the Peloponnese, in Arcadia, Megara, Phlius, Sicyon and Corinth, where the exiles who had gone to Argos after the King's Peace made an unsuccessful effort to return (Diod. xv.40). But events of greater moment were to occur in north-west Greece. As soon as the peace had been concluded, Athenian envoys went directly from Sparta to summon Timotheus home. On his way he landed some Zakynthian exiles, who had fought with him at Alyzia, on their island and established them in a stronghold (Xen. *Hell.* vi.2.2ff, Diod. xv.45.2ff). They may already have been members of the confederacy; if not, they were now admitted.[32] The accounts of subsequent developments in the region offered by our sources are so confused and contradictory that any

---

[29] Lauffer 1959 (c 38); Andrewes 1985 (b 7).   [30] Roos 1949 (c 60) 279; Ryder 1965 (c 67) 58ff.
[31] Ryder 1965 (c 67) 128.   [32] Cawkwell 1963 (c 16) 88; Mitchel 1981 (c 205).

chronology and any reconstruction must be regarded as conjectural.[33] The people of Zakynthos promptly appealed to Sparta, and the Spartans in their turn sent envoys to Athens to protest. They obtained no satisfaction, and so Sparta manned a fleet of twenty-three ships under Aristocrates, either in autumn 375 or spring 374, to go to the help of Zakynthos. Probably in the summer of 374 another appeal came to Sparta, this time from Spartan sympathizers in Corcyra, who were eager to overthrow the democracy and promised to betray the city to the Spartans if Sparta would send a fleet. Sparta was well aware of the strategic importance of Corcyra and at once sent out twenty-two ships under Alcidas. The Corcyraeans naturally turned to Athens, and the Athenians voted to help both them and the Zakynthian exiles. It may have been at this time that Corcyra joined the confederacy, as the price of Athenian aid (Tod no. 127 = Harding no. 42).[34] Ctesicles was sent out, perhaps in winter 374/3, to take command of the exiles, while preparations were begun for a major expedition to Corcyra in the spring. As was natural in view of his earlier successes in the region, Timotheus was appointed to command. But although he had been voted sixty ships, it proved impossible to man them all, and when he set out in early summer 373 ([Dem.] XLIX.6) he was forced to sail among the Cyclades in search of crews and may even have ranged as far afield as Thrace. If so, he may have played a part in the conclusion of an alliance between Athens and Amyntas of Macedon which probably belongs to the middle seventies (Tod no. 129 = Harding no. 43). The Athenians believed, or were persuaded by his enemies, that Timotheus had frittered away the sailing season, and so they deprived him of his command and recalled him (Diod. XV.47.3, [Dem.] XLIX.9). Timotheus, who had again been plagued by financial problems, returned from Calauria in the autumn of 373. He was charged with treason by Callistratus and Iphicrates, who had recently returned to Athens from Egypt after a difference of opinion with Pharnabazus, but both Alcetas and Jason – who was by now an ally of Athens, though not necessarily a member of the confederacy – spoke in his favour and he was acquitted. He was not, however, reinstated in his command and departed to serve the Persian King in his war against Egypt ([Dem.] XLIX.9ff, 22ff, [Plut.] *Mor.* 836D).

Meanwhile the summer of 373 had brought dramatic developments in Boeotia. By this time Thebes had succeeded in recovering Tanagra and Thespiae, had destroyed their walls and forced them into submission (Isoc. XIV.9, cf. 19, 35).[35] Unfortunately it is not entirely clear how the Thebans organized Boeotia in these years. There are two possibilities: either the Boeotian Confederacy was revived, much as it had been before

---

[33] Cawkwell 1963 (C 16); Gray 1980 (B 48); Tuplin 1984 (C 81).
[34] Against: Cargill 1981 (C 101) 69ff.　　[35] Tuplin 1986 (C 350).

its dissolution in accordance with the terms of the Peace of Antalcidas, or those cities which came under Theban control were absorbed by a form of synoecism into a single Boeotian state, in which Thebes predominated by weight of numbers and because the assembly met at Thebes. Certainty is impossible, but the latter alternative seems perhaps more consistent with the language of the sources.[36] After Thespiae the Thebans looked to Plataea. To save themselves the Plataeans decided to hand over their city to Athens (Diod. xv.46.4ff). We may wonder how Athens would have replied to this somewhat embarrassing offer, but the Thebans did not wait to see and attacked at once. By the terms of Plataea's surrender, its people were constrained to depart with their movable property, never to return to Boeotia. They fled to Athens, where they were granted isopolity. Plataea was razed to the ground and its land divided up among Theban owners (Isoc. xiv.7, Paus. ix.1.7f).

Not surprisingly the fate of Plataea provoked violent reactions at Athens, which are reflected in the *Plataicus* of Isocrates. The Thebans might claim that they had acted in the interests of the confederacy, since Plataea had served as a Spartan stronghold ever since the King's Peace (Isoc. xiv.11f, 21). But she had had no choice in the matter, nor had the Thebans consulted the *synedrion*; her destruction was merely the culmination of a series of violations of the autonomy clause by the Thebans (1, 5, 10). It is striking that Isocrates does not make his Plataeans appeal to Athens as the avowed champion of the peace of 375, a position which she had apparently made no attempt to claim. He argues rather that to let Thebes go unpunished would be inconsistent with the grounds on which Athens had gone to war against Sparta in 378 and with the principles proclaimed in the decree of Aristoteles (17, 44). If Athens now assumed the *prostasia* of the peace, such a stand would greatly strengthen her position and improve her image, whereas to sit back and allow the Thebans to destroy any city they pleased would have disastrous consequences (42f).

The argument was a powerful one, but to accept it would have meant too great a reversal in Athenian policy. There were still Boeotian ships in Timotheus' fleet in this year ([Dem.] xlix.14, 48f), and for all her disillusionment with Thebes, Athens would not go so far as to fight her in defence of Boeotian autonomy, or even to propose her expulsion from the confederacy. Isocrates' appeal fell on deaf ears, and the Thebans, by the summer of 371, had meted out to Thespiae the same treatment as to Plataea, though the Thespians do not appear to have been expelled from Boeotia (Xen. *Hell.* vi.3.1, Diod. xv.46.6, 51.3).[37] Yet the fate of Plataea may well have contributed to the downfall of Timotheus, who could be presented as the favourite general of the partisans of Thebes at Athens. It

[36] Thiel 1926 (c 349); Sordi 1973 (c 348).   [37] Tuplin 1986 (c 350).

is not unlikely that anger at Thebes helped to turn the people against him.

In the north west a Spartan fleet of sixty ships commanded by Mnasippus, which had set sail shortly after that of Timotheus, had reached Corcyra, gained control of the countryside and put the city under siege (Xen. *Hell.* VI.2.4ff, Diod. xv.47.2f). The Spartans had also sent to Syracuse for help, pointing out to Dionysius that it would be a bad thing if Corcyra fell into Athenian hands. The Athenians at once sent out Ctesicles with 600 peltasts, while making preparations for a more serious expedition to be commanded by Iphicrates in the spring of 372 (Diod. xv.47.4ff, Xen. *Hell.* VI.2.10ff). Ctesicles was brilliantly successful. He made his way into the city and set about improving the morale of the defenders. Meanwhile Mnasippus' troops were becoming discontented, since he ill-treated them and kept them short of pay. By spring Ctesicles was strong enough first to launch a sortie, then to fight a pitched battle against the besiegers, in which Mnasippus was killed and the Spartan camp almost captured. This defeat and rumours of Iphicrates' imminent arrival inspired the *epistoleus* Hypermenes first to ship out the booty and slaves, then to evacuate the Spartan forces to Leucas.

Iphicrates, whose fleet numbered some seventy ships, had not surprisingly sailed round the Peloponnese with all possible speed, training his men as he went (Xen. *Hell.* VI.2.27ff). At the time of Mnasippus' death he was in the neighbourhood of Pylos, though he had certain news of it only when he reached Cephallenia. There he gained control of the cities – Xenophon's language suggests the use of force – before sailing to Corcyra. A much damaged alliance between Athens and Cephallenia, which may belong to this time, makes ominous reference to garrisons and to the sending of Athenian overseers (Bengtson, *SdA* 267). Shortly after his arrival he succeeded in intercepting a squadron of ten ships which had come from Syracuse in response to the Spartan appeal and captured nine of them (Xen. *Hell.* VI.2.35, Diod. xv.47.7). But though the profits of this coup were used to pay his men, Iphicrates was still in great financial difficulties and was forced to hire his sailors out to the Corcyraeans as farm labourers. After an expedition to Acarnania to help friendly cities there, he returned to Cephallenia with a fleet that now numbered ninety ships and extracted money from the cities of the island, again using force or the threat of force where necessary. Then he set about making preparations for a campaign not only against Sparta's remaining allies in the north west but against Laconia itself. For this enterprise he asked the Athenians to send him as colleagues not only Chabrias, but Callistratus, despite the orator's reputation for hostility to him (Xen. *Hell.* VI.2.39).

But the spring of 371 saw new moves for peace, though Iphicrates

began his campaign and made some gains, even after the peace had been
concluded (Xen. *Hell.* VI.3.1ff, 4.1, Diod. XV.50.4). The Thebans too
were active, making another attempt to gain control of Phocis, to which
Sparta responded by sending out Cleombrotus as she had done in 375.
Once again the initiative for peace came from Persia (Diod. XV.50.4,
Dion. Hal. *Lys.* 12, confirmed by Xen. *Hell.* VI.3.18); whether Artaxerxes
had been prompted by yet another Spartan appeal inspired by Iphicrates'
successes of the previous year we do not know, but it is not unlikely.[38]
The Athenian motive for compliance, according to Xenophon, was
increasing discontent at the aggressive behaviour of Thebes, fanned by
the presence of the Plataean refugees in Athens, appeals to avenge the
destruction of Thespiae, and the spectacle of the new Theban invasion of
Phocis. But the Athenians still felt that they could not go so far as to
make war on Thebes, even if such a course had seemed expedient, which
it did not. So, in the somewhat optimistic hope that a renewal of the
King's Peace would put a brake on Theban expansion, despite the
precedent of Theban behaviour after the peace of 375, they persuaded
the Thebans to accompany them to Sparta. One of the Athenian envoys
was Callistratus, for Iphicrates, paralysed by lack of funds, had sent him
home to Athens to obtain money or bring about a peace.[39] That
Callistratus chose to pursue the latter course may reflect both his own
political preference and the harsh realities of Athens' financial situation.

Xenophon reports the speeches of the principal Athenian ambassadors at Sparta (Xen. *Hell.* VI.3.3ff).[40] Callias, the Spartan *proxenos*, chose
to emphasize the common ground between Athens and Sparta, the anger
both felt at the destruction of Plataea and Thespiae, while Autocles was
sternly critical of Spartan hypocrisy, pointing out the inconsistency
between her championship of the autonomy clause in theory and her
persistent breaches of it in practice. Callistratus then took up a position
between these opposing views, reminding Sparta that it was thanks to
the seizure of the Cadmea that the Boeotian cities, which she had been so
eager to liberate in 386, had again fallen under Theban domination. Nor,
he insisted, was Athens seeking peace because she feared that Sparta and
Persia would again combine against her, for Athens, who championed
autonomy and practised what she preached, could have nothing to fear
from the King. The explanation of Athens' presence at the conference
was to be found in her displeasure at the behaviour of Thebes. But if
Athens and Sparta were to settle their differences, they would have
nothing to fear from Thebes or any other Greek power and could share
the mastery of Greece as they had done in the past.

This Cimonian vision appealed to Sparta, and she voted to accept the

---

[38] Cawkwell 1972 (C 334) 258.   [39] Tuplin 1977 (C 262).
[40] Mosley 1962 (C 206); Ryder 1963 (C 245) 237ff.

peace. Its terms included not only the withdrawal of governors from the cities by both sides but also the demobilization of both military and naval forces, as well as the inevitable restatement of the autonomy clause. But if any city violated these conditions, only those who wished need go to the aid of the victims (Xen. *Hell.* VI.3.18). With this change in the customary guarantee Callistratus could be well satisfied. If Thebes proved recalcitrant, Athens could remain neutral while Agesilaus, if his health permitted, played once again the role he had performed with such gusto in 386. The Spartans, as usual, swore for themselves and their allies, while Athens and her allies took the oath individually. All now depended on the attitude of the Thebans. On the first day they allowed themselves to be listed as Thebans, but on the next they returned and demanded that Boeotians be substituted (Xen. *Hell.* VI.3.19). Their leader was Epaminondas, and his change of front drew down the wrath of Callistratus, for the altercation between the two men which Diodorus (XV.38.3) places at the conference of 375 really belongs here.[41] But an even more dramatic clash came between Epaminondas and Agesilaus. Agesilaus offered Epaminondas the choice between swearing as Thebans and exclusion, while Epaminondas declared that Thebes would leave the Boeotian cities autonomous when Sparta did the same for the cities of Laconia (Xen. *Hell.* VI.3.19, Plut. *Ages.* 27.4–28.1, Paus. IX.13.2). So Thebes was excluded from the peace, which was concluded in about July 371 (Plut. *Ages.* 28.5: 14th of the month Scirophorion 372/1).

Two explanations of the behaviour of the Thebans are possible.[42] Either their envoys were at first not all agreed that Thebes was now capable of facing Sparta alone, but Epaminondas was able to convince them overnight that the risk was worth taking, or the whole affair was deliberately stage-managed to provoke the anger of Sparta and of Agesilaus in particular and so to bring on a confrontation that Epaminondas at least was confident of winning. If Xenophon is right in saying that the Thebans departed in great gloom, then the former view is perhaps more likely. But if Epaminondas did lay a trap, Agesilaus walked boldly into it, delighted at being given another chance to humble Thebes (Plut. *Ages.* 28.2), while the Athenians too are said to have looked forward eagerly to the Thebans' seemingly inevitable humiliation (Xen. *Hell.* VI.3.20), though expectations at Athens must surely have been more complicated than that.

Events now moved swiftly, though the interval of twenty days between the making of the peace and the battle of Leuctra (Plut. *Ages.* 28.5) cannot be accepted with confidence, since it relies upon Plutarch's arbitrary equation of 5 Hippodromios in the Boeotian calendar with 5

[41] Lauffer 1959 (C 38), Cawkwell 1972 (C 334) 257.
[42] Cawkwell 1972 (C 334) 264f; Mosley 1972 (C 342); Buckler 1980 (C 329) 52f.

Hecatombaion in the Athenian.[43] However, the interval is unlikely to have been more than a month or six weeks at the most, and may have been less, since twenty days is in practice just possible.[44] The Athenians withdrew their garrisons in accordance with the terms of the peace and instructed Iphicrates to hand back everything he had acquired since the peace had been sworn. The Spartans did the same, with one significant exception: the army of Cleombrotus was not recalled from Phocis (Xen. *Hell.* vi.4.1ff, Diod. xv.51.1ff). When the king sent home for orders – that he should feel the need to do so when the terms of the peace were clear is itself remarkable – Prothous spoke in favour of disbanding the army and giving the Thebans a chance to back down. This delay should be used to encourage the cities to make contributions to a common fund and then Sparta should lead those who favoured autonomy against anyone who tried to resist. This course would have had the advantage of reaffirming Sparta's claim to sole championship of the King's Peace, but the Spartan assembly was as eager as Agesilaus to force a show-down with Thebes, and Prothous' suggestions were dismissed as nonsense. Cleombrotus was ordered to keep his army together and to attack Thebes at once if she would not grant the Boeotian cities their autonomy. The king duly sent an ultimatum, demanding not only that the Boeotian cities should be left autonomous but that Plataea and Thespiae should be refounded and their land restored to its former owners. The Theban reply was intransigent and consistent with the position taken up by Epaminondas at Sparta: Thebes had never interfered in Laconia and Sparta had no business to do so in Boeotia.

Cleombrotus promptly advanced into Boeotia. At first he did no more than cross the border and halt at Chaeronea (Diod. xv.52.1),[45] hoping perhaps that the Thebans might still have second thoughts. But they signalled their intention of resisting, and of withstanding a siege if the worst came to the worst, by voting to remove their women and children to Athens (Diod. xv.52.1). Their apparent confidence that Athens would have welcomed them is on a par with their subsequent expectation that the Athenians would be overjoyed at the result of Leuctra. It is unclear whether the plan, which Pausanias (ix.13.6) mentions only at the time of the boeotarchs' debate before Leuctra, was ever put into operation. There is no trace of Theban refugees at Athens, and it may be that, even if the evacuation was begun, the non-combatants never crossed the border into Attica. Epaminondas then led out the Theban army and took up his position at Coronea (Diod. xv.52.7). But Cleombrotus withdrew to Ambrossus in Phocis, then entered Boeotia over Mt Helicon. This route avoided the main Theban force at Coronea and was only inadequately defended by a detachment under Chaereas, which Cleombrotus wiped

---

[43] Pédech 1972 (C 343).   [44] Beister 1970 (C 322).   [45] Tuplin 1979 (C 80).

out (Paus. IX.13.3). He advanced by way of Thisbe to Creusis, where he captured the fortifications and twelve Theban ships (Xen. *Hell.* VI.4.3ff).[46] Then, moving inland along the road to Thebes,[47] he came to the plain of Leuctra and encamped on the hill to the south, while the Thebans and other Boeotians established themselves on the slope at the opposite side of the plain. Sparta's allies had expected that there would be no battle, but Cleombrotus now came under great pressure from friends and enemies alike to prove that he was able and willing to take action against Thebes.

The six boeotarchs who were with the Theban army were not in agreement as to the best course to pursue. Epaminondas and two others felt that, if they did not fight, not only would Theban control of Boeotia collapse but the city itself might turn against its present leaders (Xen. *Hell.* VI.4.6), but three were in favour either of withdrawing and choosing a more favourable site for a battle (Diod. XV.53.2ff) or of carrying out the planned evacuation of Thebes and preparing to resist a siege (Paus. IX.13.6f). The deadlock was broken on the arrival of the seventh boeotarch, Brachyllidas, who had been guarding the pass over Cithaeron. He voted to fight. Once this decision had been taken, omens of victory began to be reported from Thebes, probably engineered by Epaminondas to counter those which had accompanied the army's departure.

On the day that battle was finally joined, Epaminondas, who did not trust the loyalty of the other Boeotians, especially and understandably the Thespians, gave them permission to depart, but the Spartan mercenaries and some of their allies misguidedly drove them back into the camp (Xen. *Hell.* VI.4.9, Paus. IX.13.8). Xenophon ascribes this to the good fortune of the Thebans, as he does the allegedly excessive potations of the Spartan commanders at lunch, but he does not deny what is clear from other sources, that sound planning by the Thebans was the principal cause of their victory. The essential feature of Epaminondas' scheme was his decision to concentrate his attack, with a phalanx drawn up fifty deep, almost exclusively on the Spartan right wing and especially on Cleombrotus and his Spartiates, and so to win the battle by 'crushing the serpent's head' (Polyaen. II.3.15). Historians both ancient and modern have disagreed as to how precisely this goal was triumphantly achieved (Xen. *Hell.* VI.4.12ff, Diod. XV.55f, Plut. *Pel.* 23). Four facts stand out, to which any reconstruction must attempt to do justice. First, Cleombrotus took the unusual step of placing his cavalry in front of his infantry and the Thebans followed suit. Secondly, the Theban infantry

---

[46] Burn 1949 (c 332); Beister 1970 (c 322) 37ff; Buckler 1980 (c 329) 54ff; see also Tuplin, 'The Leuktra campaign: some outstanding problems', *Klio* 69 (1987) 72–107 at 72–7.

[47] Tuplin 1981 (B 119) 190ff.

advanced diagonally towards the Spartan line, and in response Cleombrotus tried to swing his right wing forward to envelop the Thebans. Thirdly, a cavalry skirmish took place just before the infantry made contact, in which the Spartans were quickly defeated and fell back on the hoplites behind them, causing some disruption. Fourthly, the Theban infantry encountered Cleombrotus unexpectedly quickly, partly because Pelopidas and the Sacred Band moved forward at speed from their station at the front left corner of the Theban phalanx and fell on the Spartan right wing before it could complete its intended enveloping manoeuvre.[48] Nevertheless, as long as Cleombrotus survived, the Spartans held their own, and even after he fell they were able to carry him still living from the field, but eventually they were driven back almost to their camp. The rest of the Peloponnesian army, which had hardly been engaged at all, happily followed. Some Spartans still felt that they should fight again to recover the bodies of the dead and prevent the Thebans from setting up a trophy, but the polemarchs decided to ask for a truce. Spartan casualties were in the vicinity of 1,000, including 400 of the 700 Spartiates present, and their allies had no desire to fight. Indeed, some were not ill pleased at what had happened. So the Thebans set up their trophy and the bodies were returned.[49]

News reached Sparta on the last day of the Gymnopaidia, and the ephors ordered that the celebrations be completed and forbade the relatives of the fallen to mourn (Xen. *Hell.* VI.4.16). The two remaining *morai* were then sent out, together with all available members of the *morai* that had been at Leuctra, up to forty years over the minimum military age. Agesilaus was still convalescing from his illness, so his son Archidamus was appointed to command (Xen. *Hell.* VI.4.17ff; Diod. XV.54.6, 55.1 are misplaced). Sparta was still able to secure allies from Tegea, Mantinea, Corinth, Sicyon, Phlius and Achaea, and preparations were made to ship the army across the gulf, though in the event it went by land.

Meanwhile the Thebans had sent a message to Athens immediately after the battle, to report their great victory and encourage the Athenians to join them in taking revenge for all they had ever suffered at Sparta's hands. They may have hoped that the Athenians would be carried away on a wave of emotion, or they may have been too overcome themselves to think anything coherent at all. In fact the Athenian reaction was first, inevitably, shock and then dismay. The Theban herald found the *boule* in session, but it gave no answer to his request for help and sent him on his way without even the usual courtesies. So the Thebans turned to Jason of Pherae (Xen. *Hell.* VI.4.20; Diod. XV.54.5 is misplaced). The tyrant made

[48] Tuplin 1981 (B 119) 233ff.
[49] Tod no. 130 = Harding no. 46 is, however, a gravestone, not a trophy.

a lightning march through Phocis to Leuctra, but when the Thebans urged him to join them in finishing the Spartans off, he advised them against risking a decisive engagement which, if it turned out badly, might undo all their good work. He then gave similar advice to the Spartans, telling them to wait until they had recovered some strength before taking the field again. The Spartans accepted his offer to arrange a truce, and the survivors of the battle withdrew from Boeotia, meeting Archidamus and his force at Megara.

Jason's motive in dissuading both parties from a further confrontation is plain enough. If the Thebans won, which must now be deemed the likely result, they might quickly overrun the Peloponnese and be free to turn their undivided attention northwards and lead all Sparta's former allies against Thessaly. It would be far better for Jason if Sparta remained capable of offering some resistance to Thebes, so that part at least of the Theban effort would be diverted from the temptations of expansion to the north. On his way home Jason strengthened his own position by capturing and destroying Heraclea (Xen. *Hell.* vi.4.27f), so that, should he feel inclined at any future date to march south, his path could not be blocked at that point.

After Athens had recovered from the immediate shock of Leuctra, she attempted yet again to check Theban expansion by diplomatic means, inviting to a conference at Athens all those who wanted to share in the King's Peace (Xen. *Hell.* vi.5.1ff). Xenophon presents the motive as a desire to humiliate Sparta even further and reduce her to the position that Athens had been in in 404. Some Athenians may indeed have felt like this (cf. Xen. *Hell.* vii.1.12ff). But Athenian policy was not controlled by those who were obsessed by hatred of Sparta. Athens was certainly proclaiming herself sole champion of the peace, a position she had failed to seize in 375 and which Sparta had disastrously reclaimed a few weeks before. But to close ranks in the face of the Theban threat will have been the principal object, just as it had been before Leuctra, though the urgency was now much greater, as may be seen in one of the two striking features of the terms. If any participant in the peace was the victim of aggression, from any source, the other signatories bound themselves to come to her aid. This was not far short of a defensive alliance against Thebes. The other remarkable development was that those who swore undertook to abide not only by the peace which the King sent down but also by the decrees of the Athenians and the allies. The most natural reference of this clause is to those expansions and clarifications of the original autonomy clause which had been embodied, for instance, in the decree of Aristoteles. It does not mean that all who swore to the peace became members of the Athenian Confederacy.[50] Of those present, only

[50] Hampl 1938 (C 31) 24f; Sordi 1951 (C 77); Ryder 1965 (C 67) 133.

the Eleans objected, out of reluctance to concede autonomy to Margana, Scillus and Triphylia. So, when the other cities took the oath, Elis refused to swear, from which it emerges that for the first time Sparta did not presume to swear for her allies. That Sparta herself participated in the peace should not be doubted (Xen. *Hell.* vi.5.5, 10, 36f).[51]

On paper the peace was a diplomatic triumph for Athens, and it is also of note as the first renewal of the Peace of Antalcidas in which Persia played no part. 'The King's Peace' had become no more than a name (cf. Tod no. 133.23ff). But the Thebans had of course not attended the conference, and the initiative in Greek affairs now lay not with Athens or with Sparta and her allies but with Thebes.

[51] Sordi 1951 (c 77).

CHAPTER 7

THEBES IN THE 360s B.C.

J. ROY

Thebes' victory at Leuctra allowed it to attract allies and wield influence in many parts of the Greek world. It moved quickly from a position of relative weakness to become a leading power in Greek inter-state politics, acting in central Greece, Thessaly and Macedon, the Peloponnese, and – briefly – the Aegean. The available evidence of Theban activity in these various regions is very uneven. Information is richest on events in the Peloponnese, because Xenophon, who gives the fullest ancient account of the 360s, concentrates on Peloponnesian affairs to the neglect of other parts of Greece. Even on Peloponnesian affairs Xenophon is partisan in his judgments, both political and social, and also omits major events of the first importance, such as the liberation of Messenia. None the less his account, taken in conjunction with other available evidence, offers a quantity of information on Peloponnesian affairs that we do not possess for other areas. Much remains uncertain even in Peloponnesian history, but even more in the history of other Greek areas in these years.[1]

The opportunities which opened up for Thebes in the aftermath of Leuctra were great and tempting, but not all predictable. In the Peloponnese Sparta had for long done what it could to prevent unwelcome change. Resentment had none the less developed among Peloponnesian states on a great number of issues; some of these were particular matters, such as Elis' claim to Triphylia and Mantinea's desire to refound her urban centre, while others were wider, such as a wish to create an Arcadian federal state. Many such resentments and aspirations were linked to the widespread tensions between oligarchic and democratic factions in Peloponnesian states. It was natural for those Peloponnesians hostile to Sparta to try to take advantage of Spartan weakness following the setback at Leuctra; but their attempts led with surprising rapidity to a further weakening of Sparta, and offered Thebes remarkable opportunities in the Peloponnese.

---

[1] The nature of our sources makes chronological reconstruction of these years uncertain at many points. See in general the full and reasoned discussion by Buckler 1980 (C 329) 233–62, with a survey of the available literary sources, *ibid.* 263–77. Help may also be sought in Gehrke 1986 (C 28) and Cartledge 1987 (C 284).

Likewise in central and northern Greece in 371 B.C. any prospect of expanding Theban influence seemed to be checked by the strength of the Thessalian tyrant, Jason of Pherae. His murder, however, in 370 was followed by instability in Thessaly, and similarly in Macedon the death of King Amyntas (probably in later 370) brought on an unsettled period. In both areas Thebes found opportunities to seek influence which could not have been foreseen in 371.

In northern Greece, however, Thebes had to reckon with the ambitions of Athens. Athens had to adjust to the progressive shift of power in Greece which followed Leuctra.

The Second Athenian Confederacy had been set up to oblige the Spartans to allow other Greeks peace and freedom; but after Leuctra it became clear that Athens must consider the growing power of Thebes more dangerous than Sparta's depleted strength. By 369 Sparta and Athens were allied, while opposition between Athens and Thebes grew. This opposition, a natural development of the balance of power in the years following Leuctra, was sharpened by Thebes' interest in northern Greece, since Athens was interested in the same area, particularly in Amphipolis and the Chersonese.[2]

In their several areas of activity the Thebans tended to compartmentalize their efforts rather than to combine them. Clearly the strain of sending forces simultaneously to Thessaly and Macedon and to the Peloponnese, as in 369, or to the Aegean and to Thessaly, as in 364, must have affected decision-making at Thebes; but the Theban expeditions to these several areas, even when simultaneous, are presented by our sources as separate ventures. Because of that, and because of the state of our evidence, it is convenient to survey events region by region.

I. CENTRAL GREECE

In the period after Leuctra Thebes strengthened its position both within Boeotia and across central Greece. Orchomenus, a potential rival within Boeotia, was obliged to join the Boeotian federation, and a series of states – Aetolians, Acarnanians, Aenianians, West and East Locrians, Phocians, Heracleots, Malians, and Euboeans – formed alliances with Thebes (Diod. xv.57.1; cf. Xen. Hell. vi.5.23, Ages. 2.24). It is notable that the Euboeans defected from the Athenian Confederacy to join Thebes; Theban connexions with the island are illuminated by an

---

[2] The status of Athens' claims to Amphipolis and the Chersonese is unclear because of the difficulty of identifying the diplomatic transactions in the course of which Athens' claims could have been recognized by other states as Athenian orators later asserted (Aeschin. II.31–3; Dem. VII.29; IX.16; XIX.137, 253; on the difficulties raised by these passages see Buckler 1980 (C 329) 252–4). The passage of Aeschines, if reliable, shows an Athenian claim to Amphipolis before the death of King Amyntas of Macedon (probably late in 370 B.C.).

inscription recording loans made to Carystus around 370 by individual wealthy Thebans.[3] By late 370 Thebes' network of alliances in central Greece made her secure in the area – as she had not been before Leuctra – and offered scope for further expansion of Theban influence.

Lack of evidence obscures Thebes' relationship with these allies in central Greece. They provided troops for Theban-led campaigns, although the Phocians claimed successfully in 362 that their treaty with Thebes provided only for mutual defence (Xen. *Hell.* VII.5.4). It does appear however that alliance with Thebes saved the area from being a theatre of war during the decade following Leuctra. Campaigning took place to the north and to the south, but not in central Greece. The one major and notorious exception occurred in 364, when the Thebans destroyed Orchomenus; because of a supposed plot by Orchomenian knights and Theban exiles against Thebes, the knights were executed, the other inhabitants of Orchomenus sold into slavery, and the city razed (Diod. XV.79.3–6). Otherwise only a brief flurry over Oropus is noted (Xen. *Hell.* VII.4.1). Therefore, while we do not know why the states of central Greece were willing to ally with Thebes in 371 or 370, there was eventually advantage for them in such an alliance.

Jason of Pherae, himself increasingly powerful, had been a potential obstacle to Theban ambition in this area. He however was murdered in late summer 370 (Xen. *Hell.* VI.4.28–32). His brothers Polydorus and Polyphron succeeded him, but Polydorus was soon killed, possibly by Polyphron. Polyphron himself was murdered in 369 by Alexander of Pherae, who became the leading figure in Thessaly but met fierce opposition from other Thessalians (Xen. *Hell.* VI.4.33–7). This situation allowed Thebes more chance of developing influence in the north, besides removing any Thessalian threat to central Greece.

II. PELOPONNESIAN AFFAIRS, 370–367 B.C.

Other opportunities, however, were presented to Thebes by developments in the Peloponnese in late 371 and 370 B.C. In Argos an extreme democratic movement (the *skytalismos*) broke out (Diod. XV.57.3–58.4), and there may have been attempted revolutions in Phigalea, Corinth, Megara, Sicyon and Phlius.[4] The most significant events, however, occurred in Arcadia.

The Mantineans, relying on the autonomy guaranteed by the peace at Athens, re-established a democracy and recreated their city, split up by Sparta in 384 B.C. (see above, p. 157). Sparta sent King Agesilaus to

[3] Wallace 1962 (B 181).
[4] Diod. XV.40 dates these revolutions to 375/4. Although his date has been defended (Roy 1973 (C 378)), the revolutions are often dated to the period after Leuctra.

persuade the Mantineans at least to postpone their plans, but he found no effective argument (Xen. *Hell.* VI.5.3–5). At the same time in neighbouring Tegea a violent struggle broke out between pro-Spartan oligarchs and anti-Spartan democrats; when, with Mantinean help, the democrats prevailed, the oligarchic leaders were executed and 800 of their supporters fled to Sparta (Xen. *Hell.* VI.5.6–10). A major issue in the Tegean *stasis*, according to Xenophon, was the democrats' proposal to found a federal Arcadian council. From the democrats now in control in Mantinea and Tegea came the impetus for an Arcadian federation.

It was debatable whether the Mantinean intervention in Tegea violated the peace recently concluded at Athens (cf. Xen. *Hell.* VI.5.36), but Sparta mounted an expedition against Mantinea. Many Arcadian states assembled to assist Mantinea; only Heraea and Orchomenus, in Arcadia, are known to have supported Sparta (Xen. *Hell.* VI.5.10–11). Xenophon says that Orchomenus refused to join the *Arkadikon*, thus making it clear that an Arcadian League had been created by the time Sparta attacked in late 370 B.C.[5] (The League was therefore not inspired by the Boeotians, who had not yet intervened in the Peloponnese, and indeed its constitution showed marked differences from the Boeotian federal structure.)[6] Argos, fiercely democratic, sent help to Mantinea. So too did Elis, probably not firmly democratic but undergoing tension between democrats and oligarchs, as was certainly the case in 365: Elis' main object was to recover Triphylia and Margana, removed from Elean control by Sparta in 400 B.C. (Xen. *Hell.* III.2.30, VI.5.2; see p. 41f). Presumably Arcadia, Argos and Elis formed alliances with each other, for they jointly sought an alliance with Athens against Sparta, and, when Athens refused, they similarly appealed to Boeotia, which accepted (Diod. XV.62.3; Dem. XVI.12, 19–20). These negotiations were going on while the Spartan army under King Agesilaus was in Arcadia in the winter months of late 370. When the Eleans informed the Mantineans that the Thebans would certainly come to their aid, the Mantineans and their allies waited, refusing to face Agesilaus in battle (Xen. *Hell.* VI.5.19). Agesilaus then withdrew to Sparta. On his departure the Arcadians attacked pro-Spartan Heraea in western Arcadia, and then returned to Mantinea to join the Thebans and their allies (Xen. *Hell.* VI.5.22). By this time many Arcadian states were members of the Arcadian League, and most, if not all, joined by 369 B.C.

The Thebans and their allies had come to protect Arcadia against Sparta, which was no longer necessary. Their Peloponnesian allies, however, urged that all together should now invade Laconia, and the

[5] Dušanić 1970 (C 357) 281–90 puts the formation of the Arcadian League in August or September 370, but that is too early; cf. Roy 1974 (C 379).

[6] Dušanić 1970 (C 357) 285–6.

Boeotian commanders agreed.[7] There followed a major invasion, during which Laconia suffered considerable devastation. The Spartans successfully defended the town of Sparta itself, but could not prevent attacks on many towns in Laconia and on the dockyards at Gytheum, despite help from allies in the north-east Peloponnese (Xen. *Hell.* VI.5.23–32, 50–2; Diod. XV.62.5–65.6). The invaders then moved from Laconia to Messenia; they liberated Messenia from Spartan control and founded the city of Messene (Diod. XV.66.1–67.1: there are numerous other references to these events in ancient literature, but Xenophon omits them entirely from the *Hellenica*). The creation of the new Messenian state was evidently due to Epaminondas, and as such the first Boeotian initiative in Peloponnesian affairs. During the invasion of Laconia Sparta had appealed successfully to Athens for help (Xen. *Hell.* VI.5.33–49). The Athenians sent a force to the Peloponnese under Iphicrates, but he achieved little, and the Boeotians were able to leave the Peloponnese without serious hindrance (Xen. *Hell.* VI.5.51–2).

This campaign weakened Sparta drastically and permanently. Coming soon after Leuctra, the invasion of Laconia was a severe blow to Spartan military prestige; and the losses in Laconia through looting and destruction were heavy. Of the Peloponnesian League little was left except some allies in the north-east Peloponnese (Xen. *Hell.* VI.5.29, VII.2.2), themselves now under threat. Worst of all by far for Sparta, however, was the loss of most of Messenia, and with it the Messenian land and helots. Deprived of these resources for the support of Spartiates, Sparta could not hope to recover her former strength. Moreover her neighbours to the north and west were now hostile. Sparta remained a military power of note, and within a few years Agesilaus was able to campaign in the Hellespont and Egypt; but over the next decade in mainland Greek affairs Sparta's activities were confined to the Peloponnese.

In 369 the Arcadians, Argives, and Eleans persuaded the Boeotians to undertake another campaign in the Peloponnese (Diod. XV.68.1). Sparta and Athens had meanwhile formed an alliance (Xen. *Hell.* VII.1.1–14; Diod. XV.67.1), but their forces failed to prevent the Boeotians from entering the Peloponnese (Xen. *Hell.* VII.1.15–17; Diod. XV.68.1–5). Epaminondas, after joining his Peloponnesian allies, attacked Sicyon and Pellene. Sicyon, after early losses, came to terms with Epaminondas and his allies; Epaminondas installed a garrison in the citadel but left the ruling oligarchs in control (Xen. *Hell.* VII.1.18, 2.2–3, 2.11, 3.2–4). The capitulation of Pellene is not directly attested, but it certainly joined the

---

[7] In undertaking further operations the boeotarchs somehow exceeded their authority, and Epaminondas and Pelopidas were tried as a result, but evidence for this episode is very poor: see Buckler 1980 (C 329) 138–45; Beister 1970 (C 322) 75–111.

anti-Spartan alliance (Xen. *Hell.* VII.1.18, cf. 2.2–3, 2.11–15). Then Epaminondas attacked Troezen and Epidaurus, and later Corinth, where the defence was strengthened by Athenian troops and by mercenaries sent by Dionysius of Syracuse to help Sparta (see above, p. 150). These attacks achieved nothing and brought some losses, and Epaminondas and his allies returned to their homes (Xen. *Hell.* VII.1.18–22; Diod. XV.69.1–70.1).

Also in 369, before and after the main campaign, Argos and Arcadia fought elsewhere. Argos attacked Phlius and Epidaurus (Xen. *Hell.* VII.2.2–4; VII.1.25), and evidently had hopes of expanding its power in the north-east Peloponnese. Arcadia attacked Pellene (Xen. *Hell.* VII.2.2–4; Diod. XV.67.2) and Asine (Xen. *Hell.* VII.1.25). Argos, Arcadia, and Elis together jointly tried, without success, to help democratic exiles take over Phlius (Xen. *Hell.* VII.2.5–9).

In the winter of 369/8 Philiscus arrived in Greece as an emissary of the Persian satrap Ariobarzanes, presumably to win influence for Ariobarzanes and recruit mercenaries in Greece. He organized a peace conference at Delphi attended by the major Greek states. Sparta and Thebes could not, however, agree over the status of Messene, and the talks collapsed. Before leaving Greece Philiscus handed over to Sparta 2,000 mercenaries, paid for in advance (Xen. *Hell.* VII.1.27; Diod. XV.70.2). Sparta seems subsequently to have entered into an alliance with Ariobarzanes (Xen. *Ages.* II.26).

The Boeotians did not campaign in the Peloponnese in 368, nor are the Eleans recorded as playing any part in that year's fighting. In the spring the Arcadians and Argives helped Euphron of Sicyon set up what he represented as a democratic government in Sicyon; Euphron argued that the oligarchs currently in power were liable to revert to alliance with Sparta. The initial phase of the change of government at Sicyon, despite the presence of Arcadian and Argive troops, may have seemed legitimate; but Euphron soon made himself tyrant. Relying on mercenary troops and popular support, he banished opponents and killed or exiled the other democratic leaders (Xen. *Hell.* VII.1.44–6).[8]

Strengthened by Philiscus' mercenaries and by another force sent by Dionysius of Syracuse, Sparta recaptured Caryae near the Arcadian border and invaded south-west Arcadia. Arcadia received help from Argos and Messenia. (Messenia was evidently too weak to play much part in the fighting of these years, but mobilized when – as now and in 364 (Xen. *Hell.* VII.4.27) – Sparta threatened south-west Arcadia, through which ran the main military route from Laconia to Messenia.)

[8] On the chronology of Euphron's career see Meloni 1951 (C 370). For the interpretation followed here see Roy 1971 (C 61) 579–81, but cf. the criticisms of Thompson 1983 (C 386) on that and other aspects of Arcadian federal politics.

The Arcadians and their allies cut off the Spartan army and forced a pitched battle, which they then lost. This Spartan victory at the 'Tearless Battle' had little long-term significance, but at the time it helped restore Spartan prestige and morale, and it also gratified Elis and Thebes, now somewhat mistrustful of their ally Arcadia (Xen. *Hell.* VII.1.28–32; Diod. XV.72.3).

Despite the defeat the Arcadians and Argives went on to attack Phlius yet again (Xen. *Hell.* VII.2.10). The most important act in the Peloponnese in 368 after the Tearless Battle was, however, the foundation of Megalopolis. The communities of much of south-west Arcadia, and in particular of the main Megalopolis basin (as it can now be called), were united into a single polis with a fortified urban centre.[9] Though Epaminondas received considerable credit in antiquity for the founding of Megalopolis (Paus. VIII.27.2, IX.14.4, IX.15.6), it seems to have been essentially an Arcadian creation, carried out at a time when relations between Arcadia and Boeotia were beginning to cool, though Thebes sent Pammenes with 1,000 men to help protect the building of the city (Paus. VIII.27.2). In addition to the social and economic importance of providing a major urban centre for south-west Arcadia, the new fortified city also created a serious obstacle to Sparta, as did the fortified cities of Mantinea (newly rebuilt) and Tegea, in south-east Arcadia, and Messene.

Some fighting continued in the Peloponnese in 367. Phlius was attacked yet again by Argos, Pellene, Sicyon and the Boeotian garrison in Sicyon (Xen. *Hell.* VII.2.11–15; Diod. XV.75.3). There is no record of other campaigning.

Thebes could feel reasonably satisfied with events in the Peloponnese since Leuctra. Sparta had been drastically weakened, while Thebes had formed alliances with Arcadia, Argos, Elis, Sicyon and Pellene. (It is notable that, while Thebes called on its allies from central Greece for campaigns in the Peloponnese, no attempt was made to use Peloponnesian allies outside the Peloponnese.) Though other Thebans might disagree with the policy, Thebes under the leadership of Epaminondas did not support any particular form of government among her allies, forming ties with both the democrats of Argos and Arcadia and the oligarchs of Sicyon. Elis too did not try to promote any particular form of government elsewhere; Elis' prime aim in these years was to recover

[9] The main ancient accounts of the foundation are in Diod. XV.72.4 and Paus. VIII.27.1–8; Xenophon does not mention it. Much remains controversial about both the date and the nature of the synoecism. See Moggi 1976 (C 48) 293–325 no. 45, where ancient evidence is cited and discussed; also Dušanić 1970 (C 357) 317–31; Lanzillotta 1975 (C 368); Buckler 1980 (C 329) 107–9; and, with a review of earlier arguments, Hornblower 1990 (C 366). While dates from 371 to 367 have been proposed for the foundation, the date reported by Diodorus (368) is adopted here. Pausanias lists much wider participation in the synoecism than Diodorus; it is in any case clear that some communities, intended to join the new foundation, resisted strongly (Diod. XV.94.1; Paus. VIII.27.5–6).

lost territory, but that aim was producing conflict with Arcadia. Elis sought Triphylia and Lasion, but both claimed to be Arcadian (Xen. *Hell.* VII.1.26) and were admitted to the Arcadian League; Triphylia joined by 367 at latest (Xen. *Hell.* VII.1.33, cf. Paus. VI.3.9) and Lasion by 365 at latest (Xen. *Hell.* VII.4.12), but both may have been admitted as early as 369. Elis accordingly had little left to fight for, unless it challenged its ally Arcadia. Argos and Arcadia, both themselves democratic, had shown a desire to promote democracy elsewhere, most notably at Sicyon. Argos in addition evidently had ambitions in the north-eastern Peloponnese, though these made little progress; in 366 Argos was still unsuccessfully attacking Phlius (where the defenders were then helped by the Athenian Chares (Xen. *Hell.* VII.2.18–23; Diod. XV.75.3)). Arcadia still faced a threat from Sparta, since Sparta could act in the Peloponnese only by first passing through Arcadian territory. Moreover, Arcadia held territory won from Sparta; besides Aegytis and Sciritis, incorporated in Megalopolis (Paus. VIII.27.4), the Arcadians occupied Sellasia in Laconia as late as 365 (Xen. *Hell.* VII.4.12). Arcadia, moreover, had the capacity to strike elsewhere in the Peloponnese. It was thus doubtful whether Thebes or Arcadia was the more influential in the Peloponnese, and Thebes had reason to be suspicious of Arcadian ambitions.

III. THESSALY AND MACEDON, 369–367 B.C.

North of Boeotia in 369 B.C. Alexander of Pherae was attempting to secure control in Thessaly, nominally as chief federal magistrate (*tagos*) but effectively as tyrant. His Thessalian opponents appealed to the young King Alexander of Macedon, who had succeeded his father King Amyntas, probably in later 370 (Diod. XV.61.2–3). King Alexander moved into Thessaly before the tyrant could forestall him, and took and garrisoned the Thessalian towns Larissa and Crannon before returning to Macedon (Diod. XV.61.4–5). When the tyrant's opponents also appealed to Thebes, Pelopidas was sent into Thessaly with an army. No agreement between Pelopidas, or Thebes, and King Alexander at this stage is recorded, but Pelopidas was able to take over Larissa and Crannon with an ease which suggests some previous arrangement.[10] Meanwhile in Macedon King Alexander was being challenged by a pretender, Ptolemy; both king and pretender appealed to Pelopidas, who

---

[10] See Buckler 1980 (C 329) 113–14. For the chronology of these events adopted in the text, see Buckler *ibid.* 245–9; a different view is offered by Hammond and Griffith 1979 (D 50) 180–5. Buckler (*ibid.* 247) also argues that some scattered evidence of campaigning in Thessaly by Pelopidas can be assigned to 369 B.C. It is also possible (Buckler *ibid.* 247–8) that Pelopidas initiated constitutional reforms there that year, though it is only certain that the reforms were in effect by 361/0; cf. Tod no. 147 = Harding no. 59, showing an *archon* as chief Thessalian magistrate.

marched into Macedon. There, according to Plutarch, Pelopidas arbitrated between the king and the pretender, composing their differences, while according to Diodorus he made an alliance with the king. The latter, at least, must be true, since the king handed over to Pelopidas hostages including his own younger brother Philip, the future king. Pelopidas then returned through Thessaly to Boeotia (Diod. xv.67.3–4; Plut. *Pel.* 26).

In 368 the Thessalian opponents of the tyrant Alexander of Pherae again appealed to Thebes against his conduct. Thebes decided to send Pelopidas and Ismenias as ambassadors to investigate. Once in Thessaly, however, Pelopidas, who had no Boeotian troops, found it necessary to recruit in Thessaly. Meanwhile in Macedon the pretender Ptolemy had had King Alexander murdered, and now ruled as regent for the young Perdiccas. Ptolemy was himself challenged by a further pretender, Pausanias, who captured some places at the north end of the Chalcidic peninsula. Because of interest in Amphipolis, Athens tried to profit from this uncertain situation, and sent Iphicrates with a force to the area. (He remained until replaced by Timotheus in 365 (Dem. xxiii.149).) Iphicrates drove Pausanias out of Macedon, no doubt in the hope of gains for Athens in the Chalcidic peninsula. Pelopidas, however, also entered Macedon. He had only unreliable mercenaries at his disposal, and might have found himself in a dangerous situation, had not he reached an agreement with Ptolemy. Ptolemy in fact made an alliance with Thebes much as his predecessor Alexander had done. Pelopidas then returned to Thessaly, still with no effective military force. When he and Ismenias met the tyrant Alexander of Pherae at Pharsalus, the tyrant seized the two men and imprisoned them at Pherae (Diod. xv.71.1–2; Plut. *Pel.* 27; Aeschin. 11.26–9). Thebes sent an army to Thessaly to free the two Thebans. Alexander of Pherae in the mean time had made an alliance with Athens, which sent Autocles with thirty ships and 1,000 men to Thessaly. The Theban force not only failed to overcome the tyrant and his allies, but got into serious difficulties when it tried to withdraw; Epaminondas, serving as a private soldier, succeeded in extricating it (Diod. xv.71.3–7; Plut. *Pel.* 28.1–29.1).

In spring 367 Epaminondas led a second Theban expedition to free Pelopidas and Ismenias. He proceeded cautiously in order to avoid provoking Alexander of Pherae. The tyrant had in fact recently shown his character by massacring the inhabitants of two Thessalian towns, Meliboea and Scotussa. At length Epaminondas' tactics moved Alexander to seek terms. He offered to release his prisoners in return for a treaty of peace and friendship, but Epaminondas refused to agree to more than a thirty days' truce. This was accepted, and the prisoners returned to Boeotia with Epaminondas and his army (Plut. *Pel.* 29). In

effect the truce left Alexander with his power, such as it was, intact in
Thessaly for the time being, since Thebes did not send another force into
Thessaly in 367.

The limited evidence for Theban activity in Thessaly and Macedon
from 369 to 367 makes it difficult to judge what was happening, the more
so because our sources tend to concentrate on Pelopidas and say little of
policy-making at Thebes. Thebes clearly sought to limit the power of
Alexander of Pherae; if securely in power in Thessaly he would be a
potential threat to central Greece, as Jason of Pherae had been at the end
of his life. So long as the situation in Thessaly was unstable, however,
there was the prospect of extending Theban influence; and the same was
true in Macedon so long as it too remained unstable. Athens was clearly
willing to seek advantage in such a situation, as the expeditions in 368 of
Iphicrates to Macedon and Autocles to Thessaly show (and Athens had
tried, but failed, to persuade Sparta to send Dionysius' mercenaries to
Thessaly for use against Thebes, Xen. *Hell.* VII.1.28); Thebes apparently
was equally willing to exploit the situation. Insecure rulers in Macedon
and the ineffective Thessalian opposition to Alexander of Pherae could
not, however, give Thebes secure influence in these areas, and Thebes
had achieved nothing of lasting significance there by 367.

IV. PEACE NEGOTIATIONS, 367–366 B.C.

In 367 B.C. Sparta sent an embassy to the Persian King at Susa. When the
Thebans and Athenians learnt of this, they too each sent an embassy. The
Thebans consulted their allies, and ambassadors from Elis and Arcadia
accompanied Pelopidas, the Theban representative. Thebes evidently
now felt that it was powerful enough to merit Persian support, as well as
being anxious to ensure that Sparta or Athens did not succeed in
obtaining Persian backing to an extent dangerous to Thebes. Before the
King Pelopidas could make good use of Thebes' medism during Xerxes'
invasion of Greece, and of Thebes' very recent successes. He proposed
to the King that peace be arranged in Greece on condition that Greeks
should be autonomous; that Messenia be independent; that the Athenian
fleet be beached; and that parties to the peace agree to make war on
anyone breaking it. During the negotiations Pelopidas received a
surprising degree of support from Timagoras, one of the Athenian
ambassadors. Other issues must have been discussed, but the only one
explicitly recorded is the possession of the territories disputed by Elis
and Arcadia; although Arcadia held these territories, and had in fact
chosen a man from Lepreum in the disputed area as Arcadian ambassador, the King favoured Elis, no doubt prompted by Thebes. Most such

minor issues are not recorded in the evidence. We can surmise that, from the King's point of view, there were attractions in supporting Thebes rather than Sparta or Athens, because Athens was still powerful in the Aegean through its confederacy, while Sparta had received help in 368 from the dubiously loyal satrap Ariobarzanes. Persian support for Thebes could weaken Athens and Sparta while offering no danger to Persia. Artaxerxes did, in fact, approve of the Theban proposals, and the ambassadors returned home. When they reached home, the Athenians tried and executed Timagoras for his part in the negotiations (Xen. *Hell.* VII.1.33–8, Plut. *Pel.* 30).

The embassy had lasted several months, and it was probably early in 366 that Thebes organized a congress of states in order to have the terms of the peace accepted. The congress went very badly. Thebes wanted those present to swear to the terms of the peace, which were announced by a representative of the Persian King. Some of the ambassadors objected that they were there only to listen to terms, not to swear to adopt them. The Arcadian leader Lycomedes went further and challenged the right of the Thebans to hold the congress in Thebes; he then, in the face of Theban anger, refused to take part in the congress. The congress finally failed to make any progress at all (Xen. *Hell.* VII.1.39). The Thebans then tried again to persuade Greek states to accept the terms of the peace by sending ambassadors to individual cities. Corinth, the first state so approached, refused to accept the terms, and other states in turn did the same (Xen. *Hell.* VII.1.40). Thebes' diplomatic initiative failed utterly.

V. CENTRAL GREECE AND THE PELOPONNESE, 366–365 B.C.

In 366 B.C., after Thebes' abortive diplomatic initiative, Epaminondas again led an army into the Peloponnese, in order to win over Achaea and also to gain more influence over Arcadia and the other Peloponnesian allies. The Achaean cities were oligarchic, but had so far remained neutral in the recent conflicts in the Peloponnese. Having united with his Peloponnesian allies, Epaminondas entered Achaea, where the ruling oligarchs rapidly came to terms with him. They agreed to form an alliance with Thebes provided that they remained in control in Achaea; the agreement was similar to that made by Epaminondas with Sicyon in 369. He none the less 'liberated' three strategically important places, Dyme in western Achaea and Naupactus and Calydon, both north of the Gulf of Corinth but at the time Achaean; he then returned home (Xen. *Hell.* VII.1.41–2; Diod. XV.75.2). Epaminondas' acceptance of the Achaean oligarchies roused protests from the Arcadians and 'the opponents' (presumably Achaean democrats, but possibly Theban opponents of Epaminondas), who complained at Thebes. By Theban decision Epaminondas' settlement was drastically modified. Theban harmosts were sent to Achaea, where they expelled the oligarchs and set up democracies. The exiled oligarchs, however, joined forces and marched against each city in turn, and rapidly regained control. Whereas they had been neutral before 366, once back in power they were firmly pro-Spartan (Xen. *Hell.* VII.1.43).

A surprising incident in 366 was the deposition of Euphron by the Arcadians. In 368 the Arcadians and Argives had helped Euphron establish a democratic regime in Sicyon. He had then made himself tyrant. In 366 the Arcadian federal general Aeneas of Stymphalus, thinking the situation in Sicyon intolerable, led a force to the acropolis of Sicyon, apparently with the acquiescence of the Theban governor; there he summoned the leading citizens still in Sicyon and recalled the exiles. Euphron fled, handing over the harbour at Sicyon to the Spartans before he left. It is not clear what form the government of Sicyon now took, save that oligarchs and democrats were at odds. With Arcadian help the Sicyonians recovered control of their harbour. Euphron returned with mercenaries from Athens, and with popular support again took control of the city. Unable to secure full control while a Theban governor held the acropolis, he went to Thebes in the hope of persuading the Thebans to exile the oligarchs and give him complete control. Some former exiles, however, learnt of his plan, and one of them assassinated him in Thebes. The Sicyonians took his body home and buried it with honour in the market-place (Xen. *Hell.* VII.1.44–6, 2.11–15, 3.1–12, 4.1; Diod. XV.70.3). Sicyon maintained its links with Boeotia and with its Peloponnesian allies (Bengtson, *SdA* II²285a; Diod. XV.85.2). This episode was not in itself of great political importance, but it is illuminating. Besides offering yet another example of the internal conflict so widespread in Peloponnesian communities at this time, it shows that the Arcadians, while supporters of democracy, were not prepared to tolerate a tyrant, even one acting in the popular interest.[11]

Around midsummer 366 Themison, tyrant of Eretria on Euboea, seized from Athens Oropus, which had fairly recently returned to Athenian control after periods of independence and of Theban domination. When Athens sent a force to recover Oropus, the Thebans, Themison's allies, took over Oropus to protect it, and subsequently retained possession of it, the Athenians failing to recover it in a legal

---

[11] See note 8 above. Thompson 1983 (c 386) sees the deposition of Euphron as evidence that there were in the Arcadian League two principal factions, one supporting the *demos* in Sicyon and its leader Euphron, the other supporting Euphron's opponents. He also sees these factions as having much wider significance in Arcadian affairs.

arbitration.[12] The incident poisoned the already difficult relations between Athens and Thebes, and the two states remained unfriendly until they allied against Philip of Macedon in 339. Athens was also distressed at her allies' failure to help during this incident, and Lycomedes, the Arcadian leader, profited by the situation to propose an Arcadian–Athenian alliance. Although some Athenians doubted the wisdom of forming such an alliance with Sparta's enemy while the Athenian–Spartan alliance made in 369 was still in force, there were advantages for Athens in reducing Arcadia's reliance on Boeotia, and Athens entered into a mutual defence pact with Arcadia. While returning home from these negotiations Lycomedes was murdered by Arcadian exiles (Xen. *Hell.* VII.4.2–3). The Theban–Arcadian alliance had lately been under considerable strain. The negotiations with Persia had favoured Elis over Arcadia on the Triphylian question, and Lycomedes had played a considerable part in wrecking the subsequent congress at Thebes; and then Epaminondas' settlement in Achaea, clearly unpopular with the Arcadians, would, had it lasted, have increased considerably Theban influence in the Peloponnese. Yet the Boeotian–Arcadian alliance was still in force; as Xenophon says, reducing Arcadia's dependence on Boeotia was one of Athens' motives for forming an alliance with Arcadia, and Thebes did continue to provide military support for Arcadia (e.g. in 364, Xen. *Hell.* VII.4.27; Justin VI.6.6–10). Lycomedes thus succeeded in maintaining Arcadia's alliance with Boeotia while reducing Arcadia's dependence on Thebes.

During the negotiations with Arcadia it was also proposed in Athens to ensure that Corinth could not be a threat to Athens. Corinth, hearing of the proposal, forestalled any such move by obliging all Athenian troops to withdraw from Corinth. Corinth then hired mercenaries to protect her independence, and went on to campaign against hostile neighbours (Xen. *Hell.* VII.4.4–6; cf. Plut. *Tim.* 4.1). The brief tyranny of Timophanes at this time may suggest some internal unrest in Corinth.[13] These events probably occurred over the winter 366/5 B.C.

---

[12] Xen. *Hell.* VII.4.1; Aeschin. III.85 with schol.; Diod. XV.76.1. On the date of the incident see Buckler 1980 (C 329) 250–1; on the arbitration Buckler 1977 (C 325). On the changing status of Oropus from 411 B.C. see Thuc. VIII.60 (in 411 garrisoned by Athens and captured by the Boeotians), VIII.95.1–4 (Peloponnesian base in 411); Lys. XXXI.9 (independent in 403); Diod. XIV.17.1–3 (after *stasis* and Theban intervention in 402, first independent and then incorporated into Boeotia); Isoc. XIV.20 (Oropian territory ceded to Athens) and 37 (unsuccessful Theban attempt to overthrow the Athenian claim to Oropus). Sealey 1956 (C 253) 190–2 dates the events referred to in Isoc. XIV.37 to 375/4; Oropus had evidently by then become independent of Boeotia, no doubt under the Peace of Antalcidas.

[13] Plut. *Tim.* 4; Arist. *Pol.* 1306a19–24; Nep. *Tim.* 1.1.3; Diod. XVI.65.3–5 (obviously misdated); cf. the earlier unsuccessful revolution in Corinth (Diod. XV.40.3). On the possibility that Timophanes' tyranny is evidence of unrest in Corinth, see the balanced judgment of Salmon 1984 (C 380) 384–6. Cf. below p. 709.

Corinth also initiated peace negotiations of considerable importance. After a preliminary inquiry at Thebes as to whether negotiations about peace might be fruitful, Corinth sought permission from Sparta to make peace with Thebes, and Sparta granted that permission not only to Corinth but to any of her other allies who wished to make peace. Exactly how many states made peace in spring 365 is not clear from the evidence; certainly, of Sparta's allies, Corinth, Phlius, and Epidaurus made peace with Thebes and Argos (though Argos did retain a fortress in Phliasian territory), but it is possible that on both sides others were also party to the agreements. Thebes wanted Corinth to join in an alliance, but Corinth made it plain that it wanted only peace.[14] These agreements brought to an end the Peloponnesian alliance which had been a major support of Spartan power since the sixth century B.C.; Thebes had now deprived Sparta of both Messenia and the Peloponnesian League. For the Thebans and their Peloponnesian allies the peace meant that any further warfare in the Peloponnese was essentially an Arcadian affair. The north-east Peloponnese was now at peace, and Argive ambitions in the area had to be abandoned. There remained, however, war between Sparta and Arcadia, and that was soon to be extended when Elis changed sides and, supported by Sparta and Achaea, fought Arcadia. Arcadia's allies were still committed to helping Arcadia; but such campaigns did not directly concern their own interests.

VI. NORTHERN GREECE AND THE AEGEAN, 366–364 B.C.

The background to Thebes' renewed interest in northern Greece and her unique naval venture is increased Athenian activity in and around the Aegean. In 366 the Persian satrap Ariobarzanes, then in revolt, appealed to both Athens and Sparta for help. Despite their difficulties in mainland Greece, both responded. Sparta sent King Agesilaus, who in these years sought to raise money by military service abroad, first for Ariobarzanes and later in Egypt (Xen. *Ages.* 25–31). Athens sent Timotheus with instructions to help Ariobarzanes but to avoid violating the terms of Athens' treaty with the Persian King (Dem. xv.9). Timotheus acted as an

---

[14] The nature of the peace treaty is controversial. The main sources are Xen. *Hell.* VII.4.6–11 and Diod. xv.76.3; further information comes from Isoc. VI, set during these negotiations. Xenophon's version (followed in the text) is clearly not a full account. Diodorus has only a brief statement that Persian ambassadors arrived and persuaded the Greeks to make a Common Peace. Cawkwell 1961 (C 14) argues in favour of Diodorus' version (*contra*, Buckler 1980 (C 329) 251–5); Ryder 1957 (C 66) (summarized in Ryder 1965 (C 67) 83) supports Xenophon's version, but supposes that the terms of the peace were those already unsuccessfully proposed by Thebes in the congress at Thebes in 366 B.C.; Salmon 1984 (C 380) 379–81, rejects Diodorus' version but also stresses (against Ryder) that the initiative for the negotiations came from Corinth, which wanted peace only, and not from Thebes.

opportunist, going wherever there were gains to be made.[15] He first took Samos after a ten-month siege; it had had a Persian garrison but was not protected by the King's Peace (Dem. xv.9; Isoc. xv.111). It was not a member of the Athenian Confederacy, and the Athenians felt free to expel Samians and install Athenian cleruchs (Arist. *Rh.* 1384b32–6; Diod. xviii.8.7, 18.9); even though not a breach of the rules of the confederacy, Athens' action may have worried members of the confederacy, as may the installation of another cleruchy by 361/0 at Potidaea (Tod no. 146 = Harding no. 58). After Samos, though the details and timing of his activities are unclear, it is apparent that Timotheus devoted much of his energies to Macedon and the Chalcidic peninsula on the one hand, and to the Hellespontine region on the other. In the Hellespont he took Sestus and Crithote (Xen. *Ages.* 11.26; Isoc. xv.112; Nep. *Timoth.* 1.3). In the area of Macedon and Chalcidice in a series of campaigns he took Methone, Pydna, Torone and Potidaea (Dem. iv.4; Isoc. xv.113; Din. 1.14; Diod. xv.81.6). Here the young king of Macedon, Perdiccas, had murdered his regent Ptolemy, probably in 365 (Diod. xv.77.5, xvi.2.4). He fought with Amphipolis against the Athenian forces (Aeschin. 11.29) but eventually co-operated with them (Dem. 11.14; Polyaen. 111.10.14). While Athens thus sought to extend her influence, Thebes made two attempts, one by sea and one by land, to develop her own influence.

Boeotia had never been a major naval power, although it did have ships (e.g. [Dem]. xlix.14–15, 21; Xen. *Hell.* vi.4.3). It was hampered by a lack of suitable harbours, and by the fact that from its east coast the Aegean could be reached only through the straits past Euboea. None the less Thebes decided, probably in 366, to build and launch a major war-fleet. The cost of building, equipping and manning such a fleet must have been very great, and it is entirely likely (though not attested) that Thebes, favoured by Persia in the negotiations of 367–366, received financial help from the Persian King for its navy. Epaminondas persuaded the Thebans to build 100 triremes, together with the necessary dockyards (Diod. xv.78.4–79.1). Time was obviously needed to build the ships and train the crews, and the fleet finally sailed in 364.[16] Epaminondas' plan was to win over Rhodes, Chios and Byzantium; if successful, it would have given Thebes allies at major strategic points. Epaminondas' fleet escaped from an Athenian squadron under Laches, and visited the three cities, but no lasting gains for Thebes seem to have been made, except perhaps to detach Byzantium from alliance with

---

[15] The lack of a coherent narrative of Timotheus' campaigns after the siege of Samos makes any reconstruction of them difficult. Buckler 1980 (C 329) 255–7, offers a discussion of the evidence and a reconstruction; cf. the comments by Kallet 1983 (C 180) 246 n. 24.

[16] On the date see Buckler 1980 (C 329) 257–9.

Athens.[17] Epaminondas also intervened in internal conflict at Heraclea
on the Black Sea, as Timotheus had done before him (Justin XVI.4.1–3).
It is possible, but far from certain, that a revolt from Athens on Ceos, the
second in quick succession, was inspired by Epaminondas' voyage; but
in any case the Athenians soon re-established control (Tod no.
142 = Harding no. 55). While, remarkably enough, Epaminondas was
able in 364 to sail a war-fleet across the Aegean without serious
opposition, he did not commit the fleet to any major fighting and he did
not succeed in using it as an effective diplomatic instrument. After this
one, ineffective, voyage the Theban fleet returned home and did not
venture forth again. If the fleet was in fact subsidized by the Persian
King, he may well have declined to continue paying for a fleet which
achieved so little; but this is conjecture.

On land the Thebans again marched north in 364. In his struggle
against Thessalian opposition Alexander of Pherae made progress,
capturing and garrisoning Phthiotic Achaea and Magnesia. His opponents appealed to Thebes to send a relief force under Pelopidas. Thebes
agreed, but then disbanded the army because of an eclipse of the sun (13
July 364). Pelopidas then set off with a force of volunteers and
mercenaries, and joined his Thessalian allies. When his forces met those
of Alexander in battle at Cynoscephalae, Pelopidas' men won a hard-
fought victory but he himself was killed. His death provoked an intense
reaction among his Thessalian allies, who begged for the honour of
conducting his funeral and carried it out in a rich and splendid style
(Diod. XV.80.1–5; Plut. *Pel.* 31–4). It was probably on the same occasion
that a statue of Pelopidas was dedicated at Delphi by Thessalians (*SEG*
XXII 460 = Harding no. 49 (incomplete)). Thebes, on learning of his
death, immediately sent a powerful expeditionary force, which defeated
Alexander's army in a second battle. Thebes obliged him to withdraw
from the Thessalian cities which he had occupied, and to become an ally
of Thebes (Diod. XV.80.6; Plut. *Pel.* 35.1–2). Thebes had for the time

---

[17] On these events see Diod. XV.79.1; Isoc. V.53; Plut. *Phil.* 14.1–2. There seems to be no doubt
that Rhodes and Chios remained members of the Second Athenian Confederacy until they revolted
from it in 357 (Diod. XVI.7.3). Only Byzantium may conceivably have been detached from alliance
with Athens by Epaminondas' naval efforts in 364 (so, e.g., Cargill 1981 (C 101) 169). Though
Byzantium too is described by Diodorus (XVI.7.3) as having revolted from Athens in 357, it may
already have been unfriendly to Athens in 362 ([Dem]. L.6). But, despite Hornblower 1982 (F 644)
200, there is no evidence that Byzantium formed an alliance with Thebes in 364 B.C. Tod no.
160 = Harding no. 74 shows Byzantium as friendly enough with Thebes in the period 355–351 to
send two financial contributions to help Thebes in the Sacred War. It refers to the official Byzantine
representatives as *synedroi*, but it is hazardous to conclude from this that Byzantium was part of a
Theban alliance within which member-states were represented in a *synedrion* (so now Lewis 1990 (C
341)); even if it is regarded as evidence of an alliance between Byzantium and Thebes, the alliance
need not have been formed as early as 364. Dem. IX.34 is ambiguous, and in any case refers to 341.

being achieved the dominant influence in Thessaly which it had sought since 369. Alexander was in effect a subordinate ally, and had to provide troops for Theban campaigns, as did his Thessalian opponents also (e.g. Xen. *Hell.* VII.5.4). He was so far separated from his former ally Athens, that in the late 360s he launched piratical raids in the Cyclades, attacked Peparethos and Tenos (both members of the Athenian Confederacy), and even raided the Piraeus ([Dem.]L.4; Diod. XV.95.1–2; Polyaen. VI.2.2; cf. Xen. *Hell.* VI.4.35). Finally in 361/0, when Thebes was weakened by the Battle of Mantinea, Alexander's Thessalian opponents made an alliance with Athens against him (Tod no. 147 = Harding no. 59). In 364, however, by defeating Alexander and imposing an alliance on him, Thebes had done much to counter any growth of Athenian influence in northern Greece.

VII. PELOPONNESIAN AFFAIRS, 365–362 B.C.

War between Sparta and Arcadia continued. In 365, with the help of mercenaries sent by Dionysius II of Syracuse, Sparta recovered Sellasia (Xen. *Hell.* VII.4.12). The war was soon extended, however, when Elis seized Lasion, hitherto claimed by Elis but incorporated in Arcadia, and so provoked an Elean–Arcadian war (Xen. *Hell.* VII.4.12; Diod. XV.77.1–2, confused). Athens must have regarded Elis as the aggressor, since it sent help to Arcadia under the mutual defence pact of 366 (Diod. XV.77.3; Xen. *Hell.* VII.4.29); Boeotia, Argos and – when Sparta entered south-west Arcadia in 364 – Messenia also sent troops to help Arcadia (Xen. *Hell.* VII.4.27, 29, 36; Justin VI.6.6–10). Elis had clearly broken with the Boeotian–Peloponnesian alliance, and instead formed an alliance with Sparta and Achaea (Xen. *Hell.* VII.4.17–19). Within Elis there was conflict between oligarchs and democrats; the oligarchs succeeded in taking control and expelled the democrats, who were friendly towards Arcadia (Xen. *Hell.* VII.4.15–16). During the war the Arcadians tried to establish the Elean democrats at Pylus, east of Elis, and also to promote a democratic revolution at Pellene in Achaea, but both attempts soon collapsed (Xen. *Hell.* VII.4.16–18, 26). The first Arcadian counter-attack against the Elean seizure of Lasion reached the agora of Elis itself, and thereafter the Eleans had to fight on their own territory, much of which fell under Arcadian control. Two notable incidents during the war were the capture by the Arcadians and their allies of a Spartan force at Cromnus in south-west Arcadia (Xen. *Hell.* VII.4.19–27; Justin VI.6.6–10), and a battle in the sanctuary at Olympia while the 104th Olympic games were being held (Xen. *Hell.* VII.4.28–32; Paus. VI.4.2, 8.3, 22.3; Diod. XV.78.1–3 is confused, with a doublet at

xv.82.1). With the territory captured from Elis, Arcadia created independent states in Acrorea and Pisatis; an inscription shows them as
parties to an alliance with Arcadia, Messenia and Sicyon.[18]

No further fighting in this war is recorded after the battle at Olympia
in 364. The reason appears to be that the initiative lay with the Arcadian
League, and that the league was hampered by internal dissension, at the
very time when its influence in the Peloponnese was strongest. Though
the new state of Pisatis controlled Olympia, Arcadian officials evidently
had access to treasure at Olympia, and used it to pay for the Arcadian
League's standing force (the *eparitoi*). Mantinean protests at the practice
eventually won a majority in the federal assembly, and the practice
stopped; this meant that the *eparitoi* were no longer paid, and they
dropped out, to be replaced by wealthier Arcadians. The assembly also
voted for peace with Elis. Federal officials, however, were opposed to
these tendencies, and looked for Theban support. A crisis was provoked
when the officials, with the help of the Theban commander present in
Arcadia, tried and failed to arrest their leading opponents. The Theban
commander was sent back to Thebes and an Arcadian embassy complained about his conduct. This provoked a bitter complaint from
Epaminondas that the Arcadians had made peace with Elis without
consulting Boeotia, and the threat that the Boeotians would march into
Arcadia (Xen. *Hell.* vii.4.33–40; Diod. xv.82.1–2 is confused). The split
in the Arcadian League thus brought major warfare again to the
Peloponnese.

The Arcadians opposed to Thebes, among whom the Mantineans
were prominent, allied themselves with Elis, Achaea and Sparta, and
appealed to Athens under the mutual defence pact for military help,
which was sent. The pro-Theban Arcadians, including the Tegeans and
Megalopolitans, continued to benefit from Arcadia's alliances with
Argos, Sicyon, Messenia and Boeotia. After attempts on Sparta and
Mantinea, Epaminondas and his allies faced Sparta, Athens and their
allies near Mantinea. Epaminondas' army broke the enemy line, but
Epaminondas himself was killed, and this major confrontation produced
no decisive outcome (Xen. *Hell.* vii.5 *passim*; Diod. xv.82.3–87.6).

VIII. INTERNAL POLITICAL CONFLICT IN GREEK STATES IN THIS PERIOD

It is difficult to discern the internal politics of Thebes in this period. The
available sources concentrate on the two friends and leaders Epaminondas and Pelopidas, who were in fact chosen to play a leading part in most

18 *SEG* xxii 339 = Bengtson, *SdA* 285a; see also *SEG* xxix 405, xxxii 411 (reporting a new fragment mentioning Acrorea). See also the Pisatan proxeny-decree, *SIG* 171.

of their state's campaigns and embassies abroad and therefore presumably enjoyed considerable political support at home. Plutarch singles out the opposition to Epaminondas and Pelopidas of Menecleidas, attributing it to spite (Plut. *Pel.* 25.2–7; cf. Nep. *Epam.* 5.2–6); his opposition may, however, have had a sounder political basis, and in particular a desire for less warfare. Certain incidents show that there was opposition to political leadership of Epaminondas and Pelopidas. These include the trials of Epaminondas and Pelopidas in 369, in which Menecleidas played a part;[19] and Thebes' readiness in 366 to overturn Epaminondas' agreement with the ruling Achaean oligarchs and set up democracies in Achaea. These are mere glimpses, just as there are glimpses of out-and-out hostility to the current constitution of Thebes. After political failure Menecleidas apparently attempted a revolution (Plut. *Pel.* 25.7); and Orchomenus was totally destroyed by Thebes in 364 because of a supposed plot by Orchomenian knights and Theban exiles to overthrow the Theban constitution (Diod. xv.79.3–6). It is possible that the two occasions were the same.[20] Nothing came of such attempts, and there is no reason to believe in serious political instability within Thebes.

It is in Peloponnesian states that such instability can be observed. Because of Xenophon's interest in the Peloponnese, it is in this period the area of Greece for which evidence is fullest. The number of attested cases of internal political conflict in the Peloponnese is, however, probably due not merely to the bias in the available evidence but also to the removal of Spartan control. Isocrates (vi.64–8) puts into the mouth of the Spartan prince Archidamus a bitter description of instability in the Peloponnese at this time; his words are clearly rhetorical and tendentious, but other evidence makes it clear that unrest was widespread. After the unsuccessful revolutions in Phigalea, Corinth, Megara, Sicyon and Phlius dated by Diodorus to 375/4 (Diod. xv.40), there are known cases of severe internal conflict between 370 and 365 at Argos (Diod. xv.57.3–58.4), Tegea (Xen. *Hell.* vi.5.6–10), Phlius (Xen. *Hell.* vii.2.5–9), Sicyon (Xen. *Hell.* vii.1.44–6, 3.1–12), Achaea and especially Pellene (Xen. *Hell.* vii.1.41–3, 4.17–18), and Elis (Xen. *Hell.* vii.4.15–16, 26). Several of these cases involved bloodshed and banishment on a large scale.

The fear of political instability is shown in alliances of the period. In the alliance uniting Arcadia, Sicyon, Messenia, Pisatis and Acrorea (Bengtson, *SdA* II².285a), the fragmentary surviving text shows provisions against internal revolution or unconstitutional movements. In the network of alliances linking Boeotia with Peloponnesian states, it was

---

[19] See note 7 above. Buckler 1980 (C 329) 142–5 argues for the historicity of Epaminondas' second trial (Diod. xv.72.3), questioned by others.
[20] Buckler 1980 (C 329) 147–8; see *ibid.* 130–50 on Theban politics of this period generally.

provided that exiles could be extradited from all allied states, and probably also that exiles from one allied state should be banished from all;[21] such measures limited the chance that exiled political dissidents might strike back.

Internal conflict typically took the form of a struggle, more or less acute, between two political groups, who may broadly be labelled oligarchs and democrats. These terms however are somewhat misleading, since on occasion the two factions could both pursue their political aims within a given constitution. That had presumably happened at Elis until the oligarchs took control in 365. A shift of power could take place without formal constitutional change, as at Mantinea in 370, where no such change is recorded although a democratic, anti-Spartan, group took over control (Xen. *Hell.* vi.5.3–5, 8–9). Xenophon's account of dissension in the Arcadian League in 364–362 (Xen. *Hell.* vii.4.33–40) shows how such change could occur within a constitution. It follows that the political groups engaged in such conflict were not primarily interested in establishing particular forms of government for doctrinaire reasons; but our evidence is too meagre to allow us to identify what the main issues were, although so many Peloponnesian communities were bitterly divided over them.

For any such partisan group within a community foreign alliance was an important resource. In general a group's political complexion determined where it could usefully seek allies, and, for example, the oligarchs of Achaea and Elis, when impelled to seek help against the Thebans and their allies, turned naturally to Sparta for support. It was rare for a form of constitution to be imposed because of alliance with a foreign power, although the Thebans and their allies, notably the Arcadians, did impose democracies in Achaea in 366. Although the tendency for partisan political groups to seek sympathetic foreign alliances was clear, Epaminondas did not support or exploit that tendency, but instead allied with oligarchs and democrats alike. At Sicyon in 369 and in Achaea in 366 Epaminondas used military strength to force the other side into an alliance, but in both cases he left the ruling oligarchs in control. The Arcadian League, on the other hand, sought to promote democracy abroad, in Phlius, Sicyon, Achaea and Elis, though none of these attempts was ultimately successful. Epaminondas' policy was more tolerant, but it gave Thebes allies who could not live together, as the Arcadian protest at Epaminondas' settlement in Achaea shows. This basic disagreement between Epaminondas' policy and that of his principal Peloponnesian ally was a serious disadvantage to them both.

---

[21] Xen. *Hell.* vii.3.11, discussed by Roy 1971 (c 61) 598. Cf. Lewis 1990 (c 341).

IX. THE AFTERMATH OF THE BATTLE OF MANTINEA

After the Battle of Mantinea the states of mainland Greece succeeded in composing their differences and making a common peace treaty. The one exception was Sparta. When other states, notably the Megalopolitans and other Arcadians associated with them, wanted the Messenians to be included in the peace, Sparta refused; this led finally to the exclusion of Sparta and the inclusion of the Messenians (Polyb. iv.33.8–9; Diod. xv.89.1–2, 94.1; Plut. *Ages.* 35.2–4). The text on a fragmentary inscription found at Argos and now again lost (Tod no. 145 = Harding no. 57) is usually supposed to emanate from some or all of the parties to this common peace of 362/1; in it 'the Greeks' inform the emissary of 'the satraps' (probably rebel satraps rather than a group loyal to the Persian King) that by diplomacy the Greeks have settled their differences in a common peace in order that, free from war against each other, they may make their cities prosperous; and further that they have no hostility to the Persian King and will live in peace with him if he shows no aggression and provokes no trouble. From this it appears that the Greeks achieved their common peace by their own diplomatic efforts among themselves without Persian intervention.

The peace treaty, according to Diodorus, included the provision that 'each should return to their own territory after the battle'. (Such a clause may have been intended to ensure that all armies withdrew to their home territory.) About a year after peace was made, however, some of the Arcadians who had been moved into the new foundation Megalopolis interpreted the clause to mean that they could leave Megalopolis and return to their homes. When conflict developed between them and Megalopolis, they appealed to Mantinea and the Arcadians associated with it. A Theban army under Pammenes was sent to help Megalopolis, and forced the reluctant settlers back into Megalopolis, thus averting the danger of fresh trouble in the Peloponnese (Diod. xv.94.1–3). The incident shows that the Tegea–Megalopolis fragment of the Arcadian League had maintained its alliance with Thebes (see also Dem. xvi.19, 27–9).

The states of mainland Greece, despite Spartan recalcitrance and flurries at Megalopolis, had found peace at least briefly after a decade of warfare. Some were none the less still wary, and in 362/1 the anti-Theban section of Arcadia (Mantinea and its allies), Achaea, Elis and Phlius made an alliance with Athens, pledging mutual assistance against invasion or against any attempt to subvert their respective constitutions.[22]

---

[22] Tod no. 144 = Harding no. 56, on which see also Dušanić 1979 (C 358) 128–35.

Thebes' period of greatest influence had come to an end. Thebes was much stronger and more secure in 361 than before Leuctra, and could show her strength (as in Pammenes' expedition to Megalopolis). Yet Thebes had lost some of the capacity she had had before the battle of Mantinea to initiate change in Greek inter-state politics. It is notable that Thebes now concerned herself only with central and southern Greece, and made no further attempt to manipulate affairs in Thessaly and Macedon. Indeed, the Thessalian opponents of Alexander of Pherae, still locked in conflict with him in 361/0, turned for help not to Thebes but to Athens (Tod no. 147 = Harding no. 59). In the Peloponnese Thebes' most powerful ally, the Arcadian League, had suffered a split that was to last for at least twenty years (scholion on Aeschin. III.83), and the section still allied to Thebes was too weak to give Thebes much support (just as the other group of Arcadian states was too weak for a major role in inter-state politics). Sparta, though not crushed, had been drastically and permanently weakened by Thebes. There remained Athens, still a major international power, to which the 360s had brought both gains and losses, neither spectacular enough to change markedly Athens' international standing.

CHAPTER 8*a*

ASIA MINOR

SIMON HORNBLOWER

A speaker in Xenophon's *Hellenica* describes Temnos, a small city north of Smyrna (Izmir) in the Aeolid, as a place in the Persian King's Asia 'where one could nevertheless live without being one of the King's subjects' (IV.8.5: 390s). This is a paradox: how could a city escape 'subjection' to the king in whose territory it lay? The solution lies in the nature of Persian control of Asia Minor in the fourth century. That control was indirect, respectful of (or indifferent to) local autonomy, and, by the standards of ancient imperialism, light. Because of the amount of documentary evidence, chiefly inscriptions on stone, from fourth-century Asia Minor, we are better informed about Persian rule in that part of its empire than about any other group of satrapies (which is not to say that Asia Minor conditions were reproduced elsewhere). By far the greatest part of the evidence comes from the south-west corner of Anatolia, the satrapy of Caria.[1] This region was ruled in the two generations between 400 and Alexander by a vigorous native dynasty, the Hecatomnids. The dynasty's best known member was Mausolus. But Lycia, and the area round Dascylium on the sea of Marmara (Propontis), are also rich in remains from the 200-year period of cultural confrontation with Greece (546–334), as are parts of Lydia further into the interior.

The Persian Wars of the early fifth century had added a word to the vocabulary of Greek political abuse: medism. Until then, the pro-Persian

---

[1] For archaeological evidence on Caria and the other districts of Asia Minor see Mitchell and McNicoll, 1978/9 (F 684) and Mitchell alone, *Arch. Rep. for 1984–85* (F 681) and *1989–90* (F 682). (For Turkish periodicals and reports I sometimes cite Mitchell, where full references can be found.) Mitchell has also (1980) usefully revised Bean's classic works on Ionia (F 571), Pamphylia etc. (F 573), and Caria (F 572): for Lycia see Bean 1978 (F 570). Akurgal 1985 (F 558) covers the whole of Anatolia, unlike Bean, but is less good than Bean, and the quality of the revision is uneven. For Caria see also Hornblower 1982 (F 644); for northern Caria Marchese 1989 (F 677). The epigraphy of western Asia Minor is now being covered by the ongoing series *Inschriften griechischer Städte aus Kleinasien = IGSK* (Bonn, 1972–), but see also Bibliography under Herrmann 1981–9 (F 643: N. Lydia), Crampa 1969–72 (F 619: Labraunda) and Robert (F 702–13). On western Asia Minor generally in the Greek period Cook 1962 (F 611) is brilliantly readable but getting dated; for more up to date insights by the same author see the relevant parts of Cook 1983 (F 14). Where the articles of Louis Robert could be cited by ref. to two major collections, Robert 1969–90 (B 172) or 1987 (F 712), I have not given the original publication.

209

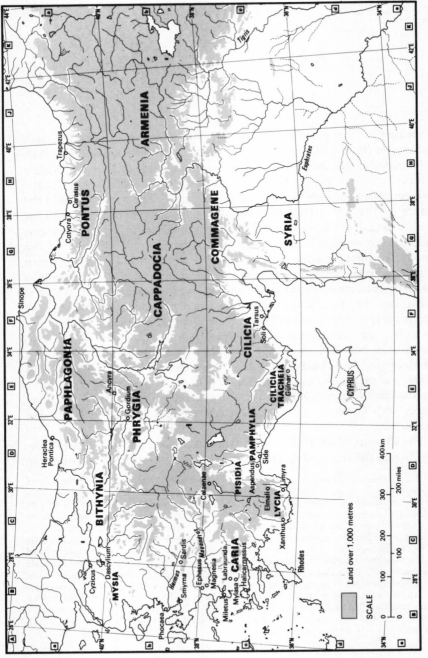

Map 4. Asia Minor.

acts and feelings, which that word denotes, were not discreditable. But even afterwards there was one part of the Greek world where Persian culture and the Persian political system continued to have its admirers, namely Asia Minor.[2] There one could live free from interference from either Sparta or Athens.

The political status of the 'Greeks of Asia' as a separate group in need of 'liberation' by their kin on the Greek mainland may date from no earlier than the diplomacy around 400.[3] This resulted in the King's Peace of 386 (see above, p. 79f), whereby Greek claims to western Anatolia were abandoned in favour of Persia. Nevertheless the history of Greek Asia is different from that of mainland Greece because of the high density of settlement by Persians and Persian favourites, and the date 400 (or 386) has no relevance to this process of uninterrupted social penetration by Persians.

A chapter of Herodotus, VI.20, may be taken as the starting point. After the failure of the Ionian Revolt (*CAH* IV[2] ch. 8) the territory of Miletus was distributed between Persians, who took the land round the city and also the plain, and Carians from Pedasa who got the hilly parts (less good).[4] This passage is important because it reminds the reader that archaic Miletus was not just a trading city but like all Greek *poleis* relied for agricultural produce on its hinterland, which in Miletus' case was unusually large and fertile.[5] One difference between archaic and classical Miletus, then, was that its ability to exploit its own territory was curtailed, as Persians were given fiefs on Milesian soil. Other cities may have suffered in this way even earlier, and the hardship so produced may have been one cause of the Ionian Revolt.

The political settlement of Ionia after the revolt (Hdt. VI.42–3) was generous: it included the limiting of the power of Persian-installed tyrants and in some cases their actual suppression. But the continuance and even stepping-up of the economic colonization of Anatolia, by Iranian individuals and groups, meant that the cities of Western Asia Minor were henceforth not fully Greek *poleis* in one important sense: after 546, and even more after 494, they were no longer in complete control of their own *chora* or territory.[6] Such enfeoffment had begun with Cyrus the Great in the sixth century, who 'gave' seven cities, that is presumably their revenues, to Pytharchus of Cyzicus. Pytharchus' signature, or perhaps a descendant's, to judge from the letter-forms of

[2] Momigliano 1979, reprinted 1984 (A 42). On Persian fief-holders in Asia Minor (Persians and Greeks) see generally Cook 1983 (F 14) ch. 17 and Sekunda 1985 (F 719) and in F 40, 175–96 and F 53, 83–143.

[3] Seager and Tuplin 1980 (C 74).

[4] Cook 1961 (F 609); *CAH* III[2].3, 211.

[5] Robert (1969–90) (B 172) I 393; Müller-Wiener 1986 (F 686); Mitchell 1989/90 (F 682) 107.

[6] Hampl 1939 (C 32) at 26f.

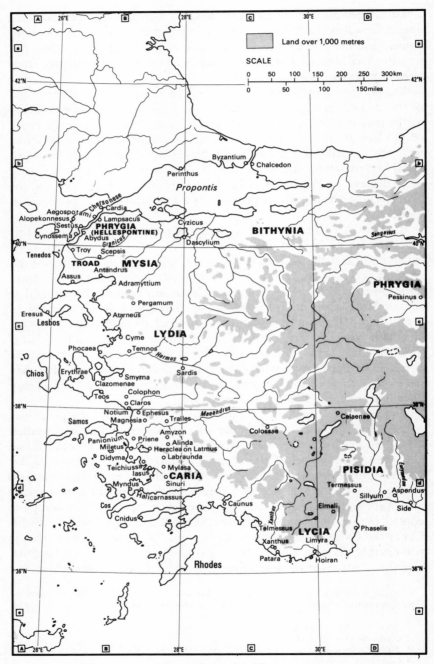

Map 5. Western Asia Minor.

the inscription, has now turned up at Persepolis.[7] The distant find-spot
of this item may mean that the older Pytharchus was an absentee *rentier*
like the Iranian owners of Egyptian estates (A31, 64).

The process of enfeoffment continued in the fifth century with the
grant of cities like Magnesia on the Maeander and Lampsacus to
Themistocles,[8] and of the revenues of Blaundus in Greater Phrygia, if
that is the right name for the city, to the son of a Macedonian princess
and an Iranian called Boubares.[9] The results were visible in Xenophon's
day, when the descendants of the 'medizers' Demaratus the ex-king of
Sparta and Gongylus of Eretria still ruled valuable holdings in the
Aeolid, given them by Xerxes as a reward for taking the Persian side in
480–479 (Hdt. VI.70.2; Xen. *Hell.* III.1.6; *An.* VII.8.8–19). The results
were still visible right up to the third century B.C. By this time the two
dynasties, like true introverted colonials, had evidently intermarried: an
inscription from Delos (*SIG* 381) honours a Demaratus son of Gorgion,
and Gorgion is the name of one of the descendants of Gongylus whom
Xenophon met. That this Demaratus is called a Spartan may show that,
like Roman colonial elites,[10] some members of the family had returned to
their origins after making good, or rather, having lived down an old
scandal. It is even possible that a third family, that of Themistocles, was
connected to the other two: the wife of Gongylus is called Hellas or
'Greece', which is just the kind of name Themistocles in exile might have
picked. He did, after all, call two of his daughters Asia and Italia.[11]
Finally, there was a marriage between Demaratus' descendants and
Hermias the ruler of a pocket kingdom at Atarneus nearby.[12] Remarkably, the philosopher Aristotle was caught up in this family network (see
below, p. 622, cf. 220).

These resident feudatories were the beneficiaries of the Persian
dispensation, profiting at the expense of the Greek cities. Many of those
cities also suffered in the fifth century from being squeezed between two
tribute-levying empires, Athens as well as Persia; it seems likely that they
were assessed for tribute simultaneously by both,[13] and perhaps they
actually paid twice over. This is one possible explanation for the material
poverty of fifth-century Ionia, and the failure of the Ionians in that
century to do much monumental building.[14] Perhaps settlement in Ionia

---

[7] Fornara no. 46; Pugliese Carratelli 1966 (F 694); Jeffery and Johnston 1990 (B 146) 474, dating
the text to the second half of the fifth century.

[8] Thuc. 1.138.5 with Hill *Sources*[2] B 122, C 10; Cahn and Gerin 1988 (F 596).

[9] Hdt. VIII.136 with Hornblower 1982 (F 644) 218 n. 2; E. Badian, forthcoming.

[10] Syme 1958 (A 58).

[11] For Hellas, Xen. *An.* VII.8; for Asia and Italia, Plut. *Them.* 32.

[12] Six 1890 (F 721) 192 n. 27; Pareti 1961 (F 689A) esp. family tree at 191; de Ste Croix 1972 (C 68)
38–40.   [13] Murray 1966 (F 687).

[14] Cook 1961 (F 610) but see Boardman 1964 (F 583) 83.

was in any case more dispersed and less polis-based than has traditionally been allowed (see below, p. 223).

But the social and religious institutions of classical Ionia did not necessarily suffer from the Persian reconquest. The settlement of 494 had provided that the cities should submit their disputes to arbitration, and a century later an inscription (Tod no. 113 = Harding no. 24) shows that there existed among the Ionian cities an elaborate system for settling disputes, with five votes per represented city. This panel had heard, reported on, and nearly decided a case between Miletus and Myus when the Myusians threw in their hand and the Persian satrap of Ionia, Strouses, had to decide the matter instead (but he would perhaps have ratified an Ionian verdict, had one been given). That this system of judges was somehow connected with the old Panionian League[15] is suggested by a fourth-century inscription rediscovered in the 1960s at the site of the league's meeting-place, the Panionion.[16] This text mentions *dikai*, lawsuits. And the continued existence of the Ionian League, as a religious institution at least, though no longer a focus for anti-Persian resistance, is attested by Thucydides III.104. This long and interesting chapter speaks of the Ionians of the 420s as gathering at the Ephesia, which on the likeliest interpretation[17] is just another name for the Panionian festival. So too the old Carian League, which figured at the end of Herodotus book V, resurfacing in the fourth century when it sent a delegation to Artaxerxes II (Tod no. 138), probably survived the fifth century intact.

The Carian League was a native, rather than a Greek, local institution, and this native element deserves a word. In addition to Persians and their favourites on the one hand, and the old-established Greek polis-dwellers on the other, there was a third group, the indigenous Anatolian peoples. Their ruling classes begin, in the second half of the fifth century, to adopt the forms of both Greek and Iranian culture. In the early fourth century, Pericles of Limyra in south-east Lycia made a metrical Greek dedication to 'Zeus, son of Kronos and Rhea, ruler of the gods'. He boldly calls himself 'king of [all] Lycia', perhaps a hit at the pretensions of the Xanthian dynasts.[18] Xanthus in the south west of Lycia was ruled, perhaps a little earlier than Pericles, by a man with a Persian-looking name, Arbinas son of Gergis, originally dynast of Tlos and a Lycian native. He celebrated in seventeen crude Greek hexameters, written by the Greek seer Symmachus of Achaean Pellane, his conquests of Xanthus, Pinara and Telmessus of the fair havens.[19] It has now been

---

[15] For which see *CAH* III².1, 749f; III².3, 217; IV² 481.   [16] Kleiner *et al.* 1967 (F 667).

[17] Hornblower 1982 (F 645); *contra*, Stylianou 1983 (F 722) but see Hornblower 1991 (B 62) 528.

[18] Wörrle 1991 (F 732) 203–17, at 213.

[19] *SEG* XXVIII 1245 (= *CEG* 2 888–9), with L. Robert 1969–90 (B 172) VII 381–426, cf. already Gergis at M–L no. 93 (with 314 of 1988 reprint); see Childs 1979 (F 598). Note that M–L no. 93 is accompanied by long inscriptions in Lycian. See now *Fouilles de Xanthos* IX (1992).

suggested that the Nereid Monument, with its massed hoplites and archers, was commissioned by Arbinas the conqueror;[20] perhaps the Mausoleum at Limyra was a kind of propagandist reply.[21] One line of Arbinas' poem is particularly remarkable: Arbinas refers to wise men, like himself, who practise archery, virtue and hunting. The allusion is surely to the description in Herodotus (1.136) of Persian education, which taught how to ride, to shoot with the bow and to speak the truth. Arbinas is therefore claiming to participate not only in the Greek *paideia* or culture of which his poem is a manifestation, but also in the value system of his Persian political masters. Arbinas' use of Greek to declare attachment to non-Greek values looks forward to such hellenistic documents as the third-century edict of Asoka from Kandahar in Afghanistan, a Greek vehicle for Buddhist sentiments: *SEG* xx 326. But in Arbinas' verses there is also a strongly emphasized native Lycian aspect: Arbinas may have struck fear into the Lycians (line 10) but he is still their glorious king (line 4; cf. n. 19 for Gergis).

In the fourth century this fusion in Anatolia between native, Greek and Persian was taken further, symbolized by the three languages – Lycian, Greek and the official Persian chancellery language, Aramaic – in which was carved the important trilingual inscription found at Xanthus and published in 1974: *SEG* xxvii 942, see below, p. 219. In the best documented satrapy, *Caria*, the process was superintended by satraps whose own indigenous origins to some extent guaranteed the preservation of the native element (see further below on this important aspect).

The appointment by Persia of a local ruling house, the Hecatomnids, to full satrapal status in a now separate Carian satrapy, falls in the decade after the end of the main Peloponnesian War and is causally related to it. The view here taken about the status of Caria as a proper satrapy is traditional, and the present writer justifies it elsewhere against a recent suggestion that the Hecatomnids merely usurped the title from an impotent Persian government.[22] It is not in dispute that the family used it on their inscriptions,[23] see above all the Aramaic text of the new trilingual inscription mentioned above: this calls Pixodarus 'satrap in Caria and Lycia'. The problem is that extant contemporary literary sources appear to avoid the word 'satrap' for the Hecatomnids, whose status was certainly unusual (joint 'satrapies', non-Iranian 'satraps',

---

[20] Coupel and Demargne 1969 (F 616) and esp. Childs and Demargne 1989 (F 600) with refs. in Mitchell 1989/90 (F 682) 116.   [21] Wörrle 1991 (F 732) 215.

[22] Petit 1988 (F 693) but note Xen. *Cyr.* viii.6.7, a satrap of Caria appointed, contrast vii.4.2, no satrap sent to Cilicia or Cyprus, which were left under native kings. This cannot be used as straightforward historical evidence for any period, but has some bearing on Xenophon's perception of the fourth-century position.

[23] *SIG*[2] 573 = Hornblower 1982 (F 644) 365 M4, cf. 364 M3; *SIG* 167 (= Tod nos. 138) and 170 = Blümel 1987–8 (F 582) 1–3, 5; Crampa 1972 (F 619) 42 = Hornblower 1982 (F 644) 366 M8. For the Aramaic text of the trilingual inscription see the full publication at Metzger *et al.* 1979 (B 158).

female 'satraps') and whose behaviour is unusually free. But unusual is not the same as impossible.

A suitable moment and motive for the creation of a new Carian satrapy is not hard to find. The early years of the fourth century are also the early years of the reign of Artaxerxes II. The revolts of Pissouthnes, Amorges and the younger Cyrus had been a warning to Persia against allowing ambitious Iranian proconsuls to profit from the opportunism of the Greek city states and the availability of their mercenaries. The support by Athens of Pissouthnes and Amorges (*CAH* v² 464–5), and, more alarming from the Great King's point of view, Sparta's support of Cyrus, had shown that western Anatolia must be secured from satrapal subversion and from Greek would-be liberators of Asia Minor. Hence the promotion of the Hecatomnids to satrapal status. Such local men could only extend their frontiers, they could not expect to succeed in a bid for the Persian throne.

In Ionia also, at any rate in the early years of the fourth century, the threat posed to Persian interests by Athens and Sparta led to some fresh thinking, but here the result took a different form, namely a degree of temporary emancipation for the Greek cities of the coast. After the Persian and Athenian victory at the battle of Cnidus in 394, Pharnabazus the satrap and Conon the Athenian promised autonomy for the Greek cities (see above, p. 74). Until recently this was thought to be palpable insincerity, since Strouses, in the inscription already cited (Tod no. 113 = Harding no. 24), is called 'satrap of Ionia' soon after, which seemed to imply outright subjection.

But a text published in 1976 from Ionian Erythrae, for which the likeliest context is shortly before the King's Peace of 386, showed Erythrae pleading with Athens not to be 'handed over to the barbarian' i.e. Persia. In other words, it was 386 not 394 which for Ionia constituted the end of liberty.[24] Strouses' competence perhaps extended only over the *chora* or countryside, not the cities, of Ionia;[25] or else 'satrap of Ionia' refers to a military authority of an overriding, non-territorial type, something found at other times.   •

After 386, Ionia, cities and territory alike, was subsumed once more under the satrapy of Sardis: Diodorus mentions Rhosaces, a 'satrap of Ionia and Lydia' in the 340s. By 334, one Spithrobates is satrap of Ionia, and this is the first unproblematic evidence for Ionia as a separate satrapy of a normal territorial type.[26]

---

[24] *SEG* xxvi 1282 = Hornblower 1982 (F 644) 369 M14 = Harding no. 28A. See Lewis 1977 (A 33) 144 n. 55.

[25] For this as a Persian distinction see Thuc. VIII.37.2 with de Ste Croix 1972 (C 68) 313–14 and Lewis 1977 (A 33) 105. *I. Labraunda* (F 619) 42 = Hornblower 1982 (F 644) 366 M8 may also be relevant, see Hornblower 1982 (F 644) 163–4 and n. 212.

[26] Diod. XVI.47 (Rhosaces); XVII.19 (Spithrobates).

Otherwise the political pattern of the Asia Minor satrapies is not different except in details in the fourth century from the fifth and sixth, though a tendency has been noted towards 'more compact and manageable satrapies';[27] see above on Caria and below on Cappadocia.

The main palatial centres continue, after the anomaly of Cyrus' accumulation of satrapies (p. 53), to be Dascylium, Celaenae and Sardis. There was a secondary centre at Magnesia on the Maeander in the fifth century at least (M–L no. 12 = Fornara no. 35 and Hdt. III.122.1)); and it has even been claimed that Tissaphernes had a residence at Miletus (at Kalabaktepe in the southern suburbs of the city).[28] He certainly had a Carian *oikos* or estate somewhere (p. 66), but Miletus, despite its Carian element,[29] is perhaps a bit far north for this. Even in the Hecatomnid period the evidence for direct satrapal control of Miletus is slight, the evidence·of the coinage being inconclusive.[30] The Carian capital was Halicarnassus on the coast, but inland Mylasa, the modern Milas, was the satrapal centre both before and after (see below) Halicarnassus' *belle époque* under the Hecatomnids.

Dascylium was the capital of *Hellespontine Phrygia*. It has been definitely located on lake Manyas, in good hunting and fishing country, as we would expect from Xenophon's description of it. Proper excavation of this satrapal palace, recently begun, may be expected to produce rich results, judging from the numerous Greco-Persian stelae or gravestones found in the vicinity.[31] The most spectacular new find is a Babylonian cylinder seal of the second millennium B.C., but there is Attic red- and black-figure pottery and Achaemenid material.[32]

Celaenae, modern Dinar, was the capital of *Greater Phyrgia* and is described by Xenophon in language as lyrical as his sketch of Dascyleum. Celaenae was always a place of military importance, the headquarters for many years of Antigonos Monophthalmos, who was one of the greatest of Alexander's immediate successors; it was also the approximate site of a famous Seleucid Apamea, a foundation of Antiochus I.[33]

Sardis was the capital of *Lydia*.[34] It had once been the royal capital of a great kingdom, the Mermnad Lydian, and can be seen as a kind of 'second city' of the western empire – Alexandria to Susa's Rome.

[27] Cook 1983 (F 14) 172.   [28] Mitchell 1989/90 (F 682) 104.
[29] For which see Hdt. 1.146 with Hornblower 1982 (F 644) 17, cf. 112 n. 42.
[30] Against Hornblower 1982 (F 644) 111 see Kinns 1986 (F 665) 249 and 1989 (F 666); also Moysey 1989 (B 210) 129–30 with n. 65.
[31] Xen. *Hell.* IV.1.15f; Mitchell 1989/90 (F 682) 89–90. Earlier work: Cook, 1959/60 (F 607) 34. Cf. Balkan 1959 (F 564) and below n. 145.
[32] Mitchell 1989/90 (F 682) 89, Lewis 1977 (A 33) 51–2, and see refs. in preceding n.
[33] Xen. *An.* 1.2.7–8; Ramsay 1895–7 (F 701) 396–450, cf. n. 72 below; Billows 1990 (F 579) 241, 246; Briant in Bilde *et al.* 1990 (F 578) 62 n. 15. For Iranians at Celaenae/Apamea see Robert 1963 (F 707) 348–9.   [34] Lewis 1977 (A 33) 52–5; Cook 1983 (F 14) 165–6; Hanfmann 1983 (F 636).

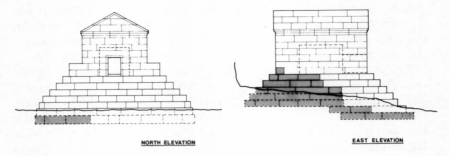

NORTH ELEVATION   **EAST ELEVATION**

Fig. 2. The Pyramid Tomb at Sardis. (Reconstruction by Christopher Ratté; see *Ist.Mitt.* 42 (1992) 135–61.)

Evidence for the Persian presence here is plentiful, not just from literary references (Hdt. v.101; vi.4) but from dedications to 'Artemis Anaitis' and to 'Persian Artemis' at Maibozani/Mermera, which was in the Roman assize district of Sardis in the imperial period; the name Maibozani is itself an Iranian survival.[35] At Sardis, as at Dascyleum, there are Greco-Persian stelae, including one with a Lydian inscription; and the Achaemenid Persian seals from Sardis are very attractive miniature art.[36] (See further below, p. 232.) The so-called 'pyramid tomb' at Sardis (Fig. 2) is in fact a tomb built to house a Persian dignitary (we may compare the 'Ptolemaion' at Rhodes, which was not Ptolemaic at all but a Persian-period tomb from the days of Hecatomnid Carian occupation).[37] This is not the only monumental 'mausoleum' in the vicinity of Sardis.[38] The area round Sardis was surely covered with villages, feudally obliged to provide a turn-out of militia, or to pay for their upkeep, when required, as in the hellenistic text from Sardis known as the Mnesimachus conveyance.[39]

Lycia, east of Caria, was always an enclave apart, isolated by mountainous barriers both from Caria and from Pamphylia on the other side. Classical Lycia was highly balkanized under a plethora of local dynasts, as the coins have always shown; inscriptions are now helping to fill in the

[35] Robert 1964 (F 708) 27; Robert 1987 (F 712) 334; Habicht 1975 (F 635) 65 (line 10); 73. The Iranians later found at Carian Aphrodisias, Robert 1987 (F 712) 349–53, must similarly represent some kind of throw-back to the Achaemenid period.

[36] Ramage 1979 (F 700); Radt 1983 (F 699); Cook 1983 (F 14) 165; Starr 1977 (C 79) 69–75, stressing that the workmanship on the seals need not be Greek at all. See n. 149 below, esp. Root 1991 (F 53) there cited, an interesting discussion of problems of 'ethnicity' in their relation to 'Greco-Persian' art. [37] Fraser 1977 (F 630) 5.

[38] Hanfmann and Ehrhardt 1981 (F 637).

[39] Buckler and Robinson 1932 (F 594) no. 1 with Billows 1992 (F 580) ch. 4, devoted entirely to this inscription.

picture of their rivalries.[40] Theopompus evidently narrated some of all this (*FGrH* 115 F 103), and it is a pity that we have only Photius' bare epitome. The remarkable hellenized decoration of the fourth-century tombs at coastal Limyra, and Hoiran to the south west (ancient name unknown) stresses warrior motifs, and reminds us of the conquests of which Arbinas boasts (p. 214); these elaborate graves look back to the important sixth- and fifth-century paintings at Elmali (Karaburun) in northern Lycia, but also forward to the Alexander Sarcophagus from Sidon.[41] Lycia was unsubdued by Persia in any formal sense in the early fourth century, as Isocrates remarked in 380; but it was eventually absorbed by the Carian Hecatomnids, as is shown by the trilingual inscription from Xanthus.[42]

The Hecatomnid Mausolus also penetrated as far east as *Pamphylia*[43] and even *Pisidia*,[44] a refractory area in the fourth century, the Afghanistan of Anatolia: first Pharnabazus, then Datames are recorded as leading raids on Pisidia without establishing Persian authority there on a permanent footing. *Lycaonia* too was hostile and recalcitrant country.[45]

Late fifth-century *Cilicia*, like fourth-century Caria, was subordinated to a native dynasty, the house of Syennesis (cf. Hdt. VII.98) but on present evidence they were unlike the Carian Hecatomnids in that they did not have the satrapal title.[46] Syennesis is not heard of after the beginning of the fourth century, in whose early decades the satraps Tiribazus, Pharnabazus and Datames coined at Cilician Tarsus. But this need not imply that Cilicia was now ruled by Iranians, to the exclusion of local appointees: at any rate we hear of the 'provincia' of the Carian-born Camisares, father of Datames, in northern Cilicia.[47] The grand Tarsus

---

[40] Isolation of Lycia: Treuber 1887 (F 723) 10–11; Robert 1969–90 (B 172) VII 389. Fifth- and fourth-century coins: Kraay 1976 (B 200) 271; Mørkholm 1964 (F 685); Mildenberg 1965 (F 680); Hornblower 1982 (F 644) 182, 170; Bryce 1982 (F 591); Zahle 1989 (F 734) and in F 53 (1991) 145–60 (taking in archaeological and epigraphic evidence as well). Inscriptions: see Robert 1969–90 (B 172) VII 381–426; Badian 1977 (B 135) and above all Wörrle 1991 (F 732).

[41] Limyra and Hoiran: Mitchell 1989/90 (F 682) 119; Borchhardt *et al.* 1984 (F 587); Elmali/Karaburun: Mitchell 1984/5 (F 681) 102, 1989/90 (F 682) 119, cf. Cook 1982 (F 14) plate 30. For the Lycian sarcophagi ('Satraps' Sarcophagus', 'Alexander Sarcophagus') see Robertson 1975 (J 35) 404 with refs.; Schmidt-Doumas 1985 (F 718).

[42] Isoc. IV.161; *SEG* XXVII 942 = Hornblower 1982 (F 644) 367 M9, from the time of Pixodarus. Already under Mausolus, Caunus, in the part of Caria closest to Lycia, was in the Hecatomnid sphere of influence. See *SEG* XII 470–1, with Bean 1953 and 1954 (F 567); and for Caunus generally Robert 1987 (F 712) 487–520; Mitchell 1989/90 (F 682) 109.

[43] Bengtson, *SdA* 367 = Hornblower 1982 (F 644) M10 (Phaselis).

[44] Steph. Byz. s.v. Σόλυμοι; Cook 1959 (F 605) 120. For Pisidia see esp. Mitchell 1991 (F 683).

[45] Polyaen. VII.27.1.

[46] Xen. *Cyr.* VII.4.2, for what it is worth, is explicit; see n. 22 above. *CAH* IV² 224 (Cilicia a satrapy) follows Hdt. III.90.3, but Hdt. is here, despite his use of the word 'satrapy', really describing financial *nomoi* or 'taxation districts', see Lewis 1977 (A 33) 52 n. 19, 118 n. 69.

[47] Nep. *Dat.* 1. For Syennesis see Xen. *An.* 1.2.

coinages[48] were perhaps struck only for military convenience at what was an obvious base for the operations being conducted at the time against Cyprus and Egypt.[49] Cilicia was perhaps not fully 'satrapal' until Mazaeus in the 340s.[50] Somewhere around this time Cilicia, as the coins suggest, was possibly amalgamated with *Syria* (which falls outside this sub-chapter); but by 334 Cilicia had again been hived off, under Arsames, and Mazaeus controlled Syria alone.[51] (See also *CAH* IV² 154.) Despite the late date at which Cilicia became a formal satrapy, there is cultural evidence of a Persian presence, for instance another Greco-Persian relief sculpture[52] (compare above for Dascyleum and Sardis).

North of Ionia were *Mysia* and the *Troad*.[53] They were still under feudal-type rule: we hear of 'Memnon's country' in this region.[54] This enclave lay in the old mainland holdings of island Tenedos. Such *peraiai* right down the coast opposite the islands Chios, Samos, Rhodes and Tenedos probably passed to Persia with the King's Peace (p. 80). We also hear of the territory of Tithraustes,[55] a Persian to judge from his name. There are also the Gongylids and Demaratids, whom we have already noticed, and full-blooded Persians like Asidates (Xen. VII.8, a splendid chapter); and a spectacular pocket principality at Atarneus in the middle of the century,[56] whose ruler Hermias was patron, father-in-law and friend of Aristotle, through whom he was connected by marriage to the Demaratids (p. 213). He engaged in anti-Persian intrigues with Philip II of Macedon, and made a treaty with Erythrae.[57] But no separate satrapy of Mysia existed, despite a doubtful reference in Diodorus to Orontes as satrap of Mysia; this is surely a slip for *Armenia* over in the eastern half of Anatolia.[58] (See ch. 3, p. 51f for the Armenian evidence from Xenophon's *Anabasis*.)

The other great satrapy in this eastern half of the subcontinent was *Cappadocia*, valuably described for us by Strabo (XI.1.1–2). Cappadocia was probably divided in two during the fourth century; Datames ruled a northern kingdom in the 360s.[59] Datames was perhaps no more than a successful rebel (for the Satraps' Revolt see ch. 3) rather than a

48 Kraay 1976 (B 200) 281.   49 Diod. XIV.39.4; XV.4.2; cf. above, ch. 3, p. 80.
50 Diod. XVI.42.   51 Bosworth 1980 (B 14) 111, 286.
52 Mitchell 1984/5 (F 681): find from Cilician Corycus; Hermary 1984 (F 642); Fleischer 1984 (F 628) at 92–8; cf. Borchhardt 1968 (F 586). Note also the Aramaic law from Cilicia at Mitchell 1989/90 (F 682) 130, promulgated by an Artaxerxes, who could however be the fifth-century Artaxerxes I, not II, III or IV (all fourth-century; for Artaxerxes IV see above, p. 50).
53 Rostovtzeff 1923 (F 715) for Mysia; Cook 1973 (F 163) for the Troad.
54 Arr. *Anab.* 1.17.   55 *FGrH* 105 no. 4 = Harding no. 72C.
56 Wormell 1935 (H 124).   57 Tod no. 165 = Harding no. 79.
58 Diod. XV.90, on which see Hornblower 1982 (F 644) 176–9. Another view: M. Osborne 1982 (B 165) II 65–72, cf. Osborne 1975 (F 689); Moysey 1989 (B 210) 123–5.
59 Division: Strabo XII.1.4 and perhaps Polyb. F 54; Datames: Diod. XV.91. For settlement in Cappadocia see Gwatkin 1930 (F 633) 18 and n. 14: Phrygian-style strongholds known as *tetrapurgiai*. See n. 72 below.

recognized satrap, and the partition of Cappadocia may have been a *de facto* affair, never formally acquiesced in by Persia: another usurper, Ariarathes, was established in the northern, Pontic, part by around 350. Certainly the south stayed in Persian hands: Mithrobouzanes is called 'satrap' in 334, and he may be identical with the unnamed Persian to whom a king Artaxerxes gave 'Cappadocia' as a reward for saving him from a lion.[60]

Paphlagonia to the west was included in northern Cappadocia by the 320s, but in the earlier fourth century, as no doubt in the fifth, this tribal enclave was first independent under a king called Gyes or some similar name;[61] then it was reduced by Datames in the 370s, but the evidence does not justify us in speaking of a satrapy of Paphlagonia at this time. By 334 Paphlagonia was subsumed under *Hellespontine Phrygia*.[62]

In this area, but wholly unique, was *Sinope*,[63] which was independent between the 430s, when the Athenian Lamachus deposed the tyrant Timesileos,[64] and the King's Peace of 386. In Xenophon's *Anabasis* (400 B.C.) it actually ranks as a minor imperial power in its own right, still levying tribute on places like Trapezus – itself a future imperial city in Byzantine times – and its own colonies Cotyora and Cerasus, the 'place of cherries'.[65] Datames held Sinope in the years after 372 (p. 85), and its inhabitants are treated by Alexander as subjects of Persia; perhaps by the middle of the fourth century it was subsumed, after an autonomous interval following the disappearance of Datames, in satrapal Cappadocia.[66] The results of excavation at the site of Sinope have not quite matched the splendour of what literary sources show was a 'golden day of autonomous prosperity' between the 440s and 386, but there have been finds of decent work of conventional classical Greek type – antefixes, egg-and-dart simas, and so on.[67]

[60] Mithrobouzanes: Arr. *Anab.* 1.16; lion: Polyb. F 54. For another king (Alexander) saved from a lion see Plut. *Alex.* 40 with Moretti *ISE* 74 (dedication by Craterus at Delphi), cf. below, p. 659f. For royal lion hunts in Macedon and Persia see Briant 1991 (F 11A).

[61] *Hell. Oxy.* XXII Bart. Cf. Xen. *An.* VI.1.2 and V.5.23; Corylas ruler of Paphlagonia *c.* 400.

[62] On Datames, see Nep. *Dat.* 2, but note that 'praefectus < Paphlagoniae >' at Trogus *Prologue* X is an editor's supplement; more could have dropped out than the supplement assumes. It does not justify us in speaking of a 'satrapy' of Paphlagonia: Bosworth 1980 (B 14) 188. For 334 see Diod. XVII.19.4.

[63] On the history and prosperity of Sinope see Robinson 1906 (F 714): Leaf 1916 (F 673); Burstein 1976 (E 222) 59 and 129 n. 57, 70 and 135 n. 15; Hind 1983/4 (E 258) 95–6; Moysey 1989 (B 210) 121–2. For Sinope's reputation for table-woods see Meiggs 1983 (I 101) 296 citing Strabo XII.3.12 and other passages. For iron from Sinope see *CAH* IV² 451. Cf. below ch. 9f.

[64] Plut. *Per.* 20.1 with *CAH* V² 146 and nn. 113 and 114, also P. A. Stadter, *Commentary on Plutarch's Life of Pericles* (Chapel Hill, 1989) 216–19.

[65] Xen. *An.* V.3 and 5; Gschnitzer 1958 (C 29A) 18–19. For Byzantine Trebizond see Gibbon (ed. Bury) VI 421 and n. 25.

[66] Burstein 1976 (E 222); Arr. *Anab.* III.24.4, a problematic passage, see Bosworth 1980 (B 14) 353. The Scythian king Scydrothemis ruled Sinope in the time of Ptolemy I Soter: Fraser 1972 (A 21) 247.

[67] Akurgal–Budde 1956 (F 559).

Further west towards Byzantium was *Heraclea Pontica*. Like Byzantium, Heraclea was a Megarian colony (but with a Boeotian element, which Xen. *An.* VI.2.1 was wrong to suppress completely). It was democratically ruled till 364, when Clearchus, a pupil of Plato, seized power. He was succeeded, after his assassination in 352, by his brother Satyrus, as regent for his sons Timotheus and Dionysius, who themselves ruled, in even more openly autocratic fashion than their father, between 346 and 305. The history of the city is, at certain phases of the classical period, closely bound up with that of the Bosporan kingdom to the north, and this aspect, and Heraclea's importance as a grain-supplier, is treated in ch. 9*f* below. But Heraclea deserves a mention here because of its 'position of unchallenged preeminence among the Greek cities of northern Anatolia'[68] in the century and a quarter after Clearchus' seizure of power. (Heraclea continued to suffer from tyranny till 281 but that phase is outside the scope of the present volume.) Our main source for the dynasty's history is the local historian Memnon, who preserves such details, interesting if true, as, that Dionysius of Heraclea bought up the household effects of Dionysius of Syracuse (*FGrH* 434 F 4.5, not saying which Dionysius. Perhaps both.) This recalls Diodorus' statement (XV.81, from the chronographic source, above, p. 9) that Clearchus imitated Dionysius I of Sicily; an analogy which the Platonic connexion would have suggested to us anyway. Clearchus went further than his Sicilian model in his claim to be son of Zeus (*FGrH* 434 Memnon F 1.1; Justin XVI.5.8) but it is hard to know what to make of this.

From polis-dwelling Greeks to Pisidian guerillas, with tribal Paphlagonians and dynastically controlled Lycians and others somewhere in between, this was a patchwork of peoples, with very different settlement habits. Numbers are impossible to determine without census records. An interesting attempt has however been made to use the old Athenian Tribute Lists (on these see *CAH* v² 55–61) for the Troad, an area of small-to-medium cities without the usual peppering of villages in between. When taken together with modern and medieval figures for what the population will support, this yields not more than 3,000–4,000 head of population per one talent of tribute, with about 5,000 per polis. But a more recent general examination of the implications of the Tribute Lists for the size and resources of Greek cities concludes that 'the assumption of a direct relationship between tribute and population does not work'.[69]

[68] For Heraclea Pontica see Burstein 1976 (E 222); quotation from 65. For its grain see Garnsey 1988 (I 55) 151, 155. This is surely relevant to the large number of Heracleots buried at Athens. For instance, they had a special precinct in the Ceramicus. For Epaminondas and Heraclea see p. 202.

[69] Tribute lists are used as indicators of population by Cook 1973 (F 613) 382, cf. 267f. See however the scepticism of Nixon and Price in Murray–Price 1990 (C 52) 146, cp. 160 nn. 38 and 40. For other indicators, e.g. ships, see Cook 1958/9 (F 604) 22 n. 55; *CAH* III².3, 217f.

As for Ionia, settlement here has traditionally been seen in polis terms; but a case has now been made for a more dispersed pattern, characterized by isolated farmsteads or *pyrgoi*. This may be right, but it is still true that most of the evidence for these farmsteads is from round Teos, a region which may or may not have been typical.[70]

Elsewhere in Anatolia, we can be a little more confident that village-based settlement was normal. It is explicitly said by ancient writers to be characteristic of Caria[71] and Greater Phrygia;[72] here the population was definitely scattered. This was something that, in western Caria at least, the Persian authorities and their delegates, anticipating more ruthless hellenistic methods, set out to adjust: it is not too much to speak of a limited policy of urbanization. The most conspicuous example is Mausolus' concentration (synoecism) of native 'Lelegian' places in the Myndus peninsula to swell the population of Halicarnassus.[73] Halicarnassus' ruler in the Persian Wars commands a mere five ships (a good index for this kind of thing,[74] as should be the figures for the battle of Lade in the mid 490s, though there are some oddities here).[75] The city's tribute to Athens is a mere $1\frac{2}{3}$ talents; however crude a pointer to population (see n. 69) this is in sharp contrast with Ephesus, which paid 6 talents. But as a result of the forcible addition in the (?)370s of hundreds of Lelegian families, whose settlements have now been meticulously studied,[76] Halicarnassus became, in the hellenistic period, a city with a maximum attested citizen population of 10,000. The evidence for this is the attendance total for its assembly, preserved on an inscription.[77] (It must however be said that another inscription records a mere 1,200 votes.)[78] Mausolus (see above) moved the capital from Milas to Halicarnassus;[79] but in the very early hellenistic period the satrapal capital was once again Milas: *SEG* XXXIII 872 = *I. Mylasa* (F 582) no. 21, dated by the satrap Asander. This may reflect some decline in Halicarnassus' fortunes after Alexander's punishing siege (for which see below, p. 802); if so it could well be that mid-fourth-century Halicarnassus had been even more populous and prosperous than it was to be in the hellenistic period.

[70] Balcer 1987 (F 563) cf. Hunt 1947 (F 648).

[71] Village-based settlement generally: Briant 1982 (F 10) 137–60. Caria: *FGrH* 26 Conon F1, cf. Hornblower 1982 (F 644) 10 and n. 46, 163.

[72] Curt. III.1.11; cf. Anderson 1897 (F 561) 412 and Ramsay 1895–7 (F 701) 123–30. For the relation between these villages and the *tetrapurgiai* or strongholds of the Celaenae area see Ramsay 1895–7 (F 701) 419–290, on Plut. *Eum.* 8.

[73] *FGrH* 124 F 25; Pliny *HN* v.107, with Hornblower 1982 (F 644) ch. 4.

[74] Hdt. VII.99 with n. 69 above. But it is relevant that Artemisia also commanded Coans and others.   [75] Hdt. VI.8 with *CAH* III².3, 217–18.

[76] Radt 1970 (F 698), building on the pioneering work of Bean and Cook 1955 (F 575).

[77] Michel 455 with Hornblower 1982 (F 644) 8 n. 38 and 102 n. 186 citing Beloch.

[78] Cousin and Diehl 1890 (F 617) 95 no. 3.

[79] Vitr. II.8.10f is explicit for a move which could anyway have been inferred by combining Strabo XIV.2.23 and Diod. XV.90.3. See Hornblower 1982 (F 644) 297–8, cf. 78 and 188.

Other sites also seem to have been physically moved, perhaps for reasons of defence, cf. Diod. xiv.36.3 for the alleged motive behind Thibron's move of Magnesia on the Maeander in 400 b.c.; or to make possible some grandiose building scheme or other (Asia Minor in the fourth century seems to have been a more prosperous place than in the fifth, cf. above, p. 213); but perhaps also with the intention of bringing a broader catch of population within the trawl of town life on the Greek model. Individual cases are sometimes controversial; the reader should be specially warned that archaeological finds and fashions are likely to upset anything said dogmatically on this topic.

At Ionian Erythrae,[80] and the Carian cities of Cnidus, Heraclea on Latmus, Bargylia and Mylasa,[81] fourth-century moves of site have been postulated, and historians have, without certainty but not without reason, detected the hand of the Hecatomnids. The position at Erythrae is archaeologically controversial,[82] and the political situation is also worth pausing over. The city was closely aligned with Mausolus and Artemisia in the 350s: Tod no. 155. But it was independent enough, about 350, to make a treaty with Hermias (p. 220 above on Tod no. 165 = Harding no. 79). It would, however, be too simple to infer from this an automatic loosening of Hecatomnid involvement, because in 1981 there was published an Erythraean inscription honouring Mausolus' younger brother Idrieus (satrap 351–344 b.c.) in terms partially similar to the honours to Mausolus: *SEG* xxxi 969 = Harding no. 28b.[83]

---

[80] For Magnesia (geographically Ionian, though ethnically Aeolian) see Bean 1980 (F 571) 248 and Demand 1990 (F 623) 165: silting may also be relevant, in addition to the military motive given by Diod. Erythrae: Hornblower 1982 (F 644) 100 with refs., cf. 102, following Cook 1958/9 (F 604). But see Mitchell 1984/5 (F 681) 83 (where 'decisive' is a little strong, see n. 82 below); Graf 1985 (F 631) 156 and n. 11. Graf is interesting on Erythrae, Phocaea and Clazomenae generally.

[81] *Cnidus*: Hornblower 1982 (F 644) 101 and n. 180, cf. 318, following Bean and Cook 1952 and 1957 (F 574 and 576) for a move from Datça to Tekir; but see Mitchell 1984/5 (F 681) 89, citing contributions on both sides of the argument; Mitchell 1989/90 (F 682) 109 cites further objectors to the move; see esp. Demand 1989 (F 622). *Heraclea on Latmus*: see Hornblower 1982 (F 644) 100–1, 321–3; Peschlow-Bindokat in Linders and Hellström 1989 (F 674) 69–76; Wörrle 1990 (F 731) 41. *Bargylia*: Bean and Cook 1957 (F 576) 141; Hornblower 1982 (F 644) 100 and 319. *Milas/Mylasa*: for the move of capital to Halicarnassus see n. 79 above, and for a possible earlier physical move from Milas to Peçin Kale see Hornblower 1982 (F 644) 99, 101; for Peçin or Beçin see also Koenigs 1980 (F 669) with Mitchell 1984/5 (F 681) 88.

[82] See n. 80. It should be emphasized that archaic material found at sites *to* which a move is postulated, such as Tekir, do not automatically disprove the hypothesis of a basic move, any more than a classical move *away* from a site is disproved by post-classical sherds or other material evidence. (Cook and Bean were well aware of some of the archaic evidence now being cited against them.) Settlement changes were not always abrupt or total, cf. Hornblower 1982 (F 644) 92–3 for evidence that some Lelegian sites synoecized by Mausolus (above nn. 73, 76) had an after-life of sorts. As for the choice of new sites, Alexander's eponymous 'foundations' were often, for good geo-political reasons, located on pre-existing settlement centres. See now Blümel's volume on Cnidus in the *IGSK* series (above, n. 1).

[83] See Varinluoglu 1981 (F 725) 45. D. M. Lewis tells me he thinks it possible that the honours to Mausolus and to Idrieus were carved on the same stone.

Honours to Idrieus in his brother's lifetime cannot be ruled out (the title
'satrap' is not used in either text). But it is surely likely that Idrieus is
being honoured during his own tenure of the satrapy. If so he is being
honoured by a city able at roughly the same period to deal with Hermias
in terms that, remarkably for a city which had been 'handed over to the
barbarian' in 386 (see above, p. 216), include pledges of mutual military
assistance. To return to the hypothetical move of the physical site, it
might, in the light of this evidence for Erythrae's relative freedom of
action, be safer to speak of Hecatomnid encouragement rather than
insistence. And that, quite apart from the archaeological uncertainties,
may go for some other places within the reach of the long but not always
overpowering arm of Mausolus.

This policy, if that is not too strong a word, looks forward to
Alexander's refoundation of ancient sites like Smyrna, Alinda, and
Priene. (But Priene may be the work of the Hecatomnids;[84] or again,
perhaps there was no single act of re-creation but a gradual physical and
social revival in the fourth century.)[85] There is certainly some reason to
believe in population growth to fill these new cities (though Mausolus
was too optimistic at Theangela, the old Syangela, and the place had to
be bisected and thus reduced in size).[86] At any rate, in the 340s, 'coastal',
that is presumably western, Anatolia provided 6,000 soldiers, not a
contemptible total, for the great Persian drive against Egypt.[87] The
prolific city-coinages of fourth-century Pamphylia and Cilicia[88] suggest
that there was progress in urbanization here as well. But more intractable
north and north-central Anatolia had to wait till the third- and second-
century hellenistic kings, or even (in Pontus) till Pompey[89] and the
Roman emperors. But Pisidia, whose citadels defied Alexander (see
below, p. 803), crystallized into a set of city states early in the hellenistic
period. It is less surprising that the more accessible and amenable Troad
made strides rather earlier than Pontus, in fact under Antigonus and
Lysimachus.[90]

Returning to Caria, the Halicarnassus synoecism did not terminate life
in the old Lelegian places, where fortifications, and archaeological traces
of habitation, prove that a life of sorts went on in the otherwise
evacuated rubble.[91] This gradualist policy towards the local, native

[84] Bean and Cook 1957 (F 576) 141, etc. For Priene see Hornblower 1982 (F 644) 323–30, more
diffident than represented by the valuable discussion in S. Sherwin-White 1985 (B 175) 88–9.
[85] Demand 1986 (F 621) and 1990 (F 623) 140–6: no 'relocation' of Priene.
[86] Bean and Cook 1957 (F 576) 94. Other explanations for the cross-wall are of course possible.
[87] Diod. XVI.44.4. See above, p. 92, and cf. Curt. VII.10.12: 4,000 Asia Minor infantry and 500
cavalry brought from Lycia under Alexander.   [88] Kraay 1976 (B 200) 275–86.
[89] A. N. Sherwin-White 1984 (F 720) 229–30; S. Mitchell, *Anatolia* i (1993) ch. 7.
[90] Pisidia: Mitchell 1991 (F 683). Troad: Cook 1973 (F 613) and 1988 (F 614).
[91] Above, n. 82.

element is confirmed by the inscriptions put up by the various *koina* or
commonalties (the word is the standard one for 'league') of Caria. The
most important and presumably biggest of these, the Carian League,
persisted through the fifth and fourth centuries as we have seen, but
other smaller leagues blossomed too. Thus Telmissus, one of the places
incorporated in Halicarnassus by Mausolus, survived as a post-Mauso-
lan *koinon*,[92] and the local communities of the Koarendeis and the
Plataseis[93] grant tax-exemptions and so forth *in conjunction* with the
Hecatomnids, thus anticipating Seleucid and general royal hellenistic
practice.[94] With this Carian evidence we may perhaps compare the
slightly earlier involvement of Pericles, the Limyran dynast, with the
koinon of the Lycian Pernitai, as attested by a badly preserved letter on
stone.[95] All this looks enlightened: here is no high-handed removal of
internal sovereignty and autonomy. So much for Alexander's claim to
have liberated Asia Minor, and to have given back its laws (cf. below, p.
868ff). The taxes of the king must be paid, but there are other taxes over
which the community has control. Thus the local 'Group of Pelekos'
grants immunity from all tax 'except the *apomoira*'.[96] This word is
interesting because it is an attested Ptolemaic royal tax (above p. 62).
And at Hecatomnid Lagina there is a mention of tax-exemption from 'all
except royal tribute'.[97] Xanthus actually grants tax-freedom unconditionally, subject only to ratification by the satrap.[98] Finally, an
inscription from the Carian sanctuary of Labraunda[99] shows that the
Plataseis controlled their own citizen-intake in the time of the satrap
Pixodarus (341–336 B.C.). Such control was an important ingredient in
any ancient notion of autonomy. Even Athens had lost it by the time of
the early Successors of Alexander (see *SIG* 315).

This generally permissive policy was confined on present evidence to
the Carian mini-empire – whose rulers' sphere of influence was,
however, large. It extended from Erythrae in the north, with evidence
for military involvement still higher up, at Assus and even Sestus.[100] It
went round to Pamphylian Phaselis and Pisidia in the south, taking in the

---

[92] Michel 459 with Hornblower 1982 (F 644) 65. For the survival of other, (?)religious leagues in
Asia Minor after the fourth century see Boffo 1985 (F 585) and Isager in Bilde *et al.* 1990 (F 578)
79–90.

[93] *SIG* 311 (Koarendeis) with Hornblower 1982 (F 644) 64; for the Plataseis grant see Crampa
1972 (F 619) no. 42 = Hornblower 1982 (F 644) 366 M8, and see Varinluoglu *et al.* 1990 (F 726) for an
early hellenistic decree of the polis of the Plataseis/Pladaseis.

[94] Hornblower 1982 (F 644) 161; Wörrle 1988 (F 730) 458; for the relation between Seleucids and
Achaemenids see generally Briant in Bilde *et al.* 1990 (F 578) 40–65; Sherwin-White and Kuhrt 1993
(F 672).   [95] Wörrle 1991 (F 732) 224–34.   [96] Robert 1940–65 (B 171) VII 63.

[97] *SEG* XXVI 1229 = Hornblower 1982 (F 644) 368–9 M13.

[98] *SEG* XXVII 942 = Hornblower 1982 (F 644) 366 M9.

[99] Crampa 1972 (F 619) no. 42 = Hornblower 1982 (F 644) 366 M8.

[100] Xen. *Ages.* II.26f; above p. 85, and F 644, 201.

Greek offshore islands Rhodes, Chios and Cos. Even Crete, as we now know, came within the sweep of Hecatomnid diplomacy.[101]

In the Greek states, Hecatomnid interference or perhaps just proximity seems to have resulted in oligarchy. Demosthenes attests it for Rhodes, Chios and Cos (n. 101 above); and a similar progression, by which Athenian democratic influence was gradually undermined, is likely at Erythrae. Here where we may contrast the democratic assembly of the 390s (Tod no. 106 = Harding no. 12D) with the formula in the honours to Mausolus later in the century: 'it seemed good to the Council, on the motion of the generals' – no mention of a sovereign *demos*, which is equally absent from the honours for Idrieus (Tod no. 155; *SEG* xxxi 969 = Harding no. 28B. The preamble to the Hermias treaty is not preserved). To this extent Persia, and specifically its agents and appointees the Hecatomnids, deserve the discredit for bringing to an end western Anatolian, and east Aegean, democracy on an Athenian model, and for helping to settle what in modern language would be called the class struggle, in favour of the men of property.[102] Five qualifications should, however, be made.

First, it is in Demosthenes' interests in the most relevant speech, that *On the Freedom of the Rhodians* (xv), to paint Mausolus very black. (See F 644, 210f, and for the general issue of Demosthenes' truthfulness, p. 17 above).

Second, distinctions between democracy and oligarchy are not absolute, and we should be specially careful how we use crude introductory formulae in inscriptions; even Athens' famous fifth-century 'support of democracies' becomes more complicated on a second look.[103]

Third, it is only fair to point out that satrapal tolerance or perhaps indifference was not confined to the native *koina*: at Iasus, a more than partly Greek city, a pro-Mausolan decree[104] has a democratic preamble with a mention of popular assembly as well as council (though this should be seen as a concession rather than as an indication of where the real power lay. It has been well said that 'assemblies often continued to meet even under tyrannies, in Sicily as elsewhere').[105] There was also assembly pay, a very democratic institution and surely a survival from the fifth-century Athenian period, at the same city as late as the third century, and so presumably in the satrapal fourth century as well.[106] And we have seen (above) that even Erythrae, where political change can be most straightforwardly correlated with the growth of Hecatomnid

---

[101] Phaselis and Pisidia: above, nn. 43 and 44; Rhodes, Chios, Cos: Dem. xv; v.25; Crete: Crampa 1972 (F 619) no. 40 = Hornblower 1982 (F 644) 366 M7. See generally Hornblower 1982 (F 644) ch. 5.
[102] de Ste Croix 1981 (C 70).   [103] See above, p. 50 n. 33.
[104] *SIG* 169 = Blümel 1985 (F 581) no. 1.   [105] Finley 1979 (G 164) 98.
[106] Michel 466 = Blümel 1985 (F 581) no. 20 with de Ste Croix 1975 (C 69).

influence, had relative freedom of diplomatic action as late as the middle of the century. But (to return to Iasus), it is significant that the hellenistic city bothered to republish a decree honouring some men known from other evidence to have been opponents of the Hecatomnids; this, it has been said, 'testifies to Iasos' lasting sympathy for Carians who were hostile to the dynasty of Hekatomnos and Mausolos'.[107] There is other, slight, evidence for strong if predictable reaction, a fragmentary inscription from Labraunda which may call one of the family 'tyrant'.[108] The date is uncertain, but nobody, surely, would have dared call Mausolus' family tyrants while they were still in power, not even in the time of Alexander's appointee Ada, who, though part of the new supposedly liberal dispensation, was nevertheless Mausolus' younger sister.

Fourth, female rulers like Ada, her older sister Artemisia, and Mania in the Aeolid, show that elite Asia Minor culture avoided one of the most basic and usual exclusions of Greek political life. But it now seems clear that the extent of Lycian 'matriarchy' was exaggerated in the nineteenth century, by over-interpretation of Hdt. 1.173.[109]

Fifth and last, if the class struggle is envisaged not just in terms of *Greek* oligarchs versus *Greek* democrats, the possibility has to be faced that native Carians, Lydians, Lycians and so on, hitherto something of an exploited class, actually had a better deal under the fourth-century satraps than either under the Athenian empire or under the Seleucids of the third and second centuries. The latter, on one extreme and admittedly controversial view, employed a mere $2\frac{1}{2}$ per cent of natives in the upper cadres of their administration.[110] When the Greeks arrived in Anatolia during the Dark and Archaic ages, they had reduced to servitude people like the Pedieis of Priene, the Mariandynoi of Bithynia, and the Lelegians of Caria.[111] Though there is evidence that, for instance, some Lelegians were still used as helots in hellenistic times,[112] still the epigraphic finds of the second half of the twentieth century have shown that some natives at least attained high office and status in Asia Minor under the Achaemenids. Thus Artemelis, a Carian name, is made garrison-commander at Xanthus;[113] Hyssollos and Obrokas, two more

---

107 *SEG* xxxviii 1059 reporting Pugliese Carratelli.

108 Crampa 1972 (F 619) no. 41 with Hornblower 1982 (F 644) 70–1 and Petit 1988 (F 693) 316.

109 Pembroke 1965 (F 692), 1967 (I 118). Note also, for female 'property power' in the Persian empire, the interesting short study by Sancisi-Weerdenburg 1988 (F 48). Mania: Xen.*Hell.*III.1.12.

110 Habicht 1958 (F 634), but see S. Sherwin-White in Kuhrt and Sherwin-White 1987 (F 671) 6. Note however the reservations on this point in the important review by Walbank 1988 (F 727) of Kuhrt and Sherwin-White. See also now Sherwin-White and Kuhrt 1993 (F 672).

111 For the evidence for such Asia Minor 'serfdom' cf. generally Jones 1971 (F 662) 384 n. 20 and J. K. Davies, *CAH* vii².1, 300 n. 264; and see Petit 1990 (F 45) 244–53 for the theoretical problems of using such feudal language in this context (also *CAH* vii².1, 300 n. 263).

112 *FGrHist* 741 Philip of Theangela F 2.

113 n. 98 above.

Carian names, feature as *archontes* at Lagina;[114] and the same office is filled by local men at the Carian sanctuary Amyzon. The same text honours Bagadates and Ariaramnes; these names are Iranian;[115] and there is a possible Iranian dedicant at (?) late fourth-century Labraunda.[116] But it is clear that native Carians, or people with Carian names, were prominent alongside those bearers of Persian names whose presence in Asia Minor, down to hellenistic and even Roman times, was constantly and rightly insisted on by the late Louis Robert (above, nn. 35 and 115).

Hecatomnid furtherance of this native Carian element is an important feature of family policy. As the present writer has emphasized elsewhere,[117] we can legitimately speak of active 'Carianization' alongside the more obvious processes of hellenization. It would certainly be wrong to 'privilege' the Greek element in the dynasty's activities and in the Caria over which they presided.

Thus Zeus Kaunios, so called from the Carian city of Caunus, gets an altar in the Xanthus trilingual, and Zeus Idrieus, whose epithet is certainly Carian, is mentioned at Iasus.[118] Obviously, none of this is crude evidence of a Hecatomnid religious, still less political, programme (see n. 117); but the blend of Greek and native elements is very striking. Negative evidence is also significant: the Hecatomnids lavishly patronized the Carian sanctuaries (Amyzon, Labraunda, Sinuri, Lagina and no doubt Kasossos) with buildings and dedications;[119] but on present evidence they made no effort whatsoever to buy and build their way into prominence at the old panhellenic sanctuaries of Greece. Even at Ionian Clarus, an oracular site which had an archaic history and featured, though not as a sanctuary, in Thucydides,[120] there is very little evidence for activity of any sort till the end of the fourth century. The Hecatomnids are equally noticeable by their absence from Didyma in Milesian territory, despite this great sanctuary's (?) Carian name.[121] This absence would be less surprising if Darius or Xerxes had indeed sacked the

---

[114] *SEG* xxvi 1228 = Hornblower 1982 (F 644) M368 M12.

[115] Robert 1983 (F 703) 97 no. 2, *SEG* xxxiii 851 (summary, no text given).

[116] Crampa 1972 (F 619) no. 28. But the Persian name is very hard to read.

[117] See Hornblower 1982 (F 644) 276, 352, 342 and *passim*. On Gunter 1985 (F 632A) see my reply at Hornblower 1990 (F 647).

[118] Zeus Kaunios: see *SEG* xxvii 942 = Hornblower 1982 (F 644) 366 M9 with 115 n. 71; Zeus Idrieus: see Pugliese Carratelli 1969/70 (F 695) 372 no. 1 = Blümel 1985 (F 581) no. 52 with Hornblower 1982 (F 644) 113.

[119] Amyzon: Robert 1983 (F 703); Labraunda: Jeppeson 1955 (F 651); Westholm 1963 (F 729); Hellström and Thieme 1982 (F 641); Hellström 1965 (F 639); Säflund 1980 (F 716); Jully 1981 (F 664); Crampa 1969 and 1972 (F 618, 619). Sinuri: Robert 1945 (F 706); Lagina: *SIG* 311; Kasossos: Robert 1945 (F 706) 17 and Wörrle 1991 (F 732) 205 n. 10.

[120] III.33.1 with my comm., Hornblower 1991 (B 62) *ad loc.* For Clarus see Robert 1989 (F 713) and Parke 1985 (F 690); Mitchell 1989/90 (F 682) 98–9.

[121] Fontenrose 1988 (F 629) 3–5; Zgusta 1984 (F 736) 162 and n. 170. The word suggests also the Greek 'twin', and was so understood by the ancients.

temple of Apollo there, as ancient sources tell us, but even this has been challenged.[122] Such revisionism is extreme; but at the very least, it has cautiously been said that 'we now have sufficient evidence of cult activity at Didyma in the period from 494 to 334'.[123] But when the Milesians wished to honour the Hecatomnid satraps Idrieus and Ada with a pair of bronze statues, they chose Delphi, not Didyma as the place to do so, suggesting that in the middle of the fourth century the city looked to Delphi as the great Apolline centre.[124] After 300 B.C., it has been observed, this statue group would certainly have stood at Didyma.[125]

Moving away from Caria, a very elegantly carved Greco-Lydian bilingual inscription records a dedication by Nannas son of Bakivas (Dionysocles) to Artemis.[126] (The name Bakivas also appears on a pyramidal seal of Persian type from this part of the world.[127]) Epigraphically attested cult titles like 'Mother of the Lydian Gods'[128] can be seen as expressive of a Lydian ethnicity surviving into the hellenistic period. We may compare Arr. *Anab.* 1.17.4 for Alexander's restoration of the 'old customs of the Lydians'. If this means anything, it ought to imply that memory of those 'customs' had survived.

The 'iranization' of Anatolia is illustrated by the 'gods of the Greeks and Persians' in the plain of Tabai in east Caria;[129] and by a fourth-century decree from Sardis standing in the name of the sub-satrap Droaphernes, and attesting the influence of Zoroastrianism.[130] Also from Sardis is a bilingual inscription in Lydian and Aramaic about the destruction of temple property, and dated to the 'Tenth Year of Artaxerxes'; but the inscription nevertheless refers to Artemis of Ephesus by that title, a Greek goddess however deep her oriental tinge.[131] There is archaeological as well as epigraphic evidence for such fusion: excavations at Sardis have brought to light a relief depicting Cybele, with lion and tympanum, side by side with Artemis, draped and carrying a hind across her chest.[132]

Hellenization in Western Anatolia is not confined to religion. Priest lists from the Carian sanctuary of Sinuri[133] show that Carian personal names give way to Greek in the course of the later fourth century, a process which can be documented elsewhere in the Hecatomnid despo-

---

[122] Tuchelt 1988 (F 724): cf. Parke 1985 (D 218) and 1986 (F 691); Mitchell 1989/90 (F 682) 105–6.
[123] Fontenrose 1988 (F 629) 15.   [124] Tod no. 161B with Parke 1985 (F 690) 35.
[125] Parke 1985 (F 690) *ibid.* For the great series of hellenistic dedications Günther 1971 (H 55).
[126] Littmann 1916 (B 675) 1 p. 38.   [127] Boardman 1970 (F 584).
[128] Robert 1987 (F 712) 323.   [129] Robert 1969–90 (B 172) V 736.
[130] Robert 1969–90 V (B 172) 485–309 and 1983 (F 703) 116. Note also Cook 1983 (F 14) 149: Oromedon, the name of the father of Syennesis of Cilicia (Hdt. VII.98) may imply 'some recognition of Ahura-Mazda west of the Euphrates before the time of Darius I'. Cf. West 1971 (H 116).
[131] Littmann 1916 (F 675) 1 p. 23.
[132] Hanfmann and Ramage 1978 (F 638) no. 20 figs. 78–83. For Artemis/Anahita Robert 1969–90 (B 172) VI 137–68 at 140–60.   [133] Robert 1945 (F 706) no. 5.

tate (though it should always be remembered that *natives* may give their children Greek-looking names).

Western Anatolia was invaded in the fourth century by a diaspora, in part the result of the collapse of the Athenian empire as paymaster, of Greek artists, sculptors, poets and intellectuals generally. Martin West has written of Hesiod's 'hob-nailed hexameters'; we might say of Symmachus, the Achaean hack poet and seer in the pay of Arbinas of Lycia, that his were Greek hexameters in Persian trousers (above, p. 214). The Hecatomnid court alone (but perhaps it *was* alone in the intensity of its patronage) played host to Eudoxus the mathematician,[134] Dexippus the doctor from Cos,[135] Aeschines the Athenian orator,[136] Theodectes the tragedian, and the numerous other performers at the cultural contest organized by Artemisia after her brother Mausolus' death.[137] .

Then there are the architects Pytheus, Satyrus, Timotheus, Leochares, Scopas and Bryaxis, most of them top artists, who built the Mausoleum – a building which blends Greek, Persian, native Carian and even Egyptian elements.[138] And Pytheus may have had a hand in the fine temple of Zeus at Labraunda,[139] a shrine spectacularly endowed by the Hecatomnids. All these visitors had their precursors in the hellenizing entourage of Pericles of Limyra, an older contemporary of Mausolus. It now seems clear that it was wrong to dismiss Pericles' hellenizing activity as just a veneer:[140] he was true to his famous name.[141] The Nereid Monument from Xanthus, now in the British Museum, was surely the work of Greek or Greek-influenced craftsmen[142] as were the Caryatids at Limyra, on display in the museum at Antalya;[143] we have seen (p. 215 above) that there may have been artistic as well as military and political competition between these cities and their respective dynasts. Lycian

[134] See generally Hornblower 1982 (F 644) ch. 12. Eudoxus: D.L. VIII.88.
[135] Suidas s.v.   [136] Philostr. *VS* para. 481 Kayser.
[137] *FGrH* 115 Theopompus T 6 a-b and F 345; Lane Fox 1986 (B 65) 108–9.
[138] Jeppesen 1958 (F 652) 1–67; 1961 (F 653); 1967 (F 654); 1974 (F 655); 1976 (F 656 and 657); 1977/8 (F 658); Jeppesen *et al.* (F 660); 1984 (F 659); Waywell 1978 (F 728); Hornblower 1982 (F 644) ch. 9. On the testimonia Jeppesen in Jeppesen and Luttrell 1986 (F 661) is unreliable, see Hornblower 1988 (F 646) 175–7. The Mausoleum is the subject of several of the papers collected in Linders and Hellström 1989 (F 674), on which see my forthcoming review in *Gnomon*. For the blend of Greek and non-Greek, specifically Persian and native Carian, elements in the Mausoleum in particular and Hecatomnid culture generally see Hornblower 1982 (F 644) *passim* esp. 246, 251 on Persia; also Hornblower 1990 (F 647) on Gunter 1985 (F 632A). See also below p. 658.
[139] Hellström and Thieme 1982 (F 641) 56; Carter 1983 (F 597).
[140] Wörrle 1991 (F 732) 216 n. 69, protesting against Asheri 1983 (F 562) 85–105 and Hornblower 1982 (F 644) 120–1. For Persian as well as Greek influence on Lycian art in the Achaemenid period Jacobs 1987 (F 649).
[141] Bryce 1980 (F 590). See also Bryce 1982 (F 591), 1983 (F 592), 1986 (F 593).
[142] Above, n. 20. Greek influence does not necessarily indicate the workmanship or even the presence of Greeks, see Hornblower 1990 (F 647) 138–9.   [143] Borchhardt 1976 (F 586A).

die-cutters imitated the finest types of Syracusan coinage.[144] But the achievement of less magnificent names, figures of minor or anonymous talent, supplements that of Pytheus and the others. There are the craftsmen who carved the Greco-Iranian stelae from Dascylium, now in Istanbul Museum;[145] these carry banqueting or funerary subjects executed in a partly Greek manner, but their Persian cultural origin is underlined by the presence of the occasional inscription in Aramaic. Or there are the Athenians, artists of no particular fame or consequence, attested as working in western Asia Minor: Philistides, at Carian Theangela, or Theodorus, who left an exquisitely carved statue-base signature at Lycian Tlos.[146]

Throughout this chapter we have discussed the evidence for cultural fusion, and used expressions like 'Greco-Persian'. These expressions are not, however, intended to beg the questions of ethnicity to which such mixed cultures give rise. It must be emphasized that it is difficult, in the Achaemenid period, to say whether an artistic product is the product of a Greek, or a Persian, or a native workshop, or what kind of clientele the object was designed for. The position at the end of the period here discussed is neatly illustrated by a text from Pamphylian Side, a place which 'discovered' its Greek origins when it was convenient to do so.[147] The text is a bilingual inscription[148] in Greek and the local Sidetan script, which may be from as early as the late fourth century. The signature, again on a statue base, runs 'Mnaseas son of Artemon, the Sidetan, made this.' What is remarkable about this is the artist's explicit assertion of a local origin. In the couple of centuries preceding Mnaseas' inscription it would often be impossible to say confidently what ethnic group the artist belonged to. Certainly we should, in trying to identify ethnic origin, beware of such assumptions as that Greek means beautiful but Persian means stiff.[149] Even the validity of the concept of hellenization, which

[144] Kraay 1976 (B 200) 271.

[145] Bernard 1969 (F 577); Dentzer 1969 and 1982 (F 625 and J 12); Starr 1976 and 1977 (C 79); Cook and Blackman 1970/1 (F 615) 60; Metzger 1971 and 1975 (F 678 and F 679); Altheim-Stiehl *et al.* 1983 (F 560); Bammer 1983 (F 565); Cremer 1984 (F 620); cf. Radt 1983 (F 699).

[146] Robert 1936 (B 169) 93–4; *TAM* I p. 25.

[147] Arr. *Anab.* I.26.4. For the allegedly Greek (specifically Argive) origins of Pamphylian Aspendus in the early hellenistic period see *SEG* XXXIV 282, cf. Strabo XIV.4.2 for both Side and Aspendus. But 'invented tradition' has been at work here: many places found it expedient to claim Argive origins after the time of Alexander, whose family also liked to think of themselves as Argives: Hdt. V.22.2. For the reality (Aspendus in the earlier fourth century not Greek at all) see Lewis 1977 (A 33) 144 n. 55. *FGrHist* 4 Hellanicus F 15 may however be relevant (fifth-century interest in Aspendus' origins).

[148] Bean 1965 (F 569) 81; cf. Woudhuizen 1988–9 (F 733).

[149] See Root in F 53 (1991) 1–29. Nothing in the present chapter should be understood to imply that the only people in Achaemenid Persia capable of turning out convincingly Greek-looking art were ethnic Greeks; cf. above, nn. 36, 117, 142 and the works there cited, and see above all Root in F 53 (1991), e.g. 18: 'the notorious circularity of discussion on "Graeco-Persian" art is caused to some degree by the refusal to relinquish the notion that only Greeks could produce Greek-style art-forms'.

once seemed unproblematic, has been challenged ('a modern idea, reflecting modern forms of cultural domination').[150] More theoretical clarification of these notions is needed, and we can be confident that new and exciting evidence will continue to emerge – and that it will continue to subvert the theories.

[150] Bowersock 1990 (A 11) xi.

CHAPTER 8*b*

MESOPOTAMIA, 482–330 B.C.

MATTHEW W. STOLPER

Xerxes and his successors succeeded in consolidating imperial control over Mesopotamia. There is, at least, no explicit record of Babylonian resistance to Achaemenid rule after the revolts in the early years of Xerxes' reign (*CAH* IV² 73–5, 133–5). Later political disturbances were not matters of provincial reaction, but struggles among members of the Achaemenid dynasty and the imperial aristocracy. Even these left few plain marks in Babylonian texts.

The available Babylonian texts are similar in kind to those from the early Achaemenid reigns, but there are fewer of them. They include few fragments of historiographic texts and royal inscriptions. Most are legal and administrative documents. Among about 1,100 published texts of these kinds from the last 150 years of the Achaemenids, a few are temple records, but most belonged to the private archives of Babylonians – in fact, nearly two thirds of them come from a single source, the Murashû archive (454–404 B.C.) – and, although they record contacts with agencies of the provincial government, they are not documents from the conduct of government as such. What they divulge is limited by the concerns of city-based businessmen. They are conservative in form, almost oblivious to political events, and often enigmatic in their allusions to contemporary institutions. They are a rich source of detail on local conditions, but an episodic source on the history of their times.[1]

I. TRACES OF POLITICAL HISTORY

As has been shown in *CAH* IV² 133–5, the classical accounts of Xerxes' reprisals after the Babylonian revolts have no counterpart in Babylonian

---

[1] Of the legal and administrative texts that do not belong to the Murashû archive, about one third can be assigned to a dozen archival groups from Babylon, Borsippa, Kish/Hursagkalama, Nippur, Ur and Uruk. Most of the published legal, administrative and epistolary documents from the period are listed in Oelsner 1976 (F 149) 312ff n. 10 and Dandamayev 1984 (F 95) 16–18. Cuneiform texts are cited in the style of the Chicago Assyrian Dictionary (F 157), with minor adaptations to *CAH* style and additional abbreviations noted in the list of abbreviations. Babylonian dates are cited in this form: day (Arabic numerals)/month (Roman numerals)/regnal year (Arabic numerals). In Babylonian chronological conventions, regnal years are coterminous with calendar years, beginning 1 Nisannu (March/April); a ruler's accession year is the balance of his predecessor's last regnal year, i.e. the period between the previous ruler's death and the next New Year. Conversions to Julian dates follow Parker and Dubberstein 1956 (F 159).

texts. If Xerxes sacked Esagil, the temple of Marduk in Babylon, the event was as transient in effect as his destruction of the Athenian Acropolis, for both property and personnel of Esagil recur in texts from later reigns.[2] The revolts and their aftermath may only have affected northern Babylonia, where all of the known texts dated by the rebel kings were drafted. Some legal archives from the northern cities came to an end at about this time (the latest available text of the large archive of the Egibi family at Babylon, for example, is dated under the rebel Shamash-erība),[3] but family archives from Ur in the south cover the period of the revolts and beyond without interruption.[4]

Nor do the changing royal titles used in date formulae tell a clear story. The element 'King of Babylon' was not dropped from the titulature at once and everywhere as a token of reprisal against the revolts. 'King of Babylon' and 'King of Persia and Media' appear intermittently in date formulae from the later reign of Xerxes, and in a few texts from the reign of Artaxerxes I, as late as 441 B.C. (*Bagh. Mitt.* 15 268 No. 4).[5] What is striking in Xerxes' titles is their variation, contrasting sharply with the mostly regular usages of legal texts from earlier and later reigns, and the introduction of 'Persia and Media' beside 'Babylon and the lands'. It is still likely that these traits and the general reduction of the title to 'king of the lands' in later reigns do indeed reflect changes in the empire's structure and the provinces' status, or at least in the view of those matters that the rulers wished to propagate. This development in royal policy, however, was not abrupt and it was not a response provoked only by the Babylonian revolts, but part of a long political process.[6]

Babylonian astronomical texts put the date of Xerxes' death in early

[2] See Stolper 1989 (F 181) 295f. The records of tithes paid for clearing debris from Esagil, dated soon after Alexander's seizure of Babylon (CT 49 5 and 6, see Oelsner 1964 (F 146) 265, McEwan 1981 (F 137) 59), along with references in an astronomical diary and two Seleucid chronicles (Sachs and Hunger 1988 (F 172) No. −321 r. 14, Grayson 1975 (F 105) no. 10 obv. 6, rev. 13, 33, 11 obv. 2) to similar clearing operations in the times of Philip Arrhidaeus and Antigonus, are not evidence of the persistent effects of Xerxes' ravages but only of building campaigns conducted and described in traditional Mesopotamian terms.

[3] *ZA* 3 157 no. 16. See Böhl 1962 (F 79) 110 for a group of unpublished texts from Babylon, covering the period between the Neo-Babylonian king Nabopolassar and the rebel Shamash-erība. The latest texts of the Ea-ilūta-bāni/Ilī-bāni family archive from Borsippa date from the final years of Darius I; the aftermath of the revolts against Xerxes may have caused the closing of the preserved part of the archive; see Joannès 1984 (F 117) 145f and 1989 (F 119) 24, 126.

[4] Texts in the group with the excavation number U.17243 (the Barber family archive in UET 4) reach through the entire Achaemenid period to the early years of Macedonian rule; texts in the group with the excavation number U.20089 include documents from as early as Neo-Assyrian times and as late as the fourteenth year of Xerxes (UET 4 115); see Figulla 1949 (F 101) 1; Van Driel 1986 (F 198) 10 and 1987 (F 197) 164–8.

[5] See Kessler 1984 (F 125) 262, Joannès 1989 (F 119A), and Stolper 1985 (F 177) 9 n. 24, with references. See also *CAH* iv² 134f; Kuhrt and Sherwin-White 1987 (F 132) 72f.

[6] But Joannès 1990 (F 121) 180 interprets the evidence to indicate a sharp break with the past and a general political reorganization in the time of Xerxes.

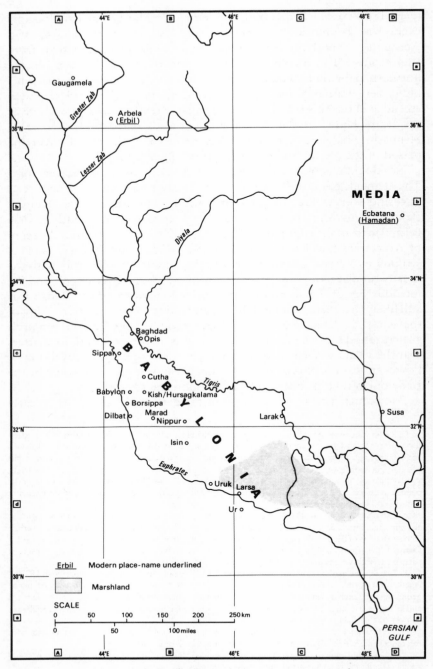

Map 6. Mesopotamia. For detail on ancient water-courses see F 73 fig. 28.

August 465.[7] The few texts that can be ascribed to the beginning of Artaxerxes' reign show no sign of disturbance during the succession.

Texts from the Murashû archive of Nippur begin in Artaxerxes' tenth year, and they show some of the local effects of imperial politics, for they name influential figures of the court, including some who participated in the events that brought Darius II Ochus to the throne. Among them are Menostanes (Babylonian Manushtānu), a nephew of Artaxerxes and son of the satrap of Babylonia, Artarius (Babylonian Artarēme); Arsames, the satrap of Egypt (Babylonian Arshamu); Ochus' queen Parysatis (Babylonian Purushâtu); the courtier Artoxares (Babylonian Artaḫsharu); and others of comparable stature. They controlled wealth and men in the region around Nippur, and although it is not likely that figures of such rank were often at their Babylonian holdings, they were still able to act on local affairs through their Babylonian agents.[8]

There are discrepancies concerning the date of Artaxerxes' death and Darius' accession, both among classical authors (Thuc. IV.50f, Diod. XI.69.6, XII.64.1, XII.71.1, Ctesias *FGrH* 688 F 14.15) and between them and Babylonian texts. The Babylonian sources, though, are consistent among themselves. According to the scribes who drafted legal texts at the time of the events and the scholars who compiled astronomical records later, Artaxerxes I died in the forty-first year of his reign, Darius II was his immediate successor, and the succession occurred between 24 December 424 and 13 February 423 B.C.[9]

No known Babylonian texts, neither legal documents contemporary with the events nor later astronomical compilations, acknowledge Xerxes II's or Sogdianus' evanescent tenure on the throne, known from non-Babylonian sources, but several texts from Nippur and Babylon explicitly treat Darius' accession year as the continuation of Artaxerxes' final regnal year.[10] Darius II Ochus was himself in Babylon very soon after Artaxerxes' death, as one of the Murashû texts (BE 10 1) indicates.

---

[7] Stolper 1988 (F 61) 196–7, disposing of contrary evidence. Cowley, *AP* 6 supplies a *terminus ante quem* of 3 January 464 for knowledge of the succession in Upper Egypt; it names Artaxerxes as King, but refers to his accession period as the balance of the twenty-first regnal year (*sc.* of Xerxes). The new king's given name is damaged in the astronomical diary Sachs and Hunger 1988 (F 172) No. –440:1. Babylonian [*Ar*]*shu*, i.e. Arses, is plausible but uncertain, since the date to which the text refers is not confirmed by the astronomical contents, and all Greek mss of Joseph. *AJ* XI.6.1 (184) have the ruler's name as 'Cyrus', commonly emended to 'Asuēros' (Gutschmid). See Sachs 1977 (F 171) 130f.; Schmitt 1982 (F 57) 83, 87; Sachs and Hunger 1988 (F 172) 61.

[8] Similar conditions may underlie earlier references to a major domo (Babylonian *rab bīti*) of Mardonius (Babylonian Mardiniya, Marduniya) in Evetts 1892 (F 100) App. 4 (Xerxes, year seven (collated, despite Graziani 1986 (F 107) 38 No. 31)) and BM 64535 (Xerxes, year eight), both from Babylon; see Stolper 1992 (F 188). If this Mardonius is Xerxes' cousin, brother-in-law, and general, the later mention of him is posthumous. A reference in Xerxes' accession year to a wet-nurse of the king's daughter (Evetts App. 2, see Graziani 1986 (F 107) 10 No. 8) at least verifies that members of the royal family were sometimes in Babylonia during tranquil times.   [9] Stolper 1983 (F 60).

[10] BE 8/1 127; BE 10 4, 5, 6, 7; PBS 2/1 3; *AMI* NF 16 233f.

Ochus' party controlled Babylonia, using it as a staging area during the succession crisis, and the Murashû archive may reflect their preparations. A sharp increase in the number of Murashû texts that record lands pawned by smallholders coincides with the period during which the succession was at issue, a phenomenon that may result from extraordinary demands for money and service that participants in the contest imposed on their subordinates. If so, local short-term circumstances were surprisingly sensitive to imperial politics, precisely because the Great Kings had granted Babylonian offices, estates and revenues to their relatives, friends and potential rivals.[11]

The astronomical texts agree with the Greek sources on the point that Darius' given name was Ochus,[12] but direct evidence of events during his reign is slight. A few Murashû texts refer to smallholders in Nippur called to arms for travel to Uruk on the King's service during the second year of the reign (BE 10 61, 62; PBS 2/1 54, 162, 194; UCP 9/3 275), but the occasion is not indicated. If Ctesias is to be believed, it was in Babylon that Darius contracted his fatal illness (*FGrH* 688 F 16. 57). In the same passage, however, Ctesias erroneously gives Darius a thirty-five year reign, while Babylonian legal texts put Darius' death in the last half of his nineteenth regnal year, between 17 September 405 and 10 April 404.[13]

Soon after the accession of Artaxerxes II,[14] the penetration of Cyrus the Younger's army to the vicinity of Babylon (p. 49), the raising and provisioning of the king's forces to oppose him, and the armed retreat of the Greek mercenaries must have caused serious local disruptions. No Babylonian texts now available record these events, but there are texts that hint at their background. Two documents (*ZKM* 2 pl. after 324 = *TSBA* 4 pl. after 256 no. 2 [12/III/17 Darius II], and *ZKM* 1 pl. after 254 = Actes du 8ᵉ Congrès International 25, [7/X/3 Artaxerxes II]) record transactions done in Babylonia by agents of a man called Bēlshunu, entitled 'governor of Across-the-River'. He was Belesys, the governor of Syria whose palace and park Cyrus' army destroyed on their march to the Euphrates (Xen. *An.* 1.4.10, cf. VII.8.25) only a few months after the later of these tablets was drafted. The same Bēlshunu had been a district governor at Babylon early in the reign of Darius II and perhaps

[11] So Stolper 1985 (F 177) 104–24; Van Driel 1987 (F 197) 174–6 and 1989 (F 200) 223–4 demurs.
[12] *LBAT* 163 and 1426 (see Sachs 1977 (F 171) 130–3) and Sachs and Hunger 1988 (F 172) No. -418B.
[13] The latest published text from the reign is Durand *Textes babyloniens* pl. 36 17603 = Joannès 1982 (F 116) 103 No. 34 (2/VI/19). CBS 1714, dated in the first year of Artaxerxes II, records a receipt of rent due for the period covering the nineteenth year of Darius and the first year of Artaxerxes, implying that the two years were contiguous.
[14] With the given name Arses (Babylonian *Aršu*): Sachs 1977 (F 171) 132–39; Schmitt 1982 (F 57) 84 and 88f.

even late in the reign of Artaxerxes I. He and his agents conducted business in Babylonia throughout this period and for at least a short time after Cyrus' invasion.[15]

The texts that mention this Bēlshunu supply a rare glimpse of a Babylonian's political career under Achaemenid rule. Bēlshunu was a member of a prosperous business house that operated at Babylon. He was recruited into government as a district official in the reign of Artaxerxes I or the early years of Darius II. He was promoted to the provincial governorship of Syria in the middle years of Darius and remained in that post until the early years of Artaxerxes II. He achieved a political rank normally occupied by members of the Iranian imperial aristocracy, and he survived two troubled royal successions. His career may reflect the monarchy's delicate political circumstances; his promotion by Darius II to the governorship of Syria came perhaps not only because Darius' Babylonian mother had given him a special regard for Babylonians, or as a reward for services rendered in Babylon during Darius' accession to the throne, but as a method of securing Darius' control by taking Syria out of the hands of an aristocratic family that was dangerous to a usurper and putting it under a man who was safer for having no ties of blood or marriage to the royal house. Bēlshunu's promotion from Babylon to Syria, at any rate, implies some tightening of the ties between the two regions in spite of their administrative separation in earlier reigns.

Astronomical diaries mention fighting in the early 360s: in April 369 troops were sent on a campaign to Razaunda (Sachs–Hunger *Diaries* No. −369 r. 8), evidently in Media (Ptol. *Geog.* VI.2.12), and in May or June 367 royal forces were engaged in battle at an uncertain location (Sachs–Hunger *Diaries* No. −366 A ii 3). If Artaxerxes II's attempts to reconquer Egypt and the revolts of the western satraps (pp. 50–64) made demands on Babylonian resources, however, known Babylonian texts do not show their effects.

Artaxerxes II died between November 359 and April 358.[16] Babylonian astronomical texts, a chronicle fragment, and a fragment of uncertain literary character confirm classical notices that the given name of his successor, Artaxerxes III, was Ochus.[17] The chronicle fragment alludes to Artaxerxes' suppression of the rebellion in Phoenicia, recording the arrival of prisoners from Sidon at the king's palace in Babylon during the autumn of 345. No Babylonian corroboration is available,

[15] Stolper 1987 (F 178).

[16] VAS 6 186 (Babylon); see Parker and Dubberstein 1956 (F 159) 19.

[17] Sachs and Hunger 1988 (F 172) Nos. −346. −343, −342, *AJAH* 2 147 (see Sachs 1977 (F 171) 138ff); Schmitt 1982 (F 57) 85 and 89f; Grayson 1975 (F 105) no. 9:1 (Sollberger *ap.* Cawkwell 1962 (C 103) 137–8 suggests that the year should be read as the fourth rather than the fourteenth).

however, for the supposition that Belesys, the governor of Syria who took part in an attempt to take Sidon in 344 (Diod. xvi.42.1), was related to the like-named Babylonian who had governed Syria fifty years earlier. The few texts that can now be assigned to the time of Artaxerxes III[18] have no clear bearing on the political events of the reign.[19] The colophon on a literary tablet from Uruk dates by the twenty-first and final year of the reign,[20] and an astronomical fragment fixes the date of this Ochus' death and the accession of his son Arses in the sixth month of that year, August–September 338 B.C.[21]

Babylonian records from the stirring times during the Macedonian advance are tantalizing. A hellenistic astronomical compilation called the Saros Canon (*LBAT* 1428) dates a lunar eclipse by Arses' first regnal year. Arses, again called the son of Artaxerxes Ochus, figures in a narrative fragment that also mentions Alexander in connexion with activities at Esagil (*AJAH* 2 146), but too little of the tablet survives for certain interpretation. The Uruk King List (UVB 18 58 W.20030,105) enters someone with a Babylonian given name (Nidin-Bēl, or Nidin-Ishtar, or Nidinti) immediately before Darius III. His identity is unexplained: he is unlikely to be Arses; he may be one of the rebels from the reign of Darius I, misplaced by manuscript corruption; but he may also be an otherwise unrecorded local usurper who claimed power in Babylon during the unstable period of the assassinations that brought Darius III to the throne.

Astronomical texts mention the first three regnal years of Darius III, supplying his given name, Artashâta.[22] A single legal text from Ur (UET 4 25) dates from the end of his fourth year, in March 331. It is a record of a routine sale, with no hint of the preparations that were under way in the months before the Battle of Gaugamela.[23]

Astronomical texts record Alexander's approach and arrival. The obverse of a diary fragment describes a pitched battle after which the army deserted the losing commander and fled to the highlands (in Babylonian, 'the land of the Gutians'), and since the event is dated to 1

---

[18] CT 49 1–4 (Babylon, years 4 and 5), UET 4 1 and 2 (Ur, year 9); perhaps VAS 6 293, OECT 12 pl. 41f B 2 and B 7 (see Joannès 1982 (F 116) 344f), and Durand *Textes babyloniens* pl. 10 AO 6027 and pl. 4 AO 2137 and CT 44 80 (all probably from Babylon or Borsippa, years 2 through 18, see Joannès 1982 (F 116) 331ff); probably VAT 16476 = w.16584 (Uruk, 10 + x/VIII/1, unpublished, see Sarkisian 1974 (F 173) 16); see Kuhrt 1987 (F 128) 152; Oelsner 1971 (F 147) 161 and 1976 (F 149) 314.

[19] The interpretation of the astronomical fragment VAT 4924 in Unger 1931 (F 192) 318 n. 3 is erroneous; see Kuhrt 1990 (F 129) 179; Stolper 1988 (F 61) 197f, and the edition of the fragment in Sachs and Hunger 1988 (F 172) No. –418.

[20] TCL 6 56; see Hunger 1968 (F 113) 47 no. 112 and Oelsner 1986 (F 153) 409 n. 571.

[21] BM 71537, courtesy of C. B. F. Walker.

[22] Sachs 1977 (F 171) 142f; Schmitt 1982 (F 57) 90f; Sachs and Hunger 1988 (F 172) Nos. –333 and –332.

[23] See Oelsner 1976 (F 149) 314f. The fragmentary ration list Durand *Textes babyloniens* pl. 77 AO 26771 may also belong to the reign of Darius III; see Joannès 1982 (F 116) 333.

October 331 B.C., the text can only refer to Darius III's defeat at Gaugamela and his flight to Arbela and Media. The reverse describes the Macedonian progress southward during the following month, to Sippar by 18 October and to Babylon on 20 October.[24] Mazaius, who had withdrawn with his contingent to Babylon after Gaugamela, led a delegation of Babylonian notables to surrender the city to the Macedonians before an assault could be launched (Arr. *Anab.* III.16.3; Curt. v.1.17ff). Babylon was an open city, and astronomical diaries record Alexander's arrival in approving terms. The Babylonians' rejoicing was an act of formal compliance with the terms of surrender, modelled on Mesopotamian precedents,[25] but their relief must have been sincere.

II. DOCUMENTATION, SETTLEMENT AND LANDSCAPE

Alexander's conquest brought him a prize that was of great value and greater potential. Archaeological surveys in Babylonia show an increase in the number and average size of settlements between the periods identified as Middle Babylonian and as Neo-Babylonian/Achaemenid, with eastern and south-eastern Babylonia undergoing an especially pronounced resurgence. These developments were part of a long trend of growth that continued until Sassanian times, but the archaeological criteria for distinguishing among Neo-Babylonian, early Achaemenid and later Achaemenid remains, and for correlating these material categories with political epochs are very insecure, and the short-term situation of late Achaemenid Babylonia is therefore not well defined by these means. There were probably temporal fluctuations in Babylonian demography that are undetectable by archaeological survey methods, and there were certainly local variations.

Ur, in the extreme south, benefited only from the beginnings of the long cycle of growth, when the Neo-Babylonian kings and Cyrus the Great sponsored the reconstruction of its temples. A shift in the main channel of the Euphrates gradually choked off the city's access to water, and the density of the urban population was low. The location of Achaemenid graves and kilns indicates the beginnings of encroachment on the precincts of the refurbished temples.[26] Nevertheless, the city was

[24] Sachs and Hunger 1988 (F 172) No. −330 (partly in Wiseman 1985 (F 207) 119–21, the date corrected by Brinkman 1987 (F 82)); see Bernard 1990 (F 78) 515–28). A passage in a literary fragment called the 'Dynastic Prophecy' (Grayson 1975 (F 106) 34 iii 1–13), widely considered to be an account of the contest between Darius III and Alexander, almost certainly refers instead to the wars for control of Mesopotamia between Antigonus and Seleucus after 310 B.C.; see Geller 1990 (F 103) 5f.

[25] Sachs 1974 (F 170) 47; Wiseman 1977 (F 206) 374, citing BM 36923 (unpublished); Kuhrt 1988 (F 130) 68–71 and 1990 (F 131).

[26] Wright *ap.* Adams 1981 (F 73) 334; Woolley and Mallowan 1962 (F 208) 49ff. Compare UET 4 11, recording an alienation of real estate described as temple property (Darius II).

occupied throughout Achaemenid times, and legal texts were still drafted there under the earliest Macedonian rulers.[27] Over fifty legal texts document the late Achaemenid occupation, most of them belonging to two family archives.[28] About a third of them deal with the possession and exploitation of agricultural property at Ur and in its hinterland, and mention properties of the same range of juridical types found in other late Achaemenid texts, located with reference to no more than six canals, three outlying settlements and five named meadows and marshlands. None deal with large-scale agricultural operations. Late Achaemenid Ur was a modest settlement, well along in its final decline.

Late Achaemenid documentation from Uruk, in south central Babylonia, is anomalous. There are thousands of published legal and administrative texts drafted there and dated in Neo-Babylonian and early Achaemenid reigns, and hundreds more from Seleucid and Arsacid reigns, but very few from the interval between Xerxes and Alexander.[29] This situation probably does not result from a historical decline in the city's fortunes, to judge by the existence of a sizeable late Achaemenid literary archive,[30] the existence of unpublished late Achaemenid legal and administrative texts,[31] and the mentions of Uruk as a military destination in texts from the Murashû archive (see above, p. 238). The network of canals developed around the city in Neo-Babylonian and early Achaemenid reigns was surely intact under the later Achaemenids and capable of supporting substantial rural and city populations. Larsa, about 20 km to the east, was probably part of Uruk's hinterland, since late Achaemenid texts from Larsa sometimes mention men who also figure in contemporary texts from Uruk.[32]

Nippur, in north central Babylonia, was surrounded by a similar grid of canals, probably linked to the network around Uruk. Extensive residential building in the city continued into the late Achaemenid reigns.[33] About 650 published texts from the Murashû archive, found at Nippur, and about 80 other late Achaemenid legal and administrative texts drafted there and at nearby towns[34] display well-developed settle-

---

[27] IM 17801 = U.17243, 16, Alexander the Great, year 12 (unpublished); UET 4 43, Philip Arrhidaeus, year 7; see Oelsner 1976 (F 149) 314 n. 15 and 1986 (F 153) 235.

[28] UET 4 *passim* and Brinkman 1976 (F 81) 44f; see Oelsner 1974 (F 148) 1056 and n. 74; Van Driel 1987 (F 197) 164–8.

[29] Stolper 1990 (F 182) 563ff nos. 1–9, 11, 13–19, 22 and other texts listed *ibid.* 560 n. 4.

[30] Oelsner 1983 (F 152) 248f, and add von Weiher Uruk 8; also *Bagh. Mitt.* Beih. 2 84; Oelsner 1986 (F 153) 94 and n. 299.   [31] See Stolper 1990 (F 182) 560 n. 5.

[32] Stolper 1990 (F 182) 576 no. 12, 585 no. 20. Similarly, a text excavated at Larsa, dated in the third year of Philip Arrhidaeus, records a debt owed by a man from Uruk (Arnaud 1985 (F 76)), and other hellenistic texts drafted at Larsa were probably found at Uruk (Oelsner 1986 (F 153) 154, 235 and n. 872.   [33] McCown *et al.* 1967–1978 (F 136) II 39–41, I 71–3.

[34] Including a small group from Shaṭir, a town probably located between Nippur and Uruk; see Joannès 1982 (F 116) 86ff. An archive of scholarly manuscripts from Nippur is also of late Achaemenid date: Oelsner 1982 (F 151) 94f and 1986 (F 153) 467 n. 870; Joannès 1982 (F 116) 6f and 73; Van Driel 1986 (F 198) 10f.

ment throughout the city's hinterland. They name six major waterways that traversed the region, forming the boundaries of administrative subdivisions and the arteries of local communication, as well as sixty derivative canals, the lifelines of agriculture. That two of the major canals are not attested before Achaemenid times (one of them not before the fifth century) signifies the continuing extension of the irrigation network under Achaemenid rule. Some of the texts found at Nippur were drawn up at fifteen smaller towns, the secondary centres of the region; others mention more than 180 outlying settlements, including villages, farmsteads and centres of estates. Many of the village names, of the type 'House of So-and-So' or 'Village of So-and-So', were no more than a generation or two old, again suggesting the shifting and probably the expansion of rural settlement. The documents include plain evidence of large- and small-scale date and cereal cultivation and of large- and small-scale herding. A few texts found at Nippur but drawn up at other cities (Babylon, Susa)[35] or mentioning property at cities from which contemporary records are unavailable (Marad, Isin, Larak), along with business records from Nippur and Babylon that mention the same individuals in both cities,[36] indicate active extra-regional contacts. The countryside around Nippur was flourishing, at least in the aggregate, through late Achaemenid times. It produced much revenue for the rulers, supported many absentee landlords and some commercial agricultural contractors, and was capable of supporting a large urban population.

Aside from the Murashû texts, the largest numbers of late Achaemenid legal and administrative documents come from the old cities on the north-western alluvium of Babylonia – Babylon itself, Borsippa, Cutha, and Hursagkalama – or from small towns in the same region. As in earlier times, these cities formed a kind of conurbation, the interactions among their propertied inhabitants often producing texts that were drafted at one town and deposited at another.[37] In this region too the Neo-Babylonian kings had refurbished most of the major temples. The irrigation network underwent a change of orientation and its eastern sections were extended during Neo-Babylonian and Achaemenid times, with a concomitant increase in the number of settlements.[38] More than 300 late Achaemenid legal and administrative texts and fragments from this region are available. Many of them record sales or leases of houses in the cities, indicating a more active urban life than the modest remains of

[35] See Donbaz 1989 (F 97) and Stolper 1992 (F 186), rebutting Dandamayev 1986 (F 96).

[36] Cited in Stolper 1988 (F 179) 141 n. 32.

[37] On this standard, Dilbat can be considered a southern extension of the region; see Stolper 1992 (F 187). According to Durand *Textes babyloniens* pl. 6 AO 2569 (dated in or after the eighth year of Darius II), a case concerning property missing from a temple in Dilbat was brought before an assembly of the temple Esagil and the district governor at Babylon.

[38] Gibson 1972 (F 104) 5of, 55ff, 253f; Adams 1981 (F 73) 191 fig. 40; McEwan 1983 (F 139) 121f.

Achaemenid residential areas excavated at Kish and Babylon would suggest.[39] Many others deal with the control and exploitation of agricultural properties, naming fifteen canals and thirty-five villages and small towns. Two archives record commercial agricultural operations of a type and perhaps of a scale comparable to the enterprise of the Murashûs at Nippur.[40] The sorts of property they deal with correspond to those mentioned in Quintus Curtius' account of events around Babylon after Alexander's death (x.8.11–13): the hinterland of Babylon was organized in villages and estates, sufficiently numerous and productive to support the city. The shift of population away from the old cities along the Euphrates may already have begun, but the demands of the provincial and imperial centres at Babylon must have retarded the process, and the general suggestion of the available texts is that much of this region was still well settled and exploited throughout the late Achaemenid reigns.

The status of Sippar, the north-westernmost of the old cities of the alluvium, is uncertain. There is archaeological survey evidence of Achaemenid settlement and irrigation at Sippar itself and in its vicinity. At Abu Qubūr, about 10 km north west of Sippar, traces of occupation in the Achaemenid period occur on all areas of a 55-hectare mound; a large public building was built there near the end of the period.[41] Known texts from the voluminous archives of the temple Ebabbar end early in Xerxes' reign, and the latest published private archival text (Durand *Textes babyloniens* pl. 1 AO 1729) is dated in Xerxes' sixth year. Yet Sippar was still an important centre at the end of the Achaemenid period, to judge by its mention in the astronomical diary that records Alexander's approach to Babylon (see above, pp. 240f). There are texts from Sippar dated as late as Artaxerxes I,[42] but since none is available, no assessment of the adjacent late Achaemenid landscape can be made. Similarly, there is no textual counterpart to the archaeological evidence for growing Neo-Babylonian and Achaemenid settlement in the Diyala region,[43] despite Strabo's allusion (xvi.1.4) to a palace of Darius I in the area between the Lower Zab and the Diyala.

In sum, most of the old cities of Babylonia were still active centres of legal and commercial activity. Traffic among them was unimpeded. Some were surrounded by well-developed hinterlands dotted with numerous villages and somewhat fewer small towns, and sustained by large, regular irrigation grids. The decline of the extreme south was

---

[39] Moorey 1978 (F 142) 179; Reuther 1926 (F 164) 34f, 147f.

[40] On the Tattannu archive, see Van Driel 1987 (F 197) 176–9 and 1986 (F 198) 10, with additions in Stolper 1990 (F 185). On the Kasr archive see Stolper 1987 (F 178) and 1990 (F 183).

[41] Adams 1981 (F 73) 191 fig. 40; Gasche *et al.* 1989 (F 102) 5, 6f, 24.

[42] Walker and Collon 1980 (F 204) 96.   [43] Adams 1981 (F 73) 192.

offset by the increasing use of lands in the east, along the Tigris. Whether or not Babylonia as a whole prospered, some elements of Babylonian society certainly did, and the region was equipped to support a large resident population, a growing number of landlords holding estates and entitlements from the imperial government, and the demands for taxes and manpower made by the imperial government itself.

III. TENURE, EXTRACTION AND CONTROL ·

One of the keys to the control and exploitation of the province was a pattern of land-grants propagated by the early Achaemenids and especially well attested in texts from later Achaemenid reigns. The relationships among its elements can be traced best in texts from Nippur, but the elements appear in late Achaemenid texts from all parts of Babylonia.

The distinctive units of this pattern were smallholdings called 'bow lands', 'horse lands', and 'chariot lands', that is, properties intended to support archers (infantrymen), cavalrymen, and chariot crews. They were occupied by groups of agnatic relatives, on condition of military service and payment of an annual tax. The regular service obligation was often commuted to equivalent payment, although actual service might still be required and some texts therefore record the provisioning of soldiers called up from such tenancies.[44] The properties could be leased or pawned, and shares in them were transmitted by inheritance, but they were not normally alienable. The few legal records in which the proprietorship of such holdings was transferred involve extraordinary circumventions.[45] Judging by the rents drawn from them, such tenancies were small.[46] The characteristic terminology that names them appears sporadically in the earliest Achaemenid reigns (*CAH* IV² 128–9), but the properties figure as the objects of legal transactions with increasing frequency in texts from the reign of Darius I on, and above all in the Murashû texts.

The Murashû texts (and a few texts from other sources) show these smallholdings and their occupants as organized into groups called *ḫaṭru*s.

[44] Cardascia 1951 (F 83) 99; Joannès 1982 (F 116) 19f. UET 4 109 (25/IV/8 Artaxerxes II), records an agreement to provision a substitute soldier to discharge obligations at a royal muster, but without explicit mention of a property encumbered by these obligations.
[45] UCP 9/3 271ff (a uniquely detailed account of the equipment for a mounted warrior called up for royal service) presupposes a prior adoption transferring a share in a 'horse land' to the Murashû family; VAS 6 188 records such an adoption, the adopted parties receiving a share of a 'bow land' in perpetuity on condition of their discharging the incumbent service obligations; Durand *Textes babyloniens* pl. 43f. AO 17611 appears to record the sale of a limited interest in a 'bow land' (see Joannès 1982 (F 116) 94ff).
[46] Durand *Textes babyloniens* pl. 52 AO 17645 records the dimensions of several parts of a single 'bow land', totalling about 13 hectares; see Joannès 1982 (F 116) 84.

The term is of uncertain etymology; it is probably an Aramaic or Iranian loan-word. It is not well attested before the reign of Artaxerxes I, so the institution that it labels may have been newly introduced (or else reorganized and renamed) under the late Achaemenids.[47] Each *ḫaṭru* was overseen by a superintendent responsible for allocating the constituent properties and for collecting the incumbent taxes and services. Texts from the Nippur region mention more than sixty such groups. Some are named for military, administrative, craft and agricultural occupations, others for estates and administrative installations to which their members were attached, and others for the local or ethnic origins of their members, including groups from Iran, India, Anatolia and other parts of the empire, but also indigenous Babylonians. This regime was extended to some of the central institutions of pre-Achaemenid Babylonian society, embracing temple personnel and property (see below, p. 250) and elements of the urban population.[48]

Many smallholders were also subject to a higher level of control. The Murashû texts mention estates, also granted by the crown, including manors called by the names of their proprietors (some of them qualified as officials or princes), manors named for social ranks ('estate of the queen', 'estate of the crown prince', without mention of the proprietors' names), and 'administrative estates', that is, blocks of property committed to the support of permanent state offices or institutions (e.g. 'equerry's estate', 'treasury'). Some *ḫaṭru*s were demonstrably subordinate to these estates.

The proprietors of such estates included leading figures in contemporary political history: Parysatis, Arsames, Menostanes and Artoxares, all active participants in the succession crisis of 425/4 B.C. In Babylonian legal transactions they were represented by their bailiffs or agents, mostly Babylonians. When the upheavals of 425/4 eliminated some courtiers and promoted others, the control of some smallholders' organizations and administrative estates was transferred from prominent supporters of the losing factions to prominent allies of the successful contender for the throne. The proprietorship of large estates and the control of administrative establishments were, if not matters of

[47] The word may occur as a common noun, without the late Achaemenid administrative connotations, as early as 544 B.C. (YOS 19 125 *ap*. Beaulieu 1988 (F 77) 38 (4/XII/11 Nabonidus)), and as a place name in the reign of Xerxes (OECT 10 184 (Hursagkalama, 4/VI/19 Xerxes), cf. Dar. 477 (19/—/18 Darius II(?)). The institution may also be older than the attested appearances of the word; see *CAH* IV² 128 n. 123 and Van Driel 1989 (F 200) 207.

[48] Stolper 1988 (F 179) 131 with references; also CT 44 82 (Babylon, 27/V/36 Artaxerxes), see Van Driel 1989 (F 200) 210. At Nippur, the men who oversaw townsmen's 'bow lands' and collected rents on them even held the same titles as the superintendents of *ḫaṭru*s (Babylonian *šaknu*); Stolper 1988 (F 179) 131–8, against Zadok 1978 (F 214) 275, Oppenheim 1985 (F 156) 569 n. 2 and others who treat the holders of this and kindred titles as city-governors.

immediate political importance to the royal court, at least among the prerogatives of political success.

While the Great Kings parcelled out some of Babylonia's real wealth and production in this way, they reserved other resources for themselves. Some texts refer explicitly to crown lands. More importantly, the crown controlled the major elements of the irrigation network, the limiting resource of all Babylonian agriculture. These properties produced crown income from the direct use or lease of land and perhaps also from the sale or lease of water-rights. Their local overseers were the crown's agents or contractors.[49]

The role of other forms of tenure in the late Achaemenid regime is less plain. Some texts mention temple lands, occasionally supervised by crown agents rather than by temple personnel. Some mention holdings called, literally, 'hand property', smallholdings assigned by the crown or by temple agencies, but without clearly documented fiscal or military encumbrances.[50] Some mention 'royal grants' of agricultural property or urban real estate, again without indication of encumbrances.[51] Still others mention land supervised by bailiffs acting for proprietors of unspecified social or political status; at least some of these proprietors were surely members of a provincial landed gentry that included both Babylonians and Iranians. Records of real-estate sales and references to them are scarce, and very few of them deal with agricultural properties, but the exceptions demonstrate the continued existence of outright private property, without restrictions on alienation, though they do not clarify the importance of such tenure in local or provincial economies.[52]

The direct exploitation of land rarely needed formal documentation. It is chiefly because proprietors sometimes leased or pawned their holdings to commercial contractors that elements of late Achaemenid tenure appear in the textual record. Some of these contractors operated on a large scale, and the best documented of them is the Murashû firm,

---

[49] The characteristic title of the lower rank of agents who controlled canals and crown lands in the Nippur region, Babylonian *ša muḫḫi sūti ša nār* NN, literally '[man] in charge of revenues [or: rents] from such-and-such a canal', is formally similar to the titles of the individuals who controlled temple *latifundia* in sixth-century Uruk and Sippar, and the latter were commercial contractors who paid annual rents to the temple administration and/or to the crown. Overseers of canals and crown properties may have stood in a similar relationship to the crown (cf. Van Driel 1987 (F 197) 173 and 1989 (F 200) 215), but no leases issued to them are extant.

[50] Ries 1976 (F 165) 38f; Joannès 1982 (F 116) 11ff.

[51] Eilers 1940 (F 18) 107, FuB 14 29 No. 21, OECT 10 192, Kelsey 89490, YBC 11586; see Stolper 1992 (F 187).

[52] E.g. Durand *Textes babyloniens* pl. 41f. AO 17612; UET 4 18; *ZKM* 4 pl. after 258, F. Cf. Oelsner 1974 (F 148) 1055f and 1987 (F 155) 122f, Stolper 1992 (F 187) 126. A text from Ur confirms that single individuals might hold both crown grants and private lands, since it includes a clause in which one party renounces any claim to the other parties' land held from the king and any property held independently of the king (UET 4 194, 5/X/39 Artaxerxes I or II).

active at Nippur in the last half of the fifth century. Members of the firm held extensive properties outright, but most of their records deal with operations of lease and credit. They rented land from smallholders and estate owners. They rented land, water-rights, and sometimes equipment and farm-hands from crown agents. They subleased these items to their own tenants, also supplying draft animals and seed. They paid rents to their landlords and they paid the taxes due from rented smallholdings. Furthermore, they supplied short-term credit to smallholders, with the use of the holdings commonly pledged to secure the debt. When debtors defaulted, more land came under the firm's control without additional costs to the firm in rents. Most of the firm's income was in the form of crops; most of its outlays were in silver. The firm therefore had some means of converting crops into cash, perhaps selling produce to the urban population, but the process is not documented.

The Murashû firm's operations made adjustments between the juridical pattern of tenure and the actual pattern of land use. They permitted some beneficiaries of crown grants to convert their holdings into sources of cash rents. They assured the regular payment of taxes, again in cash, even when the smallholders from whom the taxes were due were impoverished or indebted. And since the Murashûs could combine smaller parcels of land into larger ones without regard for juridical status and could supply them with water-rights and equipment that were difficult for small farmers to obtain otherwise, they rationalized and perhaps intensified local production.

By fostering production and facilitating extraction, the Murashûs enriched the Achaemenid government. Nevertheless, such general benefits were obtained at specific costs. Some texts deal with distrained debtors held in the Murashûs' workhouses.[53] One records litigation over the predatory, even lawless behaviour of the firm's representatives.[54] Above all, the many texts that record loans to smallholders actually reflect defaults; the smallholders were reduced to long-term indebtedness.[55] These defaults are an indication that the economic conditions under which the firm prospered kept many smallholders in precarious circumstances. If Mesopotamia experienced overall growth under the Achaemenids, the Murashû archive suggests that the results were not enjoyed equally even among direct beneficiaries of the Achaemenid government. As the firm acquired effective control over pledged smallholdings, its operations, however useful they were for the production of crops and taxes, became oppressive to the lowest order of the

[53] See Cardascia 1951 (F 83) 161–5.   [54] BE 10 9; see Cardascia 1951 (F 83) 183.

[55] Otherwise Van Driel 1987 (F 197) 175 (suggesting that many of the unpaid notes are the product of a conjectured remission of debts at the beginning of the reign of Darius II) and 1989 (F 200) 223f (suggesting that the notes are merely stale documents recording bad debts).

government's beneficiaries. Despite this contradiction, the Achaemenid government not only tolerated the firm's operations for more than thirty years, but actually fostered them, as princes and state agencies extended their patronage to the firm.

The Murashû archive may reflect some circumstances untypical of Babylonia at large, but it is clear that other firms of commercial contractors were active in Babylonia. A Murashû text (BE 9 28) refers to another such contractor in the Nippur region; the Tattannu archive documents large-scale commercial contracting of date cultivation in the vicinity of Borsippa during the reigns of Xerxes and Artaxerxes I and probably later; and the remains of a private archive from Hursagkalama, also from the reigns of Xerxes and Artaxerxes I, include texts that reflect the leasing and subleasing of property belonging to Iranian estate-holders and of temple property controlled by an individual with an Iranian name.[56] The Kasr archive includes transactions from the region around Babylon, Borsippa and Cutha, similar in kind to the Murashû firm's operations and roughly contemporary with them.

Members of leading business families sometimes travelled to the imperial residences (one of the Murashûs to Susa and one of the Tattannus to Ecbatana, both in the reign of Darius II,[57] as members of the Egibi firm had travelled to the vicinity of Persepolis in the 520s (*CAH* IV² 117)), but if political connexions or occasions lay behind these trips they are not expressed. The Kasr archive, however, is suggestive about the relationship between such businesses and the provincial government. During the Neo-Babylonian and Persian periods, the Kasr mound at Babylon had become a sort of acropolis where residential palaces and centres of government were located, and the Kasr archive is so named because it was stored there. The link between the archive and the provincial government was one of the principals in the business that produced the archive, the governor Bēlshunu (Belesys, see above, pp. 238f). Bēlshunu may have used his political status to develop the business of lease and credit recorded in the Kasr texts, but it is also possible that the business antedated his political career, that the Achaemenid rulers recruited a local entrepreneur into the upper ranks of their political administration, and that the commercial house that supported Bēlshunu thus became a functional counterpart of the Babylonian domains that supported influential aristocrats.

The status of the Babylonian temples in the late Achaemenid provincial regime is uncertain. Published legal and administrative texts from the great temple archives of Uruk and Sippar come to an end in the reigns of Darius I and Xerxes I, respectively, and no inscriptions recording late

[56] OECT 10 191 and 192; for other texts from the same archive see Joannès 1988 (F 118) 360.
[57] Stolper 1990 (F 185) and 1992 (F 186).

Achaemenid temple construction or endowments are extant. Nevertheless, late Achaemenid textual evidence on the property and personnel of Babylonian temples is ubiquitous and diverse, not only in the records of the temples themselves, but in private legal documents.[58] The disjointed information produces no orderly image of any late Achaemenid Babylonian temple. It does, however, demonstrate what the more abundant information on the temples of Seleucid and Arsacid Uruk and Babylon leads one to suppose: that established temples continued to exist throughout Babylonia under the later Achaemenids, not only as cult centres, but also as social units with dependent populations and extensive administrative staffs, and as economic units with widespread real property, diverse sources of income, and facilities for accumulating and redistributing their wealth.

The temples had long been inviting targets for royal intervention, and there was no reason for the later Achaemenids to abandon the control that their predecessors had exerted. A few documents indicate some of the means of control. In texts from the Murashû archive, the leasing of property called 'land of the god Bēl' was overseen by the same set of functionaries who handled crown lands and crown-controlled waterways, reflecting direct government claims on temple holdings.[59] Other Murashû texts record rents paid for land of oblates of the god Bēl to a supervisor of the oblates who was comparable in title and function to the supervisors of *ḫaṭru*s (PBS 2/1 94 and 211, TuM 2–3 182). Texts from Ur (UET 4 41, 42, 53) refer to land characterized simultaneously as property of the god Sin and as 'bow land', and others (UET 4 48 and 49) mention taxes due from oblates, using the Iranian loan-word (Babylonian *bāru* from Iranian *bāra-*) that elsewhere labels taxes due from the holders of 'bow lands'. A text of uncertain provenance (BM 13249) refers explicitly to 'bow lands' held by oblates of the god Bēl. This modest information suggests that the Achaemenid government incorporated some temples into a general system of government-regulated tenure, treating them as functional counterparts of the administrative estates that supported permanent state offices, allotting to temple dependants holdings of the same kinds, with the same encumbrances, as those that supported the dependants of other estates.[60] There is no evidence, however, that a significant measure of control over the temples was awarded to figures of high political rank, like those to whom other domains were granted.

The elements in this regime were not new to Mesopotamia. The assignment of income-producing allotments, the distribution of administrative prerogatives to members of a ruling elite, state intervention in

---

[58] Stolper 1989 (F 181) 295–6 with references.   [59] See Stolper 1985 (F 177) 42f.
[60] Joannès 1982 (F 116) 25 and 45 observes evidence of this process as early as the reign of Darius I. See Stolper 1988 (F 179) 139f.

temple administration, and commercial manipulations of state-controlled property were all venerable in Mesopotamian states and were constitutive features of Neo-Babylonian society and economy.[61] The nature of the regime in late Achaemenid texts, however, does not reflect the concerns of a Mesopotamian state, but those of the continental empire to which Mesopotamia was now subject.

The smallholdings supported a military reserve. Indeed, to judge by the terms for the allotments, this may once have been the primary rationale of such grants. They were also a means of placing new settlers in Babylonia, and of maintaining, monitoring and extending cultivation. Above all, they were a means of extraction: they supported labour for state agencies and for state-assigned manors, and they returned a large part of their production in taxes. A text from Nippur (Durand *Textes babyloniens* pl. 50 AO 17637) appears to list the annual taxes paid by some constituents of a single *ḫaṭru*; the total is thirty-three minas of silver. If this amount is typical, the sixty-odd known *ḫaṭru*s of the Nippur region alone paid more than 30 Babylonian talents of silver in taxes each year.

The manorial organization superimposed on the smallholdings was a distributive device. It conferred real wealth on the king's friends, it was a means of assigning the control of some locally important administrative units (such as the royal 'treasury', and the 'equerry's estate' mentioned in the Murashû texts), and it was a means of transferring some crown income – that is, the taxes and labour of smallholders – directly to members of the ruling classes without centralized redistributive agencies. It did not merely create a provincial landed gentry, but, as the Murashû texts show, it also supported members of an imperial aristocracy close to the politics of the Achaemenid court. It conferred on them wealth and administrative responsibility, and consequently some effective political power in the province.

This distribution of power must have put restraints on provincial governors. It is common to view Achaemenid satraps as virtual sovereigns in their territories, granted a high degree of political autonomy in order to ensure the internal coherence of the provinces. Nevertheless, when significant local resources were controlled by individuals like Parysatis, Artoxares, Arsames and princes of the royal house, the governor of Babylonia must have required political negotiation and competition, both in the province and at the imperial court, to maintain his control. Hence, the distribution of manors was not only a way of rewarding the king's friends but also of checking his potential rivals. (Xen. *Cyr.* VIII.6.5–20, imputes similar policies to Cyrus the Great.)

Babylonian legal texts, however, give little explicit information on

[61] Van Driel 1989 (F 200).

satrapal government, or even on the names and titles of the governors. Murashû texts from the reign of Artaxerxes I mention Artarēme, giving him no title but naming him as the father of Manushtānu, the latter entitled 'prince' (*mār bīti*, a Babylonian loan-translation from an Iranian word). This can only be Artarius, according to Ctesias (*FGrH* 688 F 14.41) the brother of Artaxerxes, the father of Menostanes, and the governor of Babylonia.[62] Murashû texts from the reign of Darius II mention Gubāru, entitled 'governor of Babylon' or 'governor of the land of Akkad',[63] possibly the Gobryas who was one of Artaxerxes II's commanders at the battle of Cunaxa (Xen. *An.* 1.7.12). No extant Babylonian texts mention the other late Achaemenid governors Herodotus names (Zopyrus III.159; Megapanos VII.62; Tritantaichmes, 1.192) – or late Achaemenid successors of the Iranian 'treasurers' attested at Babylon in earlier reigns.[64]

Moreover, the usual Babylonian terms for 'governor', like their Iranian counterpart 'satrap', may denote not only the provincial governor, but also a district subgovernor.[65] This was the case with Bēlshunu (Belesys), who held the titles 'governor of Babylon' before and during the time when Gubāru (Gobryas) was governor of Babylonia,[66] and may have been entitled 'satrap' still earlier.[67] There are a few other references to such subgovernors, also with Babylonian names.[68] The satrapal government appears, therefore, to have echoed some of the organization of aristocratic estates: as in other satrapies, the provincial governors were normally Iranians of high social rank; they delegated the routine conduct of local affairs to district officials recruited within the province.

---

[62] The earliest mention of Artarēme is BE 9 39, dated 26/VII/34 Artaxerxes I; the latest, naming a Babylonian subordinate entitled 'law-officer' (*dātabara*), PBS 2/1 185, dated 2/VII/1 Darius II, may be posthumous.
[63] The two titles were synonymous and no political significance should be imputed to the variation between them (see Stolper 1987 (F 178) 397 n. 38, against, e.g. Schwenzner 1923 (F 58) 247; Oppenheim 1985 (F 156) 564).   [64] Dandamayev 1968 (F 15).
[65] Babylonian *pīhatu*, *pāhatu* and cognate titles: see Stolper 1989 (F 181) 290f. The synonym *muma'iru* does not appear in legal texts, but its use under the Achaemenids is implicit in the mention of *muma'irūtu*, 'governorship, satrapy', beside Babylonian administrative titles (*mašennu*, *rab ummu*) in an astronomical diary from the reign of Artaxerxes II (Sachs and Hunger 1988 (F 172) No. –366 A ii 8).
[66] Earliest: YBC 11550, —/—/2 or 3 Darius II; latest; FuB 14 11 No. 1, 12/I/9 Darius II; both from the Kasr archive.
[67] McEwan LB Tablets 48, from Nippur, 18/X/35 Artaxerxes I (?); for the date see Stolper 1987 (F 178) 399 n. 47, 1988 (F 179) 150–1, 1989 (F 181) 291 n. r despite Zadok 1984 (F 217) 73f, 1986 (F 217A) 285f, and *CAH* IV² 154.
[68] A Kasr text (YBC 11554, —/XII/2 Artaxerxes II [?]) mentions Erība, entitled 'governor of Babylon'. A Murashû text (PBS 2/1 2, 11/—/accession year Darius II) mentions Ṣīhā', entitled 'satrap'. A text from Shaṭir (Durand, *Textes babyloniens* pl. 43 AO 17611, 1/IX/42 Artaxerxes II) mentions a field belonging to an unnamed 'governor', (*šakin ṭēmi*) and a text from the Murashû archive (PBS 2/1 198) mentions an 'estate of the governor' (*šakin māti*). The last two titles may be anachronisms embedded in place names.

To judge by the case of Bēlshunu, some district officials, like the supervisors of some estates and *ḫaṭru*s, might weather political disturbances more easily than their aristocratic superiors.

Yet the actual conduct of satrapal government is not well documented. Bēlshunu was involved in the adjudication of a dispute over missing temple property (see n. 37). His superior Gobryas may have supervised the crown agents who managed the use of canals and crown lands.[69] A Murashû text (PBS 2/1 21) refers vaguely to the possibility of legal action brought before 'the king, the satrap, or a judge'. Otherwise, the legal texts mention judges, law-officers, investigators, messengers and other judicial and administrative functionaries. They have both Iranian and Babylonian names, both Iranian and Babylonian titles. Some held grants of land. A few are explicitly called subordinates of the governors, and others surely belonged to bureaus of the satrapal regime. But they appear chiefly in passive roles, as witnesses to legal transactions, and the texts do not clarify the organization of government services.

This information on tenure and control does not corroborate Xenophon's schematic description of a satrapal regime (*Oec.* IV.4–11) in any detail, but it does suggest, as Xenophon does, a decentralized regime. At the apex of both provincial government and manorial tenure, imperial aristocrats tied the province closely to the Achaemenid court. At a lower level, indigenous functionaries helped to insulate provincial arrangements – and, above all, the province's ability to produce revenue – from the occasional political shocks that originated in imperial politics.

IV. BABYLONIAN SOCIETY AND CULTURE UNDER ACHAEMENID INFLUENCE

The Assyrian and Babylonian empires had brought foreign populations into Mesopotamia by immigration and deportation, and by recruiting defeated soldiers into imperial forces. The Achaemenid empire extended the areas on which these processes drew and late Achaemenid Babylonian texts are rich in evidence of foreign presence. They sometimes give individuals ethnic labels (Persian, Median, Magian, Egyptian), and sometimes mention settlements named with ethnic terms (e.g. Village of Carians)[70] or named for distant towns (e.g. Gaza, Ashkelon).[71] Some *ḫaṭru* organizations have foreign ethnic or local names (e.g. Lydians, Urartians, Melitenians, Carians, Cimmerians, Tyrians, Indians); most such groups probably began as foreign military units resettled in Babylonia. Above all, the texts abound with personal names of Iranian,

---

[69] Stolper 1985 (F 177) 48f.
[70] See *CAH* IV² 133; also OECT 10 404 (Cambyses); OECT 10 406 (Nebuchadnezzar IV).
[71] Zadok 1978 (F 213) 61.

West Semitic, Anatolian, Egyptian or other non-Babylonian origin. Such names appear throughout the Achaemenid period, but the evidence rarely fixes the date of arrival of individual groups with any precision. The growing frequency of foreign names despite signs of acculturation suggests continuous movements into Babylonia.

Names of foreign origin, though they should indicate that the individuals who bore them had some present or past connexion with immigrant groups, are doubtful indicators of ethnicity. It may be a sign of ethnic cohesion that some legal texts record transactions conducted among people with non-Babylonian names and witnessed by others with names of related linguistic origin, but apart from *ḫaṭru* names indications that foreigners formed identifiable, self-regulating ethnic enclaves are scarce.[72] Babylonian legal texts record specifically Babylonian behaviour, and individuals with foreign names appear in the same roles as individuals with Babylonian names.

The most distinctive of the foreign elements are Iranians, a small but growing minority of the Babylonian population in late Achaemenid reigns.[73] Some are named as the occupants of 'bow lands' (particularly in the Murashû texts). Many are named as landholders represented by bailiffs or stewards, the latter usually with Babylonian names. Some of these landholders and many other individuals with Iranian names were administrative or judicial officers, bearing titles of both Iranian and Babylonian origin. Occasionally, men with Iranian names appear as agents of commercial firms,[74] or as outright chattel slaves, bought and sold by Babylonians (Patiridata, McEwan LB Tablets 35). That is, by late Achaemenid times Iranians (or at least individuals with Iranian names) were to be found at almost all identifiable levels of Babylonian society. The staffs and dependants of Babylonian temples, among whom Iranian names are as yet unattested, are the only apparent exception.[75]

Iranians did not, however, monopolize any role within those areas of Babylonian society and government that are discernible in legal texts. Individuals with Babylonian names also appear as smallholders and estate owners. Among the bearers of the Iranian administrative title or honorific *ustarbaru* (of uncertain significance), men with Iranian and non-Iranian names occur in roughly equal numbers.[76] Bearers of the

---

[72] Eph'al 1978 (F 99) 76–83; cf. a possible reference to 'free citizens of Caria(?)' in VAT 16043 (cited in Eilers 1940 (F 373) 189 n. 1), and the remarks of Zadok 1984 (F 217) 67. The bond among people with Egyptian names and patronyms whose transactions with each other are recorded in a group of Babylonian texts from late Achaemenid Susa is perhaps not identification with an ethnic enclave but a common subordination to the service or household of a single official; see Joannès 1990 (F 122) 178.   [73] See Zadok 1977 (F 211) with additions in 1981–2 (F 216) 139.

[74] In the Murashû firm, Tirakam, son of Bagapanu; see Cardascia 1951 (F 83) 12.

[75] But in OECT 10 191 (Hursagkalama, 14/I/4 Artaxerxes I) land held by an individual with an Iranian name, Baḥameri, is called property of the Babylonian god Zababa, one of the principal gods of Kish.   [76] Eilers 1940 (F 18) 83–9.

Babylonian title 'judge' include men with Iranian names, but more with Babylonian names.[77] Individuals with the Iranian title *dātabara*, roughly 'law-officer', have both Iranian and Babylonian names.[78] Iranians certainly constituted the empire's ruling aristocracy, and in Mesopotamia as elsewhere they dominated the uppermost political posts, but, being a small minority in a region with well-established juridical and administrative practices, they shared lower juridical and administrative posts with Babylonians, and some of them were simply part of the subject population of the province. Like other foreign populations in Babylonia, Iranians – at least those of modest economic status – were prone to acculturation; hence, many individuals with Iranian patronyms or ethnic labels had non-Iranian given names. Acculturation was far less pronounced among Iranians of high status in Anatolia, and the same was probably true of Iranian members of the political elite in Babylonia.

The other conspicuous 'foreign' populations in late Achaemenid Babylonia were West Semites, including small numbers of Arabs (identified not only by personal names, but also by place-names and a *ḫaṭru*-name), Phoenicians, and Jews (identifiable only by their personal names), and large numbers of Arameans.[79]

The Aramaicizing of Mesopotamia had already been under way for centuries; the Achaemenid conquests had accelerated the process, spreading the use of Aramaic as a language of recording and administration. Marks of this continuing process are abundant in late Achaemenid Babylonian texts. There are frequent references to functionaries called *sepīru*, itself an Aramaic loan-word, properly indicating a scribe competent in both Aramaic and cuneiform recording, and commonly used to indicate literate administrative or commercial agents, but not applied to the scribes who drafted cuneiform tablets. Aramaic 'dockets' – short texts inked or incised on cuneiform tablets to identify or summarize their contents – are increasingly frequent on tablets of the fifth century.[80] Cuneiform texts occasionally refer to documents written on leather or parchment; these were certainly in Aramaic, and some of the lacunae in our documentation may result from the partial replacement of cuneiform recording on clay tablets with Aramaic recording on perishable materials. Nevertheless, most allusions to leather documents do not refer to legal records of the kinds represented by surviving

---

[77] Cardascia 1951 (F 83) 20f; Eilers 1940 (F 18) 108; McEwan LB Tablets 35; BM 54091 (see Stolper 1991 (F 184)).

[78] BM 30136, cited in Zadok 1977 (F 212) 107; *ZA* 5 279:19 (collated by M. A. Dandamayev); BE 9 82–84, PBS 2/1 1, 34, 185 (all referring to the same person); Stolper 1985 (F 177) Nos. 55 and 110.

[79] Coogan 1976 (F 91); Zadok 1976 (F 210), 1977 (F 212), 1981 (F 215) 69–79; Bickerman 1978 (F 362); and others.

[80] Clay 1908 (F 88); Vattioni 1970 (F 202); Jakob-Rost and Freydank 1972 (F 115); Oelsner 1987 (F 154) 40f.

cuneiform texts, but to administrative orders authorizing agents to make collections or take legal actions. Government administrative recording may have relied more heavily on perishable Aramaic records, but such documents probably formed only a small component of private Babylonian archives.

Neither late Achaemenid Babylonian texts nor the earlier administrative records from Persepolis use 'Aramean' as an ethnic label. Classical mentions of 'Assyrian characters' almost certainly refer to Aramaic, and Elamite texts from Persepolis explicitly designate as Babylonians the scribes writing on leather, presumably in Aramaic.[81] Hence, even though it is unlikely that Babylonian survived as a widely spoken language, the use of Aramaic script and language was not a marker of ethnicity but a trait of Mesopotamian behaviour. Judged by the uncertain standard of personal names, people of West Semitic extraction were always a minority in late Achaemenid Babylonia. Judged by the same standard, the majority population was Babylonian, regardless of its spoken language.

This population maintained the cuneiform writing of Mesopotamian languages both in utilitarian and in scholarly applications. Competence in cuneiform recording was not restricted to professional scribes, for late Achaemenid texts were sometimes drafted by parties to the transactions they record.[82] The continuity of scholarship is documented in archives from Borsippa, Nippur and Uruk that include manuscripts dated in late Achaemenid reigns. They are exemplars of texts from the main stream of Mesopotamian scholarly tradition: lexical texts, diagnostic omens, commentaries, hymns and rituals.[83] They prefigure the more extensive scholarly collections from Seleucid Babylonia.

Similarly, the flowering of Babylonian astronomy manifest in the astronomical texts from Seleucid and Arsacid reigns relied on developments in late Achaemenid reigns. In the larger and earlier of the two major archives of late Babylonian astronomical texts, from Babylon itself, texts increase steadily in number from the middle of the fifth century B.C. to a peak in the second century B.C.[84] In particular, although the earliest extant datable astronomical diary is from 652 B.C., diaries begin to occur in significant numbers only from the beginning of the fourth century, recording observations of astronomical and meteorological phenomena and monthly summaries of the silver prices of commodities (including records of significant intra-monthly price fluc-

---

81 Hallock 1973 (F 28) 322; Stolper 1984 (F 176) 305.

82 E.g. TuM 2–3 63 (Nippur, Xerxes; promissory note with debtor as scribe); VAS 3 189 (Borsippa, Artaxerxes); Moore Michigan Coll. 50 (Borsippa, Darius II; receipt with recipient as scribe); see Joannès 1982 (F 116) 80.

83 Hunger 1968 (F 113) Nos. 112, 119, 120f, 123–33; Joannès 1982 (F 116) 6f; Oelsner 1982 (F 151) and 1983 (F 152) 249.   84 Sachs 1948 (F 168) 271f; Neugebauer 1967 (F 145) 965 with fig. 1.

tuations), river levels, and occasional political or religious events.[85] The nineteen-year intercalation cycle – that is the Metonic cycle that persisted in Islamic and western medieval astronomy – was fixed in Babylonian calendaric notation during the first third of the fourth century, having been apparently known and followed with rare deviations since 498 B.C.[86] It is imprecise to assert that the zodiac was invented in fifth-century Babylonia, since the names of the zodiacal constellations had become traditional at least as early as the seventh century, but the division of the ecliptic into twelve houses of thirty degrees each is first attested in Babylonian texts from the second quarter of the fifth century.[87] This innovation was one of the preconditions of horoscopic astrology, and the earliest Babylonian horoscopes appear at the end of the fifth century.[88] Astronomical advances are perhaps the most important cultural contribution of late Achaemenid Babylonia, not only because they endured for so long among the foundations of science, but also because they were so widely spread among the societies of the time. Elements of Babylonian mathematical astronomy (as well as of traditional Babylonian divination) appeared in Greece, Egypt and India in the fifth and fourth centuries, transmitted by the long-range cultural exchanges that the Achaemenid empire brought into effect.[89]

The maturing of Achaemenid imperial rule left a literal imprint on Babylonian documents in the form of changes in glyptic style. While seal impressions with traditional Neo-Babylonian motifs and style persist on tablets from late Achaemenid reigns, impressions with Iranian motifs and style become common only in and after the reign of Darius I,[90] and impressions with Greek motifs and style appear sporadically on tablets from later Achaemenid reigns.[91] These gradual changes in frequency reflect increasing access to foreign craftsmen or foreign artistic models, but they must also reflect the penetration into everyday behaviour of tastes encouraged by imperial authority.

The very use of seals reflects gradual changes in legal behaviour. In late Achaemenid reigns, more seals were applied to legal texts of more diverse formal types than in earlier reigns, and the application of many witnesses' seals to individual legal tablets became prevalent.[92] These may have been internal Babylonian developments, but there are other

[85] Sachs 1974 (F 170) 44–8; Sachs and Hunger 1988 (F 172).
[86] Neugebauer 1975 (H 87) 355.
[87] Aaboe and Sachs 1969 (F 72) 12 Text B (475–457 B.C.); see Neugebauer 1975 (H 87) 593.
[88] *JCS* 6 54 and Durand *Textes babyloniens* pl. 52 AO 17649 (see Rochberg-Halton 1989 (F 167) 111–14), both 410 B.C.   [89] Pingree 1982 (F 163) 617–19.   [90] Zettler 1979 (F 218).
[91] E.g. TuM 2–3 pl. 98 No. XXVII and pl. 99 No. LV, Legrain 1925 (F 133) Nos. 971 and 972 (all from the Murashû archive); Moore Michigan Coll. 43; *FuB* 14 14 No. 4, 17 No. 7, OECT 10 140 (all from the Kasr archive); McEwan 1982 LB Tablets 35; CBS 1594; FLP 1716; HSM 8414.
[92] Oelsner 1978 (F 150).

suggestions of new legal conditions imposed by the Achaemenids. Occasional mentions of royal registries of property ownership (including chattels as well as real estate), clauses in some slave-sales requiring registration of the document of sale, and clauses in others that mention the transfer of the slaves 'in the royal revenue office' are the traces of Achaemenid taxes and institutions that anticipated the taxes on slave-sales extracted by Seleucid rulers and the *chreophylakion* where sales were registered.[93] A Muraṣhû text stipulates flogging and the plucking out of the hair and beard as a penalty for default.[94] Such a corporal penalty is not a Babylonian commonplace but a sharp departure from the fines or distraints usual in such texts. The passage is both a suggestion of new practices and a tantalizing evocation (scarcely a corroboration) of Plutarch's claim that Artaxerxes I exempted members of the ruling classes from just such punishments (*Mor.* 173D, cf. *Mor.* 565A and Amm. Marc. xxx.8.4).

The most conspicuous marks of Achaemenid influence on Babylonian institutional behaviour are the Iranian loan-words that appear in Babylonian texts from the outset of Achaemenid rule and increase in number from the late reign of Darius I on. Almost all are special to the language of legal and administrative practice: titles of officials, honorifics, names of administrative institutions or records. They reflect real innovations, since one may assume that the rich idiom of Babylonian legal recording adopted these terms only when no precise Babylonian equivalent existed. Etymologies provide approximate ranges of meaning for most of them (yielding generic translations like 'accountant', 'investigator', 'storehouse', 'registry' and so on). But most of them were never common; most label offices or practices that impinged on Babylonian business life without being a regular feature of it; hence, the real functional relationships that most connoted are uncertain. Surprisingly few survived in Seleucid Babylonian texts.[95]

Little can be said of changes in Babylonian religion under Achaemenid influence. There is no cuneiform corroboration of Berossus' statement (*FGrH* 680 F 11) that Artaxerxes II introduced a statue cult of Anahita in Babylon and in other imperial centres, nor would such corroboration be expected if the cult was meant exclusively for resident Iranian communities. The prominence of the Anu-cult in Seleucid Uruk had its beginnings in the late Achaemenid period, as the personal names that contain the divine name Anu in the late Achaemenid documents from Uruk imply.[96]

---

93 Stolper 1977 (F 175) 259ff, see *CAH* iv² 132; Stolper 1989 (F 180).
94 Stolper 1985 (F 177) No. 91 (28/—/5 Darius II).
95 Eilers 1940 (B 18); Hinz 1975 (F 35); Zadok 1976 (F 209) 213–18; McEwan 1981 (F 137) 185.
96 See Stolper 1990 (F 182) 561 and *passim*.

The evidence for gauging the overall economic standards of late Achaemenid Babylonian society is inadequate. The terms of leases from Nippur suggest normal expectations of crop yields that were good to very good in comparison to those of large-scale farming in the sixth century.[97] Farm labour was probably in short supply throughout the Achaemenid period, and leases in the Murashû archive indicate a local situation in which the rental value of land was relatively low and the costs of draft animals, water and other inputs relatively high, a situation generally unfavourable for small proprietors with limited access to capital. Occasional prices scattered among texts from other sources are in general agreement. The sale prices of slaves fell in ranges that were higher than in the Neo-Babylonian period but not much different from the range in the reign of Darius I.[98] Commodity prices indicated in astronomical diaries were subject to sharp fluctuations, but the ranges within which they varied seem to have abated slightly from the peaks of the early fifth century.[99] There is no serious evidence of sharp increases in interest rates, disruption of markets, or shortages of cash, and none to support the commonplace judgment that the period was one of economic stagnation and decay. The evidence is generally consonant with conditions of overall growth, which were accompanied by fairly high levels of taxation, and which were unfavourable for small-scale proprietors subject to juridical restraints. Secure evaluation of the information, however, is impeded by the almost complete lack of evidence on investment, wage and ration levels, the conduct of trade and manufacture, and the basic means of livelihood of any segments of the population except those with a direct interest in the exploitation of real estate.

Babylon itself was an imperial metropolis of growing importance under the later Achaemenids. Herodotus' and Ctesias' descriptions of the city include preposterous characterizations of oriental society, but accurate physical depiction, and they represent Babylon as rich and populous. A Babylonian chronicle mentions a royal palace at Babylon under Artaxerxes (see above, p. 239), and the palaces built by the Neo-Babylonian rulers were maintained by the Achaemenids and still occupied by Alexander. At some point in the Achaemenid period, a light enclosure wall was thrown around the Kasr mound, segregating the palaces, the celebrated Ishtar gate, and the processional way from the city at large. A small, elegant palace was added on the Kasr, with a columned portico and columned hall, coloured pavements, and glazed brick wall decoration. It was the work of Artaxerxes II, whose fragmentary Elamite inscription is found on pieces of black stone that belonged to the

[97] Van Driel 1989 (F 200) 216, 222, and 1990 (F 201) 241–9 expounds the grave uncertainties in this evidence and its interpretation. [98] See Stolper 1991 (F 184) 57.
[99] Oelsner 1974 (F 148) 1052f.

plinth of a column from the building; other fragments from inscriptions of Artaxerxes II were found elsewhere on the site.[100]

Imperial crises enhanced the city's importance. It was probably from Babylon that Darius II Ochus launched his successful attempt to take the imperial throne in 425/4 B.C.; Babylon was the target of Cyrus the Younger's unsuccessful attempt in 401; and in the narratives of Arrian and Quintus Curtius Babylon overshadows Susa as the principal royal residence, the command centre, and the staging area for organized Achaemenid resistance to the Macedonian invasion. When Babylon was lost, Iranian resistance stiffened, but the Near Eastern empire of the Achaemenids ceased to exist.

[100] See *CAH* iv² 115 n. 16, with references, and cf. MDP 24 127 no. 28 (= A²Sb Elamite). Also Weissbach *ap*. Wetzel *et al*. 1957 (F 205) 49 no. 6 (a fragment of an Akkadian version of the same text) and 48 no. 1 (a fragment from the processional street on the Kasr with the name of Artaxerxes in Old Persian); see also Vallat 1989 (F 194), rebutting Haerinck 1973 (F 111).

CHAPTER 8c

JUDAH

HAYIM TADMOR

This chapter was planned independently from *CAH* III².2, ch. 31, to which the reader may also refer for the period of the Restoration. It is, however, intended to be complementary to *CAH* IV² ch. 3*b*. That chapter looked at Judah as a part of the Achaemenid empire; here we try to consider its internal development during the period.

The Old Testament books which are relevant are inevitably controversial.[1] It is here assumed (see below, p. 292) that the book of Ezra-Nehemiah was put together, long after the time of the events, from the 'building blocks' which included much contemporary documentary material, including a first-person narrative by Nehemiah himself; how much Ezra had to do with his own narrative is more doubtful. The compiler did not aim at a chronological composition, and he tends to build his narrative round the major personalities; gaps and a certain amount of confusion result. We do not believe that this compiler was the same as the author of the Book of Chronicles (below, p. 293), although that used to be the dominant view.

There is little other literary material to help us. Josephus' survey of the period in the *Jewish Antiquities* is largely dependent on the edited version of the book of Ezra-Nehemiah in some form or another, and most of his variations are in general likely to arise from his attempts to resolve contradictions than from independent information. Much more help comes from contemporary material, the Elephantine papyri,[2] the Samaria papyri from Wadi Daliyeh,[3] ostraca, coins, seals and other remains of material culture.[4]

---

[1] Biblical references are primarily to the Hebrew text; references to the Authorized Version are added in brackets where necessary.

[2] Cowley 1923 (F 427); Porten 1968 (F 504); Grelot 1972 (F 443). The texts are being re-edited in Porten and Yardeni, 1986– (F 505).   [3] Cross 1969 (F 370); 1985 (F 371A); 1988 (F 371B).

[4] A major collection of the material by Stern 1982 (F 397), summarized in Stern 1984 (F 398).

I. THE RETURN

1. *The Edict of Cyrus*

Shortly after Cyrus conquered Babylon in 539, he issued an edict to the exiles of Judah in Babylon, permitting them to rebuild the Temple in Jerusalem. The context of this in his religious policy has been discussed elsewhere.[5] The original version, probably in Aramaic, has not survived. However, a brief Hebrew version, recast in the wording of a later editor, is preserved in Ezra 1:2–3: 'Thus saith Cyrus king of Persia, The Lord God of Heaven hath given me all the kingdoms of the earth and he hath charged me to build him an house at Jerusalem which is in Judah. Who is there among you of all his people? His God be with him, and let him go up to Jerusalem, which is in Judah and build the house of the Lord God of Israel, he is the God, which is in Jerusalem.' In structure, style and terminology, this Edict in Ezra resembles other documents of the period. According to the heading, it was issued in the first year of Cyrus' reign, that is, it would seem, in the first year of his reign as the king of Babylon (538 B.C.), perhaps in the spring, in the course of the New Year festivities. At the same time an Aramaic version, found in Ezra 6, was prepared for the use of the royal chancellery. It gives the measurements of the Temple and states expressly that the funds of rebuilding should be taken from the royal treasury (Ezra 6:3–5).

The Edict awakened substantial hopes. The very granting of permission to rebuild the Temple from the funds of the royal treasury was an incentive to return. As early as 538, the year of the proclamation, the first group of returnees was organized. The number recorded is 42,360 (Ezra 2:64), together with 7,337 men and women servants and more than 200 male and female musicians. These figures presumably constitute the total of the several waves of returnees during the reign of Cyrus and his successors, and some assume that they actually include the returnees down to the days of Ezra as well. It is plausible that the return ceased for some time during the wars waged by Cambyses in Egypt. Obviously, a considerable number of exiles decided to remain in Babylonia, despite the enthusiastic urging of Deutero-Isaiah: 'Go ye forth from Babylon, flee ye from the Chaldeans with a voice of singing . . .' (Isa. 48:20). In the course of fifty years in exile, the uprooted Judaeans had established themselves in their new country, and their economic situation was apparently quite favourable.

---

[5] See *CAH* IV² 40–1, 124.

2. *Sheshbazzar 'the prince of Judah'*

The returnees were headed by Sheshbazzar 'the prince (*nāsī*) of Judah' (Ezra 1:8), who is also referred to as 'governor' (*peḥā*) in a contemporary Aramaic document (*ibid.* 5:14). It was to Sheshbazzar that the Persians delivered the gold and silver vessels plundered from the Temple by Nebuchadnezzar. The return of these vessels and their restoration to their original sanctuary accords with Cyrus' policy as formulated in his proclamation to the Babylonians (*CAH* IV² 124), except that in that case it was the images of the gods which are said to have been restored to their temples, now rebuilt by royal decree.

It is probable that Sheshbazzar was a Davidite prince, most likely[6] to be identified with Shenazzar son of Jehoiachin (1 Chron. 3:18). However, the theory[7] that Sheshbazzar and Zerubbabel (see below) were one and the same must be rejected. Sheshbazzar is a Babylonian name (*Šamaš-aba-uṣur*, meaning '(the god) Shamash [pronounced Shashu] protect the father!'). Zerubbabel is also a Babylonian name (*Zēr-Bābili*, meaning: 'seed of Babylon'), and no person can have been known by two different Babylonian names. These Babylonian names should not surprise us. Princes from foreign lands, captured and deported by the Babylonians (or by the Assyrians before them), or taken as hostages, raised at the royal court and educated as courtiers loyal to the king, were customarily given Babylonian names as an indication of their prestigious new identity. This custom appears explicitly in the prose narrative of Dan. 1:7, which relates that the king's chief officer gave Daniel and his three companions Babylonian names. We may thus reasonably assume that Sheshbazzar was raised at the royal court of Babylon, like the rest of the family of the exiled Jehoiachin, who lived at court as part of the king's entourage (*CAH* III².2, 418–19).[8]

Sheshbazzar's title, 'prince (*nāsī*) of Judah', corresponds exactly to that employed by the prophet Ezekiel (34:24, 37:25, 45:17, 46:16 etc.) for the scion of the restored Davidic line. 'Prince of Judah' may therefore be considered as a Hebrew adaptation of Sheshbazzar's formal title 'governor' (*peḥā* – an Akkadian loan-word in Aramaic and late Hebrew). Although the title 'prince' could hint at Jewish hopes that the Davidic governor would ultimately restore the monarchy, it is certainly no proof of Cyrus' intentions. The Jews were authorized solely to rebuild the

---

[6] See e.g. Cross 1975 (F 371) 12 n. 43; Japhet 1982 (F 377) 96; the identification is denied by Berger 1971 (F 359); Williamson 1985 (F 400) 5.

[7] This seems to have been the view of Josephus, *AJ* XI.13–14, and is revived from time to time; see Williamson 1985 (F 400) 17.

[8] The fate of Jehoiachin of Judah was shared by the king of Ascalon; see *CAH* III².2, 420.

Temple at Jerusalem. Barring a few isolated exceptions, such as Tyre, Sidon and Lycia, the hierarchic structure of the Persian empire did not provide for vassal kings, but only for governors and satraps (some of whom may indeed have been representatives of local royal dynasties). Just as Cyrus was considered king of Media, Elam and Babylonia, he was also king of Judah.

II. CONSTRUCTION OF THE TEMPLE

1. *Zerubbabel son of Shealtiel*

Sheshbazzar apparently served only for a short time as governor, and was succeeded by Zerubbabel son of Shealtiel, grandson – or great-grandson – of Jehoiachin (cf. 1 Chron. 3:17–19).[9] The prophet Haggai, in an oracle (1:1) delivered in the second year of Darius, refers to Zerubbabel as 'governor (*peḥā*) of Judah'. However, this does not necessarily imply (as many scholars have concluded)[10] that Zerubbabel had taken up his post at Jerusalem only a short time before that date. Judging by the extent of his activities, as reflected in the book of Ezra, he had probably been in Judah for a considerable time. There are good grounds, therefore, to assume that Zerubbabel came to Judah with one of the first waves of returnees, possibly even in that led by Sheshbazzar. When Sheshbazzar died, Zerubbabel was appointed to succeed him.

This assumption allows sufficient time for Zerubbabel to have consolidated his position in Judah, as is implicit in the prophecies of Haggai and Zechariah. Moreover, in view of the disorder and grave political crises which shook the empire after the death of Cambyses, particularly from Darius' assumption of the throne to the end of his first year, it is extremely doubtful that there could have been any immigration from Babylon to Judah in that period. Babylonia was then in the throes of rebellion (*CAH* iv² 129–30), and the long roads through the empire were presumably quite unsafe, and not conducive to the free movement of civilians. In addition, a period of rebellions in the name of descendants of local dynasties (*CAH* iv² 57–63) was hardly an appropriate time to appoint a Davidite as governor of Judah.

Zerubbabel was not the only leader of the community of returnees; he shared the burden of leadership with Joshua son of Jehozadak the High Priest (Hag. 2:1–5; Zech. 3:1–4). Although a later chronicler of the Restoration in Ezra 1–5 made every effort to maintain a balance between the two leaders (like the balance between Ezra and Nehemiah evident in subsequent chapters of the work), attentive readers of the prophecies of

⁹ Japhet 1982–3 (F 377).   ¹⁰ E.g. Wanke in *CHJud* I (F 372) 164.

Zechariah detect marked tension, if not outright strife, between them at one point. Zechariah describes Joshua as 'clothed in filthy garments' and 'Satan standing at his right hand to accuse him' (Zech. 3:1–3). The prophet, hinting at the supremacy of Zerubbabel, expresses the hope that Joshua will be cleared of some unspecified accusation levelled against him and that ultimately 'the counsel of peace' will reign between him and Zerubbabel, who, according to Zechariah (6:13), is destined to occupy his throne, not merely by virtue of his position as Persian governor, but as an offshoot of the Davidic line.

Several statements in the oracles of Haggai and Zechariah, who witnessed the events personally, would seem to imply that it was not Sheshbazzar who laid the foundations of the Temple, as claimed by the elders of Judah in their letter to Tattenai, governor of Beyond the River (Ezra 5:16), but Zerubbabel. Zechariah says explicitly (4:9): 'The hands of Zerubbabel have laid the foundations of this house: his hands shall also finish it', while Haggai even specifies a date for the foundation of the Temple – 'the four and twentieth day of the ninth month' (Hag. 2:18), i.e. 30 December 521.

The events in question cannot be fully grasped without a careful study of the various chronological data embedded in the text of Haggai and Zechariah. It has been suggested[11] that the regnal years of Darius in the book of Ezra–Nehemiah are not reckoned according to the system current in Babylonia and in Beyond the River, by which every year began on the first of the month of Nisan, and by which what was designated Darius' first year did not start until 14 April 521. The dates are consistent only if we assume that Darius (and he alone) reckoned his regnal years from the death of Cambyses in July 522 or perhaps even from the accession of Gaumata (Smerdis) in March of that year. In other words, that he credited himself with an additional half-year, since the throne was occupied at the time by Gaumata, whom he considered a usurper. By this reckoning, then, Darius' first regnal year would have begun in spring or summer of 522 and not in spring 521, as customary in the Babylonian system of reckoning.

This earlier date for Darius' first year harmonizes particularly well with Haggai's hopeful references to Zerubbabel, who was to come when Darius was still struggling to subdue the last rebellion in Babylonia and Elam, in the winter of 521 (the second year of his reign, by this reckoning). The same is true of Zechariah's prophecy of 24 Shevat in the second year of Darius, which speaks of peace reigning in the land (1:11), obviously referring to the situation shortly after Darius had successfully quelled all unrest and consolidated his rule. By contrast, the chronology

---

[11] Bickerman 1981 (F 363) 23–8.

hitherto commonly accepted,[12] by which Darius' first regnal year did not begin until April 521, would imply that Haggai's oracles hinting at the fall of the Persian empire and Zerubbabel's restoration of the monarchy in Judah were delivered long after the suppression of the rebellions; such hopes would hardly have been reasonable under the circumstances.

This prophecy of Haggai, though not actually inciting rebellion, associated Zerubbabel with expectations which could not but raise Persian suspicions. This could have been a reason for removing Zerubbabel shortly afterwards from his official position in Judah. When Tattenai, the Persian governor of Beyond the River, came to Jerusalem (see below), it was not Zerubbabel who negotiated with him, but the elders of the Jews, an anomalous procedure under any administration. It would appear that Zerubbabel was not then in Jerusalem, and he may well have been deposed, never to complete the construction of the Temple.

2. Delays and completion

Why was the Temple not built immediately, at the very beginning of the Restoration, as sanctioned by Cyrus' Edict to the Jews? In Ezra 4, the ancient chronicler attributes this failure to interference by the 'adversaries of Judah and Benjamin', i.e. the 'people of the land' who had been denied participation in the building of the Temple (*ibid.* 4:1–3). They harassed the people of Judah and 'hired counsellors to frustrate their purpose' and impede completion of the work (*ibid.* 4–5). Though this account may contain grains of historical truth, it is more likely that the story reflects Nehemiah's struggle with the leaders of Samaria, or perhaps it even originates from a still later period, the time of the schism with the Samaritans in the fourth century (see below, pp. 288–90).

Another possible suggestion is that it was not only the people of Samaria who tried to prevent the building of the Temple; Persian officials in the provincial administration will have constantly put obstacles in the way of work on the Temple and the reconstruction of Judah in general. The sources tell us nothing explicit to this effect, but it is not inconceivable that the administrators and bureaucrats of the province of Beyond the River were in no hurry to implement Cyrus' edict or to render assistance to the building of the Temple.

It seems more probable, however, that the major factor in the delay was the grave economic situation in Judah at the time, possibly as a result of a long drought (Hag. 1:6). The details are supplemented by Zechariah's account (8:10), which may also hint at civil unrest. Such a

---

[12] See P. R. Ackroyd, *JNES* 7 (1958) 13–22; *CAH* III².2, 436; D. L. Peterson, *Haggai and Zachariah 1–8* (Philadelphia, 1984) 43–4.

conjunction of troubles could not but occasion widespread despair and a feeling that the time was not yet ripe for the reconstruction of the Temple.

The general mood of the people, endeavouring to explain away their failure to act, is depicted succinctly by Haggai: 'This people says: "The time has not yet come" – the time to rebuild the house of the Lord' (1:2). The term 'time' (^{c}et) here has to be understood as predestined and predetermined period of time. The idea underlying the popular slogan 'the time has not yet come' has to be explained in the context of other prophecies.[13] It surely refers to Jeremiah's prediction that the land would lie desolate for seventy years, during which it would be ruled by the king of Babylon (Jer. 25:11–12). Jeremiah interpreted these seventy years as comprising three generations, Nebuchadnezzar, his son, and his grandson, during which the people of Judah would have to serve the king of Babylon 'until the time [^{c}et] of his own land come' (Jer. 27:7), and there could be no question of deliverance before that time of retribution was over.

'Seventy years' also figures as a standard length of punishment in Isaiah's 'burden of Tyre': 'Tyre shall be forgotten seventy years' (Isa. 23:15); only after seventy years would Tyre be remembered and her commerce with all the nations be resumed. The same length of time is mentioned in a retributive context in an inscription of Esarhaddon,[14] king of Assyria (681–669 B.C.), in connexion with the destruction of Babylon by his father Sennacherib in 689 B.C. According to this text, the Babylonian god Marduk had decreed that Babylon 'would lie desolate for seventy years' but he was appeased, had mercy on the city and converted 'seventy' into 'eleven';[15] the reconstruction of Babylon was indeed initiated in the first years of Esarhaddon's reign. Predestined periods of catastrophe appear in other Assyrian and Babylonian literary works; it was an age in which prophecies and omens were taken particularly seriously, whether they involved a predetermined time (adannu in Akkadian) or not.

The significance attached by the peoples of the ancient Near East to predictions of the destruction and reconstruction of temples should not surprise us. The principle of theodicy implied that the destruction of any temple – including the House of YHWH in Jerusalem – was necessarily an expression of divine wrath. In his anger, the god orders the destruction of his temple and thus punishes his worshippers by depriving them of a legitimate place to practise their cult. A temple, once

[13] Ackroyd, *JNES* 7 (1958) 23–7; Meyers and Meyers 1987 (F 384A) 117–18.
[14] Luckenbill (who first interpreted the passage) 1927 (F 134A) 243 §643; Borger 1956 (F 80) 15; *JNES* 18 (1959) 74.
[15] Interchanging the appropriate cuneiform signs in fact changes 70 into 11.

destroyed, can be rebuilt only on the express instruction of the god, whose wrath has been appeased. In Mesopotamia such instructions were delivered through omens, interpreted by astrologers and *haruspices*. In Israel it was the prophet who announced such instructions. Jeremiah, for example, emphasizes more than once that divine retribution will be followed by redemption: Jerusalem's ruins will be rebuilt; her exiles – both those deported by the Assyrians and those now being deported by the Chaldeans – will return to their homes; the Temple will rise again and the glory of the Davidic monarchy will be restored (e.g. Jer. 33:14–18).

It was now evident to the people of Judah that, as far as the destruction of Jerusalem was concerned, Jeremiah's prophecy had been fulfilled, as befitted a genuine prophecy (so according to the concepts of that age; cf. Deut. 18:21–2). The exiles were therefore convinced that the desolation would have to last exactly seventy years; any pre-emptive action would be reprehensible. The seventy years would end in 527, if reckoned, on the more lenient view, from the deportation of Jehoiachin in 597, or in 516, if reckoned, more stringently, from the actual destruction of the Temple in 586. On either calculation, the period of retribution was near its end, and one can readily appreciate Deutero-Isaiah's impassioned appeal to the exiles in Babylon on the eve of its occupation by Cyrus, to the effect that indeed '[Jerusalem's] time of service is accomplished . . . her guilt is paid off' (Isa. 40:2), and that deliverance was now at hand.

At the beginning of Darius' reign, the 'seventy years' prophecy was again invoked, in the stricter interpretation reckoning from the destruction of the Temple. Hence, the popular slogan quoted by Haggai asserting that the time had not yet come to build the Temple. Nevertheless, Haggai and his supporters seem to have prevailed, and in that very year – the second of Darius' reign (according to the Babylonian system), the work of reconstruction began.

While the building of the Temple was in progress, apparently in the third (or fourth) year of Darius' reign, the Persian governor of Beyond the River, Tattenai, arrived in Jerusalem and demanded to know by what authorization the Jews were rebuilding their Temple. Tattenai is known to us from contemporary Babylonian documents (*CAH* IV² 154). His name is written Tattanu, and his direct superior was Uštanu, whose title in these documents is 'governor of Babylon and Beyond the River'. His visit was probably part of some reorganization of the province[16] after the suppression by Darius of revolt throughout the empire. The Jewish representatives who received him were unable to produce the required document and thus to prove that they were proceeding on

[16] It can no longer be held that Beyond the River was formally split from Babylonia at this time; see *CAH* IV² 130–1, 153–4.

the direct authorization of Cyrus. But they did tell Tattenai the story of the Edict, mentioned Sheshbazzar, and bolstered their argument with the observation that the work had actually begun under Cyrus and had never been interrupted though it had not yet been completed. Accordingly, they requested that a search be made in 'the king's treasure-house' in Babylon, where a copy of Cyrus' Edict would presumably be found. The governor passed the matter on to Darius (Ezra 5:3–17), and the King ordered a search to be made in the royal archives at Babylon. Official evidence of the Edict was indeed discovered, not in Babylon, but in the fortress at Ecbatana, the capital of the Median kingdom before its occupation by Cyrus. The document found was not the Edict itself but an internal memorandum (*dikhrōnā*) dealing with monies drawn from the royal treasury for the construction of the Temple. Darius, whose administration of the empire was governed by strict legalism and his claim to be the legitimate successor of Cyrus, authorized the completion of the work. Moreover, he took pains to order that the work be financed by royal funds in the province of Beyond the River, in accordance with Cyrus' original Edict as summarized in the memorandum. Thus the people of Judah were not obliged to bear the costs of the reconstruction, and we may assume that the provincial bureaucracy now complied with alacrity.

The work now continued uninterrupted and was soon completed, on 3 Adar in the sixth year of Darius' reign (Ezra 6:15), that is, 12 March 515 (by the Babylonian reckoning of regnal years). It is surely no accident that the work of rebuilding was thus actually completed a full seventy years after the destruction of the Temple in 586. It would seem that the returnees, having witnessed the fulfilment of Jeremiah's prophecies of doom, were intent on finishing the work at the appropriate time, as if proclaiming that the 'cup of bitterness' (Isa. 51:17) had been drained and that a new era, that of divine mercy, was about to begin.[17]

3. *Jerusalem as a temple city*

With the construction of the Temple, all the provisions of the original Edict of Cyrus had been implemented, culminating in the establishment of Jerusalem as a full-fledged temple city. This special privilege was further reinforced by a decree of Darius providing for the sacrificial cult, and in particular the sacrifice for the welfare of the King and his sons (Ezra 6:10). Cyrus, in a similar vein, had requested in his cylinder inscription from Babylon that all the gods restored to their temples by his generosity should pray to Marduk daily for the welfare of himself and his son Cambyses (*ANET* p. 316). This sacrifice for the welfare of the

---

[17] For a discussion of the physical evidence for the Second Temple, see *CAH* III².2, 437–9.

ruling power remained in effect in Jerusalem during the periods of the Ptolemies, the Seleucids and the Romans; its abolition in A.D. 68 signalled the beginning of the great revolt against Rome. It may be assumed that the Temple and its personnel were relieved of the obligation to pay taxes and participate in the various forced labour projects customary in the Persian empire. Elsewhere in the empire important temples were also given special favours and relieved of these burdens. This was a method by which the government secured the loyalty of major temples; their priests probably also received economic privileges (cf. *CAH* IV² 124–5). Thus the new status of Jerusalem and its Temple as a major centre – cultic, spiritual and even political – was not dissimilar from that of other temple cities of the period, particularly those of Babylonia. The priesthood increased its economic power, in a way which remained in effect until the economic reforms of Nehemiah. It was only natural that from this time the priests, thanks to their exclusive role in the Temple, enjoyed a much improved standing and prestige among the people of Judah. The hierarchy was headed by the High Priest, who would gradually come to be regarded as the recognized leader of the people. But, in contrast to the times of Zerubbabel and Joshua, who had shared the responsibilities of leadership, the void left by the disappearance of Zerubbabel was not at first filled by the High Priests and their families, but rather by the 'Elders of the Jews', a council which was to become a permanent instrument of government in a later phase of the Second Temple period.

Towards the end of the Persian period, additional changes took place in the organizational structure of the Temple personnel. The principal source for these changes is the book of 1 Chronicles, in which we read of twenty-four priestly divisions or courses (1 Chron. 24:7–18). This division is well documented by various Jewish sources, ranging in date from the end of the Second Commonwealth to Byzantine times.[18] Also listed in 1 Chronicles (23) are various groups of Levites, now officially constituted, such as musicians and door-keepers. Most of these changes are listed there as reforms instituted by King David, but scholars are generally agreed that their development should be ascribed to a late stage of the post-exilic period.[19]

4. From Zerubbabel to Ezra

The sixty years or so that elapsed from the completion of the Temple to the arrival of Ezra constitute one of the most obscure periods in the

---

[18] Schürer, Vermes and Millar 1973–87 (F 394) II 245–50; H. G. M. Williamson, *VTSupp.* 30 (1979) 251–68.

[19] Schürer, Vermes and Millar 1973–87 (F 394) II 251–6.

history of the Restoration. The author of the book of Ezra, faithful to his method of building his historical narrative around major personalities, has virtually nothing to say about this period. The few hints to be found in Ezra provide some evidence of tension between the returnees and certain communities in Samaria. This tension, of which we are given no details, was the motive for a letter of accusation sent to Xerxes (486–465). Its contents are not cited in the collection of documents in Ezra 4, but in that chapter another such letter, sent to Artaxerxes (465–424), is cited in full. This letter, requesting a halt to the Jews' construction of the walls of Jerusalem, was composed by Rehum, the *běʿel ṭěʿem* (*bēl-ṭēmi* in Akkadian), the officer responsible for the composition of official documents,[20] and Shimshai the scribe, on behalf of the community of Samaria, descendants of the people deported there centuries before by the Assyrians (*CAH* III².2, 342–4). The authors of the letter point out that Jerusalem had always been considered a rebellious city, and warn the King that, if the construction of the wall is completed, payment of taxes to the King will cease and the income of the royal treasury will be adversely affected (Ezra 4:7–16).

Though the events detailed at the beginning of the letter lack any known historical background, the implication is that a daring attempt had been made to rebuild the walls of Jerusalem and thus reinforce its standing as a privileged temple city. Had the work been completed, Jerusalem would have enjoyed an advantage over Samaria, which was also the seat of a governor but had no temple. Hence the leaders of Samaria were vigorously opposed to the rebuilding of Jerusalem's walls, and their petitions were indeed successful. Artaxerxes was convinced that the action of the Jews constituted a threat and commanded a halt to the building; at the same time he issued a warning against causing the Jews any harm. His orders were carried out, and the walls of Jerusalem lay in ruins until the advent of Nehemiah.

In this context, it is worth noting that Artaxerxes I must have been particularly sensitive to any hint of rebellion. His father Xerxes had been assassinated, and he himself had ascended the throne only after his elder brothers had been murdered.[21] Rebellions broke out throughout the empire. Egypt rose against the Persian overlord, aided by Athens; Athenian ships anchored off Cyprus and even approached the shores of Palestine (*CAH* IV² 144, V² 52). It is quite possible that this situation helps to explain the two major events in Jewish history in the early years of Artaxerxes' reign: the interruption of the unauthorized building of the

[20] For recent discussions of the phrase see Lewis 1977 (A 33) 10 n. 38; Stolper 1984 (F 176) 305 n. 17.

[21] Stolper 1988 (F 61) 196 gives the primary evidence (BM 32234) for the assassination. The Greek evidence has not yet been reassessed in the light of it.

Jerusalem wall and the mission of Ezra to Palestine with the express permission and assistance of the central government.

1. The authority of Ezra

Modern scholarship is divided as to the chronological sequence of the activities of Ezra and Nehemiah. Some authorities[22] maintain that the biblical date, 'in the seventh year of Artaxerxes the King' (Ezra 7:7), refers not to the reign of Artaxerxes I (465–424) but to that of Artaxerxes II (404–359), implying that Ezra arrived on the scene some fifty years after Nehemiah. Alternatively, it has been suggested[23] that the text is corrupt and should read 'in the thirty-seventh year of Artaxerxes (I)', i.e. 428, which again puts Nehemiah before Ezra. However, there seems to be no definite evidence which justifies emending the dates in the sources and inverting the sequence of events as described by the editor of Ezra-Nehemiah; it therefore seems preferable to accept this aspect of the biblical account and assume that Ezra's mission did precede that of Nehemiah.[24]

Ezra son of Seraiah was descended from a High-Priestly family (Ezra 7:5); the genealogy of Ezra 7 traces him to the Zadokite line. His other title, as specified in the King's certificate of credentials (ništĕwān, Ezra 7:12–26) is 'the scribe of the Law of the God of Heaven' (sĕphar dātā di ʾĕlāh šĕmayā, ibid. 12; dātā is an Old Persian word for 'law'). This title is very similar to the title 'scribe of the words of the commandments of the Lord' (ibid. 11). Yet another similar title for Ezra is 'a ready scribe in the Law [tôrāh, teaching, instruction] of Moses' (Ezra 7:6); 'ready scribe' (sōphēr māhīr) is an ancient title, appearing as far back as the Ugaritic documents of the thirteenth century.

It is commonly agreed that the term 'scribe' as it appears here does not have the connotation of one who copies books of the Law or other sacred texts. It should rather be understood as the official designation of a post in the imperial administration.[25] It has often been assumed that Ezra was the spiritual leader of the community and wielded both the power and the authority to assemble a large number of Jews to accompany him to Judah. The far-reaching letter of credentials he

22 The best discussions of this view are by Rowley 1952 (F 390) 131–59 and 1963 (F 391) 211–45.
23 Bright 1960 (F 366) and 1981 (F 367) 391–402, but see Emerton 1966 (F 374).
24 The corner-stone of all chronology is the belief that the Artaxerxes in whose twentieth year Nehemiah came to Jerusalem was Artaxerxes I. That Artaxerxes II and the year 385/4 cannot be ruled out of account has been argued from time to time, most recently by Saley 1978 (F 392) on the basis of the Samaria papyri. But see Blenkinsopp, JBL 106 (1987) 420; 1989 (F 365) 205.
25 Schaeder 1930 (F 393); Stolper 1989 (F 181) 298–9.

received from the King, cited in full in the book of Ezra, authorized him to appoint magistrates and judges over the community and to execute judgment in accordance with the law of his God and the law of the King. He was empowered to exact severe punishment, including the death penalty (Ezra 7:25–6). The letter extended his authority, not only over the Jews in the province of Judah, but also over all Jews resident in the satrapy Beyond the River who observed the 'Law of the God of Heaven'.[26]

The King permitted Ezra to convey to the Temple vessels of gold and silver, gifts from the King and his counsellors. He also granted him a special allowance from the royal treasury and charged the royal treasurers of Beyond the River to comply 'with all diligence' (Ezra 7:19–21). Moreover, he decreed (*ibid.* 24) that from now on the priests, Levites, singers, porters and other Temple servants would be exempted from payment of the various state taxes, 'tribute, impost or toll' (*mindā*, *bĕlō*, *hălakh*, taxes familiar from Babylonian documents of the period as *mandattu*, *biltu* and *ilku*). In short, the *ništĕwān* granted Ezra far-reaching privileges as a leader, thereby greatly enhancing the prestige of the community of the returnees and of the group which accompanied him. It is quite possible that the document, which attests familiarity with the internal affairs of the Jewish community, was originally formulated by Ezra himself.[27] The powers were broad, but one is struck by the contrast between them and the rather limited scope of his activities as described in the memoir.

2. *Spiritual awakening in Babylon*

The stormy events on the international stage and the subsequent consolidation of Artaxerxes' control were not the only factors which prompted the departure of Ezra at the head of a group of 1,754 returnees. A no less significant contribution to the organization of the move at this particular time came from within the Jewish community. Examination of the Jewish names in the documents of the house of Murashû, a family of Babylonian businessmen based at the time in the city of Nippur, has revealed an important feature, not hitherto noted in this context. It turns out that, around the middle of the fifth century, the Jews seem to have experienced a marked change of spirit; third-generation exiles began to resume the use of Jewish names with the theophoric element *yahu*,

[26] There has been some scepticism about this extension; but see H. Mantel, *Hebrew Union College Annual* 44 (1973) 63–71; H. G. M. Williamson, in R. E. Clements, *The World of Ancient Israel* (Cambridge, 1989) 154.
[27] Schaeder 1930 (F 393) 53 ff. But cf. Neh. 11:24 for a royal adviser at the King's hand in all matters concerning the people.

together with many compound names incorporating the element *hanan* ('was gracious').[28] This observation, if correct, may well indicate that the community of exiles in the region of Nippur began to evince a renewed interest in their Jewish heritage in the first half of the fifth century. If this local reawakening can be applied to the Babylonian Jewish community as a whole, we have here unique evidence of a spiritual process which culminated in the immigration with Ezra.

The Ezra memoir contains a list of heads of families of the immigrants who accompanied him, first and foremost priestly families. Ezra made special efforts to include Levites in his group; these were required in their capacity as Temple servants. In general, the returnees in this wave were members of families and circles with particularly strong ties with Jerusalem and its Temple.

The actual timing and organization of the move reveals a symbolic resemblance to the events of the Exodus from Egypt. The company set out in the first month, the same month in which the Children of Israel had left Egypt (Exod. 13:4). In addition, upon their arrival in Judah, the immigrants sacrificed bullocks, rams and he-goats, in multiples of twelve. Probably the emphasis on this number was intended to represent the participation of the entire people in the return to Zion.

3. The 'congregation of the captivity' and the 'peoples of the lands'

Despite the broad scope of Ezra's authority, his actual activities were confined to the 'congregation of the captivity' (the *gōlāh*, the community of the exiles) alone. As is evident from the fragments of Ezra's memoirs and the biblical editor's narrative, his prime concern was not for the political or social welfare of the people in Jerusalem and Judah, but for the relations between the returnees and the local inhabitants, who had not experienced the spiritual awakening of the exiles. Ezra addresses his admonitions to the 'captivity', 'the children of the captivity' or the 'congregation of the captivity' (Ezra 8:35, 9:4, 10:6, 8), while his opponents are termed 'peoples of the lands' (ʿammē hā-ʾărāṣōt, the plural of ʿam ha-ʾareṣ, 'people of the land', *ibid.* 9:1–2), a phrase having the connotation of 'gentiles'. The original connotation of ʿam hā-ʾāreṣ in First Temple times was the nation of Judah (2 Kgs. 24:14), perhaps sometimes the influential and privileged element of the population (2 Kgs. 21:24). As late as the time of Haggai and Zechariah the term was still being used in a positive sense, denoting the entire nation or an element acting on its behalf. Thus, when Haggai urges the people to build the Temple, he appeals (2:4) among others to 'the people of the land'. Similarly, Zechariah (7:5) applies the phrase 'all the people of the land' to the entire

28 Bickerman 1978 (F 362) 7 with Table 1, drawing on Zadok 1976 (F 210).

community of returnees. The Ezra narrative uses the term in a radically different sense. Ezra employs it for the inhabitants of Judah, in sharp distinction from his 'congregation of the captivity', also referred to as 'the holy seed' (9:2). The concept apparently encompasses not only the people of Judah who had not been deported to Babylonia, but also converts and neighbours of Judah who worshipped the God of Israel.

We have explicit indications of widespread religious conversion in the account of the celebration of the Passover festival in Ezra 6:19–21. The paschal lamb was eaten not only by the returnees, the 'children of the captivity', but also by 'every one who had joined them and separated himself from the pollutions of the peoples of the land to worship the Lord', that is to say, all those who had adopted the cult of the God of Israel as required by the Law. A similar term occurs in Neh. 10:28: 'all who have separated themselves from the people of the lands to the law of God', while Esther 8:11 speaks of 'many of the people of the land who became Jews' (RSV 'declared themselves Jews').

The reference here is to gentiles who had joined 'the people of Israel' and undertaken to observe the Law, for this category is mentioned after the enumeration of the various divisions of the Jews themselves: priests, Levites, porters, singers and Nethinim (Ezra 2–3). These 'converts' are referred to by the archaic term *gēr*, originally meaning 'stranger', and in the course of the Second Temple period the new meaning of 'convert' or 'proselyte' became fully entrenched. Conversion was ultimately instituted as a ritual procedure with well-defined laws and ceremonies, some of which still survive.

Ezra's primary goal, however, an integral component of his spiritual outlook, was to shape the community of returnees as a unique body, adhering as far as possible to the norms which had governed their life in Babylonia; hence his adamant demand for ethnic and religious separatism. This separatist philosophy rejected the universalistic expectations expressed by Zechariah (8:23) in the early days of the Restoration: 'Thus saith the Lord of hosts: In those days it shall come to pass, that ten men shall take hold, out of all the languages of the world, shall even take hold of the skirt of him who is a Jew, saying: We will go with you, for we have heard that God is with you.' This view, however, was rejected in favour of the isolationism of Ezra and Nehemiah, which was, it seems, the dominant outlook of the Jews in Babylonia and the Persian diaspora. Ezra's major achievement, described at length in his memoirs (9–10), was an uncompromising implementation of this separatist attitude. The situation facing him upon his arrival in Judah is described in his memoirs in the following terms:

Now when these things were done, the princes drew near unto me, saying: The people of Israel, and the priests and the Levites, have not separated themselves

from the peoples of the lands, doing according to their abominations, even of
the Canaanites, the Hittites, the Perizzites, the Jebusites, the Ammonites, the
Moabites, the Egyptians and the Amorites. For they have taken of their
daughters for themselves and for their sons; so that the holy seed have mingled
themselves with the peoples of the lands; yea, the hand of the princes and rulers
hath been first in the faithlessness.

(9:1–2)

His reaction, as described in the sequel, was dramatic: he rent his
garments, plucked out the hair of his head and his beard, and sat in
mourning and fasting. On rising from his fast, he uttered a prayer of
confession, the gist of which was that the adverse conditions in Judah
were occasioned purely by the marriage ties of 'the people of Israel' with
'the peoples of the land'. It is most instructive that this motif, as
formulated here, makes no appearance in the historical literature of the
First Temple period or even in the book of Deuteronomy, which forms
the basis for Ezra's admonition in 9:6–12. Ezra, in broadening the
biblical prohibition on marriage with Ammonites and Moabites (cf.
Deut. 23:4–7 (23:3–6)) was thus enunciating a significant new principle
of homiletic interpretation of Mosaic Law (below, pp. 284–5).[29]

He now made an impassioned appeal to 'the congregation of the
captivity' (subsequently (10:9) referred to by the archaistic term 'men of
Judah and Benjamin') and urged them to divorce their gentile wives.
The memoirs end (10:18–44) with a list of persons, mainly priests, who
had wed foreign wives, but so abruptly that it is by no means clear
whether those listed did indeed divorce their wives. An endeavour of
this magnitude, with its grave social and humanitarian implications,
required a leader of a different stamp. The necessary properties were to
be embodied in the person of Nehemiah.

<h2 align="center">IV. NEHEMIAH'S ACHIEVEMENT</h2>

<h3 align="center">1. The personality of Nehemiah</h3>

We turn now to Nehemiah son of Hacaliah, cupbearer to King
Artaxerxes I (465–424), who appointed him governor of Judah. His
achievements, which were to leave a clear imprint on the history of the
country, were founded both on his forceful personality and on the
extensive powers attached to his position. These properties were a sharp
contrast to the character of Ezra. Nehemiah's natural milieu was the
royal court at Susa, where high posts were filled by officers of noble

---

[29] The position in the development of the book of Ruth, which takes a strongly positive view of
one Moabite wife, is far from clear.

origin from the diverse nations which made up the Achaemenid empire.[30]

Nehemiah's reference (2:3) to Jerusalem as 'the city of my ancestors' graves' and the accusation made against him by his political opponents: 'You have also set up prophets in Jerusalem to proclaim about you: There is a king in Judah! . . .' (Neh. 6:7) have been taken[31] as an indication that he was of Davidic descent, although the genealogical data in 1 Chron. 3 provide no evidence to that effect. His post, cupbearer to the King, was considered a most honourable one (Hdt. III.34.1), since only the most reliable persons were permitted to approach the King, let alone serve him wine.

Nehemiah took up his post in Jerusalem as governor of Judah in 445/4, the twentieth year of Artaxerxes I.[32] It is very likely that he only remained there for a short period, a year or, at the most, two. According to Nehemiah 13:6, he returned to Persia, coming again to Jerusalem after Artaxerxes' thirty-second year. Our primary source for his activities is the book of his memoirs (Neh. 1–7:5; 12:27–13), possibly written after his second term of office. A personal document, apologetic in parts, addressed to God and to a future reader, it is the only one of its kind in biblical literature. Because of his achievements in solidifying the political fortunes of Judah and, equally importantly, the faith which pervades them, his memoirs were destined to enter the biblical canon, alongside works attributed to David, Solomon and other famous men of old. Indeed, in one later tradition which telescopes the past, Nehemiah is credited with the restoration of the Second Temple. In another, only he and not Ezra is mentioned as the leader of the community in Judah (see below, p. 285).[33]

Very little is known of Nehemiah's predecessors in the post of the governor of the province of Judah (*yĕhūd mĕdintā* in Aramaic). Nehemiah (5:15) refers to them as 'the former governors who were before me' and states explicitly that these officials imposed heavy taxes on the people and burdened them with the maintenance of the governor's household ('the bread of the governor'). Some authorities maintain that seal impressions on jar handles from the Persian period, bearing such inscriptions as *yhwᶜzr pḥwʾ* and *ʾḥzy pḥwʾ* indicate the names of some of those former governors.[34] In any case, one can no longer agree with the once common

---

[30] Bearers of such posts were often eunuchs (cf. Lewis 1977 (A 33) 20–1), and tradition affirms this of Nehemiah (see the variant in LXX II Esdras 11.11 and Origen on Matthew 19:12). But see Yamauchi 1980 (F 401).

[31] Kellermann 1967 (F 380) 156–9, but see Williamson 1985 (F 400) 179.   [32] But see n. 24.

[33] For these and other later traditions, see Blenkinsopp 1989 (F 365) 54–9.

[34] See *CAH* IV² 161 fig. 5, and Avigad 1976 (F 355) 33–5; Stern 1982 (F 397) 202–6, 237, agrees that they are governors (which is not all that certain), but dates them later.

view[35] that Judah did not constitute a separate administrative unit before Nehemiah's day, but was subordinate to the governors of Samaria. This, it was suggested, was the real background to the struggle between Nehemiah and Sanballat, the governor of Samaria, which started at the very beginning of Nehemiah's term of office. However, it appears that the reasons for this struggle were far more complex, and only partly concerned the range of Nehemiah's authority.

In the Persian empire, the governor, by virtue of his position as representative of the King, could frequently appeal directly to the royal court, bypassing his immediate superior, the satrap. This must have been particularly obvious in the case of Nehemiah, who, as the King's cup-bearer, was reckoned among the monarch's inner circle. It is not likely that Sanballat enjoyed any such standing, although he may have been superior to Nehemiah in administrative status, since Samaria was more important than Jerusalem as a centre of government and administration (cf. 'the army of Samaria', Neh. 3:34 (4:2)).

2. *Nehemiah's opponents and the refortification of Jerusalem*

The governor of Samaria already appears as Nehemiah's principal opponent at the inception of his very first project – the fortification of Jerusalem with a new wall. His Babylonian name Sin-uballit and the epithet 'the Horonite' (Neh. 2:10) may perhaps indicate that he originally came from the city of Harran in northern Mesopotamia, the cult-centre for Sin, the moon-god. Yet the Yahwistic names of his sons Delaiah and Shelemiah[36] leave little doubt that, despite his Babylonian name, Sanballat worshipped the God of Israel. Nehemiah never accuses him of idolatry or syncretism.

A second adversary mentioned in Nehemiah's memoirs (3:35 (4:3)) is Tobiah the Ammonite. Although Nehemiah refers to him as 'the Ammonite slave' (*hā-ᶜebed hā-ᶜammōnī, ibid.* 2:19, probably a word play on his official title *ᶜebed ha-melekh*, 'slave of the king'), it is very likely that he was a member of a wealthy family which, though originally from Judah, owned property and estates across the Jordan, where it wielded considerable influence.[37] This family, known from Josephus as the Tobiads, was to attain a position of some prominence in Palestine some 200 years after Nehemiah, when one of its members, Joseph son of Tobiah, played a significant part in the country's history under Ptolemaic rule. Tobiah had an office ('chamber', Neh. 13:7) in the Jerusalem

---

[35] Alt 1934 (F 354); see e.g. Smith 1987 (F 396) 149–50 and *CAH* IV² 160–1.
[36] These are mentioned in a letter of 408, Cowley, *AP* 30.29, from the Jews of Elephantine to Bagohi, governor of Judah.   [37] Mazar 1957 (F 383).

Temple; he was related by marriage to Eliashib the High Priest (*ibid.*) and to other distinguished Jerusalem families (Neh. 6:17–19).

Nehemiah (2:19) mentions yet a third opponent – Geshem the 'Arab', probably the king of the Qedarites, a tribal grouping in northern Arabia which monopolized the highly profitable incense trade.[38] His attitude to Nehemiah may have been primarily politically motivated, reflecting the threat to his position which would be posed by the strengthening of Judah and his fear of Nehemiah's ambition.

It is only natural that the powers granted the new governor and his multifaceted activities as a reformer were looked on as a threat to the social establishment throughout Palestine, not only in Jerusalem and Judah. At the very beginning of his term of office, he threatened these three influential opponents: 'But you have no portion, nor right, nor memorial, in Jerusalem' (Neh. 2:20). Thus he denied them the privileges which their administrative, social and economic status had previously given them in Jerusalem and its Temple.

Nehemiah also had to cope with antagonism from within the Jerusalem community itself, headed by the High Priest, Eliashib, related by marriage to Sanballat, but this opposition appears to have been less violent than that of Sanballat or Tobiah; Eliashib is not directly criticized in Nehemiah's memoirs.

Nehemiah's first project was the fortification of Jerusalem, a crucial step in buttressing its status as a temple city.[39] Construction of walls on such a scale required an immense labour force, part of which was supplied by families who volunteered their efforts. But these voluntary contributions were not enough, and, since large sections of the population refused to take part, Nehemiah had no choice but to exercise his authority as governor and impose corvée labour (termed *pelekh*, a Babylonian loan-word, in Nehemiah 3). The *pĕlākhīm* – teams of corvée labourers – were presumably mobilized on a territorial and administrative basis (*CAH* iv² 159 and n. 50). The work was finished in fifty-two days (Neh. 6:15).[40]

[38] For a silver bowl, found at Tell el-Maskhuta, at the eastern approaches to Egypt, bearing an inscription with the name of Qainu son of Geshem, king of Qedar, see *CAH* iv² 148, 164, *Pls. to Vol.* iv, pl. 93.

[39] Nehemiah (2:1–8) makes it clear that the rebuilding of the walls had been mentioned to the king and authorized by him. That some imperial calculation lay behind the wall-building is not to be excluded; see Lewis 1977 (A 33) 51 n. 5, 153 n. 118.

[40] Josephus (*AJ* xi.179) has it that the work took two years and four months. It has often been suggested that the two figures be reconciled by assuming that the biblical account refers only to the last stage of construction, but see Bewer 1924 (F 360).

3. *Nehemiah's social reforms*

Although the immediate goal of Nehemiah's mission was to rebuild the walls of Jerusalem, he was quick to recognize the sorry condition of the population of Judah and initiated reforms in social and economic spheres. For two generations, social polarization had been on the increase. On the one hand, the notables and senior officials (the *sĕgānīm*) and priestly families, unburdened by taxation, lived comfortably; on the other, the peasants and petty landowners were burdened by famine and exorbitant taxes, and many became destitute. Slavery and serfdom were rife, as evidenced by the people's appeal to Nehemiah:

> For there were that said: 'We, our sons and our daughters, are many; let us get for them corn, that we may eat and live.' Some also there were that said: 'We are mortgaging our fields, and our vineyards, and our houses; let us get corn, because of the dearth.' There were also that said: 'We have borrowed money for the King's tribute upon our fields and our vineyards. Yet now our flesh is as the flesh of our brethren, our children as their children; and, lo, we bring into bondage our sons and our daughters to be servants, and some of our daughters are brought into bondage already; neither is it in our power to help it; for other men have our fields and our vineyards.'

(Neh. 5:2–5)

The radical solution devised by the new governor was the remission of debts and restitution of lands to their former owners. He convened most of the people at Jerusalem in a 'great assembly' (Neh. 5:7), with the wealthy sections of the population in the minority. Speaking forcefully and persuasively, appealing both to the popular will and to his authority as governor, he proclaimed a far-reaching social reform. The wealthy were obliged, there and then, to take a public oath that they would forthwith restore fields, vineyards, olive plantations, houses, money, grain, wine and oil, to the original owners. Such radical social reforms are well attested from the history of ancient Mesopotamia, where they were not infrequent occurrences, particularly in the *andurarum* legislation of Babylonian kings. The suggestion has been made[41] that Nehemiah's reforms should be compared with Solon's in Athens in the sixth century, or, even more aptly, with his fifth-century contemporaries, tyrants in Ionia and Sicily.

Another far-reaching reform undertaken by Nehemiah was the repopulation of Jerusalem. This he achieved by issuing a decree,

[41] E.g. by Smith 1987 (F 396) 103–9. For an attempt to sketch social and economic developments in the period, see Kreisig 1973 (F 381); Japhet 1983 (F 378); J. P. Weinberg, *Klio* 34 (1972) 45–59, *VT* 23 (1973) 400–14, and in J. Harmatta and G. Komoróczy (eds.) *Wirtschaft und Gesellschaft im alten Vorderasien* (Budapest, 1976) 473–86. But see recently J. Blenkinsopp, in P. R. Davies (ed.), *Second Temple Studies*, 1 *Persian Period* (Sheffield, 1991) 22–53.

commanding that a tenth of the population of Judah should settle in the city (Neh. 11:1–21). Parallels to this legislation may again be found in Greece and in the hellenistic period, in the practice of synoecism, that is, the forced repopulation of a city by decree.[42] If the decree was to work, it was first necessary to hold a census. Genealogical lists associated with this census appear in the book of Nehemiah, in chapters 7 and 11.

The account of these activities in Nehemiah's memoirs incorporates new terms for various social groups and government offices, ḥōrīm and sĕgānīm. The first is already attested in 1 Kgs. 21, and means free men, mostly of noble birth. Its semantic parallel in contemporary temple records of Babylonia is mār banūti, meaning 'well-born' persons. The second term is a loan word from the Babylonian šaknu, which at that time denoted any appointed official of high rank (in contrast to its specific meaning 'governor' in the Assyrian period). Nehemiah does not use the term gōlāh, the community of the captivity, as Ezra had done. The general public, outside the ranks of the ḥōrīm and sĕgānīm, are categorized as 'Jews' (yĕhūdīm), priests and Levites. The first of these terms, however, carries several different connotations. It sometimes refers to the population of Judah as a whole (Neh. 3:34 (4:2), 6:6), sometimes to those who are neither priests nor Levites (ibid. 2:16), and sometimes it is used in an ethnic-religious sense and contrasted with the gentiles (ibid. 4:6 (4:12)).

4. Intervention in Temple affairs

Though not a priest, Nehemiah intervened extensively in Temple affairs and administration. He instituted improved regulations for the maintenance and upkeep of the Temple and its priests, and for its routine administration. One much needed innovation was his provision for its regular funding by official organization of the various offerings and tithes (Neh. 10:33–40 (10:32–9), 13:10–12); this measure contributed significantly to the economic independence of the Temple and its personnel. On the other hand, he did not hesitate to clash openly with the Temple leadership, as, for example, when he had Tobiah's household effects removed from the Temple and abolished his chamber there (ibid. 13:4–9, 28–31). It is noteworthy that Nehemiah, who generally reports his own actions in a rather apologetic vein (5:19; 13:14), rounds off the list of his achievements with the measures which he took to improve the lot of the priests and Levites, the lowest priestly class (13:29–30).

Nehemiah no doubt believed that by improving the status of the Temple and its priestly staff he was enhancing the prestige of Jerusalem as a whole and reinforcing the city's economic base. While decreeing regular payment of tithes (the most common form of tax in Mesopota-

[42] Smith 1987 (F 396) 109.

mian temple cities in the sixth and fifth centuries), he also instituted a
significant reform. Hitherto, priestly families had administered the
Temple finances and controlled the distribution of gifts in kind brought
to Jerusalem by the people of Judah; the Levites had been left without a
regular source of income. Wishing to provide for these Levites, the most
needy of the Temple personnel, Nehemiah designated new functions for
them in the Temple service and provided them with a permanent income
from the priests' prebend (Neh. 13:10–13).

Such actions could not fail to create an element indebted to Nehemiah
and sympathetic to his cause, through which he could exert his influence
in the Temple and pursue his struggle with the established priestly
aristocracy. From this time the Levites gained in strength, and in the
course of the Persian period they were to attain a position of respect as
door-keepers and guardians of the Temple precinct, as reflected in the
book of Chronicles (edited several generations after Nehemiah).

Another topic of particular interest to Nehemiah was the strict
observance of the Sabbath. This is not surprising, since this aspect of
religious observance had become one of the most important manifestations of faith among the Jewish community in Babylonia,[43] whereas it
was apparently less rigorously observed in Judah. Accordingly, he
ordered the gates of Jerusalem to be closed to the Tyrian tradesmen who
were accustomed to bring their wares on the Sabbath; it was the Levites
who were charged with enforcement of the day of rest (Neh. 13:16–22).
It is doubtful, however, that he was able to ensure cessation of
agricultural and other labour throughout Jerusalem on the holy day
(*ibid.* 15).

Like Ezra, Nehemiah was faced with a problem of mixed marriages,
particularly among the upper classes. In addition to the legal arguments
cited by Ezra (Ezra 9:11–12) he based the condemnation of mixed
marriages on cultural and historical considerations as well (Neh. 13:25–
7). However, his campaign against intermarriage was also motivated by
his personal conflict with the family of Eliashib the High Priest, who was
related to Sanballat by marriage and on familiar terms with Tobiah.
Nehemiah scored a victory, evicting Eliashib's grandson, Sanballat's
son-in-law, from the Temple (Neh. 13:28), but the victory was only
temporary, since at the end of Nehemiah's term of office the High Priest
regained his former position. Nevertheless, for the most part, Nehemiah's reforms had a lasting impact, though in a somewhat modified
form.

In spite of the close similarity between Ezra and Nehemiah in their
attitudes to mixed marriages, there is a certain difference between them:

---

[43] See below, p. 284. Note its importance in Isaiah 56:6, and see Smith 1984 (F 395) 247, 258, 263,
271.

whereas Ezra confined his mission to the community of the returnees, Nehemiah appealed to the entire population of Judah, though not to the inhabitants of Samaria and other territories bordering on Judah. Nehemiah considered all the Jews, whether returnees or the indigenous population who had never been deported, as an element apart, drawing a sharp line between them and the residents of the province of Samaria. Ezra's separatism was now reinforced by the injection of a political administrative dimension – the distinction between the Jews and the Samaritans.

5. Enforcement of the Law and the covenant

Interwoven with the memoirs of Nehemiah is a comprehensive account of two major endeavours credited to both Ezra and Nehemiah. Though neither mentions the other in his memoirs, they are portrayed as coming together in the context of measures taken to impose the Law in Judah. The first was a major public assembly dedicated to the reading of the Law (Neh. 8–9:1–3). The dominant figure here is that of Ezra; the reference to Nehemiah in the ceremony (*ibid.* 8:9) is doubtful and believed[44] to be an editorial addition.

At the beginning of the 'seventh month' (Tishri) (Neh. 7:73),[45] the people gathered in Jerusalem for the ceremony, which was held on the first and second of the month, and continued during the Feast of Tabernacles, reaching its peak on the twenty-fourth of Tishri (Neh. 9:1). Standing on a specially prepared wooden pulpit, Ezra read the Law to the assembled people. Simultaneously, an Aramaic translation was read and an explanation was provided by Levites, described in the text as 'they that cause the people to understand' (*ibid.* 8:7). It would appear that the comminatory sections of the Pentateuch containing the blessings and maledictions (Deut. 28 or Lev. 26) were among the passages read. The extent and content of the 'book of the Law of Moses' (Neh. 8:1) read out by Ezra are by no means clear; it would seem that the sections read to the people, which included the commandment to celebrate the Feast of Tabernacles, were selected specifically from the Priestly passages in the Pentateuch (e.g. Num. 29:12–39).

The most instructive feature of this ceremony is its treatment of the reading of the Law as a communal ritual. When Ezra opens the book, the people rise and he delivers a benediction, blessing God. The people respond 'Amen, Amen', lifting up their hands, bowing their heads, and prostrating themselves. This is the first record in Jewish history of a

[44] Williamson 1985 (F 400) 279.
[45] The relationship of this to the development of the New Year Festival is beyond our present scope, but Leviticus 23:23–6 must be relevant to this choice of date.

ritual revolving around the Law, rather than around sacrifices, and it was
to provide a model for Jewish worship throughout the Second Temple
period. Indeed, later traditions in Judaism stress the pivotal role of Ezra
in creating this new status for the book of the Law. Prominent in these
traditions is the parallel drawn between Moses and Ezra as law-givers:
'Ezra would have been worthy of the Law being given through him, had
not Moses anticipated him ' (BT *Sanhedrin* 21b).

The other major event in which Ezra and Nehemiah appear together is
the conclusion of the covenant (Neh. 9:38 (10:1); the Hebrew word used
here – *ʾămānāh* – is coterminous with *bĕrīt* in the language of the time). In
contrast with the reading of the Law, this initiative is attributed to
Nehemiah. The biblical editor placed the account of it after that of the
reading of the Law, but most scholars[46] view the covenant as a separate
entity, resembling that concluded by King Josiah upon the discovery of
the 'Book of the Covenant', usually identified with Deuteronomy (2
Kgs. 32). The covenant in Neh. 10 extended the prohibition on mixed
marriages to all 'peoples of the land'; it forbade on the Sabbath not only
labour, but also trade and commerce, which had not been explicitly
prohibited by the Law. Sabbath observance had become one of the most
characteristic marks of the Jews in Babylonia, setting them apart from
those around them. The injunction against the slightest desecration of
the Sabbath thus became one of the measures adopted to impose the
religious norms customary in the Babylonian and Persian diaspora upon
the Jews in the province of Judah.

In the covenant, the people undertook to suspend all agricultural
work and to forego the exaction of debts during the sabbatical year (Neh.
10:32), as well as to maintain the regular payment of various tithes to the
Temple and gifts to the priests and Levites. Among other things, they
were to pay an annual tax of one-third of a shekel to the Temple (*ibid.* 33)
and to bring a 'wood-offering' (*ibid.* 35). The payment of one-third of a
shekel was an innovation, ultimately raised to half a shekel, (as in Exod.
30:11–16), at which level it remained throughout the Second Temple
period; the wood-offering was intended to provide the sacrificial service
with a regular supply of fuel, a vital commodity in a country far from rich
in forests.

These last two measures are not explicitly stipulated in the Pentateuch,
but were derived from the text by the procedure later known as *midrash
halakhah*, 'interpretation of the Law'.[47] In fact, the other measures listed
in the covenant also betray evidence of the application of this procedure:
they are not formulated in the language of the biblical text, and are

[46] See Williamson 1985 (F 400) 325–31; Blenkinsopp 1989 (F 365) 311–14.
[47] Clines 1981 (F 369); M. Fishbane, *Biblical Interpretation in Ancient Israel* (Oxford, 1985) 114–27.
See also J. Liver, *Studies in Bible and Judean Desert Scrolls* (Jerusalem, 1971) 116–20 (Hebrew).

considerably broadened and extended to cases not explicitly mentioned in the Pentateuch. Hence the covenant marks the beginning of an important process, developed over the coming centuries, signalling one stage in the formulation of the Oral Law. It is highly significant that it is not Ezra, the priest and scribe, but Nehemiah, the governor, who is associated with that process. According to his memoirs, Nehemiah not only interpreted, but even enforced, some of the measures listed in the covenant (Neh. 13).

It should thus come as no surprise that historical tradition credits Nehemiah with the creation of institutions of lasting importance. Particularly striking is the attitude of Ben Sirach in his catalogue of praises of past worthies, who makes no mention whatever of Ezra (in itself a significant omission), but pays homage to Nehemiah as one 'who rebuilt our walls, which lay in ruins, erected the gates and bars and rebuilt our houses' (Ecclesiasticus 49:18–19 (49:13 NEB)). Yet another tradition even attributes the building of the Temple and the altar to Nehemiah, extolling his memory as the person who restored the eternal fire to the Temple (2 Macc. 1:18–36).[48]

6. Nehemiah's successors

After the career of Nehemiah, the influence of the governorship in the life of the community in Judah began to decline. Epigraphic sources have furnished the names of two further governors: Bagohi, approached by the Jews of Elephantine in 408 with a request that he intervene on their behalf (Cowley, *AP* 30), and Yehizkiyah, whose name appears on coins dating to the end of the Persian period.[49] Despite Bagohi's Persian name (compare Bigvai in the list of repatriates, Ezra 2:2), the fact that he was requested to assist in the repair of 'the House of YHW that is in Elephantine' seems to imply that he was a Jew; perhaps he, like Nehemiah, came to Judah from the Persian court. Some scholars[50] have suggested that the Hananiah mentioned in some of the Elephantine letters (Cowley, *AP* 21, 38) should be identified with Hananiah 'the governor of the castle' (Neh. 7:2); however, this and other names derived from the root *ḥnn* were quite common among Jews in the fifth century, so that this identification need not necessarily be valid.

As the governorship lost prestige, the priests were able to regain their former position. Instructive evidence of the political prominence of the

[48] 2 Maccabees also (2:13) attributes to Nehemiah the collection of 'the chronicles of the kings, the writings of prophets, the works of David, and royal letters about sacred offerings', to found his library. For Nehemiah in Josephus and Talmudic sources, see Blenkinsopp 1989 (F 365) 54–9.
[49] Rahmani 1971 (F 389); Naveh 1971 (F 385) 30; H. G. M. Williamson, *Tyndale Bulletin* 39 (1988) 73. [50] See Porten 1968 (F 504) 130, who offers an alternative view at 279–80.

priests comes from a coin dating to the end of the period (contemporary with the Yehizkiyah coins), bearing the inscription *ywḥnn hkwhn* (Yohanan the priest).[51] This Yohanan is not to be identified with Yohanan son of Eliashib (Neh. 12:23), who may be Yohanan, the High Priest mentioned in the petition of the Elephantine Jews to Bagohi (Cowley, *AP* 30:18). The (High) Priest of the coin presumably dates to a later period; he may have been the predecessor of Jaddua (below). Henceforth, the High Priest is leader of the community and its acknowledged representative with the government. This is reflected by the legend about the High Priest who is alleged to have welcomed Alexander the Great on the outskirts of Jerusalem in 332, at the head of a delegation of notables.[52] Josephus (*AJ* XI.302) identifies this high priest as Jaddua, but talmudic tradition (BT Yoma 69a) relates that it was Simeon the Righteous. Of the non-Jewish sources, Hecataeus of Abdera (*FGrH* 264 F 6(5)) explicitly states that the Jews were governed in their land by a High Priest. It is quite likely that the High Priest was supported in his tasks by a council of elders, the institution known in hellenistic times as the *gerousia*, but there is no direct evidence of this.

This hierarchy of government left no place for the descendants of the Davidic dynasty (though they maintained their privileged status in Babylonia – witness the later traditions of the exilarchs). That was a consequence of the imperial policy of the Persian Kings. After the disappearance of Zerubbabel, no scion of the House of David ever headed the community in Judah. Nevertheless, interest in the ancient royal house remained alive and its genealogy was preserved. Full details of the dynasty are given in 1 Chron. 3:19–24, in a register which extends several generations beyond Zerubbabel. The restoration of the Davidic monarchy was now linked to eschatological hopes, and it was to become an integral part of the messianic vision of Second Temple times.

V. THE SAMARITANS AND THE CIRCUMSTANCES OF THEIR SEPARATION

It should be clear from this survey of the history of Judah in the Persian period that the ethnic component of the population described in the sources by the adjective 'Jewish' (*yĕhūdī*, Judahite) had not been modified after the destruction of the First Temple and retained its distinctive identity through exile and restoration. The Babylonian monarchs, unlike the Assyrians, did not normally repopulate conquered territories with foreign peoples, but only uprooted the local populations

---

[51] Barag 1985 (F 356); 1986–7 (F 356A); *CAH* IV² 152 with fig. 2.

[52] No non-Jewish source knows anything about this visit, which is accepted by few. See Bickerman 1988 (F 364) 4–5 with 314.

and deported them to Babylonia. The Assyrians, by contrast, had practised the method of 'bilateral deportation', which as a matter of course ultimately produced a new ethnic entity replacing the deported nation. The new inhabitants, strangers to their new environment, were naturally dependent on the imperial authorities in all areas of economic and civil life.

This was certainly true in the case of the inhabitants of Samaria, settled there by the Assyrians after Sargon's destruction of the kingdom of Israel in 720. Sargon's inscriptions tell us that Arabs were deported to Samaria (*CAH* III².2, 436 and n. 176), as well as peoples from other lands of his kingdom who were settled in the city itself (*CAH* III².2, 342 and nn. 149, 150). Our principal biblical source on this matter, 2 Kgs. 17, does not name the Assyrian king, but provides a detailed list of those cities whose residents were transported: 'And the king of Assyria brought men from Babylon, and from Cuthah, and from Avva, and from Hamath and Sepharvaim, and placed them in the cities of Samaria instead of the children of Israel; and they possessed Samaria and dwelt in the cities thereof' (2 Kgs. 17:24).

The deportees were thus for the most part natives of Babylonia and of the regions to its east, on the border with Elam. In time, Jewish sources came to call them 'Cutheans', to the exclusion of all other names. The usual name in post-biblical sources from the hellenistic period is 'Samaritans'.[53] Surprisingly, this name is not to be found in the book of Ezra–Nehemiah, whose accounts of the controversy between the Jerusalem leaders and those of Samaria employ other names: in Ezra 4:1, they are named 'the adversaries of Judah and Benjamin', while Nehemiah's northern enemies are referred to as the brethren of Sanballat and the army of Samaria (Neh. 3:34 (4:2)).

It is quite evident that the historians and the editors responsible for the book of Ezra–Nehemiah made particular efforts to highlight the hostility between the returnees and the leaders of Judah on the one hand, and the governing circles of Samaria on the other. The circumstances which gave rise to this relationship are complex, and fall into two categories: ethnic/religious and political/administrative. We do not know when the newly arrived peoples became truly assimilated with the remnants of the indigenous population of Samaria (it is hardly likely that the entire population of the northern kingdom went into exile) nor how far-reaching this process was. It may be assumed that a considerable measure of intermixture took place. There is no doubt that the 'Samaritans', or at

[53] The word only occurs once in the Bible, in 2 Kgs. 17:29, and there refers to the former inhabitants of the kingdom of Samaria; see M. Cogan and H. Tadmor, *II Kings* (Anchor Bible) (New York, 1988), 211; S. Talmon, in *Gesammelte Aufsätze* I (Neukirchen-Vluyn, 1988), 131–4, and in S. Talmon (ed.), *Jewish Civilization in the Hellenistic-Roman Period* (Sheffield, 1991) 30–1.

least their political leadership, recognized the cultic pre-eminence of the Jerusalem Temple. Moreover, as we have already seen, Sanballat was related by marriage to the High Priest at Jerusalem; his sons were given Yahwistic names, Delaiah and Shelemiah, and were approached by the garrison of Elephantine with a request that they intervene to secure permission for the rebuilding of the 'House of YHW' at Elephantine (Cowley, *AP* 30). Thus the political and administrative rivalry between Nehemiah and Sanballat has to be seen in the light of such co-operation between the leaders of Samaria and the High Priests in Jerusalem. However, the roots of the rivalry lie farther back; they are already evident in the letter of accusation from Rehum and Shimshai to Artaxerxes (Ezra 4:8ff, above, p. 271). The writers of this letter introduce themselves to the King of Persia as descendants of exiles from Erech (Babylonian Uruk), Babylon and Susa. The reference to Susa is particularly significant, since it was the ancient capital of Elam and now one of the capitals of the empire. Thus, by stressing their Mesopotamian and eastern origins, these writers seem to be suppressing any links with Judah, at the same time as they emphasize the rebellious tendencies of Jerusalem and the dangers to the central government inherent in its fortification (Ezra 4:12–14). But it is doubtful whether Sanballat and his family, with their close ties with Jerusalem, can have belonged to this anti-Judah faction in Samaria. What is clear from the letter is that the population of Samaria consisted of several ethnic and religious groups; further details are unknown.

It is significant that an army was stationed at Samaria (Neh. 3:34 (4:2)), whereas Jerusalem did not enjoy this military–administrative privilege.[54] On the other hand, Samaria was not considered a temple city like Jerusalem, so that it is only natural that the 'Samaritans' sought to establish a foothold in the Jerusalem Temple, an attempt which continued throughout the period of the Restoration.

Ezra and Nehemiah, through their separatist policies, were determined to sever any bonds between the Jews and the 'Samaritans', but these policies had their opponents within influential circles in Jerusalem. Nehemiah used his authority as governor to dislodge Sanballat's family from its position in the Temple, evicting from it Sanballat's son-in-law, the son of the High Priest (Neh. 13:28). But this was not the final outcome. Once Nehemiah's term of office was over, the ties between the

---

[54] This proposition is not universally accepted. Tuplin 1987 (F 66) 182, 238, pointing to the fortress-commander in Jerusalem (Neh. 7:2), counts both Jerusalem and Samaria as provincial capitals with military forces attached to them, and thinks it possible that Dor, Lachish and Ashdod should be put on the same level. Whatever the eventual situation, it is by no means obvious that Jerusalem had a garrison before the completion of its wall. On the other hand, it has also been doubted (Williamson 1985 (F 400) *ad loc.*) whether *ḥyl* in Neh. 3:34 (4:2) is necessarily an official Persian force, rather than a local militia.

leaders of Samaria and the High Priest's family were resumed, and in fact the attitude of the Chronicler to the northerners implies that the people of Judah were favourably disposed towards them; they are described as worthy to participate in the Temple services at Jerusalem (see below, p. 293).

We have as yet very meagre sources for fourth-century historical developments at Samaria and Jerusalem;[55] what is clear is that the dissension finally brought on a complete rupture. According to Josephus (*AJ* XI.309–12), presumably drawing on a reliable tradition, Sanballat (now known to be the third governor of that name)[56] encouraged his son-in-law Manasseh, son of the High Priest, to establish himself in Samaria. Allegedly with the permission of Alexander, shortly after his conquest of Palestine, Sanballat built a new temple on Mount Gerizim (the mount of blessing, Deut. 27:12) and Manasseh became its High Priest.

The Samaritans claimed to be the real Israelites, worshipping the God of Israel in their new temple. In the hellenistic period an offshoot community of theirs on Delos describes itself as 'The Israelites on Delos who send their contributions to the holy shrine Argarizein'.[57] This drastic and unprecedented step of erecting a rival to the Jerusalem Temple would be inconceivable, had there not been a grave rupture between Jerusalem and Samaria. Was this rupture the result of a Judahite initiative, as in the time of Nehemiah? Did it stem from a web of family intrigue, as described by Josephus? Alternatively, perhaps the process was a gradual one: relations between the communities deteriorating to the point where the breach could not be healed, with the northern community going its separate way as a distinct national and religious body, as in the days of the ancient Kingdom of Israel. In that case, we can better grasp the significance of the recent discoveries of coins minted in Samaria at that time in the name of Jeroboam.[58] We have no way of knowing whether this personage was a governor or a High Priest, but the mere use of this archaic, historically pregnant, name may well be a demonstrative act of independence on the part of the people of Samaria: it would signify the inception of a new era, like that ushered in by

[55] There is something to be hoped for from the final publication of the Wadi Daliyeh papyri (see Cross 1969 (F 370), 1985 (F 371A), 1988 (F 371B)); the new numismatic evidence (Meshorer and Qedar 1991 (F 384)) makes a substantial contribution. It is now clear, for example, that coinage in the name of *šmryn* (the city, the province, or both?) started a few years after 375 B.C. and ran parallel to the *yhd* coinage, to which it is more closely dated; *ibid.* 66.

[56] Cross 1975 (F 371). Meshorer and Qedar 1991 (F 384) 52–3 nos. 41–5 are probably coined in his name.

[57] *SEG* XXX 810 (250–175 B.C.) and 809 (150–90 B.C.), published by Bruneau 1982 (F 368).

[58] Meshorer and Qedar 1991 (F 384), 14, 49 nos. 23–7 (five different types). They are not the first coins minted in Samaria, as originally suggested; they do not appear in the Samaria hoard, buried *c.* 345 B.C.

Jeroboam son of Nebat when he broke away from Jerusalem and the House of David (1 Kgs. 12, 2 Chron. 10).

The next, irrevocable, step in the schism was the sanctification of Mount Gerizim in writing – in the Samaritan Pentateuch.[59] A fragment of a historical work by a Samaritan author of the hellenistic period, known as Pseudo-Eupolemus (*FGrH* 724 F 1.5 *ap*. Eus. *Praep. Ev.* 9.17), relates that Abraham visited 'the temple at Argarizin (which is, being interpreted, "the mountain of the Highest") and there received gifts from Melchizedek, who was priest of the god and also king'. The process had thus come full circle: the myth associated with the new temple and its location on Mount Gerizim appropriated the entire body of traditions which had built up round Jerusalem and its Temple. However, shortly after the establishment of the temple, Samaria revolted unsuccessfully against Alexander and became the site of a Macedonian colony (Curt. IV.8.9–10, Eus. *Chron.*, Jerome p. 123 (cf. p. 365) Helm).[60] The exiled Samaritans settled around their temple, perpetuating the distinctive identity and traditions of their community and in continuing rivalry with Jerusalem.[61]

VI. LANGUAGE AND LITERATURE

1. *The vernacular as a literary language*

The destruction of the First Temple and the Babylonian exile constitute a watershed in the cultural history of Israel. The fact is evidenced, first and foremost, in a linguistic sense: Hebrew ceased to function as the exclusive vernacular tongue in Judah and a second language came into gradually increasing use – Aramaic, the lingua franca of most of the Persian empire. At that time, the importance of Aramaic was unrivalled. No longer merely a political, diplomatic language, as it had been in the Assyrian empire, it had become both the vernacular and a vehicle for literature and administration. A variety of Aramaic documents have survived: royal inscriptions, such as the Aramaic version of Darius' inscription at Behistun, literary works, like the Proverbs of Ahiqar, and legal and economic documents. Though primarily a script for the pen, on papyrus and parchment, there is plenty of evidence for its use on stone and clay as well.

It is obvious that documents on papyrus and parchment could

---

[59] For the Samaritan Pentateuch see Purvis 1968 (F 388).

[60] Whether the temple was actually built at this time seems very uncertain (Meshorer and Qedar 1991 (F 384) 26–7). But see more recently I. Magen, in F. Manns and E. Aliata (eds.), *Early Christianity in Context: Monuments and Documents*, 91–148 (Jerusalem, 1993).

[61] For later history of the Samaritans see Schürer, Vermes and Millar 1973–87 (F 394) II 16–20, with bibliography in n. 50; J. D. Purves in *CHJud* II 596–613.

withstand the ravages of time only in regions having a dry climate, primarily in Egypt, and their survival in Palestine is more or less confined to the dry regions of the Jordan Valley and adjacent areas like Wadi Daliyeh. However, other locations in Palestine, such as Arad and Beersheba, have produced numerous ostraca. It is apparent that the exigencies of everyday life compelled the inhabitants of Palestine to turn increasingly to Aramaic, which became a major unifying element, common to all the diverse administrative units and ethnic groups in the country.

As we have seen from the biblical account of reading the Law in public (Neh. 8:8), many of the Jews could not understand the original Hebrew of the text and had to have it explained in Aramaic. The very fact that the historian who compiled Ezra 1–7 frequently shifts from Hebrew to Aramaic and back attests the co-existence of the two languages in Judah during the Persian period. The items of official correspondence incorporated in the text were naturally written in Aramaic and the compiler saw no need to translate them into Hebrew. Another indication of the increasing influence of Aramaic is the large number of Aramaic loan-words and Aramaic linguistic usages in the Hebrew of the period, extending to the use of prepositions, verb forms and sentence structure.[62] However, in spite of the prevalence of Aramaic among the Jews in the Diaspora and among the returnees to Judah, Hebrew retained its vitality. Nehemiah's memoirs attest the author's excellent command of written Hebrew, despite his career at the Persian court. In Judah, where some of the population had not been deported to Babylonia and which was naturally less exposed to Aramaic influence, the level of Hebrew was considerably higher. This is evident from the books of the Restoration prophets, Haggai and Zechariah, whose language is relatively free of Aramaic influence. That Hebrew was occasionally maintained for official use can be deduced from the epigraphic evidence, such as the seal inscription *lyrmy hspr* (= *ha-sōphēr*, the scribe, not the Aramaic form *spr'* = *saphrā*) (Avigad 1976 (F 355) 7–8 no. 6), or the seal impression *[...]yhw bn [sn']blt pḥt šmrn* (Cross 1969 (F 370) no. X), in which the Hebrew forms *bn* and *šmrn* are preferred to the Aramaic *br* and *šmryn*, for 'son' and 'Samaria'. The Hebrew vernacular figures in the literary works of the period, conclusive proof that it too, not only Aramaic, was a living tongue.[63] The linguistic heritage of Hebrew was still preserved in later books, although these sometimes betray evidence of archaism.

---

[62] See A. Hurvitz, *Biblical Hebrew in Transition – A Study in Post-Exilic Hebrew and its Implications for Dating of Psalms* (Jerusalem, 1972) (Hebrew); *A Linguistic Study of the Relationship between the Priestly Source and the Book of Ezekiel*, (Cahiers de la Revue Biblique 20) (Paris, 1982); R. Polzin, *Late Biblical Hebrew – Toward Historical Typology of Biblical Hebrew Prose* (Harvard Semitic Monographs 12) (Missoula, Montana, 1976).   [63] Naveh and Greenfield 1984 (F 386) 120–2.

2. *Literature and its social context*

The most characteristic literary genre of the Persian period was historiography, represented by two major works: the book of Ezra–Nehemiah and the book of Chronicles. The book of Ezra–Nehemiah represents a new historiographic form, in which personal memoirs and original documents are incorporated into a historical narrative framework with a well-defined ideology.[64] The author of this comprehensive account, writing long after the events, begins his work with the Edict of Cyrus and concludes it with the end of Nehemiah's mission. The account has two main focuses: the beginning of the Restoration and the achievement of Ezra and Nehemiah. No attempt is made to create a continuous historical development exhibiting some coherent notion of cause and effect, as in the book of Kings; indeed, the failure to do so sets this book far apart from the mainstream of biblical historiography.

The book of Chronicles differs markedly from Ezra–Nehemiah. (The once common view that these works were written by the same author is untenable.)[65] The book relates the history of Judah and the House of David, presenting events within the context of a historical process reflecting a comprehensive philosophy of ideas. The author, known in scholarly literature as the Chronicler, draws most of his historical material from the books of Samuel and Kings, but leaves his ideological and linguistic imprint even on these borrowed passages. His ideology is concentrated on two points: glorification of the House of David, and the Temple and its cult personnel. This dual perspective had no use for the history of the northern kingdom of Israel alongside that of Judah; indeed the historical survey does not even refer explicitly to the destruction of the northern kingdom and the exile of the ten tribes. Moreover, in the Chronicler's view, the presence of the Israelites in their homeland has nothing to do with the conquest and settlement under Joshua. He traces a continuity extending from the fathers of the world, through the patriarchs of the nation, to Jacob-Israel, and, ultimately, in a direct line to David and his descendants. The history of Israel is thus envisaged as a single continuum. Even the Babylonian exile is considered a mere episode in this chain: once 'the land had been paid her sabbaths' (2 Chron. 36:21), the continuity is resumed 'to fulfil threescore and ten years'. Within such an ideological frame, Judah is the only possible protagonist in the story of Israel in its land, and the northern

---

[64] See Japhet in Tadmor 1983 (F 398A) 176–202 and the recent commentaries by Williamson 1985 (F 400) and Blenkinsopp 1989 (F 365).

[65] Japhet 1968 (F 376) and 1989 (F 379); Williamson 1977 (F 399); resistance in Blenkinsopp 1989 (F 365) 47–54.

kingdom has no part to play. As we have said, the Chronicler does not explicitly mention the destruction of Samaria and the deportation of the ten tribes, merely hinting that nothing remains to the north of Judah except a remnant that escaped 'out of the hand of the king of Assyria' (2 Chron. 30:6). This remnant is not defined as consisting of foreign peoples or their descendants, but as the brethren of the people of Judah; both Hezekiah and Josiah, kings of Judah, call on these northern remnants to participate in their purification of the cult (2 Chron. 30; 34:9, cf. 6). It follows, therefore, that those who returned as a consequence of Cyrus' edict are not the exclusive bearers of the heritage of Israel, but only one of its constituents. This attitude towards the Israelites is diametrically opposed to that of the authors of Kings and of Ezra–Nehemiah; it is certainly at variance with what Ezra, Nehemiah and their supporters consider to be the distinctive identity of the nation. The book of Chronicles may therefore have originated in those circles which opposed the separatist ideology of the returnees to Judah from Babylonia and Persia. Such oppositional views were apparently common in influential circles, including those of the High Priesthood. Thus the book throws some light on social and religious views prevalent in Judah in the days following Nehemiah, especially on the attitude towards what might have been regarded as the remnants of the northern kingdom of Israel.

Another genre which evolved during the Persian period is that of the historical novella, which derives from the literature of the ancient Near East.[66] We know several novellas written in that period, such as the older part of the book of Daniel (chapters 1–6) and the book of Esther, both included in the biblical canon, and the books of Tobit and Judith, which survive today only in translation as books of the Apocrypha. However, the only one of these works which can definitely be associated with Palestine is the book of Judith, which may even have been written there. The geographical background of the book, the Persian names of its characters and a few other features link it directly to the Persian period and its specific administrative and military milieu.

Also belonging to this genre is the book of Jonah,[67] which is essentially a pseudepigraphic work revolving, after the fashion of the period, around the person of an ancient hero, Jonah son of Amittai (compare the prophet of the same name from Gath-Hepher, 2 Kgs. 14:25). Jonah is sent to the 'great city of Nineveh'; this is not the capital

---

[66] Elements of it spread into Greek literature by way of those authors who treated Persian history, e.g. Dinon of Colophon.

[67] Bickerman 1967 (F 361) 1–49; J. Sasson, *Jonah* (Anchor Bible) (New York 1990) 26–8.

of the Assyrian empire, destroyed in 612, but the symbol of an iniquitous metropolis.[68]

The same principle of attributing a work to an ancient hero is employed in the Song of Songs, whose hero is King Solomon. This book,[69] too, is dated by many authorities to the Persian period, at least on linguistic grounds (cf. such Persian loan-words as *pardēs* (4:13) and *ʾappiryōn* (3:9)). The pseudepigraphic principle was common, not only in the literature of the Persian period, but also in that of the hellenistic age, in which it evolved still further.[70]

Yet another common literary genre in the area was wisdom literature. The creators of this literature were scribes and learned men, a small group of those who would today be called 'intellectuals', who apparently wielded no small influence in the upper ranks of society. Such literati are known from Egypt and Mesopotamia during this period. A characteristic feature of the wisdom literature of the ancient Near East, as we know it today, is its preservation of ancient traditions, which are reworked and adapted to the spirit of the period. For this reason, it is extremely difficult to determine which elements in the book of Proverbs, for example, date to the Second Temple period. A similar situation exists in the case of Job, except that the prose framework of the book (chapters 1–2, 42:7–17) reveals some characteristic features of late Hebrew and post-exilic religious concepts. The most prominent of these is the motif of Satan tempting Job, which has no parallels in the biblical literature of the pre-exilic period or in the entire literature of the ancient Near East. It is commonly agreed[71] that the concept of Satan as an independent entity took shape in the Persian period, and indeed his earliest appearance in the Bible in the role of 'Accuser' is in the book of Zechariah: 'The Lord rebuke thee, O Satan' (Zech. 3:2).

The book of Ecclesiastes[72] actually contains nothing to link it explicitly with a real Palestine. Nevertheless, it is most definitely a Second Temple work, and it has often been claimed that it was written in the hellenistic period. Some of the pessimistic attitudes expressed in it are known from various phases of wisdom literature in the ancient Near East, but their formulation in Ecclesiastes betrays clear signs of re-editing in Second Temple times. The prospective readership of the book quite obviously consisted of a well-defined circle of intellectuals and

---

[68] The literature of the period frequently uses Assyria, sometimes as a substitute for Persia, and sometimes as an abstraction of a gentile world power (cf. e.g. Ezra 6:22). The plot of Judith revolves around the killing of Holophernes, commander of the army of 'Nebuchadnezzar king of Assyria', who invades Palestine, and Tobias, the hero of the book of Tobit, is associated with the Assyrian Nineveh.   [69] Pope 1977 (F 387).

[70] For pseudepigraphy, see Bickerman 1988 (F 364) 201–4 with 322.

[71] Lods 1939 (F 382); Meyers and Meyers 1987 (F 384A) 183–6; P. L. Day, *An Adversary in Heaven* (Harvard Semitic Monographs 43) (Atlanta, 1988).   [72] Bickerman 1967 (F 361) 139–67.

thinkers; the author both refers to and contests their ideas. There is no need to assume that the conceptions of life and its futility expressed in Ecclesiastes are drawn from Greek philosophical schools; such pessimistic world-views are quite common in ancient Near Eastern literature, both in Mesopotamia and in Egypt.

The last genre of the Second Temple period to be considered is that of psalms, especially those associated with worship in the Temple. The lateness of the language of some psalms, e.g. 103, 117, 119, 125 and 143, is indisputable, and some authorities ascribe several additional psalms to this period. Many of these pertain to the Temple cult and to pilgrimage to Jerusalem. At this time liturgical song was evidently an important component of the Temple service, and entrusted to a special team of singers, some of them named after eponymous ancestors: Asaph, the sons of Korah, Heman, Ethan and Jeduthun, ancient masters of their craft.

Besides the psalms which praised God and Temple, there are others of a didactic nature, which review major events in the history of Israel according to contemporary historical and philosophic ideas. Psalm 106 is a typical example of this category, relating Israel's past sins from the Exodus to the destruction of the Temple, and ending with the entreaty 'Save us, O Lord our God, and gather us from among the nations, that we may give thanks unto thy holy name, that we may triumph in thy praise' (Ps. 106:47).

3. The cessation of prophecy

By the beginning of the Restoration, prophetic literature, so rich in the pre-exilic period and during the Babylonian exile, had already begun to decline; it was to disappear completely in the course of the Persian period.[73] The prophetic texts of that period can be divided into two: those which deal with communal or national matters, and those which were concerned mainly with the Temple. To the first category belong the prophecies of Joel and Obadiah, the contents of which, although not dated, reflect the ambience of the early Restoration years. In both books the neighbours of Judah are castigated for rejoicing at her misfortune: Obadiah predicts the utter ruin of Edom, who 'rejoiced over the children of Judah on the day of their destruction' (v. 12), and Joel preaches the great day of judgment in the Valley of Jehoshaphat, when sentence will be passed on all the nations (Joel 4:2 (3:12)).

Joel's prophecies return to the motif of 'the Day of YHWH' in its national sense, familiar from First Temple times, and at the same time

---

[73] For a recent treatment see Barton 1986 (F 357).

glorify Zion and Jerusalem: 'Then shall Jerusalem be holy, and there shall no strangers pass through her any more' (Joel 4:17 (3:17)).

The second category of prophecies and prophets manifests a concern with the Temple, either with its actual construction (Haggai and Zechariah) or with the purity of Temple worship (Malachi). Whereas First Temple prophecy was concerned with a critique of society and its mores, particularly those of its leaders, the Restoration prophets pay no attention to such matters. Their great object is to comfort the people and to encourage them to proceed with the building of the Temple. Occasionally they were consulted on cultic matters, as, for example, when Zechariah (ch. 8) was asked about the continued observance of the national fasts, once the Second Temple had been built (Ezekiel fulfilled a similar role for his contemporaries in Babylonia); Malachi gives explicit injunctions about the priestly gifts – the tithes and the heave-offerings (Malachi 3:10), and is even more emphatic in his demand for the perfection and the purity of the sacrifices, finding fault with the priests for their failure to observe these codes (*ibid.* 1:6–7). We find here a highly significant stage in the development of prophecy: while the First Temple prophets criticized the Temple cult and belittled its importance, Malachi, the last of the classical prophets, fought for the maintenance of sacrifices, tithes and other priestly gifts as enjoined in the Pentateuch. The proclamation 'Remember ye the law of Moses my servant, which I commanded unto him in Horeb for all Israel, even statutes and ordinances' (*ibid.* 3:22 (4:4)) clearly reflects the transformation of prophecy. There was no room for the prophet in the fulfilment of such demands; the 'word of the Lord' was now permanently and officially entrusted to those who had preserved and interpreted the Law of Moses. Unfortunately, we have no sources for this critical juncture in the ideological and spiritual history of Judah and the Jewish people in general, and the details of the process remain obscure. No less obscure are the details of the collection, standardization and canonization of most of the Scriptures, a process which must have been in full swing during the Persian period and was presumably completed by the beginning of the hellenistic period. This canonization, which also involved the editing of the texts, was practically the final stage in the creation of biblical literature.[74]

[74] For recent work on the formation of the canon see Beckwith 1985 (F 358); Barton 1986 (F 357); Goodman 1990 (F 375).

CHAPTER 8d

CYPRUS AND PHOENICIA

F. G. MAIER

When Cyprus and Phoenicia were incorporated into the Achaemenid empire during the later sixth century B.C. they already looked back upon long centuries of trading connexions and cultural exchanges. During the fifth and fourth centuries B.C. both areas, forming part of the Fifth Satrapy (Hdt. III.91.1), had a number of basic problems in common. Both were divided into a number of relatively small, half-independent political units. These polities were long-established monarchies: Salamis, Ceryneia, Lapethus, Soli, Marium, Tamassus, Citium, Idalium, Amathus, Curium and Paphos in Cyprus; Sidon, Tyre, Byblus and Aradus in Phoenicia.

One trend to be observed in the history of both Cyprus and Phoenicia during this period is a continuous conflict of interests between these kingdoms. Again and again local feuds arise from their attempts to extend their own territory at the cost of neighbouring states or to gain domination over the whole area. These conflicts are superseded for short periods by a common policy when the kingdoms unite in their aim to gain greater, if not absolute, independence from their Persian overlord. Such a tendency – which can be observed in all regions of the Achaemenid empire which had strong political and cultural traditions of their own – is more marked in Cyprus than in Phoenicia. The front-line position of the island during the wars between the Greek *poleis* and Persia more easily prompted attempts to shake off Achaemenid rule.

Cypriot kingdoms and Phoenician city states also confronted a number of similar social problems, not least the process of growing Hellenization with its consequences. Yet despite such common problems and tendencies the traditions and the development of Phoenicia and Cyprus are different to such a degree that it seems necessary to treat both areas separately during most of the period under review.

I. THE KINGDOMS OF CYPRUS

The local kingdom had been the dominant form of political organization in Cyprus since the Late Bronze Age, but it is difficult to assess to what

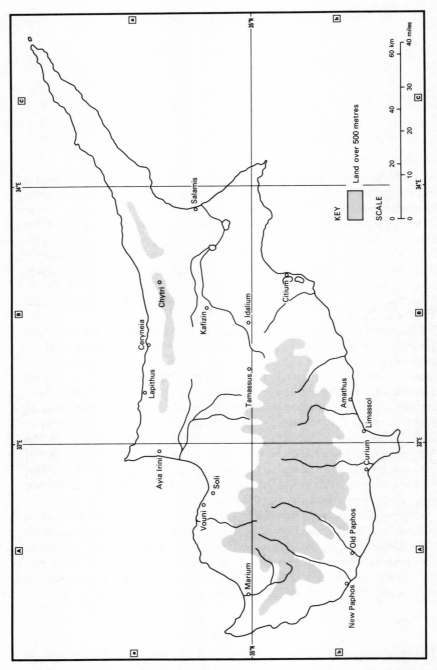

Map 7. Cyprus.

extent the traditions of Mycenaean monarchy and of Canaanite kingship were instrumental in shaping the peculiar system of Cypriot monarchy. As in Phoenicia, monarchic institutions survived throughout the archaic and classical periods, setting the island apart from the Greek world where (except for its northern fringes and Cyrene) kingship had disappeared long before. Diodorus neatly sums up the situation in the middle of the fourth century: 'in this island were nine important cities (πόλεις ἀξιόλογοι); beside them existed small towns (μικρὰ πολίσματα) which were dependent on the nine cities. Each of these cities had a king who ruled it, but was subject to the King of the Persians' (xvi.42.4).

The history of Cyprus and of its cities during the fifth and fourth centuries is difficult to reconstruct, as the evidence is extremely scanty and often confused. Yet the history of the island in the classical period has been presented in a surprisingly precise way as a conflict between the Greek dynasties and Persia, based on 'national' aspirations and cultural antagonism – assuming that Persia used Phoenician dynasties as tools, and that this led to a temporary ascendancy of the Phoenicians in the island and to a repression of the Greeks and their culture.[1] Such a view of Cypriot history is liable to impose the modern concept of nationality upon the past. Critical examination of the evidence thought to support the idea of a Greek–Phoenician antagonism shows, however, that much of it has to be discarded. The following account presents only those facts which are reliably recorded or can be inferred with a sufficient degree of plausibility.[2]

The Achaemenids had refrained from altering the existing political system and had recognized the status of the Cypriot kings. The conditions of their vassalage and the resulting restrictions of sovereignty are not known in great detail. The kingdoms had to pay a regular tribute and to contribute their contingents to the Persian fleet in case of war. On the other hand the Cypriot monarchs kept the right to issue their own coins; the royal mints were active throughout the fifth and fourth centuries B.C.

Information about the political organization of these kingdoms is very inadequate. In the fifth century it is practically confined to Herodotus who hardly records more than the bare fact of monarchic rule in the cities of Cyprus. It seems of no peculiar significance that he describes the Cypriot rulers sometimes as *basilees*, sometimes (but often in the same chapter) as *tyrannoi*: this simply denotes autocratic rule.

[1] With special emphasis in Gjerstad 1933, 1946, 1948, 1979 (F 254–7).
[2] Detailed examination of the evidence in Maier 1985 (F 285), Seibert 1976 (F 329). Yet factoids die hard. The restatement of the romantic-nationalist view of events by Stylianou 1989 (F 339) demonstrates once more how preconceived ideas impair the critical assessment of sources and research.

In the fourth century Aristotle wrote a *Kyprion Politeia*, Theophrastus *peri Kyprion basileias*. But of both treatises only one fragment of Aristotle survives, supplemented by the speeches of Isocrates and by a few fragments of Clearchus of Soli and of the comic poet Antiphanes (preserved in Athenaeus). Thus it is impossible to reconstruct in detail the internal structure of these small kingdoms, although a number of characteristic traits emerge from our sources.

The basically autocratic character of the Cypriot monarchies is confirmed by those elements of their political organization which are reliably recorded. The male relations of the ruler bore the traditional title of *anaktes*, the women were called *anassai* (Arist., F. 203). The *anaktes*, described by Eustathius (*Il.* XIII.582) as a notable class (*tagma endoxon*), seem to have wielded some degree of political influence, as the *kolakes* were directly responsible to them. These noble *kolakes*, described in some detail by Clearchus of Soli,[3] formed a secret police organization, expressly characterized as a tyrannical institution (*ktema tyrannikon*). The *kolakes* were of good family, but apart from the most prominent members of this body neither their number nor their names were known. The *kolakes* of Salamis, which may have served as a model for other courts, were divided into two hereditary branches, the *Gerginoi* and the *Promalanges*. The *Gerginoi* acted as spies and informants, listening to the talk of the people and reporting daily to the *anaktes*. The *Promalanges* investigated those cases which seemed to deserve closer scrutiny, using subtle techniques of disguise in their work.

Some fourth-century authors describe the rule of these kings as a mixture of soft living, ostentatious display of wealth and tyrannical cruelty. Princes of Paphos are depicted as lying on a silver-footed couch spread with expensive carpets from Sardis, clad in white shirt and purple robe, and attended by slaves and flattering courtiers.[4] The king of Paphos is said to keep himself cool by being fanned by doves which are attracted by the smell of Syrian perfume and shooed off by his slaves.[5] Nicocles of Salamis, on the other hand, is reported to have put to death the harpist Stratonicus and the sophist Anaxarchus for their witticism and freespoken utterance.[6] As some of these anecdotes occur in comedies and as all nicely fit the cliché of oriental despotism and decadence, they may largely be conventional. It is therefore open to question how far they depict the realities of life at the Cypriot courts of the age.

The palaces erected by Cypriot rulers during this period certainly were symbols of monarchic power, meant to impress by their splendour and wealth. The extensive palace of Vouni (Fig. 3) on the north coast of

---

[3] In Ath. VI. 255F–256B (fr. 19 Wehrli).
[4] Clearchus in Ath. VI 255E, 256F–257C (fr. 19 Wehrli).
[5] Antiphanes in Ath. VI 257D–F (fr. 200 K–A).   [6] Ath. VIII 349C–F, 352D; D.L. IX.10.58–9.

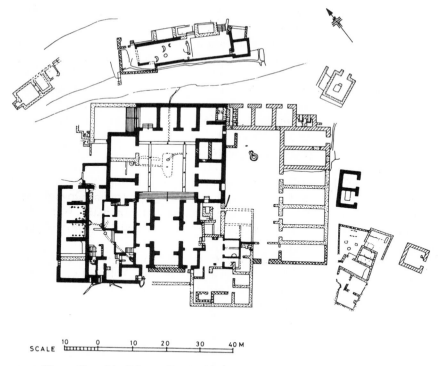

SCALE

Fig. 3. Plan of the Palace at Vouni. (After Karageorghis 1982 (F 276) 160, fig. 118.)

Cyprus was built in the early fifth century B.C. Remains of similar royal residences were recovered at Paphos and possibly at Soli.[7] At Vouni the rooms were arranged round a central colonnaded court; on its south-western side, above a flight of stairs, rose tripartite state apartments of *liwan*-type. Both Vouni and Paphos show the strong impact of contemporary oriental, especially Persian, palace architecture, but it would be rash to read details of political structures or events into the ground plans of such royal residences.[8]

To the Greeks of the fourth-century polis such institutions may have appeared strange and decidedly oriental. It is indeed obvious that the organization of the *kolakes* was modelled closely on the imperial police of Achaemenid Persia, the 'eyes and ears of the King'. The Persian *otakoustai* are indeed equated by Eustathius (*Il.* XIII.582) with the Cypriot

[7] Maier 1989 (F 286), with relevant bibliography.

[8] Gjerstad's hypothesis that the palace of Vouni was built by a persophile ruler of Marium in order to dominate a hellenophile Soli (and subsequently rebuilt by an hellenophile Marium king installed by Cimon) is far too speculative; Maier 1985 (F 285) 36–7; Maier 1989 (F 286) 18.

kolakes. But in the Greek world the Sicilian tyrants would also provide a model for autocratic forms of government.

The basic structure of a hereditary autocratic monarchy, supported by the close relations of the king, seems to have been common to all Cypriot kingdoms – whether they were ruled by Greek or by Phoenician dynasties. It survived in this form until the kingdoms were abolished by Ptolemy at the end of the fourth century B.C. Isocrates' description of the ruling methods of Evagoras, despite its openly eulogistic tendencies, in principle conforms with it (*Evag.* 20–3).

Democratic or representative institutions seem not to have developed in the island. The fifth-century bronze tablet from Idalium (*ICS* 217) mentions together with king Stasicyprus the city (*ptolis*) of Idalium. The city had to contribute to the emoluments of the physician Onasilus and his brothers and thus seems to have had a separate treasury. But it does not follow from the extant text that king and city shared the government of Idalium.[9]

At Paphos the political powers of the king were traditionally combined with the cult functions of the high priest of Aphrodite, as several inscriptions testify. In these texts the Paphian king – who wore an elaborate double crown of manifestly Egyptian inspiration – invariably styles himself *basileus* and *iereus tas Wanassas* (the traditional cult name of the Paphian Aphrodite). This combination of secular and religious powers originated from the special role of the sanctuary of Aphrodite at Paphos. There is so far no proof that the idea of sacral kingship played a role in other dynasties in the island.[10]

Hardly anything reliable is known of the social and economic structure of the Cypriot kingdoms during the classical period. Burial customs did not change markedly as compared with the archaic period. Rock-cut chamber tombs remained the burial place for the majority of people; only a number of wealthy families used more elaborate built tombs. The fourth-century Paphian kings Echetimus and Timocharis were buried in a large, elaborate chamber tomb just outside the city.[11] Limestone and marble sarcophagi became more widespread. A number of these, with the lid carved in human form, were imported from Phoenicia; later they were imitated locally, for instance at Citium. It also became a custom now to mark burial places by tombstones, partly executed in local Cypriot style, partly derived from contemporary Greek models. As regards the structure of society at the time, however, the cemeteries reveal hardly more than the basic fact that there were well-to-do as well as poorer citizens.

[9] *ICS* 217: Mitford and Masson in *CAH* III².3, 72.
[10] Maier 1989 (F 312). Inscriptions: *ICS* nos. 7, 16, 17, 90, 91; Masson 1980 (F 291). Yon 1989 (F 352) 373 and 1993 (F 353) 14 assumes a 'théocratie' at Citium.
[11] Maier and von Wartburg, *Arch. Anz.* 1992, 585–6.

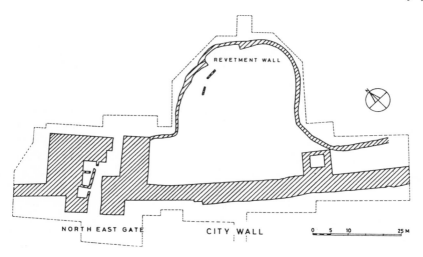

REVETMENT WALL

NORTH EAST GATE   CITY WALL   0 5 10   25 M

Fig. 4. Plan of the north-east gate at Nea Paphos in the classical period. (After Maier and Karageorghis 1984 (F 288) 209, fig.195.)

The cities of Cyprus remained, as in the archaic period, seats of government and centres of social and economic life. But except for the royal residences mentioned above, few remains of the public and private architecture of the period have been recovered so far. The cities continued to be fortified – for obvious reasons, if we consider the political situation in the island during these two centuries. Idalium built an elaborate system of fortifications in the fifth century, which was used into the hellenistic period; Golgi erected a city wall presumably in the fourth century.[12] The fortifications consisted of limestone walls with a rubble core or of mudbrick walls on a stone foundation; only parts of special importance were built of fine ashlar masonry. Thus when Paphos reconstructed its walls in the second half of the fourth century, only the North East Gate (Fig. 4) and the city wall immediately adjacent to it were built of large bossed ashlars. The plan of the gate incorporated both Near Eastern and Greek elements.[13]

Living quarters in the cities and towns – partially uncovered for instance at Idalium, Ayia Irini, Citium or Paphos – consisted of fairly modest houses with mudbrick superstructures of traditional type. The style and technique of the stone-built houses in the harbour town of Ayios Philon (in the Karpass), however, are clearly influenced by contemporary Phoenician building. In Citium workshops for the smelting of copper were still built next to the temple of Astarte – a close

[12] Idalium: BCH 98 (1974) 882; 102 (1978) 925; 103 (1979) 708–10. Golgi: BCH 95 (1971) 404–6; 96 (1972) 1073; 97 (1973) 673. Possibly also Tamassus: RDAC 1977, 303–5.
[13] Maier, RDAC 1967, 43–4; 1973, 190–2. Masson and Sznycer 1972 (F 294) 209–12.

connexion between metallurgy and religion to be observed there as early as in the Late Bronze Age.

Public architecture so far is represented mainly by sanctuaries, though there are remains of well-constructed buildings which may have served as administrative centres or official residences – such as a large Late Classical mansion with a peristyle court at Paphos.[14] Sanctuaries were as a rule constructed (or reconstructed) in the traditional form, combining a large courtyard with altars and votive gifts, a small covered *cella*, and sometimes a number of other buildings bordering the central court. Such traditional cult-places are represented by the sanctuaries of Athena at Vouni, of Aphrodite-Astarte at Tamassus, or of Heracles-Melqart at Citium-Bamboula. The dominant traditional cult in the island was still the worship of Aphrodite-Astarte with its antecedents in the fertility goddess of prehistoric Cyprus. At Citium the Phoenician temple of Ashtart, reconstructed for the last time, still flourished: an interesting painted fourth-century inscription illustrates its cult life.[15] But the centre of Aphrodite's cult remained Paphos, where the goddess was venerated as the *Wanassa* (the cult title *Paphia* does not appear before the hellenistic period). The buildings of the Archaic and Classical sanctuary at Palaepaphos were destroyed by Roman structures around A.D. 100. But a rich harvest of broken votive terracottas of the Classical period recovered from *favissae* near the temple, testifies to the flourishing life of the great sanctuary.[16]

No temples of Greek design have been discovered so far, although Ionic capitals found at Citium and Paphos may point to the existence of such buildings.[17] Greek cults – of Zeus, Hera, Apollo, Artemis, Athena or Heracles – gained popularity in the island, as coins and inscriptions demonstrate. This spread of Greek cults is but one aspect of growing Greek influence in Cyprus. Greek art was imported and imitated on an increasing scale, the bulk of Greek objects being represented by Attic pottery. The flow of such objects had already begun in the sixth century: after the Ionian Revolt it continued throughout the fifth and fourth centuries. A certain fall-off of imported Attic pottery during the first half of the fifth century – in contrast to Phoenicia or Palestine – has been attributed to the impact of the political and military situation on trading exchanges. But even if Attic pottery could be dated so precisely that the quantity of imports in the first and second half of the century could be reliably compared, such a temporary reduction in pottery imports is balanced to some degree by imported Greek sculpture, such as the

[14] Maier and von Wartburg, *RDAC* 1985, 113–17.
[15] *CIS* I 86 A-B (*KAI* 37); Chaumont 1972 (F 228); Masson and Sznycer 1972 (F 294) 21–68.
[16] Maier and Karageorghis 1984 (F 288) 182–3, 208.
[17] Nicolaou 1976 (F 308) pl. XXI 1; Maier and Karageorghis 1984 (F 288) 222–3.

famous bronze head of the 'Chatsworth Apollo' (*c.* 470–460), or the head
of a youth from the Paphian sanctuary (*c.* 480–470).[18] Cypriot sculptors
during the second quarter of the fifth century were obviously inspired by
contemporary developments in Greek art.[19]

During the second half of the fifth century, the volume of Greek trade
in the eastern Mediterranean increased perceptibly. This has been noted
also in Cyprus. At Citium nearly 50 per cent of fifth- and fourth-century
Attic pottery found so far is dated *c.* 450–400 B.C., at Salamis the largest
group of red-figure vessels belong to the years *c.* 420–370 B.C.[20]

The time-honoured arts and crafts of Cyprus, representing a highly
original blend of autochthonous, Greek and oriental elements, still lived
on. Traditional White Painted, Bichrome or Black-on-red pottery
continued to be produced in quantity. A few new types were invented,
such as jugs with a terracotta *kore* on the neck which acted as a spout. But
some of the vigour and *Kyprios charakter* of the Archaic potters seems to
be lost. Greek motifs and ornaments increasingly find their way into the
decoration of vessels. The same process can be observed even more
markedly in terracottas and jewellery.

Tradition still had a hold on the civilization of Cyprus. Amathus
seems to have been a stronghold of the authochthonous population;
Eteocypriot, written with syllabic signs, was still its official language in
the fourth century (*ICS* 190–7). The long survival of the Syllabic script is
a further proof of Cypriot conservatism. Salamis had begun to use the
Greek alphabet on coins and inscriptions by the end of the fifth
century.[21] But at Paphos alphabetic texts do not occur before *c.* 320 B.C.
(a dedication of the last king Nicocles whose other inscriptions are still
Syllabic), while at the Kafizin sanctuary in the territory of Idalium the
Syllabic script was employed for cult purposes until the late third century
B.C.

The Phoenician element in Cypriot society, religion and art was still
vigorous, radiating from Citium, the Tyrian colony on the south-eastern
coast of the island. Citium enlarged its territory, acquiring Idalium
before the middle of the fifth century, and later (about 350 B.C.) for a
short time also Tamassus. Political rule was followed by Phoenician
influences: Phoenicians lived at Idalium (as their tomb inscriptions
testify) and Melqart, Reshef-Mikal, Anat and Astarte were worshipped
in the city. But the Phoenician presence and Phoenician cults spread

---

[18] Vermeule 1976 (F 348) 15–17; Yon 1986 (F 350) 100; Maier and Karageorghis 1984 (F 288) 181 fig. 170.
[19] *Salamine de Chypre* x 1978 (F 323) 78; see also Pouilloux 1975 (F 314) 116; Yon 1974 (F 349).
[20] For Cyprus e.g. *Salamine de Chypre* IV (F 321) 71–3, 77–78, VIII (F 322) 4–9, X (F 323) 215–18; Salles 1983 (F 325) 54–8; Hermary 1989 (F 266) 189; Maier and Karageorghis 1984 (F 288) 217–18. For Phoenicia, Elayi 1983 (F 246). Short summary with bibliography up to 1985, Collombier 1987 (F 229).   [21] See the digraphic inscription of Evagoras I, *Salamine de Chypre* IV (F 321) 81–4.

beyond the zone of direct political influence, as inscriptions and other finds demonstrate. The cult of Melqart, Anat and Astarte is attested at Larnaka *tis Lapithou*; a Phoenician sanctuary existed in the early classical period in the territory of Amathus, at Limassol.[22] Phoenicians resided at Ayia Irini and at Tamassus (before *c.* 350 B.C.). The present state of evidence does not warrant the hypothesis of an 'economic expansion' aimed at exploiting the copper deposits in the Tamassus and Amathus area. Nor does it support the concept of antagonism and enmity between Greeks and Phoenicians. A number of testimonies point to a considerable degree of peaceful co-existence, mutual cultural impacts and even intermarriage between the two ethnic groups.[23] The kingdom of Lapethus possibly represented a kind of Graeco-Phoenician community; in fifth-century Salamis the presence of Phoenicians is attested by a tomb inscription recording Phoenician names in Greek language and Syllabic script.[24]

Despite Eteocypriot traditions and Phoenician presence, however, an increasing impact of Greek art, manners and religion is to be observed in the civilization of fifth- and fourth-century Cyprus. The process of Hellenization, originating from the strong ties formed between Cyprus and the Greek world in the sixth century B.C., was gathering momentum even if political developments seemed for a time antagonistic to it.

II. CYPRUS BETWEEN PERSIA AND THE GREEKS, *c.* 495–411 B.C.

The history of Cyprus between the Ionian Revolt and the middle of the fifth century is dominated by the conflict between the Achaemenid empire and the Greeks. The offensive strategy of the Delian Confederacy made the eastern Mediterranean, where an open flank of Persia could be attacked from the sea, a principal theatre of war. Cyprus, capable of supporting a large fleet, inevitably became a naval base contested by both sides. For Athens it was a necessity to secure such an advanced base; at the same time it was of the utmost importance for Persia to hold Cyprus as a base for her own fleet. In this she succeeded for most of the time, although Athens within thirty years made three attempts to gain a foothold in the island.

'After a year of freedom, the Cypriots were again reduced to slaves': Herodotus (v.116) thus sums up the consequences of the abortive rising of the kingdoms of Cyprus in 499/8 B.C.; some of the conquered cities were, as it seems, garrisoned for a time by Persian troops (Diod.

---

[22] *CIS* I 88ff. *KAI* nos. 38, 39 with Vol. III p. 64; Yon 1986 (F 350).

[23] Seibert 1976 (F 329); see also Chaumont 1972 (F 228) 179; Hadjisavvas 1986 (F 262); Michaelidou-Nicolaou 1987 (F 297); Hermary 1987 (F 265); van Berchem 1975 (F 347) 53–4.

[24] Karageorghis 1970 (F 274) 269–73.

XI.44.2).[25] We have no detailed information regarding the aftermath of the revolt, but it can hardly be doubted that the unsuccessful rising marked a turning-point in the history of fifth-century Cyprus.

The subsequent events of the Persian Wars demonstrate that Achaemenid control over the island was firmly re-established. The Cypriot kings discharged the duties to which they were bound by their allegiance to the Great King, whatever their real feelings and aspirations may have been. Already in the final stage of the Ionian Revolt Cypriot vessels formed part of the Persian fleet which defeated the Ionians in 494 B.C. at Lade, although the Cypriots (as may be inferred from Herodotus VI.6) seem not to have been very keen fighters. In 480 B.C. the Cypriot kings like other vassals had again to detail contingents to the fleet. The Cypriot ships numbered 150 and thus represented the fourth largest contingent after 300 or so East Greek, 300 Phoenician and 200 Egyptian vessels (Hdt. VII.89–90; Diod. XI.3.7).

The Cypriot ships were commanded by their own kings such as Gorgus of Salamis or Timonax, son of Timagoras (his city is not specified); the squadron of the Paphian general Penthylus numbered twelve vessels (Hdt. VII.98,195). Herodotus records that the Cypriots were clad like Greeks except for their head-dress: their kings wore a *mitra*, the others (presumably the officers) a *kitaris* (Hdt. VII.90). The *mitra* as a sovereign's headgear may have been similar to the Egyptian-style crown worn by the priest-kings of Paphos, while the *kitaris* may have resembled the head-dress of Persian satraps or that worn by a number of Late Archaic statues from Paphos.[26] Herodotus' distinction between Greeks and Cypriots represents in any case an interesting parallel to Aeschylus' famous lines (*Supp.* 288–9) referring to the *Kyprios charakter* as something definitely recognizable.

The Cypriot contingent earned little distinction in the naval war of 480 B.C. The fate of the Paphos squadron is described in some detail by Herodotus. Penthylus lost eleven of his ships before the battle during a storm off Cape Sepias. With his last vessel he was then taken prisoner at Artemisium; so was Philaon, the youngest brother of Gorgus. This shows that a number of Cypriot vessels were amongst the thirty Persian ships captured during the battle. The prisoners were sent to Corinth bound in chains, as the Greeks hoped to elicit from them information about the Persian plans (Hdt. VII.195, VIII.11).

Those Cypriot ships which were left to fight at Salamis proved to be a failure. According to Diodorus (XI.18.6–19.1) they broke first, together

---

[25] There is no proof for a Persian commander's residence at Paphos (as suggested in Schäfer 1960 (F 326)): Maier and Karageorghis 1984 (F 288) 208.

[26] Maier 1989 (F 287) 383; Maier and Karageorghis 1984 (F 288) 185 fig. 172; different interpretation, Hermary 1989 (F 266) 180; see also Gjerstad 1979 (F 257) 119 n. 4.

with the Phoenicians. It seems unlikely that the Cypriots fled on purpose, in order to help their Greek compatriots. But their not very creditable performance (Hdt. VIII.100.4) may indicate that the Cypriots were indeed disaffected. During the Persian council of war preceding the Battle of Salamis Queen Artemisia of Caria (who led her own ships with great valour and was in a position to judge) had already rated the fighting capacity of the Cypriots rather low: 'these so-called allies, Egyptians, Cypriots, Cilicians and Pamphylians, are of no use at all' (Hdt. VIII.68γ). But the Cypriots at least escaped the severe punishment meted out to some of the Phoenician commanders by Xerxes.

The defeats of 480 and 479 B.C. seem to have momentarily loosened Persian control over the kingdoms of Cyprus. Aeschylus' *Persae* (472 B.C.) implies that the cities freed from Persian rule included Soli, Salamis and Paphos in Cyprus (891–2). Such an implication, surprising at first, seems to be supported by the events of 478 B.C. In the spring of this year a Greek fleet of eighty ships, commanded by Pausanias, sailed to Cyprus and 'reduced most of it' (Thuc. 1.94); according to Ephorus in Diodorus' epitome, Pausanias 'liberated those cities which still had Persian garrisons' (XI.44.1–2). The extent and success of these operations are not recorded. But it is certain that the Greek fleet left after a short time and that Achaemenid rule not long after reasserted itself.[27]

The Persian reserve squadron of eighty Phoenician vessels which in 466 arrived too late to join the main fleet at the Eurymedon, was obviously based on Cyprus. Cimon subsequently captured this squadron off the coast of Cyprus, together with other vessels that had escaped from the Eurymedon battle but did not attack the island (Ephorus *FGrH* 70 F 192; Diod. XI.60.5–6). There were still good strategic reasons for an occupation of Cyprus, but Athens did not make a new attempt to gain control of the island before 460/59 (or 459/8) B.C. A fleet of 200 ships under Charitimides operated in the waters of Cyprus, but was soon diverted to Egypt in order to assist the revolt of Inarus (Thuc. 1.104.2). There is no record of Athenian operations in Cyprus at that time, except for the list of the members of the *phyle* Erechtheis who in 459/8 B.C. died in action 'in Cyprus, in Egypt, in Phoenicia' (M–L 33). As the Cypriots, together with Phoenicians and Cilicians, supplied the Persian fleet sailing for Egypt in the spring of 456 B.C. (Diod. XI.75.2), there can have been no lasting successes.

A last attempt to secure Cyprus as a base was made when Cimon resumed operations against Persia in the Eastern Mediterranean in 450/49. A fleet of 200 ships – 60 of which were soon detached to Egypt at the

---

[27] See also Meiggs 1972 (C 201) 56–8; the plea of Stylianou 1989 (F 339) 441–4 for Cypriot members of the Delian Confederacy is based on too many hypotheses.

appeal of Amyrtaeus, the king in the Marshes – arrived in the island in the spring of 449. The Athenian forces besieged both Marium in the west and Citium in the east, but neither the chronology nor the results of these operations are entirely clear (Thuc. I.112.2–4; Diod. XII.3–4; Plut. *Cim.* 18–19).[28] For obvious geographical reasons Marium seems to have been the first target. But it is uncertain whether the Athenian forces took the city or whether they raised the siege to proceed to the eastern coast of the island. A conquest of Marium has sometimes been inferred from Diodorus' 'he took by siege Citium and Marium' (Κίτιον μὲν καὶ Μάριον ἐξεπολιόρκησε). But as it seems certain that Citium was not taken (Thuc. I.112.4; Plut. *Cim.* 19), this sentence furnishes no positive evidence for a conquest of Marium either.

The siege of Citium met with no success and Cimon died during the operations. His death was concealed for thirty days and the siege raised. The homeward-bound Athenian fleet encountered Persian naval forces consisting of Phoenicians, Cypriots and Cilicians (Thuc. I.112.4); a combined action on land and sea was fought off Salamis. The victorious Greeks sustained such severe losses that Isocrates later compared the battle with the Athenian defeats in Egypt, Sicily, and at Aegospotami (VIII.86). Whether the battle was a chance encounter (as the text of Thucydides seems to suggest) or whether it resulted from a systematic Greek attack on Salamis, remains uncertain.

The failure of this last Athenian attempt to occupy Cyprus practically confirmed the *status quo* created by the Battle of the Eurymedon and put a definite end to the ambitious Athenian strategy in the eastern Mediterranean. Cyprus from now on remained firmly under Persian rule. Achaemenid control of the island, except for the years of Evagoras' 'Cypriot War', was not disputed until the conquest of Alexander.

Salamis was ruled by a Greek dynasty which traced its ancestry back to the legendary Teucer. King Gorgus had been dethroned when he refused in 499 to join the Ionian Revolt. He must have been re-installed after a comparatively short time as he appears in command of the Salaminian contingent in the fleet of 480. In the thirties of the fifth century the Greek dynasty was ousted by a Phoenician adventurer from Tyre (whose name is not recorded). He came to Salamis as a fugitive and won the confidence of the king but in the end 'expelled his benefactor and himself seized the throne' (Isoc. *Evag.* 19–20). Isocrates draws a gloomy picture of the usurper's rule: 'he reduced the city to barbarism (ἐξεβαρβάρωσε) and brought the whole island into subservience to the

[28] The ingenious attempts of Barns 1953/4 (F 222) and Sordi 1971 (F 330) to divide Diodorus' account into a 'lost campaign' of 460 B.C. and the events of 450/49 B.C. fail to convince; see Parker 1976 (F 309). See also *CAH* IV² 54, 501–2.

Great King' (*Evag.* 20). But apart from Cyprus having been under Persian rule for a hundred years already, archaeology has disproved his notion of a 'barbarized city' (*Evag.* 47).

The importance of Citium must have increased considerably when its Phoenician dynasty succeeded in annexing the kingdom of Idalium which bordered the Citian territory to the north. A state of conflict between the two kingdoms is proved by the Idalian bronze tablet (*ICS* 217; *CAH* III².3, 72, 78; *Pls. to Vol. III*, pl. 224) which records a siege of Idalium by 'Medes and Citians'. The date of the inscription is disputed (between *c.* 478 and *c.* 445, if not later); the circumstances of this attack are unknown. It can, however, not have been connected with the conquest of Idalium: the text shows that the siege at that time was unsuccessful and the Idalian king Stasicyprus still ruled when the inscription was set up. Idalium was definitely incorporated during the reign of King Ozbaal who styles himself 'king of Citium and Idalium', while his father and predecessor Baalmelek I was 'king of Citium' only. Ozbaal seems to have ruled shortly after the middle of the fifth century, but the precise chronology of the kings of Citium (except for Pumiathon, the last of the line) is still disputed.[29]

Next to Salamis and Citium, Paphos seems to have been the most important kingdom; it owed its special role to the famous sanctuary of Aphrodite. Yet of the history of Paphos and of other kingdoms nothing is known but the names of some rulers. The Paphian dynasty was Greek and used the Syllabic script for inscriptions and coin legends.

Marium and Lapethus present a slightly more complex situation. King Sasmas of Marium (*c.* 470/60–450?) bears a Phoenician name, and on some of his coins the Phoenician *mlk* for 'king' occurs beside the usual Syllabic signs. But as both his father Doxandrus and the later kings Stasioecus and Timocharis (second half of the fifth century?) have perfectly good Greek names, it seems difficult to decide whether he was actually a Phoenician or a Greek who was given a Phoenician name for reasons unknown to us. At Lapethus Greek and Phoenician names occur side by side in the list of kings, but in contrast to Marium their coin legends (except for the last king, Praxippus) uniformly use Phoenician signs. The population of Lapethus was primarily Greek; but there is evidence of not inconsiderable Phoenician presence. These facts, however, do not make the interpretation of the list of kings less difficult.

An unbiased assessment of our body of reliable evidence hardly supports the hypothesis of a Persian–Phoenician alliance to oppress the Greek dynasties and their populations. What can be reasonably inferred

---

[29] Recent archaeological research at Idalium has yielded important fourth-century ostraca with both Syllabic and Phoenician graffiti, and has proved that the acropolis was not destroyed suddenly, but abandoned gradually (Dr M. Hadjicosti, personal communication).

from a number of fairly isolated facts is the existence of conflicting aims and divided interests amongst the Cypriot kingdoms, which had already become apparent during the Ionian Revolt. The building and reconstruction of fortifications may be considered as additional proof for this state of affairs, although these building operations cannot be reliably connected thus far with particular events or rulers.

Political disunity facilitated Persian rule, and Phoenician kings may indeed have been more amenable at times, as they could not count on backing from outside. But one single instance of a co-operation of Persians and Phoenicians against a Greek city proves neither a general support of the Phoenicians nor a systematic anti-Greek policy of the Achaemenids. Persia did not act ideologically: no measures were taken, for instance, when the Greek Evagoras deposed the Phoenician Abdemon at Salamis in 411 B.C. There is, furthermore, no proof that Persia exchanged Greek for Phoenician rulers at Marium or Lapethus. Achaemenid rule relied on diplomacy and persuasion; it pragmatically resorted to a well-tried instrument of politics when it exploited conflicting interests of the kingdoms in order to tighten the hold on the island.

A fundamental conflict between Greeks and Phoenicians resulting from racial or cultural motives can hardly be inferred from one single instance of a Phoenician dynasty annexing a Greek kingdom (Citium would meet Greeks wherever it tried to extend its territory), and one single instance of a Phoenician pretender forcibly ousting a Greek king. The vehement anti-Greek policy of the Tyrian usurper at Salamis is alleged only by Isocrates; none of the Phoenician kings at Marium or Lapethus can be connected with such policies. Generally our sources reveal more co-existence than conflict between Greeks and Phoenicians (see above, pp. 305–6); it seems significant for the political climate in the island that a Phoenician could attain an influential position at the Greek court of Salamis.

Differences between Greeks and Phoenicians may have influenced politics to some degree. But the Greeks themselves seem rarely to have been united by national aspirations. In 499 Phoenician Citium joined the revolt, while the Greek kings of Salamis and Amathus refused to do so, and Stasanor of Curium deserted the Greek cause in battle. In the following years our sources never mention Greek Cypriot support of Athenian operations; in the battle of Salamis in 449 Cypriot contingents fought with the Persian fleet, not with the Athenians. Divided loyalties must have been even more marked in the Greek Cypriot kingdoms than in the Ionian cities of Asia Minor.

What we know for certain about the history of the Cypriot kingdoms reveals nothing but elements of inter-dynastic conflicts. Their policies aim at the extension of power, irrespective of the ethnic group: thus

Evagoras will indiscriminately attack Citium, Soli and Amathus – cities with Phoenician, Greek and 'Eteocypriot' populations.

III. THE REIGN OF EVAGORAS OF SALAMIS

A new phase in the history of Cyprus began when Evagoras seized power in Salamis in 411 B.C. The career of this outstanding monarch, who was to dominate Cypriot politics for a generation, culminated in a number of successes which made Salamis for some years a power in the eastern Mediterranean. Yet it became apparent very soon that Evagoras' rise was mainly due to a number of favourable but fleeting conditions in the foreign policy of his time. When these conditions changed, the political decline of Salamis set in and Evagoras' position dramatically collapsed within a number of years.

At Salamis a descendant of the Tyrian usurper had been murdered by another Phoenician, Abdemon, in *c.* 415 (Isoc. *Evag.* 26). Abdemon was either of Tyrian (Diod. XIV.98) or Citian origin (Theopomp. *FGrH* 115 F 103.2); as he was one of the *dynasteuontes* at Salamis (Isoc. *Evag.* 26), his career may have been similar to that of the first usurper. Evagoras, born *c.* 435, claimed descent from the royal house of Teucer (Diod. XIV.98.1; Isoc. *Evag.* 18) and seems to have lived unmolested at Salamis until Abdemon gained power. Regarded by the new ruler as a political rival, he was threatened with arrest and fled to Soli in Cilicia. From there he returned in 411 with a small group of devoted supporters to Salamis, broke at night into the city through a postern gate, attacked the royal palace and sent Abdemon into exile (Isoc. *Evag.* 26–32; Diod. XIV.98). This coup, so reminiscent of Ibn Saud's action at Riyadh in 1902, made Evagoras king of Salamis; the Greek population of the city remained remarkably indifferent (τῶν δ'ἄλλων πολιτῶν θεατῶν: Isoc. *Evag.* 31).

Evagoras consolidated his newly won power at Salamis by an extensive programme of reconstruction: he strengthened the fortifications, enlarged the harbour and built a fleet of triremes (Isoc. *Evag.* 47). Such measures were not prompted by a 'barbarization' of Salamis under Phoenician rule, as alleged by Isocrates; no decline in the arts and material culture of Salamis or Cyprus is to be observed during this period (see above, p. 306). Evagoras' basic aim was to increase the power of his kingdom: 'he caused it to become so powerful that many, who had previously held it in contempt, now feared it' (Isoc. *Evag.* 47). There is no evidence for an anti-Persian policy at that time, let alone for plans to liberate Cyprus from Achaemenid rule.[30] Evagoras' two-pronged policy during the first part of his reign shows this clearly. His one aim was to

---

[30] Costa 1974 (F 231), where Evagoras' career up to *c.* 391 is discussed.

extend the rule of Salamis, possibly over the whole island (ἅπασαν τὴν νῆσον σφετερίσασθαι: Diod. XIV.98.1): in this he eventually succeeded, partly by adroit political manoeuvres, partly by military force. At the same time he carefully inaugurated a foreign policy calculated to further his plans in Cyprus and shrewdly taking advantage of the complicated conflicts between Persia, Sparta and Athens. But this foreign policy worked for a long time in the interest of Persia, assisting her to eliminate Spartan naval power.

Persia did not react to the overthrow of Abdemon and the re-establishment of Greek rule at Salamis. From the terms concluded with the rebel Evagoras in 380/79 B.C. (Diod. XV.9.2: he submitted to the Great King 'as king to king' (ὡς βασιλεὺς βασιλεῖ) it can be inferred that he was recognized by the Great King as vassal king of Salamis from the beginning. Evagoras could hardly have acted as a mediator between Tissaphernes and Athens around 410 B.C. if he had been on strained terms with his Persian overlords. Towards the end of the century, some friction seems to have developed, for reasons we cannot verify conclusively (taking advantage of Cyrus' revolt?). But relations went back to normal when Evagoras in 398/7 agreed to pay the arrears of the customary tribute which he had obviously withheld for some years (Ctesias *FGrH* 688 F 30); until 391 he remained in principle loyal to the Great King.

The relations which Evagoras established with Athens during the first years of his reign are not easy to define. In 410 or 409 the Athenians honoured the king by a decree which survives in a very mutilated state.[31] It seems plausible that these honours were occasioned by negotiations which Evagoras conducted in the Athenian interest, and that they included a grant of citizenship (Dem. XII.10) – 'because of many great benefactions', as Isocrates records (*Evag.* 54). During the final phase of the Peloponnesian War refugees from Greece, not always of unambiguous repute, flocked to the court of Salamis (Isoc. *Evag.* 51). Prominent amongst these was the orator Andocides. His dealings with the king were not free from complications (he was imprisoned by Evagoras for a time: Lys. VI.28), but through him Evagoras in 407 supported hard-pressed Athens with grain (Andoc. II.20). The arrival of the Athenian Conon in Cyprus made a greater impact on the future policy of Evagoras. After the Athenian defeat at Aegospotami in 405 he escaped with a small squadron of eight triremes to Cyprus and stayed there for several years (Isoc. *Evag.* 52; Xen. *Hell.* II.1.29). In due time the Athenian relations of the king of Salamis gained greater political significance.

[31] *IG* I³ 113 = *Salamine de Chypre* X (F 323) 113–15 no. 247 = Osborne 1981–3 (B 165) D3; see Spyridakis 1935 (F 331) 46–50. Dated January 411 by Gregoire and Goossens 1940 (C 145); 'as late as possible in 408/7', Lewis 1977 (A 33) 130 n. 133.

The policy advocated by Conon was directed at overthrowing the Spartan hegemony over Greece and thus tried to get support from Persia. The Great King was indeed willing to back such a policy to a certain extent, as became apparent when Evagoras – won over to support Conon's claim to be appointed admiral of the Persian fleet – in 398 opened negotiations with Artaxerxes through the historian and physician Ctesias (*FGrH* 688 F 30; Isoc. *Evag.* 54–6; Diod. XIV.39). Agreement was reached after lengthy bargaining. Pharnabazus in 397 ordered the Cypriot kings to build a hundred triremes (Diod. XIV.38.2), to be commanded by Conon. The fleet finally sailed in 396 and after initial setbacks – being blockaded in Caunus where the Cypriot merce-naries mutinied (*Hell. Oxy.* xx (xv)) – in 394 won a decisive victory at Cnidus which terminated the short-lived Spartan dream of a domination of the seas. Athens in 393/2 once more decreed a number of special honours for the allied Cypriot king, including the *proxenia* and a bronze statue to be erected beside a statue of Conon in front of the *stoa Basileios* (Isoc. *Evag.* 57; Paus. 1.3.2).[32]

The co-operation between Evagoras and Conon primarily had a political function, although Diodorus mentions a friendship between the two men (XIII.106.6; also Isoc. *Evag.* 53). Evagoras seems to have had a sincere interest in assisting Athens against Sparta, but Conon may well have considered the Salaminian king (to whom he proposed a marriage-alliance with Dionysius of Syracuse, presumably in order to detach him from Sparta (see above, p. 105): Lys. XIX.19–20) merely a pawn in his game. But it is obvious that the course of events also fitted Evagoras' plans very well. Under the cover of his good relations with the Great King (whom he had assisted during the naval war against Sparta) he could reasonably expect to be given a free hand in his schemes for extending his hegemony over all kingdoms of Cyprus. The first open conflicts with other Cypriot monarchs are recorded in 398 (Ctesias *FGrH* 688 F 30). Further operations, 'by force or by persuasion', began in 393 or even earlier; by 391 only three cities still resisted: Citium, Soli and Amathus (Ephorus *FGrH* 70 F 76; Diod. XIV.98.2–3).

These three cities appealed for help to Artaxerxes. The reaction of the Great King, which seems to have come as an unexpected blow to Evagoras (Isoc. *Evag.* 58), marked the real turning-point in the career of the Salaminian king: it was the beginning of the 'Cypriot War'. Artaxerxes immediately ordered Hecatomnus, the dynast of Caria, to intervene in Cyprus; at the end of 391 Hecatomnus seems to have landed his troops in Cyprus unopposed by an apparently unprepared Evagoras

[32] *IG* II² 20 = *Salamine de Chypre* x (F 323) 117 no. 250. Two new fragments of the inscription, Lewis and Stroud 1979 (B 152) = *SEG* XXIX 86; see also Funke 1983 (C 140). For a possible portrait head of Evagoras see Hermary 1989 (F 266) 181.

(Diod. xiv.98.3–5). It is open to discussion whether the attempted conquest of the whole of Cyprus by the king of Salamis was connected with the reversal of Persia's Greek policy in 392/1.[33] But it seems to follow from our sources that Evagoras' revolt was not a planned insurrection, part of an anti-Persian 'grand design': it arose from a wrong assessment of Persian policy in Cyprus. The initiative lay with the Great King. For some years he apparently did not object to the gradual expansion of Salaminian rule. But once Sparta's offensive schemes seemed to have been effectively curbed, he decided to forestall the potential threat of a united Cyprus: 'The King, not only because he did not wish Evagoras to grow any stronger, but also because he appreciated the strategic position of Cyprus and its great naval strength whereby he would be able to protect Asia in front, decided to accept the alliance' with Amathus, Soli and Citium (Diod. xiv.98.3).

Evagoras, thanks to his diplomatic skill, was able to thwart the Great King's first measures and thus gained time to enlist support from outside. The small squadron of ten triremes which Athens sent to assist Evagoras was captured near Rhodes by a Spartan fleet. The delicacy of the situation did not escape Xenophon: Athens, still siding with Persia at that time, tried to help Persia's enemy Evagoras, while the Spartan enemies of Persia destroyed a force destined to fight the Persians (Xen. *Hell.* iv.8.24). But Evagoras managed to come to an arrangement with Hecatomnus who evacuated his forces and later secretly assisted the king with money. At the same time he consolidated his position by allying himself, not only with Athens, but with the Egyptian king Acoris (who had concluded a treaty with Athens in 388) and some other discontented Achaemenid vassals.[34]

In the spring of 387 a new Athenian fleet of ten ships, carrying 800 peltasts and commanded by Chabrias, got through to Cyprus. With the help of these forces Evagoras succeeded in subduing σχεδὸν ὅλην τὴν Κύπρον (Xen. *Hell.* v.1.10; Diod. xiv.110.5). How far his control of the island really went, is impossible to establish; we have no proof that his conquests included the cities of Citium, Soli and Amathus.[35]

The peace of Antalcidas (before the middle of 386) forced the Athenians to withdraw Chabrias with his squadron; the treaty expressly named Cyprus as an island subject to the Great King (Xen. *Hell.* v.1.31).

---

[33] Costa 1974 (F 231) 52–6. M. Yon and M. Sznycer announced in December 1991 a new Phoenician inscription from Citium, celebrating a victory of King Milkyaton over other Cypriots which may refer to the conflicts of the period.

[34] Theopomp. *FGrH* 115 F 103; Diod. xv.2.3–4; Bengtson, *SdA* nos. 234, 237.

[35] The coins of the 'Athenian king Demonicus', supposed to have been installed at Citium in 388 by Evagoras, have been shown to come from Lapethus by Schwabacher 1947 (F 328); see also Robinson 1948 (F 320) 45–7, 63–5; Masson and Sznycer 1972 (F 294) 100; Kraay 1976 (B 200) 302–3, 309.

But the King's Peace not only isolated Evagoras from his Athenian allies. It also released Persian forces to deal with the rebellious vassal ruler; and Diodorus (XIV.110.5) views the settlement precisely in this context.

For the moment, however, Evagoras' position was not impaired and the years after 386 marked the zenith of his career. The preoccupation of Persia with its Greek enemies had hitherto made possible his successes; Artaxerxes' decision to concentrate his forces against one of the areas of unrest, Egypt, gave him further respite. In secret understanding with a number of other disaffected dynasts, he built up large funds and assembled a considerable force said to have consisted of 90 triremes and 6,000 peltasts. This enabled him to extend his hegemony in Cyprus and beyond: in Phoenicia he conquered 'Tyre and some other cities' (Diod. XV.2.3; Isoc. Evag. 62; Paneg. 161). Evagoras seemed the undisputed master of the eastern Mediterranean and a threat to Persian naval power.

But a Persian expeditionary force, commanded by Orontes and Tiribazus, slowly assembled in western Asia Minor; its fleet was provided by the Greek cities under Persian rule. As in 498, Cilicia was chosen as a base of operations and the army ferried over to Cyprus from there. Evagoras, supplied with ships, grain and money by Achoris of Egypt, put up a gallant resistance on sea and land, but was defeated in a naval battle off Citium (Diod. XV.3–4). A long drawn out siege of Salamis followed, remarkable both for the courage and ingenuity of the defenders and for the discord between the Persian commanders. Despite successful intrigues (which led to the arrest of Tiribazus and the flight of the Persian naval commander Glos to Egypt) Evagoras had to come to terms in 380 or 379.[36] He was forced to give up all his conquests but retained the kingdom of Salamis, paying the customary tribute and acknowledging the suzerainty of Artaxerxes not 'as slave to master' (ὡς δοῦλος δεσπότῃ) but 'as king to king' (ὡς βασιλεὺς βασιλεῖ) (Diod. XV.8–9.3).

The final seven years of Evagoras' rule over a defeated and exhausted Salamis (Isoc. Nic. 31. 33) are not known in any detail. He was murdered, together with his eldest son Pnytagoras, in 374/3 – the victim of a court scandal according to Theopompus (FGrH 115 F 103.12). Evagoras was fortunate in finding a first-class public relations manager immediately after his death: Isocrates' Evagoras glosses over the slightly unsavoury circumstances of his end but depicts him as the image of an ideal king, worthy to rule not only over Salamis but over all Asia. There is no doubt that Isocrates wrote not history but an encomium, full of rhetorical exaggerations. But even a more sober assessment of Evagoras' life has to concede his remarkable qualities as a ruler: a shrewd politician, a skilful

[36] See for the chronology Hill 1949 (F 267) 140; Swoboda 1907 (F 341) 825–6.

diplomatist with a wide experience of the machinery of Persian government, and a bold strategist.

His career, which made Cyprus for a few years almost autonomous, once more demonstrates two points. (1) The internal policies of Cyprus were dictated not by 'national' motives but by the interests of the individual kingdoms. Evagoras impartially subdued Greek and Phoenician dynasties: adapting himself to the changing situation, he fought with his Persian overlord or against him. Independence may have been his final aim; his monarchy would hardly have conformed to the political system of Greece. Not by chance Isocrates, foremost advocate of monarchy and severe critic of Athens, was to be his panegyrist. (2) Independence from Persia was to be realized only for short periods, by taking advantage of unstable political conditions and temporary weaknesses within the Achaemenid empire. But now, as before in the fifth century, Persian rule reasserted itself in the end.

The political schemes of Evagoras failed; Cyprus gained no permanent independence. But his impact on the history of the island should not be underrated. What has been termed rather loosely his 'cultural policy' (and what was mainly the attraction of his court) had a more lasting effect than his power politics. To credit Evagoras – who in many ways remained a pure despot – with creating an 'Attic-Salaminian culture' may be an exaggeration. But philhellene he certainly was. We may believe Isocrates that Evagoras made Salamis 'inferior to none of the cities of Greece' (*Evag.* 47); he was the first king in Cyprus to use the Greek alphabet – albeit still beside the traditional Syllabary on coins and inscriptions. Greek writers, musicians and artists lived at Salamis; the marble head of Hygieia in early Praxitelean style found at Salamis may well be the work of such a resident artist. An Attic colony now formed at Salamis, with its counterpart in the Salaminian merchants living at Athens.[37] This philhellenic attitude in art, letters and life style was to be continued by Evagoras' successor Nicocles. One may still ask whether this testifies to a 'Greek national consciousness' or whether it simply represents philhellene pretensions similar to that of the Great King and many of his satraps and vassal rulers, such as the Phoenician kings. Yet in the end it emphasized and accelerated the integration of Cyprus into the Greek culture of the fourth century.

IV. THE CITY STATES OF PHOENICIA

Herodotus, who visited the country in the middle of the fifth century, defined the Phoenicians of his time as living on the coast of Syria (τῆς Συρίης οἰκέουσι τὰ παρὰ θάλασσαν: VII.89.2). Now, as in earlier centu-

[37] Pouilloux 1975 (F 314) 118–19.

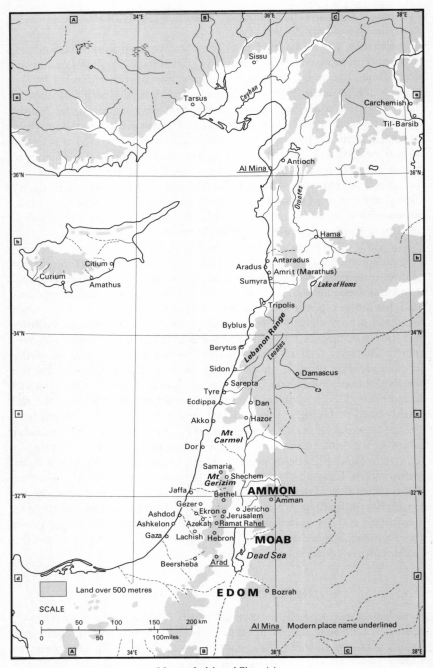

Map 8. Judah and Phoenicia.

ries, Phoenicia formed neither a geographical nor a political unit: it consisted of a string of cities on a narrow strip of the Syro-Palestinian coast, bordered by and interlocking with Syrians, Aramaeans, Hebrews and Philistines.[38] Connexions with the island of Cyprus off the Phoenician coast were long established – commercial, cultural, but also political. Citium had been colonized from Tyre and formal relations between the two cities seem to have existed as late as in the fourth century: a sarcophagus found at Citium bears the inscription of 'Eshmounadon, son of Eshmounadon, minister (*skn*) of Tyre', an official presumably accredited to the king of Citium.[39]

Phoenicia was divided politically into the city kingdoms of Sidon, Tyre, Byblus and Aradus. The history of Phoenicia is thus the history of these quasi-independent city states; but despite a number of obvious differences they share basic features of political organization, economy and civilization. These can be reconstructed only in the broadest outline, as the sources for the history of the Phoenician cities during the fifth and fourth centuries are very meagre and often conflicting. Fragmentary, often second- or third-hand, literary tradition is only very partially supplemented by inscriptions and coins. Archaeological evidence is unfortunately far less extensive than for the Bronze Age or the Hellenistic-Roman period. Thus our knowledge of the internal history of the cities, especially of their political and social systems, is severely limited; many problems remain unsolved.

Phoenicia was of special importance to Achaemenid Persia for two reasons. The country formed part of the land bridge connecting the empire's western Asian dominions with the vital province of Egypt; the fleets of the Phoenician cities with their great naval experience, suitable harbours and ample supply of ship timber were indispensable in building up a Persian navy (as Herodotus rightly implies: 1.143). The naval strength of Achaemenid Persia rested largely on the Phoenician contingents which – as a rule commanded by their own kings – formed the backbone of the fleet. That 'the whole navy was dependent on the Phoenicians' (Hdt. III.19.3) may not be an actual saying of Cambyses, but certainly formulates a basic truth of Achaemenid warfare and strategy. Phoenician warships played a decisive role in the Persian wars (Hdt. v.108, 109, 112; vi.6, 41; Paus. 1.15.3); Phoenician engineers proved to be more efficient and skilful than other units in constructing the bridge of boats across the Hellespont and in cutting the Athos canal (Hdt. vii.23).

The Phoenician contingents in the Persian fleet were usually provided by Sidon, Tyre, Aradus and Byblus. The Sidonian squadron was considered the most efficient in the fleet of 480 (Hdt. vii.96.1, 99.3) and

---

[38] For the approximate extent of Phoenicia during this period see Elayi 1982 (F 245).
[39] Masson and Sznycer 1972 (F 294) 69–75.

was in special favour with Xerxes. He reviewed his fleet at Abydus aboard a Sidonian vessel (Hdt. VII.100.2; also 128.2); during the council of war on the eve of the Battle of Salamis the commanders 'sat according to the rank assigned by the King to each; first the king of Sidon, then he of Tyre, then the others', and the king of Sidon was the first to give his opinion (Hdt. VIII.67.2 – 68.1). He must have been Tetramnestus who heads Herodotus' list of the most renowned naval commanders (VII.98).[40] The poor performance and subsequent execution, on Xerxes' orders, of a number of Phoenician crews at Salamis (Hdt. VIII.90; Diod. XI.18, 19.4) did not end the loyal service of Phoenician contingents in the Achaemenid fleet. They occur in most naval encounters of the fifth century, usually acquitting themselves bravely – helping, *inter alia*, to defend Cyprus from the Delian Confederacy or to destroy Athenian forces at Prosopitis (Thuc. 1.110.4).[41] Conon's fleet in 396 was still reinforced by 80 Phoenician triremes, commanded by the Sidonian king (*Hell. Oxy.* IX (IV).2; Diod. XIV.79.8). In Evagoras' Cypriot War, however, the Persian navy had for the first time to fight without the experienced Phoenician detachments.

To respect existing political structures as long as they were compatible with Persian rule was a constant maxim of Achaemenid policy. But the strategic role of Phoenicia may explain why her cities – similar to the kingdoms of Cyprus – obviously enjoyed a very considerable degree of local autonomy. The Achaemenid conquest of Syria and Phoenicia after the fall of Babylon in 539 caused no fundamental changes in the traditional political system of the area, which consisted of a number of hereditary monarchies. Darius I, revising in *c.* 515/14 the administrative organization of the Persian empire, incorporated Phoenicia into the Fifth Satrapy, together with 'Syria, Palestine and Cyprus' (Hdt. III.91.1).[42] In contrast to Jerusalem or Samaria no local governors seem to have been installed in the Phoenician cities. The Phoenician kings, allowed to mint their own coins, were in many ways treated rather as allies than as subjects. Their position seems to have fitted the formula of Evagoras: vassals of the Great King not 'as slave to master' but 'as king to king' (Diod. XV.8.2–3).

The Great King recognized the Phoenician rulers only on certain conditions which restricted their autonomy: to remain loyal to the Persian interest in general, and to contribute their naval forces to the Achaemenid fleet. Control was exercised by the satrap and by periodic inspections of *otakoustai*. For a long time there are no records of disaffection or insurrection. Throughout the fifth and well into the

---

[40] The king of Sidon was, however, never 'admiral' of the Persian fleet; Hauben 1970 (F 264).

[41] M–L no. 34: fifteen Phoenician ships taken by the Samians in Egypt, 460–454 B.C.

[42] The organization of the Fifth Satrapy has been discussed by Elayi 1978 (F 242); see also *CAH* IV² 153–4.

fourth century the Phoenician kings proved again and again loyal to their overlord. Only from the time of the Revolt of the Satraps did a growing hostility against Persian rule make itself felt, culminating in the Phoenician revolt following the Egyptian campaign of 351/0.

The internal situation of Phoenicia under Persian rule resembled that prevailing amongst the Cypriot kingdoms of the time: local conflicts for the extension of political power and economic influence of the individual kingdoms, during which those cities able to do so seem to have enlisted the help of Persia. According to the literary sources Sidon, Tyre and Aradus were the most important Phoenician cities during these two centuries. This is confirmed by the distribution of the cities' coins[43] and by the archaeological evidence from those sites which have been excavated so far. Byblus also was a prosperous city with imposing public architecture, but its coins did not attain the same extensive circulation as those of the three first-named cities.

Political power corresponded with wealth and prosperity of the cities: Sidon, Tyre and Aradus obviously were the kingdoms able to consolidate and to extend their rule during this period. The Phoenician states were not 'city kingdoms' in the strict sense. They consisted of the city itself and of a territory of varying extent in the coastal plain, which comprised a number of townships and villages and supplied the agricultural products needed. In only a few cases Phoenician rule extended beyond the coastal range, as (probably) with the Aradian towns of Mariamme, Marsya and Raphanea.[44] These territories were often discontinuous – a characteristic feature of Phoenician political organization made feasible by the good sea communications: Sidon ruled Dor south of Tyre, but Crocodeilon and Ashkelon south of Dor were again controlled by Tyre.

Aradian territory included, beside the towns already mentioned, Antaradus, Amrit/Marathus, Simyra (still an independent city in Assyrian times), Carne and Enhydra. Tyre won control over the coast from Sarepta in the north to the southern slopes of Mt Carmel during the fifth century; its territory also included – as just mentioned – parts of the Philistine coast.[45] Sidon was rewarded by the Great King with new territories, either in the late sixth century or in the first half of the fifth century, according to the sarcophagus inscription of King Eshmunazar II: 'and the Lord of Kings gave us Dor and Jaffa, the fine corn lands in the plain of Sharon, for the great deeds I did' (*KAI* 14.18–20).[46]

[43] Elayi 1982 (F 245) fig. 3.

[44] Elayi 1982 (F 245); Teixidor 1980 (F 345).   [45] [Scylax] (*GGM* I 78).

[46] The date – and thus the motive – is disputed: Dunand 1975–6 (F 240) 494 puts Eshmunazar II at *c.* 535–520, a date supported by recent archaeological research (R. A. Stucky, personal communication); Huss 1977 (F 268) 139 – following Assmann 1963 (F 220), Galling 1963 (F 251) – in the early fifth century; Mullen 1974 (F 306) 28 gives 465–51. If Dor really paid tribute to Athens in 459–454 (*ATL* III 174–5, 260–1, 269), this last date would seem plausible. See also *CAH* IV² 144.

The kingdoms jealously guarded their autonomy; it is characteristic that their naval contingents were usually commanded by their own leaders (Tetramnestus of Sidon, Mattam of Tyre and Marbalus of Aradus in 481/0: Hdt. VII.98). Some temporary alliances must have been formed, but none of these developed into a permanent confederation of the Phoenician cities – as is sometimes inferred from the one common action recorded of the three leading kingdoms: Sidon, Tyre and Aradus founded Tripolis in the early fourth century. The new city was divided into the three quarters "of the Aradians, of the Sidonians and of the Tyrians', but was also meant to serve as a place where 'the Phoenicians held their common council and deliberated on matters of supreme importance' (Diod. XVI.41.1). Thus the cities, at least in the fourth century, met to discuss or to concert their policies; a permanent confederation, however, does not necessarily follow from such meetings.

None of the cities, on the other hand, was ever able to impose its hegemony upon the other kingdoms. Tyre had lost its leading role in Phoenicia in the course of the sixth century,[47] while Sidon during the fifth century attained a prominent position which lasted until the revolt against Persia. This was partly due to Sidon's economic prominence, based on the rich alluvial soils of its territory and even more on its especially advantageous harbour. Sidonian trade, as demonstrated by coin finds, prospered in advance of Tyre and Aradus; in the fourth century 'in wealth and other resources the city far excelled the other cities of Phoenicia', being able to muster more than a hundred triremes and quinqueremes (Diod. XVI.44.6; also 41.4). The rich jewellery and other precious gifts found in the tomb of a Sidonian lady illustrate the enormous wealth of the city's upper classes in this period.[48] In a way Sidon's pre-eminence must have been enforced by serving – at least in times of war – as a meeting place of Persian officials and as a main garrison (Diod. XVI.41.2, 5). At the same time the special importance of the city and harbour for Persia may have made Achaemenid control over Sidon more strict than over the other cities. But our sources are insufficient to elucidate fully the complex relations between the Great King and his Sidonian vassal, and between the monarch and his Sidonian subjects.[49] Sidon's leading role seems beyond doubt, yet there is no indication that it ever amounted to a hegemony over the other cities.

The political system of the Phoenician cities during the fifth and fourth centuries can only be reconstructed in its most basic lines. The

[47] Katzenstein 1979 (F 279).

[48] Parrot, Chebab and Moscati 1977 (F 310), 107–10.

[49] It may be signficant in this context that only Sidon issued coins showing the Great King (in the fourth century). The attempt of Bondi 1974 (F 224) to demonstrate that the Sidonian kings had an especially 'persophile' policy rests on too slender evidence.

cities were ruled by hereditary kings, who dressed – as the relief of Yehawmilk shows – in Persian fashion. The surviving dynastic lists are, however, fragmentary and their chronology is still disputed.[50] It seems beyond doubt that the ruler wielded considerable powers; ladies of a dynasty could act as regents for minor sons, such as queen mother Amashtart for Eshmunazar II at Sidon (*KAI* 14). The record of Persian naval operations in the fifth and fourth centuries demonstrates that one of the chief functions of the king was to command the fleet (and most likely also the other forces) of the kingdom. Employment of mercenaries is recorded at least in the fourth century (Diod. XVI.41.4, 42.2); Phoenician defence of cities and siege warfare were of an advanced technical standard (Diod. XVII.41.4, 43.1; Arr. *Anab.* II.21.1–7).

Justice is praised as one of the king's virtues (*KAI* 10.9). But it remains uncertain whether the king acted, as at Carthage, as supreme judge (*šofet*). The king's political powers were traditionally combined with religious functions. Eshmunazar I (*c.* 479–470?) and Tabnit (*c.* 475–460?) of Sidon were 'priests of Ashtart' (*KAI* 13.1–2), King Ozbaal of Byblus (*c.* 350?) 'priest of Baalat' (*KAI* 11). Inscriptions demonstrate some of the religious activities of the kings. Eshmunazar II of Sidon (*c.* 465–451?) built or reconstructed sanctuaries for Ashtart, Eshmun and Baal (*KAI* 14, 15–18); Bodashtart of Sidon (*c.* 451–?) for Reshef and Eshmun (*KAI* 15, 16); Yehawmilk of Byblus (*c.* 450?) for Baalat, 'mistress of Byblus' (*KAI* 10.3–6).

The king's power was limited by the prerogatives of the Persian overlord and his satraps, but it seems not to have been shared – as is often assumed – with a 'council of elders'. The existence of such councils in pre-Persian times can hardly be inferred from the treaty between Asarhaddon and Baal of Tyre[51] or from a sixth-century reference of Ezekiel to Tyre (27:9). For the fifth and fourth centuries there is no proof at all of such an institution. The 100 prominent citizens King Tennes of Sidon took with him as advisers (Diod. XVI.45.1) and the *presbeis* of Tyre who pleaded with Alexander (Arr. *Anab.* II.15.6–7) were not constitutional bodies with an authority independent from the king, but ad hoc delegations formed in an emergency.[52] But those two episodes indicate that the opinion of the subjects could at times differ from the king's policy and had to be taken into account. There is hardly any doubt that the rich merchant families which formed the upper classes in the Phoenician cities (Diod. XVI.41.4, 45.6) played an important part in forming and expressing such public dissent.[53]

[50] For the reconstruction of the Sidonian king-list, see now Mullen 1974 (F 306) and Peckham 1968 (F 311) 72–6; for the fragmentary dates of the Byblus dynasty: Dunand 1965 (F 235) 35; *KAI* II 10–15; Jidejian 1968 (F 269) 211–12; Moscati 1979 (F 303) 63.

[51] Borger 1956 (F 80) 69, Rs. III 7.   [52] Bondi 1974 (F 224) 158–60.

[53] There is no conclusive evidence (despite Elayi 1981 (F 244)) for placing the often-discussed slave revolt at Tyre in such a fourth-century context.

The cities of Phoenicia benefited from Persian rule. Favoured by the Great King and profiting from peaceful conditions and good communications in the empire, their prosperity increased despite the loss of Carthage and other colonies in the West. As in earlier centuries, Phoenicia exported cedar and other hardwoods of the Lebanon; Tyrian purple; fine garments of Byblus, Tyre and Berytus; glass, faience, metalwork and salt. Phoenician shipyards were renowned for their products. At the same time the cities profited greatly from their position at the end of the caravan trade routes leading from the East through the Achaemenid empire: from their harbours the goods were shipped all over the Mediterranean. Phoenician traders were active at Ezion-Geber, a Red Sea post on the road of incense and spices;[54] a Tyrian trading colony, comprising a temple of 'Aphrodite the Stranger', was established at Memphis (Hdt. II.112.2).

Phoenicia was not only situated in the best position for trade; it formed at the same time – in a way similar to Cyprus – the crossroads of peoples and civilization. Thus in Phoenician culture now as in earlier periods foreign influences mingle with strong indigenous traditions of life and art. The luxurious courts of the kings, attracting foreign products and artists, must have promoted such exchanges to a considerable degree. Egyptian influence had been very marked from the ninth to the seventh century. During the sixth century impulses of Neo-Babylonian and Achaemenid art and architecture made themselves felt, without entirely suppressing Egyptian traditions, which are to be observed as an undercurrent until the Roman period. From the fifth century onwards the impact of Greek art slowly increased – both through Cyprus as an intermediary (as demonstrated by the import of Archaic Cypriot sculpture in the late sixth century) and through direct contacts with the Greek world.

In the monumental Phoenician architecture of the period Persian influence is dominant. The remains of a fifth-century palace at Sidon, marble capitals with bull protomai and column bases, are clearly inspired by the Achaemenid style of Persepolis and Susa, but are more vivid and naturalistic in execution. Despite Diodorus' reference to a royal park, *basilikos paradeisos*, at Sidon (XVI.41.5) it is still uncertain whether these remains belong to a palace of the Phoenician king or to the *apadana* of the Persian satrap. Achaemenid in style are also the fifth-century fortifications at Byblus. The defences of the coastal cities were a constant preoccupation of the Achaemenid kings and a common interest of both Phoenicians and Persians.[55] Remains of the strong walls of Aradus still survive; the enormous walls of fourth-century Tyre are described by Arrian (*Anab.* II.21.4).

[54] Glueck 1971 (F 258).   [55] Dunand 1968 (F 236) and 1969 (F 237).

Sanctuaries were still built in traditional form: a fairly small holy of holies enclosed by an open walled *temenos*, which sometimes contained an artificial lake as at Amrit/Marathus.[56] In the main cities, however, monumental temples were built or reconstructed in a different style. At Byblus a sanctuary of rectangular plan with two rows of pillars rose on an extensive podium, reminiscent of the podium of the reconstructed temple of Jerusalem:[57] most likely the temple of Baalat-Gebel, the 'mistress of Byblus', of King Yehawmilk's inscription (*KAI* 10). At Sidon King Eshmunazar II had reconstructed 'near the spring of Ydlal, in the mountains' (*KAI* 14.17) the temple of Eshmun. The podium of this temple, comparable to that of Pasargadae, the ashlar style of the masonry, and four marble bull protomai clearly demonstrate Persian inspiration. Some fragments of marble columns, Ionian capitals and palmetted cornices seem to be the work of Greek masons, but this is nothing foreign to the eclecticism of Achaemenid architecture. The Greek impact becomes definite only with the addition of a choreographic tribune (by King Bodashtart: *KAI* 16?); its rich sculptural decoration clearly adapts Attic models of the fourth century. Yet the early fourth-century marble votive statuettes of 'temple boys', found in the temple, still demonstrate elements of Cypro-Phoenician tradition.

In the Phoenician religion of the time a corresponding development is to be observed. The strong hold of traditional deities on Phoenician society is obvious. Sidon worships Ashtart, the Phoenician goddess of fertility, love and also war, as 'our lady'; the protective god of the city is the 'holy prince' Eshmun, the only god also venerated as a healing god in the Near East (and as such likened to Asklepios). The great god of Tyre was of old Melqart, the 'ruler of the city'; Baalat, the 'mistress', remained the goddess of Byblus. On the stela dedicated by King Yehawmilk she is characteristically represented in the form of the Egyptian Hathor-Isis.[58] But if the religion of the Phoenicians shows a strong persistence of ancestral gods, it exhibits at the same time a marked ability to adapt elements of foreign cults. Egyptian influence here gradually gave way to Greek cult names, cult objects and votive gifts.

Burial customs follow a similar trend. In contrast to the Persian models adapted in the architecture of the sixth and fifth centuries, the mummification of the dead and the forms of sepulchral art show dominating Egyptian influence. The anthropoid sarcophagi, in which the royal families and the rich were buried during the fifth and fourth centuries, are of special interest in this respect. The earlier sarcophagi of

[56] Egyptian influence in plan and construction is obvious here; the sanctuary is dated to the hellenistic period by Lézine 1961 (F 283), in contrast to Dunand 1946/48 (F 233) 106–7.
[57] Dunand 1954 (F 234) 26–41 and 1969 (F 237).
[58] There is no proof for a 'triad of divinities' at Byblus: Sznycer 1981 (F 342) 252.

this group were either imported from Egypt – as the black basalt coffin of Eshmunazar II with the king's portrait and inscription on the lid – or modelled closely on Egyptian prototypes. From the first half of the fifth century onwards the Sidonian ateliers were famous for their anthropoid marble sarcophagi which blend Egyptian and Greek elements in a way highly characteristic of Phoenician art. Egyptian traditions still survive in this local industry – sometimes in a surprising form when a head of pure Greek style displays an Egyptian plaited beard. But the influence of Classical Greek models, imitated by Phoenician craftsmen with great finesse, becomes more and more apparent especially in the treatment of the sculptured head on the lid. From the beginning of the fourth century Greek inspiration dominates Phoenician sepulchral art, as the famous relief sarcophagi from the royal necropolis of Sidon demonstrate. The sarcophagi of 'the Lycian' (*c*. 400), 'the Satrap' (*c*. 380/70), 'the Weepers' (*c*. 365/55), and the 'Alexander sarcophagus' (*c*. 333) are truly representative examples of Greek funeral art at its best.[59] The impact of Greek civilization, as reflected in sepulchral art, is also demonstrated by the steadily growing import of Attic pottery which penetrates from the coastal cities into Galilee, Samaria and even Judaea.[60]

Evagoras of Salamis had occupied Tyre and possibly some other Phoenician cities around 385 (above, p. 316). There is no further information about his operations but it is certain that his rule over parts of Phoenicia ended with the Cypriot War. After 379 all the traditional local dynasties were re-installed both in Phoenicia and in Cyprus; the state of political fragmentation which seemed most effectively to guarantee Persian control was thus restored. Conditions in both areas were similar, and so were the effects of the situation: insurrection against Persia – this time of Cypriots and Phoenicians alike.

V. CYPRUS AND PHOENICIA: FROM THE CYPRIOT WAR TO THE
PEACE OF 311 B.C.

With the end of the Cypriot War Phoenicia and Cyprus reverted to their own affairs. The traditional divergence of interests between the local kingdoms must have persisted in both areas and influenced their politics. But we have scarcely any information about actual conflicts. A state of tension between Salamis and the other Cypriot cities (Isoc. *Nic.* 33) was nothing but the natural aftermath of Evagoras' policy. The destruction

---

[59] See for the dating now Gabelmann 1979 (F 249); in general Kukahn 1955 (F 280); Fleischer 1983 (F 248). It is still questionable which Sidonian kings were buried in these sarcophagi (see now Gabelmann 1982 (F 250)) as the chronology of the kings is only provisionally established: Mullen 1974 (F 306) 28. Generally on Greek influences in Phoenicia: Stucky 1983 (F 335) and 1984 (F 336).
[60] See Stern 1982 (F 397) 136–41, 283–6.

of the palace of Vouni in the early fourth century may as well have resulted from Evagoras' actions in the nineties as from a violent settling of old scores between Marium and Soli.[61]

The only major change in the political system of Cyprus we know of was the further expansion of the kingdom of Citium-Idalium, this time by peaceful methods. The bankrupt ruler of Tamassus, Pasicyprus, sold his kingdom for 50 talents to Pumiathon of Citium around 350; he then retired to live as a private citizen at Amathus. Pumiathon henceforth styled himself 'king of Citium, Idalium and Tamassus'.[62] Thus by the middle of the fourth century the eleven kingdoms of Cyprus were reduced to nine (Diod. xvi.42.4): Salamis, Citium, Paphos, Curium, Amathus, Marium, Soli, Lapethus and Ceryneia.

Citium must have gained in political and economic power by acquiring Tamassus with its copper mines. But Salamis still seems to have retained its position as the most important city in the island. The kingdom was ruled from 374/3 onwards by Nicocles, the second son of Evagoras.[63] Nicocles' claim to fame mainly rests on his close relation with Isocrates whose disciple he may have been for a time. For which of the three Cypriot pamphlets dedicated to the king the author received 20 talents ([Plut.], *Mor.* 838A) remains uncertain. But there is no doubt that these three orations were instrumental in propagating the idea of monarchy. The *Nicocles* couples severe criticism of democracy with very outspoken defence of monarchy as a political system. The tenets of *Ad Nicoclem* were understood as guiding principles for the conduct of the 'good prince' and strongly influenced later writings on that subject, such as the treatise of the Byzantine author Agapetus.[64]

The impact of Isocrates' writings on the kings of his time is hard to gauge. One doubts whether Nicocles himself heeded the author's concept of rulership as a serious responsibility with the task 'to relieve the state from any distress, to maintain its prosperity and to enlarge it' (Isoc. *Nic.* 9), or his sensible advice 'to be a slave to no pleasure but rule over your desires even more firmly than over your people' (*Nic.* 29). It seems equally possible that he only used high-sounding principles to represent despotic government as a lawful, enlightened monarchy.

[61] Maier 1985 (F 285) 36–7.
[62] Duris *FGrH* 76 F 4. He does not mention Pasicyprus's kingdom, but the inscriptions of Pumiathon of Citium show that it was Tamassus; in his 8th year he rules Citium and Idalium only (*CIS* I 92), but in his 21st year Citium, Idalium and Tamassus (*KAI* no. 32). In his 37th year – after Alexander had transferred Tamassus to Pnytagoras of Salamis (see below, p. 333) – he is reduced again to Citium and Idalium (*KAI* no. 33). The exact dates remain uncertain, as the conventional date for Pumiathon's accession, 361, is no more than probable. Diod. xvi.42.4 seems to imply that Tamassus was sold before the revolt against Persia.
[63] Diod. xv.47.8 (Nicocles the eunuch who had Evagoras assassinated) is an obvious error.
[64] F. Dvornik, *Early Christian and Byzantine Political Philosophy* (Washington, DC, 1966) I 200–3, II 712–14. See also *CAH* VII².1, 75–7.

How far Isocrates' description of the situation at Salamis and of Nicocles' ruling methods generally depicts reality, or how far it is only an exercise in irony, is impossible to decide. The portrait of the king is certainly as strongly biased as that of his father Evagoras. Had Nicocles been such a model of virtue and justice, he could hardly have been described by contemporary historians as a tyrant living in extreme luxury and dissolution, vying in his excesses with the Sidonian King Straton (Theopomp. *FGrH* 115 F 114; Anaximenes *FGrH* 72 F 18). This image of the oriental despot again may partly be a cliché: the true character of Nicocles remains difficult to assess.

The Salaminian monarch and Straton I of Sidon (*c.* 375/4–361) obviously had more in common than a taste for debauchery and a predilection for Greek musicians, dancers and courtesans (Theopomp. *FGrH* 115 F 114). Nicocles patronized Greek literature and art, like his father. Straton I (his hellenized name: on his coins he appears as Abdashtart) was called 'Philellēn' – with good reason, as the arts and crafts of Sidon during this period demonstrate. An Athenian decree of about 364 exempts from taxes Sidonian merchants and honours Straton I as *proxenos* (IG II² 141).[65] Whether this testifies only to close commercial relations between the Phoenician metropolis and Athens or whether it possibly implies a political understanding, remains uncertain.

But it seems not impossible that opposition to Persia formed another bond between Nicocles of Salamis and Straton I of Sidon. Unfortunately we lack precise information about the relations of the Cypriot and Phoenician vassal kingdoms and their overlord at this time. But a growing hostility against Achaemenid rule, notably in Phoenicia, is to be inferred from subsequent events. Such a change of political attitude obviously resulted from an interaction of the increasing prosperity of the Phoenician cities and the harsher ruling methods adopted by the Achaemenid empire as it became more unstable.

Straton I was involved, with the help of Egyptian troops and possibly on the instigation of the Pharaoh Tachos, in the main phase of the Satraps' Revolt, *c.* 362–360.[66] The king died during the revolt, reputedly getting himself stabbed by his wife (Hieron. *adv. Jovin.* 1. 45). Nicocles also met with 'a violent death' in prison about this time (Theopomp. *FGrH* 115 F 114; Maximus Tyr. *Diss.* II.14): thus it seems not impossible that he was in some way involved too.

The Satraps' Revolt turned out to be a portent of things to come as far as Cyprus and Phoenicia were concerned. When Artaxerxes III Ochus succeeded in 359/8 he was determined to restore the Great King's rule over the territories in revolt. But disaffection had spread wide in the Persian empire and for several years Artaxerxes' measures met with

[65] Moysey 1976 (F 305).   [66] Diod. xv.90.3, 92.3–4. See p. 84.

limited success only. In 351/0 Persian forces began an attack on Egypt, the main area of revolt. The Phoenicians, at some later time, followed the example of the Egyptians: on the instigation of the Sidonians they formed an alliance against Persia, concluded a treaty with the pharaoh Nectanebus and prepared for war (Diod. XVI.40.3–41.4). Diodorus tries to explain the reasons for the rising: 'the King's satraps and generals dwelt in the city of the Sidonians and behaved in an outrageous and high-handed fashion towards the Sidonians in ordering things to be done; the victims of this treatment, aggrieved by their insolence, decided to revolt from the Persians' (XVI.41.2). This seems to be a correct assessment of the actual situation. The spirit of revolt had been fostered to no small extent by the billeting and provisioning in Phoenicia of troops destined for the Egyptian campaign.

The signal for the rising of Phoenicia was the destruction of the *basilikos paradeisos* at Sidon, combined with the burning of the fodder stored for the Persian cavalry and the arrest of the leading Persians (Diod. XVI.41.5). The Cypriots followed suit: the kings of the island 'in common agreement and in imitation of the Phoenicians revolted, and having made preparations for the war, declared their own kingdoms independent' (Diod. XVI.42.5).[67] At Salamis Nicocles had been succeeded about 360 by his son (or brother) Evagoras II who advocated a pro-Persian policy; he was dethroned and in turn succeeded by Pnytagoras. Both Cyprus and Phoenicia were rarely nearer to achieving unity of political purpose than during this short period.

Events developed in a pattern similar to the strategy adopted by Persia during the Cypriot War. As Artaxerxes' forces were fully engaged in Egypt and Phoenicia, Cyprus was for the moment being left to its own devices. In Phoenicia the revolt was led by King Tennes of Sidon who in the end betrayed his city, only to be executed himself by order of Artaxerxes.[68] The Great King crushed the rebellion in a merciless way. Sidon was destroyed by fire and (according to Diodorus) 40,000 of its inhabitants perished; 'the rest of the cities, panic-stricken, went over to the Persians' (Diod. XVI.45.4–6). Straton II succeeded Tennes as king of Sidon; the destruction of his city cannot have been as thorough as suggested by Diodorus, because only twenty years later Sidon is described as an important city with a considerable fleet.[69]

The task of recovering Cyprus was, as in Evagoras' war, entrusted to the satrap of Caria – Idrieus, the son of Hecatomnus (351/0–344/3).

[67] The exact chronology of the Phoenician and Cypriot revolts is somewhat hazy, but the relative sequence of events seems clear. For the chronology of Diod. XVI.40ff in general see Sordi 1959 (F 59A); Cawkwell 1962 (C 105).

[68] For a fuller account of the Phoenician campaign see *CAH* IV² 145–6; also Barag 1966 (F 221).

[69] Arr. *Anab.* II.20. Kahrstedt 1926 (F 272) 39 suggested that after 351 Tyre took over some Sidonian territories in the south.

Operations did not begin before 346 and ended presumably in 344/3.[70] Ironically, the force of forty triremes and 8,000 Greek mercenaries was now commanded by the Athenian Phocion, accompanied by Evagoras II bent on recovering his throne at Salamis. The Cypriot cities were reduced with comparable ease. Only Salamis under King Pnytagoras had to be invested from land and sea, while the mercenaries pillaged the island (Diod. XVI.42.6–9, 46.1). After a long-drawn, skilful defence Pnytagoras surrendered of his own will and was allowed to remain king of Salamis. Evagoras II, contrary to his plans, was not reinstated but given 'another and higher command in Asia': coin evidence seems to suggest the kingdom of Sidon. His misgovernment there lasted a few years only (c. 344/3–342/1?); he had to flee to Cyprus and was executed there (Diod. XVI.46.2–3). Sidon was again ruled – *Darei opibus adiutum* – by the local king Straton II (Curt. IV.1.16).

Persia had for a last time reasserted her rule in Phoenicia and Cyprus. Again it is obvious that neither 'national' motives nor solidarity between Achaemenid vassals were dominant factors in the politics of the time: a Carian dynast and an Athenian general combined to enforce impartially the submission of the Greek and Phoenician kingdoms of Cyprus. Artaxerxes was free now to concentrate his forces against Egypt and to crush the revolt there finally in 343/2. Persia seemed to have recovered her strength once more. Yet after the short span of a decade Alexander's campaigns put an end not only to the Achaemenid empire but also to the old-established kingdoms of Cyprus and Phoenicia.

The highly skilled Cypriot and Phoenician contingents operated for a last time with the Achaemenid navy in 333. Their presence may have prompted Alexander not to engage the Persian fleet at Miletus (Arr. *Anab.* 1.18.7) – the more so as Cypriots and Phoenicians now had in commission true quinqueremes, the most decisive innovation in sea warfare before the adoption of the naval gun.[71] When Alexander's army began its march into Phoenicia after the battle of Issus, the fleets of Tyre, Sidon, Byblus and Aradus still sailed with the Persians under Autophradates (Arr. *Anab.* 11.20.1–2). Cypriot and Phoenician ships formed part of the fleet of Amyntas heading for Egypt (Arr. *Anab.* 11.13.2–3; Diod. XVII.48.1–2).

With Alexander's advance into Phoenicia things began to change. Aradus, then Byblus and Sidon, surrendered without a fight: 'the Sidonians who loathed Persia and Darius called him in themselves' (Arr. *Anab.* 11.13.7–8, 15.6; Curt. IV.1.15–16). The feeling created by the

[70] For the chronological problems see Hornblower 1982 (F 644) 41–5. It does not follow, however, from Diod. XVI.42.6ff that Cyprus was recovered before Phoenicia; for military reasons this seems rather unlikely.

[71] Tarn 1930 (K 57) 129–32; Morrison and Williams 1968 (K 48) 183, 235, 249.

abortive revolt of 346; the shock of the Persian defeat; the absence of the kings, except for Straton II of Sidon, with the fleet (Arr. *Anab.* II.15.7, 20.1): all this may have contributed to these easy surrenders. Alexander's strategy to neutralize the Persian fleet by depriving it of its bases seemed successful beyond hope. Tyre, however, probably strengthened in its attitude by an embassy from Carthage and apparently not convinced of a final Persian defeat, was not prepared to yield its autonomy. The city offered a formal submission but refused to admit a Macedonian garrison (Arr. *Anab.* II.15.6–16.8).

Alexander, believing it imperative to secure his sea communications with Greece, considered it too great a risk to advance further in pursuit of Darius with a hostile Tyre at his rear. Thus lengthy and complicated siege operations began, described in great detail by Arrian (*Anab.* II.18–24) and Diodorus (XVII.40.2–46). The strength of the Tyrian position is neatly summed up by Arrian: 'the siege of Tyre obviously was a difficult proposition. The city was an island, strengthened with high walls on all sides; all operations from the sea were in Tyre's favour, as the Persians still controlled the sea and the Tyrians still had many ships left' (II.18.1–2). Thus it must have been a most welcome surprise for Alexander (who had secured already the assistance of the Phoenician naval forces except for those of Tyre) when the kings of Cyprus sailed into the harbour of Sidon with 120 warships, voluntarily shifting their allegiance to Macedon (Arr. *Anab.* II.20.3; Plut. *Alex.* 24.2).

The eventual success of the seven months' siege – one of the great siege operations in history – was in no small measure due to Phoenician and Cypriot assistance. The Tyrians, like all Phoenicians, were accomplished masters of defence under siege. Alexander, on the other hand, employed engineers 'from Cyprus and all Phoenicia' (Arr. *Anab.* II.21.1) to construct a mole on which to attack the island city and to drive home his assault with the most advanced siege techniques. At the same time he proceeded to blockade Tyre from the sea, combining the Cypriot and Phoenician squadrons. The Cypriot quinqueremes posted at the north wing suffered severe losses when the Tyrians made an unexpected and well-disguised sally – destroying, *inter alias*, the ships of Pnytagoras of Salamis, Androcles of Amathus, and Pasicrates of Curium.

With the fall of Tyre in July or August 332 the history of the semi-autonomous kingdoms of Phoenicia ends – even if the kings retained their thrones for the time being, except for the Persophile Straton II of Sidon whom Hephaistion replaced by Abdalonim (Diod. XVII.46.6–47; Curt. IV.1.15–26). Alexander's administrative arrangements in Syria and Phoenicia, an area of great strategic value which formed the centre of his communications, are difficult to reconstruct.[72] In December 331, control

[72] Bosworth 1974 (F 225).

over the entire area seems to have been concentrated in the hands of
Menes of Pella, appointed 'hyparchos [satrap] of Syria, Phoenicia and
Cilicia' (Arr. *Anab.* III.16.9; Diod. XVII.64.5). There are no further
records about Syria and Phoenicia until Alexander's death in June 323.
In the settlement of Babylon, Cilicia and Syria (including Phoenicia)
were made separate commands, obviously for military reasons: Syria was
given to Laomedon (Arr. *Diad.* 1.5). From a group of vassal states
governed by local rulers Phoenicia now was definitely reduced to the
status of a mere province.

The Cypriot kings' well-considered and timely move after Issus, on
the other hand, gave their monarchies another lease of semi-autonomous
life. Persian rule had ended after 200 years, but the status of the kings
with their local autonomy remained – except for the abolition of the
tribute – largely the same as under the Achaemenids, either because
Alexander wanted to acknowledge the kings' services or because the
island was of less strategic importance than Phoenicia. It seems significant, however, that the kings' traditional right to mint their own coins
was curbed; the mints of Salamis, Citium and (to a lesser extent) Paphos
now issued Alexander's imperial coinage.[73]

Cypriot and Phoenician cities had, as before, to contribute their
contingents to the fleet. Their experienced shipyards were kept busy
constructing new quinqueremes (Arr. *Anab.* VII.19.3–4). A hundred
Cypriot and Phoenician ships were requested when a naval force under
Amphoterus was sent against Sparta in the summer of 331 (Arr. *Anab.*
III.6.3). Nearchus employed Phoenician and Cypriot crews and specialists in his Indus expedition; two of his trierarchs were Cypriot princes –
Nicocles, son of Pasicrates of Soli, and Nithaphon, son of Pnytagoras of
Salamis (Arr. *Anab.* VI.1.6; *Indike* 18.8). Hieron of Soli (but he may have
come from Cilician Soli) was ordered to circumnavigate Arabia and
reached the mouth of the Persian Gulf (Arr. *Anab.* VII.20.7–8).

The Cypriot rulers attended the magnificent victory celebrations
staged by Alexander on his return from Egypt in the spring of 331,
Nicocreon of Salamis, the successor of Pnytagoras, and Pasicrates of Soli
competing as *choregoi* (Plut. *Alex.* 29.1). Alexander's entourage included
a number of noble Cypriots such as the trierarch Nicocles. One of these,
Strasanor of Soli, was appointed governor of Areia and Drangiane in
329, of Bactria and Sogdiana in 321 (Diod. XVIII.3.3). It seems not
unlikely that these Cypriot *hetairoi* were both hostages and representatives of their kingdoms at the centre of power.

In the island the contest for the leading position between Salamis and

[73] The issue of superb gold coins by Milkyathon and Pumiathon of Citium (Kraay 1976 (F 200)
307) does not warrant Tarn's assumption (*CAH* VI¹ 432) that the Cypriot kings were treated as 'free
allies', the Phoenicians as 'subject allies'.

Citium continued, the rivals as usual trying to gain the overlords' support for their own interests. This became apparent immediately when Alexander rewarded the kings who had succoured him at Tyre (Curtius IV.8.14). Pnytagoras of Salamis, who seems to have led the move, asked for and received Tamassus (Duris *FGrH* 76 F 4). This city with its copper-mining district was as valuable an acquisition for Salamis as it was a severe loss to Citium which had bought Tamassus but twenty years before. There is no reliable clue as to the reasons for Citium's fall from favour;[74] nor are any other inferences of this kind recorded in the time of Alexander. But the history of Cyprus during these years is at least as obscure as during the preceding decades.

The death of Alexander and the ensuing contest for supreme power was bound to involve Cyprus. If the Alexander coins of Nicocles of Paphos, inscribed with his own name in almost illegible miniature signs, were indeed issued immediately after 323, they may indicate a brief moment's hope of greater independence.[75] But the island was strategically the key to the eastern Mediterranean. Its ships, shipyards and ship timber were of utmost importance to all contenders, as were the coastal cities of Phoenicia.

Ptolemy, destined to annex Cyprus in the end, moved first – not least in order to secure the ship timber which Egypt did not provide. In 321 he won four Cypriot kings as allies against Perdiccas: Nicocreon of Salamis, Nicocles of Paphos, Pasicrates of Soli, and Androcles of Amathus. Other cities obviously refused an alliance, as Ptolemy dispatched a fleet of about 200 ships to besiege a city in Cyprus, while Perdiccas sent a force of 800 foot and 500 horse to its relief. Our information is so scanty (Arr. *Diad.* 24.15–28) that it is neither possible to locate the city nor to reconstruct subsequent military operations in the island. We only know that Antigonus Monophthalmus came from Cyprus to attend the conference of Trisparadisus late in 321 (Arr. *Diad.* 1.30) and that Eumenes later recruited forces in southern Asia Minor, Syria, Phoenicia and 'in the cities of Cyprus' (Diod. XVIII.61.4).

Antigonus, strongest of the pretenders after the execution of Eumenes in 316, faced a military coalition of Ptolemy, Lysimachus and Cassander in 315 (Diod. XIX.57.2). Perceiving clearly that the want of a fleet was one of his main weaknesses, Antigonus summoned the kings of Phoenicia to 'old Tyre' (the mainland suburb of the city) and inaugurated an extensive ship building programme in the yards of Tripolis,

---

[74] Pumiathon of Citium issued no coins between 332/1 and 323/2, but obviously remained 'king of Citium and Idalium', as an inscription of his 37th year (326/5?) shows (*KAI* no. 33).

[75] May 1952 (F 295). The attempt of Gesche 1974 (F 253) 113–19 to date these coins to 310/9 is subtle but not convincing. Nicocles also repaired for a last time the walls of Paphos: Maier and Karageorghis 1984 (F 288) 222.

Byblus and Sidon. His control of Phoenicia was, however, not complete: he had to take Jaffa and Gaza by storm and to besiege Tyre which only capitulated after a long fight in 314 (Diod. XIX.58–59.3, 61.5).

Parallel to securing Phoenicia and its naval resources Antigonus in 315 tried to get a hold on Cyprus by means of diplomacy. His envoy Agesilaus was able to conclude alliances with Pumiathon of Citium,[76] Praxippus of Lapethus, Stasioecus II of Marium, and the king of Ceryneia (Themison, to whom Aristotle dedicated his *Protreptikos*?); but he had to report that Ptolemy's allies stood firm (Diod. XIX.57.4, 59.1). Ptolemy, who had already sent 3,000 soldiers to Cyprus, reacted immediately and despatched a strong force of 100 ships and 10,000 men to the island, commanded by his brother Menelaus. This force encountered Seleucus, who had arrived from the Aegean with a fleet, but the leaders came to an understanding. A large part of their troops were detailed to the Peloponnese and to Caria; Menelaus and Seleucus, supported by Nicocreon and the other allied kings, proceeded to subdue those cities which sided with Antigonus. Ceryneia and Lapethus were taken after an apparently brief investment; Marium and Amathus came over without fighting; Citium, however, had to be reduced by a systematic siege (Diod. XIX.62.1–6).

Yet these successful military operations obviously did not ensure the loyalty of the former allies of Antigonus. In 312 Ptolemy, having crushed the insurrection of Cyrene, crossed in person to Cyprus to settle the affairs of the island. Harsh measures were adopted. Praxippus of Lapethus and the ruler of Cerynia, suspected of treachery, were arrested. Pumiathon of Citium, who had been found in contact with Antigonus, was executed; the temple of the city god Melqart-Heracles was destroyed, presumably also that of Ashtart.[77] Stasioecus of Marium was deposed or executed, his city destroyed, the population removed to Paphos – probably to the harbour town of Nea Paphos founded during these years by King Nicocles of Paphos. Unfortunately it is impossible to prove whether the fragment of an oath, found recently at Paphos and mentioning the king several times, is in some way connected with these events.[78] Nicocreon of Salamis was appointed *strategos* in Cyprus, receiving the cities and revenues of the deposed kings (Diod. XIX.79.4–5).

Whether Ptolemy regarded these arrangements as workable and durable we do not know. As his brother Menelaus also retained the title of *strategos* and commanded the troops in the island (Diod. XX.21.1), friction was bound to develop. Nor was Antigonus to accept the loss of

---

[76] Still referred to as 'king of Citium and Idalium' in an inscription of 320/19 (Karageorghis and Guzzo Amadasi 1973 (F 277) A 30).   [77] Karageorghis 1976 (F 275) 116, 171–2.
[78] Masson and Mitford 1986 (F 293) no. 237.

Cyprus. In the event Ptolemy's dispositions lasted only for a very short time – in the same way as the treaty of 311 between Antigonus, Cassander, Lysimachus and Ptolemy (Diod. XIX.105.1–4) proved to be nothing but an uneasy truce.

During the fourth century the kingdoms of Cyprus and Phoenicia for brief moments had hoped to gain greater, if not complete, political independence. But the change from Persia to Alexander resulted – in contrast to what some Greek cities may have expected – merely in a reduction of autonomy. The rule of the Successors finally abolished the traditional political system in both areas, although the end of the old dynasties was not everywhere as dramatic as at Salamis (Diod. XX.21.1–3).[79] Cyprus and Phoenicia became mere provinces of a hellenistic monarchy.

But Cypriots and Phoenicians were not only politically integrated into the hellenistic world. The influence of Greek art and civilization now became paramount. In the later part of the fourth century the lively economic and cultural exchanges between Greece and the Levant continued, hardly hampered by the military operations. The steady flow of Attic pottery, terracotta statuettes and other Greek imports did not diminish.[80] The products of the sarcophagus ateliers of Sidon demonstrate that the Phoenicians even surpassed the Cypriots in the masterly adaptation of Late Classical Greek art.

There are additional proofs for a close connexion with Greece. At Athens the Salaminian trading colony still flourished; in the later fourth century it formed a cult community venerating Aphrodite and Adonis.[81] King Pnytagoras, whose coins depict Athena and Artemis, was honoured at Delos as *proxenos* and dedicated a gold crown there; so did King Androcles of Amathus between 315 and 310.[82] The Citian merchant community at Athens obtained in 333/2 the right to build a temple of Aphrodite.[83] Sidonians formed another Phoenician trading colony at Athens, accorded tax privileges in the middle of the fourth century (above, p. 328). The *hieronautai* of Tyre at about the same time

[79] The end of Nicocreon and his family is still enigmatic; see Karageorghis 1969 (F 273) 151–64; Kyrris 1985 (F 281).

[80] See above n. 20.

[81] *IG* II² 1290; Pouilloux 1975 (F 314) 119–20.

[82] Pnytagoras: *Inscr. de Délos* 1409 Ba II 113–114, 1429 A I 78, 1441 A I 98–99, 1450 A 63; *IG* XI 2, 161 B 88–9. Androcles: *IG* XI 2. 135, 39–41; cf. *SEG* XXX 1571 = CEG 872. A list of *thearodokoi* from Nemea (Miller 1988 (B 159) = *SEG* XXXVI 31), dated 323/2 by its editor, includes Nicocreon and Teucer from Salamis, Pasicrates and Themistagoras from Curium, and Stasicrates from Soli (who may be identical with the Pasicrates mentioned by Plutarch; see Hill 1949 (F 267) 150 n. 5; Stylianou 1989 (F 339) 513).

[83] *IG* II² 337 = Tod no. 189 = Harding no. 111; see also the dedication by Aristoclea of Citium to Aphrodite Urania (*IG* II² 4636), and other inscriptions recording Salaminians and Citians residing at Athens in the fourth century (*IG* III² 9032–6, 10176, 10178–9, 10202–3, 10205, 10208–9, 10217/18).

dedicated at Delos two statues representing Tyre and Sidon.[84] The process of Hellenization of the Phoenicians was slower than is sometimes assumed; strong and conscious Phoenician elements are still to be observed at Citium and Lapethus in Cyprus in the third century.[85]

The process of Hellenization meant even for the Greek Cypriots the loss of some of their individuality; for the Phoenicians it meant virtually the end of their own culture. Under Achaemenid rule it had been able to develop for a last time; now the uncompromising and all-pervading standards of Greek art and literature gradually eradicated the indigenous tradition.

[84] *CIS* 1 114; Parrot, Chebab and Moscati 1977 (F 310) 461.
[85] *Studia Phoenicia* v 1987 (F 338) 15–17, 21–3; Mitford 1953 (F 301) 86.

CHAPTER 8e

EGYPT, 404–332 B.C.

ALAN B. LLOYD

I. INTERNAL HISTORY

The domestic history of Egypt during her last age of independence was dominated by power struggles both within dynasties themselves and between great families of the Delta each jealous of the other and anxious to gain possession of the crown. These dissensions were greatly exacerbated by the sectional interests of the native Egyptian warrior class or *Machimoi*, the priesthood, and the greed and jealousy of foreign mercenaries.[1]

Initially, however, the major problems confronting Amyrtaeus, the sole king of the XXVIIIth Dynasty,[2] were the expulsion of Persian forces from the kingdom and consolidation of his position as an independent ruler. It would appear that his credentials for this role were impeccable. He was certainly a Saite and probably a descendant of the brilliant and prosperous XXVIth Dynasty;[3] it has also been plausibly suggested that he was the grandson of the Amyrtaeus who succeeded Inarus as the leader of the great but abortive revolt of Egypt against Artaxerxes II.[4] For all that, his task was no easy one. His accession date can be located *c*. 404, but he was certainly not in complete control of the country until some time later; for in the Jewish colony at Elephantine Artaxerxes II was still recognized as late as 401 whilst the first document in the name of Amyrtaeus does not appear until regnal year 5 (*c*. 400).[5] Of the details of his reign virtually nothing is known. However, the *Demotic Chronicle* speaks at III.18–19 of violation of the divine law in his reign and states a little later (IV.1–2) that he was deposed as a result of this and his son not permitted to succeed.[6] The immediate change to the XXIXth Dynasty after Amyrtaeus lends credibility to these cryptic comments and suggests that we are in all probability confronted with our first example of the dynastic squabbling endemic to the period.

---

[1] Kienitz 1953 (F 463) 76–121; Gyles 1959 (F 447) 45, 67, 71–4; Drioton and Vandier 1962 (F 434) 605–14; Lloyd 1983 (F 476) 287.

[2] In general see Pietschmann, *RE* I 2012–3; De Meulenaere in Helck *et al.* 1975– (F 453) I 252–3.   [3] See below, pp. 355ff.

[4] E.g. Kraeling 1953 (F 465) 112 n. 3; Porten 1968 (F 504) 236 n. 3. For the revolt see Lloyd 1975–88 (F 473) I 38–49.   [5] See note 99.   [6] Johnson 1983 (F 459) 66.

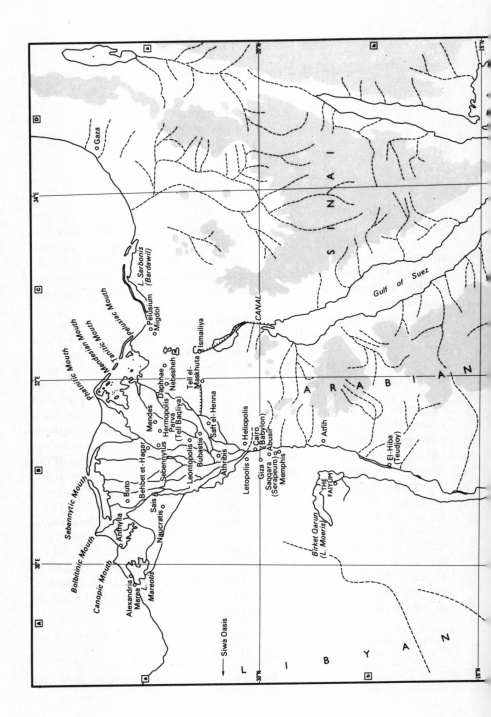

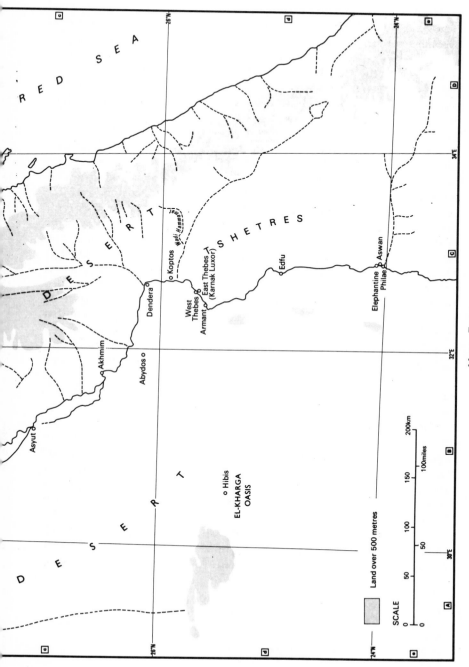

Map 9. Egypt.

The XXVIIIth Dynasty was succeeded by the XXIXth which derived from the great Delta city of Mendes. We know that its founder Nepherites received some support from the important Delta city of Letopolis[7] and, like most of his successors, was careful to foster good relations with the priesthood. He also nurtured the idea that his rule was nothing less than the restoration of the glories of the XXVIth Dynasty, a policy which he may well have taken over from Amyrtaeus and which was pursued with fervour by all subsequent Egyptian rulers until the Persian reconquest of the country.[8] A badly damaged Brooklyn Aramaic papyrus refers to Nepherites' accession, but the precise circumstances remain obscure.[9] The history of this family was clearly wracked with turmoil. The contradiction in our evidence on the order of kings is best interpreted as a reflection of recurrent internal dissension over the succession in which Nepherites' death was followed by a power struggle between three claimants, Psammuthis, Achoris and a third whose name is unknown. This was a struggle eventually won by Achoris who undoubtedly figures as the outstanding ruler of the dynasty. Even after his victory he made unusual efforts to assert and establish his legitimacy, particularly in his choice of titles. This image of instability is confirmed by the fact that only Achoris enjoyed a reign of any length (thirteen years): Nepherites I died in his seventh year; king x was deposed, if that is the correct interpretation of the opaque wording of *Demotic Chronicle* IV.6; Psammuthis had one year; and Nepherites II four months only.[10] Indeed, it is a matter of explicit comment in the *Chronicle* that Achoris completed his reign (IV.9)! In view of this lamentable history, it is not surprising to find the XXIXth Dynasty swiftly replaced, almost certainly deposed, by a rival family, this time from Sebennytus.[11]

The precise relationship between the kings of the XXXth Dynasty and those of the XXIXth has been much discussed. On the basis of Spiegelberg's translation of *Demotic Chronicle* IV.3–5, it has been claimed that Nectanebo I was a son or grandson of Nepherites I,[12] but Johnson's new rendering reveals that this view is untenable.[13] The most we can say is that he was an army commander before his accession and that his father Tachos was also a high-ranking military officer who may have been a prince.[14] Given such an ancestry and the extreme brevity of Nepherites' reign, the advent of the new dynasty looks suspiciously like a military coup, and it may well be that Nectanebo's great Hermopolis stela

7 Vercoutter 1962 (F 543) 102; Traunecker 1979 (F 538) 422.
8 Traunecker 1979 (F 538) 420–3. In general see below, p. 349ff.
9 Kraeling 1953 (F 465) 283–90 n. 13. In general see Bianchi in Helck *et al.* 1975– (F 453) IV 454–6.
10 See pp. 356f.   11 Traunecker 1979 (F 538) 436; Traunecker *et al.* 1981 (F 539) 14.
12 De Meulenaere 1963 (F 487) 90–1; Johnson 1974 (F 457) 7–9.
13 Johnson 1974 (F 457) 7–9.   14 De Meulenaere 1963 (F 487) 90–1.

actually refers to disturbances surrounding such an event (lines 8–9). However that may be, it comes as no surprise to find that the XXXth Dynasty, like its predecessor, was subject to the recurrent malady of dynastic instability.[15] This is probably the explanation for the surprising appearance of a co-regency at the end of the reign of Nectanebo I who associated his son Tachos with him in government from regnal year 16 until his death in year 19.[16] The reign of Tachos provides the best-documented example of the phenomenon in the period as a whole in the form of the civil war between Tachos and Nectanebo II. When Tachos embarked on his great expedition against Persia in Asia, he left a general in control in Egypt called Tja-ḥap-imu who was clearly his brother.[17] The latter promptly persuaded his own son Nectanebo, who was campaigning with Tachos, to rebel. Nectanebo, in turn, prevailed upon the Spartan king Agesilaus, who commanded Tachos' Greek mercenaries and harboured a personal grudge against Tachos, to join the insurgents. These multiple acts of treachery proved a signal success, and Tachos was forced to take refuge with the Great King. This was not, however, the end of the matter. An unnamed Mendesian was then declared pharaoh by a section of the Egyptian populace and rose against Nectanebo. There can be little doubt that he was a member of the royal house of Mendes making a bid to restore past glories and he certainly constituted a formidable threat since he was able to field a substantial army, presumably *Machimoi*, and forced Nectanebo and Agesilaus to take refuge in an unspecified fortified city. Nectanebo, through the excellence of his Greek troops and the generalship of Agesilaus, was able to extract himself victoriously from this crisis, but nothing can disguise the mortal danger in which he stood or the precarious nature of royal power in Late Period Egypt.[18]

One of the most intriguing aspects of the episode just described is the crucial role played by foreign troops, but the kings of this period, in their attempts to maintain control of the country, had also to cope with two important groups within the populace itself: the *Machimoi* and the

---

[15] On the history of the dynasty see Kienitz 1953 (F 463) 88–112: Drioton and Vandier 1962 (F 434) 609–12; Johnson 1974 (F 457) 10–17.

[16] Johnson 1974 (F 457) 13–17; Murnane 1977 (F 492). Since Tachos would have become co-regent in 364/3, the difficulties of Hornblower 1982 (F 644) 174f in relation to Xen. *Ages.* 11.27 would seem to disappear. If he became co-regent in that year, he may well have occupied a dominant position even before that and may, therefore, have been treated as *de facto* ruler by outside observers as early as 366.   [17] De Meulenaere 1963 (F 487) 91; von Kaenel 1980 (F 460) 40.

[18] On this episode see *IG* ii² 119; Xen. *Ages.* 11.28ff; Theopompus *FGrH* 115 F 106, 108; Nep. *Ages.* 8; Plut. *Ages.* 36–9; Diod. xv.92–3; Polyaen. 11.1.22; Lyceas of Naucratis *FGrH* 613 F 2; Paus. 111.10; Eust. *Od.* 10.515 (1642); Plut. *Mor.* 214D–E. Plutarch's figure of 100,000 men for the Mendesian's army is surely too high (cf. Diod. xv.93, where Tachos is named in error for the rebel). In addition to these classical sources we now have a fragmentary hieroglyphic inscription which refers to these events (von Kaenel 1980 (F 460)).

priests. That the *Machimoi* were a power to be reckoned with is quite certain, and it is equally clear that they were perfectly prepared to play the king-maker.[19] The ease with which Nectanebo got support c. 360 shows that they were unreliable and suggests that their services were very much at the disposal of the highest bidder; it would be very surprising if the adherents of Nectanebo's unnamed Mendesian rival were not a further illustration of this point, but paucity of evidence makes certainty in this case impossible. It is, however, noteworthy that the *Machimoi* played an extremely prominent part in the military operations of the fourth century: according to Diodorus (xv.92) Tachos had c. 80,000 in his expeditionary force; the unidentified Mendesian usurper had 100,000 men, probably mainly *Machimoi*, at his disposal in his struggle with Nectanebo c. 359 (Plut. *Ages.* 38);[20] and Nectanebo, in the defence of Egypt against Ochus, deployed 60,000 (Diod. xvi.47). We can be sure that all these figures are exaggerated, but they can nevertheless be taken with confidence to symbolize very substantial forces and generate the nagging suspicion that the kings of this period, unlike Apries in the XXVIth Dynasty, did their utmost to avoid offending *Machimoi* susceptibilities. It was clearly crucial for the royal house to keep control of this military element, and we find that it was standard practice for royal princes to serve as generals in the army.[21] The effectiveness of this policy can best be judged by considering that, of the three kings of the XXXth Dynasty, Nectanebo I probably and Nectanebo II certainly came to the throne as the result of military coups. The wealth and influence of the priesthood were also potent forces which the crown ignored at its peril.[22] Concern for the temples formed part of pharaoh's traditional priestly role and was a time-honoured expression of royal power and wealth,[23] but it would be a mistake to ignore its political ramifications.[24] Unfortunately, relations with the priesthood at this period are far from well documented, but the broad outlines are clear and present an ambiguous picture. On the one hand, we have instances of open-handed generosity. Achievements in temple-building were a pale shadow of former glories, but they became progressively more spectacular to culminate in the great temple of Behbet el-Hagar begun by Nectanebo II.[25] Furthermore, benefactions were frequently made by the crown to major shrines: e.g. an inscription at Edfu enumerates gifts conferred on the temple between the beginning of the reign of Necta-

[19] Lloyd 1983 (F 476) 309f.
[20] Diod. xv.93 erroneously names Nectanebo as the commander of this force.
[21] Clère 1951 (F 425) 135: De Meulenaere 1963 (F 487) 90, 93.
[22] Kienitz 1953 (F 463) 122–6; Lloyd 1983 (F 476) 301–9.
[23] Lloyd 1983 (F 476) 293–5; Johnson 1983 (F 459) 67ff.
[24] Kienitz 1953 (F 463) 122–6; Johnson 1974 (F 457) 11.
[25] See below, p. 353 and in general Kienitz 1953 (F 463).

nebo I and year 18 of Nectanebo II;[26] the Hermopolis stela of Nectanebo I describes in detail that king's benefactions to the deities of the city;[27] the Naucratis stela of regnal year 1 of Nectanebo I records the donation of one tenth of the royal income from imports from the Mediterranean at Henet and Naucratis to the Saite temple of Neith.[28] On the other hand, the wealth of the temples provided a capital asset which excited the acquisitive instincts of more than one ruler of the period; e.g. Tachos, under the influence of Chabrias, imposed severe pecuniary restrictions upon them in order to meet the costs of his Asiatic campaign ([Arist.] *Oec.* II. 2 (1350–1a)).[29] Such actions must have been bitterly resented by their many victims,[30] and we can hardly doubt that the ensuing priestly opposition to Tachos was a significant factor in the triumph of Nectanebo II.

When we turn to the structure of the general administration at this period we encounter a marked paucity of evidence. The residence city and centre of administration was probably Memphis, and the signs are that government functioned on traditional centralized lines,[31] and was dominated by great officers of state, such as Somtutefnakht,[32] who were capable of holding at one and the same time a wide range of offices, civil, religious and military. We know of one official bearing the title of vizier in this period, Harsiese in the XXXth Dynasty, but whether he functioned as the chief minister of state is an open question.[33] Provincial government operated on the basis of nomes which were administrative districts roughly comparable to English counties. Taxation was demonstrably a major concern of the provincial governors, or nomarchs, but we can assume that, as in earlier times, they exercised a wide range of administrative functions (cf. [Arist.] *Oec.* 2.2 (1350–1a)). On the character of the administration there is little information. Doubtless the accustomed Egyptian stance of benevolent despotism continued to operate at all levels, but there is evidence of stringent and, at times, oppressive taxation ([Arist.] *Oec.* 2.2 (1350–1a); *Demotic Chronicle* IV.4–5; Polyaen. III.11.5).

Not the least interesting feature of the Late Period is the fact that our

[26] See n. 104.   [27] Roeder 1952 (F 518) 375ff and 1959 (F 519) 91.

[28] Lichtheim 1980 (F 472) 86ff. In general see Meeks 1979 (F 481) 653ff.

[29] Will 1960 (F 550). It is now recognized, on the basis of Johnson's new translation, that *Demotic Chronicle* IV.4–5 refers to Tachos' exactions from the temples (Johnson 1974 (F 457) 7–9 and 1983 (F 459) 64).

[30] Apart from priests who officiated in the temple, many Egyptians clearly held salaried priestly offices which did not entail any duties. All would have been equally affected.

[31] Lloyd 1983 (F 476) 331–7. Inscriptions of royal officials are uncommon but do occasionally occur, e.g. Bothmer 1969 (F 414) 92ff; Traunecker 1979 (F 538) 422.

[32] His biography is preserved on Naples 1035. Discussions: Schäfer 1897 (F 520); Tresson 1930 (F 540); Gardiner 1961 (F 440) 379ff; Lichtheim 1980 (F 472) 41ff; Lloyd 1982 (F 475) 178ff.

[33] De Meulenaere 1958 (F 485); Lloyd 1983 (F 476) 332.

classical sources permit a rather clearer picture of the personal character of Egyptian kings than it is possible to gain for any earlier age. Most of them show the keenest perception of Egypt's best interests and were often adept at directing their policy to meet them, but the impression gained of some is by no means consistently flattering: Amyrtaeus emerges as ruthless to the point of treachery,[34] Tachos as obtuse and headstrong (Diod. xv.92), and Nectanebo II as a ruler in whom arrogance was alloyed with a disturbing tendency to panic or precipitate action in times of crisis which played no small part in losing him his kingdom (Diod. xv.93 – substitute Nectanebo for Tachos and the unnamed Mendesian for Nectanebo; xvi.46–51; Plut. *Ages.* 36ff; Polyaen. ii.1.22).

The impact of the Persian conquest was severe. Once Ochus gained control, he pulled down the walls of the major cities, plundered the temples, and amassed a large quantity of gold and silver. He also carried off Egyptian sacred writings, though his minion Bagoas subsequently sold them back to the priests. Egypt was then turned into a satrapy under the rule of Pherendates (Diod. xvi.51).[35] Details of its history down to 332 are severely limited. It is clear that the Persians did receive the support of some Egyptian officials like Somtutefnakht who were perfectly prepared to make the best of the situation and accepted positions in the government,[36] but Egyptian and classical sources leave us in no doubt as to the character of the administration which is described as violent, avaricious, arrogant, impious and disruptive of the norms of ordered life.[37] In consequence, when the Macedonian rebel Amyntas arrived in Egypt in 333 he was welcomed by the Egyptians who flocked to him to assist in destroying the Persian garrisons, and the arrival of Alexander the Great in 332 was greeted with equal jubilation (*POxy.* i.xii.iv; Diod. xvii.49; Curt. iv.1(5); 7(29)).[38] It is, however, possible that, even before that time, Egyptian discontent had led to open rebellion and that a short-lived independence had been wrested from the Persians by an enigmatic pharaoh called Khababash.[39]

The origin and date of Khababash have been matters of considerable debate. To judge from his name, he was not Egyptian but probably

---

[34] See below, p. 347.

[35] The tradition on the iniquities of Ochus was subsequently greatly elaborated: Schwartz 1949 (F 521).

[36] For Somtutefnakht see above, p. 343. See also Lepsius 1849–59 (F 470) vi 69 no. 162; Meyer 1915 (F 490) 291 n. 4.

[37] Petosiris inscription 81: Lefebvre 1923–4 (F 469) i 136–45, ii 53–9; Otto 1954 (F 497) 180ff with page references to discussion indexed at 128, 46; Lichtheim 1980 (F 472) 45ff; Lloyd 1982 (F 475) 178; *POxy* i xii col. IV; Diod. xvii.49; Curt. iv.7 (29).

[38] The Amyntas episode is also mentioned in Arr. *Anab.* ii.13.2–3.

[39] Kienitz 1953 (F 463) 185–9; Gardiner 1961 (F 440) 380ff; Drioton and Vandier 1962 (F 434) 612–14, 621; Lloyd 1988 (F 477).

Libyan or Ethiopian by extraction. As for chronology, the evidence is as follows: (1) The Satrap Stela of regnal year 7 of Alexander IV (312–311 B.C.)[40] informs us at lines 7 ff that, after the reign of Xerxes, a pharaoh called Khababash had given a piece of land to the gods of Buto while he was reconnoitring the northern Delta 'to keep off the fleet of the king of Asia'. These events clearly took place before the Macedonian conquest in 332; (2) A marriage contract of a minor Theban priest is dated to regnal year 1, month 3, of Khababash and is signed by the same notary as a text of the year 324;[41] (3) An Apis sarcophagus mentions regnal year 2, month 3, of Khababash.[42] The Satrap Stela clearly yields the termini 464–332, but a scribe active in 324 could hardly have been born earlier than the beginning of the fourth century and will have begun his career rather later, i.e. the Khababash whose name appears in the dating formula of P. Libbey (Spiegelberg 1907 (F 533)) can be located no earlier than the XXIXth Dynasty.[43] We must, therefore, look for him within the time-span of the XXIXth–XXXIst Dynasties. Although Khababash is regarded as a legitimate king in the Satrap Stela and Egyptian documents give him two regnal years, there is no trace of any such reign in the lists given in Manetho or the *Demotic Chronicle* for the XXIXth–XXXth Dynasties. Therefore, he was probably contemporary with the XXXIst. If so, there are several obvious dating possibilities: Khababash might have been the immediate successor of Nectanebo II, and the late date given for the conquest of Egypt in pseudo-Manetho (339/8) could reflect the defeat of Khababash, not that of Nectanebo II; alternatively, he might have rebelled on the death of Artaxerxes (338/7) or Arses (336/5).[44] There is no decisive argument to offer in favour of any of these possibilities, but it is evident that all the probabilities point to the hypothesis that Khababash was a rebel pharaoh who achieved a brief independence during the Second Persian Occupation.

II. FOREIGN RELATIONS

Our sources for Egyptian foreign relations between 404 and 332 are pre-eminently classical and reflect the interests of the classical world.[45] The

[40] Text *Urk.* 2.11ff; translations, Bevan 1927 (F 408A) 28–32; Spiegelberg 1907 (F 533) 2ff; Spalinger 1978 (F 528) 147ff and 1980 (F 529); Ritner 1980 (F 514); Lloyd 1982 (F 475) 175ff.

[41] Spiegelberg 1907 (F 533) 3; Erichsen 1950 (F 437) I 71, II 28–30; Lüddeckens 1960 (F 467) 22–3.

[42] Gunn 1926 (F 446) 86ff no. III.

[43] Since the average lifespan in ancient Egypt was less than forty years, it is probable that the scribe was born during the XXXth Dynasty.

[44] Kienitz 1953 (F 463) 187f concludes that the rebellion ran from winter 338/7 to winter 336/5, but his case is not strong.

[45] For general surveys see Kienitz 1953 (F 463) 76–112; Olmstead 1948 (F 43) 396–416; Bresciani 1969 (F 416) and in Davies and Finkelstein 1984 (F 372) 358–72; Traunecker 1979 (F 538) 396ff; Cook 1983 (F 14) 208–25; Lloyd 1983 (F 476) 337–46; Hornblower 1983 (A 31) ch. 14ff. There is much useful material in Hornblower 1982 (F 644); see his index under the relevant kings.

record is, therefore, overwhelmingly concerned with events in the eastern Mediterranean in which Greeks were closely involved and which impinged strongly on Greek historical consciousness. Indisputably, the Libyan frontier of Egypt continued to be a matter of close political, economic, and strategic concern, and it is equally clear that cordial relations existed with the Nubian kingdom to the south,[46] but, since neither area saw Greeks participating in major historical events, our information on Egypt's relations with peoples to the west and south is extremely sparse.

It is evident that the dominant issue is Egypt's relations with Persia from whom she achieved independence at the end of the fifth century but whose claims to the country were never abandoned. The Egyptian response to this problem was essentially a resumption of Saite Asiatic policy in that an attempt was made to keep the Persians at bay by two methods: dissidents in the western provinces of the Persian empire were given moral and logistic support to keep the Great King embroiled in conflicts away from the Egyptian frontier; Egyptian forces engaged in active military operations against the Persians. In this strategy the Egyptians received on many occasions the support of Sparta whose ambitions in Greece and the Aegean area frequently brought her into conflict with Persia and, *ipso facto*, created a happy community of interest with Egypt.

Egypt's Persian policy falls into four phases: (1) Initial caution (Amyrtaeus); (2) Material support of rebels against the Great King but stopping short of armed conflict (Nepherites I; the early part of the reign of Achoris); (3) Full-scale military confrontation (the second half of the reign of Achoris; Tachos); (4) A return to a policy much closer to that of phase 2 (Nectanebo II). As for the Persians, their capacity to resolve the Egyptian problem was severely impaired by their distance from Egypt and more pressing concerns nearer the heart of the empire. Nevertheless, at least four major attempts were made to bring Egypt to heel, one in the reign of Artaxerxes II (374) and three by Artaxerxes III (*c*. 354, *c*. 351, and 343–342).

It is clear that, as early as 401, the Persians were contemplating the recovery of Egypt (Xen. *An*. II.1.14; 5.13; possibly also *An*. 1.4.3 and 5), but there is no proof positive of Egyptian operations against Persia at this time. Egypt does, however, figure in the events of 400 immediately following the defeat of the rebellion of Cyrus when we are informed that Cyrus' leading supporter, Tamos, governor of Ionia, fled to Egypt,

---

[46] Lloyd 1983 (F 476) 343–6. It should be noted that the claim that Achoris' cartouche appears at the temple of Aghurmi in the Siwa Oasis (Steindorff *et al*. 1933 (F 537) 19–21; Kienitz 1953 (F 463) 83) is based on a misinterpretation of a damaged inscription (Traunecker 1979 (F 538) 418 DI). There is, however, evidence of a treaty with Barca (Theopomp. *FGrH* 115 F 103; Kienitz 1953 (F 463) 83).

taking with him most of his family as well as a fleet laden with treasure.[47] The Egyptian king, who must surely have been Amyrtaeus,[48] promptly killed his unwelcome guest and requisitioned the fleet and its cargo. The fact that Tamos fled to Egypt, together with Diodorus' cryptic comment that pharaoh was under an obligation to Tamos, suggests, in turn, that the Egyptian king may well have been giving him covert support in his rebellious activities. However, suspicions are not facts, and the most that can be said at present is that such support, if it were given, was neither sufficiently active nor obvious to make a clear impression on our sources.

We have to wait until the intensification of Sparta's military operations against Persia in 396 for the first clear evidence of Egypt's role as the paymaster of Persia's enemies. In that year, the Spartans requested an alliance from Nepherites I, who refused, but he did dispatch equipment (presumably sails and cordage) for 100 triremes and 500,000 measures of corn (Diod. XIV.79; Justin VI.6.1–5; Oros. III.1.8).[49] Nepherites' policy was initially followed by Achoris. An alliance with Athens is mentioned in Aristophanes' *Plutus* (178) produced in 388. This must be seen in the broader context of Athens' support for Evagoras of Cyprus who was in rebellion against the Persian King. Achoris' alliance with the Pisidians (Theopomp. *FGrH* 115 F 103) had a similar strategic motive. However, we do not have any evidence of a large military commitment by the Egyptians to the war. It was the Peace of Antalcidas of 386 which led to that. By this treaty the Great King removed the rebels' supporters on the mainland of Greece and was able to devote his full attention to Evagoras and Egypt (Theopomp. *FGrH* 115 F 103; Oros. III.1.25). The attack on the latter appears to have been mounted in 385. We have no unequivocal information on subsequent military operations, but if, as is probable, an enigmatic passage in Isocrates' *Panegyricus* refers to this conflict, it lasted for three years and ended in the defeat of the Persians.[50] This was soon

---

[47] This date is that of Diodorus (XIV.35) and fits the historical context well. On the career of Tamos, who came from Memphis, see Lewis 1977 (A 33) 92f, 107 n. 96, 118 nn. 72, 74.

[48] Diodorus (XIV.35) calls him 'Psammetichus, a descendant of Psammetichus'. In view of the date we should expect the king to be Amyrtaeus, and the fact that he is said to be a descendant of Psammetichus tends to strengthen this suspicion since it indicates that he was a Saite, as Amyrtaeus certainly was (cf. Drioton and Vandier 1962 (F 434) 606; Kraeling 1953 (F 465) 112 n. 3; Hall 1927 (F 448) 144; De Meulenaere in Helck *et al.* 1975– (F 453) 1 252). Given Diodorus' notorious carelessness, a mistake is perfectly feasible. Nevertheless, we cannot absolutely discount the possibility that Psammetichus was a rival of Amyrtaeus (cf. Kienitz 1953 (F 463) 76f; Traunecker 1979 (F 538) 399).

[49] Cf. Lewis 1977 (A 33) 141 n. 43. Diodorus gives the date as 396 (XIV.54), and this is compatible with other evidence.

[50] *Panegyricus* 140 speaks of a campaign conducted in the reign of Artaxerxes II by Abrokomas, Tithraustes and Pharnabazus against the Egyptians. In view of the date of this speech (*c.* 380) and the comment's historical context it is difficult to see what it can refer to except Achoris' war (cf. Kienitz 1953 (F 463) 85). It is possible that Egyptian operations in Phoenicia are reflected by the presence there of three altar bases of Achoris (Traunecker 1979 (F 538) 435; Stern 1982 (F 397) 205), but this would not be the only interpretation of the presence of such small and easily portable finds.

followed by a severe setback in the defeat of Egypt's major ally Evagoras who received rather less than total support from his Egyptian allies. In 381 we find Achoris supplying Evagoras with food, money and other resources. In addition, 50 triremes were sent, but no crews are mentioned, and it may well be that it is the vessels only which are at issue. In the following year Evagoras went to Egypt in person to persuade Achoris to prosecute the war more vigorously, but he obtained nothing but further financial support (Diod. xv.3–4, 8–9; Justin vi.6.1–5).[51] The defeat and capitulation of Evagoras in, or shortly after, 380 were in some small measure alleviated by the rebellion in the same year of Glos, son of the ill-fated Tamos, who created an anti-Persian alliance with Achoris and Sparta. Achoris mustered a large force of Greek mercenaries and also hired the services of the Athenian commander Chabrias, but the latter was soon lost to the Egyptian cause when he was recalled to Athens at the request of the Persian commander Pharnabazus (Diod. xv.9.3–5, 29).[52] We hear nothing of subsequent Egyptian military operations, though Glos and his successor Tachos are known to have maintained their rebellion for two further years.

It is hardly surprising that these events were soon followed by the first known major Persian attack on Egypt itself which fell in 374/3 B.C. during the reign of Nectanebo I. It was mounted by a massive Persian force allegedly consisting of 20,000 Greek mercenaries, 200,000 non-Greek troops, 300 triremes, 200 *triaconters* and a large supply train, and was commanded by Pharnabazus and the distinguished Greek general Iphicrates who attempted a full-scale invasion of the traditional Persian amphibious type. The operation was a complete failure. Not only did the slowness of the Persian build-up give the Egyptians ample warning, but Iphicrates and Pharnabazus were continually at loggerheads on the conduct of the expedition. These deficiencies were sufficient in themselves to breed disaster, but the Persians also had to contend with adverse geographical circumstances and an Egyptian defence conducted with consummate skill (Diod. xv.38, 41–3).[53]

Nectanebo's spectacular success in defeating this threat was doubtless a factor in inspiring his successor Tachos to resume Achoris' aggressive policy in Asia c. 360.[54] Encouraged by a large-scale rebellion against

[51] Diodorus' dates for the rebellion of Evagoras are untenable; those in the text follow the reconstruction of Beloch 1912–27 (A 5) III 2, 226–30.
[52] The military preparations described in xv.29 are dated to 377, which is impossibly late (see below, p. 358).
[53] As usual, the figures should be treated with a measure of caution. If we could accept the suggestion of Kuhlmann 1981 (F 466) that Nectanebo married a Greek woman named Ptolemais, we might well have evidence of an attempt to strengthen his hand against the Persian threat by establishing the closest connexions with the Greek world. Such a ploy is by no means improbable, but the text in question is too mutilated to justify complete confidence in its interpretation.
[54] The date is discussed by Kienitz 1953 (F 463) 180f, who opts for spring 360.

Persian authority centred on Asia Minor, he concluded an alliance with Sparta and collected together a large force of mercenaries and Egyptian troops as well as 200 triremes. The Spartan king Agesilaus was given command of the mercenaries and Chabrias of the fleet whilst Tachos assumed overall command. The force then moved north, but, when it reached Phoenicia, the entire operation collapsed owing to treachery at home aggravated by hostility between Agesilaus and Tachos which led to Tachos' deposition and the accession of Nectanebo II (Xen. *Ages.* II.28–31; Diod. XV.92–3, with confusion of Tachos and Nectanebo II at 93; Nep. *Ages.* 8; Plut. *Ages.* 36; Polyaen. III.11.7).[55] With him we revert to the more cautious policy of the beginning of the dynasty; he certainly gave some support to the great Cypro-Phoenician rebellion of the mid-340s, but his known involvement fell a long way short of full-scale commitment of all Egypt's military resources; probably the policy throughout his reign was to give the minimum assistance required by the circumstances. Be that as it may, his disruptive influence in the Levant was quite sufficient to guarantee the active hostility of Artaxerxes III who paid him the dubious compliment of mounting three determined attempts to re-establish Persian control of Egypt (Trogus, *Prol.* x (F 73 Seal)). The first, of which no details are known, was perhaps around 354; the second, apparently in 351, is alleged to have failed through the cowardice and inexperience of its leaders and seems to have made Artaxerxes something of a laughing-stock (Diod. XVI.40, 44, 48; Isoc. V.101).[56] The third was an altogether different matter. After the most meticulous preparation, Artaxerxes marched south again in 343/2, and in 341, thanks to the military incompetence of Nectanebo and treachery within the Egyptian forces, the country was once more in Persian hands, and the last native pharaoh of Egypt had been driven south into Nubia never to return (Diod. XVI.40–52).[57]

III. CULTURE

The final period of Egyptian independence, so rudely cut short by Ochus' invasion, was an age of renaissance and national rediscovery. It aimed at the revival of the great traditions of the past, particularly those of the XXVIth Dynasty, by the resuscitation of ancient norms, in the fond hope, perhaps, of recreating some small measure of the glories

---

[55] Diodorus dates all these events to 362 which is close to our date of 361/0 for the beginning of Tachos' reign (see p. 358).

[56] The date is not given by Diodorus, but must lie between 358, the year of Artaxerxes' accession, and 346, the date of the composition of *Philip* (Mathieu and Brémond, *Isocrate. Discours* IV (1962) 7f). If we assume that Diodorus' erroneous date of 351 for Artaxerxes' *third* campaign arose from confusion of the two expeditions, we get a precise fix, but this should be treated as no more than a plausible hypothesis; cf. Kienitz 1953 (F 463) 99–107.   [57] For the date see pp. 359f.

which Egypt had known before the Persian conquest of 525. This policy did not, however, result in an arid and moribund classicism, but rather engendered a culture of considerable vitality capable, at times, of surprising innovations and destined to form the basis for the civilization of the Ptolemaic period.

The concept of kingship, which provided, at all periods, the ideological basis of Egyptian civilization, exemplifies at this period a typical mixture of tradition and evolution. The last Egyptian pharaohs, as restorers of the ancient order, functioned in the main with scrupulous regard for the conceptual framework and canonical programme of action which had determined pharaoh's role as a divine king from the beginning of Egyptian history.[58] It comes as no surprise, therefore, that one of the most favoured elements in royal iconography at this time was the blue crown, the wearing of which constituted from the Second Intermediate Period onwards an emphatic claim to legitimacy.[59] Efforts are also frequently made in royal epithets to establish links with the XXVIth Dynasty which was regarded at this time as the model of all that was truly Egyptian.[60] The cult of royal statues which begins in the XXVIth Dynasty is also maintained and developed.[61] On the other hand, contemporary circumstances clearly led to a crucial modification in the Egyptian perception of kingship. Traditionally, and with few exceptions, pharaoh's omnipotence and unassailable righteousness had been undisputed, but, in our period, there is compelling evidence that a greater willingness had developed to concede dependence on the gods, and that the idea took root that the king might even be at odds with the divine will. Indeed, in the *Demotic Chronicle* this notion is developed systematically into a theory of historical causation according to which Egypt's history between Amyrtaeus and Nectanebo II was dominated by a series of expressions of divine wrath at royal iniquities.[62]

The society ruled by these kings is not copiously documented, but its general character is beyond dispute. In basic structure and conditions of life there is no reason to suspect any significant divergence from traditional practice. The population was probably below the total of around 3 millions which we have some reason to believe it attained during the Saite period, and was divided into two basic categories, free and unfree. The former included officials, priests, warriors and a proletariat made up of craftsmen, peasants and similar elements, whereas the unfree consisted of serfs and slaves. There were, in addition, large

---

[58] Otto 1954 (F 497) 102ff; Lloyd 1983 (F 476) 288–99.

[59] Davies 1982 (F 433).   [60] Traunecker 1979 (F 538) 395 ff.

[61] Otto 1957 (F 498); De Meulenaere 1958 (F 485) 233ff; Yoyotte 1959 (F 553); De Meulenaere 1960 (F 486); Traunecker 1979 (F 538) 425; von Kaenel 1980 (F 460) 40.

[62] Meyer 1915 (F 490); Johnson 1974 (F 457); Lloyd 1982 (F 474) 41–5.

numbers of foreigners, particularly Greeks, in the country.[63] This
population lived in settlements which ranged in size from individual
farms to large cities. Urban centres were usually built on a mound, most
of which normally consisted of the accumulated debris of centuries of
occupation, and these settlements would have had at least one nodal
point such as a temple, palace or large administrative complex. Towns
were protected with circuit walls and also, in some cases, boasted citadels
which would often have shown a consummate mastery of military
engineering. Sites such as Nebesheh[64] and Elephantine[65] demonstrate
that street planning could be very rudimentary, and that houses were
mainly constructed of mud brick. At Elephantine they were often two-
storey dwellings, but there is good reason to believe that taller buildings
were known elsewhere.[66] In the Delta the cemeteries were laid out in
suitable land adjacent to the settlement whereas in the valley the dead
were interred in the neighbouring deserts, usually, though far from
invariably, to the west.

The style of life presents no startling innovations. The spectacular
discoveries of the Egypt Exploration Society at the animal necropolis in
North Saqqara have significantly increased the amount of documentary
evidence for our period, though most of it still awaits publication.[67] It is,
however, already clear that it contains a wealth of detail on the socio-
economic life of Egypt at this time. As yet, nothing has emerged which
the student of earlier Egyptian history or the Ptolemaic period would
not expect, but a number of points are worthy of note: administration
was still characterized by a complex and paper-ridden bureaucracy;
oracles were an important means of extricating people from difficulties;
appeals to pharaoh at Memphis were not infrequent; and literacy was
sufficiently widespread to embrace even such people as stonemasons.[68]
Other evidence does reveal novelties of a modest nature: from c. 365 a
new type of marriage-contract appears, called the $sḫ-n-sᶜnḫ$, 'maintenance
document', which subsequently becomes very common. This type of
contract created particularly favourable conditions for the wife since it
imposed crushing financial penalties on the husband in the event of
divorce. Such a situation is certainly within the spirit of earlier Egyptian
practice, but, as far as is known, no attempt had previously been made at

---

[63] Lloyd 1983 (F 476) 299–301, 316–18.

[64] Porter and Moss (F 506) IV 7ff; Lloyd 1983 (F 476) 318–25.

[65] Porter and Moss (F 506) V 221ff; Porten 1968 (F 504) 94–102.

[66] Porten 1968 (F 504) 97. Petrie found at Memphis a Late Period house model, precise date
unknown, which shows a mud-brick town house with three storeys (Petrie 1910 (F 502) pl.
XXXVIII 6).

[67] For a useful preliminary survey of the material see Smith 1974 (F 526); cf. also Ray 1976 and
1978 (F 511–12).

[68] On literacy in ancient Egypt see now Baines and Eyre 1983 (F 407); Baines 1983 (F 406).

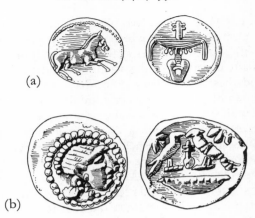

(a)

(b)

Fig. 5. (a) gold coin – horse; combination of *nb* and *nfr* signs. (b) silver coin – head of Athena; double falcon/owl with olive twigs, *nb* and *nfr* signs. (After Daumas 1977 (F 432) 433, 442, figs. 1–2; Curtis 1957 (F 429) pl. 10.2.)

such a rigorous formulation.[69] Novelty is also detectable in economic life. Payments in kind were still the basic means of achieving circulation of goods, though emmer wheat and quantities of silver measured by weight were employed as media of exchange. From the Persian period we hear of '*kite* of the treasury of Ptah' which were presumably pieces of silver weighed according to the standard used in the temple of Ptah at Memphis and stamped to guarantee the weight.[70] However, in our period for the first time we encounter native Egyptian coinage. The extant examples, inscribed in demotic or hieroglyphic, are struck in gold and silver and probably date to the XXXth Dynasty (Fig. 5). They are modelled on Greek or Macedonian prototypes, and their poor workmanship clearly betrays the inexperience of the moneyers. The rarity of these coins suggests that they never came into general use.[71] It is possible that they were intended as payment for mercenary troops, but the inconsistency in their weight and the unreliable quality of the metal would not have recommended them to foreign recipients accustomed to money of high quality, and they would probably have proved unaccept-

[69] Nims 1958 (F 496); Lüddeckens 1960 (F 467), Index, *Urk.* ID.; Pestman 1961 (F 500) Index s.v. P. Orient. Inst. 17481; Seidl 1968 (F 522) 72ff; Allam 1981 (F 403), particularly 119; Lloyd 1983 (F 476), 311–14. Whether the *sh̠ n s' nh̠* mentioned in the sixth century was of the same kind is, as yet, an open question; see Seidl 1968 (F 522) 74.

[70] Préaux 1939 (F 509) 273ff; Lüddeckens 1960 (F 467) 316ff; Pestman 1961 (F 500) 105; Porten 1968 (F 504) 62–70; Lloyd 1983 (F 476), 328f.

[71] Jenkins 1955 (B 197) 144ff; Curtis 1957 (F 429); Mørkholm 1974 (B 208); Shore 1974 (F 524); Daumas 1977 (F 432). Hoards of Greek coins continue into our period. It is clear that they were generally treated as bullion rather than as a medium of exchange. Athenian coins are particularly numerous, e.g. the Tell el-Mashkuta hoard buried *c.* 380 contained about 10,000 Athenian tetradrachms (*IGCH* 1649) (cf. Naster 1970 (F 494); Kraay 1976 (B 200) 294–5).

able. On the whole, it seems more probable that they were introduced experimentally on a small scale for native use and never achieved a wide circulation. At all events, they provide an unequivocal instance of foreign influence at this time.

Temples continue to be a dominant feature of towns and even of necropolises. Their construction and maintenance formed, at all periods, an integral part of the role of pharaoh, and the archaizing rulers of this period were inevitably active in this area.[72] The foci of interest are significant and present a consistent picture. There is a resurgence of building work on temples connected with the cult of Amon-re' at Thebes which had largely been ignored by the Persians. It begins in the XXIXth Dynasty, the most significant monument being the shrine for the sacred bark of Amon-re' west of the First Pylon. This intriguing building was possibly begun by Nepherites I, who was certainly active at Karnak, but its decoration was exclusively the work of Psammuthis and Achoris. Together with contemporary work at Medinet Habu, it formed part of the resuscitation of the ancient cult of the Theban creator gods, a cult which was intended not only to maintain the potency of the gods themselves but also to promote the demiurgic power of the king.[73] The XXXth Dynasty was equally active at Thebes. The temple of Khonsu excited its interest, but the main emphasis of its work lay in the protection of the ancient sacred areas by careful attention to the girdle walls and gateways.[74] The first archaeologically attested example of the *mammisi* or birth temple was built by Nectanebo I at Dendera,[75] though temples certainly contained some such installation at least as early as the Ramesside period.[76] These structures were to become common features of Graeco-Roman temples. The cult of Isis was also a focus of particular attention. Nectanebo I built the elegant vestibule of her temple at Philae,[77] and Nectanebo II at the very least began the large and splendid temple of Behbet el-Hagar in her honour.[78] In their devotion to this cult the kings of the XXXth Dynasty were, as often, following XXVIth Dynasty precedent,[79] but it is probable that there were also other dimensions: these kings originated in the Delta, and Isis was probably a

[72] On donations see Meeks 1972 (F 480) and 1979 (F 481) 652ff. For a key to the monuments see the royal indexes in Porter and Moss (F 506). For those of the XXIXth Dynasty see Traunecker 1979 (F 538) 407ff. Older lists are those of Petrie 1905 (F 501) 373ff; Kienitz 1953 (F 463) 190–232.

[73] Traunecker *et al.* 1981 (F 539) 89ff.

[74] Porter and Moss (F 506) II, Royal Index, s.v. Nektanebos I and II, Teos; Spencer 1979 (F 530) 73f.

[75] Daumas 1952 (F 431). Birth-temples appear in temples where triads consisting of god, goddess and child were worshipped. They function in cult as the birthplace of the infant (Bonnet 1952 (F 410) 209f and in Helck *et al.* 1975– (F 453) II 462ff).   [76] De Meulenaere 1982 (F 488).

[77] Porter and Moss (F 506) VI 206f 94.

[78] Porter and Moss (F 506) IV 40ff; cf. Clère 1951 (F 425) 136, 144ff.

[79] Lloyd 1983 (F 476) 294.

Lower Egyptian goddess; her cult was popular, and kings devoted to it inevitably increased their stock amongst the people at large; finally it was a cult closely associated with kingship. Building on behalf of sacred animal cults was also a conspicuous feature of the period:[80] there is reason to believe that kings of the XXIXth Dynasty were involved in the development of the temple area at the north end of the sacred animal necropolis of North Saqqara;[81] Nectanebo I was active on behalf of such cults at Hermopolis, Saft el-Henna, Mendes and Hermopolis Parva,[82] and Nectanebo II at the Serapeum, the North Saqqara animal necropolis, Bubastis, Heliopolis, Hermopolis, Edfu and Elephantine.[83] In part, the motivation may well have been that these cults were popular, but, since they were also distinctively Egyptian, their encouragement may perhaps be seen as promoting a sense of Egyptian national identity.[84] It should, however, also be remembered that, since the large-scale development of animal cults gathers momentum in the Saite period,[85] the last native kings of Egypt may even here be associating themselves with their great XXVIth Dynasty predecessors.

In physical structure the temple buildings of the last dynasties evidently follow standard Late Period practice, typical features of which were the use of artificial platforms and elaborate subterranean foundations.[86] Temple platforms of our period have been identified at North Saqqara;[87] the example in the great temple complex on this site was possibly begun in the time of Psammuthis and Achoris, but it was certainly the focus of considerable attention on the part of Nectanebo II.[88] Earlier Late Period temples were laid on foundations consisting of a huge pit excavated into the soil, lined with brick, and filled with sand, e.g. the Saite temple at Mendes.[89] An instance specifically of our period has yet to be identified, but there can be no doubt that this practice was followed by the rulers of the time. Both temple platforms and sand-box foundations reflect the same mythological prototype, the primeval hill or island from which all life was claimed to have emerged at the creation, i.e. all these temples, whatever their size, were regarded as being built on this island and became, *ipso facto*, centres from which demiurgic power could permeate the land of Egypt.[90] This concept of the temple may also

---

[80] Smith 1974 (F 526) 6, 85.   [81] Smith 1974 (F 526) 36f.

[82] Roeder 1940 (F 517) 78; Saft el-Henna, Roeder 1914 (F 515) 58–99; Mendes, *ibid.* 99–100; Hermopolis Parva, Porter and Moss (F 506) IV 40.

[83] Serapeum, Porter and Moss (F 506) III 2, 778; North Saqqara, *ibid.* III 2, 820f; Bubastis, Naville 1891 (F 495) 56–9; Hermopolis Parva, Brugsch 1867 (F 418) 91; Heliopolis, Bosse 1936 (F 412) 70 no. 187; Hermopolis, Chabân 1907 (F 421) 222; Edfu, Porter and Moss (F 506) VI 146; Elephantine, Honroth *et al.* 1909 (F 454) 52–9.

[84] Wiedemann 1912 (F 549) 20f; Hopfner 1913 (F 455) 25; Lloyd 1975–88 (F 473) 293.

[85] Hopfner 1913 (F 455) 23ff.   [86] Spencer 1979 (F 530) 70ff and 1979 (F 531).

[87] Spencer 1979 (F 530) 72f and 1979 (F 531) 132f.

[88] See above, n. 83.   [89] Spencer 1979 (F 530) 71.   [90] Spencer 1979 (F 531) 132f.

emerge at Hermopolis where the XXXth Dynasty enclosure wall was built of bricks laid in undulating courses which are possibly intended to imitate the waters of the primeval ocean.[91] In much of this architectural work and particularly in decoration, e.g. the use of composite palm capitals and the style of sculptural decoration,[92] the builders of this period established or confirmed the traditions to be followed by their successors in the Ptolemaic period.

Predictably, developments in the plastic arts are very much of a piece with the picture already sketched.[93] The work of the XXIXth Dynasty, though not abundant, shows that it was an important transitional phase between the Persian period and the XXXth Dynasty. The work of the latter is often of outstanding quality. It sometimes imitates that of the XXVIth Dynasty, but it also shows a taste for adaptation and innovation so that the overall impression is one of considerable diversity. It has sometimes been maintained that these developments were the result of Greek influence, but this is now generally discounted.[94] Old features continue: in sculpture in the round the Late Period tendency to greater freedom and the shift from bipartition to tripartition of the human form are continued;[95] old forms and features such as the block statue and the valanced wig are much used, and technical processes remain unchanged. On the other hand, true portraiture appears for the first time; the modelling of the body can achieve unprecedented excellence; there is an interest in unusual stones such as red breccia; and startling novelties in costume are in evidence. As for relief sculpture, the XXXth Dynasty even surpassed its Saite models. Here their work is distinguished by excellent draughtsmanship, outstanding technical mastery, and a marked taste for soft, sensuous, plastic modelling which, in the treatment of the face, can create an impression of puffiness. There is also, at times, an erotic element which shows itself in a taste for emphasizing the female genitals. In all these activities the Sebennytes, as so often, were not only preserving and developing older traditions, but established the pattern to be followed by the artists of the early Ptolemaic period.

APPENDIX: CHRONOLOGY

Chronology has been a recurrent problem in the study of this period, and we are still some way from resolving all the difficulties. Nevertheless, recent research

---

[91] Spencer 1979 (F 530) 73. [92] Stevenson Smith 1981 (F 527) 411.

[93] Bothmer 1969 (F 414); Aldred 1980 (F 402) 233ff; Stevenson Smith 1981 (F 527) 416ff.

[94] Stevenson Smith 1981 (F 527) advocated Greek influence; Steindorff 1944–5 (F 536) 58, Bothmer 1953 (F 413) 6 and Aldred 1980 (F 402) 236 contest it. On the much discussed question of Greek influence in the late tomb of Petosiris see Picard 1931 (F 503).

[95] Bipartition involves bisecting a figure along a well-marked vertical axis to create two distinct halves; tripartition involves constructing the torso out of three distinct parts, the chest, rib-cage and abdomen.

has made substantial progress in this area, particularly at the most basic level of the dating and sequence of kings.

The chronological framework for the XXVIIIth–XXXth Dynasties is provided by the king-list of the Egyptian priest Manetho supplemented by data from hieroglyphic, demotic, Aramaic and classical sources. This list was compiled in the third century B.C. and in its extant form consists simply of a catalogue of kings' names with an indication of the length of their reigns.[96] It is evident that these year-totals were calculated in terms of Egyptian civil years and generally reflect the last completed regnal year, i.e. any residual days or months in the year of a king's death were simply assigned to the first regnal year of his successor.[97] Unfortunately, the list only survives in the much later and defective excerpts of such writers as Africanus, Eusebius and Syncellus. These extracts are frequently contradictory and corrupt, but, if they are combined with other chronological data, it is possible to establish a workable king-list for the XXVIIIth–XXXth Dynasties:

XXVIIIth Dynasty. All Manetho's excerptors assign the dynasty one king called Amyrtaeus with a reign of 6 years. His position as the sole ruler is confirmed by the *Demotic Chronicle* (III.18 F.; IV.1),[98] and the reign-length is not only corroborated by the *Palaion Chronikon* (*FGrH* 610 F 2) but is also in line with an Aramaic papyrus which mentions his 5th regnal year.[99]

XXIXth Dynasty. The excerptors are contradictory:

Africanus 4 kings		Eusebius (Armenian Version) 4 kings	
Nepherites	6 years	Nepherite	6 years
Achoris	13 years	Achoris	13 years
Psamuthis	1 year	Psamuthes	1 year
Nephorites	4 months	Muthes	1 year
		Nepherites	4 months
Total: 20 years 4 months		Total: 21 years 4 months	

Eusebius (Syncellus) 4 kings		Eusebius (Jerome)	
Nepherites	6 years	Neferites	6 years
Achoris	13 years	Achoris	12 years

[96] Text in Jacoby, *FGrH* 609; translation in Waddell 1940 (F 545).

[97] Cf. Psammetichus II who is given 6 years in Manetho whereas he died in regnal year 7 (De Meulenaere 1951 (F 484) 65), and Amasis who is given 44 years whereas a regnal year 45 is certain (Lloyd 1975–88 (F 473) I 192). This system is identical to that observed in the Ptolemaic Canon (Skeat 1954 (F 525) 1ff). It was not, however, employed in the account of the XXXIst Dynasty which appears in our fragments of Manetho, but, since this section was not written by him (Waddell 1940 (F 545) 184 n. 1; Lloyd 1988 (F 477)), this anomaly need not concern us. In general see Kienitz 1953 (F 463) 153f, 168; Gardiner 1961 (F 440) 69ff.

[98] Spiegelberg 1914 (F 534); Roeder 1927 (F 516) 238ff; Bresciani and Donadoni 1969 (F 417) 55ff. Discussions in Pieper, *RE* XVI 2236f; Kaplony 1971 (F 461); Johnson 1974 (F 457); Kaplony in Helck *et al.* 1975– (F 453) I 1056ff; Johnson 1983 (F 459) and 1984 (F 458).

[99] Cowley, *AP* no. 35; Porten 1968 (F 504) 295–6, cf. 160–4, redating Cowley, *AP* no. 22 to this year.

Psammuthis	1 year	Psammuthes	1 year
Nepherites	4 months	Neferites	4 months
Mouthis	1 year	Nectanebis	18 years
		Teo	2 years

Total: 21 years 4 months

Africanus gives 4 kings and Jerome's version of Eusebius clearly reflects the same tradition, though we must correct the patent error whereby the first two kings of the XXXth Dynasty have been transferred to the XXIXth. However, the traditions of Syncellus and the Armenian version of Eusebius both add a Muthes/Mouthis to give 5 kings, though the rubrics claim that there were only 4 rulers. On the other hand, these two sources differ on the positioning of the extra king, the Armenian version placing him after Psammuthis, whilst Syncellus locates him after Nepherites.

The most obvious and attractive solution to these contradictions is to regard Muthes/Mouthis as a post-Manethonian interpolation; indeed, the similarity of his name to that of Psammuthis and the fact that both Psammuthis and Muthes/Mouthis are given the same reign-length suggest that the latter is nothing more than a ghost, the product of a scribal slip-of-the-eye, who should be removed from the list altogether.[100] If this is done, we are left with a list of 4 kings whose reign-lengths are identical in all versions except for Achoris who is given 12 years rather than 13 in Jerome's version of Eusebius, but the lamentable state of the received text of Jerome deprives this anomaly of any force; in all probability a XIII has simply been corrupted into XII in the course of transmission. Manetho's XXIXth Dynasty would then have run: Nepherites (I), 6 years; Achoris, 13 years; Psammuthis, 1 year; Nepherites (II), 4 months. However, when we turn to other sources, this scheme is contradicted. The *Demotic Chronicle* (III.18ff; IV.1ff) yields a list: Nepherites (I), *x*, Psammuthis, Achoris, Nepherites (II).[101] We are also informed that Psammuthis had a short reign and Achoris a long one, though precise figures are not given. The best solution is to argue that Achoris succeeded Nepherites and was faced at some point in his reign with a power-struggle against a rival claimant called Psammuthis who was successful in achieving some measure of autonomy for approximately a year and was then deposed to leave Achoris as undisputed pharaoh, and Demotic sources do indeed suggest that Psammuthis' reign coincided with Achoris' regnal year 2.[102]

XXXth Dynasty. Once the error in Jerome's text is rectified (see above), the excerptors are agreed on the order of kings, but reign-lengths are a matter of considerable confusion. Africanus and Jerome assign Nectanebes/Nectanebis 18 years whereas the Armenian version of Eusebius and that of Syncellus give him only 10. The essential accuracy of the former tradition is confirmed by the *Demotic Chronicle* which allots him 19 years (IV.13ff), if we assume that Manetho's

[100] Cf. Meyer 1915 (F 490) 290; Helck 1956 (F 451) 49.
[101] At II.2–4 the *Chronicle* contains an abbreviated list which omits king *x* and Psammuthis. The omissions presumably reflect an alternative tradition which denied their legitimacy.
[102] Ray 1986 (F 513).

figure means that this king's last completed regnal year was year 18 and that he died in year 19 (see above).[103] There is agreement amongst the excerptors in allotting 2 years to Teos, and this is also compatible with the *Chronicle* (IV.16–17) which assigns him one full year of independent rule, i.e. Manetho counted the year of his accession in his father's regnal year 19 as Teos' year 1 so that his last completed year would have been year 2. The excerptors disagree on Nectanebos who gets 18 years in Africanus and Jerome but only 8 in the Armenian version and Syncellus. Again the *Chronicle* vindicates Africanus, allotting Nectanebos 18 years (IV.18–19), and that figure is corroborated by a text of Edfu which gives him a regnal year 18, the highest known for this king from any monument.[104] Our list should, therefore, run: Nectanebos, 18 years, dying in his 19th; Teos, completed his 2nd year, deposed in his 3rd; Nectanebos, 18 years.

At this stage all we need in order to convert to our own chronological system is a synchronism. Until the publication of Kienitz's *Die politische Geschichte Ägyptens* (F 463) in 1953, it was generally held that this was provided by the Ptolemaic *Tale of the Dream of Nectanebo*, the narrative of which is dated to the night of the 21–22 Pharmouthis in regnal year 16 of Nectanebo II; the night in question is expressly stated to have had a full moon. This information enables us to pinpoint the date by astronomical means to 5 July 343, and, since, at this period, the Egyptian civil year began in the middle of November, Nectanebo II's 16th regnal year would have begun in November 344.[105] Computing back from this point, we can now convert our chronological data into years B.C. as follows:

Amyrtaeus	c. 404/3–398/7
Nepherites I	c. 398/7–392/1
Achoris	c. 392/1–379/8
Psammuthis	1 regnal year, probably contemporary with Achoris' regnal year 2
Nepherites II	c. 379/8. His 4-month reign would have fallen in the time-range 379–8, but its precise location cannot be established.
Nectanebo I	379/8–361/0
Teos/Tachos	361/0–359/8
Nectanebo II	359/8–342/1

Kienitz, however, discounted the evidence of *The Dream* and preferred to place the beginning of the XXXth Dynasty in 381/0. Not all his arguments need refutation, but his thesis has, on the face of it, two cogent supports: in the first

---

[103] The relevant passage has been discussed by Johnson 1974 (F 457) 13–17. Her analysis makes all previous discussions obsolete. The *Chronicle* also reveals that Nectanebo associated Tachos with himself as co-regent from regnal year 16; see p. 341.

[104] Chassinat 1932 (F 422) 239; Meeks 1972 (F 480) 133f.

[105] Text, Lavagnini 1922 (F 468) 38; discussion, Bickermann 1934 (F 409) 78f; Kienitz 1953 (F 463) 171f.

place, a Theopompus epitome (*FGrH* 115 F 103(10)) speaks of Nectanebo being king of Egypt before the end of the rebellion of Evagoras which is generally placed in 380. However, the evidence for the precise date of Evagoras' surrender is far from conclusive – a date in 379 is by no means inconceivable – but, even if we accepted 380, Theopompus could well have been referring to a position of *de facto* power acquired before Nectanebo's formal accession;[106] for there is good reason to believe that Nectanebo was in rebellion against the last ruler of the preceding dynasty before he came to the throne (see p. 340).

A second argument which can be used to support Kienitz's chronology is the fact that the invasion of Egypt by Artaxerxes III took place between November 343 and February 342, i.e. in Nectanebo's regnal year 17 by the old chronology, whereas Egyptian sources give him a regnal year 18, and a text at Edfu refers to a donation made by him in that year. This is not as damning as it looks. Regnal year 18 by the pre-Kienitz chronology would be 342/1 and would have begun about 10 months after the latest date for the invasion accepted by Kienitz. Given the defective nature of our sources, it is by no means impossible that Nectanebo II maintained, or even restored, his position sufficiently in the south in that year for such an inscription to be possible (see p. 343).

All in all, therefore, the case for abandoning the old chronology is not as cogent as has often been assumed. Since its dates are compatible with such monuments as exist and with the information available from classical sources (see below), it has been preferred in the narrative, but it should be borne firmly in mind that the matter is far from settled and is likely to remain so without the acquisition of new information.

XXXIst Dynasty. Reliable dates are, in the main, available from Babylonian chronology: Ochus, 358–337; Arses, 337–335; Darius III, 335–332.[107] The only problem here is the date of Ochus' succession *in Egypt*. There can no longer be any doubt that he gained control of the country some time between summer 343 and spring 342[108] but, according to pseudo-Manetho, he conquered Egypt in his twentieth regnal year, a date which must be expressed in terms of Babylonian chronology, i.e. 339/8.[109] If the text is correct, this claim means that, as far as some Egyptian chronographers were concerned, there was a gap of 1 or 2 years between the last year of Nectanebo II and Ochus' first Egyptian regnal year, i.e. Ochus invaded *c.* 343/2, but several years were spent bringing the country to heel, and he was only recognized as the legitimate king from 339/8.[110]

[106] On this question the comments of Cawkwell 1976 (C 112) 274 are well worth careful consideration.

[107] Parker and Dubberstein 1956 (F 159) 19, 35f. For our purposes the reign of Darius III ends with the conquest of Egypt by Alexander in 332.

[108] Bickermann 1934 (F 409) 8off; Kienitz 1953 (F 463) 170–3; Johnson 1974 (F 457) 10.

[109] Parker and Dubberstein 1956 (F 159) 35. *Pace* Kienitz 1953 (F 463) 170, it seems probable to me that ps.-Manetho's statement was based on Babylonian chronology and that the Egyptian system was only employed in such cases once the foreigner had been recognized as king of Egypt. Waddell 1940 (F 545) 185 n. 2 is equally in error in dating it to 343.

[110] The suspicion that there were different views on the question of when Ochus became pharaoh is confirmed by the manuscript variants of ps.-Manetho. Africanus' version, the most authoritative

So much for kings. When we attempt to pinpoint events within a reign we are, in general, thrown back on classical sources. Dates, when given, are expressed in terms of eponymous magistrates and Olympiad dates which can easily be converted into our system of chronology by using Bickerman's tables.[111] It should be noted, however, that serious problems arise with Diodorus Siculus, our main source for the history of the period. We must use extreme caution in dealing with his chronology and can only accept it when corroborated by other evidence.

source, gives Ochus a reign of two years which agrees with the statement that he became king in year 20; on the other hand, Eusebius, in both the Armenian and the Syncellan versions, gives him six years, despite the fact that he also dates the conquest to year 20. If Ochus is given a reign of 6 years, the conquest has to be dated to 343. Evidently, the Eusebian tradition reflects an incomplete revision of ps.-Manetho intended to bring his chronology into line with a different view of Egyptian history; cf. Lloyd 1988 (F 477).   [111] Bickerman 1968 (A 9) 146ff, 168ff.

CHAPTER 9a

CARTHAGE FROM THE BATTLE AT HIMERA TO AGATHOCLES' INVASION (480–308 B.C.)

G. CH. PICARD

I. SOURCES AND APPROACHES

The two centuries of the history of Carthage with which we deal are crucial: in this period the Tyrian colony becomes a city state important both for the expansion of her African territory to an area of about 30,000 sq.km. (equal to Roman territory in about 300 B.C.), and for her empire of the seas which is practically identical with the western Mediterranean coastal area, except for the much smaller sphere of influence of Marseilles. The acquisition and maintenance of empire were the cause of terrible wars, especially against the Sicilian Greeks. Within the city state, this period corresponds to a change from a monarchical regime to a complex aristocratic one. This evolution has been variously interpreted by modern historians;[1] many think that monarchy was the result of an irregular concentration of power in the hands of a few noble families; others, with whom I agree, consider monarchy an inheritance from the Phoenician colonists. From the religious point of view, the most important cult, which had direct ties with the city state, gave to the goddess Tanit a place at least equal to that held by her partner, Ba'al Hammon, who had previously been named alone in dedications. At the same time, Demeter and Kore were borrowed from the Greeks at the very moment of the most intense struggle between the two cultures.

We discern all these facts through a kind of mist, the result of the great weakness of our sources, composed of very diverse elements of unequal value and often contradictory. No interpretation is entirely sure; we have to appeal to hypotheses in the search for coherence. We first deal briefly with the literary and epigraphic evidence.

Punic literary texts have all perished, with the exception of one document, which raises great problems and has been interpreted in quite contradictory ways; it is in fact a Greek text, pretending to be a translation from the Punic, called 'Hanno's Periplus'. Some consider it a

---

For the earlier history of Carthage and the Punic world see *CAH* III².2, ch. 32, section III (W. Culican), and *Pls. to Vol. III* pls. 103–11 (D. Collon).

[1] Huss 1985 (G 39) 467–74.

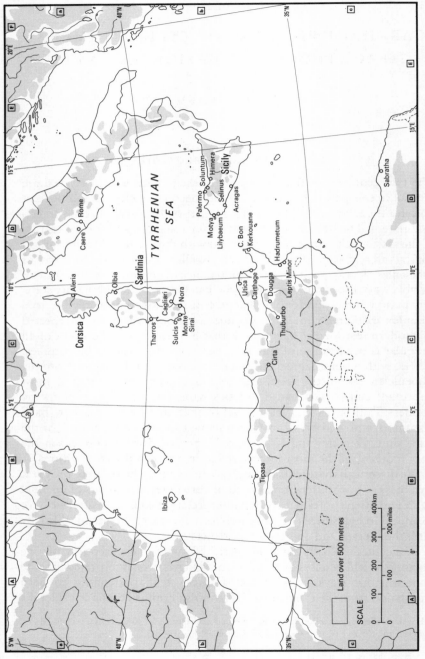

Map 10. The Punic world.

fake, others an account of an expedition on the coasts of Morocco. I think that it is a combination of two genuine Punic texts, of which the second describes a voyage around the tropical shores of western Africa at the beginning of the fifth century B.C.[2]

Punic inscriptions, especially numerous after the beginning of the fourth century, can be divided into two categories: epitaphs and votive inscriptions. The latter almost all come from the *tophet* of Salammbo, which will be briefly described in the following pages. Three or four sacrificial tariffs must be added, which may be dated in the fourth century. No proper legal text, no list of magistrates, not even a single dedication of a monument is known for our period. The historical interest of the inscriptions is practically limited to the titles of magistrates (*shophet, rab*) assumed by the dedicators themselves or by some of their ancestors.[3]

A few Greek inscriptions do mention Carthaginians, some of them historical figures. The most important is a decree of the Athenian *boule* concerning the Magonids Hannibal and Himilcon, in the last years of the fifth century (M–L 92; *IG* I³ 123).[4]

Greek and Roman authors wrote many books about Carthage. Of the few that survive we must chiefly mention sóme passages of Herodotus, of which the most important (VII.166–7) will be studied later, and books XI to XX of Diodorus of Sicily, written in the third quarter of the first century B.C. This is the essential source, not only for the wars between Greeks and Carthaginians, but also for the internal politics of Carthage during the fourth century. Aristotle devoted several passages of his *Politics* 1272b to the *politeia* of the Carthaginians; his point of view changed as he learned more of this subject, so his remarks are sometimes contradictory and generally difficult to understand.[5] Polybius, who dealt with Carthage at the time of her wars with Rome, summarizes the previous history of the city (VI.51) as a transition from a well-balanced regime with kings, senate and people to an immoderate democracy. Pompeius Trogus' *Philippic Histories*, written under Augustus' reign, are known from the prologues and a summary written by Justin. The end of Justin XVIII, and XIX–XXI are for the greater part devoted to Carthage, an essential source, especially for the story of the Magonids. Unfortunately Justin was a very bad historian, who mixes myth (for instance, that of Dido and Malchus) with fact, and distorts Punic institutions by giving them names (dictatorship, triumph) which have no meaning except in

[2] Sznycer 1978 (G 83) 478, bibl. nos. 1429–60; Picard 1982 (G 65) 175–80.
[3] Sznycer 1978 (G 83) bibl. nos. 1429–31a, 1442–4.
[4] Meritt 1940 (G 49) 247–53. A man called Iomilkos is called *basileus* in Delian inscriptions: *IG* XI,2 161 (inventory dated 279 B.C.) and 223 B 11 (dated 262 B.C.) which gives the title. He is no *shophet* as O. Masson thinks (Masson 1979 (G 47) 53–7) since these magistrates had no jurisdiction outside Carthaginian territory.   [5] Weil 1960 (B 123) 228–52.

Latin, and no equivalent in Punic. No fact attested by Justin alone can be considered trustworthy.

Archaeology offers some valuable help. At Carthage, the place where Ba'al Hammon and Tanit were worshipped, the *tophet* (a Hebrew word borrowed from the Book of Kings in the Bible) where children were sacrificed, was located in 1921 near the harbours, in the district now called Salammbo. Many monuments, once dedicated there and displaced in the Roman period, had previously been discovered. We know several hundred dedications which can be dated in the fifth and fourth centuries. We shall study the typological evolution later.

Tombs of the sixth century are numerous and rich; the relative scarcity of those of the fifth century raises problems. For the fourth, we know many cemeteries; one of them, called the *rabs*, was certainly used by the aristocracy at the end of the century and enclosed the most magnificent monuments ever built in Carthage.[6]

In Africa outside Carthage, Hadrumetum must have been occupied about 600 B.C., Kerkouane about 550, the Tripolitanian *emporia* about 500. There is no proof that Utica is older than Carthage and the story told to Pliny (*HN* XVI.216) by the warden of Apollo's temple about the age of its timbers deserves little respect. But it is true that the town had some kind of independence from Carthage, both in politics and in religion, being one of the very few African towns which lacks a *tophet*.[7]

In Sicily, Punic presence is most evident at Motya; there is a *tophet* which must be contemporary with that of Carthage, but showing marked originality in the decoration of its stelae. Dionysius of Syracuse destroyed the town in 396 B.C. It was replaced by Lilybaeum (Marsala). Palermo and Solunto are Phoenician but not Punic towns, probably founded by colonists from Lebanon. They lack a *tophet*, as well as typical Punic objects such as razors. At Selinus a mosaic with the so called Sign of Tanit attests Punic presence after the sack of 409 B.C. Untypical sites on the island have often been called Punic without reason.[8]

In Sardinia *tophets* exist at Sulcis, Monte Sirai and Nora, where a Phoenician inscription, perhaps of the ninth century, has been found.[9] Punic culture existed beside the Nuraghic and survived the Roman conquest for several centuries.

In Spain a distinctive Phoenician culture appears on several Andalusian sites, probably not before 1000 B.C. at the earliest. It differs from the Punic culture especially in its lack of *tophets* (since there was no cult of Ba'al Hammon and Tanit before the Barcids) and the persistence of red-varnished ware, originating in Lebanon, which disappears in Carthage by 700 B.C. There was only one genuine colony of Carthage, nearby on

6 Bénichou-Safar 1982 (G 9) 132–5.   7 P–W Suppl. IX s.v. 'Utica' (G. Ville).
8 Moscati 1980 (G 55) 111–49.   9 *KAI* 63, 339, no. 46.

Ibiza. Carthaginians, however, maintained strong political and economic ties with Phoenicians settled in Spain and Morocco, whom they
considered fellow-countrymen. (See also *CAH* III².2, 512–35, 540–6.)

In Italy, an important stream of commerce brought to the centre of the
peninsula fine jewellers and works of art such as the Praeneste bowl, and
established at Pyrgi a colony which played a decisive part in religion and
politics under the reign of Thefarie Veliunas (about 500 B.C.). This traffic
seems to have been controlled by the Phoenician cities in Lebanon.
However, an alliance was concluded between Carthaginians and Etruscans to resist the establishment of Phocaeans in Corsica, and was
victorious at Alalia in 535 B.C. Subsequently, this alliance played no part
in the war in Sicily during the fifth century, but it was revived in the
fourth century so effectively that Aristotle (*Pol.* 1280a 36-8) could
comment on the extreme closeness of their commercial ties. Archaeological evidence attests the strength of cultural ties between Carthage and
Etruria in the last years of the fourth century, confirming Aristotle's
observation.[10]

II. THE RULE OF THE MAGONIDS

On this evidence we have to build a largely hypothetical scheme. First we
deal with the political regime, and especially the ruling authority. No
single Punic text certainly designates the head of the state for this period,
and words used by Roman writers, such as *dictator* or *imperator* are
meaningless in any other language, as is apparent from the fact that the
translators of Punic dedications to Roman emperors could find no words
for them. We call the kings of Carthage *basileis*, the title regularly
employed by the Greeks for them, as for the absolute King of Persia. It is
most probable that the Punic equivalent was *milk*, a title given to
Thefarie Veliunas in the Pyrgi tablets.

The fundamental evidence is that of Herodotus, contemporary and
credible. He tells us (VII.166) that in 480 B.C. Hamilcar, son of Hanno of
the family of Mago, was elected as *basileus*, and this because of his valour
(*andragathia*) which proves that the *basileus* was primarily a war leader.
We know from Diodorus XIII.43.5 and Justin (XVIII.7.19) that Hamilcar's ancestor Mago, was himself (apparently the first in his family)
basileus about the middle of the sixth century.[11] We have also to account
for a very obscure and mutilated passage in Aristotle (*Pol.* 1272b 38–40):
'The advantage in Carthage (*vis-à-vis* Sparta) is that the kings are not
confined to one family, and that one of no particular distinction, and
also that if any family distinguishes itself . . .' (trans. Rackham, Loeb,

[10] Picard 1970 (G 75) 132–4.
[11] Genealogy of the Magonids: Maurin 1962 (G 48) 13, n. 2.

1959 p. 161). Aristotle speaks for his own time, when kings could be chosen from several families; but, like Herodotus, he seems to think that the *basileus* was selected in consideration of his personal qualities among his kinsmen or other nobles. This is what Samuel does, when, at the direction of the Lord, he anoints David, youngest son of Jesse, excluding his elders.[12] Such a process certainly excludes popular election, even if there was some kind of solemn recognition of the *basileus* after the choice by the people or the army. The choice itself could only be made by a select body, perhaps one of the pentarchies, which, according to Aristotle (*Pol.* 1273a 13–15), had the right of appointing the Hundred Judges (see below) and the most important dignitaries.

Even if the *basileus* was essentially a war-lord, he could not act as commander of the armies without being previously endowed with religious authority. This is clear in Herodotus: during the whole battle at Himera, Hamilcar remained in the camp, slaughtering victims and studying the omens from their viscera (VII.167). It was normal in antiquity that a general should take the omens before a battle, but it is astonishing in this case, that a man chosen especially for his valour, took absolutely no part in the action either as commander or as fighter. This shows that even the military function of the Carthaginian *basileus* consisted primarily in obtaining the favour of the gods, and this is quite in accordance with the practice of all Semitic peoples.

This religious role of the *basileus* carried with it considerable responsibilities. For this again Herodotus is informative: seeing defeat Hamilcar threw himself into the pyre and died in the flames. This version of the king's death must have been given Herodotus by the Carthaginians since the Syracusans knew nothing of it. He says also that Hamilcar was worshipped as a god or hero by his countrymen, a monument being dedicated to him in Carthage and others in each Punic colony.[13] This is confirmed by Diodorus (XIII.62.4 and cf. XI.22.1): after his revenge at Himera in 409 B.C., Hamilcar's grandson Hannibal sacrificed 3,000 prisoners in honour of his forebear. This behaviour corresponds better with theories of kingship dependent on cult, than with other explanations recently offered (suicide from remorse or 'potlatch'.[14]

Hamilcar's self-sacrifice clearly prefigures Vergil's account of Dido's voluntary death, and somewhat later Himilco's penance will be an

[12] This way of choosing the king seems very similar to the Spartan: Carlier 1984 (A 13) 248–9.
[13] A statue of the middle of the fifth century recently discovered at Motya could belong to Hamilcar's monument in the city: Falsone 1986 (G 20); 1988 (G 21).
[14] Grotanelli 1983 (G 27) 437–41; he borrowed the notion of 'potlatch' from R. Mauss, who found it in Amerindian ethnology. It describes a challenge for power in which the competitors try to outdo each other by the splendour of their gifts, the lesser eventually taking his own life. The main objections are that potlatch is attested in neither the Semitic nor the Greek world, and that it exists only within a society and not between two peoples at war, especially of different cultures.

attenuated form of the same ritual (see below). This means that there existed a tie between the myth of the origins of the city, unparalleled elsewhere and perpetuated by the cult of Dido, and the royal ideology of the Magonid period; this tie consisted essentially in the religious responsibility of the king.[15]

In the fifth and fourth centuries, the *basileus* of Carthage had no colleague. This is shown by the fact that in 407 B.C., Hannibal being already an old man, his nephew Himilco was required to assist him without having the royal title, which he received only after Hannibal's death.[16] If there had been two kings, either the second would have been able to replace Hannibal, or Himilco, being already king, would immediately have taken command after the death of his associate.

We shall see that the judicial powers of the king were practically nonexistent; the title of *shophet*, whose basic meaning is judge, is inappropriate, but, as we have observed, *milk*, attested in the Pyrgi inscription, is wholly suitable.[17]

On two occasions, Diodorus (XIII.43.5 and XIV.54.5) describes the king of Carthage as *basileus kata nomous*; the same formula is used by Thucydides (V.66.2) for the king of Sparta.[18] This means that the king of Carthage was not exactly elected, the Lacedaemonian *basileis* being hereditary, but that he had to obey the laws of the city. The *basileus* of Carthage could not in fact undertake any expedition without the agreement of the people, and some special authority to make war. Sometimes (for instance in 410) the opposition was strong enough to delay the declaration of war, or to reduce the forces granted to the king.[19] The first sentence of the 'Periplus of Hanno' is probably a version of a decision of the popular assembly defining the royal mission (foundation of colonies on the Atlantic coast of Morocco). Though we have no case of a royal trial, one of the sons of Hamilcar of Himera, Giscon, was banished for a time (Diod. XIII.43.5). It is possible that the necessity of obtaining the people's agreement to their enterprises, which perhaps included the adoption of a special title by the *basileus*, gave rise to the use by Roman writers of the word *dictator*, to translate a formula more or less analogous to the Greek *basileus autokrator*.

The main achievement of the Magonids was the establishment of empire. The story of Malchus, found in Justin XVIII.7, is entirely mythical: there is no trace of important wars in Sardinia and Sicily in the middle of the sixth century and it is quite incredible that Carthage could

[15] Picard 1954 (G 67) 27–45.
[16] Diod. XIII.43.5 says that the Carthaginians established as general Hannibal, who was already king according to the law; and in XIV.54.5, that they chose Himilcon as king according to the law in order that he could lead the war.   [17] *Pls. to Vol.* IV pl. 297, for the Pyrgi inscription.
[18] Carlier 1984 (A 13) 248.   [19] Diod. XIII.43.3; Huss 1985 (G 39) 108.

have raised an important army from her citizens at this time, since she was not able to do this even at the height of her power. The death of Carthalo, crucified by his father in his sacerdotal dress, is evidently a tale invented to justify one of the forms of the sacrifice of the king's son. At the Battle of Alalia the Punic force comprised only the fleet, the military power of the city being just sufficient to maintain its navy and to guard Carthage against the Libyans to whom tribute was still paid.[20]

The first task of Mago and his successors was diplomatic. Many important treaties were concluded in the last third of the sixth century, thanks to the activity of Mago and his son Hasdrubal. The alliance with the Etruscan League, and especially with Caere, resulted in the victory of Alalia and the driving of the Phocaeans out of Corsica (535 B.C.). Shortly after, Caere was ruled by Thefarie Veliunas, and an important Phoenician colony lived in her harbour town, Pyrgi, worshipping Astarte, assimilated to Uni. Rome was then very closely associated with Caere, and there is no difficulty in accepting the date of the first treaty she concluded with Carthage, recorded by Polybius who gives (III.22.7–9 see Walbank *ad loc.*) a detailed translation of the text (509 B.C.). Romans were forbidden to travel in Byzacium and Tripolitania, which Carthaginians were in the process of settling but they were permitted, under supervision, to sail to western Sicily and Sardinia which Carthaginians regarded as their property. Other treaties were concluded with the Persians, whose King seems to have considered Carthage as a dependency of his empire, and with the Phoenicians of Spain, which Punic forces seem to have protected against the natives. At the beginning of the fifth century, Hanno's and Himilco's expeditions must be the consequence of these agreements, but Hanno's attempt to colonize the Atlantic coasts of Morocco proved a failure. As for the Greeks, Phocaeans (including Massaliotes) on one side, and Gelon on the other, were considered as enemies, but Anaxilas of Rhegium and Terrillus of Agrigentum were friends, and Carthage protected them against Gelon and Theron of Agrigentum.

This political activity could deploy an army of a very peculiar type, created by the Magonids as a logical consequence of the shortage of manpower in the city and the relations established with a great number of 'under-developed' barbarians. The force consisted of mercenaries bred among those fierce savages who liked war and would accept relatively little pay. Only a small guard, the so-called Sacred Band, was composed of young Carthaginian nobles. Herodotus tells us (VII.165) that Hamilcar of Himera disembarked in Sicily with the Phoenicians (the guard), Libyans, Iberians, Ligyans and Elisyces (whose fatherland was Catalonia and Languedoc), Sardinians and Corsicans: on the whole, a

[20] Gauthier 1960 (G 26) 268–70; Maurin 1962 (G 48) 20–1, n. 3.

colonial army, not unlike, *mutatis mutandis*, those of France and Great Britain in the beginning of this century. This sort of army has the advantage of being relatively cheap, both in wages and weapons; but it required brave and cunning recruiting officers, who after the creation of the army remained on its staff. It restricted use of the hoplite phalanx and did not allow complicated manoeuvres. Its strength relative to Greek armies was comparable with that of the Persians relative to the Greeks, and in both cases Greeks won. Tactics and equipment seem to have improved considerably in the course of the fifth century, as is shown by the brilliant victories of Hannibal at Selinus, Himera and Agrigentum.

War and the economy are obviously related. War was expensive in antiquity but an army and navy are profitable investments for well-organized states, since looting is the greatest source of profit. However, for the state of Carthage trade was necessarily the only important source of income. At the beginning, as has been shown by C. Picard and J. Alexandropoulos,[21] the city was essentially a staging-point for ships returning from Spain, which had travelled from Lebanon to Malta, Sicily and Sardinia. Colaeus' voyage (*CAH* III^2.3, 139, 214) demonstrates the colossal profit to be gained from such voyages, but Carthage had long to be content with a tiny share of this wealth, and could expand only when she was able to enjoy most of it. This could happen when Tyre was besieged by Nebuchadrezzar (587-574) and, under the pressure of Greek competition, Carthage was better able to resist than any of the Phoenician cities.

But an ancient commercial economy is well balanced only when it controls land where trade profits can be invested in agriculture. Centuries elapsed before Carthage was able to secure such property on her very restricted peninsula. According to Justin (XIX.1.3-4), who on this occasion seems credible, the first Magonids failed to suppress the power of the neighbouring chieftains, and it was only during the period of apparent quiet after the battle of Himera that their successors (among whom was the mysterious Hanno the Great) succeeded in subduing them. Thereafter Carthage need no more fear caprices of fortune. The foundation of Kerkouane about 500 B.C., and the extraordinary expansion of the cemeteries all over Cape Bon during the fifth century, as well as the digging of quarries at El Haouaria, whose sandstone was used for every sort of building in Carthage, confirm that the peninsula was under firm control. It is quite possible that the impoverishment suggested by the tombs in Carthage herself during the fifth century was caused by the migration of some of the richest families to the newly conquered lands. The famous Punic agronomist Mago, who probably lived much later, advises the landlords to live on their estates rather than in town

[21] Picard 1982 (G 74) 161-73.

(Columella 1.1.18), and this seems to have been the usual practice. As soon as they controlled Cape Bon and the mountainous district which lies between it and the capital, Punic farmers could develop the vine and olives, which could be sold at high prices, while corn was supplied in abundance by the lower Mejerda valley and Byzacene. Land was tilled by Libyan peasants who were reduced to a very harsh serfdom, which later occasioned fierce revolts, but had the advantage of reducing the cost of labour almost to nothing.

If we examine the activities of the *basileus*, we see that he had very little time left to administèr Carthage: diplomacy, recruiting, wars and voyages kept him abroad for years. Justice, holding of the various assemblies and councils, enforcement of the laws, required a full-time magistrate. Those who admit the existence at this time of *shophets* are certainly correct; but it is impossible that the same man could have held both offices, and we have seen that there was only one *basileus*. This office was certainly distinct from the *shophet*, and the two offices were complementary. We do not know how many *shophets* were in office then, nor for how long they held office, nor how they were chosen. The tariff of Marseilles is dated by the names of two eponymous *shophets*;[22] these at least were certainly in office for one year, but the same text says that they had colleagues. It is therefore possible that from a college of several members, two had been selected each year to preside and these gave their names to the year. I think this solution more probable than the assumption that the colleagues mentioned in the text were other magistrates, elected for duties different from those of the eponymous *shophets*. However, there were certainly financial managers, municipal officers in charge of streets, markets and public buildings, controllers of the temples, officers of the police and perhaps many other civil servants. All certainly answered to the senate, which had the task of co-ordinating public activities in general, including those of the *basileus*. The poverty of the Punic language necessitated the use of very few words to name the different magistrates, instead of creating special terms for each, as in Greece and Rome. Some conclude from this that there were only as many magistrates as there were words for them, but it is quite impossible that such an important political system could have been managed like a small borough.

The astonishing strength of the Punic city state was certainly founded on the religious faith that motivated most of its citizens, which was considered by most other people as cruel fanaticism. In fact the Carthaginians had in common with most Semitic peoples a feeling for the transcendency of divinity which is lacking among Indo-Europeans. This did not, as with the Hebrews, lead to a belief in the unity of God,

[22] *KAI* no. 69; Huss 1985 (G 39) 540, n. 296.

but to a very hierarchical conception of the pantheon: only one god, or a god and his partner, were really transcendent, the others acting as mere assistants or intermediaries with the mortal world. As in Egypt, several theological systems existed, each giving the supreme role to a different god or goddess. What is characteristic of Carthage is the giving of the first rank to Ba'al Hammon, a god to whom the homeland Phoenicians paid little respect.

Our knowledge of Punic religion in this period is founded essentially on the excavation of *tophets*, of worship-places characteristic of Ba'al Hammon, though the word *tophet* itself has not been found in Punic inscriptions, but is borrowed from the Bible. Its true meaning seems to be 'the place of burning' where infants, probably previously killed with a knife, were reduced to ashes, which were sealed in a pot buried in the sacred area. Very often a stone monument was raised over the urn. Nowhere else, except perhaps at Hadrumetum has the burning place been discovered. The *tophet* of Carthage consists of a large area west of the commercial harbour. The oldest monument, called 'chapelle Cintas' after its discoverer, must be studied from his original reports which are credible,[23] and can be tested on site. It had been built at the very beginning of the cult, at least by about 750 B.C. In the period of the Magonids the votive monument standing over the urn with the ashes of the sacrificed child, sometimes mixed with those of an animal, and some offerings, is a block of sandstone, carved in the shape of a throne bearing a pillar, or a chapel resembling an Egyptian temple. Some of these monuments bear an inscription reading 'cippus dedicated (by sacrifice) *molk* to Ba'al'. No goddess is named. When the cippus is in the form of a chapel, figures are frequently represented inside it; some are symbols, the most frequent being in the form of a bottle (Fig. 6), and some in human shape. The latter are much more numerous at Motya[24] than at Carthage. Before the end of the fifth century a symbol appears composed of a triangle bearing a bar and a circle, which it is customary to call the Sign of Tanit and which probably represents the divine power (Fig. 7).[25]

III. THE DISMANTLING OF KINGSHIP

The fourth century B.C. is a deeply disturbed period in Punic history. A terrific struggle, in which neither of the adversaries could succeed, was engaged with Syracuse, which, under Dionysius' tyranny, became the champion of western hellenism. One consequence of this war was the fall of the Mago family. Other statesmen, the most illustrious being Hanno, tried in vain to restore a strong personal power. Aristocracy at last

---

[23] *CRAI* 1946, 373–4; P. Cintas, *La céramique punique* (Paris, 1950) 490; Picard 1954 (G 67) 30–1.
[24] Moscati and Uberti 1981 (G 57). [25] Picard 1978 (G 63) 91–112.

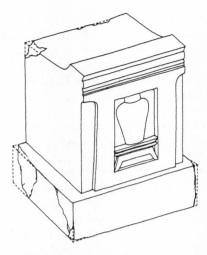

Fig. 6. Stela with 'bottle' symbol from Motya; Motya Museum. (After Moscati and Uberti 1981 (G 57) fig. 34.746.)

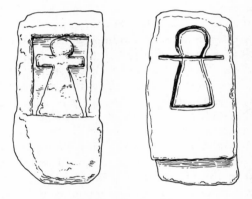

Fig. 7. Stelae with Tanit signs from Carthage; Carthage Museum.

imposed its authority through a pitiless justice. At the same time, fundamental reforms transformed religion. In the *tophet* cult the goddess Tanit took pre-eminence over her partner Ba'al Hammon. The cult of Demeter and Kore was introduced, borrowed from the Syracusans but soon punicized, while the Punic gods, Eshmun and Shadrapa, were more or less assimilated, the former to Asclepius, the latter to Dionysus. The basic spirit of Punic religion was, however, not altered since these gods were only auxiliaries of the supreme deities, and did not share their transcendence, and it is interesting to observe that the harshness of political conflict did not suppress cultural development.

The events that resulted in the institution of an aristocratic republic in Carthage belong to the first half of the fourth century. In 409 B.C. royal power was in the hands of Hannibal, grandson of the Hamilcar who perished at Himera in 480 B.C. The Athenians' expedition against Syracuse appeared to him as an opportunity to avenge a still painful defeat. Though resisted by a large body of opinion, the king succeeded not only in destroying Himera but in conquering all the southern coast of Sicily, sacking Selinus and Agrigentum. But after his natural death, his cousin and heir Himilco failed to take Syracuse. Already disagreeing on the decision to go to war, his countrymen did not judge that the penance he inflicted on himself, completed with his suicide, was enough to restore the fortunes of the dynasty,[26] especially since the threat had helped Dionysius to regain his tyranny at Syracuse, and to develop an ambitious international policy, eased by the triumph of Sparta over Athens. The destruction of Motya in 397 compensated for the loss of Selinus and Agrigentum, which remained henceforth dependent on the Carthaginian *eparchia* in Sicily. Carthage could even be vulnerable in Africa, as was shown by a terrible rising of the Libyan peasants (Diod. XV.24), which Himilco's successor, Mago, whose family is unknown to us, had to face. Just after surviving this trial, Mago had to prevent an attempt of Dionysius to unite Magna Graecia. He was able to revive the old Etruscan alliance, and it is probably then that the pact with Rome, still intimately associated with Caere, was renewed. But Mago fell in a battle with Dionysius. The two adversaries exhausted themselves without obtaining victory and a peace, quite profitable for Carthage, was concluded in 373 B.C.

External and internal problems (a new Libyan revolt broke out immediately after Mago's death) embittered contentions within the leading class. The second third of the fourth century was especially disturbed. The outstanding personality, Hanno, nicknamed the Great as had been an homonymous Magonid in the previous century, is depicted by Justin (XX.5.11; XXI.4) as a very wealthy man who was reputed to own as much money as the state. He could seek support from popular societies, and even the slaves and Libyan serfs; many of these features seem borrowed from the traditional image of the Greek tyrant, but there may be some truth in them. For instance, the banquets at which Hanno is said to have tried to poison the senators, are perhaps those public meals which Aristotle calls *syssitia* (*Pol.* 1272b). J. M. Dentzer has shown that this was an oriental institution borrowed by Greek aristocrats and tyrants, and so it is quite probable that it existed also in Carthage.[27] Traces of the practice can be found in the cities of Roman North Africa.

Hanno succeeded first in having the leader of his opponents, Eshmu-

[26] Maurin 1962 (G 48).   [27] Dentzer 1982 (J 12) 433–4.

niaton (whose name has been altered to Suniaton), sentenced to death. His victim had supported a reconciliation with Syracuse, possibly with the help of philhellenic circles. Hanno was firmly attached to national traditions, and went so far as to forbid by law the teaching of Greek, but when he tried to restore absolute power and to suppress the legal authorities, the people rose against him; taken alive, he died after terrible torture.

The fall of the Magonids and the failure of Hanno resulted in the conclusive institution of an oligarchy, which Aristotle registered among his *politeiai*, comparing it to the constitutions of Sparta and Crete. Information reached the philosopher at various times, registering situations that changed quickly. His aim and method was to generalize not analyse. This led him to compare institutions which seem to have little in common, such as the ephors of Sparta and the Court of the Hundred at Carthage, only because both exercised essentially a right of control. We must not conclude that Aristotle did not understand the laws of Carthage, but that he saw them from a point of view different from our own.

This difficulty is aggravated by the great poverty of Punic political language. Three or four words were enough to define most diverse offices. The words *rab* and *shophet* occur frequently in inscriptions; the first may apply to the chief or president of any group, club, senate or religious college, as well as the general of an army. Sometimes the meaning is made more precise by a determinative: *rab kohanim* means chief of the priests. But the dignitaries buried in the beautifully carved sarcophagus at Sainte Monique in Carthage are called *rab* without other determinative.[28] The title *rab mahanat*, which means chief of the army, has been found so far only in Punic inscriptions of the Roman imperial period, where it is translated as consul; but it would certainly be absurd to conclude that there were no generals to lead Punic armies in the fourth or third centuries.

It is certain that supreme authority lay with a senate or council, which Aristotle and Polybius compare with the Spartan *gerousia* and the Senate of Rome, though these two assemblies had little in common.[29] It is generally admitted that the members of this senate were many. We do not know anything about the mode of election. It had a board of maybe thirty men and was divided into committees of five members, called pentarchies by Aristotle, whose very imprecise remarks suggest that the selection of officers was based both on the personal qualities and the

[28] Huss 1979 (G 38) 217–32, and 1985 (G 39) 465, argues that the *rab* were the heads of the financial administration. I think this is not supported by any evidence.
[29] On the title of 'senators' (DRM or RSM) Huss 1985 (G 39) 462, n. 37. It is remarkable that there seems not to have existed a word for the 'senate' as a whole.

wealth of the candidates. Aristotle says also that the pentarchies chose the Hundred Judges (*Pol.* 1273a 13–15), whose first task was control of the magistrates who held the political and military power. We already saw that he speaks of *basileis* who were taken from several families; this agrees with the assertions of Diodorus and Justin (xxi.4.1) about Hanno the Great and Bomilcar: kingship has been dismantled rather than abolished, and the *basileis* retained the right of commanding the armies, under the rigorous control of the Hundred. The *shophets*, among whom two were eponymous, strictly had no military competence, as is shown by the fact that no one was able to face Agathocles' attack.[30] They probably dealt with non-political justice. The popular assembly could interfere only when there was a contest between the senate and the magistrates, which probably seldom occurred, since the aristocracy could easily get rid of its adversaries by the sentence of the Hundred. But the power of societies such as Aristotle's *syssitia* could eventually balance the authority of councils, as is shown by Hanno's experience. One thing is sure: until the end of the fourth century, Punic military command maintained an efficiency that was to be lost in the third, the unfortunate generals then being deprived of any authority by the tyranny of the Hundred.

There is probably some relation between political changes and religious innovation (cf. Diod. xx.14.4–7). One example is the cult of the *tophet* which, as we have seen, directly concerned the fate of the city; this appeared clearly when Carthage was for the first time besieged by Agathocles, and public opinion compelled the nobles who had managed to save their sons from the pyre to sacrifice them, arguing that their fraud was the cause of the disaster. About one century before, the monuments of the *tophet* had taken a new shape: around 400 B.C., massive cippi are replaced by stelae looking like small obelisks, topped by a pyramid and carved on their fronts with decoration almost always associated with an inscription. This is a dedication mentioning first 'the Lady Tanit, face of Ba'al' and only in second place the god Ba'al Hammon.[31] The discovery by Pritchard of a plate dedicated at Sarepta to Tanit and Ashtart solves conclusively the problem of the Phoenician origin of Tanit.[32] It is remarkable that this goddess, of apparently little reputation in Phoenicia, could rise to the first place in the Punic pantheon, overshadowing even her partner. This can only be the result of a drastic reform of which the causes remain unknown to us, but which is contemporary, on the one hand with the adoption of the cult of Demeter, on the other with the dismantling of kingship. It is hardly credible that there was no connex-

---

[30] It appears clearly from Diod. xx.6.3 that before the election of Hanno and Bomilcar as *strategoi* there was no possibility of opposing the invaders, who met no resistance at Cape Bon.
[31] Huss 1985 (G 39) 513–14.   [32] Pritchard 1982 (G 76) 83–92.

Fig. 8. Stela with priest holding child, from Carthage. (Height 1.15m; Tunis, Bardo Museum Cb 229). (After Harden 1980 (F 263) pl. 35; Picard 1976 (G 63) pl. 8.10.)

ion between these three phenomena which redefined the character of Carthage. The symbols and figures carved on the stelae are as numerous and various as the texts of their dedications are monotonous; the depiction of worship, especially the image of a priest in Egyptian linen robes and a round cap (the Phoenician national dress) holding in his arms an infant ready for sacrifice (Fig. 8), is highly impressive.

The installation of the cult of Demeter is related by Diodorus (xiv.77.5). It was intended to expiate Himilco's sacrilege, and according to the historian, priests and priestesses were chosen among Greeks living in Carthage. However, the cult very quickly became punicized, and in the Roman imperial period inscriptions distinguish the *Ceres punica* from the Greek. A *favissa* excavated by Father Delattre on the Borj Jedid hill

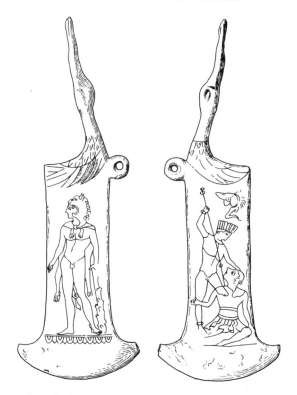

Fig. 9. Bronze razor from Carthage; Carthage Museum. (Cf. Picard 1967 (G 66) pl. 30, no. 37.)

seems to mark the place where the temple stood.[33] Demeter was accompanied by her daughter Kore, and Pluto; terracotta statues found at Cape Bon are likely to represent the cult images. A *naiskos* found in Thuburbo Maius, where Greek architectural mouldings are used in a characteristic non-Greek composition with a heavy flat entablature, is probably a model of the temple in Carthage.

All this shows that Punic society in the fourth century is relatively well known. Even the physical appearance of the Carthaginians is sketched on the stelae of the *tophet*, in silhouettes rather than portraits, and may be compared with the statues adorning the sarcophagi from Sainte Monique. These statues are the result of a cultural syncretism to which Phoenicia, Egypt, Greece and Etruria contributed. None, of course, is a portrait, even idealized, but the men wear the dress of Punic dignitaries, a long tunic with an *epitogium* on the shoulder, while the women are

[33] *CRAI* 1923, 354–66; Picard 1982/3 (G 64) 187–94.

clasped in the wings of a gigantic dove, a strange garment characteristic of Isis. Engraved finger rings bear human heads worthy of the best Greek jewellers.[34] Engraving was also used to adorn the flat sides of razors in the shape of a hatchet, which are found only in Punic tombs; some drawings are inspired by Egypt, others illustrate Greek myths or figures (Fig. 9).[35]

It was long believed that Carthage did not use coins before 400 B.C. and first used them only to pay her mercenaries, especially in Sicily. Now an issue can perhaps be dated to the end of the fifth century,[36] while Palermo and Motya already had mints, strongly influenced by Greek workshops. This Siculo-Punic coinage persisted throughout the fourth century, having as its main purpose the paying of the army. But as early as the first half of the fourth century Carthage started to issue gold coins whose weight is the Phoenician shekel, while Sicilian coins observe the drachma standard. We can see that there was a twofold stream in trade, one directed towards Sicily and the other towards the old eastern fatherland, which, after Alexander's conquest, depended upon the flourishing Lagid kingdom. We must not forget that ambitious economic plans embraced the whole far west, with Spain, the mysterious cultures of Atlantic Gaul, then withering under Celtic pressure, Morocco and even tropical Africa, the marvellous islands of the western ocean.[37]

Carthage's prosperity, which had already struck Thucydides (in the speech by Hermocrates, VI.34.2), is reflected in brilliant architecture. The building of a double harbour in the pools at Salammbo started with the digging of a large channel running from south to north, which probably began in Kram bay and went as far as the later war harbour, constructed only at the time of the wars with Rome.[38] Kerkouane, destroyed by Regulus, has preserved her double rampart, and quite hygienic and comfortable houses with bathrooms including shoe-shaped tubs.[39] Hellenistic innovations were quickly adopted: for instance, the internal courtyard becomes a peristyle, adapted to local usage.

In spite of this prosperity, the Punic city state was not spared that universal crisis of the polis which had begun in Greece. Polybius (VI.51), following Aristotle (Pol. 1316b 5), describes this as a decay, leading from well-balanced institutions to extreme democracy, which he considers as the end of the political cycle. The Achaean historian's views are biased by his conservatism, but he is right to consider that the evolution in Carthage was more rapid than in Rome. The Punic system was in fact more intricate than the Roman, and the causes of unrest more numerous.

---

[34] Quillard 1979, 1987 (G 77).   [35] Picard 1967 (G 66).
[36] Cutroni-Tusa 1983 (G 16) 40 gives the latest account of the problem.
[37] Huss 1985 (G 39) 84–5.   [38] Hurst 1983 (G 36) 603–10.   [39] Fantar 1984/5 (G 23).

In Africa, Carthage's large and well-managed territory of course procured important income, and when one walks in the streets of Kerkouane, one can see that the inhabitants of this rather modest borough were as well-off as their contemporaries in Greece or Campania. But this prosperity did not benefit the Libyan peasants who constituted the main manpower. Carthage's leaders, conscious of this problem, attempted to solve it by settling colonists in the region of the present Bou Arada, and by cultural assimilation, which succeeded in giving birth to half-breeds called by the Greeks Libyphoenicians. But frequent revolts showed that ethnic opposition remained alive. The still independent tribes were beginning to build a political organization, which obliged Carthage to keep an army on the border and to extend occupation to the west and south. In Sicily, Carthage could have taken advantage of the end of Dionysius' tyranny, but Timoleon, who tried to restore aristocracy in Syracuse, wanted to strengthen his regime by military glory, and his victory on the Crimisus, in which the elite of the Punic army was annihilated, made clear that Carthage had not solved her war problems. It is on this occasion that our sources mention for the first time the execution of incompetent or unlucky generals (Plut. *Tim.* 22). However, the military leaders had not yet entirely lost authority, and a kind of balance between the powers, highly praised by Aristotle (*Pol.* 1272b 24ff), seems to have still prevailed.

Though we are able to follow more or less the changes in Carthage's external policy, her real character remains obscure. Even the textless pictures on the stelae of the *tophet* raise many problems to which there is no logical answer. The outburst of fanaticism that resulted in the slaughter of hundreds of adult noble children, when Agathocles attacked the city, attests the existence of hidden tendencies that might be called retrograde. This means that we can draw no ready parallels with situations elsewhere and in other periods. The only certainty is that the aristocracy, which was probably not homogeneous, hardened its resistance both to personal power, lacking now the support of solid institutions and becoming a mere toy for the ambitious, and to popular aspirations. Agathocles' invasion, foolishly daring as it was, revealed in the clearest light all the weaknesses of the city state: the incapacity of the lawful holders of civil power, especially the *shophets*, to oppose the invaders with the slightest force, because they entirely lacked anything like the Roman *imperium*; the outburst of religious fanaticism; the crimes and excesses of military leaders called back from Sicily, among whom the most illustrious, Bomilcar, was perhaps an offspring of Hanno the Great; the cruelty and meanness of the aristocracy. This gloomy picture has been drawn for us by Timaeus, whom Diodorus faithfully transcribed, and Timaeus was a rhetorician. Bomilcar's speech in the agora of

Carthage (Justin XXII.7.9–11), uttered from the cross on which he died, is clearly a scholastic exercise. But even embellished or distorted facts remain facts; the very expansion of the city had destroyed the basis of legal order, as had been the case in Greece before, and as would happen later in Rome.

SOUTH ITALY IN THE FOURTH CENTURY B.C.

NICHOLAS PURCELL

The fifteen decades which elapsed between the expedition to Sicily of the Athenians during the Peloponnesian War and the war between Pyrrhus of Epirus and the Romans are something of a heroic age in Italian history. It was a time of trial during which the success or failure of communities was constantly at stake, and in which the patterns of the preceding centuries were often obliterated and those which were to endure until the late imperial period formed. The trial took the form of almost unceasing warfare, confused by continuous changing of sides according to a mutable diplomacy and the exigencies of more or less mercenary manpower. Overall, the losers were the already ancient *apoikiai*, the city states of the Greek diaspora, whose champions, whether leaders from within the body politic or *condottieri* summoned from the east, all failed to establish their power sufficiently for either their descendants or their successors to share in it. The victory went to the Italic communities, whose elites in this period provided the forebears of long lines of city aristocrats whose tradition endured until the Roman empire. That such continuity came out of this period reminds us that it was no Dark Age. The victors were not usually in a position to despoil or obliterate completely; the fighting was not genocidal. This was partly because the warfare of the time was promoted and fuelled by background social and economic conditions which were tending, despite the dangers of the time, in positive directions: demographically, Italy was regarded at this time as a place with relatively abundant manpower, and the rewards of the integration of local production systems into Mediterranean-wide networks of distribution and consumption were becoming generally more palpable. In this situation the assertiveness of the Italic

This account is intended to follow the themes of *CAH* IV² chs. 14 (Salmon) and 15 (Penney), and to replace the brief résumés of *CAH* VI¹ 127–31 (on Dionysius I in Italy) and 299–301 (on the *condottieri* at Taras). It is a slender attempt at a fusion of the themes of the political history of Megale Hellas as they were set out by Ciaceri 1927–32 (G 138) and Giannelli 1928 (G 180) with the much more recent understanding of the social and cultural circumstances of the time. I am grateful to the editors for their help, and for the facilities of the British School at Rome where much of it was composed. Readers should note that the term Italiote means a citizen of a Greek city on the Italian mainland; Italic, on the other hand, refers to the other inhabitants of the peninsula.

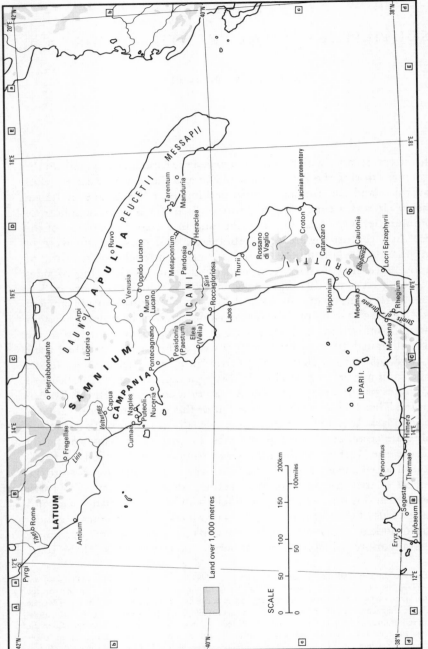

Map 11. Italy.

Fig. 10. Bronze corslet dedicated by Novius Fannius; Switzerland, private collection. (After Colonna 1984 (G 142) pl. 1.)

peoples was accompanied and tempered by their continued rapid adoption of the cultural and social institutions of the Hellenic Mediterranean *koine*, as it is sometimes called, that coalescence of local social forms into the more or less homogeneous civilization that was eventually to underlie the Roman empire. Imitation, assimilation and acculturation in fact made the ethnic stand-off less damaging, and an interactive, settled, productive social system was spreading to a greater extent, in aggregate, than it was set back by *razzia* or reprisal.

To open this account, however, it may be helpful to take three vivid individual illustrations of these wider tendencies. First, the inscriptions set up by a proud Etruscan-Roman family of Tarquinii in the first century A.D. which commemorate their early ancestors, including a chieftain whose expedition with a local contingent to a war in Sicily may plausibly be linked with the Athenians' expedition and its support from western communities.[1] This remarkable document illustrates the fortunes, centuries ahead, of those who emerged most successful from the years of turmoil at which we are looking. Second, equally remarkable, equally eloquent, the magnificent corslet (Fig. 10) of the third quarter of the fourth century taken as a prize of war against the peoples of the coast by a Samnite chieftain called Novius Fannius, as we know from the inscription he had engraved on his trophy – in Greek letters.[2] Such ornaments,

[1] Torelli 1975 (G 307); cf. Thuc. VII.53, 54, 57.11. 800 Campani in Sicily, Frederiksen 1984 (G 173) 143; Diod. XIII.44.2.
[2] Novius Fannius: *SEG* XXIX 1026; Colonna 1984 (G 142) (the object was first published in 1979).

we may guess, were not uncommon in the sanctuaries of the mountain zone, increasingly coming to resemble the shrines of the Hellenic peoples with whose goods they were now embellished. Finally we may compare with the Tarquinian document the famous painting from the tomb of the *gens Fabia* on the Esquiline Hill in Rome in which the heroic exploits of some of the Fabii in wars in the south in the early third century are depicted in ways which once again are wholly characteristic of the region in which, and to some extent against which, they were fighting: in the style of the painting, and in the details of the military equipment.[3]

In the west as in the Aegean world the third quarter of the fifth century saw a new interest in the recording and expounding of the past. Antiochus of Syracuse, whose treatise on the affairs of Italy selecting 'the most trustworthy and the clearest material' went down to 424 B.C., is the exemplar of this new concern.[4] There were indeed many lessons to learn, and many puzzling circumstances of life in the western Mediterranean, with its strange juxtaposition of peoples and traditions, which it will have seemed of the highest importance to understand and analyse. The question of the nature of the community and how it related to the practical or desirable forms of power was prominent. In many of the cities of South Italy the ideology of the ruling elite had long been shaped by a system of philosophical ideas linked with the name of Pythagoras, in which adherence to a set of distinctive intellectual, moral and spiritual principles appears to have marked out individuals worthy of political prominence and to have been used to promote their cohesion with each other to form an elite that transcended community boundaries. But violence had shown that the system was not unquestioned. We hear of an episode in which the meeting-places of the Pythagoreans were burned, killing the chief men of each city, with murder, revolution and general turmoil as the result, and cannot but liken it to the episodes of stasis which are so prominent a part of Thucydides' profile of the contemporary Greek world.[5] The question of the stability of the power of the elites remained a live one in the Italian cities throughout this period, gaining importance through the effect internal dissension had on decision-making in external politics, and through the direct influence the mutual

---

[3] Esquiline painting: Felletti Maj 1977 (G 163); Dondero, I. and Pensabene, P. (edd.), *Roma repubblicana fra il 509 a.C e il 270 a.c.* (Rome, 1982) 200f. *CAH* VII.2, 13, fig. 2.

[4] *FGrH* 555, cf. Pearson 1987 (G 92) 11–18.

[5] Polyb. 11.39.2 with Walbank 1975 (B 122) *ad loc.*; von Fritz 1942 (G 175); Minar 1942 (G 234); Guthrie 1962–81 (H 56) I 178–91. The event is hard to date but may most plausibly be assigned to the fifties or forties of the fifth century. For some sense of geographical unity among the city states of South Italy under the hegemony of Croton in the fifth century, expressed in Pythagorean thought and perhaps in the name Megale Hellas itself, Maddoli 1982 (G 221); Mele 1982 (G 231).

sympathy of aristocracies had in constructing relations between communities.

It was the question of the nature of such relations which was most pressing at the end of the fifth century. The success of the Deinomenid tyrants of Syracuse, though it had not proved very durable, was an interesting precedent, which was to be resumed in 405 by Dionysius I. More specifically, the constitutional and diplomatic initiatives which they had taken were temptingly well suited to other parts of the Hellenic west; the binding of daughter settlements to the polis, the redeployment of large populations and the use of a fluid citizenship policy, control of varied and flexible military resources, the building up of networks of client states through diplomacy which gave small communities a share in the life of the strong, and a general ability to manage the social complexities of the co-existence of native and Hellene: these were all things in which the Deinomenids had had a certain measure of success, and they were of the utmost relevance to other Greeks from the plains of Campania to the Strait of Otranto.[6] The importance of the resources of the whole region – surpluses of grain, timber for ship-building, and above all abundant manpower – was a further preoccupation. The management of these resources had already made some of these cities recognizable naval powers, a role which they would long retain.[7] Other Mediterranean states had begun to solve the problems of organization involved in the control of more than one or two cities and their territory more quickly than some of the Hellenes of the west, and that these were clearly interested in expanding their hegemony in the area made the issue more pressing. The days of complacent autonomy and purely local hostilities were over when the Athenian fleet sailed for Sicily in 415 B.C.; the Athenians – who had also intervened in the politics of the mainland – failed, but not so the Carthaginians in their war in western Sicily from 409 to 405.[8]

Carthage seems to have developed its hegemony out of the network of relations which tied a metropolis to daughter-settlements, and such a structure was not unfamiliar in the southern part of the Italian peninsula.[9] Croton had made use of a similar arrangement in her Pythagorean heyday of the first half of the fifth century, and Locri long exerted similar

[6] For the Deinomenids, see *CAH* IV² 757–80, V² 149–70.
[7] Resources of Magna Graecia: cereals, [Xen.] *Ath. Pol.* II.7; Pliny *HN* XVII.65, quoting Sophocles' *Triptolemus* (fr. 600 Radt); timber, Meiggs 1983 (I 101) 124–5; manpower, cf. below, p. 400.
[8] Athenian involvement with Artas and Iapygia, Thuc. VII.33; see Nenci 1979 (G 242) 43–4. Carthaginian war in Sicily, above, chs. 5, 9a.
[9] Structures of Carthaginian imperialism, Whittaker 1978 (G 91), tracing an economic development in some ways parallel to the experience of peninsular Italy as outlined in this chapter. See also *CAH* IV² 749–51; pp. 367–700 above.

control over her dependants.[10] Tarantine power in the fourth century, when the government of a Pythagorean ruler, Archytas, made it possible to revive in some sense the departed glory of Croton, owed something to this.

Institutional consolidation was not only an issue for the Greeks. The native peoples of the peninsula are found in the late fifth century already beginning to form federal arrangements. In Campania the Oscan peoples centred on Capua seem to have formed some precise new arrangement in 438–437, and all the Greek cities of the area except for Naples succumbed to the 'nation of the Campanians' (*Kampanon ethnos*) which resulted.[11] A similar system can be glimpsed to the south at Nuceria.[12] The Samnite League, although not specifically attested until the middle of the fourth century, may also be this early. Similarly the Lucanians, who are found causing trouble at Thurii as early as 433, may have had a corporate form by then.[13] The effectiveness of the Italici is not in doubt; by the year 390 the whole Tyrrhenian coast down to Rhegium was in their control except for Naples and Hipponium, and their influence even without conquest in those cities was great, as we shall see. What is more problematic is whether these basically federal forms can be regarded as a largely, or wholly, independent political evolution of Italic society, or whether the spirit and the forms owe something to contemporary Greek federalism.[14] This question cannot be regarded as closed.

Certainly we find the Greeks too moving in the direction of the federal solution to their problems. It should be stressed that this was neither easy nor natural. The cities were the foundations of very different and often mutually hostile communities in Greece; their geographical settings were very varied; politically, many of the cities found their principal preoccupations away from their Greek neighbours of the peninsula. Rhegium, on the Straits, and behaving frequently as if it were part of Sicily, is a case in point. A league around Croton, Sybaris and Caulonia was nevertheless formed in the years before 417 B.C. which intended to use the institutions of the Achaean League as a blueprint for creating a sense of common interest among the Italiotes.[15] The step is specifically attributed to the alarm that followed the Pythagorean crisis, but is likely

10 Crotonian hegemony: Giangiulio 1989 (G 179) 213–59.
11 Diod. XII.76.4 for the fall of Cumae (421/0), cf. Livy IV.44; Frederiksen 1984 (G 173) 139.
12 Frederiksen 1984 (G 173) 141–2.
13 The Samnite League is first attested in 351 B.C.; cf. Salmon 1967 (G 279) 95–9. 'Lucanians' as a collectivity already, however, the object of campaigns by the Spartan Cleandridas in the years after the foundation of Thurii; Polyaen. II.10.2, cf. II.10.4.
14 On Italic federalism, Salmon 1967 (G 279) 42. Note the foundation of the Bruttian state, 356 B.C. (n. 33).
15 Formation of the Italiote League, Polybius (n. 5); Giannelli 1928 (G 180) 63f; Larsen 1968 (C 37) 95–7; cf. Lombardo 1987 (G 219) 55–6 and for the problems involved in organizing common action, Sabbatini 1989 (G 278).

to have had external objectives as well. It may owe something to the diplomatic initiatives with which the Athenians attempted to make their relations with the west easier (certainly the Italiote League supported the Athenians in 415–413), but most importantly provided a bulwark against the native peoples – and against other aggressors. Certainly the effective history of the Italiote League dates from 393 when it was afforced by the inclusion of Thurii, Hipponium, Rhegium and Elea and perhaps even Naples.[16] The motive force for this step came indeed from the Italic threat, but as wielded by the then tyrant of Syracuse.

Dionysius I had wide ambitions in the southern Tyrrhenian, where the Greek cities were weak through long exposure to both seaborne hostility and to the attention of the Lucanians and Bruttians in the hinterland.[17] The improved Italiote League notwithstanding, in a series of campaigns and wars Dionysius created a Syracusan province in the Bruttian peninsula. His old ally Locri formed the core, and the other cities were disposed of in more or less generous settlements: after his victory at the Helleporus in 389 Dionysius was inclined to be lenient to the combatants, but the subsequent fate of Caulonia was more serious – her territory was assigned to Locri but, significantly, her population was removed wholesale to Syracuse.[18] Thurii was sacrificed to the Lucanians; Hipponium had a similar fate to Caulonia; Rhegium was reduced by siege in 387. Finally, after the war of 379–378 Croton too was humbled.[19] In all this the Italic peoples, especially the Lucanians, played a major role. Manpower resources, whether Greek, as in the deportation policy, or Italic, as with the soldiers who alongside Syracusans helped Sparta in 387, were the principal concern.[20] Meanwhile to the east Taras, which had also helped Syracuse during the Athenian crisis, was consolidating its power to the south over the Messapians and to the west, through her satellite Heraclea (founded 437), had more or less neutralized Metapontum.[21] The Gulf was Tarantine in more than name. The mutually

[16] Diod. XIV.91.1, cf. 101 for provisions of mutual aid against the Lucanians. On Dionysius, Caven 1990 (G 134); ch. 5 above; also Sanders 1987 (G 283); Sabbatini 1988 (G 277), both good on the historiographical tradition and with earlier bibliography.

[17] Expedition against Lipareae (389), Diod. XIV.103; against Etruscan Pyrgi (384), Diod. XV.14.3. Carthaginian involvement: Diod. XV.15.2; 24.1 (the restoration of the Hipponiates).

[18] Battles of Laus, Diod. XIV.101–2.3; of the Helleporus, Diod. XIV.104. Caulonia, Diod. XIV.106. 3; cf. Paus. VI.3.11. Also above, p. 146.

[19] Thurii, Diod. XIV.101–2; Hipponium, Diod. XIV.107; role of the Lucanians in the battle of Laian Draco, Strabo VI.1.1, cf. Diod. XIV.102. Fall of Rhegium and humiliation of its general Phyton, Diod. XIV.112. Croton, Ath. XII.541.6; [Arist.] Mir. Ausc. 196 (the cloak of Alcisthenes). For the problem of comparison with Dion. Hal. XX.7, Lombardo 1987 (G 219) 61. See now Sabbatini 1988 (G 277) for the almost continuous hostilities of this period; above, pp. 149–50.

[20] Help to Sparta: Xen. Hell. V.1.26 (ships).

[21] Taras, Heraclea and Metapontum, Brauer 1986 (G 125). Thurii–Taras treaty, Strabo VI.1.14 p. 264, VI 3. 4 pp. 280–1 refers to events during the expedition of Alexander the Molossian, Lamboley 1983 (G 208). Athenians attempt to stir up Iapygians and Messapians against Taras, Thuc. VII.33.4, with Frederiksen 1977 (G 109) 204; see also Santoro 1972 (G 286).

beneficial connexion with Syracuse made Tarantine power virtually unassailable, and it is not surprising to find that in due course this position is expressed through a hegemony of the old Italiote League. A federal coinage begins in 380, and it is tempting to see the subjugation of the League to Taras as the culminating stroke of policy of Dionysius after his long series of victories. The symbolic movement of the League's sanctuary from Croton to Tarantine Heraclea seems however to have taken place in 374.[22] The security and tranquillity of Taras in the ascendancy of Archytas, who came to power in 366, cannot be ascribed solely to Pythagorean benevolence. Taras' power remained secure even after Dionysius' death.

In terms of political history, then, from the end of the first quarter of the fourth century, the *apoikia* cities of Magna Graecia had dwindled or been eclipsed or destroyed in one way or another so as to render them second-rate powers. This is not to say that they were grass-grown ruins – Locri and Metapontum still flourished and retained not only civic continuity but even some prosperity throughout the period.[23] But two cities achieved a standing which was comparable with the greatest independent political entities of the fourth-century Mediterranean, and between them started to shape the history of south Italy: Neapolis and Taras. The importance of Neapolis is only beginning to emerge, although it has long been obscured by the brilliance of the encompassing Oscan aristocracies of Campania, with which it was in close touch, and by the vast Roman endeavours in Campania after the defeat of Hannibal and the foundation of Puteoli. Reconsideration of the texts and a better understanding of the archaeology is leading to a new emphasis on the cultural, economic and political effects of the prominence of the city in the fourth, third and second centuries.[24] One may almost guess that it was *because* there was so little antagonism between Neapolitans and Italics (and indeed Neapolis clearly became Oscanized to a considerable extent) that the stature of Neapolis has been taken less seriously than that of Taras: but if we can see the influence of the latter city so clearly in the

[22] Tarantine domination of the League, Brauer 1986 (G 125) 55 and 58–9 with nn. 29–30; Wuilleumier 1939 (G 326) 64–6. On the weakness of the tradition for Dionysius' Adriatic ambitions, Woodhead 1970 (G 325); cf. however Mambella 1986 (G 222) for cultural reflections of the influence of Sicily there. Strabo VI.4.2 p. 241, if right in claiming that Ancona was founded by refugees from Dionysius, may give a glimpse of the real complexities. See also pp. 147–50.

[23] Continuity at Locri, Musti 1977 (G 236), cf. Costabile 1980 (G 146), and De Franciscis 1972 (G 150) for the incontrovertible evidence of the Locrian tablets. Prosperity of Metapontum, Carter 1988 (G 129), estimating the surplus wheat production of its *chora* at the end of the fourth century as 235,000 medimni p.a. available for external sale, with a value of 98 talents. Decline of Croton: Mele 1984 (G 232) 79–87.

[24] Lepore 1952 (G 212) is still fundamental on the economy of hellenistic Naples. For the archaeology of the city Greco 1988 (G 188); for its influence on Rome, Baldassare 1988 (G 114); for the history of Roman intervention, Càsola 1988 (G 130), Colonna 1984 (G 142), Frederiksen 1984 (G 173), 208–12.

material evidence for the culture of its foes, we can agree wholeheartedly with the view that it is likely that 'Neapolis is a no less effective centre for the diffusion of Greekness than Taras'. However, we shall, as is appropriate, consider it in more detail alongside its contacts, turning now to the more southern metropolis.[25]

In the case of Taras there is no alternative centre to distract the attention of the historian; after the Roman settlement of 281–280 the history of the cities of the deep south is nearly a vacuum, and there is no need to refuse to fill it with some sort of a role for Taras. Archaeology is now showing increasingly, against the earlier consensus, that political eclipse by no means ended the city's influence, but that when reconsidered, the evidence of material culture across the whole spectrum from gold and silver of the utmost luxury to ceramics,[26] reveals an extended prosperity that reaches the late Republic if not the early Empire. To understand why this is such a surprise we need to consider the political history of Taras in the fourth century.

This subject has a perceptible shape in the ancient literary tradition, and it is this shape that has survived with too little scrutiny in the modern analyses. Basically, the problem is, as so often in the historiography of politics, the pattern of a hero followed by unworthy successors. The clearest statement of the whole picture is that of Strabo, which has been highly influential.[27] Enough survives of the tradition about Archytas son of Mnesagoras for it to be clear that the ancient view was hagiographical: he represented a philosopher king in a Spartan city who could be seen against the background of either the Laconian tradition or the aristocratic intellectual ideology of the Pythagoreans.[28] He could provide a foil to the vicissitudes of the pursuit of political wisdom at Dorian Syracuse, coming to the rescue of Plato in 362–360.[29] His position was all the more poignant because of the perennial tendency to *truphe* (luxurious excess in defiance of morality) in the rich lands of South Italy, which is latent in the historiography of the region, ready to be evoked in set pieces on Sybaris or Syracuse, Taras (*molle Tarentum*) or Capua.[30] The whole could readily

[25] On the Oscanization of Naples, Frederiksen 1984 (G 173) 209, 217; our quotation is from Prosdocimi 1976 (G 261) 234. For Naples as the heart of the late fourth-century cultural *koine*, Pontrandolfo (G 112) 269–71, cf. Baldassare (G 112) 222, Morel (G 112) 309–10 and 359.

[26] Continuity already adumbrated, Moretti 1971 (G 235); see now *Gli ori di Taranto* 1984 (G 185). The older view: *Atti 10 Conv.* (G 106) 280.   [27] Strabo VI.3.4 p. 280.

[28] For Archytas, Ciaceri 1927–32 (G 138) II 438–49; Lombardo 1987 (G 219) 68–75 (note 70 'Archita, autentica figura di reggitore-filosofo coerente e capace'). The biographical tradition went back to Aristoxenus; Aristotle also wrote on Archytas, but probably more on his thought than his life (D.L. v.25). For a summary of his achievements, D.L. VIII.79–82.

[29] Archytas and Plato: Plut. *Dion* 20, cf. D.L. III.22; [Plato] *Ep.* VII 338–50; cf. pp. 154–5.

[30] *Truphe* in the Taras of Archytas: Polyarchus 'Hedypathes' ('voluptuary'), in Aristoxenus, *Life* fr. 50 Wehrli; Gigante 1971 (G 181) on Aristoxenus, Archytas, the *vetus oratio* and *truphe*. In general see also Mele 1984 (G 232) on these themes in Crotoniate history, and on Archytas specifically, Mele 1981 (G 229). The tradition goes back to Antiochus: Nenci 1979 (G 242) 33–41.

be set against the perennial theme of Rome's eventual victory: what had enfeebled the Hellenes? And this question in turn was rendered poignant by the revival of another old theme, the contrast of the fortunes of East and West, going back to Herodotus on the coincidence in the timing and fortunes of the battles of Salamis and Himera, and in this case contrasting the ineffectual leaders who eventually lost to Rome with the glory of Alexander the Great and his successors. Given these interpretations we should be very cautious about accepting uncritically the pattern of Tarantine glory in the age of Archytas, followed by an age of decadence and decline when the city was reduced to seeking the disastrous help of outsiders, the five *condottieri* whose names dominate the narrative: Archidamus of Sparta, Alexander of Epirus, Cleonymus of Sparta, Agathocles of Syracuse and Pyrrhus of Epirus.[31]

In fact the ancient pattern has little to recommend it: though we should stress as usual that the authors who formulated it had more evidence at their disposal by far than they have been able to transmit to us. Archytas is attributed seven successive generalships and wars against the Messapians, but these are hard to date (the usual view, for want of another synchronism, is that they coincided with Plato's visits to the west in 366/5 and 361/0), and impossible to fit in to any sort of a framework of political and social history. Was he having a beneficial effect on Taras even before his supremacy of office? Did his influence survive his defeat? Was the felicity of Taras real? Did it derive from the successful *Realpolitik* which we have examined, linking Taras with the tyranny at Syracuse, a relationship which the Plato story shows that Archytas could still capitalize on, though it cannot have been of his creating? In what aspects of Tarantine society was the practical efficiency of Archytian Pythagoreanism found, and how transient was the phenomenon? In the absence of answers to these questions the contribution of Archytas to the prosperity of Taras over half a century should not be casually exaggerated.

Nor do we understand the chronology of the events of the second half of the century. The Roman annalistic system of the period is hotly debated, and its complexities have perplexed Diodorus Siculus, our only continuous source for the affairs of Sicily and Magna Graecia.[32] The crisis of the middle years of the century seems to have been provoked as much by events in Syracuse as by any Italian circumstances, though the organization and ambitions of the Italic peoples were continually

---

[31] Clearest presentation of the *condottieri* as a sequence: Strabo VI.3.4 p. 280. Flaws of Taras, especially commercial prosperity and theatrical life, played up in the *mise-en-scène* of the outbreak of war with Rome at Florus I.18. For the coinage of the period, Brauer 1986 (G 125) ch. 5. Cf. De Sensi Sestito 1987 (G 154).

[32] See Sordi 1969 (G 293); Frederiksen 1984 (G 173), chs. 8 and 9; Pearson 1984 and 1987 (B 91–2).

increasing – the formation of the Bruttian League is only the most visible step.[33] In 352 a revolution removed Rhegium from Syracusan control; in 345 Locri similarly abandoned Dionysius II, murdering his family.[34] The fall of the tyranny was followed by the appeal of Syracuse to Timoleon, whose arrival was just in time to save Locri from the Bruttians, who had already seized Hipponium. Taras was by then at war with the Lucanians.[35] This was the context in which the Tarantines appealed to their mother-city, and induced King Archidamus of Sparta to come to their aid; but it is not clear precisely when the appeal was made.[36] It was noted that the death of Archidamus in battle at the siege of Manduria occurred at the same instant as the great battle of Chaeronea – a sign of how eagerly parallels between East and West were observed.[37] What we do not know is whether until the unfortunate siege of Manduria he had been successful at promoting the diplomatic and military cause of the Tarantines. There is no reason to assume the worst; that it was as soon as the fourth year after that the next outsider came to lead the Tarantines suggests that the services of such leaders were considered fruitful and reappointment an urgent matter – but also that the job was not without its appeal.

The activities and chronology of the expedition of Alexander of Epirus are not clear either, 334–331 being the preferred estimate for the latter. He too died in battle, at Pandosia (identified with S. Maria d'Anglona), but had certainly by that time had a profound diplomatic impact. His contribution can have been disappointing only by the standards of his namesake. We can glimpse the extreme delicacy of his relations with Rome and the Italic peoples of the Campanian area, and observe the significance of the fact that he was operating at least briefly in the ambit of Paestum.[38] His successes were not acceptable to the Tarantines, who abandoned him. The treachery is not admirable, but it

[33] Formation of the Bruttian League, a slanted and chronologically loose account in Diod. XVI.15.1–2 under 356/5 B.C.; cf. Justin XXIII.1.3–14; Strabo VI.1.4 p. 255. See Lombardo 1987 (G 219) 73–4 and, for background on the Bretti and bibliography, Guzzo and Luppino 1980 (G 193) 865–6.
[34] Rhegium, Diod. XVI.45.9; Locri, Diod. XVI.66.6. For the close ties of Locri with Syracuse, above, pp. 144–7.   [35] Plut. Tim. 16.2; 19.2; for Taras and the Lucanians, Diod. XVI.61.4.
[36] For Archidamus Ciaceri 1927–32 (G 138) III 6–7; Diod. XVI.61–3–63.5. Diodorus is recording the fate of the sacrilegious Phalaecus (cf. p. 758), and his remarks on Archidamus need not be in their right chronological context. The appeal by Taras need not then be as early as 346/5 and his arrival can be put nearer his death at Manduria in 338. It is worth recalling that the outbreak of war between Rome and the Samnites in 343 will have made the atmosphere in the south more critical (for that war CAH VII².2, 351–9). The later date for the appeal to Archidamus means disjoining that Lucanian War from the Bruttian War of Timoleon's reinforcements.   [37] Diod. XVI.88.3.
[38] For Alexander Livy VIII.3.6–7; Justin XII.2.12; Strabo VI.1.5 p. 256; see Manni 1962 (G 223) for the date, and Ciaceri 1927–32 (G 138) III 7–16, seeing in Alexander the missed opportunity for strong unification of South Italy. D'Agostino 1974 (G 147) saw the main effect of Alexander's visit as being the realization by the peoples of Apulia that their real enemy was the Italic peoples, not the Italiotes. See also n. 21 above. For general contact between Taras and Epirus in the fourth century, CAH VII².2, 458.

seems unreasonable to blame Taras at the same time, as some are inclined to, for being craven enough to need outside help and sufficiently brazen to jettison it!

In the supposed series of props for declining Taras there is now a gap of some twenty-seven years. We may guess that both the city and potential helpers found discouraging food for thought in the double saga of Archidamus and Alexander. Sparta produced plenty of candidates, however, one of whom, Acrotatus, was briefly seen at Taras by accident in 314.[39] By 303 Taras was ready to welcome a new royal general from Sparta on its own behalf, Cleonymus, who raised an army of nearly 30,000 from mercenaries of various origins as well as from Taras itself.[40] But the sequel showed how different the world was from the experience of a generation before. The interval had seen – and perhaps been maintained by – the long struggle between Rome and the Samnites, and its ramifications in the Tyrrhenian and Adriatic areas. Rome was now on the hit list supplied to Cleonymus.[41] The other hellenic cities had now begun to wane visibly, whereas the native cities were, as we shall see in more detail shortly, increasingly homogeneous and hellenized. International politics, in the first age of the Diadochi, was a different business too, and as the concerns of Cleonymus in Corcyra showed, for example, South Italy could now be considered only part of a much greater game. Horizons were suddenly very much wider.

Cleonymus did not achieve anything very remarkable, despite a Draconian style in keeping with the swagger of the new age – he took female hostages, for example, an unprecedented and suspicious act.[42] He too was abandoned by Taras, but did not pay the price of his life. Once again the next Tarantine supporter is a quick successor, behaving in a similar way, though again in the style of the age after Alexander the Great rather than of that of Archidamus and Alexander of Epirus. The contacts of the Cleonymus episode brought in Agathocles, the new and formidable tyrant of Syracuse, following in the footsteps of the two Dionysii in supporting Taras, as in maintaining a lively Italian mercen-

---

[39] Diod. xix.70.2, with 70.7–8. Note that Agathocles' first military service was on behalf of Croton and later against it: *CAH* vii².1, 385–7.

[40] Diod. xx.104, cf. Livy x.2. On Cleonymus Ciaceri 1927–32 (G 138) iii 25–30; cf. Vattuone 1989 (G 318) 61–5; also Braccesi 1991 (G 124) for the Adriatic. A glimpse of the impact of the *condottieri* on their supporters may be had in the financial records of Locri, if De Franciscis 1972 (G 150) 75–9 is right in seeing the *basileus* to whom the Locrians contributed more than a third of their annual income as Pyrrhus in the years 280–274.

[41] In assessing this claim Roman exaggeration – and the search for a precursor for Pyrrhus – should be borne in mind. But Duris was aware of the Battle of Sentinum in 295, a sure sign of how high the stakes now were: the conflict has recently been called 'the greatest military engagement that had ever taken place in Italy' (*CAH* vii².2, 379).

[42] Ath. xiii 605e, from Book iii of Duris' Life of Agathocles (*FGrH* 76 F 18). The city in question was Metapontum.

ary policy.[43] We catch only fragments of all this; alliance with Iapyges and Peucetians, attacks on the Bruttians of Hipponium; Agathocles was a man of the widest plans.[44] Taras can scarcely be credited with the initiative in this association, but it is somewhat unreasonable for critics of the Tarantines to regard as a sign of decay an association, with a powerful Syracuse, which had also characterized an age which they regard as preceding the decadence. In many ways the scene is now being set for the first act of the new drama of Pyrrhus: the colourful populist stylishness of Agathocles, so well suited to the cities that shocked and insulted Roman ambassadors for fun; and the spreading networks of ties which precisely did include the Epirote monarchy, through the marriage to Pyrrhus of Agathocles' daughter Lanassa.[45] The Cleonymus–Agathocles–Pyrrhus story is not a tale of three more lone *condottieri*, but part of a single complex phenomenon, the near-birth of a Successor state in the west. But neither in Taras nor in Hieron's Syracuse did that ever quite come about.

The glory of the age of Archytas, then, and the mounting mollitude which succeeded it, driving the Tarantines to hire swords while they kept holiday, may be regarded as a historiographic construction of some interest but little real interpretative value. It is a *mythos*, an explanatory narrative, that is informed by another powerful antithesis, that between the pure Hellenism of Laconian Taras and the native hordes growling at the borders.[46] This is a tradition which has for many reasons long been in vogue, and the corrective now being provided by archaeology has been tardy because of the enormous prevalence in our knowledge of the antiquities of South Italy of the cemetery – and worse, of the looted contents of tombs sold to collectors: the Hellenic long dominated this type of evidence too. But it has become clear over the last three decades that there is a real possibility of tracing the realities of cultural change in the south Italian peninsula through the archaeological remains – and that to adhere to the old schematisms is not just to distort the truth, but also

---

[43] Agathocles and Italy: Ciaceri 1927–32 (G 138) III 28–33; Lombardo 1987 (G 219) 84; Vattuone 1989 (G 318). For Agathocles as heir of the Dionysii, cf. Justin XXIII.1. Even in 330 Syracuse was still continuing the policy of opposing the Italic peoples, helping Croton against the Bruttii: Diod. XIX.3.3.

[44] Diod. XXI.3.4, XXI.3.8 (perhaps of 295 and 294 B.C.). See *CAH* VII².1, 406–7; Vattuone 1989 (G 318) 71.

[45] Agathocles' buffoonish and theatrical behaviour (Diod. XX.26.2) must owe something to Duris' presentation. Compare the famous scene of the Romans at Taras, Dion. Hal. *Ant. Rom.* XIX.5.1–5, cf. Val. Max. 2.2.5. Lanassa: Diod. XXI.3.4. For Pyrrhus see now the account in *CAH* VII².2, 456–85.

[46] For these views Brauer 1986 (G 125) 53, cf. 61 (whence these phrases); note that some directions in the study of Greek art have helped the tendency to oversimplify, e.g. Carter 1975 (G 128) 7. Against the simple oppositions, Pugliese Carratelli 1972 (G 263) 38, stressing both the divisions of the Italic peoples and the ethnic complexity of the Greek cities. Note Florus 1.18 of Taras 'Civitas semigraeca', and cf. n. 53.

to miss the opportunity to examine one of the most fascinatingly complicated patterns of cultural interchange which we can perceive from antiquity.[47]

It must be conceded that the ancient sources help the simple view to survive, representing, as they do, gallant outposts of Hellenism fighting off aliens. The quotation from the contemporary Tarantine Aristoxenus observing the fate of Posidonia is well known:

> we do as do the Posidoniates who dwell in the Tyrrhenian Gulf. It has been their lot, who in the beginning were Greeks, to become completely barbarized, turning into Etruscans or Romans, and to change their language and other customs so that today they celebrate only one Greek festival. Coming together for this, they recall the ancient names and practices, lament one with another and go on their way after shedding many tears. In this way, then, says Aristoxenus, when the theatres are barbarized and the music which has spread so far has fallen into deep corruption, those few of us who survive also recall among ourselves what real music was.[48]

We have a triple picture of this phenomenon. First, texts such as the above, which form a strand in the complex historiography of social and political values that was outlined briefly above (p. 389). Second, archaeology, to which we shall return; but conscious as ever of the limitations of the deduction of ethnicity from material culture. Third is the study of language, thanks to the epigraphic habit a relatively useful tool in this operation, but one which also needs methodological care.

Through patient study of inscriptions specialists have been able to identify linguistic traditions which can be associated with various types of Oscan, and with Messapian, Peucetian and Daunian, and to trace something of the history of the interaction of these with each other and with Greek.[49] This gives us altogether a quite subtle view of one aspect of the tension between regional survival of cultural identity and incorporation in a world of wider allegiances. Two caveats are worth advancing, however. The first is that the medium of the language fragments which have come to us is always more than one step towards acculturation; even if the language is non-Greek, both the letter-forms and the very idea of the inscription are potently Hellenic.[50] The second is

[47] It is perhaps preferable, as well as in keeping with the more sophisticated notions of ethnicity now usually applied to the social history of the western Mediterranean in the first millennium B.C., to refrain from the term 'native peoples'. Cf. Adamesteanu 1974 (G 93) 187–215. For an overview of the ethnic situation Salmon 1982 (G 280) 10–21.

[48] Aristoxenus fr. 124 Wehrli, linked by Fraschetti 1981 (G 170) with the mood in Taras and south Italy in the 320s. For the nature of the hellenizing process in the case of the aristocracy of Oscan Paestum, Greco Pontrandolfo 1979 (G 257) 47, cf. 50.

[49] For recent work on the languages see *CAH* IV² ch. 15; Santoro 1978 (G 287) (Peucetian and Messapian); Pisani 1972 (G 253) (Oscan and Messapian); Prosdocimi 1976 (G 260) on the coexistence of language seen from the Roman context; Landi 1979 (G 209) 115f on the 'mondo indigeno'.

[50] Thus Adamesteanu 1974 (G 93) 209 on the Armento wreath (below, n. 54) 'in poche parole tanti errori di lingua greca': but it is in Greek, and that fact is far more important than the lapses.

that we must not unthinkingly give linguistic identity the same status among the indicators of ethnic belonging which it has in familiar modern societies. The attitude of its last speakers towards Messapian is unlikely to have resembled the defence of Scots Gaelic.[51] One case of the misuse of the linguistic argument has been analysed recently: the false antithesis between a Messapian culture surviving and maintaining stalwartly its linguistic independence, and one permeated by and heavily influenced by Greek to the extent of preserving Greek language through the Roman period and into more recent times. The point of the antithesis has been to explain the 'grico' of the Sallentino, a Hellenic dialect which has a quite different social history.[52]

However, language helps us to perceive the tension between the tendency to form common cultural traits and the underlying dividedness of the Italic peoples; and, moreover, that it is a tension evolved in a stable system and is the product of phenomena like the widespread use of mercenaries — as with the Oscan-speakers in Sicily — rather than emigration or invasion. It is now thought that there was no Oscan 'barbarian invasion', and that the fourth century is simply the last phase in a long, though not peaceful, coexistence between Hellenic and indigenous peoples (cf. *CAH* iv²). It is necessary to insist on this point, since the differences between the non-Greek populations, from the Samnites of north Campania to the Messapians of Calabria with their geographical and cultural links with Illyria, are of very great historical importance.[53] Unity eluded the Italici, paradoxically, until they adopted a sufficiently adaptable Hellenization to form social and political institutions which could transcend local differences. The race was on to see which Italic people could adopt its Hellenizing *mores* most effectively first. As we know, this race was won by Rome. It was however not an easy victory, and there were many other contenders. This means that the task of tracing the interpenetration of Hellenic elements across the southern part of the peninsula is complex to the point of despair, as we have already seen in the example of language. The same thing can be said of elaborate artefacts[54] — are they Greek or local in style? — and of the archaeology of whole communities. So the formation of nucleated settlements like Roccagloriosa in western Lucania, in their early stages, seems to respond to purely local and short-term needs; until the arrival of

[51] For 'Oscan' and 'Messapian' as different kinds of label from 'Latin' or 'Italian', Pisani 1972 (G 253). [52] Parlangeli 1970 (G 250), cf. Nenci 1979 (G 242).

[53] Illyrian connexions of the Messapians, Parlangeli and Santoro 1978 (G 250A). On differentiation between peoples, Pontrandolfo Greco 1982 (G 258) 160. Note as an additional complexity the survival until the third century of Etruscans in Campania (D'Agostino 1974 (G 147) 212); this is now known to be true further south at Pontecagnano too.

[54] Note for example the debate on the Armento wreath: is its workmanship in the Macedonian/Hellenic tradition mediated through Taras (Pontrandolfo Greco 1982 (G 258) 145) or in an Italic artisan tradition just interpreting a Greek idea (Lipinsky 1975 (G 216))?

a major fortified enceinte, which seems to hint that the whole process of nucleation might be better seen against a background of awareness of an urban ideal and the political institutions associated with it.[55] In fact a historical process *can* be seen at work which enables us to make sense of the whole of South Italy in the late fourth and early third centuries, and to get beyond the simple evolutionist perspective of analysing hundreds of local experiences in geographical order.

The principal phenomenon of the social history of South Italy in this period is cultural change, the acculturation, to put it broadly and too simply, of the indigenous peoples by the Greeks; a process which seems to reflect topography in its irradiation of the mountainous interior from the coasts by way of the greater river valleys. It is worth stating again that this is to be regarded as the principal phenomenon because it is to us the one which is visible; and to remark that it is visible to us, as not all forms of cultural change of this kind might be, because the Hellenic goal was one which, to our good fortune, was expressed in terms of material culture which has, to some extent proved durable – buildings, especially fortification and tombs, ceramics, especially in grave-deposits, and the inscriptions which convey the linguistic data to which we have already alluded. It would be easy to think of profound cultural influences which could escape the archaeological search entirely. We must also be wary, as so often in the study of acculturation, of seeing all the processes as transmission and none of them as inventive or creative.

It is not unnatural to begin by asking who was acculturated. The traces of the process are closely linked with the activities of a social elite, and one of a certain type. There is always the possibility that there was an equivalent process outside the elite by which, say, small agriculturalists of Greek territories came to influence religious or economic practices of their non-Greek neighbours through direct interchange; but such tendencies can only be guessed, since the evidence happens to be remarkably specific towards an elite: a competitive, hierarchical, image-conscious, aggressive, militaristic elite at that.[56] Since, moreover, the

---

[55] Fracchia 1983 (G 168) models Roccagloriosa as an *oppidum* of North West Europe. It is a site of the first importance, as the central place for the exploitation of the Mingardo valley; excavations are illuminating the process by which it inherited the functions and identity of the Greek *apoikia* Pyxus and passed them on to the Roman *colonia* at Buxentum (cf. Ridgway 1989 (G 275) 139): something similar may have happened in the case of Hipponium-Veipo-Vibo further south (cf. n. 69). Interesting contrast between Roccagloriosa and Moio della Civitella in the territory of Velia, assessed as more Hellenic and taken as a subsidiary of Velia because of the regularity of its plan and degree of urbanization, Greco and Schnapp 1983 (G 189); cf. Tréziny 1983 (G 310), on the problems of distinguishing it from other types of settlement. Fortifications of the late fourth century also at Laus (S. Maria del Cedro, on the hill of S. Bartolo di Marcellina).

[56] As Guzzo 1984 (G 191) puts it in the case of the territory of Sybaris 'si hanno due sibaritide . . . quella italiota, constituta della razionale città di Thurii sulla costa, e quella italica, che occupa l'interno con le sue piazzeforti e i suoi nuclei sparsi. Il collegamento e lo scambio fra le due sono costanti e continue.' On the funerary evidence see the formulation of Pontrandolfo Greco and Rouveret 1982 (G 259).

signs of acculturation are co-extensive with a social milieu we should hesitate to interpret them ethnically. When we are tempted to see a 'Samnite' cultural preserve infiltrating, as it might be, a Daunian context, we should be careful that this is not just a case of social change affecting a local elite and encouraging them to adopt the forms of behaviour of the warrior aristocracies which were most *à la mode*.[57]

To begin with the military side. The fortification of settlements in the interior proceeds rapidly towards the end of the fourth century. On the fine ashlar masonry of one case an inscription attributes the work to the *'arche* (rule, command) of Nummelos': here at Serra di Vaglio a leader is attested whose name is Italic but whose building and authority are Greek, as are the language and style of the commemoration of both.[58] The Oscan inscription at Muro Lucano attributing the fortification work to an Italic institution, the *meddikia*, is only somewhat more removed from the Hellenic sphere.[59] In some places the contemporary fortification of a cluster of strongpoints in a locality is attested, and can be linked to particular forms of regional cohesion and organization.[60] The choice of sites reflects the pattern of through high- or low-level routeways (see Map 11) which shapes the mountainous interior of the southern part of the Italian peninsula, a pattern which has been essential for the historical development of the region at all periods.[61]

So there is a new and impressive emphasis on the formation and fortification of nucleated settlements, which can in some cases amount to the spread of what it may not be too rash to call urbanism or its beginnings.[62] Even where the architecture is not devoted to overtly

[57] Thus Torelli, sensitively, on the Melfese in *Sannio* 1984 (G 285) 31: contrast the view which makes of the Period III of the Daunian culture the age – visible at Canusium from *c.* 400 onwards – of the extirpation of a distinctively Daunian culture by Samnite pressures.

[58] Nummelos at Serra di Vaglio, Adamesteanu 1990 (G 97) and 1987 (G 96): *epi tes Nummelou arches*.

[59] Note that although the title is Oscan, in terms of constitutional theory the magistracy is Greek, as is the epigraphic habit itself. The sudden boom in Oscan epigraphy (other early inscriptions, e.g. from S. Giovanni in Fonte and Atena Lucana) is a phenomenon of considerable historical importance in its own right.

[60] Fortifications at Serra, Città di Tricarico, Torretta di Pietragalla, Serra del Carpine di Cancellara, Croccia Cagnato (all possibly associated with Nummelos), Adamesteanu 1974 (G 93) 196–7. Note that earlier scholarship labelled these 'Greek': a full account in Tréziny 1983 (G 310), agreeing with Adamesteanu. The social group involved here in the Melfese may be the Utiani (Adamesteanu 1974 (G 93) 204) whose federal centre lay at the Rossano del Vaglio sanctuary. Similar fortifications among the Brettii, Guzzo and Luppino 1980 (G 193) 865–6; urbanization in Daunia, Mazzei 1984 and 1987 (G 226–7).

[61] Adamesteanu 1983 (G 95), cf. 1974 (G 93). Note especially the routes followed by the later Roman roads Via Appia and Via Annia, the Catanzaro Isthmus and the long routeway identified by Quilici *et al.* 1969 (G 270) 64–7.

[62] Changes at Ruvo and Oppido Lucano, Ridgway 1982 (G 274) 73. The late fourth-century form of Laus, regular in plan and monumental, totally eclipsed its Greek predecessor (cf. n. 55 above). Similar changes in a Hellenic context at Velia; compare the *teichopoiia* of the Locri tablets (with Musti 1977 (G 236)).

military purposes it is still connected to the maintenance of the ideology
of a warrior aristocracy, most explicitly in the great extra-urban
sanctuaries. The best known of these in the south is the *temenos* of Mefitis
at Rossano di Vaglio, but the sanctuary of Hercules at Armento in the
Agri valley is another case, and it is clear that we have here further
instances of the well-known sanctuaries of the Samnites further north at
Campochiaro or Pietrabbondante.[63] Here the trophies, of the same kind
as the breastplate of Novius Fannius (above, Fig. 10) were dedicated,
potent testimony to the source of the wealth and authority and ambition
which built these complexes. At Pietrabbondante – now clearly seen to
be a federal centre of particular importance – the sanctuary was hung
with the spoils of Taras, from the wars of the fifth century and from the
defence against the champions of the series which culminated in
Pyrrhus.[64] Similarly, the funerary ideology which can be traced in the
design of tombs and in their decoration and furnishing reinforced the
military ethos as did the practice of the cults of the new sanctuaries. Once
again, the scenes of the glorification of the individual warrior, especially
the cavalryman, and the tendency to display wealth and power through
the elaboration of the outward form also of the tomb, are found in both
the Hellenic world, imitating the rulers of Macedon and their success,
and in the territories of the indigenous peoples. Close parallels can be
drawn between the well-known Oscan cemeteries of Paestum and the
experience of Neapolis and Taras.[65] Indeed when archaeological accident deprives us of such a source, our information suffers: the abandonment of the Fornaci cemetery at Capua deprives us of much crucial
information about the early Samnite aristocracies of Campania.[66]

   This is the archaeological counterpart of the continual presence of the
mercenary theme in the literary sources, as we have already seen it
emerging: the contingents involved in the Athenian and Carthaginian
Wars in Sicily in the late fifth century, the dispositions made by the
Dionysii, the Campanian cavalry and its relationship to Rome, the forces
used by the *condottieri*, the Mamertini and the Campanian garrison of

[63] For the inscriptions of Rossano Lejeune, *Rend. Linc.* 26 (1971) 664; 27 (1972) 399; 30 (1975)
319. *Id. ap. Atti 11 Conv.* (G 107) 83 claimed, too strongly, that the sanctuary was 'immune to Greek
religious forces'. For the Serra Lustrante shrine at Armento (late fourth-century) see Pontrandolfo
Greco 1982 (G 258) 158. On the Samnite sanctuaries see now *Sannio* 1980 (G 284), esp. B.
D'Agostino, pp. 140f on the Tarantine spoils. Etruscan origin (? via Campania) for the Heracles cult,
Atti 11 Conv. (G 107) 68–9.
[64] For the particular importance of Pietrabbondante, Lejeune in *Sannio* 1984 (G 285).
[65] For this process at Paestum, Pontrandolfo Greco 1979 (G 257), Pontrandolfo Greco and
Rouveret 1982 (G 259), esp. 127–9; at Capua, Johannowsky 1972 (G 204), drawing attention to the
parallels at Taras and Neapolis. Also Pontrandolfo in *Atti 25 Conv.* 268–9. For domestic
architecture, in the case of hellenistic Locri, see Barra Bagnasco, *Studi A. Adriani* 1985. For the
military subjects of wall- and vase-paintings, Trendall 1989 (J 51).
[66] Johannowsky in *Sannio* 1984 (G 285) 52f.

Rhegium.[67] An inscription shows us a *vereia Campsanas Metapontinas*, a mercenary force of this kind, in the ailing community of Metapontum at the end of the fourth century, and perhaps the Oscans at Neapolis were not so very different in 327/6, when we hear of a Neapolitan leader with the probably Oscan name of Nymphius (cf. Nypsius the Neapolitan general of Dionysius II: Diod xvi.18.1).[68] Nor was this practice wholly land-based. Maritime power seems to have been accumulated in similar ways, and the contribution of 'pirates' of the Messapians to Agathocles was close to the more acceptable use of contingents of city naval forces (like that sent by the Tarantines with Acrotatus in 314 B.C.).[69] The use later made by the Romans of these cities as *socii navales* was nothing new.

This mercenary phenomenon both promoted the aristocratic ideal which we have noted and made more general cultural influence and exchange much easier.[70] In particular, the interesting suggestion has been made that the simple ideals of personal military excellence were infused with the legacy of the thought of the Pythagoreans, and a cultural influence can be traced extending from the Laconian background of Taras and Locri through the political interpretations of the Pythagoreans to the age of Archytas. The Pythagorean Italici, like the mysterious figure Ocellus, or the C. Pontius Herennus who conversed with Archytas and Plato at Taras, are invoked as part of this intriguing picture. Once again, the presence of similar influences at Rome may be taken as further confirmation of the general picture.[71] We certainly must not overemphasize how rough the soldierly life of the hinterland was: for alongside these military phenomena a whole range of associated cultural activities was tending to produce a *koine* across the peninsula. The life of the popular theatre and the spread of religious forms such as the mysteries of Orpheus and Dionysus may be cited as examples, known from a variety of sources but especially from painted ceramics.[72] The local styles of painted pottery, vigorous, varied and independent as they are, constitute the most impressive, and certainly the best-known

[67] Diod. xxi.3.3 (Agathocles), cf. xxi.18, their dismissal *c.* 288. Diod. xxii.1 (Decius at Rhegium); *legio Campana* in Sicily, Frederiksen 1984 (G 173) 222–3 with n. 27. Note also Diod. xiii.88.7, mercenaries in the Carthaginian War of 409–405.

[68] The contingent at Metapontum: La Regina 1981 (G 207) 135 *vereias kampsanas metapontinas*. On the *vereiia* see most recently Tagliamonte 1989 (G 303).

[69] Messapians, Diod. xxi.4; Acrotatus, Diod. xix.70.7–8. Note Agathocles' development of the port of Hipponium, a foreshadowing of the functions of Roman Vibo, Strabo vi.1.5 p. 256; cf. Dionysius II's refoundation of Rhegium as Phoebia, Strabo vi.1.6.

[70] Stressed by Lepore in Borraro 1975 (G 119) 63.

[71] Pontrandolfo Greco 1982 (G 258) 161; cf. Mele 1982 (G 231). For Rome, Fraschetti 1981 (G 170). Ocellus: D–K no. 48 (vol. 1, 440–1).

[72] Space forbids proper consideration of these themes, but note Pontrandolfo Greco 1982 (G 258) 135–6 on red-figure vases and the theatre; a useful brief overview in Trendall 1989 (J 51). Orphic tablets: a new example from Hipponium, Pugliese Carratelli 1974 and 1976 (G 264–5). Compare the Agnone tablet, Vetter 1953 (G 319) 147.

manifestation of the shared experience of the southern part of the peninsula in this period. They remind us forcefully, in their enormous quantities, of the extent of cultural sophistication and moderate means, which is salutary considering the literary concentration on war and our knowledge of the violence with which it all ended.

We cannot but revert here to the importance of manpower, fundamental to the mercenary phenomenon, and stressed by the literary sources: for example Polybius' praise of Taras as being associated with the most populous of the indigenous peoples.[73] The organization of this resource for the purposes which we have examined had a variety of other consequences, economic and social. In the Greek cities, the concentration of population seems to have given each *politeia* or state a potential human resource which would have been far less easily deployed in the more relaxed days of the sixth century, and which the Sicilian tyrants were impelled to gather by mass deportation. The phratries of Neapolis, for example, show by their names the incorporation of refugees from Cumae. But there were also, undoubtedly to the demographic gain of Neapolis, the Oscan speakers whose presence is remarked on by the sources. In a city like Posidonia/Paestum which had technically 'fallen' but which was perhaps, despite Aristoxenus' lament, not so very different in composition or social forms from the Hellenic 'survivors', the demographic resource again seems to have been exceptionally buoyant.[74] The wealth and populousness of the cities of the region in turn combined to produce an elaboration of the forms of citizen life which was unusual by contemporary Mediterranean standards; in the opulence of life at Taras and the forms it took, with spectacles and buildings for them, frequent holidays, the origins of widespread public bathing, and so on, we find not only the raw material for the tradition about immoral luxury that we have already noticed, but also for the developed Roman/Italic ideology of urban life.[75]

Such a phenomenon had its economic implications. The typical landscape of an organized society of this kind, whether the older nuclei or the increasingly self-conscious 'peoples' of the interior, with their league institutions or the increasingly elaborate Oscan constitutional ideology of the *touta* (Lat. *populus*), was a division into productive units

[73] Polyb. II.39.

[74] Cumaean refugees at Neapolis, Frederiksen 1984 (G 173) 93; incorporation of Oscan-speakers, *ibid.* 139, cf. 101. For increase in population in Campania, Johannowsky, *Sannio* 1984 (G 285) 52f. On Paestum, Pontrandolfo Greco and Rouveret 1982 (G 259); Greco Pontrandolfo 1979 (G 257) 36, 48.

[75] Praises of Taras, Polyb. II.39, cf. X.1; Plautus *Men.* prol. 27f stressing *mercatores* and *ludi*, cf. Strabo VI.3.1 p. 277; Florus I.18 'in ipsis Hadriani maris faucibus posita in omnis terras Histriam Illyricum, Epiron Achaiam African Siciliam vela dimittit'. Oscan *lavacrum* at Cumae, *Arch. Rep. for 1976-7* 45.

based on the *oikos* or household;[76] but the division was something which could be centrally controlled, and the production was increasingly oriented towards the network of consumption which spread with the formation of the larger *poleis* (city states) and the escalation of their aspirations. Meanwhile the process of exchange was being further enhanced not just by more complex systems of redistribution, but by monetization of the economy as a result of coining to pay for the mercenary activities themelves: while the fighting made available manpower in the form of slaves who were redeployable either in the pursuit of city amenities or of intensified agricultural production. So in the countryside archaeology has revealed formal or informal land division, agricultural changes across whole landscapes which must be oriented not simply to local consumption but to the opportunities provided by major changes in the redistribution-network: new forms of scattered rural settlement and distinctive farmhouse forms; and the spread of deployable coinage in the interior.[77] By the beginning of the third century, in short, a change in the whole of the southern part of the Italian peninsula had come about which affected the Greek *poleis* and their non-Greek neighbours, and which produced out of the pursuit of glorification through violence a rosy show of prosperity: big communities, strongly walled, impressive sanctuaries filled with the glitter of the trophies of war, new farmhouses in a recently ordered countryside producing the wherewithal for the comfort of the cities. But it was prosperity which was illusory to the extent that it depended on the roughly equal distribution of success, and even then could be intercepted by the practice of violence itself. When the balance of success of the pursuit of military goals began to shift finally in the direction of Rome, the other signs of prosperity, including wealth and population, began to ebb from South Italy, in a process which was exacerbated but not caused by the violence of the Pyrrhic and Hannibalic Wars. Not that the decline was irreversible or ubiquitous; we have seen how well Taras and Campania did, the latter for obvious reasons of proximity to the new centre of power. But the hectic prosperity of the fourth century, the

[76] On new forms of magistrate, the evolution of the *touta*, the *basileus* and the *meddix, oikos, ethnos* and league, the excellent account of Lepore in Borraro 1975 (G 119) esp. p. 54.

[77] Metapontum (Carter 1986 (G 129)) is the best-studied case of the spread of land-divisions; note the Roman use of the practice from 318 B.C. (Ager Falernus). The Metapontum project has shown a change to large-scale grain production at this period. Adamesteanu 1974 (G 93) 207 for new patterns of settlement in the Val d'Agri: new studies of farmhouses at Cancellara and Tolve, see Ridgway 1989 (G 275) 142. On rural slavery some of the anecdotes of the Pythagorean/Archytas tradition give us a little evidence, cf. Biliński in *Atti 10 Conv.* (G 106) 207–10. Monetization of Lucania, Adamesteanu 1974 (G 93) 187, cf. Stazio Cantilena in *Sannio* 1984 (G 285) 85f with bibliography.

fantastic product of frenetic but inconclusive military competition in an age of social and economic upheaval, was at an end.[78]

The epilogue is Roman. Not that that should lead to its exclusion, for all that has been said here goes to show how little of what Rome did in South Italy between 350 and 250 was 'really' Roman. The Roman aristocracy of this epoch is a perfect example of the new military elites, and it is no surprise to find it producing documents like the painted tomb which was one of our starting-points. It can even be argued that it shows traces of the sub-Pythagorean influence which provided the social and political ideology of the age. Ap. Claudius and M' Curius must be seen beside Ocellus and Pontius Herennius, Nummelos and Nypsius.[79] The relations of Rome with other communities, like the surrender (*deditio*) of Capua, the treaty with Naples, the network of protection celebrated by the *PISTIS* (loyalty) coinage of Locri, fit in to the voluntary associative phenomena which we have seen at work all through the period, to a world in which mercenary behaviour is fundamental and in which new opportunities for protection and power are always being sought.[80] We have seen how the associative tendencies of the elites lie behind the varied and flexible federalisms of the age; in 326 Rome's cultivation of the elite of Arpi, the rich centre of Daunia whose espousal of the Roman cause is represented as *deditio* (surrender) by Livy, is no different. Such relationships formed the position of Rome in Magna Graecia years before the time of Pyrrhus.[81] What Rome did when she was in a position of strength was again not unique – land-division, construction of military works, transfer of populations, whether her own or others, the formation of new cities to serve as strongpoints. We may think of the formation of the *tribus Falerna* (318) and the building of the Via Appia (312), the colonization of Luceria (314) and Venusia (291) as truly Roman, but they are merely larger scale applications of well-tried strategies, long familiar to the peoples of the south.[82] Rome, in fact,

---

[78] Toynbee 1965 (G 309) II ch. 1 attributed the decline of the south to the Punic Wars. Archaeology now points to earlier discontinuities: Pontrandolfo Greco 1979 (G 257) 48 (end of ex-voto offerings in territory of Paestum); Settis *Athenaeum* 43 (1965) 127 (Medma abandoned); *Atti 22 Conv.* 571 (Laos abandoned, end of third century); Adamesteanu 1983 (G 95) 157 (transience of the fortified centres of the fourth century; note that the Rossano sanctuary survives); *Atti MSMG* 23–4 (1976–7) 163 (general decline in the Potentino). The story of the settlements at Le Murge di Strongoli in the retroterra of Croton (perhaps the ancient Macalla) is typical – incipient urbanization in the fourth century, decline in the third, replacement by a neighbouring Roman centre (Petelia) thereafter; see *Stud. Etr.* 52 (1984) 491–2. Add now Ridgway 1989 (G 275) 139, destruction level at Pontecagnano *c.* 300.

[79] South Italian influences on Roman aristocracy: Fraschetti 1981 (G 170).

[80] Frederiksen 1984 (G 173) ch. 9.

[81] For Rome and Arpi, Livy VIII.25; Mazzei 1984 and 1987 (G 226–7). Moretti 1971 (G 235) 52 stresses continuity of Roman-Tarantine relations despite Pyrrhus. See also Clemente 1988 (G 140).

[82] On Roman imperialism in this period see Salmon 1982 (G 280) ch. 3; *CAH* VII².2, ch. 8. Luceria (walls *c.* 314, Ridgway 1982 (G 274) 70), colonized in 325 according to Velleius 1.14, is of central

made the grade and succeeded in applying all this as well as did the
hellenistic monarchs of the eastern Mediterranean; she attained true
modernity, the latest in state management, going further even than
Syracuse and Carthage in bringing to the west the new methods of the
hellenistic age.[83]

The results were far from good in South Italy; but – not that it will
have been a goal of the Roman aristocrats – the extension of the cultural
koine which we have studied in formation in the fourth century to form a
truly hellenistic melting-pot society was eventually achieved. That
limestone 'island' the Messapian peninsula, which had so long resisted
the influence of nearby Taras – it was here that Archidamus had died, at
the siege of Manduria only 25 km from his base – survived as a district of
independent *mores* and considerable agricultural prosperity. But it came
to form part of the Roman *koine* as it had never of the Hellenic. Direct
heirs to the prosperous and independent Messapian past, its dozen or so
solid urban communities survived to become, eventually, Roman
municipalities. Even before that, though, it was from one of them that
there came that classic figure of third/second-century Italy, speaking
Greek, Oscan and Latin and writing in them all – the epic poet Ennius.[84]

importance: centuriation Torelli 1984 (G 308) 328. *Ibid.* 329–30 for S. Salvatore votive deposit,
showing very rapid Latinization. Cf. the case of Sthenius Sthallius the Lucanian, 285 B.C., Pliny *HN*
XXXIV. 32.

[83] Adamesteanu 1974 (G 93) 215 contrasts the particularist character of the Greek and indigenous
experience of the fifth and fourth centuries with the newer and vaster vision of the Roman state in
the epoch after Alexander.

[84] Ennius: see Strabo VI.3.5 p. 281. On Messapia, *CAH* IV² 683 ff – more Corinthian than
Tarantine. Cf. [Scylax] 14 (cf. Ath. XII.523) on the Greekness of Hydruntum, on the coasting route.

CHAPTER 9c

CELTIC EUROPE

D. W. HARDING

Any synthesis of Europe north of the Alps in the first half of the first millennium B.C. is conditioned by imbalances in the archaeological record. Much of the evidence is derived from cemeteries with specialized inventories of grave-goods, or from high-status fortified sites of exceptional character and function, rather than from a full spectrum of settlement or material remains. Even these data are unequally distributed regionally, or at any rate unequally studied, and not equally represented in successive chronological phases. The effect of this imbalance and discontinuity of evidence can be the creation of artificial horizons, which may be used to justify historical episodes or socio-economic climaxes, and which compound a tendency towards a 'selected highlights' view of European prehistory.

The classification and chronology of later prehistoric Europe is still largely based upon the system devised by Reinecke at the beginning of the century, named after the Alpine type-sites of Hallstatt and La Tène. In Reinecke's scheme, Hallstatt A and B equate with the Older and Younger phases respectively of the Urnfield Culture, in absolute terms spanning the twelfth to eighth centuries B.C., whilst Hallstatt C and D, dating from later eighth to early sixth, are generally recognized as the first Iron Age in central and western Europe. The system is essentially a Central European one, with important transalpine correlations, and it has been developed in large measure from the concentration of systematic research on the rich cemetery assemblages in these regions. West of the Rhine, in both Urnfield and Iron Hallstatt phases, the cemetery inventories show a more limited range of types, with fewer examples that could be regarded as diagnostic of the Central European culture, and local regional variants that progressively lend assemblages a distinctively Atlantic aspect.

Whatever its limitations, the Reinecke system at least has the merit of underlining the element of cultural continuity from later Bronze to earlier Iron Ages, which is evident from a study of the material assemblages themselves. An older conventional view had placed great emphasis upon the novelty of the appearance of so-called Thraco-

Cimmerian equestrian equipment in chieftains' burials of the Hallstatt C phase, especially in the eastern Hallstatt zone, with an implied equation with the introduction and adoption of iron technology from regions further east around the seventh century B.C. In fact, the knowledge if not the regular use of iron is already evidenced in eastern Central Europe in the earlier second millennium, and by 1000 B.C. iron regularly appears among Urnfield grave inventories. Nor can these finds be dismissed as exotic imports, since in several instances they are unequivocally associated with the debris of local production. The commonly held view that iron was initially used for ornamental rather than functional purposes is not sustained by the presence of utilitarian artefacts such as knives and axes in assemblages as early as Reinecke A2/B1, even though they occur at this stage in very limited numbers.[1] In fact, iron is not quantitatively the dominant metal in most Hallstatt C and D cemeteries, even though that period is generally regarded as the first Iron Age of Europe. The stages in the process of adoption of iron, from the point of technological introduction to its regular or commercial exploitation, are not the concern of the present essay, however, except in so far as such a study might underline the importance of social and economic factors in its local development in Europe, in contradiction to older diffusionist models.

A primary consideration in the study of the Celtic Iron Age in Europe and its relations with the classical world must be the question, 'When did Celtic Europe become Celtic, and in what sense?' It is a common misconception, fostered by linguists, that the term can only be used correctly of Celtic-speakers, even though the earliest commentators, Hecataeus and Herodotus, writing in the sixth and fifth centuries B.C., evidently intended it as an ethnic identification of one of the major barbarian neighbours of the classical world. That these people were indeed linguistically Celtic is indicated by references to personal and tribal names in classical sources, as well as by place-names and inscriptions recorded widely throughout Europe north and west of the Alps. Furthermore, since language could only be transmitted, before the advent of literacy or telecommunications, by direct population contact, the emergence of an Indo-European language in Celtic Europe has been taken to imply some measure at least of settlement from regions further east. Given the historical references alluded to above, this episode or sequence of episodes must have preceded the middle of the first millennium B.C., and cannot be equated, for instance, with the La Tène culture which is widely regarded as synonymous with Celtic culture. In fact, the earliest Celtic settlement in Europe need not accord exclusively with any observed archaeological culture, but if such an equation were

[1] Waldbaum 1978 (E 54) 22–3.

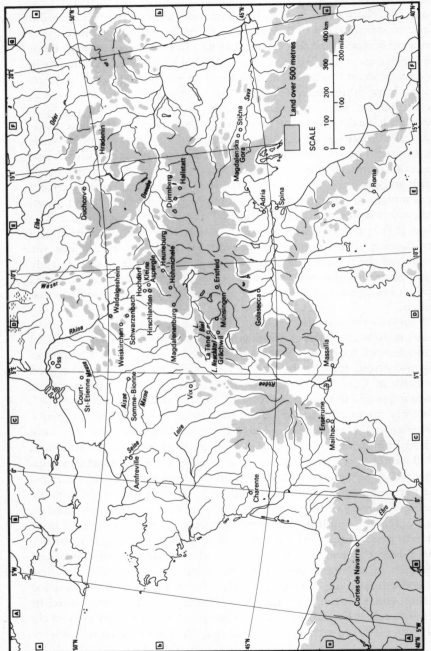

Map 12. The Celtic world.

admitted, it should be with a pan-European culture earlier than La Tène, among which the Urnfield culture might afford a possible contender. The process need not be the product of a single, simple episode but part of a progressive sequence of 'cumulative Celticity'.[2] It must, in all events, have involved people who cannot have become Celtic-speaking by a process of linguistic osmosis, or 'Celtic by accretion' extending the whole process back into remote antiquity.

In the light of the linguistic issue, the evidence for continuity of culture from Urnfield to Iron Hallstatt is particularly relevant. In fact, many types, correctly regarded in detail as diagnostically Hallstatt C, none the less have antecedents in the Urnfield sequence, including swords, horse-gear and luxury goods like beaten bronze vessels, while a comparison of south Bavarian Hallstatt C pottery types[3] with their Urnfield counterparts[4] further reinforces the essential continuity of ceramic tradition. The break in settlement continuity has been frequently remarked, though this would appear to be less applicable to open, lowland settlements than to hillforts. The major innovation of the Hallstatt C phase is the change in burial rite, with inhumation replacing inurned cremation as the dominant practice, and with the reappearance of tumulus burial, some exceptional for the wealth of their grave-furnishings and equipment.

At the top of the social order, and reviving a much older Eurasian tradition, were vehicle-burials,[5] generally of four-wheeled wagons or carriages, buried intact within a timber chamber, as in the Hallstatt C phase at Hradenin in Czechoslovakia or at Grosseibstadt in Bavaria, or even more lavishly and with the inclusion of southern imports among their grave-goods in Hallstatt D, as at Hochdorf[6] in Baden-Württemberg (Fig. 11), or at Vix,[7] where the vehicle was dismantled to accommodate the wealth of grave-goods, on the upper Seine. Though there may be a principal central burial, as at the Hohmichele[8] or the Grafenbuhl, there are commonly additional graves within the tumulus; in the case of the massive Magdalenenberg tomb[9] 126 lesser burials are disposed concentrically around the perimeter of the mound. Some tumuli were evidently marked by a stone stela, which appears to have been the function of the Hirschlanden statue, an ithyphallic figure with helmet, torc and dagger found by a Hallstatt D barrow containing more than a dozen modestly furnished inhumations. It is important to recognize, of course, that the princely tombs are a small minority of the total number of known Hallstatt burials, even in southern Germany, where cemeteries of several hundred graves are not uncommon. Less

[2] Hawkes 1973 (E 17).   [3] Kossac 1959 (E 28).   [4] Müller-Karpe 1959 (E 39).
[5] Piggott 1983 (E 44).   [6] Biel 1982 (E 1).   [7] Joffroy 1954 (E 22); cf. Pls. to Vol. III pl. 373.
[8] Riek and Hundt 1962 (E 46).   [9] Spindler 1971–3, 1976–7, 1980 (E 51).

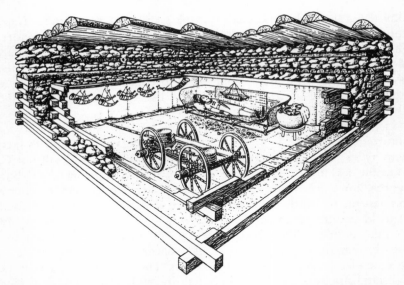

Fig. 11. Reconstruction of the burial at Hochdorf; later sixth century B.C. (After Moscati (ed.) 1991 (E 5) 86; see Biel 1982 (E 1); *Trésors* 1987 (E 52) 95–188.)

spectacular in their grave assemblages, these cemeteries are none the less equally significant in reflecting the shift to inhumation as the dominant rite, and furthermore they are crucial for determining the regular and recurrent types which distinguish Hallstatt C and D, and the sub-divisions within each phase. Whether or not the change in burial rite is attributed in part to new elements within the population, other factors, such as the exploitation of mineral resources and the establishment of trading relationships with the Mediterranean world, could have had an equally profound impact upon the social and economic patterns of Hallstatt Europe.

One region within the eastern Hallstatt province where such factors appear to have taken effect early in the first millennium B.C. is Slovenia. Here, major fortified settlements with extensive tumulus cemeteries nearby, like Stična and Magdalenska gora, were evidently dependent not simply upon the rich agricultural potential of the region, but upon its iron-ore resources which were being widely exploited by the eighth century. From this period for several centuries a pattern of trade was established in the northern Adriatic, from which the major centres of north-eastern Italy like Este received iron products in exchange for wine and other Italic and Mediterranean luxury goods, like the Etruscan bronze tripod from Novo Mesto. In the sixth century, this relationship between the Venetia region and Slovenia culminated in the distinctive style of figural art represented on sheet-bronze situlae, a remarkable fusion of central European and southern traditions.[10]

The site of Hallstatt[11] itself did not enjoy the advantages of a fertile agricultural environment; its wealth was based exclusively upon the mineral resources of the Austrian Alps, and specifically the local deposits of salt in the Salzkammergut range. Though the cemetery at Hallstatt dates mainly from the eighth century onwards, the salt-mines were apparently being worked from the late Bronze Age, perhaps initially on a seasonal basis. Of the estimated total of 2,000 or more excavated graves, a relatively high proportion was richly furnished, including a number of warrior burials, though few attain the exceptional wealth of the princely burials of Hallstatt D in the West Hallstatt province. As a community engaged in a specialized industrial economy, Hallstatt may not have been unique, though other sites do not appear to have equalled its size or importance.

By contrast, the late Hallstatt citadels of south-west Germany have been seen both as aristocratic strongholds controlling a territorial hierarchy of settlement, and as entrepreneurial centres controlling the exchange and redistribution of goods.[12] Crucial to their function and status was the introduction of Mediterranean imports, following the establishment of the Greek colony at Massilia in 600 B.C., or within the half century thereafter.[13] The distribution of amphorae of Greek type, of so-called grey Phocaean wares, and local imitations of these, suggest a hinterland which was receptive to Mediterranean fashions, and beyond that a natural corridor led via Rhône and Saône to the heartlands of Celtic Europe, to the upper Danube and Rhine, where the Heuneburg fortress[14] with its nearby cemetery of princely tombs was a major regional focus in the Hallstatt D phase, and to the headwaters of the Seine, where the Mont Lassois hillfort[15] and the burials at Vix bear witness to the imported wealth which these Celtic chieftains could command. Mediterranean influence was not restricted to the import of luxury goods, however, as can be seen by the use of mud-brick walls and bastions in the defensive circuit of the Heuneburg fortress. What was supplied reciprocally from Celtic Europe is not so obvious from the archaeological record, and presumably must have included agricultural products, raw materials and even mercenaries and slaves.

The function and status of these *Fürstensitze* have been much debated. Dehn, Kimmig and others have distinguished a hierarchy of settlement, though the criteria for defining the princely residences of the first rank have not always been consistent, nor yet susceptible to demonstration by

[10] Frey 1969 (E 10); Boardman 1971 (E 2).   [11] Kromer 1959 (E 29); Peroni 1973 (E 43).
[12] Wells 1980, 1984 (E 55–6).   [13] Kimmig 1983 (E 26).   [14] Kimmig 1983 (E 27).
[15] Joffroy 1960 (E 24).

excavation.[16] More recently, emphasis has been placed upon their function as regional territorial *foci*, or as commercial and economic centres without any necessary concomitant political role. Their relatively short-lived supremacy – few seem to have outlasted Hallstatt D – has suggested a dependency upon Mediterranean trade, though it is still unclear whether this gave them their status or whether it was simply a manifestation of their status. An instructive comparison might be drawn between the impact of Massilia upon west-central European Hallstatt society and the native communities in the hinterland of the trading settlement at Emporium. Insufficient distinction in this context is made between relatively utilitarian Greek imports, like the black-figure wares of no great distinction found on a number of late Hallstatt sites, and truly prestigious goods like the Vix crater, or the Etruscan furnishings of the Hochdorf burial. The presence of the former may reflect little more than the commercial or redistributive role of a hillfort, but the latter must surely be indicative of aristocratic status.

West of the Rhine, French archaeology since Déchelette has also recognized a two-phase division of the first Iron Age, traditionally termed Hallstatt I and II – regarding the Urnfield period simply as *Bronze Final* (I, II, III) – though more recently a threefold classification (*ancien*, *moyen*, *final*) has gained favour. In eastern France and the Jura, correlation with south-west Germany is understandably quite close, but progressively north and westwards the recognizably Hallstatt elements within assemblages of this period acquire the aspect of exotic imports rather than diagnostic types. Hallstatt assemblages in Belgium and the Netherlands, like the horse- and vehicle-gear from Court-St-Etienne[17] or the warrior-grave from Oss, have the appearance of exotic introductions, and have been seen as evidence for intrusive Celtic warlords dominating the indigenous population. Other notable regional groupings west of the Rhine include the Vixien of Hallstatt Final, characterized at the Mont Lassois hillfort by painted pottery and Italic-style brooches, and the Jogassien from the Marne,[18] named after a cemetery which like Vix included a later Hallstatt wagon-burial, but which was apparently at this time beyond the zone of high-status Mediterranean imports. To the south another distinctive regional culture, the Mailhacien, developed in the Mediterranean hinterland, taking its name from a series of sites in the vicinity of Mailhac in Languedoc.[19] Here the local sequence is unbroken from the late Urnfield cemetery at Le Moulin to the middle of the sixth century cemetery at Le Grand Bassin II, in which imported Greek and Etruscan amphorae are used as ossuaries with grave-goods including black-figure pottery, Etruscan *bucchero nero*, 'Phocaean' and native

[16] Härke 1979 (E 14).   [17] Marien 1958 (E 33).
[18] Favret 1936 (E 8); Hatt and Roualet 1976 (E 15).   [19] Louis and Taffanel 1955–60 (E 31).

pseudo-Ionian wares, together with iron antenna daggers, cross-bow brooches, and belt-hooks of late Hallstatt derivation. This combination of local Urnfield, Hallstatt and Mediterranean elements may be matched in varying degree from Provence to the Ebro, and reflects both conservatism and innovation in this important cultural interface.

Across the Pyrenees, a parallel sequence is exemplified at the settlement of Cortes de Navarra[20] on the middle Ebro. Though the stratigraphy from this type-site is far from clear in detail, the settlement like a tell with its characteristic buildings of adobe-brick construction evidently spanned a final Urnfield and Hallstatt phase into what is locally termed 'post-Hallstatt' with a final abandonment around the fourth century B.C. Conventionally, these Urnfield and Hallstatt elements south of the Pyrenees have been attributed to successive waves of migration from unspecified west-central European sources, introducing peoples who were both ethnically and linguistically Celtic. Yet the peninsular cultures have always been regarded as a fusion of indigenous and intrusive elements, with local traditions in some regions remaining dominant, as in the *castro* culture of the north west. In fact, even in the Ebro and the Meseta, Hallstatt or Hallstatt-derived types are strictly limited in number: antenna-swords, daggers, belt-clasps and certain brooch types may be cited, while ceramic influences, though generally acknowledged, are somewhat indeterminate.[21] This pattern continues into the La Tène Iron Age, with a relatively sparse distribution of types in the middle and upper Duero. The castros of the peninsular north west, in their developed and surviving form, are evidently later Iron Age in date, though their stone-built defences and circular houses may obscure earlier phases of settlement which have yet to be fully investigated. These sites have been regarded as the fortified settlements of Celtic communities, whose establishment in the region, presumably by late Hallstatt times, has yet to be demonstrated in the archaeological record.

The case for Celtic settlement south of the Pyrenees, then, rests not upon the presence of diagnostic artefact types or distinctively central European settlements or cemeteries, but upon the testimony of historical sources, particularly in reference to the wars of the second century B.C. waged by the Romans against native 'Celtiberians', and upon the evidence of place-names. Celtic elements in place-names occur in some abundance across the northern half of Spain and Portugal, in marked contrast to the south and east where Mediterranean connexions gave rise to the distinctive Iberian culture in the second half of the first millennium B.C. But the onomastic evidence is of interest as much for elements which are absent as for those, notably the suffix -*briga*, which are present, a pattern which has been taken to indicate an early introduction of Celtic

---

[20] Maluquer de Motes 1954 (E 32).   [21] Schüle 1960, 1969 (E 47–8).

Fig. 12. Bone sphinx with amber face, from Klein Aspergle; late sixth century B.C.; Stuttgart, Württembergisches Landesmuseum. (After Moscati (ed.) 1991 (E 5) 74.)

speakers into the peninsula. Closer archaeological definition of Celtiberian culture, however, is constrained here, as elsewhere in the Atlantic west, by the problems of identifying material types which might be regarded as diagnostically Celtic beyond the primary zone of Hallstatt and La Tène culture.

The transition from late Hallstatt to early La Tène has been well documented in Europe north of the Alps in terms of artefact typology, but its significance is less evident in cultural or social terms. The fifth century B.C. saw a number of important changes in settlement, burial and economy, as well as the appearance of an art-style distinctively Celtic for which local antecedents were almost totally lacking. At the same time, certain traditions continue, like that of vehicle-burial in rich graves with southern imports included among the grave-goods, though the four-wheeled wagons of the previous phase are replaced by two-wheeled chariots or carts, and the exotic grave-goods testify to the ascendancy of transalpine trade routes from Etruria rather than connexions with the Greek colonies of the Mediterranean littoral. Most striking is the shift in settlement patterns away from the late Hallstatt princely strongholds of south-west Germany to the Hunsrück-Eifel[22] and the middle Rhine, where the domination of a new regional elite is declared, not so much by prestigious fortifications as by the wealth displayed in its chieftains' burials, including a variety of Greek and Etruscan imports (Fig. 12). On the southern fringe of this group, the Klein Aspergle tomb, with its spectacular drinking service – including Etruscan stamnos, bronze beaked-flagon, bronze cordoned bucket, gold-embellished drinking horns and pair of Greek cups – is the latest of a series of princely tombs in near proximity to the Hohenasperg hillfort, suggesting that here the late Hallstatt regime may have continued into the La Tène A phase. One element in this shift may have been the increased exploitation of the local

[22] Joachim 1968 (E 21); Haffner 1976 (E 12).

iron deposits of the Hunsrück-Eifel, which could have been the basis of the region's social and economic ascendancy in the early–middle La Tène periods. Central to the interpretation of this apparent shift in locational emphasis is the chronology of the late Hallstatt–early La Tène transition, whether these phases are regarded as wholly exclusive and successive, or whether in particular the final Hallstatt (D3) phase, characterized by certain developed brooches and allied material types, is seen as overlapping and contemporary with La Tène A in adjacent regions.[23] Nor is the problem restricted to this horizon alone, for similar issues may be raised in considering the La Tène A-B sequence, particularly in the context of the development of early Celtic art. In fact, the distribution of southern imports shows marked local groupings and associations. Bronze situlae are concentrated in the Rhein–Mosel area, while Etruscan bronze-handled dishes are restricted to the Hochwald-Nahe and Rheinhessen–Palatinate regions. Only bronze beaked-flagons are found in both. Such a selective distribution may argue against a system of regional redistribution, and favour a view of independent links with individual chiefdoms which would be consistent with, and perhaps consequent upon, the decline of late Hallstatt princely centres. Any interpretation of southern imports in central Europe in the early La Tène phase, however, must be qualified by the fact that, in the absence of complementary evidence from settlements or hoards, finds derive exclusively from high-status funerary contexts, and their occurrence or survival therefore may be determined by cult requirements rather than reflecting an effective pattern of trade or exchange.

A similar shift in the focus of commercial activity at the end of the fifth century in the eastern Alps saw the decline of the salt-mines at Hallstatt and the development of a new industry at Dürrnberg-bei-Hallein,[24] not far to the west but located in a valley which was easier of access and supported by a better local agricultural potential. The cemetery at Dürrnberg was smaller than that at Hallstatt, though its grave-goods indicate that the community enjoyed a high standard of material wealth, including imports from the Mediterranean world. One warrior inhumation with a two-wheeled vehicle was accompanied by a rich assemblage of grave-goods, including weapons, helmet, a huge bronze situla 88 cm high, and an Attic cup of late-fifth-century date. A secondary burial from the same tomb accompanied by a Certosa brooch and lens-shaped pottery vessel characteristic of the fourth century indicates the continuing occupation of the Dürrnberg settlements, probably into the middle La Tène period.

In Switzerland, a prolonged period of use from La Tène A-C also

[23] Dehn and Frey 1979 (E 7); Frey and Kossack 1978 (E 11).
[24] Penninger 1972 (E 42); Moosleitner et al. 1974 (E 38); Pauli 1978 (E 41).

accounts for the size of the cemetery at Münsingen,[25] near Berne, where more than two hundred graves were excavated at the turn of the century. Study of diagnostic artefacts indicated that there had been a linear spread of burials over time from north to south, and this horizontal stratigraphy, together with the existence of good individual grave-associations, enabled a detailed typological sequence of the principal groups of artefacts to be worked out. In particular, the Münsingen type-series of brooches serves as a model for the La Tène period in Europe from Bohemia to Britain. Most enigmatic of all the Swiss La Tène sites, however, is the type-site itself,[26] situated at the north-east end of Lake Neuchâtel, where it drains into Lake Biel. The site can be classified neither as a settlement nor a cemetery, comprising a vast collection of artefacts – the estimated total of items exceeds 3,000 though the authenticity of provenance is not always established beyond doubt – recovered at various times since the middle of the nineteenth century. In addition to several hundred swords, spears and brooches, this material included domestic and agricultural utensils, and evidence for a range of related activities such as carpentry, leatherwork and basketry. Structural evidence from the vicinity included timbers of bridges, among which a number of skeletons was also recovered. The main period of use of the site was evidently the middle La Tène phase, but its function is highly problematical. It has been variously interpreted as a ritual or ceremonial site, as a kind of prehistoric supermarket, or, in view of its location between the subsequent territories of the Helvetii and the Sequani, as a frontier establishment serving a garrison or custom-post. The sheer quantity of prestige goods, however, argues that La Tène was a major centre for exchange or redistribution, a function which need not have been exclusive of other activities, economic, social or ritual.

Southern imports in the early La Tène phase were not restricted to the eastern Alpine communities, but penetrated further into east-central Europe, to the settlements of the Vltava and the tumulus burials of southern Bohemia. The initial occupation of hillforts like Zavist in the late Hallstatt–early La Tène phases may have coincided here as in the middle Rhine with the beginnings of the commercial exploitation of the iron resources of the southern highlands, providing the reciprocal basis for long-distance trade and exchange. To the north, the rich löss soils of the lowland hills of northern Bohemia had been the agricultural basis for the flourishing Bylany culture; here by the La Tène B phase, the small cremation cemeteries of late Hallstatt had given way to inhumation in flat cemeteries of the so-called 'Dux' horizon, a phase characterized by brooches of a type represented in the votive hoard from Duchcov.[27] This

[25] Hodson 1968 (E 19).   [26] Vouga 1923 (E 53); de Navarro 1972 (E 40).
[27] Kruta 1971 (E 30).

contrast in burial rite in Bohemia has been seen as an archaeological reflection of distinct cultural groupings, and even the product of migrating Celts of the fourth century as recorded in classical sources.[28] Without discounting such factors, we should exercise caution in making such a simple or direct correlation between population groups and archaeological distributions, to the neglect of other factors, environmental or economic, which may have determined the pattern of archaeological evidence.

West of the Rhine, a distinctive early La Tène culture developed in the Champagne,[29] successive to the local Jogassien late Hallstatt, and counterpart to the contemporary group of the Hunsrück-Eifel. Its cemeteries are distributed in great profusion in the valleys of the Aisne and the Marne, and include more than a hundred chariot-burials of the early La Tène warrior aristocracy. The layout of these graves sometimes provided vertical slots for the chariot-wheels and an extension for the yoke and pole, so that the vehicle bearing the dead could be lowered intact into the burial-pit. The grave-furnishings commonly include a bridle-set in lieu of the horse itself, together with pottery, weapons, ornaments and occasionally, as at Somme-Bionne and La Gorge-Meillet, imported Italic wine-flagons or Attic red-figure pottery. Lesser burials also conform to the rite of extended inhumation, though in a simple rectangular grave, sometimes grouped and encompassed by a square-ditched barrow. Grave goods are nonetheless relatively prolific, as in neighbouring north Alpine groups of the early La Tène phase. Brooches, bracelets, torcs, swords and spearheads in a range of variant forms have provided the basis of a detailed system of classification, particularly for the phases Hallstatt *Final* and La Tène *Ancienne*. In the Paris basin and northern France, early La Tène assemblages invite comparison with the more distinctive material of the Marne and Aisne, or with the contemporary *groupe de la Haine* in Belgium.[30]

In the Atlantic west La Tène types are more sparsely distributed, and in some areas are totally absent prior to La Tène 3. In Aquitaine,[31] some early La Tène types, including brooches and weapons, are represented among grave-goods in cremation barrows, but in the centre-west of France early and middle La Tène material is virtually non-existent. A notable exception is the recently discovered helmet from Charente (Fig. 13): made of iron and bronze with coral and leaf-gold ornamentation, its form and decoration are reminiscent of the helmet from the Seine at Amfreville-sous-les-Monts, and must represent a high-status import into a region otherwise largely devoid of La Tène influence. Brittany,

[28] Filip 1956 (E 9).
[29] Bretz-Mahler 1971 (E 3); Hatt and Roualet 1977 (E 16); Joffroy 1958 (E 23).
[30] Marien 1961 (E 34).   [31] Mohen 1980 (E 37).

Fig. 13. Gilt iron and bronze helmet with coral inlay, from Agris (Charente); Angoulême, Mus. de
la Soc. Arch. et Hist. de la Charente. (After Moscati (ed.) 1991 (E 5) 293.)

though peripheral to the archaeology of Celtic Europe, was doubtless
known to the Greeks through the reported trading expeditions of
Tartessians before the voyage of Pytheas in the later fourth century.[32]
The region has a distinctive Iron Age culture, exemplified particularly by
its characteristic field monuments. Burial practices reveal a measure of
continuity from late Hallstatt to early La Tène, notably in the persistence

[32] Hawkes 1977 (E 18).

of cremation alongside inhumation, though close dating is often precluded by the paucity of grave-goods. Granite stelae, frequently displaced or subject to later Christianization, though not exclusively funerary in function, are commonly found in association with these cemeteries. They assume a variety of forms, high, low or hemispherical, and may be ornamented with curvilinear designs in the La Tène style. Pottery, too, displays decorative styles paralleled in the mainstream of continental Celtic art. From the early La Tène phase the technique of stamped ornament bears a striking similarity to the stamped arc- and circle-styles of central Europe,[33] from which some direct impulse may be inferred. Other fine wares, dating from around the fourth century B.C., are decorated with vegetal and palmette-derived motifs, more usually associated with La Tène metalwork in Central Europe. Settlements have been less extensively researched, but some at least of the distinctive cliff-castles of the Atlantic and Channel coasts have revealed evidence of occupation from early La Tène times. Among the most characteristic field-monuments of western Armorica are souterrains, dating to the early and middle La Tène phases. Their function is debatable, but proximity to settlements and the occurrence in their chambers of domestic occupation debris suggest that they must have served as an adjunct to settlement, perhaps for storage of agricultural produce. Though the Armorican souterrains are distinctive in construction and layout, they none the less invite comparison with analogous underground structures in south-western Britain, Ireland and Scotland.

By contrast with continental Europe, our knowledge of the early Iron Age in Britain derives almost exclusively from the study of settlements and fortifications rather than cemeteries.[34] In consequence, though the evidence for settlement patterns and economy, particularly in southern England, is substantial, the material assemblages from these sites reveal a limited range of types and a markedly insular character compared to the extensive cemetery inventories of Central Europe. Cross-channel connexions are none the less attested from the late Bronze Age to the end of the Iron Age, the Channel itself serving as a natural route for trade and exchange rather than as a barrier to cultural communication. Population movements are notoriously difficult to substantiate archaeologically, but linguistic evidence alone requires the introduction of Celtic-speaking people into Britain and Ireland by a date which can hardly be later than the middle of the first millennium B.C. A simple equation between areas of Celtic settlement and the distribution of La Tène artefact types is plainly untenable here, since this would effectively exclude large parts of Scotland and Ireland which none the less have abundant evidence of Iron Age occupation. In Ireland, the contrast between the distribution of La

[33] Schwappach 1969 (E 49).   [34] Harding 1974 (E 13); Cunliffe 1978 (E 6).

Tène metalwork in the northern half of the country (coincident broadly
with the distribution of beehive rotary querns) and its relative absence in
the south west, where later prehistoric settlement is attested notably in
small, stone forts (cashels, cathairs), has given rise to the use of the term
'non-La Tène' Iron Age for this variant of insular Celtic culture.[35] The
origins of Ireland's Celtic settlement are contentious, since the surviving
linguistic evidence is Q-Celtic, predominantly if not exclusively, by
contrast to P-Celtic in Gaul and southern Britain. Scottish Gaelic is
generally reckoned not to have been transmitted across the North
Channel until the invasions of the Scotti around the fourth century A.D.
and thereafter, but it is not impossible that a Q-Celtic language was
introduced earlier into Atlantic Scotland along a west coast route from
Iberia and south-western Ireland. In archaeological terms, such an
Atlantic cultural axis would be essentially non-La Tène, so that La Tène
metalwork in Ireland would need to be explained as a separate introduction, perhaps involving reciprocal influences with northern England and
southern Scotland, but not necessarily requiring population movements
on any significant scale.[36]

It is the metalwork deposited in graves of the early La Tène phase
which affords the primary medium for the craftsmen who developed
from the early fifth century the distinctive style of early Celtic art.[37] The
genesis of early Celtic art has provoked a good deal of debate, not least
because it lacks any unequivocal antecedents in the local north Alpine
late Hallstatt culture, though the geometrical and rectilinear designs
which characterized Hallstatt pottery and metalwork persist in modified
form on some early La Tène ceramics. In metalwork, however, it is the
southern influences that are most apparent, as Jacobsthal amply demonstrated. His Early Style is well exemplified by the Schwarzenbach bowl
from the middle Rhine. The lower of its two main panels is composed of
alternating lotuses, complete with sepals, and pendant palmettes, here
reduced to a simple three-leafed motif: the upper panel also contains
these elements, but characteristically adapted and fragmented to produce
a less formal structure. These plant and vegetal motifs, however,
represent only part of the repertory of the Early Style. In contrast to such
classical-derived elements are those geometric, sometimes compass-
drawn, motifs which have been termed an 'arc'- or 'circle-style', and for
which Hallstatt origins have been claimed. Whereas the plant-style is
mainly represented in west-central Europe, the arc-style apparently is
concentrated further east – with the exception of the anomalous
derivative group in Brittany – forming two distinct zones within the
Early Style, though with a measure of interaction between the two. The

[35] Caulfield 1977 (E 4).   [36] Raftery 1984 (E 45).
[37] Jacobsthal 1944 (E 20); Megaw 1970 (E 35).

contrast must be qualified, however, by the fact that much of the arc-style ornament is represented on pottery, whereas the plant-style is almost exclusively limited in central Europe to metalwork. The fact that the 'arc-style' also appears on bowls of Braubach type, ornamented internally, of La Tène B raises again the question whether the La Tène A and B distinction is genuinely one of chronological sequence or one of regional variance.

A second influence upon the Early Style which has been much debated is the orientalizing element, one which was probably received indirectly through Greek or Etruscan intermediaries, though the Persian expeditions of the late sixth and fifth centuries could have provided the context for a more positive impulse into south-east Europe. For some scholars these orientalizing influences have seemed far too nebulous for serious consideration, and it is true that convincing examples represent a small minority of items within the total body of early Celtic art. Backward-looking beasts, as depicted on the Parsberg brooch, the Rodenbach armring, and on the Erstfeld torques,[38] or the strange 'Siamese-twin' creatures from Erstfeld and on the Weiskirchen belt-clasp, have prompted comparison with various Western Asiatic models. Most closely Scythian in treatment are the wolf-like beasts on the Basse-Yutz flagons, with their curled shoulder-joints and stabbed rendering of their pelts, the latter replicated also on the animals of the Parsberg brooch. Actual imports in Celtic contexts are exceedingly rare, the drinking-horn mount with its panel of sphinxes from Weiskirchen possibly reflecting Achaemenian workmanship. In general, however, it is the hallmark of Celtic art that it absorbs eastern or southern themes and transforms them freely to create a quality and style of its own.

This essential characteristic of Celtic art is best illustrated in the products of the so-called 'Waldalgesheim Style', regarded by Jacobsthal as successive to his Early Style, with a distribution somewhat complementary to it (Fig. 14). Renewed classical impulses may be detected, as for example in the star-rosette motif in the Waldalgesheim torque itself, but the diagnostic characteristics of the style are the use of continuous, free-flowing motifs, rather than simply a series of independent elements, and the use of relief to define the design so that there is no longer a reciprocal interplay between foreground and background. Recurrent among the elements incorporated in the Waldalgesheim Style are the 'fan', 'vortex' and 'swelling-leaf' motifs, and what Jope[39] has termed the over-and-under figure-of-eight pattern, not individually represented but drawn together into a continuous composition. Whether we assign an earlier or later fourth-century date to the Campanian bronze bucket from the type-site, the Waldalgesheim Style evidently belongs to the fourth

---

[38] Wyss 1975 (E 57).   [39] Jope 1971 (E 25).

Fig. 14. Ornament from gold torque, from Waldalgesheim; fourth century B.C.; Bonn, Rheinisches Landesmuseum. (After Moscati (ed.) 1991 (E 5) 202; see Jope 1971 (E 25) 169, fig. 36a.)

century and after, in turn influencing the later Swiss and Hungarian 'sword styles' of middle La Tène.

   With the decline in transalpine trade in the fourth century, there followed a period of change in central and western Europe, broadly coincident with the historical appearance of Celtic raiders in Italy and Asia Minor. In general, there is a marked absence of high-status settlements or fortifications, and of lavishly furnished burials. Cemeteries tend to be smaller than those of the preceding phases, and the flat inhumation burials less richly equipped. Grave-goods commonly include weapons – sword, spear and sometimes shield – as well as personal ornaments, and attempts have been made to distinguish social groups on this basis. The impression is, none the less, one of a warrior society with smaller, or less sedentary, communities, rather than the hierarchical society which characterized the late Hallstatt world or the developing tribal or state system which emerges in the late La Tène period, when commercial links were once again being fostered with the Mediterranean world. The causes of the Celtic migrations of the fourth century and after are not self-evident from the traditional accounts in the historical sources, nor is it easy to distinguish cause from effect in the archaeological record. The breakdown of the late Hallstatt and early La

Tène social and economic system, whether precipitated by internal factors or by the external agency of the decline in trans-Alpine trade, must have been responsible for the widespread political turmoil which for nearly two centuries continued to threaten the periphery of the classical world.

CHAPTER 9*d*

ILLYRIANS AND NORTH-WEST GREEKS

N. G. L. HAMMOND

Our concern is mainly with the area which today comprises Epirus and north-western Macedonia in Greece, Albania and the Yugoslav cantons of Metohija and Kosovo. Its geographical features have been described in Vol. III².1, 619–24. In ancient times it was inhabited by southern Illyrian tribes and north-western Greek tribes. Our knowledge of them for the period *c.* 540 to *c.* 360 B.C. is derived from some fragments of Hecataeus and some passages in Strabo and from the findings of archaeology, especially in Albania. For the subsequent period, 360–323 B.C., there is more literary evidence, and something like a consecutive story can be told. This chapter is therefore divided chronologically into two parts.

I. THE ILLYRIANS *c.* 540–360 B.C.

The lakeland area holds a most important place in the south-west Balkans economically and strategically. Three parallel ranges, running north and south, enclose Lakes Ochrid, Prespa, Little Prespa and until recently Malik (now artificially drained); and these lakes, being more than 800 m above sea level, are exceptionally rich in fish and eels. The lowlands afford excellent arable land and pasture, and the mountains are forested and abound in game. Silver was mined in antiquity by the Damastini to the east and the north east of Lake Ochrid. The economic wealth of the area is somewhat obscured today by the fact that it is divided between three countries – the former Yugoslavia, Albania and Greece. Strategically it stands at the main crossroads of the southern Balkans. Communications from north to south, running through this high corridor, are very easy because there are no considerable rivers or mountains to cross. They are threatened at only a few places beside Lake Ochrid where the passage is narrow and confined. Communications from east to west are easier here than at any point north of the Gulf of Corinth. In antiquity there were two routes: one skirting the north shore of Lake Ochrid became famous as the Via Egnatia, and the other ran beside Lake Little Prespa and then Lake Malik. The lakeland itself has a natural line of division at the southern end of Lake Ochrid, where passage on the sides is narrow and a low range of hills forms a watershed between Lake Ochrid and Lake Malik.[1]

The northern end of the lakeland was held by an Illyrian-speaking tribe which the Greeks called the Encheleae, meaning 'eel-men'. Hecataeus, writing at the turn of the sixth century B.C., mentioned them, and it was probably from him that Strabo derived his statement, that the royal house of the Encheleae claimed descent from Cadmus and Harmonia (VII.7.5). 'Next to the Encheleae', wrote Hecataeus (*FGrH* I F 103), 'the Dexari, a tribe of Chaones', and a note was added to the fragment that they lived under Mt Amyron, which is best identified with Mt Tomor. Thus the Dexari held the area which was later called Dassaretis, namely the southern part of the lakeland and the hilly country to the south west of it. The Chaones, as we shall see (pp. 434, 437), were a group of Greek-speaking tribes, and the Dexari, or as they were called later the Dassaretae, were the most northerly member of the group. We learn the names and the positions of the southern Illyrian tribes from fragments of Hecataeus and from Strabo (VII.7.4, 8, 9). The Bylliones held the hill-country on the north side of the lower Aous and were neighbours of the Greek colonial state, Apollonia. The Parthini occupied the middle Shkumbi valley, and the Taulantii the hinterland surrounding the Greek colonial state, Epidamnus, known also as Dyrrhachium. The Abri lived north of the Mati valley and their northern neighbours were the 'Illyrii proper', that is the tribe from which the generic name 'Illyrian' was taken. The Chelidonii or 'swallow-men' were inland of the Abri. The Taulantii was the name of a cluster of small tribes (two are named in *FGrH* I F 99 and F 101); and this was probably so with the Encheleae, Bylliones, Parthini and Chelidonii. Through contact with their Greek neighbours some Illyrian tribes became bilingual (Strabo VII.7.8 *diglottoi*): in particular the Bylliones and the Taulantian tribes close to Epidamnus. We hear of some Illyrian tribes in a genealogy which was probably put together by the Greek founders of Epidamnus (preserved in Appian, *Ill.* 1); for Illyrius had sons and daughters who gave their names to the Encheleae, Taulantii, Parthini, Dardanii (in Metohija and Kosovo) and four north-westerly tribes, Autariatae or Autarieis, Perrhaebi, Dassaretii and Daorsi.[2] These Dassaretii, not to be confused with the Greek-speaking Dexari or Dassaretae, lay between the Dardanii and a coastal people, the Ardiaei (Str. VII.5.12).

The natural resources of the northern part of the lakeland were exploited during the period *c.* 540–475 by two powerful dynasties, whose royal cemeteries have been excavated. The manner of burial was the same in each. The corpse was laid in a simple trench, which was filled

[1] Hammond 1974 (E 73) 66, 77; 1981 (D 93) 201ff.   [2] Hammond 1972 (D 46) 381.

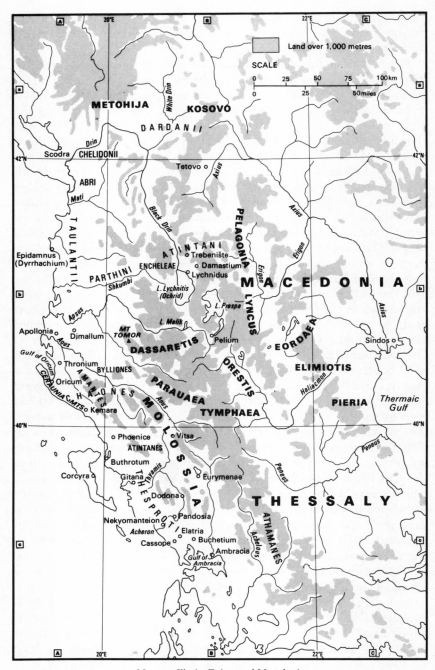

Map 13. Illyria, Epirus and Macedonia.

Fig. 15. Burial I at Trebenište. (After Filow 1929 (E 65) 4, fig. 3.)

with soil and was then covered over with a flat layer of river-bed stones. The men were buried with sword, helmet and spears, and there were fine offerings with both men and women. The richer cemetery was at Trebenište, at the very north-east corner of the lake-land basin (Fig. 15). There some of the dead wore gold death-masks (Fig. 16), gold gloves and gold sandals, and the women and the men were accompanied by gold pins and by other gold and silver ornaments. The other cemetery, at Radolište near the outflow of Lake Ochrid, had no gold objects, but in other respects the offerings with the dead were similar.[3] It is clear from the offerings that the two dynasties had very wide contacts: with the Greek world through the Greek colonies on the Adriatic coast (Epidamnus and Apollonia) and on the coast of the Thermaic Gulf (especially

[3] Lahtov 1965 (E 78) 181ff; Hammond 1967 (E 72) 437ff; *Archaeologia Yugoslavica* 5 (1964) 75. In both cemeteries the men's heads faced east and the women's west.

Fig. 16. Gold mask from Burial I at Trebenište. (After Filow 1929 (E 65) pl. 1.1.)

Potidaea), with Greek Epirus through Dodona, and with regions to the north and to the east.

The choice of Trebenište as the site of a royal cemetery is explicable only if the dynasty ruled over a wide area to the north and to the north east of it; and it was only from those directions that the gold could have come, since the nearest deposits were in Metohija–Kosovo and Kratovo. The choice of Radolište was natural to a dynasty which owned the famous fisheries at the outlet of the Lake and controlled the surrounding area. The silver which both dynasties had at their disposal came probably from the mines of the Damastini. For it is at this period that a silver coinage in large denominations was issued with the inscription *TYNTENON*, and these 'Tyntenoi' are to be identified with the Atintani who are mentioned later as living in the area to the north of Lake Ochrid (Fig. 17). Their coins reached Italy, Egypt and many parts of Asia. They belonged to the Group of 'Thraco-Macedonian' coinages of this period, and they bore the same emblems as the coins of Ichnae at the head of the Thermaic Gulf.[4]

The dynasty which buried their kings and queens at Radolište was certainly that of the Encheleae, whom Hecataeus mentioned at that time. It must have been on good terms with its richer neighbour, since Radolište and Trebenište are only some ten kilometres apart. A corrupt passage in Strabo VII.7.5, which was probably derived from Hecataeus, may help us; for it seems to record the combination of the 'Peresadyes'

---

[4] Hammond 1972 (D 46) 93, citing *Ziva Antika* 3 (1953) 261; Hammond and Griffith 1979 (D 50) 74f, 92f; Hammond 1989 (E 76) 40. Cf. *CAH* IV² 442–3.

Fig. 17. Silver triple stater of the Tynteni, about 540–511 B.C. (After N.G.L. Hammond in W.G. Moon (ed.), *Ancient Greek Art and Iconography* (1983) 247, fig. 16.3.)

and the Encheleae to create a powerful state.[5] If so, the Peresadyes was the name of the dynasty at Trebenište. The name suggests that they were Thracians, and the placing of gold foil on the face of a corpse to form either a mask or just a mouthpiece is known to have been practised in Thrace. This suggestion has been recently strengthened by the discovery of such gold death-masks, mouthpieces and pins in the warrior-graves of a dynasty at Sindos in Lower Macedonia; for this dynasty was probably that of the Thracian Edones (see *CAH* iv² 495).

The Encheleae declined first; for their cemetery went out of use early in the fifth century. The rich graves at Trebenište were followed by 'poor graves' from 475 B.C. to the end of the century; thereafter this cemetery went out of use. The silver coinage of the Tynteni ceased early in the fifth century. The period after 475 was one of comparative poverty, during which contacts were lost with mainland Greece and relations with Ionia via the Danube valley slackened. Southern Yugoslavia shared in this decline.[6]

The areas to the north and to the west of the lakeland differed from it in an important respect, the practice of tumulus-burial, which had its origins in the Bronze Age and continued in the Early Iron Age (see *CAH* iii².1, 235 and 624ff; and *CAH* iii².3, 261ff). The largest concentrations of tumuli, often numbering several hundred, were in areas attributable to specific Illyrian tribes: in the Mati valley, home of some Taulantian tribes; in the Zadrime plain, belonging probably to the Grabaei; in the Scodra region, home of the Labeatae, in the valley of the Black Drin, where the Chelidonii lived (with three great cemeteries at Çinamak, Krume and Këneta). The burials were those of warrior-rulers and their women, and the weapons and the ornaments buried with them were related not only to each other but to those in the tumulus-burials of Metohija and Kosovo, home of the Dardanii, and of central Yugoslavia, where a distinctive Illyrian culture has been called the Glasinac culture.[7]

[5] Hammond 1967 (E 72) 466; 1972 (D 46) 93; Hammond and Griffith 1979 (D 50) 63, 92.
[6] *Archaeologia Yugoslavica* 5 (1964) 78.   [7] *Iliria* 1 (1971) 348ff.

In most of these areas tumulus-burial continued into the fourth century B.C.; and it occurred less often in the hellenistic period. On the other hand, there is no evidence of any settlement worthy of the name until the second half of the fourth century B.C. Remains of a few hovels without any roof-tiles were found on the hill of Pogradec and dated by a few sherds to before 360 B.C.[8] Burials of ordinary people have not been found.

The way of life which has been associated with the practice of tumulus-burial is that form of nomadic pastoralism which engages in the transhumance of livestock, especially sheep and goats.[9] Where such pastoralism plays the major part in the economy of a country, the warrior-chiefs of the small tribes which form the individual pastoral groups are the leaders in society; and as the small tribes form into a tribal cluster, a tribal aristocracy takes control. In Illyria it seems that the warrior-chiefs dominated the settled population of agricultural peasants, because they were well armed to protect the flocks from lions, bears and wolves and to contend with their rivals. Many of those who were buried in the tumuli took with them three spears and a knife; and the richest had also a bronze helmet made in a Greek workshop and exported to Illyria, bronze greaves and occasionally a bronze cuirass.[10] We gain from Thucydides an insight into this layer of Illyrian tribal society. For in the speech which he put in the mouth of Brasidas in 423 B.C. he said of the Illyrian tribes that 'the few rule the many, the few having no other title to their despotic power than superiority in fighting' (IV.126.2 τῷ μαχόμενοι κρατεῖν). They were the terror of their neighbours in Macedonia, when they came as raiders or as mercenaries; for they were 'warrior people', ἄνθρωποι μάχιμοι (IV.125.1).

The creation of a powerful army by bringing many tribes into a single organization was achieved at the start of the fourth century by Bardylis, who seized power and set himself up as king of the Dardanii and added the lakeland to his dominions. His forces defeated the Macedonians and the Molossians time and again, and he evidently subjected the Chaonians to his rule. In 393–391 he ruled Macedonia through a puppet king; in 383–382 he overran Macedonia; and he forced the Macedonian king to pay tribute in 372 (Diod. XVI.2.2). Forming an alliance with Dionysius, tyrant of Syracuse, he killed 15,000 Molossians in battle and controlled Molossia in 385–384, until the Spartans sent an army north and drove him out (Diod. XV.13.2–3). He returned in 360 and raided far and wide. The Molossian king, Arybbas, sent the population to Aetolia and laid ambushes with his Molossian troops, who won some successes (Frontin. Str. II.5.19). Finally in 359 Bardylis killed the Macedonian king and 4,000

---

[8] *Iliria* 9/10 (1979/80) 237; cf. *Iliria* 1 (1971) 63, 67 (Rosuje); 2 (1972) 227 (Zgerdhesh); 3 (1975) 481f (Pogradec).   [9] Cf. *CAH* III².1, 235.   [10] *Iliria* 11 (1981) 46ff, 2 (1972) 460.

Fig. 18. Drachma of Damastion, about 395–380 B.C. (After N.G.L. Hammond in W.G. Moon (ed.), *Ancient Greek Art and Iconography* (1983) 254, fig. 16.21.)

of his men in battle (Diod. XVI.2.4–5), and he occupied the cities of Upper Macedonia (XVI.4.4). Although Theopompus regarded him as a mere bandit (*FGrH* 115 F 286), he was a successor to Sitalces and a forerunner of Philip II in the creation of a powerful monarchic state.[11]

Like Philip Bardylis combined military and economic developments. His subjects, the Damastini, began to issue a fine silver coinage *c.* 395, which adopted a version of the standard and some emblems of the then powerful Chalcidian League (Fig. 18). They also exported silver in ingot form. Another coinage began *c.* 365, that of 'Daparria', a mining town perhaps in Metohija–Kosovo, which used the same standard and types as the coinage of the Damastini.[12] The distribution of these coinages shows that Bardylis built up a wide region of trade within the Central Balkans and northwards to the Danube, which was quite separate from the areas of Greek trade. Dionysius of Syracuse tried to tap Bardylis' region of trade when he planted colonies in the Adriatic. It is probable that Bardylis, unlike previous Illyrian dynasts, built a few fortified cities; for Lychnidus and Pelium in the lakeland were walled sites probably before the accession of Philip.

Another area of great economic importance in Illyris was the coastal plain which afforded huge areas of excellent pasture for transhumant herds. The southern part was controlled by the Greek colonial state Apollonia, which was itself famous for its sheep. There was a well-to-do Illyrian element in the city's population (see *CAH* III².3, 267f). Apollonia maintained friendly relations with the Illyrians of the hinterland, who rented its pastures. The northern part was in dispute between the Taulantians and Epidamnus, which traded extensively with the Illyrians but seems to have been racially exclusive. In an early war the Taulantians nearly destroyed Epidamnus, and attacks by the Illyrians

[11] Hammond 1966 (E 71) 243, 248. The Dardanians were the strongest of Macedonia's neighbours, as in Justin VIII.6.3. For a different view Papazoglou 1961 (E 81) and in Garašinin 1988 (E 69) 178ff and M. B. Hatzopoulos in *ibid.*, 85ff.

[12] May 1939 (B 204); Hammond and Griffith 1979 (D 50) 189–91.

added to the horrors of the civil war of the 430s (Thuc. 1.24.4 and 6). That the influence of Apollonia was much greater than that of Epidamnus can be seen from the excavations at Belš, an open settlement almost equidistant from Apollonia and Epidamnus. The fifth century there was a transitional period during which the local 'Devolian' or 'north-west Geometric' style was dying out and imported Greek wares were being imitated, but the fourth century was marked by the dominance of imports from Apollonia.[13] The strength of Epidamnus lay in her prolific coinage, made from the silver of the Damastian mines, and the distribution of her coins shows that she traded extensively in the central and northern Balkans in the fourth century.[14]

II. THE NORTH-WEST GREEKS *c.* 540–360 B.C.

The north-west Greeks occupied a large area, extending in the west from the Gulf of Ambracia to the Gulf of Oricum and in the east to an imaginary line from the upper Achelous valley to the upper Erigon valley. Their country was well-watered, mountainous and rich in pasture and forests (see *CAH* III².1, 623f), and they engaged extensively in transhumant pastoralism. Their way of life differed little from that of the southern Illyrian tribes, and they too were organized in tribal groups (*ethne*) which were made up of constituent small tribes (*phylai*). The main groups from south to north were called Thesproti, Athamanes, Molossi, Atintanes, Chaones, Parauaei, Orestae, Elimeotae, Lyncestae and Pelagones (see *CAH* III².3, 271). The dominant groups in this period were the Chaones and the Molossi. The former were worn down by the Illyrians, especially in the reign of Bardylis, and the latter lost the last four of the groups to the rising power of Alexander I, king of Macedon, early in the fifth century.[15] But the Molossi compensated themselves by ousting the Thesproti from control of Dodona and winning the favour of Zeus (Str. VII.7.8, 11).

The importance of these tribal groups is clear from Thucydides' description of operations in 430–429 B.C. Then the Chaones took the forces of the Thesproti under their own command; the Molossi did the same with the Atintanes; and the king of the Parauaei commanded the forces of the Orestae (II.80.5–6). The command in the field was vested for the Chaones in two members of the royal house annually appointed as 'leaders' (*prostatai*); for the Molossi in the guardian (*epitropos*) of King Tharyps, who was a minor; and for the Parauaei in their king. Of the secondary groups in this coalition the Thesproti no longer had kings, the Orestae had a king who entrusted his men to the king of the Parauaei,

[13] *Iliria* 3 (1975) 444ff; 19 (1989) 205ff.   [14] Noe, *BGCH* 325.
[15] Hammond and Griffith 1979 (D 50) 63f; Strabo IX.5.11.

and we are told nothing of the Atintanes. In the coalition as a whole the Chaones took the lead in action, because they regarded themselves and were regarded by the others as the 'most warlike' (μαχιμώτατοι, 11.81.4).

The internal organization of a tribal group has become known for the Molossi (and we may extrapolate it for the others) through the publication of two inscriptions, dating to 370–368 B.C., in which citizenship was conferred by the Molossi on foreigners.[16] The officials of the Molossian state were the king, the 'leader' (*prostates*), the secretary (*grammateus*), and the ten *damiorgoi*, one each for the ten tribes which made up the group (e.g. Arctanes, Genoaei). The adult males of these tribes were the Molossi. Once a year the king of the Molossi, having sacrificed to Zeus Areios as god of war, made a formal exchange of oaths with the Molossi, he swearing to rule in accordance with the laws and they swearing to preserve the kingship in accordance with the laws (Plut. *Pyrrh.* 5.2). While the tribes shared the common name, each kept its own name, so that there were, e.g., Μολοσσοὶ Ὄμφαλες (*SGDI* 1347) and later Ὀρέσται Μολοσοί (*Ep. Chron.* 1935.248). There is an exact analogy in Macedonia, where the Orestae and the Lyncestae became 'Macedones' and were so known to Thucydides (e.g. IV.83.1 Λυγκησταὶ Μακεδόνες). There was no separate tribe named 'The Molossi'.

A later inscription, dating probably within the reign of Neoptolemus I who died *c.* 360 B.C., named the Molossian state as τὸ κοινὸν τ[ῶν Μο]λοσσῶν and mentioned not only the previous ten tribes but also five more – all from north Pindus – which had evidently entered the Molossian fold since 370–368 B.C. The state officials were now the king, the *prostates*, the secretary (*grammateus*) and a board of fifteen *synarchontes* in place of the earlier ten *damiorgoi*.[17] The kings held military command as 'Aeacidae', descended from Achilles, and they included in their genealogy one Pielus, who was a grandson of Achilles and a brother of Molossus (Paus. 1.11.1–2). This Pielus was the eponymous ancestor of the royal tribe, the Peiales, to which the royal house belonged. Similarly in Macedonia the Temenid royal house belonged to a royal tribe, the Argeadae. The credit for the enlarging of the Molossian state went to the kings in the opinion of Aristotle, who attributed to their beneficent policy the long life of the Molossian monarchy (*Pol.* 1310b35–40).

The Molossians mentioned in these three inscriptions were defined by their tribal membership only, with the exception of one man, who was cited as Ἀρκτὰν Εὐρυμεναίων. This probably means that he was a citizen of a city Eurymenae, which is known from Diod. xix.88.4–5 to have been fortified already in 312 B.C., and the inference may be made that there was no other city in the territory of the Molossian state *c.* 370–368 B.C.

[16] *ArchEph* 1956, 1ff; Hammond 1967 (E 72) 525ff; *SEG* xv 384.
[17] *Hellenika* 15, 247ff; Hammond 1967 (E 72) 527ff; *SEG* xxiii, 161; xxiv, 160f.

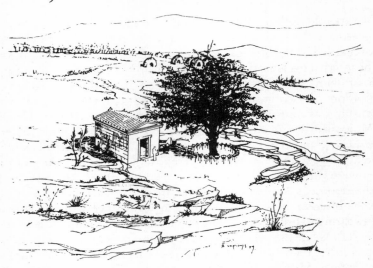

Fig. 19. The Temple of Zeus at Dodona, about 400 B.C. (After Dakaris 1971 (E 61A) 42, fig. 9.)

This is what we should expect on other grounds. Writing of the period *c*. 380–360 B.C., [Scylax] 28 and 30–2 stated that the Chaones, Thesproti, Cassopi and Molossi lived in villages (*komai*), and in 360 B.C., when Arybbas sent the population to Aetolia, he did so presumably because there were in general no fortified towns. The archaeological evidence is also clear. The earliest fortifications in the territories of the tribes were of the period 350–300 B.C. Open settlements with post-holes for round huts have been found, and the tiny village of a dozen little houses and two cemeteries at Vitsa (see *CAH* III².1, 636f) remained much the same from *c*. 900 to *c*. 300 B.C. The burial rites at Vitsa even in the fourth century[18] were as they had been at Trebeniŝte, for instance; for the men were buried with two or more spears in a shallow trench which was covered over with a layer of stones. Sanctuaries too were open. The only stone building at Dodona in this period was built *c*. 400 B.C., not as a temple but as a single room for storing votive offerings (Fig. 19), and there was no building at all at the Nekyomanteion (see *CAH* III².3, 269f).

When we turn to the northern areas, the evidence points to a similar lack of development. There was, however, a decline in tumulus-burial. This form of burial had been practised during the Bronze Age and/or Early Iron Age by those peoples who later became differentiated as Greeks, Illyrians and Thracians. This had been so in northern Epirus. The latest burials in excavated tumuli (often few out of many) indicate

---

18 *ArchDelt* 28 (1973) Chr. 402; Vokotopoulou 1986 (E 88) 328.

that the practice ceased at Bajkaj and Vodhinë *c.* 900 B.C., at Dukat *c.* 700, at Vajzë *c.* 650, at Kuç i zi *c.* 500, at Piskovë near Permet probably *c.* 300 and at Cepune *c.* 250.[19] A very large cemetery, estimated to have a hundred tumuli, is being excavated at Koutsokrano in Pogoni, the homeland of the Molossian group of tribes. It was used probably by the royal tribe of that group, the Peiales, and by the royal family, which, we may be sure, practised the same rite of tumulus-burial as their ancestor Achilles had practised in the epic poems. This cemetery was in regular use from the tenth to the fourth century inclusive.[20] Elsewhere it seems that fashion changed earlier where there was a main line of communication, and later in remote areas as at Piskovë and Cepune. Tumulus-burial lasted much longer in the territories of the southern Illyrian tribes to the north of the Via Egnatia line.

The tribal way of life which we have been describing was entirely different from that of a Greek city state. For it lacked such developments as urban life, walled fortifications, republicanism, democracy, political awareness and even hoplite warfare. Greek writers always drew the contrast between 'the Greek city' on the coast of Epirus and the inland tribes (the Greek cities being Ambracia, Buchetium, Elatria, Pandosia, Oricum and Thronium); and Thucydides, [Scylax] and [Scymnus] had no hesitation in calling the tribes 'barbarians' (Thuc. II.80.5–6 and 81.3 and 6; [Scylax] 32; [Scymn.] 444ff). On the other hand, they never called them Illyrians. That name was given by Thucydides to the Taulantii, by Herodotus to the Encheleae, by Strabo's source (perhaps Hecataeus) to the mountains north of the Shkumbi river (beside which the Via Egnatia ran; Str. VII.7.4), and by Strabo to specific tribes south of that river. Rather, the distinction was clearly maintained between three groups of people: Illyrian tribes, Epirotic tribes and Greece proper, 'Hellas', which began with the Ambraciotes and the Acarnanians (Str. VII.5.1; VII.7.1, 6; [Scylax] 33). The habitat of those Epirotic tribes was described as 'the continuous barbarous stretch between the Illyrian mountains and Hellas in the south'. 'The Macedonian tribes' were rated with the Epirotic tribes and not with Hellas (Str. VII.5.1.).

That the Epirotic tribes and the Macedonian tribes spoke Greek in the fifth century B.C., and indeed much earlier, has been argued in *CAH* III².3, 284.[21] The conclusive evidence is in the decrees of the Molossian state *c.* 369 B.C., which are entirely Greek in language, onomastics and tribal forms. The names of the persons were given to them in the fifth century, presumably by Greek parents and grandparents, and the names

---

[19] Cf. *CAH* III².1, 636; adding *Iliria* 7/8 (1977–9) 143; 11 (1981) 255 (Piskove).
[20] Preliminary reports by E. Andreou in *Archaiologia* 3 (1982) 54–60; cf. *Arch. Rep. 1985/6* 52 (Merope). For the territory of Pogoni being the Molossian homeland see Hammond 1967 (E 72) 703.
[21] Hammond 1967 (E 72) 422ff.

of the tribes had no doubt a very long history. Moreover, as the Molossian state can have formed only out of tribes of common language, it follows that the 'Thesprotian' tribes spoke Greek, as three such tribes were members of the Molossian state. At the end of the sixth century, when the Orestae and their neighbours were 'Molossian' tribes, they too must have spoken Greek to join that state. Finally, if the Amymni of one decree are the same as the Amymones, a Chaonian tribe (*FGrH* 703 (Proxenus) F 6), it follows that the Chaonian group spoke Greek, as we should indeed infer from the fact that the Greek-speaking Thesprotians accepted Chaonian command in 429 B.C., and that the Greek-speaking Epirote League later accepted the Chaonians as members. Nor was this Greek speech derived from the Corinthians and Corinthian colonists; for the dialect of the inscriptions was not Corinthian Doric (indeed even the alphabet was not Corinthian).[22] It was evidently their own traditional Greek, probably West Greek, as some recorded inquiries at Dodona seem to show.

While the Greek cities on the coast kept pace with Greek culture, the north-west tribes were utterly retarded. Local hand-made pottery, sometimes with 'north-west Geometric' decoration, continued through the fourth century alongside the first generally imported pottery, plain black-glaze. Dodona was an oasis, in that southern Greeks deposited bronze statuettes (Fig. 20) and other offerings; but even there very little imported pottery was found in extensive excavations. But the shrine's period of popularity with the southern Greeks was short, *c.* 600–470 B.C. It went out of fashion during the rest of the fifth century and recovered slowly in the fourth century. Its contacts were always strong locally and in the north. Only one form of Greek and particularly Corinthian art, namely bronze vessels of all kinds, was in constant demand. Many specimens were dedicated at Dodona, and many were placed with the dead at Vitsa (Fig. 21); and a hoard of them was found at Votonosi.[23] Metal containers have always been preferred by semi-nomadic groups of shepherds who practise transhumance, and it is no accident that Vitsa and Votonosi are high places with summer pastures. The leaders of these groups in antiquity had the means to buy fine metal ware.

By 360 B.C. inland Epirus was ready to develop. Its way of life and its tribal society were such as had existed for centuries among the Dorians of the Dark Age in the Peloponnese (see *CAH* III². 1, 703f). But the menace of Illyrian conquest under Bardylis galvanized the most vigorous of the tribes into forming a military coalition, similar in a military sense to the Peloponnesian League. But what was more important, they

[22] Dakaris 1972 (E 63) 79.
[23] Vokotopoulou 1975 (E 86) 104; N. M. Verdelis in *BCH* 73 (1949) 19f; Ph.M. Petsas in *ArchEph* 1952, 7f.

Fig. 20. Bronze figurines from Dodona: (a) horseman; mid-sixth century B.C.; Athens, National Museum. (b) Zeus; mid-fifth century B.C.; Athens, National Museum; (c) eagle from a sceptre; fifth-century B.C.; Ioannina Museum. (After Dakaris 1971 (E 61A) pls. 25, 28, 32.)

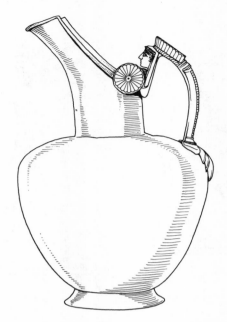

Fig. 21. Bronze oenochoe from Vitsa, 2258/T 66; mid-sixth century B.C. (After Vokotopoulou 1986 (E 88) II, fig. 29.)

created a well-knit egalitarian tribal state, which had the great superiority over the Peloponnesian League that it possessed a common citizenship.

III. ILLYRIANS AND NORTH-WEST GREEKS *c.* 360–323 B.C.

Philip's crushing defeat of Bardylis in 358 B.C. revolutionized the situation in the north-western area. The Illyrian terror of the last forty years was ended; for Bardylis accepted an ignominious peace, and Philip deprived him of the lakeland base from which he had ravaged Epirus and Macedonia. For on annexing the eastern part of the lakeland and on barring the north-eastern side of Lake Lychnitis Philip was in a position to enfilade any Illyrian force in the western lakeland. The effect on the Greek-speaking tribes was especially important. The report in Diodorus (using Ephorus) XVI.8.1 that 'Philip made all the peoples who lived there as far as the lake subject to himself' is more significant than it appears. In the last years of Perdiccas III the Pelagones were independent and hostile (*IG* II² 190 and 110), Orestis was part of the Molossian state (*SEG* XXIII.471.13; Hammond 1967 (E 72) 527f), and Lycnus was in Illyrian hands in 359 B.C. It was not enough for Philip after his victory to recover just Lyncus and create a narrow salient by advancing to Lake Lychnitis. He had to protect his flanks. Now or soon afterwards he incorporated Pelagonia and Orestis in his kingdom, and he created a new canton of Macedonia in the south-eastern lakeland.[24]

The political situation among the north-western tribes *c.* 360–355 B.C. is known from an inscription which records the hosts of sacred envoys from Epidaurus (*IG* IV² 95 II 23ff). The regional name 'Epirus', occurring here for the first time in an inscription, was applied in effect to the coastal area between the Buthrotum Channel and the western part of the Gulf of Ambracia. The other regional names were 'Corcyra', 'Chaonia' and 'Artichia'; and since they, unlike 'Epirus', provided hosts, there was some political organization behind each of them – a Greek polis in the island, a tribal state of Chaones, and a tribal state probably of Atintanes. Next there were tribal states: 'Thesproti', providing probably three hosts, and 'Molossoi' with one host, 'Tharyps', i.e. the king usually known as Arybbas. There were also Greek cities: Pandosia (one of three Elean colonies) and Ambracia. 'Cassopa', which was mentioned twice, was either the region of the Cassopaei (or Cassopi, as in [Scylax] 31) or else their centre, being a shrine rather than a town.[25]

The nature of the Thesprotian tribal state is known from an inscription found at Goumani and dated to the second half of the fourth century.[26] It was dated by the name of the 'leader of Thesprotoi' (*prostates*), evidently annually appointed, and by the name of the priest of Themis, to whom a liberated slave was being dedicated. The tribal affiliation of the liberator was given as ᾿Ικαδωτός, and this was one of the fourteen or so tribes which we know to have been members of the Thesprotian state at one time or another. For the Chaonian tribal state we have numerous inscriptions from Buthrotum, beginning in the third century, which show that they too had an annual 'leader' (*prostates*). This state too consisted of many tribes and at least one of the tribes was itself a cluster of lesser tribes.[27] We do not know the extent of the Chaonian state *c.* 360–355 B.C.

Thus the north-western area was divided between independent Greek city states on the coast; two small tribal states (Cassopaei and probably Atintanes); and three large tribal states, which had long been rivals of one another and still were. The Molossian state had recently expanded at the expense of the Macedonians by attracting the Orestae. All these states were Greek-speaking. Had it not been so, the sacred envoys would not have visited them.

Philip made marriages of state in the two years 359–357: with Phila a

[24] Hammond 1981 (D 93) 212f.   [25] Hammond 1980 (E 75) 9f.

[26] Dakaris 1972 (E 63) 86f and in Cabanes 1987 (E 59) 75.

[27] Hammond 1967 (E 72) 655; Cabanes 1987 (E 59) 186ff; *Iliria* 11 (1981) 231.

princess of Elimea, Audata an Illyrian princess, Philinna an aristocrat of
Larissa in Thessaly, and Olympias a Molossian princess. This last
marriage was accompanied by an alliance between Philip and Arybbas,
the uncle of Olympias; indeed the two kings became brothers-in-law,
because Arybbas was married to the elder sister of Olympias. Thus
Philip chose to align himself not with Chaonia or Thesprotia but with
Molossia, the strongest of the three, which was soon to be his immediate
neighbour in north Pindus. Indeed the superior economic strength of
Molossia was shown by the fact that it alone was issuing coinage at this
time. Its bronze coinage started probably when the Molossian state
entered the Athenian Confederacy c. 375 B.C. and could trade overseas;
for between 380 and 360 B.C. it acquired a strip of coast on the Gulf of
Ambracia. The start of a very short-lived silver coinage is controversial.
Who supplied the silver ore? The nearest source, the mines of Damastium, were controlled by Philip from 358 B.C. onwards, and the next
nearest, the mines of the Pelagiteis, who coined first c. 358 B.C., were
probably near Tetovo. There are resemblances between the Molossian
silver coins and the Pelagitan silver coins, and the common link may
have been Philip. It is possible, then, that Philip supplied silver ore to
Arybbas, but only for a few years after 357 B.C.[28]

Philip's other concern in his early years was Illyris. After his defeat of
Bardylis the strongest state was that of the Grabaei, ruled by a
homonymous king, Grabus, a descendant no doubt of the King Grabus
with whom Athens entered into alliance when she was active in the
region of Epidamnus in the 430s. The homeland of the Grabaei, Mirditë,
was and is rich in deposits of copper and iron, and its eastern territories
marched with Philip's sphere of influence in the western lakeland.[29]
Defeated by Philip in 358/7 Grabus allied himself briefly with the
Chalcidian League and then in 356 B.C. with Athens, Lyppeius and
Cetriporis;[30] but he was defeated that summer and compelled 'to side
with the Macedonians' (Diod. XVI.22.3). This victory isolated the
Parthini and the Taulantii, who perforce (we may infer) became allies of
Philip. He consolidated his advance by building fortified posts in Illyris.
There was truth in the remark of Isocrates in 346 B.C. that 'Philip had
become controller and master of the bulk of Illyrians apart from those
inhabiting the Adriatic' (*Philippus* 21); for the Adriatic Sea began then to
the north of the river Drin (see Str. VII.7.8, defining rivers entering the
Ionian Gulf).

Shortly after 346 B.C. Philip defeated 'the Dardani and the rest of his

[28] Hammond 1967 (E 72) 543ff; Hammond and Griffith 1979 (D 50) 668, n. 4; otherwise, Franke
1961 (E 67) 89ff.
[29] Hammond 1956 (E 70) 244; 1976 (E 74) 74f; note *homoroi* in Diod. XVI.22.3.
[30] Bengtson, (*SdA*) 2, no. 307; Tod no. 157.

neighbours' in a major campaign, which included an act of deception or treachery on his part (Justin VIII.6.3, deception as in Polyaen. IV.2.5); this brought Cleitus, son of Bardylis, into a position of dependence. Next, in 344/3, 'invading Illyris with a large force', Philip defeated the Ardiaei, whose territory extended northwards of Scodra to the river Naro (Neretva).[31] In 339 B.C. he reduced the Triballi in the area of Niš, and in 337 B.C. he fought against Pleurias, king probably of some strong tribe which lay between the Ardiaei and the Triballi.[32] Thus Philip imposed his will on the bulk of the Illyrian tribes by the only means which they respected, 'superiority in fighting' ($\tau\hat{\omega}\ \mu\alpha\chi\acute{o}\mu\epsilon\nu\sigma\iota\ \kappa\rho\alpha\tau\epsilon\hat{\iota}\nu$). In the Illyrian wars he made his victories decisive by long cavalry pursuits (e.g. Didymus *in Dem.* col. 12.64); for thereby he achieved his aim of forcing the mounted tribal aristocrats to accept his hegemony. Thereafter he let them run their internal tribal affairs, even leaving a king such as Cleitus in office; what he required was peace among the tribes, acceptance of his own foreign policy, payment especially in precious metals, and the provision of elite troops at his desire. There is no indication that he revolutionized their way of life by planting cities or encouraging native towns, as he did in Thrace, but the effects of peace and economic co-operation can be seen in a coin hoard at Rhizon in the Gulf of Kotor. Whereas the Greek cities of the north-west region adopted the Corinthian standard *c.* 350 B.C. and formed a *koine* of trade with South Italy and Sicily, the coinage of Damastium and other mines under the influence of Philip was dominant in the western Balkans, so much so that at Rhizon it had an advantage of two to one over the coinages of the Greek cities. One beneficiary was Epidamnus, which linked the two economic spheres.[33]

Philip acted differently in Epirus. Arybbas too was a wealthy and ambitious monarch, thrice victorious at Olympia and at Delphi and traditionally a close friend of Athens, the enemy of Macedon. Philip forestalled any move against himself by invading Molossia, removing Alexander, Olympias' brother, to his own court as a political pawn, and annexing Parauaea, Tymphaea and, if he had not already done so, Orestis (D. 1.13; Tod no. 173 *fin.*; Justin VIII.6.4–5). From this time, *c.* 350 B.C., it is probable that the bronze coinage of Philip was used instead of the Molossian coinage in Epirus. Philip returned in winter 343/2 B.C. He expelled Arybbas and put Alexander on the Molossian throne. Secure in his loyalty, Philip captured three Greek cities – Buchetium, Elatria and Pandosia – and incorporated them and their lands in the Molossian state, and he encouraged the Cassopaeans to form a political centre at the

---

[31] Philip was wounded while pursuing the Ardiaean king, Pleuratus; for the date see Hammond 1966 (E 71) 245.   [32] Perhaps the Autariatae; see Hammond 1966 (E 71) 245.

[33] May 1939 (B 204) 199f and Noe, *BGCH* 325.

shrine of Cassope. The Molossians, the Cassopaeans and the Eleaei (or Eleatae), who held the rich plain of the Acheron, now issued coinage as independent states, using at first the bronze coins of Philip which were overstruck with their own names.[34] Whether Philip made any attack on Ambracia is uncertain. In any case, the increasing power of Molossia and its allies, who now controlled the entry to the Gulf of Ambracia, was a threat to Ambracia. But Corinth and Athens came to its aid.

The alliance between Molossia and Macedonia was cemented in 336 B.C. by the marriage of Alexander to Cleopatra, daughter of Philip by Olympias and so a sister of the Macedonian prince Alexander. The assassination of Philip did not weaken that alliance; for the two Alexanders remained close friends. But the settlement in the Balkans was severely shaken. Alexander had to reassert Macedonia's authority by 'superiority in fighting'. He did so decisively in 335 B.C. (see below). After the decisive victory in Illyris the long pursuit by his cavalry[35] resulted in the submission of the rebellious kings, Glaucias of the Taulantians and Cleitus of the Dardanians. Meanwhile, his ally the king of the Agrianians ravaged the lands of the Autariatae, who had planned to support the rebels. In the next year he took Illyrian troops to Asia, no doubt as Philip would have done, and he summoned many others, e.g. 3,000 in autumn 331 B.C. Returning warriors brought new forms of wealth and new ideas to their tribes, and towards the end of the century small urban centres began to develop in southern Illyris, where Illyrians and Greeks were in close proximity; for instance, at Krotine (Dimale or Dimallum), Irmaj, Berat and Pogradec. The most remarkable monument of Macedonian influence is to be seen at Lower Selcë by the upper Shkumbi in the rock-cut facaded tombs which have startling similarities to the largest tomb at Vergina (Philip's Tomb) and to the 'Tomb of Amyntas' at Fethiye (Telmessus). One thinks of an Illyrian officer of Alexander's army and his descendants ruling over the Parthini.[36]

The successes of the Molossian state constituted a challenge to its rivals. The Thesprotian state began c. 335 B.C. to issue its own bronze coinage, and the first mention of the Chaonian state as ἁ πόλις ἁ τῶν Χαόνων occurs about then in an inscription at Dodona. In 334 B.C., at the invitation of the Tarentines, Alexander crossed to Italy with fifteen

[34] Hammond 1967 (E 72) 541f; Hammond and Griffith 1979 (D 50) 307f; otherwise, Franke 1961 (E 67) 44f.

[35] Hammond 1978 (K 22) 139f. For the battle being in Illyris see Hammond and Walbank 1988 (D 51) 41, n. 1. A location inside Macedonia is given by Bosworth, below, p. 796.

[36] *Iliria* 2 (1972) 48 (Irmaj); 3 (1975) 500 (Berat); 4 (1976) 367–79 (Selce); 389f (Krotine); 9/10 (1979/80) 237 (Pogradec). For 'Pithon Illyrius' see Justin XIII.4.13 and XIII.8.10; and for the predominance of Macedonian coinage and especially of Alexander's European issues in Dassaretis see *Iliria* 15 (1985) 192.

warships, some cavalry transports and many merchant vessels, and he campaigned there until his death late in 331 B.C. (see below). As Molossian king, he commanded the forces of 'The Molossians and their allies', and in Italy he coined in his own name. 'The Molossians and their allies' was a new political body, analogous to the Peloponnesian League and the Second Athenian Alliance or Confederacy. Its organization was probably bicameral, as in the Second Athenian Alliance, the Molossians as *hegemones* deliberating by themselves and the allies deliberating in their own council. It made alliances with other states, e.g. with Tarentum, which did not become members of the political body, and it had its foreign representatives; for a decree at Dodona mentions some Zacynthians as 'consuls' (*proxenoi*) of 'Molossians and allies'.[37] The Molossian state was described at this time as Μολοσσῶν τὸ κοινόν and one of its decrees was dated by king, 'leader' (*prostates*) and 'secretary' (*SGDI* 1334).

Although the overall achievements of 'The Molossians and their allies' in Italy were very remarkable, the war ended with the destruction of the Epirote army and the death of the king (Livy VIII.24.7–14). Such a total disaster shattered the prestige and crippled the strength of Molossia as the holder of the hegemony. The Molossian Alliance collapsed and a new political organisation, 'The Epirote Alliance', took its place (*SGDI* 1336 οἱ σύμμαχοι τῶν Ἀπειρωτᾶν). The date suggested by the present writer in 1967 for its emergence, between 331 and 325, has been narrowed to c. 330 by the recent publication of an inscription recording the hosts of sacred envoys from Argos, in which Ἄπειρος appears as a political unit and its representative is Cleopatra, the widow of Alexander. Thus the royal family of the Molossians still kept its privileged position and its prestige in the new state. The coinages of the tribal groups – the Molossi, Cassopaei, Eleaei and Thesproti – now came to an end, and a new coinage was issued with the legend ΑΠΕΙΡΩΤΑΝ, marking it as the coinage of 'The Epirotes'. The constitution of 'The Epirotes' was thought worthy of description by Aristotle, but his description has not survived (fr. 494, Rose).

The Epirote Alliance was evidently an equal alliance of member-states. This form of alliance involved the maintenance of the *status quo* for each member-state in relation to the other member-states. Thus the Molossian state, for instance, could not expand by attracting tribes from other member-states; rather, it was frozen at its current size within the body of the Alliance. The extent of the Alliance's territory can be inferred from the list of hosts of sacred envoys from Argos of c. 330 B.C., in which the states independent of Ἄπειρος may be restored with

---

[37] Cited with illustration by Dakaris 1964 (E 61) pl. 4.

probability as [Φοιν]ικα, [Κορκυ]ρα and ['Ωρικος.Κ]νημος.[38] The hosts at Phoenice were the representatives of the Chaonian state. Either that state or Corcyra controlled Buthrotum, since it did not figure in the list. Oricum and its harbour Πάνορμος . . . ἐν μέσοις τοῖς Κεραυνίοις ὄρεσι (Str. 324) were independent. It follows that Ἄπειρος stood for the Molossians, Thesprotians, Cassopaeans and Atintanes only.

That there was a variety of political entities, within what we call 'Epirus' in a geographical sense, can be discerned also in the arrangements made after the death of Alexander the Great in 323 B.C. When we put together the fragments of Arrian and Dexippus (FGrH 156 F 1,7 and 100 F 8,3), which came from a single source, Hieronymus of Cardia, we find that Antipater was to rule over 'Epirus extending up to the Ceraunian mountains' (Arrian) and 'as much of Epirus as he had ruled while Alexander was still alive' (Dexippus). In other words a part of Epirus (as a geographical term) was independent and had been, namely the territory of the Epirote Alliance. That part of Epirus over which Antipater had authority was, as seen from Macedonia, the area which lay between Macedonia and the Ceraunian mountains – namely the territories of the Chaonians and of Oricum. To the south of the Epirote Alliance Antipater ruled over 'all the Greeks' (Arrian and Dexippus both saying 'all'). They started with the people of Ambracia.[39]

What caused the formation of the Epirote Alliance is not known. We may suspect some prompting by Antipater, supported by Alexander, who wanted to curb the activities of the Molossian state where Cleopatra and Olympias were so influential. The function of the Epirote Alliance was to decide matters of foreign policy, control its own financial system, appoint or depose its commander-in-chief, and conduct its own diplomacy; and it had a common citizenship. But it was not a close-knit sympolity. The individual states were still too strong. They continued to be each a cluster of tribes, each tribe having its own koinon, and to manage their internal affairs. The pastoral way of life in which the tribes were rooted so firmly was still predominant, but at the very close of this period there were a few fortified sites which acted as defences for a settled population and as centres of political organization. Although the criteria for dating such fortifications are imprecise, it seems that by 323 B.C. citadels rather than wall-circuits were built at the following places within the territory of the Epirote Alliance: Cassope for the Cassopaeans, Argos Hippaton (Kastrion) and Gitana (Goumani) for the Thesprotians, and

---

[38] BCH 90 (1966) 156, 710; SEG xxiii, 189; Hammond 1980 (E 75) 14ff; Cabanes 1987 (E 59) 173ff. Professor S. G. Miller kindly informed the writer that the restoration 'Korkura' in line 13 of Charneux's text is confirmed by his unpublished Nemea text (in Hesp 47 (1979) 79, n. 19 there is an error: line 16 should be 13). This supersedes my proposed restoration 'Kemara' and Charneux's proposed 'Kassopa'.　　[39] Hammond 1980 (E 75) 472ff.

Dodona and Eurymenae (Kastritsa) for the Molossians.[40] To the north the Chaonians had expelled the Corcyraeans from their holdings on the mainland and built fortifications at Buthrotum, Kalivo and Kara-Ali-Bey; and they had a citadel at their political centre, Phoenice.[41] The state represented by 'Kemara' in the list of hosts had two centres, Himarrë and Borsh, both probably fortified, and farther north the Amantes had strong points at Kanine and at their political centre, Plocë.[42] Inland, however, in central Epirus the only fortified places were in the plain of Ioannina, the centre of the Molossian state.

Thus the north-west Greek-speaking tribes were at a half-way stage economically and politically, retaining the vigour of a tribal society and reaching out in a typically Greek manner towards a larger political organization. In 322 B.C., when Antipater banished the anti-Macedonian leaders of the Greek states to live 'beyond the Ceraunian mountains' (Plut. *Phoc.* 29.3), he regarded Epirus as an integral part of the Greek-speaking mainland. It was to prove to be so in the hellenistic world.

[40] Dakaris 1971 (E 62) 107f, 130; Hammond 1967 (E 72) 659; Dakaris 1972 (E 63) 91.
[41] Hammond 1967 (E 72) 572f.   [42] *Iliria* 7/8 (1977–9) 271; 9/10 (1979/80) 268; 2 (1972) 81.

CHAPTER 9e

THRACIANS AND SCYTHIANS

ZOFIA H. ARCHIBALD

I. THE FOUNDING RULERS OF THE ODRYSIAN KINGDOM —
TERES AND SITALCES

Following the three and a half decade occupation of its southern flanks by Persian troops, the post-war history of Thrace in the fifth century is marked by a rapid development of tribal political power, with the emergence of elite military hierarchies, distinct regional centres of authority and the assumption of regular political and trading relations with Greek cities.[1] Precisely what role the Persian campaigns played in this crystallization is disputable. The scarcity of contemporary literary references makes it difficult to assess the chronological relationship between given tribal entities and specific geographical regions. Nor is it easy to integrate historical facts with the archaeological material, which becomes increasingly more abundant from the second quarter of the fifth century onwards.

The most significant tribal group to emerge on the international stage was that of the Odrysians. Much of what is known of the founder of their ruling dynasty, Teres (Thuc. II.29.2–3) is anecdotal, whether it be his longevity (Lucian Macr. 10) or the rustic character of his preferred life-style (Plut. Mor. 174D).[2] The only detailed incident recorded from his reign, a surprise night attack by the Thyni during which Teres was deprived of his baggage train and his troops suffered heavy losses, is reported in the reminiscences of a later ruler, Seuthes II (Xen. An. VII.2.22). The dates and duration of Teres' reign are unknown and Thucydides does not make it clear whether it was he or his son Sitalces who extended Odrysian power towards the Aegean on the south and the Danube on the north (II.29.2; Diod. XII.50.1).

Herodotus' passing reference to the Odrysians in his account of

---

The author is indebted to Professor Alexander Fol for providing a draft version of this section.

[1] Danov 1976 (E 105) 282–93; Fol 1972 (E 118) 73–93, 115–27; *CAH* IV² 234–53, for the Persian Wars, though Hammond's views on the extent of Persian occupation are not shared by the present writer.   [2] Also attributed to the Scythian ruler Atheas at 792C.

Darius' progress through Thrace to Scythia (IV.92) tells us nothing of their relative power at the beginning of the fifth century, although he had obviously heard a good deal about Odrysian relations with the Scythians. Teres evidently aimed at establishing positive diplomatic links with the most powerful Scythian leader, Ariapeithes, by offering the latter his daughter in marriage. Teres' son and successor, Sitalces, did more than merely maintain this family connexion. He turned what might have been a serious political threat into a real diplomatic coup (Hdt. IV.80). Ariapeithes' son by Teres' daughter, Octamasades, did not succeed his father, and became the focus of disaffection in Scythia against the new king, Scylas, himself the son of Ariapeithes and a Greek woman from Histria. An unnamed brother of Sitalces, evidently perceived as a rival by him, joined Octamasades' circle. When Scylas sought Sitalces' support against the insurgent Octamasades, Sitalces opted for the latter. Not only did he thereby persuade his cousin to hand over the offending brother but also made Octamasades beholden to him for the legitimacy of his position. This incident seems to have taken place in Octamasades' youth and at a time when Sitalces' succession was not entirely secure. He is not designated king ($\Theta\rho\eta\ddot{\iota}\kappa\omega\nu$ $\beta\alpha\sigma\iota\lambda\epsilon\dot{\upsilon}s$) as he is, for instance, regarding the events of 430/29 (Hdt. VII.137; Thuc. II.67.1). Sitalces was a well-established monarch by the time of the Athenian alliance, so this event could date at the latest to the 440s. The marriage alliance between Ariapeithes and Teres' daughter would then belong to the 460s if not earlier.[3]

The core of Odrysian land is impossible to disengage from their later fifth-century acquisitions, but this may have included, as it undoubtedly did during the reign of Sitalces, the middle course of the Maritsa (Hebrus) river, which would have given them an economic as well as a strategic advantage.[4] The Maritsa valley is the prime thoroughfare into the east Balkans and control of its middle and lower reaches gave access to the Thracian interior and much of the hinterland besides. At Mezek, near Svilengrad, above the confluence of the Maritsa and Arda (Fig. 22), is a tumulus cemetery stretching back to the early centuries of the first millennium B.C., with elaborate built tombs and rich grave-goods dating from the fourth century B.C. The spectacular later burials almost certainly belonged to Odrysian princes, and since this is clearly a dynastic cemetery of exceptional character, is likely to represent a major Odrysian centre.[5] Traces of an earlier hillfort settlement were surveyed at the time of the cemetery excavations in the 1930s. How far Odrysian power extended into the Thracian Plain before Sitalces' reign is still a matter of dispute. The distributions both of coin hoards and of prestigious burials

---

[3] Danov 1976 (E 105) 288.   [4] Fol and Spiridonov 1983 (E 120) II 47–8 with references.
[5] Filow 1937 (E 116); Velkov 1937 (E 164).

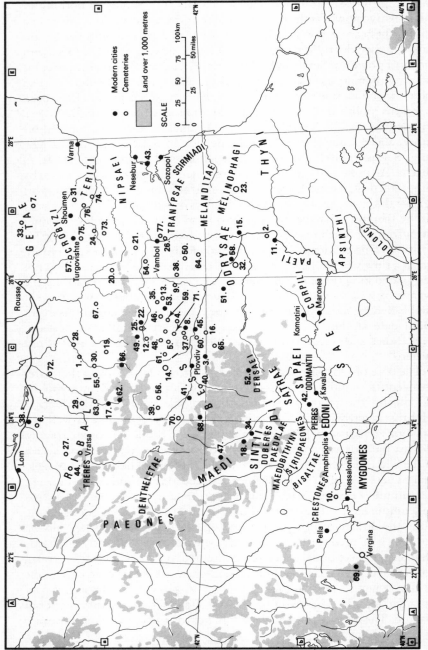

Map 14. Thrace: Thracian sites and tribal territories of the classical period. (See also Maps 16, 17, pp. 724, 740.)

1 Alexandrovo	27 Krivodol	53 Stara Zagora
2 Arzos	28 Letnitsa	54 Staro Selo
3 Asenovgrad	29 Loukuvit	55 Stojanovo
4 Bednyakovo	30 Lovech	56 Strelcha
5 Brezovo	31 Madara	57 Svetlen
6 Boukyovtsi	32 Mezek	58 Svilengrad
7 Branichevo	33 Mumdjilar	59 Sarnevets
8 Chirpan	34 Nevrokop	60 Tatarevo
9 Daskal Atanassovo	35 Nova Mahala	61 Tchernozem
10 Derveni	36 Novoselets	62 Teteven
11 Didimotikhion	37 Opulchenets	63 Toros
12 Dolno Sahrane	38 Oryahovo	64 Topolovgrad
13 Dulboki	39 Panagyurischte	65 Topolovo
14 Duvanlij	40 Pastousha	66 Troian
15 Edirne	41 Pazardjik	67 Turnovo
16 Ezerovo	42 Philippi	68 Velingrad
17 Glozhene	43 Pomorie	69 Beroea
18 Gotse Delchev	44 Pudrija	70 Vetren
19 Gradnitsa	45 Purvomaj	71 Voinitsine
20 Izgrev	46 Pustrovo	72 Vulchitrun
21 Kaloyanovo	47 Razlog	73 Vurbitsa
22 Kazanluk	48 Rozovets	74 Yankovo
23 Kirklareli	49 Seuthopolis	75 Yourukler
24 Kjolmen	50 Skalitsa	76 Zlokoutchene
25 Koprinka	51 Slavyanovo	77 Kabyle (Cabyle)
26 Kozarevo	52 Smoljan	

of the fifth century B.C. (Figs 23 & 24), suggest that the most important centres of south Thracian tribal power were concentrated here.[6]

The most detailed account of Odrysian territorial domains is found in Thucydides' description of the tribes which supplied levies for Sitalces' invasion of Macedonia in 429 (II.96ff). The historian begins with the tribal homelands (without specifying their whereabouts) and goes on to list those tribes subject to Sitalces: the Getae, north of the Haemus range, some of the 'independent' hill tribesmen, including the Dii, in Rhodope; the Paeonian Agriani and Laeaei, who obviously formed the western-most limits of Sitalces' control, with the Treres and Tilataei in the north west, Mount Scombrus (Vitosha) forming a natural boundary between these tributary groups and the independent Triballi further to the north west, as far as the Danube. Many important tribes are not mentioned in

---

[6] Domaradzki 1987 (E 109).

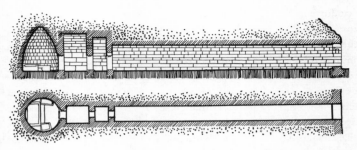

Fig. 22.   Tholos tomb at Mal Tepe (near Mezek). (After Venedikov and Gerassimov 1975 (E 171) 60, fig. 36.)

Fig. 23.   Gold ornament from Duvanlij; Plovdiv Archaeological Museum. (After Venedikov 1976 (E 170A) no. 157; Filow 1934 (E 117) pl. 2.3.)

this survey, though Thucydides states categorically that the Odrysians at this time controlled the whole coastline between Abdera and the mouth of the Danube (II.97.1).

The varied geography of the Balkan peninsula would have made so vast an area difficult to control effectively and the extent of real Odrysian authority doubtless depended on its enforceability. From this point of view, the triangle of land between the Haemus and Mt Vitosha in the north west, skirting Rhodope towards the mouth of the Hebrus in the south, formed a coherent and manageable unit. The Getae south of the Danube were apparently more accessible to southern pressures, whether through the eastern passes of the Haemus or by sea, than those tribes north of the west and central Haemus, principally the Triballi, and those

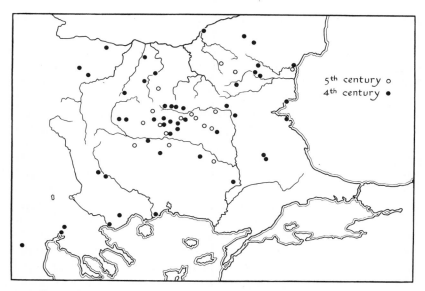

Fig. 24. Finds of imported metalware in Thrace of the fifth and fourth centuries B.C.

inhabiting the higher reaches of Rhodope. Sitalces' progress westwards in 429 suggests that, for a time at least, he was able to impose his authority over the Thracians of the middle Strymon valley, the Maedi, and south of the Rupel Pass, the Sintii and others. That Sitalces had more permanent ambitions in these regions seems clear from an earlier campaign against the Paeonians, when he cut a way through the forest (Thuc. II.98.1–2), as well as a later campaign against the Triballi in 424, in which he was killed (Thuc. IV.101.5).

Unfortunately, the historian has nothing to say about the relationship between the Odrysians and the Bessi, in the upper reaches of the Hebrus and foothills of Rhodope (Hdt. VII.110; Str. VII.331 F 48). The term Bessi may be an alternate designation for a functional group, perhaps priests and prophets, amongst the mountain tribesmen who included the Satri and Dii, united by a common lifestyle and beliefs. Later the term could even be applied to the Thracians as a whole.[7] The Satri, Dii and others are associated in the sources with the cult of Dionysus; they shared the same cult centres in Rhodope and were primarily mountain people, although archaeological evidence shows that culturally the communities of Rhodope extended into or had close links with the western parts of the Thracian Plain.[8] In Sitalces' time political control over these areas seems to have given way to that of the Odrysians, as Thucydides implies. But

[7] Sarafov 1974 (E 156), 1974 (E 157); Fol and Spiridonov 1983 (E 120) I 116 with references, II 24–5, 52–3.   [8] Gizdova 1990 (in E 162).

the exceptionally rich burials spanning the second and final quarters of the fifth century B.C. in the tumulus cemetery of Duvanlij, north of Plovdiv, indicate the continuing prosperity of a local elite which clearly enjoyed Odrysian backing, even if its members were not themselves Odrysians. The male warriors were buried with fine imported silver and bronze-ware, prestige armour and weapons both of native and imported manufacture; their female counterparts with exquisite gold jewellery, again, both imported and locally produced (Fig. 23), bronze vessels, glass and alabaster.[9] The grave goods at Duvanlij reflect both unprecedented wealth and highly specialized contacts with the Greek world. The rites and the overall character of the grave goods exhibited show many common features with other elite tumulus burials south of the Haemus range. North of the Haemus elite burials with imported Greek metalware and jewellery do occur in this period, but differences both in the range of goods and in the burial rite are far more marked. The combination of weapons and heavy body armour in many of the male burials suggests that these were cavalrymen, and that their wealth reflects the rewards of military success. The appearance of horsemen on many regal coins of the Odrysians is hardly accidental. Thucydides did not suppress his disdain for the majority of Sitalces' army, made up of infantry volunteers; but his cavalry could hold its own against the Macedonian, and this was composed almost entirely of Odrysians and Getae (Thuc. II.98.4).

Thucydides makes it clear that the Odrysians acquired their wealth through an extended system of duties and obligations (II.97.4). These were conferred not only upon the dynast himself but also upon his retainers. It was the assiduousness and efficiency with which they exacted gifts which made the Odrysians pre-eminent among the Thracian tribes. The historian mentions precious metals and fabrics. The latter have not survived but the former are well represented in rich burials (Fig. 24). Thucydides, writing from the perspective of the Greek Aegean colonies, emphasized the amount of money and goods in kind which these cities were obliged to pay the Odrysian kings, calling it 'tribute', though he does add that ordinary Thracians were also involved in this exchange of gifts. This elaborate system of gift exchange articulated social relationships within the Odrysian kingdom, with ordinary tribesmen (and visiting Greeks) offering more superior members of the hierarchy slaves, horses, fabrics as well as jewellery and tableware in precious metals (Xen. *An.* VII.3.18ff). In return they were probably entitled to expect security and the general benefits of patronage, including advantageous marriages and gifts of property (Xen. *An.* VII.2.38).

Although little is known about how Sitalces succeeded in exercising

[9] Filow *et al.* 1934 (E 117).

and retaining his power, he was clearly a man of considerable diplomatic acumen as well as military skill (Diod. XII.50.1). His interest in the territories occupied by Thracian tribes south of Rhodope may have been one of the chief motives for his acquiescence to Athenian overtures in 431, through a wealthy Abderitan, Nymphodorus, who was also Sitalces' brother-in-law (Thuc. II.29.1). An alliance was concluded between Athens and Sitalces, whose son, Sadocus, became an Athenian citizen. Sitalces was instrumental in arranging a reconciliation between Perdiccas of Macedon and Athens, with the return of Therme to Macedon as a bargaining counter. Nevertheless, the Athenians hoped to be able to use Sitalces' military support to weaken Macedonian influence in Thrace and strengthen their own (Thuc. II.29.4–7). In the summer of 430/29, Sitalces and Sadocus demonstrated their loyalty by handing over Aristeas of Corinth together with a Tegean, an Argive and three Spartan envoys, who were on their way to the Persian court but had tried to bring the Odrysians over to the Spartan side (Hdt. VII.137; Thuc. II.67).

Sitalces was no doubt keen to stress this alliance for official purposes and any genealogical propaganda which served the same cause would have been grist to the mill (Thuc. II.29.1–3), though it is unlikely that Sophocles' *Tereus*, set in Thrace, contained any direct political allusions.[10] Legendary genealogical links were a useful formal device which continued to be used by later rulers, such as Seuthes II (Xen. *An.* VII.2.31; 3.39). The success of Sitalces' policy can be judged from the fact that even in 425, when his unsuccessful Macedonian campaign would hardly have been forgotten in Athens, Aristophanes could make the Odrysian's philathenian proclivities the butt of his comic interlude with a detachment of Odomantian mercenaries (*Acharnians* 135ff). Judging by the derogatory remarks voiced by Hermippus in the *Phormophori*, ordinary Athenians took a dim view of what might be gained by closer relations with Sitalces (Edmonds *FAC* I, 304–5, F 63; Athen. I.27d–e).

II. THE NORTH AEGEAN BACKGROUND

Events along the north Aegean coast in the years following the Persian retreat are unlikely to have raised Sitalces' confidence in the genuineness of Athenian or Macedonian intentions. The recapture of Byzantium and the Hellespontine Straits, the restoration of the Chersonese to Athenian control and the establishment of a major league based at Eion were all indications of a new bid, spearheaded by Athens, to maintain a foothold on the Thracian coast (Thuc. 1.94; 98.1; Hdt. VII.106–7; Plut. *Cim.* 7–8; schol. Aeschin. II.31; Polyaen. VII.24). At the western end of the north

---

[10] Höck 1891 (E 127) 78, n. 2; P–W VAI s.v. 'Tereus'; Danov 1976 (E 105) 289, n. 19, 311; Hall 1989 (B 53) 105, 111–12, 134ff. *Contra*, Mihailov 1977 (E 142) 237–50.

Aegean, the most important tribes of the lower Strymon valley – the Pierii, Bisalti and Edoni – who had been driven out of their original homelands in lower Macedonia between the seventh and sixth centuries, came under increasing pressure from Macedon in the reign of Alexander I, who may even have held the Edonian stronghold, Enneahodoi, for a short time, although our only source is pro-Macedonian ([Dem.] XII.21).[11]

The Edoni succeeded in retaking it by ambush (schol. Aeschin. II.34) and, at the nearby site of Drabescus, destroyed, with the help of neighbouring Thracians, an Athenian force of 10,000 under the leadership of Leagrus and Sophanes, which attempted to recolonize Enneahodoi in 465 (Hdt. IX.75; Thuc. I.100.3; IV.102.2; Diod. XI.70.5; XII.68.2; Paus. I.29.4–5). The Athenians were trying to keep Alexander I, who already had the silver mines of Dysoron in Paeonia at his disposal (Hdt. v.17.2), away from the gold and silver mines, hitherto monopolized by the Thasians (Hdt. vi.46), in the area of Daton on the mainland of Thrace. The Athenians themselves were prepared to go to war with their ally Thasos in order to secure these resources (Thuc. I.100.2; 101.1–3; Diod. XI.70; Plut. Cim. 14.2; Themist. 25.2; Nep. Cim. 2.5).[12]

The precise nature of Thasian mining rights on the Thracian mainland and the identity of the Thasian mine at Skapte Hyle have long been controversial.[13] Nevertheless, they can only have been obtained with the co-operation of the local Thracian tribes, particularly the Edonians, Pierii, Odomanti and Satri (Hdt. VII.112). Such co-operation is confirmed by the existence of a joint Thraco-Macedonian minting standard, which was used by many local mints of Chalcidice and the north Aegean coast, by Thasos and her colony Neapolis, Aegae for its own and Macedonian regal issues, and also by a host of greater and lesser native tribes, both Paeonian (Letaei, Laeaei) and Thracian (Bisalti, Edoni, Orescii, Derrones, Zaeelii) some of which are only known to have existed from their coinage. Thasos and her colonies on the mainland, particularly Neapolis, whose proximity to ᵗhe island's chief mining region on the mainland soon promoted her from partner to rival, may have had a greater influence on the minting traditions of the neighbouring Thracian communities than has usually been assumed.[14] The obverse type showing a centaur carrying off a nymph is shared by Thasos, one or

---

[11] Hammond and Griffith 1979 (D 50) 102.

[12] J. Pouilloux in *Etudes Thasiennes* III 106–16, and 1990 (E 152).

[13] Koukouli-Chrysanthaki 1990 (E 136) with references; she locates Skapte Hyle in the Daton region NE of Kavalla.

[14] J. Svoronos, *L'Hellénisme primitif de la Macédoine* (Paris 1919) pls. 5, 17–24 (Orescii), 6, 11 (Zaeelii), 7. 3, 5 (Letaei), 95ff pl. 10 (Thasos); *Guide de Thasos* (1968) 185–6, pl. 1. 1–5; Price and Waggoner 1975 (B 213) 32–6, nos. 100–28; Picard 1982 (E 148) 424 and 1990 (E 144) 541–8; M. Oikonomidou, ibid. 533–40.

more unnamed mainland mints, probably in the Thasian peraea, the Orescii and Zaeelii. Other tribes stressed pastoral rather than Dionysiac themes, with a youth leading a horse or a yoke of oxen.[15] There are no reliable indicators for dating the beginning of these series; some issues may only have been produced for limited periods during the Persian wars, while many of the most prominent series with large denominations are not found in dateable contexts before the 470s and come to an end around 450, for reasons which are as yet uncertain.[16]

III. ATHENS, AMPHIPOLIS AND THRACE IN THE PELOPONNESIAN WAR PERIOD

The Athenians revived their exploration of northern strategic interest during the 440s and 430s, and redoubled their efforts to establish a personal stake on the Thracian mainland, both in the lucrative mining regions of the lower Strymon and Angites valleys, and in the Straits. Brea, known from an inscription but difficult to locate, was founded in a more co-operative spirit with the native inhabitants than any previous Athenian colony. This might be the cleruchy lodged in the land of the Bisaltians according to Plutarch's *Life of Pericles* 11.5 (Theop. *FGrH* 115 F 145; Hesychius and Steph. Byz. s.v. *Brea*).[17] Real success came only with Amphipolis (437 B.C.), a prime strategic site situated on a hill in a bend of the river Strymon, just south of Enneahodoi (identified with Hill 133 north east of the city: Thuc. IV.106; 108.1; V.11.1; Diod. XII.32.5; 68.2; schol. Aesch. II.31-4; Polyaen. VI.53; Harpocrat. s.v. *Amphipolis*; Steph. Byz, s.v. *Hagnoneia*).[18] Excavations conducted at the site since 1956 have as yet revealed little of the fifth century, though it was conceived on ambitious lines and bristled with fortifications from the start.[19] A further cleruchy in the Chersonese, sent out in 448/7 and reinforced in 443/2,[20] formed the final link in the chain of Athenian and

[15] Gaebler 1935 (B 194) pl. 12. 1–11 (Bisalti); Price and Waggoner 1975 (B 213) 38, no. 52; D. Raymond, *Macedonian Royal Coinage to 413 B.C.* (New York 1953) 100–1, nos. 54–7; Fried (B 193) and Kagan (B 198) in Carradice 1987 (B 188) 1–2, 24–5.

[16] Kraay 1976 (B 200) 131, 134, 136–41, and *Num. Chron.* 1977, 89–98; Price and Waggoner 1975 (B 213) 39; M. J. Price in Carradice 1987 (B 188) 43–7.

[17] M–L no. 49; Fornara 1983 (A 19) 110, no. 100 with references; J. Vartsos, *Archaia Makedonia* 2 (1977) 13–16; D. Asheri, *AJP* 90 (1969) 337–40 argues that the colony Brea should be located in the Chalcidic peninsula (cf. Thuc. IV.109.4).

[18] Pritchett 1965 (A 48) I 30–45, 46–7 (E. Vanderpool); D. Lazaridis, *PAE* 1960, 68–72; 1964, 39; 1965, 50–2; 1971, 58, 62, fig. 33; 1972, 70–2; 1973, 50–4; 1974, 63–4; 1975, 69–71; 1976, 94–8; 1977, 43; 1978, 58; 1979, 79; 1981, 25; 1982, 50–1.

[19] Lazaridis 1972 (E 137) and 1986 (in K 39) 31–8.

[20] Plut. *Per.* 11.5; 19.1; *IG* I² 205.29: *Neapolis ap' Athenon*; *ATL* I 376–80, III 285–90; Kahrstedt 1954 (E 133) 6ff, 15ff; A. J. Graham, *Colony and Mother City in Ancient Greece* (Manchester 1964) 178–9, 193–5. On the reinforcement of 443/2: *ATL* III 205, 289; Kahrstedt 1954 (E 133) 22, n. 56.

League bases encircling the northern Aegean; Abdera had probably been a member since the 470s, Aenus and Maronea had joined before 454.[21]

However, Perdiccas of Macedon began to encroach on this Athenian monopoly when he encouraged the synoecism of Olynthus with its neighbours in 432 B.C. (Thuc. 1.58.2). It is in this context that the Athenians approached Sitalces with offers of alliance. The principal outcome of this alliance, the joint invasion of Macedonia, planned for 429, which was to replace Perdiccas with a usurper, was in the event not supported by Athens and achieved no lasting success (Thuc. II.95–101).[22] The impressive resources in land, men and money upon which Sitalces could draw evidently caused a sensation in the Greek world (Thuc. II.101.4; Diod. XII.51.1) and may have persuaded the Athenians that their Odrysian allies were already too powerful. In fact, despite the impressive numbers – put at 150,000 by Thucydides (II.98.3) – not more than a third were cavalry troops, and no match for the practised, though less numerous, Macedonian horsemen (II.100.5). Moreover, the expedition was doomed to failure by secret negotiations between Sitalces' nephew, Seuthes, and Perdiccas, who promised Seuthes his daughter Stratonice in marriage if he could lead off the invaders (Thuc. II.101.5).

Seuthes became king after Sitalces' death in 424 and rumours circulated implicating him in the death or disappearance of his cousin, Sitalces, perhaps with Athenian connivance; Sadocus is not heard of again (schol. *Acharn.* 145; [Dem.] XII.9).[23] Seuthes' father, Sparadocus, was probably one of the most powerful princes of the royal house, the *paradunasteuontes* mentioned by Thucydides (II.97.3). A series of silver coins inscribed with his name is the earliest evidence to date of native Thracian regal coinage. The reverse types seem to have been modelled on Olynthian coins,[24] while obverses with the forepart of a horse are paralleled at Maronea.[25] It seems likely that Sparadocus held a fief within Odrysian territory, probably somewhere in south-western Thrace. The silver drachms and didrachms with reverses inscribed SEYTHA ARGURION and SEYTHA KOMMA, and a galloping horseman on the obverses, should probably be ascribed to Seuthes I, who was best known for having raised the tribute of the Greek cities to its highest rate (Thuc. II.97.3).[26] With the intensification of Athenian military ope-

---

[21] *ATL* I 517–19; III 214–23.

[22] Danov 1976 (E 105) 311–16; Hammond and Griffith 1979 (D 50) 127–32.

[23] The victim of Athenian duplicity in [Dem.] XII.9 is stated to be a Sitalces, and an Athenian citizen; this may be a mistaken reference to Cotys I and the context would suggest a fourth-century ruler (Hammond and Griffith 1979 (D 50) 314, n. 2).

[24] Casson 1926 (E 97) 196–7, 207, pl. 71; Yourukova 1976 (E 173) 9–11, pl. 4. 17–22; Gaebler 1935 (B 194) 84, pl. 17. 1–5 (Olynthus); D. M. Robinson and P. A. Clement, *Excavations at Olynthus* IX (1938) 294–7, pl. 34a–b. Baltimore.   [25] West 1929 (E 172); Schönert-Geiss 1987 (E 159).

[26] West 1929 (E 172) 97–8; Yourukova 1976 (E 173) 13, 19, pls. 5. 27, 27. 1a; Rogalski 1977 (E 155).

rations in the north following the defection of a number of Chalcidian and Thracian cities, notably Amphipolis, to Brasidas between 424 and 423 (Thuc. IV.84–123), and the renewal of hostilities between Athens and Perdiccas, the man responsible for inviting Spartan aid in the first place (IV.82), Seuthes was in a position to exploit these diversions so as to put pressure on the Greek cities further along the Aegean coast. Meanwhile, independent tribesmen joined either the Spartans, as did the Myrcini and Edoni (Thuc. IV.107.3; V.6.4) or the Athenians, as did Odomantian and other Thracian mercenaries (Thuc. IV.129.3; V.6.2) in subsequent engagements at Amphipolis.

The reduction of tribute for Delian League members in the Thrace-ward region, and the continued minting of coins in some of the northern cities, particularly Acanthus, Abdera and Maronea, have frequently been associated with measures to alleviate the tribute imposed by the Thracian kings, although many different factors are probably reflected in tribute fluctuations.[27] Amphipolis, Abdera, Maronea and the mainland colonies of Thasos and Samothrace were all protected by fortifications enclosing substantial areas of land, thereby reducing their vulnerability to surprise incursions. Excavations have confirmed their continuing prosperity during the second half of the fifth century; whatever the demands of the Delian League on the one hand, and Seuthes I on the other, these Greek communities were by no means drained of resources. On the contrary, there is growing evidence from hoards north of Rhodope that commercial relations between the coastal Greek cities and the leaders of the interior were good. Beginning some time during the second quarter of the fifth century and developing particularly towards the end of the fifth and first half of the fourth century, staters and fractions of Thasos, together with native imitations, enjoyed a wide circulation between the Strymon and Nestus valleys and as far north as Vetren, north west of Pazardjik. A similar pattern, though with a more easterly distribution, is reflected in hoards of coins from Parium and the Thracian Chersonese, found across the Thracian Plain right into the foothills of Haemus.[28]

Virtually nothing is known of Seuthes' later years and his eventual death some time between 420 and 410 B.C. There are signs of administrative strains. Rival princes of the royal house were vying for power. One of those who suffered was Maesades, father of Seuthes II, whose fief included the Melanditae, Tranipsae and Thyni in south-east Thrace (Xen. *An.* VII.2.32). The 'Delta' in the hinterland of the Propontis was in

27 P–W XX s.v. 'Phoroi' 583, 585; *ATL* I 154, 203; III 307–8; E. S. G. Robinson, *Hesperia* Suppl. 8 (1949) 324ff; M–L nos. 111–17; May 1950 (B 205) 12ff, 71–87; Danov 1976 (E 105) 293ff; other factors are discussed in *ATL* I 517–19; III 310; May 1950 (B 205) 17, 76, 81–2; Meiggs 1972 (C 201) 249–53; Lewis 1987 (C 186).   28 Domaradzki 1987 (E 109); Dimitrov 1989 (E 107).

the hands of a Teres, perhaps Sitalces' son of that name (Xen. *An.*
VII.5.1; schol. Ar. *Acharn.* 145). With the growing appreciation of the
value of mixed troops, light-armed men as well as hoplites, during the
Peloponnesian War, Thracian mercenaries appeared in increasing
numbers outside their homeland. Aristophanes' Odomanti in 425
(*Acharn.* 147–53), and the 1,300 peltasts of the Dii who were to join the
Sicilian expedition (Thuc. VII.27.1; 29), like the peltasts from Lemnos,
Imbros and Ainos sent to Sphacteria (Thuc. IV.28.4), reflect the
beginnings of major tactical changes in the art of warfare which were to
be developed fully in the fourth century.[29]

Recent archaeological discoveries are beginning to provide new
information about the background of these social and political relations
between the Greek cities and the Odrysian kingdom. The overall
increase in wealth of the Odrysian nobility is reflected in the lavish
disposal of precious metals in burials. The new wealth was directed
towards the acquisition of a wide range of imported items, symptomatic
of the growing interest in Greek customs and culture as well as in objects
which were status symbols in their own right. Some of the most
magnificent examples of fifth-century (Ionian?) Greek jewellery were
found in three successive female burials at Duvanlij (Koukuva, Musho-
vitsa and Arabadjiyska Mounds). The same is true of the gilded silver
plate from Golyama and Bashova Mounds, Duvanlij, and Dulboki near
Stara Zagora. The plate, together with some Attic black- and red-figure
cups and jars, as well as wine amphorae, reflect a new interest in Aegean
wines and the paraphernalia of the symposium. The lady buried in
Lozarskata Mogila, Duvanlij, lay on a Greek-type ash wood bed with
lathe-turned legs.[30] Of even greater potential interest is the evidence
from two recently discovered settlements. At Saadersi, near Vasil
Levsky, Karlovo district, in the foothills of the Haemus mountains,
traces of a settlement have been found with monumental dressed stone
constructions; pottery, both imported and native imitations of Attic
black glaze, painted Laconian roof tiles and other objects all of which
seem to antedate the fourth century B.C.[31]

At Adjiyska Vodenitsa, near Vetren, close to a tributary of the Maritsa
north west of Pazardjik, lies a major site spanning the fifth to third
centuries B.C. During the first three trial seasons in 1988–1990, large
quantities of pottery and tiles, both native and imported, several
hundred coins, bronze and iron implements were found together with
monumental stone-built structures. Three periods have been identified.

[29] Parke 1933 (K 50) 17–18; Best 1969 (K 8); Griffith 1981 (D 44).
[30] Filow 1930–1 (E 115) and 1934 (E 117); Archibald 1983 (E 90); Domaradzki 1988 (E 110); M. Reho, *La ceramica attica a figure nere e rosse nella Tracia Bulgara* (Rome 1990).
[31] K. Kisyov, *AOR* 1989 (1990) 41–2 (in Bulgarian).

A powerful *emplekton*-style wall of hammer-faced stone blocks backed by large undressed rocks and packed with river stones, built on a base of undressed stones 2.6–2.8 m. wide, belonged to period 1. This has been dated on the basis of stratigraphic material to the third quarter of the fifth century B.C. The site may have been a princely seat established around the middle of the fifth century, a regional capital subject to the Odrysians, as the range of coin types would indicate.[32] Other centres of power undoubtedly existed further east in the Thracian Plain but have not yet been investigated. There is new evidence of a valley settlement beginning in the fifth century B.C. at Plovdiv, perhaps associated with the sanctuary on Nebet tepe. The concentration of hoards and elite burials in the area of Stara Zagora would suggest another focus of power. In the south-eastern parts of the Thracian Plain the picture is more complicated and there may have been several centres here, including Mezek, Asara (medieval Bulgarian Simeonovgrad, near modern Dimitrovgrad); Odrin, at the confluence of the Tundja and Maritsa rivers; and Kypsela, modern Ipsala, where the later Via Egnatia crossed the Maritsa river above the delta's flood plain.[33] Recent finds bear out what we might have suspected from political affairs, namely, that relations between the Greek cities and the Odrysians (which in practice would have meant the Odrysian nobility and mercenary armies), were close-knit; that regular and sustained contacts with the Aegean made those Thracians in positions of authority familiar with Greek and Persian life-styles. Such individuals were probably responsible for the introduction of Greek masonry practices, pottery and domestic articles, new metalworking techniques and coined money. The new techniques were nevertheless envisaged in a native idiom and adapted for quite specific local purposes.

IV. AMADOCUS THE ELDER AND YOUNGER, HEBRYZELMIS AND COTYS I

During the first half of the fourth century, the Chersonese became an arena of conflict between the Greeks, the Odrysians and local Thracians. The overriding strategic importance of the Hellespontine region in the final years of the Peloponnesian War and throughout the fourth century resulted in regular expeditions, both from Athens and Sparta, to secure their respective interests.[34] This coincided with the intensification of

[32] Domaradzki and Yourukova 1990 (E 112).   [33] Domaradzki 1987 (E 109) 10–11.
[34] Xen. *Hell.* I.1.12, 32; 3.10; 4.9; II.1.25–6; Plut. *Alc.* 36–7; Lys. XIV.26, 38; Diod. XIII.74; 105.13 (Thrasybulus and Alcibiades); Xen. *Hell.* I.1.5; Thuc. VIII.80.2 (Clearchus, 411 B.C.); Xen. *Hell.* II.2.5 (Eteonicus, 405 B.C.); Plut. *Lys.* 20.7; Paus. III.18.3 (Lysander, 404 B.C.); Diod. XIV.12.1; Xen. *An.* II.6.2–5; Polyaen. II.2.6 (403 B.C.); Xen. *Hell.* III.2.2–5, 9 (Seuthes II and Dercyllidas); Xen. *Hell.* III.2.9–10; Diod. XIV.38.3–7 (Dercyllidas in the Chersonese).

Odrysian interest in the same regions, though it is not clear whether and how this is to be connected with the division of power which emerged between rival branches of the ruling dynasty.

Medocus, also called Amadocus, who succeeded Seuthes I to the royal title some time between 410 and 407 B.C. (Xen. *An.* VII.2.32; 7.3; Harpocr. s.v. *Amadokos*, Isoc. v.6),[35] was challenged by his kinsman, Seuthes II, son of Maesades, who attempted to carve out an independent kingdom based on his father's patrimony with the help of Xenophon's mercenaries (Xen. *An.* VII.2.18ff). The Athenian general Thrasybulus intervened in this dispute between the two princes, probably in 390/89, and concluded with them one of a series of alliances in the Hellespont and north Aegean which were to pave the way for a Second Athenian Confederacy (Xen. *Hell.* IV.8.26; Diod. XIV.94.2; Arist. *Pol.* v.10.24 1312a).[36]

The renewal of Athenian friendship in a treaty of 386/5 with Amadocus' apparent successor, Hebryzelmis (whose origins are not clear), seems contemporary with increased hostility to Athens on the part of Seuthes II and may have been partly responsible for it (Polyaen. VII.38; Aristides *Panath.* 172).[37] Iphicrates, sent to Sestus against the Spartan Anaxibius in 388, subsequently found his way into the service of Seuthes II and may have attacked Hebryzelmis on his behalf (Nep. *Iphicr.* 2.1).[38] He remained to fight for Seuthes' son and heir, Cotys I, and married the latter's daughter before c. 386 (Dem. XXIII.129; Anaxandrides F 41 apud Athen. IV.131; Theopomp. *FGrH* 115 F 31; Nep. *Iphicr.* 2.1). Hebryzelmis is a mysterious figure, though an alliance with Athens at a time when that city's foreign relations were constrained by the broad powers accorded to Sparta under the terms of the King's Peace indicates that he was not insignificant. A series of bronze coins found in the lower Hebrus valley and inscribed EBRY- confirms his importance in that region. The reverses show a cotyle and the letters KYPSE-, indicating their mint, Kypsela, which could also have been Hebryzelmis' seat of power.[39]

A separate but related series of bronze issues, whose types suggest a connexion with the Maronitan mint,[40] has been variously divided between Medocus-Amadocus I and Amadocus II (Theop. *FGrH* 115 F 101; Harpocrat. s.v. *Amadokos*) both of whom are usually assumed to

[35] Danov 1976 (E 105) 325ff; Fol 1975 (E 119) 103–4; Harding 1985 (A 29) no. 76.
[36] Bengtson 1975 (A 6) II 185ff., no. 238; Seager 1967 (C 250); Cawkwell 1976 (C 112) prefers winter 391; Tacheva-Hitova 1972 (E 161) 394 B.C.; Harding 1985 (A 29) no. 25; Parke 1933 (K 50) 56–9 on Chabrias' early career.   [37] Tod no. 117; Harding no. 29.
[38] Parke 1988 (K 50) 55–6.
[39] May 1950 (B 205) 186; Yourukova 1976 (E 173) 16, pl. 6. 32–6.
[40] Yourukova 1976 (E 173) 18–9, pl. 9. 51; cf. Kraay 1976 (B 200) nos. 429–30; Schönert-Geiss 1987 (E 159).

have held territories in central southern Thrace, between the lower Hebrus and Maronea (Dem. XXIII.183). Among the eleven regal coins from the preliminary excavations at Vetren, there are two bronze issues of Cotys I; one *hekte* of Thasian type has the rare reverse legend BERG-(which appears elsewhere as BERGAIOY); the remaining eight coins belong to Amadocus I and II, together with one bronze of Teres II. Among those ascribed to Amadocus I is a rare silver issue showing the characteristic reverse shared by these three rulers, a double axe with the incumbent's name, in this case ME(T)OKO, and the head of a handsome man on the obverse with short hair cut in an unusual style, a long moustache and clipped beard. It is distinctive enough as a design to suggest a conscious portrait, which would make it among the earliest known from the Aegean.[41] This and the remaining bronze coins would give weight to the idea that the western parts of the Thracian Plain, as well as its southern flanks, fell within the political ambit of Amadocus the Elder and his son of the same name, and the short-lived Teres II after them.

Minor princes of the early hellenistic period had coins minted in their own name but this was by no means a new practice. There are new silver coins from Rhodope, all small denominations, of Saratocus, who used the Maronitan- or Thasian-inspired bunch of grapes on his reverses. The finds from Vetren give more weight to the view that the 'Bergaios' coins refer neither to a Thasian moneyer, nor to a community called Berge, but to a native ruler of this name.[42] Written sources do not provide adequate information either about the dynastic relationships between Odrysian rulers of the fourth century B.C., or about the tribes and territories in their power. It is, nevertheless, clear that a fundamental division into separate regions or principalities of varying autonomy, already apparent in the latter part of the fifth century, continued through the fourth, and that the pre-eminent position of Cotys I was the exception rather than the rule.

Cotys inherited his father Seuthes' lordship over the south-eastern tribes between Apollonia Pontica and the Straits, and, whatever the status of these regions during Seuthes' troubled reign, succeeded in extending his influence as far west as the eastern bank of the Hebrus, across the whole west Pontic seaboard into the hinterland of Odessus (Dem. XXIII.181f; schol. Aeschin. II.81; Str. VII. F 48). This enlarged kingdom was inherited by Cotys' son, Cersobleptes. The relationship between this power bloc and the patrimony of Amadocus I is uncertain.

[41] Domaradzki and Yourukova 1990 (E 112) 11, fig. 4.
[42] Saratocus: Yourukova 1976 (E 173) 15, pl. 5. 28–30; cf. Kraay 1976 (B 200) no. 438 (c. 375–350 B.C.); Y. Yourukova, *Archeologiya* (Sofia) 1979, 4, 59. Bergaeus: Yourukova 1990 (E 112) 10. *Contra*, Picard 1982 (E 148), 1987 (E 149).

Amadocus II is mentioned as an independent ruler only after Cotys' death in 359 (Dem. XXIII.8,183), when he and his western colleague, Berisades, decided not to treat Cersobleptes as their overlord. But both men were past their prime in 359 and are likely to have held positions of authority for many years prior to this. Demosthenes would have us believe that the tripartite division came about only as a result of Cotys' untimely death, and was in favour of the Athenians supporting such a division. The clear implication is that under Cotys all three principalities owed allegiance, however nominal, to Cotys. The little that we know about Philip II's conquest of Cersobleptes' kingdom makes it clear that control of the Thracian Plain was of vital strategic importance. It is here that relations between two rival branches of the Odrysian dynasty, that of Amadocus and that of Cotys, would have been the most sensitive.

One of the two bronze coins of Cotys found at Vetren is a rare bronze type which has affinities with early coins of Amadocus II and Maronea.[43] Perhaps this early connexion with Maronea and the house of Amadocus holds a clue to the changing relationship between the two houses. Despite Seuthes II's endeavours, Amadocus I remained the senior prince. Cotys was probably a junior princeling like his father until he reversed the relationship by eliminating (the usurper?) Hebryzelmis and subjugating other rivals, including probably the future Amadocus II.

Cotys I, the most vigorous, skilful and astute of fourth-century Odrysian rulers, inherited his father's distrust of Athens and became a worthy match in guile and duplicity (Dem. XXIII.104, 114, 118, 129–32, 150, 153, 156–9). Some allowance has to be made for the fact that Greek writers are usually hostile towards him and his son Cersobleptes, particularly Demosthenes, whose speech *Against Aristocrates* is the most important single documentary source for this period in Thrace. A man of strong personality, he was equally capable, apparently, of vindictive cruelty and poetic inspiration (Plut. *Mor.* 174D 1–2; Athen. XII. 531e (Theopomp. *FGrH* 115 F 31), IV 131; Harpocrat. s.v. *Kotys*).

Like Hebryzelmis, he issued silver and bronze coins from the mint at Cypsela – the reverses show a cotyle like the civic issues – and introduced new iconographic types. The bronzes include an obverse showing a galloping rider with right arm outstretched, his cape blowing in the wind, which may have been modelled on coins issued by Archelaus and Amyntas III of Macedon.[44] This is a modification of the galloping rider motif familiar from fifth-century coins of Seuthes I (?) and both the earlier type and Cotys' version are reflected on native gold ring bezels

[43] Yourukova 1990 (E 112) 14–15, fig. 7.
[44] Yourukova 1976 (E 173) 17, pl. 7. 37–43, cf. 9–11 and pls. 8. 67, 10. 101–2, 27. 15–6; Head 1879 (B 195) 163, nos. 1–2 (Archelaus), 173, nos. 14–16 (Amyntas III); N. G. L. Hammond in W. Moon (ed.), *Ancient Greek Art and Iconography* (1983) 253, fig. 16. 201.

Fig. 25. Gilt silver rhyton from Borovo, inscribed; Rousse, Museum of History II–358. (After Venedikov 1976 (E 170A) no. 544; *Das Altertum* 26 (1980) 7, fig. 2.)

and were further popularized on coins of Cersobleptes, Sroios (?) and Seuthes III. During Cotys' reign the import and local manufacture of high quality luxury articles continued, judging by the quantity of gilded silverware and jewellery found in intact burials. These reflect both contemporary Aegean trends, Persian as well as mainland Greek, and features of native inspiration. The increasing popularity of built chamber tombs which could be reopened periodically means that much of this wealth has since disappeared.

A number of silver phialae from rich burials at Alexandrovo and Vratsa in north west Bulgaria, and Agighiol in the Dobrudja, as well as three vessels from a hoard found near Borovo, Rousse, close to the Danube (Fig. 25), were inscribed KOTYOS EGBEO(Y) and that from Alexandrovo, KOTYOS EGGEISTON. The first word has usually been identified with King Cotys I, by analogy with a phiale from Branichevo, inscribed with the names Amadocus and Padruteres (Amadocus II and an unknown local ruler?).[45] The significance of such inscribed vessels was confirmed by the discovery in north-west Bulgaria

[45] Filow 1934 (E 117) 180, fig. 202 and 1917 (E 114) 52; D. E. Strong, *Greek and Roman Gold and Silver Plate* (London 1966) 77, pl. 16a (Alexandrovo); Venedikov 1966 (E 169) 12; Nikolov 1967 (E 146) and 1968 (E 147) fig. 50 (Vratsa); Berciu 1969 (E 93) 222–3, fig. 5, pls. 117.1, 118.3 (Agighiol); Ivanov 1980 (E 130) figs. 1, 5, 8–11 (Borovo); Dremsizova 1962 (E 113) 175 (Branichevo); Venedikov 1972 (E 170); cf. also the Kirk kilise treasure, Hasluck 1910–11 (E 126); M. Pfrommer, *Studien zu alexandrinischen und grossgriechischen Toreutik frühhellenistischer Zeit* (Arch. Forsch. 16, 1987), and in *Journal of the J. Paul Getty Museum* 13 (1985) 9–18. Cf. *Pls. to Vol. IV* pl. 109.

of the Rogozen hoard (1985–6).[46] Thirteen phialae and one jug from among the 165 vessels it contained carried similar inscriptions. One phiale and the jug are simply inscribed SATOKO(I); one phiale carries the name Cersobleptes, ten more name Cotys, with the same accompanying legends as the vessels already described, together with new ones.

The Rogozen vessels have clarified the legends accompanying the royal or princely names: EX APRO, EX ARGISKES/ERGISKES, EG (EX) BEO, EG GEISTON, EX SAUTHABAS, must surely be the Greek preposition 'ex' = from and a geographical location,[47] referring to the place of manufacture or assembly point of such objects for tax purposes. On this reckoning the tribute collected by weight from various Greek communities, as Thucydides implies, would have been melted down and stored as tableware. The inscribed vessels, excepting the hoard from Borovo, are either undecorated or have simple tongued ornament, which makes them look like batch products. Their places of origin cannot be identified with certainty, but most can, on etymological grounds, be located in the region of the Propontis.[48] The proximity of such sites to the Greek cities may be significant. Tribute payment to the Odrysians was notorious in the days of Seuthes I, and some form of tribute continued to be paid by Greek cities of the north well into the fourth century.[49] Thracians did also contribute gifts, but these may have been paid more often than not in kind; the Odrysian kingdom had not yet become a 'money economy' in the same sense that we might apply this concept to the Greek cities, despite the circulation of bronze and small denominations of silver. Moreover, the social significance of gift-giving in Thrace would suggest that a different system may have operated with respect to the Greeks who did not belong within this framework. From the administrative angle these differences are less apparent; the Rogozen jug and bowl belonging to prince Satocus are marked in the same manner as the customized Cotys bowls inscribed with their provenance.

The final location of many of these silver vessels north of Haemus may be connected with three factors: the external relations of the Odrysian kings; the break-up of Cersobleptes' kingdom during the Macedonian conquest and the growing importance of the Triballi in present-day north-west Bulgaria. Both hoards and burials of the fourth century within and outside the confines of the Odrysian kingdom contain mixed collections of silver, consisting of imported and locally produced vessels and other objects. Silver bullion, which may often have been in the form of coins or manufactured articles, was probably melted down and reused freely unless other considerations were at play. Inscribed silverware

---

[46] A. Fol et al., The New Thracian Treasure from Rogozen (British Museum 1986); Cook 1989 (E 104).
[47] J. Hind in Cook 1989 (E 104) 38–43.   [48] Ibid. 41 and fig. 4.   [49] See note 57.

from Alexandrovo and the burials at Moghilanska Mogila, Vratsa (tomb 2) and Agighiol is either contemporary with Cotys' reign, or might have been acquired as diplomatic gifts at that time. The Rogozen hoard, packed into two bags with scrap silver and no doubt bound for the melting pot, was buried some considerable time later, and is more likely to be connected with the two latter factors.

During the fourth century the Triballi rose to become the most powerful Thracian tribe alongside the Odrysians. Sitalces had failed in his confrontation with them in 424. Thereafter they remained a challenge to the Odrysians. Tumulus burials of the fifth century show that Early Iron Age traditions of bronzeworking, including the manufacture of distinctive horse gear, continued to thrive.[50] In 375 some 30,000 Triballi are said to have attacked Abdera, apparently following a famine in their own lands. The invaders got away with great quantities of booty, but Abdera was saved by the unexpected appearance of the Athenian general Chabrias, who, with an eye to his city's interests, installed a garrison there (Aen. Tact. xv.8–10; Diod. xv.36.1–4; Aristides *Panath.* 1, 172, Dindorf XIII p. 275 & schol. *ad loc.*). The Triballi continued to flourish thereafter, as burials and hoards from the middle and second half of the fourth century from Alexandrovo, Letnitsa, Loukuvit, Stoyanovo (form. Radyuvene), Teteven, and the cemeteries around Vratsa indicate.[51] Aristides' reference to 'two kings' being reconciled by Chabrias, one of whom was the 'king of Maronea' makes some sense in view of the by now traditional association of the house of Amadocus with Maronea. According to Aristides, the Maronitans were in league with the Triballi. If there is any historical value in this story, it might be a dim echo of tensions between Amadocus II and Cotys, which erupted into the open under Cersobleptes. Abdera had had close relations with Sitalces and Cotys may have reassumed patronage – exactly the sort of move which might have been taken as a provocation by Amadocus. Cotys' Aegean ambitions should not be underestimated. Coins of Sparadocus and four fourth-century monarchs, Hebryzelmis, Cotys I, Cersobleptes and Cetriporis turned up at Olynthus. A new inscription from Vetren which stipulates legal regulations for certain colonists from Maronea and merchants from Thasos and Apollonia, in the vicinity of Pistiros (Vetren?; cf. Steph. Byz. s.v. *Pistiros*) and in certain *emporia*, refers to earlier regulations made in the time of Cotys.[52] This Aegean (rather than Hellespontine) dimension of Cotys' policy is only now becoming apparent.

---

[50] Kitov 1980 (E 135); Gergova 1986 (E 122).

[51] Venedikov and Gerasimov 1975 (E 171) figs. 231–4, 257–92.

[52] Robinson and Clement, *Excavations at Olynthus* IX, 340–1. The inscription, apparently from the third quarter of the fourth century, is to be published by V. Velkov and L. Domaradzka.

Cotys had an able lieutenant in his son-in-law, Iphicrates, who, for twenty years, helped him to affirm his authority over south-east Thrace if not beyond (Polyaen. III.9.4; 32; 41; 46; 50; 62) and to stamp out usurpers; an Adamas (Ar. *Pol.* v.10.18 1311b) and in 362 Miltocythes (Dem. XXIII.104; 114; 169f). Iphicrates' close association with Cotys *c.*383, when the Athenian general helped Amyntas III to regain Macedon (and for this was rewarded with formal adoption as Amyntas' son, Aeschin. II.28),[53] could have paved the way to a renewal of friendship between Macedon and the Odrysian kingdom. There is some evidence of a closer relationship between the two royal houses perhaps dating to the 370s.[54]

By 375, Aenus, Abdera, Dicaea, and other Greek cities on the Thracian coast had joined Perinthus and Maronea in the Second Athenian Confederacy.[55] Although some of these cities may have been providing him with tribute, Cotys resented these signs of a resurgent federalism which challenged his ability to deal with the Greek cities separately. In 367 he attacked Sestus, Athens' ally and principal naval base in the Chersonese, then Perinthus (Dem. XXIII.141–2). Timotheus succeeded in rescuing Sestus and Crithote for Athens in 364, returning with impressive spoils (Dem. XV.9; Nep. *Tim.* 1; Isoc. XV.108;112). But Cotys, now aided by the mercenary captain Charidemus of Oreus, since Iphicrates' loyalties were divided, recaptured the Chersonese in 362, and, apart from the temporary loss of Sestus in 361, both he and his son Cersobleptes successfully staved off a string of Athenian commanders for the next ten years.[56] In spite of a treaty concluded in 357, by which the Chersonese except Cardia was ceded to Athens – the most favourable arrangement the Athenians were likely to get (Dem. XXIII.104f; 173–4; [Dem.] L.4–20) – Cersobleptes disregarded these terms in the following years, laying claim to Athenian port and customs dues as well (Dem. XXIII.110; 176; Isoc. VIII.24). A final settlement was not made between him and Athens until 352, by which time the political situation in Thrace had undergone radical changes (Diod. XVI.34.3–4).

Cotys was murdered early in 359 by two citizens of Aenus, Python and Heracleides, who apparently had a personal grudge against him. The grateful Athenian *demos* voted crowns to the murderers (Dem. XXIII.119; 163; Aeschin. III.51; Ar. *Pol.* v.10.18 1311b; schol. D.L. III.46). It is unnecessary to infer collusion; Cotys was an obstacle to Athenian policy in the north Aegean and her citizens were glad to be rid of him. The

---

[53] Hammond and Griffith 1979 (D 50) 176–7.

[54] *SIG* 195; *Fouilles de Delphes* III.1 392 (proxeny decree for the sons of Cersobleptes, Iolaus, Posidonius, Medistas and Teres); J. Buckler, *Klio* 68 (1986) 2, 348–50 (date in archonship of Aristoxenus, 356 B.C.); G. Herman, *Ritualized Friendship and the Greek City* (Cambridge, 1987) 20, n. 34 and 127, n. 37.   [55] Cawkwell 1981 (C 113) 42–5.

[56] Höck 1891 (E 127) and 1904 (E 128); Cloché 1932 (E 102).

Athenians relied on short-term, piecemeal measures to maintain their northern interests. This approach was reasonably successful so long as there was no united regional opposition to their aims. They had signally failed to displace Cotys because they were either unable or unprepared to launch a properly funded expedition. The Athenian alliance of 357 with Cotys' three successors, Berisades, Amadocus II and Cersobleptes, was intended to shore up Athens' traditional policy by diplomatic means. The Athenians supported the rival claims to autonomy of Berisades and Amadocus so as to prevent Cersobleptes gaining any advantage over the other two (Dem. XXIII.8; 170; 173).[57]

V. PHILIP II OF MACEDON AND ODRYSIAN THRACE

Both the Social War with her allies and affairs at home prevented Athens from giving more than cursory attention to Thrace during the 350s. The same factors left Philip II of Macedon free to rebuild and restructure his army, consolidate his precarious hold over the kingdom and disable those of his neighbours whose collusion and aggression had kept the country weak and divided for lengthy periods during the first half of the fourth century. But Philip did not plan just to roll back the invading armies. He was determined to eliminate the conditions which made it possible for Athenians and Chalcidians or Athenians and Illyrians with sundry pretenders to ride roughshod over crown lands. Having wiped out the Illyrian Bardylis, subjugated Paeonia (Diod. XVI.4.2–7) and captured Amphipolis by outmanoeuvring the Athenians, Philip's next move was to appropriate the mining colony of Crenides, renamed Philippi, which had been attacked by Thracians, perhaps at the instigation of Cersobleptes (Steph. Byz. s.v. *Philippoi*; Dem. XXIII.9; 179; Diod. XVI.3.7;8.6).[58] Very little is known at present about Thracian communities in the Philippi plain before the Macedonian conquest. But in the first years of his reign, Alexander the Great confirmed certain rights of land use upon local, unnamed, Thracians, rights probably established by Philip II, perhaps at the time of Philippi's foundation. This clearly indicates that native Thracians continued to live in close proximity to the mining area.[59]

The identity of these Thracians is closely connected with the problem of the Thracian attack on Crenides. Although the Thasians and their mainland colonists had been operating in the mining region of Daton for

---

[57] Tod no. 151 (= Bengtson, *SdA* no. 303); *ATL* II 104, 78d; III 310 for text changes; Harding 1985 (A 29) no. 64.

[58] Collart 1932 (E 103) 39ff, 133ff, 152ff; Hammond and Griffith 1979 (D 50) 235ff, 248–9.

[59] Vatin 1984 (E 163); L. Missitzis, *AncW* 12 (1985) 3–14; M. Hatzopoulos, *Bull. Epigr.* 1987, 436–7, no. 714; 1989, no. 471.

two centuries, the foundation of Crenides signalled, to the Thracian tribes of the region, a change of relationships. In principle after 359 the south-western parts of the Odrysian kingdom were ruled as an autonomous unit, first by Berisades, and, from 356 if not earlier, by his son Cetriporis, though two younger sons, perhaps Monounios and Scostocus,[60] disputed Cetriporis' claim and appealed to Philip for arbitration (Justin VIII.3.14ff.). Unfortunately, there are few guidelines for locating this south-western kingdom; it must have included parts of Rhodope and probably the northern part of the Drama plain. Cersobleptes allegedly attacked the rulers of the other two kingdoms in 358 (Dem. XXIII.171) – hence the strict stipulations about mutual rights and obligations in the treaty of 357 and subsequent attempts to isolate him (Dem. XXIII.175; 189).

Cersobleptes might have wished to exercise the high degree of authority enjoyed by his father. We know far too little as yet about the extent of Odrysian interests in the coastal areas and the mining districts in particular. In the archaic period the mining centres of Dysoron, Pangaeum and Daton attracted a large number of coastal, inland and immigrant communities. More powerful states, Macedon and Athens, were soon drawn into the same orbit. Sitalces coveted a share but failed. During the fourth century competition for access increased, even amongst established participants. Thasos founded Crenides around the time of, or soon after, Cotys' murder. Cotys and Cersobleptes, who lost no opportunity to redirect revenues to their own treasury, are unlikely to have remained bystanders in an increasingly anarchic situation.

The occupation of Crenides by Philip polarized attitudes immediately; those who felt directly threatened united to form a four-sided alliance and pledged themselves to reverse the takeover.[61] Its members consisted of the Illyrian and Paeonian kings, Grabus and Lippieus, the sons of Berisades (Diod. XVI.22.3) and Athens, conspicuously excluding both Amadocus and Cersobleptes, as well as the Thasians of former Crenides. This alignment would confirm the idea that it was Cersobleptes who attacked Crenides; if Berisades' successors motivated the attack, they are unlikely to have been accepted into the grand alliance immediately afterwards. Moreover, Philip treated Cetriporis more leniently than the other native kings ranged against him; the colonists of Philippi needed time to become established and Cetriporis remained in nominal control of his territory, probably until 352 (Dem. XXIII.179;189).[62]

The Macedonian bided his time; Cersebleptes was still refusing to give

---

[60] Monounios: see note 61. Skostokos: Höck 1891 (E 127) 106, n. 5; Ellis 1976 (D 80) 110, n. 88; Badian 1984 (E 92) 55–7; Yourukova 1976 (E 173) 26 and 1978 (E 174).

[61] Tod no. 157 (= Bengtson, SdA II no. 309; Harding no. 70).

[62] Cawkwell 1978 (D 73) 44–5; Hammond and Griffith 1979 (D 50) 252.

ground over the Chersonese to Athens. In 353 Philip made an exploratory mission, ostensibly to escort the Theban Pammenes on his way to Asia, but more also to test Thracian reactions. Embarking from western Thrace, he was intercepted by Amadocus at Maronea (Dem. XXIII.183; Diod. XVI.34). In retaliation Philip attacked Maronea and Abdera on his return journey (Polyaen. IV.2.22). The two cities did not belong to any anti-Macedonian axis. The incident only makes sense if they were in some sense aligned with the two independent Thracian kings.

Cersobleptes' reaction to the expedition tends to confirm such an interpretation. He immediately sent a Greek envoy, Apollonides, to Philip, but evidently had no satisfactory reply. In the following year, pressed by Chares' recapture of Sestus, the Odrysian was obliged to come to terms with Athens (Diod. XVI.34.3). This provided Philip with the formal·means of treating Cersobleptes as a self-proclaimed enemy. Amadocus, caught between the hammer and the anvil, threw in his lot with Philip, thus reversing his policy of the previous year (Theop. *FGrH* 115 F 101). Together they attacked Cersobleptes, who had apparently quarrelled with Byzantium and Perinthus over 'disputed territory' (schol. Aeschin. II.81; cf. [Ar]. *Oec.* II. 27; Dem. XXIII.142,165,167). No doubt such stories were easy enough to concoct. What is interesting is that Philip felt he needed such pretexts to intervene. He did not observe such fastidiousness for protocol consistently, whether with regard to the Greek cities or non-Greek communities, but at this time he was anxious to be seen as acting according to inter-state protocol. He did not need the support of the Greek cities to achieve his programme in the region, but their enmity could upset his plans. Philip gambled on success by attacking his targets unprepared. Unforeseen delays could diminish his control of events. Cersobleptes was defeated and reduced to vassal status, one of his sons a hostage at Pella. Nothing is known about the confrontation or the campaign as a whole. Amadocus and Cetriporis were deposed (Dem. 1.13). Amadocus seems to have been replaced by Teres, perhaps a son or younger relative, whose coinage is closely derived from that of the former ([Dem.] XII.8;10).[63]

Greek written sources are particularly lacunose with regard to Philip's staged conquest of Thrace in 352, 346 and the final war of attrition between 342 and 340. The fragments of Theopompus' *Philippica* and the very brief references in Diodorus do not amount to a coherent stategy. Demosthenes' political speeches from the same period project events from an aggressively pro-Athenian perspective which is emotional, belligerent and unscrupulous. As a result it is almost impossible to make any realistic assessment of Philip's most extensive territorial conquests outside Greece. There are hints that the Greek cities of the Pontic coast

[63] Yourukova 1976 (E 173) 21, pl. 9. 58–63; Domaradzki and Yourukova 1990 (E 112) 16, fig. 10.

may have hoped to play off the native tribal leaders against him – a situation which Philip was determined to avoid. Cersobleptes was reputed to have made war on Byzantium, Perinthus and Amadocus about 'disputed territory' (schol. Aeschin. II.81 (Dindorf, 57.12)). A sudden act of aggression at this delicate juncture is implausible. More likely than not Philip exploited a long standing dispute at this time because he had managed to persuade Amadocus that they could attack Cersobleptes jointly and win (Theop. *FGrH* 115 F 101). His illness during the siege of Heraion Teichos (Dem. III.4) – undertaken, presumably, in support of Perinthus, though the causes are obscure – prevented a satisfactory resolution at this point.

In 346, while peace negotiations were in progress in Greece, Philip resumed the pacification of Thrace by capturing key forts along the Aegean coast and Chersonese, including Serrheium, Doriscus, Ergisce, Myrtenum, Ganus and Hieron Oros, most, if not all of which had been fortified or strengthened by Chares and Diopeithes in the years since 351 to give substance to the new understanding between Athens and Cersobleptes (Dem. III.15; VIII.64; IX.15; XIX.150; 156;164;334; XVIII.25;27; [Dem.] VII.36–7; Aeschin. II.90; III.83). Meanwhile, at Athens, Cersobleptes' envoy, Critobulus of Lampsacus, was deliberately excluded from becoming a signatory to the peace negotiations with Philip (Aeschin. II.81ff; III.83). This merely played into Philip's hands and enabled him to pick off Cersobleptes' forts without embarrassment. Demosthenes' frequent railings against Philip's supposed duplicity were a sham; it was he who made sure that Critobulus was not heard. Demosthenes himself must have realized earlier that the Macedonian would not accept peace proposals if he were not allowed a free hand in Thrace.

The events of 346 give some idea of Philip's methods. He proceeded slowly, capturing key strategic locations and fortifying them before moving into the Thracian plain for the final onslaught. The network of forts along the coast was mirrored further inland.[64] The campaign of 346 secured a broad fan of defensive posts stretching well into the hinterland of the north Aegean, providing the framework on which to launch a pincer movement across Rhodope towards the richest and most important centres of the Odrysians. In the Strymon valley these posts extended almost as far as the Rupel Pass; Amphipolis and Philippi dominated the Drama Plain. It was probably at this time that Philip formally moved the eastern border of Macedonia to the Nestus.[65] East of the Nestus

---

[64] Kalyva: *ArchDelt* 29 (1973/4) Chr. 2/2, 804; 30 (1976) Chr. 2/2. 300, pl. 204a; 31 (1977) Chr. 2/2, 312–13. *ArchDelt* 29 (1973/4) Chr. 2/2. 805 (Aerikon), 808 and *ArchEph* 1971, Chr. 40 (Koptero).

[65] Str. VII (C 331) F 33; VII.7.4 (C 323); May 1966 (B 206) 286ff; Hammond and Griffith 1979 (D 50) 364–5; Badian 1984 (E 92) 66, n. 54.

Macedonian strength was probably more localized and confined to the coast itself, although Antipater had certainly reached Aprus (Theop. *FGrH* 115 F 160). This would indicate that the Macedonians had succeeded in cutting Cersobleptes off from the coast well before the final campaign beginning in 442. Philip subsequently had to contend with Diopeithes snapping at his heels (Philoch. *FGrH* 328 F 158; Dem. VIII. Hypoth. 2f; 6;21;26ff; 58 (=IX.60), IX.35; [Dem.] XII. 3 and 11). But at least he would have had a cordon sanitaire separating the increasingly antagonized coastal cities from his Thracian opponents.

Virtually nothing is known about the final onslaught, which occupied Philip fully for more than two years of continuous fighting. Greek writers delighted in underscoring the grisly encounters, the harsh winters and uncompromising geography (Dem. VIII.2;14;35;44; Aen. Tact. XVI.6; Polyaen. IV.2.4;13). Philip held overall command but deployed his generals across selected regions. Antipater and Parmenion spent some time fighting the mountain tribes of Rhodope; we know of an incident in which the Tetrachoritae were involved, (Theopomp. *FGrH* 115 F 217; Polyaen. IV.4.1; Steph. Byz. s.v. *Bessi*). Alexander the Great received his first independent command at this time, taking a separate force up the Strymon valley, beyond Philip's new foundation at Heraclea Sintica through the Rupel Pass and into the territory of the Maedi. A garrison post built on a former native settlement and now housing a mixture of Macedonians, Thracians and probably Greeks, was rather proudly dubbed Alexandria (Plut. *Alex.* 9.1).

Philip's plans were ambitious. He realised that this vast region, far larger than Macedonia itself, would require the deployment of huge numbers in manpower in order to be governed effectively (Justin VIII.3.6; 3.7–6.2). South of Rhodope a dense network of new settlements arose. In Parorbelia alone Callipolis, Orthopolis. Philippopolis and Garescus (Str. VII (C331) F 36) were probably satellites of Heraclea Sintica, to which might be added forts, towers and other strongpoints. Philip undoubtedly adopted the same policy north of Rhodope. The odd names bandied about by Demosthenes were deliberately chosen to belittle the purpose of the campaign. Drongylium and Masteira might have been large villages for all we know (Dem. VIII.44; X.15). Eumolpias, renamed Philippopolis (Pliny *HN* IV.11.41; Ptol. III.11.12; Amm. Marc. XXII.2.12) was not, apparently, a princely seat. There was a sanctuary on Nebet tepe, one of the three hills which make up the acropolis, during the Early Iron Age. Later ancient as well as modern buildings overlie the fourth-century B.C. levels. No fortifications which might be associated with Philip's reorganization can be identified; it is likely that the earlier phases of existing defensive structures were obliterated in hellenistic and Roman times. But new evidence has recently been found of buildings at the foot of the acropolis' north-east side, while further south, in the area of the Roman forum, several metres of hellenistic levels, including the agora, show that the layout of the Roman city probably goes back to Philip's day.[66]

Of Philip's other named foundations, neither Binae nor Beroe have yet been identified. At Cabyle (Theop. *FGrH* 115 F 110; 220; Dem. VIII.44; X.15; Polyb. XIII.10.10; Anaxim. *FGrH* 72 F 12; Pliny *HN* III.2.12; Str. VII.6.2, 320) the hellenistic levels have not yet been reached in the lower city. But a tower superimposed on the rock sanctuary of Artemis Phosphoros on the steep acropolis, together with sections of the west wall, including a square bastion and rectangular gate built of coarsely fitted isodomic masonry, can confidently be assigned to the original fort on the basis of stratigraphy.[67] Likewise the magnificent defences of the 'Krakra' hillfort at Pernik, south-west of Sofia, probably belong to the time of Philip or Alexander, though in this case there is no stratigraphic confirmation.[68] Activity on the site suddenly expanded in the last third of the fourth century and came to an end some time early in the third. The polygonal circuit wall, originally articulated by rectangular towers only one of which survives, crowns a steep scarp in a magnificent position overlooking the upper Strymon river. As at Cabyle, the circuit has two skins, here built of finely hammered isodomic blocks on a rusticated socle. Drains, water spouts and interior staircases were built to the same meticulous standard. But a comparison of the two sites shows how variable the outward character of these frontier posts might be. Neither seems to have been in Macedonian hands for more than half a century.

The Greek sources concentrate on Philip's administrative and fiscal reorganization of the former Odrysian kingdom (Dem. VIII.44f; Diod. XVI.71.1; Arr. *Anab.* VII.9.2). The creation of a *strategos epi Thrakes* fits Philip's plans though there is no conclusive evidence of such a post before Alexander assumed control (Arr. *Anab.* I.1.6; 1.25.2; Diod. XVII.62.5; Curtius XI.44; Justin XII.2.16).[69] At Vetren phase 1 is followed by a period of Macedonian occupation. The fortification wall was modified in line with new structures, also ashlar built, but serving different functions. A new domestic quarter with houses of several rooms, clearly following Aegean patterns, and including a fine new drain, arose immediately inside the old fortification wall. But a chamber

---

[66] Botusharova 1963 (E 94) and 1966 (E 95); Botusharova and Tankova 1982 (E 96); A. Peykov in Velkov 1986 (E 167) 30–40; *AOR* 1989 (1990) 64–5; Domaradzki 1990 (E 111) 30.

[67] V. Velkov, *Klio* 62 (1980) 5–11, and 1983 (E 166), *Kabyle* I (1982); Domaradzki 1982 (E 108) and in Velkov 1991 (E 168) 54–81 for the stratigraphic evidence.

[68] Changova 1982 (E 98) 52ff.

[69] Ellis 1976 (D 80) 170, n. 60, 174, n. 64; Cawkwell 1978 (D 73) 44; Badian 1984 (E 92) 70 (Philip); Hammond and Griffith 1979 (D 50) 558–9 (Alexander).

tomb of ashlar masonry built under a mound in close proximity to the site around the turn of the fourth century follows native architectural fashions. Perhaps the local dynasty was reinstated.

VI. SCYTHIANS, TRIBALLI AND GETAE

Philip II's invasion of the Odrysian kingdom caused uproar in the territories beyond. The main beneficiaries in the first instance were the Triballi, who probably attacked a Scythian enclave near the Danube around this time (Polyaen. VII.44.1; Frontin. II.4.20).[70] The incident provides no evidence of an eastward shift of Triballian communities and demographic movement is very difficult to substantiate archaeologically. There are some similarities in finds west and east of the Iskur river, the boundary of the Triballi in Thucydides, but these may be due more to material resemblances between the dominant social groups in both areas. Wealthy tomb inventories such as that in Moghilanska Mogila, Vratsa, west of the Iskur, are paralleled by a plethora of analogous finds in the Lovech region.[71] The significance of such finds, particularly gilded parade armour and harness ornaments, is connected with the general problem of metalwork decorated in the 'Animal Style', examples of which have been found as far apart as the southern Ukraine and the Iron Gates. Warrior burials between Haemus and the Danube indicate a highly mobile, eclectic culture in the fourth century, but the nature of this society has yet to be evaluated. Triballian settlements and patterns of land use are at present completely unknown, and the same is true of the region between the Osam and Yantra rivers.

The encounter with the Scythians involved Atheas, a king whose coins, which show a bearded, long-haired bowman on horseback, have been found between the Danube and the Romanian border with Bulgaria. They were struck at Callatis and some of this city's coins were overstruck in his name.[72] Otherwise there is little evidence to associate with this Scythian enclave. It is fair to say that Scythian pottery, of a type known at Histria and its environs in the late sixth century and sometimes associated with the Scythian incursions following Darius' withdrawal, begins to reappear, and in greater quantities, in the fourth at sites in central Dobrudja. But it is absent from the excavated cemeteries of southern Dobrudja, that is, in the hinterland of Histria and Callatis.[73]

---

[70] Papazoglou 1978 (E 82) 45–63; Fol 1975 (E 119) 9–24; Fol and Spiridonov 1983 (E 120) 59–61.

[71] Dimitrov 1957 (E 106); Venedikov 1966 (E 169); Nikolov 1968 (E 147); further references in note 51; P. Alexandrescu, *Dacia* 27 (1983) 1–2, 45–66.

[72] V. A. Anokhin, *Numizmatika i Sfragistika* (Kiev 1965) II 3–15, and *Skifskye Drevnosti* (Kiev 1973) 20–41; Rogalski 1961 (E 153) and 1970 (E 154).

[73] Pippidi 1971 (E 150) 91–2, and 1977 (E 151) 386–7, n. 26; Melyukova 1979 (E 139) 137–41, 239–44.

These regions traditionally belonged to the Getae, who straddled the Danube delta. Getae and Scythians co-existed along the lower Dniester and there are definite signs of Scythian penetration, in the form of underground chamber tombs, in the Dobrudja. But the two communities maintained their separateness, at least in material terms. Soviet archaeologists have noted considerable discontinuities in the occupation of the steppe zone during the Scythian period and now believe that the Scythian tribes were for the most part small independent groups which only began to become sedentary during the fifth century B.C.[74] Whatever Atheas' power, there is nothing on the Danube to compare with the wealth of the Royal Scythians in the lower Don and Dnieper valleys, not least because Atheas' followers were still a migrant and not a settled community.

Nevertheless, it is likely that antagonism arose between such incoming groups of nomadic Scythians and the resident Getic communities. The Getae had been federated with the Odrysians in the fifth century; how these relations developed in the following century is unknown. With the fall of the Odrysian kings the Getae found themselves in an ambiguous position. As Philip's mastery over the Thracian plain became more pronounced during 341, the tribal communities outside the former Odrysian kingdom could no longer be indifferent to their new neighbour. Many Greek cities opportunistically expressed support for Macedon (Diod. XVI.71), but it would be presumptuous to assume that most wanted or were in a position to do so.

Odessus was at this time subjected, it seems, to the lordship of the neighbouring Getae and their king Cothelas (Gudila). The story is preserved in Jordanes, who cites Dio (Chrysostom), but the ultimate source may well have been Theopompus (Jord. *Get.* x, 65; cf. Theop. *FGrH* 115 F 216 (= Athen. XIV.24 p. 627d–e)). Philip, short of funds, ordered his troops to raid the territory of Odessus. To the Macedonians' surprise, the city gates suddenly opened and they were confronted by a procession of white-robed priests, intoning supplicatory prayers and strumming citharas. Instead of attacking the city, Philip concluded a treaty and made Cothelas' daughter Mēdopa his wife. This account is consistent with the list of Philip's wives as given by the early hellenistic Peripatetic biographer, Satyrus, where the Getic princess Meda, who brought with her an impressive dowry, is reported as a legitimate wife alongside Olympias (Satyrus F 5 = Athen. XIII, 557b–e). This marriage was intended to cement relations between the Macedonian crown and an important border region, analogous to Alexander's union with Bactrian Roxane. Both Jordanes and Satyrus accord this union considerable

[74] Marchenko and Vinogradov 1989 (E 138).

significance.[75] This becomes more comprehensible in the light of evidence from a growing number of sites which can be associated with Getic communities in the hinterland of Odessus. Contacts between these Getae and the Greek colonists began early on and appear to have been fluid. Sixth-century Greek pottery turns up in the cremation cemeteries of Dobrina and Ravna, while a range of rich warrior burials located between Rousse on the Danube, Haemus and Odessus, equipped with native and imported metalwork, pottery and armour reflects the aspirations of an emergent elite in the late fifth and early fourth century.[76] In the early hellenistic period this region flourished as never before. A cult complex which began to be used from the early first millennium B.C. near Sboryanovo, Razgrad, situated on the Kamen Rid ridge and extending into the valleys below, was redesigned at this time. Likewise a number of elaborate tombs in the associated tumular necropolis, including the lavishly sculptured barrel-vaulted chamber inside Ginina Mogila have illuminated the extensive cultural influences, Asiatic as well as Greek and Macedonian, which were grafted onto a very distinctive local burial tradition.[77]

VII. PHILIP II, ATHEAS AND THE TRIBALLI

The final stage of Philip's Thracian campaign was the defeat, in 339, of the Scythian leader Atheas. This incident lost some of its aura when the Triballi intercepted the returning Macedonian armies and managed to steal the entire booty, including 20,000 brood mares, as many captives and large flocks of cattle (Justin IX.3.1–3.3). There is a lack of correspondence and clarity in the sources concerning these events. Justin describes a series of negotiations between Philip and Atheas which are full of ambiguity. First the people of Apollonia are represented as requesting Philip's aid on Atheas' behalf, against 'the Histrians', with whom the Scythian is at war. Atheas ostensibly offers to make Philip his heir. Philip sends troops. Following the death of the 'rex Histrianorum', Atheas appears to change his tune; he sends back the Macedonians and denies having made requests of Philip. Philip's vow to erect a statue of Heracles at the mouth of the Danube is thus an attempt to salvage some pride from an embarrassing misunderstanding.[78]

    The marriage of Philip to Meda and his foray into Getic terrain is usually treated as a separate incident, preceding the confrontation with

---

[75] A. Tronson, *JHS* 104 (1984) 120–3; Gardiner-Garden 1989 (E 121) 29–40.
[76] Chichikova 1969 (E 99).
[77] Chichikova 1988 (E 101); Gergova 1988 (E 123); articles in *Terra Antiqua Balcanica* 3 (1988), 4 (1990).   [78] Gardiner-Garden 1989 (E 121) 33–4.

Atheas by one or two years at least.[79] The chronological relationship between the two events cannot be ascertained; but it is probable that they were connected. Both Jordanes and Justin present Philip's forays into this region as attempts to restore depleted finances. Jordanes makes no reference to Scythians, but this selectivity is characteristic of his whole work, which was conceived as an encomium of the Gothic people. Equally, Justin concentrates exclusively on the Scythians; his narrative involves the region of the Danube estuary, though we know that Atheas was also connected with Callatis (modern Mangalia), which lay south of Tomi (Costantia), in whose vicinity were the Odessitan lands raided by Philip according to Jordanes. It is difficult to believe that Philip would have concluded an important alliance with Cothelas in 341, given clear social expression in the marriage-alliance, and then envisaged partnership with a manifestly impoverished and rather insignificant Scythian leader, himself in difficulty with his neighbours, unless there were some very specific advantage to be gained thereby.

According to Clement of Alexandria, citing Aristocritus (*Strom.* v.31.3) the Scythian king Atheas threatened that if the Byzantines continued to damage his 'revenues', his horses 'would drink their water'. This may be an authentic Scythian remark,[80] and it is just possible to connect it with Philip's siege of Byzantium because of Justin's reference to demands made by Philip of Atheas towards the cost of the siege. Atheas is most unlikely ever to have been in a position to carry out these threats on Byzantine territory. The Propontis, an area patrolled by Thracian and occasionally Greek armies since the beginning of the fourth century, had been systematically strengthened by Cersobleptes since 351. Athenian commanders, particularly Diopeithes, lurked along the coast. The threats are therefore understood as indirect, aimed at Byzantine overseas interests (at Histria?)[81] or connected in some other way with Philip's siege.

Perhaps this was a plan which simply went wrong. Philip may have offered Atheas alliance knowing that the Scythian was in difficulties and then been embarrassed by a well-publicized refusal. Philip was no ally for a recently arrived migrant Scythian community proud of its independence but vulnerable to attack, whether from the Triballi or an alliance of Greeks and Getae. The 'rex Histrianorum' might well represent a Getic leader who had managed to enforce his authority over the city in the same way that Cothelas seems to have done over Odessus. Philip's Getic connexions must only have strengthened Atheas' suspicions of him. Despite the lost booty this was no negative campaign. Philip had

[79] Momigliano 1933 (E 145); Alexandrescu 1967 (E 89); Shelov 1971 (E 160); V. Iliescu, *Historia* 20 (1971) 172–85; Pippidi 1971 (E 150) 90–5, and 1977 (E 151); Hammond and Griffith 1979 (D 50) 561–3.   [80] Cf. Rolle 1989 (E 341) 109.   [81] Momigliano 1933 (E 145) 344.

the distinction of having been one of those very rare commanders who managed to defeat a Scythian army in battle, a feat which neither Darius nor any Greek general shared (Frontin. II.8.14). In the antechamber of tomb II at Vergina there was a gold-plated bow-case of a well-known Scythian type, and the kind illustrated on Atheas' coins.[82] Objects such as these might have been saved from the Triballi where slaves and animals were lost. The gold, iron-backed pectoral from the same tomb, however, has good parallels both in Thrace and Macedonia, and is probably a localized form of parade armour adapted by the Macedonians.[83]

The impressive warrior burials below tumuli which, during the fourth century, increased in size from ashlar-built cists into elaborate vaulted chambers reflect the progressive accumulation of wealth and economic power of a restricted social group throughout the Thracian tribes, but especially those in the richest agricultural lands of the Thracian plain and river valleys north of Haemus. Many of the pre-Macedonian tomb assemblages, such as the unlooted semi-underground chamber at Kaloyanovo, Sliven,[84] reflect a variety of styles and contacts, Aegean, steppe and regional Thracian, which were superseded by more eclectic and more uniform displays, such as the jewellery and horse trappings from a third-century female cremation at Kralevo, Turgovishte.[85] The circulation of Greek coins and imports such as wine amphorae (mainly from Thasos and to a much lesser extent, Chios, followed towards the end of this period by Rhodes, Cos, Heracleia Pontica and Sinope) assumed a mass character only in the second half of the fourth century, although both the volume, the rate of acquisition of such imports and their distribution has been modified significantly by evidence from settlement sites such as Seuthopolis, Kabyle, Asara and Vetren.[86]

Philip's conquest of Odrysian Thrace brought the territories south of Haemus firmly into the Greco-Macedonian political sphere. Many material features first seen in the Aegean, such as the use of ashlar masonry, wheel-turned pottery decorated with a lustrous glaze, certain vessel shapes in silver and bronze, coinage and the use of Greek as the language of diplomacy and commerce, were well established among native communities at least half a century before the foundation of Philippi. It is ironic that the monuments to Argead supremacy in these regions, military forts like Kabyle, Pernik and Philippopolis, proved the most ephemeral or were superseded by native foundations, swelled by a non-military population.

---

[82] Andronikos 1984 (D 6) 180–6, figs. 146–9; Schiltz 1979 (E 158).
[83] Archibald 1985 (E 91).   [84] Chichikova 1969 (E 100).   [85] Ginev 1983 (E 125).
[86] M. Lazarov in *Actes du II Congres Internat. de Thracologie* II (1980) 171–87 and *INMV* 18 (1982) 5–14; A. Bozhkova, *Vekove* 1988.3, 25–33.

CHAPTER 9f

THE BOSPORAN KINGDOM

JOHN HIND

I. INTRODUCTION: TOPOGRAPHY AND SOURCES

Exposed on the extreme north-eastern rim of the classical Greek, and later of the hellenistic, world, was the Bosporan state, ruled from about 438 B.C. for 330 years by dynasts bearing Greek and Thracian names – Spartocus, Leucon, Satyrus, Paerisades. The ruler styled himself '*archon* of Bosporus and Theodosia', and 'king of the Sindi, Toreti, Dandarii and Psessi', or sometimes 'king of all the Maeotians'.[1] From the early fourth century B.C. the state comprised the eastern portion of the Crimea (Kerch Peninsula) and the opposing part of the northern Caucasus (Taman Peninsula), separated by the sea current flowing through the then Cimmerian Bosporus (present-day Straits of Kerch). On the Asiatic side in Taman were once five islands in the delta of the Antikeites/Hypanis (now River Kuban); here the Sindi, agriculturally very productive, lay immediately inland of the Greek cities in the lower valley of the Hypanis. In the Kerch Peninsula a native population of sedentary Scythians, and perhaps some remaining Cimmerians left behind from their wanderings of the late eighth century B.C., exploited the area's noted fertility.

The main cities in the area were three in the Kerch Peninsula, Panticapaeum, Nymphaeum, Theodosia, which last was annexed to Bosporus some years after 390 B.C., and three on the islands and in the Kuban delta to the east of the straits, Phanagoria, Hermonassa, and Gorgippia, in the hinterland of which lay the Sindi who were incorporated in Bosporus between 400 and 375 B.C. A number of other small townships flourished by the Bosporus, situated near salt-water lakes or inlets (limans) or under rocky headlands – Porthmieus, Myrmecium, Tyritace, Cimmericum, Acra, Cytaea, and a lost Hermisium on the Crimean side.[2] On Taman were Achilleum, Patraeus, Cepi, Tyrambe, Corocondame and another missing town called Stratoclia. In the fourth century the Bosporan state comprised some 5,000 sq. km. of territory, thirty towns large and small, and a population of approximately

---

[1] Minns 1913 (E 321) 573–80; Gaidukyevich 1971 (E 241) 70–4; V. V. Struve *et al.*, *Corpus Ins. Regni Bosporani* (1965) nos. 6–10, 971–2, 1037–40; Tod no. 115, 171; Harding no. 27.
[2] Minns 1913 (E 321) 20–4; Shelov-Kovyedyayev 1985 (E 378) 24–44.

100,000–120,000 citizens and subjects. It profited from a brisk trade up-country with much of the Ukraine and the North Caucasus, then ranged and dominated by the nomad and 'Royal' Scythians.

Strabo (*c.* 64 B.C.–A.D. 21) gives the best ancient account of the natural resources of Bosporus and the prosperity flowing from them:

> The Chersonesus [the Crimea], except for the mountainous area which extends along the sea as far as Theodosia, is everywhere level and fertile and is exceedingly productive of grain; it yields thirtyfold, whatever implement is used. In earlier times the Greeks used to import their corn from there and their salted fish from Lake Maeotis. Leucon is said to have once despatched 2,100,000 medimni of grain from Theodosia to Athens.
>
> (Strabo VII.4.6)

Some four centuries before Strabo, and three quarters of a century before Leucon ruled on the Bosporus, Herodotus had noted the same basic items of trade at Olbia/Borysthenes on the joint estuaries of the Rivers Bug and Dnieper far away in the north-western corner of the Black Sea (IV.53). He describes the unparalleled pastures by the great River Borysthenes (Dnieper), a river more bountiful than any but the Nile, providing excellent and abundant fish stocks (sturgeon), salt for their preserving, and in the surrounding steppe the deep soil ideal for growing grain. Some tribes grew this specifically for sale (IV.17–18). Presumably this was marketed at Olbia/Borysthenes, the 'port of trade' (*emporion*), known to and visited by Herodotus.

These international markets merit some attention. They were not small trading posts preceding colonies proper, nor mere merchant communities dependent on neighbouring large *poleis*. A city with an exceptional trading interest might itself rather loosely be referred to as an *emporion* as well as a polis.[3] Besides Olbia/Borysthenes, another such mart is mentioned by Herodotus – Cremni, the *emporion* for the Royal Scythians, which lay on the European side of Lake Maeotis (IV.20; 110). As the Cimmerian Bosporus was another name for the mouth of Lake Maeotis, it may well be that Cremni ('the Cliffs') was the earliest Greek name for Panticapaeum itself (Mt Mithridates is almost 190 m high) or for nearby Nymphaeum, which lay on a line of cliffs, rising some 24 m above the sea and containing caves; it had a good harbour and exceptionally close links with the surrounding Scythians during the fifth century B.C.[4] The third possibility is that Cremni was at an unlocated site near Taganrog on the northern shore of Lake Maeotis (Sea of Azov), where as yet only pottery, some much eroded by the sea, but some clearly

---

[3] Hind 1985 (E 259) 105–9; Karyshkovsky 1962 (E 277).
[4] Hind 1985 (E 259) 109–16 (for Panticapaeum); Khudyak 1945 (E 280) 149; Grach 1981 (E 249), 1985 (E 251) (for the character of Nymphaeum).

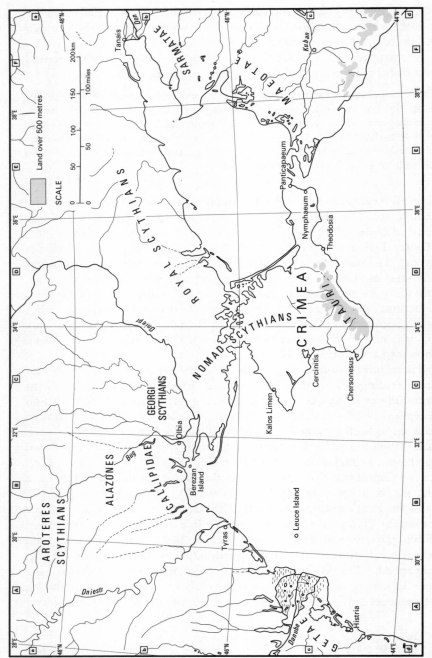

Map 15. The north coast of the Black Sea.

of the later sixth and first half of the fifth century B.C.,[5] has been found.[6] A change of name, rather than total abandonment, of the *emporion*, may best explain the disappearance of Herodotus' Cremni after the fifth century.

Later both Panticapaeum and Phanagoria became great *emporia* on the proceeds of the above-mentioned products, to which should be added furs, hides and slaves (Strabo VII.4.5). In later hellenistic times at least, and probably much earlier, Panticapaeum was the great centre for goods coming up from the Black Sea, and Phanagoria for trade with the Kuban River valley and the eastern shores of the Sea of Azov (Strabo XI.2.10; Appian *Mith.* 107–8). From the later fourth century there was also a Bosporan Greek trading settlement in the Don delta (River Tanais) at the native site of Elizavetovskoye, but it had already been destroyed by *c.* 250 B.C. Perhaps it was the 'settlement of mixed people', later given the name Alopecia by Strabo. At any rate it was overshadowed by the more regular *emporion* founded further west at Nedvigovka by the Bosporan rulers in the early third century B.C., which firmly took to itself the alternative names Tanais and Emporion (Strabo VII.4.5; XII.2.3).[7] Yet another site, Theodosia, on the Black Sea coast of the Crimea, was developed into an *emporion* between *c.* 390 and 350 B.C. by Leucon (Dem. XX.33), and later had a harbour for a hundred ships (Strabo VII.4.4).

Taken together with Herodotus and Strabo (who gives information from Ephorus, Posidonius, Apollonides and other hellenistic writers),[8] there are some forty ancient literary sources for Bosporan history of this period. They range from the sixth century B.C. (fragments of Alcaeus, Hipponax, Aristeas and Hecataeus) to the largely out-of-date material gathered in the *Res Gestae* of Ammianus Marcellinus in the late fourth century A.D. (XXII.8.26–32) and in the Anonymous Periplus (Sailing Manual) of the fifth century.[9] A valuable insight into the conditions of trade and into the 'World of the Emporion' in the fourth century B.C. is afforded by several private speeches of the Attic orators (Lys. XVI.4; Isoc. *Trap.* III.5.7; Aeschin. III.191–2; Dem. XX. *In Lept.* 20; 29–40; XXXIV *In Phorm.* 8;36–7; Dinarchus, *In Dem.* 43). There is a hostile strain in many of these references; the Bosporan rulers are barbarian tyrants, and may be enemies of Athenian interests. Yet they are also trading partners and worth heaping with honours as suppliers of corn. A series of anecdotes is set in the early-fourth-century wars of Satyrus and Leucon against Heraclea Pontica over Theodosia, and against the Maeotae over the Sindi; they have been culled from such major lost historians as Phylarchus and Hieronymus of Cardia and preserved in

---

[5] Blavatsky 1963 (E 202) 93–8; Kopylov 1990 (E 289).   [6] Boltruk and Fialk 1987 (E 208).
[7] Marchenko 1986 (E 313), 1990 (E 314); Arsenyeva and Shelov 1988 (E 183).
[8] Gratsianskaya 1988 (E 254) 34–146.   [9] Diller 1952 (B 34) 130–3.

collections of military stratagems ([Arist.] *Oec.* II.2.8; Aen. Tact. v.2; Polyaen. v.23; 44; vi.9.2–4; vii.57; Ael. *VH* vi.13; Ath. 257a; 349d).

Valuable circumstantial detail is provided by two very different works of the first century B.C. The first is a versified Periplus, which seems to owe its Pontic expertise to Ephorus, but also to local hellenistic writers, Demetrius of Callatis, and perhaps to writers about the origins of cities such as Dionysius of Chalcis and Polemo of Ilium ([Scymn.] *Ad Nicomedem Regem* 795–898).[10] The second work is the *Library of History* by Diodorus Siculus, and to it we owe our knowledge of the chronological framework of Bosporan history between *c.*480 and 264 B.C. (Diod. XII.31.1; 36.1; XIV.9.3; XVI.36; XVI.52; XX.101.7). Essentially this is a list of rulers with the numbers of years they ruled. At several points there is confusion in the number of years assigned to individuals; there is corruption of names and numerals, and misinterpretation of joint periods of rule and successive reigns. Anachronistically, all the dynasts are referred to as 'reigning' or as 'kings'. Yet this structure is our only extant framework, and once (311/10 B.C.) it burgeons into a full-scale narrative of civil war between the brothers Satyrus, Prytanis and Eumelus (Diod. XX.22–6). Some local historian, such as Syriscus of Chersonesus,[11] given wider circulation by Chrysippus, the Stoic philosopher, may have been the source of these entries (Strabo vii.4.3), and for the now lost sections of Pompeius Trogus' History – *origines et res gestae regum Bosporanorum et Colchorum* (Justin prol. xxxvii). The final episode in the history of this dynasty was the abdication of power by the last Paerisades (V) to Mithridates VI of Pontus at a time when he was hardpressed by the Scythians of the Crimea, as well as by the internal faction led by his former protégé, Saumacus (Strabo vii.3.17, 4.4, 4.7; Chersonesite decree for Diophantus).[12]

Diodorus' chronological list can be corrected by using fourth- and early-third-century decrees from Athens (*IG* ii² 212; 653). Dedications found at the international religious centres of Delphi, Delos and Branchidae give further information about the later Bosporan rulers. Their titles and the lists of their subject peoples appear in inscriptions found on the Bosporus itself. Proxeny decrees for representatives of foreign cities illustrate trading connexions. Administration, the composition of the population and the deities worshipped, likewise receive illumination from honorary decrees, grave monuments and religious dedications from a total of some 190 inscriptions of this period.[13]

There has been considerable detailed study by numismatists of the

---

[10] Diller 1952 (B 34) 168–72.
[11] Rostovtzeff 1915 (E 344) (for Syriscus) and 1931 (E 350) 112–14 (for the local Bosporan historian); Struve 1968 (E 396); Martin 1981 (D 104).   [12] Minns 1913 (E 321) 647–8, no. 18.
[13] Struve 1965, see n. 1 (inscriptions given chronologically and by site).

early silver coinage of Panticapaeum, thought to commence in the late sixth or early fifth century B.C., and of the smaller Bosporan cities of the second half of the fifth and early fourth century (Nymphaeum, Phanagoria, Theodosia and the Sindi).[14] These provide unexpected detail (and some ground for disagreement among scholars) about the political situation obtaining on the Bosporus before the unification enforced by Satyrus and Leucon. Some otherwise barely known bearers of the name Spartocus and Paerisades are given substance for us by the gold and silver 'royal' coins of the later third and second centuries B.C. In addition political influences, hints at the staple products, and traces of economic trends can be divined from the types, symbols, countermarks, denominations and weight reductions of the Bosporan coins within the long period from the early fifth to the late second century B.C.

Lastly, a century and a half of excavation on the sites of some fifteen ancient Bosporan towns, and at hundreds of rural settlements and *necropoleis* and tumuli in the Kerch and Taman Peninsulas, has amassed a vast store of material and information. Trade is largely plotted by finds of imported wine amphorae, fine decorated pottery and metalwork. But studies of burial practices, the linear defences (ditches and walls), city fortifications, town planning, and the phases of construction and destruction, have all filled out the material side of life in the Bosporan state before the coming of the Pontic and Roman intervention.[15] Most recently underwater excavations have revealed the submerged parts of cities (Phanagoria, Cepi) and of entire small towns (Acra), not to mention what are effectively small one-period sites – the ancient shipwrecks found in the Bosporus Straits or off the coasts of the Crimea.[16]

II. COLONIZATION IN THE BLACK SEA AND BY THE BOSPORUS

The Greeks of the homeland held distant, but deeply stamped, impressions of the vast area north of the Black Sea, not least that the sea itself was a wide open main, 'Pontus', with dangerous shores, coastal peoples who indulged in piracy and the wrecking of ships, and an almost total lack of islands (Xen. *An.* VII.3.16; Ath. 353c.) unlike their own Aegean. Its supposed original name *axenos*, 'inhospitable', was said to have been later euphemistically changed to *euxeinos*, 'hospitable', as it became a familiar sea ([Scymn.] 734–7; Strabo VII.3.6). However, the original name may have meant 'dark' (Iranian *akshaeina*), as does the Turkish *Kara Deniz* and Russian *Chernoye Morye*.[17]

[14] Shelov 1978 (E 372); Anokhin 1986 (E 182) 7–51.
[15] Koshelenko *et al.* 1984 (E 290) 58–98, 154–240.
[16] Peters 1982 (E 336); K. K. Shilik in *Problemy Istorii i Arkheologii Vostochnogo Kryma* (Kerch, 1984). [17] Moorhouse 1940, 1947 (E 322); Allen 1947 (E 178).

Although it was fertile and rich in natural resources, the area beyond the Black Sea was kept from easy familiarity by distance and the perception of danger. Legends floated around the area like the thick snow blizzards reported as feathers in the air too thick to permit movement (Hdt. iv.8.31). The mythical cross-continental wanderings of Io to the Caucasus and thence to Scythia were immortalized by Aeschylus (*PV* 707–35), and aetiology derived the names of the two Bosporus Straits from her passing. Heracles had been entertained and detained for a time by the Scythian snake-footed goddess (Hdt. iv.8–9), and had left his progeny as well as his footprint by the River Tyras (iv.82). The story that Iphigenia had been spirited away to the temple of Artemis among the Tauri was developed by Euripides (*IT* 85–9). Achilles lived a life after death on Leuce Island, north east of the Danube delta, and was held to race along sand spits to the east of Olbia (Alcaeus Z 31 Lobel/Page; Pind. *Nem.* iv.49–50). Hyperborean Apollo rode out on a winged griffin from the lands north of Scythia (Diod. 11.47) and gifts arrived regularly from the Hyperboreans themselves at Apollo's temple on Delos (Hdt. iv.32). By the shores of Lake Maeotis migrating Amazons were said to have mingled with a party of young Scythian men to produce the Sarmatian people (Hdt. iv.110). Eurasian shamanism seems to lie behind the story of Abaris, the Scythian, who traversed the world on an arrow (Hdt. iv.36) and that of Aristeas, a Greek from Proconnesus in the Propontis, who fell down as though dead in Cyzicus and then disappeared; he turned up seven years later and composed his poem, the *Arimaspea*, about his travels far beyond the Scythians. Among other fabulous peoples he sang of 'One-Eyed Arimaspians' and 'Griffin-Guardians of Gold'.[18] The snake-footed goddess, Amazons, griffins and Arimaspians all became favourite motifs on the metalwork of local Bosporan and Scythian artists and on the so-called 'Kerch' red-figure vases (*pelikai*) of the late fifth and fourth centuries B.C.[19] These myths and monsters were all in currency by the latter half of the fifth century. They will have entered the Greek consciousness, as the areas and peoples concerned, and their local deities, became known in the process of exploration, commercial interchange and settlement.

Greeks probably first sailed into the Black Sea in the second half of the eighth century B.C., a feat which may have later been worked up into the legend of the voyage of the fifty-oared (*penteconter*) ship Argo. Much later a 'foundation' of Sinope by crewmen of Argo was assigned by patriotic local historians to the generation before the siege of Troy ([Scymn.] 989–91). The first historical, though brief, colony at Sinope was that led by the Milesian Habron or Habrondas; the founder himself was killed and

---

[18] Dodds 1951 (H 30) 140–1; Bolton 1962 (E 207); Hommel 1980 (E 264); *VDI* 1981, 1, 53–76.
[19] Minns 1913 (E 321) 343; Kobylina 1951 (E 284).

the settlement extinguished by the Cimmerians (993–4), who were to use the Sinope peninsula as a base for their ravages of Asia Minor (Hdt. IV.12). This will have excluded the Greeks from the Pontic coast of Asia Minor for much of the seventh century. When the Milesians again looked to send colonies within the Black Sea area, after Abydus on the Hellespont and Cyzicus on the Propontis had been secured,[20] they turned at first to its west and north-west shores, probably to avoid the Cimmerians in Asia, despite the fact that the first stretch of coast northwards (Salmydessus) was harbourless and inhospitable.[21] The traditional dates for Istria (657/6 B.C.) and Borysthenes/Olbia (647/6), the one south of the Danube delta and the other on the joint estuaries of the Bug and Dniepr rivers, are given in the late chronological tables of Eusebius (in Olympiads).[22] Presumably these seemingly exact dates go back to some such relative scheme of dating as 'when the Scythians followed the Cimmerians into Asia' ([Scymn.] 768–72) and 'in the period of the Median empire' ([Scymn.] 804–12). Some time later the Milesians revived their settlement at Sinope, the Cimmerians perhaps having moved on from there to raid more lucrative targets. The oikist-founders were Cretines and Coes, exiles from Miletus, at the time 'when the Cimmerians overran Asia' ([Scymn.] 994–7). The date is presented by the late chronographic tradition as a firm 632/1 B.C. (Eusebius).[23] Subsequently a number of small cities, Sesamus, Tius, Cromna and Cytorus, were planted by Milesian colonists on the coast west of Sinope ([Scymn.] 1002–11).

Milesians proceeded to fill in uncolonized sites. On the west coast of the Crimea, near present-day Eupatoria, lay Cercinitis. Fifth-century remains have recently been found there.[24] It was a polis in Herodotus' time (Hdt. IV.55), but later came under the domination of Chersonesus. Towards the eastern side of the Crimea, on a broad curving bay, was Theodosia, a definite Milesian colony and an independent city until captured by the rulers of Bosporus (Anon. *Periplus* 50). Over on the eastern (Colchian) side of the Black Sea Milesian Greeks settled perhaps as groups of traders and artisans, as at Pichvnari near Kobuleti, rather than as *apoikoi* (colonists). 'Hellenic cities' seem to have existed from the fourth and third centuries on this coast, to judge from the literary sources, but by then a *polis hellenis* meant any Greek-style town, not necessarily an autonomous city with a true colonial foundation.[25]

[20] *CAH* III².3, 118–22. [21] Stronk 1985 (E 395).

[22] Isaac 1986 (E 129) 268–78; P. Alexandrescu and W. Schuller, *Histria: Konstanzer Althistorische Vorträge und Forschungen* 25 (1990) 50–5; Vinogradov 1989 (E 417) 33–5. For the relationship of what is now Berezan Island to Olbia see *CAH* III².3, 258 and Hind 1983/4 (E 258) 79–80.

[23] Drews 1976 (E 228); *CAH* III².3, 123; Hind 1988 (E 260).

[24] Kutaisov 1990 (E 301) and *VDI* 1986,2, 88–97.

[25] Lordkipanidze 1988 (E 308); Kacharava (E 267); Koshelenko and Kuznetsov (E 292).

The area of the Cimmerian Bosporus, with its agricultural and fishery resources, likewise did not fail to attract the Milesians. No dates, however, are given for the foundations. Panticapaeum, the later capital, was originally Milesian (Pliny *HN* iv.86), founded by driving Scythians out (Strabo xii.2.5; Ath. xii.26). Athenaeus comments in moralizing mode (following Ephorus) that in general the Milesians bestrewed the Black Sea with famous cities, expelling the Scythians, until they succumbed to luxury. For the Bosporus the truth seems to be that those sites which had been occupied in the Early Iron Age – Panticapaeum, Tyritace, Myrmecium, Nymphaeum, Cimmericum and Phanagoria – had already been abandoned by the middle of the seventh century, and that the Greek settlers would have found empty sites, or have met resistance from a weak remnant of the earlier inhabitants.[26] A curiosity in the sources is the statement that Panticapaeum was founded by a son of Colchian Aeetes on land ceded to the settlers by a Scythian king, Agaetes (Steph. Byz. 'Panticapaeum'; Eustathius, *ad Dionysium Perieget.* 311). It was named after the River Panticapes, which flowed by it. The latter was probably the Iranian name for the Bosporus itself, meaning 'fish-route' (*panti-kapa*).[27] Whether some Colchians had gone to the northern Bosporus after its vacation by the Cimmerians is unverifiable, but there were early Caucasian bronzes traded there, and later Colchian and Bosporan trading connexions in the fifth and fourth centuries are confirmed by finds of coins and pottery exchanged by both areas.[28] Perhaps the existence of the town named Cytaea south of Nymphaeum (Pliny *HN* iv.86) led some people to seek an origin for it in the legendary capital of Aeetes, Cytaean Aea.

On the eastern side of the Bosporus was Cepi ('The Gardens') also said to be Milesian ([Scymn.] 899). But other East Greek cities planted colonies here on the islands of the delta of the River Kuban. Hermonassa was settled either by Mytileneans from Lesbos, taking its name from the wife of the *oikistes*, or by unspecified Ionians from a founder named Hermon (Eustathius, *ad Dionysium* 549). To judge by the early finds from Panticapaeum, Cepi, and Hermonassa these foundations belonged to the first half of the sixth century b.c.[29] Somewhat later, *c.*545 b.c. came Phanagoria, settled by Teans, escaping from the Persian assault on their city (Hdt. 1.162–4; [Scymn.] 886–7).[30] Other towns in the Bosporus–Don delta area were either, like Cimmeris, Gorgippia and Tanais, products of later internal colonization sponsored by the 'Spartocid'

26 Shelov-Kovyedyayev 1981 (E 375) 52.
27 Abayev 1949 (E 175) 170, 175.   28 Tsetskhladze 1990 (E 403).
29 Blavatsky 1964 (E 203) 15–44; Gaidukyevich 1971 (E 241) 15–49; Koshelenko and Kuznetsov 1987 (E 291); Kuznetsov in *Tskhaltubo-Vani* vi; Zeyest 1968 (E 440); *Sov. Arch.* 1977,4, 86; Sidorova 1987 (E 385).   30 Kobylina 1983 (E 286) and 1989 (E 287).

rulers in the fourth and third centuries B.C., or towns of which tradition has recorded no origin (Myrmecium, Tyritace, Cimmericum) beyond what might be deduced from the name.

The reason for this spate of colonies can be found in lack of land, exacerbated by pressure on the mother-cities by more powerful neighbours. In Asia the Lydian kings, Gyges and Ardys, attacked a number of Ionian cities including Miletus, and their successors, Sadyattes and Alyattes fought an eleven-year-long war with her in the last quarter of the seventh century B.C. (Hdt. 1.14; 15; 17–22). During this time, no doubt, Miletus acted as a point of assembly for other refugee Ionians to go to her colonies. In addition there was the disruption caused by the Cimmerian incursions somewhat earlier in the century (Hdt. 1.6; 15–18) to cause flight from an area, Ionia, which was in normal times considered to be the ideal homeland (Hdt. 1.142). Internally there was civil strife both at Miletus and at another parent of Pontic colonies, Megara in mainland Greece; tyrants were in power in both cities in the late seventh century, Theagenes at Megara and Thrasybulus at Miletus. In the sixth century warring factions continued (*aeinautai; cheiromacha*) and threw up tyrants at Miletus, the party of Thoas and Damasenor (Plut. *Quaest. Graec.* 12; Ath. 542a).[31] With these common problems, the two mother-cities seem to have agreed to share access into the Black Sea, but to exclude others until the policy was relaxed in the interest of some smaller Ionian cities in the second quarter of the sixth century.

Miletus underwent two generations of these troubles until the men of Paros were invited to arbitrate, and moderated the strife (Hdt. v.29), by which time Miletus' position externally was much improved by a long-lasting treaty with King Croesus, and confirmed by the Persians in a way that gave her a special position among the Ionian cities (Hdt. 1.141, 143,169). In the second half of the sixth century she was the 'showpiece' of Ionian splendour (Hdt. v.28–30). She had a good friend locally in the island state of Chios, and longer-distance ties with Athens and Sybaris in South Italy (Hdt. v.21). Although the programme of colonization – some said seventy-five *apoikiai* (Sen. *Helv.* 7.2), some said ninety (Pliny *HN* v.112) – was now largely over, Miletus was deriving great profit from the extent of the network of affiliated but independent cities.[32]

One attraction to the first colonists was the fact that there was a power vacuum and relatively empty land to the north of the Black Sea in what had once been Cimmeria but was, since the early seventh century, Scythia. The Scythians themselves had spent almost a generation in Upper Asia (Hdt. 1.104–6), twenty-eight years after aiding the Assyrians against the Medians (*c.*613–585 B.C.),[33] and had returned to the steppes of

[31] *CAH* III².3, 199–201, 259.   [32] *Ibid.* 192, 217, 427–8.
[33] Grakov 1971 (E 252) 19–20; Artamonov 1974 (E 186) 56–7; Melyukova 1989 (E 320) 33.

north Caucasus and the Ukraine, only to find resistance and a war, so
Herodotus thought, with the sons of their own former ('blinded') slaves
(Hdt. IV.1–2). Even when they had proved victorious the Royal
Scythians did not seek to eliminate Greek colonies, which anyway were
rather an encroachment on the lands of some of their lesser settled
subjects than on their own nomadic range. Their rulers always tended to
expect gifts and 'protection money' from their subjects, and looked on
the Greek cities as sources of wine and luxury goods (Strabo VII.4.6). On
the Bosporus the Cimmerians and the half-Scythian slaves will have left a
remnant to be utilized by the incoming Bosporan Greeks. They also
bequeathed the names, 'Cimmerian' straits, walls, Bosporus and the two
towns, Cimmericum on the Kerch Peninsula and Cimmeris on Taman
(Hdt. IV.3.9.28).[34] The sons of the blind slaves were thought to have dug
a ditch from the Taurian mountains to the broadest part of Lake Maeotis,
by which may be meant the defensive mound and ditch, 33 kilometres
long, which connects the Sea of Azov with Cimmericum on the southern
side of the Kerch Peninsula, since there probably never was a ditch
further west near Theodosia.[35] Another inner ditch across the Kerch
Peninsula further east, of only some 10 or 11 kilometres in length, may be
one of the above-mentioned 'Cimmerian Walls' protecting a shrinking
people from the Scythians (Fig. 26).[36]

The presence of these pre-existing earthworks on the Kerch Peninsula
perhaps led the small independent Milesian and other Ionian cities to
conceive of a merger of sovereignty behind their protection. Pantica-
paeum/Apollonia, Myrmecium, Tyritace, Cepi, and perhaps Hermonassa, may have formed under the hegemony of Panticapaeum a single
Bosporan state, symbolized by the first silver coinage struck in the late
sixth century, bearing a frontal head of a lion, the lion being a natural
choice of coin type for the colony of Miletus. The mother-city's coins
bore a lion looking back and bequeathed that type to another of her
daughter-cities, Chersonesus in Thrace.[37] Perhaps the inner Cimmerian
ditch was refurbished about this time to hold back Scythian encroachments, using the aid of Sindi, whose lands were the regular targets of
winter expeditions of the Scythians across the ice (Hdt. IV.20).

Some time between c.517 and 512 B.C. the Persian King Darius
invaded Scythia across the Danube, ostensibly to punish the Scythians
for having occupied Upper Asia, but partly to punish them for
contemporary raiding and in pursuit of the dynamic of his own empire.

---

[34] Kuklina 1981 (E 299); Tokhtasyov 1984 (E 397) 142–8.
[35] Maslennikov 1983 (E 316) 14–22.
[36] Grinyovich 1946 (E 255); Sokolsky 1957 (E 390); Maslennikov 1983 (E 316) 19–22; Tolstikov 1984 (E 399) 32–7.
[37] Shelov 1978 (E 372) pl. 1.1; Anokhin 1986 (E 182) 6, pl. 1.1–8; Kraay 1976 (B 200) 158, no. 566; Shelov 1951 (E 364) 47–8.

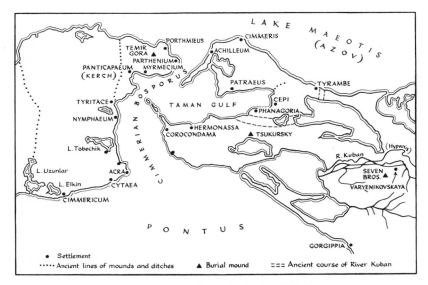

Fig. 26. Plan of the Cimmerian Straits and ditches.

Ariaramnes, the satrap of Cappadocia, is said to have been sent by Darius on a separate expedition with thirty *penteconters* across the Black Sea and to have taken Scythian prisoners (Ctesias *Persica* 16). The extent to which Darius' own expedition (700,000 men and 600 ships, according to Herodotus IV.87) penetrated into Scythia is disputed.[38] The Greek cities beyond the Danube are not brought into the story. It has been suggested that two expeditions have been conflated, a European one reaching little further than the 'Forest-Steppe' people on the middle reaches of the Dniestr river, with one starting much further east, perhaps through a Caucasus pass and reaching the rivers flowing into the Sea of Azov and the Tanais (River Don). Herodotus, without regard to distance or the large rivers between, makes the Persian army reach the Don immediately after bridging the Danube (IV.122).[39] Darius' subsequent retreat from Scythia was considered to have ended in a debacle, though it led to the formation of a satrapy in southern Thrace and Paeonia, and to the conversion of Macedon into a client-state. The Scythians' reputation rose high among the Greeks. They were overlords of all peoples as far south as the Danube, and they even drove through Thrace as far as the Chersonesus *c.*510 B.C. (Hdt. VII.40). By the early fifth century mainland Greeks felt that only the Scythians and themselves were capable of

[38] See also *CAH* IV² 234–53.
[39] Olmstead 1948 (F 43) 147; Chernenko 1982 (E 224) 3–4; and 1984 (E 225); Gardiner-Garden 1987 (E 244).

holding and then repelling the Persian threat, even of invading that empire itself (Hdt. IV.46; VI.84). The Greeks of the North Black Sea cities were now subject to the demands of an acknowledged major power. They might respond by receiving an agent or governor of the Scythian king, such as were Tymnes (Hdt. IV.76), or Eminakos, the issuer of coins at Olbia,[40] or by uniting for common safety, as the individually small townships of Bosporus seem to have done in the eastern tip of the Kerch Peninsula.

III. THE FIFTH CENTURY

Within the Black Sea area four powers played parts, after the Persian Wars had seen the repulse of Persia from Europe. The Scythian 'empire of the steppes' sometimes confronted, sometimes made alliances with, the increasingly formidable power of the Odrysian dynasty in Thrace (Sitalces c.440–424 B.C.; Seuthes 425–405), which built up an empire in the south-eastern corner of Europe, stretching from the River Strymon to the Ister (Hdt. IV.77–80; Thuc. II.100–9). The Persian empire under Xerxes (486–465), Artaxerxes (464–424) and Darius II (424–405) continued to be the standing colossus of the Near East, controlling more or less directly the lands on the southern side of the Black Sea and exerting immense cultural influence on the lands to its north. On the other hand, the political influence of the Greek mother-cities was now minimal. Miletus had been destroyed at the end of the Ionian Revolt in 494 B.C., and only very partially recovered by the 450s.[41] Megara was a minor member of the Peloponnesian League, sometimes detached to form a dependency of Athens (459–448 B.C.) or subjected to economic squeeze by her (432).[42] The Athenians took their place as the Greek power which had a long naval arm. They obtained an opening into the Pontus from about 471/0 B.C. when Byzantium was taken over at the allies' request from the Spartan 'renegade' admiral of the Greeks, Pausanias (Thuc. I.128–35; Justin IX.1.3). Previously interested in the north east though she had been, that interest had taken her no further than to plant colonies at Elaeus and Sigeum on either side of the Hellespont and to sponsor an Athenian-ruled *tyrannis* over the newly synoecized Dolonci on the Gallipoli Peninsula (c.545–493) – a state of the Thracian Chersonesus, which was defended across the isthmus by a wall built by Miltiades (Hdt. VI.36–41).[43] One wonders whether the Bosporan Greeks were not inspired by this recent example to refurbish the walls on the Kerch Peninsula and form a unified polity (see below).

---

[40] Vinogradov 1980 (E 412) 76–8, and 1989 (E 417) 103–4.
[41] J. P. Barron, *JHS* 82 (1962) 1–6; Meiggs 1972 (C 201) 36, 115–17, 562–5.
[42] Meiggs 1972 (C 201) 160–1, 190, 202–3, 430–1.   [43] *CAH* III².3, 121–2, 404–5.

How much grain was imported from the Black Sea area into Greek cities before the Persian Wars is unclear, but some idea can be gained from two incidents reported by Herodotus. About the time of the Ionian Revolt, and after the collapse (*c*.494–493 B.C.), Histiaeus of Miletus found it worth his while, along with a contingent of men from Lesbos, to waylay merchant ships sailing out of the Black Sea (Hdt. VI.5; 26). Some fourteen years later Xerxes, reviewing his army of invasion at Abydus, noticed grain ships again sailing through the Hellespont from the Black Sea and bound for Aegina and the Peloponnesus, significant enough in number, he thought, to be allowed to pass and to contribute to the supplies of his own army when it arrived in Greece (Hdt. VII.147). Athens' own need for grain may have been satisfied by sources in Sicily and Egypt initially, but after the middle of the fifth century the disastrous Egyptian expedition and the growing enmity with Corinth seem to have quickened her interest in the Black Sea lands.[44] Aristides is said to have died in the region (Plut. *Arist.* 26.1).

What drew Athens into physical intervention in the Pontus area was the attitude and course of events prevailing in two city states of local importance, Sinope and Heraclea. Sinope had by now a mini-sphere of influence comprising her tribute-paying colonists at Cotyora, Cerasus and Trapezus, and a strong trading and cultural presence in Colchis, as evidenced in the 'Greek' cemetery at Pichvnari.[45] She also had links across the Pontus (Hdt. II.34) with sister-cities, colonies of Miletus like Olbia and Istria,[46] and seems to have initiated a coinage, which had the sea-eagle (*haliaetos*) as its main type – first as an eagle's head on the obverses of Sinope itself, then as a full 'eagle on dolphin' on the reverse side of coins of Istria and Olbia, as well as the later issues of Sinope.[47] These latter coins seem to date from the second half of the fifth century B.C. and on into the latter part of the fourth. They no doubt denote a common worship of Apollo Delphinios, but also some claim that the sister-cities controlled the sea between them and ranged it like the sea-eagle and the dolphin. Another city, Megarian Heraclea, was a potential enemy to Athens,[48] and, being just to the west of the narrow waist of the Black Sea, posed a threat to the interests of Bosporus in her trade with the Athens-dominated Aegean. By the last quarter of the fifth century, if not earlier, she had her own colony, Chersonesus, on the south-western tip of the Crimea, and this led to her intervention in the north Euxine in the early fourth century.

[44] Brashinsky 1963 (E 215) 85–9; Meiggs 1972 (C 201) 264; Noonan 1973 (E 325) 241–2; Garnsey 1988 (I 55) 108–9, 117–51.

[45] J. B. Brashinsky, *Sobschenia Akademii Nauk Gruzii* 47 (1967) 3, 759–60; Kvirkvelia forthcoming (E 302).   [46] Knipovich *et al.* 1968 (E 283) 13–14; E. I. Solomonik, *Klio* 52 (1970) 427–36.

[47] Hind 1976 (E 257); P. O. Karyshkovsky, *Numismatika Antichnogo Prichernomorya* (1982) 80–98; Kraay and Hirmer 1966 (B 201) figs. 688–9.   [48] Burstein 1976 (E 222); Saprykin 1986 (E 352).

At some time close to 480 B.C. the cities of Bosporus fell under a dynasty, the Archaeanactidae, which then ruled for forty-two years, when, according to the entry in Diodorus for 438/7 B.C., they were displaced, but in circumstances unknown (Diod. XII.31.1). It is supposed that they were Milesian in origin, or Mytilenean, on the ground that an Archaeanax is known to have been active in each of these East Greek states in the sixth century B.C. (Strabo XIII.1,3B). Probably the preference should be given to the Milesian family, in view of Miletus' stronger presence on the Cimmerian Bosporus.[49] The Archaeanactidae were arguably a clan of *tyrannoi*, not unlike the Miltiades and Stesagoras dynasty on the Thracian Chersonesus. In their time a large temple dedicated to Apollo was built in the capital, Panticapaeum, which may well have been the Apollonia, of which the legend appears on some coins as APOL.[50] Early fifth-century coin-types of Panticapaeum have a lion's head on the obverse and an irregular incuse depression on the reverse, which gradually takes the form of a four-armed mill-sail. The APOL legend, when it appears, has been interpreted variously as an entirely different, though related, city Apollonia, as the name of a magistrate Apol[lonius], or as the mint of the temple of Apollo, or fourthly as an 'alliance' issue of the Bosporan cities.[51] The lion-head coin type seems to hint at the tutelary god Apollo; the dynasty of Archaeanax ('the ancient lord') may well have thought it a type appropriate to them too. Perhaps there was a brief period when exiled Apolloniatae still claimed to rule the polis, but from a different centre. But the name Panticapaeum was soon to be stressed by Spartocus and Satyrus on coins with the legend PA; PAN; PANTI, dated c.440–400 B.C. Miletus itself was divided at just this time (the 450s) into communities at Leros and Teichiussa,[52] seemingly loyal to the Athenian connexion, and those then installed in the main city who were not (see Fig. 27). According to Diodorus a certain Spartocus 'succeeded to the Archaeanactidae', leaving it open to speculation whether this was peaceful or otherwise. However, the mention elsewhere of exiles in Theodosia (Anon. *Periplus* 51) makes it likely that there was trouble leading to the change of dynasty. The date given is 438/7 B.C., but it could have been a year or two earlier, since several other events placed by Diodorus in that year are similarly misplaced. Spartocus is said to have ruled for seven years, which ought to have fallen in the 430s B.C. The date of the change-over of dynasty then was about the time of the revolt of Athens' reluctant allies, Samos and Byzantium, in 440

[49] Zhebelyov 1953 (E 442); Gaidukyevich, 1971 (E 241) 51; Vinogradov 1980 (E 412) 65–7; Shelov-Kovyedyayev 1985 (E 377) 70. For the Aeolian argument, Blavatsky 1970 (E 205).

[50] Shelov 1978 (E 372) 13–14; Anokhin 1986 (E 182) 7–10; Karyshkovsky 1962 (E 276).

[51] *Ibid.*; Shelov 1978 (E 372) 15–18; Dyukov 1975 (E 231); Gaidukyevich 1971 (E 241) 52–3; Pichikyan 1974 (E 337) 105–10; Tolstikov 1984 (E 399) 46–7, n. 95; Anokhin 1986 (E 182) 10–14, 25–6, pl. 1. 26–7, 48.   [52] Meiggs 1972 (C 201) 112.

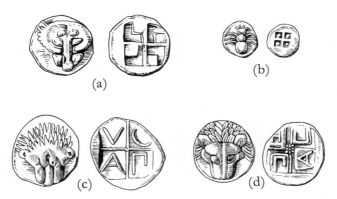

Fig. 27. Silver coins of Panticapaeum/Apollonia: (a) about 500–475 B.C.; (b) 'Myrmekion' about 475–450 B.C.; (c) about 450 B.C.; (d) about 440–425 B.C. (After Dyukov 1975 (E 231); Anokhin 1986 (E 182); see note 51.)

B.C., which was put down in the following year by Pericles himself (see also *CAH* v² 143–6).

The question of the origin of Spartocus has been much debated. It can surely be discounted that he was Greek, or Sindian, or Sarmatian, or a descendant of the Cimmerian stock still remaining on the Bosporus.[53] He was rather of Thracian origin, and not a mere mercenary, but a member of the Thracian royal family of the Odrysae tribe whose names were in several cases identical to those of the Spartocids – Spardocus, Berisades, Komosarye.[54] King Sitalces' brother was called Sparadocus (Thuc. II.100). Perhaps then the Thracians, being at the height of their power, attempted to exploit a difficult situation by supporting the installation of one of their family in answer to an appeal from the Cimmerian Bosporus.

Pericles determined to follow up in person his successes against Samos and Byzantium. Our information about the Pontic expedition of Pericles is undated, but, placed in sequence after the revolt of Samos and Byzantium, it may best be assigned to *c.*438–36 B.C.[55]

He entered the Pontus with a large, well-found fleet and accomplished everything which the Greek cities had requested of him, and established friendly relations with them. But to the neighbouring barbarian tribes, their kings and dynasts, he demonstrated the greatness of the Athenian power, their confidence and audacity in sailing wherever they wished and making themselves complete masters of the sea. He left thirteen ships and some troops under Lamachus at the disposal of the men of Sinope to deal with the tyrant Timesileos.

(Plut. *Per.* 20)

[53] Blavatskaya 1959 (E 190) 26–38; Blavatsky 1976 (E 206).

[54] Gaidukyevich 1966 (E 240) and 1971 (E 241) 66–8. Yailenko's recent work displays considerable confusion about the origins of the dynasty. They were either 'local Scythian', more precisely 'Thraco-Iranian' or 'Greco-Scythian': Yailenko 1990 (E 432) 286, 308.

[55] Meiggs 1972 (C 201) 199.

The only specific measure of Pericles that is mentioned is the ousting of Timesileos, who has now been recognized on an inscription from Olbia.[56] In a follow-up measure the Athenians passed a decree to send 600 Athenians to Sinope as colonists. These men may have aided a further Athenian colony at Amisus led by Athenocles, which was renamed Piraeus (Strabo XII.3.14), and issued coins with Athenian-type owls on the reverse side.[57] An Athenian colony was also planted at Astacus in the Propontis about this time (Strabo XII.4.2).[58]

Among the native peoples to be overawed by Pericles' expedition were no doubt the Paphlagonians inland of Sinope and the Cappadocians around Amisus/Piraeus, but the phrases 'sailing wherever they wished', and 'complete masters of the sea' imply much wider-ranging interventions. It seems at least possible that Pericles sailed across from Sinope to the Bosporus with the intention of resolving the disturbances there, and helping to power, or showing the flag to a recently installed Spartocus. Either way, the Athenians were strong enough to establish an outpost of their own at Nymphaeum, which, being just beyond the Tyritace rampart and ditch, was not within the area protected from Scythian mounted raids, and had direct contact with the Scythians, as the burial mounds around it show.[59] Nymphaeum was independent of the Bosporus until c.405 B.C. and issued coins in the last quarter of the century. It was then relinquished by the Athenian Gylon (maternal grandfather of Demosthenes) to the Bosporan tyrant in circumstances which Aeschines portrays as disgraceful, though Gylon probably had little choice, given Athens' situation at the end of the Peloponnesian War (Aeschin. III.171–2). Gylon received the gift of Cepi in lieu of Nymphaeum from the next ruler Satyrus. While Nymphaeum adhered to Athenian rule, it is said to have paid one talent annual contribution (Craterus *FGrH* 342 F 8), and there is a possibility that several fragmentary names in the Athenian Tribute Lists for 425 B.C. refer to cities north of the Black Sea.[60] Lamachus is attested to have been in the Pontus area at least once more, attempting to collect arrears of tribute in 424 B.C. from Heraclea, but it was not a signal success, as he lost his squadron of ships and had to march back overland in discomfort (Thuc. IV.75.1–2). Nevertheless Athens did for some thirty years have influence and outposts in the Black Sea area, in the afterglow of Pericles' show of force, which embraced Sinope, Amisus and the route to Colchis, as well as Bosporus, and the nearer cities of Apollonia Pontica and Heraclea.[61] Such influence as Athens had

[56] Vinogradov 1981 (E 415) and 1989 (E 417).

[57] Head 1911 (B 196) 496; Malloy 1970 (E 309).   [58] Meiggs 1972 (C 201) 198.

[59] Silantyeva 1959 (E 386) 93–7; Vickers 1979 (E 410) 9–50; Yakovenko 1981 (E 433); Tolstikov 1984 (E 399) 41–4.   [60] *ATL* I 527–9, 557; Meiggs 1972 (C 201) 328–9.

[61] *ATL* I 528, 539, no. 38; II 46, 126, fr. 38; B. D. Meritt and A. B. West, *The Athenian Assessment of 425 B.C.* (Ann Arbor, 1934) 26, 29, 68 and pl.

was obviously weakened in 411 with the Ionian Revolt; Alcibiades resorted to exacting a 10 per cent tax on trade leaving the Black Sea in 410 B.C. using a base at Chrysopolis upstream of Byzantium on the Bosporus, which probably shows a reluctance to sail in force into the Black Sea, but also an appreciation of Athens' need to secure its traffic and substantial revenues (Xen. *Hell.* 1.22). By 405 B.C. all Athenians were forced to repatriate to the home city in Lysander's sweeping-up measures after the Battle of Aegospotami. Athenian garrisons and colonists must have left by then or soon after. The loss of this vital supply-line led to the capitulation of Athens itself (Xen. *Hell.* 11.2.9).

On the Bosporus Spartocus was succeeded by his son Satyrus (Diod. XII.36.1) after ruling for seven years. He had probably been *archon* (with special powers) of the Bosporus state, but nothing is known of his title. Nor did he give his name to the dynasty in ancient times; the line was known as Leuconidae (Ael. *VH* VI.13) or the 'house of Paerisades and Leucon' (Strabo VII.414). Satyrus probably ruled alone, though with some participation in the *tyrannis* on the part of his sons, Leucon, Metrodorus and Gorgippus.

The Seleucus, who is made to rule for forty of Satyrus' forty-four years (433/2–389/8 B.C.), is doubtless an error in the manuscript of Diodorus for Satyrus himself (Diod. XIV.89.3), in spite of several attempts to create an otherwise unknown and anomalously named co-ruler of the Bosporus. There is no evidence for fully shared rule so early in the Bosporan dynasty's history.[62] Satyrus had a long and successful rule, one which coincided with Athens' increased need of negotiated contracts for a secure corn supply, but he probably profited also from the needs of other cities, e.g. Mytilene in 428 B.C. (Thuc. III.2.2). Shortly before 405 B.C. the sons of well-to-do Athenians were finding useful and welcome occupations on the Bosporus (Lysias XVI.4). By 394 'the Bosporan' was regarded as well disposed towards Athens and earned gratitude for granting special privileges to Athenian grain vessels (Isoc. XVII.3–5). The political muscle of Satyrus' state had obviously grown with the acquisition of Nymphaeum, and it by now also included not only the Milesian Cepi, but also the other colonies on the Taman Peninsula – Hermonassa and Phanagoria.

In the final quarter of the fifth century Nymphaeum struck some small silver coins (drachms, diobols and hemi-obols) in a single series, bearing the head of a nymph on the obverse and a bunch of grapes on the reverse, which ceased, probably when Gylon handed the city to Satyrus

---

[62] Werner 1955 (E 425) 418–19; Brashinsky 1965 (E 216); Grach 1968 (E 247); Tuplin 1982 (E 404) 126–7. For a recent attempt to revive not only Seleucus but also a Spartocus II, father of Satyrus, Yailenko 1990 (E 432) 286, n. 102, 307.

Fig. 28. Coins of four states of the Bosporus. (a) Nymphaeum, silver, about 425–400 B.C.; (b) Sindi, silver, about 425–400 B.C.; (c) Theodosia, silver, about 400–375 B.C.; (d) Panticapaeum, gold, about 350–325 B.C. (After Shelov 1978 (E 372); Anokhin 1986 (E 182); cf. Kraay and Hirmer 1966 (B 201) figs. 440–1.)

(Fig. 28a).[63] The Sindi put out coins between c.425 and 400 B.C., in three-obol down to quarter-obol denominations, and in three series. The types show Heracles testing the string of his bow, a head of Heracles, a bull's head, a griffin and grain of wheat on the obverse sides (Fig. 28b), and on the reverses an owl with spread wings once, and a horse's head five times, accompanied by the ethnic *Sindon* – 'Of the Sindi'.[64] The Heracles types are probably a hint at that hero's famed wanderings north of the Black Sea rather than an indication of a link with Heraclea Pontica across the sea. The griffin was the city emblem of Phanagoria's mother-city Teos, and may have been borrowed from there, but griffins were monsters famously associated with the area east of Scythia and Sindica. The grain of wheat is a symbol typical of those to be found on future Bosporan coinage, advertising local products. The Athenian colony at Amisus, or Athenian influence generally, may have inspired the Sindian owl-type, while the consistent appearance of the horse's head on the reverses might be said to make it the specific badge of that tribe, where horses were placed in profusion in chieftains' burials. These very Hellenic-looking coins seem to be the output of Greek die-makers, acting for a strongly hellenized tribe rather than of a place on the coast, called Sindicus Limen.[65] These issues ended perhaps c.400–375 B.C.

Phanagoria was a third state on the Bosporus which coined in silver in the last two decades of the century. This city may have briefly

---

[63] Shelov 1978 (E 372) 21–5; Anokhin 1986 (E 182) 15, 18, 29.
[64] Shelov 1978 (E 372) 27–31; Anokhin 1986 (E 182) 14, 19–20.
[65] Shelov 1949 (E 361); V. P. Shilov, *Sov. Arch.* 1951, 205–15; D. B. Shelov in *Tskhaltubo II 1979* 232–47; Shelov-Kovyedyayev 1985 (E 378) 126–8.

participated in the lion-head coinage in the 420s, since one such coin has the legend PHA on the reverse. Phanagoria now struck two series of coins, ranging from drachmae down to half-obols. The obverses have the head of a young or bearded Cabirus (chthonic god), wearing a conical cap and the reverses bear a bull's head and grain of wheat.[66] Perhaps the obverses bear some unexplained relation to the name of the founder, Phanagoras. This series also came to an end about the turn of the fifth to fourth centuries.

IV. THE EARLY SPARTOCIDS: *ARCHONS* OR BARBARIAN TYRANTS?

Satyrus' rule over the Bosporan state lasted until 389/8 B.C., when his son, Leucon, succeeded and ruled for a further forty years until 349/8 (Diod. XIV.93; XVI.31.6). Thereafter two of his sons ruled jointly for five years, Spartocus II and Paerisades I. After the death of Spartocus Paerisades ruled alone for a further thirty-three years. Diodorus presents the one as following the other consecutively, adding five years to the total for the dynasty (Diod. XVI.52.10), but this is an error easily corrected with the help of the Athenian decree of 347/6 B.C. (*IG* II² 212; Tod no. 167; Harding no. 82)).[67] On the death of Paerisades his three sons, Satyrus II, Prytanis and Eumelus, engaged in fratricidal war, drawing in allies from the Scythian and Sarmatian chiefs. Satyrus and Prytanis ruled jointly for nine months, Prytanis alone only very briefly. Eumelus, the eventual victor, ruled alone for five years and five months, initiating ambitious policies which embraced the whole Black Sea area, 310/9–304/3 B.C. (Diod. XX.100.7).

A further period of stability ensued with the accession of Eumelus' son, Spartocus III, who ruled now as king over all parts of his domain until 284/3 B.C.[68] By the end of this sequence the 'Leuconidae' and 'those starting with Paerisades and Leucon' had been handing down power within the family for over 150 years, through the time of the Peloponnesian War in Greece, Spartan and Theban ascendancy and the Second Athenian Confederacy, and the rule of Philip II, Alexander the Great and his first Successors, such as Lysimachus. Since Satyrus' accession hardly one *archon* had lasted for less than twenty years, except in the period during and just after the war between the brothers in 310/9 B.C.

To outsiders these rulers were either 'tyrants' or 'dynasts' and

[66] Shelov 1978 (E 372) 31–2; Anokhin 1986 (E 182) 29–30.
[67] Yailenko 1990 (E 432) 286 follows Diod. literally in making the five years of Spartocus precede the rule of Paerisades rather than making him co-ruler for that period.
[68] Using *Corpus Ins. Regni Bosporani* add. 4, p. 938, Yailenko produces a Seleucus, son of Eumelus, but this fragmentary name can hardly support the existence of a hitherto unknown ruler: Yailenko 1990 (E 432) 299–301.

barbarian ones at that, though they might be expected to be friendly or to grant Athenian merchants and shipping special concessions, and the Athenians might reciprocate with honours. They would usually be referred to as though they were private citizens and with no official title. Satyrus is referred to as 'the one in Pontus' (Lys. xvi.4), and he and his family are called 'tyrants' in the account of how they received Nymphaeum from the Athenian representative Gylon (Aesch. iii.171). Leucon and Paerisades are usually labelled 'tyrants' and 'dynasts' by Athenian writers of the time, though by writers of Roman date, dependent on hellenistic ideas of kingship, they are often called 'kings'. Only Demosthenes (xx.26, 31) comes close to the official titulature, using the term *archon*, and at the same time reflects Athens' interest, describing him as *kyrios tou sitou*, 'in control of the corn supply'.

On official inscriptions found in the Bosporus area Spartocus I and Satyrus I do not figure, but Leucon does, being at first called merely 'son of Satyrus, the Panticapaean' (*CIRB* 37), and later '*archon* of Bosporus'. He is also styled, perhaps a little later, 'archon of Bosporus and Theodosia' (*CIRB* 1111), and soon also 'king of the Sindi, Toreti, Dandarii and Psessi' (*CIRB* 6, 1037–8), or of 'the Sindi and all the Maeotae' (*CIRB* 8). Paerisades I claims these latter titles also (*CIRB* 10, 11, 1039–40), but adds the kingship of further tribes, Thatei and Doschi (*CIRB* 9, 972, 1015). The Sindi, Toreti and Dandarii are again listed separately as ruled by him (*CIRB* 1014). An inscription in verse found at Panticapaeum goes further and says of Paerisades, 'he ruled over the whole land, including the furthest bounds of the Tauri and the borders of the Caucasus' (*CIRB* 113).[69] Interestingly, however, there is never any claim to rule the Scythians, who ranged over the northern part of the Crimea and the steppes north of Lake Maeotis, so the last inscription must be referring to control of Theodosia.

Alongside these rulers were *paradynastae*, members of the 'tyrant' family, as with the Odrysian dynasty in Thrace.[70] Satyrus had a son, Metrodorus, who was handed to the Maeotae as hostage (Polyaen. viii.55). Gorgippus seems to have been given some responsibilities under Satyrus, and may have governed Sindicus Limen, renamed Gorgippia, for a long period under Leucon;[71] his daughter Comosarye married Paerisades (*CIRB* 1015). Associated with Spartocus II and Paerisades I in honours voted by Athens in 347/6 B.C. was their brother Apollonius, though he clearly did not rule (*IG* ii² 212; Tod. no. 167; Harding no. 82). His position is somewhat reminiscent of that of Hipparchus with Hippias at Athens between 528 and 514 B.C. We have

[69] Wormell 1946 (E 428) 49–71; Belova 1967 (E 187); Bosi 1967 (E 211); Tod no. 115A–C, 163, 171A–E, p. 209; Hansen 1983/9 (B 142) 885.   [70] Shelov-Kovyedyayev 1985 (E 378) 180.
[71] Kruglikova 1971 (E 293).

already seen that Spartocus II and Paerisades ruled jointly until the death of the former, and that Satyrus II and Prytanis did so for nine months, but a properly shared rule does not appear to have been the norm, and the last case, which ended in civil war, was not a good example of it. The later Spartocids ruled alone, probably because only one could take the title *basileus* at any one time. The date of adoption of the title 'king' in Bosporus, as well as over the Maeotian tribes is unknown, but it was certainly used by the time of Spartocus III, son of Eumelus, whose inscriptions have a new formula, '*archon* and king' (*CIRB* 974; 1043) and 'ruling as king' (*basileuontos CIRB* 19.) This Spartocus was also given the title 'king' in the Athenian decree of 285/4 B.C. (*IG* ii² 653). Taking the title of king was in fashion around that time, for Zipoetes of Bithynia had done so twelve years earlier (297/6 B.C.), and had produced an era, which was to be used in Pontus and on the Bosporus from the late first century B.C.[72]

The earlier practice, then, seems to be one typical of a *tyrannis* – the sole rule of the *archon* for life, with participation by one or more sons, which explains the frequent references to Bosporan 'rulers' (plural). Brothers, brothers-in-law and sons-in-law (*paradynastae*), might also act as governors of cities or regions without any actual political division of the state. Sopaeus, the father of a client of Isocrates, was just such a governor of a large territory and an army commander. He fell out of favour with Satyrus, who feared conspiracies, was returned to favour and married Satyrus' daughter (*Trap.* 3; 57). Gylon became governor of Cepi, and Stratocles (*CIRB* 6) may have given his name to the lost town, Stratoclia, as Gorgippus did to Gorgippia.

By the end of Satyrus' life, his state was of considerable importance in the Greek world, and was still expanding to east and west.[73] However, he was finding difficulties in his relations with the Sindi and with Theodosia. In Sindica he attempted to intervene in the affairs of Hecataeus, their king, offering him a marriage with his daughter, and causing a war with the Maeotae who took up arms against him on behalf of Hecataeus' wronged Maeotian wife, Tirgatao. One of Satyrus' sons, Metrodorus, was held hostage. Satyrus, with the business still unsettled, died 'in despair', says Polyaenus (VIII.54). Leucon will have brought the war to a successful conclusion with the annexation of the Sindi during the next decade or so, c.390–380 B.C.[74] Satyrus was said to have actually died in the course of the siege of Theodosia, no doubt he was attracted by the

[72] G. Perl in *Studien zur Geschichte und Philosophie des Altertums* (ed. J. Harmatta, 1968) 299–330. Amsterdam.

[73] Anfimov 1967 (E 179) 128ff; Shelov-Kovyedyayev 1985 (E 378) 89–144; Gardiner-Garden 1986 (E 243).

[74] Berzin 1958 (E 189); Ustinova 1966 (E 405); Kruskol 1974 (E 296); Shelov-Kovyedyayev 1989 (E 381).

fact that the city had a harbour less liable to icing up, and by its ability to accommodate up to a hundred ships (Strabo VII.4.4), as well as being aggravated by the gathering there of hostile refugees, if that refers to this time (Anon. *Periplus* 51).

Heraclea undertook to support Theodosia from across the Black Sea, and the war now ran through an initial phase before Satyrus' death, which saw some relief of the siege (Polyaen. v.23), and through a fairly long war in which Leucon's territories in the East Crimea were ravaged by a Heraclean fleet ([Arist.] *Oec.* II.2.8). His armies were under pressure in manning (Polyaen. VI.9.3) and on the battlefield (VI.9.4) and his finances were in difficulties; he is said to have resorted to calling in coin and reissuing it at double its former value (VI.9.1). A last episode involved Memnon of Rhodes, who played a trick on Leucon in order to discover the strength of the Bosporan army (v.44.1). The war was probably over by *c.*370 B.C. and Theodosia annexed,[75] receiving the name of Leucon's wife or sister (schol. ad. Dem. XX.33). Leucon rebuilt the harbour installations and these were impressively complete by 355 B.C. (Dem. XX.33). Heraclea's purpose had probably been to safeguard her colony, Chersonesus, further west, but also to preserve some independent access for herself to the produce of the rich area around Theodosia, and to check the aggrandizement of the rulers of Bosporus. In this she clearly failed and within a few years Heraclea herself fell under a dynasty of tyrants (from 364 B.C.).

Developments in the coinage of Bosporus reflect these events and ambitions. Theodosia's minting of autonomous coins probably ceased in the period *c.*380–375. It had issued two series of silver drachmae, diobols and half-obols, and some bronze (crisis?) coinage.[76] On the obverses were a curly-bearded head (Fig. 28c), a head of Athena in a rounded helmet and a head of Heracles, and on the reverses a bull's head, and a *boukranion* wearing a garland and a club, all with the legend THEODO. The *boukranion* may be a pun on the city's name, 'gift to the god', thus an animal sacrifice. Bosporan coinage continued to be issued in the name of the citizens of Panticapaeum. The silver still has the frontal lion's head on the obverse, and on the reverse a ram's head.[77] Later, perhaps after Satyrus' death, a satyr's head appears on the obverses of the silver; on the earliest series he wears a garland of ivy; on the reverses are either a forepart of a sturgeon, a lion stalking left, or a lion's head in profile. Here seems to be a twofold reference – far back to Milesian Apollo, the sponsor of the colony, and back to the recent founder of the state's

---

[75] Shelov 1950 (E 363) and 1957 (E 370); V. D. Blavatsky, *Sov. Arch.* 1981, 4 21–9; Burstein 1974 (E 221); Shelov-Kovyedyayev 1986 (E 380).

[76] Shelov 1978 (E 372) 25–6; Anokhin 1986 (E 182) 15, 29–30; Zolotaryov 1984 (E 450).

[77] Shelov 1978 (E 372) 14–15; Anokhin 1986 (E 182) 8–9.

prosperity, Satyrus.[78] Now from *c.*375 B.C. for some sixty years impressive gold coins (issued on an electrum system in staters and 'sixths') were struck, proclaiming the wealth of Panticapaeum under Leucon and Paerisades. They have distinctive types and are in a superb style. On the obverse is a satyr head either in profile or in a three-quarter pose, and on the reverse is a unique lion-headed, horned, griffin, in a pose *passant et regardant*, standing over an ear of wheat, and bearing a spear in its jaws (Fig. 28d).[79] The lion-headed griffin is a noted mythical enemy of the Persians, but the creature is also surely a 'gold-guarding griffin'. Carrying a spear, he is a watch-guard over the gold of the state of Panticapaeum, on one piece of which he is represented. The source of this prosperity is indicated beneath him in the ear of wheat, just as the sturgeon, used as a symbol on contemporary Panticapaean silver coins, points to its second source of wealth.[80] Indeed grain from Bosporus' own domains in the east of the Kerch Peninsula and in Sindica can explain all the influx of gold into the Bosporan coffers in the fourth century B.C. No great gathering-in of grain from wider Scythian lands by trade need be invoked.[81] Nor need the Bosporan gold used in decorative metalwork have been acquired from huge distances overland from the Agathyrsi to the west or from the Arimaspians of central Asia, though the Scythian gold treasures may have been fashioned from gold taken as 'gifts' from those sources. The Bosporan gold may rather have come as a consequence of exports of grain and salted fish to Greece, the metal ultimately coming from Thraco-Macedonian and Colchian gold sources, and the silver from Thracian and from the Athenian silver mines.[82]

Athens' position at the beginning of the fourth century was at first very weak, then partially restored after the Battle of Cnidus in 394 B.C. and much enhanced with the formation of the Second Athenian Alliance in 378/7 B.C. However, she was not able to dictate and make dispositions for corn importation into cities in the Aegean, as she had done in the fifth century in the cases of Methone (*IG* I³ 61; M–L no. 65) and Aphytis (*IG* I³ 62) almost regarding it as her right and common practice ([Xen.] *Ath. Pol.* 11.12). Now Athenians would be grateful if Satyrus and his general, Sopaeus, gave their merchant ships the right of *exagoge* in time of scarcity, when others were sent away empty (Isoc. XVII.57). Other cities were indeed in need of grain, such as Mytilene, which again is found importing from the Bosporus (*IG* XII 2.3; Tod no. 163).[83] But it is Athens which we find, down to the 350s B.C. and beyond, relying on Pontic corn

---

[78] Shelov 1978 (E 372) 83; Anokhin 1986 (E 182) 9.
[79] Shelov 1978 (E 372) 79–82; Anokhin 1986 (E 182) 32–4; Kraay and Hirmer 1966 (B 201) figs. 440–1 and pl. 15.　　[80] Hill 1923 (D 197); Shelov 1950 (E 362); Brabich 1959 (E 214).
[81] Brashinsky 1963 (E 215); Scheglov 1987 (E 356).
[82] Mantsevich 1950 (E 310) and 1962 (E 311); Zograf 1972 (E 448).
[83] Heisserer 1984 (B 144) 121.

both in normal times, and in crisis, such as famine or the defection of much of her renewed alliance (357 B.C.). The speeches of Demosthenes, *Against Leptines* (XX; *c*.355 B.C.) and *Against Phormio* (XXXIV; *c*.328/6 B.C.) and the honorary inscriptions of the Athenian people (347/6 B.C.) for the three sons of Leucon (*IG* II² 212) and the still later one (*IG* II² 653) for Spartocus III (285/4 B.C.), taken together, give abundant contemporary evidence for this trade.[84] It was reflected in the conferment of the equivalent of 'most favoured nation status' on each other. The Bosporan dynasts gave Athenians the right of pre-emption of corn, and exemption from customs dues (tax of 1/30th) in view of the guaranteed continuing demand. The Athenians in return gave the heads of the family Athenian citizenship, freedom from taxes (*ateleia*), gold crowns and statues, at first to be set up in the Agora and later on the Acropolis. They were honoured as 'guest-friends' and 'benefactors' of the Athenians, and the relationship, which began in the time of Satyrus, perhaps shortly after the Corinthian War *c*.394 B.C.,[85] gradually became one in which Athens' position grew weaker and her dependence on the ruler's goodwill more apparent.

The corn supply was not always secure, even when it was on its way to Athens, as various cities in those times of war and famine might intercept grain ships.[86] These included Byzantium, Chalcedon and Cyzicus, in the Black Sea approaches, and Chios, Cos, Rhodes and Philip of Macedon's forces in the Aegean. All intercepted grain deliveries between 362 and 338 B.C. Heraclea within the Black Sea area, under her dynast Dionysius, seized the grain shipment of a merchant on his way to Athens in 330/29 B.C. (*IG* II² 360.35–40). On the other hand Athens honoured two merchants from Heraclea (*IG*² II 408) for their services. On the Bosporus the wide range of trading interest is shown by inscriptions from the three main cities, Panticapaeum, Phanagoria and Gorgippia, where men and women from Chersonesus (*CIRB* 173), Heraclea, (*CIRB* 923, 925), Sinope (*CIRB* 218), Piraeus/Amisus (*CIRB* 1 and 249–50), Chalcedon (2), Colophon (248), Chios (1233), and Syracuse (203), are found, representing the fourth century and the hellenistic period. There is also the gold crown (*IG* II² 1485, 22) sent to Athens by Spartocus III towards the end of the fourth century (perhaps 306 B.C.), which heralds a number of such gifts sent to the major centres of Greek communications by the later hellenistic rulers of Bosporus.[87]

During the fourth century the relative importance of Olbia declined

[84] Brashinsky 1963 (E 215) 123–6.
[85] Tuplin 1982 (E 404).
[86] G. de Ste Croix, *Origins of the Peloponnesian War* (London, 1972) 47, App. VIII, 314.
[87] Burstein 1978 (E 223) 181–5; D. M. Lewis ap. Knoepfler (ed.) *Comptes et inventaires dans la cité grecque* (Neuchâtel, 1988) 303.

compared with Bosporus, mainly because she remained a single small polis open to pressure from the Scythians, but, as it was to turn out later, also from Scirians, Galatians, Thysamatae and Saudaratae, the last two of whom were probably Sarmatians.[88] But the interest of the metropolitan Greeks had turned inevitably to the larger and more assured source of supply further east. In the speech attributed to Demosthenes, *Against Lacritus* (xxxv), of *c*.341/40 B.C., sailing up the west side of Pontus (via Olbia) is an option that a merchant might take or forego. Such merchants' main medium of exchange was the Cyzicene electrum stater, which after modest representation in the fifth century is found in large hoards of coins in the fourth.[89]

Throughout much of the first half of the fourth century the Scythians were united and the major force within the immense area from the Danube to the Don. They were ruled by a nonagenarian king Atheas, who was killed in battle against Philip of Macedon, after which the grand conglomeration of Scythian tribes under the *Scythae Basileis* began to break up.[90] Paerisades had a war with the Scythians which distracted him from organizing the grain supply for Athens (Dem. xxxiv *In Phorm.* 8). Most of his activities, however, seem to have been directed against the Maeotae. Some internal colonization probably occurred now at Cimmeris ([Scymn.] 896), and a small Bosporan post (Tanais) at Elizavetovskoye was later transferred to Nedvigovka on the River Don,[91] probably in the time of Spartocus III (304/3–284/3 B.C.). Paerisades' fighting skills may have been considerable, but the anecdote of Polyaenus (VII.37) implies that his luxury exceeded them, for he is said to have had garments in which to draw up his battle line, others to fight in, and still others in which to make a quick getaway! At all events Strabo (VII.4.4) says that his reputation was so high that he was declared a god.

The next generation saw the outbreak of civil war between Eumelus, the youngest son of Paerisades, and Satyrus II and Prytanis (311/10 B.C.). Most of the action took place on the Asiatic side of Bosporus in the Kuban Valley, where Eumelus had gained most of his support from Aripharnes, king of the Thatei or perhaps, more likely, the Sarmatian Siraci (Diod. xx.22–6), who had 22,000 infantry and 20,00 cavalry.[92] Satyrus had 2,000 Greek and 2,000 Thracian mercenaries, and an estimated 20,000 Scythians on foot and 10,000 cavalry. When Satyrus

[88] Levi 1985 (E 306); D. P. Kallistov in Welskopf (ed.) 1974 (C 83) 551–86.

[89] Shelov 1949 (E 359); S. A. Bulatovich, *VDI* 1970.2, 73–86, *Sov. Arch.* 1970.2, 222–4, and *Numismatika Antichnogo Prichernomorya* (1982) 98–105.

[90] V. A. Anokhin, *Numismatika i Sphragistika* 2 (1965) 3–15; D. B. Shelov, *ibid.*, 16–40; Kallistov 1969 (E 272); Melyukova 1989 (E 320) 35; Vinogradov and Marchenko 1989 (E 418); Hammond and Griffith 1979 (D 50) 560–2; Ellis 1976 (D 80) 185–6.

[91] Marchenko 1986 (E 313), 1990 (E 314).

[92] Blavatsky 1946 (E 191); Gaidukevich 1971 (E 241) 83–4; Struve 1968 (E 396).

was killed in battle near a place called Gargaza, and Prytanis was killed at Cepi (after having been captured once, released on condition that he went into exile, and yet trying to seize power again at Panticapaeum), the civil war was over. Eumelus proved savage against the followers of Satyrus. Only the young son of Satyrus, Paerisades, escaped to find refuge with the Scythian king, Agarus. Soon, within a few decades, the remnant of the Royal Scythians would move down into Crimea under pressure from the Sarmatians, to a series of forts in the foothill part of the Taurian mountains and to a capital near Simferopol–Neapolis.[93] There they would, even in their reduced state, be an ever-present menace to both Chersonesus and the Bosporus down to the end of the second century B.C.

Eumelus was for a brief space dominant on the Bosporus and pursued a wider policy spanning the Black Sea, freeing the sea of pirates, aiding Sinope, Byzantium and Callatis, and settling 1,000 refugees from the last city at a place on the Asiatic side called Psoa, perhaps because of depopulation there caused by the warfare.[94] He had proclaimed a return to the 'ancestral constitution', calling an assembly at Panticapaeum, no doubt to ratify his taking of power, and seeking to dampen down the unpopularity arising from the blood-bath which had surrounded his route to power. What this 'ancestral constitution' was is unclear, but he was probably trying to stress the role of the citizens while retaining his own role as 'archon' of Bosporus.[95] Perhaps Satyrus had tried to style himself king in the fashion of the new hellenistic monarchs, and this had proved unpopular. Neither this Satyrus nor Eumelus have left any coins or inscriptions in their name, but a later figure of the last decade of the third century B.C., one Hygiainon, was still using the title 'archon' on gold and silver coins rather than 'king'.[96]

V. KINGS OF A DECLINING BOSPORUS

During the third and second centuries B.C. the dynasty continued with one possible short break, the period of the above-mentioned *archon* Hygiainon (*c.*220–200, or according to others *c.*150 B.C. or even later).[97] After the rule of Spartocus, son of Eumelus, the list of kings in Diodorus ceases. Official inscriptions, however, are numerous, royal stamps on tiles are fairly frequently found,[98] and gold and silver coins were struck

[93] P. N. Schultz in *Problemy Skiphskoi Arkheologii* (1979); T. N. Vysotskaya, *Neapol' – Stolitsa Gosudarstva Pozdknikh Skiphov* (1979); Melyukova 1989 (E 320) 127ff. Moscow.

[94] A. A. Neikhardt in *Drevny Mir, Festschrift V. V. Struve* (1962) 597.

[95] Gaidukevich 1971 (E 241) 85–6; Shelov-Kovyedyayev 1985 (E 378) 151.

[96] Gaidukevich 1971 (E 241) 93; Shelov 1978 (E 372) 157–9; Anokhin 1986 (E 182) 67–9.

[97] Werner 1955 (E 425) 426–7; Golenko 1982 (E 246) 55, n. 45; Yailenko 1990 (E 432) 307, n. 169 has the *archon* Hygiainon at the end of the series, c. 108 B.C., as a kind of sub-ruler under Mithridates.

[98] Gaidukevich 1958 (E 239); Shelov 1978 (E 372) 167.

in the names of several of the last kings. Paerisades II ruled from 284/3 B.C. to c.245 B.C. (*CIRB* 20–5; 822). After him for a few years came Spartocus IV (c.245–240) who is said to have been killed by his brother Leucon, on account of adultery with his wife, Alcathoe. He in turn was murdered by her c.220 B.C. (Ov. *Ib.* 309; schol. *ad loc.*). Spartocus and Leucon are known each from one Bosporan inscription (*CIRB* 24; 25), and Leucon issued bronze coins in three denominations, bearing his own name as king. Bosporan coinage in the first half of the third century had sunk to a poor state, and these unique issues seem to have been a recognition of the monetary crisis and an attempt to find a solution.[99] If Hygiainon is to be placed as *archon* after Leucon II, then the next 'Spartocid' king would be Spartocus V (*CIRB* 26; 75), perhaps son of a Paerisades, ruling from c.200–180 B.C. His daughter, Camasarye, proved a prominent figure in the reign of her husband, Paerisades III, from c.180–150 B.C., and on into that of her son Paerisades IV c.150–125 B.C., when she had a second husband, Argotes. Appropriately this Paerisades took the title Philometor to answer his mother's Philoteknos (*CIRB* 753; 1044). The last ruler, Paerisades V, reigned from c.125 B.C. down to 109, at which point he signed away his kingdom to Mithridates of Pontus.

Of these Bosporan rulers, Hygiainon, a Spartocus (either IV or V) and perhaps two Paerisades (III and IV or IV and V) issued gold coins of the type imitating 'Lysimachi' struck at Byzantium from c.210–200 B.C., and some additional silver. These coins bear a portrait of Spartocus and a bow and arrow case on the reverse, and an obverse portrait of Hygiainon with a galloping rider on the reverse.[100] Regnal years on the coinage of Paerisades go up to the figure '20'. One coin type can be eliminated from the Bosporan series, a fine gold imitation 'Lysimachus' of a king Akes, which seems to be an early imitation issued in Colchis.[101] During this time Bosporan city issues continue, notably with a series bearing the head of Apollo on the obverse and a bow and arrow case on the reverse.[102]

With the decline in the importance of Athens as a safe and sufficient market, Bosporan rulers kept a wide range of contacts in the Aegean. Sea power passed on this larger stage from Athens to Philip and Alexander, then to Antigonus and Demetrius of the immediate Successor kings, and on to the Ptolemies of Egypt and, in a more limited trading and policing sense, to Rhodes.[103] Those states outside the Black Sea area which showed interest in it were Thrace under Lysimachus c.282 B.C., and Ptolemaic Egypt and Rhodes (Dio Chrys. XXXI.103). Egypt was a

[99] Shelov 1953 (E 366), 1978 (E 372) 133–7; Anokhin 1986 (E 182) 55–6; Karyshkovsky 1960 (E 275).
[100] Zograf 1972 (E 448) 185; Shelov 1978 (E 372) 159–60; Golenko 1982 (E 246) 50, 53; Anokhin 1986 (E 182) 62–4.   [101] L. P. Kharko, *VDI* 1948,2, 147; Dundua 1987 (E 230) 88–9.
[102] Shelov 1978 (E 372) 141–5; Anokhin 1986 (E 182) 66–7.   [103] Shelov 1958 (E 371).

sufficient producer of grain for herself, overproducing massively for export, and was therefore in some sense a co-producer and could be a rival of Bosporus.

Alexandria sent a number of products, including pottery, to the north Black Sea area,[104] but on one occasion a fleet of Ptolemy Philadelphus ventured into the Black Sea to intervene on behalf of Sinope against the king of Cappadocia/Pontus (*c*.275–270 B.C. Steph. Byzant. 'Ancyra' = Apollonius of Aphrodisias). This was an even rarer intervention from outside for these times than Pericles' expedition had been in the fifth century. But the rulers of Bosporus in turn kept an interest in these major powers. Paerisades II sent an embassy to Ptolemy Philadelphus in 254 or 253 B.C.[105] He also dedicated a silver bowl at Delos *c*.250 B.C., and Camasarye (*CIRB* 75) was responsible for making dedications at the shrine of Apollo of Branchidae near Miletus (178 and 177 B.C.). An honorary decree for her and Paerisades was made at Delphi in *c*.160 B.C. Again a gold phiale was given to the Branchidae Temple in 154 B.C.[106] To be conspicuous for piety at the two Apollo shrines was an appropriate thing for rulers of a colony of Miletus, and a good advertisement among the Aegean Greeks.

Polybius summarizes for us the state of the Pontic economy with a list of imports into, and exports from, the Euxine generally at this time (IV.38.5). Slaves were a major item, with honey, wax and salted fish going into Greece, and wine and olive oil going the other way; grain was transported both ways, as need arose. The increased availability of grain from Egypt, and the reduction in produce, locally, due to instability among the peoples north of the Black Sea, had probably brought about this changed situation. The importation of wine and oil into the Bosporus area is amply illustrated by the finds of thousands of fragments of bulk-carrying amphorae from such producers as Chios, Thasos, Samos, Mende, Heraclea, Sinope, Byzantium, Rhodes, Cnidus, Cos, and others whose amphora stamps and distinctive shapes have been found in lesser numbers.[107] Recently the Egyptian connexion has been underlined by the find of a fresco in a shrine at Nymphaeum, dating to the third century B.C., on which was represented a ship sporting the name Isis.[108]

The Bosporan troubles with the Scythians were often aggravated by

[104] I. G. Shurgaya, *VDI* 1965.4, and *Klio* 61 (1979) 453–8; Yailenko 1990 (E 432) adds a Paerisades III (*c*. 225–200 B.C.) to the list on the strength of a graffito found at Nymphaeum, in which a Satyrus is mentioned, son of ? and Paerisates.

[105] H. I. Bell, *Symbolae Osloenses* 5 (1927) 36–7; Maximova 1956 (E 318) 175–6, 233–4; I. G. Shurgaya, *KSIAK* 138 (1975) 51.

[106] Rostovtzeff 1930 (E 346) 580–1; *IG* XI.2 287B (Delos); *CIG* II 2855 (Didyma); *Rev. Phil.* 22 (1898) 114 (Didyma) = *Didyma* I 463–4; *SIG* 439 (Delphi).

[107] Zeyest 1960 (E 438); Brashinsky 1980 (E 218) 209–16, pls. 1–9, and 1984 (E 219) pls. 1–32.

[108] Grach 1984 (E 250) 401.

the Sarmatians pressing behind that people. But on occasion alliances would be made with the remoter people against the nearer. A vivid instance is told by Polyaenus about the difficulties experienced by the Chersonesites when beset by the Scythians (VIII.56). They were aided by the Sarmatian queen Amage, who first ordered the Scythian king to desist, and then made a lightning foray on horseback with a small group of cavalry over a distance of 200 km to his capital. She is said to have killed the king, restored land to the citizens of Chersonesus and to have handed the kingdom to his son. This episode entirely bypassed Bosporus, but similar events, set there at about the same time (c. 150 B.C.), were worked up into historical romances, which illustrate themes of friendship or revenge among bands of horse-archers in the steppe country (Lucian, *Toxaris*; *Papyrus Soc. Ital.* VIII.981). Somewhat later, towards 120 B.C., the Scythian king, Scilurus, is found minting coins at Olbia but with a fixed capital in the foothills of the Crimea, perhaps at Kermenchik near Simferopol, which was one of three such strongholds – Neapolis, Palacium and Chabum.[109] He had up to fifty sons, one of whom, Palacus, managed to unite under him the Tauri and to draw the Sarmatian Rhoxolani into an alliance. He attacked Chersonesus and had a kind of 'fifth column' in Panticapaeum as well.

Recently, with the find of an inscription made at Panticapaeum in 1978/9, a daughter of Scilurus called Dedmotis has been shown to have resided there, married to one Heraclitus, a Bosporan Greek. She dedicated an altar table to a Scythian goddess Dithagoea.[110] Another element in the confused situation on the Bosporus was the Scythian population of the Kerch Peninsula. A Scythian, Saumacus by name, was raised at the court of Paerisades V and apparently had some expectation of succeeding to his rule. His was probably a palace faction and a racial group rather than the slave uprising some Soviet scholars have taken it to be.[111] In this situation where the threatened Bosporan Greeks were opposed to this possibility, an appeal was made across the Black Sea to Mithridates VI of Pontus. Diophantus, his general and a native of Sinope, was sent in response. He repelled the Scythians from Chersonesus and later from the western coastlands of the Crimea, and went on to rescue Theodosia and Panticapaeum from the Saumacus faction (c. 111– 109 B.C.). Saumacus himself was sent in chains to Mithridates' court at Sinope. With this act Diophantus put an end to hopes of even an adoptee and pretender carrying on an independent state of Bosporus, where a

[109] Frolova 1964 (E 232); T. N. Vysotskaya, *Pozdnye Skify v Yugo-Zapadnom Krymu* (Kiev 1972).
[110] J. G. Vinogradov *et al.*, in *Tskhaltubo III 1982* (1985) 589–610.
[111] V. F. Gaidukevich in *Antichnaya Istoria i Kultura Sredizemnomorya i Prichernomorya* (1968) 81–95; Gaidukevich 1971 (E 241) 317, n. 19; K. V. Golenko, *VDI* 1963.3, 69ff, Dundua 1987 (E 230) 102–5; Rubinsohn 1980 (E 351).

series of seventeen *archons* and kings had perpetuated the line of Leucon and Paerisades since 438 B.C. A new phase in the history of the Black Sea area was being entered upon, with Mithridates turning the Euxine into a lake dominated by the empire of Pontus (*c.*110–65 B.C.).

VI. SUCCESSFUL SYNOECISM ON THE CIMMERIAN BOSPORUS

The dynasts of the Bosporus were, in the fourth century, regarded as barbarians, as we have seen, but accepted as kings in the new hellenistic milieu from the early third century, when classical Greek titles such as *archon* lacked their former cachet. But almost uniquely the same family went on into that new world undisturbed. One strand of their inheritance was certainly Thracian and probably from the royal family, the Odrysae. But they intermarried with Bosporan Greeks and occasionally with the Sindi as well, though not, so far as we know, with Scythians, Maeotians or Sarmatians. The state, when it was fully formed, had a core of Ionian and Aeolian Greeks, with some citizens priding themselves on their origin (*Panticapaites, Cepites, Nymphaites*).[112] Scythians were located in many of the 200 agricultural and fishing, rural settlements in the Kerch Peninsula, especially in that part protected by the Cimmeric (Uzunlyarsk) bank and ditch; in addition there would be some Cimmerians, a remnant of their former subjects, left behind on the Bosporus. The Sindi of the Taman Peninsula had been incorporated *in toto*, but also some Maeotian and north Caucasus peoples had acceded to Bosporan overlordship. Individuals, like Tychon the Taurian (*CIRB* 114) and Drysanis the Paphlagonian (*CIRB* 180), who came as a mercenary, increased the racial mix. At the present time some 150 settlements are known from the Taman Peninsula, engaged in grain growing, fish-salting and cattle-rearing.[113] Local sculpture used on funerary monuments shows up a racial distinction here, where draped, half-length, rounded figures, replace the Bosporan relief stelae found elsewhere.[114] Some large-scale sculpture is good Greek in style with only a slight provincial air, or exhibiting a concern with local subjects. There is a *kouros* head probably of the early fifth century from Cepi, a Hellenistic Aphrodite found in 1963 from the same site, and a newly found (1983 and 1985) Amazonomachy relief and grave stelae of the fourth century B.C. found in the northern part of the Taman Peninsula (Fig. 29), perhaps the remains of a *heröon*. The 'monument of a Satyrus', mentioned by Strabo as being a

[112] Blavatsky 1958 (E 197); Kolobova 1953 (E 288) 60.
[113] Kruglikova 1975 (E 294); Anfimov 1977 (E 180) 6–12; Yakovenko 1981 (E 433); Paromov 1986 (E 333); Maslennikov 1989 (E 317).
[114] Ivanova 1961 (E 266); Sokolsky 1966 (E 393), and in *Le Rayonnement des Civilisations; VIII Congrès int. d'arch. classique* (Paris 1965) 473–9; Sokolov 1974 (E 389) pls. 89, 90.

Fig. 29. Grave stela from Taman. (After Savostina 1987 (E 353) 19, fig. 11.)

little further west near the strait, is a possibility for its source.[115] In some fifteen of the thirty townships of Bosporus excavations have been carried out. A monumental temple in the Ionic order was found at Panticapaeum belonging to the middle of the fifth century. An Ionic column capital from Hermonassa of even earlier date exists to prove such public buildings there; at a later date Phanagoria and Gorgippia also were well appointed.[116] The cults were from the start the common Milesian ones of Apollo Ietros and Apollo Delphinios, but deities which had a strong native content soon appear strongly, Artemis Agrotera, and the several centres of worship of Aphrodite Urania in and near Phanagoria and Cepi (Tod no. 115 B-C; 171 B-E).[117] In the 1960s excavations in Panticapaeum

[115] M. M. Kobylina, *Antichnaya Skulptura Severnogo Prichernomorya* (Moscow 1972) 20–6; N. I. Sokolsky, *Sov. Arch.* 1962.2, 132–41; Savostina 1987 (E 353); Sokolov 1974 (E 389) pls. 9, 15–18, 95–6.

[116] Pichikyan 1974 (E 337) and 1975 (E 338); Koshelenko *et al.* 1984 (E 290) pl. 90.

[117] Minns 1913 (E 321) 615–20; N. Ehrhardt, *Milet und seine Kolonien* (Diss. Frankfurt 1983).

produced a Doric-style monumental building of the second century B.C.,
which has been identified as a prytaneum, and in the years leading up to
1980 strong fortifications (tower, curtain walls and bastions) were found
on the north side of the acropolis, which dated to the period of
Mithridates and his immediate successors.[118]

Alongside the massive import of wine and oil containers already
mentioned there is a great deal of fourth-century Attic red-figure and
black pottery, including the class of 'Kerch' vases, the choice of which
for the Bosporan market may be betrayed by popular subjects on them,
especially Arimasps, griffins and Amazons. The burials of the ordinarily
well-to-do Bosporans have a generally Greek look, though the inclusion
of swords and 'Scythian-type' arrow heads in many graves modifies this
picture.[119] The imposing corbelled vaults and *dromos*-approaches of the
tombs of the nobility and rulers, however, have their best parallels in
those of Thracian dynasts and the Macedonian kings, and are even
reminiscent of the long-gone Mycenaean 'beehive' tombs. They are, in
the main, cut into the ridges approaching Panticapaeum from the West,
those on Jüz Oba perhaps representing resting places of the Bosporan
archons. That at Kul Oba and the 'Patinioti' burial will have belonged to
Scythian kings of the fourth century B.C., who had been drawn towards
Panticapaeum, as King Scyles once had been towards Olbia (Hdt.
IV.77).[120]

Bosporan metalwork in iron and, more decoratively, in bronze was
highly developed.[121] But most outstanding in an artistic sense were the
gold and silver bowls and amphorae, the war equipment and horse
accoutrements. These were produced in a Hellenic style adapted to
barbarian tastes on the one hand, but, more creatively, in a somewhat
civilized, yet highly original, barbarian 'Scythian animal style'. These
comprise ornamental shield bosses, horse frontals, scabbards, covers for
the *gorytus* (bow and arrow case; Fig. 30), gold dress-plaques in
thousands, the latter of which may imitate Greek coins, or represent
miniature beasts in combat. The animals figured may be monsters, the
by-now-familiar lion-headed or eagle-headed griffin or a snake-tailed
goddess, but the 'animal-style' proper more typically depicts fish, goats,
bears, foxes, sometimes superimposed upon the body of a larger beast.
By far the most frequent and highly developed of these motifs are a
stylized head of a bird of prey, a stag with hooves tucked up beneath its
belly and antlers often branching into minuscule beasts, and a curled

[118] Tolstikov 1984 (E 398); Marchenko 1968 (E 312).
[119] Rostowzew 1931 (E 350) 164ff; Koshelenko et al. 1984 (E 290) pl. 95.
[120] Minns 1913 (E 321) 200ff, 323ff; Rostowzew 1931 (E 350) 164–94; Gaidukevich 1971 (E 241) 256–302; Koshelenko et al. 1984 (E 290) pl. 112.
[121] Blavatsky 1959 (E 198); Treister 1988 (E 402), 1987 (E 401), and 1984 (E 400).

Fig. 30. Gold *gorytus* cover from Chertomlyk. One of four made from the same model in Scythian tombs. (After Minns 1913 (E 321) 285, fig. 206.)

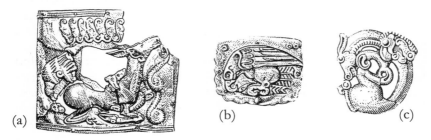

(a)   (b)   (c)

Fig. 31. Animal style plaques, fifth century B.C. (a) from Ilyicheva (East Crimea); (b) from Zavadskoye I (Dniepr bend); (c) Kovalevka (lower Bug area). (See note 122.)

predator (in some cases a wolf or wolverine, but in the hellenized examples resembling most a panther), whose paws again turn into miniatures of the whole (Fig. 31).[122] These may have been originally totemic motifs of the northern peoples, symbolic of their strength and resources. The style may well have originated in decoration of horse bridles and ornaments, and the earliest examples seem to have been carved in wood or bone. The skills of the Bosporan artists transformed these themes of their pastoralist neighbours into objects of decorative art of great beauty and elegance. At the same time they produced realistic scenes of Scythian life in the more Hellenized narrative style, a richness

---

[122] Chlenova 1962 (E 226); Onaiko 1966 (E 329); Shkurko 1969 (E 384); Artamonov 1968 (E 185) pls. 37–140; Galanina and Grach 1986 (E 242); Koshelenko *et al.* 1984 (E 290) pls. 114–16.

of creativity heavily concentrated in the Bosporan and Scythian *floruit* *c.*400 to 250 B.C.[123]

The Bosporan Greeks, their barbarian rulers and incorporated peoples, constructed a stable and original society and culture in their exposed position on both sides of the Cimmerian Bosporus. They had a unique population mixture, natural resources, and a geographical position on the European side (Kerch Peninsula), which was protected from the major threat of cavalry raids and migratory movements by the two rampart-and-ditch systems. They had durable and talented individual dynasts in the late fifth and fourth centuries, who ruled for long periods and gave Bosporus a prestige which carried it through the rather more difficult times of the first half of the third and early second centuries. Sometimes the dynasty and state is compared with its contemporary, Syracuse, under its successive rulers, the Deinomenids, Dionysius and the family of King Hieron, which yielded to Rome in 212 B.C. (Aelian *VH* vi.13). There is something parallel and similar in their development, but the great difference was the proximity of Syracuse to two major competing empires, Carthage and Rome. Bosporus was just beyond the reach of Persia's long arm, far beyond the domination of the major classical and hellenistic powers, which had an interest in the Black Sea area, and the Scythians were not interested in settling in towns in a restricted area like the Bosporus.

The idea of synoecism and communal defence of small cities behind defensive ramparts was in the air in the late sixth and early fifth centuries B.C. Pisistratus had attempted to unify mineral-rich areas of Thrace at Rhaecelus and near the gold mines of Mt Pangaeum, but gave the latter up to return to Athens. More significantly, perhaps, and in the approaches to the Black Sea, Miltiades the Elder answered the call of some Thracian Dolonci who lived in the Thracian Chersonesus and wished for protection from the more powerful Apsinthii who lived beyond the isthmus (Hdt. vi.35–40; 103; 139–40). Miltiades constructed a wall across the isthmus of this Gallipoli Peninsula and unified behind it a number of small towns – Cardia, Crithote, Madytus, Pactye, Sestus, Elaeus.[124] The dynasty lasted for about fifty years until Miltiades the Younger left for Athens some three or four years before the Persians attacked Athens in 490 B.C., but the Athenians revived the idea of control of Chersonesus with *cleruch*-settlers in the fifth and fourth centuries. Chersonesus, like Bosporus, had a tyrant dynasty, a synoecism, protection by long walls, and it was a significant producer of grain (*Agora Chersonesiton*). It even underwent a Scythian raid in the early fifth century,

---

[123] Artamonov 1968 (E 185) pls. 142–273; Sokolov 1974 (E 389) pls. 50–65.

[124] A. J. Graham, *Colony and Mother City* (Manchester 1964) 32–4, 194–7; Ehrenberg 1946 (C 133) 117–28.

though that was only a transitory thing for the Chersonesites in the Hellespont. The Bosporan state may well have been conceived on the model of that in the Thracian Chersonesus, but its very remoteness guaranteed it greater independence from Aegean states such as Athens, and from later Balkan powers such as Lysimachus or the Antigonid rulers of Macedon. It could only be absorbed by a state with a genuine Black Sea power base such as that of Mithridates' Pontus.

Whatever the origin of the idea of a Bosporan state, its history was a long one, with many original features, adapting the Greek way of life to local conditions, and having a long-range economic effect, and a certain cultural influence, on the metropolitan Greek states as well. It was even to have a second period of independence, though one of clientship to Rome, under the long dynasty (bearing once again Odrysian Thracian as well as Sarmatian names) which ruled from c.A.D. 10 to 336/7. This last amounted to a period (over three centuries) of striking symmetry to that which we have already seen (438/7–109 B.C.) in the longevity of the 'Spartocid' dynasty.[125]

[125] Gaidukevich 1971 (E 241) 333–70, 459–96; Frolova 1979/83 (E 233); Anokhin 1986 (E 182) 132–3. For Mithridates' empire around the Black Sea see *CAH* IX² ch. 5, 137–40.

CHAPTER 9g

MEDITERRANEAN COMMUNICATIONS

L. CASSON

The Greek city states clustered about the shores of the Mediterranean like 'frogs on a pond', as Plato put it (*Phd.* 109b). And the centres of greatest economic importance – not only Greek but Phoenician as well – were by and large seaports: Tyre, Miletus, Byzantium, Athens and its Piraeus, Syracuse, Carthage, Marseilles. There was good reason for this. The shortest and least arduous way of getting from one distant point to another was most often by the body of water that lay so conveniently at the centre of the Greek and Roman world. Men learned to sail on it as early as the eleventh millennium B.C.[1] and were doing so regularly by the seventh (*CAH* I³.1, 570–1).

I. COMMUNICATIONS BY LAND

Travel by sea, to be sure, had its disadvantages, as we will note in a moment, but they were far less grave than those by land. There the very possibility of movement depended squarely upon the existence of roads, and its speed on the nature of the terrain. In the flat plains of southern Mesopotamia, by the second millennium B.C., there were roads between the major city states, like those from Nippur to Ur or from Babylon to Larsa, and the international route that ran from Egypt north along the Levantine coast to Beirut dates back at least to the late second. Minoan Crete had roads between its important points, and so did Mycenaean Greece. The Assyrian empire, in the years of its greatness, *c.* 900–600 B.C., maintained an efficient government dispatch service and the network of roads that this required; both were taken over and improved by the Persians.[2]

However, a fully developed road system, one that offered all-weather paved surfaces on key highways and that laced together the entire Mediterranean area, had to await the days of the Roman empire. Before this, in mountainous regions, such as made up large parts of Greece, roads for wheeled traffic did not exist, merely paths for walkers and pack animals; for example, there was not even a proper road between Athens

[1] Renfrew and Wagstaff 1982 (I 126) 24.   [2] Casson 1974 (I 23) 25–7, 49–54.

512

and Megara until Hadrian had one built. And some of these mountain paths, including a few that linked sizeable cities – e.g. Sparta with Argos or Tegea – followed river gorges and hence must have been impassable during winter rains.[3]

Transport by land, even where suitable roads existed, was held to a minimum, particularly if the freight was heavy or bulky; the means were so primitive and the pace so slow that the cost was prohibitive. There has survived an inscription which details the expenses for putting up a building at Eleusis in the late fourth century B.C. The stone for the columns, coming from the quarries at Pentele, perforce travelled by road; an entry (*IG* II² 1673, lines 64–5) reveals that it took thirty-one teams of oxen three days to move a single drum the 30 odd km involved.

On the other hand, voyagers who were travelling light, or carriers of dispatches, might find the land as feasible as the sea, and, when the seas were closed (see below), they had no alternative. Between nearby points, even in difficult terrain, quick communication was possible through the use of professional runners, the *hemerodromoi*, 'day-runners', as the Greeks called them, from the distance they were able to cover in a day (cf. Livy XXXI.24). When pushing themselves to the utmost they could reel off 175 km, as one did when, after the Battle of Plataea in 479 B.C., he raced from Plataea to Delphi and back, but the average was very likely considerably less.[4] Between distant points, relays of runners could be used and, where terrain permitted it, relays of horsemen certainly were. The mounted relay service that is best known, thanks to a famous description in Herodotus (VIII.98; cf. V.52–3), was that maintained by the Persian Kings between Sardis and the capital at Susa; the riders went the course in about twenty days, averaging 150 km or a little less each day.[5]

II. SAILING THE MEDITERRANEAN

Whenever they had the choice travellers much preferred a sea-lane to a road. The delegations that Athens sent to the Olympic games, for example, went as far as they could by ship, keeping to a minimum the stretch they had to do by land (cf. Photius, s.v. *Paralos*). For merchants, particularly those who dealt in any of the three commodities that bulked largest in ancient commerce – grain, wine and olive oil – transport by land, except where utterly unavoidable, was out of the question; it had to be by sea. One of Demosthenes' cases involved a pair of partners who financed a shipment of 3,000 amphorae of wine from Mende to the Borysthenes (XXXV.10). It was all put aboard a standard cargo carrier, a modest-sized vessel driven by the wind and manned by a crew of perhaps

[3] Pritchett 1980 (A 48) 151–8, 164–5.   [4] Riepl 1913 (I 131) 137; Frost 1979 (K 13) 160.
[5] Pflaum 1940 (I 120) 192–205.

less than a dozen, which, given no bad luck with the weather, could make the voyage in a few weeks. To have sent it overland would have required hundreds of pack animals, a regiment of drivers, and months of provisions for both.

But sea travel, for all its convenience, had shortcomings of its own. The most serious was its limited availability, from late spring to early autumn as a rule. The rest of the year vessels went into hibernation, the smaller drawn up on beaches and the larger snugged down in the inner recesses of harbours. Ancient sailors were loath to expose themselves to winter's dangerous storms, less dependable and fiercer winds, and above all its reduced visibility. Having no such aid as the mariner's compass, they had to find their way by the stars at night and, during the day, by various time-honoured methods including the position of the sun and the sighting of heights or promontories – Mt Athos, Mt Ida, the lofty peak of Samothrace, Sunium, Malea, Taenarum and the like – that could be discerned from miles away in the clear air of a Mediterranean summer day; it was not for nothing that the Greeks planted on many of these spots temples to Poseidon or Castor and Pollux or other deities favoured by the seaman.[6] Hesiod, a lubberly peasant, timidly counselled venturing on the water only during the fifty days after the summer solstice (*Op.* 663–5); for professional sailors the season ran from late April to mid-September, at the outside from March to early November. A very few routes were exempt; thus ships plied between Rhodes and Egypt all year round. Everywhere else, voyages between October and April were strictly limited to the delivery of vital dispatches, the ferrying of urgently needed supplies, the carrying out of military movements impossible to delay.[7]

Another shortcoming of sea travel was its dependence upon the wind, first and foremost whether there was any or not and, second, its direction. During the summer, calms are discouragingly frequent throughout the Mediterranean. In the Tyrrhenian Sea, an area of prime commercial importance in ancient times, calms between May and September reach 33 per cent. In the channel between Sicily and Africa, a vital waterway for ships going from the western to the eastern basin of the Mediterranean, they reach 28 per cent. Along the coast of Asia Minor, another area thronged with traffic, calms run from 15 per cent during July and August to 21 to 26 per cent during May, June and September.[8]

When there was wind, the direction it came from was of crucial importance. Ancient sailing craft, whether Egyptian, Phoenician, Etrus-

---

[6] Semple 1931 (I 140) 587–91, 613–37.   [7] Casson 1986 (I 24) 270–2.

[8] Based on the charts in *Sailing Directions* 1975 (I 134) 37–9, 43–5. The winds in antiquity were the same as today; see Murray 1987 (I 111).

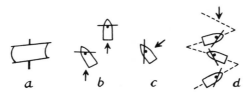

a Squaresail
b Sailing before a favourable wind
c Heading into the wind
d Tacking

Fig. 32. Modes of sailing.

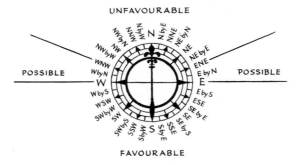

Fig. 33. Effects of wind on a ship sailing to the north.

can, Greek or Roman, were almost all equipped with squaresails (Fig. 32a). Such a rig operates very efficiently with a wind from astern or on the quarter (Fig. 32b), i.e., if a vessel is headed due north, with a wind anywhere from ESE around S to WSW (Fig. 33). It can manage with a wind on the beam (still assuming a north heading, with a wind from E or W) and even struggle with a wind somewhat forward of the beam (from ENE or WNW; Figs. 32c, 33). However, if the wind is ahead – that is, still assuming a north heading, fron ENE around N to WNW (Fig. 33) – a skipper, if he has the chance, simply stays where he is until a favourable wind begins to blow, as the skipper of St Paul's ship did at Rhegium, waiting there until a southerly sprang up to carry him to Puteoli (*Acts* 28:13). If he does not have the chance, if willy-nilly he has to sail into a head wind, he must resort to tacking, proceeding toward his destination by a series of zigzags, each at the closest possible angle to the wind. So, if his destination lay due north and if the wind was blowing from precisely that direction, he would sail for a while towards ENE, then sail for a while towards WNW, and so on (Fig. 32d). Tacking is arduous work and produces slow, often painfully slow, progress.

In many bodies of water, currents and tides are a significant consideration for navigation, but not in the Mediterranean. There both are generally too feeble to matter, save in certain narrow channels. At Gibraltar, since the level of the Atlantic is higher, its waters spill through the strait, causing a strong easterly current. At the other end of the Mediterranean a similar situation obtains: the Black Sea is higher and, as a consequence, a strong westerly current runs through the Bosporus, the Sea of Marmora, and the Dardanelles. Elsewhere currents for the most part follow the direction of the wind. One exception is the coast of North Africa, where the current from Gibraltar retains enough strength to aid easterly bound vessels as far as Tunisia.

The sole tidal currents of importance are in the Strait of Messina and the Euripus, where they are powerful enough to force vessels to wait until the flow is in the right direction before venturing through.[9]

III. THE SHIPS

The standard cargo carrier of the ancient world was the sailing ship. Inevitably, when the wind failed or came from the wrong direction, it had to stand by, its sails slatting helplessly or furled out of the way, awaiting a turn for the better. Warships, however, could not afford such idleness; they had to be able to move – to attack an enemy or flee from him, to chase after a pirate, to ferry a sorely needed batch of reinforcements, and so on – when the occasion arose, regardless of the wind. The ancients' solution was to use galleys for their naval craft, slender shallow-draft ships propelled by lines of rowers as well as by sail.

These war galleys played a role not only in battle but also in communications, for their freedom from dependence on the vagaries of the wind caused them to be pressed into service regularly as carriers of passengers or messages. For example, the officials of Athens who were sent to collect special levies from the subject cities of the empire went back and forth on triremes,[10] a type of galley powered by three superimposed banks of oarsmen that was the ship-of-the-line of the Athenian navy. Indeed, the navy maintained a pair of crack triremes, the *Paralos* and the *Salaminia*, specially for transporting important persons or delivering important dispatches. It was the *Salaminia* that met the Athenian expeditionary force at Catana in 415 B.C. with orders to bring Alcibiades back for trial (Thuc. VI.53.1); it was the *Paralos* that Conon sent flying to Athens in 405 to report the news of the disaster at

---

[9] Semple 1931 (I 140) 582–3; Le Gras 1870 (I 97) 42–3; Hodge 1983 (I 74) 74.
[10] Meiggs 1972 (C 201) 254.

Aegospotami (Xen. *Hell*. II.1.29). Both of these vessels, and probably other triremes in the fleet as well, ferried the Athenian delegations all or part way to the great international festivals at Delphi, Delos, Olympia.[11] The speed at which triremes on such duty travelled depended upon the urgency of the assignment. Those going to the festivals very likely proceeded in a leisurely manner under sail, using the oars only when necessary. Those carrying crucial messages very likely set the rowers to work the moment the wind failed or even dropped below desirable strength, and in this way might cover 100 miles or more in a long day's run. In a crisis, such as the time during the summer of 428 B.C., when the Athenians sent a trireme carrying a harsh decree against the Mytilenians and then the next day rushed another with countermanding orders (Thuc. III.49), the oars might be used the whole distance, each bank rowing in turn to keep up a steady unflagging rate. The rate under oars alone, however, would average but half of that possible under a good wind.[12]

War galleys were not designed for long voyaging, particularly over open water. With almost all available space taken up by the rowers, it was impossible to stow away enough food and water for the many mouths aboard to last for any length of time. They were for courses that permitted them to reach shore preferably every night.

Not only naval commanders but also merchants found it at times advantageous to have at their disposal carriers that did not depend exclusively on the wind. And so, alongside the war galleys, there were merchant galleys, designed for carrying passengers and cargo instead of marines and engines of war. Since the main consideration was not speed or agility, they were broader and heavier than their naval cousins and were propelled by far fewer rowers. Moreover, since they performed a wide range of duties, they varied far more in size, from very small craft driven by a handful of oarsmen to vessels capable of hauling hundreds of passengers. They travelled under sail as much as possible, running out the oars only when strictly necessary (a feature that is reflected in the Greek name for them, *histiokopos* 'sail-oar-er'), when becalmed or when entering a port or rounding a headland against a foul wind. Very likely they were slower than a sailing ship with a good wind behind it. On the other hand, they were able to keep moving under all circumstances; the service they offered may not have been quicker but it was more reliable. They tramped along coasts or between adjacent islands, picking up and depositing casual passengers and modest loads of freight.[13]

[11] Jordan 1975 (K 27) 160–4. See Pls. Vol. pl. 184.

[12] Xen. *An*. VI.4.2: from Byzantium to Heraclea Pontica (*c*. 120 nautical miles) was 'a long day's run under oars'; Xenophon must mean 'with the help of the oars' since, under oars alone, a galley could cover but half that distance in a day (cf. Rodgers 1937 (K 52) 9).

[13] Casson 1986 (I 24) 157–68.

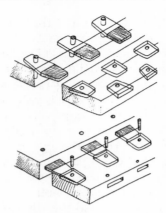

Fig. 34. The joining of ships' planks. (After Giamfrotta and Pomey 1981 (1 63) 238.)

Most cargo, and virtually all that travelled over open water, went aboard sailing ships. These ran the gamut of size from very small craft for moving goods and people about harbours to freighters capable of holding several hundred tons that hauled bulky commodities between major ports. Mediterranean shipwrights from at least the fourteenth century B.C. on constructed all their vessels, small as well as large, in a special fashion that emphasized staunchness and strength. They did not start with a skeleton of keel and frames (ribs) and pin to this a skin of planks, as has been standard practice in the western world for centuries. Instead they first built up the shell of the hull and then into this shell they inserted a set of frames. This is a well-known procedure, one employed by numerous peoples all over the globe right up to the present century. Where the Mediterranean shipwright went his own way was in the very special method he used for joining the planks to each other as he built up the shell of the hull: he set them edge to edge and fastened each to its neighbours above and below by means of closely spaced mortise and tenon joints (Fig. 34). In carefully crafted vessels these stood no more than the width of a joint apart so that each seam was linked by a serried row of them. In addition, every joint was transfixed by dowels above and below the seam to ensure that it would never come apart. On top of all this care in the binding together of the hull, a full set of frames was then inserted to stiffen it. The result was a ship of extraordinary strength and durability that needed a minimum of caulking, one well able to stand up under the loads of amphorae or building stone or other ponderous freight it was so often called upon to carry.[14]

Ancient sailing vessels were primarily for transporting cargo, not passengers – although these were often aboard. Neither the Greeks nor

[14] Casson 1986 (1 24) 201–8, 448.

the Romans had packets, ships that operated between fixed points on a regular schedule. People who needed to get to an overseas destination simply inquired at the waterfront until they found some freighter going their way. All they were generally able to book was deck passage; there was some scant cabin space available, but it was reserved for the captain, the owners of the cargo or their agents, and perhaps an occasional important personage. Passengers came abroad with their own tentlike shelters, sleeping pads, etc., and enough food to last them till the first port of call, where they could lay in supplies for the next stage.[15]

Official dispatches, like official passengers, as noted above went on special galleys. Private letters went as haphazardly as private passengers: just as travellers looked about until they found some vessel going their way, so writers of letters looked about until they found some traveller going to the required destination who would be willing, as it were, to serve as postman.[16]

And neither cargo nor passengers nor letters made their arrival in any great hurry, since the ships they went on were designed and rigged for safety and seaworthiness and not speed. On most sailing vessels, the largest as well as the smallest, the chief source of drive was a single broad squaresail carried low on a relatively short mast set amidships; foresails, though known, were not common, the mizzen seems not to have been introduced until hellenistic times, and that great advance in rigging, tiers of superimposed sails, did not come to pass until the fifteenth century of our era. The ancients' rig clearly was designed for moving before favourable winds and for moving without risk rather than quickly. Under ideal sailing conditions, their ships were capable of making between 4 and 6 knots; voyages cited as examples of record speed average no more than 6. With unfavourable winds, the rate dropped to half that or less.[17] Thus the time required to effect transport between the various shipping centres about the Mediterranean depended squarely upon the prevailing winds.

IV. THE EASTERN BASIN

When Agamemnon was ready to lead the Greek fleet out of Aulis he was held up a long time by contrary winds. The legend has a solid meteorological basis: the course to Troy from Aulis was north east, which meant a continuous fight against the Etesian winds, as the Greeks called them, the Meltem of today, the northerlies that dominate the Aegean in the summer; in July and August, the heart of the sailing season, they attain a frequency of 80 per cent or more. South of the

---

[15] Casson 1974 (I 23) 152–4.   [16] Casson 1974 (I 23) 220–1.
[17] Casson 1986 (I 24) 239–43, 282–91.

Aegean, from the Levant westward to a line just beyond the west coast of Greece, the dominant summer wind is north-westerly, and it is so frequent as almost to justify being called a trade wind; the only other winds of consequence are westerly. Nor are these winds mild. In the southern area they average close to 11 knots, and in the northern even more than that, over 12.[18]

This means that vessels travelling in any southerly direction had a quick and easy run. One of the fastest voyages on record from ancient times, reported by Pliny the Elder (xix.3–4), was made by a ship that went from the Strait of Messina to Alexandria in six days; since the distance is some 830 nautical miles, its speed works out to an average of a little less than 6 knots.[19] From the Cimmerian Bosporus to Rhodes, c. 880 nautical miles, generally took nine to ten days. From either Rhodes or the eastern tip of Crete to Alexandria, c. 325 and 310 nautical miles respectively, took about three and a half days. These work out to an average of 4 knots. Presumably ships normally travelled from the Strait of Messina to Alexandria at that rate rather than the 6 knots of Pliny's pace-setting run. No question, Greek and Roman merchantmen, with their conservative rig, were slow; sailing ships of the last century, for example, made the trip from Crete to Egypt at double the speed of the ancients, in one and a half to two days instead of three to four.[20]

To go in the other direction, from the south towards the north, since it involved a constant struggle against head winds, required twice as much time or even more. One voyager who went from Byzantium to Rhodes in five days, and from Byzantium to Gaza in ten, took exactly ten and twenty days respectively to get back; on the homecoming trips he averaged under 2 knots. It took him ten days to get from Caesarea to Rhodes; since the distance is c. 400 nautical miles, he made less than 2 knots on this run as well. The longer time was partly because the ships moved slowly through the water, but even more because they had to set a roundabout course in order to obtain a slant that would enable them to make progress against the prevailing northerlies. A significant case in point is the well-travelled route that went from Athens to Rhodes and, after Alexander's conquest of Egypt, to Alexandria. Outbound, skippers were able to shape a direct course and arrive at Rhodes in some three days (assuming they covered the c. 275 nautical miles at an average of 4 knots) and Alexandria in another three or four. However, to return home, they first had to sail, keeping the wind on or just forward of the port beam, roughly north east until past the eastern tip of Cyprus; in one reported voyage this leg alone took seven days – almost as long as the whole of the

---

[18] *Sailing Directions* 1975 (I 134) 43–5; Semple 1931 (I 140) 580–1.
[19] For citation of sources for these and the other voyages mentioned, see Casson 1986 (I 24) 282–91.   [20] Le Gras 1870 (I 97) 109.

outbound voyage (the distance is *c.* 250 nautical miles, so the speed was
well under 2 knots). They would then turn left and head almost due west
along the southern coast of Asia Minor to Rhodes. Finally, to get from
Rhodes to Athens, they had to tack laboriously through the Cyclades.

Another route of great importance was the one that connected the
Cimmerian Bosporus with Athens and numerous other centres around
the Aegean or on the islands; these lived off imported grain, and the fields
of the Ukraine, then as now, were a rich source of supply. The route
crossed the Aegean to the Dardanelles, passed through the Dardanelles,
Sea of Marmora, and the Bosporus, and then traversed the western
segment of the Black Sea. It was the outbound run that took the time.
The first part, over the Aegean, like Agamemnon's run to Troy, had to be
made in the face of the Etesian winds, the prevailing northerlies. Next
came the passage through the two straits, where ships bucked current as
well as wind: in the Dardanelles the current flows westward at a speed of
$2\frac{1}{2}$ to 3 knots, and under abnormal conditions even 5, while in the
Bosporus it is still more violent, averaging 4 to 5 knots and under
abnormal conditions going as high as 7. Fortunately the flow does not
follow the line of the channels but ricochets from shore to shore creating,
as it does, eddies with counter-currents. By taking advantage of these,
and by patiently awaiting winds from the south or west, which, though
far less frequent than those from north or east, do occur, skippers were
able to work their way through.[21] The struggle, however, did not always
end there, since the course thereafter was roughly north east, and the
Meltem in the part of the Black Sea that they had to sail over blows
prevailingly from that direction.[22] The voyage home was all downhill,
the vessels flying along with wind and current on their heels. If they had
no need to stop, they could arrive in the Aegean in less than eight days.

In effect, Greek merchants who traded with the Black Sea ports could
count on only one round trip during the sailing season, for the quick
return did not make up for the time spent on the outbound voyage. The
ships not only had to wait for favourable winds, especially at the straits,
but had to put in here and there along the way to pick up cargo that could
be sold further along or at the final port of call. The delays were such that
skippers frequently were unable to start their return until after the sailing
season had closed – so frequently that contracts for maritime loans might
include a clause raising the interest rate if the homebound trip began later
than mid-September (Dem. xxxv.10). The winds alone were enough to
put the length of the voyage beyond reasonable calculation. When Philip
of Macedon marched against Thrace, located to the north east of Athens,
he was well aware of this; as Demosthenes bitterly pointed out (IV.31),

[21] *Black Sea Pilot* 1969 (1 6) 41–2; Labaree 1957 (1 92); Graham 1958 (1 66) 28–31.
[22] *Black Sea Pilot* 1969 (1 6) 57.

'He waits for the Etesians or the winter for his attacks, when we cannot get there.' Of the two straits, the Bosporus was the more troublesome. Even sailing craft of the nineteenth century found it impossible to get through when the current was running strongly; only an agile ship aided by a good wind could succeed.[23]

To be sure, the Cimmerian Bosporus was not the only source of grain. Egypt was an important supplier, but for the Greek states the voyage there offered similar difficulty, save in reverse: as pointed out above, on this run the winds dictated a fast voyage out but a slow one back.

A third grain-producing area was Sicily. Here merchants, if they were able to effect a quick turnaround, might count on squeezing in two round trips during the sailing season. No voyages are specifically reported in our sources, but a rough estimate of the time they must have taken can be worked out. From the Piraeus to Sicily is, in very round numbers, about 500 nautical miles: 100 to Cape Malea and then another 400 westward to Sicily. Vessels would cover the 100 with the Meltem carrying them along. Trouble would start as soon as they rounded Cape Malea, for here the wind ceased being favourable. From this point on they very likely had to cope a good deal of the time with head winds, the northerlies and westerlies that prevail in the Ionian Sea, particularly in midsummer.[24] Assuming a speed of 4 knots for the quick leg and 2 for the slow, the trip would take some nine to ten days. The return would be just the reverse, 4 knots for the first 400 miles and 2 for the final 100, and take some six days.

Merchants from the Aegean whose ports of call were not in Sicily but along the west coast of Greece or up the Adriatic also had slow going once they rounded Cape Malea, inasmuch as the summer winds in the lower and middle Adriatic, like those in the Ionian Sea, tend to be northerly and north-westerly.[25] Again the sources provide no specific voyages, but a run from the Strait of Otranto to the head of the Adriatic, about 500 nautical miles, could well have required upwards of eight days, though most vessels doubtless took even longer by making stops en route.

V. THE MALTA AND SICILY CHANNELS AND STRAIT OF MESSINA

There were two ways of getting from the eastern basin of the Mediterranean to the western or vice versa: either through the Malta and Sicily channels or through the Strait of Messina.

[23] Le Gras 1870 (I 97) 193.   [24] *Sailing Directions* 1975 (I 134) 43–5.
[25] *Sailing Directions* 1975 (I 134) 37–9.

The channels are fairly broad, that between the eastern tip of Sicily and the island of Malta being about 45 miles wide and that between the western tip of Sicily and Cap Bon about 75. In both the prevailing summer winds are from the west and north west.[26] Thus ships coming from the western to the eastern basin found it advantageous to pass through the channels.[27] It follows that ships coming from the eastern to the western basin would meet head winds in the channels. Rather than fight these, they preferred to pass through the Strait of Messina, and from there they sailed along the western coast of Italy and then across the Gulf of Genoa.[28]

Ships travelling across the channels, from Italy or Sicily to North Africa or the reverse, made good time in either direction, although the run southward was somewhat the quicker. Reported voyages, for example, indicate that fast vessels could go from Ostia to Africa in two days, whereas the return took two and a half to three.

VI. THE WESTERN BASIN

A voyage from Alexandria to Marseilles that took thirty days was hailed as a most prosperous crossing. Yet the average speed works out to a mere 2 knots. Obviously the run ordinarily took even longer – and for good reason: the sail from the eastern end of the Mediterranean into the western basin had to be done for the most part against head winds.

As it happens, the westerlies and north-westerlies that made westbound sailing so difficult in parts of the eastern basin prevail in much of the western.[29] However, once a vessel was well in the western basin, these winds allowed fairly efficient movement toward the major westerly ports. Among his examples of particularly fast voyages, Pliny the Elder includes (XIX.3–4) three across this area, all westbound: Ostia to Narbo in three days, to Hither Spain in four, to the Strait of Gibraltar in seven; the speed works out to between 5 and 6 knots. The return in all three cases must have been just as fast.

Along the coast of North Africa too, travel was more or less equally efficient in both directions. Westbound traffic had the advantage of prevailingly easterly winds; thus the voyage from Carthage to the Strait of Gibraltar, like that from Ostia, took but seven days. Eastbound traffic, on the other hand, enjoyed the help of the eastward flowing current which, starting from the strait, made itself felt as far as the borders of Tunisia.[30]

[26] *Sailing Directions* 1975 (1 134) 43–5.   [27] Cf. Hodge 1983 (1 74) 75–6.
[28] Cf. Hodge 1983 (1 74) 76–7.   [29] *Sailing Directions* 1975 (1 134) 37–9.
[30] Le Gras 1870 (1 97) 41–3.

VII. PORTS

In the eastern Mediterranean, along the Levantine coast, where maritime commerce dates as far back as the third millennium B.C., men early learned to improve naturally sheltered landing places by adding break-waters and lining the shores with quays.[31] The kingdom of Ugarit in the fourteenth and thirteenth centuries B.C. had four harbours, of which that at Ugarit itself was capable of handling ships of no less than 500 tons (*CAH* II[3].2, 131). Presumably Minoan and Mycenaean Crete boasted equal facilities.[32] An Egyptian tomb painting of *c.* 1400 B.C. reveals what harbours of this age looked like: it shows a line of freighters moored, prow to, to a wharf; stevedores are busy unloading them by means of gangplanks descending to the wharf, where various figures are energetically engaged in business transactions concerning items of the cargo.[33]

The sophisticated ports of the east may well have remained in constant use. Further to the west, however, when the mists of the dark age lift, no such amenities are to be found. Ports were, and for long continued to be, little more than sites provided by nature – deep bays, mouths of rivers, the sides of a peninsula, lakes near a coast and with an outlet to the sea.[34] Vessels moored as close to the shore as they could get and took on or discharged cargo with the help of barges and other small craft. Homer (*Od.* VI.263–9, XIII.77) attributes such a harbour to the Phaeacians, those dwellers in a seafarers' paradise: he tells of a sheltered bay where the only works of man are the shacks in which shipowners stored their gear, stone bollards, probably fixed in the sand, to which ships could tie up, an area where sailmakers and shipwrights worked, and a shrine to Poseidon.

Eventually the Greeks, as their predecessors in the Near East had long before, learned to improve upon nature, to build moles for protection. The earliest example found so far, dating to the eighth century B.C., is at Delos, a ponderous structure of massive rough-hewn blocks of local granite that juts out for a length of 100 metres. By the next century other ports had received similar moles and, by the end of the sixth, there had come into being such carefully guarded harbours as that built by Polycrates for Samos; it had two mighty moles, 370 and 180 metres respectively, to protect it against the sea, and the whole complex was included in the circuit of the city's defence wall to protect it against potential foes.[35]

Athens, which in the fifth century B.C. became a great seaport, for long was a laggard. Right up to the opening decades of the century, vessels

---

[31] Cf. Blackman 1982 (I 7) 92.   [32] Cf. Blackman 1982 (I 7) 93.
[33] Pritchard 1954 (F 317) Fig. 111.   [34] Cf. Schmiedt 1975 (I 139) 152.
[35] Casson 1986 (I 24) 362.

still loaded and unloaded in age-old fashion, lying at anchor off the shore of Phalerum Bay. Then, at Themistocles' urging, perhaps as early as 493 B.C., work began on an up-to-date facility at the Piraeus. For sailing freighters and merchant galleys there were quays to tie up at, backed by an *emporion*, an extensive covered area where merchandise could be stored and business conducted. For the navy's warcraft there was a long line of shipsheds, parallel slipways or ramps, sheltered by a continuous roof, up which the galleys were drawn until they were clear of the water; like racing shells today, when not in use they were kept out of the water and protected from rain to prevent their getting waterlogged. By the fourth century B.C., when Athens' fleet was at its greatest strength, there were 372 of these slipways: 94 shared with the quays of the commercial harbour the shore around a commodious bay to the west of the peninsula, while two smaller bays to the east, with 196 and 82 respectively, served the fleet exclusively.[36]

No doubt harbours similarly equipped existed at Corinth, Miletus, Rhodes and other maritime centres that carried on an active seaborne trade and maintained a naval arm. Where terrain permitted, some had two harbours facing in different directions, so as to be accessible whatever the wind.[37] Moreover, if a centre happened to have in its vicinity a sanctuary that attracted crowds of pilgrims but was inconveniently far from the harbour, this might have a 'sacred harbour' of its own.[38]

Multiple harbours and sophisticated facilities, however, were only for ports that handled enough traffic to merit them. Elsewhere, at countless minor seaside points ships continued to load and unload as they had been doing since earliest times, by mooring close to land and counting on the aid of local small craft for transfer to the shore. Indeed, long after Athens had built up the Piraeus, some cargo vessels still preferred to discharge in this fashion off Phalerum Bay since the haul to the city was so much shorter from there. And the same sort of discharge no doubt went on at that spot, just north of the Piraeus, which smugglers so favoured that it earned itself the name 'Thieves' Harbour' (Dem. xxxv.28).

To sum up. Communication by land, particularly in mountainous areas, was slow and irregular, and this condition did not improve until the late fourth century B.C. when the Romans began their building of long-distance highways. Governments could call upon the services of special runners or relays of horsemen; the riders of the famed Persian service between Susa and Sardis could cover 150 km a day. Transport by land,

---

[36] Judeich 1931 (C 179) 425–56; Garland 1987 (I 53) 11–13, 83–100, 152–5, 160. On shipsheds, see also Blackman 1982 (I 7) 204–6.   [37] Robert 1960 (I 132); Blackman 1982 (I 7) 193.
[38] Robert 1960 (I 132) 265.

especially of bulky or heavy freight, was painfully slow and inefficient; it was avoided as much as possible.

The preferred means of communication, and the only practicable one for the transport of commodities, was the sea. Its one great drawback was its limited season, for ancient sailors restricted their operations to the time of year between March and November at the outside; voyaging during the winter months, though occasionally done, was exceptional. Governments used war galleys for sending dispatches or transporting passengers on official business over routes that followed the coast or hopped from island to island; they could cover 100 nautical miles or better in a long summer's day. Merchant galleys took care of a certain amount of cargo carrying and transport of passengers over similar routes; they were slower than warcraft but surer than sailing ships, for, when confronted with calms or contrary winds, they proceeded under their oars. Sailing ships took care of all voyaging and transport over open water. Built for safety and durability rather than speed, they were slow: an average of 6 knots was a record figure, 5 very good speed, and 2 or even less was the best they could do when fighting the wind. In the eastern Mediterranean, because of the prevailing northerlies, voyaging from north to south was quick, while going in the opposite direction might take twice as long or more. In the western Mediterranean, the northerlies are not as troublesome; there ancient sailing ships made good time on most of the major routes.

CHAPTER 10

SOCIETY AND ECONOMY

M. M. AUSTIN

The central theme of this chapter is the impact of war on the Greek world in the first half of the fourth century B.C. Thucydides described the Peloponnesian War as the greatest disturbance in Greek history, a war that came to affect almost the whole of the Greek world and part of the non-Greek world as well. His verdict was amply verified by subsequent events.

Not every Greek state was affected at once or to the same degree. The central Peloponnese, for example, was largely unscathed, and Elis was in a flourishing condition at the time of the Spartan invasion of *c.* 402 (Xen. *Hell.* III.2.21–31). Boeotia as a whole suffered only one abortive Athenian invasion in 424. In the Decelean War the Thebans enriched themselves on the plunder of Attica and acquired many of the runaway Athenian slaves (*Hell. Oxy.* XVII (XII). 3–5). The impact of the war on the society and economy of the two protagonists differed strikingly. Sparta's victory, and the role she chose to play in Greek affairs after 404, placed strains on her society which she could not withstand. Whereas the fifth-century Athenian empire had spread prosperity through all classes of Athenian society, and thus helped to cement political and social stability, the Spartan empire aggravated internal tensions and inequalities in Sparta. The gap between Sparta's ambitions, and the resources available to her, seemed dangerously wide. Sparta's decline in the fourth century, within little over a generation after her victory, followed as a long-term consequence of that victory. This was recognized by contemporary and later sources, friendly or hostile.

Athens, by contrast, adjusted to defeat much better than Sparta did to victory. Athens suffered heavy losses in manpower through war, the plague and civil conflicts. The enemy occupation of Decelea from 413 affected her economy more heavily than previous Spartan invasions of the land (Thuc. VII.27–8), and resulted in much destruction of property and the ruin of individual Athenians.[1] The reduction in silver mining at Laurium caused a break in Athens' silver coinage which was not

---

[1] Whether the agriculture of Attica suffered long-term damage is another matter: Hanson 1983 (K 24); see in general Strauss 1986 (C 259).

resumed till the late 390s (Ar. *Eccl.* 814–22). Athens lost her naval empire and with it her imperial revenues and control over her vital corn supply. She never rose again to the peak of her fifth-century prosperity, and there remained many signs of the erosion of her public and private wealth. Yet she survived the critical years after 404 and recovered as a leading power, as she was to survive again the low point of her defeat in the Social War in 355. In the time of Demosthenes Athens was still the most important, prosperous and stable state in the Greek world.

For the Greek world as a whole, the Peloponnesian War was in retrospect but one stage in a widening conflict between an increasing number of contestants. None of them had the resources to achieve a durable hegemony, until a solution was imposed from the outside by Philip of Macedon. Sparta was at war more or less continuously from 404, Athens from 396 to 386 then from 378 onwards with only brief interruptions, Thebes from 396 to 386 then almost continuously from 379. The system of alliances drew smaller states into the conflicts of the larger cities. Few states could insulate themselves from war and its effects for any length of time. External and internal events constantly interacted. The debilitating and indecisive character of the struggles for hegemony is aptly summarized by Xenophon in his comments on the battle of Mantinea in 362 (*Hell.* VII.5.26–7). Some twenty years later, Demosthenes drew a similar picture of the fragmentation and weakness of the Greek mainland, brought about by such conflicts (x. 51–3).

War was thus for most Greek states of the fourth century a virtual constant. It placed strains on their resources, human, material and financial on a probably larger scale than ever before. An analysis of the phenomenon of war and its causes in Greek history would exceed the scope of this chapter,[2] which will focus on the consequences of war for the Greek world of this period.

I. SOCIAL AND POLITICAL CONFLICTS (*STASIS*)

When Philip of Macedon organized the Greek states of the mainland into the League of Corinth in 337, one of the clauses of the new league was directed against constitutional subversion in other member states. The league officials were to ensure that there would be no sentences of death or exile in violation of the existing laws of the cities, nor confiscations of wealth, redistribution of land, cancellation of debts, nor freeing of slaves for the purposes of revolution (Tod no. 177, lines 12–14 = Harding no. 99A; [Dem.] XVII.12 and 15; *SdA* 403). There were precedents for such provisions in bilateral or multilateral treaties between Greek states (for example Tod no. 147; *SdA* 293 = Harding no. 59, the treaty between

---

[2] Finley 1985 (A 18) 67–87; Garlan 1989 (I 52) and cf. also Austin 1986 (I 4).

Athens and Thessaly of 361/0; Tod no. 144 = *SdA* 290 = Harding no. 56 the treaty between Athens, Arcadia, Achaea, Elis and Phlius of 362/1).[3] But this was the first time that legislation against internal political and social subversion had been included in a panhellenic treaty. The implication would seem to be that by this time much of the Greek world was in a state of chronic instability, and that this could only be arrested by the enforcement of the *status quo* by a dominant power.

There is much evidence to substantiate this impression. It was a theme to which the political writers of the age constantly returned. Thus Isocrates in the *Panegyricus* in 380 presents the Greek world as being in a state of political and social turmoil (IV.114–17, 167–8) and returns to the issue repeatedly in subsequent works.[4] Plato regarded the problem of the distribution of property and wealth as fundamental to the stability of the state. In the *Republic (c.* 375–370) he sought to achieve this by denying all private property to the first two classes in his ideal state, and by reserving all economic activity to the third and lowest class, itself deprived of all political power.[5] In the *Laws* (late 350s to early 340s) he accepted the principle of private property, but laid down the strictest safeguards to keep both wealth and poverty within defined limits and to prevent the development of excessive inequalities.[6] How different was the contemporary world: 'any state, however small, is in fact divided into two, one the state of the poor, the other of the rich. These are at war with one another' (*Rep.* IV.422e – 423a, cf. VIII.551d). Aristotle in the *Politics* similarly saw the Greek states as divided usually into two groups, the rich and the poor, and he devoted the whole of book V to the problem of *stasis* in its many forms, the instability of existing constitutions, and the means of ensuring their stability.[7]

It has been doubted whether such generalizations can be taken at face value.[8] On the other hand, concrete instances of outbreaks of *stasis* in the fourth century abound. One may, following the example of Thucydides (III.82–3), take the case of Corcyra as paradeigmatic. Prior to the affair of Epidamnus and the conflict with Corinth in the 430s, Corcyra had pursued a policy of aloofness *vis-à-vis* the major power blocks, and had been seemingly free from *stasis*. Her alliance with Athens in 433 changed this. What started in 427 as a struggle between rival pro-Athenian and pro-Spartan leaders escalated into full-scale class conflict between the few and the many. Further outbreaks at Corcyra are attested in 411/10 (Diod. XIII.48), in 374 and 373 (Xen. *Hell.* VI.2.3–15; Diod. XV.46–7), and in 361/0 (Diod. XV.95.3; Aen. Tact. XI.13–15).

---

[3] Gehrke 1985 (C 27) 301–4.
[4] Fuks 1972 (I 45).   [5] Fuks 1977 (H 44).   [6] Fuks 1979 (H 45).
[7] de Ste Croix 1981 (C 70) 69–80; Lintott 1982 (C 43) 239–51.
[8] Gehrke 1985 (C 27) 323–5, more fully in Gehrke 1985 (H 51).

The case of Corcyra is not an isolated one. In the Peloponnesian War and after, Greek states previously immune from *stasis* fell a victim to the disease. Corinth, a model of oligarchic stability in the fifth century, underwent a violent revolution during the Corinthian War; the oligarchic exiles took refuge with Sparta and fought on her side against their fellow-Corinthians (Xen. *Hell.* iv.4.1–13). For a few years Corinth was united in some way with Argos, though the precise nature of that union is debated.[9] The King's Peace terminated this experiment and enforced the return of the pro-Spartan exiles, and the consequent banishment of the rival leaders from Corinth (Xen. *Hell.* v.1.34). Though Corinth was thereafter submissive to Sparta till after Leuctra, underlying tensions remained. In 366 Timophanes carried out an abortive coup, with the help of a body of mercenaries recruited by Corinth, and offered according to Diodorus (xvi.65) a programme of support for the poor. Sparta's defeat at Leuctra in 371 was the signal for a general upheaval in the Peloponnese; the *demos* rose up everywhere against the pro-Spartan oligarchies (Diod. xv.40; Isoc. vi.64–7). At Sicyon, which 'up till then had been governed in accordance with traditional laws', as Xenophon puts it, Euphron, a leading citizen and former pro-Spartan, seized power *c.* 369 with the connivance of the Argives and Arcadians, the support of a mercenary army and of the lower classes, who honoured him as the 'founder' of the city after his assassination and buried him in the agora (Xen. *Hell.* vii.1.44–6; 3.1–12).

Instances could be multiplied from every part of the Greek world,[10] even though the record is necessarily incomplete and cannot by itself reveal fully how far *stasis* was an endemic condition. It is no accident that it should be precisely at the end of the fifth century that *homonoia* – concord – between citizens emerged as a political slogan (Thuc. viii.75.2 and 93.3; Andoc. 1.140),[11] to become a much used catchword of internal and external Greek politics in the fourth century and the hellenistic period.[12] 'Everywhere in Greece it is customary for the citizens to swear to preserve concord (*homonoia*) and everywhere they swear that oath' (Xen. *Mem.* iv.4.16). Aeneas Tacticus, writing around the middle of the fourth century, is a particularly valuable witness on the conditions prevailing among 'average' Greek cities. The author urges the importance of promoting concord within each city through appropriate measures (*Poliorcetica* 10.20, 14.1, 17.1, 22.21).[13] The emphasis on concord reflected its absence in reality. It is hard to point to any Greek

---

[9] Griffith 1950 (C 362); Tuplin 1982 (C 387); Salmon 1984 (C 380) 354–62, 383–6; Whitby 1984 (C 390).

[10] See the collection of material in Gehrke 1985 (C 27) part 1, with analysis at 254–61, though the survey does not include Athens, Sparta, or the western Greek world.

[11] de Romilly 1972 (C 59); Hands 1968 (I 69) 38–42.   [12] West 1977 (C 85).

[13] Whitehead 1990 (B 131) 25–33; Winterling 1991 (C 86).

state in the fourth century that was demonstrably immune from the threat of internal upheaval. The author of the *Athenaion Politeia* regarded Athens as an exception, when he commented in glowing terms on the behaviour of the restored democracy in 403 and after: 'the Athenians seem both in public and in private, to have acted in the fairest and most civic-minded way in relation to the previous misfortunes . . . they decreed an amnesty . . . whereas in the other cities the democrats, when they are victorious, far from contributing from their own funds, actually carry out a redistribution of land' (*Ath. Pol.* 40.3). Contrast Aristotle's comment in the *Politics*: 'in some oligarchies nowadays they swear "I will be hostile to the common people (*demos*) and plan whatever harm I can against them"' (*Pol.* v.1310a8–12, cf. 1307a19–20, 34–9).

While the greater extent and seriousness of *stasis* in the fourth century as compared with the fifth seem clear,[14] the character and causes of the phenomenon are more problematical. It may be observed first that *stasis* was by and large restricted to the citizen population of Greek states, and did not normally involve outsiders in an active way or in significant numbers.[15] This is the underlying assumption in the discussions of Plato and Aristotle, for example. *Stasis* was, in a sense, a privilege of the citizen, and it lasted as long as the free polis did, from the archaic age to the Roman conquest.[16] The citizen's possession of political power gave him a capacity to fight for control of the state, a capacity that was denied to outsiders. These are occasionally found involved in political conflicts: for instance, many metics sided with the democrats in the Athenian civil war of 404/3. How many may have received the reward of Athenian citizenship is unclear,[17] but in any case the institution of the *metoikia* was unaffected. Metics as a whole were not a political class, willing and able to express collective demands of their own.[18]

The same holds good for slaves, or more exactly chattel-slaves.[19] 'Freeing of slaves for the purposes of revolution' was one of the steps explicitly banned in the charter of the League of Corinth. This tactic is occasionally attested in outbreaks of *stasis*, but it was precisely a tactic, a means of enlisting extra support used by one side against the other, which did not affect the institution of slavery as such.[20] The initiative in such cases did not come from the slaves themselves, whose diverse origins and languages, social fragmentation, and lack of political power as well as of leaders, deprived them of all possibility of cohesive action. Their apparent passivity does not mean that they were necessarily

---

[14] Doubted by Lintott 1982 (c 43) ch. 8, though see the collection of material in Gehrke 1985 (c 27) part 1 with comments at 259f.

[15] Cf. Winterling 1991 (c 86) 220–2 for a different emphasis.   [16] Finley 1981 (i 38) 82.

[17] Krentz 1980 (c 181) and 1986 (c 183) on Tod 1948 (b 179) no. 100; Whitehead 1986 (c 268) 147f.   [18] Whitehead 1977 (c 265) 154–9, 174f.

[19] Vidal-Naquet 1986 (i 146) 159–67.   [20] Mossé 1961 (i 109); Garlan 1988 (i 51) 155–63.

satisfied with their lot. Given a chance, especially in war time, slaves might vote with their feet, as did the runaway Athenian slaves during the Decelean War. But they could not organize a revolt or articulate common aims.[21] Whatever was under threat in the fourth century, it was not the institution of slavery. That the legitimacy of slavery was discussed and challenged by some in this period emerges notably from book I of Aristotle's *Politics*, where Aristotle seeks to refute the challenge and demonstrate that slavery was an institution according to nature. The debate was purely intellectual in character and conducted within a very restricted circle.[22] It ended with Aristotle and the existence of the institution itself was in no way affected. Competition of slave versus free labour has been suggested as a cause of the growing impoverishment of the free poor in the fourth century, on the (questionable) analogy of the decline of the Roman Republic.[23] But there is no clear sign of any protest on the part of the free poor against this alleged competition.[24]

To return to conflicts between citizens. Thucydides provides a starting point with the example of Corcyra. As he observed (III.82–3), the spread of *stasis* was closely linked with panhellenic wars, which created opportunities for rival groups to appeal to outside powers, and pretexts for intervention by the latter. Internal and external events interacted; *stasis* fuelled war, and war fuelled *stasis*. Rivalry between Sparta and Athens in the fifth century encouraged polarization within Greek states in the Aegean. Sparta was the natural champion of oligarchies, while Athens in the fifth century became known as the champion of democracies.[25] The defeat of Athens at the end of the fifth century meant the overthrow of many democracies and their temporary replacement by Lysander's 'decarchies'. Sparta's defeat at sea in 394 led to a resurgence of the democracies in the Aegean, and Athens emerged once more as their champion. At Rhodes, for example, a democratic revolution had overthrown the oligarchy and exiled the oligarchic leaders (*Hell. Oxy.* xv [x]). In 391 they turned to Sparta for help, pointing out 'that the Spartans ought not to allow the Athenians to subdue Rhodes and gain the benefit of such an increase in power. Realizing that if the democracy prevailed the whole of Rhodes would belong to the Athenians, while if the richer classes did they would have the island, the Spartans manned eight ships, with Ecdicus as nauarch' (Xen. *Hell.* IV.8.20–4; cf. Diod. XIV.97.1–4; 99.5). The return to the divisions of the fifth century remained till at least Leuctra in 371 (Xen. *Hell.* VI.3.14; Diod. XV.45.1). Thereafter the patterns were less clear-cut, with Sparta's

21 Cartledge in Cartledge and Harvey 1985 (A 14) 16–46; Garlan 1988 (I 51) 176–200.
22 Cambiano in Finley 1987 (I 39) 22–41.   23 Pečirka 1976 (C 217) on this wider point.
24 de Ste Croix 1981 (C 70) 201f; Finley 1981 (I 38) 106f; doubted by Nenci 1978 (I 112).
25 de Ste Croix 1972 (C 68) 34–44.

decline and the Athenian alliance with Sparta in 370. Thebes became for a while the supporter of democracies in the Peloponnese against Sparta (Xen. *Hell.* VII.1.43). Athens retained to the time of Demosthenes the claim to be the natural leader and champion of democracies (Dem. XIII.8; XV.17–24), but the claim was not always borne out by events and Athens' power to intervene declined, especially after the Social War.[26]

This might seem to suggest a primarily political interpretation of the phenomenon of *stasis*.[27] Such a view gains apparent support from the fact that in the majority of known cases the initiative in action clearly belonged to small factions and groups from within the respective cities. More often than not, intervention by an outside power was invited by a faction within the state, as for example at Corcyra in 427 and in all subsequent outbreaks of *stasis* in the island. Others have followed the views of the fourth-century political writers, and have emphasized underlying social and economic problems which helped to create instability.[28] 'Redistribution of land' and 'cancellation of debts' were the twin revolutionary slogans of the Greek world, heard with increasing frequency in the fourth century, and banned by the provisions of the League of Corinth. Citizenship and ownership of land were closely associated; the demand for land runs through the whole of Greek history and was acute in this period (below). That debt was also a recurring issue is clear, for instance, from the comments of Aeneas Tacticus on the dangers facing the Greek cities of his time. He urges the importance of promoting concord within each city through suitable measures, especially the reduction or cancellation of debts (*Poliorcetica* 14.1). In practice, it does not seem possible to separate clearly a 'political' as opposed to a 'social and economic' sphere; the distinction might not have been intelligible to the Greeks themselves.

Be that as it may, there is no doubt about the effects of *stasis*. *Stasis* was a vicious circle with no solution. There was no end to the cycle of confiscations and banishments. Political exiles, that characteristically Greek phenomenon, were created in ever increasing numbers.[29] Though the initiative in outbreaks of *stasis* belonged usually to small factions, substantial numbers of the population could be affected, in extreme cases as much as a quarter of the citizen body. For example, at Samos in 412 the *demos* killed 200 of the wealthiest citizens, and exiled another 400 (Thuc. VIII.21). At Chios in 409 one group of exiles returned and expelled their opponents, 600 in number (Diod. XIII.65.4). The Spartan seizure of the

---

[26] Cf. Hornblower 1983 (A 31) 169.
[27] Thus, with varying degrees of emphasis, Ruschenbusch 1978 (c 63); Lintott 1982 (c 43) ch. 8; Gehrke 1985 (c 27) 309–53; Winterling 1991 (c 86).
[28] Fuks 1974 (I 46); de Ste Croix 1981 (c 70) 283–300.
[29] Seibert 1979 (c 75); Gehrke 1985 (c 27) 224–34.

Theban Cadmea in 382 resulted in the flight of some 300 anti-Spartans (Xen. *Hell.* v.2.31). In 370, 1,400 pro-Spartan Tegeans were expelled, and 800 of them took refuge with the Spartans (Diod. xv.59.2; Xen. *Hell.* vi.5.10). When Alexander in 324 issued a proclamation at Olympia ordering the Greek states to restore their exiles, some 20,000 men are said to have gathered to hear the proclamation (Diod. xviii.8).[30]

It is likely that even in the fifth century the Greek world had an exportable proletariate: this is implied, for instance, by the foundations at the Nine Ways, Thurii and Amphipolis, and by other settlements. One characteristic of the fourth century was the growth of a large floating population,[31] and *stasis* made the greatest single contribution to the problem. Many turned to mercenary service, a phenomenon on the increase in this period.[32] Mercenary service as such was nothing new, and it would also be misleading to suggest a single explanation for its growth. Warfare was becoming more diversified and specialized; the demand for mercenaries was increasing, in the Persian empire and among the military tyrannies of the fourth century. Some captains, many of them Athenians, such as Conon, Iphicrates and Chabrias, were in great demand in the Greek world and beyond for their skills and amassed considerable private fortunes from war. For others mercenary service might be a temporary speculative venture (cf. Xen. *An.* vi.4.8). But this does not by itself account for the scale of the phenomenon. Increased demand partly reflected an increase in the supply, and the supply always exceeded the demand: one never hears of any state or ruler being unable to raise any mercenary force required. There is no doubt that the majority of men who took up mercenary service did so because they had no alternative. Poverty was the driving force, and they were probably recruited chiefly from the lower orders of Greek society: the hostile references to them in the sources, notably Isocrates, imply as much. Conditions of service were poor, employment irregular and unpredictable, and pay frequently not forthcoming at all, particularly in the service of Greek cities.

To bring *stasis* to an end required the imposition of the *status quo* by a dominant outside power, or the creation of new sources of wealth that would be more equally distributed, and thus alleviate underlying problems of poverty and the resulting tensions. But this was not possible in the technological conditions of the ancient world. As for land, apart from a few military colonies founded by Dionysius in Sicily, it was largely unavailable for settlement within the Greek world. Nor was it

---

[30] These are of course round figures; for other figures cf. Seibert 1979 (c 75) 405f; Gehrke 1985 (c 27) 219f, 236, 360f.   [31] McKechnie 1989 (I 100).

[32] Parke 1933 (K 50); Aymard 1967 (K 7); Seibt 1977 (K 54); Perlman 1976–7 (I 119); Marinovic 1988 (K 42); McKechnie 1989 (I 100) ch. 4 with Whitehead 1991 (K 59); Garlan 1989 (I 52) ch. 7.

available in Asia so long as it was ruled by the Persians, despite the Persian King's increasing need for Greek soldiers.

If there was to be a solution, it had therefore to be an external one: foreign conquest and settlement. The wealth of Asia, on the doorstep of impoverished Greece, had long been a source of envy for the Greeks, and talk of a profitable war of conquest had been heard long before the fourth century (cf. Hdt. v.49, referring to 499).[33] The growth of the idea of a war against Persia, to be followed by Greek settlement, can be traced from Xenophon's *Anabasis* (III.2.26; v.6.15–19; vi.4.1–6 and 12–22) through to Isocrates, who from 380 onwards made the notion peculiarly his own. In Isocrates' view, the threat to social stability could only be removed through the cessation of wars between Greek states, the conquest of new territory, and exporting Greece's floating proletariate to Asia (iv.167–8; v.119–23; viii.24). The conquered Asiatics were to provide a new labour force to their Greek masters: they would be compelled to 'serve as helots' to them (*Ep.* iii.5; cf. Arist. *Pol.* vii.1329a24–6, 1330a25–31).

II. POPULATION AND MILITARY MANPOWER

No figures for the total population of the ancient Greek world are available at any period of its history, and the evidence for individual cities is scattered and fragmentary. Hence all estimates, for individual cities and for the Greek world as a whole, necessarily involve a wide margin of uncertainty.[34] The many wars and internal conflicts of the fourth century must have entailed significant human losses, though it is doubtful whether the population of the Greek world as a whole was declining. The political theorists of the age were more concerned with keeping the population within acceptable limits (Pl. *Rep.* v.549d, 461c; Arist. *Pol.* vii.1335b20–26) than with the fear of depopulation such as was voiced two centuries later (Polyb. xxxvi.17.5–10). Infanticide and exposure of unwanted children, especially daughters, were commonly practised, though perhaps less than in the hellenistic period.[35] As seen above, the outstanding demographic feature of the fourth century was the existence of a large and increasing floating population which the Greek world itself was unable to absorb.

Greek history as known to us through the ancient evidence focuses on a minority of larger and more prominent cities. The vast majority of smaller states have little active share in the record.[36] In territorial as in

---

[33] Cf. Starr 1976 (C 79) 48–61.
[34] Ruschenbusch 1984 (C 64) estimates some 3 million inhabitants for the mainland of Greece and the Aegean basin. [35] Eyben 1980–81 (I 33); Golden 1981 (I 64).
[36] Ruschenbusch 1985 (C 65) reckons about 750 *poleis* in all for the mainland and the Aegean basin.

human terms, Greek states were all small in size by modern comparisons, though the range of differences between the largest and the smallest makes it doubtful whether there was such a thing as an 'average city'.[37] Sparta controlled the largest expanse of territory of any Greek state, some 8,400 km² taking Laconia and Messenia together; Athens had about 2,650 km², rather less than the largest Sicilian cities; Syracuse with Leontini some 4,700 km²; Acragas 4,300 km². Most Greek cities had considerably less than this, many of them under four or even three figures. Similarly with population: a city with a citizen population of 5,000, such as Phlius, was already reckoned to be substantial (Xen. *Hell.* v.3.16), and the fourth-century political theorists thought in terms of a city of moderate size. Plato in the *Laws* envisaged a state of 5,040 citizen households, the number of which was to be kept constant (v.737a). Aristotle, while not laying down any precise figure, believed that a city should ideally be large enough to achieve self-sufficiency, but no more: it must be possible 'to take it in at one glance' (*Pol.* v.1326a6–1326b26). In practice only a minority of Greek states exceeded this size. In the early fourth century, out of a total of many hundreds of Greek *poleis*, there may have been only about twenty cities with 10,000 citizens or more; the vast majority of smaller cities probably had citizen populations numbering only three figures.[38] Fourth-century Athens provides a good illustration of the difficulties in assessing precisely the population of individual Greek cities. There is an unresolved debate in modern scholarship on whether the adult male citizen body of Athens numbered in this period around 20,000 or around 30,000 men; the discrepancy originates in a conflict in the ancient sources on the effects of Antipater's abolition of the democracy in 322 and his restriction of citizen rights to Athenians with property worth 2000 drs. or more. Diodorus (xviii.8.5) states that 9,000 Athenians retained their civic rights and 22,000 lost theirs, while Plutarch (*Phoc.* 28.7) gives a figure of 12,000 for the latter category; ironically both writers are drawing on a common source, and it is an open question which of the two texts needs to be emended.[39] The only figures for all categories of the population of Athens come from the census of Demetrius of Phalerum in 317–307. This yielded totals of 21,000 citizens, 10,000 metics, and (allegedly) 400,000 slaves (Ath. vi.272c from Ctesicles *FGrH* 245 F 1), and every one of these figures is open to debate and conflicting interpretation.[40]

Small in terms of territory and population, Greek cities unlike Rome

---

[37] Gehrke 1986 (C 28); Nixon and Price 1990 (I 113) 146f, 158–62 on Ruschenbusch 1983 (C 240) and 1983 (I 133) and 1985 (C 65).   [38] Ruschenbusch 1985 (C 65).

[39] Rhodes 1980 (C 227); Ruschenbusch 1981 (C 238), 1984 (C 241) and 1988 (C 244) for the lower figure; Hansen 1986 (C 165) 28f for the higher one.

[40] Hansen 1986 (C 165) 28–36; Garnsey 1988 (I 55) 136f.

found it difficult to extend their citizenship beyond a limit. Aristotle's discussion of the optimum size for a Greek city is indicative of this bias. Sparta was notoriously reluctant to grant citizen rights, even when faced with a steady decline in citizen numbers. Athens at the end of the civil war of 404/3 had both the opportunity and the need to replenish her depleted citizen body with suitably qualified metics, such as the orator Lysias, but how far the opportunity was taken is not clear (see above, p. 531 with n. 17). A proposal by Thrasybulus to extend the citizenship more generously was quashed (Arist. *Ath.Pol.* 40.2).[41] Large-scale enfranchisement of outsiders was generally a forcible measure, characteristic of tyrannies such as those in Sicily, and was almost invariably a source of tension and instability (cf. Arist. *Pol.* v.1303a28–b3). Self-governing cities resorted to this only in emergencies and with reluctance (cf. Arist. *Pol.* iii.1278a30–5). Before the battle of Arginusae in 406 Athens may have enfranchised the metics who fought there (Diod. xiii.97.1), and after the battle she gave restricted citizen rights to the slaves who had participated (Hellanicus *FGrH* 323a F 25). In 338 after the battle of Chaeronea Hyperides proposed to enfranchise the metics and free the slaves for the purposes of defence, but the proposal was resisted and it is not clear that it was implemented ([Plut.] *X orat.* 849a).[42] In some parts of the Greek world, there was experimentation with the idea of a wider, federal citizenship, to build larger and more effective power blocks, as in Boeotia (*Hell.Oxy.* xvi [xi]), or the Chalcidian federation dominated by Olynthus (Xen. *Hell.* v.2.12–19). Yet besides meeting with the determined opposition of Sparta, anxious as Athens had been in the fifth century to prevent the formation of hostile power blocks, these were ultimately of only local significance, and also met with strong local resistance.

The military manpower of Greek states was never more than a proportion of their total adult male population. The archaic age had established the predominance of the heavily armed infantryman, the hoplite, who fought in close formation, and was recruited from the property-owning section of the citizen body. The wealthiest might serve in the cavalry, militarily not usually very effective, though socially prestigious. Political power was related to the citizen's military function. The poorer citizens might be called on in an auxiliary supporting role as light-armed fighters, more or less organized and effective. Thus a general levy from Boeotia in 424 aligned 7,000 hoplites, 1,000 cavalry, 500 light-armed peltasts, and over 10,000 light-armed troops (Thuc. iv.93.3). Non-citizens and slaves had, in principle at least, no military role at all (cf. Xen. *Cyr.* vii.5.79).

[41] Davies 1977–8 (C 125).   [42] Whitehead 1977 (C 265) 162f.

In the fifth century Athens innovated in the military sphere and developed sea-power far beyond all precedents. This increased the military role and political importance of her lower classes as rowers in the fleet. Athens also had recourse to metics (who were in addition called on to provide hoplite service in accordance with their wealth), and to mercenary rowers from her allies and elsewhere. But the core of her navy was Athenian in recruitment (cf. Thuc. 1.143.1–2; Old Oligarch 1.2), and remained so in the fourth century (cf. Xen. *Hell.* VII.1.3–7).[43] The status enjoyed by the navy at Athens was unusual by Greek standards. Other naval states in Greece relied apparently to a large extent on their unfree population (cf. Thuc. 1.55.1 on Corcyra; Arist. *Pol.* VII.1327b12–16, citing Heraclea; Xen. *Hell.* VI.1.11 on Jason of Pherae's naval ambitions).[44] Athens, by contrast, only conscripted slaves for the navy on one occasion, at Arginusae in 406. The political significance of this was not lost on contemporaries: at Athens naval power and the radical democracy were linked, hence the anti-naval bias of one opponent of the democracy after another from the Old Oligarch (1.2) onwards.[45]

During and after the Peloponnesian War, increased manpower demands for war, and the changing conditions of warfare, caused the gap between principle and reality to widen further. Of all Greek states, Sparta faced the most acute manpower needs. Sparta claimed to have a natural right to lead the Greek world, yet her own military class, the *Homoioi*, was small in number and steadily decreasing. At the time of the Persian Wars there may have been some 8,000 Spartiates, 5,000 of whom fought at the Battle of Plataea. Just over a century later, there were perhaps only about 1,200 Spartiates, 700 of whom fought at Leuctra in 371, where the casualties amounted to 400 (Xen. *Hell.* VI.4.15). By the time of Aristotle, the number of Spartiates had fallen to under 1,000: 'Sparta could not sustain a single blow, but was destroyed by her lack of men' (*oliganthropia*) (*Pol.* II.1270a30–4). Spartan *oliganthropia* was well known to contemporaries (cf. Xen. *Lac.Pol.* 1.1). It was reflected in Sparta's eagerness to economize over her own human resources and her anxiety over even small losses, such as the prisoners at Sphacteria in 426 (Thuc. IV.108.7; 117.2; V.15.1) or the defeat of a Spartan *mora* at Lechaeum in 390 by Iphicrates' peltasts (Xen. *Hell.* IV.5.7–17). The causes of the problem lay in Sparta's property and inheritance institutions, as Aristotle argued in a passage which is the starting point of all modern discussions (*Pol.* II.1270a15–1270b7), but also in the competitiveness of her society which was in itself a source of inequalities, and in

[43] Amit 1965 (c 88) 30–49; Meiggs 1972 (c 201) 439–41.
[44] For the use of the unfree in naval and land warfare, Welwei 1974–77 (K 58) and Garlan 1988 (I 51) 163–76.   [45] Momigliano 1960 (c 50).

the impact that her new role from the end of the Peloponnesian War had on her society.[46]

At the time of the Persian Wars and possibly even earlier (cf. Paus. IV.6.16), Sparta had already been making use of her lower classes in a military capacity. Besides the 5,000 Spartiates at the Battle of Plataea, there were also 5,000 hoplites from the perioeci, and (allegedly) 35,000 helots, who were used not just as servants but also performed a limited combatant role (Hdt. IX.28–9). Brigaded separately at the Battle of Plataea, perioeci were by 425 and possibly earlier brigaded together with the Spartiates (cf. Thuc. IV.8.9 and 38.5; V.68), probably in increasing numbers; the intention seems to have been to conceal the Spartiates' numerical inferiority.[47] Perioeci thus conscripted did not, so far as we know, gain any further promotion within the Spartan state. Starting with Brasidas' expedition to Thrace in 424, the use of helot armies for long-distance expeditions became common (Thuc. IV.80.5; V.34.1). In 421 occurs the first mention of the *neodamodeis* (literally, 'new members of the *demos*'), a class of helots liberated by the Spartan state and used for military service (Thuc. V.34.1). This may have been an innovation of the late Archidamian War, and they were a regular feature of Spartan armies abroad for the next fifty years, last mentioned in 370/69 (Xen. *Hell.* VI.5.24). Without them Sparta could hardly have played the military role she did for a generation after 404.

What is true of Sparta's land forces applies also to her navy, though little is known of the means, human and material, whereby Sparta became the dominant naval power in the Aegean for a decade from 404 to 394, and remained a force to be reckoned with till the rise of the Second Athenian League after 378. Apart from allied contingents, Sparta's fleets seem to have been recruited largely from helots (cf. Xen. *Hell.* VII.1.12–13) though also from mercenaries, as had been the case during the Ionian War. There is little evidence to suggest that these naval helots, unlike their counterparts on land were regularly given or even promised their freedom (cf. Myron of Priene *FGrH* 106 F 1).

All this raises questions. The relationship between Spartiates and helots was generally assumed to be hostile, yet somehow a means was found of selecting, equipping and training for war helots in significant numbers (certainly thousands), and of appealing to their loyalty and self-interest. Helots used for military service abroad were never in practice a

---

[46] Among many see de Ste Croix 1972 (C 68) 331f; Redfield 1977–78 (C 311); Cartledge 1979 (C 282) 307–18 and 1987 (C 284) 395–412; Finley 1981 (I 38) 24–40; Hodkinson 1983 (C 296), 1986 (C 297) and in Powell 1988 (C 309) 79–121.

[47] The usual view (e.g. Cartledge 1987 (C 284) 40–3), though see Lazenby 1985 (C 300) 14–16.

security risk until after the Battle of Leuctra (cf. Xen. *Hell.* VI.5.28–9, during the Theban invasion of 370).[48]

While the case of Sparta was exceptional, the increase in the military role of the lower orders of society seems characteristic of fourth-century Greek warfare. This can be seen in the success and spread of a new type of infantry fighter, the light-armed peltast, from the Corinthian War onwards. The unexpected success of the well-drilled force under the Athenian Iphicrates against a Spartan battalion at Lechaeum in 390 established the peltast as a type of fighter who might be a match for the traditional heavy-armed hoplite. Thereafter peltasts were recurring participants in fourth-century warfare. The difference between peltast and hoplite was partly one of equipment and tactics (the peltast was lightly armed and more mobile), and partly one of social recruitment, which offered a new military role for men below hoplite status (cf. Xen. *Hell.* VI.1.8–9, Jason of Pherae's plans to recruit peltasts from the Thessalian perioeci). Peltasts were normally mercenary forces, and it is above all in the increased availability and use of mercenaries that the evolution in the social composition of Greek armies in the fourth century can be seen.

The extent to which Greek states relied on mercenaries varied. By the middle of the century Aeneas Tacticus assumed that any Greek state would be using them (*Poliorcetica* 10.7, 10.18–19, 12–13, 22.29), but he also assumed the continuation of Greek citizen armies.[49] Sparta employed mercenaries for her navy and her land forces intermittently, as in Asia Minor from 399 (the remnants of the 10,000), and during the Corinthian War after 394 (Xen. *Hell.* IV.4.14). Thebes, on the other hand, made little use of them in land warfare, though it may have depended on them, as well as on the Boeotian lower classes, for her attempt to become a maritime power in 364.[50] Athens in the fourth century appears to have employed them but little in her navy, less than in the fifth century, and relied primarily on her own native Athenian rowers from the thetic class. It seems in fact that the Athenians gradually became stricter in the naval demands they made on the *thetes*. They probably introduced conscription in 362, previously used only temporarily, and imposed it much more frequently.[51] On land the first significant use of mercenaries by Athens was the force of peltasts under Iphicrates during the Corinthian War. The unexpected success of that force may have encouraged the Athenians subsequently to rely on mercenaries.[52] They certainly play a

---

[48] Against the view of the helots as the 'Achilles heel' of the Spartan system (e.g. de Ste Croix 1972 (C 68) 89–94; Cartledge 1987 (C 284) 160–79), cf. Cawkwell 1983 (C 286) and Talbert 1989 (C 318).   [49] Bengtson 1962 (C 8); Whitehead 1990 (B 131) 120.
[50] Buckler 1980 (C 329) 163f.   [51] de Ste Croix 1981 (C 70) 207 and 581 n. 8.
[52] Pritchett 1974 (K 51) II 117–25.

prominent part in Athenian wars thereafter. Demosthenes, though in principle hostile to reliance on mercenary troops, for practical and ideological reasons, did assume that Athens could not do without them altogether. In the proposals he put forward in 351 for a standing army to fight against Philip (iv.19–27), he suggested a mixed force of 500 citizen hoplites, to serve in turn for seasonal campaigning, and 1,500 mercenaries for year-round operations. But the impression given by him and by Isocrates that the Athenians had come to rely exclusively on mercenaries, and that the Athenians themselves would not serve, is misleading: when required the Athenians could and did fight.[53] The major land battles on the mainland of Greece were fought and won by citizen armies (Nemea and Coronea 394, Leuctra 371, Mantinea 362, Chaeronea 338). Indeed, for most city states large-scale use of mercenaries on a long-term basis was financially not practical. To be effective it required resources which were only available to Persian Kings or satraps, or other eastern rulers (as in Cyprus and Egypt), and within the Greek world to autocrats (Dionysius of Syracuse, Jason of Pherae, Euphron of Sicyon, Clearchus of Heraclea, and others), men who were able and prepared to raise funds in ways unacceptable to city states.

III. THE FINANCES OF GREEK STATES

War was a matter of manpower, but also, and increasingly since the Peloponnesian War, a matter of financial resources (cf. the words of Pericles in Thuc. 1.141–3; 11.13). The Delian League had introduced finance as a regular part of naval warfare through annual tribute, in contrast to the tribute-free alliance of Sparta. The Athenian democracy innovated further through the creation of political pay for magistrates, members of the *boule* and of the juries, and the payment of subsistence allowances to sailors and land forces. The revenues from her empire enabled Athens to accumulate reserves on a quite unprecedented scale. The importance of all this was at first only partially grasped and admitted by the Peloponnesians (Thuc. 1.80.3–4; 83.2; 121.3 and 5), but the issue became predominant after the Sicilian disaster. Thereafter finance was an ever-recurring problem for Greek states through the hellenistic period. 'In war those on whose side Wealth sits will always prevail' (Ar. *Plut.* 184–5, in 388 during the Corinthian War, when the issue was particularly topical). The Greeks never recognized and conceptualized the economy as a separate sphere in its own right.[54] On the other hand, financial management emerged in fifth-century Athens as a branch of statecraft (cf. Xen. *Mem.* III.6.4–7). In the fourth century it acquired increasing importance: one aspect of the partial specialization of government

[53] Pritchett 1974 (K 51) II 104–10.   [54] Finley 1985 (A 18) ch. 1.

functions, seen in the separation of military and political leadership (cf. Isoc. VIII.54–5; Plut. *Phoc.* 7).[55] No Athenian politician could overlook the issue of finances, and Demosthenes constantly returns to the subject, from his very first public speech in 354 onwards (XIV.16–30; IV.28–9). Some Athenian politicians made their name as financial specialists, such as Eubulus after the Social War who 'applied himself to the finances, increased the revenues and thereby greatly benefited the city' (Plut. *Mor.* 812F).[56]

The development was not restricted to Athens: 'many cities are in need of raising funds (*chrematismos*) and sources of revenue . . . hence some statesmen even devote their activity exclusively to finance' (Arist. *Pol.* 1.1259a36–8; cf. *Rhet.* 1359b). Interest in the resources of states is seen already in Herodotus (cf. e.g. 1.64; III.57 and 89–97; V.49; VI.47; VIII.111); it is frequent in fourth-century literature. Xenophon's writings contain several examples (cf. *An.* III.2.26 on the Persian empire; *Hell.* V.2.16–17 on Olynthus; VI.1.11–12 on Jason of Pherae and Thessaly), and his last work, the *De Vectigalibus* of c. 355, offered suggestions to restore Athens to financial prosperity after the disaster of the Social War. In the late fourth or early third centuries an anonymous writer of the Aristotelian school compiled a short work entitled *Oeconomica*. Book I gives a summary description of various existing types of financial management, while book II is a compilation of fiscal devices resorted to by cities and rulers in financial difficulties.[57] The majority of the examples cited date from the fourth century, and many of them are related to war, notably the need to pay mercenary troops.

In financial as in other respects Sparta was peculiar. Although Spartan finances are largely a mystery, enough can be deduced to show Sparta's limitations here as in other respects. It is not that Sparta lacked the necessary wealth. Though a land-locked state which, unlike Athens, deliberately cut herself off from international trade, Sparta was territorially the largest Greek state and could also derive important revenues from her newly acquired empire. In the early fourth century she could be thought of as exceptionally wealthy (Pl. *Alc.* 1.122d–123a). Throughout this period considerable wealth poured into private hands, yet Sparta was unable to make that wealth serve public purposes. Bankruptcy hit Sparta during the Corinthian War, and became permanent after the Battle of Leuctra. Very striking was Sparta's attitude towards coinage (cf. Polyb. VI.49).[58] In the sixth century, when other Greek states were adopting the new invention, Sparta deliberately abstained and preserved her old-style iron currency (Plut. *Lyc.* 9). In the fourth century coinage

[55] Hansen 1981 (C 158) 368–70 and 1983 (C 162) and 1983 (C 163).
[56] Qualified in Cawkwell 1963 (C 107). [57] van Groningen 1933 (H 111).
[58] Cartledge 1987 (C 284) 88–90.

continued to spread, in the Greek world and beyond. This was caused in part by the use of mercenaries and the convention that they were normally paid in gold or silver currency: Persian satraps, the rulers of Egypt, and Carthage, issued coins for the payment of their mercenaries.[59] Sparta's establishment of a panhellenic empire in 404, which involved tribute payments from her Aegean dependants and considerable military expenditure, could have been expected to entail the creation of a specifically Spartan coinage. There is evidence of a debate in Sparta at the end of the Peloponnesian War over the acceptance of the large sums in foreign coin (Plut. *Lys.* 16–17). But the creation of a new coinage was not apparently contemplated,[60] and Sparta continued to use foreign coins for public and imperial purposes. In practice, despite the ban on their private use – searches were conducted (Xen. *Lac.Pol.* vii.6) – much found its way into individual hands (cf. Plut. *Lys.* 16). 'There is more gold and silver in private hands in Sparta than in the rest of Greece' (Pl. *Alc.* 1.122e). It was never suggested that this might be used for coinage, though elsewhere privately owned gold and silver was occasionally used in this way (cf. Din. 1.69; [Arist.] *Oec.* 11.2.19; 20a and h). Of the rest of Sparta's financial system little is known and not much can be added to the verdict of Aristotle:

Sparta's public finances are badly managed: when forced to carry on wars on a large scale Sparta has nothing in the state treasury, and the Spartiates pay war taxes [*eisphorai* – see below, pp. 546–8] badly because, as they own most of the land they do not scrutinize each other's contributions. The law-giver has achieved the opposite result to what is advantageous: he has made the city poor and the individual citizens avaricious.

(*Pol.* 11.1271b11–18)

Athens' finances, on the other hand, are known in greater detail than those of any other Greek state of the period.[61] Despite the Peloponnesian War Athens recovered to become again the most prosperous and prestigious state of the Greek world (thus frequently Demosthenes, e.g. xiv.25; iv.40; ix.40; x.16; cf. Isoc. xv.293–302). Athens and Piraeus remained the economic centre of the Greek world; both state and individuals derived important benefits and revenues from this,[62] through the flow of foreign visitors of all kinds, and the influence this could give Athens with foreign rulers desirous of Athenian approval and honours. Xenophon's suggestions in the *De Vectigalibus* are based on the premise that Athens enjoyed special advantages of this kind, which Xenophon details in his pamphlet (i–iv) as potential sources of increased

---

[59] Garlan 1989 (I 52) ch. 3.   [60] Cf. Bommelaer 1981 (C 279) 155 and n. 230.
[61] For Athens' finances in the fourth century cf. Rhodes 1979–80 (C 226) 309–15.
[62] Garland 1987 (I 53) ch. 2.

revenue.[63] Yet the losses suffered through the Peloponnesian War could only be made good in part. Political pay, introduced in the fifth century, was abolished in 411, and it is not clear how far state offices were salaried in the fourth century.[64] But a new form of pay, for attendance at the Assembly, was added in the 390s. This was required initially as a political measure, to ensure a quorum at the Assembly at a time of political and economic depression. Introduced at some time after the restoration of the democracy at a rate of 1 obol per meeting, it rose to 2 then 3 obols by the late 390s (Ar. *Eccl.* 289–310; Arist. *Ath.Pol.* 41.3). In the time of Aristotle it was paid at the rate of 1 dr. for ordinary meetings and 1½ drs. for principal ones, though only to the earliest arrivers (*Ath.Pol.* 52.2). In addition, after the Social War, Eubulus introduced pay for attendance at festival performances from the newly created Theoric Fund.

Athens' financial system, for all its scale and complexity, shared many features with other Greek states.[65] Direct taxation on the person of citizens – a poll-tax – was avoided, as a matter of social ideology; it was felt to be servile and degrading (cf. Dem. XXII.54–5), and the wealthy preferred more politically rewarding methods of contributing their wealth.[66] In Athens only metics were subjected to such a tax, the *metoikion*, at the rate of 12 drs. a year (possibly 1 dr. monthly) and 6 drs. for women who had no son paying the tax; the tax symbolized their inferior status (cf. Lys. XXXI.9).[67] Indirect taxes, on the other hand, had no such stigma, and were widely used by Greek states, in the form of harbour and market dues, taxes on sales and auctions, on all imports and exports indiscriminately, levied at a flat rate *ad valorem*. These were particularly common in maritime states with a significant flow of international trade,[68] such as Byzantium; most long-distance trade went by sea, though inland tolls were also common. These taxes generally drew no distinction between citizens and non-citizens or between free and slaves (Dem. LVII.34 is an exception); they were purely fiscal in intention and did not seek in any way to encourage or restrict economic activity as such. Trade was 'international', in character and in its personnel, and protective customs barriers were unknown. A typical illustration is the tax of 1/50th or 2 per cent, common to much of the Greek world, and levied at Piraeus on all goods imported to, or exported from, the harbour, no matter their origin or nature. The collection of such taxes was normally auctioned to private contractors. They had to provide sureties and pay a lump sum to the state, and recouped

---

[63] Gauthier 1976 (B 42).

[64] See on one side Hansen 1979 (C 157) and 1971–80 (C 151); MacDowell 1983 (C 195); and on the other Gabrielsen 1981 (C 141); Rhodes 1981 (B 94) 691–5.   [65] Jones 1974 (I 86).

[66] Veyne 1990 (I 145) 71–83.   [67] Whitehead 1977 (C 265) 75–7 and 1986 (C 269) 146.

[68] Vélissaropoulos 1980 (I 144) 205–31.

themselves by making a profit on the collection of the tax. In 400/399 it was auctioned for 30 talents, and in the next year this increased to 36 talents (Andoc. 1.133–4), an indication of the resumption of maritime trade through Piraeus not long after the end of the Peloponnesian War (cf. also Xen. *Hell.* v.1.19–24; Isoc. IV.42, in 380). The yield of the tax in normal times was probably significantly higher: Demosthenes estimates an annual yield of 200 talents from ports in the Thracian Chersonese (XXIII.110). Taxes of this kind were therefore potentially a large source of revenue (cf. Xen. *Hell.* v.2.16 on Olynthus; Dem. 1.22 on Thessaly), though the yield varied according to the level of economic activity. The system meant a financial loss to the state in relation to the real value of the tax; Callistratus in Macedon in 361/0 was able to double the revenue from a harbour tax (*ellimenion*) from 20 to 40 talents ([Arist.] *Oec.* II.2.22). On the other hand it relieved the state of the burden of collection, difficult in the absence of the necessary administrative personnel. It also circumvented the – very real – risk of corruption by officials, an obsessive preoccupation with Greek states (cf. Arist. *Pol.* v.1308b32 – 1309a14), and guaranteed to the state fixed payments at specific dates.

Aristotle describes in detail the procedure at Athens and the officials involved (*Ath.Pol.* 47.2–48.2) and lists other sources of indirect revenue: these included court fines, the sale of property confiscated by the state, rents from public and sacred lands, and the royalties on the silver mines and the sums paid for mining concessions. Athens' possession of silver mines at Laurium was to her an important though fluctuating source of revenue (cf. esp. Xen. *Vect.* IV). The state asserted ownership of the mines (though not of the land above them), but their exploitation was left to private Athenian citizens, who used slave labour on a large scale. A series of leases has been preserved on inscriptions, though in fragmentary form, the earliest list from 367/6. There is mention of an earlier list, which implies that the mode of concession was of recent introduction. The last dated list is of 307/6. The leases continue to the late fourth or early third century.[69] The Laurium mines are the only classical mines for which detailed evidence is available, from literary, epigraphic and archaeological sources. Much is known, or can be inferred, about the owners or concessionaries of mining land, many of them from the upper levels of Athenian society, about the patterns of land ownership or leasing in the mining area, about the use of slave labour and the techniques of production, about the ups and downs in mining activity and its links with political events.[70] Yet while it is known that the mines were indirectly a source of great revenue to the Athenian

---

[69] Crosby 1950 (I 29) and 1957 (I 30).

[70] Hopper 1953 (I 76) and 1968 (I 77); Lauffer 1957 (I 94) and 1975 (I 95); Conophagos 1980 (I 26); Jones 1982 (I 87); Osborne 1985 (C 212) ch. 6.

state, it is not possible to quantify precisely the benefits derived, since the exact nature and incidence of the payments recorded in the leases are not known. The revenue from all these sources could be substantial, though it fluctuated. Just after the Social War Athens' revenues are said to have fallen to a mere 130 talents (Dem. x.37), though by 346 they had risen to 400 talents annually, which was probably higher than they had been since the fifth century (Theopomp. *FGrH* 115 F 166).

The substitute for taxation on the persons of citizens was taxation assessed on their wealth, which was reckoned as capital wealth and not as income. This meant that wage-earners with little or no property would not be taxed, but these would in any case be men of modest means.[71] In the Greek world wealth was occasionally reckoned in terms of agricultural produce, as was the case with Solon's four classes (Arist. *Ath.Pol.* 7.3–4), but these were not used for taxation purposes. By the fourth century this method was obsolete; greater diversification led to its expression at Athens in monetary terms. Occasionally taxation might take the form of a quota on produce, as at Athens in the sixth century under the tyranny (Arist. *Ath.Pol.* 16.4; Thuc. vi.54.5). This lapsed after the Pisistratids and in the Greek world quotas on produce were only levied for religious dues, as for the offerings to the Eleusinian goddesses (M–L 73, *c.* 422, superseded by another law, amended in 353/2, *IG* ii².140).

A tax common to virtually all the Greek world was the *eisphora*, found even at Sparta (see above, p. 543), though most of the evidence in this period relates to Athens. There are numerous unsolved problems of detail as to its organization there,[72] but the character of the tax is clear: it was in essence an emergency levy on capital wealth for military purposes. At Athens it is first explicitly attested in the financial decrees of Callias (M–L 58 B, l.17, if correctly dated to 434/3), though it was no doubt older, and was first levied during the Peloponnesian War in 428 (Thuc. iii.19).[73] Though frequently levied thereafter, little is known of it until an important reform in 378/7, the date of the foundation of the Second Athenian League, which represented a new beginning in the financial as well as in the political and military history of Athens. It is likely that initially the Athenians did not reckon on levying regular contributions from their allies (below), and strict financial management on the Athenian side was required. At the same time they may have sought to establish a military reserve fund supplied from any surpluses of public

---

[71] de Ste Croix 1981 (C 70) 179–204.

[72] de Ste Croix 1953 (I 135); Jones 1957 (C 178) 23–9; Brunt 1966 (I 18) and de Ste Croix 1966 (I 137) on Thomsen 1964 (I 143); Davies 1981 (C 126) 15–28; Rhodes 1982 (I 127); Brun 1983 (I 17) 3–73; MacDowell 1986 (C 196); Ruschenbusch 1985 (C 242) and 1987 (C 243); Hansen 1990 (C 168) 353.

[73] Thucydides' meaning is ambiguous, Griffith 1977 (C 147).

revenue, though the sums available must have been limited.[74] Fourth-century Athens did not enjoy the benefit of large reserves as in the fifth century, and nostalgic references to the financial abundance of the past are frequent in the orators (cf. e.g. Dem. xxiii.207–10). Also in the same context there is a fragmentary epigraphic record of a law on the recalling of debts to the state (*IG* ii² 45), reminiscent of the efforts made after the end of the Social War to recover arrears of sums due to the state (Dem. xx, xxii, xxiv). Relevant too is the fresh impetus in mining activity implied by the leases (above).

The reorganization of 378/7 was based on a reassessment of the taxable wealth of both citizens and metics in Attica. The total assessment amounted to 5,750 talents (Polyb. ii.62.7), and Demosthenes in 354 mentions a total of 6,000 talents (xiv.19 and 30) – either a rounded figure, or a result of subsequent reassessments. Despite Polybius, these figures are much too low to relate to the total wealth of Attica, but refer rather to the total declared taxable wealth. This involves two restrictions: in the first place those with a property rating below a certain figure, perhaps 2,500 drs., were excluded. Whatever the number of citizens and metics liable to the *eisphora*,[75] non-contributors were in any case a majority; their exclusion probably reflects the impracticality of collecting a large number of small contributions. Second, the assessment represented the total *declared* wealth (the assessment was based on wealth both movable and immovable, i.e. it included cash, personal belongings and slaves as well as land and houses, though mining concessions may have been exempted). There was no register of landed property, still less of slaves and other chattels, and no available bureaucracy: reliance therefore had to be placed on the declaration of individuals. Under-assessment of landed wealth and concealment of movable wealth were common; an honest declaration was something to be boasted of in courts, though fear of informers and of the *antidosis* procedure (see below, pp. 550–1) will have helped to restrict evasion.

The incidence of the *eisphora* was irregular and unpredictable. After the reorganization of 378/7 it remained as before an emergency tax, raised from time to time for military purposes by decision of the Athenian Assembly, in the form of a levy on capital wealth, usually at the rate of 1 or 2 per cent, which was levied at the same flat rate on all tax-payers. Although Athens was at war almost continuously from 378, the tax was only resorted to intermittently. Between 378/7 and 355 only a little above 300 talents was raised in *eisphorai* (Dem. xxii.44): this would represent a rate of 0.25 per cent if the tax had been levied annually. Yet despite these relatively low figures, the *eisphora* was considered by the wealthy an unwelcome burden, as was the trierarchy (see below, p. 550), presumably because of the very unpredictability of the tax, which made inroads into the cash reserves of individuals, in a world with limited credit resources.[76]

The number of those liable to the *eisphora* was probably higher than those called on to perform liturgies; these may have numbered 1,200 citizens.[77] The level of wealth required to belong to the liturgical class was somewhere between 3 and 4 talents, or about 7 to 9 times as much as the minimum for liability to the *eisphora*; as with the *eisphora*, metics were also liable for liturgies.[78] The institution of the liturgy is known in great detail at Athens, but was common to many Greek states; it is attested for example even in a small island like Siphnos in the 390s (Isoc. XIX.36). It was based on the premise that the wealthy had a duty to spend from their private wealth for public purposes; the return for the spending was prestige and gratitude on the part of one's fellow-citizens. Even Sparta is known to have had liturgies – at least, the trierarchy is attested (Thuc. IV.11.4, cf. Xen. *Hell.* VII.1.12), though no details are known – but in general Sparta seems to have made much less play with the notion of using private wealth for public purposes than other Greek states.

At Athens liturgies fell into one of two groups. There were the religious liturgies, such as the *choregia*, which involved the recruiting and training of a chorus for a dramatic festival, and many others, around 100 in all, and 117 or more in a Panathenaic year;[79] this was the main method of financing and organizing Athens' festivals, renowned in the Greek world for their splendour. With the military liturgies – the trierarchy and the *proeisphora* – lists of those liable were kept and exemptions were not allowed (Dem. XX.18); they were regarded as essential for the safety of the state, though they were apt to be seen as an imposition. The trierarchy involved in theory the command and maintenance of a trireme for up to a year, though in practice the obligations and expenditure falling on trierarchs could be much more extensive (cf. esp. [Dem.] L). The *proeisphora* or 'advance payment' is not attested before 362; it affected the 300 richest Athenians who might be called upon to advance the money due for an *eisphora* from their own funds, and recover later the sums in excess of their share from the other members of their tax-paying unit (symmory). The contrast between the unpopularity of military liturgies and the popularity of festival liturgies recurs frequently in the orators (Dem. IV.35–6; XX.26).

As practised in classical Athens, the liturgy system was ambiguous in

[76] Osborne in Rich and Wallace-Hadrill 1990 (I 128) ch. 5.
[77] Against the lower figure of Davies 1981 (C 126) 15–28 cf. Rhodes 1982 (I 127) 1–5; Hansen 1990 (C 168) 353.   [78] Whitehead 1984 (C 267) 80–2.   [79] Davies 1967 (C 122).

character. The institution was aristocratic in origin, but institutionalized within a democratic framework. It both distinguished between and linked the public and private spheres (cf. Dem. XIV.28; XXII.26; X.43–5). The Athenian democracy rested on an explicit guarantee of respect for private property, yet as Socrates says to Critobulus in Xenophon's *Oeconomicus* (II.6) 'if ever you are thought to have fallen short in the performance [of your liturgical duties], I know that the Athenians will punish you just as much as if they had caught you stealing their own property'. Performance of liturgies and payment of *eisphorai* were constantly cited in court as proof of civic spirit and a claim to the jurors' indulgence (cf. e.g. Lys. XXV.12–13). Yet the same behaviour could also be construed as ostentatious spending for personal self-glorification (Lycurg. *Leoc.* 139–40). In fourth-century Athens, the words 'wealth', 'wealthy', sometimes had pejorative connotations (cf. esp. Dem. XXI).[80] A further ambiguity lay in the level of liturgical performance expected: minimum obligations were defined (the details are not known), but in practice performance varied considerably between individuals. Social pressures there certainly were, but some liturgies were highly sought after, as Aristotle also confirms in general terms (*Pol.* v.1309a17–21).

Similarly ambiguous was the institution of *epidoseis* (public contributions to the state on a nominally voluntary basis). They are attested at Athens since the Archidamian War (Plut. *Alc.* 10), then quite commonly in the fourth century and later, and are also found in other Greek states, though the evidence is most abundant for the post-classical period.[81] In Athens, *epidoseis* rested on a public decree of the Athenian people, which declared the specific purpose for which it was required (down to the time of Alexander, always a military purpose), and invited citizens and non-citizens to contribute. Individuals then announced publicly in the Assembly the gifts they intended to make (usually money), and their names might subsequently be publicly listed (cf. Isae. v.37–8; Dem. XXI.160–1). The eminently public character of benefactions in the Greek world is noteworthy: benefactors did not wish to remain anonymous, rather publicity was their reward, and *epidoseis* were boasted of in court in the same way as performance of liturgies and payment of *eisphorai*.

'When I was a boy,' wrote Isocrates in 354/3, 'being rich was considered so secure and respectable that almost everyone pretended he owned more property than was the case, because he wanted to share in the prestige it gave. Now, on the other hand, one has to defend oneself against being rich as if it were the worst of crimes' (xv.159–60). In another passage he lists the specific grievances: 'the multitude of burdens laid upon the rich, the liturgies, and all the nuisances connected with the symmories and with exchanges of property (*antidoseis* – see below, pp.

[80] Dover 1974 (H 32) 109–12. [81] Kuenzi 1923 (I 91); Migeotte 1983 (I 103).

550–1); for these are so annoying that the propertied find life more burdensome than those who are continually in want' (VIII.128). Isocrates cannot be taken to speak for all the Athenian wealthy; moreover, his complaints would carry greater conviction if his own record had been more impressive. Though a wealthy man, among the richest in Athens in his time, he seriously undervalued his own property (XV.155–8), and is known to have performed only three trierarchies (Davies 1971 (C 124) 7716). Nevertheless, his is not an isolated critique, but represents one strand of Athenian thought, first found in the Old Oligarch (1.13). It received expression notably at the time of the failure of the Social War (cf. Xen. *Vect.* VI.1), and also finds mention in Aristotle's strictures on democracy and its threats to the property of the wealthy (*Pol.* VI.1320a16–22). The wealthy, or some of them, claimed that they were overburdened by state-imposed expenses, and that their property was threatened in the courts. The accusation is heard that in times of financial stringency the popular law-courts were inclined to condemn rich defendants to confiscate their property: thus several times in the early fourth century at a time of stress (esp. Lys. XXX.22, cf. XIX.11, XXVII.1), but also in the time of Demosthenes (X.43.5).

It is difficult to assess such allegations, particularly as they involve conflicting political standpoints. A democratic sympathizer would retort with a defence of the impartiality of Athenian juries (Hyperides III.33–6). In practice Athenian democracy went a long way towards making protection of private property a corner-stone of its institutions. Every year on taking office, the *archon* would proclaim through a herald that everyone would remain in possession of all his property till the expiry of the *archon*'s year of office (Arist. *Ath.Pol.* 56.2). All Athenian jurors swore an oath which included a promise not to vote for revolutionary social and political measures of the kind later banned in the League of Corinth (Dem. XXIV.149–51). Further, there were safeguards to protect the less wealthy against an unfair burden of liturgies. The most onerous liturgy, the trierarchy, was from the late fifth century onwards frequently shared between two men, and attempts were made in the fourth century (in *c.* 357 by one Periander, in 340 by Demosthenes) to spread the costs of the trierarchy more equitably, though the exact details are disputed. In the fourth century no one was allowed (or at least could be compelled) to perform more than one liturgy at a time, nor could liturgies be performed in consecutive years. Further, any Athenian who felt that the obligation to perform a liturgy should fall on another richer than himself could take the matter to court, and challenge his opponent either to undertake the liturgy or to exchange properties (this was the procedure known as *antidosis*, or 'exchange'). The bluntness of the procedure is striking: in practice what the state wanted was to ensure the performance of the liturgy, and this was probably normally achieved without the upheaval of a literal exchange of properties, though such exchanges are known to have taken place (cf. Lys. IV.1).[82]

The laws thus provided safeguards for the protection of wealth. Nevertheless the reluctance of some of the wealthy to pay *eisphorai* and to undertake military liturgies is a fact of fourth-century history. After the failure of the Social War, a challenge to Athenian imperial policies was expressed, more clearly and openly than before, as shown by Isocrates' two pamplets *On the Peace* (VIII) and the *Areopagiticus* (VII) and Xenophon's *De Vectigalibus*. The motives of those who sympathized with this view may have been less concern for the injustices of Athenian policy, as they put it, than unwillingness to bear themselves the expenses of war. Nevertheless this revealed an important shift in attitudes. For most of the history of the fifth-century empire there is little sign of any serious challenge in Athens to it. In practice its benefits were enjoyed, collectively and individually, at different levels of Athenian society.[83] Early in the fourth century many Athenians, including the wealthy, still looked forward to a resumption of fifth-century imperialism (cf. Andoc. III.15; Isoc. IV, in 380). But in 378/7 Athens, in order to attract willing allies to her new league, was forced to renounce explicitly several features of her fifth-century league: these included the acquisition of land in allied states by Athenian individuals (Tod no. 123 lines 25–31, 35–46 = Harding no. 35; Diod. XV.29.8), widely practised by wealthy Athenians on a large scale. Henceforward, though individual Athenians might still make profits, as commanders and officials, from what was left of Athens' imperial role (implied, for instance, by Tod no. 152 = Harding no. 68),[84] the opportunities were now more circumscribed. From the point of view of the wealthy, empire could be seen to be costing more and bringing in less by way of return. The few fourth-century cleruchies of Athens benefited only the lower classes. It would be too schematic to talk of an Athenian 'war party of the poor' as against a 'peace party of the rich', but conflicts of interest were now appearing.

IV. EXTERNAL SOURCES OF WEALTH

No Greek state, however wealthy, could bear by itself the cost of large-scale military power: the fifth-century Athenian empire had to rely on regular tribute from its allies. On the other hand, the word *phoros* (tribute) acquired a stigma which fourth-century imperial attempts could not ignore. Sparta, on winning over Athens in 404, followed the Athenian formula: tribute was imposed on the Aegean states now

---

[82] MacDowell 1978 (C 194) 162–4.   [83] Finley 1981 (I 38) 41–61.
[84] de Ste Croix 1981 (C 70) 604 n. 27.

included in Sparta's maritime empire. Very little is known of this, as indeed of most forms of imperial tribute in the fourth century. References to Sparta's Aegean tribute are few and uninformative (cf. Isoc. IV.132; [Herodes] *Peri Politeias*, 24); Diodorus mentions a figure of 1,000 talents, which seems excessively large and cannot be verified (XIV.10.2). It may be in fact that Sparta sought to avoid the by now unpleasant word 'tribute' (*phoros*) and referred instead to 'contributions' (*synteleiai*) (cf. Arist. *Ath.Pol.* 39.2). After Sparta's defeat at Cnidus in 394, these will have lapsed, or at least have become much more difficult to collect. No regular tribute was imposed on the members of Sparta's old alliance, though a trend towards monetary contributions, in place of or at least in addition to providing military contingents, becomes visible after the King's Peace (Xen. *Hell.* v.2.21–2, cf. v.3.10 and 17, and the reorganization of Sparta's allies by districts mentioned by Diod. xv.31.2).

The political sensitivity attached to tribute is well illustrated by the Second Athenian League. The manifesto of the league explicitly promised to signing members that they would be free from tribute (Tod no. 123 line 23 = Harding no. 35), and it seems likely that the Athenians and their allies reckoned initially on having a viable military alliance without the need for some form of tribute. A few years of campaigning showed this to be unrealistic, yet the Athenians were tied by their original promise. Payments by the allies for military purposes are first attested in 373 ([Dem.] XLIX.49), and may have started then.[85] Significantly they were given the neutral name 'contributions' (*syntaxeis*) instead of the offending *phoros* (Theopompus *FGrH* 115 F 98; Plut. *Sol.* 15.2–3). Little is known of these fourth-century 'contributions';[86] they were probably expected from every ally of Athens and may have been in theory *ad hoc* emergency payments which gradually evolved into a regular annual obligation. A few gross sums are mentioned (Dem. XVIII.234: 45 talents; Aeschin. II.71: 60 talents), well below the figures for fifth-century tribute. The fourth-century league was not a source of wealth to the Athenian state. Of the other leading states in the period, Thebes appears to have made no attempt to impose tribute on its allies.[87] The system of contributions by Boeotian cities to the federal treasury, about which little is known (*Hell.Oxy.* xvi [xi] 4), was not apparently significantly extended during Thebes' period of predominance after Leuctra. It was only an autocrat like Jason of Pherae who could openly contemplate tribute as the normal source of his revenues, comparing his position, with no little hyperbole, to that of the Persian King (Xen. *Hell.* VI.1.12).

Formal tribute was not the only form of outside revenue. Material and financial support might be expected from friendly foreign states and

85 Wilson 1970 (C 271); Cawkwell 1981 (C 113) 48.
86 Cargill 1981 (C 101) 124–7; Brun 1983 (I 17) 74–142.   87 Buckler 1980 (C 329) 224f.

individuals on an *ad hoc* basis, a practice frequently attested. A well-known inscription (M–L 67) records donations to Sparta's war effort, probably during the Archidamian War. Sparta probably expected this from friendly states whenever possible. For example, Phlius during the war against Olynthus 'made large contributions of money, and quickly, for the expedition', and was praised by Agesipolis for doing so (Xen. *Hell.* v.3.10). In 371 the Spartan Prothous suggested, though the proposal was rejected, that each of the allies should deposit any sum they wished as a contribution to a war fund, to be entrusted to the safekeeping of Apollo at Delphi (Xen. *Hell.* vi.4.2). Another inscription (Tod no. 160 = Harding no. 74, of *c.* 355–1) records similar contributions made to the Boeotians by friendly states for the Sacred War. The distinction between 'states' and 'individuals' is in practice rather artificial. The world of the Greek cities, divided in many respects, was bound together by a large nexus of personal friendships between influential individuals or families in different Greek states, some of which extended over generations.[88] Just as a wealthy man in his home state would spend from his private wealth for public purposes, so too he might give assistance, political and material, to a city or an individual in another city with whom he had ties of friendship. Thus the metic Lysias during the civil war of 404/3 showed his support for the Athenian democracy by giving the democrats 2,000 drs, 200 shields, hiring 300 mercenaries, and also by persuading his guest friend Thrasydaeus of Elis to give a further 2 talents ([Plut.] *X orat. Lysias* 7). Athens in the fifth century deliberately exploited the support of pro-Athenians abroad: the Thessalian magnate Menon of Pharsalus gave Athens 12 talents of silver and the services of 200 cavalry recruited from his own *penestai* in 477/6 during the war against Eion (Dem. xiii.23). The orator Andocides claims that during his exile in 411 he managed to supply timber from Macedon for the Athenian fleet on the strength of his traditional guest friendship with Archelaus of Macedon (ii.11). Personal links with wealthy and influential foreigners could thus be a source of support of one's home city, as Andocides claimed (i.143). This was repeatedly illustrated in the fourth century with many of Athens' leading generals, themselves figures of great standing in the Greek world and beyond, as the careers of Conon, Timotheus, Chabrias, Iphicrates and others showed (cf. [Dem.] xlix.22–37, concerning Timotheus).

Lack of accumulated reserves in the fourth century did not mean that such reserves were non-existent within the Greek world. These were to be found in temples in the form of accumulated treasures. The economy

---

[88] Gehrke 1985 (C 27) 291–7 (in relation to *stasis*); Herman 1987 (C 34) esp. ch. 4; Cartledge 1982 (C 283) for one specific example (Sparta and Samos); Cartledge 1987 (C 284) ch. 13 for Sparta generally.

of Greek temples varied considerably in scale, given the number and diversity of Greek cults; nevertheless there were common features. First, throughout the Greek world temples and cults were under the ultimate control of a political authority: the Athenian people controlled its cults and temples, the Delians regulated their sanctuary of Apollo, the Amphictyonic Council supervised the temple at Delphi. Independent temple states, such as were common in the Near East, were unknown in the Greek world. Second, though temples frequently owned 'sacred' land, from which they drew rents, this was never on a large scale; in Greek states most agricultural land was normally in the hands of citizens. Third, where temples did possess significant wealth, it came in the form of deposits of precious objects of all kind from the outside, on a temporary or permanent basis. Some temples served as repositories for private deposits, such as Delphi where Lysander left a (modest) sum of under 2 talents (Plut. *Lys.* 18; cf. the proposal of the Spartan Prothous in 371), or the Artemisium at Ephesus which enjoyed a considerable reputation for safety (Xen. *An.* v.3.4–13, cf. Plut. *Demetr.* 30.1–2); Delos and Olympia did not apparently play this role. Most important were the innumerable gifts and dedications accumulated in the temples over many generations, from both individuals and states. The custom to dedicate in some form to the gods a tithe of the spoils of successful warfare was a source of enrichment and adornment to the gods.[89] Greek cities might also make dedications in the sanctuaries of other Greek states as a demonstration of gratitude for services received (cf. Dem. XXII.70–2, gold crowns dedicated at Athens by other Greek cities). Individuals would also make offerings, which varied widely in their motives and importance. Conon for example left a sum of no less than 16 talents 4,000 drs for dedications to Athena and to Apollo at Delphi, an indication of the great wealth he had won from his political and military activity in Persian service (Lys. XIX.39).

Considerable sums would thus accumulate in some Greek sanctuaries. Some temples engaged in money-lending activities, though there was much variety in practice.[90] Neither Delphi nor Olympia appear to have done this with any regularity, if at all. Some of the sanctuaries in Attica made loans to individuals, but the great Athenian temples in the fifth century only to the Athenian state. Further, such money-lending as was practised by temples was small in scale, and involved only a small proportion of the temple's total accumulated wealth. Personal deposits, for instance, were left untouched. The best known example in this period of the financial operations of a Greek sanctuary comes from Delos, where the temple accounts were regularly inscribed on stone. One

---

[89] Pritchett 1971 (K 51) I 93–100.   [90] Bogaert 1968 (I 10) 279–304.

preserved inscription (Tod no. 125)[91] records the transactions for the years 377/6 to 374/3 when Delos was back once more under Athenian management after the interruption at the end of the Peloponnesian War. Besides the revenues from rents on temple property (land and houses) sums were lent to individuals and, interestingly, also to states. The rate of interest at Delos was fixed at 10 per cent for religious and not economic reasons (cf. the various tithes to gods and goddesses). All the loans recorded, both to individuals and to states, were purely local among the neighbouring islands; the total sums involved were modest, some 50 talents altogether, and the largest part was lent to states. No less revealing is the constant difficulty of Delos in securing payments of arrears: not just individuals but borrowing states were defaulting in their modest debts to Apollo.

The largest part of the accumulated wealth of Greek temples was thus never put into circulation. There was a contrast between the large reserves of some temples and the chronic depletion of Greek public treasuries. The temptation to use that wealth was therefore great. From a purely economic point of view it was usable wealth, with much precious metal which Greek states were mostly very short of. The decision to use it was political, since Greek sanctuaries were under political control, but since this wealth belonged to the gods, practical considerations and religious scruples pulled in opposite directions. The suggestion of using temple wealth for political purposes is first attested in the context of the Ionian Revolt, when Hecataeus of Miletus advised the Ionians ιο melt down the offerings at Didyma to serve as a war fund – a suggestion the Ionians rejected (Hdt. v.36). At the outbreak of the Peloponnesian War, the Peloponnesians considered borrowing from Delphi and Olympia to make up for their financial weakness – but apparently never carried this out (Thuc. 1.121.3 and 143.1).[92] Pericles in 431 listed the dedications in Athenian temples as well as her moneyed reserves as Athenian resources, but specified that the Athenians should only touch these in an emergency and should replace eventually anything used up (Thuc. 11.13.4–5; cf. some fourth-century proposals to coin sacred objects in times of emergency, Dem. xxii.48 and Deinarchus 1.69). In 407/6, in the concluding stages of the Peloponnesian War, shortage of silver compelled the Athenians to introduce an emergency gold coinage minted from sacred offerings in the temples on the Acropolis (Philochorus *FGrH* 323 f 141).[93]

In the fourth century the pressures to use such treasures increased, but the religious inhibitions remained strong. Only few Greek states or rulers resorted to the expedient, notably Dionysius of Syracuse (Ael.

---

[91] Bogaert 1968 (I 10) 128–30; Migeotte 1984 (I 104) 142–4 (in part only), 151–6.
[92] Migeotte 1984 (I 104) no. 22 p. 89f.   [93] Kraay 1976 (B 200) 68–70.

VH 1.20; [Arist.] *Oec.* 11.2.20 and 41, cf. 24a on Datames) and Euphron of Sicyon (Xen. *Hell.* vii.1.46 and 3.8). Jason of Pherae was expected to help himself at Delphi (Xen. *Hell.* vi.4.30). When the Arcadians after Leuctra sought to turn themselves into a major Greek power with a standing army of 10,000, they tried to meet the inevitable financial problem by using the wealth of the temple at Olympia; this resulted in internal divisions, and the recourse to temple wealth was then abandoned (Xen. *Hell.* vii.4.33–4; Diod. xv.82.1). The most glaring case occurred in 356–346 when the Phocians seized Delphi, and by using the dedications in the temple were able to finance a large and effective mercenary force for a decade. Significantly, there are signs of hesitation on the part of the Phocian leaders (Diod. xvi.56–7). Militarily this was a unique feat for a small and relatively backward Greek people, but it was also a sacrilege for which they paid a heavy price, both financially (cf. Tod no. 172 = Harding no. 88) and politically.

There remained one major potential source of external wealth: Persia.[94] More than anything else, Persian gold had made possible Sparta's victory at sea over Athens. The lesson was not forgotten. Subsidies, frequently on a very significant scale, from the Great King or his satraps, or from other eastern rulers, played an often decisive, though spasmodic, role in the financial, military and political history of the fourth-century Greek world. They helped to bring about the coalition against Sparta in the Corinthian War through the mission of the Rhodian Timocrates; they gave a decisive impetus to the revival of Athenian power under Conon from 393 and also enabled the allies to maintain an effective mercenary force at Corinth for several years;[95] and they may have enabled Thebes to make an attempt at naval power in 364.[96] Virtually every one of the leading cities of the fourth century did at one time or other solicit, and sometimes receive, eastern subsidies (cf. Isoc. xii.159–60). However, the subsidies were politically sensitive and a matter of easy reproach on the part of other Greeks not at the time in receipt of such funds: the Persians were supposed to be the national enemy. Hesitation and obloquy over such subsidies recur through to the end of the Persian empire, as shown for instance by Callicratidas in 407/6 (Xen. *Hell.* 1.6.7 and 11), the outcry against Timocrates at the start of the Corinthian War (Xen. *Hell.* iii.5.1–2), Teleutias in 387 (Xen. *Hell.* v.1.17), or later the special pleading of Demosthenes when he suggested the possibility of Persian financial support in the conflict with Philip (x.31–4, contrast xiv.3–5, 29–32, 36–40). Moreover, the Persians only spent their money on the Greeks when it suited their interests. Unlike other past and present rulers on the fringes of the Greek world, and

[94] Lewis 1989 (C 42).   [95] Pritchett 1974 (K 51) II 117–25.
[96] Buckler 1980 (C 329) 160f.

unlike their hellenistic successors, the Persians were not interested in securing the reputation of philhellenes through generosities to the Greeks. No single state could secure effective Persian backing for any length of time. Sparta, the recipient of Persian wealth at the end of the Peloponnesian War, lost this source of revenue when she broke with the Persians. Though she eventually moved back to the Persian alliance she never received more than intermittent funds (cf. Xen. *Hell.* III.4.26, in 396; IV.8.16, in 391; Diod. XV.9.3–5, in 385; Xen. *Hell.* VII.1.27, in 368). Thereafter the Persians had no further use for Sparta until the revolt of Agis III in the time of Alexander. Athens enjoyed significant financial support from Persia in the early stages of the Corinthian War (cf. also Lys. XIX.24–6), but then forfeited that assistance when she took the side of Evagoras of Cyprus and of Egypt in revolt against the Great King. Thebes had some success with Persia in the decade after Leuctra; she (probably) received subsidies which enabled her to attempt to build a naval force in 364, and obtained a further 300 talents for the Sacred War in 351 (Diod. XVI.40.1–2). But all in all, from the Greek point of view, the Persian King was not a dependable ally or paymaster (cf. *Hell. Oxy.* XIX.2 [XIV.2] in relation to the 390s, and later Dem. XIV.36).

The military finances of Greek states thus remained haphazard and improvisatory. From the Corinthian War onwards inability to finance military forces effectively was a recurring problem. Commanders in the field, with little or no money from their cities, were frequently left to their own devices to face the problem of unpaid and discontented troops. Mercenary soldiers could be efficient and well-disciplined only if paid regularly and well treated, and Greek cities were not usually in the position to emulate the example of Jason of Pherae (Xen. *Hell.* VI.1.5–6). In these conditions, more often than not booty became in the fourth century the substitute for regular pay.[97] In 387, for instance, the Spartan Teleutias, short of funds, made a highly profitable raid on Piraeus and on merchantmen sailing to and from Athens. The Athenian Xenophon relates the raid on his native city with apparent approval, as an example of resourcefulness on the part of a commander in war (*Hell.* V.13–24). Throughout the Greek world it was assumed that armies would normally live off enemy territory. Demosthenes' proposals (in 351) for a standing Athenian army took this for granted (Dem. IV.28–9): the shortfall in financing the troops would be made up 'from the war'. Substantial sums could sometimes be raised in these ways: Agesilaus' campaigns in Asia Minor collected more than 2,000 talents' worth of booty (Xen. *Ages.* 1.34), largely at the expense of non-Greeks. Chabrias in 376 captured 3,000 prisoners at the Battle of Naxos, who were sold in Athens as slaves, which raised about 100 talents (Dem. XX.76–7). But

[97] Pritchett 1971 (K 51) I 89f.

such windfalls were unpredictable, and pillaging of Greeks was expensive in goodwill, especially of one's own allies. The ideal commander, from the point of view of a state like Athens, was one who could somehow find ways of conducting wars effectively despite lack of financial support.[98] Conon's son Timotheus was a versatile example (Davies 1971 (C 124) 13700): he spent freely from his own wealth to help finance his troops ([Dem.] XLIX), while not omitting to gain personal wealth from his campaigns, like other successful commanders. He was constantly resourceful ([Arist.] *Oec.* II.2.23), and could be presented by his mentor Isocrates as a general who was eminently good value for the little money he was given (Isoc. XV.101–39).

V. THE CORN SUPPLY OF GREEK STATES

The ideal of the self-sufficient polis was taken for granted by the fourth-century philosophers, yet both Plato and Aristotle knew that no city could cut itself off from the outside world and the need for exchanges and foreign trade, much as they would have liked to restrict this (cf. e.g. *Leg.* XII.952d–953e; *Pol.* VII.1326b26–1327a40).[99] In reality, trade between states, particularly those with access to the sea and maritime traffic, was common.[100] Total self-sufficiency had probably never been attainable, and the larger the city the more difficult it was to achieve. As the Old Oligarch said, commenting on Athens' use of her naval power in the fifth century (II.11–12), 'if some town is rich in timber for ships, where will it sell it, if it does not persuade the ruler of the sea to let it? If a town is rich in iron or copper or flax, where will it find a market, if it does not persuade the ruler of the sea to let it? [. . .] The same town does not have both timber and flax . . . nor can copper and iron be had from the same town.' The writer is referring here primarily to Athens' need for shipbuilding materials, a paradoxical weakness for a naval power.[101]

Most important, though not mentioned by the Old Oligarch, was the food supply of Greek cities, that is to say their corn supply, since grain was (with olives) the staple food of the Greek world.[102] The beginnings of the corn trade go back to the archaic age, and by the classical period it had grown into the largest international sea-borne trade of the Greek world. The most important sources of supply lay partly within the Greek world, as in Sicily and the West, and in Thessaly, and partly beyond it, in Egypt and as far as the Crimean Bosporus. These and other countries

[98] Instances of Athenian financial difficulties in de Ste Croix 1981 (C 70) 607 n. 37.

[99] Bresson 1987 (I 16).

[100] Nixon and Price in Murray and Price 1990 (I 113) 137–70, at 160; Winterling 1991 (C 86) 208f on Greek cities in Aeneas Tacticus.   [101] Meiggs 1982 (I 101) 116–32, 188–217, for timber.

[102] Heichelheim 1935 (I 72); Foxhall and Forbes 1982 (I 43); Garnsey and Whittaker 1983 (I 58); Osborne 1987 (I 115) ch. 5.

are explicitly attested as exporters to the Greek world, though the evidence, as always with economic matters, is fragmented and hapha-zard. For instance, the role of Thessaly as an occasional exporter of corn is attested casually for the fourth century by only two references in Xenophon (*Hell.* v.4.56 and vi.1.11).[103] As usual, the evidence on the corn supply overwhelmingly concerns Athens. But while Athens' dependence on foreign imports of corn was certainly exceptional, she was not alone in this position, though it is difficult to judge from scattered evidence the extent and regularity of the dependence of other Greek cities. The dividing line between sufficiency and scarcity was narrow; abundance in one region or year could be matched by shortage in another.[104] Individual cases of shortages are known (cf. e.g. [Arist.] *Oec.* ii.2.16a, at Clazomenae, cf. also Tod no. 114, ll.17–20 = Harding no. 26 of 387 B.C.; [Arist.] *Oec.* ii.2.17, at Selymbria). Crop failures, caused by disease or drought, were a recurring threat. One such failure, which resulted in widespread food shortages in the Greek world, is attested in the late 360s ([Dem.] l.6, 17 and 61); another one happened soon after, in 357/6 (Dem. xx.31–3).[105] In the time of Alexander there were repeated shortages, partly caused by the manipulations of Alex-ander's appointee in Egypt, Cleomenes ([Dem.] lvi.7–10; [Arist.] *Oec.* ii.2.23).[106] Generally, the disturbed conditions of the fourth century were liable to disrupt both agriculture and overseas trade. Ravaging of the enemy's agricultural land was a normal tactic of land warfare, regularly used for instance by Sparta during much of the Peloponnesian War and after.[107] Though the long-term effects were perhaps limited, this could induce even agriculturally self-sufficient cities to import corn on an emergency basis, as for example Argos during the Corinthian War (Xen. *Hell.* v.2.2), Thebes in 377 (Xen. *Hell.* v.4.56–7), or Phlius in 366 (Xen. *Hell.* vii.2.17–18). Where land had escaped such ravages for a long period of time this is mentioned as something unusual (Xen. *Hell.* vi.2.6, Corcyra in 373; Plut. *Ages.* 31.1–2, Laconia in 370; Diod. xvi.42.8, Cyprus in 344/3). Internal *stasis* could have the same effect, as at Abydus, where an outbreak in *c.* 360 caused the land to be uncultivated: the metics were unwilling to make any further loans to an already indebted peasantry ([Arist.] *Oec.* ii.2.18). On the high seas piracy was on the increase from the late Peloponnesian War onwards (Andoc. 1.138; Xen. *Hell.* v.1.1–13, Spartans at Aegina during the Corinthian War; Isoc. iv.115, in 380).[108] During her period of naval ascendancy Sparta made seemingly no attempt to control the problem, indeed she contributed to

103 Cf. also for later evidence Garnsey, Gallant and Rathbone 1984 (I 56).
104 Jameson in Garnsey and Whittaker 1983 (I 58) 6–16; Garnsey 1988 (I 55) part I.
105 Camp 1982 (I 20). 106 Garnsey 1988 (I 55) 154–62. 107 Hanson 1983 (K 24).
108 Garlan in Finley 1987 (I 39) 7–21; McKechnie 1989 (I 100) ch. 5.

it. The resurgent naval power of Athens after 378 sought to curb the spread of the evil, though with only partial success.[109] Piracy was not just an 'external' phenomenon, practised by individuals or peoples on the fringes of the civilized Greek world: Greek states at war employed piratical tactics against their enemies, as did the Spartans at Aegina during the Corinthian War. Also, Greek states claimed and exercised the right to 'bring to land' (*katagein*) ships passing by, especially when faced with corn shortages, to compel them to discharge their cargoes on the spot.[110] Athenian commanders at sea are even known on occasion to have extorted blackmail from maritime traders when faced with the usual problem of shortage of military funds (Dem. VIII.24–9, in 341): this despite the anxiety of Athens to safeguard the flow of maritime traffic to Athens and her occasional use of naval convoys to protect merchantmen, as in 362 and 361 ([Dem.] L.4–6, 17–23, 58–9, cf. also Dem. XVIII.73). It may be in this period – unless the 'Congress Decree' attributed to Pericles is genuine (Plut. *Per.* 17.1) – that there first developed the notion of the 'freedom of the seas', to be respected by all Greek states, a counterpart to the (no less ineffective) notion of peace among Greeks. This was first written into the Peace of Philocrates in 346 (*SdA* 329) and then again into the charter of the League of Corinth in 337 ([Dem.] XVII.19–21). The notion survived into the hellenistic period, to be championed with some success by Rhodes (Polyb. IV.47).

Athens was more dependent than any other state on foreign imports of corn from at least the time after the Persian Wars.[111] But Athens was now more vulnerable than before: the revival of her naval power in the fourth century was something of a necessity for survival (Xen. *Hell.* VI.I.11–12; Dem. XX.31), a fact sometimes forgotten by those like Isocrates who came to dream after the Social War of an Athens dissociated from the sea. Most crucial was the control of the Straits of the Hellespont, through which all the traffic from the Black Sea flowed: fear of loss of control to an enemy recurs throughout the history of classical Athens. That was how Athens lost the Peloponnesian War, and was later forced to accept the King's Peace (Xen. *Hell.* V.1.28–9).

Already in the fifth century, the food supply of Athens was one of the subjects an aspiring statesman had to be conversant with (Xen. *Mem.* III.6.13). By the late fourth century, if not earlier, it was a regular formal item on the agenda of the Athenian Assembly (Arist. *Ath. Pol.* 43.4), on the same level of importance as the defence of the territory. Athens also

---

[109] Amit 1965 (C 88) 119–21.

[110] de Ste Croix 1972 (C 68) 47, 314; Vélissaropoulos 1980 (I 144) 151–6; Garnsey 1988 (I 55) index s.v. *katagein*.

[111] Gernet 1909 (I 62); de Ste Croix 1972 (C 68) 45–9; Isager and Hansen 1975 (C 176) 11–75; Garnsey in Cartledge and Harvey 1985 (A 14) 62–75 and Garnsey 1988 (I 55) part III; cf. Millett in Cartledge, Millett and Tod 1990 (A 15) 192f on grain prices.

used her prestige, particularly with rulers on the fringes of the Greek world, in the interest of her food supply. This can be seen in her relations with the Spartocid rulers of the Crimean Bosporus. In return for honours from the Athenian state, which included Athenian citizenship, they gave Athens preferential treatment in the export of corn from the territories they controlled, and used their assets for prestige as well as for economic ends. Traders bound for Athens were exempted, perhaps since the late 390s or early 380s,[112] from the normal export-duty and provided with facilities for speedier loading (Dem. xx.29–41; Tod no. 167 = Harding 82). 'Traders bound for Athens', it will be noted, not 'Athenian traders' nor even 'traders resident in Athens'. The corn trade, as all seaborne trade in the Greek world, was international in its personnel. The bulk of the traffic was carried by Greek or non-Greek merchants from many different cities and countries.[113] No more than other Greek states did Athens have a national trade, or a merchant fleet of her own.[114] This had important consequences for Athenian policy: she had no ultimate control over foreign traders, but could only endeavour to make Athens an attractive destination for them. The need for Greek cities to attract foreign traders is a recurring theme in political literature (cf. Lys. xxii, in 386).[115] As Xenophon puts it, 'all cities always welcome those who import something' (*Hipparchicus* iv.7), and in the *De Vectigalibus* of *c.* 355 he suggested various ways of enticing back to Athens the foreign traders who were deserting her after the Social War (iii.2–5, 12–13; iv.40; v.3–4; cf. Isoc. viii.20–1 in the same context). The fear of commercial competition from outsiders was seemingly alien to the Greek world.

What legal means Athens could use to safeguard the corn supply applied largely to persons domiciled in Athens, citizens or metics, over whom she had jurisdiction. Long-distance trade by sea required financing ([Dem.] xxxiv.51–2), and this was normally met by merchants borrowing money, on the security of their ship or their cargo and at a high rate of interest (up to 30 per cent or more), which reflected the risk involved in these loans.[116] The earliest attested case of such a loan dates from 421;[117] in the fourth century it was the normal method of financing the corn trade, and was a common Greek practice, most fully attested at Athens through the speeches made in court over cases of disputed loans ([Dem.] xxxii–xxxv, lvi). The text of one contract over a maritime loan has been preserved ([Dem.] xxxv.10–13). The practice implies that

---

[112] Tuplin 1982 (E 404). [113] Reed 1981 (I 125); McKechnie 1989 (I 100) ch. 7.
[114] de Ste Croix 1972 (C 68) 393–6.
[115] Seager 1966 (C 249) and for a different interpretation of the speech Figueira 1986 (I 34).
[116] de Ste Croix 1974 (I 138); Vélissaropoulos 1980 (I 144) 301–8; Millett in Garnsey-Hopkins-Whittaker 1983 (I 57) 36–52; Mossé *ibid.* 53–63; Hansen 1984 (I 70). [117] Harvey 1976 (I 71).

traders were normally men of modest means, unable to finance long-distance journeys themselves. For those with cash to spare, maritime loans offered the possibility of a speculative investment that was considered respectable,[118] though it had a high degree of risk. The evidence from Athens shows the lenders to have included Athenians, metics and foreigners, and the lenders tended to be involved themselves in trade, or to be professional money-lenders. The extent to which bankers may have participated in commercial loans is disputed.[119] The law in Athens laid down that no one domiciled in Athens, whether a citizen or a metic, was allowed to lend money on a ship that was not commissioned to import corn to Athens ([Dem.] xxxv. 51). Further, no Athenian citizen or metic was to transport corn to any other destination than Athens ([Dem.] xxxiv. 37 and xxxv. 50; Lycurg. *Leoc.* 27). The laws are only attested in the second half of the fourth century, but may have been older. Another law may have laid down that all corn brought to Athens had to be sold there, one third at the grain market in Piraeus, and the remaining two thirds at the grain market in Athens.[120] The corn traders, or at least those over whom Athens had powers of jurisdiction, had no freedom of choice with their cargo once in Athens. On the other hand, traders had to be enticed to Athens in the first place. The most that Athens could do here was to speed up judicial procedures in the case of trials over maritime loans, to enable traders to take to the sea again with minimum delay. Such a category of suits which had to be heard within a month (or, alternatively, which were granted every month)[121] is first attested (with reference to the commercial suits, the *dikai emporikai*) in 343/2 ([Dem.] vii. 12), though it had been advocated by Xenophon (*Vect.* iii. 3) and introduced earlier, at some time after the Social War. In Athens and Piraeus the sale of corn was carefully regulated, under the supervision of the 'overseers of the mart' (*epimeletai emporiou*) and of special officials, the *sitophylakes* (Arist. *Ath.Pol.* 51. 3–4). The effectiveness of all these regulations may be doubted: much of the evidence about the laws comes from cases of their infringement. In any case, Athens could not control by law more than part of the process of importing corn: like many other Greek states, she remained at the mercy of outside conditions beyond her control, and if anything circumstances were to deteriorate even further in the hellenistic period.

[118] Millett 1990 (I 107).

[119] See on one side Davies 1981 (C 126) 60–2; Millett in Garnsey-Hopkins-Whittaker 1983 (I 57) 36–52; Bogaert 1986 (I 11) 27–9, 47–9, and on the other Cohen 1990 (I 25).

[120] Gauthier 1981 (I 59) though see the qualification in Garnsey 1988 (I 55) 140f.

[121] Cohen 1973 (C 120) 9–59 for this view, cf. Rhodes 1981 (B 94) 583f.

An analysis of the Greek polis in the fourth century, from whatever angle, political, military, social, economic, or financial, must read like a catalogue of shortcomings and failures. In retrospect the rise of Macedon and of the hellenistic monarchies after Alexander looks like a historical inevitability. The fourth century has often been seen as marking the 'crisis' or the 'decline' of the polis,[122] and the battle of Chaeronea as signalling its 'end'. According to one view, the polis was an evolutionary dead-end that was doomed to extinction.[123] The inability of the Greek world to devise a viable system of interstate relations is patent, as is the failure to translate growing aspirations for peace into practice. Yet though the difficulties of the polis were well known to contemporaries, no Greek drew the conclusion that its history was therefore at an end, least of all Aristotle, for all his activity at the court of Macedon as tutor of Alexander. Whatever the many weaknesses in practice of the polis, it remained a potent model. The search for larger and more viable polis units is an unmistakable trend from the Peloponnesian War onwards,[124] illustrated by the growth of Olynthus in Chalcidice (Xen. *Hell.* v.2.11–19), the *synoikismos* of Rhodes in 411–407, destined to a great future in the hellenistic age (Diod. XIII.75.1), or that of Cos in 366 (Diod. xv.76.2).[125] In the Peloponnese, the defeat of Sparta at Leuctra in 371 had as consequence, among others, a new impetus towards the creation of larger political entities, long held in check by Sparta. Mantinea, split up by Sparta after the King's Peace (Xen. *Hell.* v.2.7), reconstructed herself as a town (Xen. *Hell.* VI.5.3–5),[126] the Arcadians founded their new federal capital of Megalopolis (Diod. xv.72.4 and 94.1–3),[127] and Messene emerged as a new political entity (Diod. xv.66). Cities that had been destroyed in war sometimes sprang back into life, and their inhabitants returned after an absence of many years, tenacious of their identity despite the lapse of time.[128] Thus in 404 Sparta restored Aegina, Melos, and Scione to their original inhabitants (Xen. *Hell.* II.2.9; Plut. *Lys.* 14). Plataea, destroyed by Thebes in 427 (Thuc. III.68.3), was rebuilt by Sparta in 382 (Paus. IX.1.4), destroyed again in 373/2 (Diod. xv.46.4–6; Paus. IX.1.8), then restored once more in 336 by Alexander[129] together with Orchomenus and Thespiae, also destroyed by the Thebans a generation earlier (Arr. *Anab.* 1.9.9–10). In Sicily, despite two generations of tyranny, many wars and the destruction of several cities, there

---

[122] Welskopf (1974) (c 83) is an example.
[123] Runciman in Murray and Price 1990 (c 52) 347–67.   [124] Moggi 1976 (c 48).
[125] Sherwin-White 1978 (c 381) 43–81.   [126] Hodkinson 1981 (c 364).
[127] Hornblower 1990 (c 366).   [128] McKechnie 1989 (i 100) ch. 3.
[129] Martin 1940 (c 45) 322–4.

was a significant revival of the cities in the 330s when Timoleon resettled the island, partly with fresh settlers from outside Sicily, but partly also from the former inhabitants of the destroyed cities (Diod. xvi.82–3; Plut. *Tim.* 22–3, 35).[130] Furthermore, whatever the problems in the political effectiveness of the Greek city, it provided a model for the spread of urbanization, as in Caria under Mausolus,[131] or in Macedon in the reign of Philip.[132] Isocrates' conquest plans for Asia were meant to lead to the foundation of new Greek cities there, 'as a bulwark of Greece' (iv.34–5, 99; v.119–23). From the very difficulties of the Greek world a new though very different chapter in the history of the Greek city was to spring with the hellenistic foundations in the east.

[130] Talbert 1974 (G 304) 146–60.   [131] Hornblower 1982 (F 644) 79–105.
[132] Hammond and Griffith 1979 (D 50) 657–62.

CHAPTER 11

THE POLIS AND THE ALTERNATIVES

P. J. RHODES

I. FOURTH-CENTURY ATHENS: THE MACHINERY OF GOVERNMENT

Formally, Athens had the same constitution from the tribal reorganization of Cleisthenes in 508/7, or at any rate from the reform of the Areopagus by Ephialtes in 462/1, until the suppression of the democracy by Antipater at the end of 322/1: the oligarchies of 411–410 and 404/3 were brief interruptions, each ending with the restoration of the democracy. The working of this democracy in the time of Pericles has been described in the previous volume.[1] Decisions, on both domestic and external matters, were taken by an assembly of adult male citizens, which by the end of the fifth century had forty regular meetings a year: all topics on which the Assembly pronounced had first to be discussed by the Council of 500, and there were other safeguards by which the Assembly was limited, but any member could propose motions or amendments, or speak in the debate, and decisions were taken by a simple majority. It was not possible for all the citizens to be involved simultaneously in carrying out decisions, as they were all involved simultaneously in making them, but it was possible for them all to be involved in turn. The administration of the democracy was based on a large number of separate boards, usually comprising one man from each of the ten tribes, appointed by lot for one year and not eligible for reappointment to the same board; the scope for competence or incompetence was slight, and the conscientious citizen would serve on several of these boards in the course of his life. (In theory there were property qualifications for office, and members of the lowest class were not eligible for membership of the Council or any office, but by the second half of the fourth century these were ignored: *Ath. Pol.* 7.3–8.1, 47.1.) The Council of 500, likewise appointed by lot for one year (but to obtain enough members two years of service were allowed),[2] supervised the

---

[1] *CAH* v[2] 77–87.

[2] Possibly in the time of Pericles men were allowed to serve once only, in the Peloponnesian War this rule could not be maintained, and the limit of two years was set in the fourth century: Rhodes 1980 (C 227).

565

activities of the separate boards. Some appointments were more demanding than others, but all assumed that the citizen had leisure to devote to the service of the state: payments were made to the holders of civilian offices to compensate them for loss of earnings,[3] but it will still have been easier for a rich man than for one who had to work for his living to arrange his affairs so that he could play an active part in public life. Military appointments, unlike civilian, the Athenians did think should go to the best man for the job: the ten generals, and the officers under them, were elected by the Assembly and could be reelected as often as the Assembly wished.

In the law-courts as in administration the involvement of the citizens counted for more than expertise. There were no regular public prosecutors (though the Council or Assembly could appoint prosecutors on particular occasions), and no legal experts:[4] prosecution was left to the injured party on 'private' charges, to *ho boulomenos* (whoever wished) on 'public', and the litigants were expected to conduct their own cases. Private suits in which the sum at issue was not more than 10 drachmae were decided by the travelling *dikastai kata demous* (deme justices), for whom this was simply one appointment in the public service; most other suits went to jury-courts (*dikasteria*), in which an allotted official presided and the verdict was decided, without expert guidance, by the majority vote of a jury of some hundreds. The city state (polis) was the community of citizens (*politai*), and it was inconceivable that the citizens might need to be protected against the activities of the state; indeed, the state had little power to enforce its will, however justly, against a recalcitrant individual. The Athenians did not make the law-courts independent of the other organs of state, but gave their executive officials judicial powers to reinforce their administrative powers.

By no means all who lived in Athens and Attica were Athenian citizens. Only those whose parents were both citizens were entitled to citizenship:[5] in Periclean Athens, out of a total population of about 300,000, about 45,000 were adult male citizens and slightly over 100,000 were the wives or children of citizens; of the remainder, somewhat under 50,000 were metics, free men and women who had come to Athens as

---

[3] It is argued by Hansen 1971–80 (C 151) that far fewer offices were paid in the fourth century than in the fifth; the reply of Gabrielsen 1981 (C 141) is laboured but I believe correct; see however Lewis 1982 (C 185).

[4] There were professional speechwriters, and Isaeus (active in the first half of the fourth century), who specialized in inheritance cases, comes closest to being a legal expert. On speechwriters and their clients see Dover 1968 (B 35).

[5] Pericles' law of 45 1/0, limiting citizenship to those with citizen fathers and citizen mothers, was annulled or ignored towards the end of the Peloponnesian War but re-enacted after the war (Dem. LVII.30, Eumelus *FGrH* 77 F 2, Carystius fr. 11 Müller), and in the fourth century it was made an offence for an Athenian of either sex to marry a non-Athenian ([Dem.] LIX.16, cf. 52).

long-term visitors or permanent residents, and somewhat over 100,000 were slaves. The Peloponnesian War brought severe losses, and after it fewer foreigners came to Athens: *c.* 360 the population was perhaps 210,000, divided into 29,000 citizens, 71,000 citizen wives and children, 35,000 metics and 75,000 slaves.[6] Towards the end of the fifth century there was talk in intellectual circles of the artificiality of all human conventions, including these distinctions of status, but the distinctions were upheld by Plato and Aristotle in the fourth century and were never seriously challenged;[7] in Athens a proposal to reward with citizenship all non-citizens who had assisted the restoration of the democracy in 403 was ruled out of order.[8] Slaves were almost unrestrictedly at the mercy of their masters; metics unless specially privileged were taxed, more heavily than the citizens, were required to serve in the army if rich enough to qualify, were not allowed to own land or houses in Athenian territory, their rights at law were limited, and they were excluded from the Assembly and all public offices.

In the fourth century, while the basic framework remained unaltered, there were various changes within it.[9] The oligarchic revolutions of the late fifth century had drawn attention to the difficulty of discovering what the law was when decrees of the Assembly had accumulated for nearly 200 years since the legislation of Solon. The compilation of a revised code was begun in 410 and completed in 399;[10] and thereafter *nomoi* (laws), the contents of this code, and modifications of it made by a special procedure in which the last word lay not with the Assembly but with a body of *nomothetai* (legislators), were to be distinguished from *psephismata* (decrees), voted by the Council and Assembly as in the fifth century. According to the theorists, *nomoi* were to be permanent and of general application, while *psephismata* were to be subsidiary and particular: most Athenian enactments fit the theory, but there is one major exception, that all decisions in foreign affairs, even alliances which were intended to be permanent, were made by *psephisma*. In general, though we know a few *nomoi* enacted during the fourth century, *psephismata* are

---

[6] Based on Ehrenberg 1969 (c 19) 31. Higher figures for Periclean Athens are contemplated by Hansen 1981 (c 159) and 1982 (c 161), Rhodes 1988 (b 95) 271–6. Crucial to the fourth century is the question whether the number of citizens before the poorest were disfranchised in 321 was 31,000 (Diod. xviii.18.4–5) or 21,000 (Plut. *Phoc.* 28.7); the lower figure has been championed by Ruschenbusch 1979 (c 234) 133–52, the higher, more persuasively, by Hansen 1986 (c 165).

[7] All men naturally equal: Antiphon Soph. 87 b 44, lines 266–99 D–K, cf. Eur. *Ion* 854–6; some men natural slaves: Arist. *Pol.* 1 1254a17–24.   [8] *Ath. Pol.* 40.2.

[9] For a more detailed survey of the fourth-century constitution see Rhodes 1979/80 (c 226).

[10] Cf. *CAH* v² 484–5. See especially Lys. xxx, Andoc. 1.81–7, *IG* i³ 104–5 (stelae republishing old laws); Dow 1961 (c 131) (with references to fragments in *IG* i²/ii² and *Hesp.*: the pre-403 fragments are re-edited as *IG* i³ 236–41, the post-403 are all from Athens' religious calendar); Fingarette 1971 (c 135); Clinton 1982 (c 115); Robertson 1990 (c 232); Rhodes 1991 (c 230).

far more numerous.[11] By the end of the fifth century citizens could be paid for holding various civilian offices, but not for attending the Assembly: various devices were tried to increase attendance, and in 411 the oligarchs who proposed to reduce the citizen body to 5,000 alleged that (owing to the war) attendance was never as much as 5,000 (Thuc. VIII.72.1); soon after the democratic restoration of 403 payment was introduced – not for all who attended but for the first so many to arrive or for those who arrived by a certain time – and it appears that, in spite of the reduced numbers of citizens after the Peloponnesian War, attendance was somewhat better in the fourth century than in the fifth.[12]

Two organizational changes were made during the first half of the century. Perhaps after the late 390s, but before 379/8, the duty of presiding at meetings of the council and assembly was taken away from the *prytaneis*, the fifty councillors from one tribe who acted as the council's standing committee for one tenth of the year, and given to a new board of nine *proedroi* ('presidents'), one councillor picked by lot from each tribe except the current prytany, for a single day.[13] Earlier the chief secretary of the state, who kept records of the meetings of the Council and Assembly and was responsible for the publication of documents, was a member of the Council, elected (unusually), from a tribe other than the current prytany, to serve for one prytany: between 368/7 and 363/2 the post was detached from membership of the Council, and thereafter the appointment was made by lot for a whole year, with a ban on repetition.[14] Probably the purpose of the first change was to share out the work of the councillors a little more evenly, and the second was intended as a small step in the direction of continuity and efficiency.

Fifth-century finance had been based on a central state treasury; revenue was collected and paid into it by the *apodektai* ('receivers'); payments from it were made by ten *kolakretai* (literally, 'ham-collectors'), and had to be authorized, as single or recurrent items, by the Assembly. During the Peloponnesian War the *kolakretai* were abolished,[15] and soon after the beginning of the fourth century the central treasury was abolished: instead the *apodektai* made a *merismos* ('allocation') of the revenue to separate spending authorities.[16] It was

---

[11] On the fourth-century procedure for the enactment of *nomoi* see MacDowell 1975 (C 193); Hansen 1971–80 (C 150); Rhodes 1985 (C 228); Hansen 1985 (C 164); on *nomoi* and *psephismata*, Hansen 1978 (C 155) and 1979 (C 156).

[12] Payment: *Ath. Pol.* 41.3 with Ar. *Eccl.* 184–8, 293, 380–90, etc., *Ath. Pol.* 62.2; attendance in the fourth century: Hansen 1976 (C 154).

[13] *Ath. Pol.* 44.2–3 describes the new system. On the change: Rhodes 1972 (C 224) 21, 25–8; new *terminus ante quem*: Pritchett 1972 (B 167) 164–9 no. 2.

[14] *Ath. Pol.* 54.3; date: *IG* II² 104–7 (= Tod 134, 136 (Harding 52), 135, 131 (Harding 53): 368/7), against 110–11 (= Tod 143, 142 (Harding 55): 363/2); discussion: Rhodes 1972 (C 224) 134–8.

[15] Cf. *CAH* v² 485.

[16] *IG* II² 29 (= Tod no. 116). 18–22 (387/6), *Ath. Pol.* 48.2; cf. Rhodes 1972 (C 224) 98–105.

obviously sensible for the state to decide in advance how much it could afford to spend for different purposes, but when the state was short of money, as it was in the first half of the fourth century (after Attica had been devastated in the Peloponnesian War and the fifth-century empire had been lost), there were disadvantages in having a rigidly predetermined budget with what money there was scattered between different treasuries. At some time in the first half of the century an army fund (*to stratiotikon*) was created, with an elected treasurer, as one of these separate treasuries, and it was provided that when Athens was at war any surplus revenue not otherwise allocated should go to that fund. Probably in the mid 350s another fund with an elected treasurer was created, the theoric fund (*to theorikon*), and surplus revenue was diverted to this: the fund's ostensible purpose was to make payments to the citizens to cover the cost of theatre tickets at major festivals, but Aeschines claims that in the time of Eubulus (one of the creators of the fund) its treasurers 'controlled the office of the *antigrapheus* [a revenue clerk, about whom little is known], controlled that of the *apodektai*, controlled that of the dockyards, built the arsenal, were roadbuilders, and had in their hands almost the whole administration of the city' (III. *In Ctes.* 25). By increasing Athens' revenues and dissuading the Assembly from expensive but unrewarding military ventures Eubulus was able to attract to the theoric fund far more money than was needed for its original purpose and to make this money available for other purposes; also there seems to have been a constitutional change, by which the treasurer of this fund (a single official, elected and capable of being re-elected) was enabled to join with the Council in the supervision of the old financial committees, and so to gain knowledge of what was happening in every department of Athenian finance. Towards the end of the 340s political supremacy passed from Eubulus and his associates, who had aimed at financial recovery and caution in military matters, to Demosthenes and his associates, who wanted to resist Philip of Macedon whatever the cost; perhaps in 340, surplus revenue was diverted to the army fund again (Philoch., *FGrH* 328 F 56a), and in 337/6 Demosthenes himself was treasurer of the theoric fund (Aeschin. III. *In Ctes.* 24). Soon after that, modifications were made by a law of Hegemon (Aeschin. III. *In Ctes.* 25): thereafter the fund was controlled by a board (probably of ten, but still elected); tenure of that or any similar office was limited to four years, and the theoric board shared with the (still single) treasurer of the army fund its involvement in the supervision of the old financial boards. However, a new treasurer appeared to take the place of the old theoric treasurer, under the title *epi tei dioikesei* ('in charge of administration'): during the reign of Alexander this post was held by Lycurgus and his friends, and under the different regimes of hellenistic Athens the single man or the board *epi tei dioikesei* and the treasurer of the army fund were to be the state's most important financial officials.[17]

The ten generals (*strategoi*) were elected by the assembly, originally one from each tribe. By the time of Pericles, though the tribal basis was retained in principle, exceptions were allowed (probably if, on the first vote, none of the candidates in a tribe secured a majority);[18] later, probably in the third quarter of the fourth century, the tribal basis was abandoned and the generals were elected irrespective of their tribal membership.[19] In the time of Cimon and Pericles the generals had been political leaders as well as military commanders, but the split between political leadership and public office which began during the Peloponnesian War continued in the fourth century, and several of the fourth-century generals went abroad to fight as mercenary commanders when their services were not required by Athens. Within the board of generals regular responsibilities began to be defined: at the end of the 350s we encounter the *strategos epi ten choran* ('. . . in charge of the territory'), responsible for the defence of Attica (*IG* ii² 204 = Harding no. 78A, 19–20, Philoch., *FGrH* 328 F 155), and the post *epi ta hopla* ('in charge of the heavy arms'), to command on campaigns outside Attica, was presumably created at the same time; in the time of *Ath. Pol.* (61.1) there were in addition two generals responsible for the Piraeus and one for the trierarchic organization, the other five remaining free for *ad hoc* assignments; and by the end of the third century there were regular postings for all ten generals.[20]

At the beginning of the fourth century the system for the trial of private lawsuits was reorganized. The *dikastai kata demous* had presum-

[17] Cf. Rhodes 1972 (C 224) 105–8, 235–40. The treasurer of the army fund is first mentioned in *IG* ii² 1443. 12–13 (344/3), and Glotz 1932 (C 143) argued that the fund was then a recent creation; *contra*, Cawkwell 1962 (C 104). On the creation of the theoric fund the sources, mostly entries in lexica and scholia, are divided between Pericles (accepted by Pickard-Cambridge 1968 (H 94) 266–7), Agyrrhius (championed by Buchanan 1962 (C 97) 48–53) and Diophantus and Eubulus (supported by van Ooteghem 1932 (C 211); Ruschenbusch 1979 (C 235)); the silence of Aristophanes tells against the earlier attributions. On the theoric treasurers after Hegemon's law: *Ath. Pol.* 43.1, 47.2; on Lycurgus and the office *epi tei dioikesei* (not mentioned in *Ath. Pol.*): Hyp. fr. 139 Sauppe = 118 Kenyon, Dem. *Ep.* III.2, [Plut.] *X Or.* 841b–c (cf. decree ap. 852b), Diod. XVI.88.1, Dion. Hal. *Din.* 11, *SEG* xix 119.   [18] Cf. *CAH* v² 85–7.

[19] *Ath. Pol.* 61.1. It used to be thought that four of the six known generals of 323/2 were from one tribe (Sundwall 1906 (C 260) 23–4), but later prosopographical work has reduced them to two (Develin 1989 (C 127) 408; I count his 'nauarchos' as a general). The change is probably later than 357/6 (the eight known are from seven different tribes: *IG* ii² 124 (= Tod no. 153 = Harding no. 65). 19–23; it is possible that Chares should not be restored in that list but that Chabrias was accidentally inserted twice and therefore deleted once (Cawkwell 1962 (C 15) 38 n. 23), but Chares was in any case general (Dem. xxiii.173)).

[20] Hammond 1969 (C 149) 116 with n. 1 (= 1973 (A 28) 353–4 with 354 n. 1) dates the creation of the first two posts to the 470s and seeks fifth-century support in a variant reading in Lys. xxxii.5, but there is no other evidence for such titles before the late 350s. On the postings of the generals in hellenistic Athens see Ferguson 1909 (B 139) 314–23.

ably ceased to visit the demes during the last phase of the Peloponnesian War, when the Attic countryside was in Spartan hands, and the oligarchy of 404/3 made thirty an inauspicious number: in the fourth century their number was increased to forty, and they continued to work in Athens (*Ath. Pol.* 53.1). They were authorized to decide suits in which the sum at issue was not more than 10 drachmae. From 399, citizens of hoplite class and above were required to spend the last of their forty-two years of availability for military service, the year in which their sixtieth birthday fell, as arbitrators (*diaitetai*): private suits for more than 10 drachmae were referred through the Forty to an arbitrator, and came to a *dikasterion* only if one of the litigants appealed against his decision (*Ath. Pol.* 53.2–6).[21] The use of these men as arbitrators reflects the view that in domestic matters, including judicial matters, expertise was unnecessary; the purpose of the institution was probably to reduce the state's expenditure on jurors' stipends. To increase the revenues of Athens, Eubulus tried to attract larger numbers of foreign traders, and one method used was the creation of special commercial lawsuits (*dikai emporikai*), with a stream-lined procedure and monthly opportunities for initiating cases.[22] These were suits concerning overseas trade and arising from a written contract, and an unusual feature of them was that they ignored the normal status distinctions between citizens, metics and slaves, and were open to all men on equal terms.

In the *dikasteria* the principal changes had the object of making each jury a fair, random and unpredictable sample of the men registered as jurors. In the fifth century the men who volunteered were divided into ten sections each year, and each section was assigned to a particular court for the whole year (for major cases two or more sections were combined). Not every juror would attend every time his section was needed, but with that qualification litigants would know in advance who were to be the jurors in their case; it is surprising that what is said to be the first instance of a jury's being bribed should be as late as 409.[23] Early in the fourth century, sections were allotted to courts separately each day.[24] From about the 370s the jurors of each tribe were divided into ten sections, and by an elaborate procedure involving jurors' tickets (*pinakia*) and allotment-machines (*kleroteria*) juries were formed each day

[21] Date: MacDowell 1971 (C 192). *Ath. Pol.* 42, 53, implies that all citizens served as *epheboi* in the first two and arbitrators in the last of the forty-two years after coming of age, but see Gomme 1933 (C 144) 11; Rhodes 1980 (C 227) 191–4; *contra*, Pélékidis 1962 (C 215) 133–4; Ruschenbusch 1979 (C 236) and 1981 (C 238).
[22] Cf. Cohen 1973 (C 120). His views have been challenged by Hansen 1981 (C 160).
[23] *Ath. Pol.* 27.5, Diod. XIII.64.6, Plut. *Coriol.* 14.6. On fifth-century juries see Ar. *Vesp.* 303–6, 1107–9, with Harrison 1968–71 (C 172) II 239–40.
[24] Ar. *Eccl.* 681–6, *Plut.* 277, 972, with Harrison 1968–71 (C 172) II 240–1.

in such a way that an equal number served from each of the 100 sections, and an equal number from each tribe served on each jury.[25]

The council of the Areopagus, whose judicial competence had been limited in 462/1 to homicide and a few other charges,[26] was at any rate discussed *c*.400,[27] and enjoyed a resurgence in the time of Demosthenes. Isocrates in his *Areopagitic* praised the Good Old Days when the Areopagus had been an influential body; a decree of Demosthenes enhanced the Areopagus' judicial powers (Din. 1. *In Dem.* 62–3), and after Chaeronea it tried men charged with cowardice or treason (Lycurg. *Leoc.* 52–4, Aeschin. 111. *In Ctes.* 252); it intervened in political matters, to reopen questions decided by the Assembly (Dem. xviii. *De Cor.* 134–6); after some major offences it was commissioned by the Assembly to hold an enquiry, and reported in an *apophasis* ('declaration'), after which the Assembly decided whether to order a trial in a *dikasterion*.[28] Demosthenes' opponents accused him of being undemocratic, and were sufficiently alarmed to pass a law, in 337/6, which threatened the Areopagus with suspension if the democracy were overthrown (*SEG* xii 87 = Harding no. 101); but the Areopagus retained its enhanced position, and in 323, though Demosthenes was responsible for its being entrusted with the inquiry, it declared him guilty of taking some of the money brought to Athens by Harpalus.[29]

The distinction between *nomoi* and *psephismata* shows the influence of contemporary philosophy; it did not in practice detract very much from the Assembly's sovereign right of decision-making. Other changes made at the beginning of the century were true to the spirit of fifth-century democracy: payment for attending the Assembly; the use of men in their last year on the military registers as arbitrators; the new board of *proedroi* which presided in the Council and Assembly; the elaborately random system for making up juries. Later changes are less consonant with that kind of democracy: the powerful positions enjoyed by the treasurers of the theoric fund and *epi tei dioikesei* are the most striking instances, but in other matters too specialization and expertise came to be more highly valued. It became respectable to talk of the defects of extreme democracy. The democratic machinery continued to work, and, in a city which had bitter memories of the oligarchies of 411–410 and 404/3, no politician would admit to being an opponent of democracy, but there was not the same enthusiasm for democratic principles as in the second half of the fifth century.[30]

---

[25] *Ath. Pol.* 63–6; on the *kleroteria*: Dow 1939 (c 128); on the *pinakia*: Kroll 1972 (c 184).

[26] Cf. *CAH* v² 67–74.

[27] Cf. Lys, fr. 178 Sauppe ap. Harp. ἐπιθέτους ἑορτάς, decree ap. Andoc. 1.84. A later date for this fragment is suggested by Sealey 1991 (c 256).

[28] Cf. Harrison 1968–71 (c 172) 11 105; Hansen 1975 (c 153) 39–40.   [29] Cf. p. 858.

[30] For a study which stresses the continuity between the fifth-century and the fourth-century democracy see Bleicken 1987 (c 95).

II. FOURTH-CENTURY ATHENS: THE ANATOMY OF POLITICS

Until the death of Pericles the leading politicians of Athens had held the leading offices of state: originally the archonship, followed by life membership of the Areopagus; in the middle of the fifth century the generalship, to which they could be re-elected indefinitely. In the late fifth century the sophists taught the arts of argument and oratory as those particularly needed for political success, and so there appeared the politician as *demagogos* (literally, 'people-leader') or *rhetor* ('speaker'). While the generals became military specialists, willing to fight either for Athens or for a foreign employer (cf. above), the new politicians were men who regularly spoke in the Assembly, and persuaded the citizens to vote for their proposals, but did not regularly hold public office (cf. Isoc. VIII. *De Pace.* 54–5).[31] Callistratus was general in 378/7, 373/2 and 372/1, but he was influential as a politician throughout the 370s and 360s without holding office continuously; we tend to think of the partnership of Chares the general and Callistratus the politician.[32] Demosthenes served on various embassies from 346 onwards; he was a member of the Council in 347/6 (e.g. Dem. XIX. *FL* 154, 234); but otherwise he did not hold any regular office in Athens until 337/6, when he was theoric treasurer and member of an *ad hoc* board in charge of repairs to the city walls (e.g. Aeschin. III. *In Ctes.* 24, 31). Phocion, we read, wanted to return to the older habit of combining military and political leadership (Plut. *Phoc.* 7. 5–6): he was general forty-five times (8.2), but although he played some part in politics and his sympathies were clearly with Demosthenes' opponents he was not for most of his career a politician of the first rank, while like other generals he was not above mercenary service (Diod. XVI.42.7–9).[33] On the other hand, the new financial offices did tend to be held by leading politicians: Eubulus was theoric treasurer; Demosthenes was theoric treasurer in 337/6; Lycurgus was *epi tei dioikesei*; Demades is not known to have held any regular office except treasurer of the army fund.[34] Embassies again, which involved not routine administration but negotiation with other states, regularly attracted the leading politicians.

Not many of the fourth-century politicians were, like Lycurgus (an *Eteoboutades*), members of the old aristocracy, but most were from rich backgrounds, and Aeschines and Demades were unusual in their humble origins.[35] Wealth not only enabled politicians to devote much of their

---

[31] Roberts 1982 (C 231) protests that the great majority of the new-style politicians are known to have held some office; but what is significant is that they did not constantly hold some major office as Cimon and Pericles had done.

[32] For such collaboration cf. Dem. XIII.20 (with II.29), [Dem.] XII.19, Aeschin. III.7; also Isoc. XV.136.   [33] On Phocion see Tritle 1988 (C 261).

[34] *IG* II² 1493–1495 with Mitchel 1962 (C 202) (*SEG* XXI 552).

[35] Cf. Davies 1971 (C 124) 544–7, 100–1.

time to political activity, but also gave them the opportunity for self-advertisement in the lavish performance of the public services known as liturgies,[36] and in subscribing money when voluntary contributions were invited; Demosthenes reproached Aeschines with never having spent his money in the public interest (XVIII. *De Cor.* 311–13).

The Athenians did not attempt to make their judiciary independent of the other organs of state (cf. above), or to distinguish carefully between unlawful conduct and other failings in their political and military leaders. A general who did not achieve the success which had been expected of him, or a politician on whose recommendation the Assembly adopted a policy which led to disaster, might be charged with taking bribes to betray the interests of Athens;[37] opponents of a measure adopted as a *psephisma* by the Assembly or a *nomos* by the *nomothetai* might attack the measure and its author in a *graphe paranomon* ('public suit for illegality') or ... *nomon me epitedeion theinai* ('... for enacting an inexpedient law');[38] and the amateur *dikasteria* of Athens, despite an undertaking in the jurors' oath (Dem. XXIV. *Tim.* 151), did not confine their attention to the offences alleged but in general terms pronounced on the public figures brought before them. The century of the Attic orators (*c.* 420–320) is rich in political trials.[39] Aristophon claimed that he had been acquitted seventy-five times in *graphai paranomon* (Aeschin. III. *In Ctes.* 194); Demades, when war against Macedon broke out at Alexander's death,[40] was politically neutralized by incurring *atimia* (loss of civic rights) for three convictions in *graphai paranomon*.[41] Politics could be brought into charges other than the overtly political, and the leading politicians of fourth-century Athens took one another to court again and again.

Public officials had to undergo a scrutiny (*dokimasia*) before entering office (*Ath. Pol.* 55.2); in each of the ten prytanies of the year they had to present interim accounts (48.3) and face a vote of confidence (43.4, cf. 61.2, 4); on leaving office they had to present final accounts of their handling of public money (*logos*: 54.2), and to submit to a more general examination of their conduct in office (*euthynai*, literally 'straightening': 48.4–5). In spite of such charges as *paranomon*, which was available against any proposer of a *psephisma*, the new kind of politician, whose position did not depend on his holding any office, was felt to be elusive, and attempts were made to bring these men explicitly within the scope of

[36] Cf. *CAH* v² 84.

[37] Presents were common, and there is no separate Greek word for 'bribe'; cf. Lewis 1989 (C 42). On accusations of bribery see Perlman 1976 (C 221).

[38] The first was used against *psephismata* and the second against *nomoi*, whether they were charged with being illegal or inexpedient: Hansen 1978 (C 155) 325–9.

[39] Cf. Mossé 1974 (C 209); Cloché 1960 (C 118) effectively disproves what he set out to prove.

[40] Cf. p. 859.

[41] Diod. XVIII.18.1–2 (with the correct figure), cf. Plut. *Phoc.* 26.3, *Suda* (Δ 415) Δημάδης.

the law. In the consolidated *nomos eisangeltikos* ('law of impeachment') of the code completed in 399, the first two kinds of offence were defined 'If any one overthrows the democracy of the Athenians . . .', 'Or if any one betrays any city . . .', but the third clause reads 'Or, being a *rhetor*, does not speak what is best for the Athenian people, and takes money and gifts from those working against the people'.[42] Hyperides comments that the first two clauses concern offences which any one might commit, but the third is rightly directed against *rhetores*, 'with whom lies the proposing of *psephismata*; for you would have been mad if you had enacted the law in any other way than this, if the *rhetores* were to enjoy the honours and advantages from speaking but you had subjected the ordinary citizens (*idiotai*) to the risks on their behalf' (IV. *Eux.* 8–9). Similarly Aeschines ends his speech *Against Timarchus*, charged under a law which forbade those who had prostituted themselves to address the Assembly, 'For the law investigates not private citizens (*tous idioteuontas*) but politicians (*tous politeuomenous*)' (I. *In Tim.* 195). Timarchus' prostitution disqualified him from holding any public office (19–20),[43] and was included in a list of disqualifications headed *dokimasia rhetoron* ('scrutiny of speakers'), with the provision that any citizen who wished might prosecute a man who spoke in the Assembly when disqualified (27–32). *Rhetorike graphe* ('public suit concerning speakers'), found in the lexica but not in contemporary texts, may be another name for this *dokimasia*.[44] It appears from Aeschines that the *dokimasia* could be applied to any one who made a speech, even on a single occasion (ἐάν τις λέγῃ . . . , 'if any one speaks . . .': 28); but the term *rhetor* seems particularly to have been used of the proposers of decrees,[45] and if a man who was not a regular politician was challenged he might well claim that he was not a *rhetor* and the laws did not apply to him (cf. Hyp. IV. *Eux.* 30).

Thus the possibility of *dokimasia* on grounds of character or prosecution for conduct as a *rhetor* assimilated the politicians to the office-holders. In Aeschines' prosecution of Ctesiphon for his proposal to honour Demosthenes, launched in 336 and finally brought to court in 330, the principal charge was that Ctesiphon was making a false statement in a public document, by claiming that Demosthenes 'continually said and did what was best for the people' (Aeschin. III. *In Ctes.*

[42] Hyp. IV. 7–8, cf. Poll. VIII. 52, *Lex. Rhet. Cant.* εἰσαγγελία, both putting the clause against *rhetores* first.

[43] In spite of this he had twice served in the Council (§109, 80): the lack of public prosecutors meant that the law was enforced only when someone wished to enforce it.

[44] Harp. ῥητορικὴ γραφή, *Lex. Rhet. Cant.* ῥητορική, *Lexica Segueriana* (Bekker, *Anecd. Graeca* I 299, line 24). Identified with *graphe paranomon*, Hansen 1974 (C 152) 25; with *dokimasia rhetoron*, Rhodes 1981 (B 94) 660 n. 53.

[45] The word is used with this meaning in its first appearance, M–L no. 49 = *IG* I³ 46. 21 (*c.* 445), and this meaning may have been intended in the *nomos eisangeltikos*.

49). Demosthenes in the course of his reply insisted that as a *rhetor* he
could not be held solely responsible for the fate of Athens: not for the
courage of the soldiers or the fortunes of the opposing armies or the
generalship, but for foreseeing coming events, warning the citizens,
combating the slowness inherent in a city state, arousing patriotic
enthusiasm and rejecting Philip's bribes (XVIII. *De Cor.* 244–7).

Scholars are no longer tempted to suppose that the Greek city states
contained political parties like those of the modern world, groups of
citizens who have a common political viewpoint and who agree to co-
operate in the pursuit of a political programme, in particular by
sponsoring for election to decision-making bodies candidates who are
pledged to support that programme. In democratic Athens, as we have
seen, the major decision-making body was not a council of representatives but an assembly in which both voting and more active participation
were open to all citizens, and most appointments were made by lot in
such a way that all loyal citizens should take their turn in working for the
state. Since these allotted appointments were numerous and of short
duration, it is unlikely that there was strong competition for many of
them,[46] and the chief conclusions to be drawn from a man's holding a
particular post in a particular year are that he was willing to do so, and
was not disqualified by previous service. In the Council, when brothers
serve together, or father and son serve together, or several men who
have served together once do so again, we may assume that they chose to
do so and their fellow-demesmen did not stand in their way. When we
find Hyperbolus serving in 421/0, the year after Cleon's death (*IG* I³ 82, 5
with 42), and Demosthenes serving in 347/6, the year of the Peace of
Philocrates, (cf. p. 752), we may guess that they had chosen these as
particularly opportune years in which to serve.[47]

Appointment to elective posts must be interpreted with care. In the
case of generals, their competence as commanders must have been a
major consideration, especially in the fourth century when they were not
the leading political figures they had been in the fifth; but Athenian
voters could not be forced to close their minds to other considerations. It
might seem paradoxical to appoint a man to carry out a policy of which
he was known to disapprove: yet Nicias had been made one of the
commanders of the Sicilian expedition of 415, apparently to counter the
zeal of Alcibiades;[48] Phocion, who was not a supporter of Demosthenes,
was general each year from 341/0 to 338/7 (but was not at Chaeronea);
Chares was general in the early 340s, when Demosthenes' policies were
not in favour, but also in the late 340s and the early 330s, when they were

[46] But *Ath. Pol.* 62.1 shows that some men were eager to obtain some posts; and cf. pp. 577–8.
[47] Cf. Rhodes 1972 (C 224) 3–4 and 1980 (C 227) 193 n. 10, 197–201.
[48] Cf. *CAH* v² 446–7.

(and he was at Chaeronea). While the tribal basis of appointment was retained (cf. above) there may have been few good candidates for some tribes' posts. Similarly with embassies it would have been sensible to appoint men who agreed on the desired result, but this did not always happen. The embassy sent to arrange a *rapprochement* with Sparta in 372/1 included Callias, the *proxenos* of Sparta, and Callistratus, who favoured *rapprochement*, but also Autocles, who did not (Xen. *Hell*. VI.3.1–17);[49] Demosthenes was notoriously at odds with his colleagues on the embassies to Philip in 346;[50] after Chaeronea Aeschines, Demades and Phocion were sent to Philip, and Demades negotiated with Alexander in 336 and again in 335, but Demosthenes also was elected in 336 – though he found himself unable to face Alexander (Aeschin. III. *In Ctes.* 161; Diod. XVII.4.5–9). The new financial posts are a more reliable guide. Eubulus used his position as theoric treasurer to pursue a particular policy, and his re-election (we do not know for how long) was a sign of confidence in him and his policy; the election for 337/6 of Demosthenes, not known to have held any financial office before, indicates public support for him at one point in the unstable period between Chaeronea and the sack of Thebes; Lycurgus used his position *epi tei dioikesei* to pursue a financial policy. In general, however, success in elections is an unreliable guide to a man's political position or the state of public opinion.

Although there were no parties as we know them, there must have been political activity behind the scenes in addition to speech-making and voting in the Council and Assembly. The clearest evidence comes not from the fourth century but from the troubled days of the late fifth.[51] Andocides claims that the mutilation of the Hermae in 415, an act intended to shock, possibly for some political purpose, was the work of a *hetaireia* ('association') to which he belonged (1. *Myst.* 61–4 cf. 49, 54); in 411 Pisander encouraged the *xynomosiai* ('conspiracies') or *hetaireiai*, 'which already existed in the city with a view to lawsuits and offices', to join forces and work against the democracy (Thuc. VIII.54.4 cf. 65.2); in 404 the *hetaireiai* appointed five men styled ephors, 'to act as conveners of the citizens and leaders of the conspirators', and these appointed tribal agents through whom they announced how men were to vote and whom they should elect (Lys. XII. *Erat.* 43–4). In the consolidated *nomos eisangeltikos* of the new law-code (cf. above) the clause concerning conspiracy against the democracy included the words ἢ ἑταιρικὸν

---

49 Cf. p. 180.
50 Cf. pp. 756–7. It may not have been apparent when he was appointed that he would be at odds with them.
51 Cf. *CAH* v² 449–50, 472–3. On political activity in general, see Rhodes 1986 (C 229).

συναγάγῃ ('or forms a *hetaireia*').[52] In the fourth century, when there was no threat to the democratic constitution, there was less need for under-cover activity. However, Plato says that he did not pursue a political career because nothing could be done without friends and associates (*philoi* and *hetairoi*) and he could not find suitable men (*Ep.* VII.325c–d), and he mentions 'the efforts of *hetaireiai* for offices' as one of the things which the non-political philosopher avoids (*Tht.* 173d); the general Chares was alleged to have spent part of the money voted for his campaigns on 'speakers, proposers of decrees and private citizens sued in the courts' (Theopomp. *FGrH* 115 F 213, cf. Aeschin. II. *FL* 71). Euxitheus, one of the men deprived of his citizenship in the general scrutiny of 346/5, claims that the demarch Eubulides called his name last on the first day: the deme Halimus was thirty-five stades (6 km) from the city, and most members had already set out for home; 'those who remained were not more than thirty, but among them were all the men procured by him', and more than sixty votes were cast (Dem. LVII. *Eub.* 10, 13, cf. 16, 59–60).

There are various references in the orators to the friends and associates of leading figures, and it is apparent that a politician could have various grades of supporters. Aeschines ended his defence in 343 by invoking the support of 'Eubulus, from the political and prudent men; Phocion, from the generals, outstanding above all men for his uprightness; and from my friends and contemporaries Nausicles and all the others whose company I have kept and in whose activities I have shared' (II. 184):[53] Demos-thenes regarded it as a sinister sign if Eubulus was to speak for Aeschines when he would not speak for his own relatives (XIX. *FL* 289–93). In 330 Aeschines cast aspersions on those who were to speak for Demosthenes, 'whether they were fellow hunters or fellow-gymnasts of his when he was young'; but no, that was not the kind of pursuit to which Demosthenes devoted himself; rather 'when at the end of his speech he calls as supporters those who were his partners in bribe-taking' (III. *In Ctes.* 255, 257). Demosthenes refers to men who will speak for Meidias as the mercenaries (*misthophoroi*) who surround him, and in addition there is the *hetaireia* of witnesses which he had organized (XXI. *Meid.* 139).

In the earlier part of the fourth century we can detect various allegiances and antipathies, some more lasting than others;[54] some families or individuals may have maintained a consistent policy over a

52 Hyp. IV.8; not in Poll. VIII.52, *Lex. Rhet. Cant.* εἰσαγγελία; but cf. law ap. [Dem.] XLVI.26. On *hetaireiai* in the fourth century, see Pecorella Longo 1971 (C 218).

53 Compare the invocation in Andoc. I.150.

54 See Sealey 1956 (C 253) (too schematic), and, on the whole period to *c.* 320, Perlman 1967 (C 219), Rhodes 1978 (C 225).

long period,[55] but at any one time most Athenians wanted the same thing, and it was not a distinctive policy that separated one group of politicians from another. Athens was pro-Theban and anti-Spartan in the 370s, pro-Spartan and anti-Theban in the 360s: Callistratus was one of the leading proponents of both policies; after the Battle of Leuctra there was not a change by a few floating voters but a realization by most Athenians, more quickly by some than by others, that the balance of power in Greece had undergone a major change. In the reign of Philip, however, Eubulus and Demosthenes did come to stand for distinctive policies: to husband Athens' resources, whatever the cost to her independence, or to act energetically against Philip, whatever the cost to her economy. Here there are signs of consistent attachment to one side or the other, and of something approaching party discipline. In 343 Demosthenes says that he used to be on friendly terms with Pythocles, but ever since the man visited Philip he has avoided Demosthenes, or hurried away so as not to be seen talking to him, as if those who have given Philip their support must allow him to choose their friends and enemies (XIX. *FL* 225–6); in his speech of 330 he claims that it was in order to do nothing in opposition to those for whom he directed all his political activity that Aeschines never supported Athens with his wealth (XVIII. *De Cor.* 312–13).[56] We are closer to modern party politics in Philip's reign than at most times in Athenian history; for most of Alexander's reign Lycurgus was able to co-operate with Demades and his friends but the other members of Demosthenes' following were not prominent; at the death of Alexander the earlier alignments were briefly revived.

III. ALTERNATIVES TO THE POLIS

The first half of this chapter has been devoted to Athens, the only Greek state on whose internal affairs we have a substantial body of evidence; but Athens was only one state among many. In the course of the fifth century the Greeks had come to divide political constitutions into three kinds: kingdoms or tyrannies, where a single man ruled, lawfully and by inheritance or absolutely and by usurpation; oligarchies, where a few ruled; and democracies, where the many ruled. Athens had come to be

[55] Autocles, the hostile envoy to Sparta in 372/1 (cf. above), perhaps belonged to a consistently anti-Spartan family (Davies 1971 (C 124) 161–5, misdating the embassy; but the attractive revision of Xen. *Hell.* VI.3.2 by Tuplin 1977 (C 262) would eliminate his link with that family). On the other hand, Leosthenes the elder ended his life as an exile at Philip's court, but his son was staunchly anti-Macedonian (Davies 1971 (C 124) 342–4).

[56] There is an earlier complaint about the increasing organization of political support in Dem. XIII.20 (353/2?), more or less repeated in II.29 (349).

the leading exponent of democracy, a city where decisions were freely taken by assemblies of all the citizens and offices were shared out among the citizens; she encouraged, and sometimes enforced, democratic forms of government in the cities belonging to the Delian League, the alliance which she built up in the fifth century. The leading exponent of oligarchy was Sparta: there a far smaller proportion of the population than in Athens were citizens, possessing some political rights; the assembly had comparatively little business referred to it by the authorities, and was expected simply to approve or reject proposals made by the authorities; and, although the citizens were styled *homoioi* ('equals'), the authorities included a council of elders (*gerousia*) whose membership was limited to the two kings and a group of privileged families; Sparta encouraged oligarchies in the cities belonging to her alliance, the Peloponnesian League, until after the Battle of Leuctra she lacked the strength to enforce her will and the league broke up. Different degrees of democracy or oligarchy were possible: membership of the citizen body which had some political rights, the power of the citizen assembly as against the authorities, and the distribution of public offices were three basic points of contention. Individuals and cities had rallied to the two labels, but there was not in fact a sharp distinction between democratic cities and oligarchic. Moreover, Aristotle remarked that an oligarchic constitution could be administered in a democratic spirit and a democratic in an oligarchic spirit (*Pol.* IV. 1292a39–1293a34). Athens exemplified his most extreme form of democracy, in which the state's revenues allowed it to make payments for public service and the poor were enabled to exercise the rights which the constitution gave them (1292b41–1293a10). We do not know how democratic other democracies were: most states were poorer than Athens, and could not afford to pay the many stipends which she paid, but they were also smaller than Athens, and could have managed without the many officials whom she had, so it is not impossible that the Athenian kind of democracy should have been emulated elsewhere.[57]

Sparta retained her two kings, whose powers were limited by the institution of the ephors but were still considerable. Otherwise, in the fourth century, monarchy was largely confined to the fringes of the Greek world: there were kings in Macedon (cf. below) and Molossia; there were tyrants in Syracuse and other cities of Sicily, in Pherae in Thessaly (cf. below), and in Heraclea on the south coast of the Black Sea.[58] Earlier, tyrant had not invariably been a term of abuse, but in the

[57] Cf. *CAH* v² 91–5.
[58] See on Sparta this vol., ch. 5; on Syracuse, this vol., ch. 13; on Heraclea Pontica this vol., pp. 222, 498. In the heart of Greece, Euphron was tyrant of Sicyon for a few years in the 360s (Xen. *Hell.* VII.1.44–6, 2.11–15. 3.1–12); about 365 Timophanes tried to make himself tyrant of Corinth, and his

political schemes of Plato and Aristotle the tyrant was not only a usurping, but a selfish and wicked, ruler:[59] democrats and oligarchs would agree that tyranny was a state to be avoided.

Although the polis (city state) was the characteristic political unit of Greece, and was assumed by the philosophers to be the ideal unit,[60] it was not the only kind of political organization to be found in classical Greece. The Greek mainland and the western coast of Asia Minor are divided by mountains into separate, mostly small habitable regions, and the islands of the Aegean are small. Many of these regions came to be dominated by a single urban centre, an independent polis; Athens and Sparta were atypical only in that they dominated unusually large regions. There were, however, regions which contained several towns, none of them able to gain complete control over the others.

One such region was Boeotia: of the towns surrounding Lake Copais Thebes, to the south east, became the most powerful, but its claim to supremacy was resisted, especially by Orchomenus, to the north west. Instead of subjecting its neighbours, Thebes combined them in a federal Boeotian state.[61] Already in 519 there was a federation: Plataea wished to stay outside, appealed to Sparta and was advised to entrust herself to Athens; Corinth mediated, and ruled that 'the Thebans should leave alone those of the Boeotians who did not wish to contribute to the Boeotians' (Hdt. VI.108).[62] The federation perhaps broke up after the Persian Wars; and for about ten years, from 457 to 447/6, Boeotia was under Athenian control;[63] the federation was then revived, and two texts give us an analysis of its organization. There was a property qualification for full citizenship; the individual *poleis* were autonomous in their internal affairs, and in each polis the body of full citizens was divided into quarters and each quarter in turn acted as a probouleutic council. The federal organization was based not on the cities as such but on eleven regional units: Thebes formed two of these units in her own right and, after the destruction of Plataea in 427, a further two on behalf of Plataea

---

brother Timoleon was involved in his assassination (Diod. XVI.65, Plut. *Tim.* 4–5, cf. p. 199); for other possible tyrants see Berve 1967 (C 9) I 296–309 with II 673–7. It is not clear how many of the partisans of Philip whom Demosthenes calls tyrants deserve the label.

[59] E.g. Plat. *Rep.* VIII 562a–569c, *Polit.* 291d–293e, 300e–303b, Arist. *Pol.* III 1278b6–1280a6, and on tyranny IV 1295a1–24, *Eth. Nic.* VIII 1160a31–1161a9.

[60] E.g. Plat. *Rep.* II 368e–369b, *Leg.* I.626b–c, Arist. *Pol.* I 1251a1–1253a39 (beginning: 'Since we see that every polis . . .').

[61] On the Boeotian federation see especially Larsen 1968 (C 37) 26–40, 175–80; Roesch 1965 and 1982 (C 345–346); Salmon 1978 (C 347); Buckler 1980 (C 329). Coins were issued sometimes in the name of the Boeotians, sometimes in the name of Thebes or other cities, but regularly bear a distinctive shield on the obverse: Kraay 1976 (B 200) 108–14 with pll. 19–20.

[62] Cf. *CAH* IV² 298, 360. The date is derived from Thuc. III.68.5 (and some believe it to be too early). *Boiotarchoi* are attested in 480–479: Hdt. IX.15.1, Paus. X.20.3.

[63] Cf. *CAH* V² 96–7, 116, 133.

and her neighbours; other *poleis*, according to their size, formed two units or one or part of one. Each unit provided one of the eleven magistrates called *boiotarchoi*; each provided sixty members of a council of 660; the army and other institutions were based on these units (*Hell. Oxy.* XVI Bartoletti). In the federal council as in the citizen bodies of the individual cities the membership was divided into quarters, and each quarter acted in turn as a probouleutic body; there was no federal assembly (Thuc. V.38.2). The federal authorities met in Thebes (*Hell. Oxy.* XVI.4). In this organization the cities retained their local autonomy (but were all organized on the same pattern), while co-operating in a federal body for matters concerning them all, especially foreign policy. Some cities had more weight than others; Thebes not only had most weight but was recognized as the administrative capital; but citizens of all the cities were equal as Boeotian citizens: men of Tanagra were not mere *perioikoi* ('dwellers-around') of Thebes, with no say except in their domestic affairs, as men of Prasiae were *perioikoi* of Sparta.

In 392 the Spartans made their first attempt to impose on the Greeks a common peace treaty, based on the principle that all *poleis* should be independent, and the application of this principle threatened to dissolve the Boeotian federation (Xen. *Hell.* IV.8.15); in response to objections Sparta was prepared to leave the rest of the federation intact if Orchomenus might withdraw (Andoc. III. *De Pace*, 13, 20); but when peace was eventually made, in 386, Sparta did insist on the ending of the federation (Xen. *Hell.* V.1.32–3).[64] In 382 Sparta occupied Thebes; in 379/8 Thebes regained her liberty, and began to revive the federation; it was because the representatives from Thebes claimed to swear not as Thebans but as Boeotians that they were excluded from the peace of 372/1. In the revived federation we find an *archon* (apparently the formal head but not powerful: some believe that this was an old office, though not attested earlier), seven *boiotarchoi*, and not a council but an assembly (e.g. *SIG* 179 = Harding no. 48). Thebes was destroyed after her revolt against Alexander in 335, and refounded by Cassander *c.*316; but the federation survived;[65] if Alexander ordered its disbanding in 324 (Hyp. v. *Dem.*, col. 18 [fragmentary]), the order did not take effect, and there remained a federal Boeotia in the hellenistic period, based now not on the regional units but on individual cities.

Another region not dominated by a single polis was Arcadia, the mountainous centre of the Peloponnese, with a non-Dorian population:[66] the two cities of which we know most are Mantinea and Tegea, both in the south east, but there were many others. Before Leuctra 'the

---

[64] Cf. pp. 117–19 and below, 588.

[65] Roebuck 1948 (D 116) 80 n. 42 (= Perlman 1973 (D 111) 209h n. 42); *contra*, Sealey 1976 (A 53) 490–1. The sanctuary of Poseidon at Onchestus replaced Thebes as the administrative centre (Roesch 1965 (C 345) 125); by the end of the third century there was a council (*synedrion*) as well as an assembly (*ibid.* 126–33).   [66] Cf. *CAH* II².2, 702.

Arcadians' are often spoken of as such, but Mantinea and Tegea are often found on opposite sides, and evidence for a common organization is very sparse. About 491, Cleomenes tried to unite the Arcadians against Sparta, and to obtain an oath from 'the leaders of the Arcadians' that they would follow wherever he might lead (Hdt. vi.74), but he was induced to return to Sparta before he had obtained positive results.[67] There were coins issued, from three mints, in the name of the Arcadians, but they are now dated 480–418, and it is not clear how much political significance should be seen in them.[68] Herodotus' account of Tegea's claims at Plataea (ix.26–28.1) shows that the Arcadians were included in the Peloponnesian League as separate *poleis*. Mantinea, formed into a single polis by synoecism, perhaps after the Persian Wars or perhaps earlier,[69] was split into its component villages again by Sparta after the Peace of Antalcidas.[70] After Leuctra the single polis was re-formed, despite Spartan protests; then Lycomedes of Mantinea, with support from some but not all the leaders of Tegea, organized an Arcadian federation; a new city, Megalopolis, was created to be the capital of the new state, and men were drafted into it from various cities of southern Arcadia.[71] The federation could be referred to as the *koinon* ('common body': Xen. *Hell.* vii.5.1); a decree is 'resolved by the council of the Arcadians and the Ten Thousand', the former being a representative body but the latter probably an assembly open to all citizens, and is followed by a list of fifty *damiorgoi*, ten from Megalopolis and various others from nine other cities (*IG* v.ii.1 = Tod no. 132 = Harding no. 151);[72] the *archontes* of Xenophon (e.g. *Hell.* vii.4.33) may be the *damiorgoi* or a smaller body of magistrates; there was a single general (*strategos*: Diod. xv.67.2 cf. 62.1). Before long a division opened within the federation, leading to the battle of Mantinea in 362. Afterwards this division persisted: the Mantinean faction still claimed to be the Arcadian federation; and a similar claim may have been made by the rival faction,[73] but when men drafted into Megalopolis tried

---

[67] Cf. *CAH* iv² 366.
[68] Kraay 1976 (B 200) 97–8, and *CAH* v² 105; earlier the beginning of this series was connected with Cleomenes. [69] Cf. *CAH* v² 102–4. [70] Cf. pp. 157, 563.
[71] Cf. p. 193. On the Arcadian federation see especially Larsen 1968 (C 37) 180–95; Dušanić 1970 (C 357). After 418 the cities had coined individually; a Mantinean coin perhaps falls between the resynoecism and the federation; then there were federal coins; and coins of Stymphalus and Pheneus were perhaps issued when those cities did not belong to the federation (cf. Kraay 1976 (B 200) 99–102).
[72] Salmon 1978 (C 347) 5, 104–6, argues from the number of representatives that Arcadia was organized in units in imitation of Boeotia.
[73] Schol. Aeschin. iii.83 has a list including 'the Arcadians with Mantinea' and 'Megalopolis'; Dem. xix.11 mentions a meeting of the Ten Thousand at Megalopolis. That claims were made by the Megalopolitan faction is accepted by Larsen 1968 (C 37), 193, rejected by Dušanić 1970 (C 357) 307–11. Some date Tod no. 132 = Harding no. 51 after Chaeronea and claim that Philip reunited the federation (Beloch 1912–27 (A 5) III 1, 175 n. 2, 2, 173–7, Dušanić 1970 (C 357) 311–2, 336–7); *contra*, Larsen 1968 (C 37) 193 n. 4). Whatever body claimed to be the federation may have been threatened in 324 (Hyp. v. col. 18: cf. above), and is last heard of in the Lamian War ([Plut.] *X Or.* 846c–d, Plut. *Dem.* 27.4–5).

to return to their original homes Megalopolis invoked the help of Thebes and forced them to remain (Diod. xv.94.1–3).

The north and west of Greece were backward by comparison with the areas that claim most of our attention in the classical period, and there cities were slow to develop. Aetolia, north of the entrance to the Gulf of Corinth, was in the late fifth century organized not by cities but by tribes (Thuc. III.94.5, 100.1), the individual settlements being unfortified villages (*komai*: 94.4), but there was some central organization for the conduct of foreign policy.[74] The fourth century saw little development: in 335 the Aetolians sent embassies (plural) to Alexander by tribes (*ethne*: Arr. *Anab.* I.10.2),[75] and in the last quarter of the century the *poleis* of Diod. XVIII.24.2–25.1, XIX.74.6, seem little advance on Thucydides' *komai*. Yet in 367/6 there was a *koinon* to which Athens announced the Eleusinian truce and protested against the conduct of an Aetolian town (Tod no. 137 = Harding no. 54);[76] the Aetolians, collectively, were granted *promanteia* at Delphi in 338/7 (*Fouilles de Delphes* III.iv 399); the hellenistic *koinon* was organized in *poleis* and communities treated as the equivalent of *poleis*, but the *poleis* were grouped in *tele* (*SIG* 421, *B*), and it appears that the tribes became *tele* and then others were added as the federation expanded. The Aetolians had an assembly, and a smaller council (*boule* or *synedrion*), where cities were represented in proportion to their size (*SIG* 546, *B*); this was not a probouleutic body but one authorized to act between meetings of the assembly; a still smaller body, the *apokletoi*, was elected from the council (Livy XXXV.34.2, XXXVI.28.8); there was a single *strategos* (Polyb. II.2.8, 2.11–3.1). The assembly had two regular meetings a year and could have others; the autumn meeting was always at the sanctuary of Thermum (Polyb. V.8.5), but there was no fixed place for the others. The stages of Aetolia's development from a community of tribes to a federation of cities cannot be traced; by the hellenistic period it was the latter, and was an organization to which

[74] On Aetolia see especially Sordi 1953 (C 383) (rightly warning against a rigid distinction, unknown in antiquity, between primitive 'cantonal' and advanced 'federal' states); Larsen 1968 (C 37) 78–80, 195–215. Thuc. I.5.3, III.94.5, stresses the backwardness of the Aetolians. An inscribed treaty recently found at Sparta (*SEG* XXVI 461, XXVIII 408) refers in its preamble to the 'Aetolians' but in its substantive text refers apparently to the same people as the (otherwise unattested) Ἐρξαδιἐς: it is dated *c.* 500–470 on epigraphic grounds by Peek 1974 (C 306), *c.* 426–424 on historical grounds by Cartledge 1976 (C 281) (supported epigraphically by Jeffery 1988 (B 145)); Gschnitzer 1978 (C 292) repeats Peek's date without discussion, restores the name of the community in the preamble as Αἰτωλοὶ Ἐρξαδιἐς, and suspects that they were a community of Aetolians in the Peloponnese. There was no Aetolian coinage before the hellenistic period.

[75] From this Bosworth 1976 (D 20) and 1980 (B 14) *ad loc.* argues that Philip dissolved the *koinon* after 338/7 and gave each *ethnos* a separate government, and that the Aetolians re-formed the *koinon* during the reign of Alexander.

[76] In Delphic inscriptions an Aetolian may be identified by city as early as 329/8 (inscription published by Bourguet 1899 (B 136) 356–7), but by tribe as late as the second century (*SGDI* 1862.2, 1978.3).

more distant states could be attached, by *isopoliteia* ('equal citizenship') with a single city or with the whole *koinon* (e.g. *IG* IX².i 169; 173). Federal institutions are attested also in neighbouring Acarnania (Thuc. III. 105.1, Xen. *Hell.* IV.6.4, cf. after the Peace of Antalcidas *IG* II² 96 = Tod no. 126 = Harding no. 41) and in Western Locris (*IG* IX².i 665).

In the plain of Thessaly comparative newcomers had reduced the older inhabitants to subjection as *penestai*; the peoples of the surrounding mountains were *perioikoi*, whom the Thessalians controlled when they were strong enough to do so.[77] Thessaly was divided regionally into four tetrads, each of which came to be headed by a tetrarch (cf. *SIG* 274); the tetrads could combine to elect a single leader, the *tagos*, who once elected seems to have retained the position for life, but there were substantial periods when there was no *tagos*, either because Thessaly was not so unified as to feel the need for a permanent leader or because dissension prevented the filling of the vacancy.[78] During the fifth century cities developed, and the leading families had either to see their power reduced or to learn to exercise it through the cities; Thucydides lists the cities which contributed to Thessaly's support for Athens at the beginning of the Peloponnesian War (II.22.3, cf. Xen. *Hell.* VI.1.19). By the 450s the tetrarchs had been replaced by polemarchs: the change in title may have accompanied a change in power and conditions of appointment.[79] At the end of the fifth century Lycophron made himself tyrant in Pherae, and about 375 his son Jason obtained the position of *tagos* (Xen. *Hell.* VI.1.8, 18–19).[80] There followed rivalry between the tyrants of Pherae and their opponents headed by the family of the Aleuadae, based on Larissa, with first Macedon and then Boeotia intervening on behalf of the latter. Probably as a result of Boeotia's intervention in 369, the opponents of Pherae organized themselves in a *koinon*, with an *archon* as chief officer and four polemarchs (*IG* II² 116 = Tod no. 147; *IG* II² 175, probably belonging to the same occasion). In the Third Sacred War Pherae supported the Phocians and the *koinon* their enemies: in 352 Philip of

---

[77] On Thessaly see especially Westlake 1935 (C 389); Sordi 1958 (C 384); Larsen 1968 (C 37) 12–25, 281–94. Coins were issued, from the early fifth century, mostly in the name of individual cities, but sometimes in the fifth century cities co-operated to issue coins of a common design (Kraay 1976 (B 200) 215–20). See *CAH* V² 99.

[78] The first view is preferred by Westlake 1935 (C 389) 26–6 and Sordi 1958 (C 384) 337–8, the second by Larsen 1968 (C 37) 14–15. *SIG* 55. 6–7 (*c.* 450–425?) contains the phrase κὲν ταγᾶ κὲν ἀταγίαι: this appears to envisage the non-existence of a *tagos* as not abnormal; Chadwick 1969 (C 356) believes that no reference to the office of *tagos* is intended or implied, but he has not convinced Hooker 1980 (C 365).

[79] In *SEG* XVII 243 πολεμαρχεόντον τόνδε appears to be followed by two names in the genitive, then καὶ{σ} and five names in the nominative (but Sordi 1958 (C 384) 344–7 regards the first two names of the second column as further genitives before καὶ{σ}, to obtain four polemarchs); there are four polemarchs, one from each tetrad, in *IG* II² 175 (cf. below). There is no evidence for tetrarchs between *c.* 460 and *c.* 342, either in *SIG* 274 or elsewhere.   [80] Cf. pp. 32, 175.

Macedon, intervening in the war, overthrew the tyranny at Pherae, reunited Thessaly and was himself elected *archon*;[81] perhaps in 342, he replaced the polemarchs with tetrarchs appointed by himself;[82] and in 336 the Thessalians resolved that as Philip's successor Alexander should succeed to the position of *archon* (Diod. XVII.4.1, Justin *Epit.* XI.3.2).

Macedon, on the fringe of the Greek world, retained its archaic monarchy; its political institutions were rudimentary.[83] The kingship was hereditary, but a new king had to be acclaimed by an assembly of 'the Macedonians' (in practice, the army), and might not be the closest heir of his predecessor by the normal rules of inheritance (cf. Curt. x.7.1–15).[84] The king was absolute ruler, but there was a style to which he was expected to conform (cf. Arr. *Anab.* IV.11.6, Curt. IV.7.31, Polyb. v.27.7). He issued coins; he made treaties (e.g. Tod nos. 129, 158, 177 = Harding nos. 43, –, 99A).[85] The one limitation attested is an obligation to involve the assembly in the trial of capital charges (Curt. VI.8.25);[86] otherwise, no doubt, like a Homeric king he would call an assembly if and when he wished to sound out public opinion or assure himself of support. There was no formal council: inevitably the king would seek advice to some extent, but he would do so by consulting his 'companions' or 'friends' (*hetairoi* or *philoi*), men neither born to the position nor appointed by the people but chosen by himself. He had to appoint military officers, and envoys to other states; he might designate a deputy when he set out on campaign (Thuc. 1.62.2, Plut. *Alex.* 9.1); otherwise the only state officials we hear of are justices (*dikastai*), whom he could appoint and dismiss (Plut. *Reg. Imp. Apophth.* 178f). By the middle of the fourth century the plain of Lower Macedonia was urbanized, and a Macedonian could be identified by his city (e.g. *SGDI* 2759); the peoples of Upper Macedonia were organized by tribes, which before Philip's reign had had their own kings (Thuc. II.99.2), and had asserted their independence when strong enough to do so; for military purposes the whole kingdom was organized in regions (Arr. *Anab.* III.16.9, cf. 1.2.5 etc.).

The Greeks who formed a single state were, ethnically and geographi-

---

[81] Date: Hammond and Griffith 1979 (D 50) 220–3 (by Griffith); *archon* rather than *tagos*: *ibid.* 288 n. 4; *contra*, Sordi 1958 (C 384) 335–6.

[82] Dem. IX.26, Theopomp. *FGrH* 115 FF 208–9, most recently discussed by Hammond and Griffith 1979 (D 50) 523–4 (by Griffith).

[83] On Macedon see especially Hammond and Griffith 1979 (D 50) 150–66, 647–74 (by Hammond), 383–404 (by Griffith); Hammond 1989 (D 49) 49–70; Borza 1990 (D 19) 231–52; Errington 1990 (D 33) 218–50; Hammond believes in a much more formalized constitution than other scholars are prepared to accept. On the coinage of Macedon see Kraay 1976 (B 200) 141–7.

[84] Cf. p. 730, on the accession of Philip.

[85] An alliance with Athens, of the late fifth century, is followed by an extremely long list of Macedonians who swore to it: *IG* i³ 89; list lines 60ff.

[86] Brunt 1976 (B 21) xxxix observes that this was not always done.

cally, peoples who belonged together and were conscious of differing from their neighbours. In Greece proper Sparta's conquest of Messenia was the only large-scale breach of the normal limitations, and she acknowledged the limitations in the sixth century, when she abandoned the attempt to conquer Arcadia.[87] In Sicily the tyrant families of the early fifth century had used members of the family to rule more than one city;[88] Dionysius I of Syracuse at his most powerful controlled much of Sicily and the extreme south west of Italy, and three Athenian decrees give him the title *archon* of Sicily (*IG* ii² 18, 103, 105 + 523 = Tod. nos. 108, 133, 136 = Harding nos. 20, –, 52).[89] Uniquely, at the end of the 390s the cities of Corinth and Argos united to form a single polis, because the Corinthian democrats preferred union with Argos to a pro-Spartan oligarchy;[90] after the Peace of Antalcidas Sparta insisted on the separation of the two cities (Xen. *Hell.* v.1.34). The state might be an individual polis, a federation of *poleis*, a union of tribes or a Homeric monarchy; it might be ruled by the many, the few or one man; but all could be contrasted with the subjection of many peoples to one despot in the Persian empire.

However, the Greek states found it convenient to join in larger associations. Some were primarily religious, uniting those who shared an interest in a sanctuary. The twelve cities of Ionia had an association based on the sanctuary of the Panionion (Hdt. 1.143, 148): Thales' advice to make a federal state of this was not taken (1.170.3), but the association did on occasions provide a basis for joint action (1.141.4; vi.7 cf. v.109.3).[91] More extensive was the Amphictyony of Anthela and Delphi, which Boeotia exploited as a body of political importance after Leuctra:[92] twelve *ethne* (mostly from central Greece, but Athens and Sparta, and in 346 Philip, managed to gain inclusion) each sent two delegates to a council which met twice a year.

Alliances between states are a familiar institution, and from the late sixth century powerful Greek states attached others to themselves and to each other in leagues of allies: Sparta organized the Peloponnesian League *c*.505;[93] Athens formed the Delian League, against Persia, in 478/7[94] and the Second Athenian League, against Sparta, in 378/7;[95] and there are signs that after Leuctra Thebes attempted to organize her allies in the

---

[87] *CAH* iii².3, 355–6.   [88] *CAH* iv² 766–75.   [89] Cf. pp. 137–8.

[90] Xen. *Hell.* iv.4.6, 8.34, Andoc. iii.26–7, 32. Griffith 1950 (c 362) and Whitby 1984 (c 390) argue for *isopoliteia*, exchange of citizenship rights, in 392 and full union in 390; Tuplin 1982 (c 387) believes in full union in 392; Salmon 1984 (c 380) 354–62, believes in *isopoliteia* in 392 and doubts if there was ever a greater degree of union than that.

[91] Cf. *CAH* iii².3, 217, iv² 481.

[92] Cf. p. 739. On the organization of the Amphictyony see Roux 1979 (c 377) especially 1–59.

[93] Cf. *CAH* iv² 350, less confident about the clarity of the change.

[94] Cf. *CAH* v² 34–40.   [95] Cf. pp. 169–70.

same way.[96] These alliances were formed primarily for the conduct of foreign policy: in each the principal city wielded the executive power but presided over a mechanism by which the allies were involved in making decisions; in theory, though not always in practice, the allies were free to run their domestic affairs as they wished. A member state's position was thus analogous to that of a constituent city in a federal state like Boeotia: it had local autonomy, it was also part of a larger entity in the making of whose decisions it had some voice, but there was a danger that the leading city would treat the others as subjects rather than as partners. In the fourth century another form of combination was attempted, the *koine eirene* ('common peace'):[97] after an abortive attempt in 392 the first treaty was made in 386, and was followed by later, similar treaties. These were not simply treaties to end a war but were for all Greek states: they stipulated that (with a few exceptions) all were to be free and independent; and the later treaties if not the earlier tried to provide for joint action against any one who infringed the peace. In theory the common peace came to resemble a league without a dominant member; but on almost every occasion when a treaty was made or proposed there was in fact a dominant state which hoped to exploit it.

If attacked by a large army, the Greeks had to combine or submit. At the beginning of the fifth century many states did combine, in an *ad hoc* alliance, against the Persians, and the Persians were defeated and driven out; this success, and the subsequent creation of the Delian League, did much to make the Greeks aware of what they had in common. After the Peloponnesian War, in which Greeks fought against Greeks and the winners depended on Persian support, it became fashionable to call for a fresh combination against the Persians.[98] In the middle of the fourth century Philip of Macedon came not as an external invader but as one who claimed to be a Greek; he fought as an ally of the Delphic Amphictyony and was rewarded with membership of the Amphictyony; while Demosthenes called on the Greeks to unite against him, Isocrates called on him to unite the Greeks in a crusade against the Persians; there were divisions within the cities and between the cities, and in most cities there were men who looked to Philip for support. Demosthenes' opposition to Philip grew in strength, in Athens and elsewhere, though the Hellenic League under Athens' leadership, which some have postulated, is an exaggeration.[99] But Demosthenes' alliance was defeated at Chaeronea, and afterwards it was Philip who made use of the Greek

---

[96] Cf. especially Xen. *Hell.* VII.3.11 and see now Lewis 1990 (C 341).   [97] Cf. p. 6.

[98] The idea is first found in Gorgias, *Olymp.* 82 A 1 D–K (probably 392), *Epitaph.* 82 B 5b D–K (*c.* 390).

[99] Against Wüst 1938 (D 125) 118–20, and Accame 1941 (C 87) 220–1, see Ellis 1976 (D 80) 173–4 with 286–7 n. 79.

devices for combining states: there was another common peace treaty; and the Greeks were united in the League of Corinth, with Philip taking the part of the dominant state; the allies included *poleis*, federal states and tribal states, and (as in federal Boeotia) they were represented in proportion to their population.[100]

IV. THE FAILURE OF THE POLIS?

'With the bodies of [those who died at Chaeronea] was buried the freedom of the other Greeks' (Lycurg. *Leoc.* 50): this is echoed by many modern writers, and we frequently read of 'the failure of the polis'[101] or 'the crisis of the polis in the fourth century'.[102] The truth is somewhat different. Before Chaeronea the Greeks of the mainland and the Aegean (but not those of Asia Minor) had never had to acknowledge a non-Greek master, and the larger cities, particularly Sparta and Athens, had sought not only to be free from subjection to others but to make others subject to them; but within a few years all the Greeks except those of the western colonies were subjected, to a king who was not quite Greek, and thereafter until power passed to Rome they were to live under the shadow of his successors. Athens and Sparta lost for ever the absolute freedom which they had once enjoyed; but helots and perioeci had long been inferior, and even the citizens of lesser cities had not had that absolute freedom. The Greeks were incorporated in a league, not unlike the leagues which they had known before: they had a voice in making decisions, but the dominant member had the preponderant voice; they could run their domestic affairs as they wished, so long as they did not provoke the dominant member. After Alexander's death there was a plurality of kings, and in manoeuvring between these the Greek states enjoyed the kind of freedom they had enjoyed earlier in manoeuvring between Athens and Sparta.[103]

The polis was not dead: indeed it was still regarded as the ideal setting

---

[100] Cf. p. 784.

[101] E.g. Browning 1976 (c 10) 261. Cf. the first edition of this volume, where ch. xvi. 5 is entitled 'The End of the *Polis* and its Political Theory'.

[102] This is the theme of the four volumes of Welskopf (ed.), *Hellenische Poleis: Krise, Wandlung, Wirkung* (c 83), a theme received sympathetically by Browning 1976 (c 10), unsympathetically by Cassola 1976 (c 13). de Ste Croix 1981 (c 70) 293–326, writes of 'the destruction of Greek democracy' (section heading, p. 300) from the fourth century onwards. However, the failure of democracy would not be the same thing as the failure of the polis, and it is not obvious that either occurred. Gauthier 1972 (c 25) 378, thinking of judicial independence, places the end of the free city state after the Battle of Pydna (168 B.C.); and in Gauthier 1984 (c 26) he argues vigorously for the real survival of both the polis and democracy in the hellenistic period. Runciman 1990 (c 62), asking rather different questions, argues that the polis was an evolutionary dead-end, too democratic (even when under a technically oligarchic constitution) to succeed in a competitive world.

[103] Greenhalgh 1981 (a 24) 29 compares the behaviour of the Greeks in the civil war between Pompey and Caesar with their behaviour in the fifth century.

for civilized life. As a result of Alexander's campaigns, *poleis* were founded in Egypt and Asia, and organized themselves on thoroughly Greek lines. In the Greek world, as far as possible, life continued as before: *poleis* organized their own affairs, and from time to time underwent changes of constitution in response to discontent inside or pressure from outside; areas like Aetolia continued to progress from tribal institutions to city institutions; cities quarrelled or negotiated with other cities, and joined in leagues. The Aetolian and Achaean Leagues were to be important in hellenistic Greece as the Peloponnesian and Delian Leagues had been important in classical Greece, the chief difference being only that the new leagues were not the creations of single powerful cities.

Some writers detect an increasing move towards federalism and Greek unity in the fourth century, but concede that this 'could not give unity to a country desperately resolved on division'.[104] After the glory of the Persian Wars and the prolonged bitterness of the Peloponnesian War, it was easy to conclude that the Greeks' finest hour was when they were united against the barbarians, but unity is more evident in the speeches of Isocrates than in the history of his lifetime. The difference between the fifth century and the fourth is not, however, that in the fifth century Greek institutions worked but in the fourth they failed. Rather, in the fifth century Athens and Sparta were so much more powerful than any other state that they were able to divide the Greek world into two power blocs and give it a stability which was not in fact typical; when Athens had been defeated in the Peloponnesian War, and Sparta had been defeated at Leuctra, a gap was left which no Greek state was able to fill. Alliances and leagues were not new; federal states were not new; it is because this stability was removed that we hear of more, and more ephemeral, combinations of states in the fourth century; and in Philip Macedon had a king able to seize the opportunity provided.

One commentator remarks on 'a general failure of civic institutions to work, a general recourse to authoritarian rule supported by non-citizen armies, a general alienation of the citizens from participation in the affairs of their community'.[105] In fact, as we have seen, the best-known tyrannies of the fourth century were on the edges of the Greek world. In Greece proper, if upheavals in the smaller states became more frequent, this was partly because Athens and Sparta lost the power to maintain regimes congenial to themselves;[106] for Athens and Sparta the fourth century undoubtedly was less glorious than the fifth, and Isocrates in

---

[104] E. Barker, *CAH* vi¹ 506–10 (the quotation from p. 508).

[105] Browning 1976 (c 10) 261.

[106] Cf. Diod. xv.40.1–2, with the wrong date but the right explanation. For the view taken here, cf. Lintott 1982 (c 43) 255.

many passages tries to analyse Athens' degeneracy (e.g. VIII. *De Pace*, 41–56), yet these two states remained conspicuously stable. In the general unsettlement of the fourth century more men left their homes and became available for mercenary service, and, being available, they were used, but men did not cease to fight for their own states: the great majority of those who fought at Chaeronea were citizen soldiers.[107]

Philip's victory at Chaeronea, and Alexander's conquest of the Persian empire, made the Greeks part of a larger world, a world in which the individualism of the polis comes to seem increasingly parochial. This inevitably resulted in a change of atmosphere, and we need not be surprised at the disappearance of the intensity of classical Greece. But, as we have seen, cities and leagues persisted, and asserted as much independence as circumstances allowed. Greek political institutions did not fail, but showed remarkable vitality.[108]

[107] Kromayer 1903–31 (K 29) I 188–95; Beloch 1912–27 (A 5) III 2, 299–301.

[108] This chapter was originally written in 1981/2, but I have added references to important studies published since then.

CHAPTER 12a

THE GROWTH OF SCHOOLS AND THE ADVANCE OF KNOWLEDGE

M. OSTWALD AND JOHN P. LYNCH

I. ANTECEDENTS

Higher education had come to Athens with the arrival of the sophists in the third and fourth quarters of the fifth century (*CAH* v² 341–69), in order to meet the demands of a flourishing democracy for excellence in public speaking in Council, Assembly and the jury courts. Protagoras of Abdera, the earliest of these teachers to arrive in Athens, was the first to call himself a 'sophist', a term which came to be applied in a more or less loose way also to other teachers of rhetoric who appeared in Athens from abroad during the next two or three decades: Gorgias of Leontini, Prodicus of Ceos, Hippias of Elis, Thrasymachus of Chalcedon, Euthydemus and Dionysodorus of Chios, and a number of others. None of these men spent an extended period of time in Athens, and none had a fixed home there. In the course of their visits, they were entertained at the homes of prominent Athenians, would give public displays of their rhetorical skills, and accepted on an *ad hoc* basis any Athenian willing to pay a stated fee as their student. Any private home or public place (palaestra, gymnasium, or stoa) might serve as the locale of their instruction.[1]

Unlike the 'natural philosophers' of Ionia and of southern Italy, they were not interested in the pursuit of knowledge for its own sake but in preparing their students for a happy and successful life. Young upper-class Athenians believed success to be attained through the art of persuasion, and rhetoric was what the sophists delivered.

Since persuasive speaking also requires some general knowledge of historical precedent, law, literature and science to illustrate a point, Protagoras and Prodicus developed theories about the origin of civilization, Prodicus made a special study of linguistic usage, Hippias and Euenus worked out techniques for developing the memory of their students, and Hippias drew on his encyclopaedic knowledge of astronomy, arithmetic, geometry, grammar, literature, painting, sculpture, ethnography, chronography and so forth (*CAH* v² 343–51) to integrate

---

[1] For details, see Lynch 1972 (H 76) 40, n. 16.

these subjects into their teaching of rhetoric.[2] In addition, many sophists published handbooks of rhetoric and thus contributed to the development of a literate culture. Eight authors of such handbooks are mentioned by Plato alone in his *Phaedrus* (266d–267d).

The optimal common denominator of all fifth-century sophistic teaching is best summed up in the claim Plato attributes to Protagoras: 'sound judgment (*euboulia*) in personal affairs, to enable a person to run his household in the best way, and in the affairs of the city to make his contribution to civic affairs most effective in action and speech' (Pl. *Prt.* 318e–319a). Most sophists would probably also agree with Protagoras in defining this discipline, at the prompting of Socrates, as *politike techne*, 'political science' or 'art of citizenship', however divergent their views of the function of citizenship and of society might be, and however much they might differ in their perceptions of what is conducive to the welfare of the state.

It is at this point that the goals of the sophists merge with the goals of Socrates.[3] Unlike the first-generation sophists – with the exception of Antiphon – Socrates was an Athenian, who went abroad only when military service compelled him; he charged no fees for his teaching and neither gave formal instruction nor advertised his services through public displays of his skill.[4] His teaching took the form of informal discussion and debate rather than of lecture, but, like the sophists, he had no fixed locale for his sessions: any place, public or private, would do. His most faithful interlocutors were men from the upper strata of Athenian society, many of whom also associated with the sophists.

Socrates shared with the sophists the firm conviction that education beyond the conventional intellectual (*mousike*) and physical (*gymnastike*) training was required to prepare young men intelligently for the demands of life. But while the sophists looked to worldly success as the aim of education, Socrates' aim was the pursuit of a moral life ([Pl.] *Clit.* 407a–c). This does not mean that the sophists were indifferent to morality: tracts such as Prodicus' *Choice of Heracles* (Xen. *Mem.* II.1.21–34) and Hippias' *Troïkos* (Pl. *Hp.Ma.* 286a–b; Philostr. *VS* 1.11) show that they were not. But they derived their morality from traditional myths and presented it, as Prodicus did, as a simple black-and-white option between two disparate sets of rewards, or, in the manner of Hippias, as an exhortation to pursue fame. Socrates, however, rejected the pursuit of external rewards; morality itself was for him the goal of education and was based on a knowledge of absolute values. What he

[2] See Marrou 1956 (H 78) 54–6.

[3] The scholarly literature on Socrates' life and teaching is immense. Patzer 1985 (H 93) lists 2,301 items. For a working bibliography, see Vlastos 1971 (H 112) 336–9.

[4] For the practice of the sophists, see *CAH* v[2] 341–51, 354–5, 356.

tried to inculcate in his students was a desire to pursue moral excellence for its own sake.

The opposition of these two aims and the methods by which they were to be realized set the stage and the tone for the development of schools in the fourth century.

II. THE FIRST SCHOOLS

1. *The Socratics*

The idea of teaching in a fixed permanent establishment, first broached in jest in Aristophanes' *Clouds* (423 B.C.), was not translated into reality until after Socrates' death. Two of his foreign disciples returned to their homes to found schools shortly after 399 B.C., Eucleides to his native Megara, where Plato and other members of the Socratic circle are said to have joined him (D.L. II.106), and where the school he founded lasted until the end of the fourth century B.C. (D.L. II. 108–15);[5] Phaedo to Elis to found a school which survived only into the next generation.[6] No precise date can be assigned to the foundation of either school, and little is known about the way in which they were organized or functioned.

The first permanent school in Athens was opened by Antisthenes, who combined in his person characteristics of the sophists with those of Socrates. Born in Athens about 445 B.C. of an Athenian father and a Thracian mother,[7] he had been a pupil of Gorgias and a teacher of rhetoric before he made the acquaintance of Socrates to become one of Socrates' most devoted disciples (Xen. *Mem.* III.11.17, cf. II.5.2–5; Pl. *Phd.* 59b), even urging his own students to follow Socrates' example.[8] His mixed parentage suggests why he established himself in the gymnasium of Cynosarges after Socrates' death (D.L. VI.13): it was the one most closely associated with *nothoi* (bastards).[9] But he was influential enough to be attacked by Isocrates as a rival.[10] Antisthenes had no successor. His doctrines were absorbed by the 'cynic' creed, which developed soon after his death and, according to some, derived its name from the Cynosarges. Like the sophists, he seems to have charged a fee, minimal though it was, for his instruction (D.L. VI.9 = fr. 189 Caizzi with n.), and, more important, by expecting his pupils to take notes (D.L. VI.3) he attributed to the written word a greater importance than it seems to have had in fifth-century educational practice.

---

5 See Döring 1972 (H 31).   6 Rossetti 1973 (H 101) 364–81.
7 Decleva Caizzi 1966 (H 26) frr. 122A–D, 124 with p. 118.
8 Decleva Caizzi 1964 (H 25) 48–99; 1966 (H 26) frr. 125–6, 128A.
9 Cf. Humphreys 1974 (I 78) 88–95; Patterson 1990 (I 116) 40–73, esp. 63–5.
10 See Eucken 1983 (H 39) 18–27.

2. *Isocrates*

The influence of the Socratics on Athenian education is graphically reflected in the criticism levelled against them by Isocrates.[11] Isocrates was born in Athens in 436 B.C., eight years before Plato. Impoverished by the loss of his paternal estate through the Peloponnesian War, he initially earned his living by applying the lessons in rhetoric learned from Gorgias (and allegedly also from Prodicus, Teisias and Theramenes)[12] to the writing of forensic speeches, of which six survive (XVI–XXI); the latest of them, the *Trapeziticus* and the *Aegineticus*, were delivered not later than 390. But his weak voice and lack of self-assurance before a crowd soon made him forego public appearances in law-court and Assembly in favour of teaching and writing.[13] Shortly before 390 he opened a school in a private house (presumably his own) in Athens, near the Lyceum.[14] In a tract, entitled *Against the Sophists* (XIII), he states his own educational goals and criticizes those of his rivals.[15]

The 'sophists' attacked are not those maligned by Plato, but, more generally, professional educators who take pay for their services.[16] Isocrates uses the term of himself (XV *Antid.* 168–70), as well as of the earlier 'natural' philosophers such as Empedocles and Parmenides (268) and even of distinguished statesmen such as Solon (235, 313–14). The sophists attacked here have given the profession a bad name by fraudulently promising their students a knowledge that does not exist (XV *Antid.* 168, cf. 148, 199, 235; XIII *Soph.* 7–8, 11). One group among them is chastised for ignoring the importance of experience and natural talent in effective speaking and misleading their students into believing that rhetoric is a science (*episteme*) which can be taught as easily as the letters of the alphabet (9–13). A second group, 'eristics' (οἱ περὶ τὰς ἔριδας διατρίβοντες XIII.1), is attacked for claiming that there is a knowledge (*episteme*) of moral values through which happiness (*eudaimonia*) can be attained; a claim which pretends to a foreknowledge which is in fact denied to man: since each event is unique, there can be no single science of what constitutes a priori moral conduct in any and every set of circumstances (3–4). In addition, he accuses the eristics of hypocritically pretending indifference to remuneration for educating their students toward a life of righteousness, but in fact requiring them to pay their fees

---

[11] Except for autobiographical remarks esp. in XV *Antidosis*, none of the biographical data on Isocrates antedate the first century B.C.; see Westermann 1845 (B 126) 245–59. On Isocrates as educator, see Marrou 1956 (H 78) 79–91 and Wilcox 1942 (H 121) 121–55, and 1945 (H 122) 171–86. In general see Cawkwell 1982 (B 29) 313–29. [12] Blass 1892 (H 5) II 11–14.

[13] Isoc. V *Phil.* 81, XII *Panath.* 10–11, *Epp.* 1.9; 8.7.

[14] Lynch 1972 (H 76) 51–2 with n. 25; 53. [15] Cf. XV *Antid.* 193.

[16] Isoc. XIII *Soph.* 14, 19; cf. II *Nicocl.* 13; IV *Paneg.* 3; IX *Bus.* 43; XV *Antid.* 168–70, 220, 268, 313–14.

in advance (XIII.4–5). For Isocrates, as for the sophists preceding him, it was a matter of course that educators should be paid for their services (xv *Antid.* 155, 219–20, 240–1, 289).[17] Although he was said to have become rich on his fees (*ibid.* 155–8), his charges were moderate and amounted to only one tenth of what Protagoras and Gorgias are reported to have charged for their teaching.[18]

The Socratics in general and Antisthenes in particular are attacked both here and in the *Helen* some five years later (*c.* 385 B.C.) as old men who 'assert that it is impossible to make false or contradictory statements (*antilogiai*) and to speak on both sides of the same issue', and who 'persist in affirming that we are endowed with none of the virtues by nature but that one science deals with them all' (X.1). The latter charge applies to most Socratics,[19] but the former in its combination with a low fee asked for instruction (XIII.3) clearly points to Antisthenes,[20] whose school must thus by *c.* 390 have been the chief rival to the school Isocrates was about to inaugurate: Plato, the most famous champion of the Socratic doctrine that moral conduct is predicated on knowledge (*episteme*), did not open his Academy until 388/7 B.C.

Isocrates left behind no theoretical statement of his educational principles. But his views remained so remarkably consistent throughout a career spanning more than half a century[21] that he can be credited with the first programmatic statement of what we have come to regard as a 'liberal' education.[22] Isocrates appeals to an economic, not an intellectual, elite, i.e. those able to pay for their education. Like the Socratics, he believed that the cultivation of the soul (τῆς ψυχῆς ἐπιμέλεια) is the noblest pursuit to prepare the young to be useful to the city; and with the Socratics he shared the conviction that this goal can be achieved only through a dedication to 'philosophy' (φιλοσοφία).[23]

The *philosophia* of Isocrates retains the practical connotations the term

[17] Of the Socratics Aristippus was the first to teach for pay, see frr. 3–8 in Mannebach 1961 (H 77). He was followed in this by Antisthenes (below, n. 20) and Aeschines (D.L. II.62).

[18] Isocrates' 10 minae ([Plut.] *X orat.* 837d) were regarded as normal (*ibid.* 842c and [Dem.] XXXV.42); Protagoras and Gorgias demanded 100 minae (D.L. IX.52; Diod. XII.53.2; *Suda s.v.* Γοργίας; Quint. *Inst.* III.1.10).

[19] The belief that there is a teachable science of moral excellence is common to Socrates (see Guthrie 1969 (H 56) III 450–9), Euclid (see Döring 1972 (H 31) 85), the early Plato (see, e.g., *Euthphr.* 14c–d, *Lach.* 194c–d, 199c–d, *Prt.* 352b–d, 357b–e), and Antisthenes (see Xen. *Symp.* II.12; D.L. VI.10); the belief that all virtues are one is attested for Socrates (see Xen. *Mem.* III.9.5, Arist. *Pol.* I.13, 1260a20–22, cf. Pl. *Prt.* 349b–360e, *Lach.* 198d–199e, *Euthyd.* 278e–282d, 288d–293a), Euclid (see D.L. II.106), and Antisthenes (see fr. 56 [Caizzi]); and for a virtuous life as conducive to happiness, see Pl. *Grg.* 470e, *Chrm.* 171d–173d; Antisthenes at D.L. VI.11.

[20] See Decleva Caizzi 1966 (H 26), frr. 47A, 122–4 with p. 118 and Isoc. X.1, and fr. 189 with p. 128.

[21] The *Antidosis*, which was written late in his career in 354 B.C. (XV.193–4), restates the programme outlined in *Against the Sophists* (XIII.14–18) of *c.* 390 B.C. soon after the opening of his school.   [22] For the following see Mikkola 1954 (H 83), and Eucken 1983 (H 39).

[23] Cf. xv *Antid.* 304–5 with Pl. *Ap.* 29e, 30b; *Prt.* 313a; Xen. *Mem.* 1.2.4.

had in the fifth century and before,[24] encompassing any serious study conducive to fostering sound opinions and correct judgments on factors inherent in a given situation and how to cope with them. He rejects the belief that moral conduct is a science ($\epsilon\pi\iota\sigma\tau\dot{\eta}\mu\eta$), and regards 'as wise those who are able to arrive, on a non-scientific basis, at judgments ($\delta\dot{o}\xi\alpha\iota$) of what is generally the best course, and who occupy themselves as philosophers with pursuits that will most speedily make them attain this sort of discernment' (xv *Antid.* 271; cf. xiii *Soph.* 16–18). *Philosophia* includes the study of poetry (xv *Antid.* 45) as well as of statesmanship (*ibid.* 121); but it excludes geometry and astronomy, because, though useful as 'a preparation for philosophy', 'they contribute nothing useful to speech and action in a concrete situation' (*ibid.* 261–9, esp. 266; cf. xii *Panath.* 26–32).[25] Education will produce a perfect *homme d'affaires*, who will entrust his mind, already sharpened by the study of geometry and astronomy, to Isocrates for an intensive study of 'philosophy' for a period of three to four years (xv *Antid.* 87), with a view to fostering his practical ($\phi\rho\dot{o}\nu\eta\sigma\iota\varsigma$) rather than his theoretical abilities. His aim is to give competent advice ($\sigma\upsilon\mu\beta\upsilon\lambda\epsilon\dot{\upsilon}\epsilon\iota\nu$) to those who hold the reins of power.[26]

Philosophia is for Isocrates an education in *logoi*, i.e., in the faculty of rationally organizing one's thoughts and presenting them coherently to one's fellows. Because this faculty differentiates men from all other animals, it is the foundation of human civilization: 'it has made us come together to found cities, enact laws and invent skills;' 'it has laid down norms concerning what is right and wrong, base and noble' (iii *Nicocl.* 6–9, cf. xv *Antid.* 253–7).

A *logos* need not be a composition for oral delivery. Isocrates' own lack of a good voice and of self-confidence before a crowd had compelled him to abandon forensic oratory to become a publicist and pamphleteer, an author ($\pi o\iota\eta\tau\dot{\eta}\varsigma$), whose written thoughts are read by or to others (xii *Panath.* 11), rather than a litigant ($\dot{a}\gamma\omega\nu\iota\sigma\tau\dot{\eta}\varsigma$) (xv *Antid.* 48–9, 192; cf. xiii *Soph.* 15). His subjects, 'the affairs of Greece, of kings and of states', lend themselves to writing, because greater and nobler themes give higher prestige than the performances of public speakers (xii *Panath.* 11); he wishes to give advice on public issues (iv *Paneg.* 17, v *Phil.* 17, *Ep.* 1 *Dionys.* 5) and to train his students in good expression ($\epsilon\dot{\upsilon}$ $\lambda\dot{\epsilon}\gamma\epsilon\iota\nu$), convinced that this will mould their moral sensibilities. His compositions are 'political treatises' ($\pi o\lambda\iota\tau\iota\kappa o\dot{\iota}$ $\lambda\dot{o}\gamma o\iota$) (xv *Antid.* 260).

Politikoi logoi are for Isocrates discussions of issues affecting the Greek

---

[24] See Eucken 1983 (H 39) 17–18.

[25] Even more severely censured in Isocrates' early works, e.g. X *Helen* 3–6.

[26] xiii *Soph.* 15 with 8, xv *Antid.* 204, ii *Ad Nicocl.* 51–2, iii *Nicocl.* 8, v *Phil.* 82; cf. *Epp.* 6. *Jason* 6, 8. *Mytil.* 7, 9. *Archid.* 16.

world at large (xv *Antid*. 46–50, xii *Panath*. 2, 11, cf. 136, 271) rather than
public speeches in Council, Assembly and the law-courts (xiii *Soph*. 9, x
Helen 9, ii *Nicocl*. 51).[27] They are an expression of his *philosophia* devoted
to the instruction of his students, as well as directed at those in power,
offering the practical advice (συμβουλεύειν) which, he hoped, his
teaching would prepare his students to give potentates in their time.
Politikoi logoi need to be supplemented by providing models (*paradeigmata*) for both the student and statesman to imitate (μιμεῖσθαι) (xiii *Soph*.
18, cf. xv *Antid*. 188). The teacher must not only himself be a role-model
to his students, but must also provide examples of past achievement to
emulate. For the presentation of role-models, both mythical and historical, Isocrates found the encomium a most congenial form. Evagoras is
presented as a historical role-model for his son and successor Nicocles
(ix *Evag*. 12–18), just as the *Helen*, written *c*. 385 B.C. soon after the
opening of his school, is a prime example of a mythical *paradeigma* in a
politikos logos: she is praised for having inspired Theseus to bring unity,
peace and political reform to Attica (x *Helen* 16–17, 32–8), and the
Greeks to undertake a common expedition against the barbarians (*ibid*.
51–3, 67). The interlocking ideas of internal unity as a precondition of
Greek freedom and the subjugation of Persia constitute Isocrates'
political programme and animate all his writings down to the *Panathenai-
cus (c*. 342–339 B.C.) as well as his last letter to Philip, written shortly
before his death in 338.[28] What is cast in mythical terms in the *Helen*
becomes a concrete programme in the *Panegyricus*, written a few years
later, in 380:[29] Athens and Sparta are urged to reconcile their differences
and assume joint leadership in a struggle to liberate Greece from the
thraldom to Persia which the King's Peace had sealed (iv. 15–17).
Gorgias and Lysias had delivered panegyrics on similar themes at the
Olympic games of 408 and 388, respectively;[30] but by calling his
composition 'Panegyrikos' rather than 'Olympiakos' (v *Phil*. 9, xii
Panath. 172) and by proposing a specific agenda in written rather than in
oral form, Isocrates expressed his desire to reach a wider audience and to
have a more permanent impact than the speeches of predecessors had
made. The fact that Athens is envisioned as the senior partner in an
alliance (18–21, 99) that would bring immediate peace and concord to
the Greek world and add prosperity after the subjugation of the

[27] See, e.g., Pl. *Phdr*. 278e, *Menex*. 249a; [Dem.] LXI. 44, 48.

[28] See esp. Kessler 1911 (H 72), and Bringmann 1965 (H 8) 109–13. Harding 1973 (H 58) 137–49,
esp. 148–9, does not carry conviction.

[29] For the date of the *Panegyricus*, see Eucken 1983 (H 39) 141 with n. 2. See also Buchner 1958 (B
23), and Seck 1976 (H 105) 353–70.

[30] Gorgias 82 A 1.4 and B 7–8a (D–K); for the date, see Wilamowitz-Moellendorff 1893 (C 270) I
172–3 with n. 75. The date of Lysias XXXIII is assured by Diod. XIV.109.3 and Dion. Hal. *Lys*. 29, cf.
Blass 1887 (H 5) I 431 with n. 1.

barbarians (157–84) is not sufficient reason to attribute to Isocrates' influence the foundation of the Second Athenian League two years after the publication of the *Panegyricus* (see pp. 164–7) or to regard that league as a partial fulfilment of his appeal for panhellenic unity.[31] But he surely deserves credit for having correctly gauged the temper of his times. Unlike his rival Demosthenes, he recognized early that the time of the parochial pursuit by the city states each of its own interests was coming to an end, and that a larger basis for independence had to be found in order to safeguard the freedom of the Greeks.

For Isocrates the establishment of peace and concord (*homonoia*) among the Greek states was not only a political but also a moral imperative. When he recognized that neither the Second Athenian League nor the Theban hegemony[32] was capable of bringing about unity, he shifted his perspective, emphasizing the importance of internal harmony within each state and the need for a strong leader who, having brought peace to his own state, would lead the united Greeks against Persia. The shift becomes recognizable in *On the Peace*, probably composed *c.* 355 B.C. while the negotiations about the terms for ending the Social War (see pp. 736–9) were still going on (VIII.16), and more prominently in the *Areopagiticus*, which followed hard upon its heels.[33] There is no mention of the panhellenic idea; the King's Peace, condemned in the *Panegyricus* (IV.122–4), is now accepted as a sufficient guarantee of external peace (VIII.16).[34] Imperialism becomes the target of his attack in both its Spartan and Athenian form. He appeals to each city to establish peace and prosperity within its own walls and to put an end to ideological differences among its citizens; otherwise, he argues, there is no chance for good relations with other states (VIII.19–20, 75–9, esp. 133–5).

Moral leadership was for Isocrates not necessarily associated with a particular form of government. What he looked for was a government which 'habitually appoints to office and the management of affairs the most competent of its citizens, that is, those who are going to direct the affairs of state most effectively and justly' (XII *Panath.* 132). Unable to find this in a democracy or oligarchy, he finally turned to a monarch.

The idea that a monarch might be able to implement these goals first appears in an appeal to Dionysius I of Syracuse in 369/8 B.C., who, at the peak of his power when Thebes had reduced Sparta, is petitioned as 'the first of the race and as holding the greatest power' (*Ep.* 1. 7) to turn his attention to the salvation of all Greeks.[35] What form Isocrates wished

31 See Buchner 1958 (B 23) 136–8 and Bringmann 1965 (H 8) 42–6.
32 See XIV *Plataicus* and esp. VIII *De Pace* 58–50; cf. V. *Phil.* 53–5.
33 See Bringmann 1965 (H 8) 75–81.   34 See Momigliano 1966 (C 51) 457–87, esp. 475.
35 For Athens' relations with Dionysius at this time, see above, pp. 150–1 and Bringmann 1965 (H 8) 54–5.

Dionysius' leadership to take we do not know, since the letter breaks off after its introduction; any concrete recommendations it may have contained were frustrated by Dionysius' death a year later. Isocrates directed a similarly futile appeal to the young Spartan king Archidamus in the midst of the Social War in 356 (*Ep.* 9 *Archid.* 1, 14, 17–18).

Finally, Isocrates took the controversial step of turning to Philip of Macedon.[36] He saw in the Peace of Philocrates of 346 an opportunity to promote through Philip's external pressure that peace and unity among the Greeks which his appeal to other powers and potentates had failed to secure (v *Phil.* 14–16). Neither Philip nor Isocrates lived to see the implementation of this plan by Alexander.[37]

Through his students, many of whom came from abroad (xv *Antid.* 39, 146, 164, 224), Isocrates left an imprint on the politics of his own city and time. Among the roughly one hundred pupils he taught in the course of his life,[38] Isocrates gives pride of place to Timotheus son of Conon, one of the great Athenian generals and statesmen of the Second Athenian League (see above, n. 38 and pp. 174–5), whom he accompanied on several missions ([Plut.] *X orat.* 837c). To Timotheus and Conon Isocrates will have owed his introduction to Evagoras and Nicocles, close relations with whom are attested by his Cyprian tracts (II, III, and x; cf. xv *Antid.* 40). Less well known to us are seven pupils who, Isocrates boasts, were rewarded with golden crowns for their service to Athens (xv *Antid.* 93–4).[39] Lycurgus allegedly was a pupil of both Plato and Isocrates[40] before he became a prominent spokesman for financial reform and opposition to Macedonian expansion, and the Atthidographer Androtion had studied with him (*Vita Isoc.* III.95–6). Leodamas,

---

[36] The date is established by the references to the Peace of Philocrates at v *Phil.* 7. For the historical circumstances, see Cloché 1963 (c 119) 101–16; Ellis 1976 (d 80) 128–30. In his critique of this tract, Speusippus states in his *Letter to Philip* 13 (text in Bickermann and Sykutris 1928 (d 64)) that Isocrates had in the past sent similar tracts to Agesilaus, Dionysius and Alexander of Pherae.

[37] According to tradition (DH *Isoc.* 1.5, [Plut.] *X orat.* 837e and 838b, Paus. 1.18.8, Lucian, *Macrobioi* 23), Isocrates starved himself to death a few days after learning of the defeat at Chaeronea (or on the day of the funeral of its dead).

[38] [Plut,.] *X orat.* 837c with Johnson 1957 (H 68). On their known names, see Blass 1892 (H 5) II 52–61.

[39] Eunomus, general in 388/7 B.C., was defeated off Aegina by the Spartan Gorgopas (Xen. *Hell.* v.1.5–9); and was with Conon ambassador to Dionysius of Syracuse in 393 B.C. to negotiate a marriage-alliance with the family of Evagoras (Lys. XIX.19). Lysitheides and Callippus are best known to us from [Dem.] LII of 369/8 B.C., in which the latter appears as prosecutor of Apollodorus, son of the banker Pasion, for their friendship with Isocrates see *ibid.* 14–15, 30; Lysitheides was syntrierarch in 355 B.C. on the ship that took ambassadors to Mausolus (Davies 1971 (c 124) 356–7). Onetor and Philonides were brothers, the former made famous through a lawsuit launched against him by Demosthenes (Dem. XXX and XXXI), see Davies 1971 (c 124) 423. Philomelus undertook liturgies as *choregos* and trierarch from the early 370s until his death in 336/5 B.C. (Davies 1971 (c 124) 548–9), and Charmantides was *choregos* and trierarch *c.* 366 B.C. (Davies 1971 (c 124) 573–4).

[40] [Plut.] *X orat.* 841b; *Vita Isocratis* III.93 (= Westermann 1845 (B 126) 256). For Lycurgus, see Davies 1971 (c 124) no. 925.

prominent in Athens between 375 and 355 as an advocate for good relations with Boeotia, is included by [Plutarch] (*X orat.* 837d) among Isocrates' pupils, as is Lacritus, against whom a speech ascribed to Demosthenes is directed.[41] Python of Byzantium, who represented Philip in Athens in 344/3 in the renegotiation of the terms of the Peace of Philocrates, was the most eminent foreign politician to have studied under Isocrates.[42]

The most innovative historians of the fourth century, Ephorus of Cyme and Theopompus of Chios, were contemporaries at Isocrates' school and became historians at their teacher's prompting (*FGrH* 70 T 3 [a]–[c]).[43] According to some sources, Ephorus was the first to attempt to write a comprehensive Universal History from the beginning of intelligible history – in his view, the return of the children of Heracles – down to his own time. Twenty-nine books took his narrative as far as the siege of Perinthus in 341 B.C.; a thirtieth, continuing the account to the end of the Sacred War, was added by his son Demophilus.[44] Only fragments remain of his work; but we can form some idea of it from the work of Diodorus, especially his books XI–XVI, which are heavily indebted to Ephorus. More of a compiler of earlier historians than an original researcher, he tried, not always successfully, to harmonize differing accounts, sometimes by inventing facts and figures, but with little understanding of historical problems.

Theopompus began his career with an attempt to complete Thucydides' history. The fact that the twelve books of his *Hellenica* took him only from the battle of Cynossema in 411/10 to the battle of Cnidus in 394 B.C. indicates expansiveness in style and subject-matter. This will as well have characterized his *Philippica* in fifty-eight books, original in that it made one outstanding man the centrepiece of a historical era. Unlike his teacher, he regarded Philip as too morally depraved to implement ideas of a cultural panhellenism.[45] Since only sixteen of the fifty-eight books seem to have dealt discursively with Philip, it is difficult to detect Isocrates behind the rambling discussions of Sicily, of a utopian myth ascribed to Silenus, of Zoroastrianism, of Athenian demagogues, Illyrians, Etruscans, and so forth. Since the remains of these two historians

41 [Dem.] xxxv, where Lacritus is described as a pupil of Isocrates at §15 (cf. also 41). On what grounds [Plut.] loc. cit. calls him ὁ νομοθέτης 'Αθηναίοις we do not know.
42 *Vita Isocr.* III.97 (= Westermann 1845 (B 126) 257). For his activities, see Ellis 1976 (D 80) 143–7, and Cawkwell 1978 (D 73) 123–6. Less credible is the tradition that Isaeus and Hypereides ([Plut.] *X orat.* 837d; *Vita Isocr.* III.93 (Westermann 1845 (B 126) p. 256)) had been Isocrates' students.
43 For the ancient evidence see Jacoby *FGrH* 70 T 1, 2 (a), 3 (a)–(c), 4, 5, 8, and 28 (a)–(b); and 115 T 1, 5 (a), 6 (b), 20 (a), 24, 37, and 38.
44 See Barber 1935 (B 11).
45 The view that Theopompus was a panhellenist (see Momigliano 1931 (B 80) 230–42, 335–53) has been convincingly refuted by Connor 1967 (B 31) 133–54; Shrimpton 1977 (D 118) 123–44; and Lane Fox 1986 (B 65) 105–20.

are too fragmentary[46] to state what influence Isocrates may have exerted on them, we may assume that he influenced their literary style, which is no longer accessible to us, but was accessible to their ancient critics,[47] who contrasted Theopompus' bold and lively style with Ephorus' hesitant and low-key manner of writing (Cic. *De Or.* III.36).

[Plutarch] (*X orat.* 837c) alleges two literary figures to have been pupils of Isocrates, Asclepiades of Trogilus, who was the first to compose a work on tragic themes (*Tragoedoumena*) in eleven books, of which some fragments survive,[48] and Theodectes of Phaselis, a pupil also of Plato and Aristotle. He not only wrote speeches and a handbook of rhetoric, but also produced fifty tragedies (*Suda s.v.* Θεοδέκτης).

Isocrates' claim to fame rests only in part on the influence he exerted on politics, rhetoric, history and literature through the pupils he trained in the fifty-two years of his activity as a teacher. More notable is his transformation of rhetoric from an art of argumentation and debate into a powerful educational tool for civilizing and cultivating future generations: 'proper speech we regard as the surest evidence of sound thinking, and speech, when truthful, lawful and just, is the image of a good and trustworthy soul' (III *Nicocl.* 7). His *logos* lives in the written rather than the spoken word, as literature to be circulated and read time and again rather than as a statement of a position on a single transient issue. His *politikoi logoi* address principles which, he believed, should animate the life of all civilized society. He was an elitist in that only members of the upper classes could afford to become his pupils. But through their leadership, he hoped, culture would spread from Athens to encompass all mankind: 'her disciples have become teachers of the rest, and she has brought it about that "Greek" is no longer regarded as the name of a race but a way of thinking, and those are called "Greeks" who share our culture rather than our common origin' (IV *Paneg.* 50). The creation of a cultural rather than a social elite was Isocrates' aim, and it is this image of Greece that he has bequeathed to later generations.

III. PLATO'S ACADEMY

1. *Plato*

The foundation of the Academy, opened by Plato shortly after his return from his first visit to Sicily in 387 B.C. (D.L. III. 7) disillusioned with the politics of his time, signalled the first serious challenge to

---

[46] Jacoby *FGrH* 70, attributes 236 fragments to Ephorus, and *FGrH* 115, 409 fragments to Theopompus.

[47] Jacoby, *FGrH* 70 T 3 (b) and (c), 11, 22, 24 (b), 28 (a)–(b); 115 T 20 (a) 9, 34, 36, 37. Schwartz 1907 (B 102) 1–16, seems to be going too far in using this basis to reject the tradition of a student–teacher relationship. On Theopompus' style, see Roberts 1908 (B 96) 118–22.

[48] Müller, *FHG* II.301ff.

Isocrates' school.[49] Our knowledge of its place in Plato's life depends largely on the *Seventh Letter*, which purports to be Plato's response, written *c.* 353 B.C., to a request for support from Dion's followers in Sicily.[50]

Born in 427 B.C. into an aristocratic family that traced its lineage to the last Athenian king, Codrus, on his father's side and to Solon's associate Dropides on his mother's (D.L. III.1–2), Plato expected to embark on an active political career.[51] But the regime which his uncle Charmides and his mother's cousin Critias invited him to join degenerated into the autocratic government of the Thirty and 'soon showed the preceding government to have been an age of gold' (*Ep.* VII.324b–d). Not long before this disenchantment, allegedly at the age of twenty (D.L. III.6), Plato had met Socrates, whose impact on him reinforced his aversion to a democracy, which had brought to trial and condemned to death for impiety the man 'whom I should hardly blush to call the justest man of his time', and alienated him still further from participating in political affairs.

Upon Socrates' death, Plato joined Eucleides and other members of Socrates' circle in Megara (D.L. III.6; II.106), then went to Cyrene to visit the mathematician Theodorus, and finally to southern Italy and Sicily, where he established contact with local Pythagorean communities and became friendly with Archytas, the Pythagorean tyrant of Tarentum, and with Dion, who invited him to the court of his father-in-law and brother-in-law, Dionysius I, tyrant of Syracuse (*c.* 388 B.C.), where the *dolce vita* made him despair of finding anywhere the kind of moral atmosphere which, he believed, is a precondition of stable government (*Ep.* VII.326b–d).

Accordingly, upon his return to Athens he purchased a small estate adjacent to a public park just outside the city near the Colonus Hippius, named 'Academy' after a local hero. From early times on, the Academy had contained a gymnasium, sacred olive trees, the oil from which was used at the Panathenaic festivals, and, like all public areas in Athens, a number of shrines to various divinities.[52] Since it was public property,

[49] Argued in detail by Eucken 1983 (H 39) 36–43.

[50] The question of Plato's authorship (still doubted by some scholars) is of little historical importance, since it is generally conceded that its author must have been intimately familiar with Plato's life and thoughts in 353 B.C. See Morrow 1962 (H 85) 3–16; Thesleff 1982 (H 110) 200–1 (with n. 71 for the controversy); 233–5; de Blois 1979 (G 118A).

[51] For details, see Guthrie 1975 (H 56) IV 8–32.

[52] D.L. III.5 and 7. For the Academy before Plato, see Ar. *Nub.* 1002–8 with schol. on 1005. For shrines to Prometheus, Athena and Hephaestus, see schol. on Soph. *OC* 56. Paus. 1.30.2 also mentions altars to the Muses and to Hermes just outside the Academy and a recent altar to Heracles within; according to the *Vita Platonis* 154–5 (Westermann 1845 (B 126) p. 393), Plato dedicated the precinct to the Muses in front of the school. There was also a statue of Eros in or near the Academy, dedicated in honour of Charmus by either Pisistratus or Hippias (Plut. *Sol.* 1.7, Paus. 1.30.1, Athen. XIII.609d, cf. 561d–3).

neither Plato nor his successors could ever appropriate any of its grounds, but they were as free to use its facilities as was any other person (Epicrates, fr. 10 K–A). The estate, however, was Plato's personal property, of which he made personal disposition in his will along with the rest of his assets (D.L. III.41–3).

2. The Academy

Plato's Academy had no formal corporate structure. It was neither a cult-group (*thiasos*),[53] nor was it modelled on such esoteric communities as the Pythagorean schools which Plato had encountered in southern Italy: it was open to anyone and attracted even two women, Lasthenea of Mantinea and Axiothea of Phlius (D.L. IV.2). There were no fees, but only those with sufficient private means not to have to work for their living could afford to join it.[54] The tradition that Plato delivered a public formal lecture on the Good (Aristox. *Harm.* II.30–1),[55] constitutes no evidence that he gave other lectures, public or within the Academy, or that either he or any other members of the school taught on a regular, systematic basis.

We have no information about the internal organization of the school or its admission policy, apart from the fact that Plato was its head (*scholarchos*), who 'determined its structure and set problems' for the other members to pursue.[56] We hear of no official division into faculty and students, or distinction between senior and junior members, although some differences in status must have been recognized. The fact that many of his pupils entered a life of active politics after they left the Academy suggests that Plato hoped that his school would contribute to the betterment of society (Plut. *Mor.* 1126c–d).[57] But many other intellectual activities are attested, most notably co-operative work on mathematical problems, suggesting that Plato's Academy consisted of persons of similar, but not identical, interests; it fostered togetherness (*synousia, Ep.* VII.341c) and tried to 'orient young men toward goodness and justice, and to establish in each case mutual friendship and fellowship among them' (*Ep.* VII.328d). There may have been lectures, 'seminars', public readings and the like, but none are explicitly attested.[58] No orthodoxy was propounded or expected to be followed: the mathematician Eudoxus, whose views often differed from Plato's, was

[53] The old contrary view (Guthrie 1975 (H 56) IV 19–22) has been convincingly refuted by Lynch 1972 (H 76) 108–18; cf. also Thesleff 1982 (H 110) 31–2.   [54] See Lynch 1972 (H 76) 54–63.
[55] See Gaiser 1980 (H 48) 5–37.   [56] Mekler 1902 (H 80) 15–16.
[57] See Chroust 1967 (H 18) 25–40.
[58] Cherniss 1945 (H 13) 1–30, denied the tradition of oral, unwritten Platonic doctrines any authenticity; the so-called 'Tübingen' school goes to the other extreme of basing its interpretation of Plato largely on the 'unwritten' doctrines; see Gaiser 1963 (H 46), and Krämer 1959 (H 73).

placed in charge of the school when Plato revisited Sicily, and Plato designated his nephew Speusippus as his successor, despite the fact that he rejected Plato's theory of Forms. The Academy perpetuated the informality of Socrates' teaching, except that it provided a permanent home to a narrower circle of interlocutors than Socrates had done. But this was not the only – or the most important – sense in which Plato saw the Academy as perpetuating Socrates' legacy.

3. *Plato at the Academy*

Plato's earliest writings – *Apology*, *Crito*, *Ion* – probably written within a decade of Socrates' death and before the opening of the Academy, are best understood as preserving authentic Socratic traits refracted through Plato's vision: a preoccupation with moral problems and 'the conception of philosophy as psychic therapy or "tendance for one's soul", regularly exercised in *elenchos* or cross-examination, and supported by a central core of paradoxes: no one does wrong voluntarily, it is better to suffer than to do wrong, virtue is knowledge, and no evil can happen to a good man'.[59]

Plato's own preoccupations first intrude themselves in the *Gorgias*, probably published about the time of the opening of the Academy.[60] Its confrontation of an active political life with a life of philosophy seems to reflect the conflict of Plato's early adult life more than Socrates'. In treating active politics as the outcome of the teaching of rhetoric (*Grg.* 471e–472d, 482e–486d, 490a, 491c–492c), Plato may well have been training his sights on the *politikoi logoi*, with which Isocrates tried to prepare his pupils for an active political life. To Isocrates' censure of the Socratic claim to be purveying a science (*episteme*) of moral conduct, Plato responded with a counter-attack on rhetoric as no more than the knack (*empeiria*) of flattering an ignorant mob (462b–463a, cf. 459a). The sharpness of Plato's barbs leaves little doubt that Isocrates' manifesto *Against the Sophists* was their target, perhaps to herald the opening of the Academy as a rival to Isocrates' school.[61]

The *Protagoras* appears to have been written between *c.* 385 and 380 B.C. to give content to the moral principles espoused but never satisfactorily defined by Socrates. Socrates is portrayed as convincing the earliest and most successful fifth-century exponent of moral relativism not only of the unity of all virtues but also of their dependence on

[59] Kahn 1981 (H 69) 305–20 with quote on p. 319.
[60] For the priority of *Grg.* to *Prt.* see Thesleff 1982 (H 110) 118, 125–34, and Kahn 1988 (H 70) 69–102 (with earlier discussions cited in both). However, a date after Plato's return from Sicily seems preferable to a date before his departure..
[61] See Eucken 1983 (H 39) 36–43, and Thesleff 1982 (H 110) 126–7.

knowledge (*Prt.* 330c–334c, 349d–358d): unless human excellence is conceived as based on knowledge, it cannot be taught (360e–362a). The question whether or not moral values (*aretai*) are objects of knowledge is raised in the *Meno*, which demonstrates that knowledge of mathematical absolutes and 'of everything that can be learned' (τῶν ἄλλων μαθημάτων ἁπάντων) is 'recollection' (*anamnesis*) of what the soul had seen before its incarnation in its present body (Pl. *Meno* 80d–86c). The question whether virtue is teachable, i.e. similarly capable of being 'recollected' (87b–d) is temporarily shelved, but it is answered positively in *Phaedo, Symposium* and *Republic* through the theory of Forms.[62]

Plato takes the existence of Forms (*eide, ideai*) for granted even when he first describes them in the *Phaedo* as the only knowable moral and mathematical attributes, differentiating 'the just itself', 'the noble itself', 'the equal itself', etc.[63] as entities independent of the objects or actions in which they are manifested: 'we affirm that there is something "equal"', not in the sense that I call two sticks or two stones or anything of that sort equal to one another, but something beyond these things and different from them: the equal itself' (Pl. *Phd.* 74a). These entities are apprehended directly by the soul, which has gained knowledge of them before we were born and can retrieve this knowledge by 'recollection' (*anamnesis*) (72e–76d). Sense perceptions (*aistheseis*) trigger recollection, because the absolute entities 'participate' in physical objects and give them whatever knowable quality (good, just, beautiful, large, small, etc.) they possess (99d–100e). How sense perceptions can make us embark on the quest for knowledge of absolute values is shown in the *Symposium* through the example of Beauty (209e–211b): Love (Eros), which motivates this quest, marks the true philosopher (203d–204b).

The *Republic*, published after c. 377/6,[64] explores the ramifications of the theory of Forms to make it the most magnificent compendium of Plato's philosophy. Its only substantive addition to the theory itself is an all-pervasive Form of the Good as the source of what is 'good' in each virtue, placed 'beyond reality' (ἐπέκεινα τῆς οὐσίας, 509b) and giving reality not only its intelligibility but its very existence (502c–509c). Thus enlarged, the theory becomes the underpinning of all his moral and political philosophy, including metaphysics, ontology, epistemology, psychology, and a theory of education; *philosophia* assumes a new meaning, which at once defines the general aim of the Academy and sets

---

[62] On the priority of *Symp.* or *Phd.*, see Guthrie 1975 (H 56) IV 325 with n. 1, and Thesleff 1982 (H 110) 142–3. The *Symp.* can be dated after 384/3 but before 378 B.C. (see Thesleff 117 with n. 4, 135). I find the arguments of Kapp 1968 (H 71) 55–150, esp. 60–1, 90, 115, for the priority of *Phd.* to *Symp.* compelling.

[63] Variously expressed as, e.g., αὐτὸ τὸ δίκαιον, τὸ δίκαιον αὐτὸ καθ'αὑτό, αὐτὸ τὸ ὅ ἔστι δίκαιον, etc. The fullest list, given at *Phd.* 75c–d, includes the equal, the greater, the lesser, the noble, the good, the just and the pious.   [64] See Kapp 1968 (H 71) 89.

the agenda for all subsequent philosophical inquiry in the Western tradition. In complete opposition to Isocrates (e.g. xv *Antid.* 271), the activity of the philosopher is removed from the realm of the senses in which we live (ὁρατὸς τόπος) and trained entirely on the realm of the mind (νοητὸς τόπος), where absolute moral norms are to be found. The philosopher as the expert in moral and political matters is the precondition of good government: his word is law and must be accepted without question by the governed. When Plato deals with the problems faced by the philosophic ruler in gaining acceptance of his rule (*Rep.* vi.484a–497a), the blame for his failure falls on the ignorant mob, not on any lack of persuasion on his part. The philosopher so conceived is far from the Solon he was in Herodotus or the *homme d'affaires* whom Isocrates wanted to educate.

Although there is no evidence that the educational programme proposed in the *Republic* (vii.521c–541b) for raising the philosopher's mind from the sensible to the intelligible world was ever intended as a blueprint of a curriculum for the Academy, it will surely reflect Plato's priorities and interests as a teacher, and may be taken as evidence for the kind of studies in mathematics, astronomy and musical theory pursued with his encouragement at the Academy, perhaps in part even as an advertisement for the solid geometry (vii.528a–d) which was being pioneered there.[65] Above all, it attests the supreme value Plato attached to abstract philosophical discussion, dialectic, which the *Republic* presents as the high point of philosophical studies.

The works published after the *Republic* reflect a concern with bringing philosophy closer to the realities of life, as a result, we may presume, of discussions both within and outside the Academy. The *Phaedrus*[66] applies the moral Forms for the first time to the practical end of formulating correct principles for the teaching of rhetoric, and in such a way that the dialogue as a whole can be interpreted as a manifesto of an oral against the written culture of which Isocrates was the most articulate exponent at this time.[67]

Plato's disparagement of writing (274b–277a) also affords us some insight into the way he envisaged his own role at the Academy. True learning requires a living context; writing is useful only as a pastime (*paidia*) and as an *aide-mémoire*; it is no substitute for memory and is not suitable as a vehicle for teaching and communicating truthful knowledge

[65] See Fowler 1987 (H 41) esp. pp. 106–54.

[66] For the date of *Phdr.* after *Rep.* between 372 and 368 B.C., see Howland 1937 (H 59) 151–9, esp. 159 n. 1; cf. also de Vries 1969 (H 113) 7–11.

[67] See above, pp. 595, 597–8. Cf. also Howland 1937 (H 59); de Vries 1969 (H 113) 15–19 with bibliography p. 15, n. 1; Eucken 1983 (H 39) 115–20, 270–4, and Connors 1986 (H 21) 38–65. On the complimentary yet patronizing remark on Isocrates at 279a: φύσει γάρ . . . ἔνεστί τις φιλοσοφία τῇ τοῦ ἀνδρὸς διανοίᾳ, see Eucken 1983 (H 39) 273–4.

(276d). What, then, are we to make of Plato's own writings? Nothing in his statement permits us to consider his published works as in any sense different from or inferior to what he may have communicated orally to the members of the Academy. But painfully aware that writing can not express all that can be said about a given subject, he chose the give-and-take of the dialogue as the literary form for his philosophy to indicate that he regarded discussion as open-ended, and perhaps that he wanted to keep the record of a subject discussed at the Academy as a stimulus to further investigation.[68]

Lively debates and disputes about the range and validity of the Forms within the Academy can be detected in the *Parmenides* and the *Theaetetus*, written in rapid succession in the early 360s.[69] New Forms of Likeness and Unlikeness, Plurality and Unity, and Motion and Rest, introduced in the *Parmenides* (128e–129e), raise fundamental questions about the relation between Forms and things (130c–e). No answer is given, but it is agreed that without Forms no knowledge, thought, or discourse is possible (134e–135c). The *Theaetetus* demonstrates negatively that neither sense perception nor true belief can by itself result in knowledge (*Tht.* 385cd). Like the later *Sophist*, this dialogue celebrates the memory of a great mathematician, whose considerable mathematical proficiency influenced epistemological discussions in the Academy in the early 360s, and who had recently died of wounds sustained in an Athenian encounter with Corinth in 369 B.C.[70]

We get some further insight into the life of the Academy from Plato's arrangements for the two periods of his absence in Sicily on his disastrous mission to educate young Dionysius II into a philosopher king.[71] During the first (367–365 B.C.), Eudoxus of Cnidus served as temporary scholarch;[72] it was under his stewardship that Aristotle came to the Academy from his native Stagira at the age of seventeen; during the second (361–360), Heraclides of Pontus was its acting head.[73] Neither of these men was an Athenian citizen, and neither of them was a Platonist in a strict sense of the word. Eudoxus, who had already made remarkable discoveries in mathematics, which he applied to studies in astronomy and geography, and had founded a school in Cyzicus before coming to the Academy,[74] diverged from Plato in challenging the theory

---

[68] See de Vries 1969 (H 113) 21 with n. 2.
[69] On the dates, see Thesleff 1982 (H 110) 152–61, 188. The most useful commentaries on these two dialogues are still those of Cornford 1939 (H 24); and 1935 (H 22).
[70] See Bulmer-Thomas 1976 (H 10) 301–7.
[71] Pl. *Ep.* VII. 327b–330b, 337e–340a, 344d–350b; Plut. *Dion* 17.1; see Guthrie 1975 (H 56) IV 24–31.
[72] Philochorus 328 F 223 (*FGrH*) (= *Vita Marciana* 11 in Düring 1957 (H 36) 99).
[73] Heraclides Ponticus, fr. 2, in Wehrli 1969 (H 115a), with Lynch 1972 (H 76) 82 with n. 20.
[74] See Huxley 1971 (H 61) 465–7, and Guthrie 1978 (H 56) V 447–57; for his achievements in mathematics and astronomy, see Fowler 1987 (H 41) 122–30 and 'Index of Names' *s.v.* 'Eudoxus'.

of Forms (Arist. *Metaph.* A.9, 991a17; fr. 189) and in identifying pleasure as the Good (Arist. *Eth. Nic.* 1.12, 1101b27–31; x.2, 1172b9–15).

Heraclides of Heraclea in Pontus, who had entered the Academy about 365/4 B.C., was as versatile as Eudoxus in his interests, but less profound and more dependent on Plato's thinking.[75] Most of the forty-seven works attributed to him (D.L. v.87–8) were, like Plato's, written in dialogue form, and his astronomy and physics take doctrines found in the *Timaeus* as their starting-point.[76] He stayed at the Academy until after the death of Speusippus in 338. When Xenocrates defeated him by a narrow margin in the election to succeed Speusippus as scholarch, he returned to his native Heraclea (fr. 9 Wehrli).

The same free and wide-ranging intellectual life shown in these appointments is also reflected in Plato's own last works, written after his return to the Academy in 360, *Sophist, Statesman, Philebus, Timaeus, Critias* and the *Laws*,[77] which, as a group, give us Plato's most comprehensive view of the nature of life in the visible world in which we live. The *Timaeus* is the only extant part of a trilogy, projected to encompass also the (unfinished) *Critias* and a *Hermocrates*, which was never written (*Tim.* 20a, 27a; *Criti.* 108a), which proposes to set the problem of good government into a cosmic context, beginning with the origin of the universe, man's place in it, the development and degeneration of social and political life, and its restoration after a general cataclysm.[78] While this grandiose and imaginative scheme must be entirely Plato's, there can be no doubt that the *Timaeus* owes much to the research of and discussion with other members of the Academy in the 350s, especially mathematicians and astronomers.

Already before writing the *Timaeus*, Plato had given up the hope that human ills can be cured by a philosophic ruler: in the *Statesman* good government does not depend on an intellectual vision, but on the managerial skills of a knowledgeable ruler. The *Laws*, Plato's last work, which was completed by his pupil and secretary, the mathematician and astronomer Philip of Opus (D.L. III.37),[79] despairs even of the possibility that an expert of this sort can be found; it proposes instead the enactment of a detailed code of laws, which are observed through the suasion of elaborate preambles rather than by coercion, and which are periodically reviewed by a Nocturnal Council.

However, frustrations such as these never shook Plato's belief in the existence of absolute moral values. In the *Statesman*, these are embodied

75 Fragments in Wehrli 1969 (H 115a) VII; full discussion in Gottschalk 1980 (H 54).
76 Gottschalk 1980 (H 54) 58–87, esp. 82–3.
77 See Thesleff 1982 (H 110) 70–1. Owen's arguments (1953 (H 89) 79–95) for dating *Tim.* and *Criti.* with *Resp.* and *Phd.* in the middle group have been decisively rebutted by Cherniss 1957 (H 14) 225–66, and 1957 (H 15) 18–23.   78 Cornford 1937 (H 23) 1–8.
79 See von Fritz 1938 (H 42) 2351–66.

in the good ruler's knowledge of 'the truest standard of correct administration of the state' (Pl. *Plt.* 296e), which laws can at best only imitate (*ibid.* 300e); in the *Laws*, where even the possibility of government by an expert is relegated to a long-lost past (Pl. *Lg.* iv.713a–e, ix.853c), a lawgiver's expertise provides him with 'a truth he can hold on to' (*ibid.* iv.709c), with a vision of virtue as a whole (*ibid.* iii.688b, iv.714b–c), and with a standard of justice and injustice that will help him in framing laws for his community (*ibid.* iv.714b, 715b). Plato never gave up his belief that knowledge of moral values can be attained, presumably through the Forms; but access to it is so restricted that its implementation can only be left to an institution, such as a code of laws supervised by a Nocturnal Council.

4. *Plato's successors*

Unlike the schools of Antisthenes and Isocrates, Plato's Academy was able to continue as a philosophical school after Plato's death in 347 B.C.[80] How and why Speusippus, the son of Plato's sister Potone and Eurymedon of Myrrhinous,[81] was chosen to take over the Academy at the age of over sixty has been a matter of considerable speculation.[82] He was one of the very few native Athenians who had been associated with Plato's Academy from its inception. Though a loyal supporter of Plato's efforts, he frequently disagreed with his uncle on issues as central as the theory of Forms (cf. Arist. *Metaph.* Z. 2, 1028b18–24).[83]

Proclus (*In Euc.* 1. 77–8) mentions Speusippus as a leading mathematician at the Academy. Titles and fragments of his writings corroborate a particular interest in number theory and in Pythagorean mathematics. But his philosophical interests also included ethical tenets, among them his celebrated view, articulated in opposition to Eudoxus and for which he was frequently ridiculed, that pleasure (*hedone*) was an evil that ought to be avoided. This reflects debates in the Academy on the role of pleasure in human life, which also provide the background for Plato's *Philebus*.

Of the thirty titles ascribed to Speusippus by Diogenes Laertius (iv.4–5), the work on classifications entitled *Homoia* ('Similar Things') (in ten books) was influential in arguing for the need for an exhaustive classification of all things, and prefigured the classification scheme later used by Aristotle in his *Historia Animalium*. It was possibly influenced by

---

[80] Cf. Lynch 1972 (H 76) 75–7. Cf. Gaiser 1988 (H 50) 356–7, 365–6.
[81] See Tarán 1981 (H 109) 175–6.
[82] See Chroust 1971 (H 19) 170–6 with Tarán 1981 (H 109) 8–11. For the fragments, see also Isnardi Parente 1980 (H 63).   [83] See Tarán 1981 (H 109) chs. 2–4 and p. 177.

the empirical studies of Aristotle and Theophrastus going on in the Academy even during Plato's lifetime.[84]

Speusippus became an intimate friend of Dion of Syracuse during his visit to the Academy (Plut. *Dion* 17 and 22), and when Dion sailed back to Sicily, he gave Speusippus a country estate which he had acquired during his stay. Speusippus later accompanied Plato to Sicily on his third and last journey in 361/0 B.C. and, according to Plutarch, actively supported Dion's attempt to free Sicily from tyranny.

When Speusippus died, Aristotle was probably not seriously considered as his successor because he had moved back, or was engaged on a mission, to Macedonia. The favoured candidates, Menedemus of Pyrrha, about whose long career at the Academy not much is known,[85] and Heraclides of Pontus lost the vote by a narrow margin to Xenocrates of Chalcedon, who had left Athens in the company of Aristotle when Plato died.[86] Disappointed, Heraclides and Menedemus left the Academy, Heraclides to return to his native Heraclea and Menedemus to 'establish another *peripatos* and *diatribe*' elsewhere, though we are not told where.

Xenocrates, as well as his successor Polemon of Athens, occupied as scholarch the same dwelling as Plato (Plut. *De exil.* 10, *Mor.* 603B-C), perhaps through some special arrangement with Plato's heir, his grand-nephew Adeimantus (D.L. III.41–44).[87] We are told that Xenocrates refused offers of Athenian citizenship[88] and that on one occasion, when he was to be sold as a slave for failing to pay his metic-tax (*metoikion*), Demetrius of Phalerum paid the money to redeem him (D.L. IV.14).[89]

A pupil of Plato's from his youth (D.L. IV.6), Xenocrates was about fifty-seven years old when he was summoned to take over the Academy. Comparing him with the younger Aristotle, with whom Xenocrates was closely associated for much of his career, Plato is said to have likened him to a donkey that needs the spur and Aristotle to a horse that needs the curb (D.L. IV.6). In his twenty-five years as scholarch, Xenophanes is said to have visited the centre of Athens only to see the new tragedies at the Dionysia festival. In 322 B.C., he took part in an embassy to Antipater on behalf of Athens.[90]

Xenocrates was a prolific writer on a wide range of philosophical

---

[84] On these points, see Cherniss 1945 (H 13) 31–59 and 1944 (H 12) 44–8.

[85] Testimonia and fragments in Lasserre 1987 (H 75).

[86] Philodemus' *Index Academicorum*, cols. VI. 28–VII. 17, pp. 37–40 Mekler 1902 (H 80), with Merlan 1946 (H 81) 103–11.

[87] Adeimantus may have been Xenocrates' pupil (*Index Academicorum*, col. IV, 10–11, p. 45 Mekler 1902 (H 80)).

[88] Plut. *Phoc.* 29.4, and the *Index Academicorum*, col. VIII. 1–15, p. 42 (Mekler 1902 (H 80)).

[89] See Whitehead 1981 (H 119) 235–8.

[90] See Whitehead 1981 (H 119) 238–41.

subjects, focused particularly on systematizing knowledge.[91] His close association with Aristotle in the Academy and Asia Minor after Plato's death exposed him to the kind of systematic empiricism which character-ized Aristotle's work. What differentiates his thinking and writing from Aristotle's is a particular interest in demonology, which is attested by the interest Neoplatonists took in his work. Many titles suggest that Xenocrates continued the Academy's interest not only in mathematics but also in the work of the Pythagoreans who pioneered in applying the insights of mathematical knowledge to *philosophia* in its widest sense as a means to understanding the proper conduct of life.

It is intriguing to speculate, why Aristotle, when he returned to Athens in 335, did not rejoin the Academy under the leadership of Xenocrates but instead chose to found his own school. A tradition, preserved in the ancient *Lives* of Aristotle, saw the two schools as complementary branches rather than rivals.[92] Whatever the reasons for the separation of the two philosophical communities at Athens, it is worth emphasizing that Xenocrates' twenty-five years of leadership provided continuity and stability to the Academy during a period of considerable political turmoil.

5. Other members of the Academy: the extent and character of the philosophical community

Aside from the one contemporary glimpse in the fragment of the comic poet Epicrates (fr. 11 K), the oldest source on the Academic community is from the first century B.C., composed by the Epicurean Philodemus, who lived in Herculaneum and whose work on the history of the Academy survives in a fragmentary papyrus from Herculaneum, the so-called *Academicorum Philosophorum Index Herculanensis* (= *P. Herc.* 1021).[93] Though its fragmentary state does not make it always easy to interpret, Philodemus' *Index Academicorum* has proved to be a most reliable and synthetic source of information on twenty members of the Academy in Plato's lifetime, based on older and generally trustworthy evidence, possibly including an account by Hermodorus of Syracuse, a mathematician associated with the school.[94] With additions from later

---

[91] For Xenocrates' fragments, see Isnardi Parente 1982 (H 64).

[92] *Vita Marciana* 24 (p. 101 in Düring 1957 (H 36)); cf. *Vita Latina* 24 (p. 154 Düring); *Vita Vulgata* 18 (p. 134 Düring). For Aristotle's foundation of a separate school as a disloyal and ungrateful secession from the Academy, see Düring 1957 (H 36) 465.

[93] The standard edition has been that of Mekler 1902 (H 80). Cf. also Gaiser 1988 (H 50), which also includes a short related papyrus, *P. Herc.* 164, re-edited by Dorandi.

[94] Testimonia in Isnardi Parente 1982 (H 64) 157–60; cf. also Lasserre 1987 (H 75) 217–23 and 667–80.

lists over seventy-five names can now be associated with the Academy during its first forty years.

These names make the foreign cast of the Academy's make-up particularly apparent. In Philodemus' *Index Academicorum* Speusippus emerges as the only Athenian among the twenty names associated with the Academy in Plato's lifetime. To him may possibly be added from Plutarch (*Adv. Colotem*, 32, Mor. 1126C–D)[95] the generals Chabrias and Phocion. Both were, like Speusippus, kinsmen of Plato and their association with the Academy, if historical, must date soon after its opening in 387. Plutarch lists as politically active members of Plato's Academy Dion, hailed as the liberator of Sicily, and the Academic brothers Python and Heraclides of Aenus, who assassinated the tyrant Cotys of Thrace; Academics who served as law-givers mentioned by Plutarch are Aristonymus, sent by Plato to his home state of Arcadia to reform the constitution, Phormio who did the same in his native Elis, Eudoxus in Cnidus and Aristotle in Stagira. Xenocrates of Chalcedon is mentioned as a political adviser to Alexander, while Delius (or Dias) of Ephesus is described as having played a vital role as an emissary to Alexander on behalf of the Greeks of Asia Minor.

Athenaeus' *Deipnosophistae* (XI. 508c–509e), written a full century after Plutarch, lists a number of Academics, known also from Philodemus' *Index Academicorum* and other lists,[96] for their meddling in politics. It is allegedly based on a contemporary work *Against Plato's School*, written by Isocrates' pupil Theopompus of Chios (508c, see pp. 601–2 above). Almost all the names in these two lists are corroborated by the more comprehensive *Index Academicorum* or by some other credible source.[97]

Of two later lists, that given in Diogenes Laertius' *Life of Plato* (III.46) contains the well-based information, attributed to Aristotle's pupil Dicaearchus (cf. fr. 44 Wehrli), that Plato's Academy included Lasthenea of Mantinea and Axiothea of Phlius.[98]

The other list, found in Proclus' *Commentary on Euclid's Book 1*, is based

---

[95] On Plut. *Adv. Colotem* as a source, see Westman 1955 (B 129).
[96] Negative political examples include Euphraeus of Oreus, Callippus of Athens, Euagon of Lampsacus, Timaeus of Cyzicus, and Chaeron of Pellene. Euagon must be identical with Euaion of Lampsacus in the list of Diogenes Laertius; Timaeus with the Timolaos of Cyzicus in Diogenes' list and in the *Index Academicorum* (III.46 Mekler 1902 (H 80)). See Wörle 1981 (H 123). Cf. also Lynch 1972 (H 76) 59, n. 32.
[97] Neither Plutarch nor Athenaeus mentions the Academics Chion and Leonides of Heraclea, who assassinated the tyrant Clearchus of Pontic Heraclea in 352 B.C., both of whom appear in Philodemus' *Index Academicorum*, col. VI, p. 35 Mekler 1902 (H 80).
[98] See also Philodemus' *Index Academicorum* (col. VI, p. 37 Mekler 1902 (H 80); cf. *P. Herc.* 164, fr. 1 Dorandi). Themistius, the orator of the fourth century of our era, says that Axiothea came to the Academy at Athens after she had read Plato's *Republic* and that she attended the Academy disguised as a man for a long time before she was discovered (*Or.* XXIII.295c–d).

on reliable 'school' sources from the fourth and early third century B.C. and includes Philip of Opus, Plato's secretary in the Academy, and Eudemus of Rhodes, a member of the Peripatos, who composed an early history of mathematics.[99]

Among the *mathematikoi* said to have 'lived with one another in the Academy, making common inquiries' (Proclus, pp. 67–8) are the distinguished mathematician and philosopher Eudoxus of Cnidus, Amyclas of Heraclea, Menaechmus and his brother Deinostratus (both of Alopeconnesus), Theudius of Magnesia and Athenaeus of Cyzicus. Hermotimus of Colophon, Theaetetus (of Sunium), and Philip of Mende (= of Opus)[100] are all mentioned in the same context and may be safely inferred to have participated in mathematical inquiries attested for Plato and Eudoxus in the Academy. Many of the foreign *mathematikoi* mentioned by Proclus are likely to have come to Athens as followers of Eudoxus from his school in Cyzicus, in the Propontis, and at the court of Mausolus in Caria (D.L. VIII.87).[101] An interesting passage in Plutarch (*Marc.* 14.5–6) tells us that Plato objected to the use made by Eudoxus and his circle, as also by Archytas and his, of mechanical models in solving mathematical problems on the grounds that such methodology 'destroyed and corrupted the good of geometry by having recourse to sense-perceptions instead of using incorporeal, abstract thought processes and, on top of that, by employing concrete devices, which required a considerable amount of commercial activity and of manual labour'.

Plato's sharp dichotomy between sophists and philosophers blurs the fact that, despite some mutual rivalry and hostility, the school of Isocrates and the Academy of Plato also engaged in intellectual exchange and dialogue, and the result was to raise the level of discussion on a range of philosophical issues. Some members of the Academy are even reported to have studied with Isocrates·and his students. Helicon of Cyzicus was a student of Eudoxus as well as an associate of one of Isocrates' students and also of Polyxenus, one of Bryson's followers (Pl. *Ep.* XIII.360c), and is called 'one of Plato's intimates' by Plutarch (*Dion* 19). An interesting 'crossover' figure is Theodectes of Phaselis (in Lycia), who is several times mentioned with respect in Aristotle's *Rhetoric*. He is described as 'a student of Plato and of Isocrates and of Aristotle', who wrote encomia, tragedies, an *Apology of Socrates*, a rhetorical handbook in verse, and some treatises in catalogue form (see

[99] On Philip, see Tarán 1972 (H 108) 124–5 and 128–39. For Eudemus, see Wehrli 1969 (H 115A) VIII frr. 133–41.   [100] See Tarán 1972 (H 108) 125–7.
[101] See Merlan 1960 (H 82) 98–104. Cf. also Huxley 1963 (H 60) 83–96, and above, n. 74; and Lasserre 1966 (H 74).

Suda s.v. Θεοδέκτης). One of Aristotle's lost works was entitled *Compendium of the Rhetorical Handbook of Theodectes* (D.L. v.25).

The visit of an unnamed Chaldaean[102] may be related to astronomical researches and interest in calendar reform within the Academy initiated by Eudoxus and Callippus of Cyzicus. Callippus was an astronomer, who followed Eudoxus to Athens 'and lived with Aristotle, correcting and amplifying with Aristotle's help discoveries made by Eudoxus' (Simpl. *in Cael.* p. 493, 5–8). He became famous for making significant advances in calendar reform over the late fifth-century theories of Meton and Euctemon.

The intellectual, cultural and geographical variety of the Academy opened the road to a wide range of possible relationships among individuals of different purposes, interests and personal motivations. It was a centre of intellectual challenge and accommodation, not a homogeneous group with a fixed set of philosophical positions to propagate. The community was predominantly (perhaps as high as 90 per cent) non-Athenian; many members came from northern and central Greece, the Peloponnesus, Propontic and Pontic cities, the coast of Asia Minor, and the Greek West (southern Italy and Sicily). Others found their way from places which had Pythagorean brotherhoods, from cities in Asia Minor where Eudoxus and other itinerant teachers had taught, or from commercial centres located along familiar trade routes such as existed between Athens and the port cities of the Propontis and Pontus. Thus, the Academy was not a product of a particular individual or a particular polis, but a response to the need of the larger Greek world for putting the educational process and political, scientific and other sorts of philosophical questions into a panhellenic framework. Like the sophists, the Academy took advantage of public space in a highly visible urban centre and circulated philosophical writings to attract attention and build up a following. Unlike inward-looking Pythagorean brotherhoods (and, to some extent, the later school of Epicurus at Athens), participation in the Academy did not involve any prescribed initiation procedures, rites of passage, sacred or secret oaths, dietary rules, or common markings that served to distinguish an insider from an outsider in relation to the surrounding community. As an institution it was a further development of the kind of school that Isocrates and various followers of Socrates had already formed (despite Socrates' own resistance to separating philosophical education from everyday life in the city); as Isocrates and others had already begun to do, Plato reconfigured the old

102 *Index Academicorum*, col. III, 36–41, p. 13 Mekler 1902 (H 80); cf. Westerink 1962 (H 117) I.6, p. 15. Cf. Tarán 1972 (H 108) 116; cf. 124–5, esp. n. 519 (Philip of Opus, Test. v).

inter-city institution of guest-friendship, *xenia*,[103] formed through traditional family-ties, as his principal mechanism to create a more complex community, dedicated to learning, teaching and research, that looked beyond the polis even to the non-Greek world.

IV. ARISTOTLE AND THE PERIPATOS

1. *Aristotle in the Academy*

Aristotle, 'the most genuine of Plato's students', according to some ancient sources, was born in 384 B.C. in the northern Greek coastal village of Stagira, an Ionic-speaking colony on the Thracian peninsula of Chalcidice that had been settled by immigrants from the islands of Euboea and Andros.[104] He had two siblings, a sister Arimneste and a brother Arimnestus. The latter died childless, and Aristotle provided in his will for a statue to be set up in his memory.[105] Aristotle's father Nicomachus was a member of the medical guild of the Asclepiadae and become the court physician to Amyntas III, king of Macedonia, father of Philip and grandfather of Alexander the Great. Aristotle's mother, Phaestis, came from a family also associated with the Asclepiadae in Chalcis on Euboea, where she owned an ancestral estate. Despite these medical connexions, it is doubtful that Aristotle was exposed in any significant way to the practice or profession of medicine as a child, since his parents both died when he was very young. He was raised by his legal guardian, Proxenus of Atarneus, who had married Aristotle's sister Arimneste.

More significant for Aristotle's subsequent philosophical career is the fact that he was born and raised among 'outsiders', in a family professionally associated with the Macedonian court in Pella but whose connexions, cultural traditions and intellectual heritage (including their native dialect of Greek) were 'foreign' in the eyes of Macedonian society. For most of his adolescent and adult life he was to lead the life of a foreigner, a resident but never a citizen in the society in which he was living.

There are no clues to explain Proxenus' reasons for sending the young Aristotle, at the age of seventeen, to Athens to further his education at the Academy, which had become known for mathematical, political,

---

103 For this important institution, see Herman 1987 (C 34). See also McKechnie 1989 (I 100).

104 The most important discussions of Aristotle and his thought are Düring 1966 (H 37), and 1957 (H 36), which modify the influential work of Jaeger 1948 (H 67) (originally published in Berlin, 1923). For a recent treatment of Aristotle, see Rist 1989 (H 99).

105 For Aristotle's will, see Chroust 1973 (H 20) 183–231; Gottschalk 1972 (H 53) 314–42; and Düring 1957 (H 36) 263–4.

epistemological and ethical inquiries, but not for any interest in medicine, biology, or – the staple of higher learning in other institutional settings – rhetoric. In the twenty-year history of the Athenian Academy no other Macedonians are known to have come to the Academy in quest of higher learning, nor did Aristotle's career initiate a connexion with the Athenian Academy that later residents of Macedonia were to follow on. It is not even certain where Aristotle lived or what he did before he moved to Athens: a reasonable guess is that he came to Athens as a prestigious cultural centre from the home of his brother-in-law and sister in Atarneus.[106] Perhaps the circulation of some of Plato's Socratic dialogues had attracted the attention of Proxenus or of Aristotle himself.

When the young Aristotle came to the Academy in 367 B.C., Plato, now over sixty years old, was in Sicily introducing young Dionysius II to a life of philosophy, and the Academy was in the hands of the scientifically inclined Eudoxus of Cnidus (see above, p. 608). He and his follower Callippus of Cyzicus, who lived with Aristotle in Athens, may well have provided the most important early instruction for Aristotle, though presumably the writings of Plato, circulating and discussed in the community, would have influenced his intellectual development as well. Aristotle later praised Eudoxus for his self-control, which made persuasive the argument that pleasure is the good, since it did not appear to be a self-serving view: 'Eudoxus' arguments gained credence more because of his excellent character than on their own merit' was Aristotle's verdict on this debate in the early Academy (*Eth. Nic.* x, 1172b 9–17).

At the time of Aristotle's arrival most of the associates of the Academy were foreigners pursuing mathematics and astronomy, who had originally followed Eudoxus from his school in Cyzicus to Athens (see above, pp. 608–9, 614–15); others, among them Aristotle's friend Eudemus of Cyprus, came to engage in ethical and political discussions, sometimes, one suspects, because of negative political circumstances in their home states. Eudemus became a political activist against tyranny in exile after he had become its victim in his native Cyprus. He took ill and narrowly escaped death in the Thessalian town of Pherae, which he lived to see liberated from the cruel regime of the tyrant Alexander; but his dream of returning some day to a Cyprus similarly liberated from tyranny was cut short in Sicily, where he joined up with Dion, Timonides of Leucas, and other Academics *c.* 354 B.C. in their attempt to overthrow Dionysius II. Aristotle's own relationship to this political catastrophe

---

[106] This might explain why he went to Atarneus when he left Athens twenty years later. That he felt close to Proxenus is shown by his adoption of Nicanor, son of Proxenus and Arimneste, and, in the absence of a legitimate son of his own, making him his legal heir and prospective husband for his daughter Pythias. See Düring 1957 (H 36) 271–2.

remained at a literary level in that he memorialized his friendship with the slain Eudemus in a dialogue entitled *Eudemus* or *On Grief*. Why his early work on ethics also bears Eudemus' name, we do not know.

The evidence about Plato's personal relationship with the twenty-year-old Aristotle upon his return to the Academy in 364 B.C. is largely anecdotal, at best suggestive, at worst nothing but pure fancy or bias.[107] The biographical tradition stresses fundamental intellectual disagreements between the two from their earliest encounters rather than an intellectual dominance of the master over a subordinate pupil. Some sources see the disagreements as indicating personal tension or hostility, others acknowledge the existence of friendship between the two despite their intellectual differences. One anecdote suggests that Plato found Aristotle from the start to be someone who fiercely struggled for intellectual independence: 'Aristotle kicked against me as a colt kicks against his mother', Plato is reported to have said of his distinguished pupil. Even if the anecdote is a complete fabrication, the comparison is apt. It was not long before Aristotle was acting not as an apprentice in philosophy subordinate to Plato and the older philosophers at the Academy, but was teaching in the Academy, not only as the leader of his own circle within the school but also as an advocate of a subject previously neglected, even forbidden, within the Academy: rhetoric.

Attention to rhetoric as a legitimate subject represented a major departure from what the Academy stood for as an educational institution: in polemical opposition to Isocrates and his school, rhetoric was, in Plato's view, not an area of inquiry that could be isolated and studied apart from the content of what was being discussed. Aristotle disagreed: 'It would be shameful to remain silent and let Isocrates speak,' he is reported to have announced programmatically (and coltishly), signalling his lifelong interest in the subject of rhetoric in his early (perhaps his earliest) dialogue *Gryllus*, or *On Rhetoric* (dated *c.* 361 B.C.). The Academy needed to rival the success of Isocrates' school in providing counsel to rulers and men of influence. In Cicero's dramatic formulation of this major step in Aristotle's thinking, Aristotle 'suddenly changed his whole method of teaching' (*repente mutavit totam formam disciplinae suae*).[108]

The surviving fragments of the *Gryllus* suggest that it discussed critically the many encomia and funeral speeches written by Isocrates and others in honour of Xenophon's son Gryllus, who had been killed in the battle of Mantinea in 362; in opposition to Plato and in critique of Isocrates, Aristotle contended that rhetoric was not only an art worthy of study in its own right but also that its political and dialectical

---

[107] See Düring 1957 (H 36) 315–36 and Riginos 1976 (H 98) 129–34.
[108] See Düring 1957 (H 36) 311–14. For Aristotle's lost works, see Bignone 1936 (H 4). Cf. also Berti 1962 (H 3).

implications require close examination and study (*Gryllus*, fr. 2), which, if philosophers do not use or understand, they run the risk of having used against them. The *Gryllus* prompted an elaborate response, four books in length but now lost, from Isocrates' pupil Cephisodorus.

Aristotle's *Protrepticus*, or 'Exhortation to Philosophy', may be read as a challenge to Isocrates' political influence, patronage and intellectual following on the island of Cyprus (see above, p. 600). Having befriended and memorialized Eudemus, a political exile from Cyprus, Aristotle seems to have taken it upon himself to try to counteract Isocrates' standing among the Cypriot Evagorids by offering to Themison, a prince or minor Cypriot king, a vision of *paideia* and the philosophical life different from that presented by Isocrates in his *Antidosis* of 353 by emphasizing the primacy of the 'theoretical' over the 'active' life, the possibility of precise knowledge about human values analogous to mathematical knowledge, and the pleasure of devoting one's energy and life to intellection (*phronesis*).[109]

Only few fragments survive of the dialogues Aristotle wrote during his twenty years in the Academy. Like Speusippus and Xenocrates, he wrote a treatise *On the Pythagoreans* and one on the contemporary head of the Pythagorean brotherhood at Tarentum, Archytas. Most dialogues seem to have been heuristic, protreptic and introductory by design, with no pretence of being systematic or even consistent with one another. Small fragments survive of a *Symposium*, a *Sophistes*, a work *On Justice* (in four books), and *On Pleasure*, all preoccupied with Platonic themes. Fragments of his *Eroticus*, a dialogue on love partially preserved in an Arabic manuscript,[110] show Aristotle himself engaged in dialogue with an assembly of students, on behalf of whom 'his (Aristotle's) pupil Issos speaks'. That, unlike Plato, Aristotle introduced himself as an interlocutor in his own dialogues is attested by Cicero (*ad Att.* XIII.19.4) and is also exhibited in a fragment of his dialogue *On Philosophy* (fr. 10 Ross), which, as well as *On Ideas*, deals critically with the theory of Forms, making it clear that from his early writing to the end of his career Aristotle never accepted any version of the theory which posited Forms as transcendent.

Empirical research underlying his later systematic works may also have been begun during his twenty years in the Academy, such as the technical work on rhetoric that later formed the basis of his three books of *Rhetorics*. As part of his interest in rhetoric Aristotle is likely to have taught, discussed and done research in logical argumentation, laying the foundations of the *Topoi* and *Categories*, which led in turn to the whole

[109] See Düring 1961 (H 36A), and Chroust 1966 (H 16) 202–7.
[110] The *Codex Tübingen Weisweiler*, no. 81, *Erotikos*, fr. 4 Ross; English translation in Ross 1952 (H 100) 26. See also Walzer 1939 (H 114) 414–22.

series of logical treatises collected by his later followers under the name of *Organon* ('Tool'). His passion for collection and systematic classification is attested in a fragment by Isocrates' pupil Cephisodorus, in which he accused the young Aristotle of banality for collecting proverbs, the preservation of which from Greek antiquity we owe in fact largely to the efforts of Aristotle and his followers.[111]

Although Aristotle kept a low profile on political issues in Athens and those involving Athens and other states, towards the end of his twenty-year career in the Academy he got nevertheless caught up in the events of the day. When Olynthus fell to Philip II in 348 B.C., anti-Macedonian sentiment, stirred up by the ascendancy of Demosthenes and other politicians opposed to Philip, made Aristotle's situation at Athens uncomfortable if not fearful. As a metic with Macedonian connexions and as an intellectual in a city where most intellectuals were more favourably disposed to Macedon than to Persia, Aristotle became a target of political hostility. It is possible that he was forced to flee Athens some months before Plato's death in 347 B.C.[112]

2. *Aristotle's* Wanderjahre: *Assus, Mytilene and Macedonia*

The next thirteen years of his career (age 37 to 49) Aristotle spent away from Athens, first in Atarneus in the Troad, the dominion of the tyrant Hermias and home of his brother-in-law Proxenus.[113] It is possible that Hermias had visited Athens within the previous decade and had heard both Plato and Aristotle in the Academy.[114] *Epistle* VI, purported to have been addressed by Plato 'to Hermias, Erastus and Coriscus' *c.* 351/0 B.C., gives the impression that former long-time associates of Plato's Academy, the brothers Erastus and Coriscus from near-by Scepsis in the Troad, were establishing themselves as philosophical counsellors to Hermias and were starting a group to carry on discussions of the sort they had engaged in at the Academy.[115] Soon after his arrival, Aristotle, probably together with Xenocrates, Theophrastus and other companions from the Academy joined (or helped to develop) a circle of philosophers in the coastal town of Assus, which had come under Hermias' control,[116] and where he now provided the philosophers from

---

[111] See Ath. II. 60 d–e with Düring 1957 (H 36) 379–80 and 389–91. D.L. v. 26 lists a book entitled *Paroimiai.*

[112] See Chroust 1973 (H 20) ch. IX, 'Aristotle leaves the Academy', (pp. 117–24).

[113] For this phase of Aristotle's career see Wormell 1935 (H 124) 55–92, and Mulvany 1926 (H 86) 155–68. For Hermias' relation to Aristotle see Düring 1957 (H 36) 272–83.

[114] Strab. XIII.1.57 with Düring 1957 (H 36) 276 and 279.

[115] D.L. III.46 lists Erastus and Coriscus among Plato's students; Strabo (XIII.1.54) calls them *Sokratikoi.* For Erastus, see also [Pl.] *Ep.* XIII.362b.

[116] See Düring 1957 (H 36) 272–7 with Gaiser 1988 (H 50) 380–6.

the Academy with a place and 'all the necessities' for their community; here 'they spent their time (*diatribontes*) philosophizing, coming together at a *peripatos*', which suggests institutional arrangements and practices like those to which they had become accustomed in the Academy.[117] It was probably in this community that Aristotle's nephew, Callisthenes, began his philosophical education.[118]

After three years at Assus, Aristotle went across to Mytilene on Lesbos to continue his research and teaching, probably in a philosophical community that included Theophrastus, a native of the island.[119] After approximately three years, Aristotle was called by Philip to become the tutor of Alexander, then in his fifteenth year. Presumably Philip's choice was influenced not only by Aristotle's early association with the Macedonian court but also by the recommendation of Hermias, who was a Macedonian sympathizer and ally. According to Plutarch (*Alex.* 7.4), upon Aristotle's arrival, 'Philip assigned as a school (*schole* ... *kai diatribe*) to Aristotle and Alexander the nymphaeum at Mieza, where up to this day [early second century of our era] people point out the stone seats and shady walks (*peripatoi*) of Aristotle.' How long this paedagogical arrangement lasted, what Aristotle did after it ended, and where he went to live are not precisely known; but it is clear that he stayed in Macedonia for eight years and perhaps became a Macedonian citizen. He may have taken up residence for a time in his father's home in Stagira, his native town (now part of Macedonia), which had been destroyed by Philip II in 348 and which Aristotle may have persuaded Philip to rebuild.[120] He was still in Macedonia when Speusippus died in 339,[121] and Xenocrates, who also had left the Athenian community and was still living abroad at the time, was elected as scholarch of the Academy (see above, p. 611).

During his second year in Macedonia Aristotle experienced the painful loss of his former colleague, patron and friend, Hermias of Atarneus, who fell victim to his political position between his greater proximity to Persia and his greater admiration for Macedon. He was captured and executed by the Great King in 341 B.C. Grief-stricken, Aristotle dedicated a cenotaph to Hermias at Delphi and composed in his honour a hymn to *Areta* ('Excellence').[122] The execution of Hermias undoubtedly had an effect on the development of Aristotle's negative views of Persian culture and rule, with its correlative conviction of the

---

[117] See *Ind. Acad.*, col. v. 1–23, p. 23 Mekler 1902 (H 80); cf. Gaiser 1988 (H 50) 161–2.

[118] See Düring 1957 (H 36) 294–7; cf. Gaiser 1985 (H 49).

[119] For the chronology, see D.L. v.9–10 and Dion. Hal. *Ep. ad Amm.* 5, p. 727, with Düring 1957 (H 36) 253–6 and 463 and Jacoby, *FGrH* 244 F 38.

[120] See Düring 1957 (H 36) 290–4; cf. also Gottschalk 1972 (H 53) 324, n. 5.

[121] See *Ind. Acad.*, col. VII, 1–2, p. 38 Mekler 1902 (H 80); cf. Gaiser 1988 (H 50) 193 and 467–9.

[122] Preserved in D.L. v.6 and in the Didymus papyrus, see Düring 1957 (H 36) 59–60 and 274–7.

superiority of Greek to barbarian. Soon after Hermias' death Aristotle married Pythias, Hermias' niece and adopted daughter.[123]

In addition to teaching among other philosophers, offering political counsel to rulers, and privately tutoring a Macedonian prince, Aristotle was also busily engaged in empirical research on natural phenomena of all sorts. His biological writings contain abundant references to geographical places associated with his years away from Athens, where he with the help of Theophrastus and other philosophical associates did much of the collection, observation and close study that went into the composition of his systematic treatises on zoology and natural history.[124] With Callisthenes he did archival and field research into the Pythian games, compiling a list of victors and organizers 'from the beginning', in response to an invitation from the amphictyons of Delphi; for their work they were publicly honoured by the Delphic priesthood with a crown and a laudatory decree that was put up in the sanctuary of Delphi (Tod no. 187 = Harding no. 104).[125]

3. *Aristotle's return to Athens in 335* B.C.

Aristotle's reasons for returning to Athens after eight years in high Macedonian circles are far from clear, especially since anti-Macedonian sentiments were running high after Alexander's recent destruction of Athens' ally, Thebes. Equally obscure are his reasons for setting up a school of his own in the Lyceum rather than coming back to the Academy under the leadership of Xenocrates.[126] His moving elegy on Friendship (Φιλίη), dated to the year 334 B.C., suggests that Aristotle regarded his 'return to the famous soil of Cecropia' not as triumphant, polemical or political, but as pious, deeply personal and motivated by his admiration for some of Plato's philosophical principles.[127]

Aristotle, now forty-nine years of age, will have been celebrated at Athens as a philosopher, but will also have been well known as the teacher of the newly ascended king (age twenty-one), whose father Philip II had been assassinated the previous year. In addition, his close association with Antipater, the Macedonian regent over Greece,[128] made Aristotle and his school depend as non-citizens 'from the very first on Macedonian rule.'[129] Aristotle successfully took a very visible and public

---

[123] Düring 1957 (H 36) 267–8. Cf. also Gottschalk 1972 (H 53) 322, n. 1.
[124] See Lynch 1972 (H 76) 72, n. 6; cf. also Gaiser 1985 (H 49) and Düring 1966 (H 37) 510, and for chronology *ibid.* 49–52 and Rist 1989 (H 99) 283–7.   [125] See Düring 1957 (H 36) 339–40.
[126] See Lynch 1972 (H 76) 73.   [127] See Jaeger 1927 (H 65) 13–17.
[128] See Plezia 1977 (H 95) 18–19.
[129] Lynch 1972 (H 76) 94–5. For Aristotle as a metic, see Whitehead 1975 (H 118) 94–9. On the foreign origins of his followers see Jaeger 1948 (H 67) 316.

stand to honour Hermias' memory against anti-Macedonian slanders against his father-in-law. Aristotle was publicly honoured on the Acropolis by the people of Athens with an inscription acknowledging that he 'had served the city well by doing good and by the great number of his own acts of assistance and beneficence, and by all his services to the people of Athens, especially by intervening with King Philip for the purpose of promoting their interests and securing that they were well treated'.[130]

Although ancient sources unanimously credit Aristotle with establishing his own school in the Lyceum at Athens and with leading it for thirteen years,[131] some modern scholars have argued that the Peripatetic School in the institutional sense was not established until after Aristotle's death by his pupil and successor Theophrastus,[132] because the earliest mention of the *peripatos*, after which the philosophical community in the Lyceum came to be named, may be that in Theophrastus' will, referring to part of the *kepos* given to him by Demetrius of Phalerum through a grant of *enktesis* (D.L. v.39 and 52). But since the ownership of property, as we have noted, was in antiquity not a precondition for the operation of a philosophical school by a metic, there is no reason to reject the more obvious possibility that the *peripatos* which gave its name to the school was, as Diogenes Laertius reports (v.2), the *peripatos* in the public Lyceum gymnasium, rather than that in Theophrastus' private *kepos*.

Aristotle's school in the Lyceum produced among its students Demetrius of Phalerum, who had earned the epithet *Peripatetikos* before he entered political life and arranged the grant of *enktesis* for Theophrastus ([Plut.] *X orat.* 850c).[133] Diogenes Laertius' *Life* does not include a list of Aristotle's students but says that there were 'many', of whom Theophrastus was 'the most distinguished' (v.35). To Theophrastus the *Vita Marciana* (44, pp. 105–6 Düring) adds: Phaenias (of Eresus on Lesbos, Theophrastus' home city), Eudemus (of Rhodes), Clytus (of Miletus), Aristoxenus (of Tarentum) and Dicaearchus (of Messene).[134]

Like the Academy, Aristotle's school was organized as a community consisting of a number of older members, mainly concerned with teaching and research, and younger members, who were more in a

---

[130] *Vita Marciana* 20 in Düring 1957 (H 36) 100, and more fully in the Arabic life of Usaibia, *ibid.* 215–16.   [131] Lynch 1972 (H 76) 68–9 and 106–8.

[132] Argued by Brink 1940 (H 9) col. 905. Düring 1957 (H 36) 346; cf. 361, 405–6, and 461.

[133] On Demetrius of Phalerum see below, n. 152. On the term *Peripatetikos*, see Lynch 1972 (H 76) 72–5.

[134] On these students of Aristotle, see Wehrli 1967–69 and Supplements, 1974 and 1978 (H 115A). Phaenias and Theophrastus together are credited by Plutarch with removing the tyrants from their native city (fr. 7 Wehrli). Very little is known of Clytus except that he wrote a book *On Miletus* (Ath. XII.540c; cf. XIV.655b). The lists in non-Greek versions of Aristotle's Life are either selective or corrupt, see Düring 1957 (H 36) 188 (*Vita Syriaca*), 200 (Mubashir), 218 (Usaibia).

position of apprenticeship and learning.[135] But, unlike the Academy, Aristotle's school thought of itself more as an institution in the sense of a collective within which groups could be identified. Aristotle is reported to have borrowed the idea for administering his school from the Academy under Xenocrates in that he 'made it a custom in his school to appoint someone leader (ἄρχων) every ten days' (D.L. v.4). This suggests that the scholarchs of the Academy and Lyceum functioned more as *primi inter pares* than as heads of the school in a strictly hierarchical sense. This kind of administrative arrangement not only ensured efficiency in operating the school but it also fostered a sense of belonging to the group and 'a spirit of intellectual independence alien to schools of the sophistic type'.[136]

Aristotle's school did not try to perpetuate an orthodoxy or fixed ideology but rather included a range of philosophical viewpoints. Eudemus of Rhodes was called 'the most genuine of Aristotle's pupils' (fr. 59 Wehrli), the one 'who followed Aristotle in all things' (fr. 44 Wehrli), whereas Theophrastus was an independent and original thinker, who often went beyond and sometimes explicitly rejected Aristotle's views.[137] Dicaearchus of Messene, regarded as a student of both Aristotle and Theophrastus in the Lyceum, is known to have disagreed fundamentally with both of them in privileging the practical over the theoretical life (fr. 25 Wehrli). Some, such as Cleitarchus, of the Cyrenaic school, and Simmias (of Syracuse) left Aristotle's school to join the Megarian school under the leadership of Stilpo; such movements continued when Theophrastus took over the school (D.L. II.113). Though the philosophical differences between known members of the Peripatos are perhaps less striking than those among the associates of Plato's Academy, the group that formed around Aristotle was open enough intellectually to include a maverick like Aristoxenus of Tarentum, known as ὁ Μουσικός because of his preoccupation with harmonics, rhythm and other musical subjects. He had studied with a variety of teachers, including Xenophilus the Pythagorean, before he settled down to work with Aristotle in the Lyceum at Athens (fr. 1 Wehrli). A prodigious writer with 453 books attributed to him and one of the early practitioners of the genre of learned, gossipy biography, Aristoxenus 'had a great reputation among the students of Aristotle', so much so that he was bitterly disappointed and took to abusing Aristotle when he was passed over and the school was left to Theophrastus instead (fr. 1 Wehrli).

---

[135] See the wills of Theophrastus and Lyco (D.L. v.53, 70–1); for the Academy, see *Ind. Acad.* col. VI. 41, p. 38 and col. XVIII. 1–8, p. 67 Mekler 1902 (H 80) and the comic fragment of Epicrates (above, p. 612).   [136] See Lynch 1972 (H 76) 82–3 and Gaiser 1988 (H 50) 356–7 and 365–6.

[137] See Regenbogen 1940 (H 96) cols. 1389–1395.

Like Plato, Aristotle established his school to be an ongoing enterprise, both in his absence and beyond his lifetime; he was concerned that the work of the community should not depend on a living and present individual. According to Aulus Gellius (*NA* XIII.5), when Aristotle withdrew from Athens to Chalcis and his health started to fail, his followers approached him with the request that he choose a successor. Among the 'many good men at the time in the school', Aristotle is said to have expressed a preference for the sweet wine from Lesbos (Theophrastus) over the full-bodied and pleasant wine from Rhodes (the more orthodox Eudemus).[138]

Like Plato, too, Aristotle did not charge any fees for instruction or for participation in the philosophical community at any level. In contradistinction to the sophists, Isocrates and other professional teachers, he objected to turning philosophy into a business, believing that the value of philosophical teachers could not be measured in money or in honours; but he did not object to accepting voluntary contributions from those anxious to express a debt felt owed to their teachers (cf. *Eth. Nic.* IX.1, 1164a). Plato, too, may have accepted, and even solicited, gifts of money from supporters outside the school and treated such funds as his own personal money, not as the collective money of the school (*Ep.* XIII), as was noted above. But Speusippus was censured – perhaps slanderously – for introducing fees for study at the Academy (D.L. IV.2). Beyond this, very little is known about the financial arrangements of the fourth-century philosophical schools. The kind of elaborate researches carried on by Aristotle and his associates in the Lyceum will have required more financial resources than what would be needed to make a philosophical community like the Academy work. When he settled in Athens, Aristotle was probably well off financially; his will written just twelve years later suggests that he had inherited from his family and acquired through his career considerable financial assets, with much more to bequeath to his heirs than Plato possessed to leave to his. He was said to have been compensated royally for tutoring Alexander (cf. Plut. *Alex.* 7), and his powerful, imperial student is reported to have been one of his major financial supporters. In addition to monetary support from Macedon, Pliny the Elder states that Alexander put 'thousands of men' at Aristotle's disposal to subsidize his zoological investigations.[139]

Soon after his return to Athens, Aristotle, now over fifty years old, had a daughter named Pythias after his wife, who died soon after. To have an heir to his property, Aristotle adopted his nephew Nicanor, although it is not certain when. A few years before his death Aristotle

138 See Wehrli VIII. Eudemus (H 115A) fr. 5 with p. 78.
139 Pliny *HN* VIII.16.44; Ath. IX. 398e; and Ael. *VH* IV.19. On Macedonian subsidies see Düring 1957 (H 36) 288–9.

had a biological son by a servant woman, Herpyllis, from his native Stagira, whom he had freed before he died and for whom he provided substantial support in his will (D.L. v.13–14). Though his natural son was illegitimate and could not be his heir, Aristotle named him Nicomachus after his own father and provided for him and his half-sister prudently in his will, appointing his adopted son and heir Nicanor the guardian of his two children (both of them were still *paides* at the time of his will). Further, he arranged for Nicanor to marry Pythias when she would come of age;[140] if anything should happen to Nicanor (before or after his marriage to Pythias) to prevent him from having children or otherwise to fulfil the expectations of the will, Aristotle's student and long-term colleague Theophrastus – despite the vast age differential between him and Aristotle's baby daughter – was named as an alternative possibility for marrying Pythias and carrying out the terms of his teacher's will (v.12). These arrangements reflect Aristotle's meticulous caution in the face of an uncertain and dubious legal situation. As a non-citizen in most of the places in which he resided throughout his life and as a man of considerable means and variously located real estate without a straightforward biological male heir, Aristotle could not depend on social custom and local laws to ensure that his property would be appropriately divided for the benefit of his surviving family. As a result, the back-up possibilities were particularly needed in light of contemporary political instability and the dangerous military career (in the service of Macedon) of his adoptive son Nicanor. Most prudently, Aristotle appointed as executor of his will the Macedonian regent Antipater, since he could not rely on the complex international terms of the will to be carried out by any local authorities in any polis. It is noteworthy that the will says nothing about school arrangements; perhaps they had been worked out before Aristotle fled from Athens in 323 B.C. and, since they involved no common assets or private ownership of property, may not have been thought appropriate matters to be handled in his will anyway. It is clear from the story about the fate of his library that Aristotle's books, though not mentioned in his will, ended up in the personal possession of Theophrastus.

While leading his school at Athens, Aristotle experienced another personal loss. His nephew, pupil and long-time associate Callisthenes of Olynthus had not followed him to Athens in 335/4 B.C. but had chosen to stay in the company of Alexander, possibly on Aristotle's recommendation. He subsequently fell out of favour with Alexander, we are told, because of his negative views on Alexander's adoption of the oriental practice of worshipful prostration before rulers. Charged with plotting

---

[140] See Jaeger 1948 (H 67) 320 and Guthrie (H 56) vi 45. For Nicanor and Nicomachus, see above, n. 106 and Gottschalk 1972 (H 53) 322–5; on Pythias and Herpyllis, see Düring 1957 (H 36) 267–70.

to assassinate Alexander, Callisthenes was executed by Alexander's order in 327/6 B.C. From that point on, Alexander's image changed to a radically unfavourable one in Aristotle's school and its hellenistic continuation.[141] To commemorate the event, Theophrastus composed a work entitled *Callisthenes or On Grief* (D.L. v.44).

Alexander now shifted his support from Aristotle's school to two other philosophers, Anaximenes of Lampsacus and Xenocrates, scholarch of the Academy (D.L. v.10). Anaximenes, master of invective and the most notable pupil of the Cynic Zoilus of Amphipolis, was the author of historical works, including one on the achievements of Alexander (D.L. II.3), and perhaps also produced the *Rhetorica ad Alexandrum*, which survives among Aristotle's own works. Two other philosophers who found greater favour with Alexander after the Callisthenes affair are Anaxarchus of Abdera and his pupil Pyrrho of Elis, the founder of Pyrrhonian scepticism. Both accompanied Alexander on his Asian campaigns and are said to have come in contact at that time with the Indian gymnosophists and with the Magi (D.L. IX.58 and 61). Aristotle vigorously opposed the sceptical tendencies of these thinkers and doubtless found regrettable the influence they were gaining in the contemporary political world (D.L. IX.65).[142] The competition between philosophers for influence with, and financial support from, major powers continued to grow in intensity with the increase in the number of philosophical schools.

4. *The achievements of the Peripatos*

While contemporaries are likely to have perceived Aristotle's new philosophical community in the Lyceum as an extension of the Academy, it is clear that it was as different institutionally as Plato and Aristotle are different from each other philosophically. Plato and many of his followers were committed to the ultimate accessibility of transcendent truths, and much of their philosophical discussion was in search of context-free indices and measurements of the universe of human perceptions and values. Aristotle, on the other hand, was inclined to 'put the chicken before the egg' and to proceed from that assumption. The major innovations represented by Aristotle's school are summed up by Ingemar Düring as 'a systematic collecting of the previous literature, which was thoroughly worked up. A wide and likewise systematic amassing of information and material for certain purposes, generally in order to make possible a survey of a whole field of knowledge. Close cooperation between the head of the school and his fellow-scholars. And

---

[141] See Düring 1957 (H 36) 294–6 and 58–61, and Jacoby 1919 (D 200), cols. 1674–1707. See also Guthrie (H 56) VI 38 n. 1. [142] On Pyrrho, see Decleva Caizzi 1981 (H 27).

finally, most important of all, the scientific outlook and the strictly scientific method.'[143]

A number of well-known passages in Aristotle's works from his Lyceum period lay out the methodological principles guiding empirical researches: for example, the introduction to De Partibus Animalium (I.1, 639a1–642b4), his protreptic discourse on the beauties of nature in the same work (I.5, 644b22–646a4), and the celebrated opening to book II of the Metaphysics (993a30–b31) all show that for Aristotle the progress of philosophia was less the result of 'much interaction' in a dialectical community than the outcome of individual contributions and co-operative efforts whose consequences had a cumulative effect.[144]

The co-operative projects in which Aristotle and his followers in the Lyceum were engaged include the collections of archival materials such as the records of Athenian dramatic performances (Didaskaliai), the list of Olympic victors (Olympionikai), an ethnographical collection of customs among barbarian peoples (Nomima Barbarika), and the constitutions of 158 states, which included also constitutions of non-Greek states such as Carthage, whose mixed form of government Aristotle found praiseworthy in many respects (Pol. II.11, 1272b24–1273b26). The Athenaion Politeia is the only complete surviving example of this kind of collection, but his Politics are informed by detailed knowledge of the constitutions which various states had developed. In addition, Aristotle and his followers continued the collection of data on natural history, which had been going on intensively during his years away from Athens. It was based not only on direct observations of natural phenomena but also on information gathered from hunters and fishermen, who had practical experience in the natural world (Eth. Nic. VI.11, 1143b11–13; cf. also Top. 1.14, 105a34–b37). The results of these collections were published in what came to be regarded as the most characteristic type of Peripatetic writing, the synagoge or systematic collection of material on a given theme.[145] Nevertheless, Aristotle and his followers also relied heavily on books and secondary sources of information. Still, the scale of what was being investigated by the members of his school can also be underestimated, since less than 25 per cent of the titles attributed to Aristotle have survived. According to Strabo (XIII.1.54), Aristotle was the first to organize a systematic collection of books into a library, an activity that gave meaning to the verb aristotelizein (ibid.); and it was this same vision of philosophia which Epicurus and followers attacked in their polemics against the polymathia and enkyklika mathemata of the Lyceum.[146]

[143] Düring 1950 (H 33) 37–70, esp. 57–8; and 1954 (H 35) 61–77.
[144] Lynch 1972 (H 76) 85–7.   [145] See Düring 1957 (H 36) 32–52.
[146] See Bignone 1936 (H 4) 58 and Düring 1957 (H 36) 306–7.

In literary terms Aristotle's writing during this period, at least in the form in which it has survived in the *Corpus Aristotelicum*, was very different from the dialogues and treatises he and his fellow associates in the Academy had produced for a wider audience as well as for discussion within the school during his first residence in Athens.[147] These works have survived only in random quotations and paraphrases in later authors, but are works of 'a new mode of expression, scientific prose'.[148] Plato's Academy avoided the lecture as a paedagogical technique in favour of discussion and close interaction among friends; Aristotle, however, regularly lectured to students of the school in the morning, and in the evening addressed a wider public, a form of instruction which was known as his 'exoteric' teaching.[149]

The existing *Corpus Aristotelicum* consists of a later edition of what survived from the school literature or *pragmateiai*. These *pragmateiai* were 'written entirely without literary ambitions, which . . . does not at all mean that they . . . lack literary quality. Unlike Plato's or Aristotle's own dialogues, they were not protected by any literary proprietorship . . . [They consisted of] notes, revised from time to time to be kept up to date with new results and achievement . . . [They represented] an oral tradition in written form. Aristotle and his fellow scholars were continually working with this material. Their contributions take the form of additions and amplifications.'[150] Accordingly, the Peripatos produced a vast quantity of oral and written teaching very different in style and content from what the Academy had been offering. What survives as Aristotle's work is often very technical because it was not intended for circulation to a wider reading public; some of the *Corpus Aristotelicum* may be lecture notes, either Aristotle's own or those taken by his students; some notes appear to be different versions of the same theme, worked up for different audiences or as revisions of earlier versions in Aristotle's lifetime or after his death. But it is clear that Aristotle and his school were developing materials meant to communicate and teach as unambiguously and directly as possible, however complicated and technical the subject may have been; the intention was to make information, arguments, ideas, and, above all, causes (*aitiai*) available and accessible, not to restrict them to those willing to participate in a community of interpretation.[151]

Aristotle's Lyceum differed from the Academy in a number of other

---

[147] The best introduction to the major divisions of the *Corpus Aristotelicum* are the four volumes of *Articles on Aristotle*. ed. by Barnes, Schofield, and Sorabji 1975–79 (H 1).

[148] Düring 1957 (H 36) 360.

[149] See Aul. Gell. *NA* xx.5 and Arist. *Eth. Eud.* 1.8, 1217b17–26.

[150] Düring 1950 (H 33) 58–9. For the list of Aristotle's writings in D.L. v.24, see Düring 1957 (H 36) 68 and Moraux 1951 (H 84).

[151] See Mubashir's *Life of Aristotle* 37 (p. 201 Düring) as quoted in Lynch 1972 (H 76) 92 n. 37.

important ways. Less is known about individuals and individual contributions in the Peripatos, because it emphasized co-operative rather than proprietary efforts, so that much of what has come down to us as the work of Aristotle was probably the result of group investigation. Negative views on barbarian cultures permit the inference that Aristotle's school was less open to non-Greeks, and there is no evidence to suggest the involvement of anyone like the Chaldaean who came to the Academy. In addition, Aristotle's views on the position of women in society (cf. *Pol.* 1.13, 1260a20–b24), help explain why no tradition associates any women with the Peripatos. There may also have been within the Peripatos fewer homosexual couples than in the Academy, since Aristotle – in contrast to Plato – married, produced children, and appears to have been somewhat suspicious of the paedagogical value of homoerotic relationships.

It is no accident that in the ancient lists of Aristotle's writings the political writings are comparatively meagre. Despite his philosophical interests in both rhetoric and politics, as a foreigner Aristotle had to refrain from active involvement in politics, although he did have experience as a counsellor to political powers. Political theory was for him a form of political action rather than matter for contemplation; for him the word informed the deed: it was neither opposed to it nor a substitute for it. Distrustful of rapid and revolutionary change, Aristotle believed that to change the terms in which people talk and think about politics was also to change the way they would operate in the political arena. Like the Academy and like Isocrates' school, Aristotle's school had as its reference point issues in the international world of states, not local Athenian political issues. The prominent exception among his pupils was Demetrius of Phalerum, the orator and politician, who was the only Athenian citizen known to have been associated with his school and also the only person in either Plato's Academy or Aristotle's Lyceum who is singled out as 'not well-born'.[152] Composed largely of noncitizens and unprotected by any legal charter, the Lyceum was always in a vulnerable political situation.

Apprehensions were justified. The inscription honouring Aristotle for his services to Athens is said to have been hurled off its column on the Acropolis by the anti-Macedonian politician Himeraeus (brother of the Peripatetic Demetrius of Phalerum). The tradition, however suspect, is likely to contain elements hard to account for as fictions.[153] An attempt was made to rescind the decree (see above, p. 622) to honour Aristotle and his nephew Callisthenes at Delphi for their investigations into the Pythian games. Aristotle reacted in a letter to Antipater: 'As to the

[152] See Gehrke 1978 (C 142) 149–93; for a collection of his fragments, see Wehrli 1968 (H 115A) IV.
[153] See Düring 1957 (H 36) 232–6; cf. Chroust 1967 (H 17) 244–54.

honours voted to me at Delphi, of which I have been deprived, my present state of mind is such that I am not terribly concerned about them but not completely unconcerned.'[154] Worse was yet to come. After Alexander's sudden death at the age of thirty-two was announced in Athens (323 B.C.), Aristotle became the target of another anti-Macedonian attack. Having been indicted on the charge of impiety by the hierophant Eurymedon (and perhaps by a certain Demophilus),[155] he fled to his family estate in Chalcis – with a pointed allusion to the death of Socrates – 'so that the Athenians might not have the chance to sin a second time against philosophy'. To substantiate the charge of impiety, Eurymedon is said to have cited the hymn to *Areta* which Aristotle wrote in honour of Hermias and the inscription he composed for Hermias' monument at Delphi (D.L. v.5), but there can be little doubt that the charges were prompted by Aristotle's ties to Antipater and Macedonian hegemony.[156] He died some months later in Chalcis at the age of sixty-three.[157] Theophrastus of Eresus, his most distinguished pupil and long-time associate, succeeded him as head of the school he had founded in the Lyceum (D.L. v.36). Despite periods of instability and unrest in Athens, Theophrastus managed to develop the Peripatos as an institution during his thirty-five years of leadership, writing prolifically, extending the empirical researches of the community even beyond the areas of his teacher, and making the school at Athens an important instrument of hellenistic *paideia*.[158]

V. CONCLUSIONS

When we speak of 'philosophical schools' in the fourth century B.C., we are not referring simply to schools or traditions of thought in the abstract sense that later doxographers, historians and biographers often assumed them to be. What was characteristic of the age was the founding of schools in the concrete sense, groups of teachers, learners and researchers who were joined in a common enterprise, organized in a common administrative structure, and defined spatially by a common physical location.

The foundation of schools of higher learning, both in Athens and in other cities in the Greek world, is one of the most distinctive phenomena of the fourth century B.C. and surpasses all other forms of intellectual and creative activity in contributing to the cultural formations of the age. As the movement increased, the polis as a whole could no longer claim to be

---

[154] Ael. *VH* xiv.1.　[155] D.L. v.5 with Düring 1957 (H 36) 59.
[156] Düring 1957 (H 36) 344.　[157] Düring 1957 (H 36) 343–4 and 345–8.
[158] For a brief account of the workings and political circumstances of the Peripatos during Theophrastus' scholarchy (323/2–287/6 B.C.) see Lynch 1972 (H 76) 97–105.

the educator of the intellectual elite of the day. An educational system was forming that was not an arm of the political system. Separate institutions, independent of the polis and its regulations, now gave more concentrated effort and attention to what had earlier been only a small part of a city state's overall socialization process: *philosophia* in its general sense as the content of higher learning and education. The loss of faith this represented in the capacity of the city state to provide an adequate education did not make the foundation of schools in the fourth century B.C. a separatist movement, inward-looking, secretive, or detached from the world. Though not established to serve the needs of a particular city state, the schools were located in public buildings and, as outward-directed communities, concerned with the welfare of the polis. Their operation assumed that some of those educated would return to improve their home-states by counselling rulers, by teaching citizens through philosophical discussion, writing and instruction, and even at times by taking direct political action informed by philosophical reflection. The writings and students produced in the schools of Isocrates, Plato and Aristotle at Athens not only dominate the cultural landscape of the century but also were both directly and indirectly involved in the political history of the age.

In giving permanent homes to what had been a panhellenic network of itinerant sophists, the schools of Isocrates, Plato and Aristotle were international in scope, in their intellectual interests and in membership, widening the focus of inquiry beyond the issues and concerns of the individual polis. The range of possibilities they offered for philosophical education was not limited by the boundaries of the city state. Since the schools were open to all comers, since citizenship was not a criterion for participation, and since school-founding was not inhibited by the legal or proprietal constraints of a particular city state, the success of schools diminished the importance of citizenship as a precondition of meaningful association between adults.

The secular nature of these philosophical schools, which has sometimes been called into question by modern scholars, was critical to the way they operated and developed. Unlike *thiasoi* or other religious associations, schools were open, flexible and informal institutions which did not separate an insider from an outsider. The different kinds of relationships among individuals and the institution ensured the development of the schools less as communities perpetuating fixed orthodoxies than as heuristic learning communities characterized by a common concern for critical thinking and open, free inquiry. Their secular nature made for a free association of foreigners, resident aliens and citizens alike. This in turn gave philosophical inquiry a more cosmopolitan character, free from parochial concerns. The secularity of the schools also allowed them to be more exportable, extendable and replicable in other Greek city states, adding a certain dynamism to the process of school-founding, and insured that the institutionalization of higher education led to the development of an intellectual class independent of religious affiliation.

At the end of the fifth century B.C. the dominant teacher in Athens resisted the institutionalizing tendencies in sophistic education, particularly the use of writing to propagate ideas and the founding of schools to give greater regularity and a shared purpose to the process of higher education. It was Socrates' position that philosophical education ought to be pursued in human, face-to-face encounters and living conversations. Though Socrates opposed what he perceived to be the sophists' professionalization and commodification of education by writing treatises, founding schools and taking pay, his death dramatically demonstrated the limitations of his personal, charismatic approach to philosophy. There was a danger that philosophy as he understood it could have died with him, since it was dependent on oral transmission. If the kind of inquiry that Socrates initiated was to be carried on over generations and continue to be an educational force beyond his lifetime, instruments of institutional memory needed to be developed to overcome the fragility of individual memory. Many of Socrates' close followers, including Plato, ended up not only founding schools but discovering the power of the written word to preserve and propagate *philosophia*. It continued as learning and research through vicissitudes and over generations in the more complex, less traditional, and often unstable social order of the fourth century B.C. and as a heritage to later generations.[159]

---

[159] For a useful account of the continuing development of philosophical schools in Athens at the end of the fourth century B.C. and beyond see Habicht 1988 (H 57).

CHAPTER 12*b*

MEDICINE

G. E. R. LLOYD

The sources available for the reconstruction of the exciting developments that took place in Greek medical thought and practice in the late fifth and fourth centuries B.C. are extensive, although in places defective and in places biased. They fall into three main categories, first the extant treatises of the Hippocratic Corpus, second other literary sources, and third the inscriptional evidence, and a summary analysis of each in turn will serve to illustrate both the range and the limitations of the information they provide.

The great majority of the sixty or so treatises in the so-called Hippocratic Corpus date from the later part of the fifth or from the fourth century. The main exceptions are a handful of works, such as *On Nutriment, On Sevens* and some of the treatises on medical ethics, that show Stoic or Epicurean influence,[1] and one, *On the Heart*, that is generally thought to be approximately contemporary with the work of the Alexandrian biologists Herophilus and Erasistratus.[2] Even when we discount these few later works, the variety within the Hippocratic Corpus is very great, and the treatises – all of them anonymous – are evidently the work of many different authors representing, in some cases, radically divergent shades of opinion. Whether Hippocrates himself was responsible for any of them is controversial.[3] Although Hippocrates is occasionally referred to in contemporary or near contemporary writers, notably Plato, Aristotle and Aristotle's pupil Meno, the medical historian whose work is excerpted in the papyrus Anonymus Londinensis, they provide only very limited, and in places conflicting, evidence concerning the medical theories and practices he upheld, though they confirm the admiration and respect in which he was held already in the fourth century. Many attempts have been, and continue to be, made to establish the genuine works of Hippocrates himself in the

---

[1] See Mansfield 1971 (H 217) for *On Sevens* (contrast Roscher 1913 (H 239)), and Diller 1936–7 (H 144), Deichgräber 1973 (H 137); and Joly 1975 (H 179) for *On Nutriment*.

[2] See Lonie 1973 (H 213).

[3] See, for example, Pohlenz 1938 (H 237); Edelstein 1939/1967 (H 153); Herter 1976 (H 175); Smith 1979 (H 250); Joly 1983 (H 182 and 183); Mansfeld 1983 (H 220); Lloyd 1991 (H 211) ch. 9.

collection which has, since Alexandrian times, carried his name. But none commands very widespread support: in the absence of convincing evidence for authenticity scholars have all too often fallen back on the assumption that Hippocrates is responsible for those works they themselves happen to admire most. In any case the bid to identify the productions of one particular doctor, however famous at the time and subsequently, is of secondary importance in comparison with the analysis of the contents of the Corpus as a whole.

This comprises works of many different types. These include, among the most important distinguishable, though at times overlapping, groups: (1) exhibition pieces, lectures given by men who may or may not themselves have been medical practitioners, addressed to a general audience, that is both 'lay' and 'professional', though it must be stressed first that that contrast was far less sharp than it is today, and secondly that a far greater interest was shown in medical matters among those who had no intention of practising medicine: even Plato saw fit to include a theory of diseases in the *Timaeus* 81e ff and Aristotle notes the overlap between the study of medicine and the inquiry into nature in general (*De sensu* 436a17ff, *De Respiratione* 480b26ff). The exhibition pieces in the Corpus deal with such general themes as the validity of the medical art, as in the treatise *On the Art*.[4] (2) Mainly theoretical works, dealing in general terms with medical method, or the constitution of the human body, or the origins of diseases, or setting out the main types of diseases and their treatments: examples are *On Ancient Medicine*, *On the Nature of Man*, *On Airs, Waters, Peaces*, *On Affections*, *On Diseases* I.[5] (3) More specialized works treating of a particular department of medical theory or practice, notably dietetics (as in *On Regimen*), prognosis and diagnosis (*Prognostic*), surgery (*On Fractures*, *On Joints*, *On Wounds in the Head* and so on),[6] embryology (*On the Seed*, *On the Nature of the Child* and *On Diseases* IV)[7] and gynaecology (for example *On the Diseases of Women* I and II and *On Sterile Women*).[8] (4) Mainly descriptive or empirical works, containing individual case histories together, sometimes, with descriptions of 'constitutions' – that is general accounts of particular epidemics, including their climatic conditions (the seven books of *Epidemics*).[9]

---

[4] See Gomperz 1910 (H 157). On exhibition pieces, see Lloyd 1979 (H 208) 88ff; Lloyd 1987 (H 210) 61ff.

[5] See, for example, Edelstein 1931 (H 150); Jones 1946 (H 184); Festugière 1948 (H 155); Bourgey 1953 (H 127); Wittern 1974 (H 263); Potter 1988 (H 237A).

[6] See E. T. Withington, *Hippocrates* (Loeb) 3 (1928).

[7] See most recently Lonie 1981 (H 215).

[8] See, for example, Diepgen 1937 (H 141); Trapp 1967 (H 256); Hanson 1975 (H 166); Grensemann 1982 (H 162); Campese *et al.* 1983 (H 132); King 1983 (H 188); Lloyd 1983 (H 209) part 2, ch. 2; Hanson 1990 (H 168).

[9] See, for example, Deichgräber 1933 (H 134); Diller 1964/1973 (H 143); Baader and Winau 1989 (H 126); Langholf 1990 (H 201).

(5) Collections of aphorisms, brief statements setting out observations or recommendations covering almost every aspect of medicine (*Aphorisms* and *Coan Prognosis*).

Some of these works, as we said, envisage a general audience, but others are directed at the writers' colleagues, being intended as manuals to be used in medical practice, or engaging in debate on points of theory, while others again may have been meant to serve as introductory guides for pupils (though none is clearly entitled 'for beginners', as some of Galen's works were to be). Apart from the exhibition pieces, few have any literary pretensions. Indeed many are not literary unities at all, but multi-author works, collections of material from different hands (as in categories (4) and (5) especially).[10]

One characteristic that many works of different types exhibit is a certain combativeness, to be connected, in part, with the competitiveness of Greek medicine in the fifth and fourth centuries.[11] This combativeness may take the form of explicit condemnations of other styles of healing. The work called *On the Sacred Disease* aims to establish that that disease (roughly, epilepsy) has a natural cause and can be treated and cured by ordinary methods, and to refute the claims of the 'purifiers', 'charlatans' and 'quacks' (as the writer calls them) to the effect that the gods are responsible for the complaint and that it should be treated by the use of charms and ritual purifications. None of the Hippocratic works advocates such methods of treatment.[12] But other Hippocratic treatises attack theories and practices that can be exemplified from within the Corpus itself. This applies particularly to those that deal with the origin of diseases in general, where a multitude of theories was on offer and where some writers were at pains to undermine rival views that figure elsewhere in our extant treatises. Thus *On the Nature of Man* (chs. 1–8) attacks those who suggested that the human body consists of a single elemental substance, whether earth, water, air or fire, or one of the humours, blood, phlegm, bile and black bile – while we find the work *On Breaths* (chs. 2–5) claiming, precisely, that man consists of air alone and that air is the origin of all diseases. *On Ancient Medicine* similarly condemns theories based on what the writer calls hypotheses or postulates, unsupported, indeed unverifiable, assumptions, in medicine, especially those that invoked the hot, the cold, the wet and the dry. While no extant treatise actually advocates a monistic or dualistic physiological or pathological doctrine based on hot or cold, there are many (including not just *On Breaths*, but also *On the Nature of Man*) that propose theories of a broadly similar speculative and dogmatic type.[13] Moreover the concern

[10] See Lloyd 1991 (H 211) 209ff.   [11] See Lloyd 1987 (H 210) ch. 2.
[12] See Miller 1953 (H 228); Thivel 1975 (H 254); Grensemann 1968 (H 160); Lloyd 1979 (H 208) ch. 1.   [13] See Lloyd 1991 (H 211) ch. 3.

to criticize the bad practices of fellow-physicians can be illustrated also in the surgical works. *On Fractures* and *On Joints* repeatedly condemn what the authors represent as the useless or positively harmful surgical treatments commonly used by their colleagues.

Our second main source for fourth-century Greek medicine consists of other literary works. Just as in the fifth century, Herodotus, the tragedians and Aristophanes especially provide important insights both into beliefs about diseases, including what we would call mental as well as physical illness, and into medical practice, so too in the fourth we can use not just the fragments of New Comedy, but also the orators and philosophers, especially Plato, Aristotle and Theophrastus, to supplement the picture provided by the Hippocratic treatises. One work of special interest that has already been mentioned is the summary of Meno's history of medical theory that is preserved in Anonymus Londinensis.[14] This confirms and extends the impression the Hippocratic treatises themselves give, of a formidable array of competing explanations of diseases, some based on elemental substances, others on opposites, others again on humours, and yet others on the role of other pathogenic substances, for example 'residues'. In addition to two divergent accounts of Hippocrates' ideas, and a précis of Plato's theory of diseases from the *Timaeus*, the document reports the views of a variety of medical theorists, some comparatively well-known figures, such as the Pythagorean philosopher Philolaus, others otherwise completely unknown: nor should we assume that the twenty or so theorists mentioned by Meno go far towards exhausting the list of those who made some contribution to speculations in pathology in the period down to the end of the fourth century.

Apart from his extensive use of the doctor–statesman and doctor–philosopher analogies, Plato is an important source for medical traditions other than those represented by Hippocratic writers. Passages in the *Republic* (364bff) and the *Laws* (909a–d, 933aff) criticize those who purveyed charms and purifications: the type of person envisaged is broadly comparable with those attacked in *On the Sacred Disease*. Here is good evidence that it was not just those who themselves offered a rival style of treatment – and who may thus be thought to have competed for clients – who were critical of some apparently quite widespread beliefs and practices.

The evidence in Theophrastus' botanical treatises is even more valuable for the light it throws on popular ideas and on the practices of the 'root-cutters' and 'drug-sellers'.[15] Although several Hippocratic

[14] See Jones 1947 (H 185).   [15] See Lloyd 1983 (H 209) part 3, ch. 2.

works, notably some of the gynaecological treatises, frequently pre-
scribe the use of plants or plant products as medicines, none comments
either positively or negatively on any special rituals to be observed in
their collection or preparation. Yet Theophrastus' botanical works,
especially book IX of the *Historia Plantarum*, contain many reports
concerning the avoidance behaviour or other rituals that some said had
to be observed when collecting or handling a wide variety of plants such
as mandragora, hellebore, 'all-heal', the peony γλυκυσίδη and so on.
Theophrastus himself is sometimes more, sometimes less, critical of
these practices, some of which he categorizes as 'far-fetched', 'absurd' or
'superstitious'. He remarks that some stories about the marvellous
properties of plants originate with people who were seeking to 'glorify
their own crafts', though on several occasions he expresses a certain
hesitation about the extent to which what was reported was to be
believed. Yet while the Hippocratic doctors often use the very same
plants that Theophrastus discusses, they omit any reference to such
practices: we would never have gathered from them that there were any
such rituals. Their account is entirely naturalistic: yet while they show no
signs of subscribing to beliefs in the magical powers of plants, we may
imagine that their clients often did, and this is clearly a factor that should
not be discounted when assessing the popularity of some of the remedies
that the rationalist doctors recommend.[16]

Our third principal source is the inscriptional evidence. This consists
first of a number of honorific decrees that testify to the regard with which
individual practitioners were held. Secondly and more importantly,
there are inscriptions, dating mostly from the fourth century B.C. at the
earliest, that relate to the practice of temple medicine. From the earliest
times certain gods and heroes had been associated with local healing
cults. But from the late fifth century the cult of Asclepius especially
achieved unprecedented popularity and success. His cult was introduced
into many cities, including Athens, and from the fourth century on
imposing shrines were founded, notably at Epidaurus and on Cos.
Literary sources, such as Aristophanes' *Plutus*, provide good early
evidence about some aspects of temple medicine, for example for the
practice of 'incubation', where the patient slept in the shrine hoping to be
sent a dream by the god which, when suitably interpreted, might reveal
the cause of the illness or its treatment. For temple medicine in late
antiquity we have extensive material in the orator Aelius Aristides
(second century A.D.). But one of our principal direct sources for the cult

[16] See Stannard 1961 (H 251); Scarborough 1978 (H 242); Harig 1980 (H 170); Scarborough 1983
(H 243); Lloyd 1983 (H 209) part 3, ch. 2.

of Asclepius in the fourth century B.C. is the set of inscriptions from
Epidaurus that deal with a series of particular cases.[17]

These show first that the clientele was varied; second that the types of
complaints dealt with ranged from acute conditions, such as epilepsy and
consumption, to the mundane – headaches and insomnia (and indeed the
god was also asked for and gave help on non-medical matters as well,
such as finding a lost child or recovering a deposit); third that the god
was represented as insisting on the need for faith and as a stickler for due
recompense for the services he rendered (as in one case where a man who
was cured for blindness but omitted to make his thank-offering became
blind again, to be healed once more by the god after incubation); and
fourth that the god, through his representatives, claimed many notable,
indeed sensational, successes.[18] Not a single failure, nor even partial
failure, is hinted at, which is not surprising if, as seems likely, the main
function of the inscriptions was to publicise the shrine's successes,
although the contrast with some of the Hippocratic writings should be
noted: for all *their* concern to advertise the treatment *they* offered, the
authors of the *Epidemics* record failures as often as they do successful
cures and the writer of the surgical treatise *On Joints* (ch. 47) expressly
remarks that he describes an unsuccessful attempt to reduce a case of
congenital humpback so that others might learn from his experience.[19]
While we are clearly in no position to evaluate most of the claims for cure
made at Epidaurus in the fourth century, some evidently belong to the
realm of the fantastic, as for example in some of the 'surgical' cases where
a cure is achieved after the god has been seen, in a dream, performing
extraordinary feats manipulating the internal organs of the patient's
body.

The evidence our three main types of source yield is rich and the
inadequacies of one source can sometimes be supplied from another. We
must, however, observe that while what may broadly be called the
rationalist tradition or traditions are comparatively fully documented,
for many aspects of popular and religious healing our information is
scanty, indirect and in places suspect. The inscriptional and literary
evidence for established temple medicine leaves many questions unans-
wered and unanswerable. The itinerant purifiers attacked by Plato and in
On the Sacred Disease cannot speak for themselves. Nor can the drug-
sellers and root-cutters mentioned by Theophrastus and others, nor yet
the midwives and women healers referred to by, for instance, the
Hippocratic gynaecological treatises (themselves all written by men).
Much of the day-to-day treatment of the sick was, we must suppose, in

[17] See Herzog 1931 (H 176) and compare Edelstein and Edelstein 1945 (H 149); Sherwin-White
1978 (C 381).   [18] See Herzog 1931 (H 176); Lloyd 1979 (H 208) ch. 1.
[19] See Lloyd 1987 (H 210) ch. 3.

the hands of men and women who were far removed from the learned traditions of Hippocratic or even of temple medicine. The gradations from a person carrying out a simple treatment for himself or herself, or going to someone with a local reputation for special knowledge of drugs or of healing in general, all the way to a consultation at a shrine, or with a literate and articulate rationalist medical theorist, were infinitely various, and we must recognize the bias introduced by the fact that our knowledge relates quite disproportionately to the literate end of that spectrum.[20]

Claims for the originality of Greek medicine of the classical period must acknowledge first that much of the actual medical practice was popular and unsystematic in character. Moreover much within the specifically rationalist strands of Greek medicine can be compared with what we know of ancient Near Eastern, especially Egyptian, medicine.[21] It has, indeed, been suggested that parts of Greek medicine are directly indebted to Egypt or to Babylonia, for example the use of particular drugs, or the attention paid to residues as pathogenic substances, or again the use of certain tests to determine whether a woman can conceive or whether a pregnant woman will bear a boy or a girl. Thus one test recorded in *On Sterile Women* (ch. 214) involves inserting garlic in the vagina overnight: if in the morning the woman's breath smells, she is thought able to conceive, the underlying idea being that there are channels through the woman's body which prevent conception if they are obstructed. A similar, though not exactly parallel, test occurs in the Egyptian medical document, the Papyrus Carlsberg, and some have argued that Egypt is the source of this idea, as also of the common Greek belief that the womb moves round the woman's body and so causes diseases.[22] Yet even though similarities are sometimes striking, the possibility that they are fortuitous usually remains open. In any case we are generally dealing with notions that are widespread in many different parts of the world and for which the hypothesis of independent development is often as plausible as that of diffusion from a single source.

More importantly, certain aspects of the methods frequently thought central to Greek rationalist medicine are foreshadowed, at least up to a point, in the ancient Near East. The case histories in the *Epidemics*, especially books I and III, are often hailed, quite rightly, for their

[20] See Lonie 1983 (H 216).

[21] See, for example, Grapow 1954–73 (H 159); Lefebure 1956 (H 203); Steuer and Saunders 1959 (H 252); Wilson 1962 (H 262); Oppenheim 1962 (H 233); Saunders 1963 (H 241); Goltz 1974 (H 156); Harig and Kollesch 1977 (H 171).

[22] See Steuer and Saunders 1959 (H 252); Saunders 1963 (H 241).

thoroughness and meticulous attention to detail, with a whole range of diagnostic signs subject to careful examination from the look of the patient's face and the texture of the skin to the character of the stool, urine, sputum, vomit, and including also what we should call psychological factors, the patient's thoughts and courage or despondency in the face of disease. The daily condition of individual patients is recorded, with occasional observations in some instances up to the 120th day from the onset of the disease. Yet the recording of case histories can be traced in Egyptian medical papyri long before Hippocratic medicine began. The Edwin Smith papyrus, which dates from around 1600 B.C. but which contains much earlier material, sets out a number of surgical cases and makes suggestions for their treatment that are almost wholly free from references to charms, incantations and the like.[23] The originality of Greek medicine when contrasted with Egyptian must then be nuanced. It is certainly not the case that Greek doctors were the first to engage in careful observation of their patients and to make records of the changes in their condition: the difference is rather a matter of degree than one of kind, a question of the extent to which the Greeks undertook this systematically and in accordance with an explicit methodology.

Again on the question of 'magic' and 'superstition' – the appeal to supernatural agencies causing diseases and the use of spells and rituals and the like in treatment – it would be quite mistaken to represent the *whole* of ancient popular medicine as 'mystical' in character. It is true that the reference to divine or demonic forces is very common in extant Babylonian medical texts particularly.[24] But it is also clear that much Egyptian medicine, especially, was naturalistic. Conversely we have noted that religious beliefs form an important part of certain strands of Greek medicine in the fifth and fourth centuries B.C. What marks out certain rationalist Greek doctors (by no means all those who practised medicine) is the explicit attack on what *they* called 'magic' and the attempt to demonstrate that every disease has a natural cause, together with the resolution, in treatment, to stick to the usual naturalistic methods, such as the control of diet and exercise, even though in such an instance as epilepsy it may be doubted whether these were of any use.[25]

The very proliferation of different traditions is undoubtedly one of the most striking features of fifth- and fourth-century Greek medicine. It was possible for anyone to set up as a doctor. There were no legally recognized professional qualifications, and the reputation of each doctor depended largely on his actual or supposed success or failure in practice. It helped, to be sure, to have been connected with or taught by a well-

---

[23] See Breasted 1930 (H 129); compare Grapow 1954–73 (H 159).
[24] See Oppenheim 1962 (H 233).
[25] See Joly 1966 (H 178); Kudlien 1968 (H 194); Lloyd 1979 (H 208) ch. 1.

known physician, many of whom, including Hippocrates himself, earned fees from instructing pupils. The Hippocratic *Oath* sets out certain obligations the apprentice had to his teacher (though we should not imagine that all those represented by the treatises in our Corpus subscribed to the *Oath* in one or other of its forms).[26] But neither Cos, famous for its doctors, nor anywhere else had any equivalent to a modern teaching hospital (there were in any case no hospitals); ancient medical 'schools' were no more than, at most, loose associations of doctors who shared approximately the same approach and were prepared to teach it.[27]

The aspiring medical practitioner was faced, as we have seen, with an intensely competitive situation, with rivalry both within the rationalist tradition and between it and others. No doubt the challenging of traditional and popular beliefs about diseases may be seen as part of a more general development of critical thought, in philosophy, in 'history' and in political life, in Greece from the fifth century onwards. Certainly the search for naturalistic explanations in medicine may be related to the earlier development of similar investigations in Presocratic natural philosophy. Again Hippocratic techniques of argument owe much specifically to philosophy and have much in common with those deployed in the fields of politics and the law. As the writer of *On Diseases* I makes clear, the Hippocratic doctor could expect an interested and critical audience, not just on the occasions of general lectures on physiology and pathology, but in clinical practice. This text gives advice to the doctor not only about how to question the patient about his complaint, but also about how to deal with the questions that patients and their relatives and friends would put to the doctor. This challenging of the doctor to justify his diagnosis and his treatment is a distinctively Greek phenomenon and one that has to be understood in part at least against the general background of Greek political and legal experience, the examination of litigants in lawsuits, the scrutiny of magistrates on leaving office, as well as the debates in the arena of the Assembly.[28]

In a certain style of Greek medicine the ability to give reasons for a point of view was at a premium. Skill in argument was an important, indeed essential, asset in a wide variety of contexts, to persuade the patient to accept treatment and indeed to win clients, in joint consultations between several doctors called in on particular cases, or in public debates between theorists discussing such topics as the nature of man or the origins of diseases – or the validity of the 'art' of medicine. There

[26] See Deichgräber 1933 (H 137); Edelstein 1967 (H 152) 3ff; Harig and Kollesch 1978 (H 172).
[27] See, for example, Smith 1973 (H 249); Jouanna 1974 (H 186); Grensemann 1975 (H 161); Kudlien 1977 (H 197); Lonie 1978 (H 214); Sherwin-White 1978 (C 381); Smith 1979 (H 250); Di Benedetto 1980 (H 139); Thivel 1981 (H 255); Grensemann 1987 (H 163).
[28] See Lloyd 1979 (H 208) ch. 4, and compare Ducatillon 1977 (H 146).

were, to be sure, distinctions between medical practitioners and professional educators ('sophists'), but also an important possible overlap
between the two broad categories, and some of those represented in the
Hippocratic Corpus combine both roles. In Plato's *Gorgias* (456bc) the
sophist of that name is made to say that he could outdo any ordinary
doctor both in persuading patients to accept treatment and in convincing
the Assembly that he should be employed as a public doctor (an
appointment offered by some states, largely, it seems, to guarantee that
some medical help was available). Although the claim may seem absurd
to us and was no doubt meant by Plato to seem excessive, it only has
point if it has some plausibility in an ancient context and indeed, to judge
from some of our Hippocratic texts, there were many rationalist Greek
doctors whose skill in argument would not have compared unfavourably even with a Gorgias.[29]

   While the contrasts between rival styles of medicine, and the existence
of a significant degree of pluralism in this context, are striking, there are
also important points of overlap or common ground between some of
the competing traditions. The rationalists are often strident in their
claims for their own originality and for the distinctiveness of their
practice of the medical art.[30] Yet in some respects they stayed closer to
other traditions than might be expected, both in the terms in which they
described some of their aims and procedures and in some of their
procedures themselves. It was not just in temple medicine that dreams
were sometimes used in diagnosis, for some of the rationalists held that
dreams were signs of physical disturbances in the body.[31] Again
prognosis, the ability to predict the outcome of a disease, was sometimes
referred to in terms that suggested a parallelism with divination. In
words that echo the description of Calchas in *Iliad* I (70) and the Muses in
Hesiod's *Theogony* (38 cf. 32) the writer of the treatise *Prognostic* (ch. 1)
says that the doctor should 'tell in advance' 'the present, the past and the
future' in the presence of his patients. More generally, not only is the
chief word for drug (and poison), φάρμακον, also commonly used for
spells, but where the ritualist healer spoke of 'purifying' the patient, the
rationalist too sometimes used the very same term, 'purification',
κάθαρσις, for what he aimed to bring about, even though by this he
meant the physical evacuation of the body to be brought about by
purging it.[32] Though there was no need for any patient to be confused,
both styles of healing might exploit the common ground represented by
an indeterminate expectation that a cure was to be effected by a cleansing
or purification.

[29] See Lloyd 1979 (H 208) ch. 2.   [30] See Lloyd 1987 (H 210) ch. 2.
[31] See Lloyd 1987 (H 210) ch. 1.
[32] See Lloyd 1979 (H 208) ch. 1, and compare Parker 1983 (H 91).

On the side of the relationship between medical theories and philosophy there are again suggestive similarities and differences. Both Hippocratic writers and Presocratic natural philosophers sought, we said, naturalistic explanations of diverse phenomena, and in both cases the fertility of their speculative imagination often far outran their sense of self-criticism. As in philosophy a wide variety of explanations of varying degrees of plausibility was on offer for phenomena such as earthquakes or lightning, to the point where the impression is sometimes given that some theorists were satisfied with almost any account provided only that it met the requirement of being naturalistic, so too in medicine the accounts of particular diseases or of disease in general usually went far beyond the evidence on which they were based. From the observation that bile and phlegm are excreted in certain conditions, some concluded that they caused them: indeed *On Affections* (ch. 1) and *On Diseases* I (ch. 2) claimed that bile and phlegm are the cause of all diseases, or at least of all internal ones. Similarly from the observation of changes in temperature and humidity in diseases others concluded that the hot, the cold, the dry and the wet were themselves responsible.

At the same time there was this important difference between early Greek natural philosophy and medicine, that eventually – even if not initially, in the context of some public debate – the physicians were confronted with the practical task of attempting to cure the sick. To be sure, this did not invariably lead to the adoption of a more cautious, less dogmatic, attitude. Yet some writers did attack the more extreme speculative tendencies (even if they are not always free from such tendencies themselves) and several point to particular difficulties in the matter of establishing the causes of individual complaints. *On Regimen* II (ch. 70) remarks that patients are often mistaken in blaming their illness on whatever they happened to do at the time of its onset. *On Ancient Medicine* (ch. 21) says that doctors too, as well as laymen, tend to ascribe complications in a disease to a particular activity that has been indulged in, and the same treatise stipulates the criteria that a cause must fulfil (ch. 19): 'the cause of these maladies is found in the presence of certain substances which, when present, invariably produce such results'.

As for the actual treatments the Hippocratic doctors disposed of, these fall into a very few general types, most of them available already in popular Greek medicine. Apart from a variety of drugs, mostly plants, but some animal products and some minerals and metals including arsenic, they used baths, fomentations, ointments and plasters and practised venesection. Many of the surgical techniques they employed, including trepanning and cauterization, can be traced back long before the fifth century, but they elaborated some new methods, especially in the treatment of fractures and dislocations, where the discussion in the major Hippocratic surgical treatises is full of good sense. Those works warn, however, against the development of newfangled techniques, especially complex mechanical devices, designed to impress clients. They criticize, too, as we noted, the common use of methods they considered harmful or useless, although that does not stop them endorsing others that appear equally alarming: the gynaecological treatises even recommend the succussion of the patient, upside down on a ladder, for certain cases of prolapse of the womb and of difficult delivery.[33]

The control of regimen, the balance of diet and exercise, was the focus of particular attention. Again much of the advice given was sound, though what begins as a sensible principle was sometimes subject to massive theoretical over-elaboration, with some authors engaging in quite arbitrary analyses of particular kinds of food and of the effects of different types of exercise. One common idea was that opposites are cures for opposites, but this had a vast number of different applications, depending on which 'opposites' were thought significant and on how they were supposed to be brought into balance: how 'hot' was to be used to counteract 'cold' was often no simple matter, no more was how a state of 'repletion' was to be 'evacuated' or vice versa. The Greek doctors had, of course, no antibiotics, and no very reliable anaesthetic or antiseptic agents. In many cases, particularly in acute diseases, the most they could do was to let nature take its course, keeping the patient as comfortable as possible and doing nothing to exacerbate his or her condition, but with little hope that the diet or drugs prescribed would bring about a cure. In this context the defensive principles expressed by several Hippocratic authors are readily understandable. The dangers of doing positive harm to the patient with the wrong treatment are often referred to. From the *Aphorisms* (Sec. 6, 38) we may note: 'it is better not to treat those who have internal cancers since, if treated, they die quickly: but if not treated, they last a long time'. *Epidemics* I ch. 5 (Littré II 634 8f) sums up: 'Practise two things in your dealings with disease: either help or do not harm the patient.'

If in view of the limitations of our evidence we have to renounce any attempt to evaluate Greek medicine as a whole in the fourth century, we may, nevertheless, in conclusion, offer an overview of the principal Hippocratic contributions. In each of three main areas, the deployment of argument, the development of empirical techniques, and the expression of the methods and aims of the medical art, the record is a complex one.

[33] See Lloyd 1987 (H 210) 68ff.

Many Hippocratic writers were quick to expose the weaknesses in other theorists' ideas, but this was often not matched by any corresponding talent or willingness to subject their own theories to radical scrutiny. The deployment of critical and destructive argument was a prerequisite for the development of alternatives to popular and religious medicine. How much was lost in that process it is impossible to say, though temple medicine at least survived and flourished alongside the rationalist tradition until the end of antiquity. The pervasive tendency in many Hippocratic authors to act as advocates for a point of view is readily understandable in terms of the competitiveness of medicine which in turn may be related to both the pluralism and the agonistic character that mark Greek culture as a whole so strongly. Yet while the ability in debate is one of the great strengths of Hippocratic medicine, it has its corresponding negative features, in the degeneration of that ability into blinkered partisanship.

Painstaking observations were again one of the most remarkable features of some Hippocratic work, yet the limitations of the contexts in which they were carried out must be noted. In clinical studies some of the extant treatises not only set out in great detail the signs that are to be taken into account but implement these principles fully in their practice. Here, where the doctors were concerned, among other things, to establish the periodicities of acute diseases, there was a particular incentive to undertake *daily* observations of the changes in a patient's condition. Yet in anatomy, for instance, the picture is very different. Although there are occasional references to dissection, this was not used systematically by Hippocratic writers of the fifth or fourth centuries, indeed by no one before Aristotle.[34] Here the Hippocratic doctors were satisfied to base their ideas concerning the internal structure of the body on external inspection, or on observation of lesions, even on inferences from the practice of venesection.[35]

Finally the Hippocratic writers originate a fundamental methodological debate, on the aims of medicine and on the procedures to be adopted in its practice. They often express their confidence that medicine has progressed and will advance further, that diseases are investigable, that cures will be found. Paradoxically, however, this very confidence – so important for sustaining the rationalist tradition – was, at the time, based largely on wishful thinking, if not on bluff, for it far outstripped the very limited actual understanding of the causes of diseases and the even more limited actual ability to cure.[36]

[34] See Edelstein 1932–3/1967 (H 154); Kudlien 1967 (H 193), 1969 (H 195); Mansfeld 1975 (H 218); Lloyd 1991 (H 211) ch. 8.   [35] See Lloyd 1991 (H 211) 179ff.

[36] The text of this section was completed in September 1982.

CHAPTER 12c

GREEK ART: CLASSICAL TO HELLENISTIC

J. J. POLLITT

I. STYLE AND ICONOLOGY

Greek art in the fourth century B.C. is made up of two distinct strands –
one, an external set of stylistic mannerisms derived from the art of the
fifth century B.C. and the other, an inner spirit that anticipates the art of
the hellenistic period – and it is these two strands, woven together, that
give the monuments of the period their particular character.

Greek sculptors of the fourth century, for example, frequently
adopted the elegant, calligraphic style of Attic art of the later fifth
century as their point of departure. At other times they reached back
beyond this style to the serene and balanced style of the Parthenon frieze
or to the formal harmony of Polyclitus. These prototypical styles were
further developed, naturally, in ways that make works of the fourth
century recognizable and distinctive, but a sense of formal continuity
with the past nevertheless always remains strong in them. On the basis of
certain votive reliefs and grave stelae, in fact, it can even be argued that
neoclassicism, that reverence at a distance for the art of the high Classical
period as a moment of perfection which can only be emulated because it
cannot be surpassed, had its origin in the fourth century. On the other
hand, if one looks at the content of fourth-century sculpture, at the
attitudes and feelings that it is used to express, one finds a new interest in
the personal experience of the individual as an appropriate subject for the
visual arts and, with it, a rejection of the more impersonal, group-
oriented themes connected with the life of the polis that had been the
concern of much of the art of the fifth century. Above all it is the interest
in expressing personal emotions – anguish, fear, pain, humour, amorous
yearning, and a sense of religious mystery – that comes to typify the
sculpture of the time.

To the degree that its development can be traced from the limited
surviving monuments, the same dichotomy seems to have been characteristic of fourth-century painting. The Kerch style of red-figure vase

A further account of art of the later Classical period will be found in the *Plates Volume* (B. A.
Sparkes). The notes to this section include accessible illustrations and comment. See also the
Bibliography, Section J.

painting, for example, was essentially an elaboration on the elegant style of late fifth-century artists like the Meidias Painter.[1] On the other hand, literary sources describing the works of some of the prominent painters of the time suggest the presence of a new spirit of pathos (e.g. Pliny's description, *NH* xxxv.98, of the painting by Aristides the Younger of Thebes of the sack of a city) that would seem to have had no parallel in the fifth century. Even Greek temple architecture, with its increasing emphasis on the elaboration of interior space, can be said to appeal to, and attempt to provoke, the personal religious sensitivity of the individual rather than the group spirit of liturgical state religion.

This dual nature of the art of the fourth century can be understood as a reflection of diverging currents in Greek society as a whole. On one side, up until the time when Philip II began to intervene in Greek affairs, the life of the different *poleis* went along much as it had in the past. Old systems of government, intermittently interrupted by civil quarrels, survived; new alliances were formed; new wars were fought; old festivals and rituals continued, and so on. Yet in the intellectual and even in the religious history of the period one can detect a disenchantment with the polis and its institutions as the central focus of life. Plato and later Aristotle established schools which made it possible to draw back from the hubbub of city life and to think and study in an atmosphere conducive to the contemplation of far-reaching philosophical and political questions. This move toward withdrawal from the affairs of the community culminates around the middle of the century in the espousal of the Cynic way of life by Diogenes of Sinope and his followers. By renouncing the life, values and aspirations of the ordinary citizen, flouting authority, ridiculing social conventions, and taking to a mendicant's way of life, the Cynics hoped to find peace of mind and independence *as individuals*. It was their personal experience, not that of society as a whole, that mattered.

In other areas of daily life where there is evidence that makes it possible to form a judgment, the same drift toward emphasizing personal experience at the expense of communal experience is detectable. In the theatre, for example, the fourth century witnessed a striking change in the nature of comedy. What had been a bawdy ritual intensely bound up with the politics and personalities of a particular city was metamorphosed, by the time of Menander, into a form of light melodrama which explored the emotions that might typify private life anywhere. In the religious life of Greece the most revealing development of the fourth century is the growth in popularity of the cult of Asclepius, the god who cared about individuals and could miraculously intervene in their lives in order to soothe their private afflictions.

[1] Burn 1987 (J 10); Boardman 1990 (J 6) 144–7; Robertson 1992 (J 35A) 237–41.

It is no doubt significant that one of the earliest and most important large monuments of the fourth century, a temple at Epidaurus decorated with impressive architectural sculptures, was dedicated (*c.* 380 B.C.) to Asclepius.[2] These sculptures typify the art of the fourth century in much the same way that those of the temple of Zeus at Olympia and the Parthenon typify the Early and High Classical periods respectively. One group of them, the acroteria, carry on elements of the elegant style of late fifth-century Attica and represent the backward-looking strain in the art of the period; another group, the pedimental sculptures, have a pathos and dissonance that looks to the future (Pls. Vol., pl. 10). The acroteria from Epidaurus consist of a figure of Nike in the centre of each gable and female figures (Nereids? Aurae?) riding on horses at the corners at each end. Their emphasis on relatively large, smooth planes, where drapery is blown flat against the body, interspersed with eddies and furrows, derives from very late works of the fifth century like the frieze of the Erechtheum. Occasional disharmonies in these figures, it is true, give hints of a new taste for internal tension that characterizes the pedimental sculptures (e.g. the stiff postures of the riding figures and sudden, almost harsh, shifts in the drapery patterns), but overall the effect of the acroteria is one of traditional grace and elegance.

A building inscription connected with the temple of Asclepius records that one set of acroteria, probably those on the west, was done by a sculptor named Timotheus, apparently the same artist who subsequently became famous as one of the sculptors of the Mausoleum of Halicarnassus and whose reputation lived on among later writers on Greek art.[3] Because of Timotheus' later fame, it is sometimes assumed that he must have been the master sculptor of the whole Epidaurus project. The evidence of the inscription does not seem to support this contention, however, and it is more likely that if the Timotheus who worked at Epidaurus was the same as the artist whom Pliny and others remembered, he was a relatively young man at the time. He may have been an *émigré* from Athens, one of what seems to have been a substantial group of artists trained in Attica who migrated to other areas during the later stages of the Peloponnesian War and afterwards, in search of richer opportunities for employment.[4] Other works that have been associated with Timotheus, although in an admittedly very speculative way, such as

---

[2] Crome 1951 (J 11); Burford 1969 (J 9); Robertson 1975 (J 35) 397–402; N. Yalouris 1986 in (J 1) 175–86.   [3] Schlörb 1965 (J 44); Stewart 1990 (J 48) 273–4.

[4] It was probably the dispersal of these artists that accounts for the appearance of the Attic style in such disparate places as the Peloponnese, southern Italy, non-Greek areas of Asia Minor such as Lycia and Caria, and even Phoenicia. In the east, while working for non-Greek patrons, they produced what have become the best-known works of their diaspora, e.g. the Nereid Monument at Xanthus (now in London; Stewart 1990 (J 48) 171–2, pls. 461–74) and the Satrap and Lycian sarcophagi at Sidon (now in Istanbul; Robertson 1975 (J 35) 404–5).

a figure of Hygieia from Epidaurus and Roman copies of a group of Leda and the Swan bear the strong imprint of the Attic sculptural style, and it is tempting to think that it was Timotheus who brought this style to Epidaurus.[5]

In the pedimental sculptures from the temple of Asclepius the harmony and graceful lines of earlier Attic art, although they can be detected in some details, are greatly attenuated in favour of stylistic mannerisms designed to evoke a sense of stark pathos. The east group represented the sack of Troy with the death of Priam at its centre; the west group was an Amazonomachy. Many of the fragmentary torsos from both combats show bodies contorted by sharp angles and punctuated by stark anatomical divisions. The uncomfortable, beleaguered feeling that they convey purely by composition is made explicit in the pain and pathos of one crucial fragment, the head of Priam, whose anguished expression puts it at the head of a long line of monuments that culminates in the sculptures of the Altar of Zeus at Pergamum. In this head, and in the pathetically twisted figure of a dead warrior from the corner of one of the pediments (which one is disputed) we encounter the first mature examples of the ability of fourth-century sculptors to identify personally with intense emotion and to convey that emotion to their audience on a basic human level, unmodulated by grand civic themes. An otherwise unknown artist named Hectoridas, whose name is recorded as the designer of one of the pediments in the building accounts of the temple, may deserve credit for turning the art of his time in a new direction.

Another more famous sculptor, Scopas of Paros, perhaps had his early training at Epidaurus. In any case, he above all others seems to have carried forward the innovations of the Epidaurian pediments later in the century. The key monuments for the study of Scopas' career and style are the fragmentary pedimental sculptures (their subjects were the combat of Telephus with Achilles and the Calydonian boar hunt) from the temple of Athena Alea at Tegea in Arcadia.[6] Pausanias (VIII.45.4ff) records that Scopas was the architect of the temple, and it is natural to assume that his influence, if not his actual hand, shaped its sculptures. The impassioned expression that typifies the heads from the pediments, particularly a head with a lion-skin cap which may be that of Heracles or Telephus (Pls. Vol., pl. 12), an expression achieved through deep carving around the eyes and a compressed, almost cubic set of proportions, is their most distinctive feature and may have been a kind of signature of Scopas' work.

[5] Robertson 1975 (J 35) 402, pl. 129d.
[6] Dugas *et al.* 1924 (J 16); Arias 1952 (J 2); Norman 1984 (J 23); Robertson 1975 (J 35) 452–7; Stewart 1977 (J 47) and 1990 (J 48) 284–6.

The date of Scopas' career clearly ranged from *c.* 360 B.C. to *c.* 330, but whether the Tegea sculptures stand near the beginning or after the middle of that period is disputed. After he visited Asia Minor to work on the Mausoleum at Halicarnassus (*c.* 353–351 B.C.) and also visited Cnidus, there is some reason to think that he came under the influence of the style of Praxiteles and perhaps also of Leochares and that his own work took on a somewhat more eclectic character. If this is true, the Tegea sculptures, because of their clear link with Epidaurus, may belong to a relatively early phase of his work.

Although it cannot be attested in the battered fragments from Tegea, a second distinctive trait of the style of Scopas seems to have been the use of complex contrapposto compositions to achieve an effect of restlessness and tension. Such composition, at any rate, is characteristic of many of the works preserved in Roman copies that have been ascribed to him on the basis of literary references. Of these, the most impressive, as well as the most plausible, is the Dancing Maenad in Dresden, which conveys its frenzied state both through pathetic facial expression and twists of the body that border on contortion.[7]

While the expression of anguish, achieved through deep carving around the eyes and other devices, seems to have been particularly prevalent in the work of Scopas, it is clear that other sculptors of the middle of the fourth century also made use of it and that, to a greater or lesser degree, it became a hallmark of the period. The general appeal of dramatic facial expression to the emotional climate of the time is attested by its adoption on relatively modest monuments like Attic grave stelae. These stelae continued in an unbroken series from the late fifth century down to 318 B.C. when they were judged to be a form of extravagance and outlawed by Demetrius of Phalerum. Because they were purchased and set up by private individuals, they serve as an informative indicator of popular taste. Among those which reflect the spread of Scopaic pathos, the most striking is the 'Ilissus Stela' in the National Museum in Athens (Pls. Vol., pl. 17).[8]

In the work of another great artist of the period between 360 and 330 B.C., the Athenian sculptor Praxiteles, the interest in appealing to general human experience rather than to communal ideals took a different turn.[9] The literary sources about Praxiteles depict him as an easy-going personality who was fond of pleasure and amusement, and this picture seems to be confirmed by a certain humour, playfulness, languor, and sensuousness bordering on eroticism in those of his works that can be reconstructed and appreciated in Roman copies. His Apollo

[7] Robertson 1975 (J 35) pl. 143a; Stewart 1990 (J 48) 286.
[8] Robertson 1975 (J 35) 382; Stewart 1990 (J 48) 92–4, pls. 517–19.
[9] Rizzo 1932 (J 33); Robertson 1975 (J 35) 386–96; Stewart 1990 (J 48) 277–81.

Sauroctonus,[10] for example, seems to parody the sobriety of Archaic religious poetry and Classical religious sculpture by converting the dragon-slayer of Delphi into a languid youth who barely has the energy to swat a small, ordinary lizard. The famous Hermes at Olympia[11] enjoys a small joke by showing the amused god dangling a bunch of grapes before the infant Dionysus in order to test the child's innate propensities. Both of these figures also display the distinctive Praxitelean S-curve, a sinuous hipshot pose that was probably designed to show the sculptor's disdain for the studied balance so highly prized in the Polyclitan tradition.

The most notable and notorious exemplar of the sensuous and erotic strain in Praxiteles' art was the renowned figure of Aphrodite at Cnidus, a work that influenced ancient artistic taste to an extent rivalled by few other sculptures (Pls. Vol., pl. 35).[12] The enticing effect of the nude goddess, discovered but not disturbed as she disrobed for a bath, apparently tapped a spring of general erotic appeal that the largely male-dominated, tightly ordered life of the classical and archaic polis had kept for the most part buried. In the wake of the Cnidia Hellenistic and Roman sculptors turned out what seem like myriads of nude Aphrodites to meet the demands of an insatiable market.

Although the evidence is as usual limited, it seems that much of the humour and charm of Praxitelean sculpture also pervaded the painting of the middle and second half of the fourth century. Amorous themes and a particular interest in nude female figures characterize the work of some of the better painters who developed the Kerch style in late Attic red-figure vase painting, e.g. the Helena and Marsyas Painters.[13] And in Pliny's varied comments on works by the major painters of the time we read of obvious parodies (e.g. 'Zeus suffering labour pains at the birth of Dionysus' by the painter Ctesilochus, *HN* xxxv.14); of satyric carica-tures, like the 'Grylloi' of Antiphilus (*HN* xxxv.114); of paintings of flowers and flower girls by Pausias of Sicyon (*HN* xxxv.125); and of a famous nude Aphrodite rising from the sea by Apelles (*HN* xxxv.91, also mentioned by many other writers). The last of these, according to Athenaeus (590F), used for its model Praxiteles' alluring and notorious mistress, Phryne. Apelles in particular, among all the artists whose work is described by ancient writers, seems to have been something like Praxiteles' counterpart in painting. He himself is said to have cited a certain 'grace' or 'charm' (χάρις) as the distinguishing feature of his style.[14]

10 Robertson 1975 (J 35) 388–9; Stewart 1990 (J 48) 178–9, pl. 509.
11 Robertson 1975 (J 35) 386–8, pl. 125b; Stewart 1990 (J 48) pls. 607–9.
12 Robertson 1975 (J 35) 390–4; Stewart 1990 (J 48) pls. 502–7.
13 Boardman 1990 (J 6) 190–2; Robertson 1992 (J 35A) 280–8.   14 Robertson 1975 (J 35) 491–4.

Religious imagery and architecture provide still another field in which the fourth-century artist's effort to instil a more private tone into familiar forms can be felt. Just as the communal spirit of the religious atmosphere of the fifth century was in many ways crystallized in Phidias' Athena Parthenos, so too the more personal spirit of the fourth century is captured in representations of Asclepius – in votive reliefs, in works of the Roman period that seem to go back to fourth-century originals, and possibly in the great head in the British Museum known as the Asclepius Blacas.[15] A downward-directed glance, which seems to make the majestic god look with sympathy toward the devotees who approach him, is characteristic of these images and was clearly intended to bring out that possibility of personal communion between man and god which gave the cult its appeal.

The continuing interest which architects of the fourth century showed in designing elaborate new decorative schemes for the interiors of temples was probably also prompted, as noted earlier, by a desire to stimulate the individual devotee's sense of religious mystery. The subject, it is only fair to add, is a speculative one, since no ancient literary sources deal with the topic. Unlike churches, synagogues or mosques, the interiors of Greek temples were not intended for group worship (public functions that were part of a temple's cult took place at exterior altars) and hence whatever religious meaning, effect or atmosphere a worshipper absorbed from the inner *naos* (*cella*) of a temple was purely a private matter. Up until near the end of the fifth century B.C. it seems that the *naos* was thought of primarily as a secure chamber for votive treasures and for the god's image (itself a kind of votive object). Late in the century, however, in the surprisingly elaborate and original interior of the temple of Apollo at Bassae, the evidence of a desire to capture the attention and stir the emotions of potential viewers is unmistakable (Pls. Vol., pl. 9).[16] With its unusual two-part *naos*, one section of which was illuminated by a side door, its engaged Ionic columns with their unique profiles, its interior frieze, and above all its Corinthian columns, the inner space of the Bassae temple had no precedent. Pausanias (VIII.41.9) ascribes the temple to Ictinus, the architect of the Parthenon, and if his information is correct, it suggests that Ictinus lived well beyond the time of the Parthenon and absorbed, or helped to create, an architectural style, such as one also finds in the Erechtheum, which used lavish, jewel-like ornament and unusual forms to evoke an atmosphere of numinous, mysterious forces.

Features of the Bassae temple's interior, particularly its use of the Corinthian order, were widely adopted in the fourth century, both in

---

[15] Stewart 1990 (J 48) 191, pl. 574.
[16] Robertson 1975 (J 35) 356–9; Stewart 1990 (J 48) 169–70, pls. 448–54.

major temples and also in a group of shrines with circular ground-plans (*tholoi*) that, for reasons unknown, enjoyed a particular vogue at this time. Scopas' temple of Athena at Tegea employed engaged Corinthian columns in its *naos* and also, like Bassae, had a side door. In the temple of Zeus at Nemea (*c.* 330 B.C.),[17] the last important Doric temple built on the Greek mainland, a U-shaped pattern of free-standing Corinthian columns framed the cult image and served as a partial screen for a mysterious subterranean *adyton* at the far end of the *naos*. The three major *tholoi* – one in the sanctuary of Athena Pronaea at Delphi, designed *c.* 390 B.C. by Theodorus of Phocaea (Vitruvius VII. *praef.* 12); another at Epidaurus, designed by Polyclitus the Younger *c.* 350 B.C. (Pausanias II.27.5); and a third, known as the Philippeum, constructed in the sacred precinct at Olympia around 338–335 B.C. (Pausanias V.20.9) – all used Corinthian columns in their interiors.[18] The Philippeum, begun by Philip II and completed by Alexander, seems to have served as a *heröon* for members of the Macedonian royal family, and it is possible that the other *tholoi* also served hero cults, i.e. cults of a chthonic character devoted to gods and demigods who were considered once to have been mortals. (There is no evidence for the building at Delphi, but the fact that the *tholos* at Epidaurus may have housed Asclepius' sacred snakes suggests the possibility that it was devoted to the heroic aspect of the deity. Snakes were attributes of heroes, and Asclepius was viewed as an originally mortal physician who eventually achieved the status of a divinity.) In any case, their interiors, particularly that at Epidaurus with its lush floral ornament, may have been intended to evoke an awesome feeling of burgeoning chthonic forces.

A final example of the ways in which the artists of the fourth century focused their attention on the individual, in this case not so much his experience as his nature, can be found in the art of portraiture. As the century went along, there was a gradual movement away from portraiture which celebrated the public image and role of its subjects toward portraits which were designed to capture the individual personalities and inner natures of the people whom they represented. To some extent this movement in fourth-century portraiture can be seen as a revival of, or an intensification of, elements of Early Classical portraiture that had been suppressed by the idealistic strain in High Classical Greek art. Essentially the 'role portrait', exemplified by the 'Olympian Pericles' of Cresilas, is a High Classical form (Pls. Vol., pl. 26b); the 'character portrait', typified by the Alexander portraits of Lysippus and the Demosthenes by Polyeuctus, is an early Hellenistic creation; and the portraits of the first

---

[17] Hill *et al.* 1967 (J 18).
[18] Robert 1939 (J 34); Dinsmoor 1950 (J 14) 234–6; Lawrence 1983 (J 22) ch. 17.

seventy years of the fourth century form a transitional phase between the two.[19]

There is some evidence that the school of Polyclitus played an important part in expanding the range and popularity of portraiture in the fourth century. Pliny itemizes a substantial number of disciples and followers of the famous Argive master (*HN* xxxiv.50). In some respects these seem to have been conservative sculptors who kept up Polyclitus' interest in formal theory and like him made a particular speciality of statues of victorious athletes in the panhellenic sanctuaries.[20] It is probable, though the point is controversial, that works like the Youth from Anticythera in the National Museum in Athens were typical of their style (Pls. Vol., pl. 38).[21] There is no evidence, in any case, that they were concerned with the emotionalism of Scopas or the sensuousness of Praxiteles. Their response to the climate of their time may have come out, however, in an enthusiasm for designing portraits. Literary sources make it clear, at least, that the commissions which they received gave them ample opportunity to develop the genre. It was mainly followers of Polyclitus like Dameas of Cleitor and Alypus of Sicyon who worked on the elaborate sculptural group set up at Delphi by the Spartans to commemorate their victory in the Peloponnesian War (Pausanias x.9.7), a monument that contained portraits of Lysander and of as many as thirty other Spartans. Portraits by other prominent artists of the school, like Naucydes of Argos and Daedalus of Sicyon, are also recorded.

Athenian sculptors, beginning with the elusive Demetrius of Alopece whom Quintilian cites as an arch-realist (*Inst.* xii.10.10), also seem to have played an important role in the development of fourth-century portraits, and in one case it is possible to form an impression of what one of the works of a particular artist looked like. Diogenes Laertius (iii.25) refers to a portrait of Plato by the sculptor Silanion set up in the Academy, and a number of replicas dating from the Roman period, of very uneven quality, seem to derive from this original.[22] These copies preserve a common set of physiognomical characteristics that give the feeling of having been distinctive not only of an individual, unidealized face but also of a unique, pensive personality.

By the second half of the fourth century portraiture also came to be an important genre of painting. According to Pliny, some of Apelles' portraits were so vivid that fortune-tellers who were adept at reading the future from physiognomical features could make accurate predictions

---

[19] Richter 1965/1984 (J 31) 173–4, 225–8, 109–13; Alexander portraits – Pollitt 1986 (J 29) ch. 1; A. Stewart, *Faces of Power* (Los Angeles, 1993).   [20] Arnold 1969 (J 3).

[21] Robertson 1975 (J 35) 409, pl. 148b; Stewart 1990 (J 48) 185, pl. 550.

[22] Richter 1965/1984 (J 31) 181–6.

from his paintings (*HN* xxxv.88). Even if that story is fanciful, it is clear from what we hear of Apelles' portraits of Alexander and from other commissions that he received that he was a powerful portraitist. Other painters of his time such as Protogenes (*HN* xxxv.106), Antiphilus (*HN* xxxv.114) and Aristolaus (xxxv.137) were also admired for their skill in portraiture, and earlier in the century the Isthmian Euphranor, who seems to have worked mostly in Athens, incorporated portraits of Epaminondas and others into a large painting of the battle of Mantinea (362 B.C.) in the Stoa of Zeus Eleutherios in Athens (Pausanias 1.3.4). The appearance of these portraits is, of course, lost, but Pliny's observation, made in connexion with the painter Aristides of Thebes, that 'characters', *ethe*, played an important part in the paintings of the period (*HN* xxxv.98) was probably particularly true of painted portraiture.

II. ARTISTS AND PATRONS

The intellectual self-consciousness and self-assertiveness that had begun to be typical of Greek artists in the fifth century, and also the social recognition that had begun to come to them (see *CAH* v² 180–3), continued to grow in the fourth century. Not only did a number of artists become celebrities of a sort (e.g. Apelles and Praxiteles) but some of them became influential purveyors of cultural standards whose influence went beyond the immediate circle of their professional contemporaries (e.g. the painter Pamphilus, see below).

One obvious symptom of the fourth-century artists' claim to intellectual importance was their continuation of the practice of writing treatises about the more technical aspects of their craft – *symmetria*, colour and design – that laymen might not readily appreciate. These seem to have been particularly popular among painters. Euphranor wrote *volumina de symmetria et coloribus* (Pliny *HN* xxxv.129), and Asclepiodorus, Apelles and Melanthius also wrote about their art '(Pliny *HN* xxxv index; Diogenes Laertius IV.18). It seems likely that these treatises contained not only technical information but also expressions of taste and judgment. Apelles, for example, seems to have discussed *charis*, the special quality of his own style, in his book and also to have evaluated the particular virtues that were characteristic of the art of his contemporaries, Protogenes, Asclepiodorus and Melanthius (*HN* xxxv.80). Several architects of the period also put their theories into writing (see Vitruvius VII. *praef.* 12), and in these works too expressions of personal taste seem to have played a role. Pytheus, the architect of the Mausoleum of Halicarnassus, for example, inaugurated a tradition of criticism which condemned the Doric order as inherently imperfect and led to its being largely abandoned as an order for major temples. Only one specific treatise by a sculptor of the fourth century (by Silanion, Vitruvius VII. *praef.* 14) is recorded, but Pliny's discussion of Lysippus' views about *symmetria* (see below) indicates that there was an active interchange of ideas among sculptors, and it is likely that documents, in the tradition of Polyclitus' famous *Canon*, were in circulation, at least among sculptors themselves.

Another indication of the expanding intellectual influence and social importance of artists in the fourth century can be found in the formation of artistic schools, that is, organizations of artists who shared both a common geographical centre and also a certain body of doctrine (Pliny *HN* xxxv.75). The most significant of these was the Sicyonian school of painting, which, because of the reputation for great learning of one of its foremost members, Pamphilus, and because of the popularity of Pamphilus' chief pupil, Apelles, left a distinct mark on the intellectual life of Greece. 'Pamphilus was the first painter', says Pliny (*HN* xxxv.76–7), 'who was erudite in all branches of knowledge, especially arithmetic and geometry, without which, he held, an art could not be perfected . . . As a result of his prestige it came about that, first in Sicyon and later in all of Greece, free-born boys were given lessons in drawing on wooden tablets, a subject previously not taught, and thus painting was received into the front rank of the liberal arts.' The importance which the Sicyonian school attached to learning can also be said to have had a long-range influence on adult education in that it seems to have led to the creation of art history as a discipline. What appear to have been the first histories of painting and sculpture were written in the late fourth or early third century B.C. by a sculptor named Xenocrates, who is cited by Pliny and whose thoughts lie embedded in Pliny's chapters on art. Xenocrates' histories seem to have had a strong Sicyonian bias, and he himself was probably a member of the school.

To understand art and be able to make discriminating judgments about it became as important for patrons in the fourth century as technical competence was for artists themselves. The growing importance of connoisseurship as one of the credentials of an educated, cultured person comes out not only in Pliny's testimony, mentioned above, about the new role of drawing in education but also in anecdotes that he recounts about the artistic sensitivity, or lack thereof, of particular patrons, e.g. Demetrius Poliorcetes' appreciation and protection of Protogenes and his work, even in the midst of a military campaign (*HN* xxxv.105), and Apelles' taunting of Alexander for the latter's failure to grasp the fine points of painting (*HN* xxxv.85).

One way in which patrons could demonstrate their knowledge and taste in the arts was by hiring artists whose work was widely respected and brought prestige with it. Mausolus and Artemisia were probably trying to confirm their credentials as cultured philhellenes when they retained Scopas, Leochares, Timotheus and Bryaxis to do the sculptures of the Mausoleum,[23] and Philip may have had a similar motive when he hired Leochares to execute the portrait sculptures in the Philippeum. Whether it was because he was concerned about his reputation as a connoisseur or whether, as seems more likely, he recognized the importance of art as a medium for conveying a ruler's public 'image', Alexander made himself the single most influential patron in the Greek world by giving long-term appointments to the sculptor Lysippus, the painter Apelles, and a gem-carver named Pyrgoteles as 'court artists' and thus culminating the process by which artists came to be accepted as prestigious figures.

As patrons became, or were expected to become, better informed and more discriminating about the arts, it may be that there was a reciprocal effect which prompted artists to give their works a more obviously learned 'content'. In the hellenistic period it became quite normal for artists and writers to design works that were directed at a select, sophisticated, elite group rather than at the entire population of a community. Poets like Callimachus and the artists like the gem-carver who created the cameo bowl in Naples known as the 'Tazza Farnese'[24] took for granted a high level of subtlety on the part of their audience and a preparedness to catch meanings, particularly allegorical meanings, that would not be obvious to the less educated. Even though the art of the fourth century was still much more closely tied to the life of the average citizen than was much of the art of the Hellenistic period, foreshadowings of an elitist tendency of this sort can be found in it. An early example is the Eirene and Ploutos by the sculptor Cephisodotus, the father of Praxiteles, a group set up on the Areopagus in Athens c. 375 B.C. and now known through Roman copies (Pls. Vol., pl. 33).[25] On an immediate level it represented a maternal figure holding a child and looking at it with affection, just the sort of subject that would appeal to the fourth-century taste for familiar human emotions in art. On a second, more cerebral level, however, the group could be read as a simple allegory: Wealth, Ploutos, is born from and nurtured by Peace, Eirene. This didactic use of personifications perhaps had a special charm in Athens,

---

[23] Pliny *HN* XXXVI.30–1 says that the artists were retained by Artemisia after Mausolus' death (352 B.C., although Pliny gives 351) and that after her death they finished their work without a fee, simply for the glory. It is more likely, however, that the tomb was begun before Mausolus' death as part of an ambitious new urban plan for Halicarnassus and that work on it went forward for a number of years in the 360s and 350s. For the sources and probabilities see P–W s.v. 'Pytheos' (H. Riemann). Also, Robertson 1975 (J 35) 447–63; Waywell 1978 (J 52); Stewart 1990 (J 48) 281–2; Pls. Vol., pl. 11.   [24] Pollitt 1986 (J 29) 257–9; *Plates to Vol.* VII.1 pl. 7.

[25] Stewart 1990 (J 48) 173–4, pls. 485–7.

where the intellectual segment of society was slowly becoming adjusted to a more bookish, abstruse type of learning than had been common in earlier centuries. Euphranor's Theseus, Democracy, and Demos, painted around the middle of the century in the Stoa of Zeus Eleutherios in the Athenian Agora (Pausanias 1.3.3), and the relief of Democracy crowning Demos on an Athenian stela of 336 B.C. recording a decree against tyranny[26] seem to show that a substantial number of Athenians were becoming accustomed to 'reading' such works.

III. LYSIPPUS

Virtually all of the aspects of the art of the fourth century that have been discussed in this chapter came together in the art of Alexander's court sculptor, Lysippus of Sicyon. His long career, which began as early as the 360s or even the 370s and continued as late as the 320s or even beyond, both culminated the development of Classical sculpture and inaugurated many features of Hellenistic sculpture.[27]

In the early stages of his career Lysippus seems to have been an essentially conservative technician and theoretician who specialized in statues of victorious athletes and was concerned, like Polyclitus before him, with canons of proportions. His own canon, as described by Pliny (*HN* xxxiv.65), with its leaner proportions, greater spatial freedom, and interest in optical effects, was clearly innovative and influential, but the fact that he was concerned with canons at all can be viewed as an essentially backward-looking trait. At a slightly later stage of his development he may have done some eclectic dabbling in other contemporary styles. His Eros at Thespiae, for example, probably designed to compete subtly with the earlier Eros by Praxiteles in the same sanctuary, seems to have fused Praxitelean charm with Lysippus' own multifaceted style of spatial composition. When he was singled out as Alexander's court sculptor, however, he became the most forward-looking artist of his time. His renowned portraits[28] of Alexander, in capturing the king's restless *ethos* in a dramatic way, culminated the quest among portraitists of the fourth century for a style that could express personal emotion and capture individual characters; at the same time they established a new genre, the heroic ruler portrait, that was to have a long life in Hellenistic and Roman art. The same was true of Lysippus' two great historical groups, the 'Granicus Monument' at Dion, which commemorated the Companions of Alexander who had fallen in his first major battle against the Persians, and the 'Craterus Monument' at

---

26 *Athenian Agora* XIV (1972) pl. 53a.
27 Johnson 1927 (J 20); Sjöqvist 1966 (J 45); Robertson 1975 (J 35) 463–76; Stewart 1990 (J 48) 289–94; Pollitt 1986 (J 29) ch. 2.   28 See n. 19.

Delphi, which showed the king engaged in a lion hunt. In one respect these groups continued the fourth century's exploration of dramatic pathos, and in another they inaugurated a major category of Hellenistic royal iconography, i.e. monuments which glorified the exploits of the heroic ruler. Whether the elaborate figure of Kairos, 'Opportunity',[29] at Sicyon was an early or a late work is not certain, but in any case it too, by bringing the fourth century's fondness for personifications to a new level of complexity, capped an earlier tradition and served as a prototype for the learned art of the Hellenistic period.

In some of what appear to have been later works of Lysippus there are indications of a certain theatricality and even sensationalism that were essentially Hellenistic in character. His interest in colossal statuary, for example, like the Zeus and Heracles at Tarentum, and in miniatures, like the Heracles *Epitrapezios*, suggest a desire to startle the viewer and arrest his attention purely by the manipulation of mass and scale. A number of his pupils and followers, like Chares of Lindus, the sculptor of the Colossus of Rhodes, followed his example. Perhaps they foresaw that in the mixed and mobile population of Hellenistic cities appeals to a mass audience would have to become more obvious than they had been in the past, just as appeals to a learned audience would have to become more recondite.

[29] Stewart 1990 (J 48) 187–8, pl. 555.

CHAPTER 12*d*

GREEK AGRICULTURE IN THE CLASSICAL PERIOD

ALISON BURFORD

I. INTRODUCTION

Throughout Greek antiquity the ownership and cultivation of the land remained fundamental preoccupations at all levels of society, no less during the fifth and fourth centuries than at any other period. The Homeric scene of 'two men with measures in their hands, quarrelling over boundaries in the shared ploughland' finds its counterpart in the fourth-century lawsuit between neighbours in Attica concerning flood damage caused by one to the other's property.[1] Instructions in the Athenian decree *c.* 422 for Demeter's cult at Eleusis, that 'first-fruits of the harvest are to be offered to the Goddesses according to ancestral custom and the oracle at Delphi' stem from the same concerns which prompted Hesiod's precept to his brother, 'Work, so that hunger may hate you and revered Demeter may love you and fill your barn with food.'[2] If basic preoccupations remained unchanged, the question then arises whether or not agricultural methods and results underwent any transformation in the classical period. If they did, was this in part a response to developments in scientific thought? to increasing demand for food and growing pressure on the land? to progress made elsewhere in the ancient world? or simply to changes in climate and physical environment? If, on the other hand, they did not, was this mainly because there was no need for change, in that increased demand (generally assumed to have occurred) was satisfied by cultivating marginal land, by emigration, or by importing grain? Or, if change was needed but did not occur, was this due to the Greeks' failure to advance technologically, or to an ingrained conservatism that preserved traditional farming practices even in the face of repeated shortfalls? Or did the proverbial poverty of Greek farmland and the harshness of the climate make further modification of technique impractical before the development of modern farm machinery and fertilizers? Had Greek agriculture already progressed as far as it could?[3]

[1] *Il.* XII. 421ff; Dem. LV.   [2] M–L no. 73, 4–5; Hes. *Op.* 298–301.

[3] The fullest survey remains Guiraud 1893 (I 67); see also Jardé 1925 (I 83). Material is usefully collected in Michell 1957 (I 102) 38–88. For the earlier period, see Richter 1968 (I 129). White 1970 (I 148) and Frayn 1979 (I 44) provide valuable insights from the Roman period. See in general Finley 1985 (I 36) ch. 4.

Definitive answers to such questions require quantitative evidence of the kind which is largely unavailable. Despite our best guesses many factors remain beyond calculation – such as the average yield of ancient crops from grain fields, orchards, vineyards and gardens; the area of land actually under cultivation in antiquity; the size of the population; and nutritional needs in the Greek world, together with the degree of dependence on alternative sources of food, such as animal herding, hunting, fishing and the gathering of wild plants.[4] The sources vary considerably in character and content, from Theophrastus' scientific analyses *Historia plantarum* and *De causis plantarum*, neither of which was written with agriculture the primary consideration, to Xenophon's philosophical *Oeconomicus*, on household and estate management, and scattered references throughout Greek literature, which may be supplemented by the largely fragmentary records of the lease regulations for the tenants of sacred and public estates.[5] Nevertheless, we can partially discern how Greek farmers were attempting to fill their barns with food in the classical period, the outlines of the farming landscape, who actually laboured on the land, and even perhaps whose points of view shaped agricultural technique, and theory too, such as it was conceived to be.

II. THE CULTIVATION OF CROPS

The purpose of agriculture is, as Theophrastus says, to provide plants with the two most beneficial elements, nourishment and the will to grow (*Caus. Pl.* III.2.1). For both Theophrastus and Xenophon, the farmer's first duty is to understand the environment in which he works. The geology and geography of much of the Greek world are such that the full range of farmland may often occur within the same small region, from coastal or alluvial plain to well-drained slope or arid hillside; that in its natural state the soil is often thin and stony; and that a large proportion of the land has always been incultivable. But it is as important to realize that much of the land farmed in the classical period had long been under continuous cultivation, and that the soil if properly treated thereafter

---

[4] Comparative studies of agricultural conditions in the modern Mediterranean world provide certain insights into the circumstances of ancient farming, but see Halstead 1987 (1 68) for pertinent criticism of this approach, and Hodkinson 1981 (c 364), for a judiciously cautious relation of modern data to the ancient situation. On food consumption, see Foxhall and Forbes 1982 (1 43); Crawford 1979 (1 28); J. M. Frayn, *JRS* 65 (1975) 32–9; Garnsey 1988 (1 55).

[5] The best discussion of Theophrastus on plants is Einarson's introduction and comments in his edition of *Caus. Pl.* (Loeb edn. 1976, 1990). See also Hort, introduction to his edition of *Hist. Pl.* (Loeb edn. 1916); O. Regenbogen, P–W Suppl. 7 (1940) 1354–62; Sarton 1952 (H 103) 551–8. Of the inscribed leases the most informative are *IG* II² 1241, 2492–5 and 2498 (Athens); *SIG* 963 (Amorgos); *IG* XIV 645 (Heraclea in Lucania – see Uguzzoni and Ghinatti 1968 (G 316)). See also Kent 1948 (1 90), on the Delian material.

would continue to be usefully productive; soil exhaustion has too readily been seen as a root-cause of the weaknesses presumed to have pervaded the Greeks' agricultural economy.[6] The range of crops grown within any given area, even within a single farm, would have been largely determined by soil type and situation; some regional or local specialization there might have been, but rather because local conditions suited one crop better than another, than because of any official agricultural policy advocating monoculture rather than mixed farming.[7] For example, barley remained an important crop in Attica despite the advantages of wheat, while millet never became more than a minor factor; and olives were restricted to lowland and coastal areas.[8]

Mixed farming is in fact no less apparent in the evidence of the classical period – the lease inscriptions, the Attic orators' speeches and the Delian sanctuary's inventories of its estates – than in the Homeric poems. Classical farms would generally have included arable, for cereals (various strains of barley and wheat) and legumes (beans, peas, lentils), a grove of olive trees, a vineyard, an orchard of fruit and nut trees, and a vegetable plot or garden with nursery beds, herbs, shrubs and flowering plants (medicinal, culinary and perhaps ornamental too).

Xenophon gauges nicely the degree of general interest in the quality of farmland by his reference to even fishermen's assessing accurately the potential of the coastal fields they happen to be sailing past (*Oec.* XVI.7). Elsewhere he insists that the owner of a new farm take specific note of what crops are doing well on neighbouring land, and cultivate his fields accordingly (*Oec.* XVI.2–5). Methods too must be adapted to local requirements, as Theophrastus emphasizes in his cautionary tale of the immigrant farmer at Syracuse who, by clearing the ground of stones as had been his practice at Corinth, caused the crop to fail for lack of protection from frost (*Caus. Pl.* III.20.5).

The arable generally lay fallow every other year, with repeated ploughing to clear it of exhausting grass and weeds. The soil might be improved by mixing in different earths from elsewhere, or by stirring up the subsoil (*Caus. Pl.* III.20.3–4). The removal of earth (presumably topsoil) from the estate was specifically prohibited in various land leases, which indicated the importance attached to tilth. The application of manure was considered essential; Theophrastus lists various kinds in order of strength – human, pig, goat, sheep, ox and horse-donkey-mule,

[6] Cf. Gallant 1982 (I 47) 116; and on exaggerated views of damage done by grazing, see Rackham 1983 (I 124).

[7] Solon's law restricting the export from Attica of natural products to olive oil (Plut. *Sol* 24.1) has often been taken to mean that Solon intended the increase of olive production at the expense of cereals. See e.g. the comments of Bravo 1983 (I 14) 21–2, and Garnsey 1988 (I 55) 74ff.

[8] Pritchett 1956 (I 123) 186 suggests that millet was an Athenian crop (although it might have been an imported consignment for horse-feed). On olive trees, see Forbes and Foxhall 1978 (I 42).

with the comment that 'the same measure is not good for all' (*Hist. Pl.*
II.7.4, VII.1.8, 5.1, cf. *Caus. Pl.* II.6.1–2, 9.1–3). Draught animals and
sheep might be pastured on stubble and fallow land, as they sometimes
were on crops which had grown too fast (*Caus. Pl.* III.23.3), and perhaps
through groves and orchards too. The importance attached to manure is
evident in a land lease from Amorgos, which stipulates that the tenant
must not only bring in 150 baskets annually, but also check the final
instalment measure by measure in the presence of the sanctuary officials.[9]
Other means of fertilizing the land included either burning the stubble or
adding it to the compost heap to be dug in when rotted – but, says
Xenophon, 'some do not take the trouble' to collect compost (*Oec.*
XVIII.2; XX.10–11). One could also plough under grass, weeds and even
the newly sprouting crop if it came up too fast (*Oec.* XVI.12). Another
means of restoring the soil was to plant a crop of pulses, beans in
particular, which happen to increase the nitrogen content of the soil; in
Macedon and the grain lands of Thessaly, beans were planted simply in
order to be ploughed in (*Hist. Pl.* VIII.9.1). There are also hints, not only
in Theophrastus but also in two Athenian land leases, that the advantage
was recognized of rotating crops of cereals with pulses rather than
letting the arable lie strictly fallow every other year (*Caus. Pl.* III.20.7).[10]
Possibly this was a new idea tentatively acted on here and there during
the classical period; however, pulses had been cultivated since before the
Bronze Age, and it would not be surprising if the benefits of rotating
cereal crops with pulses had been suspected quite early, and practised
when or where considered suitable. Alternatively, intensive cultivation
with the regular re-application of manure might well have enabled
farmers of small holdings to get regular annual crops.[11]

The farmer's implements remained little changed – wooden ploughs,
usually with iron-tipped share, drawn by oxen, mules or even donkeys;
and equally important, mattocks, spades, hoes and rakes wielded by
hand. The extent to which intensive manual labour was applied to every
crop at every stage of its cultivation cannot be over-emphasized. The
grinding weariness of the farm labourer's lot was keenly felt – 'This hoe
weighs half a ton, it will kill me,' says Sostratus before work, and 'My
back, my neck, my whole body!' after it (Menander *Dyscolus* 390–1,
523–5).[12]

[9] *SIG* 963, 21–6 and 41–4. On the whole question of manure see Hodkinson 1988 (I 75).
[10] *IG* II² 1241. 21–3; 2493. 8–11.
[11] Thus Jardé 1925 (I 83) 86 regards planting pulses as an occasional alternative to complete
fallow, not a move towards a regular rotation of crops such as came into use in many (but not all)
parts of medieval Europe. On the likelihood of annual cropping, see Hodkinson 1988 (I 75) 39; on
fallow, Garnsey 1988 (I 55) 93f.
[12] Cf. Aeschylus, fr. 196 (*TGF*), wistfully commenting on 'the happy land where things grow
copiously, unsown and without ploughing or hoeing'. See Pritchett 1956 (I 123) 180–203, 255–61,
287–306, for the produce and the modest equipment of a 'large' estate.

But however well prepared the soil might be, 'it is the year which bears, and not the field', says Theophrastus (*Hist. Pl.* VIII.7.6), meaning that the weather ultimately decides the size of the harvest. In the Mediterranean climate, the rainy season is mainly confined to the winter months, and the summer is generally dry. Although some irrigation was practised, dry-farming was the method by which field crops and fruiting trees and shrubs were usually cultivated. This is why so much care had to be taken in preparing the soil so that it would not only be full of nourishment but would also retain as much moisture as possible; and why so much labour must be expended on tending the crops as they grew, to reduce the competition for moisture from weeds and excess foliage, in pulverizing the surface-soil to prevent capillary evaporation, in maintaining ridges and furrows or laying round stones and potsherds whereby moisture would be retained and shade provided for the roots of the plants.[13]

The arable farmer's year began with the winter sowing, between the final (third or fourth) ploughing of the fallow and the start of the winter rains. Sowing was best done over a period, not all at once, so that the whole crop would not be lost in a period of bad weather (*Oec.* XVII.6). Of the two cereals commonly raised, winter barley was the more widely cultivated if only because it was better suited than wheat to regions where a strictly Mediterranean climate prevailed, and where the soil was comparatively poor.[14] Attica in particular was good for a barley which yielded more meal, proportionately, than any other (*Hist. Pl.* VIII.8.2). Theophrastus distinguishes barleys otherwise by colour, the number of grainrows in the ear, and other such characteristics (*Hist. Pl.* VIII.4.1–3). Given the prevalence of barley it is at first sight surprising that he has much more to say about wheat and its peculiarities. The reason must be partly that wheat had long been the preferred grain – wheat flour makes better bread, among other things – and partly that although some areas favoured it, such as Thessaly, Sicily, and territory in southern Russia, in many other places to be able to grow wheat at all was probably still a matter for experiment as well as congratulation. Theophrastus certainly suggests the development of several distinct variations in type, presumably through both accidental and intentional selection and planting.[15]

Spring barley and wheat were also cultivated, but on a smaller scale.

---

[13] Xen. *Oec.* XIX.14, Theophr. *Caus. Pl.* III.5.5. See Forbes and Foxhall 1976 (1 41).

[14] Jasny 1941–2 (1 84), 1944 (1 85).

[15] Of the various grains mentioned by Theophrastus, *puros* may perhaps be identified as the commonest wheat grown in Greece, 'spelt' or *tr. vulgare* (Hort, *Hist. Pl.* Index); *tiphe* as 'one-grained' wheat, *tr. monococcum*; *zeia*, 'rice-wheat', and *olyre*, 'emmer', both *tr. dicoccum*. *Olyra* was the wheat widely cultivated in Egypt (so Hdt. II.193) until the introduction there of *tr. durum*, either during the Ptolemaic period (Crawford 1979 (1 28)), or by the Arabs (Watson 1983 (1 147)). Cf. Rickman 1980 (1 130) 4–7.

References to 'three-month' cereals are made, and Theophrastus remarks on grains of supposedly even quicker maturation (*Hist. Pl.* VIII.1.4, 2.8–9, 4.4–5); even if they are merely the reflection of farmers' boasts, they at least indicate an interest in developing new and better kinds.

In addition to cereals, the winter sowing might include some pulses – beans, chickpeas, and perhaps lupines and vetches for animal or even human consumption. Chickpeas were supposed to exhaust the soil, unlike other legumes, so that it must be restored afterwards (*Hist. Pl.* VIII.7.2). Other spring-sown crops were millet and pulses such as peas and lentils. Cereals were perhaps interplanted, as in Roman Italy, among well-spaced olive trees, if not in other crops, but Theophrastus mentions the practice of setting barley and beans among rows of young vines only as a means of taking up excess moisture, not of using farmland more intensively (*Caus. Pl.* III.15.4).

Olive groves and orchards required equally careful preparation, but less often than the arable. Olive trees were best suited to low ground and to the stony, calcareous soil found in much of the Greek world. They were propagated not by seed, which produced wild stock, but by grafting (sometimes of cultivated stock onto a mature wild tree); from cuttings; or by setting chunks of an old tree trunk to sprout. They benefited from good manure and occasional pruning (*Hist. Pl.* II.7.3, IV.16.1). A major drawback was that it takes several years for new trees to become fully productive, but unless they were rooted up or burnt entirely, they could last for three or four centuries; even if they were cut down by enemy raiders, they could recover – indeed it was recommended treatment to reduce old trees to hand-high stumps so that they would sprout afresh.[16]

A worthwhile vineyard need take up little space. Land grants of a mere 0.3 ha were made for this purpose to new settlers on Corcyra Nigra.[17] But vines called for much more intensive cultivation than olive trees. Plants had to be replaced more often; propagated by grafting or from cuttings (again, not from seed), they were set in well-dug trenched earth, with adequate manure and water.[18] If the ground was wet, excess moisture must be removed (see above). Mature vines also had to be dug round twice a year, and their roots must be protected from the sun – but farmers disagreed as to whether dust should be applied, or weeds removed (*Hist. Pl.* II.7.5, and *Caus. Pl. passim*, on viticulture). Their roots and upper branches required careful pruning, a job which may sometimes have

---

[16] *IG* II² 2492, 41–5. On the olive tree in general see Foxhall and Forbes 1978 (I 42); on its powers of endurance, see Hanson 1983 (K 24).   [17] *SIG* 141, 11–13.

[18] Some vineyards may have been irrigated, as at Heraclea in Lucania where they lay close to the river – see Uguzzoni and Ghinatti 1968 (G 316) 176.

been left to itinerant specialists, like the 'vine dresser' called in to treat all the vines on rented land belonging to an Athenian deme.[19]

Of the other commonly cultivated fruit – fig, apple, pear, quince, sorb, plum, pomegranate, almond (probably a recent introduction from Asia) – the fig was the most important source of food. It was easily propagated, but presented cultivators with the difficulty that it tended to drop its fruit prematurely. Wild figs however did not do so, the ostensible reason being that wasps from galls on other wild trees got into the immature fruit. The remedy known as caprification had long been applied to cultivated figs; farmers planted wild trees with galls and their wasps upwind of their orchards, or fastened wild fig-galls onto the cultivated trees. In Herodotus' day the process was already described in terms of 'male' galls and 'female' fruiting trees (1.193.4–5); Theophrastus considered that the wasp, engendered from the seeds of the 'male' gall, drained and ventilated the 'female' fruit, which could then ripen (*Hist. Pl.* II.8.1–3, *Caus. Pl.* II.9.5–14). In fact the wasp pollinated the cultivated fig so that the flower set and the fruit matured.[20]

The garden plot was prepared in much the same way as the arable, with the plough where space permitted, otherwise by hand. Biennial fallow was sometimes recommended, as in an Athenian garden lease.[21] Manure was applied to garden plants more generously than to cereals or fruit trees. Most vegetables required regular and abundant water, best provided by irrigation. That this was widely practised is suggested by the Athenian lease (see above) and by Aristotle's comparison of the body's blood vessels to 'the water channels which are connected in gardens from one source to many gulleys' (*Part. An.* 668a14–18).

Vegetables and a wide variety of herbs were sown and transplanted throughout the year – for example, cabbage, radish, turnip, beets, lettuce, garlic, onion, rocket, mustard, coriander and dill in winter; leeks and celery in spring; cucumber and gourd, basil, purslane and savory in summer (*Hist. Pl.* VII.1–2). Other plants grown in the garden might have included oil-producers like sesame (exhausting to the soil – *Hist. Pl.* VIII.9.3) and perhaps wild flax; poppies (honeyed seeds of which, with flax or linseed, were brought by divers to the Spartans trapped on Sphacteria); and roses, mints and myrtles.[22] The arrangement of the garden might be assisted by lettuce-stalk trellises (*Hist. Pl.* VII.4.5). Different varieties of vegetable were clearly distinguished, as both Theophrastus and the wealth of vegetable references in comic poetry suggest; this diversity would have arisen simply from differences in the

19 *IG* II² 2492. 17–19; cf. *IG* II² 1557. 44 and 91, and Amphis, fr. 3 (Edmonds).
20 Sarton 1952 (H 103) 309, 555–6. See also Georgi 1982 (I 60).
21 *IG* II² 2494. However, the text is extensively emended, without explanation.
22 Thuc. IV.26.8. On gardens – Ar. *Birds* 259–60; Dem. LIII.16.

soil of one area or another, so that care must therefore be taken to sow 'foreign' seed in a place as similar to its original home as possible, otherwise its nature would alter (*Hist. Pl.* viii.8.1). It seems from this and other observations that Greek farmers were experimenting with strains imported from elsewhere not only of vegetables but, more important, of cereals too (*Hist. Pl.* viii.4.5). There can be little doubt that they recognized the benefit of selecting the best seeds for sowing, and of encouraging plants to produce good seeds (*Hist. Pl.* vii.5.3–4).[23] It is also probable that useful wild plants were still being brought into the garden, if not for domestication then at least to have them conveniently near (*Hist. Pl.* vii.6, 7).

But no farmer, however careful in selecting seed or cultivating crops, could prevent natural disasters such as flood, drought, gales, cold mists, frosts, plagues of insects, rodents, or disease. The common understanding according to Theophrastus was that rain falling on the dropping blossoms of olives and grapes meant that the immature fruit fell too; wind damaged grain crops when they were flowering and when the grain was ripening; cold winds 'scorched' figs and olives most of all fruit trees; hot winds harmed mature grapes and olives; at Tarentum, a sudden sea mist could blight olive flowers; sun and a southerly wind inflicted caterpillars on vines, as at Miletus; pulses generally were attacked by grubs, caterpillars and spiders; and all crops, barley especially, were subject to 'rust' (*Hist. Pl.* viii.10.1–2). The conviction also prevailed that cereals could degenerate into unprofitable weeds (*Hist. Pl.* viii.8.3). Few preventative measures could be taken, other than to plant chill-prone trees away from low-lying and enclosed places, and to sow barley on windy slopes if possible; degeneration might be checked by attention to soil and cultivation (*Hist. Pl.* viii.8.2); and destructive sea mists could be warded off by sacrifice (*Caus. Pl.* 11.7.5). Insect pests may have been removed by hand when feasible; but specific remedies included hanging dead crabs in fig trees to distract the deadly *knips* from interfering with the gall wasps (see above), and interplanting vetch with radishes to do down spiders (*Hist. Pl.* vii.5.4).

Harvesting had usually to be done both timely and quickly. On a mixed farm it would have recurred at intervals throughout the summer and autumn. Crops were harvested with minimal assistance from even animal power – cereals reaped with sickles and knives; grapes and other fruits plucked by hand; olives and nuts cudgelled out of the trees; vegetables and herbs dug up or cut, as the case might be – and all loaded onto carts or into baskets to be carried by man or pack-animal to the threshing floor, barn or farm workroom. Xenophon remarks that grain

---

[23] Guiraud 1893 (I 67) 478 assumes that Greek cereals were improved through selection. Jardé 1925 (I 83) 14 thinks not. See White 1970 (I 148) 187–8.

was threshed by draught animals' hoofs (*Oec.* XVIII.3), but flailing by hand must have been as common; chaff was winnowed manually, with fan or basket. Only the final phases of preparing grain, olives and grapes for consumption involved the use of mechanical devices such as mills and presses.

Storage raised problems, even for a farmer who intended to sell part of his harvest immediately. Wheat could be left heaped up in the open temporarily, but like barley it eventually became susceptible to mildew, dust and insects. The structures suitable for long-term grain storage might be dry, unplastered chambers in farmhouse or farm tower, storage pits, or *pithoi*, the large ceramic jars used for many other kinds of dried or preserved foodstuffs too.[24] Nevertheless grain stores, like growing crops, were liable to attack by mice, as Aristotle points out (*Hist. An.* 580b10–28).

The arable farmer was also a stockman, if only in that he generally kept a yoke of plough animals; prosperous farms would have included pack-animals too.[25] They contributed motive power and fertilizer, but they also competed for use of the land in requiring fodder, whether they were mostly stall-fed on barley, millet or field crops such as vetches, lupines or straw and hay, or were pastured on green fallow, stubble land, and wherever grazing was available, in incultivable scrub or marsh.

Pressure on the land in Attica and many other places too did not permit of large tracts of pasture for dairy or beef cattle.[26] Like horses, they were generally confined to comparatively lush regions such as Boeotia, the uplands round Delphi, and Epirus, where there were good grass and abundant water. Sheep and goats, on the other hand, were raised everywhere; nevertheless few farmers could afford to keep more than a small flock on home-grown grain, grasses, stubble or garden refuse, and fewer still would have included in their holding much if any permanent rough grazing. In summer sizeable flocks might go to rented pastures in the hills where arable farming was impracticable, and return to their farms to be stall-fed or grazed about the fields in winter.[27]

Poultry and pigs could doubtless be maintained in small numbers by many households with little strain on field and garden products. But beekeeping was the most economical of all the farmer's concerns;

---

[24] On storage, see Xen. *Oec.* VIII.3, Theophr. *Hist. Pl.* VIII.11.1. For towers, granaries and pits, see *IG* II² 1672. 292; *IG* I² 76. 10; Young 1956 (1 151); Kent 1948 (1 90) 295. Towers present problems not only as to their original purpose in the agricultural infrastructure, but also as to their date, and function. On rural structures generally, see Osborne 1985 (1 114) and 1987 (1 115).

[25] Like Phaenippus' estate – Dem. XLII.

[26] Nausicydes, the rich barley miller who bred cattle and pigs (Xen. *Mem.* II.7.6), was perhaps exceptional.

[27] On cattle, Arist. *Hist. An.* 522b15–25, 595b5–11. On pasture, see Burford Cooper 1977–8 (1 27) 72–4; Georgoudis 1974 (1 61); Hodkinson 1988 (1 75).

although he must take some trouble in setting up the hives, and in encouraging and controlling the bees as the weather and their own life cycle dictated, the production of honey did not tax his land in any way, unless he planted flowering shrubs especially for their benefit. And of course the bees encouraged pollination, even if this return-kindness was not fully appreciated in antiquity.[28]

III. THE AGRICULTURAL LANDSCAPE

Most farms in the Greek world were small. In Attica even the largest privately owned estates were generally no more than 30 ha or so, while farms 4–6 ha and upward seem to have constituted the basic one-family holding; barely-subsistence plots of 2 ha or so were not unknown, either. This scale of land holding was widespread; in Attica, most of the big estates we hear of consisted of several scattered plots, perhaps each of them formerly a 'one-family' farm.[29] But bigger units also existed – certainly, estates owned by various sanctuaries and rented to wealthy tenants; some Spartan citizens' properties in Laconia and Messenia; and individual holdings in the grain lands of Thessaly. However, even in a place like Chersonesus in the Crimea, where conditions might also have favoured big estates, investigation so far reveals that few farms exceeded 35 ha.[30]

The dimensions of the agricultural landscape in Attica were such that neighbour could easily observe neighbour. A quarrel between two brothers over the division of the family land, which resulted in the death of one, was witnessed by fellow-demesmen 'who were cultivating their land at the time' (Isaeus IX.17–18); and a farm slave could see furniture being carried off from a house on the next farm (Dem. XLVIII.60–1). The outlines of farms would be determined largely by incidental geographic features, but in level plains the rectangular pattern of an early land distribution might be retained; in either case boundaries would have become fixed by established roadways, water courses, walls, marker-stones or tree stumps, and by usage. Fields within the farm might also have retained the same outlines for generations, just as the location of vineyard, orchard or garden might have become hallowed by tradition as well as, or in spite of, agricultural considerations.[31]

---

[28] On bees, see Arist. *Hist. An.* 553a17ff, 623b6–627b22; Jones *et al.* 1973 (I 89) 397–414, 443–52.

[29] Andreyev 1974 (I 2) 14–15; Burford Cooper 1977–8 (I 27) 168–71; de Ste Croix 1966 (I 136); Osborne 1987 (I 115) 37–40, 71–4, on fragmented holdings.

[30] Dufkova and Pečirka 1970 (E 229).

[31] For rectangular land division, at Metapontum, see Adamesteanu 1973 (I 1) and Carter 1980 (I 21); in the Crimea, see Dufkova and Pečirka 1970 (E 229); in Attica, Bradford 1957 (I 13) 29–34. See also Boyd and Jameson 1981 (I 12). Rural boundaries could have endured for centuries; it seems that in Britain some did so from the Celtic to the Anglo-Saxon period if not beyond; see C. C. Taylor, in *Romano-British Countryside* (ed. D. Miles, 1982).

The impact of farming on the landscape would also be evident in essential structures such as the threshing floor, storage places (stone-built towers, for instance, standing alone or within the farm-building complex), and stables and shelter for the farm labourers, in places where workers and draught animals did not customarily return to town or village every evening.[32] The extent to which farmers actually lived on the land they worked is difficult to gauge. In some small city states, like Phlius or Plataea, cultivators could have reached even the furthest cultivable areas daily from the city; and in Attica too the centres of habitation – the city itself, and the deme villages – were so distributed that many Athenian farmers could have lived 'in town' and still have been no more than two hours' walk (10 km) from their land.[33]

It can be argued that the few literary references to landowners living in the country show not exceptions to but examples of the rule, and that of the few farmhouses known from inscriptions or excavations, if some were labourers' barracks or merely seasonal dwellings, others were the permanent residences of landowners. Farmhouses are known to have stood on various sanctuary estates.[34] Among Athenian landowners, one we know had lived in the country ever since his father's death (Dem. LIII.4), and had experienced a severe drought while living on one of his farms (Dem. L.61), and another had lived since boyhood on the land which he farmed near the Hippodrome (Dem. XLVII.53).[35] Thucydides emphasizes the general distress caused by the evacuation of the Athenian countryside in 431, not least to the wealthy families which lost rich and well-furnished country houses (II.14.2; 65.2). Aristocratic enthusiasm for country life is also reported from Mantinea in 384 when, says Xenophon, the great landowners were pleased to return to their estates at the (temporary) dissolution of the polis (*Hell.* V.2.7). And Xenophon himself lived for some time on his estate in Elis (*An.* V.3).

Although few farmhouses have so far been located, enough is known to suggest the existence of a common type. The features mentioned in the Delian inscriptions – a dwelling house with a courtyard surrounded by farm buildings often including a tower – are exemplified in Attica by the farming complexes found in southern Attica and elsewhere; at Chersonesus they are known in some number (where, as it happens, the

---

[32] See n. 24.

[33] A distance of 5 km has been widely accepted as the realistic limit for subsistence farmers, but this is now in question – cf. Hodkinson 1981 (C 364) 281 and n. 142.

[34] Delos – see Kent 1948 (I 90); Heraclea in Lucania – see Uguzzoni and Ghinatti 1968 (G 316). See also Osborne 1985 (I 114) and 1987 (I 115) on residence patterns.

[35] The estate near the Hippodrome can only have been 5 km at most from the city (see Gernet, Budé edn. on the location).

distance between farm and city was in many cases considerably less than 10 km).[36]

IV. LANDOWNERS AND LABOURERS

But far more important is the extent to which the owner participated actively in farming his land, wherever he lived, and who actually did the work.[37] The *autourgoi*, men who worked for themselves, must surely have comprised the largest group of landowners in Greek society. Their circumstances would have differed considerably; the owner of a very small farm must, if that was his only resource, work it himself *on his own*, with only the assistance of family members, because he could not afford to hire or buy labourers. His way of life was synonymous with that of utter wretchedness such as Menander's Dyscolus brings upon himself by obstinately working his hill farm alone; so Xenophon measures the misfortune of a household by the fact that the son must farm *autourgos* (*Cyrop.* VIII.3.37–8).

A more prosperous man could supplement his own and his family's efforts with hired or slave hands, as Hesiod prescribes. Hired labourers are not much in evidence; they were most likely employed casually, for harvesting in particular.[38] The poorest *autourgoi* perhaps figured among them, together with landless unemployed citizens and bankrupt metics. There may have been a few itinerant professionals, free and slave, specializing in processes such as vine dressing (see above). Two hired slaves are heard of, owned and let out for reaping and fruit picking by the Athenian Arethusius (Dem. LIII.21). The economic advantages of hiring labourers for seasonal work over maintaining purchased slaves all the year round may have been realized, but they may have been offset in any case by the unreliability of hired labour; if the harvest was ready local poor farmers would be engrossed with their own problems, and itinerant hirelings would frequently be working somewhere else just when needed. The economic disadvantages of slave labour – the difficulty of keeping them all fully employed throughout the year – were perhaps less keenly appreciated. The concept of underemployment, often made a

---

[36] Delos – Kent 1948 (1 90); Attica – Jones *et al.* 1962 (1 88) and 1973 (1 89) (neither establishment quite qualifies as a working farmhouse, however cf. *CAH* v² 200–1); Young 1956 (1 151); Langdon and Watrous 1977 (1 93). Chios – Boardman 1956 (1 8) and 1958 (1 9). Chersonesus – Dufkova and Pečirka 1970 (E 229). See also Pečirka 1973 (1 117); Humphreys 1978 (1 79) 109–29; White 1970 (1 148) ch. 13 and 419.

[37] Cf. Mossé 1973 (1 110); Ehrenberg 1951 (1 32) 73–94. The important question of the proportion of slaves to others working on the land cannot be discussed adequately here – see Heitland 1921 (1 73) for the literary evidence; Jameson 1977–8 (1 81) and Wood 1983 (1 150) and *Peasant-citizen and slave* (London 1988) for argument; and cf. Finley 1985 (1 36).

[38] But see Garlan 1980 (1 48). Gallant 1982 (1 47) 124 comments on the Athenian attitude to working for hire.

point of criticism against ancient farming methods, in that more man-hours were applied to farming than the results justified, was much less potent in the ancient view. If there were numerous jobs that could usefully be done in the quieter seasons of the year, it went without saying that there were many long moments in which farmers and labourers 'just sat'.[39]

How many labourers were considered necessary to work a farm of given type and size, we do not know. As to conditions of work, it can at least be said that agricultural slaves working for an *autourgos* had the benefit of their employer's personal attention. If they needed to be taught a technique, it was the owner of the land, the plant or the animal who instructed them. Slaves working on a farm where the owner merely supervised or rarely put in an appearance would be directed by a slave or freedman bailiff, whose main concern was to satisfy the owner with good returns; his methods would not necessarily be the most beneficial in the long run for either the workers or the land. Xenophon therefore recommends, for the owner who can afford and who chooses to have his land managed by others, close supervision reinforced by the ability to train the bailiff in the right ways himself; only then can he hope to have his land worked properly.[40]

Farm labour in many parts of the Greek world included another element, dependent labour. In various places round the Black Sea, indigenous non-Greeks had fallen into this state, like the Mariandyni at Heraclea Pontica; and so it seems to have been in the farm lands of some Greek cities in south Italy and Sicily. Their precise origins aside, their position was in some ways similar to that of the *penestai* of Thessaly, the *klarotai* of Crete and the helots of Sparta – all stood 'between free men and slaves'.[41] Their conditions of employment probably resembled the helots', who were tied from generation to generation to estates belonging to Spartan citizens; they were obliged to surrender a fixed amount from each harvest in good years and bad – but the surplus was at their disposal. They therefore had some incentive to work the land well, whatever their relations with its proprietor. If it was never actually said of a helot, some *penestai* in Thessaly were reported to have become wealthier than their masters.[42]

Yet another alternative was to let one's land. Some owners may have kept close watch on what their tenants did, but the main danger in private tenancies was that both landlord and tenant might be quite

[39] Cf. Bean 1978 (F 570) 5, on the habits of isolated Turkish farmers.
[40] See Audring 1973 (I 3). Bailiff-run estates should not be understood entirely as a new feature of Xenophon's time; Plut. *Per.* 16 provides one earlier example.
[41] See Pippidi 1973 (I 121), and Lepore 1973 (I 98); Lotze 1959 (I 99); Garlan 1988 (I 51).
[42] Garlan 1988 (I 51) 102.

careless of the long-term interests of the land, especially in short leases, as Theophrastus says of rented orchards on Thasos: the owners cared only that they got back the same trees at the end of the leases as had been there at the beginning, 'and even welcome bad husbandry' (*Caus. Pl.* ii.11.3), since trees which have been encouraged to fruit well do not last as long as neglected trees, and newly planted saplings could not be represented to the next tenant as being fully productive. The tenant might lose income from poor harvests, but he was saved the bother of pursuing correct arboriculture and the expense of replacing worn-out trees.

Lessees of sacred and public land were formally bound by very specific instructions to work the estate properly, often under the lessors' eye and on pain of fine. If we are to take the leases literally, the tenants were certainly expected to replace old trees, and often given no choice as to the crops they could plant, even when the lease was to run for thirty or forty years or 'for ever'. While these regulations may have been in some instances specific responses to previous mismanagement of the land, they did not ordain drastic and radical departures from traditional farming, but *reform* simply. What little is known of the tenants suggests that they were generally prosperous performers of public service, who would probably have done the right thing by sacred and public land in any case.[43]

V. THE CHARACTER OF GREEK AGRICULTURE

Good farming, says Xenophon, results *not* from applying new ideas and clever inventions, but from hard work along traditional lines.[44] Sloth, not ignorance, is the cause of agricultural failure (*Oec.* xx *passim*). So that when Ischomachus buys land to improve, he chooses not already well-worked properties, to be enhanced by new methods, but neglected farms which he simply brings up to the mark by farming them in the usual way (*Oec.* xx.22–4). The whole point of Xenophon's discussion is that landowners needed no special training in order to farm well, because the traditional skills were accessible to everyone through observation and experience. The same impression is given by Theophrastus whenever he mentions farming procedure, but especially when he comments on the differences in the scientific approach and the farmers' – 'There is an explanation of each thing which contains its own cause, and it should not be overlooked. The farmer who acts in ignorance of it, following custom

[43] Andreyev 1974 (i 2) 43; Kent 1948 (i 90) 320–37.

[44] So Jardé 1925 (i 83) 194 – 'It is through an illusion that some have depicted Greek agronomy as being in a state of perpetual progress.' See also Finley 1985 (i 36) 108–9. M. N. Tod, *CAH* v² 13, speaks of the 'backward' fifth century, while M. Cary, *CAH* vi¹ 57, sees 'agricultural advance' in the fourth.

and the way things happen to be, may accidentally do the right thing, but as in medicine he may not understand the reason why; complete possession of the art comes from both' (*Caus. Pl.* III.2.3). His own aims are of course directed towards improving not agriculture but botanical definition; he does not recommend so much as report what are the accepted farming procedures as he has found them.[45]

These depended on traditional precepts constantly retaught and revised. Experiment and development were not excluded, but occurred gradually as a natural part of the farming process, just as they surely had since the earliest days of plant domestication anywhere. It is thus impossible from our perspective to detect precisely what adjustments were made within the classical period to the methods evolved by earlier farmers in the Greek world. What does not seem to have happened is, any vast change in crop yields or crops grown, methods, or tools employed, which would have sharply differentiated classical from earlier farming. The only obvious difference was that more land had come under cultivation, the marginal areas or *eschatiai*, which in Attica were surely already being worked in Pisistratus' time (*Ath. Pol.* XVI.6). Good farmers had always got the best out of their land by the best means available – the question is, how good were they? If we are to take Theophrastus, Xenophon and the evidence of the leases seriously, the Greeks' methods stand comparison with those of Chinese farming, in their likeness to careful gardening rather than to agriculture as it is understood in the modern world, and in the painstaking application of intensive labour at every stage. Of course the Greek farmer did not get quite the same results, owing to the considerable differences between the two regions in climate and the fertility of the soil, but that need not have been through want of trying.[46] To what extent superstition and obstinate adherence to irrational practices, in the face of commonsense improvements, held farming back, it is impossible to say. The few examples mentioned by Theophrastus, such as cursing cumin seed as it was sown, or having seers deflect sea mists from vulnerable olive trees with sacrifices, need have wasted little energy or productivity.[47]

It goes almost without saying that there were always slothful and inefficient farmers whose land was not made to yield its full potential, even under the pressure of hunger which must have been the spur for most farmers to work harder than they liked. We may not hear of any city actually confiscating privately owned land for neglect, but the communal concern for the land's productivity, ritually expressed in such ways as

---

[45] For discussion of Theophrastus' aims and methods, see n. 5.

[46] The history of Chinese agriculture is comprehensively surveyed by Bray 1984 (I 15).

[47] Bray 1984 (I 15) mentions various instances of the ancient Chinese peasants' refusal to adopt new and more sensible methods proposed by efficiency-seeking officials.

the offering of first-fruits at Eleusis, may have found practical expression in public reproof of bad farmers. It is easy to imagine, if so, how neighbours would inform on one another; in any case, lawsuits arising from damage caused by neglect to a neighbour's farm or to an estate claimed by rival relatives might result in some corrective measures being taken.[48]

Furthermore, the increasing importation of foreign grain, widespread by the fourth century if not earlier, might have prompted many cities to review the land's potential and to take some political decisions as to its use. Whether or not Solon's legislation had included any strict guidelines for Athenian agriculture, all new settlers at Corcyra Nigra were allotted land some of which was specifically for vine-growing. The small territory of Phlius was known to both Homer and Pausanias for its viticulture (as it is today); possibly the city had decided at some point to extend vineyards at the expense of other crops, for certainly pressure on the arable was such that we hear of grain being grown on the acropolis itself. The Phliasians could maintain horses enough to muster a small cavalry troop, but given the limitations of their agricultural production, they may only have been able to do so because they had surplus wine to dispose of for grain from elsewhere.[49] The Mantineans, on the other hand, appear to have been so restricted that they had been forced to give up horses altogether; there could be no question of putting aside land even for fodder crops such as alfalfa.[50]

How many inhabitants of Mantinea continued to go hungry even so is another matter. If outright famines occurred rarely in the Greek world, the gap between hunger and sufficiency was probably a narrow one in most communities much of the time; so the many references to food in comedy suggest, as do Theophrastus' remarks on the flavour and digestibility of vetch, proverbially a famine-food, and his recipes for asphodel, also commended by Hesiod and Plutarch but dismissed by Galen as edible only if one is starving.[51] Desperate measures were taken to counter the fact that in some way the land did not always satisfy its population's needs – by the city through promoting overseas settlements (for example, the Athenian cleruchies), and by individuals, through emigration, mercenary service, or infanticide.

Whether or not sheer agricultural shortages, in and of themselves,

[48] Part of the case against Macartatus was that he and his father had uprooted 1,000 olive trees unnecessarily on the estate of Hagnias (Dem. XLIII.69–70).

[49] On wine-production at Phlius – Paus. II.13.4 and P–W s.v. 'Phlius' 269–90; grain on the Acropolis – Xen. *Hell.* VII.2.8; Paus. II.13.3 (a sanctuary of Demeter?). The strength of the cavalry is put at 60 during the 360s (Xen. *Hell.* VII.2.2).   [50] Hodkinson 1981 (C 364) 278–9.

[51] On vetch – Theophr. *Hist. Pl.* II.4.2 and VIII.5.1; Dem. XXII.15. On asphodel – Hes. *Op.* 41 and West's commentary with further references. Cf. Jameson 1983 (I 82) and Garnsey 1983 (I 58) for discussion of alternative foods.

were the main reasons for such steps, is a large question which can only be answered here in the form: probably not. The importation of wheat, on the other hand, would appear to bear directly on the adequacy or otherwise of Greek farming and, it could be argued, was a most desperate step for an agriculturally based society to take. But grain imports were made possible partly, and in some places largely or solely, because other agricultural surpluses could be exchanged for them, directly or indirectly; they indicate not the wholesale collapse of cereal agriculture in Greece but the existence of alternatives open to communities and individuals – not an utter neediness but a freedom of choice (for some sections of the population, at least) between old-fashioned barley-porridge and more delicate wheat bread. Domestic grain production continued in Attica as elsewhere. The specialization which produced surpluses of other crops to be traded for grain was an equally long-standing feature of Greek agriculture determined in the first instance by what the land would and would not bear.

Communities into which grain was being imported in the fifth and fourth centuries were faced with a situation familiar in this sense too: climatic variations constantly caused fluctuations in the size of harvests from one year to the next, and from one region of the country to another, even during the same season.[52] Shortfall and surplus were recurrent factors in every farmer's calculations, whatever the scale of his farm.[53] The disposal of a surplus from one crop to offset a shortage of another was as much a part of the pattern of agriculture as any other activity, for all but the most isolated or obstinately 'self-reliant' landowner, so that in this sense the importing of grain during the classical period was not a new phenomenon, but the extension or intensification of a familiar practice.

For all its drawbacks, then, landed property of all kinds continued to be the most sought-after form of wealth. There was no revolutionary movement which did not call for the redistribution of the land, and scarcely a returning exile who did not expect to have house, land and garden restored to him.[54]

[52] For Greek dependence on imported grain, see Finley 1985 (I 36) 131–2, and Garnsey 1983 (I 58). [53] Jameson 1983 (I 82). See Garnsey et al. 1984 (I 56).
[54] As at Tegea in 324 – Tod, GHI II no. 202, 9–13 (the Exiles' Decree).

CHAPTER 12e

WARFARE

Y. GARLAN

The fifth century opened with the Persian Wars, which epitomized the superiority over the barbarian of the citizen-soldier, that ideal type which was to flourish in Periclean Athens, the newly dominant city state of Greece. As an institution and in terms of official ideology (as expressed in funeral orations, for example),[1] this ideal was to remain unchallenged until the end of the classical period. In some respects it was even reinforced after the Peloponnesian War by the admission of *thetes* to the ranks of the hoplites and again, in the time of Lycurgus, by improvement in the military training of *epheboi*.[2]

In fact, however, the situation was already changing, for although it is true that citizens continued to the last to mobilize without too much reluctance for decisive battles, at other times in the fourth century they were only too ready to entrust their overseas campaigns to mercenaries,[3] to the despair of those who looked back with nostalgia to the days of Athenian greatness and ancestral tradition. The same process was at work, although in varying degrees, in the majority of cities, particularly those, like the Syracuse of Dionysius I and Pherae under Jason, where the power of the tyrant could in this way be increased. It applied even to Sparta, which witnessed a dangerous diminution in the number of its Equals – not to mention the Great King and his western satraps, who were always seeking 'men of bronze' to settle their differences for them and to intervene in Mediterranean affairs.[4] The result was that henceforth these *misthophoroi* (mercenaries) could be counted in tens of thousands; they were also called *xenoi* (foreigners) or quite simply *stratiotai* (basically, 'soldiers') and included both Greeks who were impoverished or exiled or simply lured by the prospect of plunder, and the more or less hellenized 'barbarians', especially natives of the Balkans and of Anatolia. From this blight, which was denounced unceasingly by

---

[1] Loraux 1981 (C 190).
[2] Pelekidis 1962 (C 215); Reinmuth 1971 (B 168).
[3] Parke 1933 (K 50); Griffith 1935 (K 20); Marinovic 1975 (K 42). On population and military manpower see also above, pp. 535–41. [4] Seibt 1977 (K 54).

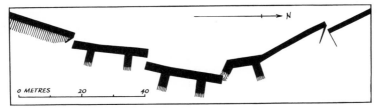

Fig. 35. Sally ports in the Dema wall at the foot of Mt Parnes, Attica. (After *BSA* 52 (1957) 157, fig. 3.IV.)

Isocrates, there was no escape, except in a few outlying regions such as Aetolia where warlike traditions prevailed unchanged, and some cities which, on the model of Sparta, preferred to devote to the pursuit of arms a selection of their citizens. Such was the Sacred Band, constituted by the Thebans in 379 out of an already existing regiment of 300 foot-soldiers who enjoyed the Homeric title of *hemiochoi* and *parabates*; or the 'public guardians' called *eparitoi* maintained by the Arcadian League about 365, and, to a lesser degree, elite troops (*epilektoi*) recruited almost everywhere either from volunteers or from a selection of those available for service.[5] Such measures were completely in accordance with the precepts of reforming philosophers like Hippodamus of Miletus and the Plato of the *Republic*, who commended the creation of a professional military caste maintained by the community.

Reflecting as it did if not a crisis then at least a total change of outlook in the cities, an analysis of which lies outside the present discussion, this development of professionalism perfectly complemented the new demands imposed by military operations. For even though the final outcome was still frequently determined by pitched battles in open country, henceforth they constituted only one element in a strategy which was more complex than it had been in the past, being both differentiated and progressive, aimed at establishing control not only over useful territory but also over walled cities and increasingly well-fortified frontier zones (such as the Attic 'Dema' wall built between Mts Parnes and Aegaleus; Fig. 35). Hence more sophisticated and varied tactics were evolved, requiring the combined use of specialized forces (integrated on the model of the human body) and based on a professional concept of military leadership and prowess.[6]

This development provoked the appearance, in the first half of the fourth century and probably under the influence of the sophists, of a body of technical literature, from which there have survived the *Art of Horsemanship* and the *Cavalry Commander* of Xenophon and, in particular, the *Poliorcetica* of Aeneas Tacticus, in which considerable attention is

[5] Andrewes 1981 (K 5).   [6] Garlan 1974 (K 17) 19–103; Hanson 1983 (K 24).

paid to stratagems and treason. And to these we might add the second book of the pseudo-Aristotle *Economics* which enlightens us about the financial stratagems to which employers of mercenaries were often obliged to have recourse. Practical lessons were taken by qualified instructors, in, for example, hoplite-fighting or in tactics (that is, in the Greek sense of the term, the art of drawing up soldiers in order of battle), who went about hiring their services to all alike, whether cities or satraps. At the same time the image of the military leaders was correspondingly modified,[7] although the manner of their appointment remained on the whole unchanged. They too increasingly assumed the appearance of experts, assigned peremptorily or as circumstances demanded to functions which were more and more specifically defined with only an indirect bearing on political life, through the medium of the public orators who made common cause with them. Moreover the most celebrated of them, men like the Athenians Conon, Timotheus, Iphicrates, Chabrias and Chares, contaminated by their association with mercenaries, served by turns their homeland and foreign masters, who were often 'barbarians'. They occupied an ambiguous position in relation to their own city, belonging at the same time inside and outside it, acting sometimes as public servants and sometimes in a private capacity, without ever losing sight either of their own advantage or of the interests of their troops.

Such, briefly summarized, are the institutional, social and ideological factors which appear to the writer to have influenced the development of the art of war among the Greeks in the fourth century – in the obviously varied and ever-changing circumstances which gave pre-eminence to those states able to muster the greatest effort in war.

In the event of a pitched battle, phalanxes of hoplites, drawn up eight, twelve or sixteen ranks deep, continued to play an essential part in the centre of the line.[8] However, the hoplites themselves were less heavily armed than they had been at the close of the archaic period and had in some instances given up their *knemides* (greaves) and generally exchanged their metal 'muscle-corslets' for a linen or leather coat or even a simple tunic, with only a light helmet or leather cap (*pilos*). The phalanxes were also more loosely deployed, manoeuvring in a less uniform fashion. Thus at the battle of Leuctra in 371 the Theban general Epaminondas, being sufficiently adaptable to learn from experience (or perhaps acting on certain Pythagorean theories which tended to detract from the sanctity of space),[9] achieved a spectacular and astonishing victory over the Lacedaemonians. He held back his right wing, which

[7] Lengauer 1979 (K 38).   [8] Snodgrass 1967 (K 55); Anderson 1970 (K 3).
[9] Lévêque and Vidal-Naquet 1960 (K 40) 294–308.

traditionally marched into the attack, and deployed on the left wing his elite troops fifty ranks deep.

The superiority of the hoplite phalanx over light infantry was, however, coming increasingly under threat, especially for siege operations and guerrilla attacks in frontier areas, the importance of which, as has been noted, continued to grow. The defeats inflicted in 426 on the Athenian general Demosthenes by the light Aetolian infantry and on a battalion of 600 Spartan hoplites by the mercenary peltasts of Iphicrates, near the Corinthian port of Lechaeum in 390, made a strong impression on contemporary opinion and resulted in the promotion of these troops, who took their name from their light shield (*pelte*) of Thracian origin.[10] Although they had previously been content to recruit from the Balkans, the Athenians henceforth began to make use of this equipment themselves, modifying it from time to time to suit circumstances. Iphicrates, commissioned by the Persians to lead an army of Greek mercenaries against the Egyptian pikemen, was thus to equip his troops with *peltai*, as well as with lances and with swords appreciably longer than those of hoplites and, in addition, those 'light and comfortable boots which are still called Iphicratides in memory of their inventor' (Diod. xv.44.4).

The effectiveness of the cavalry, which was sometimes equipped with spurs and light corslets, but never with stirrups or fixed saddles, was restricted by the vulnerability of the horses, and recruitment was deterred by the high cost of maintenance. It was not used on a grand scale except in traditional areas where its numbers were at least one-sixth of the hoplite force: for example in Boeotia where we hear also of hoplites mounted pillion (*dimachai*), in Thessaly, or on the rich plains of south Italy (Campania) and Sicily. Otherwise it performed only secondary functions of reconnaissance and harassment.[11] However, the Athenians, for their part, were far from losing interest in it.[12] This is shown by the concern of Xenophon in about 360 that the body of a thousand horsemen created by Pericles should be reinforced both in numbers and in quality, by the creation of a unit of scouts (*prodromoi*) attributed to the time of Iphicrates, and by the care taken by the *boule* over the expenditure (*katastaseis*) on horses and their inspection. (The characteristics of the horses were committed to lead tablets, numerous examples of which, belonging to the middle of the fourth century, have recently been discovered in the Agora; Fig. 36.)[13] The organization by the Lacedaemonians in 424, 'contrary to their custom' (Thuc. iv.55.2), of a force of 400 horsemen and archers had already indicated a similar interest at Sparta.

It goes without saying that the outlying Greek cities which were permanently in contact with one or other of the 'barbarian' peoples had

---

[10] Best 1969 (K 8). Pls. Vol. pls. 187–8.   [11] Anderson 1961 (K 2) and 1978 (K 4).
[12] Bugh 1988 (K 10).   [13] Kroll 1977 (K 28).

682   12*e*. WARFARE

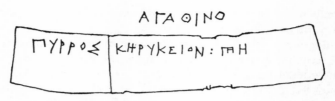

Fig. 36. Lead tablet recording an Athenian name (outside), the colour, brand and value of his horse (inside) – 'Of Agathinos'; 'Chestnut (πύρρος), *kerykeion*, 600 drachmae'; fourth century B.C. (After Kroll 1977 (κ 28) 110. fig. 2.14.)

to modify their military practices in many other respects, as did, for their part, the native principalities which were in process of becoming hellenized, such as those of Lycia where the cavalrymen were equipped with leather aprons of eastern origin. This accounts for the infinite diversity in matters of detail to be observed in texts and in figurative representations, generally in the direction of a lightening of armour and increased flexibility in fighting methods.

It was, however, more particularly in the art of capturing cities, *poliorketika*,[14] that the most striking innovations were to occur. The tendency was always to substitute attack for the traditional methods of laying siege, and especially attack in relays, which was achieved by committing to battle only a fraction of the forces available at any one time and perpetually renewing them.

In about the middle of the fifth century, the Greeks did not risk their forces in this way, save in quite exceptional and isolated circumstances when they had recourse to certain elementary *mechanai* – 'machines' (in the original sense of stratagems, devices, artificial means by which man was able to infringe the laws of nature). Whether or not Pericles was the first to have battering-rams and testudos constructed (under the supervision of Artemon of Clazomenae) for the attack on Samos, it is certain that a ram-head in bronze, dedicated in the sanctuary at Olympia, dates from this period.[15]

The ruthless siege of Plataea by the Lacedaemonians at the beginning of the Peloponnesian War was the occasion for fresh experiments, described in detail by Thucydides, such as the construction of an assault-ramp, promptly undermined by the defenders, the setting-up of battering-rams, which were caught by slip-knots and crushed by huge beams, and the invention of an incendiary machine which Brasidas made use of again, a few months later, at Lecythus. However, the decisive move in this direction was made only at the very beginning of the fourth century, by Dionysius I of Syracuse, who was engaged in a merciless struggle against the Carthaginians and was in a position to impose on his

[14] Garlan 1974 (κ 17).   [15] Kunze 1956 (κ 31). Pls. Vol. pl. 208.

compatriots an unprecedented war-effort. Diodorus has left us a description of his preparation in 399–398, so vivid that it can only have been based on the account of an eye-witness such as Philistus:

At once he gathered skilled workmen, commandeering them from the cities under his control and attracting them by high wages from Italy and Greece as well as Carthaginian territory . . . After collecting many skilled workmen, he divided them into groups in accordance with their skills, and appointed over them the most conspicuous citizens, offering great bounties to any who created a supply of arms. As for the armour, he distributed among them models of each kind, because he had gathered his mercenaries from many nations; for he was eager to have every one of his soldiers armed with the weapons of his people, conceiving that by such armour his army would, for this very reason, cause great consternation, and that in battle all of his soldiers would fight to best effect in armour to which they were accustomed. And since the Syracusans enthusiastically supported the policy of Dionysius, it came to pass that rivalry rose high to manufacture the arms. For not only was every space, such as the porticoes and back rooms of the temples as well as the gymnasia and colonnades of the market place, crowded with workers, but the making of great quantities of arms went on, apart from such public places, in the most distinguished homes. In fact the catapult was invented at this time in Syracuse, since the ablest skilled workmen had been gathered from everywhere into one place. The high wages as well as the numerous prizes offered the workmen who were judged to be the best stimulated their zeal. And over and above these factors, Dionysius circulated daily among the workers, conversed with them in kindly fashion, and rewarded the most zealous with gifts and invited them to his table. Consequently the workmen brought unsurpassable devotion to the devising of many missiles and engines of war that were strange and capable of rendering great service.

(XIV.41.3–42.2: trans. C. H. Oldfather, Loeb edn)

The catapult (for arrows) was in fact a new machine,[16] unknown to the Carthaginians, despite their having inherited all the devices of oriental siegecraft. It may have consisted of a simple cross-bow (*gastraphetes*), the composite bow of which was stretched taut by a windlass, or it may from the outset have been provided with independent 'arms' for propulsion, these being inserted into tightly twisted skeins of hair, horsehair or sinews. Its effectiveness would in any case have been limited, if the Syracusans had not simultaneously put into operation all the traditional methods of laying siege, such as tunnels, assault-ramps, battering-rams, testudos and wooden towers, to which they had probably made several improvements. In particular mention must be made of six-storied siege-towers on wheels, provided with flying bridges which were mounted against Motya in 397. It was then also that the Sicilian Greeks, finding themselves under siege, followed the Carthaginian example and began to

---

[16] Marsden 1969–71 (K 45).

take active defence measures, using massed sorties to repel the approach of enemy war-machines.

In addition to the catapult, the craftsmen assembled by Dionysius I invented, according to Diodorus, ships with four (quadriremes) and five (quinqueremes) 'banks' of rowers; the rowers were probably seated several to each oar, since it is scarcely conceivable that more than three banks of oarsmen could be superimposed one above another, as in triremes, the 'queens of the seas' in the century before.

What is at first sight surprising is that none of these inventions appears to have been rapidly taken up in the Greek homeland.[17] Thus in 325, at a time when the main force of the Phoenician and Cypriot fleets was composed of quinqueremes, the Athenian fleet contained only 2, as against 50 quadriremes and 360 triremes. Progress in technique was held back by the weight of tradition or by financial problems (if not even by the quality of the crews) and fighting at sea continued to be directed to the ramming of the enemy after collective manoeuvres designed to break the enemy's line (*diekplous*) or encircle it (*periplous*), tactics mainly inspired by fighting on land. With regard to catapults, they are only mentioned by Aeneas Tacticus as it were incidentally (xxxii.8: as an example, like slings, of offensive weapons with a longer range than the bow, and suitable for use from assault-towers); elsewhere there are only scant references to them – from about 370 in certain Athenian inventories, during the siege of Samos in 366–365, and in the reaction of Archidamus, king of Sparta from 361 to 338, who, at the sight of a catapult introduced for the first time from Sicily, apparently exclaimed: 'O Heracles, this is the end of courage in men!' (Plut. *Mor.* 191E and 219A).

It is true that in the *Poliorcetica* of Aeneas and the accounts of historians there is often discussion of other machines and counter-machines employed for assault, but assault tactics had not altogether superseded the operation of laying siege. It would seem, therefore, that in the first half of the fourth century the majority of Greek cities had scarcely felt the need or been in a position to follow the example of Syracuse and carry out systematic modernization of their siege equipment. Similarly it does not appear that the art of building fortifications had undergone any important changes,[18] despite an appreciable increase in their numbers (particularly in country districts and frontier zones). Nevertheless it may be conceded that, in certain constructions in the Peloponnese during the years 370–360 (for example, Mantinea, Messene, Megalopolis, Gortys in Arcadia), there was a growing tendency to build in stone rather than unbaked brick, to pay more attention to unevenness of ground (with a

---

[17] Taillardat 1968 (K 56); Morrison and Williams 1968 (K 48); Casson 1986 (I 24); Jordan 1975 (K 27). [18] Winter 1971 (K 60); Lawrence 1979 (K 33).

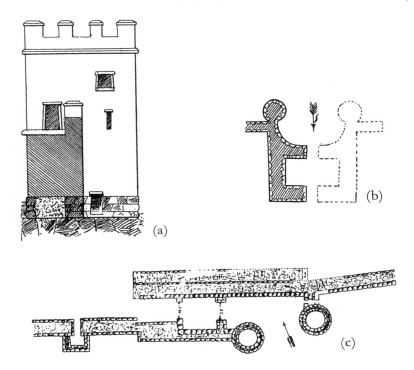

Fig. 37. Fortifications of Mantinea: (a) postern tower with section of wall, restored; (b) Gate A; (c) Gate D. (After G. Fougères, *Mantinée* (Paris, 1898) 149–55, figs. 25b, 27, 29.)

disproportionate extension of the perimeter to be defended), to increase the number of sallyports and flanking towers, to give gates additional protection by means of overlaps and outer courts and to increase the solidity of parapets by the addition of buttresses (Fig. 37).

Aristotle, in the passage of the *Politics* dated about 330, where he praises the urban fortification vilified by Plato, was nevertheless clearly aware of the progress which had recently been made in siege tactics:

As regards walls, those who aver that cities which pretend to valour should not have them, hold too old-fashioned a view – and that though they see that the cities that indulge in that form of vanity are refuted by experience. It is true that against an unevenly matched foe and one little superior in numbers it is not honourable to try to secure oneself by the strength of one's fortifications; but as it may possibly happen that the superior numbers of the attackers may be too much for the human valour of a small force, if the city is to survive and not to suffer disaster or insult, the securest fortification of walls must be deemed to be the most warlike, particularly in view of the inventions that have now been made in the direction of precision with missiles and machines for sieges . . . If then this is so, not only must walls be put round a city, but also attention must be paid to them in order that they may be suitable both in regard to the adornment of the city and in respect of military requirements, especially the new devices recently invented. For just as the attackers of a city are concerned to study the means by which they can gain advantage, so also for the defenders some devices have already been invented and others they must discover and think out; for people do not even start attempting to attack those who are well prepared.

(VII.1330b–1331a: trans. H. Rackham, Loeb edn.)

At about the same time Demosthenes, in his *Third Philippic* (47–50), was warning his compatriots against new devices introduced into the art of war by the king of Macedon:

For my own part, while practically all the arts have made a great advance and we are living today in a very different world from the old one, I consider nothing has been more revolutionized and improved than the art of war. For in the first place I am informed that in those days the Lacedaemonians, like every one else, would spend the four or five months of the summer 'season' in invading and laying waste the enemy's territory with heavy infantry and levies of citizens, and would then retire again; and they were so old-fashioned, or rather such good citizens, that they never used money to buy an advantage from anyone, but their fighting was of the fair and open kind. But now you must surely see that most disasters are due to traitors, and none are the result of a regular pitched battle. On the other hand you hear of Philip marching unchecked, not because he leads a phalanx of heavy infantry, but because he is accompanied by skirmishers, cavalry, archers, mercenaries and similar troops. When, relying on this force, he attacks some people that is at variance with itself, and when through distrust no one goes forth to fight for his country, then he brings up his artillery and lays siege. I need hardly tell you that he makes no difference between summer and winter and has no season set apart for inaction.

(trans. J. H. Vince, Loeb edn.)

The orator perhaps puts too much emphasis on treason, but he was only too well aware of the profound changes in the art of war brought about by the king of Macedon.

In this respect it was the reign of Philip II which constituted the most important landmark.[19] Whatever may have been the reforms initiated by his immediate predecessors, or, more particularly, pursued by his son in his Asiatic campaign,[20] it is to Philip II that the fundamental innovations must be attributed, whether suggested to him by Epaminondas and Pelopidas during his visit to Thebes or inspired by the memory of Iphicrates, Dionysius I and Jason of Pherae.

The distinctive feature, henceforth to be characteristic of the Macedonian infantry, who were recruited from the peasantry of the kingdom, was the long pike called a *sarissa*, 12 cubits (about 5.50 metres) in length

---

[19] Hammond and Griffith 1979 (D 50) 405–49.   [20] Milns 1976 (D 216) 87–136.

and equipped, as has been learned from a find in a tomb at Vergina,[21] with an iron point 50 cm long, together with a butt-end, also in iron, of 45 cm and a central dowel for reinforcement. Since it could not be wielded without the use of both hands, the diameter of the shield had at the same time to be reduced (possibly to 60–80 cm) and, probably for reasons of economy, the remaining dress was only a simple leather jacket and helmet and greaves of bronze. A small sword was provided in case of hand-to-hand combat.

The Macedonian phalanx of Foot-Guards (*pezetairoi*) was drawn up at a depth of eight, ten or sixteen, but sometimes even of thirty-two ranks, the first five of which carried their pikes point-forward, and was subdivided into six battalions (*taxeis*), each of 1,500 men. At the start of Alexander's campaign it was supported by three chiliarchies of hypaspists (shield-bearers). Although there is still uncertainty about the armament of this last category (it was probably similar to that of the phalanxes) and about the circumstances in which it appeared, there can be no doubt that they were special units, one of which, bearing the name of *agema*, provided the royal bodyguard.

It was around this mass of semi-heavy infantry, set in the centre of the line of battle, that the remainder of the troops formed. On the right it was usually flanked by some 1,800 Companions (*hetairoi*) recruited from the Macedonian nobility; these were horsemen in helmets and corselets, armed with lances and swords and always ready to charge, in wedge formation, into the slightest breach to rout the enemy. On the left were posted 3,000 or 4,000 more lightly armed horsemen, some of them of Macedonian origin (scouts, *prodromoi* or pikemen), but mainly drawn from allies, such as Greeks, Thessalians, Thracians and other Balkan peoples, while on the extremity of the flank and at other points as required by the course of events were various units of light infantry, armed with javelins, bows and slings. Many of these were also recruited in Macedonia and in the Balkan countries, for example Illyrians, Thracians and Agrianians, but they also included such mercenaries as had not been allocated to garrison service. As for the 7,000 Greek hoplites who, within the framework of the Confederacy of Corinth, accompanied Alexander into Asia, there is little mention of them in the accounts of the campaign before their wholesale conversion into mercenaries.

The first easterners to come under Macedonian command were to appear very soon in the capacity of specialist troops. They included Cypriot and Phoenician seamen in 333, javelin-throwers and mounted archers after about 330, Persian cavalry in 329 and subsequently

---

21 Andronicos 1970 (K 6); Markle 1977 (K 43) and 1978 (K 44).

Arachosian, Bactrian, Scythian, Sogdian and other horsemen. Henceforward increasing numbers of them were also absorbed into the
Macedonian phalanx and cavalry, or formed into parallel units armed in
Macedonian fashion. The most spectacular enactments (and the ones
most strongly opposed by the Macedonian soldiers) promoted in 327 the
recruitment and training of 30,000 young Iranians described as *Epigonoi*
and the integration in 323 of 20,000 Persians into the phalanx – those
conquered peoples who were regarded as the most suitable to support
their conquerors.

Any attempt to describe more precisely the organization of the armies
of Philip and Alexander would be in danger of losing its way among the
innumerable controversial points of detail which abound in this battle-
ground for historians: some are rewarding, making it possible, for
example, to establish that the honorary title of *asthetairoi* ('best companions' or 'companions of the cities'?) was conferred by Alexander on
certain battalions of *pezetairoi*.[22] Many others, however, lead nowhere,
through the lack of accurate sources as well as the complexity of the
subject itself. For these were armies which were still very indeterminate
institutionally and their structure, or perhaps simply their nomenclature,
was being constantly revised (especially during the campaign of Alexander) by the king quite arbitrarily, in accordance with military exigencies and the political interests of the time.

Generally speaking, it is advisable to guard against any too modern
concept of the Macedonian 'war machine', particularly as regards the
high command, which was assumed by the king in person. From his
position on the right flank, he directed the tactical moves to the best of
his ability and then, at the decisive moment, usually himself assumed the
leadership of his Companions to break the enemy lines or to strike at the
very centre where their General Staff were located.[23] The celebrated
confrontation between Alexander and Darius on the battlefield of Issus
may be recalled: it is the subject of the famous mosaic at Pompeii which
was probably inspired by a painting by Philoxenus of Eretria, dating
from the early hellenistic period. It was essential for the king to
demonstrate his personal courage by brilliant deeds, even at the risk of
no longer being able to control the deployment of his left flank and the
utilization of his reserves during the final stages of battle. What was true
of the commander-in-chief applied also to his subordinate officers of all
ranks, among whom the hierarchy remained ill-defined and fluctuating,
being largely determined by the favour conferred by the king on
individuals in recognition of their prowess.

[22] Milns 1981 (K 47).
[23] Fuller 1958 (K 14); for a study of a particular battle (Gaugamela), Marsden 1964 (D 212).

The army of Alexander was also quite traditional in its commissariat.[24] As soon as it ceased marching in line with its fleet along the coastal areas of the Mediterranean, it was in effect obliged to live off the land (either by forcible means or after coming to an agreement with the natives), and was reduced to independent supplies for only four or five days' march. Consequently, over the immense tracts of Asia, they were subject to severe strategical constraints, which were impossible to overcome without a good intelligence service and a fairly drastic reduction of the mass of non-combatants, such as valets, traders, women and entertainers of all kinds, which accompanied the army on its travels. Following the example of his father, Alexander usually reduced their numbers to a half or a third of the fighting forces (at a time when they were often equal in the Greek and Persian armies).

In spite of the weight of his effective forces, which generally numbered between 30,000 and 50,000 men and could even have totalled 120,000 at the time of his Indian campaign, Alexander was thus able to make an impact by his mobility and swiftness in action, regardless of the terrain and the time of year: these were the essential attributes of his phalanx and, shortly before his death, he must have planned to increase its flexibility still further by replacing the centre ranks with archers and light infantry. It was with the same object of efficiency that the kings of Macedon imposed such intensive training on their troops, together with the adaptation of their arms to the particular mission contemplated – as, for example, the formation of commando units composed of hoplites and hypaspists without the encumbrance of their *sarissae* – and, especially, the co-ordinated action of units specializing in one type of operation or another.

It was, however, in siege warfare that the military superiority of the Macedonians was most brilliantly demonstrated (despite their setbacks at Perinthus and Byzantium in 340): this may have been because, in the words of Philip II, there was no citadel to which one could not 'send up a little donkey laden with gold' (Cic. *ad Att.* 1.16.12), but it was also, and particularly, due to the vigour with which the attack was carried out and to the importance attached to the construction of machines.[25]

In this field Philip II was regarded as a worthy successor to Dionysius of Syracuse by the Hellenistic, Roman and Byzantine manufacturers of military machines, who derived their inspiration largely from the work of his principal engineers: Polyidus the Thessalian, who wrote a treatise *On Machines* and took part in the siege of Byzantium, and his pupils Charias and the Thessalian Diades, who also both wrote treatises with the same title and accompanied Alexander into Asia. There was also a

---

24 Engels 1978 (D 172); rev. N. G. L. Hammond, *JHS* 100 (1980) 256–7.
25 Marsden 1977 (K 46); Lendle 1981 (K 36) 330–56.

Macedonian by the name of Posidonius and a certain Philippus who was present at the banquet given by Medius in 323. Groups of expert craftsmen, such as were only obtainable at great expense, were set to work under their instructions: for the capture of Tyre, Alexander procured them from Cyprus and from all over Phoenicia.

In addition to his javelin-throwers, archers and slingers (who at Olynthus in 348 employed missiles appreciably heavier than those of the defenders), Philip II also made early use of a large number of different types of catapult, which were probably more powerful than any which had been made before. It may well have been in his time and not under Dionysius I that their projectile force was beginning to be generated by means of twisted skeins (possibly of the new type described as 'Macedonian' by Pollux 1.139). One thing which is certain is that at the beginning of Alexander's campaign 'stone-throwers' made their appearance; they were called *petroboloi* or *lithoboloi* and were capable not only of inflicting injury on the persons besieged but also of damaging the weaker points of the fortifications, such as doors, roofs or parapets.

Complementary to the adoption of catapult batteries was the construction and emplacement of wooden towers, which made it possible for attacks to be concentrated on the upper levels of the city walls. In 340 Philip II was engaged in erecting against Perinthus towers which rose to a height of 37 metres. At Halicarnassus in 333 Alexander must have done even better, for the defenders had to construct on their side a tower of 46 metres to oppose him. Against Tyre the towers equalled the height of the rampart, which, according to Arrian, amounted to 46 metres. There is also evidence of towers having been used in many other places, such as Gaza, Artacana, the Rock of Nautaca, Massaga and Aornus. For the first time some of these works of Diades and of Charias lend themselves to being reconstructed with relative precision. Three examples have survived, about 27, 40 and 54 metres high respectively, with 10, 15 and 20 storeys, the highest of which measured a fifth of the area of the base, mounted on six or eight wheels and provided at the top with flying bridges (which Diades claimed, erroneously it seems, to have invented). A giant tower constructed by Polyidus against Byzantium in 340 earned – perhaps more for its complexity than for its size – the flattering name of Helepolis ('Taker of Cities'). It is possible to form some idea of it from the description by Biton of the tower which the Macedonian Posidonius had invented for Alexander: this was 23 metres in height and rested on a rectangular base of 15.40 by 18.50 metres, supported by wheels 2.80 metres in diameter which could be operated from the inside by great 'squirrel-cages'.

Other traditional devices for siege warfare included assault-ramps, which reached unheard of dimensions against Tyre and Gaza, mines,

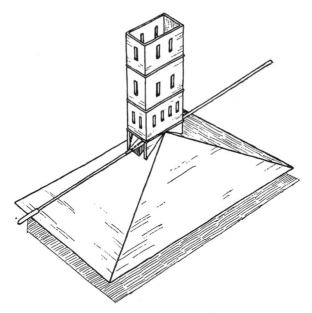

Fig. 38. Reconstruction of the 'ram-tortoise' designed by Diades. (After Lendle 1975 (K 35) 43, fig. 78.)

which were particularly effective in Asia against walls of unbaked brick, and finally battering-rams, to which Polyidus must have contributed some refinements, combined with wooden shelters known as 'tortoises'.[26] The most celebrated of these was the 'ram-tortoise' of Diades, 18 metres long, with its striking beam suspended, although that of the drill attributed to the same engineer rested on rollers (Fig. 38).

These same machines, protected from incendiary missiles by coverings of hide or metal, were often to be found in use by the besieged also, as well as a whole panoply of more or less sophisticated *antimechanemata*, such as Diodorus attributed to the ingenious inhabitants of Tyre:

Against the projectiles from the catapults they made wheels with many spokes, and, setting these to rotate by a certain device, they destroyed some of the missiles and deflected others, and broke the force of all . . . They forged great tridents armed with barbs and struck with these at close range the assailants standing on the towers. These stuck in the shields, and as ropes were attached to the tridents, they could haul on the ropes and pull them in . . . They fashioned shields of bronze and iron and, filling them with sand, roasted them continuously over a strong fire and made the sand red hot. By means of a certain apparatus they then scattered this over those Macedonians who were fighting most boldly and brought those within its range into utter misery . . . They let

[26] Lendle 1975 (K 35) and 1983 (K 37).

down long poles or spars equipped with concave cutting edges and cut the ropes supporting the rams, thus rendering these instruments useless. With their fire-throwers they discharged huge red-hot masses into the press of the enemy, and where so many men were packed together they did not miss their mark. With 'crows' and 'iron hands' they dragged over the edge many who were stationed behind the breastworks on the towers.

(XVII.43–4: trans. C. B. Welles, Loeb edn)

The art of fortification was bound, sooner or later, to undergo corresponding changes. Thus Philo of Byzantium (83.7–10) attributes to Polyidus the saw-tooth trace especially recommended for erection on the side of jagged cliffs, and Pausanias (x.36.3–4) regarded as a masterpiece the 'double wall' (?) constructed by the Thebans around Ambrysus in Phocis, shortly before the battle of Chaeronea. In view of the uncertainty and inaccuracy which continue to inhibit the dating of military outworks, not to mention the traditional time-lag to which they were always subject in relation to methods of attack, it is more difficult to assess on site the originality of what was achieved during the period of Philip II and Alexander – including, perhaps, the indented trace of the fortress of Gortys or of the southern face of the city wall at Priene; the excavation of new ditches, 4 metres deep and 10 metres wide, outside certain sectors of the walls of Athens and, according to Arrian (*Anab.* 1.20.8), 6.75 metres deep and twice as wide outside Halicarnassus just before the siege of 333; the existence of outer walls (*proteichismata*) at Athens in 337 and at Thebes in 335; the severance of structural ties between towers and their adjacent curtains, which was so complete that at Myndus one of them 'in its fall did not strip the wall' (Arrian *Anab.* 1.20.7); the adaptation of some towers and upper parts of ramparts for the installation of catapult batteries. It seems likely that the decisive changes in this sphere took place somewhat later, in the time of the Successors of Alexander and especially during the third century, one reason being that in the preceding century the Greek cities had been incapable of taking appropriate defensive measures and of matching the high level of Macedonian military technique in all its aspects – witness the paucity of the artillery listed in the maritime inventories of Athens between 330–329 and 323–322.

In all fields of military activity, even in the maritime where Macedon had begun to rival Athens since the reign of Philip II,[27] the Greek cities in the fourth century found themselves in a position of increasing inferiority despite some attempts to adapt. It is difficult not to see in this, if not the prime cause, then at least a major indication of their progressive decline, in a world which was being permanently reshaped by the exercise of open and unabashed force.

[27] Hauben 1972 (K 26) and 1976 (D 194).

CHAPTER 13

DION AND TIMOLEON

H. D. WESTLAKE

A. SICILY, 367–354 B.C.

I. SOURCES[1]

The content of the two books which Philistus devoted to Sicilian history during the five years after the accession of the younger Dionysius is not determinable, though his presentation of the tyrant whom he served can hardly have been unfavourable. Evidence is also meagre on the whole decade to 357 B.C., apart from information about the relations of Dionysius with Dion and Plato. On the other hand, the crusade led by Dion, which liberated Syracuse from tyranny but terminated after three stormy years in failure and death, proved attractive to contemporaries and posterity alike, largely because of his friendship with Plato and the part played by members of the Academy. Contemporary writers tended to be prejudiced in favour of Dion, and most secondary authorities echo this prejudice, but there are also traces of a tradition hostile towards him.

The earliest extant record of his career is provided by the Platonic Epistles, especially the Seventh and Eighth. Although the vexed question of their authenticity has not been satisfactorily resolved, their value as historical evidence is indisputable. If they were not written by Plato himself, the author must have been a contemporary with an exhaustive knowledge not only of Plato and his experience in Sicily but also of his later dialogues and intellectual outlook. Features of these two Epistles indicating the genuineness of their substance are their uneasily defensive tone and the not wholly unfavourable presentation of the younger Dionysius. They are, however, by no means objective.[2]

Another contemporary who wrote about Dion was Timonides of Leucas (*FGrH* 561), a member of the Academy, who took part in the expedition against Dionysius and sent a report on its military operations to Speusippus at Athens. Although not extant, this account evidently underlies much of the military narrative in the *Dion* of Plutarch.

---

[1] See also pp. 1–23. The texts of literary sources for this period are collected, with an introduction, by Sordi 1983 (G 298).

[2] See Westlake 1983 (G 323) 163 n. 9. I follow de Blois 1979 (G 118A) in dating the Seventh Letter to 354/3, when Callippus still held Syracuse (see pp. 704–5), and Aalders 1969 (G 91A) in dating the Eighth Letter after his expulsion.

Timonides was devoted to Dion and hostile to Heraclides, so that his testimony, though that of an eye-witness, cannot have been above suspicion. He seems also to have eulogized the mercenaries of Dion and depreciated the Syracusans. A totally different picture was evidently drawn by the Syracusan Athanis (*FGrH* 562), another contemporary, who continued the work of Philistus. He held office as a colleague of Heraclides during the eclipse of Dion and was presumably a supporter of the former and an opponent of the latter. The partisanship of Athanis may be responsible for the disparaging treatment of the final stages in the career of Dion found in the biography by Nepos.

Ephorus (*FGrH* 70) and Theopompus (*FGrH* 115), who included sections on Sicily in their voluminous histories, could have used oral reports from eye-witnesses on the period ending with the death of Dion, though neither had close links with the West. The presentation of Dion by Ephorus, if the narrative of Diodorus is based mainly upon it, was moderately laudatory but without bias against Heraclides. Theopompus probably treated Dion unfavourably, but his main theme was apparently the fall of the tyrant house through the vices of its members. This attitude influenced later writers, including Aelian and Justin. Aristotle *Pol.* 1312a 26–39, 1312b 16–21 refers to the expulsion of Dionysius by Dion as a courageous enterprise against a contemptible tyrant whose personal defects had cost him the goodwill of his subjects.

Although Timaeus (*FGrH* 566) dealt with this period in some detail, his opinions about its leading characters are unknown. His hatred of tyrants doubtless led him to welcome the expulsion of Dionysius, and he may have approved of Dion, but he certainly did not praise him as extravagantly as he praised Timoleon. Unfortunately his sources and the extent of their influence upon him cannot be traced, but the influence of his own work upon the literary tradition was considerable.

The fullest, though not the oldest, extant narrative of this period is provided by the *Dion* of Plutarch. Because much of its content is derived, directly or indirectly, from the Platonic Epistles and the report by Timonides, the treatment of Dion is very favourable. Plutarch, however, with his philosophical interests, had personal reasons for paying homage to a friend and disciple of Plato, who was believed to have based his political leadership on Platonic doctrine. The influence of Timonides is doubtless responsible for the presentation of Heraclides as a self-seeking villain. The closing phase in the career of Dion is recorded briefly and vaguely by Plutarch, who, while admitting that his hero was unapproachable, seems reluctant to acknowledge that he was guilty of autocratic behaviour.

The narrative of Diodorus (xvi. 5–20) on this period differs substantially in tone from that of Plutarch. While Dion is praised and his philosophical training is mentioned, his friendship with Plato and the contribution of the Academy to his enterprise are ignored. Heraclides also is very differently presented. Diodorus does not regard his rivalry with Dion as reprehensible but gives him credit for his naval victory and even states that some Syracusans supported him because he was not expected to aspire to a tyranny. The narrative breaks off abruptly after recording the final military victory of Dion, whose death is mentioned only in a brief note derived from the chronographical source. It is probable that Diodorus has based his account mainly upon that of Ephorus, though he may have drawn some material from Timaeus.[3]

The brief *Dion* by Nepos, probably a summary of a hellenistic biography,[4] is interesting because, whereas the first half extols the character and achievements of Dion, the second half presents him as a despot who treated even his friends and supporters autocratically. This damning picture may be derived ultimately from Athanis.

II. DIONYSIUS, DION AND PLATO, 367–360 B.C.[5]

The younger Dionysius, who must have been a little under thirty when he became tyrant, did not inherit the dynamic personality of his father. He had not received much education and hardly any training in statecraft, so that he was ill equipped for the task of discharging the onerous responsibilities bequeathed to him. He was not without intelligence, showing at times a capacity for subterfuge, and in the period immediately after his accession he apparently did not indulge in the vices traditionally associated with tyranny, including drunkenness, for which he later became notorious. He was, however, an unstable character, though on several occasions he displayed surprising resilience in adversity. The principal reasons for his failure to maintain his autocracy were that he was deficient in vigour, enterprise and the ability to impose his will upon others.

For a time after his accession, he was disposed to relax somewhat the 'fetters of steel' with which his father was popularly reputed to have held the tyranny secure.[6] This inclination to adopt a more liberal regime doubtless influenced his assent to a plea by Dion that he should invite Plato to visit Syracuse again and to give him political advice. Plato accepted, though with some misgivings, and arrived in the summer of 366. Meanwhile Philistus had been recalled to Syracuse, where he led a

---

[3] See pp. 8–10. [4] Voit 1954–5 (G 320).

[5] The most useful detailed account of events down to Dion's death is Berve 1956 (G 117), where fuller references may be sought; some differences with him are picked out in Westlake 1983 (G 323).

[6] Initially he continued the foreign policy of his father (p. 149) by sending a small force to support Sparta (Xen. *Hell.* VII.4.2) but it was soon withdrawn, and he apparently took no further action.

faction determined to preserve the tyranny in its existing form and therefore hostile to Dion. As normally occurs when a despotism is in weak hands, a struggle developed between rival groups at court, each striving to exert a dominant influence over the despot. Philistus and his associates suspected, or affected to suspect, that Dion had brought Plato to Sicily with the intention that Dionysius, captivated by philosophical teaching, might renounce control of the state, which Dion himself would assume and then hand over to his nephews, the sons of the elder Dionysius and Aristomache. There may have been a grain of truth in these suspicions.

Some three months after the arrival of Plato, when he was already finding the tyrant a difficult pupil, an episode occurred which fundamentally turned the scale in the conflict between the factions of Philistus and Dion. A letter was secretly shown to Dionysius which Dion had written to plenipotentiaries from Carthage negotiating peace terms: in it he urged them not to confer with Dionysius in his absence, since he alone could secure for them an agreement without modifications. After consulting Philistus, Dionysius deported Dion to Italy without giving him an opportunity to defend himself. Unless the letter was a forgery, which seems unlikely, Dion was engaging in underhand contacts with an enemy which he sought to conceal from the head of the state. He could well have been impeached for high treason and may be thought fortunate to have escaped with his life. Dionysius, however, perhaps afraid of reactions by the supporters of Dion, denied that he had banished him and allowed his family to send some of his movable property to him in the Peloponnese.

Dionysius now tried to supplant Dion in the affections of Plato, but there was no longer any prospect that he would accept political reforms involving the relaxation of his autocratic powers. Plato, feeling that his mission had failed, wished to go home but found himself virtually a prisoner. Only when Dionysius was preoccupied with renewed hostilities against Carthage did he permit Plato to leave. Their parting was outwardly amicable. An agreement was reached whereby Plato was to return as soon as possible and to be accompanied by Dion. Dionysius probably had already made up his mind never to reinstate Dion and had no intention of honouring this agreement.

Meanwhile Dion had been warmly welcomed in Greece. Because of his wealth he could live in considerable style and be generous to his friends. His years of virtual exile were spent mainly at Athens, where he strengthened his ties with the Academy, and at Corinth, but he visited other cities and at Sparta was granted citizenship. Though familiar with the untrustworthiness of Dionysius, he was at first hopeful of a peaceful return to Sicily through the intercession of Plato.

At the end of 363, when Syracuse was no longer at war, Dionysius invited Plato to visit him again but postponed the recall of Dion for a further year. Plato declined the invitation both on account of his age and because it did not comply with his agreement with Dionysius. When the invitation was repeated a year later, so much pressure was brought upon him that he felt unable to refuse, though dismayed by the prospect of another visit. He accepted largely in the hope of helping Dion, especially as Dionysius made abundantly clear that, if this second invitation was declined, Dion must expect harsh treatment. Another consideration was that reports from Syracuse credited Dionysius with remarkable progress in philosophical studies. Plato was doubtless sceptical but felt that if any hope, however slender, remained of redeeming the ill success of his previous mission, the opportunity must not be missed.

Although he received a cordial welcome on arrival at Syracuse (spring, 361), this final visit proved wholly abortive. Dionysius soon showed that he would never put Platonic theory into practice to the extent of renouncing his tyranny. He also became increasingly intransigent in his attitude towards Dion. He now refused to allow the revenue from his property to be any longer sent to the Peloponnese, doubtless fearing that it might be used to hire mercenaries for service against himself. Later, after lengthy wrangles with Plato, he sold the entire property and appropriated the proceeds. Plato, already embittered and without hope of benefiting Dion, longed to leave Sicily before the onset of winter but found himself compelled to remain until the following year.

His relations with Dionysius continued to deteriorate.[7] A crucial rupture was caused by an incident involving Heraclides, a prominent Syracusan who was to play a leading role in the liberation of his native city. He held high rank in the army and was a friend of Dion, with whom he had been suspected of favouring the abolition of the tyranny. Mercenaries of Dionysius now mutinied because he proposed to reduce their pay. Heraclides, believed to have instigated the mutiny, went into hiding, and when his uncle was pleading with Dionysius on his behalf, Plato happened to be present and heard assurances given that Heraclides would not be put to death. On the next day, because troops continued to search for the fugitive, Plato infuriated Dionysius by accusing him of breaking his promise. While Dionysius may have been unduly suspicious of Heraclides as a friend of Dion, the charge of bad faith seems hardly justified. The episode had far-reaching consequences. Heraclides escaped and resumed his association with Dion in the Peloponnese,

---

[7] If there is any truth in a statement of Plutarch (*Dion* 22.2–3) that Speusippus, who accompanied Plato to Sicily, conducted inquiries to discover how far intervention by Dion would receive popular support, Dionysius had every reason to complain that his hospitality was being abused.

while Plato was dismissed from the palace precincts and sent to live
among the mercenaries, where he felt his life to be in danger. Eventually
(spring, 360) he was permitted to leave Sicily. It is questionable whether
Dionysius acted generously in sanctioning his departure when he could
have detained him as a security against intervention by Dion. Dionysius
was susceptible to public opinion, and the whole Greek world would
have condemned him if any harm had befallen its most eminent
philosopher.

Plato met Dion at the Olympic festival and gave him news from Sicily.
Dion was now determined to take military action against Dionysius,
who had now inflicted upon him the crowning indignity of compelling
his wife to marry another man. Plato refused to give personal support to
the use of force against his former host but sanctioned the enlistment of
any friends wishing to lend assistance to the enterprise. The die was cast.

III. THE EXPEDITION OF DION AND ITS SEQUEL, 360–355 B.C.

Dion, in partnership with Heraclides,[8] began his preparations for
military intervention in 360 but did not sail for Sicily until the summer of
357. A combination of factors led to this long delay. He had to recruit
mercenaries surreptitiously, like Cyrus, in order to escape detection; he
was not openly sponsored by any major city; despite reports from Sicily
promising local support, his enterprise was thought to be hazardous;
finally, his motives were not above suspicion. This last factor doubtless
contributed to the scantiness of support from Syracusan exiles: some
probably felt that the aim of Dion was merely to supplant Dionysius as
tyrant, while others may have feared that the participation of the
Academy in the undertaking might lead to an experiment in Platonic
statecraft not at all to their liking.

Friction which, according to Plutarch (*Dion* 32.4), developed between
Dion and Heraclides in the Peloponnese may have arisen because the
latter resented the influence of the Academy, with which he apparently
had no links and no sympathy. This discord was probably not, as some
scholars have thought, dishonestly antedated by the prejudiced Timonides. It is, however, exaggerated by Plutarch when he alleges that the
ships and troops commanded by Heraclides constituted a separate and
independent expedition. This force could hardly have been maintained
without support from the wealth of Dion, and after Heraclides arrived at
Syracuse, there was initially some semblance of harmony between them.
According to Diodorus (xvi. 6.5), Dion left Heraclides behind to bring

---

[8] Heraclides does not seem to have been in any way subordinate to Dion. Their names appear
together in an inscription naming persons honoured by the sanctuary of Asclepius at Epidaurus (*IG*
IV² 95.39–40).

triremes and some other craft later. The separate departure of the two forces may indeed have been the outcome of strategic planning.

When Dion sailed from Zakynthos for Sicily in August, his force consisted of 800 mercenaries, two merchant ships and three smaller vessels. To avoid interception off Iapygia he chose to cross the open sea, but his fleet was carried to Africa by a storm and after some adventures made a landfall at Carthaginian Minoa in south-western Sicily. Here, profiting from earlier links with Carthage, he was welcomed by the garrison commander and soon set out for Syracuse. On the march he was joined by some Siceliots and received the welcome news that Dionysius had recently left for Italy with a strong fleet. The mercenaries of the tyrant guarding Epipolae were lured away by a false report that Dion would attack their homes at Leontini. Reaching Syracuse unopposed, he received a tumultuous welcome from the citizens, who, when he proclaimed his intention to liberate the Siceliots from tyranny, appointed him and his brother Megacles generals with full powers (*strategoi autokratores*; see p. 701). Soon the whole city was in his hands, apart from Ortygia held by the troops of the tyrant.

When Dionysius returned with his fleet, he professed willingness to abdicate, but while negotiations were in progress, he treacherously ordered his mercenaries to deliver an attack, which was with difficulty repelled, largely through the heroism of Dion. Further negotiations followed in which Dionysius craftily exploited the suspicion felt by the Syracusan populace towards Dion because of his close associations with the tyrant house. Thereafter his prestige as a liberator began to wane. Heraclides now arrived with twenty triremes and 1,500 mercenaries. After being delayed by storms, he was able to take the normal coast-hugging route unopposed because the naval forces of the tyrant had been withdrawn from Italy to confront Dion at Syracuse. The Syracusans appointed him admiral, but Dion protested that his own authority was infringed thereby and proceeded to nominate Heraclides on his own initiative. In taking this action, which, though legally justifiable, was somewhat high-handed, Dion displayed, not for the last time, some lack of judgment. Nothing was more likely to draw the Syracusan populace and Heraclides into partnership against him, and Heraclides, being more approachable than the austere Dion, soon outstripped him in popular favour.

The mercenaries brought by Dion from the Peloponnese soon suffered a loss of popularity similar to that of their leader. Their upkeep imposed a financial strain upon the impoverished city, and their pay was already in arrears. Their services began to be considered unnecessary, especially when the fleet, manned mostly by Syracusans and commanded by Heraclides, won a victory which resulted in the death of Philistus.

The loss of his ablest general caused Dionysius to offer to surrender Ortygia if he were permitted to withdraw to Italy with his mercenaries and his property. Dion recommended acceptance, but the Syracusans rejected the offer. Dionysius then stole away by sea, leaving his son Apollocrates to continue the defence of Ortygia. Heraclides incurred temporary odium because as admiral he failed to prevent the escape of the tyrant.

At this point efforts to complete the liberation of Syracuse were hampered by the outbreak of a bitter conflict between rival factions of the would-be liberators, whose interpretations of what was meant by liberty were basically incompatible. The supporters of Dion, apart from his mercenaries and some members of the Academy, consisted of prosperous, landed Syracusans who planned to replace the rule of the tyrant-house by a republican regime which would leave the ownership of land and property virtually unchanged. The opponents of Dion, who looked to Heraclides as their leader, were drawn mostly from the poorer classes, including the crews of the fleet. Their claims were voiced by an extreme democrat named Hippon, who proposed a redistribution of all land and property, involving the dismemberment of large estates belonging to the rich in fertile areas (see p. 703). The statement of Plutarch (*Dion* 37.5), presumably derived from Timonides, that Heraclides incited Hippon to make this proposal in order to divert from himself the resentment aroused by the escape of Dionysius is probably a calumny. It should not, however, be assumed that Heraclides was necessarily a sincere devotee of extreme democracy.[9] He may well have become the champion of the proletariate for other reasons, either because he genuinely suspected Dion of aiming at a tyranny or merely as a means of enhancing his own power and prestige. The conviction attributed to his supporters by Diodorus (xiv.17.3) that he would never seek to make himself tyrant seems to be well founded.

Despite opposition by Dion the assembly approved the recommendations of Heraclides to put into operation the agrarian scheme of Hippon, to discontinue the payment of the mercenaries and to elect a board of twenty-five generals. This election (summer, 356) terminated the dictatorship of Dion, and he was not among the newly elected generals, whereas Heraclides was. Most of the mercenaries reacted angrily and were inclined to take violent action against the Syracusans. Rejecting surreptitious offers of citizenship, they remained loyal to Dion, who led them away towards Leontini and easily repelled harassment by the Syracusans. The Leontines, themselves mostly retired mercenaries,

[9] If at the time of his alleged involvement in the mutiny by the mercenaries (see above, p. 699), he had been regarded as a would-be demagogue, it is unlikely that Plato would have been so willing to plead on his behalf, thereby aggravating his own already strained relations with Dionysius.

warmly welcomed Dion and his men, undertaking to provide pay and offering them citizenship. They also sent a protest to Syracuse, which was later endorsed by a meeting of Siceliot allies.

Meanwhile the garrison of Ortygia was on the point of surrender when Nypsius, an Italian *condottiere* employed by Dionysius, arrived bringing welcome supplies. The Syracusan fleet failed to intercept this relieving squadron but then made an unexpected attack and won a victory. The Syracusans indulged in immoderate celebrations, not for the first time, and neglected to post an adequate guard on the wall dividing Ortygia from mainland Syracuse. Nypsius, seizing the opportunity, led a night attack in which his troops caused widespread slaughter and destruction. So panic-stricken were the Syracusan masses that, in spite of their hostility towards Dion, they were induced by the upper classes and the allies to send an urgent plea for help to Leontini. Dion accepted at once, partly through patriotism but partly because he saw the prospect of regaining his lost authority. His mercenaries consented to accompany him. When the troops of the tyrant withdrew from mainland Syracuse, the democrats had second thoughts and cancelled their appeal, but an even more destructive attack by Nypsius, in which much of the city was burned, caused them to renew it. The arrival of Dion and his men led to a violent battle, graphically described by Plutarch, in which they eventually thrust the enemy back behind the fortifications of Ortygia.

Dion was the hero of the hour and could now undoubtedly have made himself tyrant if he had so wished. The democratic leaders fled, but Heraclides, to his credit, submitted to Dion, acknowledging his own culpability. The friends of Dion urged him to rid himself of Heraclides, but he chose to pardon him, evidently expecting that he could at last secure the acceptance of his own political views without democratic opposition. At an assembly Heraclides moved the appointment of Dion as *strategos autokrator* by land and sea. While the upper classes supported this proposal, the poorer citizens objected because it would have deprived Heraclides, their champion, of his authority as admiral. Thereupon, in a further effort to achieve harmony, Dion nominated Heraclides as admiral, but on the controversial issue of land distribution he refused to compromise and vetoed the entire scheme. This action was autocratic, perhaps even illegal, and Heraclides, when he had sailed to Messene, which was apparently threatened by Dionysius, exploited it by declaring to his sailors that Dion was seeking a tyranny.

The next development was a surprising intervention by the Spartan government. This puzzling episode is recorded by Plutarch alone (*Dion* 48.7–49.7), and the probable reason for its obscurity is that it was not altogether creditable to Dion. A Spartan named Pharax was sent, perhaps at the request of Heraclides, to act as a mediator. He initiated secret negotiations between Dionysius and Heraclides, who was still at Messene and evidently hoped to steal a march upon Dion. The proposed settlement was, however, shelved when friends of Dion serving at Messene informed him of the negotiations. Pharax then supported Dionysius wholeheartedly, helping him to regain some parts of Sicily. When Dion and a Syracusan army suffered a minor defeat near Acragas at the hands of Pharax, Heraclides, who was in command of the fleet there, sailed back towards Syracuse with the alleged intention of seizing the city and excluding Dion. The charge of disloyalty was not put to the test, since Dion forestalled him in returning to Syracuse. Pharax must have been recalled, having probably furthered his personal interests and neglected his instructions. Another Spartan agent named Gaesylus now arrived at Syracuse, claiming to have been sent, as Gylippus had been, to assume command of the Siceliots. Heraclides tried to exploit this new development to his own advantage, but Dion, himself a Spartan citizen, refused to renounce his dictatorship, and Gaesylus withdrew after negotiating an uneasy reconciliation between the rival leaders. Dion was not, however, willing to trust Heraclides, for he induced the Syracusans to disband their fleet. This measure, though justifiable on financial grounds, was politically advantageous to Dion because it divested Heraclides of his office as admiral and also weakened the extreme democratic faction.

The garrison on Ortygia was now becoming mutinous through shortage of food. Apollocrates, doubtless with the consent of his father, concluded a settlement whereby he was permitted to sail unopposed to Italy with five ships. At long last (autumn, 355) Syracuse was fully liberated, and Dion was reunited with his family. His fundamental disagreement with the populace remained unresolved.

IV. THE FALL OF DION, 355–354 B.C.

By overthrowing the Syracusan tyranny Dion won the acclaim of the Greek world, but the aftermath of his achievement brought him deepening disillusionment and eventually despair. From the inadequate evidence on this last phase of his career it transpires both that he was unfortunate in being confronted with a most intractable situation and that he committed grave errors in his attempts to deal with it.

After the withdrawal of Apollocrates the various groups drawn into uneasy partnership by the military struggle to oust his mercenaries from Ortygia no longer had a common cause. Not only was the democratic faction even less disposed to accept the authority of Dion, but disunity and bitterness developed among his own supporters. There was a conflict of interest between the richer Syracusans and the mercenaries, both expecting their wishes to be granted in return for past services. The members of the Academy also doubtless claimed that their views should be respected. A hoplite class of small proprietors, which might have been expected to favour Dion, scarcely existed at Syracuse at this time.

The discontent among his former supporters was partly the result of financial difficulties. He is reported to have rewarded friends, allies and mercenaries so lavishly that he overspent his resources, while later he first seized the property of his adversaries, which he distributed to the soldiers, and next, when this expedient proved inadequate, subjected his aristocratic friends to similar confiscations. He thus seems to have initially expected that the mercenaries would continue to be maintained from the public revenue but found that, when their services were no longer required against the forces of the tyrant, the assembly refused to shoulder this burden any longer and that he had to pay them from whatever funds he could muster. The result was that he could not now count upon the backing of the richer Syracusans, while the mercenaries, denied any prospect of winning booty, became less favourably disposed towards him because of anxiety about their pay.[10]

Information on the political measures taken by him at this time is meagre, and even less is known about the programme of constitutional reform which his death left unfulfilled. He did not resign his special powers. His retention of office might be held to be necessary until Greek Sicily was wholly liberated and political stability restored at Syracuse, but he thereby strengthened the suspicion, encouraged by the democratic faction, that he was seeking a tyranny. This faction was again led by Heraclides, who declined a conciliatory invitation from Dion to join his council, preferring to exercise the political rights open to any member of the assembly. Heraclides also attacked Dion for refusing to demolish the stronghold of the tyrants and the tomb of the elder Dionysius. Another accusation was that Dion by sending to Corinth for advisers to help in the work of political reconstruction was insulting the Syracusans. Democratic antagonism towards Dion had intensified since he vetoed the scheme for the redistribution of land, but the principal source of resentment was his manifest determination to impose upon Syracuse a constitution incompatible with the principles of extreme democracy.

Neither the composition nor the function of the council on which Heraclides refused to serve is at all clear. It was seemingly established by Dion without the sanction of the assembly. Plutarch (*Dion* 53.2) implies that the advisers from Corinth were to serve as members, so that it was presumably a temporary body appointed to frame a permanent constitu-

---

[10] Here the best evidence is provided by Nepos *Dio* 7, who describes how he alienated his former supporters and became increasingly desperate.

tion. Dion certainly contrived to ensure that it would produce a constitution consonant with his own views. His reason for seeking advisers from Corinth is stated to have been that the government there was an oligarchy which seldom consulted the assembly. How much progress the council made before his death is not recorded.

His friendship with Plato and association with the Academy has prompted the belief that he intended the constitutional reform at Syracuse to be modelled upon Platonic political doctrine. The Seventh and Eighth Epistles undoubtedly suggest that such was his intention, and they are widely thought to represent his plans in outline. The case can be neither proved nor disproved, since the evidence is insufficiently specific. These Epistles lay down principles rather than convey practical advice. Their most positive recommendation occurs in the Eighth Epistle (355e–357a), setting out a mixed constitution which the friends of Dion are urged to adopt. This constitution is framed to meet circumstances which had altered considerably since Dion died. It is, however, in accord with his ostensible views: though in theory mixed, it entrusts control of the state largely to a narrow oligarchy, while extreme democracy is totally rejected. On the other hand, the keynote of the Eighth Epistle is compromise and reconciliation, even with Dionysius, which Dion could hardly have been willing to accept, however desperate his own prospects might have become. There seems no reason to believe that he exploited his links with Plato to gain personal advantages, but whether he consciously sought to base his programme of reconstruction upon what he had learned through those links cannot be determined.

Whatever his aims may have been, progress was constantly hampered by violent opposition from Heraclides and the democrats. Eventually he yielded to persistent pressure from his supporters and allowed them to murder Heraclides. This decision was a fatal blunder. On earlier occasions, when machinations by Heraclides could have been considered treasonable, action against him might have been justifiable, but he was now only exercising his rights as a citizen. The murder created widespread apprehension and encouraged the belief that Dion had become a tyrant in all but name, a sober tyrant supplanting a drunken one. Undoubtedly he tried to impose his own views by using his special powers: his haughty temperament did not permit him to make concessions. Increasingly distrusted not only by democrats but also by aristocrats and mercenaries, he became more and more isolated and seems to have eventually become conscious of irretrievable failure. Feelings of guilt for the murder of Heraclides added to his depression.

It was now inevitable that an attempt would be made to bring about his downfall. Yet some surprise may be felt that the originator of the movement against him was the Athenian Callippus, a close friend, who had links with the Academy and had won distinction as a military leader. This conspiracy, which was widely supported, culminated in the murder of Dion (summer, 354) by some Zakynthian mercenaries who, after long service under his command, now turned against him. Throughout his dictatorship he apparently made little effort to ensure his personal safety, perhaps hoping to avoid the stigma of adopting tyrannical methods, but now neither his guards nor his friends attempted to rescue him, and some may have been guilty of betraying him. Callippus doubtless claimed, and may genuinely have believed, that drastic action was necessary if the dangerous drift towards anarchy was to be halted. He must, however, have been influenced also by personal ambition, since he evidently took over the dictatorial powers of his victim. If he tried to heal the dissensions between the rival factions at Syracuse, he certainly did not succeed. The tradition favourable to Dion naturally presents him as a traitor, a villain and a usurper.

Dion remains an enigmatic figure. His ultimate aims are largely un-known because they were never achieved and are nowhere unequivo-cally recorded. Although his plans for the reform of the Syracusan state were certainly influenced by his association with Plato and the Academy, there is, as has been noted, no conclusive evidence that he envisaged what could properly be termed a Platonic experiment in statecraft. While he may be acquitted of seeking to supplant Dionysius as tyrant, personal ambition undoubtedly exerted a profound influence upon him. His intention seems likely to have been to retain virtual control of state policy through an oligarchical council composed of his most trusted supporters.

He had many admirable qualities: high moral principles, patriotism, physical courage, an intellect which impressed Plato. As a military leader he displayed a capacity for strategic planning and for retaining the loyalty of mercenary troops not normally amenable to discipline. He also inspired devotion in a circle of friends who remained for years faithful to his memory. Endowed with these qualities, he might appear to have been excellently equipped not only to liberate Syracuse from tyranny but also to enact a political settlement whereby the liberated city was given the opportunity to enjoy harmony and prosperity. His efforts in fact led to a decade of anarchy and impoverishment. It is true that Siceliots had a reputation for political irresponsibility and unruliness and that he was faced with the exceptional problems discussed above.[11] Nevertheless his failure as a statesman was mainly the result of his own shortcomings. These were partly a legacy from his long period of service to the tyrant

[11] The highly centralized empire of the elder Dionysius was too dependent on his own vigorous personality, and the weakness of his successor inevitably led to its rapid disintegration.

house. He had no practical experience of any political environment in which a leader could not hope to implement any policy unless prepared to make strenuous efforts to win preponderant support for it. Probably for the same reason he was intolerant of opposition and tried to enforce unpopular measures by taking arbitrary and even illegal action. His failure should not, however, be attributed wholly to his association with tyranny but rather in some degree to the less laudable features of his character. He was dogmatic, inflexible, withdrawn, lacking in geniality except perhaps to his closest friends. A proverb, 'Haughtiness has isolation for her companion', is applied to him in the Fourth Epistle, and the stricture contained in this passage (321b–c), whether or not originating from Plato himself, is fully substantiated by the record of his career.

B. SICILY, 354–330 B.C.

I. SOURCES

The period of Sicilian history in which Timoleon was the central figure is fraught with intractable problems arising mainly from the tantalizing defects of the literary tradition. On the earlier stages of his mission the evidence, though adequate in volume, fails to provide satisfactory answers to fundamental questions, while on the close of the period it becomes deplorably scanty. There is also sôme conflict between the two principal authorities, Plutarch and Diodorus, on crucial issues. Another stumbling-block is the flagrant bias in favour of Timoleon, originating partly from the success of his own propaganda and even more marked than in the tradition on Dion. Accordingly the motives attributed to his opponents are highly suspect. Finally, there are no references to him in extant works produced not long after his death, though Greeks in the homeland must have contrasted their own failure against Macedonian imperialism with his success in Sicily. This phenomenon, even if influenced by the accident of survival or the parochial outlook of many Greeks, is nevertheless very puzzling.

Five historians wrote accounts of his career, or part of it, within a generation or two after his death and might therefore have had access to oral sources. They are Athanis, Theopompus, Ephorus, Diyllus (*FGrH* 73) and Timaeus. It is unfortunate that their few surviving fragments relating to Timoleon are singularly uninformative, and there is no means of establishing how favourably or unfavourably any of them, apart from Timaeus, presented him. Timaeus, being the son of Andromachus, the first and most loyal ally of Timoleon, was doubtless influenced by information from his father and perhaps by his own youthful memories, so that he represented Timoleon as a blameless and divinely inspired hero. This encomiastic picture evoked violent and probably unfair censure from Polybius (XII.23.4), whose attacks on Timaeus damaged the reputation of Timoleon. The interest felt for Dion as a Platonist did not apply to Timoleon, who, except to writers closely studying his career, came to rank as a not very important or distinctive figure absurdly praised by Timaeus.

Among surviving accounts of his achievements the most detailed is the *Timoleon* of Plutarch. As a biography it has much the same virtues as the *Dion* and as a historical source much the same defects. It is deeply imbued with eulogistic colouring derived from Timaeus, whose work Plutarch seems to have used both directly and through a hellenistic biography. Convinced that Timoleon was an essentially virtuous man and a darling of the gods, Plutarch, who looked for goodness almost more than for greatness, tends to gloss over, or even ignore, episodes which could be thought discreditable to Timoleon because he either was unsuccessful or acted harshly.

The *Timoleon* of Nepos, which is too brief to be of much value, differs from his *Dion* in being laudatory throughout. Its affinity with the *Timoleon* of Plutarch suggests that both authors used the same hellenistic biography, which was for Nepos his sole source.

The account of Sicilian history by Diodorus on the period dominated by Timoleon (XVI.65–73, 77–83, 90) is less detailed and less personal than that of Plutarch but on the whole more trustworthy. While Diodorus presents Timoleon favourably, his eulogy is relatively muted: no attempt is made to conceal the failures or the unscrupulous actions of Timoleon, and not much prominence is given to the belief that he was providentially fortunate. There are, however, important issues on which Diodorus, or perhaps his source, has erred and the conflicting version of Plutarch is to be preferred. The source, or sources, on which he based his narrative of this period cannot be identified with any confidence. It is hardly credible that Timaeus was his sole authority, since the differences between his account and that of Plutarch are such that they cannot have been caused merely by differences of outlook or interpretation.[12] There are also good reasons for concluding that he cannot have depended exclusively upon Theopompus throughout. He may here, as perhaps in his preceding section on Sicilian history, have used more than one source.[13]

[12] Meister 1967 (B 74) 123–9, believed in use of an intermediate source based on Timaeus, rightly doubted by Pearson 1987 (B 92) 212–25, who nevertheless allows considerable use of Timaeus.
[13] Westlake 1953–4 (B 128) against Hammond 1938 (B 56).

II. TURBULENT INTERLUDE, 354–345 B.C.

After the death of Dion Sicily continued to be torn by unrest leading to impoverishment and depopulation. The hordes of mercenaries brought to Sicily by the elder Dionysius, mostly barbarians from Italy, were a constant source of disruption because of their need to maintain themselves. Any ambitious leader able to muster a band of mercenaries might dominate a town where he could sustain his authority and support his troops by financial levies upon its inhabitants and by raids on other districts. Whether such adventurers should be termed tyrants is debatable; that they had a pernicious influence is beyond dispute.[14]

Callippus controlled Syracuse for one year, overcoming opposition from the friends of Dion, who fled to Leontini. From there Hipparinus, a son of the elder Dionysius and nephew of Dion, presumably with their assistance, captured Syracuse by surprise, while Callippus was absent, and held it for two years. His successor was his brother Nysaeus, who remained in power for five years. A hostile tradition labels both brothers as tyrants and charges them with the vices associated with tyranny, but the friends of Dion did not apparently leave Syracuse or become estranged from either of his nephews. In 346 Dionysius, who had been living mainly at Locri, ousted Nysaeus by treachery, and the friends of Dion again fled to Leontini, the traditional rallying-point of Syracusan exiles. Hicetas, a Syracusan and once a staunch supporter of Dion, had established himself there with a strong mercenary force. Whether he ranked as a tyrant was perhaps a matter of opinion, but the Syracusan exiles, mostly aristocrats, needed military support and appointed him to be their general. They had accepted Hipparinus and Nysaeus and could not afford to be fastidious. Their next step suggests that they owed no allegiance to Hicetas but rather claimed to be the legitimate government of Syracuse in exile.

This momentous step was to appeal for help to Corinth as the metropolis of Syracuse. Hicetas, perhaps already insincere, associated himself with their appeal. Although the substance of this appeal is not precisely known, it was very probably for a general and an expeditionary force to assist in liberating Syracuse from tyranny. Its originators were doubtless aware that Carthaginian intervention in Sicily was expected, but mention of this additional hazard would scarcely have enhanced the prospect of a favourable response.

It is indeed remarkable that the response was at all favourable, since politically and economically Corinth had long been in decline. Yet the Syracusan aristocrats cannot have derived much satisfaction from the

---

[14] On 'tyrants' see in general Westlake 1952 (G 321). Other aspects of Timoleon: Sordi 1961 (G 292); Talbert 1974 (G 304).

news that the expedition mustered by Corinth after some delay consisted of only 700 mercenaries and ten ships. As Greece had a surfeit of unemployed mercenaries, the attitude of the Corinthians was evidently lukewarm. The choice of a leader points in the same direction: they appointed Timoleon, an elderly member of a distinguished family who had lived in retirement for twenty years and apparently had little experience of military command at a high level. His only palpable qualification was that he had been largely instrumental in expelling a tyrant. His brother Timophanes, entrusted with the command of a mercenary force, had established a tyranny and put many political opponents to death. Timoleon, after vainly remonstrating with his brother, conspired with two associates who killed the tyrant while he himself stood aside. Some Corinthians applauded the action, but, because others condemned his part in it as impious, he withdrew from public life and was still in retirement when the Syracusan appeal was received.[15]

Developments in Sicily while the expedition was being prepared were inauspicious. Hicetas, though professing support for the appeal to Corinth, had expected it to be rejected. Its acceptance was prejudicial to his ambition ultimately to supplant Dionysius as tyrant at Syracuse, and he now sought to further this intention through association with the Carthaginians, who were showing an interest in Sicily after a long interval. Their aims in mobilizing a powerful force in the winter of 345–344 for service in Sicily are not precisely known, but their intervention was doubtless encouraged, as on other occasions, by reports of Siceliot weakness and instability. While their initial action, against Entella, a town in the west occupied by Campanians, was to restore their authority in their own zone, their negotiations with Hicetas and other adventurers attest plans to intervene in eastern Sicily. Hicetas expected to exploit their naval power to prevent Timoleon from landing, and some assistance from them against Dionysius might be needed, though he appreciated the danger of becoming too heavily indebted to them.

When the Corinthian expedition was on its way, Hicetas, maintaining his pose as a would-be liberator, led his mercenaries to Syracusan territory, where he established a fortified base. Any hopes of provoking a popular rising were disappointed, and lack of supplies forced him to withdraw. Pursued by the army of Dionysius, his troops counter-attacked and killed 3,000 of the enemy. They then pursued their

---

[15] The accounts of these events by Plut. *Tim.* 3.2–5.4, 7.1–2, and by Nep. *Tim.* 1.3–6 are closely parallel. Diod. XVI. 65.3–8 gives a fundamentally different version: Timophanes had not actually become tyrant; Timoleon killed him with his own hand; the episode occurred, not twenty years before the Syracusan appeal, but shortly before the arrival of the envoys, when Timoleon was about to stand trial. On all these points the version of Diodorus is almost certainly erroneous.

surviving pursuers back to Syracuse, where the whole city except
Ortygia fell into their hands. No adequate account of this engagement
has survived, but it had far reaching consequences. Dionysius, in
addition to territorial losses, had his mercenaries reduced to 2,000 and
was closely besieged by the superior forces of Hicetas, now perhaps
aided by the local population.

III. THE LIBERATION OF SYRACUSE

Although Timoleon exploited various phenomena during his voyage to
suggest that his mission enjoyed divine support, his arrival in Italy was
unpropitious. At Metapontum Carthaginian envoys warned him not to
land in Sicily, and at Rhegium a much superior Carthaginian squadron
intercepted him, bearing a demand from Hicetas that the Corinthians
should return home. Timoleon professed acquiescence, but with Rhe-
gine collusion devised a ruse whereby his ships slipped away, evading
the Carthaginians. At Tauromenium he was welcomed by Andromachus, who was reputed to be an enemy of tyrants and now provided the
Corinthians with a defensible base.

Overtures made by Timoleon to Siceliot cities were everywhere
rejected through mistrust of self-styled liberators, except by one faction
at Adranum, a town on the slopes of Etna. The opposing faction called in
Hicetas, who arrived with 5,000 men while Timoleon with only 1,500
was still some distance from Adranum after a forced march from
Tauromenium. Ordering his tired troops to press on, Timoleon took the
mercenaries of Hicetas by surprise and decisively defeated them,
capturing their camp.[16]

This initial success won the support not only of Adranum but also of
Tyndaris on the north coast and of Catana, which was ruled by
Mamercus. Besides being a tyrant, Mamercus was of Italic origin and had
apparently served as a commander of Campanian mercenaries. At this
stage, however, Timoleon was in desperate need of allies, and Catana
later proved a valuable base.

The effect of the events of Adranum upon the situation at Syracuse
was sensational. Dionysius concluded an agreement with Timoleon
whereby he himself was smuggled out of Ortygia and command of his

---

[16] According to Diod. XVI. 68.11, 69.3, the victors pressed on at once to Syracuse and arrived
there unexpectedly, outstripping fugitives from the battlefield, with the result that, while Ortygia
was occupied by Dionysius and Achradina and Neapolis by Hicetas, Timoleon held the rest of the
city. A forced march of some 85 km is not a physical impossibility, even after fighting a battle. In this
period, however, any mainland areas of the city outside Achradina and Neapolis were small and not
easily defensible. Even if the meagre forces of Timoleon could have held such positions for many
months against heavy odds, it is not clear what advantage they would have gained thereby. The
account of Diodorus must be rejected.

mercenaries there was assumed by two Corinthian officers sent with 400 men, who made their way in small groups into the fortress. This decision by Dionysius, if unexpected, was not unreasonable. After his defeat by Hicetas he had only 2,000 mercenaries and could not hope to hold out indefinitely, especially as the blockade was likely to be tightened by the arrival of more Carthaginian ships. He could rest assured that Timoleon would guarantee his personal safety in return for a foothold at Syracuse, whereas Hicetas would show no mercy. Plutarch states, doubtless accurately, that the agreement was implemented within fifty days after the Corinthian landing, but his further claim that within the same period Dionysius was sent off to the Peloponnese (*Tim.* 16.2) may well originate from the propaganda of Timoleon. Dionysius, who had shown some diplomatic skill, is unlikely to have abdicated unconditionally at this stage. More probably he regarded Timoleon as an easily corruptible mercenary captain resembling others who had come from Greece in the past. He may well have lingered at the Corinthian base for a considerable time until, appreciating the determination and astuteness of Timoleon, he consented to go into exile at Corinth. To Timoleon the advantages of gaining Ortygia with its stores of arms and money outweighed the risk of incurring discredit by concluding a pact with the tyrant against whom his mission was primarily directed. He recognized that Hicetas and the Carthaginians had become the principal obstacles to the liberation of Syracuse.

The first response of Hicetas to this dramatic development was to plot the assassination of Timoleon. When this attempt failed, he abandoned his policy of limiting his obligations to the Carthaginians and invited their general Mago to bring a powerful force to Syracuse. Throughout the winter of 344–3 the defenders of Ortygia suffered from constant attacks and from shortage of food, but they resisted successfully, supported by supplies brought from Catana on small craft which in bad weather could normally run the blockade.

The remarkable success of Timoleon encouraged the Corinthians to adopt a more enthusiastic attitude towards his mission, which hereafter received their wholehearted support. They now prepared a second expedition consisting of 2,000 hoplites, 200 cavalry and ten ships, which apparently left Corinth in the spring of 343 but was unable to proceed beyond Thurii because it was intercepted by a Carthaginian squadron. In the same spring Mago brought a large armament to Syracuse. Nevertheless he and Hicetas were unable to reduce Ortygia, and when they sailed off to attack Catana, the source of supplies for the besieged, the Corinthian commander of the garrison captured Achradina by a sudden sortie. Mago and Hicetas hastened back from their fruitless expedition. Relations between them cannot have been altogether harmonious because their aims were irreconcilable, but Mago became even more distrustful when told of fraternization between the Greek mercenaries on each side. The defenders of Ortygia, probably on instructions from Timoleon, sought to undermine the loyalty of their adversaries by pointing out the disadvantages to all Greeks if Syracuse fell into Carthaginian hands. Alarmed by these reports and by news that Timoleon was approaching, Mago withdrew his entire force to western Sicily despite expostulations from Hicetas.

On the next day Timoleon reached Syracuse from Messene, where he had met the Corinthian reinforcement after it had marched overland to Rhegium and succeeded in crossing the straits. His present army, presumably including contingents from Messene, which had joined him, and other allies, numbered 4,000, while the garrison of Ortygia amounted to some 2,500. Although corresponding figures for the army of Hicetas are not attested, it probably outnumbered that of Timoleon. According to Plutarch (*Tim.* 21.2–5) Hicetas was determined to resist, but the Corinthians, attacking at three different points, overran the strong positions held by the enemy without sustaining a single casualty. Plutarch characteristically attributes this astonishing feat to the good fortune of Timoleon, but the circumstances suggest rather that under an agreement, kept secret because not very creditable to either party, Hicetas was permitted to withdraw his forces to Leontini intact. One factor influencing the willingness of Hicetas to negotiate probably was that he had forfeited the sympathy of most Syracusans. Their hostility towards himself and support for Timoleon as their new liberator would, if he had remained, have rendered his position precarious. Thwarted of his ambition to become tyrant of Syracuse, he could confidently expect, with his military strength unimpaired, to maintain a tyranny at Leontini.

IV. THE PERILS OF LIBERATED SYRACUSE

Timoleon could now inaugurate a scheme for social and political reconstruction, which will be considered below. A more urgent task was to destroy the physical manifestations of tyranny, thus clearing himself of the odium incurred by Dion, who had refused to take this action. At his invitation the Syracusans demolished the fortress of the Dionysii together with their houses and tombs. Danger still remained, however, from external enemies: hostile tyrants controlled powerful forces, and Carthage was known to be preparing to avenge the humiliation resulting from the debacles of Mago.

An offensive against tyrants launched in the summer of 342 won only limited success. Timoleon attacked Leontini, and when his troops were repulsed, he led them against Leptines, tyrant of Engyum and Apollonia,[17] both apparently Sicel towns. Hard pressed at Engyum, Leptines capitulated and was exiled to the Peloponnese. Meanwhile Hicetas attempted to besiege Syracuse but sustained heavy casualties and had to withdraw.[18] Financial stringency caused Timoleon to send a mercenary force to plunder the Carthaginian zone, where enough booty was seized to cover at least arrears of pay and Entella and other towns, barbarian and Greek, were won.

In the spring of 341 the expeditionary force which the Carthaginians had been preparing landed at Lilybaeum. The army, said to have amounted to 80,000, had been exceeded in numbers by earlier expeditionary forces, but, most exceptionally, it included an elite corps of 2,500 Carthaginian citizens, the Sacred Band. The primary duty of the generals was to restore Carthaginian authority in the west, and their first move was probably against Entella, now in Greek hands.

Timoleon had already taken steps to meet this crisis. He patched up his quarrel with Hicetas, who could expect no sympathy from the Carthaginians and therefore contributed a contingent to the army being mobilized for the defence of Greek Sicily. This army numbered only 12,000, including 3,000 Syracusans and 4,000 mercenaries, but Timoleon adopted the astonishingly bold strategy of making a forced march into the Carthaginian zone, evidently intending to surprise the enemy in the broken country of the interior. His strategy was indeed too bold for some of his mercenaries, of whom 1,000 mutinied near Acragas and deserted him. Yet he pressed on undismayed. On a hazy June day, as his troops reached the hill on which Entella was situated, they saw, at first indistinctly, the Sacred Band in the valley below crossing the river Crimisus.[19] Because of the haze on the heights they were not themselves visible until, led by Timoleon in person, they launched their attack towards the river bank. The heavily armed Carthaginian citizens resisted staunchly but were eventually driven back, their retreat hampered by the river bed. A second phase now began when the main force of the enemy, including hordes of mercenaries, poured across the river and seemed about to engulf the Greeks through weight of numbers. At that moment

---

[17] He was a Syracusan who had once been an associate of Callippus (Diod. XVI. 45.9), but later murdered him (Plut. *Dion* 57.6). He may have been a nephew of the elder Dionysius: if so, his career illustrates how members of the tyrant house exploited the turbulence of eastern Sicily in pursuit of personal ambitions.

[18] The account of Diod. XVI. 72.2–5 is here accepted. According to Plutarch (*Tim.* 24.1–2), Hicetas agreed to abdicate and live as a private citizen at Leontini. This version seems irreconcilable with later developments; it may reproduce an offer made to Hicetas at some stage but rejected.

[19] Identification of the site is not beyond doubt and at one time gave rise to much controversy. Strong arguments have, however, been produced, especially by Chisesi 1929 (G 136), for believing that the battle was fought in the valley of the Belice sinistro below the Rocca d'Entella. The features of this site tally with the accounts of Diodorus and Plutarch. Recently discovered inscriptions (p. 153) confirm that ancient Entella was situated at modern Rocca d'Entella.

a violent thunderstorm broke with rain and hail beating on the faces of the Carthaginians and turning the river into a torrent. Impeded by their armour and struggling in the mud, many were swept away and drowned or trampled under foot. The rest fled in panic across the waterlogged plain. More than 10,000 were said to have died and 15,000 to have been captured. For Carthage the worst feature of the disaster was that the Sacred Band was almost annihilated. The Carthaginian camp and vast quantities of booty fell into Greek hands, and Timoleon sent home to Corinth a thank-offering to the gods.[20]

While he was undoubtedly lucky in being favoured by the haze and the thunderstorm of that June day, he deserves credit for taking the enemy by surprise and creating the conditions in which he could exploit his good fortune. Credit is also due to the fighting qualities of his small army, especially his mercenaries, who confirmed that the professional Greek hoplite had no equal in the Mediterranean world.

V. THE LIBERATION OF GREEK SICILY

The military career of Timoleon became less spectacular after his major victory. For this reason, and through the reluctance of a prejudiced tradition to dwell upon some setbacks and some possibly deceitful manoeuvres, evidence is regrettably meagre. It was, however, no mean achievement that before his retirement he had purged Greek Sicily of its tyrants and protected it by a satisfactory peace with Carthage.

The completeness of his victory at the Crimisus evoked a resumption of the association between Carthage and the tyrants because Timoleon was their common enemy. Mamercus allied with Hicetas and probably others in an effort to safeguard their dictatorships, and the Carthaginians, determined to restore their own prestige, mobilized another expeditionary force which included Greek mercenaries. In the absence of Timoleon two of his mercenary contingents suffered defeats, probably in 340, the first by Mamercus with Carthaginian support near Messene, now held by a tyrant named Hippon, and the second in the Carthaginian zone. Timoleon was hard-pressed for a time, but the enemy coalition was not wholly effective, and Hicetas seems to have derived only indirect benefit from it. Later, perhaps in 339, while Timoleon was operating with a small army against Calauria, an unidentified place near the route from Syracuse to Leontini, Hicetas made a fruitful raid into Syracusan territory. As he was returning with his booty, Timoleon pursued him

[20] A fragmentary inscription (Kent, *Corinth* VIII part 3 (1966), no. 23), from a monument erected at Corinth to celebrate the victory, lists contingents forming the Greek army; see also Hansen *CEG* II 809.

leading a force of cavalry and light-armed, which won a decisive victory at the river Lamyrias. The young cavalrymen mainly responsible for this success must have been Syracusan aristocrats and not mercenaries. The mercenaries of Hicetas, of whom some had served under Timoleon at the Crimisus, then mutinied, their loyalty doubtless undermined by propaganda. They delivered Hicetas, his son and his cavalry commander to Timoleon, who had them executed at Leontini. The wives and daughters of Hicetas were tried at Syracuse, and Timoleon receives a rare rebuke from Plutarch for having allowed them to be put to death.

His last pitched battle was fought at the river Abolus, apparently near Catana, against Mamercus, who was defeated and lost more than 2,000 men, many of them mercenaries provided by Carthage. Mamercus suffered an even more crippling blow when the Carthaginians abandoned him and sued for peace. In desperation he tried to enlist the support of the Lucanians, but he was deserted by his own men, who surrendered Catana to Timoleon, though he himself escaped and took refuge with Hippon at Messene.

The Carthaginians had allied with the tyrants to keep Timoleon occupied in eastern Sicily while they restored their authority in the west. This aim they had now fully achieved, and the extent of their recovery is deducible from a clause in their treaty with Timoleon fixing the boundary between the Carthaginian and Greek zones at the river Halycus near Heraclea Minoa. The Carthaginians undertook to withdraw their support from the tyrants and to allow Greeks in their zone to emigrate to Syracuse. A final clause stipulating that all Greek cities should be free refers presumably to cities in the Greek zone and may have been inserted at the insistence of Carthage as a safeguard against any future resurgence of a Syracusan empire. The treaty, concluded perhaps in 338, was a reasonable compromise, which gave an opportunity for economic recovery throughout the island.

Deprived of Carthaginian support, the cause of the tyrants was now doomed. Two minor despots, Nicodemus of Centuripa and Apolloniades of Agyrium, were expelled and immigrants were settled in their territories. The Campanians of Aetna were savagely punished, perhaps for supporting their fellow-countryman Mamercus. Timoleon conducted his last campaign against Hippon at Messene. Since his base was as far away as Mylae, he apparently adopted the same method as against Leontini and Catana, trusting mainly to the growing unpopularity of the tyrant to evoke insurrection. Mamercus somehow contrived a personal surrender on conditions which Timoleon may have violated. He was impeached before the Syracusan assembly and, anticipating condemnation, attempted unsuccessfully to commit suicide. He was then executed by a horrifying method normally reserved for brigands.

Hippon was treated similarly: after trying in vain to escape by sea, he was tortured to death publicly by the Messenians in their theatre.

Timoleon was usually careful to leave the punishment of tyrants to be determined by a public assembly. At the end of his career, however, when he could afford to dispense with their aid, he endeavoured to establish the principle that tyranny was a heinous crime, deserving savage punishment, and that any method of suppressing it, however unscrupulous, was perfectly legitimate. Mamercus was perhaps treated with exceptional ruthlessness as a representative of the Campanians, whose presence in Sicily had long been a major source of its decay.

VI. SOCIAL AND POLITICAL RECONSTRUCTION

The success of Timoleon was not confined to delivering the Siceliots from enemies and oppressors by his able generalship and astute diplomacy. An almost greater achievement was that by his policy of reconstruction he created conditions in which they might again enjoy some degree of security and prosperity. This policy involved programmes of repopulation and political reform.[21]

The upheavals which had plagued Sicily for more than a decade had depleted the populations of Syracuse and other cities. Many Siceliots had been killed, and far more had left their homes through oppression, fear or economic stress. As soon as the liberation of Syracuse was completed, some citizens returned home, but their number was insufficient, and Timoleon at once appealed to Corinth for assistance in remedying the dearth of population. The Corinthians issued a proclamation offering to repatriate Syracusans and other Siceliots resident in the Aegean area. The initial response was disappointing, and the invitation was extended to all Greeks in this area, whatever their provenance might be. To them and to others willing to emigrate to Syracusan territory from elsewhere in Sicily and from Italy plots of land and citizenship of Syracuse were offered. The progress of this scheme was disappointing at first, and success was achieved only after peace with Carthage and the eradication of tyranny had removed the strongest deterrents. Settlers from Greece, including returning exiles, amounted to 10,000, a surprisingly modest figure in view of the prevalent overpopulation there combined with the Macedonian menace. The response of Sicily and Italy was more enthusiastic, and eventually the overall number reached 60,000 according to the contemporary testimony of Athanis (*FGrH* 562 F 2).[22] Some

---

[21] On constitutional matters see now also Manni 1985 (G 224).

[22] This figure has been considered by some scholars to be an exaggeration, but the archaeological evidence attesting the prosperity of Sicily after the death of Timoleon (see below, pp. 719–20) suggests that it may be too low.

immigrants, perhaps a quarter, were settled at a distance from Syracuse in the Symaethus basin and at Camarina. Schemes to attract settlers to Acragas and Gela were independent of the main programme and completed later.

To ensure an equitable distribution of land and property was rendered almost impossible by the circumstances in which the programme was conducted. The population came to be composed of three groups: citizens who had remained in their homes, citizens who had gone away and now returned, and Greeks who had not previously lived at Syracuse. The influx of the second and third groups must have been spread unevenly over a number of years. Plots of land were apparently allocated without payment, but all houses were put up for sale. Since former owners were entitled to buy back houses in which they had lived, they must, except where the houses were in densely built up areas, have been allowed to regain at least some of the adjacent land. Despite efforts to achieve fairness, former citizens were certainly favoured at the expense of newly enfranchised immigrants, who would mostly be poor, and the inequity of the system probably contributed to the class warfare which had developed twenty years later (see *CAH* vii^2.1,384).

No surviving evidence defines precisely the authority whereby Timoleon was empowered to serve as commander-in-chief and to carry out his reconstructive programmes. It is, however, virtually certain that the Syracusan assembly conferred upon him the office of *strategos autokrator*, probably in 343 when the liberation of the city was complete, and that he retained his dictatorial authority until his retirement. That the Corinthians granted him any official status is most improbable. They had no power to nominate him to hold office in the Syracusan state, and their lukewarm attitude towards his expedition at the outset hardly suggests that they appointed him to any office in their own. On his arrival in Sicily he was only a commander of mercenaries, and the widespread distrust of his mission was perfectly reasonable.

He evidently felt that, if liberated Syracuse was to be safeguarded against a recurrence of the recent anarchy, political reform was as urgently needed as repopulation. Both Diodorus and Plutarch credit him with having established a democratic constitution, but the term had come to denote any regime that was not monarchical. Although there is evidence that the popular assembly debated important issues and took decisions, it was not necessarily in effective control of state policy and could have served as a mere facade, as under the tyrants. The political sympathies of Timoleon, as a citizen of oligarchical Corinth, may have lain with oligarchy, and Cephalus and Dionysius, his advisers on constitutional and legal reforms, were both Corinthians. Nevertheless the constitution in operation when he retired was almost certainly a democracy, though belonging to the most moderate type. The only recorded opposition to his policy was voiced by two demagogues.

The principles of moderate democracy rather than those of oligarchy or extreme democracy seem to have determined the method adopted for appointment to the only magistracy on which evidence survives, the Amphipolia of Olympian Zeus. Candidature was restricted to three families, and after one candidate from each family had been selected by vote the final choice was made by lot. The eponymous Amphipolos was nominally political as well as religious head of the state, but he appears to have been little mòre than a figurehead and his duties mainly formal. While the Amphipolia outlived the rest of the constitution by several centuries, no holder of it is known to have been politically influential.[23]

Of other elements in the constitution of Timoleon no trace has survived. After his resignation a board of *strategoi* was presumably elected annually with military and civilian duties, and even earlier a council of some sort was almost certainly instituted. Twenty years later a fervently oligarchical body known as the Six Hundred was involved in violent conflicts with Agathocles and his democratic supporters. This body may initially have been a council recruited by Timoleon mainly from the aristocratic families responsible for the appeal to Corinth. These aristocrats perhaps became increasingly disillusioned when his moderate democracy came to be dominated by incomers, and they may have tried to seize control of the state. Nevertheless, while the Six Hundred at one time ranked as an official council (Diod. xix.5.6; Justin xxii.2.11) before becoming a factional clique (Diod. xix.6.4), this body was not necessarily instituted by Timoleon.

When the liberation of Siceliot cities was completed, Timoleon might have tried to establish a new Syracusan hegemony embracing the entire Greek zone, unless a clause in the treaty with Carthage, as mentioned above, is to be interpreted as specifically precluding any such object. If some Syracusans urged him to adopt an imperialist policy, evading any treaty obligations, he must have resisted their demands. Syracuse controlled the Symaethus basin, where many immigrants to whom citizenship was granted were settled, but Acragas, Gela and Camarina were independent both in his lifetime and twenty years later. It is, however, probable that he maintained a loose alliance of autonomous cities under Syracusan leadership after the menace from tyrants and Carthage was removed.

---

[23] Among the honours paid to Timoleon the Syracusans decreed that, in the event of a war against foreigners, they would appoint a Corinthian as their general. Only one such appointment is recorded.

VII. ECONOMIC RECOVERY

Like most employers of mercenaries, Timoleon suffered acutely from financial embarrassment. His difficulties were not relieved by the liberation of Syracuse because the whole area had become severely impoverished. Spoils from the Crimisus and proceeds from the sale of houses eased the situation somewhat, but when he retired the war against the tyrants had been concluded very recently, and the Siceliot economy was still precarious. He had, however, provided the basic stability upon which prosperity could be rebuilt. Siceliots, and also Sicels, evidently felt some confidence that his peace with Carthage would safeguard them from foreign invasion, while his severity towards the Campanians, who, brought in by the tyrants, had caused so much unrest, must have been widely welcomed. Almost all the evidence for the revival of the Sicilian economy is to be dated after the death of Timoleon, but, once started, progress was rapid. Throughout its chequered history Sicily has often shown a remarkable capacity for recovering quickly from devastation and neglect.[24]

Some light is thrown upon this revival by literary and numismatic evidence. According to Diodorus (XVI.83) the restoration of peace led to an enormous increase in agricultural production, and the sale of the surplus resulted in widespread prosperity. Athens is known to have regularly imported corn from Sicily, especially during a period of famine beginning about 330, and corn and other products were doubtless exported to other parts of mainland Greece, though no information has survived. The evidence of coinage points in the same direction. A very high proportion of the silver coins circulating in Sicily during the half century from about 340 B.C. and found in local hoards bear the emblem of the Corinthian Pegasus. Most of these Pegasi were issued by Corinth and some by Corinthian colonies in north-western Greece, but a mint was established at Syracuse, probably by Timoleon using booty won at the Crimisus, and at a few other Siceliot cities. Although these Pegasi may have been initially coined to provide pay for mercenaries, their abundance in eastern Sicily over a long period does suggest a substantial revival of commercial activity, including the exportation of agricultural produce to the Greek homeland. A feature of Sicilian bronze coinages in the same period is that several small towns minted, apparently for the first time, an indication of independence and perhaps of prosperity.

Another source of information about this economic resurgence has been developed to a remarkable degree by archaeologists in the last

---

[24] What follows draws heavily on Talbert 1974 (G 304); it can be supplemented by reading of *Arch. Rep. for 1981–82* and *1987–88.*

thirty years. The excavation of urban and rural sites, especially in southern Sicily, has revealed a hitherto unsuspected revival of prosperity which appears to belong largely to the half century after the death of Timoleon. Dating tends to be uncertain, and some of the archaeological evidence should perhaps be assigned to a later period, but Gela and Acragas, which had remained unfortified villages since their destruction by Carthage, certainly became once more prosperous and powerful cities at this time. As already noted, each had its population greatly increased by the influx of former citizens and colonists in large numbers, and the success of this programme is abundantly confirmed by recent excavation. Because Gela was abandoned before 280, the construction of a most impressive city wall together with public buildings and large numbers of private houses can certainly be dated within the period after the death of Timoleon. The excavation of small towns and agricultural buildings in the fertile interior north of Gela provides further evidence of renewed prosperity. Another southern city which was resuscitated, though on a modest scale, was Camarina, while Megara Hyblaea, uninhabited for about a century and a half, was now reoccupied. Even Heraclea Minoa, which was in the Carthaginian zone before the peace concluded by Timoleon and was soon to become Carthaginian once more, enjoyed a brief resurgence as a Greek city.

VIII. EPILOGUE

While Timoleon was at Mylae conducting his offensive against Hippon and Mamercus, his eyesight began to fail, and he soon became totally blind. This last campaign completed, he returned to Syracuse and resigned his command. He chose to spend the remainder of his life in Sicily and not in Greece, but he was already an old man, and his death occurred apparently not very long after he retired. The *Timoleon* of Plutarch concludes with an encomium which may be thought somewhat extravagant in tone, but the catalogue of distinctions showered upon him during his retirement and after his death attests the gratitude felt towards him by the Syracusans. Among these distinctions were their practice of consulting him on important issues when he had become a private citizen, the magnificent funeral granted to him culminating in burial in their agora, and finally their decree in his honour 'because by having overthrown the tyrants, defeated the barbarians and repopulated the greatest of Greek cities, he was responsible for the liberation of Siceliots' (Diod.XVI.90.1).

The remarkable achievement of Timoleon is attributed by the literary authorities mainly to providential good fortune. He was perhaps lucky on some occasions, but the record of his mission, if carefully analysed, shows rather that his personal qualities were to a large extent responsible for his success. Among these qualities was his determination in refusing to be deterred from pursuing his aims when the odds against him seemed overwhelming. In the military sphere the boldness of his strategy was based on the conviction that, when his forces were heavily outnumbered, as at Adranum and at the Crimisus, grave risks must be accepted in order to take the enemy by surprise. He must have been an inspiring leader, since he gained, and almost continuously retained, the devoted support of experienced mercenaries, who were not conspicuous for discipline or for loyalty to their commanders, especially if pay tended to be irregular and opportunities for enriching themselves limited. The literary tradition is inclined to slur over setbacks sustained by Timoleon, but its assertion that his troops were less effective when not serving under his personal leadership appears to be authentic. It was, however, his astuteness in the field of diplomacy, perhaps more appropriately termed intrigue, that contributed most to his success. In seeking to liberate Greek Sicily from domination by military adventurers he did not hesitate to adopt their ruthless methods and indeed showed himself to be as unscrupulous as any of them. His ultimate accomplishment in eradicating them was the outcome of a policy designed to weaken and isolate them which he conducted for several years with masterly skill. As a political leader, he won the hearts of most Syracusans, and though his political settlement lasted only two decades, it provided a welcome respite from internal strife and was probably as effective as any that could have been devised in the prevailing circumstances. The contemptuous verdict of Polybius on his career in Sicily is amply refuted by the recently discovered archaeological evidence of renewed prosperity.

The situation in Sicily in 344 was not an exact replica of that in 357, so that the problems experienced by Timoleon differed somewhat from those experienced by Dion. Nevertheless the similarity between the backgrounds to the two enterprises is sufficiently close to prompt the question why Timoleon produced at least a temporary remedy for the troubles of Greek Sicily, whereas Dion was almost wholly unsuccessful. In 344 Dionysius was much weaker than he had been in 357, especially after his defeat by Hicetas, but in the intervening period political and economic disintegration had accelerated and become more widespread, many cities had been seized by military adventurers, and a resumption of Carthaginian intervention after a long interval had become imminent. While Timoleon initially had to contend with the distrust felt towards emissaries from the Greek homeland, he apparently enjoyed an advantage over Dion in not being a Siceliot and certainly in having no links with the Syracusan tyrant house, so that he was far less vulnerable to charges of seeking a tyranny for himself. Yet the fundamental reason for the disparity between the ultimate fortunes of the two leaders is to be found in the disparity between their personalities. In the turmoil of fourth-century Sicily Dion was handicapped both by the rigidity of his principles and by his unapproachability. Timoleon was much better equipped to solve the problems arising from such conditions by his capacity for improvisation and intrigue and by his sympathetic understanding of human nature.

CHAPTER 14

MACEDON AND NORTH-WEST GREECE

J. R. ELLIS

I. THE MACEDONIAN BACKGROUND

Macedonia had been by the middle of the fifth century a large and populous country:

. . . of Lower Macedonia the ruler was Perdiccas. The Macedonians however also encompass Lyncestae, Elimiotae and other upland tribes which, though allied and subject to them, have kings of their own. The coastal part of the country, known as Macedonia, was first won by Perdiccas' father Alexander and his forebears, originally Temenids from Argos. They became sovereign over the land by defeating and expelling the Pierians . . . and the Bottiaeans and they acquired the narrow strip of Paeonian territory [Amphaxitis] running along the River Axius from inland to Pella and the sea; beyond the Axius they hold the area of Mygdonia as far as the Strymon . . . From the district now known as Eordaea they expelled the Eordaeans . . . and from Almopia the Almopians. These Macedonians also mastered, and still hold, a number of areas once belonging to other tribes: Anthemus, Crestonia, Bisaltia . . . The whole is now called Macedonia, and Perdiccas, son of Alexander, was its king [in 429/8].

Thucydides' summary (II. 99) well describes the kingdom at the death of Alexander I and during Perdiccas II's reign (c. 454–413).

Topographically Lower Macedonia might be described as a three-quarter circle centred approximately on the head of the Thermaic Gulf, which bites a substantial segment from its south-eastern quarter.[1]

The main continuous source for the period 360–336 is Diodorus XVI, which provides, despite many chronological problems, at least a spare framework. Justin (VII-IX) offers a highly abbreviated account characterized by misunderstanding, inaccuracy and rhetoric. A number of fragments survive from lost fourth-century historians, especially Theopompus of Chios (*FGrH* 115), Ephorus of Cumae (*FGrH* 70) and Philochorus of Athens (*FGrH* 328). The speeches of Demosthenes and Aeschines and the later writings of Isocrates provide often detailed supplementation. Contemporary inscriptions, though mostly from Athens and Delphi, have survived in reasonable number, and the volume of archaeological evidence continues to increase – particularly, over the last few years as well as in prospect, for the Macedonian kingdom. Three of Plutarch's biographies (*Phocion, Demosthenes* and *Alexander*) preserve a good deal of information, some going back to contemporary sources. On the whole, though, there are very many gaps. Three treatments of Philip's reign have appeared recently: Ellis 1976 (D 80) Cawkwell 1978 (D 73) and Hammond and Griffith 1979 (D 50). These deal more or less comprehensively with the material treated here in Chapters 14 and 15.

[1] The image is from Edson 1970 (D 27) p.19.

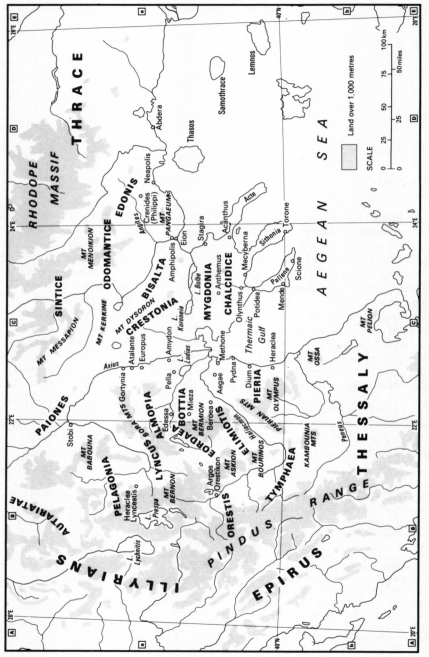

Map 16. Macedonia and Chalcidice.

Framing the alluvial coastal plain is an intermittent circuit of higher land and mountains, behind which a second and concentric ring of smaller plains is broken and confined by taller, more impenetrable ranges. Before Philip II's reign (360–336) much of the eastern half of the outer circle, dominated by the spacious but marshy Strymonic plain, was not within Macedonian control; but its western half, mostly smaller plains 600 metres or so above sea-level and often separated as much from each other as from the foreign tribal areas beyond the mountain-ranges, was Upper Macedonia.

A great diversity of resources abounded in this large region, fertile plains and rich forests, a variety of livestock in horses, cattle, sheep and goats, and a wealth of minerals in copper, iron, silver and gold. The area was self-sufficient, virtually or wholly independent of foreign trade, though of considerable interest to foreign traders, above all for its exceptionally good shipbuilding timber. Yet until Philip's reign such abundance did not produce a strong, stable kingdom. Only implied by Thucydides' sketch, but essential to the Macedonian background, is the gulf between the western highlanders of Upper Macedonia and the inhabitants of Lower Macedonia. The coastal plain was the kingdom's heartland, its people (no longer the pastoralists who had first overrun the lowlands from the mountains above the Pierian plain) exploiting the fertile soil, the alluvium of its great rivers. Like all cultivators they were more settled and therefore more vulnerable, more easily subject to central rule. The rugged uplands and their plains, by contrast, were cut off from the sea's moderation, the communities, with their grazing herds of goats and sheep, driven by harsh winters down from the mountain slopes into the protection of the valleys. Of necessity more self-reliant, hardier and less open to outside influences, the Upper Macedonians traditionally stood apart from their lowland relatives. The internal history of the kingdom between the invasion of Xerxes, when the uplands were first nominally annexed by Alexander I, and their final annexation by Philip II is, so far as it can be recovered, in large part shaped by this fundamental cleavage. Successive Macedonian rulers strove to make or keep the highland tribes subject; the local princes in their highland enclaves fiercely resisted. The tensions so generated both consumed much Macedonian energy and laid the kingdom open to those outsiders prepared to exploit division to their own ends. Such underlay, for example, much of the documented series of interventions by Peloponnesian and Athenian forces just before and during the Peloponnesian War, when Perdiccas and later Archelaus (c. 413–399) were at least periodically at odds with the monarchies of Elimea, Lyncus and perhaps others. Similar signs of divisiveness appear in the early fourth century, exacerbated by and probably contributing to the dynastic difficulties that followed the deaths of Archelaus and his young successor Orestes in the early 390s.

In its pre-Philippic days Macedonia was at its greatest in the reign of Archelaus, a time of consolidation of the territorial gains of earlier generations. It was Archelaus who removed the seat of the monarchy from the old capital, Aegae (at modern Vergina), to marshy Pella on the northern shore of Lake Ludias (at that time actually a northwestwards extension of the gulf). Here, despite the summer's steamy heat, was a better location, well placed in the lowland plain, remarkably close, as a modern map shows, to the centrepoint of the whole of the great circle of Macedonia. Two Greek colonies on the Pierian coast (Pydna and Methone) lay dangerously close to the old capital, which may help to account for the transfer. Yet Aegae retained many of its special associations in religion and tradition. There many royal and sacred occasions were celebrated. There the kings were buried. Recent excavations have confirmed its location, revealed several royal tombs and given promise of much greater knowledge and understanding of the classical Macedonians and their kingship and culture. The elevation of Pella, within a generation of its foundation the largest of Macedonian cities (Xen. *Hell.* v.2.13), seems to have been part of a reorganization of the national administrative structure, a necessary task in view of the piecemeal acquisition over several generations of the territory and peoples between the central plain and the Strymon, to the east, and of the nearer parts of Upper Macedonia in the west. Lower Macedonia and the newer eastern territories were organized into a series of districts named after, dominated by and administered from central towns (such as Pella, Aegae, Beroea, Alcomenae, Aloris: Arr. *Indike* 17). They served as recruitment zones for the army, and Archelaus improved communications with them by roadbuilding and erected fortresses at strategic points, especially, it is presumed, in the Axius valley, then as now the main avenue of access into Macedonia from the north. Though the details are uncertain, this king also made some changes and improvements to the military forces (Thuc. II.100); significant enough to catch Thucydides' attention (in the mid-390s), they seem not to have survived the difficult decades that followed. During that time and until Philip's reforms the cavalry seems, as before, to have been the only effective military unit. The Macedonian defences on the whole remained weak.

The reign of Amyntas III, though lengthy (393–369), was far from stable. This was the time when first the Olynthus-dominated Chalcidian League and then Athens' new alliance gained strength as Sparta's post-war expansionism wilted. At the same time, far northern population movements were transmitting unrest through the Balkans: under the strong leadership of Bardylis the Dardanian Illyrians looked increasingly southwards for living-space (see ch. 9*d*, pp. 428–9). Macedonia, squeezed by the two pressures, sought accommodation where possible, depending usually on concession and submission for survival. Amyntas' sons Alexander II (369–366) and Perdiccas III (365–360), and the intervening regent Ptolemy (368–365), faced similar problems, particularly as the resurgence of Athenian ambitions focused particularly on the recovery of Amphipolis, just beyond Macedonia's eastern frontier. Later in his reign Perdiccas, banking on the poor relations between Athens and the Chalcidic League, turned against the Athenians, lending troops to Amphipolis for its defence. Then he marched, too confidently, into the northwestern mountains to do battle with Bardylis, to whom his predecessors had paid tribute for three decades (Diod. XVI.2.2). The Macedonian army was overwhelmingly defeated. The king and 4,000 of his men were killed. The Illyrians prepared to push downwards into Macedonia and, further east, on the upper Axius, Paeonian tribesmen began to pillage Macedonian settlements. The Thracian king Cotys lent support to a pretender to the throne, one Pausanias. The Athenians pinned their hopes on the candidacy of Argaeus, who in the late 380s had ruled for two years, with Amyntas III in exile, as puppet of the Olynthians. Such was the heritage of Philip II (Diod. XVI.2.4–6).

II. MACEDONIAN SOCIETY

Macedonian society was anomalous by the more familiar Athenian standards, sharing many traditions and institutions with the Upper Macedonian princedoms and their neighbours on both sides of the Pindus range and with the non-Greek tribes to the east, north and north-west. The Makedones proper, the warrior males, retained in many ways the style of the small, tight-knit group they had once been, before their expansion from the seventh century onwards. This not only made them backward (hence 'barbarian') in the eyes of some Greek sophisticates but produced anomalies in the structures of a populous society now occupying an extensive area. The traditional intimacy would be further strained and would eventually break down under the massive enlargement of the kingdom and its subject territories under Philip and especially Alexander the Great (336–323).

From the earliest times until the death of Alexander IV (311 B.C.) all kings were of the Temenid family, ruling house of the dominant Argead clan, tracing their ancestry back through the Argive hero-king Temenus to Heracles (Hdt. v.20, 22, Thuc. II.99.3, v.80.2). The king stood in a close and rather informal relationship with his people (in practice, mostly, with the adult males; that is with his warriors) as the expression and 'delegate' of their religious, social and military cohesion. It was not unlike (and was perhaps precisely) what Thucydides had in mind when writing of the archaic 'hereditary kingships based on defined prerogatives' (1.13.1; cf. Arr. *Anab.* IV.11.6), here as elsewhere in his *Archaeology* (e.g., 1.6.1–2) reconstructing the past from contemporary survivals. The Makedones were a warrior people, their leader a warrior king; they served, other than in exceptional circumstances, under his direct command. The expression of the popular voice, however limited, was the military assembly; by tradition it was 'the Makedones' and in practice that could hardly be otherwise. Although its vote might be canvassed in a poll of the popular will, the army enjoyed, so far as we know, but two formal rights.[2] It elected the king by acclamation (and *very* occasionally deposed him) and it investigated cases of treason, the two matters in which the state was more obviously vulnerable in the very person of its head. In practice in the former the choice of the 'Macedonians under arms' was in most cases uncontroversial, given an evident traditional preference for the firstborn son; in the latter the king's advantages, as at once plaintiff, commander-in-chief of the jurors and high priest, no doubt usually ensured the verdict he wished. (Curt. VI.8.25 puts it formally.) Despite the qualifications, the theoretical limitations on the king well represented the kind of relationship existing between ruler and ruled. Closest to the king were his councillors, or 'Companions' (*hetairoi*), those who fought alongside him on horseback. In that he alone selected them, they were perhaps not wholly a hereditary nobility; yet since we know of nothing to suggest that the status of the traditional nobility might lapse or that sons were not raised to their fathers' standing, the term is not seriously inappropriate. From them he took advice and selected his officers and administrators. They accompanied him, apparently by law but at any rate by custom (Curt. VIII.1–18), on the hunt and, by right, on formal and ceremonial occasions. Their sons, at least with the institution of the Royal Pages (firmly attributed to Philip by Arrian *Anab.* IV.13.1),[3] were educated with his. They and their families occupied large estates, the gifts of the king.

Outside this class were the ordinary Macedonian soldier citizens, who served when required in the infantry. They were smaller landholders and it was important to avoid placing too many and heavy demands on them; for this reason it must have been much more difficult to assemble them. Presumably since the earliest days they could never have met *en masse*, even when assemblies were called on matters of importance. But they

---

[2] The question of the army's (or the people's) rights has long been contentious. The extreme positive position is represented, and was first advanced by, Granier 1931 (D 39), the negative, for example, by Lock 1977 (D 210), for the sources and literature. The most comprehensive discussion is by Briant 1973 (D 22) 237–350. And see now Anson 1985, (D 8).

[3] The attribution has been challenged (Hammond and Griffith 1979 (D 50) 168 and n.1) on – in the present author's view – insufficient grounds.

would be represented by those actually in military attendance on the king. Finally, since large numbers of men could be called upon, sometimes for extended service, it is apparent that there must have been a labouring class, probably composed of the indigenous populations subsumed during the kingdom's growth. In the military context it played a role too in the groomsmen, servants, drivers, labourers and so on. If somewhat lesser, possibly, than full citizens, such people seem not to have been as lowly as Athenian slaves; they were somewhat akin, perhaps, to Thessalian *penestai*.

The society was hardy, tough and male-dominant. The citizens of any Greek polis counted military service among their civic obligations, but here the nexus between citizenship and arms-bearing was especially close, a function of the traditionally tight relationship between king-commander and followers. Although by the fifth and fourth centuries most Lower Macedonians were dependent on agriculture, in some places hunting still formed a part of the economy, as it did generally in Upper Macedonia. The hunt also retained its social role in the training of the young for manhood and in the relaxation of the warriors. The man, it was said, who had not killed his first boar must sit at table instead of reclining (Ath. 1.18a), as in early times the horseman who had not slain his first enemy must wear his halter for a belt (Arist. *Pol.* VII.2,1324b 15–17). Feasting with male companions and courtesans was a common pastime; the drinking of mead, beer and especially unmixed wine could be heavy, as more squeamish outsiders liked to point out (Dem. II.18–19, *FGrH* 115 Theopomp. F 81, 224, 225, 236). The society was deeply religious, as is seen not only in the range of Greek and more ecstatic Thracian cults but at least as much in the rigorous care given on campaign to ritual sacrifice. In all of this the king was a man among men, standing higher than others in that his sacred, judicial and military responsibilities were paramount, yet entering with them, especially with his Companions, into the pursuits of war, public life and leisure.

It is too easy to be seduced by sophisticated authors into the view that the Macedonians were no more than illiterates from the backwoods. Some were, no doubt, as were some Attic peasants, and undoubtedly the proportion was much higher. But traditionally the ruling family and its closer retainers had fostered contacts with the learning and art of elsewhere in Greece. Names like Euripides, Agathon, Zeuxis, Timotheus of Miletus, Callistratus of Aphidna, Euphraeus of Oreus, the Cretan Nearchus, Theopompus and Aristotle himself emerge fitfully from the obscurity of the kingdom's internal history. Royal princes were – to judge by Alexander – educated in the best regarded of Greek culture; and, at least from the institution by Philip of the Royal Pages, selected sons of the Companions shared in this. Men of the calibre of Antipater,

Philip's leading administrator and diplomat, author of a (lost) history of Perdiccas III's Illyrian wars and close friend and correspondent of Aristotle, could be produced by the court. The degree to which general Hellenic culture pervaded other levels of society seems high, though certainty is difficult,[4] but the spate of recent discoveries of Macedonian tombs is likely to make some answers possible.

III. PHILIP'S EARLY REIGN, 360–357 B.C.

With Perdiccas dead there was only one practical course open to the army. A son, Amyntas, was a mere child. The surviving brother, Philip, last of Amyntas III's three sons by Eurydice, was acclaimed, but whether as king or as regent is disputed.[5] Almost all evidence points to that smooth continuity one imagines was earnestly desired by the embattled Macedonians in late 360 B.C.[6] One author (Justin v.7.9–19) mentions a regency, but no other source, directly or by inference, offers the slightest support. Quite possibly, as is common enough in Justin, this is some kind of embroidery on a misunderstanding; the subject must have been discussed, but apparently nothing more.

Philip was by this time twenty-two or twenty-three years old (b. 383 or 382). In his teenage, either in the reign of his brother Alexander or in the regency of the Alorite Ptolemaeus, he had been turned over as hostage with other young Macedonians to Thebes' general Pelopidas and remained in Thebes for two or three years. (The evidence is confusing and ultimately inscrutable; its main effect has been to license ancient and modern speculation over unconfirmable friendships and influences.) After his return we hear only that he held some kind of estate during Perdiccas' reign (Ath. XI. 506 ef, 508 de, Pl. *Ep.* v, Speus. *Ep.* XII), perhaps entailing a junior or local command. Whether other claimants to the throne were formally considered at the time of Philip's accession is uncertain. There were rivals, Pausanias and Argaeus, from collateral branches of the dynasty, but their claims relied upon force. Three 'half-brothers' of Philip, the sons of Amyntas by another wife, Gygaea, were on the scene but, if claimants, were passed over without strain. (A few years later the eldest, Archelaus, was executed and the others fled,

---

[4] The evidence for the language of the Macedonians has been reviewed and discussed recently by Kalleris 1954, 1976 (D 54) and Hammond and Griffith 1979 (D 50) 43–54, both contending that it was a dialect of Greek, a view now opposed by Badian 1982 (D 12). The increasing volume of surviving public and private inscriptions makes it quite clear that there was no written language but Greek. There may be room for argument over spoken forms, or at least over local survivals of earlier occupancy, but it is hard to imagine what kind of authority might sustain that. There is no evidence for a different 'Macedonian' language that cannot be as easily explained in terms of dialect or accent.

[5] For a detailed defence of the regency see Prestianni Giallombardo 1973/4 (D 113); cf. Ellis 1971 (D 28) and Hammond and Griffith 1979 (D 50) 208–9, 702–3.

[6] For the dates of Philip's accession and death see Hatzopoulos 1982 (D 95).

finding refuge at Olynthus when Chalcidic relations with Macedon were breaking down, probably in 350 or 349.[7] What this implies for their birth and status may only be surmised. Had Gygaea's marriage antedated Eurydice's in the late 390s – likely on the face of it, for Amyntas was into his forties by 390 – then at least one of her sons ought probably to have succeeded before at least one of Eurydice's, but did not. However, if we retreat to the position that Gygaea was married later, her sons born, say, in the 370s and therefore too young for consideration in 360, we might also provide a plausible framework for the fraternal rift of the later 350s, when the young men were passing into adulthood.)

In the weeks after the Macedonians' crushing defeat by the Illyrians, with usable manpower seriously depleted and morale at its lowest, Philip's army was of little use. Apart from its reconstruction, there were two immediate necessities. First, some priority had to be found in dealing with many demands. Second, with throne, frontiers and sovereignty all under challenge, Macedonia had an insistent need of friends. The last years of Perdiccas' reign had left her with few, and that, together with his great defeat, had exposed her to the hostility of all.

Philip's first months were thus taken up with a flurry of morale raising and diplomacy (Diod. XVI.3). His success against such odds offered a striking foretaste of the dominant methods and the remarkable achievements of his reign. Within a very short time he was in contact with Cotys, in Thrace, who withdrew his support from Pausanias. Almost simultaneously he negotiated a peace with the victorious Dardanian king,[8] presumably at the price of at least the cession of part of Upper Macedonia. No evidence remains of such a treaty, only of an imprecisely dated marriage to Philip of Bardylis' daughter or niece, Audata: but how otherwise to explain the sudden suspension of the Illyrian conflict, which, despite the tribesmen's earlier impetus, was not resumed for a year or more – and then on Philip's initiative? It cannot have been an honourable peace; this was a Macedonia, it could be said, 'enslaved to the Illyrians' (Diod. XVI.1.3). The Paeonian marauders too were held back by negotiation and bribery. The troops lent by Perdiccas to Amphipolis were recalled now or soon afterwards. No doubt they were required at home, but there was in any case no profit in continuing to antagonize the Athenians needlessly. Philip let it be known that he wished to be Athens' friend.

Time and energy, over the autumn and winter of 360/59, went into beginning the healing of Macedonia's wounds. Diodorus (XVI.3), in a relatively detailed account probably from the contemporary writer

[7] Discussed by Ellis 1973 (D 79) and Hammond and Griffith 1979 (D 50) 699–701.

[8] See Ellis 1976 (D 80) 47–8. A more cautious view is advanced by Hammond and Griffith 1979 (D 50) 211.

Ephorus, mentions a succession of assemblies exhorted by the king, constant military training and drilling and certain changes to the military organization (see below, pp. 734–36).

The first use of the army was in a skirmish during the following spring (359) when the pretender Argaeus made his bid for power, with equivocal support from 3,000 Athenian hoplites under Mantias' command. Most Athenians went no further than the landing-point, Methone, while the pretender, with his mercenaries, fellow exiles and some Athenian volunteers, tramped the fifteen or so kilometres to Aegae in an attempt to bring out the old capital in revolt. He was rebuffed and, on his retreat to the coast, caught and defeated by royal troops. Acknowledging the implications of Athens' restraint, Philip ordered her captured citizens to be released without ransom and with compensation for their losses.

There remained no obstacle in the way of Athenian and Macedonian concord. Such damage as Perdiccas had inflicted by his support for Amphipolitan independence Philip had already neutralized. Now he had demonstrated that he was in effective control of the kingdom. For the Athenians there was in fact an alternative: Olynthian envoys, apparently in a rival bid, arrived in the city asking for alliance on behalf of the Chalcidic League. But a decade of exceptionally bad relations with Olynthus combined with the new prospects for Amphipolis to win over the Athenian Assembly. Of the terms of the alliance we know little. The one datum laying serious claim to substance (Dem. 11.6) is too compressed to be comprehensible, if not too prejudiced to be believed, beyond the implication that Amphipolis was a central matter discussed, whether or not the subject of formal covenant.[9] It was not Philip's to give and probably Athens required of him little if anything more than an affirmation that Amphipolis was independent of the Macedonian kingdom.

Under the umbrella of Athens' friendship, which should keep at least the Olynthians in check, Philip turned to unfinished business. Since their earlier contact, Cotys had died, his kingdom by now partitioned among three successors. In (probably) the summer of 359 Philip led his forces northwards against the Paeonian tribesmen, whose king Agis had also just died, in and around the upper Axius valley. Less organized than the Illyrians of Bardylis they were a useful training target. Macedonia's victory was followed up, now and in succeeding years, by the foundation of a string of military fortresses along the passageway of the Axius.

Either later in 359 or possibly early in 358 the more difficult enemy was confronted. Bardylis' victory of a year or so earlier had given the Illyrians control of much of at least the more northerly of Upper

---

[9] See de Ste Croix 1963 (c 246).

Macedonia's valleys. But he was a very old man, his judgment apparently defective. Perceiving Philip's preparations and realizing that a levy of 10,000 foot and 600 horse meant serious danger, he could nevertheless bring himself to offer nothing more realistic than that each side keep what it then held. The battle was fought near Heraclea Lyncestis in the Erigon valley. A few particulars survive, indicating that, for the first time ever (to our knowledge), the Macedonian infantry played an important role, aided by storm tactics on the flanks by the cavalry (see ch. 9d, pp. 436–7).

Much more significant than the battle itself was the access it gave to Upper Macedonia. The Illyrians were pushed back and further territory annexed as far as Lake Lychnitis. Then inside that more defensible frontier Philip began the tasks of disentangling the mixed stock of peoples in those parts of the uplands, which had been subject for decades to Illyrian incursion, and of consolidating and fortifying the old and new Macedonian areas. The process must have been lengthy, involving attitudes as much as controls, but, given its urgency, probably a considerable start was made in 358 and 357. Details must largely be extrapolated from snippets of evidence relating to Macedonian border peoples at other times in the reign. Marriage-alliance may have played a part: it may be now that we are to date Philip's marriage to Phila, a princess of the Elimiote royal house (although this may antedate his accession). The resettlement, or 'transplantation', of favourable or unfavourable population groups so as to enhance support or neutralize opposition, a feature of his activities elsewhere, was probably effected here. The local monarchies were presumably dissolved at this time, but many of their leading figures became Companions of Philip. Fortified towns were established in the small highland valleys and populations manipulated and fortresses built along the frontiers themselves (Arr. *Anab.* VII.9). Necessary for the security of the highlands against foreign penetration, such foundations served too as a basis for internal control. In the longer run positive measures counted for more, especially the expansion of the army and the successful inculcation into it of national ideals and aspirations, Philip's massive enlargement of the noble *hetairos* class and his creation of the Royal Pages from sons of the old and new nobility. For seventy years from this time there is no known resurgence of the old highland particularism or of the past cleavage between Upper and Lower Macedonia.

It is unlikely to be fortuitous that the first steps in two relationships that would serve Macedonia long and well, and were of immediate relevance to the settlement of Upper Macedonia, were taken in those years. In 358 the king responded to an appeal from the Aleuadae of Larissa, the dominant noble family of the leading city of the Thessalian

League, for assistance against the tyrant of Pherae. With difficulties of his own and limited in what he could provide, he could nevertheless not overlook Thessaly's importance for the southerly land approaches to the kingdom. His marriage to Philinna, a daughter of the Aleuadae, marked the beginning of a close involvement with Thessaly.[10] What aid he gave is not known. In the following year he married Olympias, a princess of the dominant Molossian tribe in Epirus. The victory over Bardylis made him an attractive ally to the Epirotes, who too had suffered at the Illyrians' hands, and his recent alignment with Athens neatly complemented a long-standing Epirote link with her. For Philip the new ally provided useful support beyond the Pindus range. Moreover, it was most likely now that Orestis, which had moved into the league of Molossian tribes probably a decade ago, rejoined the Macedonian kingdom by amicable agreement between Philip and the Molossian king Arybbas, Olympias' uncle. Both alliances, each strengthened by intermarriage, seem closely related to the final annexation of Upper Macedonia.

By now Philip had married four women, Audata, Phila, Philinna and Olympias (see ch. 9d, pp. 437–8). Their status before marriage varied, but this will not have governed their position in the king's household, where they were all his wives. What did matter was whether they bore children for their husband and master, daughters to serve the same diplomatic function as their mothers, sons to guarantee the family's continuity. Bearing the eldest son could alone elevate one wife above the others; and even that might not have counted for a great amount until that son himself became king. It is evident that Philinna's son Arrhidaeus may have been older than Olympias', Alexander, born in 356. If so, since Arrhidaeus proved to be mentally defective, Alexander was regarded and treated, as far back as we can trace, as heir to his father.

IV. THE MACEDONIAN ARMY

Both the recent military success and Philip's growing appeal as an ally may be attributed largely to the army itself.[11] Our major source for the early reign (Diod. XVI.2–4) lays overmuch emphasis on the first weeks and months of what can only have been a gradual and lengthy process of innovation and training. None the less, much that went further than inspiration and encouragement was achieved early on, as the total defeat of the Dardanians indicates. Of all innovations the most significant, and gradual, was simply expansion. The levy of 10,000 foot and 600 horse in 359 (Diod. XVI.4.3) was certainly the maximum in the circumstances;

[10] No intervention at this time is documented. See Ehrhardt 1967 (D 77) and Griffith 1970 (D 91).
[11] The best general treatment of the army is now Hammond and Griffith 1979 (D 50) 405–49.

twenty-four years later, figures above 30,000 + 4,000 (Diod. XVII.17) were possible. The annexations of 358 and succeeding years will not alone account for the difference, nor for the greatly improved ratio of cavalry to infantry. Natural population increase during a reign that brought unprecedented security; rising prosperity as a further consequence, with a higher proportion of citizens able to afford arms and equipment; land grants from the conquered territories, made certainly to those of Companion status and apparently to those below it; such factors must have been critical. The Macedonian infantry soldier, too, more closely akin to the Thracian peltast, faced relatively less expense than the hoplite in fitting himself out: his shield was appreciably smaller and he wore no costly breastplate.

The organization and characteristics of Philip's military innovations have been discussed above.[12] What is of interest to us here is that he offered inducements for advancement to his troops on every level. An infantryman of the line by outstanding service might win a place among the Foot-Companions, so embarking on a virtually professional career and receiving a salary raised above that of his erstwhile colleagues in the *ad hoc* levies. Such appellations as 'double pay men' and '10 stater (= 40 drachmae) men' point to other kinds of inducement. Not long after Philip's death the rate for a Foot-Companion (called Hypaspist by then?) was 30 drachmae per month (Tod no. 183 = *IG* II[2] 239 = Harding no. 102); the ordinary phalangite perhaps earned 25. There were of course the normal attractions of promotion. Basically, six company commanders (*lochagoi*) stood above probably ninety-six decadarchs in each battalion, and the range of other rank nomenclature suggests a variety of opportunities for advancement. Similar inducements presumably operated within the heavy cavalry and the more lightly armed *sarissophoroi* ('spear-bearers'), or *prodromoi* ('scouts'), though evidence is lacking. Whether advancement was possible into the elect Companion Cavalry, where nobility was a complicating qualification, is not quite certain; yet under Philip Companion status did not remain exclusive, for one contemporary (Theopomp. F 224) points out that it was held by Thessalians and other Greeks as well as by Macedonians. Even that, it seems, was attainable through merit. With it went the royal grant of estates from the conquered territories.

The rewards of service were thus considerable, necessarily so in view of the heavy training in weaponry and manoeuvre required of the Macedonians. It was the rigour of this training, along with relatively simple improvements in its armoury, that lifted the Macedonian army above all its contemporaries. The stern regime, shared by the king himself, helped create a powerful unit bound by close personal allegiance

[12] See above, ch. 12e. pp.686–8.

to the leader, who, unless the forces were divided, always took command, and from the front. Constant drilling made it efficient and manoeuvrable and allowed single elements to act independently where circumstances dictated.

This was a versatile army, made even more so by the use of lighter infantry, peltasts, javelin-men, slingers and archers, some of them poorer Macedonians, others levied or hired from allied and other states where such units were specialties. Complementing the whole, at least from the late 350s onwards, was an increasingly important department, the engineers. This corps was responsible for a good deal of development during Philip's reign in siege machinery and torsion artillery.

V. THE SOCIAL WAR AND ITS CONSEQUENCES, 357–355 B.C.

The Odrysian kingdom was at this time governed by three kings: Berisades in the area west of the Nestus and adjacent to Macedonia, Amadocus in central Thrace and Cersobleptes east of the Hebrus. In summer 357 Athens, her allies restless and her finances tightly stretched, made alliance with all three (Tod no. 151 = Harding no. 64), in the hope of containing, with their assistance, the spread of rebellion in the Hellespont and Black Sea region. There Byzantium's influence was strong and Athens' corn route was at its most vulnerable. But it was too late. Revolt broke out and Athens went to war.[13] For Macedon, which depended on her for protection, the dilemma was serious. For two years or so Philip had been able to concentrate on his highland territories and inland frontiers behind the shelter, on his Aegean-side, of the Athenian alliance. With that at risk he was obliged to reconsider. It will not have occurred to him to stand alone; no Macedonian foreign policy could promise safety which did not reckon with either Athens or the Chalcidic League. In the late autumn or winter he made the decision to switch allies. Bringing up siege-engines he invested Amphipolis and quickly took it.

In the captured city a decree was immediately passed exiling Philip's opponents (Tod no. 150 = Harding no. 63). Probably not very many were affected, since the Attic element had never been especially large and decades of resistance to Athens cannot have left many of her partisans untouched. Undue harshness in any case would likely frighten the Chalcidic cities. In Athens war was declared but the demands of the Social War gave her no opportunity to act. Philip then seized Pydna, a city close to the Pierian coast and long semi-independent of the kingdom.

Some were alarmed. In western Thrace Berisades and his sons, who

[13] The main source for the Social War is Diod. XVI.7.21–2.

succeeded him on his death at about this time, feared the consequences for their own territory in the Amphipolitan region. Grabus, an Illyrian king, perhaps of the Grabaei, began negotiating with Olynthus, probably offering to re-establish the Chalcidic link with the silver mines of Damastium near Lake Lychnitis, severed by Philip's recent annexation of the area. But Philip was ready to bid high for Olynthus' friendship. He undertook to cede his Chalcidic frontier territory Anthemus to the league and to help coerce Potidaea (nominally independent but since 361 an Athenian cleruchy) back into membership. Attractive too were the prospects of profit for the Chalcidic trading cities from Macedonia's large natural resources. As early as 360 or 359 Philip had ordered his mint at Pella to abandon the 'Persic' standard, on which Macedonian coins had been struck since Archelaus' reign, and to employ instead the standard (now called 'Thraco-Macedonian') in use among the Chalcidic towns. Olynthian dealings with Grabus were terminated and a treaty with Philip signed (Tod no. 158 = Harding no. 67, Diod. XVI.8.3ff, Dem. II.6ff, VI.20, XXIII.107f, Libanius *Hypothesis* to Dem. I).

For the king, with Athens still preoccupied, it was possible to proceed further with the strengthening of Macedonia's defences. At this time Cersobleptes, of eastern Thrace, seeking eventually, so it was thought, to reunite Cotys' kingdom under his own rule, advanced on Crenides, a small but attractive cluster of mining settlements in western Thrace only 15 kilometres from the Athenian ally Neapolis. The Crenideans appealed to Philip, who drove Cersobleptes back, drew the settlements into one town and heavily fortified it. Under a new name, Philippi, the foundation took in a number of Macedonian settlers. This was the first of the long series of colonies founded by Philip and Alexander the Great. The area of Amphipolis and Philippi, containing the gold and silver mines of Mt Pangaeum, was a prolific source of revenue (producing, with more effective mining and processing, state royalties of 1,000 talents annually) and an ideal Macedonian outpost in this region, within a short distance of the sea but not directly exposed to naval attack. The marshy Angites valley, at whose head Philippi stood, was drained, its forests cleared and the soil tilled. The new colony, which continued to issue coinage under its own name until the early 320s, became and remained a Macedonian showpiece, retaining something of its original colonial status long after the surrounding parts of western Thrace were attached to Macedonia in the 340s. Why it was not simply annexed can only be guessed: at the outset, probably, because Philip did not wish to alarm his new allies. In any case it served, along with the Chalcidic, Thessalian and Epirote alliances, as one of the series of breakwaters beyond the existing frontiers.

There were repercussions close at hand. Cetriporis in western Thrace found allies in the Illyrian Grabus and in Lyppeius, the Paionian successor to King Agis, who were joined – mainly as declaration of intent, since she could scarcely honour such a commitment – by Athens (Tod no. 157). The three kings prepared to concert their forces against Macedonia. Again Philip moved swiftly, dividing his army and striking or deterring the allies before they could organize. Immediately he marched on Potidaea in fulfilment of his promise to the Chalcidians, investing the city in about July 356. The timing – this was the first of many occasions on which it would be demonstrated – was carefully managed: the Etesian Wind was by now blowing strongly from the north and aid from Athens, finally stung to action, arrived too late. Potidaea capitulated in the autumn. According to Plutarch (*Alex*. 3), just afterwards word reached Philip of three successes, Parmenion's victory over Grabus, the triumph of Philip's horse in competition at the Olympic festival and the birth of a son, Alexander, by his new Molossian wife, Olympias. There must be some licence here, since the birth is dated to July 356 and the Olympia was held in August or September, but the preceding twelve months, since the decision to align Macedonia with the Chalcidic League, had indeed been fruitful in every way. As the Macedonian year ended (*c*. October) the Athenian cleruchs at Potidaea were released without penalty or ransom (Diod. XVI.8.5), perhaps as a token for the future, for Athens' Social War would not last for ever and no one could tell, at that point, in what condition she would emerge from it. The Potidaeans themselves were sold into slavery by their Macedonian and Chalcidic conquerors and the town and district taken over by the league.

The next year (355) saw further consolidation of the Macedonian-eastern frontier. Between the mouths of the Strymon and the Nestus, apart from the thriving Neapolis, there were several trading towns, mostly nestling below Mt Pangaeum. They had usually been associated with the islanders of Thasos and were, as a result, in alliance with Athens. Two, Apollonia and Galepsus, were now destroyed and a third, Oesyme, only 20 kilometres west of Neapolis, was converted into a Macedonian base, renamed Emathia, after the sandy (*amathos*) plain at the heartland of the kingdom (Strabo VII.331 F 35, Scymn. 656ff). The noose was tightening around Neapolis and in early summer envoys sought aid from Athens. Though well received (Tod no. 159) they could not expect any substantial help. When it did fall to Philip is not known. But given its importance to him (it was Philippi's natural port), an early date, in 355 or 354, is most likely.[14]

In midsummer the Social War ended. When the Athenian navy, as usual starved of funds, had been used by its commander Chares earlier in

[14] Contrast Hammond and Griffith 1979 (D 50) 364–5.

the year to assist a satrapal revolt against King Artaxerxes – successfully, as far as it went and producing handsome profit – the Athenians were at first elated (Diod. XVI.22, Plut. *Arat.* 16). But when the King's official protest was delivered and rumours circulated that 300 Persian ships would be offered to Athens' disaffected allies, the will to fight dissipated. The assembly accepted the secessions of Chios, Cos, Rhodes and Byzantium and most other allies opted to follow suit. There remained, of any significance, only Euboea, the northern Aegean islands of the transmarine corn route and a handful of towns on the Thracian littoral, shelters on the coastal corn route followed when bad weather made the more direct passage risky. Athens' financial exhaustion was extreme, her morale abysmal and her prestige at its lowest. Philip's policy of the past two years had been vindicated and the way was open to him to press it further.

VI. THE EARLY YEARS OF THE SACRED WAR

The deaths of Thebes' two great generals, Pelopidas and Epaminondas, may have brought about a short-lived pause in her ambitions. But there were other fine commanders and the public mood changed little. Smarting under Athens' recovery of control over Euboea in 357, Thebes now sought other means of extending her sway in central Greece. There, despite the successes of the previous decade as far afield as the Peloponnese and Macedonia, her influence was patchy, countered largely by the neighbouring Phocians and by the Thessalian League. The tensions were reflected in the organization and decisions of the Amphictyonic League (literally 'neighbours'), an old and primarily religious grouping of tribes centred upon the Thermopylae region but by now extended to include various Peloponnesian states (as members of the Dorian tribe), Athens (Ionian) and others. The Amphictyony had often in the past been the political field on which central Greek power games had been played out, and Thebes now determined to use it again for that purpose.[15]

At the Council's spring meeting (*pylaia*) in 356 the Theban delegates and their supporters procured the passage of a decree declaring war if fines incurred by certain Phocians, including well-known anti-Thebans, were not paid forthwith. A second resolution denounced all, notably including the Spartans, who owed debts to the patron deity, Apollo. The decisions in fact reiterated previous judgments, but their passage, amidst disagreement and ill-feeling, openly confronted both Phocians and Spartans with a choice between humiliation and war. In Phocis an anti-

---

[15] The main source for the Third Sacred War is Diod. XVI.23–38, 56–61. For the basis of the chronology see Hammond 1937 (B 55).

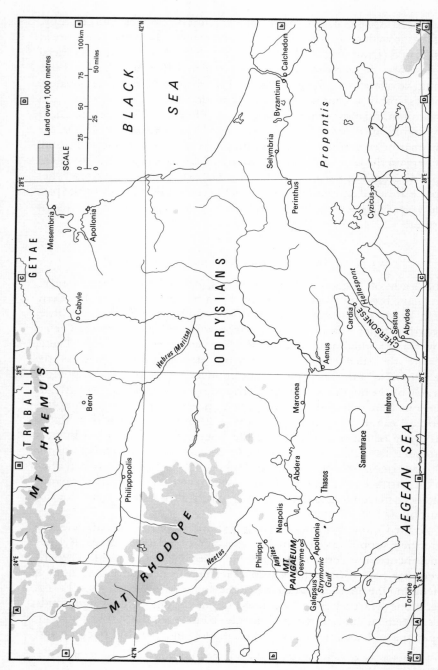

Map 17. Thrace: the political structure.

Theban, Philomelus, was elected commander of the army and, receiving private guarantees of money and mercenaries from King Archidamus of Sparta, captured Delphi, the Amphictyony's administrative and religious centre, then despatched embassies to various states to argue the justice of the cause and to re-state an old Phocian claim on the sacred city.

There was no immediate response. The Thessalian League, which could normally be counted upon to oppose Phocis, was heavily preoccupied with the continuing war against the rebel city of Pherae. The success of Phocian diplomats in winning alliances with Athens, Sparta, and probably Argos, Sicyon, and Corinth probably deterred many. But when in midsummer 355 the Social War ended and it quickly became clear that Athens could contribute little to central Greek military affairs and when, as it seems, some temporary accord was reached between the Thessalian League and the tyrant house at Pherae, Thebes again took up the initiative. At the autumn 355 *pylaia*, held perhaps in the original Amphictyonic centre of Anthela, near Thermopylae, and comprising naturally a reduced membership, sacred war was declared on Phocis. Hemmed in at Delphi and deciding that sacrilege in a 'just' cause would not much affect the military balance, Philomelus and his Phocians began using funds from the treasuries of Apollo to attract mercenaries with an unusually high wage. In spring 354 he defeated a Locrian and Boeotian force and cut off and vanquished 6,000 Thessalians moving into Locris. But when Boeotian reinforcements arrived in the autumn and engaged him in pitched battle in Neon, Philomelus was killed and his army defeated. His fellow commander Onomarchus and the remnants withdrew to reorganize.

The Amphictyonic position now seemed strong – and that must account for a puzzling Theban resolution now, perhaps to replenish her funds, to despatch a general, Pammenes, with 5,000 troops to Asia Minor in support of the revolt against Artaxerxes by his Phrygian satrap Artabazus (winter 354/3). It was a foolish move, not only because Pammenes despite some initial success was shortly dismissed by the satrap (Thebes' traditional sympathy for the Persian monarch perhaps made him unfairly suspect) but because in the consequent lull in the Sacred War the Phocian position was effectively restored. Onomarchus kept up at least some of the affairs at Delphi of what we might call the 'rebel' Amphictyony, in which Athens, Locris, Megara, Epidaurus, Sparta, Corinth, Phocis, Delphi and others took part.[16] Then in a series of campaigns through the spring and early summer of 353 he captured two important strategic points, Amphissa in Locris and Thronium near Thermopylae, ravaged parts of Doris and even took Boeotian Orchome-

---

[16] The named members contributed to the Board of Naopoioi through the early years of the war (*Fouilles de Delphes* III 5 No. 19); some are given as allies of Phocis by Diod. XVI.29.1.

nus, turning back only when he failed to capture Chaeronea and was defeated by a Theban force.

VII. PHILIP AND THESSALY

In late 355 Philip laid siege to Methone. What caused him to interrupt his coastal campaign in Thrace we do not know. The town lay uncomfortably close to Aegae and Dium, but its people had apparently kept very quiet since 359, when they played host to Argaeus and Mantias. The attack and Methone's determination to resist may go back to some now-lost source of friction. When his invitation to surrender was turned down, Philip began an extended assault on the walls, in the course of which he was wounded in and lost his right eye. In the spring (354), probably, Athens despatched aid, but it arrived too late. When the city capitulated its citizens were expelled, the walls and buildings destroyed and the land distributed among Macedonians.

Early in the following year Philip returned to Thrace, this time pushing along the coast beyond the Nestus to Abdera and Maronea, wealthy towns on high ground above the soggy central Thracian coastline and allies of Athens. For the first time known to us, his army was on this occasion accompanied by a fleet, whose function was evidently limited to the transport of supplies and equipment. If the expedition was aimed at the capture of the two towns, it failed, although their land was wasted (Polyaen. IV.2.22); certainly Maronea and possibly both were still allies of Athens in 340 ([Dem.] XII.17). At the time Pammenes and his 5,000 happened to be in the area on their way to Phrygia; Thebes either was already or became at this time the ally of Macedon. Denied further progress by the army of Amadocus, king of central Thrace, Philip made contact and some kind of treaty with Cersobleptes in eastern Thrace, using Pammenes as intermediary, but then turned immediately for home on receipt of an urgent appeal from Thessaly and Thebes for assistance against Pherae. On the voyage it was learnt that Chares, with a squadron of twenty ships, was lying in wait off Neapolis. But Philip, with no wish to face him, managed to slip past by first decoying the Athenians away.

The history of Philip's interventions in Thessaly is highly conjectural – unfortunately so, for his relationship with the Thessalians was soon to become remarkably close, and there were presumably substantial reasons for that. In central Greece in early 353 Onomarchus' campaigns were making good the Phocian losses in men and morale at Neon. By then, it is clear, he was acting in concert with the Pheraean tyrant Lycophron, and it may have been this convergence which had prompted the new appeal.

The initial campaign seems to have gone well, for Lycophron was forced to turn for assistance to Onomarchus, who despatched his brother Phayllus with troops into Thessaly. Philip defeated and drove him back, but at this point Onomarchus, following his setback at Chaeronea, abandoned the Boeotian campaign and in autumn 353 brought his whole force, including artillery, to the aid of Phayllus and Lycophron. Stone-throwing catapults were as a rule too unwieldy for use in the field and probably accompanied the Phocians primarily for use against Thessalian cities, but Onomarchus cannily devised a means of bringing them into play against Philip. Concealing the machines around the slopes of a blind valley, he made a token stand, then feigned retreat. When the Macedonians followed, without first scouting the flanks, the catapults inflicted heavy casualties. As his first known defeat in six or so years, it was disaster for Philip, the more so because it had been the result of his own carelessness. His soldiers, this once during his reign, blamed him wholly and were only with difficulty held back from revolt. Withdrawing to winter at home, Philip promised – all that was left for him after the humiliation – to return 'like a ram to butt harder next time'.

The repercussions were felt far beyond the army, and even beyond the Macedonian frontiers. During the autumn the Athenian Chares descended upon the Chersonese and captured Sestus, slaughtering the men and enslaving women and children. Since the Thracian treaty with Athens in 357 Cersobleptes had done nothing to give the Athenians any confidence in him. In coming to terms with Philip in early 353 he had automatically raised fears in their minds over the Chersonese; now, despite their post-Social War weakness, they were determined to signal that no defection would be tolerated in that vital area. Cersobleptes lost his entitlement, conceded in the treaty of 357, to draw an annual revenue of thirty talents from the peninsula and, isolated now by Philip's setback in Thessaly, relinquished all claims on it beyond Cardia, at its narrow neck. Athenian cleruchs were shortly sent to Sestus and elsewhere (Diod. XVI.34.3, Dem. XXIII.14, 103, 110, 177, 181). At such a display of Athenian will, and perhaps feeling equally exposed by its ally's defeat in Thessaly, the Chalcidic League (or at least its leading city) declared friendship for Athens and proposed the negotiation of an alliance (Dem. XXIII.107ff). Olynthus' pro-Athenians, though not very influential earlier in the 350s, evidently found the new circumstances propitious. While Athens evinced little interest at this stage, the Olynthian realignment towards her continued. This was not all. In a largely sequential list of Philip's campaigns given by Demosthenes (I.12–13), actions involving the Illyrians, Paeonians and King Arybbas are apparently (the last certainly) dated approximately to the period 351–349. In that case they too were probably responses to similar backsliding in the aftermath of the disaster of 353.

As spring (352) arrived, or even earlier, Onomarchus prepared for his

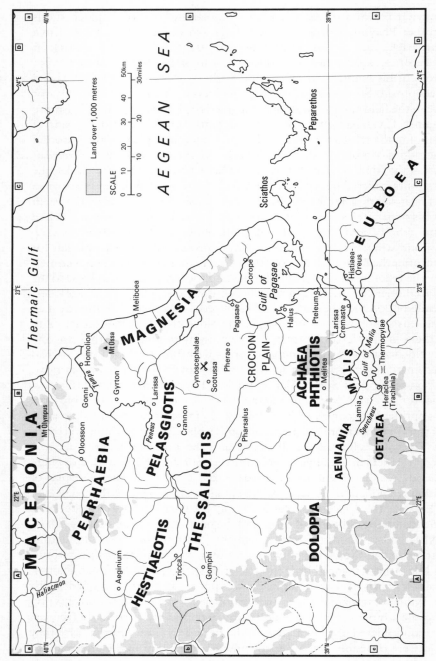

Map 18. Thessaly.

return to Thessaly, launching a new campaign into Boeotia, during which he took Coronea and, perhaps at this time, two small towns, Corsiae and Tilphosaeum. His immediate goal was to weaken Theban control over those Boeotian cities which resented her domination and so to make it unsafe for the despatch of Theban troops into Thessaly. The Athenians ordered Chares and his fleet to the Gulf of Pagasae to give naval support to the rebel armies.

For Philip the situation was critical. His Thessalian alliance was all-important; other problems must wait. Combining forces with the League (to a total of some 20,000 foot and 3,000 horse) he made speedily for Pagasae to cut off any aid from Chares. He took the port, pinned down the Pheraeans and then turned to face the forces of Onomarchus some 30 km away on the coastal plain west of the Gulf of Pagasae. This would inevitably be a significant battle, not only for the obvious reasons but because it would be fought on behalf of Amphictyons some of whom would themselves be fearful of Macedonian ambitions in the central Greek area. The king instructed his troops to don crowns of laurel, 'as if avenging an act of sacrilege' (Justin VIII.2.3), and went into battle as the defender of Apollo. In the fighting, in early summer 352, Philip's massive cavalry forces, exploiting Onomarchus' foolhardiness in joining battle on level ground, drove the Phocians back on the gulf coast, where some tried to swim out to Chares' ships, cruising offshore. Some 6,000 were killed and 3,000 prisoners were taken. The former were ritually thrown, or the latter driven (or both: Diod. XVI.35.6 is unclear),[17] into the sea as temple robbers. Onomarchus was killed either in battle or afterwards. Lycophron in desperation offered Pherae to Philip and departed under truce with 2,000 mercenaries.

The Thessalian League elected the king to its archonship,[18] an office of some weight in federal matters, involving military command and lifelong tenure. Its conferment on a foreigner was unprecedented and remarkable, prompted in part no doubt by gratitude and in part, possibly, by internal rivalries between major cities which made a native appointment difficult. Whatever the practical limitations on its powers, the office marked Philip's very great standing among the Thessalians. He was granted the proceeds of the Thessalian harbour and market taxes, probably for the military expenses of the archonship. Pagasae, the league's best harbour, now released from Pheraean control, was ceded to him. With the Pheraeans themselves he negotiated a settlement on the league's behalf and, in the Macedonian royal fashion, contracted a marriage with a local noblewoman, one Nicesipolis. (Their daughter would be aptly named Thessalonice.) The tyrants and their adherents

---

[17] See the discussion by Hammond and Griffith 1979 (D 50) 276–7.
[18] The date of the election is unknown; 352 was proposed by Sordi 1958 (C 384) 249 ff.

could have been destroyed but only at high cost to those obliged to follow their orders; for the sake of future relations with the Pheraeans, and at some potential risk to himself, Philip allowed them to escape, as six years later he would free the Phocian leaders and mercenaries to avoid a general massacre of the Phocian people. Sections of two Thessalian perioecic territories, Perrhaebia and Magnesia, were also ceded to Philip, who fortified key towns and, in at least one case, that of Gonnoi, created a new Macedonian colony along the lines of Philippi four years earlier.

Two or three months after the battle ('the Battle of Crocus Field', as it is often called, after the Crocion Plain, on which it was probably fought) Philip marched southwards towards Thermopylae. It is a mark of the seriousness with which he took his Thessalian archonship that he had delayed over its problems while the initiative against the Phocians slipped away and while his own difficulties in the north went unresolved. Following their release under truce Lycophron and his retainers had gone no further than central Greece, where they had joined Phayllus, who held Thermopylae against Philip. By the time the Macedonians arrived in the vicinity, around midsummer 352, there were other allies of Phocis at the pass, Athenians, Spartans and Achaeans. Under these circumstances an assault on Thermopylae would be difficult and, at best, costly in time and lives. Central Greece would have to wait (Diod. XVI.37–8, Dem. XIX.84, Justin VIII.2.8–12).

By November Philip was campaigning nearly 700 km away at Heraeum on the Propontine coast near Perinthus. With Athenian control firmly re-established in the Chersonese, Cersobleptes had reverted, with tacit Athenian approval, to his plans to bring the central Thracian kingdom of Amadocus under his own rule. By the time of Philip's arrival Amadocus with the cities of Byzantium and Perinthus were in league against Cersobleptes. The allies gladly accepted the Macedonian offer of assistance. Learning of the king's appearance so far east the Athenian Assembly resolved on a substantial force to trap him away from home and reinforcement. But, perhaps as it became clear that his forces were far from alone, Athens' ardour cooled; in any case, Cersobleptes' record and interests were hardly such as to guarantee his reliability. The expedition lapsed and Athens waited, impotent. The siege was a long one and in its course Philip dealt with other matters in the eastern Thracian area, evidently making certain changes to the local leadership in some parts. Around July or August 351 news reached Athens that he was ill, even that he was dead. A small fleet was detailed to reconnoitre once it was safe to do so. In August or September Philip accepted Heraeum's surrender, handed it back to Perinthus and began the march home (schol. Aeschin. II.81, Dem. 1.13, III.4–5, IV.10–11).[19]

[19] The chronology adopted here is based on Ellis 1977 (D 81).

En route he detoured into the Chalcidic peninsula. Whether he engaged in any military action or simply paraded his victorious troops before Olynthus is unclear from the evidence; what is certain is that he was not yet prepared for a major encounter and hoped that his recent successes would be enough to bring this ally back into line (Dem. xxiii.107–8, *FGrH* 115 Theopomp. f 127). As soon became obvious, he was wrong. Perhaps his own burgeoning power, of a scale six years earlier to be useful yet not threatening to his neighbour, was now seen as a danger by the Chalcidic League.

VIII. THE FALL OF OLYNTHUS

That such campaigns as Philip appears to have carried out in Paeonia and Illyria in 350 are passed over almost without notice in our sources is not really surprising. The reason may be that the distant mountain areas were of little interest to most Greeks. Philip kept such territories under control by means of periodic brief military actions rather than by the kind of governmental and administrative reorganization devoted to Thessaly and Thrace. The distinction, it seems, is between areas useful as buffers, but otherwise peripheral, and those in and beyond which Macedonia's interests were inevitably involved. So far as we know, no machinery of administration was established anywhere in Illyria, Paeonia or the far north of Thrace. Local kings continued to rule as clients of the Macedonian throne. The defeat of Grabus in 356, followed by the present expedition, extended Macedon's domination well towards the Adriatic, north of Epirus, as Isocrates (v.21) was to point out in his pamphlet, the *Philippus*, in 346. He writes too of the Paeonians' coming under Philip's yoke, referring perhaps to two requirements on their king Lyppeus which may have been imposed now, to pay a tribute to Macedonia and to provide troops when called upon. (Alexander would take a small contingent with him in 334.)

With Epirus, by contrast, Philip worked at building the same kind of relationship as he enjoyed with the Thessalians, and for much the same reasons (see ch. 9*d*). Beyond the obvious, the security of Macedonia's southern and south-western flanks, Thessaly and Epirus offered control over the two land passages, on either side of the Pindus range, between northern and central Greece. The alliance in 357 with Arybbas, the Molossian king in Epirus, had made a promising beginning there, but this too had been set back, it seems, by the Thessalian defeat of 353. Philip's Epirote campaign of 350 is undocumented in its detail and perhaps was little more than another demonstration that his power was undiminished. But on his return he brought to the Macedonian court Arybbas' young nephew and ward, Alexander, the brother of Olympias.

At Pella Philip would see to his safety, his education and no doubt his allegiance. In eight or nine years he would in fact install him on the Molossian throne in place of Arybbas. Although he presumably gave no indication yet of any such plan, the likelihood must have been obvious enough.

The actions in Illyria, Paeonia and Epirus may have taken up much of 350 and perhaps early 349. Meanwhile in central Greece Phocian fortunes had not prospered since mid-352. Financial advantage, from the use of Delphic treasure, had been neutralized by the dogged strength of Thebes. In 351 Phayllus died and was succeeded by one Mnaseas, who was killed in a Boeotian attack soon afterwards. The new leader, Phalaecus, son of Onomarchus, was no more able to make any advance, indeed lost control of the Phocian bases in Boeotia. The war tailed off in minor skirmishes, neither side capable of ending it (Diod. XVI.38).

The cause of the final breakdown between Philip and the Chalcidic League is somewhat obscure. Certainly by now the Macedonian army was a most effective weapon and the kingdom, since neither its economy nor its defences rested upon the sea, was consequently no longer vulnerable to an Athenian navy deprived of its north-western Aegean bases – unless Athens, that is, were to operate in league with an ally of some strength. Philip, in other words, no longer needed the Chalcidic alliance, and the Olynthians' movement in recent years towards Athens made them especially dangerous. Some indications of Macedonian interference in Olynthus not long after the brief Chalcidic campaign of 351 (Dem. LIX.90–1, IX.56–66, VIII.40) suggest that at that point Philip still thought a political settlement possible, though perhaps only that he hoped thus to delay while dealing with more urgent matters first. The actual *casus belli*, it seems (Justin VIII.3.10), was the Olynthian refusal to surrender to Philip his two half-brothers (see above) who had taken refuge there, presumably after the 351 campaign. That the Olynthians allowed this to become an issue is surprising. Just conceivably, they had the same kind of plan for Menelaus and Arrhidaeus as they had effected in the mid-380s, when they were able to install Argaeus temporarily on the Macedonian throne in place of Amyntas III. But things were very different now, and that hardly seems credible. At any rate, their reception of the refugees and refusal to hand them over showed the gulf between Macedon and Olynthus to be unbridgeable.

In the late summer or early autumn of 349 Philip's army crossed the Macedonian frontier and laid siege to the small Chalcidic town of Zeira (or Zereia), a place unknown to us but in or near Anthemus. When it capitulated it was destroyed as a warning. Some, perhaps all, of its neighbours surrendered and Olynthus' league began to fall apart (Diod. XVI.52.9). As Philip moved towards them, the Olynthians hastily sent envoys to beg Athens for alliance. Under pressure from, among others, Demosthenes (in his *Olynthiacs*) the Athenian Assembly eventually complied, but somewhat less than enthusiastically, despatching little more than a token force (Philoch. F 49–51). In any case there was now a lull in the campaign, for Philip was distracted by trouble in Thessaly.

At some time during 349 Peitholaus, brother of Lycophron, managed to recover control of Pherae (Diod. XVI.52.9), probably with Phocian assistance. The threat to Philip's settlement, as well as to the revenues he drew from the Pagasaean harbour and to his control of Magnesia, which had been part of the Pheraean tyrant's domain, could not be ignored. Whether that was the whole problem or there was (as Demosthenes claims: II.11, 1.22) a more general Thessalian dissatisfaction – perhaps over Philip's lengthening absence from the demands of the Sacred War, or even over his failure to prevent the tyrant's return – his intervention was imperative and took precedence over the Chalcidic campaign. How precisely he settled the difficulties we do not know, but we see no further sign of unrest in Thessaly for five years thereafter. But the impetus in the Chalcidice was lost. Athenian support, modest as it was, encouraged the Olynthians to refuse terms, even when Athens too became embroiled in military action elsewhere.

When in 357 the Athenians had expelled a Theban force from Euboea it had been with strong local support. That enthusiasm had however waned as Athens refused to act against an increasingly unpopular tyrant in Eretria, one Plutarch. Then in very early 348 Plutarch himself, facing a popular rising, appealed to the Athenians for aid. It is a measure both of Euboea's strategic importance to them that intervention was prompt and of Athens' insensitivity that it was made in Plutarch's favour. The Athenian commander, Phocion, soon perceived the error, but he was recalled and the campaign continued until Athens was defeated. A few months later she was obliged to accept a costly and humiliating settlement guaranteeing the islanders' independence (Plut. *Phoc.* 12–14, Aeschin. III.86–8). Only Carystus, at the southern tip, remained her ally. Meanwhile a second force, under Charidemus, had gone to Olynthus and joined in ravaging the areas which had previously gone over to Philip. The Macedonian campaign would virtually need to begin over again.

When about March 348 Philip pushed down towards Olynthus, again many (and perhaps all) of the communities on his route capitulated without resistance. The surrender of her port, Mecyberna, and of Torone left Olynthus exposed and she was invested. Another plea for Athenian help was somehow sent, but there was still division among the Olynthians. Not many now had confidence that Athenian aid would amount to much against Philip's strength. A substantial part of the cavalry defected. Soon afterwards, in the autumn, the city fell (Diod.

XVI.53–5). A third force from Athens, again under Chares and slightly more substantial than its predecessors, arrived too late, probably slowed by the Etesian Wind. Olynthus was sacked, the captured Athenians imprisoned and the inhabitants sold into slavery. The Chalcidic peninsula became part of Macedonia. It was a harsh end for a city which had become great as Spartan and Athenian power declined in the earlier fourth century. Its fate would serve as an example, no doubt, for the Olynthians had been friends uncoerced and had turned on their ally.

The chill was felt in Athens. Nothing could be done beyond applying the usual salves to injured pride: refuge and even citizenship were granted to those Olynthians who had escaped, those who had defected were condemned and reprehension was heaped on the Athenian generals. After their nine years of war with Macedon ('the war over Amphipolis', as Athenians continued to say), mainly in the north and mostly with little direct contact between Macedonians and Athenians, Philip suddenly seemed much closer. Nothing now stood between him and Thermopylae. Surprisingly, however, news had reached Athens in June, via Euboean intermediaries, that he no longer wished to be at war (Aeschin. II.12). Given the timing, it had seemed calculated only to weaken the Athenians' resoluteness, such as it was, over Olynthus. Then in July, during the Olympic truce, an Athenian trader had been captured by pirates and ended up in Macedonian hands. Arranging his own ransom Phrynon returned home insisting on official action over the truce violation. Ctesiphon was sent and returned (by now after the fall of Olynthus) successful, with further assurance of Philip's good will. Philocrates rose in the Assembly to propose that Philip be invited to send envoys to discuss terms. The people assented, which did not prevent Philocrates' impeachment, probably because the late Athenian–Olynthian alliance would have forsworn any negotiation with the common enemy without both parties' agreement. Defended by Demosthenes, he was overwhelmingly acquitted (Aeschin. II.12–14). Yet in this sudden turnabout there was only relief, not conviction, for Philocrates' decree was simply not put into effect. There turned out, temporarily, to be more beguiling alternatives to a peace on Philip's terms and the Athenians eagerly seized upon them.

On the motion of Eubulus, envoys were despatched far and wide to see whether a common anti-Macedonian alliance could be assembled (Dem. XIX.10–11, 303–7).[20] It could not. Thirty years earlier many Greeks, suffering at Sparta's calloused hands, had been prepared to join Athens, given firm assurances that the proposed *hegemon* would not do worse than the common enemy. In the end those guarantees had proved

---

[20] For an alternative date for this decree see Cawkwell 1960 (C 102); cf. Markle, 1970 (C 198) and 1974 (D 103) and Hammond and Griffith 1979 (D 50) 330 n. 1.

to be worth little; who would accept them again, when this was Athens' war, no one else's? The envoys returned weeks or months later without a shadow of support. A second possibility presented itself, but some context is required to make sense of it.

IX. PHILIP'S POLICY AND THE PEACE OF PHILOCRATES

In central Greece the Sacred War had subsided almost to nothing. The Phocian funds, although more Delphic treasures were plundered, seem to have been drying up. Thebes was too exhausted to take advantage. Early in 347 Phalaecus was moved from the command. Three new leaders, Dinocrates, Callias and Sophanes, sallied into Boeotia, evoking a Theban appeal to Philip for aid. But his response was half-hearted. Under (probably) Parmenion, Macedonian troops assisted in beating the Phocians back from Abae, but lack of strength or Macedonian hesitancy held the allies back from any sequel. Philip was not yet ready for a full commitment to this war. The delay was to allow other arrangements to fall into place; and his concurrent overtures to Athens were the key to that.

Hindsight suggests (contrary to the oppressive insistence of our hellenocentric – mostly Athenian – sources) that it was not Greece but the spaciousness and relative wealth of Asia Minor that attracted Philip. Here was a succession of targets worthy of a great warrior-king and a great army, here a source of rewards, in prestige, booty and tribute, to repay the effort. The builder of a large militia, however much concerned with the fostering of local security and social unity, can not afford to ignore the dangers of an army unoccupied with the kinds of campaign that provide self-respect, incentive and profit to its members. Only recently Pammenes' initial successes in support of the rebellious Phrygian satrap Artabazus had pointed to the advantages of well-trained and disciplined Greek troops in the Persian King's outer dominions. Asia Minor had always been a difficult area for the monarchy to control, mixed in population, volatile and given to local revolt. That attempt had eventually failed but in late 353 or early 352 Artabazus and his Rhodian brother-in-law Memnon had found refuge at Pella. Philip was by now, we may assume, well informed about Persian strengths and weaknesses beyond the Hellespont and knew the gains to be made there. But the Hellenic mainland could not be ignored, since the demands of Macedonian defence, largely secured by 348, had already brought commitments to allies as vital as Thessaly and conflicts with those southern states, especially Athens, accustomed to exploiting the northern Aegean's resources in harbours, minerals, timber and food. A reliable Hellenic settlement was essential if Philip was to be free to turn eastwards.

There were two difficulties. Athens was still able, given sufficient stimulus, to launch a great navy. That alone could not much damage Macedonia, but in combination with an effective army was a formidable weapon. Thebes, again given the stimulus, could put such an army into the field. That alone could have little hope of reaching Macedonia through Thessaly in fit condition to overthrow the defenders. But ally it with an experienced navy and things might be different. Common action by Athens and Thebes was not often possible, for the two neighbouring powers were more naturally rivals than allies. But need had driven them together before and might again – *would*, indeed, in the analogous circumstances of 339. For Philip it was essential to prevent that, and in particular to block the recovery of Theban power, at present inhibited by Phocis with its purloined wealth and its mercenaries. Hence his desire now to win Athens' friendship and his refusal to end the Phocian War without it. With Athens' co-operation, to be secured by the prospect of rewards for her trade reaped by penetration into Asia Minor, the Theban hold over Boeotia, the main source of her power, and her influence in central Greece might be broken. The Greek mainland might be maintained peaceful and secure.

It was desirable, therefore, that Philip win the allegiance of Athens, a difficult task after nearly a decade of antagonism, and to do so without alienating the existing ally, Thebes, until it was too late for her to resist.[21] In both respects the nature of the settlement pursued in the Sacred War would be critical: on the one hand, to destroy Phocis would both provoke Athenian hatred and remove the most useful counter to Theban recovery in central Greece; on the other, to give notice of any resolution which denied Thebes the satisfaction of vengeance on the Phocians would alienate her at the outset. Subterfuge was necessary and timing critical. And, lest the primary scheme fail, there must be a contingent strategy.

In Athens nothing of this was known. Philip would enter central Greece at his allies' behest, unless distracted by difficulties in the north, or unless Phocian strength could be augmented sufficiently to keep him out. Even if Athens could effect neither, and must therefore negotiate, she might at least in the mean time improve her bargaining position. Two leading politicians, Demosthenes and Philocrates, procured for themselves seats on the executive Council of 500 in midsummer 347. A number of resolutions, moved by Eubulus, Aristophon and Diopeithes, authorized the despatch of a force to the Chersonese (Dion. Hal. *Letter to Ammaeus* 1.11, Dem. XVIII.70). Its commander, probably Chares, made

---

[21] For the following interpretation of Philip's aims in the Peace of Philocrates and the settlement of the Sacred War see especially Rohrmoser 1874 (C 233), Markle 1970 (C 198) and Ellis 1982 (D 83); cf. Cawkwell 1978 (C 17) and Hammond and Griffith 1979 (D 50) 345 n. 1.

contact there with Cersobleptes and a number of garrisons were jointly established along the coasts of the north-east Aegean and the Propontis (though, more likely than not, few if any Athenians were actually left to operate them). In Phocis the new leaders cast about for support. To Athens and Sparta they proposed to hand over Nicaea, Alponus and Thronium, the fortress towns controlling Thermopylae. Both accepted and in Athens an expedition was prepared by Proxenus to occupy the pass and the Malian Gulf (Aeschin. II.132–4, Diod. XVI.59.1). Further north Halus, a small pro-Athenian town on the Gulf of Pagasae, was at loggerheads with Pharsalus and might, in order to exacerbate Philip's difficulties, be supplied by Athens from the sea (Dem. XIX.36 with schol.; XIX.163). In the Athenian Assembly, at the end of 347 or in January 346, a new decree was passed inviting all Greek states to join in deliberating on war with Philip or, if it seemed preferable, peace (Aeschin. II.57–60, Dem. XIX.16). This, it seems, was the second reason for Athens' delay in responding to the Macedonian peace feelers.

Philip worked to counter these moves, directly and indirectly. He may have made contact (possibly as early as the Macedonian intervention of 347) with Phalaecus and others with a view to the deposed leader's restoration. To a request from Athens for the release of her citizens imprisoned at the fall of Olynthus he assented on condition that she agree to peace. When word of this was suppressed back in Athens he released a prisoner to convey it. At an Assembly in late January or early February the report was made and, at the same time, the citizens learned that Phalaecus was again in command in Phocis and had repudiated the offer to surrender the Thermopylae fortresses. No options remained and no further delay was safe. Philocrates moved to have an embassy go immediately to discover Philip's terms. Ten Athenians, plus one representative of the allies, were selected and departed. Among them, its two most junior members, were Demosthenes and Aeschines (Aeschin. II.15–19).

In Pella the envoys, after consultation, each made a formal speech defining Athens' interests and requirements. After retiring to deliberate Philip answered each in turn, graciously and meticulously, as they later agreed (Aeschin. II.20–39). Demands over the independence of the Thracian forts and of Halus were presumably dismissed uncompromisingly; they involved Philip's allies and he would make no concessions over them. As the envoys could see for themselves, his preparations for an expedition to punish Cersobleptes were complete. The Chersonese was different: Philip did not dispute Athens' claim to it; he guaranteed not to set foot there while deliberations lasted and the treaty would protect it thereafter. He would even undertake to cut a channel across its narrow neck to enhance its defensibility and to provide a safer shortcut for Athens' corn ships in bad weather (Aeschin. II.81–2, Dem. VI.30). He would demand no ransom for the prisoners taken at Olynthus; they would be returned on the conclusion of peace (Aeschin. II.100). There were other offers: to restore Athenian influence in Euboea, to take Oropus from Thebes and hand it back to Athens and to repopulate Thespiae and Athens' old ally, Plataea, destroyed by the Thebans at the height of their power (Dem. V.10, 15, VI.30, XIX.20–1). But much of this depended upon the settlement of the Sacred War. The proposals must be secret, or at least unofficial. Philip's intention was to resolve the conflict by punishing the Phocian leadership and their mercenaries, but not the common people, for it was the reduction of Thebes, not of Phocis, that he desired (Aeschin. II.119). It would be the envoys' task, difficult but not impossible, to convey to their co-citizens the flavour of his proposal; his own communications must be limited to generalities for fear of driving the Thebans into open opposition too soon ([Dem.] VII.33). Above all, since Athens' hoplites might be useful and her visible support would be vital, he required assurance that she would give military assistance when called upon: peace and alliance, not peace alone (Dem. XIX.40). The audience over, on or about 18 March, the envoys turned homeward.

Whether excited over the prospects of co-operation in a great eastern expedition or merely relieved that Philip appeared genuine in his wish for *rapprochement* with Athens, all envoys were convinced that peace was necessary. With one possible exception, the allied representative, they also accepted that, if Philip wanted peace and alliance, then to peace and alliance Athens must agree. But, although no breach in their ranks was yet evident, there was one fundamental dissenter. Demosthenes was opposed to the destruction of Theban power not (probably) out of any particular love for that city but because, like Philip, he saw alliance with Thebes as Athens' last resort, and did not trust the Macedonian.

The Thracian campaign prospered. Within three months Cersobleptes was defeated and brought to heel and the new bases were dismantled (Aeschin. II.90–2, Dem. XIX.156–8). It may be that when in 351 Philip had fought with Amadocus and the Pontic allies against Cersobleptes he had also annexed western Thrace, from the Strymon to the Nestus; if not then, certainly now. Amadocus' successor, Teres, probably fought alongside Philip ([Dem.] XII.8). Cersobleptes was not removed from his throne, though that must have been possible and in some respects desirable. At this stage Philip evidently still planned to keep Thrace under control through the agency of Thracian clients and friends.

In Athens dates had been set for two assemblies to discuss and decide upon the terms once Philip's ambassadors were present. In the Council a preliminary motion (*probouleuma*) was formulated, under Philocrates'

name, setting out the conditions. But when debate opened, on *c.* 15 April
(18 Elaphebolion),[22] there were two opposing resolutions before the
people, that of Philocrates and one proposed by the naval allies that no
decision be taken until the envoys despatched some three months before
to seek out Hellenic support had returned, and that the agreement then
be in the form of a Common Peace, without alliance, open to the
participation of all Greeks. In the face of strong public support for the
allies' motion the envoys left the hard realities to Macedon's ambassadors. On the next morning Demosthenes disingenuously demanded of
their leader, Antipater, whether Philip would accept the alternative
motion. As all the envoys knew, he would not, and, when Antipater had
made this clear, a number of influential Athenians, including Eubulus
and two of the embassy-members, Aeschines and Ctesiphon, put the
options bluntly. Athens must either return to war immediately, alone
and close to home, or accept Philip's terms. Philocrates' motion was
carried, but with one unavoidable concession to popular disquiet: a
clause specifically excluding Phocis, Halus and Cersobleptes from the
allies of either party was deleted. That deficiency, which Philip could not
accept, was remedied only five days later when the oaths of the Athenians
and their allies were given and signed, for no representatives of those to
be excluded were recognized. The exclusion clause was in effect
reinstated. From beginning to end, as a Council member, as a speaker in
the Assembly, even its president at the oath taking, Demosthenes played
his part in ensuring that Philip's terms were the ones agreed to (Aeschin.
II.60–8, III.68–75, Dem. XIX.13–16, 291).

A week later a directive of the Council of 500, moved by Demosthenes, despatched the same ten Athenians immediately on a second
embassy. Yet there had been no hurry. It was known that Philip was still
campaigning in Thrace. There was no point in pursuing him, for he
would certainly brook no interference with his plans there. Demosthenes' haste may be seen, in retrospect, as suspicious – as is the fact that
his motion ordered the envoys to seek Philip 'where he might be found'
(Dem. XIX.154). As yet, however, his colleagues were aware of nothing
more than an increase in his personal abrasiveness. They made their way
slowly to Macedonia, not Thrace, and there waited for three or four
weeks until Philip returned, around 17 June. Other envoys too were
present, from Thebes, Sparta, Thessaly, Phocis and perhaps elsewhere.
Word was evidently circulating that the proposed settlement contained
unexpected elements, as the presence of Phocians implied. The Theban
ambassadors in particular were seriously worried and the Thessalians
appeared to know something their Theban counterparts did not (Aes-

chin. 11.136–7). Nine of the Athenians were surprised to learn that Demosthenes' aims seemed at odds with theirs. While they were happy, in accord with Philip's wishes, to discuss Phocis and Thebes, he insisted on making an issue of the Athenian prisoners, even offering to ransom them himself (with, Aeschines says at 11.100, a laughably small amount of money). He well knew that the king had promised to release them gratis by the Panathenaic festival (August). But he also saw that Philip would now be obliged either to weaken his own bargaining position by releasing them immediately or to risk a charge of bad faith if he held to his schedule. In refusing to alter his decision Philip took the step that more than any other destroyed the settlement he desired.

Although his primary plan entailed dishonouring his alliance with the Thebans, he had some legal grounds for such a change in public policy. All Amphictyons were sworn to hold inviolate the cities of their co-members and to punish any who defiled the Delphic shrine of Apollo. It was easy to point to Boeotian cities, Amphictyons all, some depopulated, others with their walls razed by Thebes in order to maintain her domination over the Boeotian Confederacy (Aeschin. 11.14–19). Phocis was undeniably guilty of sacrilege at Delphi, but to distinguish between its leaders, with their mercenaries, and the common people would be relatively simple – and desirable, for a good many Greek communities (Athens, Sparta, Corinth, Epidaurus, Megara, Sicyon, Phlius and probably Argos, at least) would be appalled if the Phocians were treated savagely. The Thebans would not, but that did not matter. Neither would the Thessalians and some other Amphictyons, but they were Philip's allies and could be offered compensatory gains.

Something of what was afoot was known, or suspected, by the various embassies in Pella (Aeschin. 11.136–7). Parleys were held between Philip and those of Athens and Sparta, with the Thebans excluded. All could see that, although Athens had been required to omit the Phocians from her treaty with Philip, she had not been ordered to repudiate her own alliance with them. As the envoys all moved off towards the south in the company of the king, who held back from supplying his own and his allies' signatures, the Phocians present were being treated as if they too were already Philip's allies (Dem. IX.11). In Thebes, now or soon afterwards, the full military levy was called out (Aeschin. 11.137).

At Pherae a halt was made. With only two days' march remaining to Thermopylae, Philip could not be kept from the pass. The oaths of the Macedonians and selected allies were given, signed and passed to the Athenian embassy. Yet while Philip continued to delay, probably as he negotiated with Phalaecus, the envoys were still detained, not, other than in Demosthenes' case, against their will. When they left, Philip led his army towards Thermopylae and, on his arrival – whether 'at', 'in' or 'inside' (= 'beyond') is not clear from the evidence – was ready to put the strategy into effect (Dem. XIX.58, 174, 323, Diod. XVI.59). A Spartan force was standing in the vicinity, ready to assist. On 11 or 12 July he sent a request to Athens for troops.

On the second embassy's return home arrangements had gone smoothly enough, although Demosthenes had begun openly distancing himself from his colleagues and casting doubt on Philip's good faith (Dem. XIX.17–18, 31–2). When the Assembly met on *c.* 10 July it was already known that the Macedonians were at Thermopylae and the envoys' assurances as to his intentions easily carried the day. Peace and alliance with Philip were confirmed and extended to his descendants in perpetuity. A final clause was added, in appropriately vague terms: 'if the Phocians do not act correctly and surrender the temple to the Amphic-tyons, the people shall send aid to achieve this against *those who prevent it*' (Dem. XIX.47–9). Rather than merely waiting on Philip's request for troops, however, the Athenians were persuaded (by whom we do not know) to send off the same envoys to convey word of the decree to the king. Now Demosthenes struck, declining service on the third embassy. After the Assembly broke up, the other envoys met in consternation. Although Demosthenes' precise intention may not yet have been apparent, it was clear that since his return from the second embassy he had done his best to dampen the popular enthusiasm for Philip and his treaty. He could not be left unopposed. Aeschines, a popular ex-actor and competent orator, was chosen and a physician procured to certify his unfitness to travel (Aeschin. II.94–5, Dem. XIX.121–2). The others departed on their unimportant mission, probably on the same day as Philip's messenger left Thermopylae. On 13 July the request arrived and a special Assembly was scheduled for the following day.

But by now everything had gone wrong. Many factors were involved, not least the ease with which public fear could be aroused of the man who had taken Amphipolis and had been Athens' enemy for a decade. More particularly, if the king so respected Athens and intended to favour her interests in the coming settlement, why did he still hold her citizens prisoner? Would he not kidnap her hoplites too? So Demosthenes and others argued. Against them stood Aeschines' credibility; Demosthenes and a colleague, Timarchus, promptly laid a charge of *parapresbeia* ('treasonous embassy-service') against him (schol. Aeschin. 1.169). When the Assembly convened, it rejected Philip's summons to action (Aeschin. II.137).

At Thermopylae stresses were already evident. The week's delay and the passage of heralds between Philip and Phalaecus were causing unease among even the staunchest allies. Daily the danger from the Theban levies grew (Aeschin. II.137, 140–1). Then, when word of Athens' default reached him by his own messenger, on *c.* 16 July, Philip knew that his plan had to be aborted. Behind the Theban position, apart from the small Spartan contingent, only some of the Boeotian cities favoured an anti-Theban war, and any battle at all would be so bloody as to risk forfeiting much of the goodwill he stood to gain. So he reverted to the alternative scheme. Accepting the surrender of Phalaecus and his mercenaries he allowed them to leave under truce, thus forestalling armed conflict and deflecting Amphictyonic vengefulness to the Council chamber, where he might personally keep it within bounds. The reduction of Theban power would have to await another occasion. The king then called for an extraordinary meeting of the Amphictyonic Council.

The meeting was probably held at Thermopylae in late July or early August. Philip formally turned over the Phocian state to the Council and discussions began. The Phocians were barred from the shrine of Apollo and their Amphictyonic membership was cancelled; their two tribal votes went to Philip, not (though this is debatable) in person but as the expression and representative of the Macedonian kingdom.[23] For the first time now the people of Delphi itself were given full voting status, the Perrhaebians and Dolopians each relinquishing one vote to that end. But the most difficult business was to consider the Phocian punishment, in particular to tone down the more extreme demands, there being one, at least, that all adult males be hurled from a clifftop. In the end the prescriptions were as moderate as was practicable in the circumstances (Diod. xvi.60). Aeschines, a member now of a fourth embassy despatched to observe proceedings, added his voice to those urging restraint. Demosthenes again did not serve.

Phocian territory was neither confiscated nor its crops harmed, the population neither slaughtered nor enslaved. Those who had fled were cursed and made subject to automatic arrest. (Some were harboured in Athens despite Amphictyonic protests.) The Amphictyons estimated the value of the pillaged Delphic treasures and imposed annual reparations on the state, but the first repayments were deferred. (It is uncertain whether the annual amount was fixed at 30 talents, but doubled in 343/2 and 342/1 to compensate for the moratorium, or at 60 talents, then halved from 341/0. At some time between 337 and 334 it was reduced to 10 talents per annum.) No levy was made for the war costs of the opposing side, despite (no doubt) Theban protests. The Phocians were forbidden to own horses or weapons. Their towns were to be razed and replaced by villages limited in size and proximity. This, the most dangerous imposition for the Phocians, was carried out by, among

---

[23] On the relationship between king and state see note 2, to which add Aymard 1950 (D 10), Errington 1974 (D 30) and Hammond and Griffith 1979 (D 50) 383–92.

others, Theban soldiers, but in the company of Macedonians who will
have been under orders to prevent atrocities (Diod. xvi.60, Dem. xix.81,
v.19).

The settlement had not been what Philip wished. There were
appreciable gains in the widespread acclaim of his bloodless success and
perhaps of his moderation, in his membership of the Amphictyonic
Council, and in his presidency of the forthcoming Pythian festival at
Delphi, to which he was now appointed. Yet the benefits were offset by
losses. His relationship with the Thebans, who must have been certain
sooner or later about what he had planned and infuriated over the
leniency of the Phocian punishment, could never again be easy. At the
same time, the outcome had thwarted and angered the Athenians,
Spartans and others, regardless of where the blame for it lay. That
smaller states increasingly came to look to him as a protector was some
compensation, but his best diplomacy would be called for if he was to
have any hope of turning the settlement of 346 into the kind of
arrangement he had desired.

CHAPTER 15

MACEDONIAN HEGEMONY CREATED

J. R. ELLIS

I. AFTERMATH OF THE PEACE OF PHILOCRATES

Most Athenians had not been privy to the detail of what had happened. Their conviction of Macedonian perfidy had been mitigated somewhat during the two or three months of the middle of 346, but was now redoubled by the settlement of the Third Sacred War. The foreshadowed benefits were not, could not be, delivered: Oropus remained in Theban hands, Euboea under Theban influence, Thespiae and Plataea depopulated. What the Athenians did not see was that their expectations were beyond reach, since Philip must not drive Thebes, already disaffected, into open opposition while Athens' adherence remained any less than certain. Those like Demosthenes declined to point this out, and their credibility, in the circumstances, stood high. Philip, for his part, if he was serious about a settlement based on Athens, must devote himself more than ever to courting the disenchanted inamorata. Generous diplomacy would have to accomplish, if anything could, what artifice had not. It is not that Philip was without supporters in Athens. Nine of the ten envoys of 346, all but Demosthenes, continued to support the new peace as the vehicle of potential Macedonian benefaction, refusing to repudiate it or its architect. In the current climate that may have seemed foolish, certainly suspect. They believed, so we must infer, what he had told them about his interests and intentions and judged, presumably, that they would eventually be vindicated. Aeschines, who had successfully countercharged Timarchus with immorality, thus temporarily invalidating the charge of *parapresbeia* against him, was prominent among them. Their opponents, foremost among them Demosthenes, while realizing that for safety's sake the peace must be upheld since the alliance was now a dead letter, were nevertheless determined that any further Philippic overtures must be rejected. The *status quo* well suited their goal; then let Athenian resentment and Theban rancour do the rest.

In time for the Panathenaea (*c.* mid-August) the Athenian prisoners were set free and Philip assured the Athenians in a letter that their fears of him were unjustified. Few were mollified. When the time came for the

For a note on sources see the beginning of ch. 14.

Pythian festival at Delphi, in September, the assembly refused to make the usual arrangements for the city's participation, even giving notice of resignation from the Amphictyony in protest over the Phocian settlement. But, when an embassy arrived from that body to demand a retraction, most even of the extremists realized that there was no choice. Demosthenes (*On the Peace*) argued that, bad as things were, the settlement must stand along with the peace, and Athens could not yet afford to shed that. Under its protection she could prepare herself and her allies for war with Philip, but, pragmatically, over some issue that would not rank all of the Amphictyony on his side. The citizens agreed. But indignation and fear remained strong.

After the Pythia and the autumn meeting of the Amphictyony (October and November) Philip departed from central Greece, leaving only one obvious sign of the new dispensation, a Thessalian garrison at Nicaea to guard Thermopylae. At about this time he let it be generally known that his object was to launch an expedition into Asia Minor. There was no timetable since no one could imagine that he would turn his back on Greece in its present state, but word of the intention might allay some fears.

II. ISOCRATES AND PANHELLENISM

Neither Aeschines' nor Demosthenes' policy was unhazardous or wholly pragmatic. On the one hand, it was not yet clear that Philip's more or less confidentially expressed plans for Macedonia and Athens were what he really had in mind. On the other, a programme which denied co-operation, and sought to sabotage all that might lead to it, was very likely to provoke the enmity its proponents assumed, and professed to fear, was already there. A third view, refreshingly panhellenic, was also abroad in Athens, represented in our extant literature by its most famous exponent, Isocrates, an aged and influential rhetorician and writer little involved in day-to-day politics but well informed on and deeply concerned about some of the major problems of fourth-century Greece. He was neither overly hopeful that the settlement of 346 could serve as a basis for Hellenic stability nor yet wholly inclined to despair of its author. In a series of pamphlets over some four decades he had expressed his pessimism over the ability of the Hellenic states to co-exist without external motivation in a reasonable state of peace. From the Peloponnesian War onwards, through a period of almost constant conflict, he had seen tyrants rise with mercenary assistance to disrupt the peace of the mainland with no major power strong enough to impose a benign hegemony over the whole. In the 380s he had hoped that Athens and Sparta might jointly provide and enforce stability. As new powers and ephemeral leaders arose in the ensuing decades he had pinned his hopes on one, then another. In 346, as the settlement of the Sacred War was in course, he wrote a new pamphlet, the *Philippus*, addressed to Philip, in which he now urged the Macedonian king to unite all the Hellenes not by force but by mounting a national crusade against the Persian realm. He expressed his approval of the peace (writing shortly before the reversal at Thermopylae), but warned that many Athenian orators had no interest in its maintenance. He feared that at the same time some of the king's advisers were urging him to press onward towards domination of the Hellenic peninsula and that Greek social and political instability could only encourage and facilitate such a course. In the Peloponnese hatred of Sparta was so entrenched that there were many who would try to contrive the king's entry. Nor could many forget the Theban interventionism of the 370s and 360s. Those who had suffered would naturally hail Philip as champion of the weak. But if he were to resist such lures and instead devote himself to an eastern expedition, the rewards in Greek unity and Macedonian prestige would be unsurpassable.

III. REORGANIZATION IN MACEDONIA AND THESSALY

Between the end of the Sacred War and the Illyrian campaign of 345 Justin (VIII.5.7–6.2) describes, in a famous passage (it was familiar to Machiavelli, for example), Philip's resettlement of population groups from some parts of the kingdom into others. While, for both social and strategic reasons, such 'transplants' undoubtedly occurred on a number of occasions during the reign, this expansive and emotive account in a mostly cryptic narrative may mean that in 346/5 examples occurred on a considerable scale. No source lends precision to Justin's melodrama, but we may guess at the reality. For the first time since 348 Philip had the leisure to make what must have been extensive arrangements entailed in the annexation of the Chalcidic peninsula. At least the Olynthian territory was granted in estates to Macedonians, and it is likely that some of the previous inhabitants, those not detained to work the land under new masters, were relocated in areas where they could not organize as a dissident faction. By now, too, Philip was planning a campaign to the more distant Illyrian areas, and it may be that by resettlement and fortification he was bolstering the north-western frontiers and securing the communication lines in the adjacent passes.

It was probably against the Ardiaei, one of the three greatest Illyrian tribes, normally occupying an area of the Gulf of Rhizon on the Dalmatian coast, that Philip marched in 345. No source supplies a reason, but Macedonians were very much better aware than most Greeks of movements among the Balkan tribes to their north. Their victories of 359/8, 356 and *c.* 350, while suppressing trouble in the nearer regions, may at the same time have made these same neighbours more vulnerable to those beyond. Probably Ardiaean influence, as a result, had been felt closer to Macedonia than usual and ought to be dealt with before instability spread as far as her frontiers. The campaign was successful and profitable, although Philip in battle against King Pleuratus sustained a serious wound to the lower right leg. In a letter (*Ep.* 2.3) Isocrates chided him for running such risks when so much was at stake.

To those with a grudge against the Athenians the Amphictyony was, to all appearances, a body worth exploiting. Most will have expected Philip, and therefore the Thessalians, Magnesians, Perrhaebians and others, not to mention the Thebans, to be sympathetic. In early 345 the islanders of Delos, though not themselves members, appealed to the Council against Athenian control over their temple of Apollo. For Athens the issue was potentially dangerous, so soon after her Amphictyonic confrontation of the previous September. The Assembly chose Aeschines as advocate, presumably hoping that he would be more acceptable to Philip. But the Areopagus intervened, quashing the appointment in favour of Hyperides, one of the orators best known for opposition to the Peace of Philocrates. Aeschines was too closely associated at Delphi with the Phocians. If that is the reason for the reconsideration, it implies that the Areopagites were confident enough of Philip's support to leave it out of the reckoning. At the spring *pylaia* the Delian plaint was dismissed, and we can hardly imagine that could happen without Macedonian assent.

Important as Athens was to Philip in the long run, by almost every criterion Thessaly was more so, and difficulties there now temporarily distracted him from all else. Their origin is obscure. The Thessalians, said Isocrates (*Ep.* 2.20), were awkward, arrogant and seditious; and, unless we dismiss this as the sycophant's rationalization, we should wonder rather that Philip's relations with Thessaly were mostly smooth than that they went through rougher times. It may be that some Thessalians, now that the profits were in, began to resent the cost of the investment in Philip: his possession of Pagasae especially may have rankled, his holdings in Perrhaebia and Magnesia too. The trouble seems to have come mostly from Pherae and Larissa. Of the former it is more easily understandable; but Larissa's involvement was very serious, for that city, with its dominant Aleuad nobility, had admitted Philip to Thessalian influence in the first place. It is clear that in 344 the special relationship between the king and the Aleuadae broke down utterly. In response to some local *stasis*, the leading oligarch, Simus, had been given a 'mediating' or 'neutral' magistracy backed by mercenary troops. When with his supporters he began to take on the trappings of tyranny, issuing coinage in his own name, Philip 'expelled the tyrants', as Diodorus (XVI.69.8) puts it, so 'winning popularity among the Thessalians'. In Pherae, following this third intervention in eight years, he replaced the local government with a decadarchy ('board of ten') supported by a garrison of Macedonian troops (Dem. VI.22).

Such disruptions were symptomatic of more general weaknesses in Thessalian government, and Philip decided now to reorganize the system more drastically. Thessaly proper, a federation (*koinon*) of four tribal territories, or tetrads (Thessaliotis, Pelasgiotis, Hestiaeotis and Phthiotis), was in origin a Dorian feudal kingdom whose aristocratic families with their retainers controlled large numbers of pre-Dorian indigenes (*penestai*) as serfs of their land. The monarch's place had been taken by the elected federal *archon* (*tagos*, in traditional terminology), who stood, in the now limited federal sphere, above the local magistrates, four tetradic commanders (tetrarchs). For at least military purposes he also held some authority over the perioecic subject territories of Achaea Phthiotis, Magnesia and Perrhaebia. But in most matters the cities and their surrounding estates were dominant and the great old families (the Aleuadae at Larissa or the Daochidae at Pharsalus, for instance) were their rulers; the revolt of Simus probably merely emphasized a problem that was ubiquitous. And perhaps it had been the strain of reaching agreement among such local dynasts which elevated Philip to the federal archonship in 352. It is unlikely that any at that time had been able to foresee that the king's expanding involvement in central Greece would dampen his enthusiasm for the role of figurehead in Thessaly and prompt him to impose a polity in which internal affairs could be made to coincide more smoothly with the *archon's* interests.

Thessalian cities had too long been fundamental to the region's social and economic conditions to be simply submerged in a new federal administration. Since coinage began it had been minted by the major cities, a good indicator (so we assume) of where power traditionally lay. In the later 370s, with Jason of Pherae as *tagos* the confederacy had flowered briefly, but after his death the headship had quickly withered in his kinsmen's less capable hands. In the 360s Pelopidas' reforms had been cosmetic, little affecting the cities' predominance; the only apparent survivals of his intervention were in changes of nomenclature (*archon* for *tagos, polemarchos* for *tetrarchos*). Philip, accepting the realities, did not attempt to change the political basis of Thessalian society; the cities remained its structural modules. The tetrarchs recovered their ancient title, which altered little; but their powers were markedly augmented. (One, Thrasydaeus, could be referred to, however hyperbolically, as 'tyrant' over his people (Theopomp. F 209).) This was to the *archon's* indirect advantage, since the tetradic leaders were the deputies of the federal organization. No doubt their selection was especially important, and the inclusion of the only two known to us from 344 in Demosthenes' famous catalogue of 'sycophants and traitors' (Dem. xvIII.295 f; cf. Polyb. xvIII.13 ff) will mean, as we would expect, that they were pro-Macedonian. Two cities in particular, Larissa and Pharsalus, had been outstanding in the past decades and appear to have retained some of their traditional superiority. They provided, for example, two each of the eight Thessalian seats in the Board of Naopoioi of the Amphictyony, not in itself particularly important but presumably reflecting something more significant. Much work is still to be done on the Thessalian coinages of the period, especially the smaller denominations, but it is clear that at least Larissaean silver drachms (a well-established issue) continued to be minted through Philip's reign in the absence of any federal silver coinage. Whether the *koinon* issued smaller denominations in bronze is uncertain (a group referring to the 'Petthaloi' has been proposed)[1] but plausible. Although so much regarding this important reorganization is unknown to us, it seems fair to characterize it in general as a compromise: primarily the promotion of national unity (with obvious benefits for the archonship at its head) by giving substance to the old forms of the *koinon*; this, however, modified by a pragmatic maintenance of the important role of the major Thessalian cities in the society and its economy.

IV. THE COURTING OF ATHENS

Since 346 Macedonian influence had grown perceptibly in the Peloponnese. Alliances were by 344 in force between Philip and Messene, Argos and probably Megalopolis. To the Athenians, whose own sympathies for the anti-Spartan movement had been at best ephemeral, this was especially ominous. Demosthenes himself (vI.19–25) on a recent embassy had berated the Messenians on the dangers of their new association. In this reaction was the danger for Philip, for, much as he might have relished the role of protector, he risked raising thereby too great a fear in Athens for pro-Macedonian opinion makers to counter. For that reason he proved, over these years, to be a disappointing ally to the Peloponnesians. Thus when, a little earlier than 344, Messene and Megalopolis had applied to the Amphictyony for membership, he declined to procure their admission. They were technically unqualified and that probably served as the rationale; but he could not allow the august body, and hence himself, to be dragged down into the rough and tumble of Peloponnesian politics. Before long, in any case, the Spartan

[1] Franke 1970 (C 361).

issue was temporarily eased: King Archidamus, with Spartan and other troops, departed in 343 or 342 in the service of local causes in Crete and Southern Italy (Diod. XVI.62.4). The Lacedaemonians, well aware by now that Philip's attitude towards them had changed since 346, that his interests now lay on the side of their enemies, were backing down as gracefully as possible, at least, perhaps, until Archidamus should win sufficient funds to pay for more active resistance.

About late summer 344 Philip's Byzantian friend Python arrived in Athens at the head of a mission of Macedon's allies, including Argos and Messene. The king regretted, they announced, that his detractors insisted upon misrepresenting him. If the Athenians were disturbed by the friendship shown by the Hellenes to him, then let Athens join him in extending the bilateral arrangement into a common peace open to all who wished to belong. Indeed he would consider whatever amendments to the existing peace she might propose. Common peace was, after all, what her citizens had overwhelmingly desired in Elaphebolion 346. It had been an unpractical instrument of his plans then, but circumstances were different. The reaction, it seems, was at first positive. The treaty, the Assembly recommended, should be open to all and should contain a guarantee (standard, though little honoured, in the terms of previous common peaces) by the participants to respect and defend the autonomy of every co-member.

The anti-Macedonians were not deterred by their fellows' enthusiasm. They proposed additional amendments shrewdly calculated to deadlock the negotiations. It was not difficult to find support for a clause guaranteeing to each party not 'what it possessed' but 'what was its own'; if Philip was in so generous a mood, he might even agree to apply that principle to Amphipolis! Moreover the Thracian fortresses jointly established by Cersobleptes and Chares in 347, but lost to Philip in the next year, might in the same way be recovered. Lastly, Halonnesus, a small island long under Athens' control but recently captured by pirates, who had then been expelled by Philip, might now be returned to its rightful owners. To the king such proposals were unacceptable. By now the mining area between Amphipolis and Philippi was Macedonia's largest source of revenue, returning upwards of 1,000 talents per year (Diod. XVI.8.6). He could not, would not, hand this part of what was now eastern Macedonia to anyone, and the claim of the Athenians, who had held Amphipolis for thirteen years nearly a century before, was laughable. Even if it had been conceivable, Philip could not agree, any more so than the Athenians themselves if they were being serious, to a principle which would inevitably set every member of the common peace at each other's throat. In practice 'to each its own' could mean nothing less than 'to each whatever it could claim to have held at any

THE COURTING OF ATHENS

time'. There could be no state, large or small, without a whole string of consequent claims to make or losses to contemplate or both simultaneously. When Hegesippus led an embassy to Pella in autumn or winter to convey the Athenian resolutions officially to the king, he was received as coolly as he ought to have expected (Dem. XIX.331). Again Philip had been forced to retreat from an arrangement he himself had proposed.

At the same time as Python's embassy (Philoch. F157, in context at Did. *in Dem.* x.34 col. 8.5 ff) the Athenians had also received envoys from Artaxerxes asking for Hellenic troops for a massive campaign, planned for the following year, to bring Egypt back under the Persian yoke. In Asia Minor some cities, with less option, complied; in Greece Thebes, as usual, and, with Spartan troops now committed to southern Italy, Argos too. But in Athens the request was frostily dismissed. Athenian friendship for the King would last as long as he attacked no Greek city; but if he should interfere with any, the decree added, Philip and the rest of the Hellenes were bidden to make common cause against him. That Philip should be so mentioned (if we can trust the source of that clause, Philip himself: [Dem.] XII.6) at the very time of Python's embassy suggests that there had indeed been some chance of public favour at the time. Athenians en masse were evidently not yet irremediably opposed to Macedon. Although once again Philip had been made to seem false, he kept open the offer of renegotiation.

Until this point, despite the Amphictyons' judgments of July or August 346, no Phocian reparation had yet been collected. That was perhaps no more than realistic, considering that resettlement in villages would entail the disruption of Phocian society; but certainly news of the moratorium would have been well received in Athens. Not in Thebes, though, and the recent negotiations in Athens had renewed Theban fears. There was even a rumour abroad that Philip intended to fortify Elatea, barring the road into Phocis (Dem. VI.44). Amphictyonic disgruntlement will not have been confined to Thebes alone, and, especially following the rebuff of his attempts at reconciliation with Athens, Philip must have been under some pressure. At probably the spring 343 meeting of the Amphictyons in Delphi arrangements were made to collect the first instalment at the following *pylaia*.

The effect in Athens was predictable. Shortly afterwards Hyperides impeached Philocrates, the envoy of 346 whose name had been most closely linked with the peace with Philip. The charge: he had 'made proposals, as the result of bribes, inimical to the public good'. A show trial might rid its promoter and his associates of one of their leading opponents and would provide a convenient forum for anti-Macedonian sentiment. Philocrates, all too likely in this atmosphere to become the public whipping-boy, fled from the city and was condemned *in absentia*.

Those, like Aeschines, who might have defended him were left dis-
armed, as his flight could so easily be taken for a confession of guilt. Yet
at the trial, in response to a challenge by Demosthenes, no envoy stood
to repudiate Philocrates. They were not so obviously implicated as he in
the discredited peace and it might be that to acknowledge Philocrates'
guilt in a lawsuit in which they could not effectively defend themselves
would be more incriminating than silence. Yet it is instructive that
neither now nor, to our knowledge, at any other time did any one of the
envoys (Demosthenes notably excepted) condemn the peace or Philip.

When Timarchus and Demosthenes had laid the similar charge against
Aeschines in July 346 their intention had been to discredit his opposition
to Demosthenes' immediate plans. There had been no need to continue
to the actual point of trial, and in any case Aeschines' successful
countercharge had deprived Timarchus of the capacity to proceed. But
in the more than two years since then Aeschines had been prominent
among those favouring the peace. Now was the time to strike. Demosthenes revived the indictment. At about this time, at any rate within the
next year, the Athenian general Diopeithes, an associate of Hegesippus,
was sent to the Chersonese at the head of a new detachment of cleruchs.

Meanwhile, in the summer of 343, *stasis* broke out in both Elis and
Megara, caused, according to Demosthenes (xix.294–5), by aristocratic
factions favouring Philip. In neither case was there any direct Macedonian intervention; Demosthenes' evidence (for example, at ix.27: 'he *has
hold of* the important city of Elis') on such matters at this time is highly
suspect.[2] But in many places the king's partisans were at a solid
advantage in domestic politics, no matter how far away their nominal
benefactor. Certainly while he still hoped to win Athens he avoided any
real and conspicuous involvement. But every time his mere influence
could be seen, or credibly alleged, his credit correspondingly fell in
Athens. In Euboea, too, endemic *stasis* furnished Demosthenes with all
too credible stories of direct Macedonian intervention. In fact Athens' ill
judged interference in the island's affairs in 349/8 had much diminished
her influence there and favoured those who claimed Philip's friendship.
In at least Eretria and Oreus they were dominant.

When Aeschines was prosecuted in autumn 343 the circumstances
were thus even worse for him than they had been for Philocrates. In his
trial there were two crucial issues: whether the peace was now in such
bad odour as to taint anyone not yet dissociated from it, and whether
Aeschines in 346 had taken Macedonian bribes to promote it to Athens'

---

[2] A different view of the degree of Philip's involvement in the Peloponnese and Euboea in 343
may be found, for example, in Hammond and Griffith 1979 (D 50) 496–504). The interpretation
followed here is that of Cawkwell 1963 (C 106) II.

detriment. Over the former he very nearly fell; his patent innocence of the latter just barely saved him. The golden words of the greatest of Athenian orators (Dem. xix) may blur but cannot obscure the fact that on every substantial matter the evidence is with Aeschines (Aeschin. ii). On a charge less transparently false he would certainly have been convicted. To Philip's supporters and to Philip himself the message was clear. As the time of the Amphictyons' autumn *pylaia* arrived, and 30 talents were received from Phocis, their standing in Athens slipped even further.

In Epirus, as the young Alexander, Olympias' brother, now in Macedon, approached the age at which he could become king of the Molossians, Arybbas' position had become increasingly difficult (see ch. 9*d*). What prompted Philip's intervention at this time is unknown but, given its awkwardness for his relations with Athens, it is probable that the initiative came from Arybbas. Setting out across the Pindus in autumn/winter 343, Philip despatched a final communiqué to the Athenians. Again he invited his ally to agree to extend the treaty to all interested participants. Again he referred to the benefits his friendship would bring. He would give her Halonnesus; if she insisted that it be 'returned', he was prepared to submit to arbitration for definition of its present ownership. So too over the issue of the Thracian fortresses. A more recent question, a territorial dispute between the newly arrived Athenian cleruchs in the Chersonese and his allies at Cardia, was similarly something for a legal settlement, with which, if necessary, he would compel the Cardians to comply. Macedonian envoys had already recently proposed establishing a Macedonian-Athenian legal procedure for hearing cases arising out of commercial disagreement. Such was proper for allies, and the offer remained open. Finally the king proposed a joint campaign to rid the Aegean of pirates, a much more serious problem since the virtual collapse of the Athenian naval alliance in 355.

It was an attractive package but probably nothing could have turned the tide at this stage. It was not difficult to distort every unencumbered offer and lay stress on those matters over which Philip was not wholly free, Halonnesus in particular, 'to return' which would be to concede that loss did not affect ownership. Halonnesus, which neither side much wanted, was made to stand in Athens for Philippic rapacity and dishonesty ([Dem.] vii, *On Halonnesus*).

In Epirus Philip met no opposition. Arybbas capitulated and went into exile to Athens, where he was granted citizenship (Tod. no. 173). Alexander, now twenty years old, became king in his place. At the same time the southern frontier of the Molossian kingdom was extended and strengthened: three or four Cassopian towns north of the Ambracian Gulf were forced to surrender to Alexander, who annexed them. The relationship between Macedon and Epirus was now, it seems, quite closely analogous to that between Macedon and Thessaly.

The Athenians had almost certainly over-reacted in response to what they took, in the Epirote intervention, to be a Macedonian threat to Ambracia, actually sending a force to Acarnania which 'prevented' Philip's 'invasion' ([Dem.] VII.32, Dem. XLVIII.24, IX.72). Nevertheless they, and others, did have cause for disquiet. Either then or within the next year Philip negotiated some kind of agreement with the Aetolians, promising to return to them, when he could, their port Naupactus, at present in Achaean hands. Soon afterwards, the Achaeans and their neighbours in northern Arcadia and Mantinea were in alliance with Athens. More serious still, so were the Argives, Messenians and Megalopolitans. This was not in breach of their treaties with Philip, since he too was technically Athens' ally, but it at least indicated that his failure to intervene in the Peloponnese on behalf of his friends was resented. The Peace of Philocrates was clearly beyond all hope. Sooner or later Philip must go to war with the Athenians. In the mean time he need no longer be overly attentive to their sensitivities.

V. ARISTOTLE AND HERMIAS

Shortly after the fall of Olynthus and the death of his mentor, Plato's greatest pupil had left Athens at the end of some twenty years of study under the old man's direction. Speusippus, Plato's nephew, was the new head of the Academy. Aristotle had travelled to Assus, in the Troad in north-western Asia Minor, settling in the company of two fellow alumni, Erastus and Coriscus, from nearby Scepsis (see ch. 12a, pp. 620–1). There he became the close friend of their philosophical associate, another ex-academician, the local dynast, Hermias of Atarneus. Not long afterwards he had married the prince's niece and adopted daughter. For three years he then combined (especially zoological) study, teaching and political discussion in this congenial company, but in 344 moved to Mytilene, probably at the instigation of a younger associate, Theophrastus. Hermias' position of relative independence in the earlier 340s, with Persia much preoccupied with plans for recapturing Egypt and with revolt in Phoenicia and Cyprus, had been assured during Aristotle's time with him, but following the recapture of the three provinces (343–342) he was obliged to look about for support. By 341 he was in alliance with Philip and the origins of the connexion are not hard to guess, since Aristotle was the son of Nicomachus, once the personal friend and physician of Philip's father, Amyntas III. The date of the alignment – whether before or after Aristotle's appointment as tutor of Alexander in

342 – is uncertain, but it presumably signifies, in view of Hermias' danger, his confidence that the Macedonian plans for Asia Minor were not far from fruition. Otherwise, one would imagine, there were much safer courses open to him.

In the summer of 342 Aristotle, now in his early forties and a man already of some stature and reputation, was invited to Macedon. Just before Philip's final Thracian expedition began, by June, the philosopher was established with his young charge, and a number of others including probably Hephaestion, Ptolemy, and some of Antipater's sons, near Mieza in the 'Gardens of Midas' on the forested slopes of Mt Bermion. In a complex of caves and shaded walks known as the Precinct of the Nymphs, Aristotle continued the education of the prince and his companions away from the steamy heat of Pella's summer. There may have been many pupils. It was Philip, we are told (Arr. *Anab.* IV.13.1, Ael. *VH* XIV.48), who instituted the Royal Pages, sons of the king's leading Companions, as personal attendants on himself. They spent their teenage at the court, sharing the education of the king's own sons and receiving a suitable training in the responsibilities of administrative and military command. There were evident virtues in the early cultivation thus of tomorrow's leaders, not least in that they were isolated from familial and local contacts in an atmosphere controlled largely by the king and by those he regarded as appropriate influences.

VI. EUBOEA

As clearly as the Thracian campaign, actions elsewhere in Greece indicate that by this summer Philip had given up hope of reconciling Athens by friendly generosity. Whether he believed by now that war was the only option or hoped, by denying Athens support, to provoke the same rush of realism among her citizens as the defection of Phalaecus had in the winter of 347/6, we cannot be sure. As would again become clear after 338, though it might be overlooked now, he still saw Athens, not Thebes, as his best southern Greek ally. But the more immediate and critical sphere of Macedonian interest was the northern Aegean. Thessaly and Epirus were quiet and secure. But Thrace, especially with Persia now renascent and Asia Minor potentially vulnerable to tighter control than had been possible for several decades, could not wait. Even as the campaign began, the Macedonian presence in central Greece too became more apparent.

Athenian hamfistedness in the early 340s and Theban quiescence during and after the Third Sacred War had encouraged a growing impetus among the Euboean cities towards independence. The practical difficulty was that no single city of the island was sufficiently dominant to give a firm lead, while inter-polis rivalries inhibited co-operation. Hence, no doubt, the high level of civil discord already in Eretria and Oreus; hence too the bitterness of the conflicts between pro-Macedonians and their opponents.

A short time before, perhaps only a year, a prominent Euboean, Callias of Chalcis, had sought Philip's support for a Euboean League strong enough to wipe Theban and Athenian influence from the island. Philip had turned him down; such flagrant interference would have undermined his negotiations with the Athenians. But by the time the Thracian campaign began there were Macedonian troops, probably mercenaries, posted on the mainland opposite northern Euboea. Over the following few months three of Philip's leading generals would serve with their troops on the island, probably in brief forays from Achaea Phthiotis or Pagasae. And in the autumn, at the Pythian festival at Delphi, Antipater, in the king's absence, would advertise the Macedonian presence south of Thermopylae. It began to seem the Athenians would not much longer be able to get away with undermining Philip's interests under the protection of his alliance.

At the time of Callias' vain plea for Macedonian support for Chalcis, while Carystus at the southern tip had remained committed to Athens, the other two major towns, Eretria and Oreus, had been in the hands of their pro-Macedonians. For the rest of 343 pro-Athenian refugees from Eretria had held its port, Porthmus, unmolested. In the summer of 342 Hipponicus with 1,000 mercenaries destroyed the walls and ejected their defenders in an attempt to confirm the dominance in Eretria of the pro-Macedonian leaders, Hipparchus, Automedon, and Clitarchus. But this was not enough to resolve their difficulties, for on two subsequent occasions Eurylochus and Parmenion found it necessary to intrude in order to suppress opposition. Parmenion also intervened against some opposition to secure Macedonia's partisans in Oreus. Why the movement of the previous year in those two places was now under challenge is not obvious. But from the fact that there was no similar intervention in Chalcis or Carystus, where there had been no comparably strong 'philippizing' tendency, we might infer that the open interventions of 342 were intended to confirm the dominance of those with genuine support rather than to elevate clients with no power base. Against that gain, however, Philip had to set the risk that the appearance of actual Macedonian troops might chill the ardour even of some of those Euboeans happy to call him friend at a moderate distance. It was, in the event, a miscalculation, especially in view of the calibre of opponents like Demosthenes and of their growing influence among the uncommitted of Athens and elsewhere.

VII. THRACE, PERINTHUS AND BYZANTIUM

The main objective of the great Thracian expedition was an ambitious one. According to a brief allusion by Diodorus (XVI.71.1) the 'Greek cities on the Hellespont' were under attack, presumably by Cersobleptes; and in the early stages of the war Philip seems to have visited at least Cardia and Aenus. But Thrace was very much more than its coastline, extensive as that was, and he spent a good deal of time and effort on the interior. His alliance with Cothelas, king of the Getae, whose territory stretched from northern Thrace to the Danube in the area of the Schipka Pass is perhaps to be dated in late 342. His daughter Meda became Philip's sixth wife. Born out of an initial opposition (Jordanes *Getica* 10–65, corrected by Theopomp. F 217) the entente was useful, erecting a northern barrier against which Philip might if necessary batter those resisting him in the difficult region of Mt Rhodope and the river Hebrus.

About the warfare itself we know next to nothing. With Cersobleptes and his colleague Teres in central Thrace cordoned off on all sides by Philip and his coastal allies, there may have been no major battles. We hear of various actions, all practically undatable and not all successful, perhaps mainly against pockets of resistance in the mountains of the interior. In some such areas outposts were established and fortified with Macedonian garrisons and mixed colonists. Two of those in the far north, Beroe and Philippopolis, were especially successful and remain, in modern Stara Zagora and Plovdiv, major populations in the fertile catchment between Mt Haemus and the northern reaches of the Hebrus.

Western Thrace was already, at least in effect, part of Macedonia; the central and eastern kingdoms now became a Macedonian subject territory, paying an annual tribute of one tenth of the produce and administered (though this is not documented until Alexander's early reign) by a Macedonian general over Thrace. By the spring of 341, despite the successes, Philip had been ill for some time, according to news reaching Athens. How seriously we cannot tell. But the long absence in inaccessible places heartened the king's opponents and dismayed his adherents. In the Chersonese the territorial dispute between the Athenian cleruchies and Cardia flared into activity. Philip joined the Cardians in appealing to Athens to submit her arguments to arbitration. She declined and gave at least tacit encouragement to her freebooting general Diopeithes, whose actions around the Chersonese were becoming highly provocative. Already in winter 342/1 he had seized a Macedonian herald and had him conveyed to Athens, where he was imprisoned and his dispatches were read publicly. Philip ordered a small force of mercenaries to Cardia to keep the peace. In the early months of 341 Diopeithes led troops into Thrace, destroying crops and carrying off the people of two towns into slavery. A second envoy sent to bid for their release was captured, tortured and held to ransom. Diopeithes shored up his finances by impounding merchant ships, either for their cargoes or for ransom.

In central and southern Greece opposition gathered. In spring or early summer Callias of Chalcis sent envoys to Athens proposing equal alliance (by contrast with the earlier hegemonial relationship) with the goal of establishing a Euboean League under Chalcis, which would in return support an anti-Macedonian coalition. Swallowing their pride the Athenians accepted the reality of Euboean 'nationalism'. Over the next months Oreus and Eretria were successfully assaulted by the Athenian generals Ctesiphon and Phocion and obliged to enter alliance with both Chalcis and Athens.

By this time, too, although Demosthenes (VIII.14–15) could still count Byzantium as Philip's, there were signs of disquiet there ([Dem.] XII.2–3). But Philip turned to the north, to the coast of modern Bulgaria, where the grain of the Maritsa and Danube basins was channelled to the Greek merchant fleets. The purpose of this venture is unknown. One effect is clear, though: when Demosthenes travelled as far as Byzantium in the autumn, it was because he was aware that disquiet over the recent activities could be exploited there. A simultaneous embassy, apparently under Hyperides, to Chios and Rhodes, Byzantium's allies in the Social War, increased the pressure. Old grudges could be overlooked when the corn route seemed under threat.

During the Persian reconquest of Egypt (Diod. XVI.40–51)[3] in the winter of 343/2, Mentor, an able mercenary commander from Rhodes, had distinguished himself in the Persian royal service and had then been set the task of tightening the imperial control over Asia Minor. Securing Artaxerxes' pardon for his kinsmen Memnon and Artabazus, in exile in Pella since 353, he had invited them to join him, undoubtedly learning whatever could be learnt of Philip's hopes with regard to Asia Minor. Although there can have been as yet few concrete plans, Mentor had evidently heard enough to worry him. Promising to obtain Artaxerxes' pardon for Hermias of Atarneus too, he lured the hapless dynast to a meeting and seized and delivered him in chains to the King. Steadfast to the end under torture, Hermias had finally been killed. In Macedon in summer 341 Aristotle mourned the death of a philosopher and friend. In Athens Demosthenes exulted over it and recommended that his fellows swallow their prejudice and seek the aid of Artaxerxes. In the same autumn an Athenian embassy at the King's court found him sympathetic.

---

[3] Diodorus' chronology of the final campaign in Egypt is seriously awry; see Cawkwell 1963 (C 106) 1 and now, for a proposed redating, Markle 1981 (C 197).

During the winter Demosthenes continued to lobby potential allies, helped by Callias. Reporting to the Athenian Assembly in late winter 340 the two men claimed to have discerned a marked increase in general anti-Macedonian sentiment. The details are obscure, coming mostly from a version (Aeschin. III.91 ff) which set out to denigrate their achievement by *amplificatio ad absurdum*. The Euboean League, at least, was now set under way: on Demosthenes' motion Chalcis was authorized to convene a *koinon* and levy contributions on the Euboean towns to finance it. Megara must also have been already Athens' ally, co-operating with her in the Euboean campaign several months earlier (Charax, *FGrH* 103 F 19); similarly the Acarnanians and probably the Achaeans (schol. Aeschin. III.83). There had been other alliances too in recent years, but the extent to which these could be used against Philip is, and no doubt was, debatable. This was hardly a 'Greek League'.[4] Nonetheless there *was* support, substantially more than might have been expected by Philip five years earlier and quite enough to raise Athenian hopes.

No further delay was possible. Philip dropped his operations in the far north east and returned to the Pontic coast. Byzantium, with Athenian, Chian and Rhodian support, encouragement from its neighbours Perinthus and Selymbria, and promises of money and men from Persia, had now turned to opposition. The implications for the Thracian settlement, for Philip's longer term plans, and for his need to isolate the Chersonese were extremely serious. Byzantium's defences were formidable (Paus. IV.31.5), so in spring 340 the Macedonian army struck at Perinthus, the lesser target but still one posing great difficulty both for the troops and for the engineering section Philip had established in the late 350s under the brilliant Thessalian, Polyidus (Diod. XVI. 74–6). The commonplace achievement from Alexander the Great's reign onwards of taking walled cities by assault had been exceptional in earlier times, and the difference may be explained in large part by the developments by Philip's technicians of sapping skills, of torsion artillery and of the engines, rams and towers of siegecraft.

Perinthus stood heavily fortified on a high peninsula, its buildings rising up the slopes behind the walls like the tiers of a theatre inside out. In this siege 40-metre towers bearing catapults were winched into place to give covering fire to the Macedonian sappers as they sought to undermine the walls. Breaches were made but gained little, as the Perinthians, by blocking the laneways between their houses, were able to fall back to successively higher barricades. Byzantium, at first holding back probably out of fear that this was a diversion, subsequently agreed to send men, catapults and missiles. By now Diopeithes was dead, but his

---

4 See Ellis 1976 (D 80) 173–4, which may be oversceptical; cf. Hammond and Griffith 1979 (D 50) 551.

successor in the Chersonese, Chares, had enough ships to keep Philip's small fleet (c. 40 ships?) out of the Propontis and enough men to deter it from beaching in self-defence. By mid-summer, as Byzantian aid continued, the siege began to look hopeless. So Philip ordered a detachment of troops onto Chersonesan territory to escort his own ships, under Alcinus, through the Hellespont. It is doubtful whether it was a deliberate act of war, as the Athenians thought. While Philip no longer scrupled to damage their interests, there was as yet no advantage for him in open conflict. He needed his fleet and, if the Athenians held it from him, he must take the risk of war and at the same time try to minimize the damage.

He despatched a letter to Athens ('Philip's Letter' = [Dem.] XII). It was not a declaration of war, even a final ultimatum, though some of its language is very blunt (esp. § 23). It firmly condemns Athenian belligerence since late 342 and deals sharply with her protests over the king's activities in Thrace, Cardia and the Chersonese. It represents Athens as wholly in the wrong and Philip as acting from necessity, not unjustly, since, from the beginning of the frankly anti-Macedonian embassies and Diopeithes' attacks from the Chersonese, there had been no doubt that Athens was at war in all but name, yet without renouncing the Peace of Philocrates. Philip, for his part, had until this point given her no direct ground. Now in the letter he appealed for restraint to those who would listen. In the Athenian Assembly no official commitment to war was made.

Even without direct Athenian intervention Philip found his position at Perinthus deteriorating further as, on Artaxerxes' instructions, the Persian satraps of Asia Minor began to pour in mercenary troops and supplies. His own fleet, while of nuisance value, could not prevent these from reaching the beleaguered city. One option remained. Byzantian aid had evidently depleted that city's resources (Diod. XVI.76.3). So, leaving a part of his army (now some 30,000-strong) at Perinthus to keep his own supply lines open, and for the same reason detaching troops to Selymbria, Philip advanced on Byzantium. He offered terms, but in vain. By now, August or September 340, a large corn fleet was mustering at Hieron, whence it would be escorted by Chares to the Aegean. As chance had it, the Athenian commander was called away for discussions with local Persian officials, and Philip's fleet swooped on the merchantmen. Fifty neutral ships he released. The rest, apparently 180 Athenian vessels, furnished a great haul in booty plus timber and supplies for the siege of Byzantium. Again Philip wrote to Athens, maintaining that her merchantmen had been engaged in supplying his enemies without even the pretext of an alliance.[5] We do not know whether the charge, however

---

[5] Not the letter ([Dem.] XII) referred to above, preserved in the corpus of Demosthenic speeches. See Wüst, 1938 (D 125) 139 and Hammond and Griffith 1979 (D 50) 577–8.

plausible, was true. In either case, so clear a challenge to the Athenians' most vital interests could only produce the most direct reaction from them; the rationalization was a waste of effort so far as they were concerned. But it was perhaps aimed more at others, at those less sympathetic to Athens' preoccupations and more inclined, if given a usable excuse, to stand back and let her fend for herself.

VIII. WAR

Such, at any rate, was the result. Athens took few allies of significance – no more than the remnants of her naval alliance – to war with her in October 340. Chios, Rhodes and Cos, Byzantium's allies, served (Diod. xvi.77.2, Tod no. 175 = Harding no. 97). Persia did not, partly, it may be, because with the approach of winter it was a poor time for assembling new levies. There is some evidence, too, of diplomatic contacts at about this time between Persia and Macedon (Plut. *Mor.* 342 B.C., *Alex.* 5.1, 9.1), but none that they had any issue.[6] Perhaps the explanation is simply that, with Athens now fully committed, Artaxerxes saw no reason to continue his subsidies.

Chares, with his forty ships, went to the relief of Byzantium, and drove the Macedonian fleet back into the Black Sea. Philip applied himself to the siege as winter began, but found neither force nor stealth effective. A second Athenian squadron under Phocion arrived, but the Macedonian effort was already faltering. Meanwhile in Macedon Alexander, now at the age of sixteen Philip's regent at home, was enjoying every success. To deal with a revolt by the Maedi, a troublesome Paeonian tribe on the upper Strymon, he led a force up the Axius, cut across eastwards and swooped on the Maedic territory, suppressing the revolt and, after his father's example, founding a military colony which he named Alexandropolis (Plut. *Alex.* 9.1). As spring (339) approached, Philip abandoned the siege of Byzantium. Just south of the Danube in the modern Dobrudja, a Scythian ruler, Atheas, had recently appealed for help against Istrus and other Greek foundations near the Danube mouth. But by the time Macedon's troops arrived, Atheas had already resolved his problems and dismissed them without even paying expenses. The settlement of northern Thrace and the alliance with Cothelas both dictated that the slight be requited; the failures at Perinthus and Byzantium made success imperative. First Philip extricated his fleet by strategem from the Pontus (Frontin. *Strat.* 1.4.13), this time his troops, as they escorted it along the Chersonesan coast, ravaging the land as they went. Perinthus and Byzantium, though still unconquered, had now been left isolated and there is reason to think that, once

[6] The common belief, based on bad evidence (Arr. *Anab.* ii.14), that Philip at some time made alliance with Persia, has been decisively refuted. See now Hammond and Griffith 1979 (D 50) 484–6.

the second siege was raised, Philip was able to renegotiate his alliances with them, as well as with Chios and Rhodes.[7]

En route to the Danube the king sent ahead a request for unhampered passage to erect a statue of his ancestor Heracles at the river mouth. Atheas refused. In a single battle the Macedonians vented the frustrations of the past year on their opponents, then loaded themselves with booty – prisoners, brood mares and cattle – and made their way westwards towards the upper Strymon (Justin IX.2). But slowness made them vulnerable and, before they had passed out of the Danubian plain, they were attacked by Triballian tribesmen. Philip himself was severely wounded in the thigh, losing consciousness; his men, at first thinking him dead, abandoned the booty (Justin IX.3). Then they bore him home to recover. The Thracian campaign, from mid-342 until July or August 339, had been long and arduous, on both counts probably much more so than expected. Despite the failures, Thrace's vastness was at Macedonia's disposal as a source of soldiers and revenue; the primary goal had been won. Provided that Greece could be made secure, none of the setbacks need much matter in the longer term. But now Greece was the problem.

In Philip's absence the Delphic Amphictyony's old internal rivalries had reappeared. At the spring *pylaia* in 339 an Amphissaean motion had condemned Athens over the text of a recent rededication of Persian War trophies; the terms tactlessly listed Thebes on the Median side and are probably to be dated to the period of the Third Sacred War. An Athenian counterclaim made by Aeschines (III.115–24) had successfully diverted the Amphictyons' ire back onto Amphissa. Following an initial skirmish, a general assembly in Delphi had then set the date for a special convention to discuss the issue, probably a month or so later, in June.

It was known that Thebes favoured Amphissa and would, so both Aeschines and (back in Athens) Demosthenes suspected, support the minority cause. The Athenian position therefore had become critical. Some, including Demosthenes, saw the matter in the context of the existing war. For them any breach between their city and the Thebans must be avoided. For, in effect, what had come about fortuitously was a recreation of the expected situation of July 346, with Thebes manoeuvred onto the weaker side in a general Amphictyonic war. At first the Athenians had resolved to support the cause, but Demosthenes had managed to get the resolution reversed (Aeschin III.125–8, Dem. XVIII.143–50). Like Thebes, Athens sent no delegates to the extraordinary meeting at Thermopylae. The Thessalian Cottyphus had been appointed general with authority to levy an Amphictyonic force, and he passed through Thermopylae, imposed a fine on the Amphissaeans and expelled the leaders guilty of the impieties. Up to this point the Theban position was not finally clear; she could simply have advised Amphissa to accept the punishment rather than provoke something much more serious. But Athens' defection must have been encouragement enough, for the Thebans now seized Nicaea, in effect closing Thermopylae to Cottyphus and Philip and daring them to do their worst. The Amphissaeans recalled their exiles and expelled some restored by the Amphictyons (Aeschin. III.129, Dem. XVIII.150-1).

It was soon after this that Philip returned to Pella. Two months later, at the autumn *pylaia*, the Council commissioned him to fight a new sacred war. In that he could now legitimately march into central Greece, it was convenient, but the alignments there were not propitious. Thebes and Athens had a common cause; the goal towards which Demosthenes had striven since 346, carefully and against much anti-Theban prejudice, was finally within reach. Quickly, to deter their combination, Philip marched south, bypassing Thermopylae, through the mountains of Oetaea to Heraclea in Trachis and thence to Dorian Cytinium. Behind him and westwards were allies, Thessaly, Oetaea, Doris itself, Achaea Phthiotis, Dolopia, Aeniania and Aetolia; to his east, via the upper Cephisus valley in Phocis, the Boeotian frontier. Leaving men to hold Cytinium, he turned into Phocis, seized Elatea and sent an embassy of allies to Thebes (Plut. *Dem.* 18.1, Philoch. F 56). There were only two demands: surrender Nicaea and either join him in attacking Attica or at least give him unhindered passage. Neither was difficult to concede if the Thebans wished to avoid war. The question of Amphissa was not broached. Nicaea would on its surrender be taken over by the Epicnemidian Locrians, whose claim to it had been ignored when it was taken from Phocis in 346; in any case, it was no longer relevant to this campaign.

Meanwhile in Athens, with Philip two days' march from the frontier, terror expunged in a moment the anti-Thebanism of generations past (Dem. XVIII.169-79, Diod. XVI.84-5). Demosthenes proposed his strategy. First: to advertise Athens' commitment, despatch a full levy to Eleusis, on the road to Boeotia. Second: send envoys with negotiating powers to accompany the generals to Thebes, there to conclude alliance and to plan jointly the coming campaign. As a sop to Athenian pride and prejudice he represented the alliance as Athens' beneficence to a stricken, needy neighbour. In Thebes itself, diplomacy would demand a much more mendicant approach.

There the embassy, led by Demosthenes himself, countered Philip's ultimatum by renouncing all of Athens' past demands for Boeotian autonomy, and by offering Thebes the full command by land with one third of the costs and assuming on Athens' behalf the full cost of the fleet and two thirds of the land command. The 'war-office' would be at

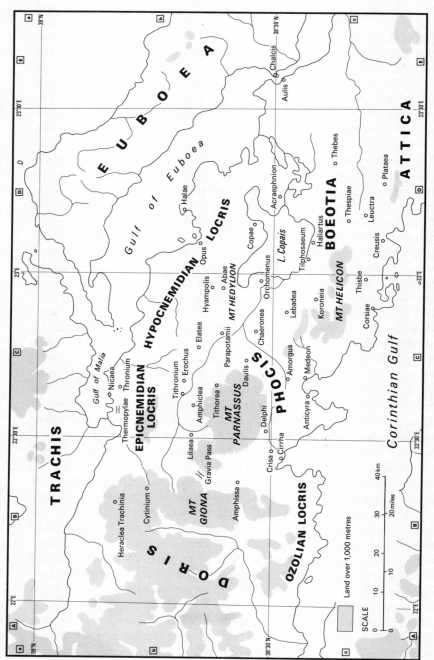

Map 19. Central Greece.

[a] 39°N
[b]
[c] 38°30'N
E 23°30'E
D
[A] 39°N
[B]
[C] 38°30'N

E U B O E A

Gulf of Euboea

Chalcis
Aulis

HYPOCNEMIDIAN LOCRIS

Halae

Opus

Copae

Acraephnion

Thebes

L. Copais

Tilphosaeum

Haliartus

BOEOTIA

Thespiae

Leuctra

Plataea

ATTICA

MT HEDYLION

Abae

Hyampolis

Orchomenus

MT HELICON

Koroneia

Creusis

Elatea

Parapotamii

Chaeronea

Lebadea

Thisbe

Corsiae

Gulf of Malia

Nicaea

Thronium

EPICNEMIDIAN LOCRIS

Tithronium

Erochus

Amphiclea

Amorgus

Medeon

Anticyra

PHOCIS

Thermopylae

Tithorea

Daulis

MT PARNASSUS

Delphi

Crisa

Cirrha

Corinthian Gulf

TRACHIS

Heraclea Trachinia

Cytinium

Lilaea

Gravia Pass

MT GIONA

Amphissa

DORIS

OZOLIAN LOCRIS

23°30'E
23°E
22°30'E
22°E

SCALE

Land over 1,000 metres

0   10   20   30   40 km

0   10   20 miles

Thebes, jointly commanded (Aeschin. III.142–51). It was enough. Philip's embassy was dismissed and the new allies prepared their defences. Philip made no further move; although his speed had carried him to within striking distance of both Amphissa (and thence the Corinthian Gulf and his Peloponnesian allies) and Boeotia, he continued with attempts to parley while his opponents made their dispositions unhindered. Sending out appeals for assistance, they moved up troops into the Gravia Pass, north of Amphissa, and to Parapotamii, in the narrow path of the Cephisus between the Phocian and Boeotian plains, and fortified such more southerly Phocian posts as Lilaea and Ambrysus in order to block the high passes across Mt Parnassus.

Philip's loss of the initiative may seem surprising. Over the winter he made no more than a few tentative probes to test the defences. But we should not from hindsight underestimate his dilemma. He had hitherto done everything possible to avoid fighting Thebes and Athens combined, and now he continued in his endeavours to stave off the event. His Peloponnesian allies, actual or potential, were cut off from him by Achaea, Megara, Corinth and Attica, and were obliged, despite his requests, to declare themselves neutral. Further he had, even if successful, to consider the post-war situation. It may be that he was treating with some states with that in mind – for instance, promising, and even beginning, to reconstruct that major part of Phocis now in his hands. He did not fail to see that victory, if bloody, might so disturb even his friends as to render co-operation very difficult.

At the end of winter he acted, perpetrating much the same hoax on those in the Gravia Pass as had extricated his fleet from the Black Sea. Feigning withdrawal from Cytinium, Parmenion waited for the defenders to relax, then pounced at night and broke through to Amphissa (Polyaen. IV.2.8), at a stroke turning the coalition's defences in the Parnassian passes and at Parapotamii. The Thebans and Athenians fell back to Chaeronea, just inside Boeotia. For four months Philip made no serious move, merely reopening negotiations. As midsummer passed, however, it became plain that all depended on battle. The course of the engagement, in August 338, on the Attic date 7 Metageitnion, is virtually impossible to recover. The sheer weight of Macedonia's cavalry, apparently led by Alexander, and the superior skill and tactics of the phalanx seem to have been decisive (Diod. XVI.86). The Thebans suffered massive casualties and Athens lost 1,000 dead and 2,000 were taken prisoner. The fugitives were not pursued and gathered disconsolately at Lebadea.

IX. SETTLEMENTS AND COMMON PEACE

As became apparent very shortly after the battle, the diplomatic dealings of the next months would rest upon almost exactly the same basic assumptions as had underlain Philip's intended, but aborted, resolution of the Third Sacred War in 346. Again the sharp distinction between Athens and Thebes: it was the one's co-operation he sought, the other's suppression. After eight years of disillusionment, the ties this time would be tighter, the guarantees more binding. But the principle and the aim of making Greece secure for his absence, were unchanged.

Finding Demades, a leading politician, among the prisoners, Philip sent him home to convey word to the Athenians of the king's wish for peace. On his heels went Alexander, Antipater and Alcimachus, escorting the Athenian dead and bearing an offer to return the prisoners gratis. By contrast, Thebes was to recover her dead and captives only on payment of ransom, to receive a Macedonian garrison on the Cadmea, to reinstate her exiled pro-Macedonians and to suffer government by an oligarchy of 300 such men. In Athens panic gave way to hope. Demades, Aeschines and Phocion were ordered to Chaeronea to negotiate, there learning how generous the settlement was to be. Oropus would be severed from Boeotia and returned to Athens. Although her naval alliance would be finally dissolved she would keep Lemnos, Imbros and Scyros as her possessions; Samos and Delos would be under her control. Despite the recent delinquency, her status in the Amphictyony would not change. She need accept no garrison or occupying force and would remain (in theory) free and autonomous, unregulated in at least her internal affairs.

Yet an apparent enthusiasm in Athens for the 'Peace of Demades', born largely of relief, was not the whole story. Demosthenes had prudently secured for himself an overseas commission after Chaeronea. But on his return, though others were hounded in the law-courts, he escaped conviction and continued to hold public office, and was even chosen to deliver the public funeral oration. Similarly, while the people erected an equestrian statue of Philip in the Agora and granted him and Alexander the citizenship of Athens, they also bestowed citizen rights on refugees from Thebes, a snub Philip seems to have accepted with good grace.

The treaties with the two erstwhile coalition partners were elements in a much larger pattern affecting most Greek states.[8] Probably the Euboean alliances with Athens were cancelled. The new Euboean

---

[8] The evidence for the detail of the settlements is surprisingly scant. For the best reconstruction see Roebuck 1948 (D 116) and, for a convincing modification regarding Naupactus and the Aetolian League, Bosworth 1976 (D 20).

League apparently remained, though some of its leaders, whether under coercion or from discretion, departed and were received as refugees in Athens. Similarly, in central Greece, the Boeotian towns destroyed and depopulated by Thebes were reconstructed; the Plataeans, in exile in Athens since 373, were restored. The Boeotian League remained intact but with a more genuinely federal character, the body forged as the vehicle of Theban power now becoming an instrument of her enfeeblement. The rehabilitation of Phocis went into effect, if not actually before the battle; soon the league of its towns was operating in something like the old form. Elsewhere, particularly in the west, in Acarnania and perhaps Leucas, Cephallenia and Corcyra, the need for intervention was reduced or negated by natural political shifts, as Macedonian partisans were swept to power. In Ambracia, to fortify the fragile southern Epirote frontier, stabilize western Greece and secure the western north–south route, Philip installed a garrison.

Later in 338 he entered the Peloponnese and received the immediate surrender of both Corinth and Megara, where news of Chaeronea had probably propelled pro-Macedonians into power. Both retained membership of the Amphictyony, but nothing else is known of their treaties, save that Corinth was garrisoned (the third, and last, at this time, of the 'fetters of Greece').[9] Some Peloponnesians (the Achaeans and the towns of the Acte peninsula, in particular) had recently been Philip's enemies; others (Elis, Argos, Arcadia and Messenia), though neutral in the war, previously allies. In many cases the desired change in the political balance probably occurred naturally; in others, at least Troezen (Lycurgus *Leocr.* 42), not without outside help, or coercion. Sparta had remained aloof from Hellenic affairs since Archidamus' departure for Tarentum in the late 340s, but no settlement could fail to take into account the Peloponnesian arrangements she had been able to guard or salvage from the Theban intervention of the late 370s and the 360s. Philip issued a warning to Sparta to surrender territories claimed by her neighbours and, rebuffed, invaded Laconia (though not Sparta itself). Then he turned over to the Argives, Megalopolitans, Tegeans and Messenians the areas in dispute, so constricting the Spartan state tightly within a circle of grateful beneficiaries. The general settlement, by now about to be unveiled at Corinth, would give these preliminary dispositions full and binding legal sanction.

Delegates of all states were summoned to Corinth in winter or spring 337.[10] All but Sparta responded. To the assemblage the king's plans were

---

[9] It is possible that there was a fourth garrison at Chalcis (Polyb. XXXVIII.3.3, Strabo X.1.8), but that was more probably established after the destruction of Thebes in 335. See Ellis 1976 (D 80) 202–3, 296–7, Hammond and Griffith 1979 (D 50) 612 n. 3.

[10] On the dating of the two conventions at Corinth see Hatzopoulos 1982 (D 94).

announced. A Common Peace was to be set up on the pattern of the 'King's Peace' of 387/6 and its increasingly ineffective successors of the next twenty-five years. But the new peace differed in two ways. This time Philip, and not the barbarian King would be its ultimate guarantor, its executor a properly constituted general synod of all signatories. And this time, unprecedentedly, a Common Peace would confirm an existing state of peace, rather than attempt to impose it. Member states were to participate on a proportional basis, each accorded delegates and votes proportional to its achievable military contribution. Each state would bind itself to take no belligerent action, by war or subversion, against another. The synod would arbitrate on violations and disturbances of the peace, elect a military commander and levy appropriate forces to serve under him if action proved necessary. The oaths of participation (as we see from [Dem.] XVII = *On the Treaty with Alexander* and Tod no. 177 = Harding no. 99, heavily restored) would also require signatories to uphold the existing constitutions of fellow members and to eschew within their own territories such revolutionary actions as unlawful execution, expulsion or confiscation, redistribution of land, debt cancellation, or emancipation of slaves. In effect, that is, the Common Peace would maintain and protect those balances which had fallen into place in many cases as the results of natural political realignments following Chaeronea, and it would crystallize the separate settlements made, some by treaty and some perhaps informally, over the same three or four months. It would enshrine in all states the existing forms of government, but not necessarily their political composition, though in practice the governing body, suitably prompted, might on occasion decide to equate the two. In the cities and tribal centres the oaths were taken and recorded (for Athens: Tod no. 177 = Harding no. 99). In spring or early summer (337) the appointed delegates gathered again at Corinth for the constitution of the general synod. From all of this Sparta still stood apart, frustrated utterly by the collision of pride and impotence but, for the time being, spared from *force majeure* perhaps as testimony to the peace's supposedly voluntary nature, or as a reminder to the hesitant of the old order, but certainly because the last thing the settlement needed was a baptism in blood. A standing committee of *proedroi* was set up and a *hegemon*, Philip, elected. Then delegates turned to the first proposal: that the Hellenes ought now to punish Persia for the destruction of their sanctuaries 150 years earlier. It was a notion to appeal to the romantic, perhaps. Philip's own goals were no doubt different. There would be great wealth for Macedonia, whose revenues were considerable, but no greater than recent expenditures, from both the booty of conquest and (on the Thracian analogy) the ensuing tithe of produce. There would be military activity aplenty for the Macedonian army, by now the most vital element not only of the kingdom's security but also of its social cohesion. The king might win, what no one before had achieved for long, despite all the lip service paid to the cause, the liberation of the Greeks of Asia Minor. For some other participants there would be similar gains, especially for the Athenians, from the increased area of trade opened up. But the first, practical intention of the stated goal, to punish the Persians for impiety, was to provide a formal means of activating the new Hellenic League in the absence of any actual breach of its charter. Wholesale sacrilege, committed no matter when, might be said while unrequited to remain a cause of the gods' displeasure and thus injurious to the general well-being. The synod, with no alternative, accepted the proposal, approved the levy of a common force and conferred on the *hegemon* full authority to take the necessary measures. The convocation then adjourned, probably to reconvene at the Nemean festival at Argos in the next autumn. Philip returned to Macedonia after midsummer.

X. PREPARATIONS

The eastern offensive was to begin in the following spring, its initial phase executed, however, by a relatively small force. Meanwhile, the Illyrian region, the only large part of the Macedonian sphere not under some stable form of supervision or control, drew Philip away at some time during the summer of 337 on a final, pre-emptive strike to deter the tribespeople from rising in his absence. Possibly Pleurias, the chief opponent in the action, was leader of the Autariatae, the last of the three great Illyrian kingdoms remaining untouched.[11]

But other preparatory matters demanded Philip's attention. For all parties to the recent peace a period of stable continuity was essential. The eastern campaign ought to have a unifying influence but there were grave dangers in it, especially if anything were to go seriously wrong. Most obvious was the risk to Philip's own life. Others were having analogous thoughts, as we see in the case of a leading Macedonian general, Attalus, who married a daughter of Parmenion apparently at this time. Philip himself by now had engaged in six marriages (Athen. XIII.557 bd), at least some of them concurrently; there may still have been as many as five in force. But the traditional royal polygamy had not achieved its expected end for Philip, for six wives had borne him only three daughters (Cynna, or Cynnane, born 359–356 to Audata; Cleopatra, born 355–352 to Olympias; Thessalonice, born 351–350 to Nicesipo-

---

[11] Some scholars have not accepted the authenticity of the evidence for this campaign. For bibliography see Hatzopoulos 1982 (D 94) 64 nn. 7–8.

lis) and only two sons (Arrhidaeus, born 357–354 to Philinna; Alexander, born 356, again to Olympias), the former of whom, possibly the elder, had proved to be mentally retarded. Apparently none was yet married, though the two elder daughters were of age: one element in the king's planning was to choose suitable husbands for them. His nephew Amyntas married Cynna and, in mid-336, Alexander of Epirus married Cleopatra (see ch. 9*d*). In conventional manner the female children thus advanced the king's interests, strengthening the bonds of loyalty and alliance. Sons might serve similarly, and as deputies and advisers. The role of the firstborn as the likely successor was special. Alexander had been treated as the heir as far back as we are able to trace, receiving honour and bearing responsibility from the earliest possible days. His mother by consequence also enjoyed higher status (though later, as 'queen mother', she was even more influential), one which no subsequent wives, however fecund, could diminish while Alexander lived; thus Nicesipolis and Meda had been in no sense and at no stage her 'competitors'.

Should Philip die in Asia there might be frightening consequences in the expeditionary force, at home and in Greece generally. Alexander no doubt was to participate in the crusade too, as he had at Chaeronea, where he probably led the Companion Cavalry. But if he, or (worse) he *too*, were to lose his life, there would be no better alternative than Arrhidaeus. Hence the need for the tightest possible network of marriage-alliances within the kingdom to link the surviving members of the Argead royal family to its staunchest and most powerful aides. Hence, too, the aim of siring more sons through a new marriage.

So Philip chose to take a seventh wife, Cleopatra, the niece and adopted daughter of Attalus, recently or soon-to-be son-in-law of Parmenion.[12] As the result of Attalus' later actions and of the propaganda aimed at Alexander and, more particularly, Olympias as the dynasty neared collapse in the years after 323, a number of stories in our sources suggest that the marriage entailed sinister consequences for the heir and his mother. But little credible evidence supports them. Accounts of Attalus' opposition to Alexander before his accession (Plut. *Alex.* 9, Athen. XVIII.557 de, Justin IX.7.3–5) are both implausible and internally inconsistent and are more likely rationalizations designed to explain his dubious loyalty and to justify his murder in the traumatic eighteen months following Philip's assassination. A tale (Plut. *Alex.* 10) linking the Carian dynast Pixodarus with Alexander in circumstances implying insecurity on the latter's part is internally unconvincing and

[12] The reconstruction proposed here of the circumstances of Philip's final marriage and murder is based on the argument in Ellis 1981 (D 82) and 1982 (D 171). Cf. Badian 1963 (D 62).

chronologically implausible.[13] The misapprehension in Justin's account (IX.5.9, 7.2, XI.11.5) that Olympias was 'divorced' and banished arises from false Roman assumptions about Macedonian marriage. There may have been some kind of disruption to Philip's court resulting in the exile of some of Alexander's contemporaries (Arr. *Anab.* III.6.5–6), but even this is far from certain. In general terms, to imagine that after carefully grooming his successor for years Philip decided at this most critical time of all to abandon him is almost impossible. Alternatively, that the king, now at the height of authority and prestige, fell suddenly vulnerable to others' pressure is no more credible. Philip's seventh marriage, like those of two of his daughters and of leading commanders, fits comfortably into the context of preparations for an inevitably protracted and dangerous campaign. It was celebrated probably in October 337. As it happened, it failed in its primary end, for only a daughter, Europe, was born from it, who, like her mother, lost her life in the troubles of Alexander's early reign. (A putative son, 'Caranus', is the invention of a later tradition apparently seeking, in ignorance of Macedonian marriage customs, to make sense of the tangle of propaganda that came long after the event to surround Philip's murder and the reasons for it.)

XI. A BEGINNING IN ASIA AND AN END IN MACEDON

In 338, soon after Chaeronea, Artaxerxes III (Ochus) had fallen, after a twenty-one year reign, to the poison of his vizier, the eunuch Bagoas. Placing Arses, the youngest son, on the throne, Bagoas had resisted the older claimants, disposing of them all by the winter. Through 337 discontent had intensified in the court and among the aristocracy, as he manipulated the young king, the last of the direct Achaemenid line. Despite Artaxerxes' campaigns of the 340s, disaffection was general in some provinces, notably Phoenicia, Cyprus and Egypt. For such reasons the time was ripe for the Hellenic expedition. Persia's response would inevitably be slow and hesitant. In spring 336 an advance force of 10,000 Macedonians and mercenaries was ferried across the Hellespont to Abydus under the command of Parmenion, assisted by his son-in-law Attalus and by Amyntas the Lyncestian. Coastal Anatolia, populated by ·many Greek communities, would first be liberated relatively easily and cheaply and with no need of the large army required to push into the interior towards Persia's western strongholds. After a successful campaign at his own expense, in the process winning new allies in Asia Minor and the plaudits of mainland Greece, Philip would be in a strong

---

[13] See also Hatzopoulos 1982 (D 94).

position to requisition the necessary money and men from the Hellenic League to sustain the main force.

Since much of this, owing to Philip's death, did not happen and since altered circumstances drew a different strategy from Alexander in 334, such inferences are speculative, in common with much else in this confusing year. Recent work on the chronology of Philip's death seems to exclude any possibility that the main expedition was to begin later in 336.[14] By October, the probable time of the assassination, it was already too late for that year. And the absence of any indication whatsoever that the allied levies had even been ordered, let alone raised, by that time confirms that the launch was not planned for earlier than the following spring. As it happened, in about June 336 Bagoas sent Arses the way of his father, replacing him with a prince of a collateral line who took the name Darius (III). Wisely the new ruler was quick to eliminate the hated vizier, but the new disruptions could only further hamper an effective Persian response to the invasion.

No evidence survives of the general extent of Philip's territorial aims in the east, as also Alexander's initial aims, though for different reasons, remain a matter of modern opinion. Perhaps the king would have been happy to make serendipity his personal guide. But it is hard to believe that he gave no public indication of the likely limits. His army would within reason follow its leader where he led, but not anywhere at all nor indefinitely. The king must have given some clue to the Hellenic states as to what constituted a proper punishment for Persian sacrilege. The liberation of the Greeks of Asia Minor might have been said to suffice, but that had to be accompanied by an assessment of what further conquest would be necessary before the vulnerable coastal strip could be held against Persia's reaction. With Alexander the difficulty is to focus on what might have been aspired to whilst dazzled by the glare of what was ultimately won. With Philip it is both that any intentions were completely unrealized and that our sources were too distracted by the assassination and by Alexander's accession to be much interested.

The only helpful testimony comes from Isocrates' *Philippus* of 346, not because Philip is at all likely to have been charmed by a rhetorician's homily but because that document alone represents a contemporary view of what might be possible. At the very least, advised Isocrates (v *Phil.*119 ff), Philip ought to free 'the cities on the coast of Asia'. Above all he might conquer 'the whole empire of the King'. But the possibility to which he devoted most space was the conquest of Asia Minor as far as the line 'from Cilicia to Sinope', roughly speaking, as far as the Taurus Mountains. By settling dispossessed populations and unemployed mercenary bands from Greece in fortresses deep in the interior, especially in

[14] Hatzopoulos 1982 (D 95).

the Taurus passes, Philip might at once eradicate a serious social and political problem from the homeland and in effect 'fix the boundary of Hellas' by means of such a series of buffers (*ibid.* 122). Against obsequious expressions of the king's opportunity to right the imbalance in status and wealth between the children of Heracles and the descendants of the castaway child Cyrus, and against the dismissive reference to the coastal cities, it is the discussion of practicalities that carries some conviction. That is not to prove that Philip's assessment and Isocrates' desires coincided. But the circumstantial evidence, that with this area Darius later tried to buy off Alexander and that Parmenion, Philip's leading general and military adviser, considered the offer reasonable and counselled Alexander to accept it, lends support. Asia Minor, reason might suggest, was a goal both praiseworthy and conceivable.

Of Philip's own activities in the spring and summer of 336 we know nothing. (Possibly the Illyrian campaign, assigned above to 337, belongs here.) By autumn, as the time of Macedonia's Olympia approached, preparations were in hand for an especially lavish celebration of the festival at the old capital of Aegae. Despatches were arriving from Parmenion with news of successes in the east. As many Macedonian guest-friends as possible from the Greek states, as well as official representatives, were invited to attend the festivities. At the same time the marriage of Philip's daughter (and Alexander's full sister) Cleopatra to Philip's brother-in-law Alexander, king of the Molossians, would be enacted. Shortly beforehand, the king's sixth (and last) child, a daughter named Europe, was borne by his seventh wife.

By now Parmenion's force had pushed southwards from Abydus down the coast, where, just as on the mainland after Chaeronea, partisans in many Greek cities rose against pro-Persian governments and welcomed their deliverer. Some of the islands came over: perhaps Tenedos, probably Chios and certainly Lesbos, where the victorious democracy at Eresus expressed its feelings in the erection of altars dedicated to Zeus Philippios, in Philip's honour. In Ephesus a statue of Philip was placed in the temple of Artemis. At Erythrae there were similar celebrations. We need not deny the sincerity of such responses but should allow too that for communities so exposed to the Persian counteroffensive, when it inevitably came, it would be politic to impress the new defender with their loyalty.

At the Olympia, despite the accretions of superstition and romance, it is clear that things mostly went as Philip hoped. He was the man of the hour. (But a story that he had a statue of himself associated with the images of the twelve Olympian gods is more likely the invention of later moralists seeking to rationalize what followed.) From all over Greece guests and heralds converged on Aegae, in some (and perhaps all) cases conveying honours to the host. From Athens came word of the people's grant to him of a golden crown and an undertaking that no one who plotted against him would be given refuge. For a short time amidst the fervour it must have seemed that a new panhellenic era had dawned. Probably some were able to keep it all in proportion, Philip himself, even. But a young man of the royal bodyguard, Pausanias, an Orestian with a personal grudge against him, at a moment when the guard had been ordered to stand back as Philip and the two Alexanders, son and son-in-law, entered the theatre, rushed forward and killed him. In the shock and confusion the assassin too was killed as he tried hopelessly to escape.

In the circumstances the assassination seemed inexplicable. So rationalizations multiplied, interlacing sexual jealousies, high politics and dynastic rivalries. At the time one thing was certain, Alexander's status as heir, and one uncertain, whether he too was at risk. Antipater quickly presented him to the army, which acclaimed him king. Presumed accessories were seized and executed, notably two brothers from Lyncus, but there was no confidence as to the assassin's motivation or his accomplices, if any. As Alexander saw hurriedly to Philip's funerary rites, revolt was already breaking out in Thrace, Illyria and even Thessaly; the Macedonian garrisons were ejected from Thebes and Ambracia; in Athens the Assembly turned promiscuously from flattery of Philip to an official vote of praise to his murderer. In Asia Minor Parmenion hesitated and Macedonia's friends took fright. In Macedonia itself stunned amazement gave way to fear as Philip's achievements threatened to crumble in the hands of his successor, only twenty years old. In such uncertainty and insecurity the new reign opened.

Despite its end, Philip's kingship had been a time of surprising achievement: unification as an accomplished fact for the kingdom itself and as some kind of possibility in principle for the whole mainland; the creation of an army able to effect the most brutal imperialism but equally able to defend the peninsula against invasion from outside and to maintain a reasonable degree of peace among the restive inhabitants. Above all the Macedonians gained a level of security and prosperity never before attained in this kingdom pressed between exploitive fellows to the south and the hardy tribespeople of the Balkans; and the Greeks as a whole the promise of a growth in trade and commerce unparalleled since Athens' rise in the middle decades of the fifth century.

CHAPTER 16

ALEXANDER THE GREAT PART 1: THE EVENTS OF THE REIGN

A.B. BOSWORTH

I. THE ACCESSION, 336–335 B.C.

This and the following chapter are intended to provide an outline survey of the reign of Alexander.[1] The king himself is central to the narrative, for the vast preponderance of the source tradition deals explicitly with his actions. Events, however important, in which he was not the protagonist depend on chance testimonia. The subject of this first chapter is the campaign and court history of the reign, the details of the process of conquest. That provides the thread of continuity for the historical interpretation of the reign and records the imperial expansion of Macedon, the most obvious – and important – aspect of the period, as well as the increasing autocracy and elimination of dissent around the person of Alexander. The next chapter deals more with the effect of Alexander: the impact of the new universal empire upon the traditional world of Greek city states and the organization of the territories and peoples acquired by conquest. The approach is encapsulated in the final section, where I examine Alexander's claims to divine status, possibly the starkest illustration of the gulf which he had created between subject and sovereign. Although the exposition is by necessity centred around Alexander, I have tried to avoid value judgments and psychological speculation. The besetting sin of traditional Alexander scholarship has been an obsession with the person of the king, who becomes less a historical figure and more a symbol of contemporary aspirations. In Droysen's hands he was the embodiment of Prussian imperialism, in Tarn's a liberal humanitarian. The dangers of distortion and subjective evangelism are pervasive and insidious, and in my opinion they can only be avoided by concentration upon the historical context. I have therefore attempted to explain the career of Alexander strictly as a phenomenon of the fourth century, leaving the reader to draw the analogies (which are legion) with the modern world.

[1] For a more general appreciation of Alexander within the fourth century see the Epilogue, pp.876 ff. I would also refer the reader to my recent monograph, Bosworth 1988 (D 159) for fuller discussion and documentation than is possible here.

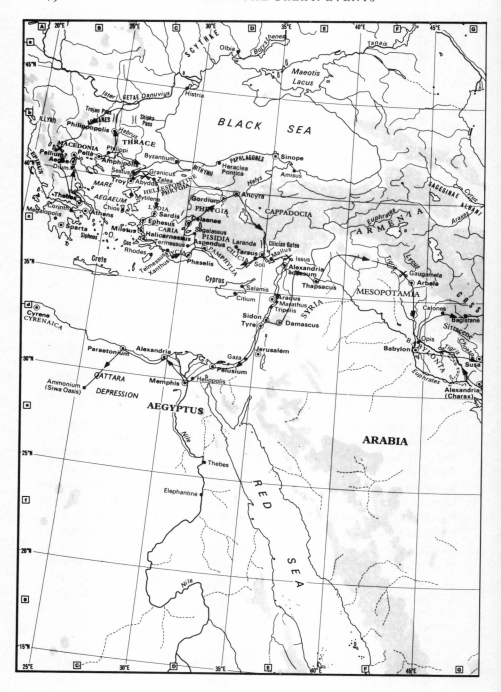

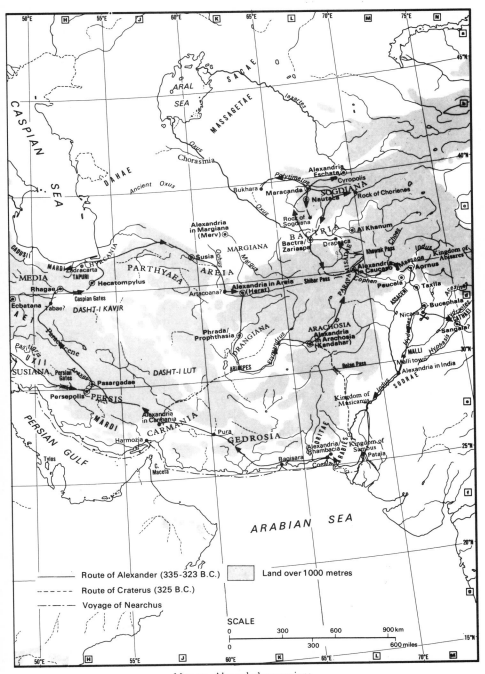

Map 20. Alexander's campaigns.

The reign began with crisis, swiftly resolved. After his father's assassination Alexander succeeded to the throne in tantalizingly obscure circumstances.[2] The sources hint at civil war, narrowly averted by ruthless massacre. Whether or not they were involved in the murder of Philip, two of the sons of Aeropus (princes of the mountain canton of Lyncestis) were immediately arrested and executed at the funeral some days later. A third brother, Alexander, attached himself to the crown prince and helped him secure the palace at Aegae. That may have been the key event. The seizure of the palace was probably followed by a meeting of the commons at which Alexander was saluted as king. A public meeting certainly followed at which Alexander presented himself as king, underlining his inheritance from Philip and promising to act as his father's son. His filial piety was publicized directly at the funeral, when his father was cremated and interred in state and the assassins were duly punished.[3]

More personal acts of vengeance followed. In particular the family of Attalus, Alexander's avowed enemy, was eradicated. Attalus himself was murdered in Asia Minor with the connivance of his fellow-commander, Parmenion. His niece, Cleopatra, the tragic last bride of Philip, was also done to death along with her infant daughter. In this instance the murder was perpetrated not by Alexander but by his mother, the vindictive and jealous Olympias. The young king expressed horror at the deed, but he had done nothing to protect the victims and their demise made his position more secure. It was more secure still after the elimination of his cousin. Amyntas, son of Perdiccas III, had been the ward of Philip and had some entitlement to the kingship. He certainly had a faction and was potentially dangerous. Soon after Alexander's accession he was killed (his wife was available for remarriage by summer 335), and the only male survivor in the royal house was the mentally incapacitated Arrhidaeus, who was to live out Alexander's reign in peaceful obscurity. There will have been lesser casualties of the accession, men who were simply suppressed or, like Amyntas, son of Antiochus, went into exile to serve with Persian forces against the man they regarded as an usurper. For

---

[2] For the background see Badian 1963 (D 62); Bosworth 1971 (D 66); Ellis 1971 (D 28), 1981 (D 82); Kraft 1971 (D 207), 11–42; Fears 1975 (D 86); Hammond 1978 (D 47); Develin 1981 (D 76).

[3] Diod. XVII.2.1; Plut. *Alex.*10.7. The scene is described in the fragmentary papyrus epitome *POxy.* 1798 (for improved text see Parsons 1979 (D 108)). Much has been written on the magnificent Tomb II of the Great Tumulus which many have identified as Philip's burial chamber (Andronikos 1979, 1980, 1984 (D 4,5,6); Hammond 1982 (D 48); Green 1982 (D 40); Borza 1981–82 (D 15). Prag *et al.* 1984 (D 59) give a very adventurous reconstruction of the head of the male occupant, complete with damaged eye socket.) Doubts, however, subsist and have tended to become more insistent. The identification of the female remains in the antechamber has posed an intractable problem. If it was Cleopatra who shared the tomb, it was a surprising legitimization of a union which Olympias and Alexander had opposed and abhorred. The question is as yet unresolved but fortunately it has no repercussions upon the historical interpretation of Alexander's reign.

many the new reign had produced death or alienation. For others it brought promotion. The senior statesman and the senior general of Philip's reign, Antipater and Parmenion, had both backed the rising star. Parmenion indeed had helped eliminate Attalus, his own son-in-law (Curt. VI.9.17), and it is not surprising that he and his sons dominated the command structure of the army in the early years of the reign. Similarly Antipater was the natural choice as regent of Macedonia in Alexander's absence.

After the eradication of his immediate rivals Alexander felt secure enough to leave the kingdom for prolonged campaigns. The winter of 336/5 saw the suppression of unrest and dissidence in southern Greece (see below, pp.847–8). A bloodless campaign resulted in his confirmation as his father's successor, both *hegemon* of the Corinthian League and supreme commander in the war of revenge against Persia. His authority established in the south, he could turn to unfinished business, in particular the subjugation of the Triballian kingdom, centred around the confluence of the Danube and Oescus rivers. That was where Philip had been wounded and defeated in 339,[4] and there was prestige to be restored. In the spring of 335 Alexander led a Macedonian expeditionary force from Amphipolis, forging north through the Rhodope range to the Hebrus valley and then to the passes of the central Haemus range, where there were still tribes (perhaps the Treres and Tetrachoritae) which were free of Macedonian control. These passes (either the Trojan or the Shipka)[5] were forced with little effort and minimal losses, and Alexander continued inexorably northwards into Triballian territory. A preliminary encounter with Triballian forces at the river Lyginus resulted in another victory; the lightly armed Triballians were helpless against the massed cavalry and phalanx assault from the Macedonians. The Triballian king, Syrmus, had evacuated his non-combatants to the large island of Peuce, where the combination of steep banks and rapid current frustrated direct ship-borne attacks. But he had evacuated the countryside and the ripening harvest was at the mercy of the invaders. That was a lesson Alexander was quick to impart. A threatening demonstration by the Getic peoples north of the Danube gave him the pretext to transport a substantial number of troops across the river under cover of night. He then used the phalanx to ravage the maturing grain and looted a small town in the vicinity before recrossing the river without a single casualty. The invading army was demonstrated to be irresistible, and capitulation inevitably followed. Syrmus was duly

---

[4] Justin IX.3.1–3; Didymus *in Dem.* col.13, lines 1–7; cf. Hammond and Griffith 1979 (D 50) II.559, 583; Gerov 1981 (E 124).

[5] On the route see Neubert 1934 (D 217); Bosworth 1980 (B 14) 54; Gerov 1981 (E 124) 488; *contra*, Papazoglou 1977 (E 82) 29–30.

enrolled among the friends and allies of the Macedonian king and submitted a contingent to Alexander's invasion army in 334. Other peoples in the region followed his example, notably the Celtic tribes which were pressing eastwards from the Adriatic coast to the Danube valley. Even they felt it prudent to conciliate the young king.

The central Danube lands were now a Macedonian protectorate, virtually an annexe of Thrace. But the success was immediately imperilled by events in the south, as the enemies of Macedon attempted to exploit the absence of its king. The most serious danger was a joint invasion of northern Macedonia by two Illyrian tribes, the Taulantii from the north west and the people of Cleitus (probably the Dardani) from the north. That threatened to repeat the events of 359 when Cleitus' father had destroyed a Macedonian army and overran the upper provinces. Alexander heard the news on his march south from the Danube, while he was being entertained by his ally, Langarus, king of the Agrianians. From Langarus' realm in the upper Strymon valley, he marched at speed to the Axius and continued westwards to the upper reaches of the Erigon (Crna). Somewhere in the Macedonian borderlands Cleitus had occupied a fortress. The topographical details given by Arrian are vague[6] and do not permit a precise location; but it seems to have been in the vicinity of Eordaea and its occupation imperilled the whole of north-west Macedonia. Alexander began operations by confining Cleitus' army in the captured fortress but he was forced to withdraw in the face of the Taulantian reinforcements. For a moment he was on the defensive, his army placed between the invaders and the Macedonian lowlands. Two days after his retreat he launched a meticulously planned night attack against the Illyrian camp and massacred the invaders. The survivors either made their way into the fortress or attempted to reach the western mountains under constant harassment. That marked the effective end of troubles with the Illyrian kingdoms, and the Triballian contingent of 334 was matched by one of Illyrians.

The Theban crisis (see below, p.848) curtailed the mopping-up operations. At the news of the revolt and the attack upon his garrison on the Cadmea Alexander left Cleitus to limp home with his surviving forces. He himself, his army intact, drove south over the plateaux of Upper Macedonia. He reached Pelinna in northern Thessaly within a week, and five days later arrived at Onchestus, three hours march from Thebes, before the rebels were aware of his approach. That effectively isolated the Thebans from any support from potential allies, and, once they had rejected his overtures, they were doomed. Even though slaves and metics were enlisted (Diod. XVII.11.2), the Thebans could not expect

---

[6] Arr. *Anab.* 1.5.5. The main crux, the location of the fortress that Arrian names 'Pellium', is discussed by Bosworth 1982 (D 157) (*contra*, Hammond 1974 (E 73); 1980 (D 190) 49–57).

to defeat Alexander's Macedonian troops outside the city. Their only hope was to defend the city and prevent the Macedonian garrison on the Cadmea joining forces with Alexander. The south side of the citadel formed part of the defensive circuit of Thebes and that sector was the major problem for the defenders. Outnumbered and desperate, the Thebans established a double palisade south of the Cadmea and prepared at all costs to prevent liaison between Alexander and the garrison. The attack that followed was ferocious and, at first, the Theban defences held. Thanks to the palisades the cavalry could not be used and the phalanx could not advance *en masse*. But ultimately the resistance was futile. It ended either when Alexander took the field in person and forced the defenders back into the city (Arrian) or when a diversionary force made a surprise irruption through an unguarded postern (Diodorus).[7] Once the walls were breached there was general carnage, as the garrison joined the action from the Cadmea and helped break the Theban last stand at the Ampheión, immediately north of the citadel. Six thousand defenders fell at a cost of 500 Macedonians and 30,000 survivors were enslaved. The city ceased to exist, and its destruction effectively suppressed the unrest in southern Greece (see below, p.848). It was late September. Alexander could now return home and prepare for the full-scale invasion of Asia the following spring.

II. THE CONQUEST OF THE AEGEAN COAST, 334–333 B.C.

The invasion of 334 came at a crucial moment. The time of troubles that had reached its climax in Persia when Darius III seized the throne in 336 had now passed. Darius rapidly secured his position by the tactical execution of Bagoas, the Grand Vizier who had procured him the throne, and proceeded to suppress native revolts in Egypt and (prob-ably) Babylonia. By the end of 335 the dynasty of Khababash was terminated and Egypt again suffered occupation after some three years of independence. Darius could turn his attention further west, and by the summer of 334 an armada of 400 warships was mobilized in the Levant for action in the Aegean. In that sector the Macedonian expeditionary force, strikingly successful in 336, had been largely confined to the Troad and Hellespont during the campaign of 335. There was a gradual mobilization of Persian satraps throughout Asia Minor, and there was increasing military activity. Memnon of Rhodes, son-in-law of the great

---

[7] Arr. *Anab.* 1.8.1–5; Diod. XVII.11.3–12.4 (cf. Polyaen. IV.3.12). Arrian's account is explicitly based on Ptolemy and may be biased against his later rival, Perdiccas, who is represented leading an unauthorized and unsuccessful attack (Bosworth 1980 (B 14) 80–1; *contra*, Roisman 1984 (B 97) 374–6). In Diodorus (XVII.12.3) it is Perdiccas who makes the decisive manoeuvre, occupying the side postern.

Persian noble, Artabazus, operated with great effectiveness at the head of a small mercenary army, attacking Cyzicus unexpectedly and driving Parmenion himself from his siege of Pitane in the Elaitic Gulf.[8] The advent of 334 saw the crossing points secured at the Hellespont but little or no territorial gains in the interior.

Alexander began his march east in early spring. With him was an invasion army comprising 32,000 infantry and some 5,000 cavalry. If one adds the contingent in Asia with Parmenion, his forces came close to 50,000.[9] Twenty days and 500 km of marching brought them to the Hellespont, after symbolically retracing the invasion route of Xerxes via Philippi, Abdera and Maronea. The symbolism continued more explicitly at the Hellespont, where the main army was slowly transported across the narrow strait (seven stades wide) between Sestus and Abydus. Alexander and his immediate entourage diverged to Elaeus at the southern tip of the Chersonese, where he sacrificed at the shrine of Protesilaus, which had been plundered during Xerxes' invasion. That sacrifice was followed by solemn libations in mid-crossing and a sacrifice to Poseidon and the Nereids (a far cry from the scourges and fetters of Xerxes), and then with his royal squadron Alexander made a landfall at the Achaeans' Harbour near Ilium, the scene of the greatest previous panhellenic expedition into Asia. He leaped ashore like Protesilaus and, according to Diodorus, he made a spear cast into the beach, claiming Asia as spear-won territory.[10] If authentic, the story proves what is obvious, that he had territorial ambitions, but it gives no hint how comprehensive those ambitions were. At Ilium he enlisted the support and sacred armour of Athena and commemorated both sides of his ancestry, honouring both Achilles and Priam with offerings. The descendant of Neoptolemus and Andromache (thanks to the Molossian royal lineage) would lead all Hellenes against the common enemy, avenging the sacrilege of the past.

The enemy forces were waiting, conveniently assembled at Zelea, near the mouth of the Aesepus river. A council-of-war had decided on a joint strategy. Against the urging of Memnon, who wished to avoid battle and deny the Macedonians the means of supply, the Persian commanders opted for a full-scale engagement and took a defensive position above the plain of Adrastea, blocking any Macedonian advance eastwards to Cyzicus. The exact movements were secret, even though Alexander was

---

[8] For details of the campaign see Diodorus XVII.7.3–10; Polyaen. v.44.4–5; with Badian 1966 (D 137) 40–2; Goukowsky 1969 (D 178); Ruzicka 1985 (D 116A).

[9] On the source divergences, which are complex, see Berve 1926 (D 146) I 177–8, Brunt 1963 (D 162) 32–6; Bosworth 1980 (B 14) 98–9. For full discussion of the composition of the army see Bosworth 1988 (D 159) 259–66.

[10] Diod. XVII.17.2 (cf. Justin XI.5.10). For various interpretations see Schmitthenner 1968 (A 52); Mehl 1980–1 (A 36); Hammond 1986 (F 29).

aware that the Persian forces were concentrated in a single mass. He therefore proceeded cautiously to the head of the Hellespont, branching inland south of Parium to avoid the rough coastline.[11] A contingent of scouts (*prodromoi*) surveyed the ground ahead of his advance and reported the Persian army in the plain of Adrastea, occupying the foothills (near modern Dimetoka) which rose above the river Granicus. The river was the obstacle, sunk between steep banks some 3 to 4 metres high, which precluded a concerted assault by cavalry or infantry phalanx.

The Persian position is difficult to establish with accuracy, thanks to the vague and conflicting reports of our authorities. There is agreement that the Persian cavalry, allegedly 20,000 strong and the flower of the army, was placed ahead of the modest infantry force of mercenaries, which again numbered 20,000 and could not match the Macedonian forces either in manpower or fighting calibre. Arrian, however, represents the Persian cavalry lined up along the edge of the Granicus, where it was impossible to charge. Diodorus has them deployed along the foothills, $1\frac{1}{2}$ km east of the river, but his account is brief and rhetorical, stating that Alexander crossed the river at dawn without opposition, whereas Arrian speaks of the *rejection* of Parmenion's advice to wait for the dawn. Alexander, Diodorus claims, attacked immediately in the face of the Persian army.[12] Both traditions are to some degree garbled by rhetorical oversimplification or propagandist exaggeration, and the truth is largely irretrievable. It does appear likely that the Persian cavalry was positioned away from the river, so as to generate a full-blooded charge violent enough to overrun the Macedonians as they regrouped after the crossing. That was elementary tactical logic and the general picture is confirmed by two passages of Arrian (*Anab.* 1.15.3,7) where the action seems to leave the banks and the Persians do charge at speed.

Alexander's strategy, according to Arrian, was simple. A contingent of cavalry (the scouts, Paeonians and a squadron of Companions) was sent across the river to advance as far as possible and sustain the Persian counter-charge while the bulk of the army crossed. This group forged diagonally across the Granicus, making use of the gravel slopes which, then as now, facilitated access to the stream bed.[13] It was followed by Alexander and the Companion Cavalry, and the rest of the army gradually filtered across in column as the cavalry battle raged on the opposite plain. Alexander's vanguard was forced back to the river, but

[11] Arr. *Anab.* 1.12.6 (a problematical passage). For the problems involved see Foss 1977 (D 174) 496–8; Bosworth 1980 (B 14) 107–9; Seibert 1985 (D 233) 30–2.

[12] Arr. *Anab.* 1.13.2–7, 14.4–5; Diod. XVII.19.2–3 (cf. Polyaen. IV.3.16). Cf. Badian 1977 (D 140) 272–4; Hammond 1980 (D 192) 73–4; Bosworth 1980 (B 14) 115–16.

[13] Arr. *Anab.* 1.14.7. Compare Badian 1977 (D 140) 286–9 with Hammond 1980 (D 192) 75–6. For the gravel banks, first pointed out by Janke 1904 (D 201), see Foss 1977 (D 174) 502; Badian 1977 (D 140) 281–2.

the Companions had the opportunity to form their battle order. Despite a desperate suicide attack on his person by a son-in-law of Darius and members of the satrapal family of Sardes, Alexander escaped death (thanks to the intervention of Cleitus the Black) and was able to force the Persian cavalry inexorably away from the river. The Macedonian lances of cornel wood were dramatically effective against the light javelins of the Persians, and the opposition was decimated. Eight commanders at least fell in battle and the line broke in the centre. As a result the entire Macedonian army crossed the river and reformed, infantry as well as cavalry. By this time the Persian horse was in full flight, but the mercenary infantry stood its ground, to parley for an armistice. They were disappointed (Plut. *Alex.* 16.13; cf. Arr. *Anab.* 1.16.2). Phalanx at the front, cavalry at the flanks, they were enveloped by the Macedonians in battle fury and massacred. Only 2,000 survived, to be sent in chains to forced labour in Macedon. They were punished for their defiance of the decrees of the Corinthian League, and the punishment had the predictable effect of stiffening the resolve of their fellows in Persian service to fight to the last.

The victory was quickly won and decisive. Hellespontine Phrygia lay open to Alexander, and its satrap, Atizyes, committed suicide to expiate his part in the disaster. The other satraps withdrew their cavalry contingents to defend their provinces. Alexander duly buried his dead, with especial honour to the men of the vanguard, the architects of his victory, and dedicated 300 Persian panoplies on the Athenian Acropolis. The first fruits of revenge went to the chief victim of Xerxes and were won, so the inscription ran, by Alexander and all the Greeks except the Spartans (Arr. *Anab.* 1.16.7; Plut. *Alex.* 16.18). But there was no time for extended celebration. The Persian fleet was expected imminently in the southern Aegean and it was vital to move south to counter the threat. Alexander quickly occupied Dascyleum, the satrapal capital of Hellespontine Phrygia and annexed the territory in his own name (see below, pp. 859f.). The new Macedonian satrap would maintain control of the area with his modest mercenary army while he continued the campaign on the Aegean coast. From the Propontis he followed the inland route to the Hermus valley and the central fortress of Sardis, a march of some 270 km. Despite its strength (perched on an outlier of Mt Tmolus 200m above the city proper) the citadel of Sardes was surrendered without a blow by its Persian commander, Mithrenes, so that Alexander simultaneously acquired the strongest fortress and the richest treasury in Asia Minor. He imposed his own garrison and treasury officials and declared the native Lydians free under their own laws – to be governed directly by his satrap. That was a propaganda gesture which meant nothing in practice.

Similar gestures followed at Ephesus, four days later. Alexander entered the city in the wake of the Persian evacuation and intervened to stop the worst excesses of factional conflict, as members of the Persian-backed oligarchic junta were summarily lynched. He oversaw the restoration of democracy (see below, p.869) and endowed the sanctuary of Artemis with the tribute previously paid to the Great King. These were real benefactions, conceded in the face of the advancing Persian fleet, and they were echoed in the commission given to Alcimachus (Arr. *Anab.* 1.18.1–2) to establish democracy, restore autonomy and remit tribute in the northern areas of Ionia and Aeolis where there were still Persian garrisons. How successful Alcimachus was there is no way of guessing, but any short-term gains he made must have been lost later in the year, when the Persians were dominant in the area.

The two fleets at last made contact at Miletus. There Alexander arrived a matter of days before the Persians, and his fleet was able to establish a firm base on the island of Lade, denying access to the Persian fleet. Despite their numbers and the quality of the crews (from Cyprus and Phoenicia) the Persian commanders could not impinge on the action. Their base was 15 km from the city, on the foothills of Mt Mycale, and they could only follow the siege as observers, keeping their triremes at sea in a threatening but futile demonstration (Arr. *Anab.* 1.19.2). Meanwhile Alexander had blockaded Miletus, rejected an offer by the ruling oligarchy to open the city to both sides and began siege operations on the narrow isthmus connecting city and mainland. The combination of missile catapults and rams quickly stripped the walls of defenders and opened a breach. That brought immediate capitulation by the civilian population, which was spared the enslavement and destruction visited upon them after the Ionian Revolt. The predominantly Persian garrison bore the brunt of the capture, massacred to a man except for 300 who took refuge on an offshore islet. Now the humiliation of the Persian fleet was compounded, when a cavalry and infantry force under Philotas prevented the crews drawing water at the mouth of the Maeander and it was forced to revictual in Samos (Arr. *Anab.* 1.19.7–8).

As a result Alexander disbanded his own fleet, except for a small transport squadron.[14] It was obviously no match for the Persian fleet in open waters, and he considered that he could continue to frustrate the enemy naval operations by the tactical use of land forces. That was one of his few military blunders. It proved impossible to prevent the Persians landing, except in the immediate area controlled by his army; and in the spring of 333 he tacitly admitted his mistake by commissioning a new fleet. The error was soon apparent in the actions at Halicarnassus. There,

[14] Arr. *Anab.* 1.20.1; Diod. XVII.22.5–23.3. Cf. Hauben 1976 (D 194) 80–1; Bosworth 1980 (B 14) 141–3.

802 16. ALEXANDER THE GREAT: EVENTS

in the natural theatre with its formidable Hecatomnid fortifications,[15] Memnon organized the land defence, concentrating all the local city garrisons. He was supported by sea from the island of Cos, and had no worries about provisioning. Alexander therefore had to take the city by storm. It was a vast and expensive exercise. The main attack focused on the north-east salient of the walls, around the Mylasa gate, and every contemporary refinement of siege technique was employed. The defenders countered a threatened breach with a secondary lunette of brick, bulging inward to entrap the attackers in a killing ground as they pressed through the outer wall. There were also a number of sorties by the Persian commanders which were technically unsuccessful but slowed the siege operations and inflicted heavy casualties.[16] Ultimately the defence was untenable. After the failure of the last great sortie and the death of the Athenian mercenary commander, Ephialtes, the Persian command set fire to the arsenals and their defensive outworks and left Halicarnassus to conflagration. The defending forces contracted to the two inner citadels, Salmacis at the western extremity of the walls and the island fortress of Zephyrium. Alexander could and did occupy Halicarnassus but the strategic situation was unchanged. The Persian forces remained in their citadels, held in check by a small garrison of 3,000 foot and 200 horse, but Memnon and his fellow commanders could deploy their fleet and attack the coast and islands almost at will.

The siege at Halicarnassus ended the campaigning season of 334. During the following winter Alexander's forces were dispersed. A group of Macedonians who had married immediately before the campaign was sent home for recreation and procreation, and their leaders, senior phalanx officers, were instructed to levy troops to compensate for the losses of the summer. The rest of the army left the Aegean coast; Parmenion went via the Hermus valley to campaign in Phrygia with the allied troops, while Alexander and the bulk of the army pushed through the interior of Lycia. Arrian (*Anab.* 1.24.3) suggests that his intention was to neutralize the area against the Persian fleet, but his operations in Lycia did not touch the sea. He moved inland from Xanthus through the mountain district of Milyas, only descending to the coast at Phaselis. No garrisons were apparently installed and the Persians operated with impunity on the Lycian coast. Alexander had other reasons for his actions. He had now certainly decided to challenge the Great King for his empire and he was annexing as much of his territory as he could before pressing east in the spring. At the same time the war-

[15] Cf. Bean and Cook 1955 (F 575) 89–91; Hornblower 1982 (F 644) 295–302.

[16] Diod. XVII.25.5–6, 26.3–27.4. Arrian's account minimizes the Macedonian setbacks and makes light of the difficulties (*Anab.* 1.20.9–10, 21.1–3, 22.1–6; cf. Bosworth 1976 (B 12) 21–2).

torn Aegean coast was spared the burden of sustaining his forces for the winter.

The two army groups moved separately to the liaison point at Gordium. There was some communication, dramatically illustrated by Arrian's story of the capture of an emissary of the Great King. Sisines, commissioned to collaborate with Atizyes, Darius' satrap of Phrygia, was arrested by Parmenion's forces and sent under escort for interrogation by Alexander. Later it was alleged that he gave incriminating evidence against Alexander's namesake, the Lyncestian prince who conspired against Philip and now commanded the elite Thessalian cavalry with Parmenion. The facts of the matter are uncertain, bedevilled as so often by source conflict,[17] but the Lyncestian was deposed from his command in 333 and kept under close arrest. If information was given, it was not damning. More importantly Alexander and Parmenion were in contact during the winter and co-ordinated their actions. The king led his staff along the narrow shoreline from Phaselis to Pamphylia while the main force traversed a specially constructed road through the mountainous interior. Here there was no military challenge. The rich Pamphylian plain sustained the army for a brief period while Alexander made a brief tour, coercing the city of Aspendus into submission and leaving the garrison at Sillyum (which offered resistance) to be reduced by his friend Nearchus, the new satrap of Lycia and Pamphylia.

Towards the beginning of spring 333 Alexander moved north from Perge. He traversed the mountain area of Pisidia at speed. An attack on Termessus was abortive; he lacked the time and the siege train to capture its formidable citadel. Sagalassus to the north fell to direct assault, as did other lesser fortresses, but Alexander's transit of the area had little lasting effect. He passed equally rapidly through Phrygia, touching on the salt expanse of Burdur Gölü before pausing briefly at the satrapal capital of Celaenae (Dinar). Once again Alexander backed away from a full-scale siege of the citadel and agreed to a conditional capitulation by its Carian and Greek garrison. Antigonus was consequently left with a force of 1,500 mercenaries to receive the promised surrender and govern Phrygia as satrap, a post he held with distinction until Alexander's death. A month later Alexander reached Gordium, and according to schedule he joined forces with Parmenion and the newly married men with their large complement of reinforcements from Macedonia (3,000 infantry and 500 cavalry).

At Gordium Alexander was at last forced to take steps to counter the

---

17 Arr. *Anab.* 1.25.2–9 locates the arrest in Phrygia; Diod. XVII.32.1 places it on the eve of Issus. The tradition may be muddied by the allegations made against the Lyncestian when he was eventually brought to trial in late 330.

Persian offensive in the Aegean. The Persian naval supremacy had been crushing. Chios fell without a blow to Memnon, as did most of the cities of Lesbos. Mytilene held out, thanks to a garrison installed by Alexander, and it was blockaded by land and sea. It was captured in the summer of 333 after Memnon himself had died of illness, and his nephew and successor, Pharnabazus, pressed the offensive towards the Hellespont, occupying the island of Tenedos, which surrendered with considerable reluctance. The Aegean was practically in Persian hands. Miletus had been lost to Alexander by late 333 and the Persians were able to sail at will in the Cyclades. One small squadron under Datames was surprised off Siphnos and lost eight triremes (Arr. *Anab.* II.2.4–5), but that is the only recorded setback and the only Macedonian initiative. But, even before Memnon's death, Darius had apparently decided to withdraw military forces from the Aegean. Thymondas, another nephew of Memnon, was commissioned to escort mercenaries from the west. He duly went to Lycia, where he took over command of the forces requested. That was shortly after the fall of Mytilene. Two hundred ships may have been taken from the Aegean fleet, an action that irretrievably weakened the Aegean offensive from the late summer of 333.

Alexander did not know the future at Gordium, and he commissioned a new fleet with separate commanders for the Hellespont and Ionian coast.[18] Despite the considerable money expended it was many months before an effective fleet was amassed, and, if Darius had not reduced his forces, there would have been complete Persian dominance in the Aegean, perhaps even (as was rumoured) an attack on Macedon itself. Alexander had good reason to be concerned, and it was at this critical time that he visited the palace at Gordium and inspected the purported waggon of Gordius. That venerable relic boasted a complex yoke fastening of cornel bark, and, according to local legend, the person who unfastened it would become lord of Asia. Propaganda demanded the prophecy be fulfilled, and fulfilled it was, by somewhat dubious means. The more popular version was that Alexander cut through the fastening; Aristobulus claimed that he removed the yoke pin and pulled the yoke from its pole, fastening and all.[19] Whatever the truth of the matter, the unyoked waggon was put on display and a timely thunderstorm confirmed Zeus' approval. The auspices for the next campaign were demonstrably favourable.

[18] Curt. III.1.19–20; cf. Hauben 1976 (D 194) 82–7.
[19] Arr. *Anab.* II.3.6–7 (*FGrH* 139 F 7); Curt. III.8.16; Justin XI.7.4; Plut. *Alex.* 18.2; Marsyas *FGrH* 135–6 F 4. Cf. Fredricksmeyer 1961 (D 176); Kraft 1971 (D 207), 84–92; Bosworth 1980 (B 14) 184–8.

III. FROM CILICIA TO EGYPT, 333 AND 332 B.C.

Towards the end of May 333 B.C., Alexander led his united army out of Gordium. He drove quickly across Anatolia via Ancyra and (probably) Tyana. There was no fighting. Paphlagonia was peacefully absorbed into the satrapy of Hellespontine Phrygia and a native dynast was placed over southern Cappadocia (the north was left to its own devices). By the end of summer the Macedonian army had forced the Cilician Gates (south of Pozanti), easily overrunning a weak Persian defence, and occupied the satrapal capital of Tarsus, so forestalling a Persian attempt to devastate the countryside. Cilicia was occupied intact and placed under Macedonian control as far as the coastal defiles of the south. It was to be the base for Alexander's defence against the Grand Army that Darius had mustered in Babylon.

Darius had gathered a formidable army, which included the greatest number of Greek mercenaries ever assembled in Persian service (30,000 according to the ancient sources). He also mobilized the entire levy of Persis and Media. Pressure of time prevented his use of the crack cavalry from Bactria and the north-east frontier, but even without it his superiority in cavalry was overwhelming and contemporaries expected Alexander to disappear under the Persian hooves (Aeschin. III.164). His strategy, which had been bitterly contested,[20] was to force a full-scale decisive battle, and by the early summer he had begun his march north. Hampered by a baggage train replete with treasure and the court harem, he progressed slowly to Thapsacus on the Euphrates. After the crossing he moved to a base camp at Sochi in the Amik plain while his baggage train diverged southwards to Damascus.

It was now September. Alexander had fallen ill in Cilicia after an imprudent swim in the proverbially chilly waters of the river Cydnus. He was in high fever for a considerable time and his life was in question. Intrigue was probably rife at court, but its only echo in the sources is Arrian's brief report of the flight of the treasurer, Harpalus.[21] That is a mysterious episode, but it was clearly not a serious threat to Alexander, for Harpalus was reinstated in the spring of 331 after a year's exile in the Megarid. Whatever the background to his desertion, it is clear that he had little faith in Alexander's recovery. But Alexander did recuperate, after his court physician administered a drastic purge, and he used his

[20] Curt. III.2.10–19; Diod. XVII.30 (Charidemus' argument for a division of forces); Arr. *Anab.* II.6.3–6; Plut. *Alex.* 20.1–4 (Amyntas' advice not to leave the base at Sochi).

[21] Arr. *Anab.* III.6.7. The report is too brief to permit any detailed explanation of Harpalus' actions. See, however, Badian 1960 (D 133); Heckel 1977 (D 196); Jaschinski 1981 (D 203) 10–18; Kingsley 1986 (D 206).

convalescence to consolidate his base in Cilicia. A seven-day campaign west of Soli guaranteed that there would be no raids from the tribesmen of the Taurus. Soli itself was garrisoned and fined 200 talents for alleged Persian sympathies, whereas Mallus, closer to the Persian advance, had its tribute remitted in recognition of its Argive origins (which Soli also claimed).[22] At Mallus Alexander received the news that Darius had encamped at Sochi, and he moved rapidly first to Castabulum and then to Issus, where he left his sick and wounded. A waiting game developed,[23] as each king took position in the terrain that best suited his forces, Darius in the open Amik plain and Alexander in the coastal defiles south of Issus. Eventually he took a position south of the Pillar of Jonah, blocking the Royal Road through the Belen Pass to Cilicia.

Ultimately it was Darius who changed his ground. He led his army on a flanking march of some 150 km through the northern Bahçe Pass and the narrows of Toprakkale. This route was undefended and the move took Alexander by surprise. It severed his communications with Cilicia and forced him to give battle, but on the other hand the Persian army had been drawn into his preferred terrain, confined in the narrow plain between the sea and the Amanus range. Darius, the sources claim, believed that Alexander would not dare to face his army in the Amik plain, and, given the time that must have elapsed between his arrival at Sochi and the battle proper, he may have been justified in his belief. At all events he could not feed his vast army indefinitely in the Amik plain, rich though it was, and the logistical pressure weighed more heavily on him than on Alexander. The Persian army had forged south of Issus and took up position north of the river Pinarus (perhaps in the vicinity of the present day Kuru Çay).[24] There the plain is relatively narrow, some 4 km wide, a distance compatible with the 14 stades given by Callisthenes (Polyb. XII.17.4).

As at the Granicus, the Persian position was defensive, along the line of the Pinarus. Cavalry were massed to the right; mercenary infantry held the centre, while the Persian national infantry continued the line into the foothills of the Amanus. The rest of the native levies were massed in depth to the rear of the line. Meanwhile Alexander began his approach at dawn, filtering his army through the narrows below the Pillar of Jonah

[22] Arr. *Anab.* II.5.5, 9; Curt. III.7.2; cf. Bosworth 1980 (B 14) 195. For the Argive origins of the Cilician cities see Stroud 1984 (B 178) 201–3; Bosworth 1988 (D 159) 254–5.

[23] Curt. III.7.8–10. Arrian (*Anab.* II.6.1–2) states that Alexander was eager to come to grips with Darius but was frustrated by the elements. The common view that he went some 120 km, from Mallus in Cilicia to Myriandrus, south of the Pillar of Jonah, in two days rests on an over-literal reading of Arr. *Anab.* II.6.2 (see Atkinson 1980 (B 8) 177; Bosworth 1980 (B 14) 199–200). For the various interpretations of strategy see Seibert 1972 (D 232) 99ff; Bosworth 1980 (B 14) 199–201; Engels 1978 (D 172) 42–53; Hammond 1980 (D 190) 94–110.

[24] For the location, still highly controversial, see Janke 1904 (D 201) 2–74; Seibert 1972 (D 232) 99–100, Atkinson 1980 (B 8) 471–6.

and gradually widening the phalanx as the plain broadened. There was a distance of 40 stades to be covered in extended line, and progress was necessarily slow as the army crossed the numerous deep stream beds that intersected the plain. The phalanx, now eight deep, held the centre of the line with cavalry on either side, Thessalians and allies to the left and Macedonians to the right. A formation of light infantry and mercenaries was thrown back obliquely to counter the Persian troops massed in the foothills. Alexander himself was at the head of the Macedonian cavalry, immediately to the right of the phalanx.

Early in the afternoon Alexander launched the attack. He himself was at the apex of his cavalry and charged across the Pinarus as soon as he came within missile range. His opponents were the Persian native infantry, the Cardaces, who may have been armed with specially lengthened scimitars (Curt. III.3.6) as well as their lances and bows, but they had no effect against the onslaught of the Companions. How exactly Alexander broke the line we are not told, and there is no word about the difficulties which a river crossing at speed must have caused. We have only the bare fact that the battle was effectively won by Alexander and the Companions. Elsewhere the situation was dangerous. The right wing of the Macedonian phalanx was exposed as Alexander broke away to charge and, as its alignment was disrupted by the river crossing, it came close to dismemberment by the mercenary hoplites in Darius' service. On the left the sheer weight of the massed Persian cavalry forced the Thessalians into retreat. As his line wavered, Alexander pressed his attack towards Darius, who was highly visible in an elevated war chariot towards the centre of his line. The Persian guard fell in defence of their king, who escaped capture by flight.[25] That was the decisive moment. The whole of the Persian left followed Darius in retreat and Alexander could continue leftwards into the flank of the mercenary phalanx. The phalanx, caught between the Macedonian cavalry and the infantry *sarissae*, folded from the right, and the retreat became general, as the victorious Persian cavalry gave up the engagement on the left. As the retreating cavalry trampled down the infantry in their path the retreat became a shambles, and spectacular numbers of Persian troops were crushed in the press. The propaganda figures in our sources list some 100,000 Persian casualties to 500 Macedonian.

The disastrous retreat, which the Macedonians harassed until nightfall, prevented the Persian army regrouping. Darius withdrew across the Euphrates with all the stragglers he could muster. The rest of the army

---

[25] Arr. *Anab.* II.11.4, suggesting that Darius led the rout. Diod. XVII.34.2–7, Curt. III.11.7–12, and Justin XI.9.9, perhaps more plausibly, suggest that he resisted spiritedly. The latter tradition seems to have inspired the battle scene on the Alexander Mosaic (cf. Rumpf 1962 (J 39); Seibert 1972 (D 232) 55–8).

dispersed. One substantial contingent forced the Cilician Gates and caused havoc in Cappadocia and Paphlagonia (Curt. IV.1.34); it took a year of campaigning and three battles before Antigonus contained the threat.[26] A large group of refugee Greeks, 8,000 strong, took ship from Tripolis to Cyprus, where they divided forces, one group making an abortive attack on Egypt, while another joined the Spartan operations in Crete (see below, p.853). At the news of Issus the Persian offensive in the Aegean foundered. The spring of 332 saw the disintegration of their fleet, as the city contingents from Phoenicia and Cyprus withdrew to make their peace with Alexander, and the newly constituted Macedonian fleet under Hegelochus and Amphoterus quickly occupied the Aegean coast and the islands from Tenedos to Cos. The remains of the Persian fleet took refuge in Crete, which became the only focus of resistance in the west.

Alexander was left the undisputed master of the Syrian coast, and also master of the Persian treasure at Issus and Damascus. In the process of acquiring the baggage train the princesses of the royal household were captured. Stateira and Sisygambis, Darius' wife and mother, fell into Alexander's hands after the battle, and the conqueror treated them with extreme deference, retaining their royal appurtenances but refusing ransom. He assumed the duties of Darius and claimed to be the proper king of Asia. Those claims were explicitly voiced in the aftermath of the battle when he categorically refused Darius' diplomatic overtures. In response to a letter requesting peace, alliance and the restoration of the royal ladies he bluntly demanded total surrender; Darius was an usurper and the aggressor in the war, whereas he was now the legitimate ruler of Asia.[27] This exchange, in which Alexander addressed himself as master to subject, ended Darius' efforts at diplomacy, and he began mustering his forces for the defence of Mesopotamia.

The winter of 333/2 was spent in Phoenicia. Alexander received the surrender of Aradus, Byblus and Sidon, changing the regime at Sidon but confirming the ruling houses elsewhere. At Tyre he met his first opposition, where the city authorities (headed by the crown prince in the absence of King Azemilk) refused to admit Alexander into their island citadel to sacrifice to the local deity Melqart (whom he identified with his Argead ancestor, Heracles). His proposed visit coincided with the main festival of Melqart, in February 332,[28] and the Tyrians refused to

[26] Curt. IV.1.34–5, 5.13. Cf. Burn 1952 (D 164) 82–4; Briant 1973 (D 22) 53–80.
[27] Arr. *Anab.* II.14; Curt. IV.1.7–14; Diod. XVII.39.1–2. On the problems of the sources see Bosworth 1980 (B 14) 227–30; Atkinson 1980 (B 8) 271–7 and, on specific details, Griffith 1968 (D 184); Mikrogiannakis 1969 (D 214).
[28] Curt. IV.2.10; cf. Menander of Ephesus *FGrH* 783 F 1. For the siege in general see Arr. *Anab.* II.18.3–24.6; Curt. IV.2.8–4.18. Diod. XVII.40.4–46.6 (cf. Bosworth 1976 (B 12) 16–25; Atkinson 1980 (B 8) 315–19).

delegate the ceremonial to an alien sovereign. It was a fateful decision. Alexander would brook no challenge to his claims of kingship, and, once the siege was committed, he could not raise it without his military credibility suffering. At first the story of the siege of Halicarnassus was repeated. Alexander constructed a siege mole between Old Tyre on the mainland and the island city 4 stades out to sea, concentrating his attack on a narrow sector of the walls, which the Tyrians had ample time to make impregnable. At the same time Tyre was supplied by sea and the defenders could launch shipborne attacks on the advancing causeway. The turning-point came in early summer, when eighty Phoenician ships returned from the Aegean. They joined the siege operations along with 120 other ships from Cyprus, whose city kings offered formal submission. From that moment the blockade of Tyre was complete, and, once the siege-engines had been constructed (the famous ship-borne towers with scaling bridges),[29] the final massed attacks were launched. In July the city was subjected to constant battering from rams mounted on warships. The walls were breached to the south, but the first use of the scaling bridges was unsuccessful. Two days later the breach was extended, and the hypaspists were able to cross the scaling bridges and control the adjacent walls. The battlements were occupied from the sea, and the attackers stormed down into the palace and the lower city. In the carnage that followed 8,000 defenders perished and a further 2,000 were allegedly crucified along the coast. Tyre was cleared of its former population and resettled from the hinterland under a resident garrison and a Macedonian commander.

After the siege Alexander duly sacrificed to Melqart/Heracles and celebrated with a grand procession and an athletic festival (Moretti, *ISE* no.113). The interior of Syria had already been pacified by Parmenion, and he was able to march south without incident. The only recorded resistance was at Gaza, where the city commander, Batis, had hired mercenaries and laid in provisions. Another siege ensued, this time of two months' duration, and it took the entire siege train, transported from Tyre by ship, to breach the walls. Bombardment and mining were finally effective. Alexander and his hypaspists again led the assault on the broken battlements, and the fighting population of Gaza was massacred. Like Tyre, the city was repopulated and reconstituted as a citadel on the Egyptian border. As the year ended, a recruiting expedition, led by the phalanx commander Amyntas, was sent to Macedon.[30] The losses incurred by a year's siege warfare needed to be redressed, and Amyntas' ten triremes were committed to the winter seas on a mission of urgency.

---

[29] Marsden 1969–71 (K 45) I 62–3, 102–3; 1977 (K 46).

[30] Diod. XVII.49.1; Curt. IV.6.30–1, VII.1.37–40. Cf. Bosworth 1986 (D 21) 6–7; 1988 (D 159) 267–8.

IV. EGYPT TO PARTHYAEA, 331–330 B.C.: THE END OF DARIUS

Egypt lay open to the conqueror. Darius' satrap, Mazaces, had certainly been in communication with Alexander, and the great fortress complex of Pelusium (at the eastern extremity of the Delta) offered no resistance, admitting the Macedonian fleet before the land forces had crossed the coastal desert. Welcomed by the Egyptian populace as liberators, the Macedonian forces moved by land and water to Memphis, where Mazaces surrendered the city and its treasury intact. Alexander duly sacrificed and held athletic and musical games, paying special honour to Apis in conscious contrast with Cambyses and Artaxerxes III, both of whom were reputed to have killed the current Apis bull, the god's earthly manifestation. The king himself assumed the conventional pharaonic titles: king of Upper and Lower Egypt, son of Ra, beloved of Amun. There may even have been an official investiture in Egyptian style.[31] But Alexander's stay in the capital was brief, and there is no evidence that he was influenced by Egyptian beliefs or institutions.

The greater part of Alexander's stay in Egypt was devoted to his visit to the sanctuary of Ammon, in the oasis of Siwah. For Alexander this deity was a local manifestation of Zeus (Callisthenes in fact termed him Zeus) and, disposed as he now was to view himself as the son of Zeus, he had long intended to visit the sanctuary. It was an oracular cult familiar in the Greek world since the fifth century B.C., and its most famous offshoot, the temple of Zeus Ammon at Aphytis in Chalcidice, was presumably well known to him. There was also a tradition that his Argead ancestors, Heracles and Perseus, had both consulted the god.[32] That reinforced his determination to make a personal visit. Accordingly he sailed down the Nile to its Canopic mouth, taking a select force of infantry and cavalry. After a tour of Lake Mareotis and inspecting the narrow isthmus to the north that was to be the heart of his first great city foundation, he struck westwards along the coast, to Paraetonium (Mersah Matruh).

Alexander paused briefly to receive a delegation from Cyrene, with which he concluded a treaty of friendship and alliance. Then he plunged south west into the desert, following the 260 km route to Siwah across the Libyan plateau. Callisthenes and later historians traced the providential hand of Zeus in the journey: the discomfort of the southern sirocco was eased by a winter rainstorm and a pair of desert crows guided the party to Siwah. The phenomena, common enough in the desert, were

---

[31] [Call.] 1.34.2 (very questionable context); see Koenen 1977 (F 464) 30–1.

[32] Callisthenes, *FGrH* 124 F 14a; Arr. *Anab.* III.3.1–2; Curt. IV.7.8. For literature see in general Seibert 1972 (D 232) 116–25. Note particularly Wilcken 1970 (A 64) 1 260ff; Tarn 1948 (D 239) II 353–9; Bosworth 1977 (D 154) 69–75.

elaborated to display the concern of the god for his self-proclaimed son. Once safely at Siwah, Alexander consulted the oracle in the central sanctuary at Aghurmi. As pharaoh he received privileged treatment, questioning the oracle within the sanctum while his staff remained outside. The whole procedure remained secret. Later tradition concocted a series of questions concerning world empire and divine paternity, but Ptolemy and Aristobulus merely stated that the king was satisfied with the (unspecified) answers he received (Arr. *Anab.* III.4.5). All that can be said with reasonable certainty is that the officiating priest addressed Alexander directly as the son of the god (see below, p.872). Whatever was meant by the title, the king accepted it as direct testimony that he was the actual son of Zeus Ammon, and to the end of his reign his words and actions reflected his belief in a divine paternity.

From Siwah Alexander returned to Egypt, probably (as Aristobulus alleged) retracing his steps via Paraetonium.[33] On his way back to Memphis he laid out the site of Alexandria, and the date of the city's foundation was later celebrated on 7 April (25 Tybi).[34] Soon afterwards he revisited the capital and sacrificed in grand style to Zeus the King, whose son he claimed to be. That formally concluded the stay in Egypt. His army, refreshed by a winter's rest in the Nile valley, was ready for the decisive campaign against Darius. Some time in April Alexander led his army from Egypt. After a brief punitive campaign in Samaria (see below, p.861) he installed himself at Tyre, where he held a second festival for Melqart, eclipsing in splendour the Panhellenic games of Greece. He also took measures to contain the increasingly threatening situation in the west. His admiral, Amphoterus, fresh from his successes in the Aegean, was sent with a fleet of more than a hundred ships to contain the troubles in Crete and bolster Macedonian allies in the Peloponnese. At the same time Athenian sensibilities were conciliated by the release of the prisoners-of-war captured at the Granicus. Alexander had no intention of sending troops home or even of suspending Amyntas' recruiting mission in Macedonia. His encounter with Darius was of paramount importance, and the concerns of the west were secondary.

Alexander remained proof against overtures from Persia. During the siege of Tyre Darius had renewed his offer of ransom and ceded the old territories of Lydia west of the Halys river. More seriously, in the summer of 331, he renounced all lands as far as the Euphrates, together with an offer of 30,000 talents' ransom for his family.[35] There must have

33 Arr. *Anab.* III.4.5; cf. Borza 1967 (D 150); Bosworth 1976 (B 13) 136–8.
34 [Call.] I.32.10. Cf. Welles 1962 (F 547) 284; Bagnall 1979 (F 405); Badian 1985 (D 142) 500–1; *contra*, Fraser 1972 (A 21) II. 2–3.
35 Plut. *Alex.* 29.7–8; Diod. XVII.54.1–5; Curt. IV.11.1–22; Justin XI.12.9–15. See also Arr. *Anab.* II.25 (dated to 332 B.C.). For discussion see Mikrogiannakis 1969 (D 214) 87–106; Bosworth 1980 (B 14) 228–9; Atkinson 1980 (B 8) 320–4, 395–6.

been strong pressure on Alexander to conclude at least a temporary peace and enjoy the fruits of victory. Parmenion apparently argued that Darius' terms be accepted, and he was crushingly answered that the king would do so, were he Parmenion. The tradition of the debate, which probably derived from Callisthenes, is strongly biased against Parmenion, but there is little doubt that he was spokesman for a significant part of the army (cf. Diod. XVII.54.3–4). Alexander's uncompromising rejection of the Persian overtures was by no means universally popular.

The Persian army had long been mustering at Babylon. Its numbers were vast, but hardly the wildly inflated totals which appear in the extant sources.[36] Alexander was certainly outnumbered, perhaps greatly outnumbered, but the forces he faced were of variable quality. Only a small contingent of Hellenic infantry remained from the great phalanx that fought at Issus, and the native infantry at Darius' disposal was largely ineffectual. His strength was in cavalry, particularly the great contingent from Bactria and Sogdiana, augmented by Saca cataphracts (mailed cavalry) from the steppes and auxiliaries from India. Led by their satrap Bessus, a relative of the Great King, they formed a coherent body comparable in calibre to Alexander's Companions. These forces needed flat open terrain to be effective, and Darius thought it best to prepare his defence away from Babylon, which had taken the burden of the muster. Accordingly he sent out a reconnoitring party under Mazaeus, his former satrap of Syria, and moved north to occupy a position in old Assyria. This was north of Arbela, between the river Bumelus (Gomil) and an advance outlier of the Zagros, the Jabal Maqlub.[37] There Darius prepared the ground for attacks by cavalry and scythed chariots, which he hoped would dislocate the Macedonian battle line.

In midsummer 331 Alexander marched west from Tyre to the Euphrates. As he crossed at Thapsacus over two pontoon bridges, the Persian scouts under Mazaeus withdrew to the main Persian army with news of his advance. That was in an unexpected direction, some 440 km across the plains of northern Mesopotamia.[38] In all probability he went via Harran and Nisibis to the Tigris, which he crossed slightly north of modern Mosul. Contrary to information pressed from captured Persian scouts, the river was not defended. The Macedonian army forded the river, which was at low water but still maintained a strong current. Two days of rest supervened, and on the evening before Alexander resumed his march (at 9 p.m. on 20 September) there was a lunar eclipse, a portent of disaster for Darius. Four days later he was encamped some 30 km from

---

[36] For discussion see Brunt 1976–83 (B 21) 1.511; Bosworth 1980 (B 14) 293. There is a highly speculative reconstruction by Marsden 1964 (D 212) 32–7.

[37] Schachermeyr 1973 (D 231) 270, correcting Stein 1942 (D 237).

[38] Strabo II.1.38. Cf. Marsden 1964 (D 212) 18–21; Engels 1978 (D 172) 68–70.

the Persian lines, having ascertained from stragglers the exact position of the enemy. After another rest period he established his main camp below the summit of the Jabal Maqlub and observed the Persian dispositions at leisure from the height of the massif.[39] Those dispositions according to Aristobulus (*FGrH* 139 F 17) were committed to writing by Darius and were captured after the battle. In the centre was Darius with his royal guard and the vestigial Greek phalanx. To his right were predominantly cavalry forces from Syria, Mesopotamia and the highlands of Media and the Elburz, and to his left, where Alexander was expected to attack, came the horsemen of the north-east satrapies under the command of Bessus. On both wings and in the centre there were scythed chariots, poised to create gaps in the Macedonian lines.

Alexander devoted a day to reconnaissance and tactical planning. Then at dawn on 1 October he marshalled his forces on the plain. His formation was roughly rectangular and occupied a narrow front.[40] The front-line troops were as usual the men of the Macedonian phalanx with the Companion Cavalry to the right and the Thessalian and allied cavalry to the left. A second parallel line consisted of mercenaries and Hellenic infantry from cities of the Corinthian League. On each flank the gap between the two lines was closed by light infantry contingents, Agrianians to the right and Thracians to the left; and on both sides there was a screen of cavalry. The inevitable result was that the Macedonian army was vastly outflanked, but it was prepared for attack from any angle.

The Persian line was static, and Alexander began the encounter by advancing – diagonally to the right. At the earliest stage he faced Darius in the centre of the Persian line but, as he moved rightwards, his entire army assumed an oblique alignment and the Companion Cavalry moved beyond the prepared ground, the only terrain on which the scythed chariots could operate. At the same time the Macedonian left was practically enveloped by the enemy forces. Alexander needed to break the Persian line in his sector of the field while his left sustained the storm as best it could. The climactic time of the battle came quickly. The Bactrian and Saca cavalry wheeled forward to prevent Alexander's line advancing further, and a heated engagement developed between the Macedonian cavalry guard and Bessus' heavy cavalry. The action threw more and more of the Bactrian cavalry to the Macedonian flank, where the mercenary cavalry and Paeonians came under increasingly heavy pressure. At the same time the massed charge of scythed chariots was

---

[39] There are problems in Arrian (*Anab.* III.9.1–2), barely elucidated in Curtius. For discussion of the various *cruces* see Bosworth 1980 (B 14) 294; Atkinson 1980 (B 8) 486–7; Wirth 1980–1 (D 248) part 2, 23–31.

[40] Arr. *Anab.* III.12.1–5; Curt. IV.13.30–2. Cf. Griffith 1947 (D 182) 77–9; Devine 1975 (D 166) 374–8.

ineffectual. Alexander himself was already outside their killing ground, and the charge itself was easily neutralized by a group of Agrianians and javelin men which immobilized the majority of the chariots before they reached the Macedonian line. The rest passed harmlessly through. Alexander was left unscathed at the head of the royal squadron, perfectly poised to exploit the gap in the Persian line which had been created by the leftward motion of the Bactrian cavalry. He led the crucial charge at the apex of the Companions, now massed in a great wedge.[41] The Persian line collapsed at the point of impact and, caught between the Macedonian cavalry pressing into the flank and the *sarissae* of the phalanx advancing frontally, the defence gradually disintegrated. As the Persian centre came under threat, Darius again took flight and once again a general rout developed.

But there were difficulties on the Macedonian side. As Alexander pressed on the pursuit of the Persian centre, determined to capture his rival, it was impossible for his entire front to advance as a whole. The left wing under Parmenion had been under sustained attack since the opening of the battle and could hardly hold its ground, let alone advance. Inevitably the Macedonian line broke in its turn, the majority of the phalanx forging on with Alexander while the two leftmost battalions maintained their linkage with the left. Fortunately the Persian centre was already in chaos. A few units of Persian and Indian cavalry penetrated the gap and had to be neutralized by the reserve phalanx to the rear,[42] but the majority of the Persian forces followed Darius in retreat. The Macedonian left remained enveloped, threatened by the Persian cavalry under Mazaeus, and Parmenion (it is unanimously stated)[43] sent an abortive message requesting help from his king. Most probably the courier never reached Alexander, who pursued the fugitive Persians until the onset of evening, while the news of the Persian discomfiture gradually filtered to his beleaguered left. The Thessalians then counter-attacked and Mazaeus' cavalry withdrew from the field. When Alexander at last returned from his pursuit, cutting his way through a large contingent of Parthyaeans and Persians in retreat from Darius' centre (Arr. *Anab.* III.15.1–2), he found his forces in control of the battlefield.

The victory at Gaugamela was decisive. Alexander probably inflicted fewer casualties and sustained more than he had at Issus. The cavalry screen at the right had been badly mauled, and the left, under pressure for the entire battle, must have suffered considerably. But Darius left the

---

[41] Arr. *Anab.* III.14.1–2; Curt. IV.15.20–1. Cf. Schachermeyr 1973 (D 231) 237; Bosworth 1980 (B 14) 307; Devine 1983 (K 11) 214–16.

[42] Arr. *Anab.* III.14.4–6. On the problems see Griffith 1947 (D 182) 84–5; Burn 1952 (D 164) 88–90; Wirth 1980–1 (D 248) 41–8; Welwei (D 243) 1979, 225–8; Bosworth 1980 (B 14) 308–9.

[43] Plut. *Alex.* 33.9–10; Arr. *Anab.* III.15.1–2; Curt. IV.16.1–7; Diod. XVII.60.7. On the problems and the relevant literature see Bosworth 1980 (B 14) 309–11.

arena of hostilities, fleeing to Arbela at breakneck pace and immediately crossing the Zagros into Media. With him was his royal guard, the surviving Greek mercenaries and the Bactrian cavalry under Bessus, which had left the field intact when the Persian centre disintegrated. The rest of the survivors dispersed, the largest group falling back to Babylon with Mazaeus. That drew Alexander's attention southwards. Renouncing for the moment the pursuit of Darius, he moved to annex the rich satrapy of Babylonia and enter the first of the great Achaemenid capitals to fall in his path.

As in Egypt, Alexander was welcomed as a liberator. The Persian garrison at Babylon could not withstand an attack from outside the city walls. As Alexander approached he received the official surrender which was offered by Mazaeus himself. The husband of a Babylonian lady and a Persian noble in his own right, he was a most appropriate person to welcome the conqueror; he was seconded by the Persian garrison commander and by representatives of the Babylonian priesthood. The king entered his capital on a carpet of flowers, to take possession of the palace and treasury. He sacrificed to Bel-Marduk, the city god and, like his Achaemenid predecessors, was invested as king of Babylon. As a gesture to the native populace he promised to restore the dilapidated temple complex of Esagila. That project was to await his return from the west (see below, p.843). For the moment the beneficiaries of conquest were his own troops, who received cash gratuities and enjoyed a month's recreation in Babylon.

The next capital, Susa, was acquired with equally little effort. The Persian satrap, Abulites, opened his gates and treasury to an emissary of Alexander, and in November he marched to take possession. It was a leisurely journey of twenty days through the well-provisioned province of Sittacene, where his army was swelled by the great convoy of reinforcements, more than 15,000 strong, which Amyntas had finally brought from Macedonia. At the river Choaspes (Karkheh), 3 km west of Susa, Alexander was received by Abulites in person and introduced to the capital and its treasury, which contained accumulated reserves of 40,000 talents of gold and silver bullion and 9,000 talents in gold darics. With this vast sum in hand he was able to transfer 3,000 silver talents to the Syrian coast to be used (in part) as a subsidy for the war against Agis which was now at its height.[44] Persian money continued to finance warfare in the Aegean but now it supported the Macedonian hegemony.

The next target was Persis, the heartland of the empire. Alexander moved quickly from Susa, keeping close to the foothills of the Zagros. His march took him through the territory of the Uxii, some of whom led a pastoral existence in the mountains; others were sedentary in the plains.

---

[44] Arr. *Anab.* III.16.10. See below, p.854.

Both groups caused trouble. The mountain Uxii demanded passage money and were subjected to a ravaging attack by a mobile Macedonian infantry column, which terrorized them into submission and tributary status. Somewhere near the border with Susiana the governor of the lowland Uxii, Medates, attempted to block the highway but was outmanoeuvred by Alexander and forced to capitulate.[45] These were separate incidents, of nuisance value but of no military significance. The real test came when Alexander attempted to force the Persian Gates. He had sent his baggage and heavy transport along the carriage way to Persepolis, while he made a direct push through the central Zagros with his Macedonian forces. The exact route is not precisely identifiable, but the most likely (which was certainly used in the Achaemenid period) is the track from the Fahlian valley to the plain of ʿAliabad, which rises through a long narrow gorge to a watershed at 2,167 metres.[46] Here (or in a similar position) the Persians had installed a strong army under the satrap Ariobarzanes. Alexander's first attempt at a frontal attack up the gorge failed miserably. His troops were demoralized by a rain of missiles from the surrounding heights and retreated, leaving their dead in the defiles. At that critical stage the history of Thermopylae was re-enacted. Local informants revealed a turning path, which allowed both infantry and cavalry to make an encircling movement (over the Bolsoru pass and south east along the base of the Kuh-i Rudian). The assault groups travelled over two nights and attacked the Persian encampment at the head of the gorge, while Craterus led a second push up the defiles. The dawn attack threw the Persians into a panic and they were routed with considerable loss of life.

Persepolis lay open to the invaders. Its citadel commander promptly made his peace with Alexander, refusing to admit the fugitive Ariobarzanes and inviting the king to take possession of the treasury. This he did, occupying the great palace complex of Darius and Xerxes and sacking the private homes of the Persian nobility. The war of revenge was now consummated, as Xerxes' capital was plundered and Persis itself turned into a satrapy under a permanent garrison of Hellenic troops. During the next four months Persepolis was host to Alexander's army, and its enormous reserves of bullion (estimated by some sources at 120,000 talents) were gradually redirected to Mesopotamia. There was also a small-scale campaign, thirty days long, against the Mardi of the southern Zagros. Finally the palace was stripped of its treasure, and it

---

[45] Curt. v.3.12–15; cf. Arr. *Anab.* III.17.6 (citing Ptolemy). On the difficulties and source divergences see Bosworth 1980 (B 14) 323–4; Briant 1982 (F 10) 161–73; *contra*, Badian 1985 (D 142) 441.

[46] Stein 1940 (D 236) 18ff; Hansman 1972 (F 32). There are criticisms and another location in an article to be published shortly in the *American Journal of Ancient History* by Henry Speck.

was then burned. The conflagration took place at a celebrated feast, allegedly at the instigation of the Athenian courtesan, Thais, and the troops indulged themselves in an orgy of destruction. The destruction was commemorated in Alexander's propaganda, which stressed the appropriateness of the act of revenge – a useful theme to air while Antipater was still embroiled with Agis in Greece; but there is some indication that it was an act of wanton vandalism which Alexander certainly lived to regret.[47]

Early in May Alexander led his forces north from Persepolis, taking with him the remains of the palace treasure. Darius had wintered in the Median capital, hoping for reinforcements from the eastern satrapies. He was disappointed, and, once travel was feasible, he left Ecbatana with his modest forces (3,300 cavalry, mostly Bactrian, and a somewhat larger force of infantry) and moved north east to the Caspian Gates, the complex of defiles that separated Media from the eastern satrapies. At the news of Darius' flight, which reached him near the Median border, Alexander reduced his forces to a minimum (cavalry, the bulk of the phalanx, and light infantry) and diverged from the main road to Ecbatana,[48] striking north eastwards to Rhagae (12 km south of Tehran) in the hope of intercepting his fugitive rival. Parmenion was detached (for the last time) to ensure that the rest of the army and the convoy of bullion reached the Median capital safely. Ten days of forced marches brought Alexander to Rhagae, where he learned that Darius had passed through the Caspian Gates. The pursuit resumed in earnest a little over a week later, at the news of a bitter power struggle in Darius' camp. Bessus, the most powerful of the eastern satraps, was intriguing to assume Darius' military command. He was supported by the chiliarch Nabarzanes but opposed by the westernized Artabazus. The dissension slowed the Persian progress and vastly increased the tide of desertions. Now Alexander began the most celebrated pursuit of his reign, which was to cover nearly 200 km in four nights and three days, from Choarene (immediately east of the Caspian Gates) to the borders of Parthyene.[49] The final stage was reserved for cavalry only, the pick of the infantry mounted for the last effort. Shortly after dawn the Macedonian column sighted the first Persian stragglers. Darius was already a prisoner of

[47] Arr. *Anab*. III.18.11–12 (revenge motive); Diod. XVII.72.1–5; Curt. v.7.2–7; Plut. *Alex*. 38.1–8 (role of Thais, originally in Cleitarchus, *FGrH* 137 F 11). For various interpretations see Seibert 1972 (D 232) 132–4; Wirth 1971 (D 246) 149–52; Borza 1972 (D 151); Badian 1985 (D 142) 443–6.
[48] Curt. v.13.1. Arr. *Anab*. III.19.5 states that Alexander actually entered Ecbatana; that is probably a misunderstanding (Bosworth 1976 (B 13) 132–6; see, however, Badian 1985 (D 142) 447).
[49] Arr. *Anab*. III.21.3–10; Curt. v.13.3–13. Calculation of the route is difficult, given the vagueness of the sources and the prevailing tendency to exaggerate marching distances. The sole key is the location of Hecatompylus, the terminal point of the pursuit (see below, n. 50). For detailed discussion see Radet 1932 (D 224); Bosworth 1980 (B 14) 336–8; Seibert 1985 (D 233) 112–14.

Bessus, confined in golden chains, and at the first sight of the Macedonian advance he was stabbed to death. The actual assassins were Satibarzanes and Barsaentes, satraps of Areia and Arachosia; the primary instigators were Bessus and Nabarzanes.

In every sense the war of revenge was complete. Alexander at last was master of his rival, whose body he sent for royal burial at Persepolis. That marked an epoch, and Alexander emphasized the message by ordering the demobilization of the entire contingent of troops from the Corinthian League. They were conveyed from Ecbatana, flush with a discharge bonus of 2,000 talents, to be shipped from Syria to Euboea. That evoked a powerful reaction from the Macedonians who saw no reason to continue the war after its objectives were realized. They were disinclined to promote Alexander's regal ambitions by indefinite campaigning, and it took all his rhetoric − and promises of generous donatives − to reconcile them to the next advance. The opposition was serious and it was to gather momentum.

V. THE CONQUEST OF EASTERN IRAN AND THE BACTRIAN LANDS, 330–327 B.C.

After the pursuit Alexander concentrated his scattered forces at the city of Hecatompylus (recently located at Shahr-i Qumis).[50] His first concern was to deal with the remnants of Darius' army, which had taken refuge in the Elburz mountains. To that end he invaded Hyrcania, crossing the mountain via the Shamshirbun Pass, while Craterus and Erigyius took other routes. There was little or no resistance, but a stream of Persian refugees made cautious overtures. The regicide Nabarzanes made contact at the first halting-place by the river Rhidagnus, and after receiving reassurances he made a formal surrender at the Hyrcanian capital. Similarly Phrataphernes, the Hyrcanian satrap, offered submission. As the campaign continued to the west of Hyrcania Artabazus and his sons attached themselves to the Macedonian court, where they were warmly welcomed. Loyalists and regicides alike were accepted into the service of Darius' successor. Finally the Greek mercenaries who had served with Darius made their peace and were incorporated in the army of their victor. The Hyrcanian campaign was a triumphal tour, the only serious fighting a five-day campaign against the independent Mardi towards the south-west of the satrapy. It climaxed in a fifteen-day stay at Zadracarta, the Hyrcanian capital, where the king held sacrifices and games for his recent successes. He then recrossed the Elburz and marched east to Areia. At Susia (now Tus, near Meshed) he received the satrap and regicide, Satibarzanes, and confirmed him in office.

[50] Hansman 1968 (F 31); Hansman and Stronach 1970 (F 33).

Now came a challenge. Bessus, safely home in Bactria, assumed the upright tiara, the insignia of kingship, and termed himself Artaxerxes. A relative of Darius, he was now arrogating the Achaemenid monarchy, implicitly branding Alexander an alien and usurper. Alexander reacted by himself adopting some elements of Persian court dress: the diadem, the striped tunic and the girdle, which he combined with the Macedonian hat (*kausia*) and cloak.[51] At the same time he gave senior Companions the scarlet robes of Persian courtiers and added Darius' brother to his entourage. He was adapting to the institutions of the throne he had acquired, but he risked alienating the more conservative-minded Macedonians, who had just completed the mission of vengeance.

Alexander began his march to Bactria, intending to invade the satrapy from the west after traversing the piedmont area north of the Kopet Dag massif. Once he was out of Areia, Satibarzanes renounced his allegiance and massacred the tiny force of cavalry that was left as a garrison. That ensured Alexander's return and his vengeance. A column of Companion Cavalry and picked infantry covered 600 stades in two nights and days, and confined the insurgents to a hill citadel near Artacoana (Herat).[52] Satibarzanes himself prudently left his satrapy and took refuge with Bessus. Alexander placed another Iranian, Arsaces, over the satrapy and moved south to Drangiana, the realm of the other regicide, Barsaentes. Bessus' challenge had changed his attitude. Now the punishment of Darius' murderers was a sacred duty, and his *pietas* might weaken local support for Bessus. In the face of the invasion Barsaentes took flight to India, and the Macedonian army occupied the Drangian capital of Phrada (Farah).

At Phrada the rift between Alexander and the family of Parmenion emerged sensationally to public view.[53] Philotas, Parmenion's eldest son and commander of the Companions, had recently returned to court after conducting the obsequies of his brother, the hypaspist commander Nicanor, who had died on the northern borders of Areia. In his absence a conspiracy had matured at court, centred around the figure of Demetrius the bodyguard. It was betrayed during the stay at Phrada, and Philotas was accused of complicity. He was not a principal, but it was alleged that he failed to act on a report of the imminent assassination. The last point is

[51] Diod. XVII.77.4–7; Curt. VI.6.1–10; Justin XII.3.8–12; cf. Plut. *Alex.* 45.1–2; Arr. *Anab.* IV.7.4–5. See Ritter 1965 (A 50) 31–55; Bosworth 1980 (D 155) 4–8.

[52] Diod. XVII.78.2; Curt. VI.6.22–32; cf. Arr. *Anab.* III.25.7. For the location of the fortress see Seibert 1985 (D 233) 120, *contra*, Engels 1978 (D 172) 87–91; Badian 1985 (D 142) 451.

[53] Arr. *Anab.* III.26–7 (apologetically slanted and based on Ptolemy and Aristobulus); Curt. VI.7.1–VII.2.38 (detailed and rhetorically embellished); Diod. XVII.79–80; Plut. *Alex.* 48–9; Justin XII.5.1–8; Strabo XV.2.10. For source analysis see Goukowsky 1978–81 (B 45) II 118–34. Modern reconstructions begin with Badian 1960 (D 132), the seminal work. See also Hamilton 1969 (B 54) 132–8; Schachermeyr 1973 (D 231) 326–36; Heckel 1977 (D 195).

emphasized in all the otherwise divergent sources, and it is agreed that he was at least guilty of passive disloyalty. That was enough to ensure his arrest, and the following day he was tried and condemned by the army present with Alexander, which was far from its full strength.[54] Rhetoric and blatant stage management succeeded in convincing the common soldiers that he was an instigator of the conspiracy. The trial completed, he was put to extreme torture in an attempt to incriminate his father. Admissions of a sort were extorted, but they were not substantial enough for a formal indictment. Parmenion was simply murdered. The king sent secret messages by racing camel, and on his instructions the mercenary commander at Ecbatana (who was the brother of Coenus, one of Philotas' enemies) cut down the old general, isolated as he was after the departure of his phalanx infantry to join the main army. In Drangiana Philotas and the convicted conspirators were executed by stoning, and in the highly charged emotional atmosphere the Lyncestian prince, Alexander, was brought to trial and put to death after three years of close confinement (see above, p.803).[55] That removed a potential threat, at the risk of antagonizing his father-in-law, Antipater, the regent of Macedonia. The king had served notice that disloyalty would not be tolerated, and he had eradicated the group which had been most antipathetic to his policies. Critics of a humbler station were relegated to a special disciplinary company known as 'the unit of insubordinates' (Diod. XVII.80.4). On the other hand the men who had engineered Philotas' downfall reaped the rewards of his demise. The cavalry command was divided between Alexander's favourite, Hephaestion, and the veteran general, Cleitus the Black, and the command of army divisions was almost monopolized by a small group of marshals: Craterus, Hephaestion, Perdiccas, Coenus and Ptolemy son of Lagus, a boyhood friend of Alexander who now replaced Demetrius as bodyguard. The king was surrounded by his intimates, and disagreement was both difficult and dangerous to voice.

The army now moved south to the land of the Ariaspians, where the river Helmand discharges into a complex of fresh-water lakes. This was one of the granaries of ancient Iran, and Alexander's forces stayed in the area for some sixty days. Meanwhile Bessus had fomented unrest in the northern satrapies, supporting Satibarzanes in a second invasion of Areia and sending troops along the northern corridor from Bactria to Media. There followed nearly two years of unrest. Satibarzanes himself was killed in the summer of 329, falling in hand-to-hand combat with

---

[54] According to Curt. VI.8.23, the assembly which convicted Philotas numbered only 6,000. The phalanx contingent with Parmenion in Media, again 6,000 strong, was in transit and reached the main army when Alexander was in Arachosia (Curt. VII.3.4; cf. Arr. *Anab.* III.19.7).

[55] Curt. VII.1.5–9; Diod. XVII.80.2; cf. Berve 1926 (D 146) 2. no. 548; Badian 1960 (D 132) 335–6.

Erigyius who commanded a punitive force sent by Alexander. But the troubles continued. Stasanor, Alexander's new satrap, had a struggle to establish himself in Areia, and in Parthyaea Bessus had backed a certain Brazanes, who managed to elude capture until 328.[56] Despite the turmoil in the north (which was not dissimilar to the situation in the Aegean in 333) the king moved on to settle accounts with Bessus. In late winter he led his united forces up the Helmand valley, struggling against deep snow and lack of provisions. The passes of the Hindu Kush were blocked, and he had to wait for at least a month in the vicinity of Kabul, provisioning his army from the well-stocked villages and founding a new Alexandria near modern Begram to control access to the strategic Shibar and Khawak passes.[57]

The following season saw the downfall of Bessus, who was unable to mobilize the Bactrian nobility under his leadership. He fell back north of the river Oxus (Amu Darya), hoping to make Sogdiana his base. Meanwhile Alexander crossed the Hindu Kush. The only difficulties were the absence of food and timber in the high country, and there was no military opposition. Bactria lay open to him, and he occupied the major citadels with his own troops, placing Artabazus over the entire satrapy, which was deceptively peaceful. The capture of Bessus was the first priority. The army traversed the 75 km of waterless desert between Bactra (Balkh) and the Oxus with considerable losses from thirst and exposure. Then came the river crossing, on improvised rafts of stuffed hides, and the final push against Bessus. There was little more to do. The self-styled Artaxerxes V was Alexander's target, and by welcoming deserters from his camp Alexander had indicated that his quarrel was with Bessus alone. Accordingly his Sogdian supporters, Spitamenes and Dataphernes, arrested him as he had previously arrested Darius and conveyed him under guard to Alexander's camp.[58] In compliance with Alexander's instructions he was naked and fettered, to be first scourged, then remitted to Bactra where he was later mutilated, and finally executed at Ecbatana in a great public spectacle. It was overtly punishment for the murder of Darius; in practice Bessus suffered the dreadful treatment meted out to pretenders to the Achaemenid throne.

The king continued his royal progress to the satrapal palace at

[56] On these events see Bosworth 1981 (D 156) 21–4.

[57] For the chronology, complicated by the fact that Strabo xv.2.10 implies that Alexander spent the winter near Begram, see Jones 1935 (D 204); Hamilton 1969 (B 54) 98–9; *contra*, Badian 1985 (D 142), 455. On the reconstruction given in the text the setting of the Pleiades, which Strabo claims coincided with Alexander's passage of Parapamisadae, must be the spring setting, in early April 329. Strabo may imply only that Alexander *saw the winter out* in the Kabul valley.

[58] This is the version of Aristobulus (in Arr. *Anab.* III.30.5; see also Curt. VII.5.36–42; Diod. XVII.83.8). Ptolemy gave a highly colourful account of a breakneck chase across Sogdiana to snatch Bessus from his captors (Arr. *Anab.* III.29.7–30.3). In all probability he greatly exaggerated his exploit. Cf. Welles 1963 (B 124) 109–10; Seibert 1969 (B 108) 14–16; Bosworth 1980 (B 14) 376–7.

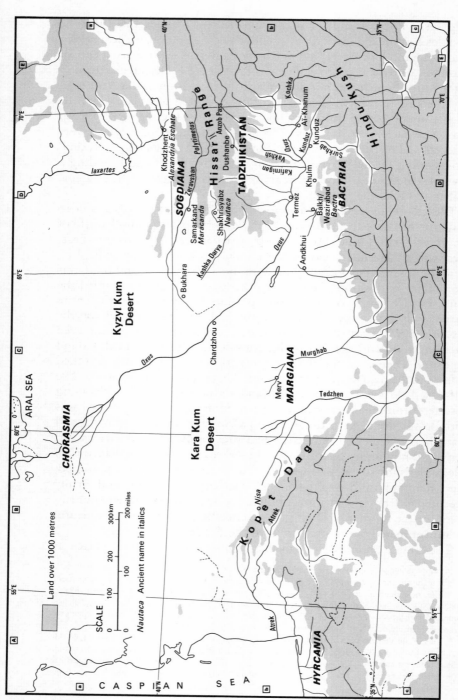

Map 21. Chorasmia, Margiana, Sogdiana and Bactria.

Maracanda and then to the banks of the modern Syr Darya. The river was known locally as the Iaxartes, but Alexander and his staff considered it the same river as the European Tanais (Don). He assumed that he had come to the traditional boundary between Europe and Asia and was encouraged in his belief by the abundant stands of silver fir which were reminiscent of the European trees. Later there was more elaborate speculation, and Alexander sent an expedition to determine whether the Caspian and the Sea of Azov were interconnected lakes, as one geographical hypothesis demanded. In 329, however, he simply assumed that in reaching the Tanais he had reached the limits of Asia, and he concluded treaty relations with the Saca tribes north of the river, considering them outside the boundary of his empire. Consistently with this concept he founded a new frontier city, Alexandria Eschate, on the south bank of the river, in the vicinity of the modern city of Khodzhent (Leninabad).

At this point Alexander was rudely surprised by an insurrection which began in Sogdiana and rapidly spread to Bactria, encouraged by Spitamenes and Dataphernes. Macedonian garrisons were massacred, and the rebellion extended to the border district where the king was operating. He reacted with predictable ferocity, reconquering seven fortresses close to the Syr Darya and punishing the insurgents with massacre and enslavement. North of the river his new foundation was threatened by hordes of Saca cavalry, ready to profit from his discomfiture. That threat was neutralized by a river crossing under the protection of an artillery barrage which did much to demoralize the enemy. There followed a cavalry engagement in which archers and light infantry protected the flanks from the wheeling attacks of the enemy while the bulk of the Companions, massed in column, broke the main Saca formation. The result was an extended pursuit, interrupted only when the king was incapacitated by dysentery. His opponents promptly offered submission.

That was only the first act of what proved a bitter campaign of reprisal. Alexander had sent a small force of mercenary cavalry and infantry to relieve the capital, Maracanda, which was undergoing siege. In that they were successful. The insurgent commander, Spitamenes, withdrew westwards with his forces; but with the help of Saca auxiliaries, who joined him near the frontier, he laid an ambush. Outnumbered and debilitated by fatigue, the Macedonian expeditionary force, whose commanders had unwisely continued the pursuit from Maracanda, were driven to panic and largely massacred.[59] It was a psychological blow to

---

[59] The details are controversial, differently reported by Ptolemy and Aristobulus, both of whom alleged incompetence among the Macedonian commanders (Arr. *Anab.* IV.5.2–9 – Ptolemy; 6.1–2 – Aristobulus; cf. Curt. VII.7.31–9).

the invaders, and the siege of the capital resumed. Alexander himself marched south with half the Companions and the pick of the infantry. He covered the 290 km to Maracanda at a furious speed, relieved the citadel and systematically devastated the western part of the Zeravshan valley in a campaign of terror calculated to eradicate all resistance. By mid-winter the western portion of Sogdiana had been crushed and Alexander withdrew to the secure base of Bactra.

In the spring of 328 he turned to the east. His united army followed the course of the Oxus, probably as far as the confluence with the Kokcha, the site of Ai-Khanum.[60] Here he divided his forces, four phalanx commanders being left to garrison Bactria while his main army, divided into five separate columns, reduced to submission the lands between the Oxus and the Hissar range. It was a grim business of siege, massacre and forcible resettlement, the highlight a spectacular climb by an elite group of mountaineers to force the surrender of a seemingly impregnable rock citadel. As summer ended[61] the various army groups converged on Maracanda, where Alexander rested his men and received a visit from the most powerful local dynast, Pharasmanes, the king of the independent land of Chorasmia (in the lower reaches of the Syr Darya). A treaty of peace and alliance effectively denied his support to the insurgents, and Alexander himself tactfully avoided an invitation to use his army to expand the Chorasmian domains (Arr. *Anab.* IV.15.4–6; Curt. VIII.1.8).

At Maracanda occurred the sensational killing of Cleitus the Black. Alienated by the increasingly oriental trappings of the court and (perhaps for that reason) nominated satrap of Bactria and Sogdiana, he gave vent to his feelings at a banquet and symposium in honour of the Dioscuri. The extant accounts of the scene differ markedly,[62] but it is relatively clear that Cleitus reacted against the court flattery which gave Alexander divine status and denigrated others, notably the commanders who had perished at the Zeravshan. In contrast Cleitus emphasized Alexander's obligations to others, notably Philip and himself, and quoted a particularly wounding passage of Euripides' *Andromache* (693 ff). Abuse turned to violence, and in the end Alexander seized a weapon from a guard and struck down Cleitus. Remorse, which appears genuine, came immediately. Alexander fasted in his tent for three days, his self-reproach causing increasing worry to both court and rank and file. He was (allegedly) consoled by the political philosophy of Anaxarchus of Abdera, who claimed that Alexander as the earthly counterpart of Zeus

---

[60] For details see Bosworth 1981 (D 156) 23–9. For other views see (e.g.) Schachermeyr 1973 (D 231) 349; Engels 1978 (D 172) 104–5; Seibert 1985 (D 233) 138.

[61] The chronology adopted here is based on Curt. VII.11.1ff, which is more coherent and plausible than Arr. *Anab.* IV.16.1ff. See for detailed argument Bosworth 1981 (D 156) 29–39.

[62] See particularly Aymard 1967 (A 2) 51–7; Brown 1949 (D 161) 236–8; Hamilton 1969 (B 54) 139–46; Bosworth 1977 (D 20) 62–4.

was the very embodiment of justice; and he emerged from his tent to general relief. Cleitus was buried, his killing (maybe) exonerated by the army (Curt. VIII.2.12), but the opposition he had voiced was not forgotten.

The Sogdian insurrection was now approaching its bitter end. Alexander moved south to his winter quarters at Nautaca, where the local ruler, Sisimithres, was blockaded in his citadel and shocked into submission by the Macedonian expertise in siege engineering. At the same time Coenus continued operations from Maracanda and heavily repulsed an invasion by Spitamenes and his nomad allies. The insurgency collapsed. Spitamenes was killed by his own allies, who sent his head to Alexander. At the same time the satraps of Parthyaea and Areia announced the end of operations in their territories. For the first time in nearly two years the eastern satrapies were relatively quiet. Bactria and Sogdiana were organized under a new satrap, Amyntas, and a large network of military colonies supported by a native agrarian work force. A large number of the native cavalry was enlisted for Alexander's army and a further 30,000 of the local youth were earmarked for training in Macedonian style. The prime of the military population would eventually leave for service elsewhere. At the same time Alexander took a Bactrian wife, Rhoxane. She had fallen into his hands during 328 and her father, Oxyartes, had collaborated with him. Early in 327 the marriage took place – in Macedonian style.[63] Like his father Alexander had married for strategic reasons, but the act doubtless exacerbated the tensions that had already been manifested in Cleitus' death.

The trouble worsened at Bactra, where Alexander began his preparations for the invasion of India as his lieutenants cleaned up the two remaining pockets of rebellion (led by Catanes and Austanes). There the king made his famous abortive experiment with *proskynesis* (see below, p.873), and the debacle was followed immediately by the Pages' Conspiracy. That was a serious attempt on the king's life, initiated from his closest entourage. The ringleader, Hermolaus son of Sopolis, had a personal grudge against Alexander and recruited a small group of intimates (seven are named) to assassinate him while they shared the guard of his bedchamber. Before the plan could be executed, it was betrayed. All the conspirators were arrested, admitted their guilt under torture and were stoned to death. The affair remains a mystery, the political motivation of the Pages (if any) a matter of guesswork – although the experiment with *proskynesis* may well have been a catalyst. Callisthenes, the king's historian, was suspected of complicity and, although no admission of his guilt could be extracted from the wretched

---

[63] Arr. *Anab.* IV.19.5; Curt. VIII.4.21–30; Plut. *Alex.* 47.7–8; Strabo XI.11.4; cf. Bosworth 1980 (D 155) 10–11.

Pages, he too was arrested, tortured and executed.[64] He had been familiar with some of the conspirators and it was easy to suggest guilt by association. His death was a stark illustration of the perils of opposing the current trends at court, and the critics of the self-proclaimed son of Zeus and King of Asia were silenced – for the moment.

VI. THE INDIAN CAMPAIGNS, 327–325 B.C.

The invasion of India had been maturing for some time with the encouragement of Indian refugees, notably Sisicottus who had served with Alexander throughout the Sogdian revolt. Interested rulers from the Indus valley, notably the prince of Taxila, had also intrigued with the conqueror, hoping to use his army for their own purposes. But no encouragement was needed. As Alexander surely knew from Herodotus, the Indus valley had been acquired for the Persian empire by Darius I, and the inhabitants of the Kabul valley at least had sent cavalry and elephants to the Persian grand army at Gaugamela.[65] There was also the factor of emulation. Greek tradition knew of the exploits of the legendary Babylonian queen Semiramis and her conquests in India; and, more pertinently, there was already a legend in vogue that Dionysus had begun his triumphal progress in the eastern lands. Alexander's staff was ready to find and create evidence for the presence of both Heracles and Dionysus. Most conveniently a small community which surrendered to him in the mountains between the Choes and the Kunar valley was identified as the birthplace of Dionysus. Nearby was a mountain whose local name recalled the Greek *meros* (Dionysus was reputed to have been concealed in the thigh ($\mu\eta\rho\acuteo\varsigma$) of Zeus), and there were abundant growths of ivy and bay trees. That encouraged the presumption that the inhabitants worshipped Dionysus and were descended from the god's entourage. They were accordingly granted their freedom (under the supervision of Alexander's satrap) with high commendation of their aristocratic government.[66]

Other communities were less fortunate, and the record of the campaign in Gandhara makes grim reading. Alexander began his invasion from Parapamisadae, after reinforcing his new Alexandria (Begram) with extra settlers. Half the Macedonian troops and all the mercenaries followed Hephaestion and Perdiccas along the main road to the Indus. The elite troops left with Alexander campaigned in the

[64] Arr. *Anab.* IV.14.3 (Ptolemy); cf. Curt. VIII.8.21. For the apologetic versions of Aristobulus (F 33) and Chares (F 15) see Hamilton 1969 (B 54) 156; Badian 1981 (D 141) 50–1; 1985 (D 142) 459.
[65] Arr. *Anab.* III.8.3,6. See further Badian 1985 (D 142) 462.
[66] On this episode see Goukowsky 1978–81 (B 45) II 21–33; Brunt 1976–83 (B 21) II 437–42; Bosworth 1988 (B 15) 70–2. It was mentioned as early as Theophrastus (*Hist. Pl.* IV.4.1).

mountain districts, in what is now Bajaur and Swat. The pattern was set in the valley of the Choes (Alingar?),[67] where resistance was punished by massacre and destruction. Some settlements capitulated, but most of the populace took refuge in the mountains until the storm passed. Alexander overran the territory, took numerous prisoners when he came into contact with the fugitive population and established military settlements at strategic sites. The methods devised for the Sogdian insurgency were employed again in India.

The most determined resistance came from the Assaceni of the Lower Swat. The local ruler had a moderate army (30,000 foot and 2,000 horse) which he strengthened with mercenaries from the plains and distributed around his strongholds. It was futile. The largest city, Massaga, had fortifications of mud brick and stone which quickly gave way before the Macedonian artillery barrage. On the verge of capture the city was surrendered under guarantee that the mercenary garrison would join Alexander's army. The mercenaries were in fact massacred under mysterious circumstances, possibly through a misunderstanding; and the city was then taken by assault. That did not encourage surrender elsewhere. The neighbouring cities, Ora and Bazira, held out until Ora was taken by storm. Bazira was evacuated, and the population at large took refuge in the mountain fortress of Aornus. It was associated with the Indian deity Krishna, whom Alexander's staff identified as Heracles, and it was allegedly impregnable – even by Heracles. That inspired Alexander to emulate and surpass. Unlike Heracles he had the most modern anti-personnel catapults, and, helped by local guides, he occupied a position high on a saddle threatening the citadel.[68] A siege mound was then constructed to support his siege artillery and its relentless advance forced the defenders first to capitulation and then to flight. The most formidable natural fortress of the area was captured relatively quickly and with a modest force of light infantry and phalanx troops. After this shock the resistance collapsed. The last enemy forces under arms left the mountains of Buner to find refuge with Abisares, prince of Hazara to the east of the Indus.

Meanwhile Hephaestion and Perdiccas had pushed forward to the Indus, capturing the capital of Peucelaotis (Charsadda) en route.[69] Even before Alexander began his siege of Aornus, they had bridged the Indus. To the west Gandhara was quiet under a Macedonian satrap, subdued by

---

[67] The topography of the early campaign is in dispute. I follow in the main the reconstruction of Eggermont 1970 (D 168) 108 (cf. Goukowsky 1978–81) (B 45) II.23–4; *contra*, Stein 1929 (D 234) 41; Seibert 1985 (D 233) 150–1.

[68] Identified attractively by Sir Aurel Stein as the ridge of Pir Sar, a level plateau with wheat fields (Stein 1929 (D 234) 131–2). For an alternative suggestion (Mt Ilam) see Eggermont 1984 (D 169A); Badian 1987 (D 143) 117.

[69] Arr. *Anab.* IV.22.8. See Wheeler 1968 (F 70) 95–8; Badian 1987 (D 143).

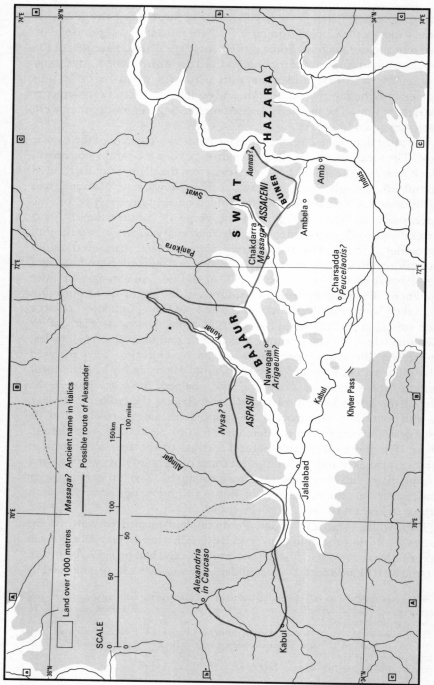

SCALE

Land over 1000 metres

Massaga? Ancient name in italics

Possible route of Alexander

0
0   50   100   150km
0   50   100 miles

Kabul

Alexandria
in Caucaso

Jalalabad

Alingar

Nysa?

Kunar

ASPASII

BAJAUR

Nawagai
Arigaeum?

Kabul

Khyber Pass

Charsadda
Peucelaotis?

Ambela

Amb

Pankkora

Chakdarra
Massaga? ASSACENI

BUNER

Aornus?

Swat

S W A T

H A Z A R A

Indus

Map 22. The Kabul valley.

an autumn and winter of terror and repression. Now, in the spring of 326, Alexander crossed the Indus near Ohind, where he met Omphis (Ambhi), the prince of Taxila. The submission formally offered in Sogdiana was renewed, and he was confirmed in his princedom under the satrap appointed by Alexander. The union was celebrated by sacrifices and games at Taxila itself, while emissaries visited the neighbouring princes. Abisares was prudent enough to offer submission, but Porus, ruler of the rich country between the Hydaspes (Jhelum) and Acesines (Chenab), rejected the overtures and prepared to defend his realm.

The campaign of the Hydaspes ensued. Alexander immediately led his army from Taxila, intent on reaching the river before it was in full spate. He crossed the Great Salt Range[70] and established his base camp on the river bank in the face of Porus' army, which held the eastern side, its elephants in full view. The strategic problem was the river crossing. Alexander kept his forces in constant motion, at the same time transporting a flotilla by land from the Indus and giving the impression that he was prepared to wait until the river reached low water in September. During these manoeuvres he had identified a crossing point where the Hydaspes flowed around a densely wooded headland and an island was conveniently placed to conceal the fleet. Under the cover of a spring thunderstorm he made his crossing, while divisions of the army made ostentatious manoeuvres to distract the enemy from the main striking force. This, it seems, was relatively small: 6,000 foot and 5,000 horse (half the Companions and Bactrian and Saca cavalry from the north-east frontier). Even so Porus' forces were outmatched and maybe even outnumbered. He had other fronts to cope with and could not concentrate his army at a single point.

At dawn the Macedonian army reached the east bank and began its advance to the main Indian army, fording a secondary channel of the Hydaspes at the expense of considerable time and trouble. A detachment of Indian cavalry and war chariots under the command of one of Porus' sons was easily routed, the cumbersome six-man chariots foundering in the rain-soaked mud. The fugitives alerted Porus, who deployed his forces, stationing his elephants at intervals along his line of infantry, with cavalry and war chariots at the flanks (Fig. 39). The elephants were intended to win the battle, smashing the phalanx infantry as Darius had hoped his scythed chariots would at Gaugamela. But the Macedonians now had experience of elephants, and there had been ample time before the battle to refine tactics. Alexander used his cavalry (which was

---

[70] For the various locations of the campaign see Seibert 1972 (D 232) 158–60; 1985 (D 233) 156–7. Given the gradual changes of the river system since antiquity, it is unlikely that certainty will ever be achieved – unless Alexander's commemorative foundations are one day unearthed.

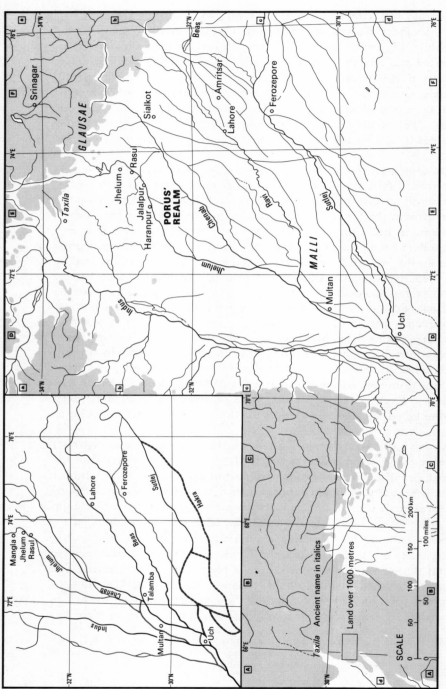

Map 23. The Punjab. The main map illustrates the present-day topography. The map in the inset is a conjectural approximation of the river system in the eighth century A.D. In Alexander's day the main rivers are likely to have flowed still further to the east.

Fig. 39. Designs from five-shekel coins struck by Alexander in Babylon, about 323 B.C. Horseman (Alexander?) attacking a war elephant; Alexander holding the thunderbolt, crowned by Nike. (Cf. Goukowsky 1972 (D 179) 478, figs. 1–3; M.J. Price, *The Coinage in the Name of Alexander* (London, 1991) 33, 452–3, pl. 159g–h.)

numerically and qualitatively superior) to cause the maximum disruption.[71] The Indian cavalry on Porus' left wing was attacked by the bulk of the Macedonian horse led by Alexander. An onslaught by massed mounted archers created confusion which he exploited by a full charge at the head of the Companions. The vortex this produced attracted cavalry reinforcements from the right of the Indian line, and, while they were in transit Coenus struck at the right with a compact cavalry force, two hipparchies strong. Caught between hammer and anvil, the Indian cavalry was forced back into Porus' infantry column. Meanwhile the elephants were largely neutralized, as the Macedonian phalanx opened its ranks, disabled the drivers and stabbed upwards at the beasts. Eventually they were driven upon their own line, an increasingly chaotic amalgam of infantry, cavalry and elephants, under constant harassment from the Macedonian cavalry, now united in one body. The final act came when the elephants, mostly out of control, began to trample their own troops. Then the phalanx pressed the attack frontally in close formation while the cavalry virtually enveloped the rear of the Indian line. From that point it was a massacre; the few survivors who broke the cordon were hounded to annihilation by the fresh forces under Craterus who crossed the river when victory was assured and began the pursuit.

The victory was complete, celebrated by games at the site and by new city foundations, Bucephala (located at the base camp) and Nicaea on the field of battle.[72] Later it was to be celebrated in two great coin series issued from the Babylon mint, tetradrachms and decadrachms, the latter

[71] Arr. *Anab.* v.16.3 (cf. Curt VIII.14.15; Plut. *Alex.* 60.10). For the difficulties of Arrian's language see Hamilton 1956 (D 186) (*contra*, Tarn 1948 (D 239) II 193–8).

[72] Arr. *Anab.* v.19.4; Strabo xv.1.29; cf. Radet 1941 (D 226) *contra* Tarn 1948 (D 239) II 236–7.

depicting a mounted Alexander armed with a *sarissa* and attacking Porus' war elephant. After Alexander the main beneficiary of the battle, paradoxically, was Porus. He had fought to the last and thrown himself on the victor's mercy. Impressed by his courage and his physique (he was over 2 metres tall), Alexander confirmed him in his realms and took his enemies as his own, just as he had done with the ruler of Taxila. While a fleet was being constructed in the timber-rich country of the Glausae (which he added to Porus' domains), he moved against Porus' eastern neighbour, a homonymous cousin, who had offered submission before the Battle of the Hydaspes but took flight with his army at the news of Porus' promotion. There was comparatively little resistance as the army proceeded across the Acesines and then the Hydraotes (Ravi), but the advance was seriously complicated by the event of the monsoon rains. The Hydaspes had been crossed in May against a background of spring thunderstorms, and by late June, when the army reached the Acesines, the monsoon deluge was in full spate and lasted until the rising of Arcturus, late in September.[73] After the annexation of the lands of Porus' cousin, the king crossed the Hydraotes to attack the autonomous Indians. Their chief stronghold, Sangala (near Lahore and Amritsar), was captured and destroyed after a brief siege; the populations of neighbouring cities were evacuated and ruthlessly harried in flight. Porus yet again was conceded sovereignty, placing garrisons in the surviving cities.

Alexander intended to go further. How far we cannot determine. The vulgate tradition, based on Cleitarchus, suggests that he had heard rumours of the realm of the Nandas, far away on the eastern Ganges (their capital, Pataliputra, lay near the modern city of Patna).[74] Arrian (*Anab.* v.25.1) speaks of an aristocratically governed people, rich in elephants. Perhaps we have in the two reports a short-term or long-term objective – or a stated end and a rumoured ambition. Whatever the case, the army had had enough. At the banks of the Hyphasis (Beas) the long simmering dissatisfaction coalesced in informal meetings and complaints by the rank and file. Alexander tested the sentiments of his officers, only to be told bluntly by Coenus, one of the most senior of the phalanx commanders, that the troops would go no further east.[75] A second meeting was no more successful, and Alexander retired to his tent with the threat that he would go on alone, if necessary. This time his

---

[73] Strabo xv.1.17–18 (Aristobulus F 35, Nearchus F 18). In Arrian (v.29.15) there is one retrospective reference to the monsoon conditions.

[74] Diod. xvii.93.2–4; Curt. ix.2.2–7; Plut. *Alex.* 62.2–3. The tradition was apparently familiar to Hieronymus of Cardia (Meyer 1927 (D 213); Hornblower 1981 (B 60) 84–6). Cf. Schachermeyr 1955 (D 229); Brunt 1976–83 (B 21) II 463–5; Kienast 1965 (D 205).

[75] On the sources and the character of the reported speeches see now Bosworth 1988 (B 15) 123–34.

bluff was called. The troops waited in silence for three days while he nursed his wrath. Then he capitulated, ostensibly finding the omens for crossing unfavourable, and announced that he would turn back. His men were jubilant, but he never forgot the humiliation and, as his reign progressed, he deliberately reduced his dependence upon them. Perhaps significantly, their spokesman, Coenus, died within days of the reconciliation and Alexander's entourage increasingly comprised only men who would approve his ambitions.

At the Hydaspes, where Alexander returned late in September, he found a fleet under construction in his new foundations of Bucephala and Nicaea. It was a great assembly of light transport craft, mainly two-banked *triaconters*, designed to convey horses, men and provisions to the southern Ocean. Under the command of his boyhood friend, Nearchus of Crete, seconded by the royal helmsman, Onesicritus of Cos, the fleet began its voyage, carrying a large proportion of the cavalry as well as the hypaspists and archers. The rest of the army, including 200 elephants, moved along the banks to right and left under the command of Craterus and Hephaestion. There was a minor debacle at the confluence of the Acesines and Hydaspes, where the strong current caused a good deal of damage and delayed the advance. The main thrust of Alexander's campaign in this area was directed against the Oxydracae (Ksudrakas) and Malli (Malavas), who were determined to resist invasion and had begun concentrating the population in defensible strongholds. Their territory was located on the lower reaches of the Hydraotes, and, while the fleet and the main army column continued the journey down the Acesines, Alexander led a mobile striking force across desert terrain to attack the Malli from the north.[76] He took them completely by surprise, cutting off assistance from the Oxydracae. The depressing policy of terror was again employed. Citadels which held out against him were stormed and the defenders massacred; and the refugees who sought sanctuary in the desert were relentlessly harassed.

Finally the surviving Malli warriors crossed the Hydraotes and made a last stand in a neighbouring fortified city. The walls were captured easily and the inner citadel alone withstood the attack. Here the assault flagged and Alexander, who had detected loss of morale in an earler siege, decided to set an object lesson. He scaled the wall and with a handful of companions, notably Peucestas, he stood there isolated and exposed, while his hypaspists tried vainly to reach him. At this point he leaped down inside the citadel, to become the single target of the defenders. He

[76] The campaign is known only from Arrian (*Anab.* VI.6-10) whose account is unitary and derived from Ptolemy (cf. VI.10.1). Though detailed, the report is not based on autopsy, since Ptolemy was not personally involved in the attack on the Malli. See, for full discussion, Bosworth 1988 (B 15) 75–83.

received a serious arrow wound when his right chest was penetrated, and his immediate bodyguard were hard put to protect him until the hypaspists stormed the wall and killed every living person. The king came close to death before he was rescued by the surgery of Critobulus of Cos; and the news of his peril caused panic among the rank and file, who had a realistic appreciation of their future in hostile territory with no obvious successor to the command. There were scenes of high emotion when he appeared alive and apparently sound in the base camp. During his convalescence he received the formal submission of the Malli and Oxydracae, and the territory south to the confluence of the Acesines and Indus was consolidated under the satrapal authority of Philip, son of Machatas. The fleet now moved on to Sind, which was proclaimed a satrapy under Peithon, son of Agenor. Many of its peoples had already capitulated. Those who had not, notably Musicanus and Oxycanus, were rapidly terrorized into submission. Revolts, like that of Sambus in the western mountains, were dealt with savagely, and the Brahman ascetics, who inspired and encouraged resistance, received special attention. Musicanus, who revoked his allegiance, was crucified in his capital along with his Brahman advisers. As Alexander approached the southern province of Patalene, the populace fled in terror before his advance, and he found the capital Patala an empty shell. His repression had been all too effective, and he was forced to give guarantees of safety before he could recruit the native labour force he required for his projects. The Indian lands had accepted the fact of conquest but it was a grudging acquiescence which turned into active hostility after Alexander and his army moved west.

VII. THE LAST YEARS, 325–323 B.C.

Patala, which the Macedonians occupied in July 325, was the centre of Alexander's preparations for his return west. Determined now to abandon further conquest in the Indian lands, he had already detached a large part of his army to traverse southern Iran. Three phalanx battalions, the entire complement of elephants and all Macedonian troops considered unfit for active service were placed under Craterus' command and sent directly west over the Bolan Pass to the Helmand valley and from there via Sistan to Carmania.[77] Alexander himself decided to take the much more arduous route along the Makran coast, which he would traverse by land while a fleet, again under Nearchus, was to conduct a detailed reconnaissance of the coast. He was to some degree aware of the dangers of his chosen route and made the most meticulous

---

[77] Arr. *Anab.* VI.17.3–4 (cf. VI.15.5 with Bosworth 1976 (B 13) 127–9); Strabo XV.2.4; XV.2.11; Justin XII.10.1–2. On the route see Goukowsky 1978–81 (B 45) II 105–7.

preparations. Patala at the head of the Indus delta became a fortress complete with dockyards; and Alexander painstakingly investigated the two main branches of the river to east and west. His first venture, down the western arm, was plagued by gales and extreme tides, but he reached the Ocean and sacrificed solemnly to Poseidon and the gods of the sea. The eastern arm proved less intractable, with a large saline lake which he turned into a second naval station. His land forces dug wells along the coast and stockpiled grain at Patala to sustain Nearchus and the fleet through the monsoon period. The winds which hampered his progress to the Ocean would intensify and render navigation impossible until the setting of the Pleiades (c. 5 November).

Alexander went ahead with the majority of his land forces: the Macedonian troops not included in Craterus' column, the Hellenic mercenaries, the auxiliary cavalry from the north-eastern satrapies and a host of non-combatants – merchants, concubines and children of the camp. They skirted the foothills of the Kirthar Range to the mouth of the Arabis (river Hab), and while a fatigue party continued the work of sinking wells, Alexander went ahead to attack the Oreitae, an independent Indian people domiciled in what is now Las Bela in Baluchistan. Three columns ravaged the plain, and Rhambaceia, the chief village of the area was marked for resettlement as another Alexandria, its rural populace recruited from Arachosia to the north.[78] Offering only a token resistance, the Oreitae surrendered, after a futile attempt to block the passes into the Makran. They were put directly under a satrap, Apollophanes; and a mobile force of Agrianians, archers and mercenaries which remained in Oreitis after Alexander's departure kept the district quiet while the grain harvest matured. In November their commander, the bodyguard Leonnatus, supervised the concentration of the produce in a depot by the coast and crushed an uprising by the Oreitae, who were probably desperate at the loss of their subsistence crop (Arr. Indike 23.5). His efforts had secured (if not depopulated) the district, and Nearchus was able to reprovision his fleet from the accumulated supplies.

By then Alexander was long gone. He had crossed the passes into the Kolwa valley early in October and began his march through the desert country of Gedrosia. According to Nearchus he was reacting to the stories that Semiramis and Cyrus the Great had lost armies there and planned to succeed where they had failed.[79] He also wished to provision the fleet, but that was a secondary motive. The provisioning was best

[78] Arr. Anab. VI.21.5; Curt. IX.10.7. Cf. Stein 1943 (D 238) 213–16; Engels 1978 (D 172) 138–9; contra, Hamilton 1972 (D 188); Seibert 1985 (D 233) 173–4.

[79] Arr. Anab. VI.24.2–3; Strabo XV.1.5, XV.2.5. See Strasburger 1982 (A 57) I 458; Badian 1985 (D 142) 471–3. Nearchus' evidence has often been discounted for more 'rational' motives (cf. Kraft 1971 (D 207) 106–18; Engels 1978 (D 172) 110–17).

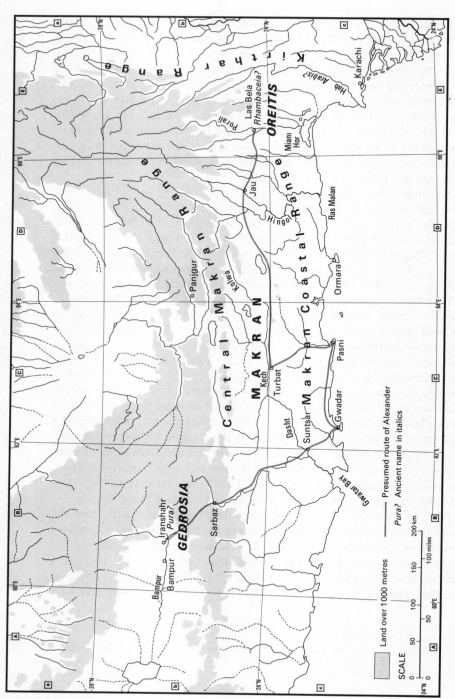

Map 24. Las Bela and the Makran.

achieved by a small column; the large force he actually led inevitably took the lion's share of the scanty supplies available. There is no obvious reason why he took the main army with its straggle of camp followers, unless (as Nearchus suggests) it was a primary objective in itself. The hardships caused by his ambition were extreme and unnecessary, and they are luridly documented in complementary passages of Arrian and Strabo, which almost certainly derive from Nearchus.[80] But the loss of life may have been largely confined to the non-combatants. There is no evidence of a sudden shortage of troops; the Macedonian infantry at Opis the following summer still numbered 18,000.[81] It is moreover clear that the first stages of the march were relatively well provided for. Alexander commandeered the crops which had grown and matured during the monsoon period (nowadays harvest comes in late October or early November) and the wells and cisterns that existed were full. By the time he reached the oasis of Turbat, some 400 km from Las Bela, Alexander had a surplus of provisions. This was transferred to the coast but consumed in transit by the famished guards. The relatively abundant conditions were only found in the area affected by the rain shadow of the monsoon. In the western Makran the season had been arid, the winter rainfall only beginning in November, and the army was progressively affected by drought and famine as it struggled for seven days along the coast from Pasni and through the Dashtiari plain to the Bampur valley. During the latter stages the baggage animals were slaughtered, and the morale of the troops disintegrated. After sixty days in the Makran it was a rabble that limped into the palace complex of Pura, where an emergency supply of grain was waiting, transported on camel from Sistan. A few days later Alexander pushed west through the Jaz Murian depression to the borders of Carmania, where fresh supplies converged from the central satrapies. That allowed a systematic carouse for seven days, in which the army, consoled by the local food and wine, forgot some of the horrors of the desert.

As he traversed Carmania, Alexander carried through one of the most dramatic police actions of his reign. His absence in India had witnessed an alarming amount of native insurrection, one of which had recently been crushed by Craterus as he passed through Arachosia and Drangiana. There had also been widespread insubordination among the satraps, many of whom had not expected Alexander to return from the east. As a result Astaspes, the incumbent satrap of Carmania, was executed during the seven-day revel. He was followed by the European generals in Media, who had been summoned (probably while Alexander

80 See particularly Strasburger 1982 (A 57) I 449–70; Brunt 1976–83 (B 21) II 475–6. For the less likely attribution to Aristobulus, see Pearson 1960 (B 90) 178; Schachermeyr 1973 (D 231) 464.
81 Bosworth 1986 (D 21) 3–4. Plut. *Alex.* 66.4–5 gives a massively inflated total of casualties.

was still in India) to bring their military forces from Ecbatana to Carmania. On their arrival they were accused by Median notables of offences including sacrilege and rape. Cleander (the brother of Coenus) and Sitalces were arrested and executed, and 600 of their army shared their fate (see below, p.864). At the same time, according to Diodorus, the king sent written instructions to his satraps, demanding that they disband their mercenary forces.[82] That had the effect of breaking up the private armies in the provinces. The troops so demobilized were earmarked for Alexander's service, and in the next eighteen months a vast number of men was conveyed from the outlying satrapies to the central capitals. Many refused to be so conscripted. A considerable number followed the Athenian Leosthenes, who led them from Asia to the great mercenary depot at Taenarum in Laconia (see below, p.859). Others simply became renegades, living off the countryside by force and intimidation. It was a security measure which swelled the royal army at the cost of empire-wide tension and insecurity. An immediate consequence was the flight of the royal treasurer, Harpalus, from Babylon.[83] He was a compatriot of Cleander (from Elimiotis) and had been responsible for the administration of the Median treasury. Whether or not he was implicated in Cleander's machinations, he had certainly lived as a despot in the central satrapies and had reason to fear reprisals. He fled to the west with 5,000 talents and a small army of mercenaries, and in the spring of 324 he impinged dramatically on the Greek mainland (see below, pp.856 ff).

By winter 325/4 Alexander reached the Carmanian capital, some five days journey from the coast. There he held an athletic and musical festival during which he heard of the safe arrival of Nearchus' fleet at Harmozea, the main sea-port of Carmania. If we may believe Nearchus' version of events, he reported in person, after a chequered journey inland, and was welcomed with joy and relief.[84] Despite the lack of provisions on the coast, pressure from hostile Indians in Patalene which drove him prematurely to the ocean and adverse monsoon winds blowing until November, he had taken the fleet practically unscathed along the arid coast, populated by the primitive Fish Eaters. The fleet covered some 1,300 km in around sixty days; and the prevailing south-easterlies, as had been predicted, brought it hungry and intact to Harmozea.[85]

---

[82] Diod. XVII.106.3, 111.1. See particularly Badian 1961 (D 134) 26–8; Jaschinski 1981 (D 203) 45–61.

[83] The seminal article is Badian 1961 (D 134). See further Seibert 1971 (D 232) 167–9 with Jaschinski 1981 (D 203) 23–44; Goukowsky 1978–81 (B 45) II.72–7; Ashton 1983 (D 128).

[84] Cf. Pearson 1960 (B 90) 134–5; Badian 1975 (B 9) 160–2.

[85] For bibliography see Seibert 1972 (D 232) 163–5. See particularly Schiwek 1962 (F 55); Eggermont 1975 (D 169) 33–55; Brunt 1976–83 (B 21) II.518–25.

Consequently Nearchus had his commission extended, to explore the coastline between Carmania and Susa. His success may have had far-reaching effects. He had shown the effectiveness of a fleet, even without land support, in reconnoitring a desert coast. Now, it seems, Alexander was inspired to devise almost megalomaniac plans of conquest and exploration which involved the circumnavigation of Africa and the conquest of the southern Mediterranean. While in Carmania he allegedly commissioned the construction of warships in Cilicia and Phoenicia, to be transported in sections to the Euphrates and floated to Babylon. This fleet was to be used for colonization and conquest in the Persian Gulf.[86] Then part of it would diverge to circumnavigate the coast of Africa, while the main army would move north to the Mediterranean coast to expand the empire westwards. The details of these projects are controversial and have aroused much speculation and scepticism; but there is no doubt that the last years of Alexander's reign saw a massive military accumulation. A vast new harbour, built to accommodate 1,000 warships, was ready near Babylon in the spring of 323, and the timber resources of Cilicia and Phoenicia were systematically depleted to provide collapsible vessels which could be transported in segments to the Euphrates for the Arabian campaign. More conventional warships, of quadrireme size and above, were reserved for use in the western offensive. Carthage, which had adversely attracted his attention in 332, was earmarked for conquest, while the fleet proved that the circumnavigation of Africa was feasible. These plans would be refined over the next eighteen months in the light of reconnaissance expeditions in the Persian Gulf, but their nucleus was conceived in Carmania.

From the Carmanian capital Alexander moved directly to Pasargadae, the old capital of Persis, while the baggage train with Hephaestion took a less exacting route closer to the coast. There the incumbent satrap, Orxines, who had usurped the position after the death of Alexander's nominee, Phrasaortes, was received politely but immediately discarded. The tomb of Cyrus the Great at Pasargadae was opened for Alexander's edification and found in a state of dilapidation and disrepair that suggested violation.[87] Orxines was cleared of suspicion on that score, but later, at Persepolis, he was accused of sacrilege and misgovernment and summarily executed. He was of royal lineage and his usurpation of government could not be tolerated. His successor was Macedonian,

[86] Plut. *Alex.* 68.1–2; Curt. x.1.19; Arr. *Anab.* vii.1.1–3. Cf. Diod. xviii.4.4 for the so-called Last Plans. For discussion see Wilcken 1970 (A 64) ii 369–84; Schachermeyr 1954 (D 228); Badian 1968 (D 138); Bosworth 1988 (B 15), 185–211. Contrast the scepticism of Tarn 1948 (D 239) ii.378–98; Andreotti 1957 (D 127) 133–40; Kraft 1971 (D 207) 119–27.

[87] Arr. *Anab.* vi.29.4–8; Strabo xv.3.7 (Aristobulus F 51). Cf. Bosworth 1988 (B 15) 46–55.

Peucestas (Alexander's saviour at the Malli town). Although European, he adopted Persian dress, learned the Persian language and by 317 had won the respect and loyalty of his subjects. His orientalism evoked resentment among the Macedonian rank and file and it was not the general fashion, but it helped keep the old Persian heartland tranquil and acquiescent under the new regime.

At Persepolis Alexander was reunited with Hephaestion, and the army took the royal road to Susa, arriving at the capital in March 324. Nearchus was waiting with the ocean fleet, which he had taken up the river system to the vicinity of Susa. Land and sea forces combined in a merry meeting with sacrifices and games. That was the prelude to a more brilliant celebration. Alexander and ninety-one other members of his court took wives from the Persian aristocracy in a five-day ceremony, graced by actors, dancers and musicians recruited from the entire Greek world. The king himself married two royal princesses, the eldest daughter of Darius and the youngest daughter of Artaxerxes III. Hephaestion and Craterus took Drypetis and Amastris, a daughter and niece of Darius. All the bridegrooms received a dowry and all Macedonians who had Asian concubines were paid a gratuity. The weddings echoed the earlier ceremonies in Bactria in 327, but this time the unions were solemnized according to Persian ritual.[88] It was a demonstration that the conquerors had become the ruling class of the Persian empire, and it went hand in hand with the investiture of Hephaestion as chiliarch (Grand Vizier) and the distribution of the Achaemenid court regalia to the Companions. There was not, as has often been suggested, a conscious policy of fusion, a placing of Macedonians and Persians on the same footing. Only a handful of Persians was assimilated into the Macedonian court and army structure, and the character of the satrapal governors was stubbornly European (see below, p.864). The Susa marriages proclaimed the fact that Alexander's nobles were the lords of Asia and would be increasingly identified with the Asian empire. The recipients of his largesse were hardly enthusiastic. They accepted their wives during the king's lifetime, but it was only Seleucus' wife, Apame, who played any dynastic role in the age of the Successors. The rank and file were more dissatisfied, alienated by the increasingly oriental trappings of Alexander's court and threatened by the new levies of recruits from the eastern satrapies. Some 30,000 Iranian youths, trained in Macedonian arms and tactics, had recently converged on Susa. Their drill was impressive, their name (*Epigoni*) ominous, suggesting that they

---

[88] Arr. *Anab.* VII.4.1–8; Plut. *Alex.* 70.3; Diod. XVII.107.6; Justin XII.10.9–10. Chares (F 4 = Athen. 538B) gave a particularly vivid eye-witness description. For a review of the problems see Bosworth 1980 (D 155), arguing against the 'policy of fusion' expounded in German scholarship (cf. Berve 1938 (D 147); Schachermeyr 1973 (D 231) 479–87).

might replace the traditional Macedonian phalanx.[89] The Macedonian infantry was now profoundly disenchanted, and complaints were bitter and vocal.

The unrest reached its climax in the summer of 324. Alexander first took a select body of troops down the river Karun to the ocean and then cut across to the mouth of the Tigris, where he founded another Alexandria, at the later site of Spasinou Charax. From there he moved upstream, demolishing the system of artificial cataracts that closed the river to navigation and preparing the way for his fleet to launch its offensive into the Persian Gulf. By midsummer the army had reached Opis, on the middle reaches of the Tigris. Here the discontent erupted into near mutiny. Alexander had announced the repatriation of all Macedonians unfit for service and their ultimate replacement by fresh blood from Macedon.[90] The effect was galvanic. All the troops, whether retained or discharged, joined in a general demand for repatriation, which was coupled with outright abuse – let Alexander continue the campaign with his father, Ammon. This time the king was determined to assert his royal authority and redress the debacle at the Hyphasis. He executed the ringleaders, subjected the rest to an angry harangue and declared roundly that, if they deserted him, he would turn to the conquered peoples.[91] Secluded in the palace, he received selected Persians to offer them commands and announced the transfer of Macedonian military titles to Persian units. At this all resistance was broken. The Macedonians sued for forgiveness in the most abject terms and Alexander accepted their homage magnanimously. There followed a great banquet of reconciliation, attended by 9,000 guests, and, duly surrounded by his Macedonians, he prayed solemnly for 'concord and community in empire for Macedonians and Persians'.[92] That was a formal announcement that the time of tension was over; in future the two peoples should coexist peacefully, fighting side by side in the grand army.

The demobilization now took place. Ten thousand veterans received their gratuities and were placed under Craterus' leadership. Their destination was first Cilicia, to supervise the construction of the armada for the west, and then Macedon. Craterus was to replace Antipater as regent in Europe, while Antipater led an army of prime recruits into

---

[89] Arr. *Anab.* VII.6.1; Diod. XVII.108.1–3; Curt. VIII.5.1; Plut. *Alex.* 71.1. Cf. Briant 1982 (F 10) 30–9; Bosworth 1980 (D 155) 17.

[90] Arr. *Anab.* VII.8.1; Plut. *Alex.* 71.2–9; Diod. XVII.109.2–3; Curt. X.2.8–30; Justin XII.11. Cf. Wüst 1953–4 (D 250); Badian 1965 (D 135).

[91] Speeches are given by Arrian (VII.9–10) and Curtius (X.2.15ff). On the question of authenticity see Wüst 1953–4 (D 251); Bosworth 1988 (B 15) 101–13.

[92] Arr. *Anab.* VII.11.8–9. For criticism of the more extreme interpretations of the prayer (in particular the views of Tarn) see Andreotti 1956 (D 126) and Badian 1958 (D 131).

Asia.[93] Antipater's supersession was the climax of a period of tension during which he had been virulently attacked by Alexander's mother and sister and had withheld reinforcements from Alexander (whether by policy or by necessity we cannot say). Relations had certainly soured. Antipater's eldest son, Cassander, was treated with brutal ferocity when he came to court to represent his father, and the relations between king and regent had deteriorated to the extent that, when Alexander died, it was immediately rumoured that Antipater had had him poisoned.[94] The crisis did not mature, since Craterus was (quite legitimately) delayed in Cilicia and did not challenge Antipater for his position, but there was deep uncertainty which must have cast an ominous shadow on Alexander's last transactions.

From Opis the army moved from Mesopotamia to spend the autumn at Ecbatana, the summer capital of the Persian Kings. That was the scene of protracted celebrations; Atropates, the satrap of Media, was careful to see that the court lacked nothing. At this point war with Athens seemed inevitable after the city's reception of Harpalus (see below, p.857) and there were extravagant promises of armaments for the anticipated campaign[95] – which came to nothing after Harpalus' arrest and escape. The war fever encouraged wild drinking, and the royal favourite, Hephaestion, fell ill during the symposia and died after seven days of fever. The shock seems to have affected Alexander's mental balance. His grief was Homeric in its extravagance, with a three-day fast over the corpse. Hephaestion himself received a heroic cult, and his mortal remains were to be conveyed to Babylon, to be deposited on a colossal funerary monument, a vast brick cube some 70 metres high. Its base was to be surrounded by the gilded prows of quinqueremes, its walls decorated by friezes. This monstrosity was never completed – it was quashed after Alexander's death by the Macedonian army, along with other architectural follies.[96] But it was seriously planned and craftsmen had been summoned from the entire civilized world. The measure of Alexander's grief was extravagantly superhuman.

The winter brought a fresh campaign, against the independent Cossaeans of the Zagros. Alexander invaded their territory with his army divided into columns and forced some at least of the tribes into

[93] Arr. *Anab.* VII.12.1–4; Justin XII.12.7–10. For Craterus' commission in Cilicia see Diod. XVIII.4.1, 12.1 (with Bosworth 1988 (B 15) 207–11), and on the deterioration of relations with Olympias Arr. *Anab.* VII.12.5–7; Plut. *Mor.* 180E, *Alex.* 68.4–5.
[94] On this tradition see Bosworth 1971 (D 152) 113–16; 1980 (B 15) 175–6; Merkelbach 1977 (B 75) 164–92.
[95] Ephippus, *FGrH* 126 F 5 (Athen. 538 A–B). For a defence of the tradition (against (e.g.) Pearson 1960 (B 90) 64–5; Errington 1975 (C 360) 54–5) see Heisserer 1980 (B 143) 169–93.
[96] Diod. XVII.115.1–5; Plut. *Alex.* 72.5; Arr. *Anab.* VII.14.8; Justin XII.12.12 (cf. Wüst 1959 (D 252)). For the quashing of the project see Diod. XVIII.4.2, with Badian 1968 (D 138); Bosworth 1988 (B 15) 202–7.

submission. Military settlements were imposed here, as in Sogdiana and India, with a reluctant agrarian population of Cossaeans, transformed by royal edict from pastoralists to tillers of the soil.[97] By 317, when they re-emerge in history, the Cossaeans had reverted to their old lifestyle (Diod. XIX.19.2–8); the effects of Alexander's invasion were evidently ephemeral. There was also intense diplomatic activity. As he advanced on Babylon Alexander was approached by a host of embassies from the west. On his way into the plain he received overtures from Libyans, Bruttians, Lucanians and Etruscans, all peoples likely to be affected by his projected conquests in the Mediterranean. At Babylon itself there were representations from mainland Greece, from the cities immediately affected by the Exiles' Decree (see below, p.855), as well as Carthage and the northern Balkans.[98] All had their interests to defend, particularly Carthage which was threatened with immediate invasion, the European Scyths who had crushed an expedition by the Macedonian general, Zopyrion (c.326), and the Odrysian Thracians who had rebelled and reconstituted their traditional monarchy. It seems that the delegations which submitted and sent tokens of submission were received favourably. Those with objections were placed firmly at the bottom of the list. Alexander was not interested in compromise, and there was no suggestion that he would cancel, let alone defer, his plans of conquest. What he required was unqualified obedience to his will.

The native astrologers warned him against entering Babylon and, according to Aristobulus (F 54), he followed their advice, attempting to make a detour by way of the north and east of the city. He was obstructed by marshland and finally approached Babylon by the regular entrance. It was a mysterious episode which was later interpreted as a portent of death, while Ptolemy (Arr. *Anab.* VII.17.1–4), perhaps rightly, suggested that the Babylonian priesthood had its own corrupt motives for denying access to the capital. Once there Alexander began work clearing the ground for the reconstruction of Esagila (and also for Hephaestion's monument). But his major concern was the forthcoming invasion of Arabia. He had already sent reconnoitring expeditions under Archias, Androsthenes and Hieron of Soli, which visited the islands of Icarus (Failaka) and Tylus (Bahrain) and penetrated as far as the Musandam peninsula. The favourable reports fuelled his determination to conquer and colonize the western shore of the Persian Gulf, a plan that ultimately

[97] Arr. *Anab.* VII.15.1–3; (Ptolemy); *Indike* 40.8 (Nearchus); Diod. XVII.111.6; Plut. *Alex.* 72.4. Cf. Briant 1982 (F 10) 57ff.

[98] Arr. *Anab.* VII.15.4–6; Diod. XVII.113.1–4. On these embassies see now Bosworth 1988 (B 15) 83–93. The Roman embassy recorded by Cleitarchus (*FGrH* 137 F 31) is probably authentic (cf. Schachermeyr 1970 (D 230) 218–23; Weippert 1972 (D 242) 1–10) but was insignificant at the time, perhaps a late arrival (Bosworth 1988 (B 15) 90). The episode later acquired considerable propaganda value.

saw fruition in the Seleucid foundation on Failaka.[99] He was also intent on conquering the legendary spice lands, giving the pretext that the Arabs had paid him no act of homage. Aristobulus adds, perhaps correctly, that he intended to guarantee their autonomy (under his sovereignty) and win acceptance as the third god in the Arabian pantheon.[100] This campaign, which was expected to subjugate the entire Arabian peninsula, at least round to the Yemen, was planned on a vast scale. Alexander would take the first wave from Babylon, but there would be subsequent fleets to help occupy and secure the conquests. Miccalus of Clazomenae recruited seamen, both slave and free, to man the ships which would gather in the great new harbour at Babylon (Arr. *Anab.* VII.19.4–5). This was the first stage of the western plans. Later stages were already in prospect, and Heraclides of Argos was commissioned to build a war fleet on the Caspian and determine finally whether it was a gulf of Ocean or an affluent of the Black Sea (Arr. VII.16.1–2) – necessary knowledge if Alexander was to link his European domains with the north east of his Asian empire (see above, p.823).

While his invasion fleet was massing, Alexander was active on the Euphrates, ensuring that the river and its major canals were navigable, and planning the last of his Alexandrias near the ocean. When he returned to Babylon, he found massive native levies from Persis and the Zagros highlands, levies which he amalgamated with the remnants of his Macedonian phalanx to create a strange composite entity: three ranks of Macedonians at the front and one at the rear enclosed twelve ranks of Persians, armed with their native bows and javelins. It eked out the scanty reserves of Macedonian infantry and created a massed, variegated phalanx which would be more than a match for the lightly armed Arabs. But the experiment was never tested in the field. The welcome news from Siwah that the hero cult of Hephaestion had been approved by Ammon was the trigger for prolonged festivities. The royal symposium was prolonged into a private party hosted by Medius of Larissa. The drinking there was prodigious; and, according to the *Ephemerides*, the day to day account edited by the chief secretary, Eumenes of Cardia, Alexander had developed a fever by the time it ended.[101] The fever intensified over ten days and the king finally sank into a coma. Before the

[99] Arr. VII.20.3–8. Cf. Jeppesen 1960 (B 147); Roueché and Sherwin-White 1985 (B 173) (on Failaka).

[100] Arr. *Anab.* VII.20.1; Strabo XVI.1.11. See Högemann 1985 (D 198) esp. 120–35.

[101] Arr. *Anab.* VII.25.1; Plut. *Alex.* 76.1 (*FGrH* 117 F 3). On the composition of this document and its apologetic nature see Bosworth 1988 (B 15) 157–84 (with full citation of literature). For the more traditional view, that the Ephemerides were an 'official' court journal, available for the entire reign, see (e.g.) Kaerst, RE V.2749ff; Berve 1926 (D 146) 1.50–1; Hammond 1983 (B 57) 4–11. The vulgate tradition is more sensational and gave rise to allegations of poisoning (Diod. XVII.117.1–3; Justin XII.13.7–10; Plut. *Alex.*75.5, Arr. VII.27.2; Ephippus, *FGrH* 126 F 3: cf. Merkelbach 1977 (B 75) 164ff).

end his troops solemnly filed past his bedside, and on the following day, 28 Daesios (10 June) by the Macedonian calendar, death supervened. The exact cause will never be known. The attested symptoms are consistent with a malarial attack, possibly assisted by the regular and epic carouses at court symposia. Foul play was inevitably insinuated, and allegations of poisoning, directed at Antipater's family and the guests at Medius' banquet, were rife within a year of the king's death.[102] It is not impossible, but proof is totally beyond our grasp.

Alexander died after a reign of twelve years and eight months, leaving a pregnant wife, a coterie of rival marshals and no designated heir. His apocryphal prophecy of a great funeral contest over his body would have been amply justified. His body in fact became a catalyst for civil war and separatist ambition. At Babylon it was first decided to send it to Siwah (as Alexander himself may have requested),[103] but there was a delay of nearly two years while an elaborate (and colossally expensive) funeral carriage was built.[104] When the cortège eventually left Babylon, its destination was the royal burial ground at Aegae (Paus. 1.6.3), but Ptolemy was able to intercept it in Syria and divert the body to Egypt, as a first stage to the fulfilment of the original plan.[105] That provoked Perdiccas' fateful invasion of Egypt which resulted in his defeat and assassination and the transference of the regency to Antipater. Ptolemy remained plenipotentiary in Egypt, satrap in name but monarch in reality. The body of Alexander was installed first at Memphis and ultimately at Alexandria, where it stood on display in a gold sarcophagus, housed in a special mausoleum (the *sema*) and venerated as the talisman of Ptolemaic monarchy. The dead Alexander had come to symbolize the dismemberment of his own life's work.

[102] [Plut.] Mor. 849F; cf. Onesicritus, *FGrH* 134 F 37. See fully Bosworth 1971 (D 152) 113–16.
[103] Diod. XVIII.3.5, 28.3; Justin XIII.4.6; Curt. X.5.4; cf. Badian 1968 (D 138) 185–9; *contra*, Hornblower 1981 (B 60) 90–2.   [104] Diod. XVIII.26.1–28.2; cf. Miller 1986 (D 215).
[105] Arr. *Successors* F1.25, 24.1 (Roos); Diod. XVIII.28.3; Strabo XVII.1.8. See further *CAH* VII.1, 35–6.

CHAPTER 17

ALEXANDER THE GREAT PART 2: GREECE AND THE CONQUERED TERRITORIES

A.B. BOSWORTH

A. MAINLAND GREECE IN ALEXANDER'S REIGN

I. THE DOMINANCE OF THE CORINTHIAN LEAGUE, 336-330 B.C.

During Alexander's reign the Greek world was controlled by the political system established after Chaeronea, which modern scholars have conveniently labelled the Corinthian League.[1] This was primarily an alliance under the leadership of the Macedonian king, in which all states which had individual treaties with Macedon were organized in a single structure, directed to the war against Persia. The corollary of alliance was peace. All contracting states committed themselves to a wide-ranging common peace, affirming freedom and autonomy for all and renouncing subversion of any participating government. The implementation of these two general aims was in the hands of a council (*synedrion*) to which all states in the alliance sent representatives. The council made general enactments about the war, prohibiting service under the Persian King, and it policed the common peace, with the ultimate power to declare war against any transgressor, a war in which all contracting states were obliged by oath to participate. It might even act as a court of arbitration, ruling on disputes between member states before they endangered the peace (Tod no. 179). But the executive power was vested in the *hegemon*, the Macedonian king whose monarchy all states were bound to uphold. Inevitably the system would be geared to Macedonian interests. Sympathetic regimes could expect the support of the *synedrion*, whereas, if a state antagonistic to the Macedonian king suffered a change of government, it was unlikely that complaints would be effectively voiced. At democratic Pellene the famous wrestler, Chaeron, was established in power, exiling his opponents with the connivance of the Macedonian general in the Peloponnese;[2] and at Athens the law of Eucrates, passed in the early summer of 336, explicitly

---

[1] For bibliography and discussion see Seibert 1972 (D 232) 76–7; Hammond and Griffith 1979 (D 50) II 604–46. The position adopted in the text is more fully documented in Bosworth 1980 (B 14) 46–9. [2] [Dem.] XVII.10; Paus. VII.27.7; Athen. 509 B. Cf. Berve 1926 (D 146) II no.818.

prohibited all attempts to subvert the democracy.[3] There was evidently little faith in the guarantees of the common peace.

Our evidence for the operation of the peace is admittedly one-sided, based largely on a fiery speech in the Demosthenic corpus (XVII) which indicts the Macedonians for systematic abuse of the treaty. It was probably delivered in 331[4] and may be the work of Hyperides: and it is clearly biased and exaggerated. But in one respect it can be checked. The speaker complains that the regime of the tyrants of Antissa and Eresus (in Lesbos) had been terminated as an abomination even though it was underwritten by the common peace. That statement is illustrated by an extensive dossier from Eresus which deals with the fate of various oligarchic juntas, notably that of Agonippus and Eurysilaus which had aligned itself with Philip and erected altars to Zeus Philippios. In 333, during the island war (see above, p.804), the junta invited Persian forces into the city and collaborated against Alexander. Consequently, when the city was recaptured in 332, the oligarchy was transformed into democracy, and the newly sovereign *demos* (on instructions from Alexander) tried and condemned the previous oligarchical leaders. The king operated directly, without apparent consultation of the *synedrion*, and tampered with the political structure as he saw fit.[5] The same applied at Chios, where Alexander established a democracy and set up a committee of legislators to remove any obstacle to the new constitution. The *synedrion* of allies is only mentioned as a court, which would try delinquent oligarchs.[6] It had no say in the constitutional changes. In the war situation (as one would expect) Alexander made unilateral rulings which suited his long-term military ends. The fact that they were technical violations of the common peace was immaterial.

It was evident from the beginning of Alexander's reign that a large number of the league members were reluctant allies. Philip's assassination provoked open breaches of the treaty. Athens attempted to enlist other cities in the cause of freedom and opened negotiations with Attalus in Asia; and there was agitation in Thebes and the Peloponnese. In the west the Aetolians reconstituted their federal organization,[7] while in Ambracia the Macedonian garrison was expelled and democracy restored (Diod. XVII.3.3). This first spate of unrest was contained by rapid

[3] *SEG* XII 87. Cf. Ostwald 1955 (C 213) 119–28; Sealey 1967 (C 255) 183–5; Will 1983 (D 245) 28–30.

[4] Cawkwell 1961 (D 165). For other suggestions see Will 1982 (B 132); 1983 (D 245) 28–30; Culasso Gastaldi 1984 (B 32).

[5] [Dem.] XVII.7; Tod no. 191 = Harding no. 112 (cf. Heisserer 1980 (B 143) 27–78; Bosworth 1980 (B 14) 178–80).

[6] Tod no. 192 = Harding no. 107 (cf. Heisserer 1980 (B 143) 79–95). For the ultimate fate of the oligarchs see Arr. *Anab.* III.2.7.

[7] Diod. XVII.3.3; Arr. *Anab.* I.10.2; cf. Bosworth 1976 (D 20)

action on Alexander's part. At the head of his army he invaded Thessaly and with the help of skilful propaganda secured election as *hegemon* of the common peace. The scenario was repeated in central Greece, where the Amphictyonic Council gave its recognition to the new king, and in Corinth the *synedrion* formally confirmed him in the office created by Philip – leader in the war against Persia (and simultaneously chief executive officer of the common peace). The Athenians had already renewed their alliance, and their embassy, diplomatically deserted by Demosthenes, was graciously received. Alexander was now universally confirmed in his father's position.

Consent was not universal, as was dramatically revealed in 335, when Alexander's prolonged absence in the north (see above, p.795) gave rise to speculation that he had been killed. At Thebes the rumour led to insurrection, as a group of exiles entered the city by night and inaugurated revolution. The oligarchy imposed by Philip was overthrown and the Thebans laid siege to the Macedonian garrison on the Cadmea. The revolutionary mood was infectious. At Athens the *demos*, encouraged by Demosthenes and Lycurgus, voted assistance and sent funds (but not troops) which enabled the Thebans to mobilize their entire citizen body. The Arcadian League even sent an expeditionary force to the Isthmus, where it remained passively awaiting events (Din. 1.18–21). In the event Alexander's lightning march south prevented the disaffection spreading. The Arcadians left the Isthmus and the Thebans were isolated. Even so they resisted Alexander's overtures, inverting the conventional propaganda and appealing to all mankind to join them and the Persian King in destroying the tyrant of Greece (Diod. XVII.9.5). That sealed their fate. The city was stormed and destroyed (see above, p.797). The survivors were enslaved on the verdict of an *ad hoc* council of allies present with Alexander,[8] and the judges solemnly took vengeance for Thebes' medism in 480. Performed by proxy and represented as an act of piety, the destruction of Thebes was calculated terrorism. As such it was immediately efficacious. The sedition in Elis, Arcadia and Aetolia ended abruptly, while the Athenians abandoned the celebration of the Great Mysteries and evacuated their countryside. An Athenian embassy was roughly treated. Alexander demanded the surrender of eight prominent statesmen and generals, including Demosthenes, Lycurgus and the distinguished general Charidemus.[9] That provoked a passionate debate at Athens, with the veteran general Phocion arguing for submission. Eventually (perhaps with Macedonian collusion) a compromise motion was passed, offering to punish the men demanded – if they

[8] Arr. *Anab.* 1.9.9; Justin XI.3.8; *contra*, Diod. XVII.14.1. Cf. Bosworth 1980 (B 14) 89–90.

[9] Plut. *Dem.* 23.4 (there are other, interpolated lists in Arr. *Anab.* 1.10.4; Plut. *Phoc.* 17.2 and the 'Suda' s.v. Ἀντίπατρος). Cf. Bosworth 1980 (B 14) 92–5; Will 1983 (D 245) 43–7.

deserved punishment. That was sufficient. Alexander accepted the proposal, insisting only that Charidemus be exiled. Otherwise the Athenian statesmen were untouched. The city resumed its symmachical obligations and supported Alexander in his renewal of the traditional crusade against Persia.

In 334 Alexander crossed the Hellespont to begin his campaign. With him were 7,000 infantry and 600 cavalry from his Greek allies in discharge of their treaty obligations, which had been promulgated by Philip (Plut. *Phoc.*16.4). They were an effective pool of hostages, an implicit sanction against unrest. There was also the machinery of the common peace, confirmed and reinforced by the campaigns of 336 and 335. The *hegemon* moved into Asia, leaving Antipater as his deputy for European affairs. His command, as defined for Craterus, his nominated successor (Arr. *Anab.* VII.12.4), covered Macedonia, Thrace and Thessaly and involved protection of the freedom of the Hellenes. As regards Macedonia and its annexes, Antipater was apparently plenipotentiary. He acted as regent with the king's power of command, and the general of Thrace was directly subordinate to him. Accordingly we find him levying troops in his own right and dispatching reinforcements to the royal army in Asia (his reluctance to send native Macedonians led to friction with Alexander later in the reign). There is a strong possibility that his command was extended to Epirus after the death of King Alexander in Italy, his writ extending as far north as the Ceraunian Mountains.[10] In Greece proper Antipater deputized for his king as president of the *synedrion* of the Corinthian League, and he exercised effective control of its mechanisms. As a matter of course he commanded the allied forces which crushed the Spartan offensive against his Peloponnesian allies (see below, pp.854 f) and he formally committed the question of reprisals to debate by the *synedrion*. He might also act on his own initiative. In 333 we find a certain Proteas operating from Chalcis with instructions from Antipater to raise a fleet to protect the Cyclades against Persian attack (Arr. *Anab.* II.2.4–5). His activities could be less benign. Together with the garrison commanders in southern Greece[11] he could foment revolution in cities which were unsympathetic to Macedonian hegemony, secure from effective opposition in the *synedrion*. Alexander commissioned him to apply force to the cities which resisted the Exiles' Decree (Diod. XVIII.8.4; see below, p.855), knowing that he had the political and military resources to constrain recalcitrants.

10 Dexippus *FGrH*100 F 8 (3); Arr. *Succ.* F 1.7 (Roos); cf. Plut. *Phoc.* 29.4. For a somewhat different view of Antipater's position see Hammond 1967 (E 72) 558–9 (modifications in Hammond 1980 (D 190) 471–6).
11 They were presumably 'the people placed over the common defence', referred to in passing by [Dem.] XVII.15. For other, more elaborate, explanations see Hammond and Griffith 1979 (D 50) II 639–42; Culasso Gastaldi 1984 (B 32) 67–72.

Antipater had regal power in every sense, and his regency in Alexander's reign enabled him to create a dynasty. Not surprisingly, his powers and his exercise of them earned him the jealousy and lasting enmity of the formidable women of the court, Alexander's mother and sister; and Olympias at least used her native Epirus as a refuge, undermining the authority of Antipater as far as she was able. Alexander himself may have later regretted the complex of powers he had vested in his regent (see above, p.842), but in the context of 334 there was little alternative. The senior statesman of Philip's reign became supreme in Europe. That solved the immediate problems of security, internal and external. The future problems posed by Alexander's over-mighty subject could be dealt with when (and if) they arose.

Of the old city states of Greece Athens was the most powerful and the most volatile. During Alexander's reign she achieved a peak of material prosperity and her military potential became formidable. That was largely due to the financial administration, controlled over twelve continuous years by the Eteobutad aristocrat, Lycurgus son of Lycophron. Much is obscure about the nature of his office, and the evidence is often ambiguous. In practice Lycurgus controlled the finances of Athens, operating with the existing financial organs, the theoric commission and the stratiotic fund but directing the surplus as he considered proper. In effect he had inherited the role of the theoric commission in the previous generation, perhaps as a result of the legislation of Hegemon which restricted the powers of the theoric officials. From (probably) 336 to his death in 325/4 Lycurgus was the financial overlord,[12] serving in his own right for the statutory limit of five years and then operating through various proxies, whom he effectively controlled. One of them, Xenocles of Sphettus, is attested in office during the period.[13]

The revenues distributed were enormous. The total sums handled by Lycurgus were estimated in antiquity between 14,000 and 18,900 talents, and the annual revenues during his administration are said to have been 1,200 talents, triple the income in 346. This vast increase is attributed to Lycurgus' initiative, and there is some evidence of his efforts to secure the bases of indirect taxation. Metics and foreign traders were attracted to the city by favourable legislation (Tod no. 189 = Harding no. 111), and in this period the Athenians were prepared to establish a colony in the Adriatic with the explicit aim of securing commerce (Tod no. 200 = Harding no. 121 lines 217–20). Increased commerce brought increased

---

[12] [Plut.] *Mor.* 841B–C; 852 B (based on the decree of Stratocles, which survives in part as *IG* II² 457). The dating here preferred is argued by Cawkwell 1963 (C 107) 54–5 and Rhodes 1981 (B 94) 515–17. For the more traditional dating of 338–326 see Mitchel 1970 (C 203) 12; Will 1983 (D 245) 22–4.

[13] [Plut.] *Mor.* 841C. For Xenocles see Meritt 1960 (B 155) 2–4, no.3; Mitchel 1970 (C 203) 29.

harbour and sales taxes, as well as the standard *metoikion* paid by aliens who opted to reside in Athens. The legislation also helped create goodwill, which was invaluable during the great famine of the 320s when imported grain was at a premium. Then the *demos* might intervene politically to secure the business interests of favoured aliens like Heraclides of Salamis (*IG* II².360), and piracy was discouraged by military force (*IG* II².1623, lines 276–308). In Attica itself the exploitation of the silver mines continued to be carefully policed, and the income from the estates of convicted delinquents was distributed among the *demos*.[14] Indeed the revenue from successful prosecutions may not have been an inconsiderable factor during this period; there are contemporary allegations of malicious accusations (by Lycurgus among others), motivated primarily by the wealth of the defendants. The sources of public income were multifarious and complex, but the sums involved were impressively large.

Expenditure is a simpler matter. Under Lycurgus' administration there was a planned military build-up. By 330/29 the inventories of the naval curators record a total of 392 triremes, most of them allegedly in battle readiness ([Plut.] *Mor.* 852C). The quadriremes, which were increasingly in vogue in the eastern Mediterranean, reached a total of fifty in 325/4,[15] while the triremes declined from 392 to 360. At the same time the new arsenal and dockyards were brought to completion, and the navy was superbly housed. The *ephebeia* was also reorganized. From 336/5 service became compulsory for all Athenians in the two years after their reception into the citizen body.[16] Subsidized by the state and armed at public expense, they were trained intensively in their first year, then delegated to frontier service. There was a deeply patriotic streak to the training, symbolized in the ephebic oath (Tod no. 204 = Harding no. 109), and the system of tribal messes inculcated an ethos of solidarity. The *demos* as a whole profited from a programme of public architecture, which affected all the main civic institutions: the theatre of Dionysus was rebuilt and extended, and there was new construction on the Pnyx, the council complex and the law courts. The younger population enjoyed the wrestling school and gymnasium in the Lyceum.[17]

There was a good deal of political motivation behind this expenditure. Athens was prepared for war but was not involved in war; and the *demos* had a positive inducement to avoid military adventures. Distributions from the theoric fund, the so-called cement of democracy, were sometimes substantial (Plut. *Mor.* 818E), and there were *ad hoc* donatives,

---

[14] [Plut.] *Mor.* 843D. Cf. Hyper. *Eux.* 35–6.
[15] *IG* II² 1629, line 811. Cf. Schmitt 1974 (C 248); Ashton 1977 (D 9) 3–7, 1979 (C 91).
[16] Reinmuth 1971 (B 168): cf. Mitchel 1975 (C 204); Ruschenbusch 1979 (C 236).
[17] Full details and references in Will 1983 (D 245) 79–93.

like the 160 talents which accrued from the condemnation of Diphilus ([Plut.] *Mor.* 843D). This was a deterrent against frivolous adventures, which would jeopardize the public largesse; and the traditional sentiment of the propertied classes continued to be averse to war. That was so even after the death of Alexander, when the ground swell of popular feeling against Macedon was countered by the men of property (Diod. XVII.10.1). This group included the veteran general Phocion and his associates, all of whom had a pressing interest to avoid the capital expenses of a major war. That reluctance would have been still more evident during Alexander's lifetime. There were also individual contacts with Macedon and the royal court. The ties of *proxenia* were as strong in that respect as they were with members of city states. Accordingly Demades moved the conferment of honorary citizenship and *proxenia* upon prominent Macedonians, including Alcimachus and Antipater, while Phocion had close contacts with Harpalus and Alexander himself. Even Demosthenes made overtures to Hephaestion (cf. Aeschin. III.162). These contacts were important. Hostile critics could malign them as treasonable, but in practice, once war came, there was almost complete solidarity. Pytheas and Callimedon were the only Athenians to desert their city in 323 (Plut. *Dem.* 27.2), and their desertion was not apparently motivated by Macedonian sympathies. But on the other hand, while peace subsisted, the personal contacts had a moderating influence, and Phocion's political caution may well have been influenced by his contacts with court.

By and large the prevailing mood at Athens was pacific, particularly after the destruction of Thebes. Individual politicians might argue for military intervention in specific crises, but until the promulgation of the Exiles' Decree (see below, p.856) the material interests of the *demos* were not threatened and there was no general will for war. The principal centre of opposition after 335 was Sparta. That city had acquiesced perforce when Philip invaded Laconia after Chaeronea and annexed her border territories (see above, p.783). But, despite the coercion, Sparta kept aloof from the Corinthian League and took no part in the war of revenge, much to the chagrin of Alexander who pointedly commemorated her abstention in his first victory dedication (Arr. *Anab.* 1.16.7; Plut. *Alex.* 16.18). Her ambition was to regain the lost territories, the Laconian borderlands and ultimately Messenia, and that was totally incompatible with the common peace, which guaranteed Messenian autonomy. Conflict with the ruling power was therefore inevitable.

At first the Spartans needed time to recover from the demoralization of Philip's invasion and the death in Italy of the veteran king Archidamus. Under the monarchy of Agis (the Agiad king, Cleomenes II, reigned for sixty years and ten months and left no other trace on the historical record) they maintained a diplomatic neutrality in the troubles of 336 and 335. The success of the Persian offensive in the Aegean offered the opportunity of more radical action, and in 333 the Spartans sent an envoy to the Persian court.[18] By the end of the campaigning year King Agis had conferred with the Persian admirals at Siphnos, soliciting military and financial support for war in the Peloponnese (Arr. *Anab.* II.13.4). The news of the Macedonian victory at Issus aborted those immediate plans, Agis received minimal assistance (30 talents and ten triremes) and instructed his brother Agesilaus to begin operations not in the Peloponnese but in Crete. That was a useful arena in which to deploy and acquire mercenary forces. The Cretan cities were not apparently signatories to the Corinthian League, and they had been involved in internecine war for decades. Like his father Archidamus (Diod. XVI.62.4) Agis probably intervened in the interests of Lyttus, which claimed to be a Spartan colony, and attacked Cnossus, exploiting the endemic hatred between the two states. In 332 the Spartan forces were joined by some 8,000 Greek refugees from Darius' army at Issus (Curt. IV.1.39; Diod. XVII.48.1), and the remnants of the Persian fleet in the Aegean eventually regrouped in Crete. This combined army held at bay Macedonian forces sent to help the other side, and by the end of the summer it controlled the greater part of the island. By the spring of 331 Alexander himself was sufficiently worried to send a large naval squadron under Amphoterus with orders to clear Crete of the hostile Spartan presence and simultaneously strengthen Macedonian allies in the Peloponnese who were in danger of subversion. He did not formally declare war upon Sparta, hoping to isolate her and destroy the base in Crete.[19]

The mission of Amphoterus came too late. War broke out in the Peloponnese during the summer of 331, a peculiarly propitious time for Agis.[20] The military reserves of Macedon had been depleted by the recruiting of Amyntas (see above, p.815) which had taken 6,000 infantry from Macedonia and 4,000 mercenaries from the Peloponnese. At roughly the same time Antipater was distracted by a mysterious revolt in Thrace which engaged his entire army (Diod. XVII.62.6).[21] Seizing the opportunity the Spartan government declared itself for liberty and

[18] Arr. *Anab.* II.15.2–5; Curt. III.13.15. On the complex source problem see Bosworth 1980 (B 14) 233–4; Atkinson 1980 (B 8) 261–2.

[19] Arr. *Anab.* III.6.3; Curt. IV.8.15; cf. Bosworth 1975 (D 153); Atkinson 1980 (B 8) 484–5.

[20] The chronology is difficult, but there is a growing tendency to date the end of the war to spring 330, in the light of Aeschin. III.133 (see below, p.854): cf. Cawkwell 1969 (C 108) 170–3; Bosworth 1975 (D 153); Badian 1985 (D 142) 446–7. The other view, based on Curtius' unacceptable synchronism of the end of the war with the battle of Gaugamela (Curt. VI.1.21), is less tenable. For bibliography see Will 1983 (D 245) 76–7.

[21] Cf. Berve 1926 (D 146) 2 no. 499; Badian 1967 (C 277) 179–80; Bosworth 1988 (D 159) 201.

appealed for help throughout Greece, while Agis transferred his mercenary army from Crete and began operations in the Peloponnese. A Macedonian general, Corrhagus, was defeated and allies rapidly accrued. Elis, unstable under a Macedonian-backed oligarchy, expelled its government and joined Sparta, as did the Achaean League (Pellene excepted) and all the Arcadian cities but Megalopolis. The alliance mustered a formidable army, 20,000 infantry and 2,000 cavalry, with a large proportion of battle-hardened mercenaries, and it soon controlled the majority of the Peloponnese. By autumn Agis had laid siege to Megalopolis and inaugurated the recovery of the lost territories.

The movement, as it transpired, was confined to the Peloponnese. At Athens the Spartan embassies proved ineffectual. There was certainly a mood for war, expressed trenchantly in the speech on the treaty with Alexander ([Dem.] XVII) which was most probably delivered at this time. That uncompromising call to arms was resisted by many leading politicians, notably Demosthenes, who had never been sympathetic to the hegemonial aspirations of Sparta.[22] His verbal dissuasion was supported more effectively by Demades who (in February 330) quashed public agitation to send triremes by threatening to finance the operation from the theoric fund (Plut. *Mor.* 818E-F). As in 335 the Athenians refrained from active intervention and conserved their resources.

That was fatal. Antipater was able to come to terms with the rebels in Thrace, and in the early spring of 330 he moved south with a vast army 40,000 strong. The Macedonian nucleus was swelled by mercenaries and citizen troops supplied by allied states (Diod. XVII.63.1), presumably the Thessalians and the peoples of central Greece. Agis' forces were outnumbered, and he could only await events in the vicinity of Megalopolis. There the final engagement took place, on restricted ground which favoured the smaller Spartan army (Curt. VI.1.10), and after a hard-fought battle Agis' troops were routed. The king was wounded and died in retreat, defending himself to the end, and 5,000 dead remained on the field of battle.

That ended the campaign. The fate of the insurgents was referred to the *synedrion* of the Corinthian League, which imposed an indemnity on Elis and the Achaeans. The Spartans, non-members of the league, were sent to plead their cause before Alexander. In the mean time they surrendered fifty hostages (after protest), and by the late summer of 330 hostages and embassy were about to begin their long journey east (Aeschin. III.133). There is no record of the ultimate settlement, but, now that Sparta was militarily crushed, it is unlikely to have been harsh. The city could be left, benignly neglected, to its decline. Under Agis'

---

[22] His opposition is documented (rather puzzlingly) by Aeschin. III.165–7. For his earlier views see Dem. XVI. esp. 19–22.

successor, his youngest brother Eudamidas, and the ageing Cleomenes
Sparta remained quiet for the rest of Alexander's reign and preserved her
neutrality during the Lamian War. For all his courage and planning Agis
had been unable to build a sufficiently strong coalition, and the stubborn
siege of Megalopolis was probably a fatal error. It recalled the Spartan
imperialism of the past, which most states found less palatable than the
Macedonian protectorate of the present.

II. THE EXILES' DECREE AND THE ORIGINS OF THE LAMIAN WAR

After 330 the main stimulus for political turmoil came from Alexander
himself. The policies which he initiated after his return to Mesopotamia
in 324 unleashed general dissatisfaction and unrest. His death was the
signal for open war. The focus of the discontent was the so-called Exiles'
Decree, which was promulgated at the Olympic games in the summer of
324. His emissary, Nicanor of Stagira, delivered a royal letter, announc-
ing the restoration of exiles throughout the Greek world, and it was read
out to an appreciative audience comprising more than 20,000 exiles
(Diod. xviii.8.3–5). As quoted by Diodorus (from the contemporary
Hieronymus of Cardia), the letter briefly disclaimed responsibility for
the exiles, guaranteed return to all but those guilty of sacrilege and
threatened the coercion of any city reluctant to comply. It was a
staggering exhibition of autocracy, a total abrogation of the common
peace which had prohibited the return of exiles.

According to Diodorus (xviii.8.2) the Decree was motivated by
Alexander's desire for glory and the practical need to have his own
partisans in every city. That is credible enough. Alexander had been
solicited by many specific groups of exiles, in particular those from
Samos and Heraclea Pontica,[23] and he was well aware of the advantages
they might confer if restored. Many, as we know from the contemporary
Tegean inscription (Tod no. 202 = Harding no. 122, lines 48–57), had
been generations in exile (the Samians had been refugees since 365), and,
if restored, they would be strangers in their own cities, dependent upon
the power that had restored them. What is clear is that Alexander did not
rehabilitate the people exiled by his own actions. Many, particularly
those convicted of medism during the Aegean War, could have been
considered guilty of sacrilege, and, as far as the Thebans were concerned,
their restoration was not considered before Cassander invaded Boeotia
in 316. When Polyperchon re-enacted the Decree in 319, he explicitly
restored the people exiled since Alexander's invasion of Asia (Diod.

[23] Memnon, *FGrH* 434 F 1 (4.1). Compare Alexander's interventions at Amisus (App. *Mith.* 83.374).

xviii.56.4); they had evidently not been covered by the amnesty of 324. The exiles who received Alexander's benefaction were the victims of his father and of earlier political conflict. Their restoration jeopardized Philip's settlement, but Agis' War had shown how precarious that settlement had been, in the Peloponnese at least.

The Decree was conceived in Mesopotamia, about the time of the mutiny in Opis,[24] and the contents of Nicanor's letter were public knowledge from the time he began his journey to Greece, around May 324.[25] The news unleashed a hectic round of diplomatic negotiations which climaxed early in 323 with the reception of various embassies of protest (Diod. xvii.113.3). There was some success. The Tegeans at least were able to modify the full rigours of the Decree. Their objections were confirmed by a royal rescript (Tod no. 202 = Harding no. 122, lines 2–4), and the rights of the exiles to restitution of property were prudently circumscribed. We hear most about the two states most directly affected, the Aetolians who were commanded to vacate the Acarnanian city of Oeniadae and the Athenians whose cleruchies on Samos were threatened. The restoration of the Samians had been pressed at court by prominent citizens of neighbouring Iasus, Gorgus and Minnion, and, sometime in the spring or summer of 324, Alexander made a formal announcement 'in the camp' that he was giving back Samos to the Samians.[26] That ruling was to dominate political decisions at Athens for the rest of the reign.

The situation was further complicated by the movements of Harpalus. In the spring of 324 the fugitive treasurer manned a flotilla of thirty ships in Cilicia and voyaged west to the mainland. His course took him first to Athens, where he had honorary citizenship, and he arrived off Sunium around May, when the Greek world was in suspense at the news of Nicanor's mission.[27] At first his request for asylum was rejected categorically, perhaps because of Athenian suspicions of his good faith, given the size of his squadron. Harpalus had no choice but to transfer the bulk of his forces to the great mercenary depot at Taenarum, and he returned to Athens with three ships and an ample supply of money. That

[24] Diod. xvii.109.1–2; Curt. x.2.4–7. There is no record in Arrian, but the Decree may have been mentioned in the great lacuna (cf. vii.12.7), where (we happen to know) he dealt with the flight of Harpalus.

[25] The commission included some obscure instructions dealing with the federal assemblies of the Achaeans and Arcadians (Hyper. *Dem.* col. 18: supplements presupposing a third state cannot be imposed upon the scanty traces of the papyrus). Some restrictive legislation is highly likely: see Badian 1961 (D 134) 31; *contra*, Aymard 1937 (D 130) 7–10.

[26] *SIG* 312. For the date see Heisserer 1980 (B 143) 183–9; Ashton 1983 (D 128); *contra*, Errington 1975 (C 360) 53–5.

[27] Hyper. *Dem.* col. 18. Harpalus' name is supplied in the context, but there is no plausible alternative.

was less threatening. Philocles, the general in charge of the docks, now admitted Harpalus to the city.[28] His entry was controversial. Demosthenes at first claimed that it would lead to general war; on the other hand it was argued that it would encourage further refugees to transfer funds and mercenaries from Asia. In the course of the debate Harpalus' money, generously distributed, made him more welcome, and Demosthenes acquiesced in his presence. But it was a dangerous move. When the news of Harpalus' reception reached Alexander in Ecbatana, the king seriously planned an expedition against the city, and Athens' enemies gave him every encouragement.[29]

The crisis came to a head as demands were made for Harpalus' extradition by Antipater, Olympias and even Philoxenus, the satrap of Caria. But, on Demosthenes' instigation, the *demos* ruled that Harpalus could only be surrendered to emissaries sent by Alexander himself. In the mean time the fugitive was to be interned; his monies (which he estimated at 700 talents) were lodged on the Acropolis. That kept the options open. Harpalus might be surrendered if it were diplomatically desirable, or he might be enlisted as an ally if the negotiations over Samos foundered. Meanwhile Demosthenes led an embassy to Olympia, where he had discussions with Nicanor and presumably raised the issue of Harpalus. Soon after, if not simultaneously, Harpalus was allowed to escape custody and leave Athens. He withdrew his forces to Crete, where he was murdered by his lieutenant Thibron, no later than October 324. His mercenary army was retained by exiles from Cyrenaica and ceased to be a factor in Greek affairs.[30]

Harpalus' monies remained – or rather a fraction of them. An inventory revealed that only 350 of the original 700 talents was actually on the Acropolis. The revelation inspired a political furore, in which it was claimed that Harpalus' monies had been corruptly dissipated in bribes.[31] In the face of the outcry Demosthenes, who was particularly vulnerable to the accusations, demanded an investigation by the Areopagus; on past performance it would be sympathetic to his interest. In fact he could not deny having received money, but he claimed that he received it as a loan to the theoric fund and disbursed it in the interest of the *demos*. There may be some truth in this. In the latter part of 324 Leosthenes, the mercenary commander at Taenarum, was retained for Athens after secret negotiations with the *boule* (Diod. XVII.111.3;

---

[28] Din. III.1–5. See further Bosworth 1988 (D 159) 293–4.
[29] Curt. x.2.1–2; cf. Ephippus, *FGrH* 126 F 5; Justin XIII.5.7, on which see above, p.841.
[30] For the events in Cyrenaica and their chronological implications see Bosworth 1988 (D 159) 291–2.
[31] Hyper. *Dem.* col. 7; cf. Din. 1.68–9. On the development of the scandal see in particular Badian 1961 (D 134) 32–6; Goldstein 1968 (B 43) 39–63.

XVIII.9.2).[32] There may have been unofficial initiatives by Demosthenes, using Harpalus' money (in part) for preliminary, unreceipted payments. But such secret negotiations were not susceptible of proof, and it was wise to delay the reckoning until the immediate passions of the *demos* had cooled.

The Areopagus did its work well. It took six months to publish its findings, by which time the public anger had dissipated. Around March 323 it submitted a list of recipients of money from Harpalus. Demosthenes headed the list with twenty talents. Other delinquents included Demades, Philocles and Charicles (Phocion's son-in-law). The culprits were tried before a court of 1,500 jurors, with ten prosecutors ranged against each defendant. From the surviving speeches of Dinarchus and Hyperides it seems that it was relatively hard to arouse the jurors' emotions. Convictions were made, but the penalties were not draconian. Demosthenes suffered a fine of 50 talents, not the death penalty he had invoked against himself if convicted. Imprisoned as a public debtor, he was allowed to escape and lived miserably in exile, first at Troezen and then at Aegina. Demades, however, was apparently able to pay his fine, for he was active in Athens at the time of Alexander's death. There were other casualties, notably Philocles, but we do not know the penalties inflicted.

The scandal over Harpalus' monies had long been overshadowed by the greater events associated with the Exiles' Decree. Athens herself faced the imminent prospect of the return of exiles, now gathered as a group in Megara and alleged to be a threat to the democracy (Din. 1.58,94). There was also trouble in Samos, where a group of exiles crossed from Anaea and came into conflict with the Athenian cleruchs there. Some were captured by the Athenian general in Samos and referred to Athens, where they were first condemned by the *demos* and then ransomed through the good offices of Antileon of Chalcis. The dating of this episode is controversial, but it is perhaps best placed in the last months of Alexander's reign, when the Athenians were determined to protect their interests but preferred to avoid an atrocity which might alienate sympathy.[33] Meanwhile they intrigued with the Aetolian League, which was openly at loggerheads with Alexander because of its determination to retain possession of Oeniadae.[34] There would ultimately be a reckoning, and the Aetolians were happy to receive the Athenian overtures, which were made discreetly and indirectly through

---

[32] On the problems involved and the distinction of Leosthenes the mercenary commander from Leosthenes, son of Leosthenes, who is attested (in an Oropian dedication) as *strategos* in charge of the *chora* (Reinmuth 1971 (B 168) no 18), see Jaschinski 1981 (D 203) 51–4; Bosworth 1988 (D 159) 293–4.

[33] Habicht 1957 (B 141) 156–69, nos. 1–2. On the dating see further Errington 1975 (C 360) 55; Badian 1976 (B 134); Rosen 1978 (D 227) 26.

[34] Diod. XVIII.8.6; Plut. *Alex.* 49.15; cf. Mendels 1984 (C 371) 129–49.

Leosthenes, the mercenary commander at Taenarum. There was discontent elsewhere, notably in Thessaly, which was faced with the mass return of the families exiled during the long struggle between the Thessalian League and the tyrants of Pherae. It was a direct threat to the ruling families, particularly those of Pharsalus and Larissa, who had been most favoured by Philip. When war eventually came, after Alexander's death, the Thessalians changed sides *en masse* and the centre of the agitation was Pharsalus (Diod. XVIII.11.1,12.3).

Alexander's actions had been ruinous. He died only ten months after the proclamation of the Decree, when the political ferment it caused was unresolved. But he had effectively undermined the common peace, the corner-stone of Philip's settlement. Instead he had enlisted the old dispossessed in his service and imposed their return by royal edict and threat of force. Autonomy was a dead letter; the façade of consensus which Philip had created was demolished, and it was evident that there was little distinction in Alexander's mind between allies and subjects. His death accordingly provoked a strong general reaction. The Athenians formalized their relations with the Aetolians and concluded a regular alliance, at the same time declaring their championship of the common freedom of Greece.[35] Their appeal for allies was enthusiastically received in central Greece and the Peloponnese, and Antipater faced a general rising, a war which the participants dubbed the 'Hellenic War'.[36] Alexander's autocracy had created a spirit of national resistance, with Macedon identified as the common enemy, the very situation that his father had devoted decades of diplomacy to prevent.

B. KING AND EMPIRE

I. THE APPOINTMENT OF SATRAPS

When he invaded Asia, Alexander had no model for action, no system inherited from his father. He came not merely to avenge past delicts but also to conquer. According to one tradition[37] his first gesture on disembarking in the Troad was to make a spear cast and claim the land as 'spear won'. The story is to some degree corroborated by his first administrative acts, which were to place his own men over the existing satrapies (with the title of satrap). In Hellespontine Phrygia he appointed Calas, one of the commanders of the expeditionary force as satrap and

---

[35] Diod. XVIII.11.1. For the Aetolian alliance see *SEG* XXI 299 = Moretti, *ISE*, no. 1 with Mitchel 1964 (B 160).

[36] *IG* II² 448, lines 43–4; 505 line 17. On this and other evidence see Ashton 1984 (C 92).

[37] Diod. XVII.17.2; Justin XI.5.10: see above, p.798.

maintained the level of tribute imposed by the Persians (Arr. *Anab.* 1.17.1). Similarly in Lydia he retained the Persian division of command, with the great citadel of Sardis under a separate Macedonian commander, while the satrap, Asander, son of Philotas, had an independent force of cavalry and light armed foot. Precedent was also observed in Caria, where Alexander vested the satrapy in the senior member of the Hecatomnid house, the princess Ada, who had reigned for four years under Achaemenid sovereignty.[38] But here he left a Macedonian general, Ptolemy, who commanded a mercenary army 3,200 strong (Arr. *Anab.* 1.23.6). In theory the area had a native ruler. In practice the general was independent – in the military sphere at least. During the Aegean War Ptolemy acted as a free agent, operating on equal terms with the Macedonian satrap of Lydia.

Alexander felt free to depart from precedent when it served his interests. That was evident in his settlement of Lycia, which under Achaemenid rule had become absorbed by the satrapy of Caria.[39] Alexander passed through the area in person and may have been requested to remove the Hecatomnid supervision. That he did but created an entirely new satrapy, combining Lycia and Pamphylia. For the duration of the Aegean War the coastline between Telmissus and Side was placed under a single commander, Alexander's friend Nearchus. After he was recalled to court in 330/29, the area became annexed to Antigonus' command in Greater Phrygia. It was no longer strategically important. Alexander's concentration on the immediate present was particularly evident in 333. Intent on the encounter with Darius, he made only the most perfunctory settlement of central Asia Minor. Antigonus was installed at Celaenae, the satrapal capital of Phrygia, with a modest force of 1,500 mercenaries. Otherwise peoples like the Paphlagonians, who submitted, were annexed to existing satrapies or, as happened in southern Cappadocia, a native ruler was imposed without any military support. Consequently Cappadocia remained a no man's land. Antigonus won three victories against Persian refugees from Issus and clearly controlled the royal road between Sardis and the Cilician Gates, but he was unable to enforce control of Cappadocia. That region, together with Paphlagonia, was classed as unconquered territory in·323 and assigned to Eumenes.

The year 332 witnessed more complex administrative arrangements, as Alexander fought his way down the Levantine coast. Cilicia, which was a coherent geographical entity with clear-cut borders, he placed

---

[38] Arr. 1.23.7–8; cf. Bosworth 1980 (B 14) 152–3; Hornblower 1982 (F 644) 45–57.

[39] On the direct control exercised over Xanthus see the trilingual inscription (Metzger *et al.* 1974 (B 157) 82–149, and 1979 (B 158) redated by Badian (B 135) 1977). See above, p.219. For relations with Phaselis see Hornblower 1982 (F 644) 122–3.

under a royal bodyguard, Balacrus son of Nicanor, who was both satrap and general. Syria was a far less homogeneous area with a huge range of political systems. Here Alexander imposed commanders as suited the military situation. North Syria, the coastal area between Cilicia and Phoenicia, he placed under Menon, son of Cerdimmas, with a modest force of mercenary cavalry. To the south the city states of Phoenicia remained under their local kings, who were confirmed in office except in Sidon, where a member of a collateral branch of the royal house was installed. Tyre after its capture became an enclave of direct rule, with a Macedonian garrison under Philotas. Similarly in Samaria the hereditary ruler, Sanballat III, was confirmed, as apparently was the priestly government in Jerusalem. But there was a military commander, Andromachus, who continued the work of pacification in the south. Andromachus was burnt alive early in 331 by Samaritan insurgents, and after a brief campaign of reprisal Alexander replaced him with Menon, whom he transferred from the north. When he moved from the area early in 331, he left two Macedonian commanders, Asclepiodorus in the north and Menon in the south. Late in the same year a bodyguard of high standing, Menes, was sent from Susa to act as *hyparch* of Cilicia, Syria and Phoenicia. It was obviously a major military post, and it is possible (though unprovable) that he replaced the former satraps. Certainly the two Syrian commanders were recalled to escort mercenary forces to the army in Bactria, and by 323 Syria (like Cilicia) was governed as a single satrapy.[40] The division of command designed for a war situation in 332/1 was no longer necessary in the more settled conditions at the end of the reign.

The administration of Egypt is more complex but better attested. Here Alexander retained the immemorially old division of the upper and lower kingdoms with separate armies and separate Macedonian military commanders.[41] There was at first no satrap as such. Alexander appointed native Egyptian *nomarchs* to head the civil administration. They may have been supported (and supervised) by Macedonian advisers. Power clearly resided with the Macedonian officials, and the role of the Egyptian *nomarchs* was largely cosmetic, to satisfy national aspirations and delegate instructions to the native governors of the forty-two nomes, the administrative subdivisions of Egypt. One of the nominated *nomarchs*, Petisis, in fact refused his commission, and his colleague, Doloaspis, received the entire administration. It cannot have been too onerous. The most important figure in Egypt was Cleomenes, a Greek

[40] On the complex evidence see Bosworth 1974 (F 225); Brunt 1976–83 (B 21) I 278–9, 360–1. See also the views of Leuze 1935 (F 282) 436ff; Tarn 1948 (D 239) II 176–8.
[41] Cf. Bosworth 1980 (B 14) 275–7; Atkinson 1980 (B 8) 365–7 on Arrian and Curtius. For a contemporary order by Peucestas, commander in lower Egypt, see Turner 1974 (F 542).

from Naucratis, who was appointed to the Arabian command in the east, centred at Heröopolis. But at the same time he was placed over the entire fiscal system of Egypt, receiving tribute from the local officials. That gave him control of public expenditure, the payment of royal garrisons and armies and the building of Alexandria. During the great famine of the 320s he used his fiscal power to control the sale of Egyptian grain which he sold for export at the colossal price of 32 drachmae per measure. The profits in part were used in the grandiose public buildings of Alexandria, which impressed the city's founder. Arrian (*Anab.* VII.23.7–8) cites a notorious letter in which Alexander instructed Cleomenes to build *heroa* for Hephaestion, promising immunity for all his delicts, past and future. Peculation could be condoned if it resulted in sufficiently impressive profits for the government. Cleomenes himself was ultimately recognized as satrap, a position he had held *de facto* from the outset as a consequence of his fiscal control. His status was finally regularized when he had proved his worth to Alexander, even though his authority had been largely usurped. Egypt remained a satrapy at the death of Alexander, when Ptolemy secured it as the price for his support of Perdiccas. Cleomenes survived – for a time – as his lieutenant (*hyparch*), to be eliminated on the eve of Perdiccas' invasion on suspicion of collaboration.[42] He had ensured that the two kingdoms were an administrative unity, with an impressive financial reserve of 8,000 talents (Diod. XVIII.14.1). It meant that Ptolemy could recruit mercenaries on a large scale from the moment of his arrival and enjoyed the vast centralized revenues of Egypt. By 321 the territory was his personal fief, which he regarded as 'spear won' after his repulse of Perdiccas, and the foundation of a lasting monarchy was laid.[43]

After Gaugamela Alexander experimented with satraps selected from the Persian nobility who held office alongside Macedonian generals and garrison commanders. At Babylon Mazaeus, satrap of Cilicia and Syria from the early days of Artaxerxes III, led the surrender of the city and was rewarded with the satrapy of Babylon (he probably had a Babylonian wife). He controlled the administration and even struck coins (initially bearing his own name),[44] but his activities were circumscribed by the appointment of a separate official to collect the tribute. Two Macedonians of high rank, Agathon and Apollodorus, controlled the citadel of Babylon and the armed forces of the satrapy. There were similar arrangements in Susa and even in Persis. The main problem was loyalty. Would the Persian satraps support their new king in times of trouble? In Media and Parthyaea the first satraps, although they had suffered

42 Paus. 1.6.3; Arr. *Succ.*, F 1.5 (Roos); cf. Seibert 1969 (B 108) 51, 112.
43 See *CAH* VII².1, 122–33, with Seibert 1969 (B 108) 74–5; 1983 (A 54) 222–6.
44 Bellinger 1963 (B 187) 60–8; cf. Badian 1965 (D 136) 171; Bosworth 1980 (B 14) 315.

disgrace under Achaemenid rule, were found wanting during Bessus' vigorous counter-offensive of 329 (see above, p.821). Both were replaced by the former incumbents, Atropates in Media and Phrataphernes in Parthyaea, who maintained their loyalty to Darius to the bitter end. They showed equal devotion to Alexander and retained their satrapies honourably until the end of the reign.

Other territories were more troublesome. In Areia Satibarzanes collaborated openly with Bessus and waged a guerilla war against Alexander for nearly a year. His successor and rival, Arsaces, was no more successful and was replaced by a Companion, Stasanor of Soli, who finally pacified the satrapy. The vital corridor of Arachosia was also placed under a Macedonian, Menon. Bactria and Sogdiana also saw a change of policy. After the easy occupation of the territory south of the Oxus he appointed as satrap the Persian noble Artabazus, a declared enemy of the previous satrap, Bessus. But the ease of conquest was illusory, as the general revolt of summer 329 starkly revealed. After a year of harsh, repressive warfare Artabazus abdicated his command, to be replaced (evanescently) by Cleitus the Black and then by Amyntas, son of Nicolaus. The satrap commanded the largest regional force in the empire, 10,000 infantry and 3,500 cavalry, and supervised a regular network of Greco-Macedonian city foundations (see below, p.867). Individual Iranian barons, like Chorienes of Paraetacae, might be confirmed in their domains, but the actual government was firmly in Macedonian hands.

The Indian lands lay outside the recent boundaries of Achaemenid rule, and Alexander had no established system of satrapies to deal with, rather a multitude of native princes, often at loggerheads with each other. In the Kabul valley, the scene of bitter fighting in 327, Alexander appointed a Macedonian satrap, who had an appropriately large garrison force to continue the work of pacification. Under his control were a number of Indian hyparchs, some of whom were expatriates restored to power by Alexander men like Sangaeus in Peucelaotis (Arr. *Anab.* IV.22.8) or Sisicottus at Aornus (Arr. *Anab.* IV.30.4). They would have performed much of the civil government. In India proper another satrap, Philip, son of Machatas, had the general supervision of the area west of the Hydaspes and south to the confluence of the Indus and Acesines. Once again the local rulers were subordinate, notably Taxiles, who had invited Alexander into India but had tribute imposed upon him and a garrison in his capital. The great beneficiary of conquest was Porus, who had his own realm expanded to the banks of the Hyphasis. He may have had the title satrap (Plut. *Alex.* 60.15), but in practice he was plenipotentiary, operating without Macedonian troops or Macedonian commanders. In Sind there was another satrap, Peithon son of Agenor, who had military command from the Acesines confluence to the Ocean, controlling the vassal princes forced into subjection by the terror campaign of 325.

The Indian settlement was not lasting. Late in 325 Philip, who now commanded the Cophen valley as well as northern India, was assassinated by his mercenary troops (Arr. *Anab.* VI.27.2: Curt. X.1.20–1). That forced the king to contract his command system. Preoccupied as he was by his western plans, he had little desire for further involvement in India. Accordingly he withdrew direct satrapal control to the Kabul valley, transferring Peithon from what had been the southern satrapy. The lands between the Indus and Hydaspes were delegated to Taxiles, who ruled with a Macedonian lieutenant, Eudamus, while Porus' lands were extended still further, down to Patala and the Ocean.[45] That formed a vast buffer zone, where even Porus' writ may have been largely disregarded. India was largely evacuated, except for the city foundations which remained as bulwarks of conquest. Only the Kabul valley remained under strict control, heavily garrisoned, a frontier province and a gateway for any future invasion.

The final developments came after Alexander's return to the west in the winter of 325/4. In his absence there had been a number of nationalistic uprisings in central Iran, with trouble recorded in Media and Arachosia. Satraps had tended to act as independent despots or even usurp power, as Orxines had done in Persis after the death of Alexander's first satrap, Phrasaortes. Accordingly there was a series of purges, as over-mighty satraps were executed on charges of misgovernment, which came easily to hand.[46] Astaspes was executed in Carmania, Orxines in Persis, Abulites in Susiana. Their successors were Macedonians of unimpeachable loyalty. In Persis the king's saviour, Peucestas, took over the satrapy, with his active encouragement to learn Persian and assimilate himself to the local culture, while in Carmania Tlepolemus had the benefit of years of experience as military supervisor in Parthyaea. By contrast in Media it was the Macedonian commanders who were subverted. Cleander and Sitalces were accused of sacrilege and misgovernment and executed. Again there is evidence of insubordination. They had behaved as quasi-independent monarchs (cf. Curt. X.1.7) and that was unpardonable in Macedonian or oriental. On the other hand Atropates, the Iranian satrap of Media, retained his office with distinction. As usual Alexander worked on the short term. It is hard to see any wider policy beyond the basic requirements that the satrapies should remain peaceful with the minimum of expense and that his kingship should be universally and unconditionally accepted.

[45] Arr. *Succ.* F 1.36 (Roos); cf. Berve RE XIX.219; Bosworth 1983 (D 158).
[46] Documentation in Badian 1961 (D 134) 17–23; cf. 1985 (D 142) 474–9.

II. FINANCIAL ADMINISTRATION

Finance was rarely a problem for Alexander. The expenses of his campaign were met either on the spot or from the immense accumulated reserves of bullion that he found in the Persian treasuries.[47] By and large the satraps were left to collect their own tribute, as had been the rule in Achaemenid times; and given the prevalence of local wars and rebellion there may have been little surplus over the costs of administration and the standing armies. Some satrapies which were especially wealthy or complex had separate financial officials. Nicias in Lydia had responsibility for 'the assessment and the collection of tribute' (Arr. *Anab.* 1.17.7).[48] Babylonia also had a separate official to manage its taxation, as did the cities of Phoenicia. The monies they controlled gave them power. We have seen how Cleomenes became *de facto* satrap of Egypt through his manipulation of the tribute. There may be a parallel in the case of Philoxenus in southern Asia Minor. Appointed in 331 to collect tribute 'this side of the Taurus' (Arr. *Anab.* III.6.4), a commission which probably covered the satrapies of Caria and Phrygia, he became one of the most influential men of the sub-continent and it was probably he who succeeded the old princess Ada as satrap of Caria.[49]

The most important financial official was undoubtedly Harpalus, who had control of the central treasuries of the empire. From 330 to his self-imposed exile in late 325 he supervised the collected reserves first at Ecbatana and then at Babylon, and his competence extended over the central provinces. His successor, Antimenes of Rhodes (who was certainly no more powerful), was able to give direct instructions to satraps and successfully reimposed an obsolete Babylonian import tax on visiting satraps and ambassadors.[50] Harpalus was virtually a despot, behaving like a king and supervising royal treasuries as far afield as the Levantine coast. No mere satrap could withstand the king's friend and controller of the king's money, and his functions gradually expanded beyond simple control of money. In 326 he was responsible for sending a mercenary army from the central satrapies to India (Curt. IX.3.21; Diod. XVII.95.4) together with a vast quantity of arms and medicine (but not apparently coin); and it looks as though he gave general logistical

---

[47] Strabo XV.3.9 gives a figure of 180,000 talents for the accumulated reserves at Ecbatana. See also Diod. XVII.80.3; Justin XII.1.3 and, for discussion of discrepancies, Bellinger 1963 (B 187) 68–70; Bosworth 1980 (B 14) 330.

[48] For interpretation see Bosworth 1980 (B 14) 130; *contra*, Griffith 1964 (D 183), Wirth 1972 (D 247).

[49] Argued by Bosworth 1980 (B 14) 281–2. Other interpretations presuppose *two* men named Philoxenus (with overlapping spheres of competence): a satrap of Caria and a supervisor of the Greek cities of Ionia (cf. Berve 1926 (D 146) II nos. 793–4; Bengtson 1937 (D 145); Badian 1966 (D 137) 56–60). [50] ARIST. *Oec.* 132b28–53a4. See Berve 1926 (D 146) II no. 89.

support, co-ordinating the resources of the central empire, manpower as well as money.

One of the principal functions of Harpalus, and probably of the other financial officials based on minting centres, was the striking of the royal coinage. At first Alexander issued exclusively from the royal mints of Pella and Amphipolis.[51] The famous tetradrachms with the head of Heracles and the seated Zeus went side by side with gold staters bearing the head of Athene and a winged Nike. After Issus production was supplemented from mints on the Levantine coast (Tarsus, Myriandrus, Byblus and Sidon) and, after Gaugamela, the Babylon mint also came into operation. Sometimes, as happened in Sidon and the cities of Cyprus,[52] the royal coinage totally displaced local issues as an act of policy. Elsewhere the local currency continued. It did so in Cilicia, where Balacrus, like his Achaemenid precursors, minted coins in his own name. The same happened in Babylon where Mazaeus first issued lion staters in his own name but after four issues struck them without legend.[53] Local issues might continue but they would become anonymous. By contrast Alexander's coinage was standard, empire-wide and explicitly his own, bearing his name and proclaiming his universal monarchy.

III. THE CITY FOUNDATIONS

The cities founded by Alexander were probably his most lasting memorial. In a famous passage Plutarch (*Mor.* 328E) accredits him with the establishment of seventy cities among barbarian peoples, centres of civilization and culture for the peoples of Asia. The number is probably exaggerated, the effect certainly so. For the most part Alexander's foundations were military control centres, garrison points in unquiet territory. His activity began in his father's lifetime, in 340 B.C., when he followed the pattern established by Philip in Thrace, evacuating the capital of the insurgent Maedi (in the upper Strymon) and resettling it with a heterogeneous immigrant population. It was named Alexandropolis on the analogy of Philippopolis.[54] Something similar took place after the sieges of Gaza and Tyre, when the gutted cities were repopulated from native perioeci under the supervision of a Macedonian garrison. But these were not new foundations and the permanent citizen body was not distinctively Hellenic.

By contrast Alexandria in Egypt was a completely new city, superim-

---

[51] On the dating problems see Bellinger 1963 (B 187) 3–13 and the exchange between Zervos 1982 (B 217) and Price 1982 (B 212).
[52] Cf. Newell 1916 (B 211); Merker 1964 (B 207); Mørkholm 1978 (B 209) (*contra*, Gesche 1974 (F 253)).   [53] Von Aulock 1964 (B 184) (Balacrus); Bellinger 1963 (B 187) 70–7 (Mazaeus).
[54] Plut. *Alex.* 9.1. Cf. Hammond and Griffith 1979 (D 50) II 557–9.

posed on the old harbour village of Rhacotis. Here there is no suggestion of military calculations. The sources stress the magnificence of the site, blessed with a uniquely salubrious climate, with rich agricultural territory and well placed for commerce with the hinterland.[55] From the beginning Alexander took a strong personal interest in its development (Arr. *Anab.* VII.23.7) and probably saw it as a foundation to eclipse his father's Philippi. It was a Greek foundation, as Alexander demonstrated by his personal selection of an agora and temple sites for predominantly Hellenic deities (Arr. *Anab.* III.1.5); and Greek settlers were attracted from the mainland, from Egypt and Cyrenaica. The Egyptian populace formed a sub-class, attached to the new foundation by synoecism, and provided the workforce for the generous agricultural lands which afforded subsistence for the new city.

The next foundations came late in 330, when Alexandria in Areia (Herat) and Alexandria in Arachosia (Kandahar?)[56] were established to help contain the unrest provoked by Bessus. We have explicit evidence for Alexandria in Caucaso (Begram), in the central Hindu Kush, where Alexander settled 3,000 Greek and Macedonian troops alongside 7,000 of the local population. The site was enlarged in 327 with the addition of more discharged troops and more native peoples. This pattern was developed in Bactria and Sogdiana. The new foundation of Alexandria Eschate, established as a defence point to repel nomad incursions across the Iaxartes, was populated from prisoners-of-war captured during the revolt of 329. They were 'liberated' to provide the rural workforce of the new city, the citizen body of which comprised Greek mercenaries and discharged Macedonian veterans.[57] That, like the numerous other new 'cities' of the area, was in essence a garrison, the elite Hellenic fighting body supported by members of the native population who had been transplanted by force from their old domicile. The process is well illustrated by the French excavations at Ai-Khanum, probably the site of Alexandria on the Oxus. The new foundation there was established in a plain already watered by an existing network of canals. The area was clearly under intensive cultivation, but there is no trace of earlier settlement (there may have been a garrison on the acropolis).[58] It seems that the city proper was a Greek implant, complete with gymnasium, theatre, a *heröon* for its founder and a palace for its military ruler which dwarfed even that at Vergina. But the principal buildings belong to the third century and later. The community established by Alexander probably lived in pioneer simplicity.

[55] Cf. Fraser 1972 (A 21) I 5–7, II 4–10; Cavenaile 1972 (F 420); Jähne 1981 (F 456) 68–72.
[56] On the identification see Fischer 1967 (D 173); Fraser 1979–80 (B 140).
[57] Curt. VII.6.27; Justin XII.5.12; Arr. *Anab.* IV.4.1. Cf. Briant 1982 (F 10) 244–7.
[58] Bernard 1973 (F 5A) I 69ff; 1980 (F 6) 435ff.

Similar foundations were established in the latter years of the campaign wherever Alexander met spirited resistance or rebellion. At least one city was founded in the Cophen valley; and in the Indus plain twin cities, Nicaea and Bucephala, were established on opposite sides of the Hydaspes, to serve as frontier defences after the eastern regions had been ceded to Porus. In Sind a similar process began, but the foundations there were rudimentary when Alexander left for the west and probably did not survive the transfer of the satrap, Peithon, to the Cophen valley (see above, p.864). But the repressive philosophy continued. In Oreitis the largest village of the territory, Rhambaceia, was resettled as an Alexandria, with a population drawn in part from Arachosia to the north; and in the Zagros there were a number of foundations in Cossaean territories, with the local nomads serving as a very reluctant agrarian populace. Other cities, like the foundations towards the mouths of the Tigris and Euphrates, were not garrison centres as such but were strategically placed to service the Arabian expedition, which in its turn was to colonize the Persian Gulf (see above, p.844). These cities were naturally a hardship to the local inhabitants. They were also unpopular with the Hellenic settlers, who were held in place by fear of Alexander. At his death more than 20,000 of them banded together in the far east and made for the Levantine coast 'out of longing for the Greek manner of life' (Diod. XVIII.7.1). It took a vicious massacre by Macedonian troops sent from Babylon to convince them that their residence was permanent. It remained for Seleucus to make colonization an attractive prospect and initiate the huge programme of city foundations that led to the partial hellenization of the Near East.

IV. THE GREEKS OF ASIA MINOR

The Greek cities of Asia Minor were an anomaly within the empire. Their liberation was an avowed object of the war with Persia (Diod. XVI.91.2; XVII.24.1), but on the other hand they were strategic pawns in a war zone and could not be given unrestricted autonomy. If the fortunes of war were unfavourable and there were no mitigating circumstances, they might suffer enslavement, as did the little Aeolic community of Gryneum, which was stormed by Parmenion in 335.[59] On the other hand Miletus, which surrendered at the last possible moment, was granted its liberty – or dispensation from slavery. That is an important qualification. Liberation could in practice mean little, merely the cessation of Persian government. The native Lydians, for instance, were declared free under their ancestral laws – to pay tribute under the sway of a

---

[59] Diod XVII.7.9. Gryneum had been one of the fiefs granted to the medizer Gongylus of Eretria (Lewis 1977) (A 33) 54. Like the Branchidae of Sogdiana (Bosworth 1988 (D 159) 108–9) its population may have been visited with the sins of a previous generation.

Macedonian satrap (Arr. *Anab.* 1.17.4,7). All settlements with Greek cities, however liberal, were imposed by the king, and autonomy, when it was awarded, was his personal gift. Formal treaties, such as those with the Chorasmians of the far east (Arr. *Anab.* IV.15.2–4) or the Greek communities of Cyrenaica, were concluded with peoples outside the empire proper. Within it Alexander acted as victor and benevolent despot, dictating the terms he considered proper. Ilium, the spiritual centre of the war of revenge could bask in his favour, adjudged free and immune from tribute (Strabo XIII.1.26). On the other hand, at Ephesus, which had suffered an oligarchic counter-revolution and mass exile of Macedonian sympathizers, Alexander intervened to prevent a total massacre of the oligarchs and supervised the installation of a democracy. The tribute previously paid to Persia was diverted to the great temple of Artemis.[60] However favourable the final settlement, Alexander imposed it as a despot.

From Ephesus Alexander sent out Alcimachus son of Agathocles to operate in the areas of Aeolis and Ionia which were under Persian occupation, with instructions to install democracies, restore autonomy and remit tribute (Arr. *Anab.* 1.18.2). This is a famous episode, but it should not be taken as a universal manifesto. It was rather a gesture to win over areas threatened by the Persian fleet. Democracy was a predictable reaction against the oligarchic regimes favoured by Persia. Alexander may have represented it as the natural form of government for the Ionian cities, whose common ancestor was Athens, just as he claimed that democracy was the ancestral constitution of Pontic Amisus (App. *Mith.* 8.24, 83.374). Later Erythrae and Colophon were to boast of the freedom conferred by Alexander.[61] It was in their interest to make the most of the benefaction, and in the war situation of 334/3 autonomy was necessarily qualified, not least by the imposition of protective garrisons. But the demands of the campaign inclined Alexander towards generosity. The cities between Miletus and Halicarnassus, threatened by the Persian fleet, received grants of autonomy and immunity from tribute, and we have specific evidence of democracy confirmed at Iasus under the benevolent supervision of two of its magnates, Gorgus and Minnion, who had acquired the king's ear and favour.

There is detailed evidence only for Priene, where the king rededicated the temple of Athena Polias in his own name, honouring the patroness of his crusade of vengeance. Part of an archive survives, which begins with extracts of a decree of Alexander in favour of the city.[62] The fragmentary remains of the text deal with autonomy and land occupation. Citizens of

---

[60] Arr. *Anab.*1.17.10–12. Cf. Badian 1966 (D 137) 47; Heisserer 1980 (B 143) 58–9.

[61] *OGIS* 223 (= Welles, *RC* 15), line 22 (Erythrae); *AJP* 56 (1925) 361 (Colophon).

[62] Tod no.185 = Harding no. 106 = Heisserer 1980 (B 143) 142–68. The stone is re-edited, with emphasis upon its archival nature, by Sherwin-White 1985 (B 175) esp. 80–7.

Priene resident in the harbour town of Naulochum are declared free and
autonomous, in contrast with some non-Prienian group whose autonomy was restricted. Certain domains in the hinterland are arrogated as
royal land, subject to tribute (*phoroi*). By contrast the city of Priene was
exempted from the *syntaxis* – a difficult expression which has been
interpreted as a recurrent payment or as a single levy for the purposes of
the campaign.[63] Whatever the meaning, it is clear that Priene was
exempted from an imposition which was otherwise fairly regular, and
the community, as it proclaimed, was indeed highly favoured. The king
had organized their affairs very favourably, but, given other circumstances, his edict could be far less palatable. That the Aspendians of
Pamphylia discovered when they surrendered and requested that no
garrison be imposed upon them. Alexander's price was 50 talents'
immediate donation for the army's expenses and the continuation of the
tribute of horses paid to the Persian King. When the Aspendians resisted
they were subjected to direct satrapal control, had their levy doubled,
and a monetary tribute was imposed (Arr. *Anab.* 1.26.3, 27.4). Favourable or unfavourable, the terms of settlement were autocratically
imposed and could change with the military situation.

It is most unlikely that the Greek cities were included in the formal
framework of the Corinthian League.[64] There is, as we have noted, no
explicit record of any treaty or alliance. Admittedly it would have been a
nice propaganda gesture to include the Greeks of Asia, who would be
represented joining their liberators in the crusade. But there is no trace of
such propaganda in our sources and, given the sensitivity of Ptolemy and
Aristobulus to royal apology, that is a significant omission. Until new
evidence emerges, it will be best to regard the Greek cities as largely
autonomous entities within subject territory, dependent on continuing
royal favour. By 331 Alexander considered the Greek cities liberated,
and after Gaugamela he proclaimed that all tyrannies were abolished and
autonomy prevailed (Plut. *Alex.* 34.2). After that the problems of the
Greeks of Asia were not a primary concern, and the majority of the
evidence about the coastal cities relates to a mysterious Philoxenus, who
was active on the coast of south-west Asia Minor. It is the most
economical hypothesis that he was the fiscal superintendent (see above,
p.865) who occupied Caria after the death of Ada. As satrap he probably
intervened on Rhodes to arrest Harpalus' treasurer (Paus. II.33.4). He
also asserted his will on 'autonomous' Ephesus, occupying the city after
the murder of a certain Hegesias, the dominant Macedonian partisan. He
introduced a garrison, arrested the culprits and sent them to the prison at

[63] For differing explanations see Badian 1966 (D 137) 48; Bosworth 1980 (B 14) 166, 281; Sherwin-
White 1985 (B 175) 84–6.
[64] A most contentious issue; for bibliography see Seibert 1972 (D 232) 85–90.

Sardes, to await trial by Alexander.[65] That was hardly an isolated episode. In the confusion of the Aegean War satraps may have felt themselves entitled to impose their wills, by force of arms if necessary, and the habit of intervention, once established, would have been hard to eradicate. That illustrates the precarious nature of the cities' status. No declaration of autonomy guaranteed against coercion if it suited the king or his satraps. The Greeks of Asia were certainly privileged, but they were also subjects.

V. KING AND GOD

The reign of Alexander marks a watershed in the development of the ruler cult. Before him the examples of divine honours for living men are few and controversial; later they are almost commonplace. But Alexander's actions and beliefs did not spring out of nothing. The original absolute distinction between mortality and immortality had been shaken in various ways. The language of Pindar, so eloquent about the ephemeral nature of human life and success, does suggest that there are fleeting moments in the exaltation of victory when man comes close to the divine. That embryonic thought was taken further in the fourth century B.C., when Isocrates (IX.72) eulogized Evagoras of Cyprus as a god among men. More pertinently for Alexander, Aristotle could envisage an ideal monarchy, in which the ruler appeared so superior to his coevals as to appear a god among men, and he is overtly sympathetic to the popular saying that men become gods by a surpassing display of excellence.[66] Occasionally, if very rarely, actual honours (divine as opposed to heroic) might be offered to a living man. According to Duris of Samos Lysander was the first of the Greeks to receive altars and sacrifices; and what he says about the renaming of the Samian national festival as the *Lysandreia* is now epigraphically confirmed.[67] It was Lysander's temporal power, supreme after Aegospotami, that was worshipped in this way, and there were similar, if not identical, honours paid to Philip. His statue (not a cult statue) was installed in the temple of Artemis at Ephesus (Arr. *Anab.* 1.17.11); and, more significantly the people of the little city of Eresus erected altars to Zeus Philippios, associating the Macedonian king intimately with the cult of Zeus (Tod no.191 = Harding no.112 B, line 6). By his death, if we may believe Diodorus (XVI.92.5, cf. 95.1), he was disposed to associate himself with

[65] Polyaen. VI.49. On the historicity of the story see Badian 1966 (D 137) 56–7, 64; *contra*, Tarn 1948 (D 239) II 174–5.

[66] Arist. *Pol.* 1284a10–11, 1332b16–22; *NE* 1145a19–27.

[67] Plut. *Lys.* 18. 5–6 (*FGrH* 76 F 71). On the Lysandreia see Habicht 1970 (A 26) 243–4; Badian 1981 (D 141) 33–8.

the twelve Olympian deities.[68] That was probably the culmination of a long process of public decree and private flattery. It would not be surprising if Philip thought himself more than human.

From his earliest years Alexander laid stress on his heroic lineage, from Aeacus and Achilles on his mother's side and from Heracles on his father's. He believed in it implicitly and was always eager to emulate his forebears, following Heracles and Perseus to the oasis at Siwah and embarking on the siege of Mt Aornus because of the local tradition that Heracles had failed to capture it. But Alexander felt that he was far more than the distant descendant of Zeus through his heroic ancestors. It was suggested that he was the direct son of the god. The stories that Olympias was impregnated by Zeus (in the guise of a thunderbolt or a serpent) were closely imitated by Seleucus I, who claimed that his mother, Laodice, was visited by Apollo.[69] They were obviously contemporary; and, after Alexander's accession (before which time it was dangerous to hint at any father but Philip), it became fashionable to argue that he had a dual paternity, comparable to that of Heracles. Such speculation resulted in the Milesian oracles delivered to Alexander early in 331, which dealt explicitly with his supposed birth from Zeus (Callisthenes, *FGrH* 124 F 14a). Arrian (*Anab.* III.3.2) indeed states that Alexander believed that his own origins were due to Ammon, the Libyan manifestation of Zeus, and the idea probably took shape in his mind even before his visit to Siwah (see above, p.811). The consultation of the oracle had a profound effect upon him. Callisthenes emphasized that the officiating priest greeted him publicly as son of Zeus, and all sources represent divine sonship as the central theme of the consultation. Later the king's relationship with Zeus Ammon was a commonplace at court, prominent in the flattery which enraged Cleitus at Maracanda and in the insults of the mutineers at Opis which provoked Alexander's wrath (Arr. *Anab.* VII.8.3). By 324 Demosthenes could propose ironically that Alexander should be son of Zeus or Poseidon, if he wished (Hyper. *Dem.* col.31), and the pretensions were clearly universal knowledge.

Being a son of a god did not in itself imply divinity. But Heracles had transcended that barrier from an early date, a hero god (Pindar *Nem.* III.22), who after his deeds on earth went to Olympus to live in bliss as the husband of Hebe. The idea of apotheosis was current in Alexander's day and was debated at court as early as the Sogdian campaigns of 328/7, when the king was favourably compared with the Dioscuri. It is also one of the leading themes of the debate on *proskynesis* as reported by Arrian (*Anab.* IV.10.5–7) and Curtius (VIII.5.8). That is one of the most curious

---

[68] For the highly questionable evidence of cult at Athens (Clem. Al. *Protr.* IV.54.5) see Fredricksmeyer 1979 (D 87); Badian 1981 (D 141).

[69] Justin XV.4.2–9; cf. Günther 1971 (H 55) 66–73; Hadley 1974 (A 27) 58.

episodes of the reign. In the late spring of 327 Alexander experimented with the aspect of Persian court protocol which the Greeks termed *proskynesis*. In the Persian court the act of homage, whether it involved a slight stooping forward or total prostration, was purely secular, found at all levels of Persian society.[70] In the Greek world, however, *proskynesis* was a cult act, performed to the gods – generally in a standing position but occasionally kneeling (a posture sometimes ridiculed as undignified).[71] There was general disquiet at Persian *proskynesis*, which Greeks tended to regard as intolerably servile, incompatible with any concept of freedom and there were clearly religious scruples about *their* honouring a mortal man with an act associated with worship. Barbarians could revere their kings as they pleased.

Alexander, it seems, did attempt to impose *proskynesis* on both Greeks and Macedonians, and he aroused determined opposition, represented and articulated by Callisthenes of Olynthus. Two episodes are recorded, which (contrary to the general belief) are both credible and consistent.[72] One, recorded by the court chamberlain, Chares of Mytilene, concerns a symposium with a few intimate participants. All drank a toast, performed *proskynesis* and received a kiss from the king. Callisthenes, however, attempted to avoid *proskynesis* but was detected and denied his kiss. He left the symposium in high dudgeon, but the rest of the guests apparently complied and might have encouraged Alexander to extend the experiment. A more public ceremony followed at a general banquet, when the king encouraged debate among the Greek intellectuals. Our sources have clearly embellished their material with the rhetorical jargon of the Roman empire, but there is a substratum of common material which comes from the primary tradition. The imposition of *proskynesis* is justified and attacked on religious grounds, the proponents arguing that the king had excelled Heracles and Dionysus and his achievement raised him to divinity. Callisthenes insisted on the strict division of mortal and divine honours and defended Greek traditions of liberty against an egregious affront. His speech was greeted with approval, particularly among the older Macedonians, and the public rejection was compounded by ridicule, when a senior Companion burst out laughing at a particularly profound abasement by a Persian noble. The experiment was dropped, never to be revived, and *proskynesis* was confined to the king's barbarian subjects – as were his kisses (Arr. *Anab.* VII.11.1,6).

---

[70] Hdt. 1.134; for details see Bickerman 1963 (D 148); Frye 1972 (F 20).

[71] D.L. VI.37–8; for full documentation see von Straten 1974 (H 106).

[72] Plut. *Alex.* 54.4–6; Arr. *Anab.* IV.12.3–5 (Chares F 14); Plut. *Alex.* 54.3; Arr. *Anab.* IV.10.5–12.2; Curt. VIII.5.8–24 (banquet scene). Of the two versions Chares has usually been accepted against the other tradition (cf. Brown 1949 (D 161) 244; Balsdon 1950 (D 144) 379–82; Hamilton 1969 (B 54) 152–3). Badian 1981 (D 141) 48–54 has dismissed Chares as apologetic fiction. For acceptance of two separate episodes see Goukowsky 1978–81 (B 45) I 185; Bosworth 1988 (B 15) 113–23.

Why Alexander attempted the innovation is a mystery. It is at least possible that he now believed the court flattery that elevated him above Heracles and Dionysus. The act of homage he received as a matter of course from his Persian subjects might be extended to the rest of the court, to emphasize the universality of his monarchy. If it implied recognition of his divinity, it was all the more appropriate.

In his later years Alexander's behaviour became more extravagant. As Ephippus (*FGrH* 126 F 5) claimed and the posthumous coinage of Lysimachus unforgettably demonstrates, he assumed the horns of Ammon as a recognizable feature of his dress. The court artist Apelles painted a celebrated portrait of Alexander with the thunderbolt of Zeus and was handsomely rewarded for doing so (Pliny *HN* xxxv.92). That may well have been the model for Alexander's own decadrachms, minted at Babylon, which depict him in military dress, crowned by victory and grasping a thunderbolt in his right hand.[73] At court he was treated with all the reverence due to a god, and Arrian somewhat ironically describes the Greek embassies at Babylon as for all the world like sacred envoys (*theoroi*). They may not have offered actual worship, but they treated Alexander with the awe they would a god.[74]

After the death of Hephaestion in late 324 Alexander became more explicit in his demands. He established a hero cult for his friend and had it ratified by an oracle from Siwah. It became ritual at court and was instituted elsewhere by men like Cleomenes of Naucratis, who dedicated a *heröon* in Alexandria. There seems to have been an element of compulsion. Hyperides complained that the Greeks had to countenance the scrupulous maintenance of temples and altars to living men and were forced to honour their servants as heroes. This can only refer to the worship of Alexander as a god and the simultaneous hero cult of Hephaestion.[75] Only the latter institution is compulsory. Hyperides implies that the cult of Alexander was practised to the detriment of traditional deities but was not formally prescribed.

The question of the worship of Alexander was certainly raised at Athens before the trial of Demosthenes (see above, p.858), but it remains disputed whether there was an explicit demand.[76] At the very least it was notorious that the king greatly desired to be treated as a god and, when he sent instructions (or a request) to institute the hero cult for

[73] Cf. Bellinger 1963 (B 187) 27; Kaiser 1962 (B 199); Goukowsky 1978–81 (B 45) I 61–4.
[74] Arr. VII.23.2. Cf. Badian 1981 (D 141) 55–9; *contra*, Fredricksmeyer 1979 (D 177); Goukowsky 1978–81 (B 45) I 185.
[75] Hyper. *Epitaph.* 21; cf. Bickerman 1963 (D 149); Habicht 1970 (A 26) 29–32, 219.
[76] The supposed demand was long a dogma of scholarship, particularly in Germany (cf. Wilcken 1970 (A 64) II 391; Schachermeyr 1973 (D 231) 525–31) and some bizarre political consequences have been adduced (cf. Tarn 1948 (D 239) I 370–3, following a suggestion of Eduard Meyer). For a more sceptical approach see Balsdon 1950 (D 144) 383–8; Badian 1981 (D 141) 54–8.

Hephaestion, he might have suggested the recognition of his own divinity. The issue was debated, perhaps inconclusively, in both Athens and Sparta. At Athens Demades moved a decree proposing divine honours in some form: a statue to 'king Alexander the invincible god' was mooted (Hyper. *Dem.* col.33). Demosthenes was grudgingly prepared to accept divine sonship, whereas Lycurgus expressed abhorrence at the very idea of worship ([Plut.] *Mor.* 842D). Some honours may have been voted, in the hope of winning some advantage in the Samian dispute (see above, p.856), but they certainly lapsed at the beginning of the Lamian War, when Demades was heavily fined and suffered *atimia*.

Other cities which were more friendly or pliable voted cults with alacrity. The process can be traced in Asia Minor and the islands, where several cults are attested. In the first generation after his death Alexander was honoured with a festival at Thasos, and Erythrae had a priesthood for 'king Alexander' by 270 B.C. The Ionian *koinon* held a regular annual festival which provided the model for honours to Antiochus I (*OGIS* 222) and was still observed in Strabo's day (Strabo XIV.1.31). These honours are most likely to have originated in Alexander's lifetime, while he was exercising power, but they cannot be precisely dated.[77] There is no record of any divine honour in the early years of the reign, and the oracles sent to Memphis in 331 are the first attested recognition of the king's godhead. It is likely enough that the later heroization of Hephaestion evoked the same type of proposals as are attested in Athens.

In 323 the god died. The fiction soon developed that he had been translated to heaven like Heracles (*OGIS* 4, line 5; Diod. XVIII.56.2). His progress was complete. Beginning as a Heraclid and descendant of heroes, he had became first a son of Zeus and finally a god manifest on earth. The precedent for the worship of a living man was firmly established, a precedent which his Successors were irresistibly driven to emulate.

[77] Cf. Habicht 1970 (A 26) 17–25; Badian 1981 (D 141), 59–63.

CHAPTER 18

EPILOGUE

SIMON HORNBLOWER

In the three quarters of a century between Lysander of Sparta and Alexander the Great – the period covered by this volume – the classical world had expanded and changed spectacularly, above all by the overthrow of the Achaemenid empire. The aim of this Epilogue is to put that, the biggest single change, into historical context.

Much of the present volume may seem to have been, in one way or another, preparation for Alexander the Great, who has himself filled the two preceding chapters. Philip, the subject of chs. 14 and 15, most obviously invites comparison with Alexander. Alexander's army was Philip's and so were its commanders, that is, Alexander's initial advisers. The deification of Alexander had a precedent in Philip's, and Philip the city-founder was, together with the Elder Cyrus, Alexander's likely model. Most important of all, it is arguable that Alexander conquered the Persian empire only because Philip had planned its conquest. (See further below.)

And behind Philip stand some autocrats of an earlier, but still fourth-century, generation. Dionysius I of Syracuse is the prototype (see ch. 5 above). He was a forceful military despot who concentrated power in his own hands and was effective simply by knowing where he was going – the secret of political power and success in all periods and under all forms of government. Both Philip and Dionysius had features in common with yet other fourth-century rulers such as the Bosporan kings of south Russia (ch. 9f) or Mausolus the semi-autonomous satrap of Caria (ch. 8a). For instance, they all had to balance their roles as ruler of freedom-conscious Greeks and as more absolute master of non-Greeks. One way of doing this was to adopt different titulature to express one's relationship to those different groups.

Other aspects of Alexander's career are prefigured in the traditional Greek polis. For instance, there are traces of personality cult – the issue which brought Alexander into collision with his more conservative-minded entourage – even in (among other places) that most traditional of all Greek states, Sparta.[1] (See p. 29 for the honours to Lysander.)

So there are ways in which Alexander is a kind of climax to, or culmination of, already discernible tendencies. This creates a danger that Alexander's success may seem more inevitable than it really was, a danger compounded by our calling him 'the Great'. It is easy to slide from calling a person 'great' to thinking of that person as somehow born with a 'mission'. The slide is particularly noticeable in the nineteenth- and twentieth-century German reception of Alexander.[2] It is therefore important to remember that to his contemporaries Alexander was Alexander the Macedonian, or just Alexander, not Alexander the Great. That is a title first explicitly attested for him in Roman sources, though there is indirect evidence that it was current among hellenistic Greeks.[3]

The title 'Alexander the Great' perhaps carries, with its strong individualist emphasis, the further suggestion that Alexander was impelled chiefly by the power of his own personal motivation; in fact that he was, in psychological language, inner-directed rather than other-directed. As for Alexander's own psychology, the state and character of the literary tradition means that we are almost wholly in the dark, apart from obvious points such as, that he imitated the heroes of Homeric epic. But this theme may have been exaggerated by ancient writers who were themselves imitating Homer. So it is not safe to impute to him even this rather special brand of 'other-directedness'.

This Epilogue will attempt, briefly and speculatively, to go a little further into the motives for Alexander's expedition. Why did he act as he did? Why did Macedon invade Asia?

If we leave aside the unanswerable question of Alexander's personal psychology, there are three ways of looking at the problem. Each takes us progressively further back in time from Alexander himself, and they

---

[1] For Lysander see Badian 1981 (D 141) 37–8; honours perhaps only posthumous. For Spartan kings see the discussion between Parker 1988 (H 92) and Cartledge 1988 (H 11). For Dion of Syracuse see Habicht 1970 (A 26) 8–10. There are other interesting honours to individuals, see Lintott 1982 (C 43) 353, cf. 233f. and de Ste Croix 1981 (C 70) 297 for Euphron of Sicyon (posthumous heroic honours). For Philip, Diod. xvi.92 and now *SEG* xxviii 658 (possibly posthumous). For the fifth century note Pouilloux 1954 (C 376) 63ff: Theagenes of Thasos, and see Thuc. v.11 (Hagnon at Amphipolis). For Mausolus see *CR* 1982, 110. For Alexander's difficulties with his entourage on this issue see above all Plut. *Alex.* 47 and above, p.873.   [2] Wailes-Fairbairn 1990 (D 241A).

[3] Pfister 1964 (D 222) 37–79. The so-called Heidelberg Epitome. *FGrHist* 155, calls Alexander 'the Great', and would be the first source to do so if we could be sure that it was early hellenistic (it cannot be *very* early hellenistic because it mentions events of 301 B.C.). However, Demetrius the Besieger is called 'the Great' on an inscription of about 303/2, perhaps with Alexander in mind (*ISE* no.7). The Seleucid king Antiochus III was called 'the Great' in his own lifetime, at the end of the third century B.C, see Robert 1983 (F 703) 164; and it is tempting to think that this was in direct imitation of Alexander. (Antiochus took the title after his Alexander-like expedition to the 'upper' or eastern satrapies.)

can thus be called the short-term, the medium-term and the long-term explanation. Taken together, they may help to place Alexander's achievements in their context within fourth-century (and earlier) Greek and Macedonian history.

First, Philip's inheritance. It was public knowledge that Philip had planned a Persian expedition; indeed the first steps had been taken by 336,[4] and for Alexander to have aborted the expedition at that point would itself have required a definite decision. (If he wanted to avoid the particular 'other-directedness' of completing the project of a father with whom his relations were equivocal, he could always have gone west against Italy, rather than east. About now, energetic Spartan and Epirote leaders did just that.) But Alexander went ahead with the Persian project. How far Philip himself was influenced by Greek theorists telling him that Persia was ripe for Greek takeover – my guess would be, not very far – or by the partial success of Xenophon and the Ten Thousand, we have no way of knowing. They surely counted even less with Alexander, by whose time the plan already had its own momentum.

What happened, in strategic detail, after the initial spear-throw by which Alexander claimed Asia as conquered territory (Diod. XVII.17) was with one important exception merely dictated by the moves of the Persian enemy. Alexander's campaigns up to Gaugamela resemble a game of chess, with the opposing king as the prize whose few and majestic movements dictate the lines of penetration and pursuit. The important exception, determined by basically economic considerations as far as we can see, was the gamble represented by Alexander's decision to swing temporarily west not east after the Battle of Issus. His aim (religious hankerings apart) was presumably to annex the resources of Egypt, so economically valuable to Persia and individual Persians. After Gaugamela and the capture of the king, phases like the guerrilla warfare against Spitamenes were simply imposed on Alexander, the new Great King of Persia. By the Indian phase, it might seem that he was free to do what he liked, but by that time the army was already getting mutinous and he was ultimately 'directed' by external reverse propulsion. Nevertheless, however far Alexander's territorial ambitions and his self-image developed in the decade since that first Homeric spear-throw, it must not be forgotten that Philip's precedent and planning had given the original impulse. This, then, is the short-term explanation for Alexander's invasion of the Persian empire.

The second or medium-term explanation is in terms of revenge for Persian aggression and impiety in 480 B.C. Dismissed as a mere pretext by Polybius (III.6.13), this motif is certainly all but invisible in the pre-350 writings of Isocrates where we would expect it. Modern historians have

[4] Ruzicka 1985 (D 116A).

therefore been tempted to wonder[5] whether it was the amphictyonic precedent, i.e. the Sacred War brought to an end in 346, which first put the idea of another, bigger Sacred War into the mind of Philip, or of his historian Callisthenes. This is an attractive idea, and may be right – up to a point. But on the other hand, the Persian Wars were never out of Greek thoughts at any time from 479 B.C. to the Roman period. Plataea is the paradigm case. The Plataeans, said an early hellenistic traveller, have nothing to say for themselves except that they are colonists of the Athenians (wrong, as it happens) and that the battle between the Greeks and Persians took place on their territory: Austin no. 83. Thucydides plays down this general theme, as he plays down so much else that is backward-looking or sentimental, but even he attests a cult of Zeus the Liberator at Plataea (II.71.2) and some kind of hostel for pilgrims, also at Plataea (III.68.3). Philip's offer to rebuild Plataea, destroyed by Thebes in 373, and Alexander's actual rebuilding of it (Paus. IV.27 etc.; Arr. *Anab.* I 9.10) thus acquire special point, on the eve of the new crusade.

So too, Philip's choice of Corinth as the seat of his new league in 337 can be explained not merely by the city's central position and obvious strategic importance, or even by the precedent of the 'Council in Corinth' which masterminded the Corinthian War in 395 B.C. (Diod. XIV.82.2), but by Corinth's role in the most recent and spectacular Greek repulse of a barbarian power: Timoleon's defeat of Carthage at the river Crimisus (above, p.713). It is true that there is no direct ancient evidence for this aspect to the League of Corinth, but the suggestion is ingenious and plausible.[6] So what we have here is the motif of a crusade against the barbarian. And we should perhaps place in this category such texts as the Themistocles decree (M–L no.23 = Fornara 55), which rallies Greeks against barbarians and was probably conceived in the age of Philip, whatever view one takes of the authenticity of its precise contents. There are other such texts,[7] all tending to show that the tradition about the Persian Wars still mattered to fourth-century Greeks, whether that tradition was real, invented, or (the best view perhaps) a real tradition subject to accretions and embellishment: there is after all Thucydides' evidence for Plataean cult of some sort.

We noticed above the (false) Plataean claim to be colonists, i.e. kin, of the Athenians. Kinship of this sort was a powerful concept in the fourth-century world, and is related to, though distinct from, the Greek–barbarian opposition. Alexander, says Arrian, sought to rival Perseus and Heracles, because he was descended from both (*Anab.* III.3.2). Now one Greek view held that Perseus was the founder of Persia as well as of

[5] Momigliano 1934 (D 106) 165.   [6] Lane Fox 1973 (D 208) 93.

[7] Habicht 1961 (B 52). Note also Grafton 1991 (B 46A) for the fourth century as the beginning of the heyday of literary forgery.

Argos from whose royal line Alexander claimed descent (Hdt. VII.150, actually attributing this view to the Persians!). So one reason for Alexander's stress on Perseus is the idea of kinship between Persia and Macedon, kinship which would legitimate his rule over Persia.[8] Kinship as a justification for empire was hardly a new idea (see Thuc.1.95.1), but kinship or *syngeneia* becomes a leading theme in Hellenistic history and epigraphy. (The classic text is now *SEG* XXXVIII 1476: Cytenians and Lycian Xanthus.) Colonial ties, especially with Macedon's ultimate 'metropolis' Argos, were exaggerated or invented in profusion: see for instance Tod no. 194 where Nicocreon of Cyprus claims Argive origins, or *SEG* XXXIV 282, making the same claim for Pamphylian Aspendus. Archaic Argos was not a colonizing power, and these claims are frankly usurped, or at best derived from vague traditions about prehistoric migrations from the Argolid. But the fourth-century (and later) Greek fondness for exploiting real or fictitious genealogies and colonial relationships[9] helps us to understand certain aspects of Alexander's expedition: above all, the tenderness with which he treated Ionian cities, especially those which had been prominent in the Ionian Revolt of 499. The war was, in fact, a war to liberate Greek kinsmen in Persian bondage.

We can conclude that Polybius may have dismissed the revenge-against-the-barbarian motif a touch too easily.

A third, even more long-term approach is possible, but it needs a word of general introduction, because it involves the abandonment of the notion of the city state or polis as the essential up-to-date unit of organization. An earlier chapter of the present volume (ch. 11) examined the alternatives to the polis. We saw there that one of those alternatives was the tribe or *ethnos*; work on early Greek ethnicity has tended to challenge the assumption that there was anything intrinsically backward about the *ethnos*.[10] Certainly the great hellenistic groupings with which the Romans would later have to deal, the Achaeans, Aetolians and so forth, emerged from *ethnos* not polis structures. It might then be argued that if there was actually more potential energy in the *ethnos* than the polis, it is not surprising that Alexander's background was closer to the former than to the latter. This is not to advocate a return to the position of J.G. Droysen, for whom the polis was obsolete[11] and Alexander did the world a favour by superseding Athens at the level of power politics (nor should we follow Droysen in his fantastic idea that Alexander's 'mission' was to be a kind of fully militarized John the Baptist, preparing the way for Christianity).

[8] Bosworth 1980 (B 14) 270.
[9] Bickerman 1952 (A 8); Robert 1983 (F 703) 162–3; 1987 (F 712) 477–90.
[10] Morgan 1991 (A 44) 131–63, mostly about Achaea; cf. also Runciman 1990 (C 62) at 353.
[11] Wailes-Fairbairn 1990 (D241A). The polis not 'dead': see above, pp. 563, 589.

So, having accustomed ourselves to the idea that Macedon may have possessed greater vigour precisely because it was organized on a non-polis footing, we may turn to our third line of explanation, which runs like this. The war against Persia was (it could be held by an ethnologist impatient with literary themes like revenge and kinship or inherited wars) nothing more than a repetition of the response of the inhabitants of Macedon, in about 800 B.C, to a sudden surge in human resources comparable to that experienced by fourth-century Macedon. The *ethnos* constituted by the Phrygian occupants of Macedonia had spilled over into Anatolia at an earlier phase of Balkan history – half a millennium, in fact, before Philip and Alexander. These groups of migrants founded the Phrygian kingdom of Asia Minor centred on Gordium[12] (Bryges is the Macedonian equivalent of Phryges).

Perhaps these migrants, the approximate contemporaries of Homer, claimed Asia and its riches as 'spear-won territory' – and spear-won booty. Alexander's campaigns have been called 'two things rolled into one, a booty raid on an epic scale and the permanent conquest of vast tracts of territory'.[13] The booty aspect is an enduring feature of ancient warfare (it is candidly given by Thucydides, VI.24, as one major motive for the Sicilian expedition) and reminds us that there were more prosaic and ordinary aspects of Alexander's motivation.

So we might wish to minimize the global significance of the individual Alexander. His contemporaries did not agree: Ptolemy of Egypt hijacked Alexander's body and its tremendous funeral-carriage (one of the wonders of the hellenistic age. It was described in a famous passage by Hieronymus of Cardia, the Thucydides of the early hellenistic age.[14] Diod. XVIII.26–8.) The body itself was placed in a glass[15] coffin (Strabo XVII.1.8), providing a kind of permanent photo-opportunity for the young man who had so skilfully silenced the grumblings of his army by his theatrical disappearances and reappearances. Like many other of Alexander's successors Ptolemy put the effigy of his head on his coins.[16] History and historiography recovered swiftly from the end of the Athenian empire, the event which closed our volume v²; the effect of Alexander's equally dramatic demise[17] would be less easy for the world to digest.

---

12 For all this see Hammond 1972 (D 46) 410–14.
13 Austin 1986 (I 4) 454; see also 464 on the special bellicosity of *young* kings, who needed to prove themselves; Alexander himself is an obvious case in point.
14 J. Hornblower 1981 (B 60).
15 Unless the word ὑαλίνη here means (translucent?) alabaster; Fraser 1972 (A 21) 15 and n.79.
16 Smith 1988 (J 46) 17, and (for portrait coins) 58ff.
17 O'Brien 1992 (D 217A) now argues that alcohol abuse was the key to Alexander's premature death, and to much of his behaviour in his lifetime.

CHRONOLOGICAL TABLE

Persian empire	Greece and the Aegean
405–4 Death of Darius II; accession of Artaxerxes II	
c. 404–3 Revolt of Egypt under Amyrtaeus II	404 (spring) Fall of Athens
	(summer) Lysander captures Samos
	Establishment of Thirty at Athens
	Death of Alcibiades
	403 (spring) Fall of Thirty
	(summer) Agis intervenes in Athens
	(September) Athenian exiles return; democracy restored at Athens
	Ephors abolish Lysander's decarchies
	402–400 Spartan war against Elis
401 (spring) Cyrus collects his army at Sardis	401 Independent state at Eleusis suppressed
(summer) Battle of Cunaxa	
400 Sparta declares war on Tissaphernes	400 (early summer) Death of Agis
	Succession of Agesilaus
c. 398–7 Nepherites king of Egypt	399 Thibron's campaign in Asia
	Conspiracy of Cinadon
	399–7 Dercyllidas' campaigns in Asia
	397 Conon appointed to command Persian fleet
396 First campaign of Agesilaus in Phrygia etc.	396 (autumn) Mission of Timocrates to Greece
Nepherites assists Sparta	
395 Agesilaus attacks Sardis and Phrygia	395 (summer) War between Phocis and Locris, Theban invasion of Phocis, outbreak of Corinthian war, Battle of Haliartus
	Work begun on Long Walls
	395/4 (winter) Recall of Agesilaus from Asia
394 Agesilaus recalled to Greece	394 (spring) Battle of Nemea (Corinth)
	(August) Battle of Cnidus; Battle of Coronea
	(summer) Conon and Pharnabazus operate in the Aegean
393 (winter) Embassy of Antalcidas to Tiribazus	393 (spring) Conon and Pharnabazus to Greece
	(summer) Conon in Athens, assists in the rebuilding of the Long Walls
	392 (spring) Revolution at Corinth; union of Corinth and Argos
	(summer) negotiations between Antalcidas and Tiribazus
	Spartan capture of Lechaeum
	Arrest of Conon
c. 392–1 Achoris king of Egypt	392/1 (winter) Peace conference at Sparta
	Allied recovery of Lechaeum

Sicily and South Italy	Art, philosophy, literature
	c. 425–395 Zeuxis painter
409 Carthage invades Sicily; fall of Selinus and Himera	
407 Hermocrates returns to Sicily	
406 Second Carthaginian invasion; fall of Acragas	
405 Dionysius elected *strategos autokrator* Fall of Gela Treaty between Carthage and Syracuse Dionysius tyrant	405 Aristophanes, *Frogs*
	401 Posthumous production of Sophocles, *Oedipus at Colonus*
	400 Andocides, *De Mysteriis*
	399 Death of Socrates
397 War declared on Carthage Siege of Motya	
396 Himilco attacks Syracuse Plague in Carthaginian army Suicide of Himilco	*c.* 396 Antisthenes opens school
	394–3 Dexileos gravestone, Athens
393 Dionysius honoured at Athens	
c. 392 Mago's campaign Renewal of peace	392 Aristophanes, *Ecclesiazusae*

Persian empire	Greece and the Aegean
391 Evagoras of Cyprus revolts from Persia in alliance with Athens and Achoris	391 (spring) Spartan invasion of the Argolid and recapture of Lechaeum
	(summer) Tiribazus replaced by Struthas, expedition of Thibron
	(autumn) Expedition of Ecdicus
	390 (spring) Expedition of Teleutias to Rhodes
	(summer) Spartan capture of Piraeum; defeat of Spartan *mora* by Iphicrates Thrasybulus active in Thrace, Hellespont
	389 (summer) Spartan invasion of Acarnania Death of Thrasybulus; fighting between Iphicrates and Anaxibius Fighting on Aegina
	388 (spring) Spartan invasion of the Argolid Reappointment of Tiribazus
	(summer) Mission of Chabrias to Cyprus Second mission of Antalcidas to Persia
	387 (spring) Teleutias' raid on the Piraeus
	(summer) Antalcidas operating in the Hellespont
	(autumn) Peace negotiations at Sardis
386 The King's Peace	386 (spring) King's Peace concluded at Sparta
	?386 (summer) Refoundation of Plataea Alliance between Sparta and Thebes
c. 385 Evagoras in Tyre	385 (summer) Spartan attack on Mantinea
385–3 Artaxerxes at war with Egypt	385/4 (winter) Dioecism of Mantinea
	384 Return of exiles to Phlius Alliance between Athens and Chios
c. 382 Unsuccessful attack on Cyprus by Tiribazus	382 (summer) First Spartan expedition to Olynthus Seizure of Cadmea
	(autumn) Teleutias to Olynthus
c. 381 Evagoras' fleet defeated by Persians	381 (spring) Death of Teleutias; Agesipolis to Olynthus
	(summer) Death of Agesipolis Siege of Phlius begins
	(?autumn) Polybiades to Olynthus
c. 380 Peace made between Evagoras and Persians	?380 Spartan alliance with Glos
	379 (summer) Surrender of Phlius Surrender of Olynthus
379–8 Death of Achoris. Accession of Nectanebo I	379/8 (winter) Liberation of Cadmea Cleombrotus invades Boeotia
	378 (spring) Foundation of Second Athenian League Raid of Sphodrias Athens declares war on Sparta Admission of Thebes to league
	(summer) Agesilaus invades Boeotia
	377 (spring) Decree of Aristoteles Agesilaus invades Boeotia, falls ill
	(summer) Chabrias in Euboea and Cyclades

Sicily and South Italy	Art, philosophy, literature
391 Dionysius invades Italy Alliance between Dionysius and Luca- nians	
390 Lucanians attack Thurii Peace between Italiotes and Lucanians Dismissal of Leptines Battle of the Eleporus Destruction of Caulonia	*c.* 390 Isocrates opens school (*Against the Sophists*) Temple of Apollo, Bassae 'Nereid Monument', Xanthus
388/7 Siege of Rhegium	388 Aristophanes, *Plutus* Lysias, *Olympiacus* (but see p. 139 n.82) Plato's first visit to Sicily
387 Dionysius sends help to Sparta	*c.* 387 Plato starts Academy
?386 Crisis at Syracusan court	386 'Old tragedy' introduced at Dionysia
?385 Dionysius' Adriatic ventures	
?383 Renewal of war with Carthage	384 Birth of Aristotle and Demosthenes
	380 Isocrates, *Panegyricus* 380–60 Temple of Asclepius, Epidaurus after 377 Plato, *Republic*
?378 Peace with Carthage	

Persian empire	Greece and the Aegean
	376 (spring) Cleombrotus fails to invade Boeotia
	(September) Battle of Naxos
	375 (summer) Battle of Tegyra
	Chabrias in Thrace and Hellespont
	periplous of Timotheus; Battle of Alyzia
	Theban invasion of Phocis; Cleombrotus to Phocis
	King's Peace renewed at Sparta
	375–4 (autumn-summer) Spartan expeditions to Zakynthos and Corcyra
374–3 Iphicrates helps Pharnabazus in unsuccessful expedition in Egypt	?374 (winter) Ctesicles to Zakynthos
Death of Evagoras	373 (summer) Timotheus fails to assist Corcyra
	Thebes recovers Tanagra, Thespiae, destroys Plataea
	(autumn) Trial of Timotheus
	Mnasippus in control of Corcyra
	Ctesicles to Corcyra
	372 (spring) Death of Mnasippus
	Iphicrates to Corcyra
	?372 or 371 Destruction of Thespiae
	371 (spring) Theban invasion of Phocis, Cleombrotus to Phocis
	(summer) King's Peace renewed at Sparta
	Battle of Leuctra
	King's Peace renewed at Athens
	370 Jason of Pherae murdered
	Mantinea refounded
	Formation of Arcadian League
	Alliance of Arcadia, Argos, Elis and Boeotia
	370–369 (winter) Epaminondas' first Peloponnesian campaign, invasion of Laconia, liberation of Messenia and foundation of Messene
	369 Alliance of Athens and Sparta
	Epaminondas' second Peloponnesian campaign
	Pelopidas' first campaign in Thessaly and Macedon
	368 Arcadia and Argos help Euphron to power in Sicyon
	Pelopidas in Thessaly and Macedon: Pelopidas imprisoned by Alexander of Pherae
	Spartan victory over Arcadia, Argos and Messenia at the Tearless Battle
	Foundation of Megalopolis
	367 (spring) Liberation of Pelopidas
	Embassies of Pelopidas and others to the Persian King

Sicily and South Italy	Art, philosophy, literature
	375–60 Cephisodotus sculptor, *Eirene and Ploutos*
	373 Isocrates, *Plataicus*
369 Dionysius sends help to Sparta	
368 Further help to Sparta Renewal of war with Carthage Dionysius sends embassy to Athens	
367 (spring) Death of Dionysius I Dionysius II succeeds	367 Aristotle joins the Academy 367–6 Plato in Sicily; Eudoxus temporary scholarch of Academy

Persian empire	Greece and the Aegean
	366 (spring) Congress at Thebes rejects peace terms proposed by Thebes and approved by the Persian King
	Epaminondas' second Peloponnesian campaign, alliance Thebes–Achaea, overthrow and restoration of Achaean oligarchies
	Timotheus sent by Athens to help Ariobarzanes, siege of Samos (366–5)
	Deposition, return, and murder of Euphron of Sicyon
	(summer) Oropus lost by Athens to Thebes
	Alliance Arcadia–Athens
c. 365 Ariobarzanes, followed by other satraps (Asia Minor, Cilicia, Phoenicia), revolts from Persia	365 (spring) Thebes, Corinth and other states make peace
	Elis–Arcadia war begins
	364 (or 365) Alliance of Elis, Achaea and Sparta
	364 Epaminondas' naval expedition in Aegean
	Pelopidas' campaign in Thessaly and death, Theban defeat of Alexander of Pherae, alliance of Thebes and Alexander of Pherae
	364 (or 363) Beginning of dissension in Arcadian League over use of Olympic funds
	(?)363 (autumn) Peace Arcadia–Elis
	362 Epaminondas' fourth Peloponnesian campaign, Battle of Mantinea and death of Epaminondas
	362/1 Common peace among states of mainland Greece, except Sparta
	Alliance of Athens, Arcadia (Mantinea and associated states), Achaea, Elis and Phlius
361–0 Death of Nectanebo I. Accession of Tachos	361 Expedition of Pammenes to Megalopolis
	361/70 Alliance of Athens and the Thessalian League (opposed to Alexander of Pherae)
c. 360 Death of Ariobarzanes and Datames Persian authority restored in Asia Minor	360 Death of Agesilaus
	Death of Perdiccas III of Macedon; accession of Philip II
	Philip's first diplomacy with northern powers
359–8 Accession of Nectanebo II in Egypt Death of Artaxerxes II; accession of Artaxerxes III	359 Philip defeats Argaeus
	Athenian–Macedonian alliance
	Philip defeats Paeonians
	358 Philip defeats Bardylis
	Final annexation of Upper Macedonia begins
	? Philip aids Aleuadae of Larissa against Pherae

Sicily and South Italy	Art, philosophy, literature
366 Plato visits Syracuse Peace between Syracuse and Carthage Exile of Dion	366 Isocrates, *Archidamus*
365 Dionysius II assists Sparta	
	c. 364 Lysippus sculptor, statues of Thebans
361–0 Plato revisits Syracuse	361–60 Plato in Sicily; Heraclides temporary scholarch of Academy
	358–30 Theatre of Epidaurus built

Persian empire	Greece and the Aegean
	357 Athens expels Thebans from Euboea
	Macedonian–Epirote alliance; Philip marries Olympias
	Outbreak of Social War
	Philip takes Amphipolis; Athens declares war
c. 356 Revolt of Artabazus	356 Philip takes Pydna
	First Phocian events leading to Sacred War
	Thracian kings and Athens in coalition against Macedonia
	(*c.* July 20) Birth of Alexander
	Philip takes Potidaea; Parmenion defeats Grabus
	Athens defeated in battle off Embata
	355 Social War ends
	Amphictyony declares sacred war on Phocis
	Philip invests Methone
?354 ?First invasion of Egypt by Artaxerxes	354 Methone falls to Philip
	Battle of Neon; Philomelus killed and succeeded by Onomarchus
353 Artabazus helped by Thebes	353 ? Macedonian–Boeotian alliance
	Philip in Thrace
	Military successes of Onomarchus
	Philip returns from Thrace, evading Chares off Neapolis
	Chares captures Sestus
	Athens sends cleruchs to Chersonese
	Olynthus declares friendship for Athens and requests alliance
	352 Philip defeats Onomarchus at Crocus Field
	Philip elected archon of Thessalian League
	Philip advances to Thermopylae, finds it guarded and retires
	(November) Philip at Heraeum in Thrace, in alliance with Byzantium, Perinthus and Amadocus against Cersobleptes
c. 351 Second invasion of Egypt by Artaxerxes	351 Philip successful in Thrace despite illness
	Philip's warning to Olynthians
	351/0 (winter) Demosthenes *First Philippic* (Dem. IV)
	350 Philip in Epirus

Sicily and South Italy	Art, philosophy, literature
357 Return of Dion to Syracuse	
356 Dion besieges Ortygia Arrival of Nypsius at Syracuse	
355 Fall of Ortygia	355 Isocrates, *On the Peace* Xenophon, *Revenues* 355–35 'Kerch style' of Athenian red-figure
354 Dion murdered Callippus tyrant at Syracuse	354 Isocrates, *Areopagiticus* Isocrates, *Antidosis*
352 Hipparinus succeeds Callippus	352–1 Mausoleum, Halicarnassus
351 Nysaeus tyrant at Syracuse	
	350–30 'Darius painter', Apulian red-figure 350–20 Apelles painter *c.* 350 Praxiteles sculptor, *Aphrodite* at Cnidus, *Apollo Sauroctonus* *Demeter* at Cnidus

Persian empire	Greece and the Aegean
	349 (late summer) Macedonian campaign in Chalcidice begins
	Demosthenes *Olynthiacs* (Dem. I–III)
	? Return of tyrant family to Pherae
	First Athenian aid to Olynthus, under Chares
	Philip re-expels tyrants of Pherae
	348 Rising in Euboea against Plutarch; Athenian intervention
	(?September) Olynthus falls to Philip
	Eubulus' decree seeking general alliance against Macedon
	347 Phalaecus removed from command in Phocis
	Demosthenes and Philocrates enter Council of Five Hundred
	Athens co-operates with Cersebloptes in setting up Thracian fortresses
	Small Macedonian force in central Greece
	Phocis offers Thermopylae to Athens and Sparta
	346 (January) Athenian decree inviting Hellenes to join in war or peace
	Phalaecus recovers Phocian command
	(February) First Athenian embassy travels to Pella
	(March) First embassy returns to Athens
	Philip's Thracian campaign begins
	(April) Athenian Assembly votes for peace and alliance with Philip (18–19 Elaphebolion)
	Surrender of Cersobleptes to Philip (23 Elaphebolion)
	Athens and allies swear to alliance (24 Elaphebolion)
	(May) Second Athenian embassy leaves for Macedonia (3 Munychion)
	(June) Philip returns from Thrace to Pella (*c.* 22 Thargelion)
	(July) Philip at Thermopylae
	Second embassy returns to Athens (13 Scirophorion)
	Athenian Assembly confirms treaty (16 Scirophorion)
	Third embassy leaves for Thermopylae (*c.* 17 Scirophorion)
	Timarchus and Demosthenes impeach Aeschines
	Philip's request for Athenian hoplites rejected

The fullness in detail in the 340s is a function of the abnormal character of the evidence.

Sicily and South Italy	Art, philosophy, literature
	347 Death of Plato; Speusippus head of the Academy
346 Dionysius expels Nysaeus and recovers Syracuse	346 Isocrates, *Philippus*
	346–25 Rebuilding of Temple of Apollo, Delphi

Persian empire	Greece and the Aegean
	Phocians surrender to Philip (23 Scirophorion)
	Special Amphictyonic meeting
	(September) Philip presides over Pythian festival
	Amphictyons demand Athenian assent; Demosthenes *On the Peace* (Dem. v)
	Autumn *pylaia* at Delphi
	Aeschines counter-prosecutes Timarchus (Aesch. I)
345 Revolt of Tennes of Sidon	345 Philip moves population-groups in Macedonia
	Philip campaigns in Illyria against Pleuratus
	Messene and Megalopolis refused Amphictyonic membership
344 Capture of Sidon	344 Philip puts down revolts in Thessaly, garrisons Pherae, and reconstructs tetrarchic national government
Persian appeal to Greece for help	Demosthenes travels in Peloponnese
	Python's embassy to Athens
	Demosthenes *Second Philippic* (Dem. vi)
	Athens rebuffs Persian embassy
343–2 Persian reconquest of Egypt	343 Thebes presses for Phocian repayments to begin
	Philocrates impeached and flees from Athens
	Stasis in Elis and Megara
	Pro-Macedonians dominant in Eretria and Oreus
	Trial of Aeschines (Dem. xix, Aesch. ii)
	Philip makes final offer to Athens (including Halonnesus) and leaves for Epirus
342 (winter) Mentor captures Hermias	342 Arybbas of Epirus exiled; Alexander becomes king
	Hegesippus *On Halonnesus* ([Dem.] vii)
	Athens sends troops to Acarnania and seeks alliances
	(*c.* June) Philip's final Thracian campaign begins
	Macedonian interventions in Euboea
	Violence between Cardians and Athenian cleruchs
	341 Philip sends troops to Cardia
	Diopeithes takes two towns in Thrace, and tortures Philip's envoy
	Alliance of Athens and Chalcis
	Demosthenes *On the Chersonese* (Dem. viii)

Sicily and South Italy	Art, philosophy, literature
345 Syracusan appeal to Corinth Hicetas intrigues with Carthaginians	345–30 Scopas sculptor Temple of Athena Alea, Tegea
344 Timoleon sails for Sicily Battle of Adranum Surrender of Dionysius II to Timoleon	
343 Mago in Sicily Timoleon settles affairs at Syracuse	343 Aristotle becomes tutor to Alexander
342 Timoleon's raid on the Carthaginian province Archidamus of Sparta helps Tarentines against Lucanians and Messapians	342 Isocrates, *First Letter to Philip* 342–1 Birth of Menander and Epicurus
341 Arrival of Carthaginian force in Sicily Battle of the Crimisus	

Persian empire	Greece and the Aegean
	Demosthenes *Third* and *Fourth Philippics* (Dem. ix–x)
	Philip defeats and deposes Teres and Cersobleptes
	Athens captures Oreus and Eretria
	Philip campaigns on Black Sea coast
	Demosthenes and Callias canvass support in west Greece and Peloponnese
	340 Demosthenes and Callias report massive support; Athens approves Euboean League under hegemony of Chalcis
	Philip attacks Perinthus, which is supported by Persia
	Philip's letter to Athens ([Dem.] xii)
	Philip invests Selymbria and attacks Byzantium
	(autumn) Philip captures corn fleet
	(October) Athens declares war
	Alexander defeats Maedi and founds Alexandropolis
	Chares drives Macedonian fleet into Black Sea
	Phocion arrives at Hellespont
	? Philip's troops rebuffed by Ateas the Scythian
	339 Philip retires from Byzantium and extricates fleet from Black Sea
	Philip's Scythian campaign
	Dispute over Amphissa begins at Delphi
	(*c.* June) Amphictyonic meeting at Thermopylae
	After Triballian defeat Philip returns home wounded
	(autumn) Amphictyons appoint Philip *hegemon* for sacred war against Amphissa
	(November) Philip takes Cytinium and Elatea
	Macedonian and Athenian envoys at Thebes
	Theban–Athenian alliance
	Philip fails in skirmishes on River Cephisus
338 (August) Artaxerxes III murdered; Artaxerxes IV becomes King	338 Philip and Parmenion trick Chares and Proxenus in Gravia Pass
	Parmenion captures Amphissa and Naupactus
	Coalition troops fall back to Chaeronea

Sicily and South Italy	Art, philosophy, literature
339 Execution of Hicetas	339 'Old comedy' introduced at Dionysia Xenocrates succeeds Speusippus as head of the Academy Isocrates, *Panathenaicus*
338 Peace between Timoleon and Carthage Battle of Mandonium; Archidamus killed	338 Isocrates, *Second Letter to Philip* Death of Isocrates

Persian empire	Greece and the Aegean
	(*c.* 22 August) Battle of Chaeronea
	Philip reaches settlements with Athens and Thebes
	Philip in the Peloponnese; further settlements
	337 Common Peace proposed in Corinth
	First meeting of Hellenic League declares war on Persia
	Philip returns to Macedonia
	(autumn) Philip marries Cleopatra
	336 ? Philip's campaign against Pleurias
	Pixodarus seeks alliance with Philip
	(?October) Philip assassinated at Aegae; accession of Alexander
	Alexander elected general of the Greeks
336 (spring) Parmenion in Asia Minor	336–26 Lycurgus in control of Athenian finance
Artaxerxes IV murdered; Darius III becomes King	
	335 Alexander in Thrace and Illyria
	Destruction of Thebes
334 Battle of Granicus	334 Alexander embarks on Persian campaign
Democracies set up in Ionia	
Sieges of Miletus and Halicarnassus	
334–3 Conquest of Lycia, Pamphylia and western Pisidia	
333 Conquest of Cilicia	
Battle of Issus	
332 Siege and capture of Tyre	
Siege and capture of Gaza	
332–1 Alexander's conquest of Egypt	
331 Submission of Cyrene	331 Revolt of Agis
(April) Foundation of Alexandria	Battle of Megalopolis; death of Agis
(1 October) Battle of Gaugamela	
(20 October) Alexander occupies Babylon	
Alexander occupies Susa	
330–29 Alexander winters in Persepolis	
330 Alexander at Ecbatana	330 The *Crown* trial at Athens
Death of Darius	330–26 Corn shortage in Greece
Murders of Philotas and Parmenion	
329 Conquest of Bactria	
328 Conquest of Sogdiana	
Murder of Cleitus	
The Pages' conspiracy; death of Callisthenes	
327 Alexander invades India	
326 Alexander crosses the Indus	326 Death of Lycurgus
Battle of the Hydaspes	
Mutiny at the Beas	
Voyage of Nearchus down the Hydaspes	
Conquest of the Malli	

Sicily and South Italy	Art, philosophy, literature
c. 337 Retirement of Timoleon	
	336 Tomb of Philip II, Vergina
	335 Aristotle settles at Athens
334–1 Alexander of Epirus in South Italy	334 Monument of Lysicrates, Athens
	c. 330 Lysippus sculptor, *Heracles*, *Kairos* Leochares sculptor, *Ganymede*, '*Apollo Belvedere*'
	327 Philemon's first victory

Persian empire	Greece and the Aegean
325 (July) Nearchus reaches Patala Alexander in Gedrosia (October) Nearchus in the Persian Gulf 324 Alexander in Carmania Satraps ordered to dismiss mercenaries (March) Alexander reaches Susa Restoration of Greek exiles Mutiny at Opis Death of Hephaestion 323 Alexander at Babylon (June) Death of Alexander	325–4 Harpalus admitted at Athens and escapes 324 Athens founds colony on Adriatic Exile of Demosthenes 323 Outbreak of Lamian War Alliance of Athens and Aetolia Demosthenes returns to Athens Antipater besieged in Lamia Death of Leosthenes 322 Athenian fleet defeated at Amorgos (August) Battle of Crannon Change of constitution at Athens

Sicily and South Italy	Art, philosophy, literature
c. 325 Exile of Agathocles	
	?324 First production of Menander
c. 322 Agathocles returns to Syracuse	322 Hyperides, *Funeral Oration*
	Death of Aristotle, Demosthenes and Hyperides
	321 Menander's first victory
	c. 320 Lysippus sculptor, *Apoxyomenus*
	End of Athenian red-figure
	317 Sculptured tombs banned at Athens
	c. 300 End of South Italian red-figure

BIBLIOGRAPHY

Abbreviations

AAA	*Athens Annals of Archaeology*
Abh. Ak. Mainz	Abhandlungen der geistes- und sozialwissenschaftlichen Klasse, Akademie der Wissenschaften und der Literatur, Mainz
Abh. Sächs.	Abhandlungen der sächsischen Akademie der Wissenschaften zu Leipzig
Act. Ant. Hung.	*Acta antiqua Academiae scientiarum Hungaricae*
ADFU	Ausgrabungen der Deutschen Forschungsgemeinschaft in Uruk-Warka
AfO	*Archiv für Orientforschung*
Agora	*The Athenian Agora: Results of Excavations*
AHR	*American Historical Review*
AIIN	*Annali: Istituto Italiano di Numismatica*
AION	*Annali dell'Istituto Universitario Orientale di Napoli: archaeologia e storia antica*
AION (Ling)	*Annali dell'Istituto Universitario Orientale di Napoli (sezione linguistica)*
AJA	*American Journal of Archaeology*
AJAH	*American Journal of Ancient History*
AJP	*American Journal of Philology*
AMI	*Archäologische Mitteilungen aus Iran*
Anc. Mac.	*Ancient Macedonia*
AncSoc	*Ancient Society*
AncW	*Ancient World*
ANET	J. B. Pritchard, ed., *Ancient Near Eastern Texts relating to the Old Testament.* 3rd edn. Princeton, 1974
Annales ESC	*Annales, Economies, Sociétés, Civilisations*
Ann. Serv.	*Annales du Service des antiquités de l'Égypte*
ANSMN	*American Numismatic Society: Museum Notes*
ANRW	*Aufstieg und Niedergang der römischen Welt*
Ant. Class.	*Antiquité classique*
Ant. Kunst	*Antike Kunst*
AOR	*Archeologicheskige Otkritya i Razkopki* (Archaeological Discoveries and Excavations)

ARCE	*American Research Center in Egypt*
Arch. Anz.	*Archäologischer Anzeiger*
ArchDelt	Ἀρχαιολογικὸν Δελτίον
ArchEph	Ἀρχαιολογικὴ Ἐφημερίς
Arch. Rep.	*Archaeological Reports*
AS	*Assyriological Studies*
ASAA	*Annuario della Scuola Archaeologica di Atene*
ASNP	*Annali della Scuola Normale Superiore di Pisa, Classe di Lettere e Filosofia*
ATL	B. D. Meritt *et al.*, *The Athenian Tribute Lists* I–IV. Cambridge, MA – Princeton, 1939–53
Atti MSMG	*Atti e Memorie della Società Magna Grecia*
Austin	M. M. Austin, *The Hellenistic World from Alexander to the Roman Conquest: A Selection of Ancient Sources in Translation.* Cambridge, 1981
Bagh. Mitt.	*Baghdader Mitteilungen*
BAR	British Archaeological Reports
BASOR	*Bulletin of the American Schools of Oriental Research*
BCH	*Bulletin de correspondance hellénique*
BE	Babylonian Expedition of the University of Pennsylvania, Series A: Cuneiform Texts
BEFAR	*Bibliothèque des écoles françaises d'Athènes et Rome*
BEFEO	*Bulletin de l'Ecole française de l'extrême orient*
Bi.Ar.	*The Biblical Archaeologist*
BICS	*Bulletin of the Institute of Classical Studies, University of London*
Bi. Or.	*Bibliotheca Orientalis*
BJ	*Bonner Jahrbücher*
BRGK	*Bericht der Römisch-Germanischen Kommission des Deutschen Archäeologischen Instituts, Berlin*
BS	*Balkan Studies*
BSA	*Annual of the British School at Athens*
BSOAS	*Bulletin of the School of Oriental and African Studies*
BT	Babylonian Talmud
Bull. Epigr.	*Bulletin Epigraphique*
Bull. Inst. fr. Caire	*Bulletin de l'institut français d'archéologie orientale, Le Caire*
CAH	*The Cambridge Ancient History*
CEG	P. A. Hansen (ed.) *Carmina Epigraphica Graeca* I. II. Berlin, 1983, 1989
CHIran	*The Cambridge History of Iran*
Chron. d'Eg.	*Chronique d'Egypte*
CIRB	Struve, V. V. *et al. Corpus Inscriptionum Regni Bosporani.* Moscow–Leningrad, 1965
CIS	*Corpus Inscriptionum Semiticarum*
CJ	*Classical Journal*

ClAnt   *Classical Antiquity* (formerly *California Studies in Classical Antiquity*)
Class. et Med.   *Classica et Mediaevalia*
Cl. Phil.   *Classical Philology*
Cowley, *AP*   A. Cowley, *Aramaic Papyri of the Fifth Century* B.C. Oxford, 1923
CQ   *Classical Quarterly*
CR   *Classical Review*
CRAI   *Comptes-rendus de l' Académie des inscriptions et belles lettres*
CSCA   *California Studies in Classical Antiquity*
CW   *Classical Weekly*

DAIR   Deutsches Archäologisches Institut, Rom
DGE   E. Schwyzer (ed.), *Dialectorum Graecorum Exempla Epigraphica Potiora*. Leipzig, 1923
DHA   *Dialogues d'histoire ancienne*
Dial. di Arch.   *Dialoghi di Archeologia*
D–K   H. Diels and W. Kranz, *Die Fragmente der Vorsokratiker*. 6th edn. Berlin, 1951–4

EMC/CV   *Echos du Monde Classique/Classical Views*
Ep. Chron.   Ἠπειρωτικὰ Χρονικά

FGrH   F. Jacoby (ed.), *Fragmente der griechischen Historiker*. Berlin and Leiden, 1923–58
FHG   C. Müller (ed.), *Fragmenta Historicorum Graecorum*, Paris, 1841–70
Fornara   C. W. Fornara (ed.), *Translated Documents, Archaic Times to the End of the Peloponnesian War*. 2nd edn. Cambridge, 1983

GGM   *Geographi Graeci Minores*
GM   *Göttinger Miszellen, Beiträge zur ägyptischen Diskussion*, Göttingen
GNAMP   *Godišnik Narodnija arheologičeski musej*, Plovdiv
Gött.Nachr.   *Göttinger Gelehrte Nachrichten*
G&R   *Greece & Rome*
GRBS   *Greek, Roman and Byzantine Studies*
GSU   *Godišnik na Sofiyskija Universitet*
Gymn.   *Gymnasium*

Harding   P. Harding, *From the Peloponnesian War to the Battle of Ipsus* (Translated Documents of Greece and Rome 2), Cambridge, 1985
Hesp.   *Hesperia*
Hicks and Hill   E.L. Hicks and G.F. Hill (eds.), *A Manual of Greek Historical Inscriptions*. Oxford, 1901
Hist. Fil. Medd.
Dan. Vid.   *Historisk-filologiske Meddelelser udgivnet af det Kongelige Danske*
Selsk.   *Videnskabemes Selskab*

Hist. Zeitschr.	*Historische Zeitschrift*
HSCP	*Harvard Studies in Classical Philology*
IBAI	*Izvestya na Bulgarskiya Archeologicheski Instituta*
ICS	O. Masson, *Les inscriptions chypriotes syllabiques*. Paris, 1961; 2nd edn. 1983
IEJ	*Israel Exploration Journal*
IG	*Inscriptiones Graecae*, Berlin, 1873–
IGCH	M. Thompson, O. Mørkholm and C. M. Kraay, *Inventory of Greek Coin Hoards*. New York, 1973
IMYB	*Izvestya na Muzeite v Yozhna Bulgariya*
INMV	*Izvestija na Narodnija muzej Burgas*
Inscr. Délos	F. Durrbach (ed.), *Inscriptions de Délos*. Paris, 1926–37
IOS	*Israel Oriental Studies*
IOSPE	V. V. Latyshev, *Inscriptiones Orae Septentrionalis Ponti Euxini*. Petropoli, 1885–1916
Ir. Ant.	*Iranica Antiqua*
ISE	L. Moretti, *Iscrizioni storiche ellenistiche*. 2 vols. Florence, 1967–75
Ist. Mitt.	*Istanbuler Mitteilungen, Mitteilungen des Deutschen Archäologischen Instituts, Abteilung Istanbul*
IVAD	*Izvestija na Varnenskoto archeologicesko drazestvo*
JBL	*Journal of Biblical Literature*
JCS	*Journal of Cuneiform Studies*
JDAI	*Jahrbuch des deutschen archäologischen Instituts*
JEA	*Journal of Egyptian Archaeology*
JHS	*Journal of Hellenic Studies*
JNES	*Journal of Near Eastern Studies*
JNG	*Jahrbuch für Numismatik und Geldgeschichte*
JÖAI	*Jahreshefte des Österreichischen archäologischen Instituts, Wien*
JRGZM	*Jahrbuch des Römisch-germanischen Zentralmuseums, Mainz*
JRS	*Journal of Roman Studies*
JSOT	*Journal for the Study of the Old Testament*
JTS	*Journal of Theological Studies*
JWI	*Journal of the Warburg Institute*
KAI	H. Donner and W. Röllig, *Kanaanische und aramäische Inschriften*. 2nd edn. Wiesbaden, 1966–9
KSIA	*Kratkie Soobshcheniya Instituta Arkheologii*
KSIAK	*Kratkie Soobshcheniya Instituta Arkheologii, Kiev*
KSIIMK	*Kratkie Soobshcheniya o Dokladakh i Polevikh Issledovaniakh Instityta Istorii materialnoi Kulturi*
Kuml	Kuml: Årbog for Jysk Arkaeologisk Selskab (Århus)
Kupr. Spoudai	Κυπριακαὶ Σπουδαί
LCM	*Liverpool Classical Monthly*
LEC	*Les Etudes Classiques*

MDAIK	*Mitteilungen des deutschen archäologischen Instituts, Abteilung Kairo*
MEFRA	*Mélanges de l'Ecole française de Rome, Antiquité*
Mem. Ac. Inscr.	
B. L.	*Mémoires de l'Académie des Inscriptions et Belles Lettres*
Mem. Linc.	*Memorie dell'Academia nazionale dei Lincei*
MIA	Materialy i Issledovaniya po Arkheologii SSSR
Michel	C. Michel (ed.), *Recueil d'inscriptions grecques.* Brussels, 1900–27
MIFAO	Mémoires de l'Institut français d'archéologie orientale
M–L	R. Meiggs and D. M. Lewis, *Greek Historical Inscriptions.* Oxford, 1969 rev. edn 1988
Mus. Helv.	*Museum Helveticum*
NABU	*Nouvelles assyriologiques brèves et utilitaires*
NNM	Numismatic Notes and Monographs
Noe, *BGCH*	S. P. Noe, *A Bibliography of Greek Coin Hoards.* 2nd edn. New York, 1937
Num. Chron.	*Numismatic Chronicle*
OCD	*Oxford Classical Dictionary*
OGIS	W. Dittenberger (ed.), *Orientis Graecae Inscriptions Selectae.* 2 vols. Leipzig, 1903–5
OIP	Oriental Institute Publications
OJA	*Oxford Journal of Archaeology*
OMRO	*Oudheidkundige mededelingen uit het Rijksmuseum von Oudheden te Leiden*
Opusc. Archaeol.	*Opuscula Archaeologica*
Opusc. Athen.	*Opuscula Atheniensia*
PAE	*Πρακτικὰ τῆς ἐν Ἀθήναις Ἀρχαιολογικῆς Ἑταιρείας*
PBA	*Proceedings of the British Academy*
PBF	Prähistorische Bronzefunde
PCPhS	*Proceedings of the Cambridge Philological Society*
PP	*Parola del Passato*
Proc. Mass. Hist. Soc.	*Proceedings of the Massachusetts Historical Society*
PSBA	*Proceedings of the Society of Biblical Archaeology*
RA	*Revue d'Assyriologie et d'archéologie orientale*
RB	*Revue biblique*
RC	C. B. Welles (ed.), *Royal Correspondence in the Hellenistic Period.* New Haven, 1934
RDAC	*Report of the Department of Antiquities, Cyprus*
RE	A. Pauly and G. Wissowa, *Real-Encyclopädie der classischen Altertumswissenschaft*, 83 vols. Stuttgart, 1894–1980
REA	*Revue des études anciennes*
Rec. Soc. Bodin	*Recueil de la Société Bodin*
REG	*Revue des études grecques*

REL   *Revue des études latines*
Rend. Linc.   *Rendiconti dell' Accademia nazionale dei Lincei*
Rev. Arch.   *Revue archéologique*
Rev. Arch.
l'Est et C-Est   *Revue archéologique de l'Est et du Centre-Est*
Rev. d'égyptol.   *Revue d'égyptologie*
Rev. Hist.   *Revue historique*
Rev. Phil.   *Revue de philologie, de littérature et d'histoire anciennes*
Rh.Mus.   *Rheinisches Museum*
RIDA   *Revue internationale des droits de l'antiquité*
Riv. di Filol.   *Rivista di filologia e d'istruzione classica*
Riv. stor. ant.   *Rivista storica dell'antichità*
Röm. Mitt.   *Römische Mitteilungen*
R. Stud. Fen.   *Rivista di Studi Fenici*

SAK   *Studien zur altägyptischen Kultur*
SBAk. Berlin   *Sitzungsberichte der Akademie der Wissenschaften zu Berlin*
SBAk. Wien   *Sitzungsberichte der Österreichischen Akademie der Wissenschaften*
Schweiz. Num.
Rundschau   *Schweizerische numismatische Rundschau*
SCI   *Scripta Classica Israelica*
SdA   *Die Staatsverträge des Altertums* II^2, *Die Verträge der griechisch-römischen Welt von 700 bis 338 v. Chr.*, ed. H. Bengtson, Munich, 1975; *Die Verträge der griechisch-römischen Welt von 338 bis 200 v. Chr.* ed. H. H. Schmitt. Munich, 1969
SEG   *Supplementum Epigraphicum Graecum.* Leiden, 1923–
SGDI   H. Collitz and F. Bechtel, *Sammlung der Griechischen Dialekt-Inschriften i-iv.* Göttingen, 1885–1910
Sic. Gymn.   *Siculorum Gymnasium*
SIG   W. Dittenberger (ed.), *Sylloge Inscriptionum Graecarum.* 3rd edn. Leipzig, 1915–24
SIMA   *Studies in Mediterranean Archaeology*
SO   *Symbolae Osloenses*
Sov. Arch.   *Sovetskaya Archeologiya*
Stud. Clas.   *Studii clasice*
Stud. Etr.   *Studi Etruschi*

TAM   *Tituli Asiae Minoris.* Vienna, 1901–
TAPA   *Transactions and Proceedings of the American Philological Association*
TAVO   *Beihefte zum Tübinger Atlas des Vorderen Orients*
TGF   A. Nauck (ed.), *Tragicorum Graecorum Fragmenta*, 1889
TLS   *Times Literary Supplement*
Tod   M. N. Tod, *A Selection of Greek Historical Inscriptions* ii. Oxford, 1948

UCP   University of California Publications in Semitic Philology
Urk.   K. Sethe, *Hieroglyphische Urkunden der Griechisch-Römischen Zeit.*

Heft 1: historisch-biographische Urkunden aus den Zeiten der makedonischen Könige und der beiden ersten Ptolemäer (Urkunden des ägyptischen Altertums), Leipzig, 1904

VDI	*Vestnik drevnei istorii*
VT	*Vetus Testamentum*
We. Or.	*Die Welt des Orients*
Wien. Stud.	*Wiener Studien*
WVDOG	Wissenschaftliche Veröffentlichungen der Deutschen Orient-Gesellschaft
WZKM	*Wiener Zeitschrift für die Kunde des Morgenlandes*
YCS	*Yale Classical Studies*
ZA	*Zeitschrift für Assyriologie*
ZÄS	*Zeitschrift für ägyptische Sprache und Altertumskunde*
ZAW	*Zeitschrift für die Alttestamentliche Wissenschaft*
ZDMG	*Zeitschrift der deutschen morgenländischen Gesellschaft*
ZDPV	*Zeitschrift des deutschen Palästina Vereins*
Zeitschr. für die österr. Gymn.	*Zeitschrift für die österreichischen Gymnasien*
ZKM	*Zeitschrift für die Kunde des Morgenlandes*
ZOAO	*Zapski Odesskogo Arkheologicheskogo Obschestva*
ZPE	*Zeitschrift für Papyrologie und Epigraphik*

A. GENERAL

1. Andrewes, A. *The Greek Tyrants*. London, 1956
2. Aymard, A. *Etudes d'histoire ancienne*. Paris, 1967
3. Badian, E. (ed.) *Studies in Ancient Society and Institutions presented to Victor Ehrenberg on his 75th Birthday*. Oxford, 1966
4. Beloch, K. J. *Die Bevölkerung der griechisch-römischen Welt*. Leipzig, 1886
5. Beloch, K. J. *Griechische Geschichte*. 2nd edn. 4 vols. in 8. Strasburg–Berlin/Leipzig, 1912–27
6. Bengtson, H. *Die Staatsverträge des Altertums*, II: *Die Verträge der griechisch-römischen Welt von 700 bis 338 v. Chr.* 2nd edn. Munich, 1975
7. Bengtson, H. (ed.) *The Greeks and the Persians from the Sixth to the Fourth Centuries*. London, 1969
8. Bickerman, E. J. 'Origines gentium', *Cl.Phil.* 47 (1952) 65–81
9. Bickerman, E. J. *Chronology of the Ancient World*. London, 1968 (revd edn 1980)
10. Boardman, J. *The Greeks Overseas*. 2nd edn. London, 1980
11. Bowersock, G. W. *Hellenism in Late Antiquity*. Cambridge, 1990
12. Brunt, P. A. 'Politics and patronage in the "Verrines"', *Chiron* 10 (1980) 273–89

13. Carlier, P. *La royauté en Grèce avant Alexandre*. Strasburg, 1984
14. Cartledge, P. and Harvey, F. D. (eds.) *Crux. Essays presented to G. E. M. de Ste Croix on his 75th Birthday*. London, 1985
15. Cartledge, P., Millett, P. and Todd, S. (eds.) *Nomos, Essays in Athenian Law, Politics and Society*. Cambridge, 1990
16. Droysen, J. G. *Geschichte des Hellenismus:* I. *Geschichte Alexanders des Grossen*. 2nd edn Gotha, 1877. 3rd edn Basel, 1952
17. Fieldhouse, D. K. *Colonialism 1870–1945*. London, 1981
18. Finley, M. I. *Ancient History: Evidence and Models*. London, 1985
18A. Finley, M. I. *The Use and Abuse of History*. 2nd edn. London, 1986
19. Fornara, Ch. *Archaic Times to the End of the Peloponnesian War* (Translated Documents of Greece and Rome 1). Cambridge, 1983
20. Francisci, P. de. *Arcana Imperii*, II. Milan, 1948
21. Fraser, P. M. *Ptolemaic Alexandria*, I–III. Oxford, 1972
22. Garnsey, P. D. A. and Whittaker, C. R. (eds.) *Imperialism in the Ancient World*. Cambridge, 1978
23. Glotz, G. and Cohen, R. *Histoire grecque*, III. Paris, 1936
24. Greenhalgh, P. A. L. *Pompey*, II. *The Republican Prince*. London, 1981
25. Grote, G. *History of Greece*. 10 vols. London, 1846–56
26. Habicht, Chr. *Gottmenschentum und griechische Städte* (*Zetemata* 14). 2nd edn. Munich, 1970
27. Hadley, R. A. 'Royal propaganda of Seleucus I and Lysimachus', *JHS* 94 (1974) 50–65
28. Hammond, N. G. L. *Studies in Greek History*. Oxford, 1973
29. Harding, P. *From the End of the Peloponnesian War to the Battle of Ipsus* (Translated Documents of Greece and Rome 2). Cambridge, 1985
30. Henrichs, A. 'Three approaches to Greek mythography', in H 7, 242–77
31. Hornblower, S. *The Greek World, 479–323 B.C.* London, 1983 (revd edn 1991)
32. Kinzl, K. (ed.) *Greece and the Ancient Mediterranean in History and Prehistory* (Studies presented to F. Schachermeyr). Berlin, 1977
33. Lewis, D. M. *Sparta and Persia* (Cincinnati Classical Studies n.s. 1). Leiden, 1977
34. Luttwak, E. N. *The Grand Strategy of the Roman Empire*. Baltimore, 1976
35. Mazzarino, S. *Introduzione alle guerre puniche*. Catania, 1947
36. Mehl, A. 'Δορίκτητος χώρα: kritische Bemerkungen zum "Speererwerb" in Politik und Völkerrecht der hellenistischen Epoche', *AncSoc* 11/12 (1980/1) 173–212
37. Meyer, E., *Geschichte des Altertums* III. Stuttgart–Berlin, 1901
38. Meyer, E. *Geschichte des Altertums* V *Das Perserreich und die Griechen: viertes Buch, der Ausgang der griechischen Geschichte*. 3rd edn. Stuttgart–Berlin, 1921
39. Millar, F. *The Emperor in the Roman World*. London, 1977
40. Millar, F. 'The world of the Golden Ass', *JRS* 71 (1981) 63–75
41. Momigliano, A. *Alien Wisdom*. Cambridge, 1975
42. Momigliano, A. 'Persian Empire and Greek freedom', in Ryan, A. (ed.), *The Idea of Freedom: Essays in honour of Isaiah Berlin*, 139–51. Oxford, 1979

(= *Settimo contributo alla storia degli studi classici e del mondo antico*, 61–75. Rome, 1984)

43. Moretti, L. *Olympionikai, i vincitori negli antichi agoni olimpici* (*Mem. Linc.* ser. VIII, VIII, 2 (1957) 53–198)

44. Morgan, C. 'Ethnicity and early Greek states: historical and material perspectives', *PCPhS* 37 (1991) 131–63

45. Mosley, D. J. *Envoys and Diplomacy in Ancient Greece* (*Historia* Einzelschr. 22). Wiesbaden, 1973

46. Murray, O. περὶ βασιλείας. Unpub. Oxford D.Phil. thesis, 1971

47. Niese, B. *Geschichte der griechischen und makedonischen Staaten seit der Schlacht bei Chaeronea*. Gotha, 1893

48. Pritchett, W. K. *Studies in Ancient Greek Topography* I–V (University of California Publications in Classical Studies 1, 4, 22, 28, 31). Berkeley–Los Angeles, 1965–85

49. Richardson, J. S. *Hispaniae: Spain and the Development of Roman Imperialism 218–82 B.C.* Cambridge, 1986

50. Ritter, H. W. *Diadem und Königsherrschaft* (Vestigia 7). Munich, 1965

51. Rostovtzeff, M. I. *The Social and Economic History of the Hellenistic World*. 2nd edn. Oxford, 1953

52. Schmitthenner, W. 'Über eine Formveränderung der Monarchie seit Alexander d. Grossen', *Saeculum* 19 (1968) 31–46

53. Sealey, B. R. I. *A History of the Greek City States, ca. 700–338 B.C.* Berkeley–Los Angeles, 1976

54. Seibert, J. *Das Zeitalter der Diadochen* (Erträge der Forschung 185). Darmstadt, 1983

55. Seibert, J. 'Heeresseuchen und Kriegsverlauf', in Heinen, H. (ed.), *Althistorische Studien H. Bengtson . . . dargebracht* (*Historia* Einzelschr. 40, 1983), 78–91

56. Sherwin-White, A. N. Review of A 22, *TLS* 1980, 447

57. Strasburger, H. *Studien zur Alten Geschichte* (ed. W. Schmitthenner and R. Zoepffel). Hildesheim, 1982

58. Syme, R. *Colonial Elites*. Oxford, 1958

59. Tscherikower, V. *Die hellenistischen Städtegründungen von Alexander dem Grossen bis auf die Römerzeit* (Philologus Suppl. 19.1). 1927

60. Tuplin, C. J. 'The Treaty of Boiotios', in F 51, 133–53

61. Westlake, H. D. *Essays on the Greek Historians and Greek History*. Manchester–New York, 1969

62. Westlake, H. D. *Studies in Thucydides and Greek History.* Bristol, 1989

63. Whitehead, A. N. *Process and Reality: An Essay in Cosmology*. Cambridge, 1929

64. Wilcken, U. *Berliner Akademieschriften zur alten Geschichte und Papyruskunde* 2 vols. (1883–1942) Leipzig, 1970

65. Wittfogel, K. *Oriental Despotism*. New York, 1957

B. SOURCES

I. LITERARY SOURCES

1. Africa, T. W. *Phylarchus and the Spartan revolution*. Berkeley, 1961
2. Africa, T. W. 'Ephorus and Oxyrhynchus Papyrus 1610', *AJP* 83 (1962) 86–9
3. Albini, U. [*Erode Attico*] περὶ πολιτείας. Florence, 1968
4. Anderson, J. K. 'The Battle of Sardis in 395 B.C.', *CSCA* 7 (1974) 27–53
5. Andrewes, A. 'Thucydides and the Persians', *Historia* 10 (1961) 1–18
6. Andrewes, A. 'Lysias and the Theramenes Papyrus', *ZPE* 6 (1970) 35–8
7. Andrewes, A. 'Diodorus and Ephorus: one source of misunderstanding', in Eadie, J. W. and Ober, J. W. (eds.) *The Craft of the Ancient Historian: Essays in Honor of Chester G. Starr*, 189–97. Lanham Md., 1985
8. Atkinson, J. E. *A Commentary on Q. Curtius Rufus' Historiae Alexandri Magni Books 3 & 4* (London Studies in Classical Philology 4). Amsterdam–Uithoorn, 1980
9. Badian, E. 'Nearchus the Cretan', *YCS* 24 (1975) 147–70
10. Baladié, R. *Le Péloponnèse de Strabon: étude de géographie historique*. Paris, 1980
11. Barber, G. L. *The Historian Ephorus*. Cambridge, 1935
12. Bosworth, A. B. 'Arrian and the Alexander Vulgate', *Entretiens Hardt* 22 (1976) 1–46
13. Bosworth, A. B. 'Errors in Arrian', *CQ* n.s. 26 (1976) 117–39
14. Bosworth, A. B. *A Historical Commentary on Arrian's History of Alexander* I. Oxford, 1980
15. Bosworth, A. B. *From Arrian to Alexander. Studies in Historical Interpretation*. Oxford, 1988
16. Bosworth, A. B. 'Nearchus in Susiana', in Will, W. and Heinrichs, J. (eds.), *Festschrift G. Wirth zum 60 Geburtstag am 9.12.86*, 541–67. Amsterdam, 1988
17. Bowie, E. L. 'Greeks and their past in the Second Sophistic', in M. I. Finley (ed.) *Studies in Ancient Society*, 166–209. London, 1974
18. Brown, T. S. *Onesicritus: a Study in Hellenistic Historiography*. Berkeley, 1949
19. Brown, T. S. *Timaeus of Tauromenium* (University of California Publications in History 55). Berkeley–Los Angeles, 1958
20. Bruce, I. A. F. *An Historical Commentary on the 'Hellenica Oxyrhynchia'*. Cambridge, 1967
20A. Brunt, P. A. 'Notes on Aristobulus of Cassandria', *CQ* 24 (1974) 65–9
21. Brunt, P. A. *Arrian: History of Alexander and Indica* (Loeb Classical Library) I–II. Cambridge, MA, 1976–83
22. Brunt, P. A. 'On fragments and epitomes of historians', *CQ* 30 (1980) 477–94
23. Buchner, E. *Der Panegyrikos des Isokrates* (*Historia* Einzelschrift 2). Wiesbaden, 1958

24. Cawkwell, G. L. 'A diet of Xenophon', *Didaskalos* 2.2 (1967) 50–8
25. Cawkwell, G. L. Introduction and notes to revd edn of Xenophon, *The Persian Expedition*, trans. R. Warner. Harmondsworth, 1973
26. Cawkwell, G. L. Introduction and notes, and appendix, to revd edn of Xenophon, *A History of My Times (Hellenica)*, trans. R. Warner. Harmondsworth, 1979
27. Cawkwell, G. L. Review of B 42, *CR* 29 (1979) 17–19
28. Cawkwell, G. L. Review of B 122A, *CR* 29 (1979) 214–17
29. Cawkwell, G. L. 'Isocrates', in Luce, T. J. (ed.), *Ancient Writers: Greece and Rome*, I. 313–29. New York, 1982
30. Chrimes, K. M. T. The *Respublica Lacedaemoniorum Ascribed to Xenophon*. Manchester, 1948
31. Connor, W. R. 'History without heroes: Theopompus' treatment of Philip of Macedon', *GRBS* 8 (1967) 133–54
32. Culasso Gastaldi, E. *Sul trattato con Alessandro*. Padua, 1984
33. Davidson, J. 'Isocrates against Imperialism: an analysis of the De Pace', *Historia* 39 (1990) 20–36
34. Diller, A. (ed.) *The Tradition of the Minor Greek Geographers*. Lancaster, PA–Oxford, 1952
35. Dover, K. J. *Lysias and the Corpus Lysiacum* (Sather Classical Lectures 39). Berkeley–Los Angeles, 1968
36. Dover, K. J. *Aristophanic Comedy*. Berkeley–Los Angeles, 1972
37. Ellis, J. R. 'The order of the Olynthiacs', *Historia* 16 (1967) 108–12
38. Errington, R. M. 'Bias in Ptolemy's History of Alexander', *CQ* n.s. 19 (1969) 233–42
39. Forni, G. and Bertinelli, M. G. A. 'Pompeio Trogo come fonte di storia', in *ANRW* II. 30. 2 (1982) 1298–362
40. Fraser, P. M. 'Eratosthenes of Cyrene', *PBA* 1971, 3–35
41. Fraser, P. M. Review of B 45, (I) *CR* 30 (1980) 246–8 and (II) 34 (1984) 345–6
42. Gauthier, P. *Un commentaire historique des Poroi de Xénophon*. Paris–Geneva, 1976
43. Goldstein, J. A. *The Letters of Demosthenes*. New York, 1968
44. Gomme, A. W., Andrewes, A. and Dover, K. J. *A Historical Commentary on Thucydides I–V*. Oxford, 1945–1981
45. Goukowsky, P. *Essai sur les origines du mythe d'Alexandre*, I–II. Nancy, 1978–81
46. Gould, J. *Herodotus*. London, 1989
46A. Grafton, A. T. *Forgers and Critics*. Princeton, 1991.
47. Gray, V. J. 'Two different approaches to the battle of Sardis in 395 B.C.', *CSCA* 12 (1979) 183–200
48. Gray, V. J. 'The years 375–371 B.C.: a case study in the reliability of Diodorus and Xenophon', *CQ* n.s. 30 (1980) 306–26
49. Gray, V. J. *The Character of Xenophon's Hellenica*. London, 1989
50. Grayson, C. 'Did Xenophon intend to write history?', in Levick, B. M. (ed.) *The Ancient Historian and his Materials: Essays in Honour of C. E. Stevens*, 31–43. Farnborough, 1975

51. VACAT
52. Habicht, C. 'Falsche Urkunden zur Geschichte Athens im Zeitalter der Perserkriege', *Hermes* 89 (1961) 1–35
53. Hall, E. *Inventing the Barbarian: Greek Self-Definition through Tragedy.* Oxford, 1989
54. Hamilton, J. R. *Plutarch Alexander: a Commentary.* Oxford, 1969
55. Hammond, N. G. L. 'Diodorus' narrative of the Sacred War', *JHS* 57 (1937) 44–78
56. Hammond, N. G. L. 'The sources of Diodorus Siculus XVI', I and II, *CQ* 31 (1937) 79–91, 32 (1938) 137–51
57. Hammond, N. G. L. *Three Historians of Alexander the Great: The so-called Vulgate Authors, Diodorus, Justin and Curtius.* Cambridge, 1983
58. Henrichs, A. 'Zur Interpretation des Michigan–Papyrus über Theramenes', *ZPE* 3 (1968) 101–8
59. Hirsch, S. W. *The Friendship of the Barbarians: Xenophon and the Persian Empire.* Hanover, NY–London, 1985
60. Hornblower, J. *Hieronymus of Cardia.* Oxford, 1981
61. Hornblower, S. Review of B 57, *CR* 34 (1984) 261–4
62. Hornblower, S. *Commentary on Thucydides* I: *Books I–III.* Oxford, 1991
62A. Jacoby, F. *Griechische Historiker.* Stuttgart, 1956
63. Kebric, R. B. *In the Shadow of Macedon. Duris of Samos.* (*Historia* Einzelschr. 29). Wiesbaden, 1977
64. Kornemann, E. *Die Alexandergeschichte des Königs Ptolemaios von Ägypten.* Leipzig–Berlin, 1935
65. Lane Fox, R. 'Theopompus of Chios and the Greek world, 411–322 B.C.', in Boardman, J. and Vaphopoulou-Richardson, C. E. (eds.), *Chios: A Conference at the Homereion in Chios, 1984,* 105–20. Oxford, 1986
66. Laqueur, R. 'Timaios', *RE* 6A (1937) cols. 1075–203
67. Laqueur, R. 'Diodorea', *Hermes* 86 (1958) 257–90
68. Lauritano, R. 'Sileno in Diodoro', *KOKALOS* 2 (1956) 206–16
68A. Lefkowitz, M. *The Lives of the Greek Poets.* London, 1981
68B. MacDowell, D. *Demosthenes Against Meidias.* Oxford 1990
69. Maclaren, M. Jr. 'On the composition of Xenophon's Hellenica', *AJP* 55 (1934) 121–39, 249–62
70. MacMullen, R. 'The Epigraphic habit in the Roman Empire', *AJP* 103 (1982) 233–46
71. Manni, E. 'Da Ippi a Diodoro', *KOKALOS* 3 (1957) 136–55
72. Manni, E. 'Sileno in Diodoro?', *Atti . . . Palermo* 18.2 (1957–8) 81–8
73. Manni, E. 'Ancora a proposto di Sileno-Diodoro', *KOKALOS* 16 (1970) 74–8
74. Meister, K. *Die sizilische Geschichte bei Diodor von den Anfängen bis zum Tod des Agathokles. Quellenuntersuchungen zu Buch IV–XXI.* Diss. Munich, 1967
75. Merkelbach, R. *Die Quellen des griechischen Alexanderromans* (Zetemata 9). 2nd edn. Munich, 1977
76. Merkelbach, R. and Youtie, H. C. 'Ein Michigan–Papyrus über Theramenes', *ZPE* 2 (1968) 161–9
77. Meyer, E. *Theopomps Hellenika.* Halle, 1909

78. Milns, R. D. 'Some critical observations on Ephorus, Fragments 119, 111 and Testimony 23 (Jacoby)', in Marshall, B. (ed.), *Vindex Humanitatis: Essays in Honour of John Huntly Bishop*, 46–57. Armidale, 1980

79. Missiou, A. *The Subversive Oratory of Andokides: Politics, Ideology and Decision-Making in Democratic Athens*. Cambridge, 1992

80. Momigliano, A. 'Teopompo', *Riv. di Filol.* n.s. 9 (1931) 230–42, 335–53

81. Momigliano, A. 'La valutazione di Filippo il Macedone in Giustino', in *Quarto Contributo alla storia degli studi classici e del mondo antico*, 225–38. Rome, 1969

82. Momigliano, A. *The Development of Greek Biography*. Harvard, 1971

83. Momigliano, A. 'Le fonti della storia greca e macedone nel libro XVI di Diodoro', in *Quinto Contributo alla storia degli studi classici e del mondo antico*, 707–27. Rome, 1975

84. Momigliano, A. 'Second thoughts on Greek biography', in *Quinto Contributo alla storia degli studi classici e del mondo antico*, 33–47. Rome, 1975

85. Momigliano, A. *Essays in Ancient and Modern Historiography*, Oxford, 1977

86. Momigliano, A. *The Classical Foundations of Modern Historiography*. Berkeley–Los Angeles–Oxford, 1990

87. Montgomery, H. *The Way to Chaeronea: Foreign Policy, Decision-Making and Political Influence in Demosthenes' Speeches*, Bergen–Oslo–Stavanger–Tromso, 1983

88. Murray, O. 'Greek Historians', in Boardman, J., Griffin, J. and Murray, O. (eds.) *The Oxford History of the Classical World* 186–203. Oxford, 1986

89. Nouhaud, M. *L'utilisation de l'historie par les orateurs attiques*. Paris, 1982

90. Pearson, L. *The Lost Histories of Alexander the Great* (Philological Monographs 20). New York, 1960

91. Pearson, L. 'Ephorus and Timaeus in Diodorus. Laqueur's thesis rejected', *Historia* 33 (1984) 1–20

92. Pearson, L. *The Greek Historians of the West*. Atlanta, 1987

93. Pédech, P. *Historiens compagnons d'Alexandre*. Paris, 1984

94. Rhodes, P. J. *A Commentary on the Aristotelian* Athenaion Politeia. Oxford, 1981

95. Rhodes, P. J. *Thucydides, History II*. Warminster, 1988

96. Roberts, W. Rhys. 'Theopompus in the Greek literary critics', *CR* 22 (1908) 118–22

97. Roisman, J. 'Ptolemy and his rivals in his history of Alexander the Great', *CQ* n.s. 34 (1984) 373–85

98. Sacks, K. S. *Diodorus Siculus and the First Century*. Princeton, 1990

99. Sanders, L. J. 'Diodorus Siculus and Dionysius I of Syracuse', *Historia* 30 (1981) 394–411

100. Schwartz, E. 'Kallisthenes' Hellenika', *Hermes* 35 (1900) 106–30

101. Schwartz, E. 'Diodoros', *RE* 5 (1903) 663–703 (= B 104, 35–97)

102. Schwartz, E. 'Ephoros', *RE* 6 (1907) cols. 1–16 (= B 104, 3–26)

103. Schwartz, E. *Gesammelte Schriften*, II. Berlin, 1956

104. Schwartz, E. *Griechische Geschichtschreiber*. Leipzig, 1957

105. Sealey, R. 'Dionysius of Halicarnassus and some Demosthenic dates', *REG* 68 (1955) 77–120

106. Sealey, R. 'Pap. Mich. Inv. 5982: Theramenes', *ZPE* 116 (1975) 279–88
107. Seel, O. *Eine römische Weltgeschichte. Studien zum Text der Epitome des Iustinus und zur Historik des Pompejus Trogus* (Erlanger Beiträge zur Sprach- und Kunstwissenschaft 39). Nuremberg, 1972
108. Seibert, J. *Untersuchungen zur Geschichte Ptolemaios' I* (Münchener Beiträge zur Papyrusforschung und antiken Rechtsgeschichte 56). Munich, 1969
109. Shrimpton, G. S. *Theopompus the Historian.* London–Buffalo, 1991
110. Stadter, P. A. *Arrian of Nicomedia.* Chapel Hill, 1980
111. Stevenson, R. *Greek Historiography about Persia.* Forthcoming
112. Stylianou, P. 'Commentary on Diodorus xv', Unpubl. Oxford D. Phil. thesis, 1985
113. Syme, R. 'The date of Justin and the discovery of Trogus', *Historia* 37 (1988) 358–71
114. Tatum, J. *Xenophon's Imperial Fiction: On The Education of Cyrus.* Princeton, 1989
115. Thiel, J. H. 'De Dinone Colophonio Nepotis in Vita Datamis Auctore', *Mnemosyne* 51 (1923) 412–14
116. Thomas, R. *Oral Tradition and Written Record in Classical Athens.* Cambridge, 1989
117. Thompson, W. 'Andocides and Hellanicus', *TAPA* 98 (1967) 483–90
118. Tuplin, C. J. 'Pausanias and Plutarch's *Epaminondas*', *CQ* 34 (1984) 346–58
119. Tuplin, C. J. 'Xenophon's Hellenica: introductory essay and commentary on VI 3–VI 5', Unpub. Oxford D.Phil. thesis, 1981
120. Vidal-Naquet, P. *Flavius Arrien entre deux mondes: postface à l' "Histoire d'Alexandre" d'Arrien.* Paris, 1984
121. Volquardsen, C. A. *Untersuchungen über die Quellen der griechischen und sizilischen Geschichten bei Diodor, Buch XI–XVI.* Kiel, 1868
122. Walbank, F. W. *A Historical Commentary on Polybius.* 3 vols. Oxford, 1957 (I); 1967 (II); 1979 (III)
122A. Wankel, H. *Demosthenes, Rede für Ktesiphon über den Kranz.* 2 vols. Heidelberg, 1976
123. Weil, R. *Aristote et l'histoire: essai sur la Politique.* Paris, 1960
124. Welles, C. B. 'The reliability of Ptolemy as an historian', in *Miscellanea di studi alessandri in memoria di A. Rostagni* 101–16. Turin, 1963
125. West, M. L. *Hesiod, Works and Days.* Oxford, 1978
126. Westermann, A. *Biographi Graeci Minores.* Braunschweig, 1845
127. Westlake, H. D. 'The Sources of Plutarch's *Pelopidas*', *CQ* 33 (1939) 11–22
128. Westlake, H. D. 'The Sicilian books of Theopompus' *Hellenica*', *Historia* 2 (1953–4) 288–307 (= A 61, 226–50)
129. Westman, R. *Plutarch gegen Kolotes. Seine Schrift 'Adversus Colotem' als philosophiegeschichtliche Quelle.* (Acta Philosophica Fennica, fasc. 7). Helsinki, 1955
130. Wevers, R. F. *Isaeus: Chronology, Prosopography, and Social History.* The Hague–Paris, 1969
131. Whitehead, D. *Aineias the Tactician. How to Survive under Siege.* Oxford, 1990

132. Will, W. 'Zur Datierung der Rede Ps.-Demosthenes XVII', *Rh. Mus.* 125 (1982) 202–13
132A. Wyse, W. *The Speeches of Isaeus.* Cambridge, 1904
133. Zoepffel, R. 'Untersuchungen zum Geschichtswerk des Philistos von Syrakus'. Diss. Freiburg i. Br., 1965

II. EPIGRAPHY

134. Badian, E. 'A comma in the history of Samos', *ZPE* 23 (1976) 289–94
135. Badian, E. 'A document of Artaxerxes IV?', in A 32, 40–50
136. Bourguet, E. 'Inscriptions de Delphes sur trois archontes du IVᵉ siècle', *BCH* 23 (1899) 353–69
137. Bousquet, J. (ed.) *Corpus des Inscriptions de Delphes* II: *Les comptes du quatrième et du troisième siècle.* Paris, 1989
138. Clark, M. 'The date of *IG* II² 1604', *BSA* 85 (1990) 47–67
139. Ferguson, W. S. 'Researches in Athenian and Delian documents, III', *Klio* 9 (1909) 304–40
140. Fraser, P. M. 'The son of Aristonax at Kandahar', *Afghan Studies* 2 (1979/80) 9–21
141. Habicht, Chr. 'Samische Volksbeschlüsse der hellenistischen Zeit', *Ath. Mitt.* 72 (1957) 152–274
142. Hansen, P. A. *Carmina Epigraphica Graeca* I, II. Berlin, 1983, 1989
143. Heisserer, A. J. *Alexander the Great and the Greeks: the Epigraphic Evidence.* Norman, OK, 1980
144. Heisserer, A. J. '*IG* XII, 2.1 (The monetary pact between Mytilene and Phocaea)', *ZPE* 55 (1984) 121–2
145. Jeffery, L. H. 'The development of Lakonian lettering: a reconsideration', *BSA* 83 (1988) 179–81
146. Jeffery, L. H. *The Local Scripts of Archaic Greece* revd A. W. Johnston. Oxford, 1990
147. Jeppesen, K. 'A royal message to Ikaros: The Hellenistic temples of Failakā', Kuml (1960) 174–87
148. Knoepfler, D. (ed.) *Comptes et inventaires dans la cité grecque.* Neuchâtel, 1988
149. de La Coste-Messelière, P. 'Listes amphictioniques du IVe s.', *BCH* 73 (1949) 200–47
150. de La Coste-Messelière, P. 'Les naopes à Delphes au IVe s.', *Mélanges helléniques offerts à Georges Daux*, 199–211. Paris, 1974.
151. Lewis, D. M. 'The epigraphical evidence for the end of the Thirty', in Piérart, M. (ed.), *Aristote et Athènes.* Fribourg, 1993
152. Lewis, D. M. and Stroud, R. S. 'Athens honors King Euagoras of Salamis', *Hesp.* 48 (1979) 180–93
153. Maier, F. G. *Griechische Mauerbauinschriften* I. Heidelberg, 1959
154. Matthaiou, A. P. and Pikoulas, G. A. '"Εδον τοῖς Λακεδαιμονίοις ποττὸν πόλεμον', *ΗΟΡΟΣ* 7 (1989) [1991] 77–124
155. Meritt, B. D. 'Greek inscriptions', *Hesp.* 29 (1960) 1–27

156. Meritt, B. D. and West, A. B. *The Athenian Assessment of 425 B.C.* Ann Arbor, 1934

157. Metzger, H., Laroche, E. and Dupont-Sommer, A. 'La stèle trilingue récemment découverte au Letôon de Xanthos', *CRAI* (1974) 82–93, 115–25, 132–49

158. Metzger, H., Laroche, E. and Dupont-Sommer, A. *Fouilles de Xanthos 6: La stèle trilingue du Létoon.* Paris, 1979

159. Miller, S. G. 'The Thearodokoi of the Nemean Games', *Hesp.* 57 (1988) 147–63

160. Mitchel, F. W. 'A note on *IG* II² 370', *Phoenix* 18 (1964) 13–17

161. Moysey, R. '*IG* II² 207 and the Great Satraps' revolt', *ZPE* 69 (1987) 93–100

162. Nenci, G. 'Sei decreti inediti da Entella', *ASNP* ser. III, 10 (1980) 1271–5

163. Nenci, G. Various articles on the inscriptions of Entella, in *ASNP* ser. III, 12 (1982) 769–1103

164. Osborne, M. 'Athens and Orontes', *BSA* 66 (1971) 297–321

165. Osborne, M. J. *Naturalization in Athens*, 4 vols. in 3 (Verhandlingen van de Koninklijke Academie voor Wetenschappen, Letteren en Schone Kunsten van België, Klasse der Letteren, 43, 1981, no. 98, 44, 1982, no. 101, 45, 1983, no. 109)

166. Petrakos, B. Ch. ''Επιγραφαὶ 'Ωρωποῦ', *ArchDelt* 21 (1966) 45–7

167. Pritchett, W. K. 'Lucubrationes Epigraphicae', *CSCA* 5 (1972) 153–81

168. Reinmuth, O., *The Ephebic Inscriptions of the Fourth Century B.C.* (*Mnemosyne* Suppl. 14). Leiden, 1971

169. Robert, L. *Collection Froehner 1. Les inscriptions grecques.* Paris, 1936

170. Robert, L. *Etudes épigraphiques et philologiques.* Paris, 1938

171. Robert, L. *Hellenica.* 13 vols. Paris–Limoges, 1940–65

172. Robert, L. *Opera minora selecta.* 7 vols. Amsterdam, 1969–90

173. Roueché, C. and Sherwin-White, S. 'Some aspects of the Seleucid Empire: the Greek inscriptions from Falaika, in the Arabian Gulf', *Chiron* 15 (1985) 1–39

174. Rougemont, G. *Corpus des Inscriptions de Delphes* I. *Lois sacrées et règlements religieux.* Paris, 1977

175. Sherwin-White, S. M. 'Ancient archives: the edict of Alexander to Priene, a reappraisal', *JHS* 105 (1985) 69–89

176. Stroud, R. S. 'Greek inscriptions, Theozotides and the Athenian orphans', *Hesp.* 40 (1971) 280–301

177. Stroud, R. S. 'An Athenian law on silver coinage', *Hesp.* 43 (1974) 157–88

178. Stroud, R. S. 'An Argive decree from Nemea concerning Aspendos', *Hesp.* 53 (1984) 193–216

179. Tod, M. N. *A Selection of Greek Historical Inscriptions*, II. Oxford, 1948

180. Walbank, M. B. 'The confiscation and sale by the Poletai in 402/1 B.C. of the property of the Thirty Tyrants', *Hesp.* 51 (1982) 74–98

181. Wallace, W. P. 'Loans to Karystos about 370 B.C.', *Phoenix* 16 (1962) 15–28

182. West, A. B. and Woodward, A. M. 'Studies in the Attic treasure-records II', *JHS* 58 (1938) 69–89
183. Woodward, A. M. 'An Attic treasure-record: the Hekatompedon-list for 402/1 B.C.', *ArchEph* (1953–1954 B' [1958]) 107–12

III. NUMISMATICS

(See also B 144, B 177, E 67, E 107, E 109, E 148, E 149, E 153, E 154, E 155, E 159, E 172, E 173, E 174, E 214, E 232, E 233, E 245, E 246, E 257, E 275, E 309, E 359, E 360, E 361, E 362, E 364, E 365, E 366, E 367, E 369, E 370, E 372, E 376, E 383, E 447, E 448, E 450, F 223, F 260, F 295, F 298, F 299, F 320, F 327, F 328, F 356, F 384, F 389, F 429, F 432, F 524, F 557, F 665, F 666, F 685, G 16, G 125, G 161, G 178, G 200, G 201, G 202, G 203, G 300, G 313, I 142)

184. Aulock, H. von. 'Die Prägung des Balakros in Kilikien', *JNG* 14 (1964) 79–82
185. Bellinger, A. R. 'The Thessaly hoard of 1938', *Congresso internationale di numismatica: Roma* 2 (1961) 57–60
186. Bellinger, A. R. 'Philippi in Macedonia', *ANSMN* 11 (1964) 29–52 and plates 6–11
187. Bellinger, A. R. *Essays on the Coinage of Alexander the Great* (Numismatic Studies No. 11). New York, 1963
188. Carradice, I. (ed) *Coinage and Administration in the Athenian and Persian Empires. The Ninth Oxford Symposium on Coinage and Monetary History* (BAR International Series 343). Oxford, 1987
189. Cawkwell, G. L. 'A note on the Heracles Coinage Alliance of 394 B.C.', *Num. Chron.* (1956) 69–75
190. Cawkwell, G. L. 'The ΣYN coins again', *JHS* 83 (1963) 152–4
191. Cook, J. M. 'Cnidian *peraea* and Spartan coins', *JHS* 81 (1961) 56–72
192. Franke, P. R. 'Geschichte, Politik und Münzprägung im frühen Makedonien', *JNG* 314 (1952) 99ff
193. Fried, S. 'The Decadrachm hoard: an introduction' in B 188, 1–20
194. Gaebler, H. *Die antiken Münzen Nord-Griechenlands,* III: *Makedonia und Paionia.* Berlin, 1935
195. Head, B. V. *Catalogue of Greek Coins, Macedonia etc.* British Museum, London, 1879
196. Head, B. V. *Historia Numorum.* Oxford, 1911
197. Jenkins, G. K. 'The Greek coins recently acquired by the British Museum', *Num. Chron.* (1955) 131–56
198. Kagan, J. 'The Decadrachm hoard: chronology and consequences', in B 188, 21–8
199. Kaiser, W. B. 'Ein Meister der Glyptik aus dem Umkreis Alexanders', *JDAI* 77 (1962) 227–39
200. Kraay, C. *Archaic and Classical Greek Coins.* London, 1976
201. Kraay, C. M. and Hirmer, M. *Greek Coins.* London, 1966
202. Le Rider, G. *Le monnayage d'argent et d'or de Philippe II frappé en Macédoine de 359 à 294.* Paris, 1977

203. Martin, T. R. *Sovereignty and Coinage in Classical Greece*. Princeton, 1985
204. May, J. M. F. *The Coinage of Damastion*. Oxford, 1939
205. May, J. M. F. *Ainos: its History and Coinage*. Oxford, 1950
206. May, J. M. F. *The Coinage of Abdera*. London, 1966
207. Merker, L. 'Notes on Abdalonymus and the dated coins of Sidon and Ake', *ANSMN* 11 (1964) 113–20
208. Mørkholm, O. 'A coin of Artaxerxes III', *Num. Chron.* (1974) 1–4
209. Mørkholm, O. 'The Alexander coinage of Nicocles of Paphos', *Chiron* 8 (1978) 135–47
210. Moysey, R. 'Observations on the numismatic evidence relating to the Great Satraps' revolt', *REA* 91 (1989) 107–39
211. Newell, E. T. *The Dated Alexander Coinage of Sidon and Ake*. New Haven, 1916
212. Price, M. J. 'Alexander's reform of the Macedonian regal coinage', *Num. Chron.* (1982) 180–90
213. Price, M. J. and Waggoner, N. *Archaic Greek Coinage: the Asyut Hoard*. London, 1975
214. Robert, L. *Etudes de numismatique grecque*. Paris, 1951
215. Schlumberger, D. *L'argent grec dans l'empire achéménide*. Paris, 1953
216. Thompson, M., Mørkholm, O. and Kraay, C. M. *An Inventory of Greek Coin Hoards*. New York, 1973
217. Zervos, O. H. 'Notes on a book by Gerhard Kleiner', *Num. Chron.* (1982) 166–79

C. THE GREEK STATES

I. GENERAL HISTORY, CONSTITUTIONS, PEACES, ETC.

1. Accame, S. *Ricerche intorno alla guerra corinzia*. Naples, 1951
2. Andrewes, A. and Lewis, D. M. 'Note on the Peace of Nikias', *JHS* 77 (1957) 177–80
3. Asheri, D. *Distribuzioni di terre nell'antica Grecia* (Memoria dell'Accademia delle scienze di Torino 4a, No. 10). Turin, 1966
4. Aucello, E. 'Ricerche sulla cronologia della guerra corinzia', *Helikon* 4 (1964) 29–45
5. Aucello, E., 'La genesi della pace di Antalcida', *Helikon* 5 (1965) 340–80
6. Barbera, L. 'Il problema interpretativo del trattato conchiuso a Tebe nel 366/5 a.C.', *Helikon* 9–10 (1969–70) 460–74
7. Bauslaugh, R. A. *The Concept of Neutrality in Classical Greece*. Berkeley–Los Angeles–Oxford, 1991
8. Bengtson, H. 'Die griechische Polis bei Aineias', *Historia* 11 (1962) 458–68
9. Berve, H. *Die Tyrannis bei den Griechen*. 2 vols. Munich, 1967
10. Browning, R. 'The crisis of the Greek city – a new collective study', (Review of C 83) *Philologus* 120 (1976) 258–66
11. Bruce, I. A. F. 'Internal politics and the outbreak of the Corinthian war', *Emerita* 28 (1960) 75–86

12. Buckler, J. 'Dating the peace of 375/4 B.C.', *GRBS* 12 (1971) 353–61
13. Cassola, F. 'La polis nel IV secolo: crisi o evoluzione?' (Review of C 83) *Athenaeum* ser. 2, 54 (1976) 446–62
14. Cawkwell, G. L. 'The Common Peace of 366/5 B.C.', *CQ* n.s. 11 (1961) 80–6
15. Cawkwell, G. L. 'Notes on the Social War', *Class. et Med.* 23 (1962) 34–49
16. Cawkwell, G. L. 'Notes on the peace of 375/4', *Historia* 12 (1963) 84–95
17. Cawkwell, G. L. 'The Peace of Philocrates again', *CQ* 28 (1978) 93–104
18. Cawkwell, G. L. 'The King's Peace', *CQ* n.s. 31 (1981) 69–83
19. Ehrenberg, V. L. *The Greek State.* 2nd edn. London, 1969
20. Ehrhardt, C. 'The third sacred war', Unpub. B. Litt. thesis. Oxford, 1961
21. Ferrill, A. 'Herodotus on tyranny', *Historia* 27 (1978) 385–98
22. Frolov, E. 'Die späte Tyrannis im balkanischen Griechenland', in C 83, 1, 231–400
23. Fuks, A. *Social Conflict in Ancient Greece* (Jerusalem–Leiden, 1984)
24. Funke, P. *Homónoia und Arché (Historia* Einzelschr. 37). Wiesbaden, 1980
25. Gauthier, P. *Symbola: Les Etrangers et la justice dans les cités grecques.* (Annales de l'Est, Mémoires 42). 1972
26. Gauthier, P. 'Les cités hellénistiques: épigraphie et histoire des institutions et des régimes politiques' in *Proceedings of the Eighth Epigraphical Congress, Athens, 1982,* 1, 82–107. Athens, 1984
27. Gehrke, H.-J. *Stasis. Untersuchungen zu den inneren Kriegen in den griechischen Staaten des 5. und 4. Jahrhunderts v. Chr.* (Vestigia 35). Munich, 1985
28. Gehrke, H.-J. *Jenseits von Athen und Sparta: das dritte Griechenland und seine Staatenwelt.* Munich, 1986
29. Gernet, L. 'Mariages de tyrans', in *Hommage à Lucien Febvre, Eventail de l'histoire vivante,* 41–53. Paris, 1953 (= id. *Anthropologie de la grèce antique,* 344–59)
29A. Gschnitzer, F. *Abhängige Orte im griechischen Altertum* (Zetemata 17). Munich, 1958
30. Hamilton, C. D. 'Isocrates, *IG* II² 43, Greek propaganda and imperialism', *Traditio* 36 (1980) 83–109
31. Hampl, F. *Die griechischen Staatsverträge des 4. Jhdts. v. Chr. Geb.* Leipzig, 1938
32. Hampl, F. 'Poleis ohne Territorium', *Klio* 32 (1939) 1–60
33. Heintzeler, G. *Das Bild des Tyrannen bei Platon.* Stuttgart, 1927
34. Herman, G. *Ritualised Friendship and the Greek City.* Cambridge, 1987
35. Kagan, D. 'The economic origins of the Corinthian war', *PP* 16 (1961) 321–41
36. Larsen, J. A. O. *Representative Government in Greek and Roman History.* Berkeley–Los Angeles, 1955
37. Larsen, J. A. O. *Greek Federal States: Their Institutions and History.* Oxford, 1968
38. Lauffer, S. 'Die Diodordublette xv 38 = 50 über die Friedensschlüsse zu Sparta 374 und 371 v.Chr.', *Historia* 8 (1959) 315–48
39. Lehmann, G. A. 'Spartas ἀρχή und die Vorphase des korinthischen Krieges in den Hellenica Oxyrhynchia', *ZPE* 28 (1978) 107–26; 30 (1978) 73–93

40. Levi, M. A. 'Le fonti per la pace di Antalcida', *Acme* 8 (1955) 105–11
41. Lewis, D. M. 'Democratic institutions and their diffusion', *Proceedings of the Eighth Epigraphical Congress, Athens, 1982*, 1, 55–61. Athens, 1984
42. Lewis, D. M. 'Persian gold in Greek international relations', *REA* 91 (1989) 227–35
43. Lintott, A. W. *Violence, Civil Strife and Revolution in the Classical City, 750–330 B.C.* London, 1982
44. Londey, P. D. 'Panhellenic representation at Delphoi in the fourth century B.C.' Ph.D. thesis, Monash University, Melbourne, 1982
45. Martin, V. *La vie internationale dans la Grèce des cités.* Paris, 1940
46. Martin, V. 'Le traitement de l'histoire diplomatique dans la tradition littéraire du IVe siècle avant J.C.', *Mus. Helv.* 1 (1944) 13–30
47. Martin, V. 'Sur une interprétation nouvelle de la "paix du roi"', *Mus. Helv.* 6 (1949) 127–39
48. Moggi, M. *I sinecismi interstatali greci*, 1: *Dalle origini al 338 a. C.* Pisa, 1976
49. Momigliano, A. 'La κοινὴ εἰρήνη dal 386 al 338', *Riv. di Filol.* n.s. 12 (1934) 482–514
50. Momigliano, A. 'Sea power in Greek thought', in *Secondo contributo alla storia degli studi classici*, 57–68. Rome, 1960
51. Momigliano, A. 'Per la storia della pubblicistica sulla κοινὴ εἰρήνη nel IV secolo a.C.', in *Terzo contributo alla storia degli studi classici e del mondo antico*, 457–87. Rome, 1966
52. Murray, O. and Price, S. (eds.) *The Greek City from Homer to Alexander.* Oxford, 1990
53. Niese, B. 'Chronologische und historische Beiträge zur griechischen Geschichte der Jahre 370–364 v. Chr.', *Hermes* 39 (1904) 84–132
54. Nolte, F. *Die historisch-politischen Voraussetzungen des Königsfriedens.* Bamberg, 1923
55. Ostwald, M. *Autonomia: its Genesis and Early History.* Chico, CA, 1982
56. Perlman, S. 'The causes and outbreak of the Corinthian war', *CQ* n.s. 14 (1964) 64–81
57. Perlman, S. 'Panhellenism, the polis and imperialism', *Historia* 25 (1976) 1–30
58. Rice, D. G. 'Xenophon, Diodorus and the year 379/378 B.C. Reconstruction and reappraisal', *YCS* 24 (1975) 95–130
59. Romilly, J. de. 'Vocabulaire et propagande: ou les premiers emplois du mot *homonoia*', *Mélanges de linguistique et de philologie grecques offerts à P. Chantraine*, 199–209. Paris, 1972
60. Roos, A. G. 'The peace of Sparta of 374 B.C.', *Mnemosyne* ser. 4, 2 (1949) 265–85
61. Roy, J. 'Arcadia and Boeotia in Peloponnesian affairs, 370–362 B.C.', *Historia* 20 (1971) 569–99
62. Runciman, W. G. 'Doomed to extinction: the *polis* as an evolutionary dead-end', in c 52, 347–67
63. Ruschenbusch, E. *Untersuchungen zu Staat und Politik in Griechenland vom 7.–4. Jh. v. Chr.* Bamberg, 1978
64. Ruschenbusch, E. 'Die Bevölkerungszahl Griechenlands im 5. und 4. Jh. v. Chr.', *ZPE* 56 (1984) 55–7

65. Ruschenbusch, E. 'Die Zahl der griechischen Staaten und Arealgrösse und Bürgerzahl der "Normalpolis"', *ZPE* 59 (1985) 253–63
66. Ryder, T. T. B. 'The supposed common peace of 366/5 B.C.', *CQ* n.s. 7 (1957) 199–205
67. Ryder, T. T. B. *Koine Eirene.* London, 1965
68. de Ste Croix, G. E. M. *The Origins of the Peloponnesian War.* London, 1972
69. de Ste Croix, G. E. M. 'Political pay outside Athens', *CQ* n.s. 25 (1975) 48–52
70. de Ste Croix, G. E. M. *The Class Struggle in the Ancient Greek World.* London, 1981
71. Schaefer, A. *Demosthenes und seine Zeit*, I–III. 2nd edn. Leipzig, 1885–7
72. Schehl, F. 'Zum korinthischen Bund vom Jahre 338/7 v. Chr.', *JÖAI* 27 (1932) 115–45
73. Seager, R. 'The King's Peace and the balance of power in Greece, 386–362 B.C.', *Athenaeum* 52 (1974) 36–63
74. Seager, R. and Tuplin, C. J. 'The freedom of the Greeks in Asia', *JHS* 100 (1980) 141–54
75. Seibert, J. *Die politischen Flüchtlinge und Verbannten in der griechischen Geschichte* (Impulse der Forschung 30). Darmstadt, 1979
76. Sinclair, R. K. 'The King's Peace and the employment of military and naval forces 387–378', *Chiron* 8 (1978) 29–54
77. Sordi, M. 'La pace di Atene 371/0', *Riv. di Filol.* 79 (1951) 34–64
78. Sordi, M. 'La fondation du collège des naopes et la renouveau politique de l'amphictionie au IVe siècle', *BCH* 81 (1957) 38–75
79. Starr, C. G. 'Greeks and Persians in the fourth century B.C. A study in political contacts before Alexander', *Ir. Ant.* 11 (1976) 39–99 and 12 (1977) 49–116
80. Tuplin, C. J. 'Two proper names in the text of Diodorus book 15', *CQ* n.s. 29 (1979) 347–57
81. Tuplin, C. J., 'Timotheus and Corcyra: problems in Greek history 375–373 B.C.', *Athenaeum* 62 (1984) 537–68
82. von Stern, E. *Geschichte der spartanischen und thebanischen Hegemonie.* Dorpat, 1884
83. Welskopf, E. C. (ed.) *Hellenische Poleis: Krise, Wandlung, Wirkung.* 4 vols. Berlin, 1974
84. West, A. B. *The History of the Chalcidic League.* Madison, 1918
85. West, W. C. 'Hellenic *homonoia* and the new decree from Plataea', *GRBS* 18 (1977) 307–19
86. Winterling, A. 'Polisbegriff und Staatstheorie des Aeneas Tacticus. Zur Frage der Grenzen der griechischen Polisgesellschaft im 4. Jahrhundert v. Chr.', *Historia* 40 (1991) 193–229

II. ATHENS

87. Accame, S. *La lega ateniese del secolo IV a.C.* Rome, 1941
88. Amit, M. *Athens and the Sea. A Study in Athenian Sea-Power* (Collection Latomus, LXXIV). Brussels, 1965

89. Anderson, J. K. 'The statue of Chabrias', *AJA* 67 (1963) 411–13
90. Andrewes, A. 'Philochorus on phratries', *JHS* 81 (1961) 1–15
91. Ashton, N. G. 'How many *pentereis*?', *GRBS* 20 (1979) 237–42
92. Ashton, N. G. 'The Lamian war – *stat magni nominis umbra*', *JHS* 104 (1984) 152–7
93. Barbieri, G. *Conone*. Roma, 1955
94. Beloch, J. *Die attische Politik seit Perikles*. Leipzig, 1884
95. Bleicken, J. 'Die Einheit der athenischen Demokratie in klassischer Zeit', *Hermes* 115 (1987) 257–83
96. Bruce, I. A. F. 'Athenian embassies in the early fourth century', *Historia* 15 (1966) 272–81
97. Buchanan, J. J. *Theorika*. Locust Valley, 1962
98. Buckler, J. 'A second look at the monument of Chabrias', *Hesp.* 41 (1972) 466–74
99. Burnett, A. P. 'Thebes and the expansion of the second Athenian confederacy: *IG* II² 40 and *IG* II² 43', *Historia* 11 (1962) 1–17
100. Burnett, A. P. and Edmonson, C. M. 'The Chabrias monument in the Athenian agora', *Hesp.* 30 (1961) 74–91
101. Cargill, J. *The Second Athenian League*. Berkeley–Los Angeles–London, 1981
102. Cawkwell, G. L. 'Aeschines and the Peace of Philocrates', *REG* 73 (1960) 416–38
103. Cawkwell, G. L. 'Aeschines and the ruin of Phocis', *REG* 75 (1962) 453–9
104. Cawkwell, G. L. 'Demosthenes and the stratiotic fund', *Mnemosyne* ser. 4, 15 (1962) 377–83
105. Cawkwell, G. L. 'The defence of Olynthus', *CQ* n.s. 12 (1962) 122–40
106. Cawkwell, G. L. 'Demosthenes' policy after the Peace of Philocrates' I and II, *CQ* 13 (1963) 120–38, 200–13
107. Cawkwell, G. L. 'Eubulus', *JHS* 83 (1963) 47–67
108. Cawkwell, G. L. 'The crowning of Demosthenes', *CQ* 19 (1969) 163–80
109. Cawkwell, G. L. 'The fall of Themistocles', *Auckland Classical Studies Presented to E. M. Blailock*, 39–58. Auckland, 1970
110. Cawkwell, G. L. 'The date of *I.G.* II² 1609 again', *Historia* 22 (1973) 759–61
111. Cawkwell, G. L. 'The foundation of the second Athenian confederacy', *CQ* n.s. 23 (1973) 47–60
112. Cawkwell, G. L. 'The imperialism of Thrasybulus', *CQ* n.s. 26 (1976) 270–7
113. Cawkwell, G. L. 'Notes on the failure of the second Athenian Confederacy', *JHS* 101 (1981) 40–55
114. Cawkwell, G. L. 'Athenian naval power in the fourth century', *CQ* 34 (1984) 334–45
115. Clinton, K. 'The nature of the late fifth-century revision of the Athenian law code', *Hesp.* Suppl. 19 (1982) 27–37
116. Cloché, P. *La restauration démocratique à Athènes en 403 avant J.-C.* Paris, 1915

117. Cloché, P. *La politique étrangère d'Athènes de 404 à 338.* Paris, 1934
118. Cloché, P. 'Les hommes politiques et la justice populaire dans l'Athènes du IVᵉ siècle', *Historia* 9 (1960) 80–95
119. Cloché, P. *Isocrate et son temps.* Paris, 1963
120. Cohen, E. E. *Ancient Athenian Maritime Courts.* Princeton, 1973
121. Coleman, J. E. and Bradeen, D. W. 'Thera on I.G. II², 43', *Hesp.* 36 (1967) 102–4
122. Davies, J. K. 'Demosthenes on liturgies: a note', *JHS* 87 (1967) 33–40
123. Davies, J. K. 'The date of *IG* ii.² 1609', *Historia* 18 (1969) 309–33
124. Davies, J. K. *Athenian Propertied Families, 600–300 B.C.* Oxford, 1971
125. Davies, J. K. 'Athenian citizenship: the descent group and the alternatives', *CJ* 73 (1977–8) 105–21
126. Davies, J. K. *Wealth and the Power of Wealth in Classical Athens.* New York, 1981
127. Develin, R. *Athenian Officials 684–322 B.C.* Cambridge, 1989
128. Dow, S. 'Aristotle, the Kleroteria and the Courts', *HSCP* 50 (1939) 1–34
129. Dow, S. 'The Athenian law codes', *Proc. Mass. Hist. Soc.* 71 (1953–9) 3–36
130. Dow, S. 'The Athenian calendar of sacrifices: the chronology of Nikomachos' second term', *Historia* 9 (1960) 270–93
131. Dow, S. 'The walls inscribed with Nikomakhos' law code', *Hesp.* 30 (1961) 58–73
132. Dušanić, S. 'Plato's Academy and Timotheus' policy, 365–359 B.C.', *Chiron* 10 (1980) 111–44
133. Ehrenberg, V. 'Early Athenian colonies', in *id.*, *Aspects of the Ancient World* (1946) 117–28
134. Ellis, J. R. 'The date of Demosthenes' *First Philippic*', *REG* 79 (1966) 636–9
135. Fingarette, A. 'A new look at the wall of Nikomachos', *Hesp.* 40 (1971) 330–5
136. Fisher, N. R. E. *Social Values in Classical Athens.* London–Toronto, 1976
137. Foucart, M. P. 'Les athéniens dans la Chersonèse de Thrace au IVe s.', *Mém. de l'acad. de l'insc.* 38 (1909) 83–120
138. Fuks, A. 'Notes on the Rule of the Ten at Athens in 403 B.C.', *Mnemosyne*⁴ 6 (1953) 198–207 (= C 23, 289–98)
139. Fuks, A. *The Ancestral Constitution.* London, 1953
140. Funke, P. 'Konons Rückkehr nach Athen', *ZPE* 53 (1983) 149–61
141. Gabrielsen, V. *Remuneration of State Officials in Fourth Century B.C. Athens* (Odense U. Cl. Stud. 11). Odense 1981
142. Gehrke, H.-J. 'Das Verhältnis von Politik und Philosophie im Wirken des Demetrios von Phaleron', *Chiron* 8 (1978) 149–93
143. Glotz, G. 'Démosthène et les finances athéniennes de 346 à 339', *Rev. Hist.* 171 (1932) 385–97
144. Gomme, A. W. *The Population of Athens in the Fifth and Fourth Centuries B.C.* (Glasgow U. Pub. 28). Oxford, 1933
145. Grégoire, H. and Goossens, R. 'Les allusions politiques dans l'*Hélène* d'Euripide', *CRAI* 1940, 215–27

146. Griffith, G. T. 'Athens in the fourth century', in A 22. 127–44
147. Griffith, J. G. 'A note on the first *eisphora* at Athens', *AJAH* 2 (1977) 3–7
148. Hall, L. G. H. 'Ephialtes, the Areopagus and the Thirty', *CQ* n.s. 40 (1990) 319–28
149. Hammond, N. G. L. 'Strategia and hegemonia in fifth-century Athens', *CQ* n.s. 19 (1969) 111–44 (= 'Problems of command in fifth-century Athens', in A 28, 346–94)
150. Hansen, M. H. 'Athenian *nomothesia* in the fourth century B.C. and Demosthenes' speech against Leptines', *Class. et Med.* 32 (1971–80) 87–104
151. Hansen, M. H. 'Perquisites for magistrates in fourth-century Athens', *Class. et Med.* 32 (1971–80) 105–25
152. Hansen, M. H. *The Sovereignty of the People's Court in Athens* (Odense U. Cl. Stud. 4). Odense, 1974
153. Hansen, M. H. *Eisangelia* (Odense U. Cl. Stud. 6). Odense, 1975
154. Hansen, M. H. 'How many Athenians attended the *ecclesia*?' *GRBS* 17 (1976) 115–34
155. Hansen, M. H. '*Nomos* and *psephisma* in fourth-century Athens', *GRBS* 19 (1978) 315–30
156. Hansen, M. H. 'Did the Athenian *ecclesia* legislate after 403/2 B.C.?' *GRBS* 20 (1979) 27–53
157. Hansen, M. H. '*Misthos* for magistrates in classical Athens', *SO* 54 (1979) 5–22
158. Hansen, M. H. 'Initiative and decision: the separation of powers in fourth century Athens', *GRBS* 22 (1981) 345–70
159. Hansen, M. H. 'The number of Athenian hoplites in 431 B.C.', *SO* 56 (1981) 19–32
160. Hansen, M. H. 'Two notes on the Athenian dikai emporikai', *Scientific Yearbook of the Graduate School of Political Sciences 'Panteios'* (1981) 167–75
161. Hansen, M. H. 'Demographic reflections on the number of Athenian citizens, 451–309 B.C.', *AJAH* 7 (1982) [1985] 172–9
162. Hansen, M. H. '*Rhetores* and *strategoi* in fourth century Athens', *GRBS* 24 (1983) 151–80
163. Hansen, M. H. 'The Athenian "politicians" 403–322 B.C.', *GRBS* 24 (1983) 33–55
164. Hansen, M. H. 'Athenian *nomothesia*', *GRBS* 26 (1985) 345–71
165. Hansen, M. H. *Demography and Democracy. The Number of Athenian Citizens in the Fourth Century B.C.* Herning, 1986
166. Hansen, M. H. 'Demography and democracy once again', *ZPE* (1988) 189–93
167. Hansen, M. H. *Three Studies in Athenian Demography* (Hist. Fil. Medd. Dan. Vid. Selsk. 56, 1988)
168. Hansen, M. H. Review of C 210, *CR* n.s. 40 (1990) 348–56
169. Harding, P. 'The Theramenes myth', *Phoenix* 28 (1974) 101–11
170. Harding, P. 'Androtion's political career', *Historia* 25 (1976) 186–200
171. Harrison, A. R. W. 'Law-making at Athens at the end of the fifth century B.C.', *JHS* 75 (1955) 26–35

172. Harrison, A. R. W. *The Law of Athens*. 2 vols. Oxford, 1968–71
173. Hatzfeld, J. *Alcibiade*. Paris, 1951
174. Hignett, C. *A History of the Athenian Constitution*. Oxford, 1952
175. Humphreys, S. C. 'Lycurgus of Butadae: an Athenian aristocrat', in Eadie, J. W. and Ober, J. (eds.) *The Craft of the Ancient Historian: Essays in Honor of Chester G. Starr*, 199–252. Lanham Md., 1985
176. Isager, S. and Hansen, M. H. *Aspects of Athenian Society in the Fourth Century* B.C. Odense, 1975
177. Jaeger, W. *Demosthenes: the Origin and Growth of his Policy*. Cambridge, 1938
178. Jones, A. H. M. *Athenian Democracy*. London, 1957
179. Judeich, W. *Topographie von Athen (Handbuch der Altertumswissenschaft* III.2.2). 2nd edn. Munich, 1931
180. Kallet, L. 'Iphikrates, Timotheos, and Athens, 371–360 B.C.', *GRBS* 24 (1983) 329–52
181. Krentz, P. 'Foreigners against the Thirty: *IG* 2² 10 again', *Phoenix* 34 (1980) 298–306
182. Krentz, P. *The Thirty at Athens*. Ithaca–London, 1982
183. Krentz, P. 'The rewards for Thrasyboulos' supporters', *ZPE* 62 (1986) 201–4
184. Kroll, J. H. *Athenian Bronze Allotment Plates* (Loeb Cl. Monographs). Cambridge, MA, 1972
185. Lewis, D. M. Review of c 141, *JHS* 102 (1982) 269
186. Lewis, D. M. 'The Athenian coinage decree', in B 188, 53–64
187. Lewis, D. M. 'Oligarchic thinking in the late fifth century', in *Nomodeiktes: Essays presented to Martin Ostwald*. Ann Arbor, 1993
188. Loening, T. C. *The Reconciliation Agreement of 403/402 B.C. in Athens: Its Content and Application (Hermes* Einzelschr. 53). Stuttgart–Wiesbaden, 1987
189. Loeper, R. 'The Thirty Tyrants', *Zhurnal Ministerva Narodnogo Prosvescheniya* (May–June 1896) 90–101
190. Loraux, N. *L'invention d'Athènes. Histoire de l'oraison funèbre dans la cité 'classique'*. Paris–The Hague, 1981. (Eng. trs. *The Invention of Athens*. Cambridge, MA—London, 1986)
191. McCoy, W. J. 'Aristotle's *Athenaion Politeia* and the establishment of the Thirty Tyrants', *YCS* 23 (1975) 131–45
192. MacDowell, D. 'The chronology of Athenian speeches and legal innovations in 401–398 B.C.', *RIDA* ser. 3, 18 (1971) 267–73
193. MacDowell, D. 'Law-making at Athens in the fourth century B.C.', *JHS* 95 (1975) 62–74
194. MacDowell, D. *The Law in Classical Athens*. London, 1978
195. MacDowell, D. Review of c 141, *CR* n.s. 33 (1983) 75f
196. MacDowell, D. 'The law of Periandros about symmories', *CQ* n.s. 36 (1986) 438–49
197. Markle, M. M. III. 'Demosthenes' "Second Philippic": a valid policy for the Athenians against Philip', *Antichthon* 15 (1981) 62–85

198. Markle, M. M. III. 'The Peace of Philocrates'. Ph.D. thesis, Princeton, 1970
199. Markle, M. M. III. 'Support of Athenian intellectuals for Philip: A study of Isocrates' Philippus and Speusippus' Letter to Philip', *JHS* 96 (1976) 80–99
200. Marshall, F. H. *The Second Athenian Confederacy*. Cambridge, 1905
201. Meiggs, R. *The Athenian Empire*. Oxford, 1972
202. Mitchel, F. W. 'Demades of Paeania and *IG* ii² 1493, 1494, 1495', *TAPA* 93 (1962) 213–29
203. Mitchel, F. W. *Lykourgan Athens: 338–322* (Lectures in Memory of Louise Semple Taft, 2nd series). Cincinnati, 1970
204. Mitchel, F. W. 'The so-called earliest ephebic inscription', *ZPE* 19 (1975) 233–43
205. Mitchel, F. W. 'The Nellos (IGII² 43 B 35–38)', *Chiron* 11 (1981) 73–7
206. Mosley, D. J. 'The Athenian embassy to Sparta in 371 B.C.', *PCPhS* 188 (1962) 41–6
207. Mosley, D. J. 'Athens' alliance with Thebes in 339 B.C.', *Historia* 20 (1971) 508–10
208. Mossé, C. *La fin de la démocratie athénienne*. Paris, 1962
209. Mossé, C. 'Die politischen Prozesse und die Krise der athenischen Demokratie', in c 83, I. 160–87. (French trans. 'Les Procès politiques et la crise de la démocratie athénienne', *DHA* 1 (1974) 207–36)
210. Ober, J. *Mass and Elite in Democratic Athens*. Princeton, 1989
211. Ooteghem, J. van. 'Démosthène et le théoricon', *LEC* 1 (1932) 388–407
212. Osborne, R. G. *Demos: the Discovery of Classical Attika*. Cambridge, 1985
213. Ostwald, M. 'The Athenian legislation against tyranny and subversion', *TAPA* 86 (1955) 103–28
214. Ostwald, M. *From Popular Sovereignty to the Sovereignty of Law*. Berkeley–Los Angeles–London, 1986
215. Pélékidis, Ch. *Histoire de l'éphébie attique des origines à 31 avant Jésus-Christ* (Ec. Fr. d'Athènes, Travaux et Mémoires 13). Paris, 1962
216. Parke, H. W. 'Athens and Euboea, 349/8 B.C.', *JHS* 49 (1929) 246–52
217. Pečírka, J. 'The crisis of the Athenian *polis* in the fourth century B.C.', *Eirene* 14 (1976) 5–29
218. Pecorella Longo, C. *'Eterie' e gruppi politici nell' Atene del IV sec. a.C.* (U. Padova, Pubb. Fac. Lett. e Fil. 48). Florence, 1971
219. Perlman, S. 'Political leadership in Athens in the fourth century B.C.', *PP* 22 (1967) 161–76
220. Perlman, S. 'Athenian democracy and the revival of imperialistic expansion at the beginning of the fourth century B.C.', *Cl. Phil.* 63 (1968) 257–67
221. Perlman, S. 'On bribing Athenian ambassadors', *GRBS* 17 (1976) 223–33
222. Pickard-Cambridge, A. W. *Demosthenes and the Last Days of Greek Freedom*. New York–London, 1914
223. Pohlenz, M. 'Philipps Schreiben an Athen', *Hermes* 46 (1929) 41–62

224. Rhodes, P. J. *The Athenian Boule*. Oxford, 1972. Rptd with additions 1989

225. Rhodes, P. J. 'On labelling fourth-century politicians', *LCM* 3 (1978) 207–11

226. Rhodes, P. J. 'Athenian democracy after 403 B.C.', *CJ* 75 (1979/80) 305–23

227. Rhodes, P. J. 'Ephebi, bouleutae and the population of Athens', *ZPE* 38 (1980) 191–201

228. Rhodes, P. J. '*Nomothesia* in fourth-century Athens', *CQ* n.s. 35 (1985) 55–60

229. Rhodes, P. J. 'Political activity in classical Athens', *JHS* 106 (1986) 132–44

230. Rhodes, P. J. 'The Athenian code of laws, 410–399 B.C.', *JHS* 111 (1991) 87–100

231. Roberts, J. T. 'Athens' so-called unofficial politicians', *Hermes* 110 (1982) 354–62

232. Robertson, N. 'The laws of Athens, 410–399 B.C.: the evidence for review and publication', *JHS* 110 (1990) 43–75

233. Rohrmoser, J. 'Kritische Betrachtungen über den philokrateischen Frieden', *Zeitschr. für die österr. Gymn.* 25 (1874) 789–815

234. Ruschenbusch, E. *Athenische Innenpolitik im 5. Jahrhundert v. Chr.: Ideologie oder Pragmatismus?* Bamberg, 1979

235. Ruschenbusch, E. 'Die Einführung des Theorikon', *ZPE* 36 (1979) 303–8

236. Ruschenbusch, E. 'Die soziale Herkunft der Epheben um 330', *ZPE* 35 (1979) 173–6

237. Ruschenbusch, E. 'Die soziale Zusammensetzung des Rates der 500 in Athen im 4. Jh.', *ZPE* 35 (1979) 177–80

238. Ruschenbusch, E. 'Epheben, Bouleuten und die Bürgerzahl von Athen um 330 v. Chr.', *ZPE* 41 (1981) 103–5

239. Ruschenbusch, E. 'Noch einmal die Bürgerzahl Athens um 330 v. Chr.', *ZPE* 44 (1981) 110–12

240. Ruschenbusch, E. 'Tribut und Bürgerzahl im ersten athenischen Seebund', *ZPE* 53 (1983) 125–43

241. Ruschenbusch, E. 'Zum letzten Mal: die Bürgerzahl Athens im 4. Jh. v. Chr.', *ZPE* 54 (1984) 253–69

242. Ruschenbusch, E. 'Ein Beitrag zur Liturgie und zur Eisphora', *ZPE* 59 (1985) 237–52

243. Ruschenbusch, E. 'Symmorienprobleme', *ZPE* 69 (1987) 75–81

244. Ruschenbusch, E. 'Demography and democracy. Doch noch einmal über die Bürgerzahl Athens im 4. Jh. v. Chr.', *ZPE* 72 (1988) 139f, and 'Stellungnahme', *ibid.* 194–6

245. Ryder, T. T. B. 'Athenian foreign policy and the peace-conference at Sparta in 371 B.C.', *CQ* n.s. 13 (1963) 237–41

246. de Ste Croix, G. E. M. 'The alleged secret pact between Athens and Philip II concerning Amphipolis and Pydna', *CQ* n.s. 13 (1963) 110–19

247. Salmon, P. 'L'Etablissement des Trente à Athènes', *Ant. Class.* 38 (1969) 497–500

248. Schmitt, J.-M. 'Les premières tétrères à Athènes', *REA* 87 (1974) 80–90
249. Seager, R. 'Lysias against the corn-dealers', *Historia* 15 (1966) 172–84
250. Seager, R. 'Thrasybulus, Conon and Athenian imperialism 396–386 B.C.', *JHS* 87 (1967) 95–115
251. Sealey, R. 'Athens after the Social War', *JHS* 75 (1955) 75–81 (= C 255, 164–82)
252. Sealey, R. 'Proxenus and the Peace of Philocrates', *Wien. Stud.* 68 (1955) 145–52
253. Sealey, B. R. I. 'Callistratos of Aphidna and his contemporaries', *Historia* 5 (1956) 178–203 (= C 255, 133–63)
254. Sealey, R. '*IG* II² 1609 and the transformation of the second Athenian sea-league', *Phoenix* 11 (1957) 95–111
255. Sealey, B. R. I. *Essays in Greek Politics*. New York, 1967
256. Sealey, R. '*Ath. Pol.* 25.2 and Lys. fr. 178: "additional" functions of the Areopagite Council', *JHS* 111 (1991) 210
257. Sinclair, R. K. *Democracy and Participation in Athens*. Cambridge, 1988
258. Stone, I. F. *The Trial of Socrates*. Boston–London, 1988
259. Strauss, B. S. *Athens after the Peloponnesian War*. London–Sydney, 1986
260. Sundwall, J. *Epigraphische Beiträge zur sozial-politischen Geschichte Athens im Zeitalter des Demosthenes* (*Klio* Bhft. 4). 1906
261. Tritle, L. A. *Phocion the Good*. London, 1988
262. Tuplin, C. J. 'The Athenian embassy to Sparta, 372/1', *LCM* 2 (1977) 51–6
263. Tuplin, C. J. 'Lysias XIX, the Cypriot war and Thrasybulus' naval expedition', *Philologus* 127 (1983) 170–86
264. Usher, S. 'Xenophon, Critias and Theramenes', *JHS* 88 (1968) 128–35
265. Whitehead, D. *The Ideology of the Athenian Metic* (*PCPhS* Suppl. vol. 4). Cambridge, 1977
266. Whitehead, D. 'The tribes of the Thirty Tyrants', *JHS* 100 (1980) 208–13
267. Whitehead, D. 'A thousand new Athenians', *LCM* 9 (1984) 8–10
268. Whitehead, D. *The Demes of Attica 508/7 – ca. 250 B.C.: A Political and Social Study*. Princeton, 1986
269. Whitehead, D. 'The ideology of the Athenian metic: some pendants and a reappraisal', *PCPhS* 212 (1986) 145–58
270. Wilamowitz-Moellendorff, U. von. *Aristoteles und Athen*, I. Berlin, 1893
271. Wilson, C. H. 'Athenian military finances, 378/7 to the peace of 375', *Athenaeum* 48 (1970) 302–26
272. Woodhead, A. G. '*IG* II² 43 and Jason of Pherae', *AJA* 61 (1957) 367–73
273. Woodhead, A. G. 'Chabrias, Timotheus and the Aegean cities, 375–373 B.C.', *Phoenix* 16 (1962) 258–66

III. SPARTA

274. Andrewes, A. 'The Government of Classical Sparta', in A 3, 1–20
275. Andrewes, A. 'Two notes on Lysander', *Phoenix* 25 (1971) 206–26
276. Andrewes, A. 'Spartan imperialism?', in A 22, 91–102 with 302–6
277. Badian, E. 'Agis III', *Hermes* 95 (1967) 170–92

278. Bockisch, G. 'Harmostai (431–387)', *Klio* 46 (1965) 129–239
279. Bommelaer, J.-F. *Lysandre de Sparte. Histoire et traditions* (*BEFAR* 240). Paris, 1981
280. Buckler, J. 'Plutarch and the fate of Antalkidas', *GRBS* 18 (1977) 139–45
281. Cartledge, P. A. 'A new 5th-century Spartan treaty', *LCM* 1 (1976) 87–92
282. Cartledge, P. A. *Sparta and Lakonia*. London, 1979
283. Cartledge, P. 'Sparta and Samos: a special relationship?', *CQ* n.s. 32 (1982) 243–65
284. Cartledge, P. A. *Agesilaos and the Crisis of Sparta*. London–Baltimore, 1987
285. Cawkwell, G. L. 'Agesilaus and Sparta', *CQ* n.s. 26 (1976) 62–84
286. Cawkwell, G. L. 'The decline of Sparta', *CQ* n.s. 33 (1983) 385–400
287. Coldstream, J. N. and Huxley, G. L. (eds.) *Kythera: Excavations and Studies Conducted by the University of Pennsylvania Museum and the British School at Athens*. London, 1972
288. David, E. 'The influx of money into Sparta at the end of the fifth century B.C.', *SCI* 5 (1979/80) 30–45
289. David, E. *Sparta betweeen Empire and Revolution, 404–243 B.C. Internal Problems and their Impact on Contemporary Greek Consciousness*. New York, 1981
290. Finley, M. I. 'Sparta' in Vernant, J.-P. (ed.), *Problèmes de la guerre en Grèce ancienne*, 143–60. Paris, 1968 (= Finley, M. I., *The Use and Abuse of History*, 161–77. London, 1975)
291. Graefe, F. 'Die Operationen des Antalkidas im Hellespont', *Klio* 28 (1935) 262–70
292. Gschnitzer, F. *Ein neuer spartanischer Staatsvertrag und die Verfassung des Peloponnesischen Bundes* (Beiträge zur klassischen Philologie 93). Meisenheim am Glan, 1978
293. Hamilton, C. D. 'Spartan politics and policy 405–401 B.C.', *AJP* 91 (1970) 294–314
294. Hamilton, C. D. *Sparta's Bitter Victories. Politics and Diplomacy in the Corinthian War*. Ithaca–London, 1979
295. Hamilton, C. D. *Agesilaus and the Failure of the Spartan Hegemony*. Ithaca, 1991
296. Hodkinson, S. 'Social order and the conflict of values in classical Sparta', *Chiron* 13 (1983) 239–81
297. Hodkinson, S. 'Land tenure and inheritance in classical Sparta', *CQ* n.s. 36 (1986) 378–406
298. Hodkinson, S. 'Inheritance, marriage and demography: perspectives upon the success and decline of classical Sparta', in C 309, 79–121
299. Kelly, D. H. 'Agesilaus' strategy in Asia Minor, 396–395 B.C.'. *LCM* 3 (1978) 97–8
300. Lazenby, J. F. *The Spartan Army*. Warminster, 1985
301. Lotze, D. *Lysander und der peloponnesischer Krieg* (*Abh. Sächs.* 57 (1964))

302. MacDonald, A. 'A note on the raid of Sphodrias', *Historia* 21 (1972) 38–44
303. McQueen, E. J. 'Some notes on the anti-Macedonian movement in the Peloponnese in 331 B.C.', *Historia* 27 (1978) 40–64
304. Ollier, F. *Le mirage spartiate*. I, Paris, 1933; II (Annales de l'université de Lyon III, 13, 1943)
305. Parke, H. W. 'The development of the second Spartan empire', *JHS* 50 (1930) 37–79
306. Peek, W. *Ein neuer spartanischer Staatsvertrag Abh.* (Sächs 65.3 (1974))
307. Poralla, P. *Prosopographie der Lakedaimonier bis auf der Zeit Alexanders des Grossen.* Breslau, 1913
308. Pouilloux, J. and Salviat, F. 'Lichas, Lacédémonien, archonte à Thasos et le livre VIII de Thucydide', *CRAI* (1983) 376–403
309. Powell, C. A. (ed.) *Classical Sparta. The Techniques Behind her Success.* London, 1988
310. Rawson, E. D. *The Spartan Tradition in European Thought.* Oxford, 1969
311. Redfield, J. 'The women of Sparta', *CJ* 73 (1977–8) 146–61
312. Rice, D. G. 'Agesilaus, Agesipolis and Spartan politics, 386–379 B.C.', *Historia* 23 (1974) 164–82
313. Ryder, T. T. B. 'Spartan relations with Persia after the King's Peace: a strange story in Diodorus 15.9', *CQ* n.s. 13 (1963) 105–9
314. Sansone, D. 'Lysander and Dionysius, Plut. *Lys.* 11' (with an addendum by R. Renehan), *Cl. Phil.* 76 (1981) 202–7
315. Seager, R. 'Agesilaus in Asia: propaganda and objectives', *LCM* 2 (1977) 183–4
316. Smith, R. E. 'Lysander and the Spartan Empire', *Cl. Phil.* 43 (1948) 145–56
317. Smith, R. E. 'The opposition to Agesilaus' foreign policy, 394–371 B.C.', *Historia* 2 (1953/54) 274–88
318. Talbert, R. J. A. 'The role of the Helots in the class struggle at Sparta', *Historia* 38 (1989) 22–40
319. Thompson, W. E. 'Observations on Spartan politics', *Riv. stor. ant.* 3 (1973) 47–58
320. Tigerstedt, E. N. *The Legend of Sparta in Classical Antiquity.* Uppsala, 1965–74
321. Whitehead, D. 'Sparta and the Thirty Tyrants', *AncSoc* 13/14 (1982–3) 106–30

IV. BOEOTIA AND THEBES

322. Beister, H. 'Untersuchungen zu der Zeit der thebanischen Hegemonie', Diss. Munich, 1970
323. Beister, H. 'Ein thebanisches Tropaion bereits vor Beginn der Schlacht bei Leuktra', *Chiron* 3 (1973) 65–84

324. Buckler, J. 'Theban treaty obligations in *IG* ii² 40: a postscript', *Historia* 20 (1971) 506–8

325. Buckler, J. 'On Agatharchides F. Gr. Hist. 86 F 8', *CQ* n.s. 27 (1977) 333–4

326. Buckler, J. 'The Thespians at Leuctra', *Wien. Stud.* 90 (1977) 76–9

327. Buckler, J. 'Plutarch on the trials of Pelopidas and Epaminondas (369 B.C.)', *Cl. Phil.* 73 (1978) 36–42

328. Buckler, J. 'The re-establishment of the *boiotarchia* (378 B.C.)', *AJAH* 4 (1979) 50–64

329. Buckler, J. *The Theban Hegemony, 371–362 B.C.* (Harvard Historical Studies 98). Cambridge, MA–London, 1980

330. Buckler, J. 'The alleged Theban–Spartan alliance of 386 B.C.', *Eranos* 78 (1980) 179–85

331. Buckler, J. 'Alliance and hegemony in fourth-century Greece: the case of the Theban hegemony', *AncW* 5 (1982) 79–89

332. Burn, A. R. 'Helikon in history: a study in Greek mountain topography', *BSA* 44 (1949) 313–23

333. Carrata Thomes, F. *Egemonia beotica e potenza maritima nella politica di Epaminonda*. Turin, 1952

334. Cawkwell, G. L. 'Epaminondas and Thebes', *CQ* n.s. 22 (1972) 254–78

335. Cloché, P. *Thèbes de Béotie*, Namur, 1952

336. Fortina, M. *Epaminonda*. Turin, 1958

337. Gullath, B. *Untersuchungen zur Geschichte Boiotiens in der Zeit Alexanders und der Diadochen*. Frankfurt am Main–Bern, 1982

338. Hack, H. M. 'Thebes and the Spartan hegemony, 386–382 B.C.', *AJP* 99 (1978) 210–27

339. Hammond, N. G. L. 'The two battles of Chaeronea (338 and 86 B.C.)', *Klio* 13 (1938) 186–218

340. Judeich, W. 'Athen und Theben vom Königsfrieden bis zur Schlacht bei Leuktra', *Rh. Mus.* N.F. 76 (1927) 171–97

341. Lewis, D. M. 'The synedrion of the Boeotian alliance' in Schachter, A. (ed.), *Essays in the Topography, History and Culture of Boiotia* (*Teiresias* Suppl. 3, 1990), 71–3

342. Mosley, D. J. 'Theban diplomacy in 371 B.C.', *REG* 85 (1972) 312–18

343. Pédech, P. 'La date de la bataille de Leuctres', *Riv. stor. ant.* 2 (1972) 1–6

344. Pritchett, W. K. 'Observations on Chaeronea' *AJA* 62 (1958) 307–11

345. Roesch, P. *Thespies et la confédération béotienne* (U. de Lyon, Institut F. Courby). Paris, 1965

346. Roesch, P. *Etudes béotiennes* (U. de Lyon, Institut F. Courby). Paris, 1982

347. Salmon, P. *Etude sur la confédération béotienne (447/6–386): son organisation et son administration* (Ac. Roy. Belge, Mem. Class. Lett. (8°)² 63.3). 1978

348. Sordi, M. 'La restaurazione della lega beotica nel 379–8 a.C.', *Athenaeum* 51 (1973) 79–90

349. Thiel, J. H. 'De synoecismo Boeotiae post annum 379 peracto', *Mnemosyne* ser. 2, 45 (1926) 19–28

350. Tuplin, C. J. 'The fate of Thespiae during the Theban hegemony', *Athenaeum* 64 (1986), 321–41

351. Westlake, H. D. 'Xenophon and Epaminondas', *GRBS* 16 (1975) 23–40
352. Wiseman, J. 'Epaminondas and the Theban invasions', *Klio* 51 (1969) 177–99

V. OTHERS

353. Braunert, H. and Petersen, T. 'Megalopolis: Anspruch und Wirklichkeit', *Chiron* 2 (1972) 57–90
354. ·Brunt, P. A. 'Euboea in the time of Philip II', *CQ* n.s. 19 (1969) 245–65
355. ·Cawkwell, G. L. 'Euboea in the late 340s', *Phoenix* 32 (1978) 42–67
356. Chadwick, J. '*Ταγά* and *ἀταγία*', *Studi linguistici . . . V. Pisani* (2 vols.), I. 231–4. Brescia, 1969
357. Dušanić, S. *Arkadski savez IV veka*. Belgrade, 1970 (*The Arcadian League of the 4th century*. In Serbian, with an extensive and detailed English summary at pp. 281–345)
358. Dušanić, S. 'Arkadika', *Ath. Mitt.* 94 (1979) 117–35
359. ·Dunant, C. and Pouilloux, J. *Etudes Thasiennes: Recherches sur l'histoire et les cultes de Thasos* II. Paris, 1958
360. ·Errington, R. M. 'Samos and the Lamian War', *Chiron* 5 (1975) 50–7
361. Franke, P. R. '*ΦΕΘΑΛΟΙ – ΦΕΤΑΛΟΙ – ΠΕΤΘΑΛΟΙ – ΘΕΣΣΑΛΟΙ*. Zur Geschichte Thessaliens im 5. Jh. v. Chr.', *Arch. Anz.* (1970) 85–93
362. Griffith, G. T. 'The union of Corinth and Argos (392–386 B.C.)', *Historia* 1 (1950) 236–56
363. Helly, B. *Gonnoi (Thessalie)*, I: *La cité et son histoire*. Amsterdam, 1973
364. Hodkinson, S. and H. 'Mantineia and the Mantinike: settlement and society in a Greek polis', *BSA* 76 (1981) 239–96
365. Hooker, J. T. 'Thessalian *ταγά*', *ZPE* 40 (1980) 272
366. Hornblower, S. 'When was Megalopolis founded?', *BSA* 85 (1990) 71–7
367. Kahrstedt, U. 'Chalcidic studies', *AJP* 57 (1936) 416–44
368. Lanzillotta, E. 'La fondazione di Megalopoli', *RSA* 5 (1975) 25–46
369. Legon, R. P. 'Phliasian politics and policy in the early fourth century B.C.', *Historia* 16 (1967) 324–37
370. Meloni, P. 'La tirannide di Euphrone I in Sicione', *Riv. di Filol.* 79 (1951) 10–33
371. Mendels, D. 'Aetolia 331–301: frustration, political power and survival', *Historia* 33 (1984) 129–80
372. Moggi, M. 'Il sinecismo di Megalopoli', *ASNP* 4 (1974) 71–107
373. Morrison, J. S. 'Meno of Pharsalus, Polycrates, and Ismenias', *CQ* 36 (1942) 65–76
374. Niese, B. 'Beiträge zur Geschichte Arkadiens', *Hermes* 34 (1899) 520–52
375. Piccirilli, L. 'Fliunte e il presunto colpo di stato democratico', *ASNP* ser. III. 4 (1974) 59–70
376. Pouilloux, J. *Etudes Thasiennes*. III: *Recherches sur l'histoire et les cultes de Thasos* I. Paris, 1954
377. Roux, G. *L'Amphictionie, Delphes et le temple d'Apollon au IVe siècle* (Collection de la Maison de l'Orient méditerranéen 8). Lyon, 1979

378. Roy, J. 'Diodorus Siculus xv 40 – the Peloponnesian revolutions of 374 B.C.', *Klio* 55 (1973) 135–9

379. Roy, J. 'Postscript on the Arcadian League', *Historia* 23 (1974) 505–7

380. Salmon, J. B. *Wealthy Corinth: A History of the City to 338 B.C.* Oxford, 1984

381. Sherwin-White, S. M. *Ancient Cos: An Historical Study from the Dorian Settlement to the Imperial Period* (Hypomnemata 51). Göttingen, 1978

382. Shipley, G. *A History of Samos 800–188 B.C.* Oxford, 1987

383. Sordi, M. 'Le origini del koinon etolico', *Acme* 6 (1953) 419–45 (= Gschnitzer, F. (ed.) *Zur griechischen Staatskunde*, 343–74. Darmstadt, 1969)

384. Sordi, M. *La lega tessala fino ad Alessandro magno* (Rome: *Stud. Ist. Ital. Stor. Ant.* 15). 1958

385. Thompson, W. E. 'The politics of Phlius', *Eranos* 68 (1970) 224–30

386. Thompson, W. E. 'Arcadian factionalism in the 360s', *Historia* 32 (1983) 149–60

387. Tuplin, C. J. 'The date of the union of Corinth and Argos', *CQ* n.s. 32 (1982) 75–83

388. Wade-Gery, H. T. 'Kritias and Herodes', *CQ* 39 (1945) 19–33 (= *Essays in Greek History*, 271–92. Oxford, 1958)

389. Westlake, H. D. *Thessaly in the Fourth Century B.C.* London, 1935

390. Whitby, L. M. 'The union of Corinth and Argos: a reconsideration', *Historia* 33 (1984) 295–308 •

391. Whitehead, D. 'Euphron, tyrant of Sicyon: an unnoticed problem in Xenophon, *Hell*.7.3.8', *LCM* 6 (1980) 175–8

392. Zahrnt, M. *Olynth und die Chalkidier*. Munich, 1971

D. MACEDON

I. GENERAL

1. Adams, W. L. 'The royal Macedonian tomb at Vergina', *AncW* 3 (1980) 67–72

2. Adams, W. L. and Borza, E. N. (eds.) *Philip II, Alexander the Great and the Macedonian Heritage*. Washington, DC, 1982

3. Andronikos, M. 'Vergina: the royal graves in the great tumulus', *AAA* 10 (1977) 1–40 (In Greek), 40–72 (In English)

4. Andronikos, M. 'The finds from the Royal Tombs at Vergina', *PBA* 65 (1979) 355–67

5. Andronikos, M. 'The Royal Tomb at Vergina and the problem of the dead', *AAA* 13 (1980) 168–78

6. Andronikos, M. *Vergina. The Royal Tombs and the Ancient City*. Athens, 1984

7. Andronikos, M. 'Some reflections on the Macedonian tomb', *BSA* 82 (1987) 1–16

8. Anson, E. M. 'Macedonia's alleged constitutionalism', *CJ* 80 (1985) 303–16

9. Ashton, N. G. 'The *naumachia* near Amorgos in 322 B.C.', *BSA* 72 (1977) 1–11

10. Aymard, A. '*Βασιλεὺς Μακεδόνων*', *RIDA* 4 (1950) 61–97 (= A 2, 100–22)

11. Aymard, A. 'Sur l'assemblée macédonienne', *REA* 52 (1950) 115–37 (= A 2, 143–63)

12. Badian, E. 'Greeks and Macedonians', in D 13, 33–51

13. Barr-Sharrar, B. and Borza, E. N. (eds.) *Macedonia and Greece in Late Classical and Early Hellenistic Times* (Studies in the History of Art 10). Washington, 1982

14. Borza, E. N. 'Some observations on malaria and the ecology of central Macedonia in antiquity', *AJAH* 4 (1979) 102–24

15. Borza, E. N. 'The Macedonian royal tombs at Vergina: some cautionary notes', *Archaeological News* 10 (1981) 73–87; 11 (1982) 8–10

16. Borza, E. N. 'The history and archaeology of Macedonia: retrospect and prospect', in D 13, 17–30

17. Borza, E. N. 'The natural resources of early Macedonia', in D 2, 1–20

18. Borza, E. N. 'The royal Macedonian tombs and the paraphernalia of Alexander the Great', *Phoenix* 41 (1987) 105–21

19. Borza, E. N. *In the Shadow of Olympus: The Emergence of Macedon.* Princeton–Oxford, 1990

20. Bosworth, A. B. 'Early relations between Aetolia and Macedon', *AJAH* 1 (1976) 164–81

21. Bosworth, A. B. 'Alexander the Great and the decline of Macedon', *JHS* 106 (1986) 1–12

22. Briant, P. *Antigone le Borgne: les débuts de sa carrière et les problèmes de l'assemblée macédonienne.* Paris, 1973

23. Carney, E. D. 'Alexander the Lyncestian: the disloyal opposition', *GRBS* 21 (1980) 23–33

24. Casson, S. *Macedonia, Thrace and Illyria.* Oxford, 1926

25. Cloché, P. *Histoire de la Macédoine.* Paris, 1960

26. Dell, H. J. (ed.) *Ancient Macedonian Studies in Honour of Charles F. Edson* (Institute of Balkan Studies 158). Thessaloniki, 1981

27. Edson, C. F. 'Early Macedonia', *Anc. Mac.* 1 (1970) 120–38

28. Ellis, J. R. 'Amyntas Perdikka, Philip II and Alexander the Great', *JHS* 91 (1971) 15–24

29. Ellis, J. R. 'The dynamics of fourth-century Macedonian imperialism', *Anc. Mac.* 2 (1977) 103–14

30. Errington, R. M. 'Macedonian "Royal Style" and its historical significance', *JHS* 94 (1974) 20–37

31. Errington, R. M. 'The nature of the Macedonian state under the monarchy', *Chiron* 8 (1978) 77–133

32. Errington, R. M. *Geschichte Makedoniens.* Munich, 1986

33. Errington, R. M. *A History of Macedonia.* Berkeley–Los Angeles, 1990

34. Fredricksmeyer, E. A. 'Again the so-called tomb of Philip II', *AJA* 85 (1981) 330–4

35. Fredricksmeyer, E. A. 'Once more the diadem and barrel-vault at Vergina', *AJA* 87 (1983) 99–102

36. Fredricksmeyer, E. A. 'Alexander and Philip: emulation and resentment', *CJ* 85 (1990) 300–15

37. Geyer, F. 'Makedonia', *RE* 14.1 (1928) coll. 638–771
38. Geyer, F. 'Makedonien bis zur Thronbesteigung Philipps II' (*Hist. Zeitschr.* Beiheft 19) Berlin–Munich, 1930
39. Granier, G. *Die makedonische Heeresversammlung: ein Beitrag zum antiken Staatsrecht* (Münchener Beiträge zur Papyrusforschung 13) 1931
40. Green, P. 'The royal tombs at Vergina: a historical analysis', in D 2, 129–51
41. Greenwalt, W. S. 'The introduction of Caranus into the Argead king list', *GRBS* 26 (1985) 43–9
42. Griffith, G. T. '*MAKEΔONIKA*: notes on the Macedonians of Philip and Alexander', *PCPhS* (1956–7) 3–10
43. Griffith, G. T. 'The Macedonian background', *G&R* 12 (1965) 125–39
44. Griffith, G. T. 'Peltasts and the origin of the Macedonian phalanx', in D 26, 161–7
45. Hammond, N. G. L. 'The archaeological background to the Macedonian kingdom', *Anc. Mac.* 1 (1970) 53–67 and plates 4–5
46. Hammond, N. G. L. *A History of Macedonia* 1. Oxford, 1972
47. Hammond, N. G. L. ' "Philip's Tomb" in historical context', *GRBS* 19 (1978) 331–50
48. Hammond, N. G. L. 'The evidence for the identity of the Royal Tombs at Vergina', in D 2, 111–27
49. Hammond, N. G. L. *The Macedonian State: The Origins, Institutions and History*. Oxford, 1989
50. Hammond, N. G. L. and Griffith, G. T. *A History of Macedonia*, II: *550–336 B.C.* Oxford, 1979
51. Hammond, N. G. L. and Walbank, F. W. *A History of Macedonia* III. Oxford, 1988
52. Hoffmann, O. *Die Makedonen, ihre Sprache und ihr Volkstum*. Göttingen, 1906
53. Kahrstedt, U. 'Städte in Makedonien', *Hermes* 81 (1953) 85–111
54. Kalleris, J. N. *Les anciens Macédoniens*, 1–11. Athens, 1954, 1976.
55. Kanatsulis, D. 'Antipatros als Feldherr und Staatsmann', *Ellenika* 16 (1958/9) 14–64
56. Lehmann, P. W. 'The so-called tomb of Philip II – a different interpretation', *AJA* 84 (1980) 527–31
57. Lehmann, P. W. 'The so-called tomb of Philip II – an addendum', *AJA* 86 (1980) 437–42
58. Musgrave, J. 'The skull of Philip II of Macedon', *Current Topics in Oral Biology*, 1–16. Bristol, 1985
59. Prag, A. J. N. W., Musgrave, J. H. and Neave, R. A. H. 'The Skull from Tomb II at Vergina: King Philip II of Macedon', *JHS* 104 (1984) 60–78
60. Prestianni Giallombardo, A. M. and Tripodi, B. 'Le tombe regali di Vergina: quale Filippo?', *ANSP* ser. III. 10 (1980) 989–1001
61. Samuel, A. E. 'Philip and Alexander as kings: Macedonian and Merovingian parallels', *AHR* 93 (1988) 1270–86

II. PHILIP

62. Badian, E. 'The death of Philip II', *Phoenix* 17 (1963) 244–50
63. Badian, E. 'Eurydice', in D 2, 99–110
64. Bickermann, E. and Sykutris, J. *Speusipps Brief an König Philipp* (Berichte über die Verhandlungen der Sächsischen Akademie der Wissenschaften zu Leipzig. Philol.-Hist. Kl. 80. 3). Leipzig, 1928
65. Borza, E. N. 'Philip II and the Greeks'. Review of D 80, *Cl. Phil.* 73 (1978) 236–43
66. Bosworth, A. B. 'Philip II and Upper Macedonia', *CQ* n.s. 21 (1971) 93–105
67. Buckler, J. *Philip II and the Sacred War*. Leiden, 1989
68. Burstein, S. M. 'The tomb of Philip II and the succession of Alexander the Great', *EMC/CV* 26 (1982) 141–63
69. Calder, W. M. III. 'Diadem and barrel-vault: a note', *AJA* 85 (1981) 334–5
70. Calder, W. M. III. '"Golden diadems" again', *AJA* 87 (1983) 102–3
71. Carapanos, C. *Dodone et ses ruines*. Paris, 1878
72. Carney, E. D. 'Olympias', *AncSoc* 18 (1987) 35–62
73. Cawkwell, G. L. *Philip of Macedon*. London, 1978
74. Cloché, P. *Un fondateur d'empire: Philippe II, roi de Macédoine*. St-Etienne, 1956
75. Crum, R. H. 'Philip II of Macedon and the Greek city-state'. Ph.D. thesis, Columbia, 1966
76. Develin, R. D. 'The murder of Philip II', *Antichthon* 15 (1981) 86–99
77. Ehrhardt, C. 'Two notes on Philip of Macedon's first intervention in Thessaly', *CQ* n.s. 17 (1967) 296–301
78. Ellis, J. R. 'Population-transplants by Philip II', *Makedonika* 9 (1969) 9–17
79. Ellis, J. R. 'The stepbrothers of Philip II', *Historia* 22 (1973) 350–4
80. Ellis, J. R. *Philip II and Macedonian Imperialism*. London, 1976
81. Ellis, J. R. 'Philip's Thracian campaign of 352–351', *Cl. Phil.* 72 (1977) 32–9
82. Ellis, J. R. 'The assassination of Philip II', in D 26, 99–137
83. Ellis, J. R. 'Philip and the Peace of Philocrates', in D 2, 43–59
84. Ellis, J. R. and Milns, R. D. *The Spectre of Philip*. Sydney, 1970
85. Errington, R. M. 'Review-discussion: four interpretations of Philip II', *AJAH* 6 (1981) 69–88
86. Fears, J. R. 'Pausanias, the assassin of Philip II', *Athenaeum* 53 (1975) 111–35
87. Fredricksmeyer, E. A. 'Divine honours for Philip II', *TAPA* 109 (1979) 39–61
88. Fredricksmeyer, E. A. 'On the final aims of Philip II', in D 2. 85–98
89. Geyer, F. 'Philippos', *RE* 19 (1938) coll. 2266–303
90. Glotz, G. 'Philippe et la surprise d'Elatée', *BCH* 33 (1909) 526–46

91. Griffith, G. T. 'Philip of Macedon's early interventions in Thessaly (358–352)', *CQ* n.s. 20 (1970) 67–80
92. Hamilton, C. D. 'Philip II and Archidamus', in D 2, 61–83
93. Hammond, N. G. L. 'The western frontier of Macedonia in the reign of Philip II', in D 26, 199–217
94. Hatzopoulos, M. B. 'A reconsideration of the Pixodaros affair', in D 13, 59–66
95. Hatzopoulos, M. B. 'The Oleveni inscription and the dates of Philip II's reign', in D 2, 21–42
96. Hatzopoulos, M. B. and Loukopoulou, L. D. (eds.), *Philip of Macedon*. Athens, 1980
97. Hauben, H. 'Philippe II, fondateur de la marine macédonienne', *Anc Soc* 6 (1975) 51–9
98. Heckel, W. 'Kleopatra or Eurydike?', *Phoenix* 32 (1978) 155–8
99. Heckel, W. 'Philip II, Kleopatra and Karanos', *Riv. di. Filol.* 107 (1979) 385–93
100. Hogarth, D. G. *Philip and Alexander of Macedon*. London, 1897
101. Kelly, D. H. 'Philip II of Macedon and the Boeotian alliance', *Antichthon* 14 (1980) 64–83
102. Kienast, D. *Philipp II von Makedonien und das Reich der Achaimeniden* (Abhandlungen der Marburger Gelehrten Gesellschaft 6). Marburg, 1973
103. Markle, M. M. III. 'The strategy of Philip in 346 B.C.', *CQ* 24 (1974) 253–68
104. Martin, T. 'Diodorus on Philip II and Thessaly', *Cl. Phil.* 76 (1981) 197
105. Milns, R. D. 'Philip II and the hypaspists', *Historia* 16 (1967) 509–12
106. Momigliano, A. D. *Filippo il Macedone*. Florence, 1934
107. Montgomery, H. 'The economic revolution of Philip II – myth or reality?', *SO* 60 (1985) 37–47
108. Parsons, P. J. 'The burial of Philip II', *AJAH* 4 (1979) 97–101
109. Perlman, S. 'Isocrates' "Philippus" – a reinterpretation', *Historia* 6 (1957) 306–17
110. Perlman, S. 'The coins of Philip II and Alexander the Great and their panhellenic propaganda', *Num. Chron.* (1965) 57–67
111. Perlman, S. (ed.) *Philip and Athens*. Cambridge, 1973
112. Pohlenz, M. 'Der Ausbruch des zweiten Krieges zwischen Philipp und Athen', *Gött. Nachr.* (1924) 38–42
113. Prestianni Giallombardo, A. M. 'Aspetti giuridici e problemi della reggenza di Filippo II di Macedonia', *Helikon* 13/14 (1973/4) 191–209
114. Prestianni Giallombardo, A. M. '*ΦΙΛΙΠΠΙΚΑ* I: sul "culto" Filippo II di Macedonia', *Sic. Gymn.* 28 (1975) 1–57
115. Prestianni Giallombardo, A. M. '"Diritto" matrimoniale, ereditario e dinastico nella Macedonia di Filippo II', *Riv. stor. ant.* 6/7 (1976/7) 81–110
116. Roebuck, C. 'The settlements of Philip II with the Greek states in 338 B.C.', *Cl. Phil.* 43 (1948) 73–92 = D 111, 209a–18
116A. Ruzicka, S. 'A note on Philip's Persian war', *AJAH* 10 (1985) 84–95

117. Schwahn, W. *Heeresmatrikel und Landfriede Philipps von Makedonien* (*Klio* Beiheft 21). 1930

118. Shrimpton, G. 'Theopompus' treatment of Philip in the Philippica', *Phoenix* 31 (1977) 123–44

119. Sordi, M. 'La terza guerra sacra', R*iv. di. Filol.* 36 (1958) 134–66

120. Tronson, A. 'Satyrus the Peripatetic and the marriages of Philip II', *JHS* 104 (1984) 116–26

121. West, A. B. 'The early diplomacy of Philip II of Macedon illustrated by his coins', *Num. Chron.* (1923) 169–210

122. Wilcken, U. 'Philipp II von Makedonien und die panhellenische Idee', *SBAk. Berlin* (1929) 291–318 (= D 111, 181–206)

123. Willrich, H. 'Wer liess König Philipp von Makedonien ermorden?', *Hermes* 34 (1899) 174–82

124. Wirth, G. *Philipp II* (Geschichte Makedoniens I). Stuttgart–Berlin–Köln–Mainz, 1986

125. Wüst, F. R. *Philipp II. von Makedonien und Griechenland in den Jahren von 346 bis 338* (Münchener Historische Abhandlungen 1.14). Munich, 1938

III. ALEXANDER

126. Andreotti, R. 'Per una critica dell'ideologia di Alessandro Magno', *Historia* 5 (1956) 257–302

127. Andreotti, R. 'Die Weltmonarchie Alexanders des Grossen in Überlieferung und geschichtlicher Wirklichkeit', *Saeculum* 8 (1957) 120–66

128. Ashton, N. G. 'The Lamian War: a false start', *Antichthon* 17 (1983) 47–61

129. Atkinson, K. M. T. 'Demosthenes, Alexander and asebeia', *Athenaeum* 51 (1973) 310–35

130. Aymard, A. 'Un ordre d'Alexandre', *REA* 39 (1937) 5–28

131. Badian, E. 'Alexander the Great and the unity of mankind', *Historia* 7 (1958) 425–44

132. Badian, E. 'The death of Parmenio', *TAPA* 91 (1960) 324–38

133. Badian, E. 'The first flight of Harpalus', *Historia* 9 (1960) 245–6

134. Badian, E. 'Harpalus', *JHS* 81 (1961) 16–43

135. Badian, E. 'Orientals in Alexander's army', *JHS* 85 (1965) 160–1

136. Badian, E. 'The administration of the empire', *G&R* 12 (1965) 166–82

137. Badian, E. 'Alexander the Great and the Greeks of Asia', in A 3, 37–69

138. Badian, E. 'A King's notebooks', *HSCP* 72 (1968) 183–204

139. Badian, E. Review of D 207, *Gnomon* 47 (1975) 48–58

140. Badian, E. 'The battle of the Granicus: a new look', *Anc. Mac.* 2 (Thessaloniki) (1977) 271–93

141. Badian, E. 'The deification of Alexander the Great', in D 26, 27–71

142. Badian, E. 'Alexander in Iran', in Gershevitch, I. (ed.), *Cambridge History of Iran* II, 420–501. Cambridge, 1985

143. Badian, E. 'Alexander at Peucelaotis', *CQ* n.s. 37 (1987) 117–28
144. Balsdon, J. P. V. D. 'The "Divinity" of Alexander', *Historia* 1 (1950) 363–88
145. Bengtson, H. 'Φιλόξενος ὁ Μακεδών', *Philologus* 92 (1937) 126–55
146. Berve, H. *Das Alexanderreich auf prosopographischer Grundlage* I–II. Munich, 1926
147. Berve, H. 'Die Verschmelzungspolitik Alexanders des Grossen', *Klio* 31 (1938) 135–68
148. Bickerman, E. J. 'A propos d'un passage de Chares de Mytilène', *PP* 18 (1963) 241–55
149. Bickerman, E. J. 'Sur un passage d'Hypéride', *Athenaeum* 41 (1963) 70–83
150. Borza, E. N. 'Alexander and the return from Siwah', *Historia* 16 (1967) 369
151. Borza, E. N. 'Fire from heaven: Alexander at Persepolis', *Cl. Phil.* 67 (1972) 233–45
152. Bosworth, A. B. 'The death of Alexander the Great: rumour and propaganda', *CQ* n.s. 21 (1971) 112–36
153. Bosworth, A. B. 'The mission of Amphoterus and the outbreak of Agis' War', *Phoenix* 29 (1975) 27–43
154. Bosworth, A. B. 'Alexander and Ammon', in A 32, 51–75
155. Bosworth, A. B. 'Alexander and the Iranians', *JHS* 100 (1980) 1–21
156. Bosworth, A. B. 'A missing year in the history of Alexander the Great', *JHS* 101 (1981) 17–39
157. Bosworth, A. B. 'The location of Alexander's campaign against the Illyrians in 335 B.C.', in D 13, 75–84
158. Bosworth, A. B. 'The Indian satrapies under Alexander the Great', *Antichthon* 17 (1983) 37–46
159. Bosworth, A. B. *Conquest and Empire. The Reign of Alexander the Great.* Cambridge, 1988
160. Breloer, B. *Alexanders Kampf gegen Poros* (Bonner Orientalische Studien 3). Stuttgart, 1933
161. Brown, T. S. 'Callisthenes and Alexander', *AJP* 70 (1949) 225–48
162. Brunt, P. A. 'Alexander's Macedonian cavalry', *JHS* 83 (1963) 27–46
163. Brunt, P. A. 'Alexander, Barsine and Heracles', *Riv. di Filol.* 103 (1975) 22–34
164. Burn, A. R. 'Notes on Alexander's campaigns 332–330 B.C.', *JHS* 72 (1952) 81–91
165. Cawkwell, G. L. 'A note on Ps.-Demosthenes 17.20', *Phoenix* 15 (1961) 74–8
166. Devine, A. M. 'Grand tactics at Gaugamela', *Phoenix* 29 (1975) 374–85
167. Edmunds, L. 'The religiosity of Alexander', *GRBS* 12 (1971) 363–91
168. Eggermont, P. H. L. 'Alexander's campaign in Gandhāra and Ptolemy's list of Indo-Scythian towns', *Orientalia Lovaniensia Periodica* 1 (1970) 63–123
169. Eggermont, P. H. L. *Alexander's campaigns in Sind and Baluchistan* (Orientalia Lovaniensia Analecta 3). Louvain, 1975

169A. Eggermont, P. H. L. 'Ptolemy the Geographer and the people of the Dards', *Orientalia Lovanensia Periodica* 15 (1984) 191–233

170. Ehrenberg, V. *Alexander and the Greeks*. Oxford, 1938

171. Ellis, J. R. 'The first months of Alexander's reign', in D 13, 69–73

172. Engels, D. W. *Alexander the Great and the Logistics of the Macedonian Army*. Berkeley–Los Angeles, 1978

173. Fischer, K. 'Zur Lage von Kandahar an Landverbindungen zwischen Iran und Indien', *BJ* 167 (1967) 129–332

174. Foss, C. 'The battle of the Granicus: a new look', *Anc. Mac.* 2 (Thessaloniki) (1977) 495–502

175. Fraser, P. M. 'Current problems concerning the early history of the cult of Serapis', *Opuscula Atheniensia* 7 (1967) 23–45

176. Fredricksmeyer, A. E. 'Alexander, Midas and the oracle at Gordium', *Cl. Phil.* 56 (1961) 160–8

177. Fredricksmeyer, E. A. 'Three notes on Alexander's deification', *AJAH* 4 (1979) 1–9

178. Goukowsky, P. 'Un lever de soleil sur l'Ida de Troade', *Rev. Phil.* 43 (1969) 249–54

179. Goukowsky, P. 'Le roi Poros et son éléphant', *BCH* 96 (1972) 473–502

180. Green, P. *Alexander of Macedon*. Harmondsworth, 1974

181. Green, P. 'Caesar and Alexander: aemulatio, imitatio, comparatio', *AJAH* 3 (1978) 1–26

182. Griffith, G. T. 'Alexander's generalship at Gaugamela', *JHS* 67 (1947) 77–89

183. Griffith, G. T. 'Alexander the Great and an experiment in government', *PCPhS* 10 (1964) 23–39

184. Griffith, G. T. 'The letter of Darius at Arrian 2.14', *PCPhS* 14 (1968) 33–48

185. Hamilton, J. R. 'Alexander and his "so-called" father', *CQ* n.s. 3 (1953) 151–7

186. Hamilton, J. R. 'The cavalry battle at the Hydaspes', *JHS* 76 (1956) 26–31

187. Hamilton, J. R. 'Alexander and the Aral', *CQ* n.s. 21 (1971) 106–11

188. Hamilton, J. R. 'Alexander among the Oreitai', *Historia* 21 (1972) 603–8

189. Hamilton, J. R. *Alexander the Great*. London, 1973

190. Hammond, N. G. L. *Alexander the Great: King, Commander and Statesman*. Park Ridge, NJ, 1980

191. Hammond, N. G. L. 'Some passages in Arrian concerning Alexander', *CQ* 30 (1980) 455–76

192. Hammond, N. G. L. 'The battle of the Granicus river', *JHS* 100 (1980) 73–88

193. Hampl, F. 'Alexanders des Grossen *Hypomnemata* und letzte Pläne', in *Studies Presented to D. M. Robinson* II, 816–29. St Louis, 1953

194. Hauben, J. 'The expansion of Macedonian sea-power under Alexander the Great', *AncSoc* 7 (1976) 79–105

195. Heckel, W. 'The conspiracy against Philotas', *Phoenix* 31 (1977) 9–21

196. Heckel, W. 'The flight of Harpalus and Tauriskos', *Cl. Phil.* 72 (1977) 133–5

197. Hill, G. F. 'Alexander the Great and the Persian lion-gryphon', *JHS* 43 (1923) 156–61
198. Högemann, P. *Alexander der Grosse und Arabien* (Zetemata 82). Munich, 1985
199. Instinsky, H. U. *Alexander der Grosse am Hellespont*. Godesberg, 1949
200. Jacoby, F. 'Kallisthenes', *RE* 10 (1919) cols. 1674–707 (= B 62A, 288–305)
201. Janke, A. *Auf Alexanders des Grossen Pfaden. Eine Reise durch Kleinasien.* Berlin, 1904
202. Janke, A. 'Die Schlacht bei Issos', *Klio* 10 (1910) 137–77
203. Jaschinski, S. *Alexander und Griechenland unter dem Eindruck der Flucht des Harpalos* (Habelts Dissertationsdrucke, Reihe alte Geschichte 14). Bonn, 1981
204. Jones, T. B. 'Alexander and the winter of 330/29 B.C.', *CW* 28 (1935) 124–5
205. Kienast, D. 'Alexander und der Ganges', *Historia* 14 (1965) 180–8
206. Kingsley, B. M. 'Harpalos in the Megarid and the grain shipments from Cyrene', *ZPE* 66 (1986) 165–77
207. Kraft, K. *Der 'rationale' Alexander* (Frankfurter Althistorische Studien 5). Kallmünz, 1971
208. Lane Fox, R. *Alexander the Great*. London, 1973
209. Lane Fox, R. *The Search for Alexander*. Boston, 1980
210. Lock, R. A. 'On the Macedonian army assembly in the time of Alexander the Great', *Cl. Phil.* 72 (1977) 91–107
211. Markle, M. M. III. 'Macedonian arms and tactics under Alexander the Great', in D 13, 87–111
212. Marsden, E. W. *The Campaign of Gaugamela*. Liverpool, 1964
213. Meyer, E. 'Alexander und der Ganges', *Klio* 21 (1927) 183–91
214. Mikrogiannakis, E. I. Αἱ μεταξὺ ᾽Αλεξάνδρου Γ´ καὶ Δαρείου Γ´ διπλωματικαὶ ἐπαφαί. Athens, 1969
215. Miller, S. G. 'Alexander's funeral cart', *Anc. Mac.* 4 (1986) 401–11
216. Milns, R. D. 'The army of Alexander the Great', in *Alexandre le Grand* (Entretiens Hardt 22), 87–136. Vandoeuvres–Geneva, 1976
217. Neubert, M. 'Alexanders des Grossen Balkanzug', *Petermanns Mitteilungen* 80 (1934) 281–9
217A. O'Brien, J. M. *Alexander the Great: the Invisible Enemy*. London, 1992
218. Parke, H. W. 'The Massacre of the Branchidae', *JHS* 105 (1985) 59–68
219. Pearson, L. 'The diary and the letters of Alexander the Great', *Historia* 3 (1954–5) 429–39
220. Petsas, Ph. M. 'Pella: literary tradition and archaeological research', *Balkan Studies* 1 (1960) 113–28
221. Petsas, Ph. M. *Pella: Alexander the Great's Capital*. Thessaloniki, 1978
222. Pfister, F. 'Alexander der Grosse. Die Geschichte seines Ruhms im Lichte seiner Beinamen', *Historia* 13 (1964) 37–79
223. Radet, G. *Alexandre le Grand*. Paris, 1931
224. Radet, G. 'La dernière campagne d'Alexandre contre Darius', *Mélanges Glotz* (Paris) II (1932) 765–78

225. Radet, G. 'Alexandre et Porus: le passage de l'Hydaspe', *REA* 37 (1935) 349–56
226. Radet, G. 'Les colonies macédoniennes de l'Hydaspe', *REA* 43 (1941) 33–40
227. Rosen, K. 'Der "göttliche" Alexander, Athen und Samos', *Historia* 27 (1978) 20–39
228. Schachermeyr, F. 'Die letzten Pläne Alexanders', *JÖAI* 41 (1954) 118–40
229. Schachermeyr, F. 'Alexander und die Ganges-Länder', *Innsbrucker Beiträge zur Kulturgeschichte* 3 (1955) 123–35
230. Schachermeyr, F. *Alexander in Babylon und die Reichsordnung nach seinem Tode (SBAk. Wien* 268.3). Vienna, 1970
231. Schachermeyr, F. *Alexander der Grosse: das Problem seiner Persönlichkeit und seines Wirkens (SBAk. Wien* 285). Vienna, 1973
232. Seibert, J. *Alexander der Grosse* (Erträge der Forschung 10). Darmstadt, 1972
233. Seibert, J. *Die Eroberung des Perserreiches durch Alexander den Grossen auf kartographischer Grundlage* (TAVO Reihe B, Nr. 68). Wiesbaden, 1985
234. Stein, A. *On Alexander's Track to the Indus.* London, 1929
235. Stein, A. 'The site of Alexander's passage of the Hydaspes and the battle with Porus', *Geographical Journal* 80 (1932) 31–46
236. Stein, A. *Old Routes of Western Iran.* London, 1940
237. Stein, A. 'Notes on Alexander's crossing of the Tigris and the battle of Arbela', *Geographical Journal* 100 (1942) 155–64
238. Stein, A. 'On Alexander's route into Gedrosia. An archaeological tour in Las Bela', *Geographical Journal* 101 (1943) 193–227
239. Tarn, W. W. *Alexander the Great* I–II. Cambridge, 1948
240. Tibiletti, G. 'Alexandro e la liberazione delle città d'Asia Minore', *Athenaeum* 32 (1954) 3–22
241. Unz, R. K. 'Alexander's brothers?', *JHS* 105 (1985) 171–4
241A. Wailes-Fairbairn, F. M. 'Alexander the Great: A Case Study in German Attitudes to Greatness between Napoleon and Hitler', Unpub. Oxford D.Phil. thesis, 1990
242. Weippert, O. *Alexander-imitatio und römische Politik in republikanischer Zeit.* Augsburg, 1972
243. Welwei, K. W. 'Der Kampf um das makedonische Lager bei Gaugamela', *Rh. Mus.* 122 (1979) 222–8
244. Wilcken, U. *Alexander the Great* (with preface, notes and bibliography by E. N. Borza). New York, 1967
245. Will, W. *Athen und Alexander* (Münchener Beiträge zur Papyrusforschung und Rechtsgeschichte 77). Munich, 1983
246. Wirth, G. 'Dareios und Alexander', *Chiron* 1 (1971) 133–52 (= D 249, pp. 92–111, 160–7)
247. Wirth, G. 'Die συντάξεις von Kleinasien 334 v. Chr.', *Chiron* 2 (1972) 91–8 (= D 249)
248. Wirth, G. 'Zwei Lager bei Gaugamela', *Quaderni Catanesi di Studi Classice e Medievali* 2 (1980) 51–100; 3 (1981) 5–61
249. Wirth, G. *Studien zur Alexandergeschichte.* Darmstadt, 1985

250. Wüst, F. R. 'Die Meuterei von Opis', *Historia* 2 (1953–4) 418–31
251. Wüst, F. R. 'Die Rede Alexanders des Grossen in Opis', *Historia* 2 (1953–4) 177–88
252. Wüst, F. R. 'Zu den Hypomnematen Alexanders: das Grabmal Hephaistions', *JÖAI* 44 (1959) 147–57

E. THE NORTH

I. CELTIC EUROPE

1. Biel, J. 'Ein Fürstengrabhügel der späten Hallstattzeit bei Eberdingen-Hochdorf, Kr. Ludwigsburg (Baden-Würtemberg)', *Germania* 60 (1982) 61–104
2. Boardman, J. 'A southern view of Situla art', in Boardman, J. *et al.* (eds.) *The European Community in Later Prehistory*, 121–40. London, 1971
3. Bretz-Mahler, D. *La civilisation de La Tène 1 en Champagne; le facies Marnien*. Paris, 1971
4. Caulfield, S. 'The beehive quern in Ireland', *Journal of the Royal Society of Antiquaries of Ireland* 107 (1977) 104–38
5. *The Celts*, edd. S. Moscati, E. Arslan and D. Vitali (Exhibition catalogue). Venice–London, 1991
6. Cunliffe, B. W. *Iron Age Communities in Britain*. 2nd edn. London, 1978
7. Dehn, W. and Frey, O.-H. 'Southern imports and the Hallstatt and early La Tène chronology of Central Europe', in Ridgway, D. and Ridgway, F. (eds.) *Italy Before the Romans*, 489–511. London, 1979
8. Favret, P.-M. 'Les nécropoles des Jogasses à Chouilly (Marne)', *Préhistoire* 5 (1936) 24–119
9. Filip, J. *Keltove ve Stredni Europe*. Prague, 1956
10. Frey, O.-H. *Die Entstehung der Situlenkunst*. Berlin, 1969
11. Frey, O.-H. and Kossack, G. *Acten des Kolloquiums über das Problem Hallstatt D3/La Tène A, Hamburger Beiträge zur Archäologie* (1978), 2, 2
12. Haffner, A. *Die Westliche Hunsrück-Eifel Kultur*. Berlin, 1976
13. Harding, D. W. *The Iron Age in Lowland Britain*. London, 1974
14. Härke, H. *Settlement Types and Settlement Patterns in the West Hallstatt Province* (BAR Int. Ser. 57). Oxford, 1979
15. Hatt, J-J. and Roualet, P. 'Le cimitière des Jogasses et les origines de la civilisation de la Tène', *Rev. Arch. l'Est et C-Est* 27 (1976) 421–504
16. Hatt, J-J. and Roualet, P. 'La chronologie de la Tène en Champagne', *Rev. Arch. l'Est et C-Est* 28 (1977) 7–36
17. Hawkes, C. F. C. 'Cumulative celticity in pre-Roman Britain', in Duval, P.-M. (ed.), *Actes du IVe Congr. Internat. d'Etudes Celtiques, Rennes, 1971* (*Etudes Celtiques* XIII, Vol. 2). Paris, 1973
18. Hawkes, C. F. C. *Pytheas: Europe and the Greek Explorers*. London, 1977
19. Hodson, F. R. *The La Tène Cemetery at Münsingen-Rain, Acta Bernensia* V. 1968

20. Jacobsthal, P. *Early Celtic Art*. Oxford, 1944
21. Joachim, H.-E. *Die Hunsrück-Eifel Kultur am Mittelrhein*. Cologne–Graz, 1968
22. Joffroy, R. *Le Trésor de Vix*. Paris, 1954
23. Joffroy, R. *Les sépultures à char du premier age du fer en France*. Paris, 1958
24. Joffroy, R. *L'Oppidum de Vix et la civilisation hallstattienne finale dans l'est de la France*. Paris, 1960
25. Jope, E. M. 'The Waldalgesheim Master', in Boardman, J. *et al*. (eds.), *The European Community in Later Prehistory*, 165–80. London, 1971
26. Kimmig, W. 'Die griechische Kolonisation im westlichen Mittelmeergebiet und ihre Wirkung auf die Landschaften des westlichen Mitteleuropa', *JRGZM* 30 (1983) 3–78
27. Kimmig, W. *Die Heuneburg an der oberen Donau*. 2nd edn. Stuttgart, 1983
28. Kossack, G. *Südbayern während der Hallstattzeit*. Berlin, 1959
29. Kromer, K. *Das Gräberfeld von Hallstatt*. Florence, 1959
30. Kruta, V. *Le trésor de Duchcov dans les collections tchécoslovaques*. Usti nad Labem, 1971
31. Louis, M. and Taffanel, O. and J. *Le premier age du fer Languedocien*, I–III. Bordignesa, 1955–60
32. Maluquer de Motes, J. *El Yacimiento Hallstattico de Cortes de Navarro*. Pamplona, 1954
33. Marien, M.-E. *Trouvailles du Champ d'Urnes et des tombelles hallstattiennes de Court-St-Etienne*. Brussels, 1958
34. Marien, M.-E. *La période de la Tène en Belgique: le groupe de La Haine*. Brussels, 1961
35. Megaw, J. V. S. *Art of the European Iron Age*. Bath, 1970
36. Megaw, R. and V. *Celtic Art*. London, 1989
37. Mohen, J.-P. *L'Age du fer en Aquitaine*. 1980
38. Moosleitner, F., Pauli, L. and Penninger, E. *Der Dürrnberg bei Hallein*, II. Munich, 1974
39. Müller-Karpe, H. *Beiträge zur Chronologie der Urnenfelderzeit nordlich und südlich der Alpen*. Berlin, 1959
40. de Navarro, J. M. *The Finds from the Site of La Tène*, I. London, 1972
41. Pauli, L. *Der Dürrnberg bei Hallein*, III. Munich, 1978
42. Penninger, E. *Der Dürrnberg bei Hallein*, I. Munich, 1972
43. Peroni, R. *Studi di Cronologia Hallstattiana*. Rome, 1973
44. Piggott, S. *The Earliest Wheeled Transport from the Atlantic Coast to the Caspian Sea*. London, 1983
45. Raftery, B. *La Tène in Ireland: Problems of Origin and Chronology*. Marburg, 1984
46. Riek, J. and Hundt, H.-J. *Der Hohmichele*. Berlin, 1962
47. Schüle, W. 'Probleme der Eisenzeit auf der Iberischen Halbinsel', *JRGZM* 7 (1960) 59–105
48. Schüle, W. *Die Meseta Kulturen der Iberischen Halbinsel*. Berlin, 1969
49. Schwappach, F. 'Stempelverzierte Keramik von Armorica', in Frey, O.-H. (ed.), *Marburger Beiträge zur Archäologie der Kelten*, 213–87. Bonn, 1969

50. Shefton, B. B. 'Zum Import und Einfluss Mediterraner Güter in Alteuropa', *Kölner Jahrbuch für Vor- und Frühgeschichte* 22 (1987) 207–20
51. Spindler, K. *Magdalenenberg. Der Hallstattzeitliche Fürstengrabhügel bei Villingen im Schwarzwald*, I–VI. Villingen–Schweningen, 1971–80
52. *Trésors des Princes Celtes* (Paris Exhibition 1988). Paris, 1987
53. Vouga, P. *La Tène.* Leipzig, 1923
54. Waldbaum, J. *From Bronze to Iron: the Transition from the Bronze Age to the Iron Age in the Eastern Mediterranean* (Studies in Mediterranean Archaeology, 54). Göteborg, 1978
55. Wells, P. *Culture Contact and Culture Change: Early Iron Age Central Europe and the Mediterranean World.* Cambridge, 1980
56. Wells, P. *Farms, Villages and Cities: Commerce and Urban Origins in Late Prehistoric Europe.* New York, 1984
57. Wyss, R. *Der Goldfund von Erstfeld; frühkeltisches Goldschmuck aus den Zentralalpen.* Zurich, 1975

II. NORTH-WESTERN GREEKS AND ILLYRIA

Excavation reports for sites in Albania are to be found in *Iliria* (with French summaries), *Buletin Arkeologjik* (in Albanian only), and *Monumentet* (with some French summaries). For further bibliography see *CAH* III².3, 496ff.

58. Cabanes, P. *L'Epire de la mort de Pyrrhos à la conquête romaine.* Paris, 1976
59. Cabanes, P. (ed.) *L'Illyrie méridionale et l'Epire dans l'antiquité.* Adosa, 1987
60. Cross, G. N. *Epirus: a Study in Greek Constitutional Development.* Cambridge, 1932
61. Dakaris, S. I. οἱ γενεαλογικοὶ μῦθοι τῶν Μολοσσῶν. Athens, 1964
61A. Dakaris, S. I. *Archaeological Guide to Dodona.* Athens, 1971
62. Dakaris, S. I. *Cassopaea and the Elean Colonies.* Athens, 1971
63. Dakaris, S. I. Θεσπρωτία. Athens, 1972
64. Dell, H. J. 'The origin and nature of Illyrian piracy', *Historia* 16 (1967) 344–58
65. Filow, B. *Die archaische Nekropole von Trebenischte.* Berlin, 1929
66. Franke, P. R. *Alt-Epirus und das Königtum der Molosser.* Erlangen, 1954
67. Franke, P. R. *Die antiken Münzen von Epirus.* Wiesbaden, 1961
68. Franke, P. R. 'Pyrrhus', in *CAH* VII².2 (1990) 456–85
69. Garašanin, M. (ed.) *Les Illyriens et les Albanais.* Belgrade, 1988
70. Hammond, N. G. L. 'The colonies of Elis in Cassopaea', 'Αφιέρωμα εἰς τὴν Ἤπειρον, εἰς μνήμην Χρίστου Σούλη. Athens, 1956
71. Hammond, N. G. L. 'The Illyrian kingdoms, *circa* 400–167 B.C.', *BSA* 61 (1966) 239–53
72. Hammond, N. G. L. *Epirus: the Geography, the Ancient Remains, the History and the Topography of Epirus and Adjacent Areas.* Oxford, 1967
73. Hammond, N. G. L. 'Alexander's campaign in Illyria', *JHS* 94 (1974) 66–87

74. Hammond, N. G. L. *Migrations and Invasions in Greece and Adjacent Areas.* New Jersey, 1976

75. Hammond, N. G. L. 'The hosts of sacred envoys travelling through Epirus', *Ep. Chron.* 22 (1980) 9ff

76. Hammond, N. G. L. 'The Illyrian Atintani, the Epirotic Atintanes, and the Roman Protectorate of 228 B.C.', *JRS* 79 (1989) 11–25

77. Hammond, N. G. L. 'The relations of Illyrian Albania with the Greeks and the Romans', in Winnifrith, T. (ed.), *Perspectives on Albania*, 29–39. London, 1991

78. Lahtov, V. *Problem Trebeniske Kulture.* Ochrid, 1965

79. Lepore, E. *Ricerche sull'antico Epiro.* Naples, 1962

80. Luka, Kolë. *Les Illyriens et la genèse des Albanais.* Tirana, 1971

81. Papazoglou, F. 'Les origines et la destinée de l'état illyrien', *Historia* 14 (1961) 143–79

82. Papazoglou (Papazoglu), F. *The Central Balkan Tribes in Pre-Roman Times.* Amsterdam, 1978

83. Papazoglu, F. 'Politarques en Illyrie', *Historia* 35 (1986) 438–48

84. Stipčević, A. *The Illyrians* (transl. S. C. Burton). New Jersey, 1977

85. Treves, P. 'The meaning of "consenesco" and King Arybbas of Epirus', *AJP* 63 (1942) 129–43

86. Vokotopoulou, I. Χαλκαὶ Κορινθιουργεῖς Πρόχοι. Athens, 1975

87. Vokotopoulou, I. 'Phrygische Helme', *Arch. Anz.* (1982) 497ff

88. Vokotopoulou, I. Βίτσα ι–ιι. Athens, 1986

III. THRACIANS AND SCYTHIANS

89. Alexandrescu, P. 'Ataias', *Stud. Clas* 9 (1967) 85–95

90. Archibald, Z. H. 'Greek imports: some aspects of the Hellenic impact on Thrace', in Poulter, A. G. (ed.), *Ancient Bulgaria, Papers presented to the International Symposium on the Ancient History and Archaeology of Bulgaria, University of Nottingham, 1981* 1, 304–15. Nottingham, 1983

91. Archibald, Z. H. 'The gold pectoral from Vergina and its connections', *OJA* 4 (2) (1985) 165–85

92. Badian, E. 'Philip II and Thrace', *Pulpudeva* 4 (1984) 51–71

93. Berciu, D. 'Das thrako-getische Fürstengrab von Agighiol in Rumänien', *BRGK* 50 (1969) 209–65

94. Botusharova, L. 'Stratigrafskye razkopki na Nebet Tepe' (Recherches stratigraphiques à Nebet Tepe), *GNAMP* v, 61ff; *ibid.*, 77ff, 'Krepostnata stena na Filipopol po severnite sklonove na Nebet Tepe' (La muraille de Philippopolis sur les versants nord du Nebet Tepe). 1963

95. Botusharova, L. 'Antichnyat Filipopol na novite archeologicheski razkopki', in *Archeologicheski prouchvaniya za istoryata na Plovdiv i Plovdivski kray*, 40–55. Plovdiv, 1966

96. Botusharova, L. and Tankova, V. 'Materiali za archeologicheska karta na Plovdiv' (Materials for an archaeological map of Plovdiv), *IMYB* 8 (1982) 45–67

97. Casson, S. *Macedonia, Thrace and Illyria*. Oxford, 1926
98. Changova, J., Lubenova, V., Gerasimova-Tomova, V. and Yourukova, Y. *Pernik* 1. Sofia, 1982
99. Chichikova, M. 'Nouvelles fouilles et recherches de nécropoles thraces du Ve – IIIe siècles av.n.è.', in *Actes du 1ier Congrès Internationale des Etudes Balkaniques et Sud-Est Européennes*, 365–73. Sofia, 1969
100. Chichikova, M. 'Trakiyska mogilna grobnitsa ot s. Kaloyanovo, Slivenski okrug', *IBAI* 31 (1969) 45–89
101. Chichikova, M. 'The Sveshtari tomb – architecture and decoration', *Terra Antiqua Balcanica* 3 (1988) 125–43. (In Bulgarian)
102. Cloché, P. 'Athènes et Kersobleptes de 357/356 à 353/352', *Mélanges G. Glotz* 1, 215–26. Paris, 1932
103. Collart, P. *Philippes, Ville de Macédoine*. Paris, 1932
104. Cook, B. F. (ed.) 'The Rogozen treasure', *Papers of the Anglo-Bulgarian Conference, 12 March, 1987 (British Museum)*. London, 1989
105. Danov, Chr. *Drevna Trakya*, Izsledvaniya varhu istoryata na Bulgarskite zemi, Severna Dobrudja, Iztochna Egeyska Trakya IX do III vek pr.n.e. Sofia. Tr. as *Altthrakien*. Berlin–New York, 1976
106. Dimitrov, D. P. 'Materialnata kultura i izkoustvo na Trakite prez rannata elinisticheskata epoha, IV–III v. pr.n.e.', in *Archeologicheski Otkritya v Bulgariya*, 63–91. 1957
107. Dimitrov, K. 'Treasures of autonomous coins, trade relations and infrastructure of Thrace during IVth century B.C.', *Istoricheski Pregled* 45 (1989) 21–35. (In Bulgarian)
108. Domaradzki, M. 'Trakiyskite ukrepitelni suoruzhenya' (Thracian methods of fortification) in E 165, 44–60
109. Domaradzki, M. 'Les données numismatiques et les études de la culture thrace du second âge du fer', *Numizmatika* (Sofia) 21, 4 (1987) 4–18. (In Bulgarian)
110. Domaradzki, M. 'Rich Thracian burials', *Terra Antiqua Balcanica* 3 (1988) 78–86. (In Bulgarian)
111. Domaradzki, M. 'Trakiyskata kultura prez kasnozhelyaznata epoha v Rodopite i gornite porechya na Maritsa, Mesta i Struma' (Thracian culture during the Late Iron Age in the Rhodopes and upper reaches of the Maritsa, Mesta and Struma rivers), in E 162, 29–44
112. Domaradzki, M. and Yourukova, Y. 'Nov tsentar na trakiyskata kultura – s. Vetren, Pazardjishko' (Nouvel centre de la culture thrace – Vetren, la région de Pazardjik (notes préliminaires)), *Numizmatika* 3 (1990) 1–19
113. Dremsizova, Tsv. 'Mogilnyat nekropol pri s. Branichevo' (Necropole tumulaire près de Branichevo), *IBAI* 25 (1962) 165–86
114. Filow, B. 'Denkmäler der thrakischen Kunst', *Röm. Mitt.* 32 (1917) 21–73
115. Filow, B. 'Antichnata grobnitsa pri s. Dulboki, Starozagorsko', *IBAI* 6 (1930–1) 45–56
116. Filow, B. 'Kupolnite grobnitsi pri Mezek', *IBAI* 11 (1937) 1–116
117. Filow, B., Velkov, V. and Mikov, V. *Die Grabhügelnekropole bei Duvanlij in Südbulgarien*. Sofia, 1934

118. Fol, Al. *Politicheska istoriya na Trakite ot kraya na II hil. pr.n.e. do kraya na V v.pr.n.e.* Sofia, 1972
119. Fol, Al. *Trakya i Balkanite prez rannoelinisticheskata epoha.* Sofia, 1975
120. Fol, Al. and Spiridonov, T. *Historicheska Geografiya na Trakiyskite Plemena do III v. pr.n.e.* I–II. Sofia, 1983
121. Gardiner-Garden, J. 'Ateas and Theopompus', *JHS* 109 (1989) 29–40
122. Gergova, D. 'Früh- und altereisenzeitlichen Fibeln in Bulgarien', *PBF* 14, 7 (1986). Munich
123. Gergova, D. 'The Thracian site in the Kamen Rid locality near the village of Malak Porovec – excavations, results, problems', *Terra Antiqua Balcanica* 3 (1988) 165–72
124. Gerov, B. 'Zum Problem der Wohnsitze der Triballen', *Klio* 63 (1981) 485–92
125. Ginev, G. *Sakrovishteto ot Kralevo.* Sofia, 1983
126. Hasluck, F. W. 'A tholos tomb at Kirk Kilise', *BSA* 17 (1910–11) 76–9
127. Höck, A. 'Das Odrysenreich in Thrakien', *Hermes* 26 (1891) 76–117
128. Höck, A. 'Zur Geschichte des Thrakerkönigs Kotys I', *Klio* 4 (1904) 265ff
129. Isaac, B. *The Greek settlements in Thrace up to the Macedonian Conquest.* Leiden, 1986
130. Ivanov, D. 'Le trésor de Borovo', *Actes du IIe Congrès International de Thracologie, 1976* I, 391ff. Bucarest, 1980
131. Ivanov, T. (ed.) *Kabyle* I. Sofia, 1982
132. Kacharava, D. 'Archaeology in Georgia 1980–1990', *Archaeological Reports* 37 (1990–91) 79–86
133. Kahrstedt, U. *Beiträge zur Geschichte der thrakischen Chersones* (Deutsche Beiträge zur Altertumswissenschaft 6). Baden-Baden, 1954
134. Kitov, G. *Trakiyski Mogili kray Strelcha.* Sofia, 1979
135. Kitov, G. *Trakite v Loveshki Okrug.* Sofia, 1980
136. Koukouli-Chrysanthaki, H. 'Ta "Metalla" tis Thasiakis Peraias', in E 144, 493–514
137. Lazaridis, D, Ἀμφίπολις καὶ Ἄργιλος (Ancient Greek Cities 13). Athens, 1972
138. Marchenko, K. and Vinogradov, Y. 'The Scythian period in the northern Black Sea region (750–250 B.C.)', *Antiquity* 63, 241 (1989) 803–13
139. Melyukova, A. *Skifya i frakiyski mir.* Moscow, 1979
140. Mihailov, G. 'La Thrace aux IVe et IIIe siècles avant notre ère', *Athenaeum* 39 (1961) 33–44
141. Mihailov, G. 'La Thrace et la Macédoine jusqu'à l'invasion des Celtes', *Anc. Mac.* 1 (1970) 76–85
142. Mihailov, G. 'Sitalcès et la Macédoine, Athènes et la guerre du Peloponnèse: histoire et poésie', *Anc. Mac.* 2 (1977) 237–50
143. Mikov, V. 'Proizchod na kupolnite grobnitsi v Bulgariya', *IBAI* 19 (1955) 15–48
144. Μνήμη Δ. Λαζαρίδη. Πόλις καὶ χώρα στὴν ἀρχαία Μακεδονία καὶ Θράκη (Πρακτικὰ Ἀρχαιολογικοῦ Συνεδρίου, Καβάλα, 9–11 Μαρτίου 1986).

Thessaloniki, 1990

145. Momigliano, A. 'Dalla spedizione scitica di Filippo alla spedizione scitica di Dario', *Athenaeum* n.s. 11 (1933) 336–49

146. Nikolov, B. 'Grobnitsa 3 ot Mogilanska Mogila, Vratsa', *Archeologiya* 9, 1 (1967) 11–18

147. Nikolov, B. *Archäologisches Museum Vratsa.* Sofia, 1968

148. Picard, O. 'Monnayage Thasien', *CRAI* (1982) 412–44

149. Picard, O. 'Monnaies et gravure monétaire à Thasos à la fin du Ve s.', in Φίλια ἔπη εἰς Γ. Μύλωνας (Βιβλιοθήκη τῆς ἐν Ἀθήναις Ἀρχαιολογικῆς Ἑταιρίας 103) 150–63. 1987

150. Pippidi, D. M. *I Greci nel basso Danubio.* Milan, 1971

151. Pippidi, D. M. 'Les Macédoniens en Scythie Mineure de Philippe II à Lysimache', *Anc. Mac.* 2 (1977) 381–96

152. Pouilloux, J. 'Pariens et Thasiens dans le Nord de la Grèce à l'époque archaique', in E 144, 485–9

153. Rogalski, A. 'Moneti z imeneto na skitski tsar Atea', *IVAD* 12 (1961) 23–7

154. Rogalski, A. 'Au sujet de quelques monnaies antiques de la péninsule balkanique prétendues fausses IV. Les monnaies à legende ATAIAS et ATAIA sont-elles fausses?', *INMV* 6, 21 (1970) 3–17. (In Bulgarian)

155. Rogalski, A. 'Sur les monnaies aux legendes SEYTHA KOMMA et SEYTHA ARGURION', *Thracia* 4 (1977) 259ff

156. Sarafov, T. 'L'étymologie du nom de la tribu thrace BESSOI, Bessi', *Thracia* 3 (1974) 135–8

157. Sarafov, T. 'Trakiyskite Satri. Prinos na etnogeneza na trakiyskite plemena', *GSU FIF* 67, 1 (1974) 121–91

158. Schiltz, V. 'Deux gorytes identiques en Macédoine et dans le Kuban', *Rev. Arch.* (1979) 305–10

159. Schönert-Geiss, E. *Griechisches Münzwerk: die Münzprägung von Maroneia* I–II. Berlin, 1987

160. Shelov, D. B. 'Der Skyther-Makedonier Konflikt in der Antike', *Eirene* 9 (1971) 31ff

161. Tacheva-Hitova, M. 'Vzaimnootnosheniya mezhdu Odriskite vladateli i gretskite polisi prez IV v. pr.n.e.', *Vekove* 3 (1972) 17–21

162. *Trakiyskata kultura v Rodopite i gornite porechiya na Maritsa, Mesta i Struma.* Conference Smolyan, October, 1990

163. Vatin, Cl. 'Lettre adressée à la cité de Philippes par les ambassadeurs auprès d'Alexandre', *Proceedings of the Eighth Epigraphical Congress, Athens 1982*, 1, 259–70. Athens, 1984

164. Velkov, I. 'Razkopkite okolo Mezek i gara Svilengrad prez 1932–1933', *IBAI* 11 (1937) 117–66

165. Velkov, V. (ed.) *Poselishten zhivot v Trakya* (Settlement life in Thrace) Symposium, 14–17 September 1982, Yambol. Yambol, 1982

166. Velkov, V. 'The Thracian city of Kabyle', in *Ancient Bulgaria. Papers Presented to the International Symposium on the Ancient History and Archaeology of Bulgaria. University of Nottingham, 1981*, 233ff. Nottingham, 1983

167. Velkov, V. (ed.) *Poselishten zhivot v Trakya*. Vtori Symposium, 6–9 October 1986, Yambol. Yambol, 1986
168. Velkov. V. *et al. Kabyle* II. Sofia, 1991
169. Venedikov, I. 'Novootkrito trakiysko mogilno pogrebeniye v Vratsa', *Archaeologiya* 8, 1 (1966) 7ff
170. Venedikov, I. 'Nadpisite varhu trakiyskite fiali' (Les inscriptions sur les phiales thraces), *Archaeologiya* 14, 2 (1972) 1ff
170A. Venedikov, I. *Thracian Treasures from Bulgaria*. London, 1976
171. Venedikov, I. and Gerasimov, T. *Thracian Art Treasures*. London, 1975
172. West, A. B. 'Fifth and fourth century gold coins from the Thracian coast', *NNM* 40 (1929) 1–183
173. Yourukova, Y. *Coins of the Ancient Thracians* (BAR Int. Series 4). Oxford, 1976
174. Yourukova, Y. 'Contribution à la numismatique thrace. Les monnaies de Skostokos', *Studies in Honour of Veselini Beshevliev*. Sofia, 1978

IV. THE BOSPORAN KINGDOM

175. Abayev, A. *Osyetinsky Yazyk i Folklore–Skifsky Yazyk* Moscow–Leningrad, 1949
176. Agbunov, A. 'Classical archaeology and palaeogeography', *KSIA* 191 (1987) 3–6 (In Russian)
177. Alexandrescu, P. and Schuller, W. (eds.) *Histria* (*XENIA* 25). Constanz, 1990
178. Allen, W. S. 'The name of the Black Sea in Greek', *CQ* 41 (1947) 86–8
179. Anfimov, N. V. 'The Maeotae and their relations with the Bosporus in the period of the Spartocids', *Antichnoye Obschestvo*, 128ff. Moscow–Leningrad, 1967 (In Russian)
180. Anfimov, N. V. 'Agriculture among the Sindi', *Istoria i Kul'tura Antichnogo Mira*, 6–20. Moscow, 1977 (In Russian)
181. Anokhin, V. A. *The Coinage of Chersonesus: IV Century B.C. – XII Century A.D.* (BAR Int 69), 1980
182. Anokhin, V. A. *Monyetnoye Dyelo Bospora*. Kiev, 1986
183. Arsenyeva, T. M. and Shelov, D. B. 'Das antike Tanais – Forschungen und Geschichte', *Klio* 70 (1988) 2, 372–403
184. Artamonov, M. I. 'Towards the question of the origin of the Bosporan Spartocids', *VDI* (1949) 1, 36 (In Russian)
185. Artamonov, M. I. *Treasures from the Scythian Tombs*. Prague, 1968
186. Artamonov, M. I. *Cimmeriitsy i Skiphy*. Leningrad, 1974
187. Belova, N. S. 'A new inscription from Hermonassa', *VDI* (1967) 1, 60–9 (In Russian)
188. Berenbeim, D. Y. 'The Kerch straits in the time of Strabo in the light of data concerning the changing level of the Black Sea', *Sov. Arch.* (1959) 4, 42–52 (In Russian)
189. Berzin, E. O. 'Sindica, Bosporus and Athens in the last quarter of the fifth century B.C.', *VDI* (1958) 1, 124–9 (In Russian)

190. Blavatskaya, T. V. *Ocherki Politicheskoi Istorii Bospora v V – IV vyekakh do n.e.* Moscow, 1959

191. Blavatsky, V. D. 'The battle on the R. Thates and tactics in the fourth century B.C.', *VDI* (1946) 1, 101–6 (In Russian)

192. Blavatsky, V. D. 'The Cimmerian problem and Panticapaeum', *Vestnik Mosk. Universiteta* 8 (1948) 12 (In Russian)

193. Blavatsky, V. D. 'Bosporus in archaic times', *MIA*, 33 (1953) 7–44 (In Russian)

194. Blavatsky, V. D. *Zemlyedyeliye v Antichnykh Gosudarstvakh Severnogo Prichernomorya.* Moscow, 1953

195. Blavatsky, V. D. *Ocherki Voyennogo Dyela v Antichnykh Gosudarstvakh Severnogo Prichernomorya.* Moscow, 1954

196. Blavatsky, V. D. 'Slavery and its sources in the ancient states of the North Black Sea area', *Sov. Arch.* 20 (1954) 31–56 (In Russian)

197. Blavatsky, V. D. 'On the ethnic composition of the population of Panticapaeum in the IV–III centuries B.C.', *Sov. Arch.* 28 (1958) 97–106 (In Russian)

198. Blavatsky, V. D. 'Industry on the Bosporus', *Sov. Arch.* 29–30 (1959) 42–57 (In Russian)

199. Blavatsky, V. D. 'Le processus du développement historique et le role des états antiques situés au nord de la Mer Noire', *XI Congrès International des Sciences Historiques, Stockholm*, Rapports II, 98–116. Uppsala, 1960

200. Blavatsky, V. D. 'Il periodo del Protoellenismo sul Bosporo', *Atti del Settimo Congresso di Archaeologia Classica* III, 51ff. Rome, 1961

201. Blavatsky, V. D. 'The first mention of Sindike', *Izvestia v Chest' Akad. D. Decheva*, 703–8. Sofia, 1961 (In Russian)

202. Blavatsky, V. D. 'An underwater expedition to the Azov and Black Seas', *Archaeology* 16.2 (1963) 93–8

203. Blavatsky, V. D. *Pantikapei.* Moscow, 1964

204. Blavatsky, V. D. 'Le rayonnement de la culture antique dans les pays de la Pontide Nord', *Le rayonnement des civilisations grecque et romaine sur les Cultures Périphériques*, 393–403. Paris, 1965

205. Blavatsky, V. D. 'Zur Herkunft der Bosporanischen Archaianaktiden', *Klio* 52 (1970) 33–6

206. Blavatsky, V. D. 'On the names of the Spartocïds', *Khudozhestvyennaya Kul'tura i Arkheologia Antichnogo Mira*, 56–8. Moscow, 1976 (In Russian)

207. Bolton, J. D. P. *Aristeas of Proconnesus.* Oxford, 1962

208. Boltruk, Y. V. and Fialk, E. E. 'On the site of Kremnoi harbour', *Skify Severnogo Prichernomorya*, 40–8, Kiev, 1987 (In Russian)

209. Boltunova, A. I. 'A proxeny decree from Anapa and some questions concerning the history of the Bosporus', *VDI* (1964) 3, 136–49 (In Russian)

210. Boltunova, A. I. and Knipovich, T. N. 'An outline of the history of Greek lapidary script on the Bosporus', *Numismatika i Epigraphika* 3 (1962) 3–16

211. Bosi, F. 'Note epigrafiche bosporane', *Epigraphica* 29 (1967) 131–44

212. Bouzek, J. 'Athènes et la Mer Noire', *BCH* 113 (1989) 249–59

213. Bouzek, J. *Studies of Greek Pottery in the Black Sea Region*. Prague, 1989
214. Brabich, V. M. 'Griffins on the coins of Panticapaeum in the fourth century B.C.' *KSIA* 9 (1959) 90–2 (In Russian)
215. Brashinsky, J. B. *Athiny i Severnoye Prichernomorye v VI–II Vyekhakh do n. e*. Moscow, 1963
216. Brashinsky, J. B. 'On some dynastic peculiarities in the rule of the Bosporan Spartocids, *VDI* (1965) 1, 118–27 (In Russian)
217. Brashinsky, J. B. 'Epigraphic evidence on Athens' relations with the North Pontic Greek states', *Acts of the Fifth Epigraphic Congress, Cambridge, 1967*, 119–23. Cambridge, 1971
218. Brashinsky, J. B. *Grechesky Keramichesky Import na Nizhnyem Donu v V–III Vyekhakh do n. e*. Leningrad, 1980
219. Brashinsky, J. B. *Methody Issledovania Antichnoi Torgovli*. Leningrad, 1984
220. Brashinsky, J. B. and Marchenko, K. K. 'Elizavetovskoye on the Don – a settlement of city-type', *Sov. Arch*. (1980) 1, 211ff (In Russian)
221. Burstein, S. M. "The war between Heraclea Pontica and Leucon I of Bosporus', *Historia* 23 (1974) 401–16
222. Burstein, S. *Outpost of Hellenism – The Emergence of Heraclea on the Black Sea* (U. Cal. Pubs: Class. Studies, 14). Berkeley–Los Angeles, 1976
223. Burstein, S. 'IG II² 1485A and Athenian relations with Lysimachus', *ZPE* 31 (1978) 181–5
224. Chernenko, E. V. 'The expedition of Darius into Scythia', *Drevnosti Stepnoi Skifii*, Kiev, 1982 (In Russian)
225. Chernenko, E. V. *Skifo-Persidskaya Voina*. Kiev, 1984
226. Chlenova, N. L. 'The Scythian stag', *MIA* 115 (1962) 187–205 (In Russian)
227. Dovatur, A. N., Kallistov, D. P. and Shishova, I. A. *Narody Nashei Rodiny v Istorii Gerodota*. Moscow, 1982
228. Drews, R. 'The earliest Greek settlements on the Black Sea', *JHS* 96 (1976) 18–32
229. Dufkova, M. and Pečirka, J. 'Excavations of farms and farmhouses in the Chora of Chersonesos in the Crimea', *Eirene* 8 (1970) 123–74
230. Dundua, G. F. *Numismatika Antichnoi Gruzii*. Tbilisi, 1987
231. Dyukov, Y. L. 'On the lion-head coins with the legend APOL', *VDI* (1975) 4, 71–5 (In Russian)
232. Frolova, N. A. 'The coins of the Scythian king Scilurus', *Sov. Arch*. (1964) 1, 45–55 (In Russian)
233. Frolova, N. A. *The Coinage of the Kingdom of Bosporus*. BAR Int. Series, 56 (1979), 166 (1983)
234. Fyodorov, P. V. 'Post-glacial transgression of the Black Sea and the problem of changes in sea-level in the last 15,000 years', *Kolebania Urovnya Moryei i Oceanov z 15,000 lyet*, 154. Moscow, 1984 (In Russian)
235. Gaidukyevich, V. F. 'Ceramic architectural materials from the Bosporus', *Izvestia Gosudarstvennoi Akademii Istorii Material'noi Kul'tury* 104 (1935) 211–311 (In Russian)
236. Gaidukyevich, V. F. 'New data concerning the Bosporan tile factories in the period of the Spartocids', *KSIIMK* 17 (1947) 22–7 (In Russian)

237. Gaidukyevich, V. F. *Bosporskoye Tsarstvo*. Moscow–Leningrad, 1949
238. Gaidukyevich, V. F. 'The history of the classical cities of the north Black
      Sea area', *Antichnye Goroda Severnogo Pricharnomorya*, 95–122. Moscow–
      Leningrad, 1955 (In Russian)
239. Gaidukyevich, V. F. 'Epigraphic data on Bosporan tile factories', *Sov.
      Arch.* 28 (1958) 123–35 (In Russian)
240. Gaidukyevich, V. F. 'A votive made by Heraios from Myrmekion', in
      Boltunova, A. I. (ed.) *Kul'tura Antichnogo Mira*, 70–6. Moscow, 1966
241. Gaidukyevich, V. F. *Das Bosporanische Reich*. Berlin, 1971
242. Galanina, L. and Grach, N. *Scythian Art: the Legacy of the Scythian World,
      from the mid-seventh century to the third century B.C.* Leningrad, 1986
243. Gardiner-Garden, J. 'Fourth century conceptions of Maeotian
      ethnography', *Historia* 35 (1986) 192–225
244. Gardiner-Garden, J. 'Dareios' Scythian expedition and its aftermath',
      Klio 69 (1987) 326–50
245. Golenko, K. V. 'Two coins of Panticapaeum of the second century B.C.',
      Numismatika i Epigraphika 5 (1965) 56–61 (In Russian)
246. Golenko, K. V. 'A new coin of King Spartocus', *Numismatika
      Antichnogo Prichernomorya*, 50–5. Kiev, 1982 (In Russian)
247. Grach, N. L. 'On Gorgippus and some dynastic peculiarities of the early
      Spartocids', *Antichnaya Istoria i Kul'tura Sredizemnomorya i Prichernomorya
      – Sbornik v Chest' S. Zhebelyova*, 108–14. Leningrad, 1968 (In Russian)
248. Grach, N. L. 'On the find of a Sindian coin in Nymphaeum', *VDI* (1972)
      3, 133 (In Russian)
249. Grach, N. L. 'On the ethnic composition of the population of
      Nymphaeum in the sixth–fifth centuries B.C.', *Tskhaltubo II, 1979*, 260–66.
      Metsniereba, Tbilisi, 1981. (In Russian)
250. Grach, N. L. 'The discovery of a new historical source at Nymphaeum',
      VDI (1984) 1, 81–8. (In Russian)
251. Grach, N. L. 'Nymphaeum in the fourth–first centuries B.C.', *Tskhaltubo
      III, 1982*, 333–41. Metsniereba, Tbilisi, 1985. (In Russian)
252. Grakov, B. N. *Skiphy*. Moscow, 1971
253. Gratsianskaya, L. I. 'The place of political history of the Bosporus in the
      Geography of Strabo', *Drevnyeishiye Gosudarstva na Territorii SSSR* I
      (1976) 11–15 (In Russian)
254. Gratsianskaya, L. I. 'The geography of Strabo – problems in source
      study', *Drevnyeishiye Gosudarstva na Territorii SSSR* (1986), 6–175.
      Moscow, 1988. (In Russian)
255. Grinyovich, K. E. 'Linear defences of the Cimmerian Bosporus', *VDI*
      (1946) 2, 160–4 (In Russian)
256. Hind, J. G. F. 'Greek colonisation of the Black Sea area in the Archaic
      and Classical periods' Unpublished Ph.D. Thesis. Cambridge, 1969
257. Hind, J. G. F. 'The eagle-head coins of Sinope', *Num. Chron.* (1976) 1–6
258. Hind, J. G. F. 'Greeks and barbarian peoples on the shores of the Black
      Sea', *Arch. Rep. for 1983–84* 71–97
259. Hind, J. G. F. 'Colonies and ports of trade on the northern shores of the
      Black Sea – the cases of Olbiopolis and Kremnoi', *Thracia Pontica II*, 105–
      18. Iambol, 1985

260. Hind, J. G. F. 'The colonisation of Sinope and the south-east Black Sea area', *Tskhaltubo-Vani IV, 1985*, 207–23. Tbilisi, 1988

261. Hind, J. G. F. 'Herodotus' geography of Scythia: the rivers and the Rugged Peninsula', *Tskhaltubo-Vani V, 1987*. Tbilisi, 1990

262. Hind, J. G. F. 'Map resources for the North Black Sea area in the Graeco-Roman period', in Harris, W. V. (ed.), *Map Resources for the Graeco-Roman World*. New York (in press)

263. Hind, J. G. F. 'Greeks and barbarians around the Black Sea', *Arch. Rep. for 1992–93*, 82–112

264. Hommel, H. *Der Gott Achilleus*. Heidelberg, 1980

265. Ilyinskaya, V. A. and Terenozhkin, A. I. *Skiphia v VII–IV vyekakh do n.e.* Kiev, 1983

266. Ivanova, A. P. *Skul'ptura i Zhivopis' Bospora*. Kiev, 1961

267. Kacharava, D. D. 'Greek imports in Colchis', *Colchis and the Greek World* (Bristol Class. Press, forthcoming)

268. Kallistov, D. P. *Ocherki po Istorii Severnogo Prichernomorya Antichnoi Epokhi*. Leningrad, 1949

269. Kallistov, D. P. 'The treachery of Gylon', *VDI* (1950) 27–36 (In Russian)

270. Kallistov, D. P. *Severnoye Prichernomorye v Antichnuyu Epokhu*. Moscow, 1952

271. Kallistov, D. P. 'The Bosporan decree of Pairisades concerning the grant of proxeny to a Peiraean', in *Problemy Sotsialnoi Ekonomicheskoi Istorii Drevnyego Mira*, 317–38. Moscow–Leningrad, 1963 (In Russian)

272. Kallistov, D. P. 'Strabo on the Scythian King Ateas', *VDI* (1969) 1, 127–8 (In Russian)

273. Kallistov, D. P. 'Zur Stellung der Poleis im Bosporanischen Reich', in C 83, 11, 587–607

274. Kamenetsky, I. S. 'The Maeotians and Greek colonisation', *Tskhaltubo-Vani IV, 1985*, 82–97. Tbilisi, 1988 (In Russian)

275. Karyshkovsky, P. O. 'On the history of coin circulation in the North Black Sea area in the third century B.C.' *ZOAO* 1 (1960) 112–23

276. Karyshkovsky, P. O. 'Concerning the inscriptions on the early coins of Olbia', *Materialy po Arkheologii Severnogo Prichernomorya* 4 (1962) 226ff

277. Karyshkovsky, P. O. 'Notes on Olbia and Borysthenes', *Kratkiye Soobschenia Gos. Arkh. Mus. Odessa*, 2 (1962) 85ff

278. Karyshkovsky, P. O. and Kleiman, I. B. *Drevny Gorod Tyras*. Kiev, 1985

279. Kastanayan, E. G. *Lepnaya Keramika Bospora*. Leningrad, 1981

280. Khudyak, M. M. 'Work of the expedition at Nymphaeum', *Trudy Gosudarstvennogo Hermitagea* 1. Leningrad, 1945 (In Russian)

281. Khudyak, M. M. *Iz Istorii Nympheya VI–III vyekov do n. e.* Leningrad, 1962

282. Kleiman, L. B. 'On the date of foundation of Tyras', *Vani* VI (1990) In press

283. Knipovich, T. N. and Levi, E. I. *Inscriptiones Olbiae 1917–1965*. Moscow–Leningrad, 1968

284. Kobylina, M. M. 'Late Bosporan Pelikai', *MIA* 19 (1951) 136–70 (In Russian)

285. Kobylina, M. M. *Divinités orientales sur le littoral nord de la mer noire*. Leiden, 1976

286. Kobylina, M. M. 'Pages from the early history of Phanagoria', *Sov. Arch.* (1983) 2, 51–61 (In Russian)

287. Kobylina, M. M. *Phanagoria*. Moscow, 1989

288. Kolobova, K. M. 'The political position of the cities in the Bosporan state', *VDI* (1953) 4, 47–71 (In Russian)

289. Kopylov, V. P. 'Periodisation of Greek colonisation of the North-East Azov Sea area', *Myezhdunarodnye Otneshenia v Basyeinye Chernogo Morya v Drevnosti i Sredniye Vyeka*, 9–10. Rostov-on-Don, 1990 (In Russian)

290. Koshelenko, G. A., Kruglikova, I. T. and Dolgorukov, V. S. (eds.) *Antichnye Gosudarstva Severnogo Prichernomorya*. Moscow, 1984

291. Koshelenko, G. A. and Kuznetsov, V. D. 'Greek colonisation of the Bosporus', *Tskhaltubo-Vani* v (1987). Tbilisi, 1990 (In Russian)

292. Koshelenko, G. A. and Kuznetsov, V. D. 'Colchis and Bosporus: two models of colonisation', *Colchis and the Greek World*, Bristol, forthcoming

293. Kruglikova, I. T. 'Gorgippia in the time of the Spartocids', *VDI* (1971) 1, 89–100 (In Russian)

294. Kruglikova, I. T. *Sel'skoye Khozyaistvo Bospora*. Moscow, 1975

295. Krushkol, J. S. *Drevnyaya Sindika*. Moscow, 1971

296. Krushkol, J. S. 'Die griechischen und autochthonen Städte der Sindike (Nordkaukasien) im Bosporanischen Reich im 4 und 3 Jh. v.u. Z.', in c 83, II, 608–47

297. Kryzhitsky, S. D. *Zhilye Doma Antichnykh Gorodov Severnogo Prichernomorya*. Kiev, 1982

298. Kublanov, M. M. 'Towards the history of the Asiatic side of the Bosporus', *Sov. Arch.* 29–30 (1959) 203–26 (In Russian)

299. Kuklina, I. V. 'Early reference to the Scythians and Cimmerians', *VDI* (1981) 2, 162–73 (In Russian)

300. Kuklina, I. V. *Etnogeographia Skiphii po Antichnym Istochnikam*. Kiev, 1985

301. Kutaisov, V. A. *Antichny Gorod Kerkinitida v VI–II vyekakh do n.e.* Kiev, 1990. (In Russian)

302. Kvirkvelia, G. T. 'Sinope, Colchis, Bosporus – Problems of interrelationships', *Colchis and the Greek World*. Bristol, forthcoming

303. Latyshev, V. V. *Inscriptiones Orae Septentrionalis Ponti Euxini*. Petropoli, 1885–1916 = *IOSPE*

304. Latyshev, V. V. 'Towards the history of the Bosporan Kingdom', *PONTIKA*, 176ff. St Petersburg, 1909 (In Russian)

305. Lazarov, M. 'Excavations at Varna', *Tskhaltubo-Vani v, 1987*. Tbilisi, 1990

306. Levi, E. I. *Ol'via – Gorod Epokhi Ellinizma*. Leningrad, 1985

307. Lordkipanidze, O. D. 'On the question of the relations of Colchis with the North Black Sea area in the sixth to fourth centuries B.C.', *Istoria i Kul'tura Antichnogo Mira*, 112–15. Moscow, 1977 (In Russian)

308. Lordkipanidze, O. D. 'The Graeco-Roman world and ancient Georgia', *Modes de Contacts et Processus de Transformation dans les sociétés, Collection de*

L'Ecole Française 67 (1988) 123–42

309. Malloy, A. G. *The Coinage of Amisos.* South Salem, 1970
310. Mantsevich, A. P. 'The comb and phiale from Solokha', *Sov. Arch.* (1950), 196ff (In Russian)
311. Mantsevich, A. P. 'The gorytus covers from Chertomlyk Ilyintsy and the Five Brothers tumuli', *Trudy Gosudarstvennogo Hermitagea* 7 (1962) 107–119 (In Russian)
312. Marchenko, I. D. 'Excavations at Panticapaeum in 1958–64', *Soobschenia Gosudarstvyennogo Muzeya Izobrazityelnykh Izkusstv imeni Pushkina* 4. Moscow, 1968, 27–53 (In Russian)
313. Marchenko, K. K. 'Die Siedlung von Elizavetovka – griechisches-barbarisches Emporion im Dondelta', *Klio* 68 (1986) 2, 377–98
314. Marchenko, K. K. 'Bosporan settlements on the territory of Elizavetovskoye gorodische on the Don', *VDI* (1990) 1, 129–38 (In Russian)
315. Maslennikov, A. A. *Naseleniye Bosporskogo Gosudarstva v VI–II vyekakh do n.e.* Moscow, 1981
316. Maslennikov, A. A. 'Once more on the Bosporan "dykes"', *Sov. Arch.* 1983, 14–22 (In Russian)
317. Maslennikov, A. A. 'A typology of the agricultural settlements of the Bosporus', *Sov. Arch.* (1989) 2, 66–79 (In Russian)
318. Maximova, M. I. *Antichnye Goroda Yugo-Vostochnogo Prichernomorya.* Moscow–Leningrad, 1956
319. Melyukova, A. I. 'The peoples of the North Black Sea littoral on the eve of and in the period of Greek colonisation', *Tskhaltubo-Vani IV, 1985,* 8–27. Tbilisi, 1988 (In Russian)
320. Melyukova, A. I. (ed.) *Stepi Europeiskoi Chasti SSSR v Skipho-Sarmatskoye Vremya.* Moscow, 1989
321. Minns, E. H. *Scythians and Greeks in South Russia.* Cambridge, 1913
322. Moorhouse, A. C. 'The name of the Euxine Pontus', *CQ* 34 (1940) 123–8; 41 (1947) 59–60
323. Moschinskaya, V. I. 'On the Sindian State', *VDI* (1946) 3, 203–8 (In Russian)
324. Newskaja, W. P. *Byzanz in der Klassischen und Hellenistischen Epoche.* Leipzig, 1955
325. Noonan, T. S. 'The grain trade of the Northern Black Sea in antiquity', *AJP* 94 (1973) 231–42
326. Noonan, T. S. 'The origins of the Greek colony at Panticapaeum', *AJA* 77 (1973) 77–81
327. Ognyenova-Marinova, L. 'Thracia Pontica', *Thracia Pontica* 1 1979, 69–79. Sofia, 1982
328. Onaiko, N. A. *Antichny Import v Pridnyeprovye i Pobuzhye v VII–V vyekakh, Arkheologia SSSR D 1–27.* Moscow, 1966
329. Onaiko, N. A. 'On the centre of production of the gold scabbards and sword-hilts found in the Dniepr area', *Kultura Antichnogo Mira,* 159–176. Moscow, 1966 (In Russian)
330. Onaiko, N. A. *Antichny Import v Pridnyeprovye i Pobuzhe v IV–II vyekakh do*

n.e. Moscow, 1970

331. Onaiko, N. A. 'Die Lokalisierung von Bata bei Strabo', *Klio* 59 (1977)
332. Onaiko, N. A. *Arkhaichesky Torik: Antichny Gorod na Severo-Vostokye Ponta*. Moscow, 1980
333. Paromov, Y. M. 'A survey of the archaeological remains on the Taman peninsula in 1981–3', *KSIA* 188 (1986) 69–76 (In Russian)
334. Paumenko, P. I. 'The exploitation of the mineral wealth of the Kerch-Taman region in ancient times', *Geologichesky Zhurnal* 39, Kiev (1979) 56–62 (In Russian)
335. Pečirka, J. 'Country estates of the polis of Chersonesus in the Crimea', in *Ricerche storiche ed economiche in memoria di C. Barbagallo* 1, 459–77. Naples, 1970
336. Peters, B. B. *Morskoye Dyelo v Antichnykh Gosudarstvakh Severnogo Prichernomorya*. Moscow, 1982
337. Pichikyan, I. D. 'An Ionic capital from Kerch', *VDI* (1974) 2, 105–10 (In Russian)
338. Pichikyan, I. D. 'Ordered architecture of the sixth–fifth centuries B.C. from the North Black Sea area', *VDI* (1975) 1, 120–6 (In Russian)
339. Podosinov, A. V. *Proizvedenia Ovidia kak istochnik po istorii Vostochnoi Europy i Zakavkazya*. Moscow, 1985
340. Reho, M. 'Ceramica di tipo greco-orientale ad Apollonia', *Thracia Pontica* III 1985. Sofia, 1986
341. Rolle, R. *The World of the Scythians*. London, 1989
342. Rostovtzeff, M. I. 'Strabo as a source for the history of the Bosporus', *Sbornik Statei v Chest' V. P. Buzeskula*, 370. Kharkov, 1914 (In Russian)
343. Rostovtzeff, M. I. 'Amaga and Tirgatao', *Zapiski Odesskogo Obschestva Istorii i Drevnostei* 32 (1915) 66–7 (In Russian)
344. Rostovtzeff, M. I. 'Syriscus – historian of the Tauric Chersonesus', *Zhurnal Ministerstva Narodnogo Prosvyescheniya* (1915) 151–7. St Petersburg, 1915 (In Russian)
345. Rostovtzeff, M. I. *Iranians and Greeks in South Russia*. Oxford, 1922
346. Rostovtzeff, M. I. 'The Bosporan kingdom', *CAH* VIII[1] (1930) 561–89
347. Rostovtzeff, M. I. 'The state and culture of the Bosporan kingdom', *VDI* (1989) 2, 183–97 (In Russian)
348. Rostovtzeff, M. I. 'The state, religion and culture of the Scythians and Sarmatians', *VDI* (1989) 1, 192–206 (In Russian)
349. Rostovtzeff, M. I. *VDI* (1990) 1, 173–83
350. Rostowzew, M. I. *Skythien und der Bosporus*. Berlin, 1931
351. Rubinsohn, W. Z. 'Saumacus, ancient history, modern politics', *Historia* 29 (1980) 50–70
352. Saprykin, S. Y. *Gerakleya Pontiiskaya i Khersones Tavricheský*. Moscow, 1986
353. Savostina, E. 'Trouvaille de reliefs antiques dans un établissement agricole du Bosphore cimmérien (Taman)', *Rev. Arch.* (1987) 1, 3–24
354. Scheglov, A. N. *Polis i Khora*. Simferopol, 1976
355. Scheglov, A. N. *Severo-Zapadny Krym v Antichnuyu Epokhu*. Leningrad, 1978

356. Scheglov, A. N. 'The North-Black Sea grain trade in the second half of the seventh to the fifth centuries B.C. – written sources and archaeology', *Tskhaltubo-Vani v, 1987*. Tbilisi, 1990 (In Russian)

357. Sekerskaya, N. M. 'Archaic pottery from Niconium', *Materialy po Arkheologii Severnogo Prichernomorya* 8 (Odessa, 1976) (In Russian)

358. Sekerskaya, N. M. *Antichny Nikonii i yego Okruga*. Kiev, 1989

359. Shelov, D. B. 'Cyzicene staters on the Bosporus', *VDI* (1949) 2, 94–7 (In Russian)

360. Shelov, D. B. 'On the question of the coins of the Bosporan cities Apollonia and Myrmekion', *VDI* (1949) 1, 143–53 (In Russian)

361. Shelov, D. B. 'The coins of the Sindi', *KSIIMK* 30 (1949) 111–18 (In Russian)

362. Shelov, D. B. 'On the interaction of Greek and local cults in the North Black Sea area (The satyr and griffin on the gold staters of Panticapeum in the fourth century B.C.)', *KSIIMK* 34 (1950) 62–9 (In Russian)

363. Shelov, D. B. 'Theodosia, Heraclea and the Spartocids', *VDI* (1950) 168–78 (In Russian)

364. Shelov, D. B. 'On the representation of the lion's head on the early Bosporan coins', *KSIIMK* 39 (1951) 45–52 (In Russian)

365. Shelov, D. B. 'The monetary system of the Bosporan cities in the sixth and fifth centuries B.C.', *MIA* 19 (1951) 125–35 (In Russian)

366. Shelov, D. B. 'The monetary reform of Leucon II', *VDI* (1953) 1, 30–9 (In Russian)

367. Shelov, D. B. 'Coin minting and coin circulation on the Bosporus in the third century B.C.' *MIA* 33 (1954) 58–70 (In Russian)

368. Shelov, D. B. *Antichny Mir v Severnom Prichernomorye*. Moscow, 1956

369. Shelov, D. B. *Monyetnoye Dyelo Bospora*. Moscow, 1956

370. Shelov, D. B. 'The emergence of Theodosia', *Numismaticbesky Sbornik* 2 (1957) 19–26 (In Russian)

371. Shelov, D. B. 'On the question of contacts between Rhodes and Bosporus in the Hellenistic period', *Sov. Arch.* 28 (1958) 333–6 (In Russian)

372. Shelov, D. B. *The Coinage of the Bosporus in the VI–II centuries B.C.* (BAR Int. Ser. 46) 1978

373. Shelov, D. B. 'Der nördliche Schwarzmeerraum in der Antike', in Heinen, H. (ed.), *Die Geschichte des Altertums im Spiegel der Sowjetischen Forschung*, 341–402. Darmstadt, 1980

374. Shelov, D. B. 'The Sindi of the Kuban region and Greek colonisation', *Thracia Pontica* 1, Iambol (1982) 31–8 (In Russian)

375. Shelov-Kovyedyayev, F. V. 'The inclusion of Nymphaeum in the Bosporan State', *Tyezisy Dokladov Nauchnoi Sessii v Pushkinskom Muzeye Iskusstv 1980*, 46–9. Moscow, 1981 (In Russian)

376. Shelov-Kovyedyayev, F. V. 'On the interpretation of the coins with the inscription SINDŌN', *Antichnaya Balkanistika*, 52–3. Moscow, 1984 (In Russian)

377. Shelov-Kovyedyayev, F. V. 'New Bosporan decrees', *VDI* (1985) 1, 58–74 (In Russian)

378. Shelov-Kovyedyayev, F. V. 'Istoria Bospora v VI–IV vyekakh do n.e.', *Drevnyeishiye Gosudarstva na Territorii SSSR* 8, 3–187. Moscow, 1985 (In Russian)

379. Shelov-Kovyedyayev, F. V. 'La structure politique et sociale de la tyrannie du Bosphore Cimmerien', *DHA* 12 (1986) 173–82

380. Shelov-Kovyedyayev, F. V. 'Die Eroberung Theodosias durch die Spartokiden', *Klio* 68 (1986) 367–76

381. Shelov-Kovyedyayev, F. V. 'Once more on the state of the Sindi', *Klio* 71 (1989) 216–25 (In Russian)

382. Shilik, K. K. 'Researches at Akra', *AOR 1985*, 632. Moscow, 1987 (In Russian)

383. Shilov, V. P. 'The coins of the Sindi', *Sov. Arch.* 15 (1951) 205–15 (In Russian)

384. Shkurko, V. I. 'On the curled predator in Scythian art of the wooded steppe area', *Sov. Arch.* (1969) 1, 31–40. (In Russian)

385. Sidorova, N. A. 'Archaic pottery from the excavations at Hermonassa', *Soobschenia Gosudarstvyennogo Museya imeni Pushkina* 8 (1987) 110ff. (In Russian)

386. Silantyeva, L. F. 'The necropolis of Nymphaeum', *MIA* 69 (1959)

387. Skorpil, V. V. 'The Archaeanactidae', *Izvestia Tavricheskoi Uchenoi Arkhivnoi Komissii* (1918) 58ff. (In Russian)

388. Skrzhinskaya, M. V. *Severnoye Prichernomorye v Opisanii Plinia Starshego.* Kiev, 1977

389. Sokolov, G. *Antique Art on the Northern Black Sea Coast; Architecture, Sculpture, Painting, Applied Arts.* Leningrad, 1974

390. Sokolsky, N. I. 'The dykes in the system of defences of the Cimmerian Bosporus', *Sov. Arch.* 27 (1957) 91–106. (In Russian)

391. Sokolsky, N. I. 'On the question of mercenaries on the Bosporus in the fourth and third centuries B.C.', *Sov. Arch.* 28 (1958) 298–307. (In Russian)

392. Sokolsky, N. I. 'The city of Cepi', *Archaeology* 18 (1965) 181–6

393. Sokolsky, N. I. 'On the question of Sindian sculpture', *Kultura Antichnogo Mira*, 243–58. Moscow, 1966. (In Russian)

394. Sokolsky, N. I. *Dyerevoobrabatyvayuscheye Remeslo v Antichnykh Gosudarstvakh Prichernomorya.* Moscow, 1971

395. Stronk, J. 'Wreckage at Salmydessus', *Thracia Pontica* III (1985) 203–15

396. Struve, V. V. 'The earliest historian of the USSR', *Etyudy po Istorii Severnogo Prichernomorya, Kavkaza i Srednei Azii – Sbornik v Pamyati Akademika I. Y. Krachkovskogo*, 146–58. Leningrad, 1968. (In Russian)

397. Tokhtasyov, S. A. 'Cimmerian toponyms', *Etnogenes Narodov Balkan i Severnogo Prichernomorya*, 142–8. Moscow, 1984. (In Russian)

398. Tolstikov, V. P. 'Fortifications on the acropolis of Panticapaeum', *Soobschenia Gosudarstvyennogo Muzeya Izobrazityelnykh Izkusstv imeni Pushkina* 7. Moscow, 1984. (In Russian)

399. Tolstikov, V. P. 'Towards the problem of the formation of the Bosporan state', *VDI* (1984) 3, 27–45. (In Russian)

400. Treister, M. Y. 'New data on artistic metalworking on the Bosporus', *VDI* (1984) 146–59. (In Russian)

401. Treister, M. Y. 'Bronze casting on the Bosporus in the fourth century', *KSIA* 191 (1987) 7–13. (In Russian)
402. Treister, M. Y. 'Bronze casting on the Bosporus in the sixth and fifth centuries B.C.', *Eirene* 25 (Prague, 1988) 45–67
403. Tsetskhladze, G. R. 'The North and East Black Sea areas in the VI–I centuries', *Arkheologia* (1990) 86–97. (In Ukrainian)
404. Tuplin, C. J. 'Satyros and Athens: *IG* ii² 212 and Isokrates 17.57', *ZPE* 49 (1982) 121–8
405. Ustinova, V. A. 'On the annexation of Sindica to the Bosporan state', *VDI* (1966) 4, 128ff. (In Russian)
406. Vasilyev, A. N. 'The events of 438 B.C. on the Bosporus', *Problemy Otyechestvyennoi Istorii*, 2, 154–76. Moscow–Leningrad, 1976. (In Russian)
407. Velkov, V. 'Pontic Thrace and its interrelations with the Greek world', *Tskhaltubo-Vani IV, 1985*. Tbilisi (1988) 264–80
408. Venedikov, I. *et al. Apolonia.* Sofia, 1963
409. Venedikov, I., Ognenova-Marinova, L. and Cimbuleva, J. *Nesebre I.* SOFIA, 1969; II, Sofia, 1980
410. Vickers, M. *Scythian Treasures in Oxford.* Oxford, 1979
411. Vinogradov, Y. G. 'The problem of the political status of the cities in the Bosporan state in the fourth century B.C.' *Osnovnye Problemy Razyitia Rabovladelcheskoi Formatsii, Tyezisy Dokladov Konferentsii*, 22–5. Moscow, 1978. (In Russian)
412. Vinogradov, Y. G. 'Die historische Entwicklung der Poleis des nördlichen Schwarzmeergebietes im V. Jahrhundert v. Christ', *Chiron* 10 (1980) 63–100
413. Vinogradov, Y. G. 'The ring of King Skyles', *Sov. Arch.* (1980) 3, 92–100. (In Russian)
414. Vinogradov, Y. G. *Olbia. Geschichte einer Altgriechischen Stadt am Schwarzen Meer* (XENIA I). Konstanz, 1981
415. Vinogradov, Y. G. 'Sinope and Olbia – problems of political structure', *VDI* (1981) 2, 65–90. (In Russian)
416. Vinogradov, Y. G. 'The historical fate of the poleis of the North Black Sea area in the fifth century B.C.', in *Istoria Antichnoi Gretsii* I, 363–420. Moscow, 1983. (In Russian)
417. Vinogradov, Y. G. *Politicheskaya Istoria Ol'viiskogo Polisa VII–I vv do n.e.* Moscow, 1989
418. Vinogradov, Y. G. and Marchenko, K. K. 'Das nördliche Schwarzmeergebiet in der Skythischen Epoche', *Klio* 71 (1989) 539–49
419. Vinogradov, Y. G. and Zolotaryov, M. I. 'Archaic Chersonesus', *Tskhaltubo-Vani v, 1987* Tbilisi, 1990
420. Wasowicz, A. 'La campagne et les villes du littoral septentrional du Pont-Euxin (Nouveaux témoignages archéologiques)', *Dacia* 13 (1969) 87–9
421. Wasowicz, A. 'Traces de lotissements anciens en Crimée', *MEFRA* 84 (1972) 1, 209–11
422. Wasowicz, A. 'L'aménagement de l'espace de l'état grec: Olbia Pontique, Chersonèse Taurique, Royaume du Bospore', *Rendiconti, Classe di Lettere, Istituto Lombardo di Scienze e Lettere* 109 (1975) 226–41

423. Wasowicz, A. *Olbia Pontique et son Territoire*. Paris, 1975
424. Wasowicz, A. 'Les facteurs de la civilisation et de l'urbanisation des côtes de la mer noire a l'époque de la colonisation grecque', *La Città antica come fatto di cultura – Atti del Convegno di Como e Bellagio, 16–19 giugno 1979*, 67–77. Como, 1983
425. Werner, R. 'Die Dynastie der Spartokiden', *Historia* 4 (1955) 412–44
426. Werner, R. 'Das Bosporanische Reich', in von Barloewen (ed.) *Abriss der Geschichte Antiker Randkulturen*, 143ff. 1961
427. Werner, R. 'Die griechische Schwarzmeerkolonisation und Bosporanisches Reich', *Handbuch der alten Geschichte Russlands*, 1.2. 153–72. Stuttgart, 1978
428. Wormell, D. E. W. 'Studies in Greek tyranny, ii: Leucon of Bosporus', *Hermathena* 68 (1946) 49–71
429. Yailenko, V. P. *Grecheskaya Kolonizatsia VII–III vyekakh do n.e.* Moscow, 1982
430. Yailenko, V. P. 'Archaic Greece', in *Istoria Antichnoi Gretsii* i, 137ff. Moscow, 1983. (In Russian)
431. Yailenko, V. P. 'On the identification of the rivers and peoples of Scythia in Herodotus', *Sovietskaya Etnografia* (1983) 1, 54–65. (In Russian)
432. Yailenko, V. P. 'The Bosporan state', in Golubtsova, E. S. (ed.), *Ellinizm, Ekonomika, Politika, Kultura*, 283–309. Moscow, 1990. (In Russian)
433. Yakovenko, E. V. 'On the ethno-cultural identity of the population of the Khora of the European side of the Bosporus', *Tskhaltubo-Vani ii, 1979*, 248–59. Tbilisi, 1981. (In Russian)
434. Zedgenidze, A. A. and Antonova, I. A. 'The foundation date of Chersonesus', *KSIA* 159 (1979) 27–30. (In Russian)
435. Zedgenidze, A. A. and Antonova, I. A. *Khersones-Putyevoditel'*. Simferopol, 1985
436. Zeyest, I. B. 'New data concerning contacts of the Cimmerian Bosporus with the southern shores of the Black Sea', *VDI* (1951) 1, 106–16. (In Russian)
437. Zeyest, I. B. 'On the question of trade between Phanagoria and the Kuban river valley', *MIA* 19 (1951) 107–18. (In Russian)
438. Zeyest, I. B. *Keramicheskaya Tara Bospora – Materialy i Issledovaniya po Arkheologii SSSR* 83 (1960)
439. Zeyest, I. B. 'The archaic layers at Hermonassa', *KSIA* 83 (1961) 53–8. (In Russian)
440. Zeyest, I. B. 'On a special feature of the economic development of Hermonassa', *Antichnaya Istoria i Kul'tura Sredizemnomorya i Prichernomorya*, 144–53. Leningrad, 1968. (In Russian)
441. Zhebelyov, S. A. 'Bosporan studies', *Severnoye Prichernomorye*, 159–95. Moscow–Leningrad, 1953. (In Russian)
442. Zhebelyov, S. A. 'The Bosporan Archaeanactidae', *Severnoye Prichernomorye*, 21–8. Moscow–Leningrad, 1953. (In Russian)
443. Zhebelyov, S. A. 'The last Pairisades and the Scythian revolt on the Bosporus', *Severnoye Prichernomorye*, 82–115. Moscow–Leningrad, 1953. (In Russian)

444. Zhebelyov, S. A. 'The main lines of the economic development of the Bosporan state', *Severnoye Prichernomorye*, 116–58. Moscow–Leningrad, 1953. (In Russian)
445. Zhebelyov, S. A. 'The rise of the Bosporan state', *Severnoye Prichernomorye*, 49–73. Moscow–Leningrad, 1953. (In Russian)
446. Zhebelyov, S. A. 'The rise of Chersonesus Taurica', *Severnoye Prichernomorye*, 74–81. Moscow–Leningrad, 1953. (In Russian)
447. Zograf, A. N. 'Antichnye Monyety', *MIA* 16 (1951)
448. Zograf, A. N. *Ancient Coins*, BAR S 33, 1972
449. Zolotaryov, M. I. 'New data on the ancient sea routes on the Euxine Pontus', *Tskhaltubo-Vani I, 1977*, 94–100. Tbilisi, 1979. (In Russian)
450. Zolotaryov, M. I. 'Two types of rare coins of Theodosia dating to the fourth century B.C.', *VDI* (1984) 1, 89–92. (In Russian)

F. THE EAST

I. PERSIA AND THE PERSIAN EMPIRE

1. Altheim, F. and Stiehl, R. *Die Aramäische Sprache unter den Achaemeniden* II. Leipzig, 1963
2. Austin, M. 'Greek Tyrants and the Persians, 546–479 B.C.', *CQ* n.s. 40 (1990) 289–306
3. Badian, E. 'The Peace of Callias', *JHS* 107 (1987) 1–39
4. Badian, E. 'The King's Peace', in Flower, M. and Toher, M. (eds.), *Georgica: Greek Studies in Honour of George Cawkwell*, 25–48. London, 1991
5. Balcer, J. *Sparda by the Bitter Sea: Imperial Interaction in Western Anatolia.* Chico, 1984
5A. Bernard, P., Desparmet, R. and Gardin, J.-C. *Fouilles d'Aï Khanoum* I. Paris, 1973
6. Bernard, P. 'Campagne de fouilles 1978 à Aï Khanoum', *CRAI* (1980) 435–59
7. Bickerman, E. J. 'The Seleucids and the Achaemenids', in *La Persia e il Mondo Greco-Romano* (Accademia Nazionale dei Lincei, Anno 363, N. 76, 1966), 87–117
8. Bidez, J. and Cumont, F. *Les mages hellenisés.* 2 vols. Paris, 1938
9. Briant, P. *Etat et pasteurs au Moyen-Orient ancien.* Cambridge–Paris, 1982
10. Briant, P. *Rois, tributs et paysans* (Annales littéraires de l'Université de Besançon, 269 (Centre de Recherche Ancienne, 43)). Paris, 1982
11. Briant, P. *L'Asie central et les royaumes proche-orientaux du premier millénaire (c. VIIIe–IVe siècles avant notre ère).* Paris, 1984
11A. Briant, P. 'Chasses royales macedoniennes et chasses royales perses: le thème de la chasse au lion sur *la chasse de Vergina*', *DHA* 17 (1991) 211–55
12. Cameron, G. *Persepolis Treasury Tablets.* Chicago, 1948
13. Cawkwell, G. L. 'The power of Persia', *Arepo* 1 (1968) 1–5
14. Cook, J. M. *The Persian Empire.* London, 1983
15. Dandamayev, M. A. 'Bagasarū ganzabara', in Mayrhofer, M. (ed.) *Studien zur Sprachwissenschaft und Kulturkunde (Gedenkschrift für Wilhelm*

Brandenstein) (Innsbrucker Beiträge zur Kulturwissenschaft 14), 235–9. Innsbruck, 1968

16. Dandamayev, M. and Lukonin, V. G. *The Culture and Social Institutions of Ancient Iran.* Cambridge, 1989
17. Davis, E. W. 'The Persian battle plan at the Granicus', *James Sprunt Studies in History and Political Sciences* 46 (1964) 34–44
18. Eilers, W. *Iranische Beamtennamen in der keilschriftlichen Überlieferung* 1 (all pubd) (Abhandlungen für die Kunde des Morgenlandes 25/5). Leipzig, 1940
19. *Fouilles d' Aï Khanoum* 1 (Mémoires de la délégation archéologique française en Afghanistan 21). Paris, 1973
20. Frye, R. N. 'Gestures of deference to royalty in Ancient Iran', *Ir. Ant.* 9 (1972) 102–7
21. Frye, R. N. *The Heritage of Persia.* London, 1976
22. Gardin, J.-C. 'L'archéologie du paysage bactrien', *CRAI* (1980) 480–501
23. Gardin, J.-C. and Gentelle, P. 'Irrigation et peuplement dans la plaine d'Ai Khanoum de l'époque achéménide à l'époque musulmane', *BEFEO* 63 (1976) 59–99
24. Gardin, J.-C. and Lyonnet, B. 'La prospection archéologique de la Bactriane orientale', *Mesopotamia* 13/14 (1978/9) 99–149
25. Gershevitch, I. (ed.) *The Cambridge History of Iran* 11: *The Median and Achaemenian Periods.* Cambridge, 1985
26. Graf, D. F. 'Greek tyrants and Achaemenid politics', in Eadie, J. W. and Ober, J. (eds.), *The Craft of the Ancient Historian (Essays in Honor of Chester G. Starr),* 79–123. Lanham, Maryland, 1985
27. Hallock, R. *Persepolis Fortification Tablets* (OIP 92). Chicago, 1969
28. Hallock, R. T. 'The Persepolis Fortification Archive', *Orientalia* n.s. 42 (1973) 320–3
29. Hammond, N. G. L. 'The kingdom of Asia and the Persian throne', *Antichthon* 20 (1986) 73–85
30. Hansman, J. 'Charax and the Karkheh', *Ir. Ant.* 7 (1967) 21–58
31. Hansman, J. 'The problems of Qūmis', *JRAS* (1968) 111–39
32. Hansman, J. 'Elamites, Achaemenians and Anshan', *Iran* 10 (1972) 101–25
33. Hansman, J. F. and Stronach, D. 'Excavations at Shahr-i Qūmis', *JRAS* (1970) 29–62
34. Herzfeld, E. *The Persian Empire: Studies in Geography and Ethnography of the Ancient Near East.* Wiesbaden, 1968
35. Hinz, W. *Altiranisches Sprachgut der Nebenüberlieferungen* (Göttinger Orientforschung, III. Reihe (Iranica), 3). Wiesbaden, 1975
36. Hornblower, S. Review of F 47, F 51 and F 40, *CR* n.s. 40 (1990) 89–95
37. Hornblower, S. Review of F 69, *CR* n.s. 40 (1990) 363–5
38. Joannès, F. 'La titulature de Xerxès', *NABU* 1989 No. 2, 25 sub 37
39. Kent, R. G. *Old Persian, Grammar, Texts, Lexicon* (American Oriental Series 33). 2nd edn. New Haven, 1953
39A. Koch, H. 'Steuern in der achämenidischen Persis', *ZA* 70 (1980) 105–37

39B. Koch, H. *Verwaltung und Wirtschaft im persischen Kernland zur Zeit der Achämeniden* (Beihefte zum Tübinger Atlas des vorderen Orients B89). Wiesbaden, 1990

40. Kuhrt, A. and Sancisi-Weerdenburg, H. *Achaemenid History* III: *Method and Theory*. Leiden, 1988

41. Moysey, R. 'Greek relations with the Persian Satraps, 371–343 B.C.', Diss. Princeton, 1975

42. Murison, J. A. 'Darius III and the battle of Issus', *Historia* 21 (1972) 399–423

43. Olmstead, A. T. *History of the Persian Empire*. Chicago, 1948

44. Petit, T. 'Karanos: étude d'une fonction militaire sous la dynastie perse achéménide', *LEC* 51 (1983) 35–45

45. Petit, T. *Satrapes et satrapies dans l'empire achéménide de Cyrus le Grand à Xerxès*, Ier: Bibliothèque de la faculté de Philosophie et Lettres de l'Université de Liège, fasc. 254. Paris, 1990

46. Root, M. C. *The King and Kingship in Achaemenid Art*. Leiden, 1979

47. Sancisi-Weerdenburg, H. (ed.) *Achaemenid History* I: *Sources, Structures and Synthesis*. Leiden, 1987

48. Sancisi-Weerdenburg, H. *'ΠΕΡΣΙΚΟΝ ΔΕ ΚΑΡΤΑ Ο ΣΤΡΑΤΟΣ ΔΩΡΟΝ*: a typically Persian gift (Hdt. ix 109)', *Historia* 37 (1988) 372–4

49. Sancisi-Weerdenburg, H. and Drijvers, J. W. (eds.) *Achaemenid History* V: *The Roots of the European Tradition*. Leiden, 1990

50. Sancisi-Weerdenburg, H. and Drijvers, J. W. *Achaemenid History* VII: *Through Travellers' Eyes*. Leiden, 1991

51. Sancisi-Weerdenburg, H. and Kuhrt, A. (eds.) *Achaemenid History* II: *The Greek Sources*. Leiden, 1987

52. Sancisi-Weerdenburg, H. and Kuhrt, A. (eds.) *Achaemenid History* IV: *Centre and Periphery*. Leiden, 1990

53. Sancisi-Weerdenburg, H. and Kuhrt, A. (eds.) *Achaemenid History* VI: *Asia Minor and Egypt: Old Cultures in a New Empire*. Leiden, 1991

54. Scheil, V. *Actes juridiques susiens (suite), Inscriptions des Achéménides (Supplément et suite)* (Mémoires de la Mission Archéologique de Perse 24). Paris, 1933

55. Schiwek, H. 'Der persische Golf als Schiffahrts- und Seehandelsroute', *BJ* 162 (1962) 4–97

56. Schmitt, R. 'Thronnamen bei den Achaimeniden', *Beiträge zur Namenforschung* NF 12 (1977) 422–5

57. Schmitt, R. 'Achaemenid throne-names', *Annali dell'Istituto Orientale di Napoli* 42 (1982) 83–95

58. Schwenzner, W. 'Gobryas', *Klio* 18 (1923) 41–58 and 226–52

59. Sekunda, N. 'Notes on the *Life* of Datames', *Iran* 26 (1988) 38–53

59A. Sordi, M. 'La cronologia delle vittorie persiane e la caduta di Ermia di Atarneo in Diodoro', KOKALOS 5 (1959) 107–18

60. Stolper, M. W. 'The death of Artaxerxes I', *AMI* NF 16 (1983) 223–36

61. Stolper, M. W. 'Some ghost facts from Achaemenid Babylonian texts', *JHS* 108 (1988) 196–8

62. Strassmaier, J. N. 'Arsaciden-Inschriften', *ZA* 3 (1888) 129–58

63. Stronach, D. *Pasargadae*. Oxford, 1978
64. Syme, R. 'The Cadusii in history and fiction', *JHS* 108 (1988) 137–50
65. Tuplin, C. 'The administration of the Achaemenid Empire', in B 188, 109–66
66. Tuplin, C. J. 'Xenophon and the garrisons of the Achaemenid Empire', *AMI* 20 (1987) 167–245
67. Walser, G. *Die Völkerschaften auf den Reliefs von Persepolis*. Berlin, 1966
68. Walser, G. (ed.) *Beiträge zur Achämenidengeschichte* (*Historia* Einzelschrift 18). Wiesbaden, 1972
69. Weiskopf, M. *The So-called "Great Satraps' Revolt", 366–360 B.C.: Concerning Local Instability in the Achaemenid Far West* (*Historia* Einzelschrift 63). Stuttgart, 1989
70. Wheeler, M. *Flames over Persepolis*. New York, 1968
71. Widengren, G. *Der Feudalismus im alten Iran*. Cologne, 1969

II. BABYLONIA

72. Aaboe, A. and Sachs, A. 'Two lunar texts of the Achaemenid period from Babylon', *Centaurus* 14 (1969) 1–22
73. Adams, R. McC. *Heartland of Cities: Surveys of Ancient Settlement and Land Use on the Central Flood Plain of the Euphrates*. Chicago, 1981
74. Adams, R. McC. and Nissen, J. H. *The Uruk Countryside: the Natural Setting of Urban Societies*. Chicago, 1972
75. Anonymous. 'Babylonian contract tablets, presented to the Society of Biblical Archaeology, 6th April, 1875, by Lady Tite', *Transactions of the Society of Biblical Archaeology* 4 (1876) 257
76. Arnaud, D. 'Note annexe: Trouvailles épigraphiques de la 10e Campagne (1983) à Tell Senkereh/Larsa (Iraq)', *Akkadica* 44 (1985) 18
77. Beaulieu, P. 'An early attestation of the word *ḫadru*', *NABU* 1988 No. 3, 37–39 sub 54
78. Bernard, P. 'Nouvelle contribution de l'épigraphie cunéiforme à l'histoire hellénistique', *BCH* 94 (1990) 513–41
79. Böhl, F. M. Th. de L. 'Die babylonischen Prätendenten zur Zeit des Xerxes', *Bi. Or.* 29 (1962) 110–14
80. Borger, R. *Die Inschriften Asarhaddons Königs von Assyrien (AfO* Beih. 9). Graz, 1956
81. Brinkman, J. A. 'Cuneiform texts in the St. Louis Public Library', in Eichler, B. L., Heimerdinger, J. W. and Sjöberg, A. W. (eds.). *Kramer Anniversary Volume* (*Cuneiform Studies in Honor of Samuel Noah Kramer*) (Alter Orient und Altes Testament 25), 41–52. Kevelaer and Neukirchen-Vluyn, 1976
82. Brinkman, J. A. 'BM 36761, the Astronomical Diary for 331 B.C.', *NABU* 1987 No. 3, 34 sub 63
83. Cardascia, G. *Les archives des Murašû, une famille d'hommes d'affaires babyloniens à l'époque perse (455–403 av. J.-C.)*. Paris, 1951
84. Cardascia, G. 'Le fief dans la Babylonie achéménide', *Rec. Soc. Bodin* 1² (1958) 55–88

85. Cardascia, G. 'Ḫaṭru', *Reallexikon der Assyriologie* 4/2–3 (1973) 150–1
86. Cardascia, G. 'Armée et fiscalité dans la Babylonie achéménide', in *Actes du Colloque Armées et fiscalité dans le monde antique* (Colloques Nationaux du Centre National de la Recherche Scientifique 936), 1–11. Paris, 1977
87. Clay, A. T. *Business Documents of Murashû Sons of Nippur Dated in the Reign of Darius II (424–404 B.C.)* (BE 10). Philadelphia, 1904
88. Clay, A. T. 'Aramaic endorsements on the documents of the Murašû Sons', in Harper, R. F., Moore, G. F. and Brown, F. (eds.), *Old Testament and Semitic Studies in Memory of William Rainey Harper* 1, 287–321. Chicago, 1908
89. Clay, A. T. *Legal and Commercial Transactions Dated in the Assyrian, Neo-Babylonian and Persian Periods, Chiefly from Nippur* (BE 8/1). Philadelphia, 1908
90. Clay, A. T. *Business Documents of Murashû Sons of Nippur Dated in the Reign of Darius II* (University of Pennsylvania, The Museum, Publications of the Babylonian Section 2 No. 1). Philadelphia, 1912
91. Coogan, M. D. *West Semitic Personal Names in the Murašû Documents* (Harvard Semitic Monographs 7). Missoula, Montana, 1976
92. Dandamayev, M. A. 'Die Lehnsbeziehungen in Babylonien unter den ersten Achämeniden', in Wiessner, G. (ed.), *Festschrift für Wilhelm Eilers*, 37–42, Wiesbaden, 1967
93. Dandamayev, M. A. 'Achaemenid Babylonia' in Diakonoff, I. (ed.), *Ancient Mesopotamia*, 296–331. Moscow, 1969
94. Dandamayev, M. A. 'On the fiefs in Babylonia in the early Achaemenid period', in Koch, H. and Mackenzie, D. N. (eds.) *Kunst, Kultur und Geschichte der Achämenidenzeit und ihr Fortleben* (*AMI* Ergänzungsband 19), 57–9. 1983
95. Dandamayev, M. A. *Slavery in Babylonia from Nabopolassar to Alexander the Great (626–331 B.C.)*. Rev. edn., trans. V. A. Powell, ed. M. A. Powell and D. B. Weisberg. DeKalb, Illinois, 1984
96. Dandamayev, M. A. 'Šušan in the Murašû Documents', in De Mayer, L., Gasche, H. and Vallat, F. (eds.), *Fragmenta Historiae Elamicae (Mélanges offerts à M.-J. Stève*, 289–90. Paris, 1986
97. Donbaz, V. 'The question of the Murašû texts dated at Susa', *NABU* 1989 No. 4, 59 sub 1
98. Durand, J.-M. *Textes babyloniens d'époque récente*. Paris, 1981
99. Ephʿal, I. 'The Western minorities in Babylonia in the 6th–5th centuries B.C.: maintenance and cohesion', *Orientalia* n.s. 47 (1978) 74–90
100. Evetts, B. T. A. *Inscriptions of the Reigns of Evil-Merodach, Neriglissar and Laborosoarchod* (Babylonische Texte, III Heft 6B). Leipzig, 1892
101. Figulla, H. H. *Business Documents of the New-Babylonian Period* (Ur Excavations, Texts 4). London, 1949
102. Gasche, H. Hermann, Warburton, D., *et al.* 'Abu Qubūr 1987–1988, Chantier F. La Résidence Achéménide', *Northern Akkad Project Reports* 4 (1989) 3–43
103. Geller, M. J. 'Babylonian astronomical diaries and corrections of Diodorus', *BSOAS* 53 (1990) 1–7

104. Gibson, McG. *The City and Area of Kish*. Coconut Grove, Florida, 1972
105. Grayson, A. K. *Assyrian and Babylonian Chronicles* (Texts from Cuneiform Sources, 5). Locust Valley, 1975
106. Grayson, A. K. *Babylonian Historical-Literary Texts* (Semitic Texts and Studies, 3). Toronto–Buffalo, 1975
107. Graziani, S. *I Testi Mesopotamici datati al Regno di Serse* (*Annali dell'Istituto Universitario Orientale, Napoli* 46 fasc. 2, Suppl. 47). Rome, 1986
108. Grotefend, G. 'Urkunden in babylonischer Keilschrift, erster Beitrag', *ZKM* 1 (1837) 212ff
109. Grotefend, G. 'Urkunden in babylonischer Keilschrift, zweiter Beitrag', *ZKM* 2 (1839) 177–85
110. Grotefend, G. 'Urkunden in babylonischer Keilschrift, vierter Beitrag', *ZKM* 4 (1842) 43–57
111. Haerinck, E. 'Le palais achéménide de Babylone', *Ir. Ant.* 10 (1973) 108–32
112. Hilprecht, H. V. and Clay, A. T. *Business Documents of the Murashû Sons of Nippur, Dated in the Reign of Artaxerxes I (464–424 B.C.)* (BE 9). Philadelphia, 1898
113. Hunger, H. *Babylonische und assyrische Kolophone* (Alter Orient und Altes Testament 2). Neukirchen–Vluyn, 1968
114. Hunger, H. *Spätbabylonische Texte aus Uruk, Teil I* (ADFU 9). Berlin, 1976
115. Jakob-Rost, L. and Freydank, H. 'Spätbabylonische Rechtsurkunden mit aramäischen Beischriften aus Babylon', *Forschungen und Berichte* 14 (1972) 7–35
116. Joannès, F. *Textes économiques de la Babylonie récente*. Paris, 1982
117. Joannès, F. 'Les archives d'une famille de notables babyloniens du VIIe au Ve siècle avant Jésus-Christ', *Journal des Savants* (Juillet-Décembre 1984) 135–50
118. Joannès, F. Review of F 140, *Bi. Or.* 45 (1988) 358–64
119. Joannès, F. *Archives de Borsippa, La famille Ea-ilûta-bâni, Etude d'un lot d'archives familiales en Babylonie du VIIIe au Ve siècle av. J-C.* (Ecole pratique des Hautes Etudes, IVe Section, Sciences historiques et philologiques, II: Hautes Etudes Orientales 25). Geneva and Paris, 1989
119A. Joannès, F. 'La titulature de Xerxès', *NABU* 1989 No. 2, 25 sub 37
120. Joannès, F. *Les tablettes néo-babyloniennes de la Bodleian Library conservées à l'Ashmolean Museum (Neo-Babylonian Tablets in the Ashmolean Museum)* (Oxford Editions of Cuneiform Texts 12). Oxford, 1990
121. Joannès, F. 'Pouvoirs locaux et organisations du territoire en Babylonie achéménide', *Transeuphratène* 3 (1990) 173–89
122. Joannès, F. 'Textes babyloniens de Suse d'époque achéménide', in Vallat, F. (ed.), *Contribution à l'histoire de l'Iran. Mélanges offerts à Jean Perrot*, 173–80. Paris, 1990
123. Joannès, F. 'Les archives de Ninurta-ahhê-bulliṭ' (Proceedings of the Rencontre Assyriologique International, Philadelphia, July 1988) (forthcoming).
124. Kennedy, D. A. *Late-Babylonian Economic Texts* (Cuneiform Texts from Babylonian Tablets in the British Museum 49). London, 1968

125.   Kessler, K. 'Duplikate und Fragmente aus Uruk, Teil II', *Bagh. Mitt.* 15 (1984) 261–72

126.   Klengel-Brandt, E. 'Siegelabrollungen aus dem Babylon der Spätzeit', *Oriens Antiquus* 8 (1969) 329–36

127.   Krückmann, O. *Neubabylonische Rechts- und Verwaltungstexte* (Texte und Materialien der Frau Professor Hilprecht Collection of Babylonian Antiquities im Eigentum der Universität Jena 2/3). Leipzig, 1933

128.   Kuhrt, A. 'Survey of written sources available for the history of Babylonia under the later Achaemenids (concentrating on the period from Artaxerxes II to Darius III)', in F 47, 147–57

129.   Kuhrt, A. 'Achaemenid Babylonia: sources and problems', in F 52, 177–94

130.   Kuhrt, A. 'The Achaemenid Empire: a Babylonian perspective', *PCPhS* 214 (n.s. 34) (1988) 60–76

131.   Kuhrt, A. 'Alexander and Babylon', in F 49, 121–30

132.   Kuhrt, A. and Sherwin-White, S. M. 'Xerxes' destruction of Babylonian temples', in F 51, 69–78

133.   Legrain, L. *The Culture of the Babylonians from their Seals in the Collections of the Museum* (University of Pennsylvania, The Museum, Publications of the Babylonian Section 14). Philadelphia, 1925

134.   Lenzen, H. J. *XVIII. vorläufiger Bericht über die von dem Deutschen Archäologischen Institut und der Deutschen Orient-Gesellschaft aus Mitteln der Deutschen Forschungsgemeinschaft unternommenen Ausgrabungen in Uruk-Warka, Winter 1959/69*. Berlin, 1962

134A. Luckenbill, D. *Ancient Records of Assyria and Babylonia* II. Chicago, 1927

135.   Lutz, H. F. 'An agreement between a Babylonian feudal lord and his retainer in the reign of Darius II' (UCP 9 No. 3). 1928

136.   McCown, D. E. *et al. Nippur, I: Temple of Enlil, Scribal Quarter, and Soundings* (OIP 78). Chicago, 1967. *Nippur, II: The North Temple and Sounding E* (OIP 97). Chicago, 1978

137.   McEwan, G. J. P. *Priest and Temple in Hellenistic Babylonia* (Freiburger Altorientalische Studien 4). Wiesbaden, 1981

138.   McEwan, G. J. P. *The Late Babylonian Tablets in the Royal Ontario Museum* (ROM CT 2). Toronto, 1982

139.   McEwan, G. J. P. 'Late Babylonian Kish', *Iraq* 45 (1983) 117–23

140.   McEwan, G. J. P. *Late Babylonian Texts in the Ashmolean Museum* (Oxford Editions of Cuneiform Texts 10). Oxford, 1984

141.   Moore, E. W. *Neo-Babylonian Documents in the University of Michigan Collection*. Ann Arbor, 1939

142.   Moorey, P. R. S. *Kish Excavations, 1923–1933*. Oxford, 1978

143.   Nasgowitz, D. W. 'The rise of Aramean script in Mesopotamia and its environs', Unpublished M.A. thesis. Chicago, 1966

144.   Neugebauer, O. 'The "Metonic Cycle" in Babylonian Astronomy', in Ashley Montagu, M. F. (ed.), *Studies and Essays in the History of Science and Learning Offered in Homage to George Sarton*, 435–48. New York, 1946

145.   Neugebauer, O. 'Problems and methods in Babylonian mathematical astronomy. Henry Norris Russell Lecture, 1967', *Astronomical Journal* 72

(1967) 964–72

146. Oelsner, J. 'Ein Beitrag zu keilschriftlichen Königstitulaturen in hellenistischer Zeit', *ZA* 56 (1964) 262–74

147. Oelsner, J. Review of Kennedy 1968 (F 124), *ZA* 61 (1971) 159–70

148. Oelsner, J. 'Krisenerscheinungen im Achaimenidenreich im 5. und 4. Jahrhundert v.u.Z.', in C 83, II, 1041–73

149. Oelsner, J. 'Zwischen Xerxes und Alexander: babylonische Rechtsurkunden und Wirtschaftstexte aus der späten Achämenidenzeit', *We. Or.* 8 (1976) 310–18

150. Oelsner, J. 'Zur neu- und spätbabylonischen Siegelpraxis', in Hruška, B. and Komoróczy, G. (eds.), *Festschrift Lubor Matouš* (Assyriologia 5), II, 167–86. Budapest, 1978

151. Oelsner, J. 'Spätachämenidische Texte aus Nippur', *RA* 76 (1982) 94–5

152. Oelsner, J. Review of Hunger 1976 (F 114), *Orientalistische Literaturzeitung* 78 (1983) 246–50

153. Oelsner, J. *Materialien zur babylonischen Gesellschaft und Kultur in hellenistischer Zeit* (Az Eötvös Loránd Tudományegyetem Ókori Történeti, Assziriológiai és Egyiptológiai Tanszékeinek Kiadváyai 40, Assyriologia 7). Budapest, 1986

154. Oelsner, J. 'Aramäisches aus Babylon–Notizen am Rande', in *Der Vordere Orient in Antike und Mittelalter (Festgabe für H. Simon)*. (Berichte der Humboldt-Universität zu Berlin, Sektion Asienwissenschaften, Bereich Westasien 7. Jg. (1987), Heft 10), 38–46

155. Oelsner, J. 'Grundbesitz/Grundeigentum im achämenidischen und seleukidischen Babylonien', in Brentjes, B. (ed.), *Das Grundeigentum in Mesopotamien (Jahrbuch für Wirtschaftsgeschichte*, Sonderband), 117–34. Berlin, 1987

156. Oppenheim, A. L. 'The Babylonian evidence of Achaemenid rule in Mesopotamia', in F 25, 529–87

157. Oppenheim, A. L. (ed.) *The Assyrian Dictionary of the Oriental Institute of the University of Chicago*. Locust Valley, NY, 1956–

158. Oppert, J. and Ménant, J. *Documents juridiques de l'Assyrie et de la Chaldée*. Paris, 1877

159. Parker, R. A. and Dubberstein, W. H. *Babylonian Chronology 626 B.C.–A.D. 75* (Brown University Studies 19). Providence, 1956

160. Pinches, T. G. Untitled communication, *PSBA* 5 (1883) 103–7

161. Pinches, T. G. *Miscellaneous Texts* (Cuneiform Texts from Babylonian Tablets in the British Museum 44). London, 1963

162. Pinches, T. G., Strassmaier, J. N., Sachs, A. and Schaumberger, J. *Late Babylonian Astronomical and Related Texts* (Brown University Studies 18). Providence, 1955

163. Pingree, D. 'Mesopotamian astronomy and astral omens in other civilizations', in Nissen, H.-J. and Renger, J. (eds.), *Mesopotamien und seine Nachbarn, Politische und kulturelle Wechselbeziehungen im alten Vorderasien vom 4. bis 1. Jahrtausend v. Chr.* (Berliner Beiträge zum Vorderen Orient, 1), II, 613–31. Berlin, 1982

164. Reuther, O. *Die Innenstadt von Babylon (Merkes) (Ausgrabungen der Deutschen Orient-Gesellschaft in Babylon* 3) (WVDOG 47). Berlin, 1926

165. Ries, G. *Die neubabylonischen Bodenpachtformulare* (Münchener Universitätschriften, Juristische Fakultät, Abhandlungen zur rechtswissenschaftlichen Grundlagenforschung 16). Berlin, 1976

166. Rochberg-Halton, F. 'New evidence for the history of astrology', *JNES* 43 (1984) 115–40

167. Rochberg-Halton, F. 'Babylonian horoscopes and their sources', *Orientalia* n.s. 58 (1989) 102–23

168. Sachs, A. 'A classification of the Babylonian astronomical tablets of the Seleucid period', *JCS* 2 (1948) 271–90

169. Sachs, A. 'Babylonian horoscopes', *JCS* 6 (1952) 49–75

170. Sachs, A. 'Babylonian observational astronomy', in Hodson, F. R. (ed.), *The Place of Astronomy in the Ancient World*, (Philosophical Transactions of the Royal Society of London, A 276), 43–50. 1974

171. Sachs, A. 'Achaemenid royal names in Babylonian astronomical texts', *AJAH* 2 (1977) 129–47

172. Sachs, A. J. and Hunger, H. *Astronomical Diaries and Related Texts from Babylonia,* 1 = *Diaries from 652 B.C. to 262 B.C.* (Österreichische Akademie der Wissenschaften, Ph.-Hist. Kl., Denkschriften 195). Vienna, 1988

173. Sarkisian, G. Kh. 'New cuneiform texts from Uruk of the Seleucid period in the Staatliche Museen zu Berlin', *Forschungen und Berichte* 16 (1974) 15–76

174. Sayce, A. H. 'Babylonian contract-tablet belonging to the Imperial Academy of Sciences at St. Petersburg', *ZA* 5 (1890) 276–80

175. Stolper, M. W. 'Three Iranian loanwords in late Babylonian texts', in Levine, L. D. and Young, T. Cuyler Jr. (eds.), *Mountains and Lowlands: Essays in the Archaeology of Greater Mesopotamia* (Bibliotheca Mesopotamica 7), 251–66. Malibu, 1977

176. Stolper, M. W. 'The Neo-Babylonian Text from the Persepolis Fortification', *JNES* 43 (1984) 299–310

177. Stolper, M. W. *Entrepreneurs and Empire: the Murašû Archive, the Murašû Firm, and Persian Rule in Babylonia* (Uitgaven van het Nederlands Instituut voor het Nabije Oosten 54). Leiden, 1985

178. Stolper, M. W. 'Bēlšunu the Satrap', in Rochberg-Halton, F. (ed.) *Language, Literature, and History (Assyriological and Historical Studies in Honor of Erica Reiner)* (American Oriental Series 67), 389–402. New Haven, 1987

179. Stolper, M. W. 'The *šaknu* of Nippur', *JCS* 40 (1988) 127–55

180. Stolper, M. W. 'Registration and taxation of slave sales in Achaemenid Babylonia', *ZA* 79 (1989) 80–101

181. Stolper, M. W. 'The governor of Babylon and Across-the-River in 486 B.C.', *JNES* 48 (1989) 283–305

182. Stolper, M. W. 'Late Achaemenid legal texts from Uruk and Larsa', *Bagh. Mitt.* 21 (1990) 559–622

183. Stolper, M. W. 'The Kasr Archive', in F 52, 195–205

184. Stolper, M. W. 'A property in Bit Paniya', *RA* 85 (1991) 49–62
185. Stolper, M. W. 'Tobits in reverse: more Babylonians at Ecbatana', *AMI* NF 23 (1990) 161–76
186. Stolper, M. W. 'The Murašû texts written at Susa', *RA* 86 (1992) 69–77
187. Stolper, M. W. 'Late Achaemenid texts from Dilbat'. *Iraq* 54 (1992) 119–39
188. Stolper, M. W. 'The estate of Mardonius'. *Aula Orientalis* 10 (1992)
189. Strassmaier, J. N. 'Einige kleinere babylonische Keilschrifttexte aus dem Britischen Museum', *Actes du 8e Congrès International des Orientalistes, tenu en 1889* . . . , Part 2, Section I B, 281–3 and plates 1–35. Leiden, 1892–3
190. Strassmaier, J. N. *Inschriften von Darius, König von Babylon . . . (Babylonische Texte* 10–12). Leipzig, 1897
191. Thureau-Dangin, F. *Tablettes d'Uruk à l'usage des prêtres du temple d'Anu au temps des Seleucides* (Musée du Louvre, Département des Antiquités Orientales, Textes cunéiformes, 6). Paris, 1922
192. Unger, E. *Babylon, die heilige Stadt nach der Beschreibung der Babylonier.* Berlin and Leipzig, 1931
193. Ungnad, A. *Neubabylonische Contrakte* (Vorderasiatische Schriftdenkmäler der Königlichen Museen zu Berlin 3–6). Leipzig, 1907–8
194. Vallat, F. 'Le palais d'Artaxerxes II à Babylone', *Northern Akkad Project Reports* 2 (1989) 3–6
195. Van Dijk, J. 'Die Inschriftenfunde', in F 134, 39–62
196. Van Dijk, J. J. and Mayer, W. R. *Texte aus dem Reš-Heiligtum in Uruk-Warka* (*Bagh. Mitt.* Beiheft 2). Berlin, 1980
197. Van Driel, G. 'Continuity or decay in the late Achaemenid period: evidence from southern Mesopotamia', in F 47, 159–81
198. Van Driel, G. 'Neo-Babylonian texts from the Louvre', *Bi. Or.* 43 (1986) 5–20
199. Van Driel, G. 'Neo-Babylonian agriculture', *Bulletin on Sumerian Agriculture* 4 (1988) 121–59
200. Van Driel, G. 'The Murašûs in context', *Journal of the Economic and Social History of the Orient* 32 (1989) 203–29
201. Van Driel, G. 'Neo-Babylonian agriculture, III. Cultivation', in *Irrigation and Cultivation in Mesopotamia*, II (*Bulletin on Sumerian Agriculture* 5, 1990) 219–66
202. Vattioni, F. 'Epigrafia Aramaica', *Augustiniànum* 10 (1970) 493–532
203. von Weiher, E. *Spätbabylonische Texte aus Uruk, 2* (*ADFU* 10). 1983
204. Walker, C. B. F. and Collon, D. 'Hormuzd Rassam's excavations for the British Museum at Sippar in 1881–1882', in De Meyer (ed.) *Tell ed-Dēr,* III: *Sounding at Abū-Ḥabbah (Sippar)*, 93–114, Leuven, 1980
205. Wetzel, F. *et al. Das Babylon der Spätzeit* (WVDOG 62). Berlin, 1957
206. Wiseman, D. J. Review of F 106, *BSOAS* 40 (1977) 373–5
207. Wiseman, D. J. *Nebuchadrezzar and Babylon* (The Schweich Lectures 1983). Oxford, 1985
208. Woolley, C. L. and Mallowan, M. E. L. *Ur Excavations* IX: *The Neo-Babylonian and Persian Periods.* London, 1962

209. Zadok, R. Review of F 35, *Bi. Or.* 33 (1976) 213–19
210. Zadok, R. *The Jews in Babylonia in the Chaldean and Achaemenian Periods in the Light of the Babylonian Sources.* Tel-Aviv, 1976 (In Hebrew). English translation: *The Jews in Babylonia during the Chaldaean and Achaemenian Periods according to the Babylonian Sources* (Studies in the History of the Jewish People and the Land of Israel 3). Haifa, 1979.
211. Zadok, R. 'Iranians and individuals bearing Iranian names in Achaemenian Babylonia', *IOS* 7 (1977) 89–138
212. Zadok, R. *On West Semites in Babylonia during the Chaldean and Achaemenian Periods.* Jerusalem, 1977
213. Zadok, R. 'Phoenicians, Philistines, and Moabites in Mesopotamia', *BASOR* 230 (1978) 57–65
214. Zadok, R. 'The Nippur region during the Late Assyrian, Chaldaean and Achaemenian periods, chiefly according to written sources', *IOS* 8 (1978) 266–332
215. Zadok, R. 'Arabians in Mesopotamia during the Late-Assyrian, Chaldean, Achaemenian and Hellenistic periods, chiefly according to the Cuneiform sources', *ZDMG* 131 (1981) 42–84
216. Zadok, R. 'Iranian and Babylonian notes', *AfO* 28 (1981–2) 135–9
217. Zadok, R. 'New documents from the Chaldean and Achaemenian periods', *Orientalia Lovaniensia Periodica* 15 (1984) 65–75
217A. Zadok, R. 'Archives from Nippur in the first millennium B.C.', in Veenhof, K. R. (ed.), *Cuneiform Archives and Libraries* (Papers read at the 30ᵉ Rencontre Assyriologique Internationale, Leiden, 4–8 July, 1983), 278–88. Leiden, 1986
218. Zettler, R. 'On the chronological range of Neo-Babylonian and Achaemenid seals', *JNES* 38 (1979) 257–70

III. SYRIA, PHOENICIA AND CYPRUS

219. Ap-Thomas, D. R. 'The Phoenicians', in Wiseman, D. J. (ed.), *Peoples of the Old Testament*, 259–86. Oxford, 1973
220. Assmann, J. C. 'Zur Baugeschichte der Königsgruft von Sidon', *Arch. Anz.* 1963, 690–716
221. Barag, D. *The effects of the Tennes revolution on Palestine*, *BASOR* 183 (1966) 6–12.
222. Barns, J. 'Cimon and the first Athenian expedition to Cyprus', *Historia* 2 (1953/4) 163–76
223. Betlyon, J. W. *The Coinage and Mints of Phoenicia: The Pre-Alexandrine Period* (Harvard Semitic Monographs, no. 26). Chicago, 1982
224. Bondi, I. F. 'Istituzioni e politica a Sidone dal 351 al 332 av. Cr.', *R. Stud. Fen.* 2 (1974) 149–60
225. Bosworth, A. B. 'The government of Syria under Alexander the Great', *CQ* n.s. 24 (1974) 46–64
226. Bunnens, G. *L'expansion phénicienne en Méditerranée.* Paris, 1979

227. Caubet, A. *Les sanctuaires de Kition à l'époque de la dynastie phénicienne*, *Studia Phoenicia* IV (1986) 153–68

228. Chaumont, M. L. 'Chypre dans l'empire perse achéménide' Πρακτικά τοῦ Πρώτου Διεθνοῦς Κυπριολογικοῦ Ζευνεδρίου I, 179–89. Nicosia, 1972

229. Collombier, A. M., 'Céramique grecque et échanges en Méditerranée orientale', *Studia Phoenicia* V (1987) 239–48

230. Contenau, G. *La civilisation phénicienne*. 2nd edn. Paris, 1949

231. Costa, E. A. Jr. 'Euagoras I and the Persians, ca. 411 to 391 B.C.', *Historia* 23 (1974) 40–56

232. Destrooper–Georgiades, A. 'La Phénicie et Chypre à l'époque achéménide. Témoignages numismatiques', *Studia Phoenicia* V (1987) 337–55

233. Dunand, M. 'Les sculptures de la favissa du temple d'Amrit', *Bull. Mus. Beyrouth* 7 (1944/45) 99–107; 8 (1946/48) 81–107

234. Dunand, M. *Fouilles de Byblos II*. Paris, 1954–8

235. Dunand, M. *Byblos. Son histoire, ses ruines, ses légendes*. Beirut, 1965

236. Dunand, M., 'La défense du front méditerranéen de l'empire achéménide' in Ward, W.A. (ed.) *The Role of the Phoenicians in the Interaction of Mediterranean Civilizations*, 45–9. Beirut, 1968

237. Dunand, M. 'L'architecture à Byblos au temps des Achéménides', *Bull. Mus. Beyrouth* 22 (1969), 93–9

238. Dunand, M. 'Byblos, Sidon, Jerusalem. Monuments apparentés des temps Achéménides', *VT* Suppl. XVII (1969) 64–70

239. Dunand, M. 'Le temple d'Echmoun à Sidon. Essai de chronologie', *Bull. Mus. Beyrouth* 26 (1973) 7–25

240. Dunand, M. 'Les rois de Sidon aux temps des Perses', *Mélanges de l'Université Saint-Joseph Beyrouth* 49 (1975–6) 489–99

241. Dunand, M. and Saliby, N. *Le temple d'Amrith dans la pérée d'Aradus*. Paris, 1985

242. Elayi, J. 'L'essor de la Phénicie et le passage de la domination assyro-babylonienne à la domination perse', *Bagh. Mitt.* 9 (1978) 33–6

243. Elayi, J. 'The Phoenician cities in the Persian period', *Journal of the Ancient Near Eastern Society of Columbia University* 12 (1980) 13–38

244. Elayi, J. 'La révolte des esclaves de Tyr relatée par Justin', *Bagh. Mitt.* 12 (1981) 139–50

245. Elayi, J. 'Studies in Phoenician geography during the Persian period', *JNES* 41 (1982) 83–110

246. Elayi, J. 'L'importation de vases attiques en Phénicie à l'époque perse', in G 4, 227ff.

247. Elayi, J. *Sidon, cité autonome de l'empire perse*. 2nd edn. Paris, 1990

248. Fleischer, R. *Der Klagefrauen Sarkophag aus Sidon* (Ist. Forschungen 34). Tübingen, 1983

249. Gabelmann, H. 'Zur Chronologie der Königsnekropole von Sidon', *Arch. Anz.* 1979, 163–77

250. Gabelmann, H. 'Die Inhaber des Lykischen und des Satrapensarkophags', *Arch. Anz.* 1982, 493–5

251. Galling, K. 'Eshmunazar und der Herr der Könige', *ZDPV* 79 (1963) 140–51
252. Ganzmann, L., Van der Meijden, H. and Stucky, R. A. 'Das Eschmunheiligtum von Sidon', *Ist. Mitt.* 37 (1987) 81–130
253. Gesche, H. 'Nikokles von Paphos und Nikokreon von Salamis', *Chiron* 4 (1974) 103–25
254. Gjerstad, E. 'Further remarks on the Palace of Vouni', *AJA* 37 (1933) 589–98, 658–9
255. Gjerstad, E. 'Four kings', *Opusc. Archaeol.* 4 (1946) 21–4
256. Gjerstad, E. 'The Cypro-Classical period', in *The Swedish Cyprus Expedition* IV 2, 479–507. Stockholm, 1948
257. Gjerstad, E. 'The Phoenician colonization and expansion in Cyprus', *RDAC* (1979) 230–4
258. Glueck, N. 'Tell-el-Kheleifeh inscriptions', in Goedicke, H. (ed.), *Near Eastern Studies in Honor of F. W. Albright*, 225–42. Baltimore, 1971
259. Grass, M., Rouillard, P. and Teixidor, J. *L'univers phénicien.* Paris, 1989
260. Hackens, T. (ed.) *Phoenician and Punic Numismatics and Economic History.* Louvain, 1988
261. Hadjikyriakou, K. ''Η ἀρχαία Κύπρος εἰς τὰς 'Ελληνικὰς πηγάς', I–IV. Nicosia, 1971–80
262. Hadjisavvas, S. 'Greek and Phoenician influences on Cyprus as evidenced in the necropolis of Kition', *Acts of the International Symposium 'Cyprus between the Orient and the Occident'*, 361–8. Nicosia, 1986
263. Harden, D. *The Phoenicians.* 2nd edn. London, 1980
264. Hauben, H. 'The king of the Sidonians and the Persian imperial fleet', *Anc. Soc.* 1 (1970) 1–8
265. Hermary, A. 'Amathonte de Chypre et les Phéniciens', *Studia Phoenicia* V (1987) 375–88
266. Hermary, A. 'Témoignage des documents figurés sur la société chypriote d'époque classique', in F 312, 180–96
267. Hill, G. F. *A History of Cyprus* I. Cambridge, 1949
268. Huss, W. 'Der "König der Könige" oder der "Herr der Könige"', *ZDPV* 93 (1977) 131–40
269. Jidejian, N. *Byblos through the Ages.* Beirut, 1968
270. Jidejian, N. *Tyre through the Ages.* Beirut, 1969
271. Jidejian, N. *Sidon through the Ages.* Beirut, 1971
272. Kahrstedt, U. *Syrische Territorien in hellenistischer Zeit.* Berlin, 1926
273. Karageorghis, V. *Salamis in Cyprus. Homeric, Hellenistic and Roman.* London, 1969
274. Karageorghis, V. *Excavations in the Necropolis of Salamis II.* Nicosia, 1970
275. Karageorghis, V. *Kition. Mycenean and Phoenician Discoveries in Cyprus.* London, 1976
276. Karageorghis, V. *Cyprus. From the Stone Age to the Romans.* London, 1982
277. Karageorghis, V., and Guzo Amadasi, G. 'Un iscrizione fenicia da Cipro', *Riv. Stud. Fen.* 1 (1973) 129–35
278. Katzenstein, H. J. *The History of Tyre.* Jerusalem, 1973
279. Katzenstein, H. J. 'Tyre in the early Persian period', *Bi Ar.* 42 (1979) 23–34

280. Kukahn, R. *Anthropoide Sarkophage in Beyrouth und die Geschichte dieser sidonischen Sarkophagkunst.* 1955
281. Kyrris, C. P. *History of Cyprus.* Nicosia, 1985
282. Leuze, O. *Die Satrapieneinteilung in Syrien und im Zweistromland von 520–320* (Schriften der Königsberger Gelehrten Gesellschaft; Geisteswiss. Kl. 11). 1935
283. Lézine, A. *Architecture punique.* Paris, 1961
284. Lipinski, E. 'La Carthage de Chypre', *Studia Phoenicia* II 209–34 (1983)
285. Maier, F. G. 'Factoids in ancient history', *JHS* 105 (1985) 32–9
286. Maier, F. G. 'Palaces of Cypriot kings', in *Cyprus and the Mediterranean in the Iron Age,* 16–27. London, 1989
287. Maier, F. G. 'Priest kings in Cyprus', in F 312, 376–91
288. Maier, F. G. and Karageorghis, V. *Paphos.* Athens, 1984
289. Maier, F. G. and von Wartburg, M.-L. 'Reconstructing history from the earth, c. 2800 B.C.–1600 A.D.: Excavating at Palaepaphos, 1966–1985' in *Archaeology in Cyprus 1960–1985,* 142–72. Nicosia, 1985
290. Masson, O. 'Cultes indigènes, cultes grecs et cultes orientaux à Chypre', in *Eléments orientaux dans la religion grecque ancienne,* 129–42. Paris, 1960
291. Masson, O. 'Une nouvelle inscription de Paphos concernant le roi Nikokles', *Kadmos* 19 (1980) 65–80
292. Masson, O. *Les inscriptions chypriotes syllabiques.* Paris, 1961, 2nd edn, 1983
293. Masson, O., and Mitford, T. B. 'Les inscriptions syllabiques de Kouklia-Paphos' in *Ausgrabungen in Altpaphos auf Cypern* 4 (Konstanz, 1986)
294. Masson, O. and Sznycer, M. *Recherches sur les Phéniciens à Chypre.* Geneva–Paris, 1972
295. May, J. M. F. 'The Alexander coinage of Nikokles of Paphos', *Num. Chron.* (1952) 1–18
296. Mazza, F., Ribichini, S. and Xella, P. *Fonti classiche per la civiltà fenicia e punica I: Fonti letterarie greche dalle origini alla fine dell'età classica.* Rome, 1988
297. Michaelidou-Nicolaou, I. 'Repercussions of the Phoenician presence in Cyprus', *Studia Phoenicia* V (1987) 331–8
298. Mildenberg, L. *Baana.* 'Preliminary studies of the local coinage in the Fifth Persian Satrapy: Part 2', *Eretz-Israel* 19 (1987) 28–35
299. Mildenberg, L. 'Gaza mint authorities in Persian times', *Transeuphratène* 2 (1990) 137–46
300. Mitford, T. B. 'Nikokles King of Paphos', in W. M. Calder and J. Keil (eds.), *Anatolian Studies presented to W. H. Buckler,* 197–9. London, 1939
301. Mitford, T. B. 'The character of Ptolemaic rule in Cyprus', *Aegyptus* 33 (1953) 80–90
302. Mitford, T. B. and Masson, O. 'The Cypriot Syllabary', *CAH* III² 3, 71–82
303. Moscati, S. *Il mondo dei Fenici,* new edn. Milan, 1979
304. Moscati, S. (ed.) *The Phoenicians.* Milan, 1988
305. Moysey, R. 'The date of the Strato of Sidon decree (IG ii² 141)', *AJAH* 1 (1976) 182–9

306. Mullen, E. T. J., Jr. 'A new Royal Sidonian inscription', *BASOR* 216 (1974) 25–30

307. Müller, V. 'The palace of Vouni in Cyprus', *AJA* 36 (1932) 408–17; 'A reply', *AJA* 37 (1933) 599–601

308. Nicolaou, K. *The Historical Topography of Kition*. Göteborg, 1976

309. Parker, S. T. 'The objectives and strategy of Cimon's expeditions to Cyprus', *AJP* 97 (1976) 30–8

310. Parrot, A., Chebab, M. H. and Moscati, S. *Die Phönizier*. Munich, 1977

311. Peckham, J. B. *The Development of the Late Phoenician Scripts*. Cambridge MA, 1968

312. Peltenburg, E. (ed.) *Early Society in Cyprus*. Edinburgh, 1989

313. Petit, T. 'Présence et influences perses à Chypre', in F 53, 161–78

314. Pouilloux, J. 'Athènes et Salamine de Chypre', *RDAC* (1975) 111–21

315. Pouilloux, J. 'L'hellénisme à Salamine de Chypre', *BCH* 100 (1976) 449–60

316. Pouilloux, J. 'La rencontre de l'hellénisme et de l'orient à Chypre entre 1200 and 300 av. J.-C.', in *Assimilation et resistance à la culture gréco-romaine dans le monde ancien*, 449–60. Paris, 1976

317. Pritchard, J. B. *The Ancient Near East in Pictures Relating to the Old Testament*. Princeton, 1954

318. Pritchard, J. B. *Recovering Sarepta, a Phoenician City*. Princeton, 1978

319. Rey-Coquais, J. P. *Arados et sa pérée aux époques grecque, romaine et byzantine*. Paris, 1974

320. Robinson, E. S. G. 'Greek coins acquired by the British Museum 1938–1948, I' (with Appendix: 'Kings of Lapethos'), *Num. Chron.* (1948), 43–65

321. *Salamine de Chypre IV*: Anthologie Salaminienne. Paris, 1973

322. *Salamine de Chypre VIII*. Jehasse, L. *La Céramique à vernis noir du rampart méridional*. Paris 1978

323. *Salamine de Chypre X*. Chavane, M. J. and Yon, M. *Testimonia Salaminia 1*. Paris, 1978. See also *Salamine de Chypre XIII*. Pouilloux, J. Roesch, P., and Marceillet-Jaubert, J. *Testimonia Salaminia 2*. Paris, 1987

324. *Salamine de Chypre. Etat des Recherches* (Colloques Internationaux du CNRS, No. 578, 1978). Paris, 1980

325. Salles, J.-F., 'Les égouts de ville classique', in *Kition-Bamboula II* (Lund, 1983), 54–8

326. Schäfer, J. *Ein Perserbau in Alt-Paphos?* (Opusc. Athen. 3), 155–75. 1960

327. Schwabacher, W. *The coins of the Vouni treasure* (Opusc. Archaeol. 4), 25–46. 1946

328. Schwabacher, W. 'Contributions to Greek Numismatics from Stockholm', *Nordisk Numismatisk Årsskrift* 1947, 78–108

329. Seibert, J. 'Zur Bevölkerungsstruktur Cyperns', *AncSoc* 7 (1976) 1–28

330. Sordi, M. 'La vittoria dell'Eurimedonte e le due spedizioni di Cimone a Cipro', *Riv. stor. ant.* 1 (1971) 33–48

331. Spyridakis, K. *Euagoras I. von Salamis*. Stuttgart, 1935

332. Spyridakis, K. 'Μικραὶ συμβολαὶ εἰς τὴν ἱστορίαν τῆς ἑλληνιστικῆς

Κύπρου. (A) *Νικοκλῆς ὁ Πάφιος', Κυπρ. Σπουδαί* 3 (1939) 1–11
333. Spyridakis, K. '*Μικραὶ συμβολαὶ εἰς τὴν ἱστορίαν τῆς ἑλληνιστικῆς Κύπρου.* (B) *Νικοκρέων ὁ Σαλαμίνιος* (331–311 π.χρ.)', *Κυπρ. Σπουδαί* 6 (1942) 71–82
334. Spyridakis, K. *Κυπριοὶ Βασιλεῖς.* Nicosia, 1963
335. Stucky, R.A. *Ras Shamra, Leukos Limen (Mission Archéologique de Ras Shamra* 1). Paris, 1983
336. Stucky, R. A. *Tribune d'Echmoun. Ein griechischer Reliefzyklus des 4. Jahrhunderts v.Chr. in Sidon.* Basel, 1984
337. *Studia Phoenicia* IV: *Religio Phoenicia.* Namur, 1986
338. *Studia Phoenicia* V: *Phoenicia and the Eastern Mediterranean in the First Millennium B.C.* Leuven, 1987
339. Stylianou, P. 'The age of the kingdoms. A political history of Cyprus in the Archaic and Classical periods', *Μελεταὶ καὶ 'Υπομνήματα* 2 (1989) 1–156
340. *The Swedish Cyprus Expedition* II–IV (2). Stockholm, 1935–48
341. Swoboda, H. 'Euagoras', *RE* 6 (1907) 820–8
342. Sznycer, M. 'Phéniciens et Puniques' in Bonnefoy, Y. (ed.), *Dictionnaire des mythologies et des religions des sociétés traditionelles et du monde antique* Paris, 1981
343. Tatton-Brown, V. 'The Classical period', in D. Hunt (ed.), *Footprints in Cyprus*, 84–97. Rev. edn. London, 1990
344. Teixidor, J. 'Les fonctions de Rab et de Suffète en Phénicie', *Semitica* 29 (1979) 9–17
345. Teixidor, J. 'L'assemblée législative en Phénicie d'après les inscriptions', *Syria* 56 (1980) 453–64
346. *Transeuphratène: Etudes sur la Syrie-Palestine et Chypre à l'époque Perse*, 1–4. Paris, 1989–1991
347. van Berchem, D. 'Le cadre historique' in *Chypre des origines au moyen-âge* (Geneva, 1975) 51–77
348. Vermeule, C. C. *Greek and Roman Cyprus.* 1976
349. Yon, M. *Salamine de Chypre* v. Paris, 1974
350. Yon, M. 'Cultes phéniciens à Chypre. L'interpretation chypriote', *Studia Phoenicia* IV (1986) 127–52
351. Yon, M. 'Le royaume de Kition. I. Epoque archaique', *Studia Phoenicia* V (1987), 357–74
352. Yon, M. 'Sur l'administration de Kition à l'époque classique', in F 312, 363–75
353. Yon, M. 'Le royaume de Kition. II. Epoque classique', *Studia Phoenicia* IX, 243–59. 1992

IV. JUDAH

354. Alt, A. 'Die Rolle Samarias bei der Entstehung des Judentums', in *Festschrift Otto Procksch* (Leipzig, 1934), 5–28 = *Kleine Schriften zur Geschichte des Volkes Israel* (Munich, 1953–59) II 316–37

355. Avigad, N. *Bullae and Seals from a Post Exilic Judean Archive* (Qedem IV). Jerusalem, 1976

356. Barag, D. 'A silver coin of Yohanan the High Priest', *Bi. Ar.* 48 (1985) 166–9

356A. Barag, D. 'A silver coin of Yohanan the High Priest and the coinage of Judaea in the fourth century B.C.', *Israel Numismatic Journal* 9 (1986–87) 4–21 and Pl. 1

357. Barton, J. *Oracles of God: Perceptions of Ancient Prophecy in Israel After the Exile.* London, 1986

358. Beckwith, R. *The Old Testament Canon of the New Testament Church and its Background in Early Judaism.* London, 1985

359. Berger, P. R. 'Zu den Namen ššbṣr und šn'ṣr', *ZAW* 83 (1971) 98–100

360. Bewer, J. A. 'Josephus' account of Nehemiah', *JBL* 43 (1924) 224–6

361. Bickerman, E. *Four Strange Books of the Bible.* New York, 1967

362. Bickerman, E. J. 'The generation of Ezra and Nehemiah', *Proceedings of the American Academy for Jewish Research* 45 (1978), 1–28 (= *Studies in Jewish and Christian History* III (Leiden, 1986), 299–326)

363. Bickerman, E. J. 'En marge de l'Ecriture I. Le comput des années de règne des Achéménides (Néh., i, 2; ii, 1 et Thuc., viii, 58)', *RB* 88 (1981) 19–23 (= *Studies in Jewish and Christian History* III (Leiden, 1986), 327–36)

364. Bickerman, E. *The Jews in the Greek Age.* Cambridge MA–London, 1988

365. Blenkinsopp, J. *Ezra–Nehemiah.* London, 1989

366. Bright, J. 'The date of Ezra's mission to Jerusalem', in M. Haran (ed.), *Yehezkiel Kaufmann Jubilee Volume*, 70–87. Jerusalem, 1960

367. Bright, J. *A History of Israel.* 3rd edn. Philadelphia–London, 1981

368. Bruneau, P. '"Les Israélites de Délos" et la juiverie délienne', *BCH* 106 (1982) 465–504

369. Clines, D. J. A. 'Nehemiah 10 as an example of early Jewish biblical exegesis', *JSOT* 21 (1981) 111–17

370. Cross, F. M., Jr. 'Papyri of the fourth century B.C. from Daliyeh', in Freedman, D. N. and Greenfield, J. C. (eds.), *New Directions in Biblical Archaeology*, 45–69. Garden City, NY, 1969

371. Cross, F. M., Jr. 'A reconstruction of the Judean restoration', *JBL* 94 (1975) 4–18 (*Interpretation* 29 (1975) 187–203)

371A. Cross, F. M., Jr. 'Samaria papyrus 1: an Aramaic slave conveyance of 345 B.C.E. found in the Wâdi ed-Dâliyeh'. *Eretz Israel* 18 (1985) 7–17

371B. Cross, F. M., Jr. 'A report on the Samaria Papyri', *VTSupp.* 40 (1988) 17–26

372. Davies, W. D. and Finkelstein, L. (eds.) *The Cambridge History of Judaism* I. Cambridge, 1984

373. Eilers, W. 'Kleinasiatisches', *ZDMG* 94 (1940) 189–233

374. Emerton, J. A. 'Did Ezra go to Jerusalem in 428 B.C.?', *JTS* 17 (1966) 1–19

375. Goodman, M. 'Sacred scripture and "Defiling the Hands"', *JTS* 41 (1990) 99–107

376. Japhet, S. 'The supposed common authorship of Chronicles and Ezra–Nehemiah investigated anew', *VT* 18 (1968) 330–71

377. Japhet, S. 'Sheshbazzar and Zerubbabel', *ZAW* 94 (1982) 66–98, 95 (1983) 218–29
378. Japhet, S. 'People and land in the Restoration Period', in G. Strecker (ed.), *Das Land Israel in biblischer Zeit*, 103–23. Göttingen, 1983
379. Japhet, S. *The Ideology of the Book of Chronicles and its Place in Biblical Thought* (Beiträge zur Erforschung des Alten Testaments und des antiken Judentums Bd. 9). Frankfurt am Main, 1989
380. Kellermann, U. *Nehemia: Quellen, Überlieferung und Geschichte* (Beihefte zu *ZAW* 102). Berlin, 1967
381. Kreisig, H. *Die sozialökonomische Situation in Juda zur Achämenidenzeit* (Schriften zur Geschichte und Kultur des alten Orients 7). Berlin, 1973
382. Lods, A. 'Les origines de la figure de Satan; ses fonctions à la cour céleste', in *Mélanges syriens offerts à R. Dussaud* II 649–60. Paris, 1939
383. Mazar, B. 'The Tobiads', *IEJ* 7 (1957) 137–45, 229–38
384. Meshorer, Y. and Qedar, S. *The Coinage of Samaria in the Fourth Century B.C.E.* Beverly Hills, CA, 1991
384A. Meyers C. L. and Meyers E. M., *Haggai, Zechariah 1–7* (Anchor Bible). Garden City, NY, 1987
385. Naveh, J. 'Hebrew texts in the Aramaic script in the Persian period?' *BASOR* 203 (1971) 27–32
386. Naveh, J. and Greenfield, J. C. 'Hebrew and Aramaic in the Persian period' in F 372, 115–29
387. Pope, M. H. *The Song of Songs* (Anchor Bible). New York, 1977
388. Purvis, D. J. *The Samaritan Pentateuch and the Origins of the Samaritan Sect.* Cambridge, MA, 1968
389. Rahmani, L. Y. 'Silver coins of the fourth century B.C. from Tel Gamma', *IEJ* 21 (1971) 158–60
390. Rowley, H. H. *The Servant of the Lord and other Essays on the Old Testament.* London, 1952
391. Rowley, H. H. *Men of God.* London, 1963
392. Saley, R. J. 'The date of Nehemiah reconsidered', in Tuttle, G. A. (ed.), *Biblical and Near Eastern Studies. Essays in Honor of William Sanford LaSor*, 151–65. Grand Rapids, 1978
393. Schaeder, H. *Ezra der Schreiber* (Beiträge zu historischen Theologie 5). Tübingen, 1930
394. Schürer, E. *The History of the Jewish People in the Age of Jesus Christ*, revised by G. Vermes, F. Millar and M. Black. Edinburgh, 1973–87
395. Smith, Morton. 'Jewish religious life in the Persian period', in F 372, 219–78
396. Smith, Morton. *Palestinian Parties and Politics that Shaped the Old Testament*, second corrected edition. London, 1987
397. Stern, E. *The Material Culture of the Land of the Bible in the Persian Period 538–332 B.C.* Warminster, 1982
398. Stern, E. 'The archaeology of Persian Palestine', in F 372, 88–114
398A. Tadmor, H. (ed.) *The Restoration – The Persian Period.* Jerusalem, 1983 (In Hebrew)
399. Williamson, H. G. M. *Israel in the Books of Chronicles.* Cambridge, 1977

400. Williamson, H. G. M. *Ezra and Nehemiah* (Word Biblical Commentary 16). Waco, 1985
401. Yamauchi, E. M. 'Was Nehemiah the cupbearer a eunuch?', *ZAW* 92 (1980) 132–42

V. EGYPT

402. Aldred, C. *Egyptian Art*. London, 1980
403. Allam, S. 'Quelques aspects du mariage dans l'Egypte-ancienne', *JEA* 67 (1981) 116–35
404. Badawy, A. M. 'The approach to the Egyptian temple in the Late and Graeco–Roman periods', *ZÄS* 102 (1975) 79–90
405. Bagnall, R. S. 'The date of the foundation of Alexandria', *AJAH* 4 (1979) 46–9
406. Baines, J. 'Literacy and Ancient Egyptian society', *Man* n.s. 18 (1983) 572–99
407. Baines, J. and Eyre, C. J. 'Four notes on literacy', *GM* 61 (1983) 65–96
408. Barguet, P. 'Quelques fragments nouveaux au nom de Nekhthorheb', *Kêmi* 13 (1954) 87–91
408A. Bevan, E. *A History of Egypt under the Ptolemaic Dynasty*. London, 1927
409. Bickermann, E. 'Notes sur la chronologie de la XXXe dynastie', *Mélanges Maspero*, 77–84. Cairo, 1934
410. Bonnet, H. *Reallexikon der ägyptischen Religionsgeschichte*, Berlin, 1952
411. Bonnet, H. 'Herkunft und Bedeutung der naophoren Statue', *MDAI(K)* 17 (1961) 91–8
412. Bosse, K. *Die menschliche Figur in der Rundplastik der ägyptischen Spätzeit von der XXII. bis zur XXX. Dynastie* (Äg. Forsch. 1). Glückstadt–Hamburg–New York, 1936
413. Bothmer, B. V. 'Ptolemaic reliefs. III. Deities from the time of Ptolemy II Philadelphus', *Bulletin of the Museum of Fine Arts* 51 (1953) 2–7
414. Bothmer, B. V. *Egyptian Sculpture of the Late Period, 700 B.C. – 100 A.D.* Brooklyn Museum, 1969 (repr. of 1960 edn with addenda and corrigenda)
415. Bothmer, B. V. 'Apotheosis in late Egyptian sculpture', *Kêmi* 20 (1970) 37–48
416. Bresciani, E. 'Egypt in the Persian empire', in A 7, 333–53
417. Bresciani, E. and Donadoni, S. *Letteratura e poesia dell' Antico Egitto*. Turin, 1969
418. Brugsch, H. 'Das ägyptische Troja', *ZÄS* 5 (1867) 89–93
419. Cavaignac, E. 'La milice égyptienne au VIe siècle et l'empire achéménide', *Revue égyptologique* n.s. 1 (1919) 192–8
420. Cavenaile, R. 'Pour une histoire politique et sociale d'Alexandrie – les origines', *Ant. Class.* 41 (1972) 94–112
421. Chabân, M. 'Fouilles à Achmounéin', *Ann. Serv.* 8 (1907) 211–23
422. Chassinat, E. *Le temple d'Edfou* (Mém. miss. arch. franç. 24), VII. Cairo, 1932

423. Chevrier, H. 'Rapport sur les travaux de Karnak, 1948–1949', *Ann. Serv.* 49 (1949) 241–67

424. Clère, J. J. 'A propos de l'ordre de succession des rois de la XXXe dynastie', *Rev. d'égyptol.* 8 (1951) 25–9

425. Clère, J. J. 'Une statuette du fils aîné du roi Nectanabô', *Rev. d'égyptol.* 6 (1951) 135–56

426. Corteggiani, J.-P. 'Documents divers: 1. Un poids de 12 deben au nom de Teôs', *Bull. Inst. fr. Caire* 73 (1973) 143–4

427. Cowley, A. *Aramaic Papyri of the Fifth Century* B.C. Oxford, 1923

428. Cruz-Uribe, E. 'Papyrus Libbey: a reexamination', *Serapis* 4 (1977–8) 3–9

429. Curtis, J. W. 'Coinage of Pharaonic Egypt', *JEA* 43 (1957) 71–6

430. Daressy, G. 'La chapelle de Psimaut et Hakoris à Karnak', *Ann. Serv.* 18 (1919) 37–48

431. Daumas, F. 'La structure du mammisi de Nectanébo à Dendera', *Bull. Inst. fr. Caire* 50 (1952) 133–55

432. Daumas, F. 'Le problème de la monnaie dans l'Egypte antique avant Alexandre', *MEFRA* 89 (1977) 425–42

433. Davies, W. V. 'The origin of the blue crown', *JEA* 68 (1982) 69–76

434. Drioton, E. and Vandier, J. *L'Egypte*, 4th edn. Paris, 1962

435. Driver, G. *Aramaic Documents of the Fifth Century* B.C. Oxford, 1957

436. Emery, W. B. North Saqqâra excavation reports in *JEA* 51 (1965) 3–8; 52 (1966) 3–8; 53 (1967) 141–5; 54 (1968) 1–2; 55 (1969) 31–5; 56 (1970) 5–11; 57 (1971) 3–13

437. Erichsen, W. *Auswahl frühdemotischer Texte*, 1, *Texte*. Copenhagen, 1950

438. Erman, A. and Wilcken, U. 'Die Naukratisstele', *ZÄS* 38 (1900) 127–35

439. Gabra, G. 'A lifesize statue of Nepherites I from Buto', *SAK* 9 (1981) 119–23

440. Gardiner, Sir Alan H. *Egypt of the Pharaohs*. Oxford, 1961

441. Gauthier, H. *Le livre des rois d'Egypte* (MIFAO 17–21), 5 vols. Cairo, 1907–17

442. Gauthier, H. 'Les nomes d'Egypte depuis Hérodote jusqu' à la conquête arabe', *MIE* 25 (1935)

443. Grelot, P. *Documents Araméens d'Egypte*. Paris, 1972

444. Grimm, A. 'Ein Statuentorso des Hakoris aus Ahnas el-Medineh im Ägyptischen Museum zu Kairo', *GM* 77 (1984) 13–17

445. Guilmot, M. 'Le Sarapieion de Memphis: étude topographique', *Chron. d'Eg.* 37 (1962) 359–81

446. Gunn, B. 'The inscribed sarcophagi in the Serapeum', *Ann. Serv.* 26 (1926) 82–91

447. Gyles, M. F. *Pharaonic Policies and Administration 663 to 323* B.C. (James Sprunt Studies in History and Political Science 41). Chapel Hill, 1959

448. Hall, H. R. 'Egypt to the coming of Alexander', in *CAH* VI¹, 137–66. Cambridge, 1927

449. Halm-Rasmussen, T. 'Nektanebos II and Temple M at Karnak (North)', *GM* 26 (1977) 37–41

450. Harrison, M. 'Excavations at Mendes', Newsletter *ARCE* 107 (1978/9) 15–17

451. Helck, W. *Untersuchungen zu Manetho und den ägyptischen Königslisten* (Untersuchungen 18). Berlin, 1956
452. Helck, W. *Die altägyptischen Gaue (TAVO Reihe B (5))*. Wiesbaden, 1974
453. Helck, W. *et al.* (eds.) *Lexikon der Ägyptologie* I–. Wiesbaden, 1975–
454. Honroth, W., Rubensohn, O. and Zucker, F. 'Bericht über die Ausgrabungen auf Elephantine in den Jahren 1906–1908', *ZÄS* 46 (1909) 14–61
455. Hopfner, T. *Der Tierkult der alten Ägypter* (Denkschriften Wien 57 (2)). Vienna, 1913
456. Jähne, A. 'Die 'Αλεξανδρέων χώρα', *Klio* 63 (1981) 63–103
457. Johnson, J. H. 'The Demotic Chronicle as an historical source', *Enchoria* 4 (1974) 1–17
458. Johnson, J. H. 'Is the Demotic Chronicle an anti-Greek tract?', in Thissen, H.-J. and Zauzich, K.-T. (eds.), *Grammatika Demotika* (Festschrift für Erich Lüddeckens zum 15. Juni 1983), 107–24. Würzburg, 1984
459. Johnson, J. H. 'The Demotic Chronicle as a statement of a theory of kingship', *The SSEA Journal* 13(2) (1983) 61–72
460. Kaenel, F. von. 'Les mésaventures du conjurateur de Serket, Onnophris et de son tombeau', *BSFE* 87–8 (1980) 31–45
461. Kaplony, P. 'Bemerkungen zum ägyptischen Königtum, vor allem in der Spätzeit', *Chron. d'Eg.* 46 (1971) 250–74
462. Katznelson, I. S. 'Kambesweden et Khababash', *ZÄS* 93 (1966) 89–93
463. Kienitz, F. K. *Die politische Geschichte Ägyptens vom 7. bis zum 4. Jahrhundert vor der Zeitwende*. Berlin, 1953
464. Koenen, L. *Eine agonistische Inschrift aus Ägypten und frühptolemäische Königsfeste* (Beiträge zur klassischen Philologie 56). Meisenheim am Glan, 1977
465. Kraeling, E. G. *The Brooklyn Museum Aramaic Papyri*. New Haven–London, 1953
466. Kuhlmann, K. P. 'Ptolemais – queen of Nectanebo I. Notes on the inscription of an unknown princess of the XXXth Dynasty', *MDAIK* 37 (1981) 267–79
467. Lüddeckens, E. *Ägyptische Eheverträge* (Ägypt. Abhandl. 1). Wiesbaden, 1960
468. Lavagnini, B. *Eroticorum Fragmenta Papyracea*. Leipzig, 1922
469. Lefebvre, G. *Le tombeau de Petosiris*, 3 vols. Cairo, 1923–4
470. Lepsius, K. R. *Denkmaeler aus Aegypten und Aethiopien*, 12 vols. Berlin, 1849–59
471. Lichtheim, M. 'The Naucratis Stele once again', in Johnson, J. H. and Wente, E. F. (eds.), *Studies in Honor of George R. Hughes* (Studies in Ancient Oriental Civilization 39), 139–46. Chicago, 1976
472. Lichtheim, M. *Ancient Egyptian Literature, III: The Late Period*. Berkeley–Los Angeles, 1980
473. Lloyd, Alan B. *Herodotus Book II*, Leiden, 1975–88
474. Lloyd, Alan B. 'Nationalist propaganda in Ptolemaic Egypt', *Historia* 31 (1982) 33–55

475. Lloyd, Alan B. 'The inscription of Udjaḥorresnet: a collaborator's testament', *JEA* 68 (1982), 166–80

476. Lloyd, Alan B. in Trigger, B, Kemp, B. J. and O'Connor, D. J. *Ancient Egypt, a Social History*, 279–348. Cambridge, 1983

477. Lloyd, Alan B. 'Manetho and the thirty-first dynasty', in Baines, J., James, T. G. H. and Leahy, A. (eds.), *Pyramid Studies*, 154–60. Oxford, 1988

478. Malinine, M. 'Un contrat de vente d'emplacements à construire de l'époque du roi Achoris (Pap. Lille no. 26)', *Rev. d'égyptol.* 7 (1950) 107–20

479. Malinine, M., Posener, G. and Vercoutter, J. *Catalogue des stèles du Sérapéum de Memphis.* Paris, 1968

480. Meeks, D. *Le grand texte des donations au temple d'Edfou* (Bibliothèque d'étude 59). Cairo, 1972

481. Meeks, D. 'Les donations aux temples dans l'Egypte du 1er millénaire avant J-C', in Lipinski, E. (ed.), *State and Temple Economy in the Ancient Near East*, II, 605–87. Leuven, 1979

482. Mekhitarian, A. 'La porte aux deux Nectanébo à Karnak', *Chron. d'Eg.* 24 (1949) 235–9

483. Menu, B. 'Deux contrats de vente datés du regne de Nectanébo II (P. Dem. IFAO 901 et 902)', *Bull. Inst. fr. Caire* 81 (1981) 45–52

484. Meulenaere, H. De. *Herodotos over de 26ste Dynastie (II, 147–III, 15)* (Bibliothèque du Muséon 27). Leuven, 1951

485. Meulenaere, H. De. 'Le vizir Harsiêsis de la 30e Dynastie', *MDAIK* 16 (1958) 230–6

486. Meulenaere, H. De. 'Les monuments du culte des rois Nectanébo', *Chron. d'Eg.* 35 (1960) 92–107

487. Meulenaere, H. De. 'La famille royale des Nectanébo', *ZÄS* 90 (1963) 90–3

488. Meulenaere, H. De. 'Isis et Mout des mammisi', in Quaegebeur, J. (ed.), *Studia Paulo Naster Oblata.* II. *Orientalia antiqua* (Orientalia Lovaniensia Analecta 13), 25–9. Louvain, 1982

489. Meyer, E. *Der Papyrusfund von Elephantine.* Leipzig, 1912

490. Meyer, Eduard. 'Ägyptische Dokumente aus der Perserzeit', *SBAk Berlin* (1915) 287–311

491. Meyer, Ernst. 'Zur Geschichte der 30. Dynastie', *ZÄS* 67 (1931) 68–70

492. Murnane, W. J. *Ancient Egyptian Coregencies* (Studies in Ancient Oriental Civilisation 40). Chicago, 1977

493. Muszynski, M. 'Les papyrus démotiques de Ricci', *Enchoria* 6 (1976) 19–27

494. Naster, P. 'Karsha et sheqel dans les documents araméens d'Eléphantine (Vᵉ s. av. J.C.)', *Revue belge de numismatique* 116 (1970) 31–5

495. Naville, E. *Bubastis (1887–1889).* London, 1891

496. Nims, C. F. 'A demotic document of endowment from the time of Nectanebo I', *MDAIK* 16 (1958) 237–46

497. Otto, E. *Die biographischen Inschriften der ägyptischen Spätzeit* (Probleme der Ägyptologie 2). Leiden, 1954

498. Otto, E. 'Zwei Bemerkungen zum Königskult der Spätzeit', *MDAIK* 15 (1957) 193–207
499. Perry, B. E. 'The Egyptian legend of Nectanebus', *TAPA* 97 (1966) 327–33
500. Pestman, P. *Marriage and Matrimonial Property in Ancient Egypt*. Leiden, 1961
501. Petrie, W. M. F. *A History of Egypt. III. From the XIXth to the XXXth Dynasties*. London, 1905
502. Petrie, W. M. F., MacKay, E. and Wainwright, G. *Meydum and Memphis III*. London, 1910
503. Picard, C. 'Les influences étrangères au tombeau de Pétosiris: Grèce ou Perse?', *Bull. Inst. fr. Caire* 31 (1931) 201–27
504. Porten, B. *Archives from Elephantine*. Berkeley–Los Angeles, 1968
505. Porten, B. and Yardeni, A. *Textbook of Aramaic Documents from Ancient Egypt*. Jerusalem: Vol. I, *Letters*, 1986; Vol. II, *Contracts*, 1989
506. Porter, B. and Moss, R. L. B. *Topographical Bibliography of Ancient Egyptian Hieroglyphic Texts, Reliefs and Paintings*, 2nd edn, I–II. Oxford, 1960–72. Vol. III, revised and augmented by J. Malék, Oxford, 1974–. Vols. IV–VII, 1st edn. Oxford, 1934–51
507. Posener, G. 'Notes sur la stèle de Naucratis', *Ann. Serv.* 34 (1934) 141ff.
508. Posener, G. 'Achoris', *Rev. d'égyptol.* 21 (1969) 148–50
509. Préaux, C. *L'économie royale des Lagides*. Brussels, 1939
510. Raven, M. J. 'The 30th dynasty Nespamedu family', *OMRO* 61 (1980) 19–31
511. Ray, J. D. *The Archive of Ḥor*. London, 1976
512. Ray, J. D. 'The world of North Saqqâra', *World Archaeology* 10 (1978) 149–57
513. Ray, J. D. 'Psammuthis and Hakoris', *JEA* 72 (1986) 149–58
514. Ritner, R. K. 'Khababash and the satrap stela – a grammatical rejoinder', *ZÄS* 107 (1980) 135–7
515. Roeder, G. *Naos* (Cat. gén. des antiquités égyptiennes du Musée du Caire). Leipzig, 1914
516. Roeder, G. *Altägyptische Erzählungen und Märchen*. Jena, 1927
517. Roeder, G. 'Vorläufiger Bericht über die deutsche Hermopolis–Expedition 1938 und 1939', *MDAIK* 9 (1940) 40–92
518. Roeder, G, 'Zwei hieroglyphische Inschriften aus Hermopolis (Ober–Ägypten)', *Ann. Serv.* 52 (1952), 315–442
519. Roeder, G. *Hermopolis 1929–1939* (Pelizaeus-Museum zu Hildesheim, Wissenschaftliche Veröffentlichung 4). Hildesheim, 1959
520. Schäfer, H. 'Noch einmal die Inschrift von Neapel' in *Aegyptiaca (Festschrift für Georg Ebers)*, 92–8. Leipzig, 1897
521. Schwartz, J. 'Les conquérants perses et la littérature égyptienne', *Bull. Inst. fr. Caire* 48 (1949) 65–80
522. Seidl, E. *Ägyptische Rechtsgeschichte der Saiten- und Perserzeit* (Ägyptologische Forschungen 20), 2nd edn. Glückstadt, 1968
523. Sethe, K. *Urkunden II. Hieroglyphische Urkunden der griechisch–römischen Zeit I–III*. Leipzig, 1916

524.   Shore, A. F. 'The demotic inscription on a coin of Artaxerxes', *Num. Chron.* (1974) 4–8

525.   Skeat, T. C. *The Reigns of the Ptolemies* (Münchener Beiträge zur Papyrusforschung und antiken Rechtsgeschichte 39), rev. edn. Munich, 1954

526.   Smith, H. S. *A Visit to Ancient Egypt. Life at Memphis and Saqqara (c. 500–30 B.C.)*. Warminster, 1974

527.   Smith, W. Stevenson. *The Art and Architecture of Ancient Egypt*, revised with additions by W. Kelly Simpson. Harmondsworth, 1981

528.   Spalinger, A. 'The reign of king Chabbash: an interpretation', *ZÄS* 105 (1978) 142–54

529.   Spalinger, A. 'Addenda to "The reign of king Chabbash: an interpretation"' (*ZÄS* 105, 1978, pp. 142–54)', *ZÄS* 107 (1980) 87

530.   Spencer, A. J. *Brick Architecture in Ancient Egypt*. Warminster, 1979

531.   Spencer, A. J. 'The brick foundations of Late-Period peripteral temples and their mythical origin', in Ruffle, J., Gaballa, G. A. and Kitchen, K. A. (eds.), *Orbis Aegyptiorum speculum. Glimpses of Ancient Egypt (Studies in Honour of H. W. Fairman)*, 132–7. Warminster, 1979

532.   Spencer, A. J. *Death in Ancient Egypt*. Harmondsworth, 1982

533.   Spiegelberg, W. *Der Papyrus Libbey* (Schriften der Wissenschaftlichen Gesellschaft in Strassburg). Strasburg, 1907

534.   Spiegelberg, W. *Die sogenannte Demotische Chronik des Pap. 215 der Bibliothèque National zu Paris* (Demotische Studien 7). Leipzig, 1914

535.   Spiegelberg, W. 'Reliefbruchstücke aus der Zeit der 30. Dynastie', *ZÄS* 65 (1930) 102–4

536.   Steindorff, G. 'Reliefs from the temples of Sebennytos and Iseion in American collections', *The Journal of the Walters Art Gallery* 7–8 (1944–5) 39–59

537.   Steindorff, G., Ricke, H. and Aubin, H. 'Der Orakeltempel in der Ammonsoase', *ZÄS* 69 (1933) 4–24

538.   Traunecker, C. 'Essai sur l'histoire de la XXIXe dynastie', *Bull. Inst. fr. Caire* 79 (1979) 395–436

539.   Traunecker, C., Le Saout, F. and Masson, O. *La chapelle d'Achôris à Karnak*, II (Recherche sur les grandes civilisations, Synthèse no. 5). Paris, 1981

540.   Tresson, P. 'La stèle de Naples', *Bull. Inst. fr. Caire* 30 (1930) 369–91

541.   Tresson, P. 'Sur deux monuments égyptiens inédits de l'époque d'Amasis et de Nectanébo Iᵉʳ', *Kêmi* 4 (1931) 126–50

542.   Turner, E. G. 'A commander-in-chief's order from Saqqâra', *JEA* 60 (1974) 239–42

543.   Vercoutter, J. *Textes Biographiques du Sérapéum de Memphis* (Bibliothèque de l'école des hautes études, IVᵉ section, 316 fasc.). Paris, 1962

544.   Vittmann, G. 'Zwei Königinnen der Spätzeit namens Chedebnitjerbone', *Chron. d'Eg.* 49 (1974) 43–51

545.   Waddell, W. G. *Manetho*. Cambridge, MA, 1940

546.   Weinreich, O. *Der Trug des Nectanebos, Wandlungen eines Novellenstoffs*. Leipzig and Berlin, 1911

547. Welles, C. B. 'The discovery of Sarapis and the foundation of Alexandria', *Historia* 11 (1962) 271–98

548. Wessetzky, W. 'Zur Deutung des "Orakels" in der sogenannten Demotischen Chronik', *WZKM* 49 (1942) 161ff

549. Wiedemann, A. *Der Tierkult der alten Ägypter* (Der Alte Orient 14, 1). Leipzig, 1912

550. Will, E. 'Chabrias et les finances de Tachôs', *REA* 62 (1960) 254–75

551. Winnicki, J. K. 'Die Kalasirier der spätdynastischen und der ptolemäischen Zeit', *Historia* 26 (1977) 257–68

552. Winter, E. 'Die Tempel von Philae und das Problem ihrer Rettung', *Antike Welt* 7(3) (1976) 2–15

553. Yoyotte, J. 'Nectanebo II comme faucon divin', *Kêmi* 15 (1959) 70–4

554. Zauzich, K.-Th. 'Ein Kaufvertrag aus der Zeit des Nectanebos', *MDAIK* 25 (1969) 223–9

555. Zauzich, K.-Th. 'Ein demotisches Darlehen vom Ende der 30. Dynastie', *Serapis* 6 (1980) 241–3

VI. ASIA MINOR

556. *Actes du colloque sur Lycie.* Paris, 1980

557. Akarca, A. *Les monnaies grecques de Mylasa.* Paris, 1959

558. Akurgal, E. *Ancient Civilisations and Ruins of Turkey.* Istanbul, 1985

559. Akurgal, E. and Budde, L. *Sinope: Vorläufiger Bericht über die Ausgrabungen in Sinope* (Türk Tarih Kurumu Yayinlarindan 5, series 14). 1956

560. Altheim-Stiehl, R., Metzler, D. and Schwertheim, E. 'Eine neue gräko-persische Grabstele aus Sultaniye Köy und ihre Bedeutung für die Geschichte und Topographie von Daskyleion', *Epigraphica Anatolica* 1 (1983) 1–23

561. Anderson, J. G. C. 'A summer in Phrygia', *JHS* 17 (1897) 396–424

562. Asheri, D. *Fra ellenismo e iranismo.* Bologna, 1983

563. Balcer, J. M. 'Fifth-century Ionia: a frontier re-visited', *REA* 87 (1985) 31–42

564. Balkan, K. 'Inscribed bullae from Daskyleion-Ergili', *Anadolu* 4 (1959) 123–30

565. Bammer, A. 'Architecture et société en Asie mineure au ive siècle', in *Architecture et société de l'archaisme grec à la fin de la république romaine, Actes du colloque 1980*, 271–300. Paris, 1983

566. Barron, J. P. 'Milesian politics and Athenian propaganda c. 460–440 B.C.', *JHS* 82 (1962) 1–6

567. Bean, G. E. 'Notes and inscriptions from Caunus', *JHS* 73 (1953) 10–35 and 74 (1954) 85–110

568. VACAT

569. Bean, G. E. *Side Kitabeleri: The Inscriptions of Side.* Ankara, 1965

570. Bean, G. E. *Lycian Turkey.* London, 1978

571. Bean, G. E. revised Mitchell, S. *Aegean Turkey.* London, 1980

572. Bean, G. E. revised Mitchell, S. *Turkey beyond the Maeander.* London, 1980

573. Bean, G. E. revised Mitchell, S. *Turkey's Southern Shore.* London, 1980

574. Bean, G. E. and Cook, J. M. 'The Cnidia', *BSA* 47 (1952) 171–212
575. Bean, G. E. and Cook, J. M. 'The Halicarnassus peninsula', *BSA* 50 (1955) 85–171
576. Bean, G. E. and Cook, J. M. 'The Carian coast III', *BSA* 52 (1957) 58–146
577. Bernard, P. 'Les bas-reliefs gréco-perses de Dascylion à la lumière de nouvelles découvertes', *Rev. Arch.* (1969) 17–28
578. Bilde, P., Engberg-Pedersen, T., Hannestad, L. and Zahle, J. (eds.) *Religion and Religious Practice in the Seleucid Kingdom.* Aarhus, 1990
579. Billows, R. A. *Antigonos the One-Eyed and the Creation of the Hellenistic State.* Berkeley–Los Angeles–London, 1990
580. Billows, R. A. *Macedonian Imperialism: Structures and Effects.* Berkeley–Los Angeles–London, 1992
581. Blümel, W. *Inschriften griechischer Städte aus Kleinasien, 28: Die Inschriften von Iasos.* 2 vols. Bonn, 1985
582. Blümel, W. *Inschriften griechischer Städte aus Kleinasien, 34: Die Inschriften von Mylasa.* 2 vols. Bonn, 1987–8
583. Boardman, J. Review of F 611, *CR* 14 (1964) 82–3
584. Boardman, J. 'Pyramidal stamp seals in the Persian Empire', *Iran* 8 (1970) 19–45
585. Boffo, L. *I re ellenistici e i centri religiosi dell' Asia minore.* Florence, 1985
586. Borchhardt, J. 'Epichorische, gräko-persische beeinflusste Reliefs in Kilikien: Studien zur Kunst an den Satrapenhöfen Kleinasiens', *Ist. Mitt.* 18 (1968) 161–211
586A. Borchhardt, J. *Die Bauskulptur des Heroons von Limyra.* Berlin, 1976
587. Borchhardt, J., Neumann, G. and Schulz, K. *Das Grabmal des Sohnes des Da aus Hoiran im Zentrallykien. JÖAI* 55 (1984) Beibl. 69–132
588. Bousquet, J. 'Arbinas, fils de Gergis, dynaste de Xanthos', *CRAI* (1975) 138–48
589. Briant, P. 'Les Iraniens d'Asie Mineure après la chute de l'empire achéménide (A propos de l'inscription d'Amyzon)', *DHA* 11 (1984) 167–95
590. Bryce, T. 'The other Pericles', *Historia* 29 (1980) 377–81
591. Bryce, T. 'A ruling dynasty in Lycia', *Klio* 64 (1982) 329–37
592. Bryce, T. 'The arrival of the goddess Leto in Lycia', *Historia* 32 (1983) 1–13
593. Bryce, T. *The Lycians* I. Copenhagen, 1986
594. Buckler, W. H. and Robinson, D. M. *Sardis, Publications of the American Society for the Excavation of Sardis* VII.1. *Greek and Latin inscriptions.* Leyden, 1932
595. Buresch, K. *Aus Lydien: epigraphisch-geographische Reisefrüchte.* Leipzig, 1898
596. Cahn, H. and Gerin, D. 'Themistocles at Magnesia', *Num. Chron.* (1988) 13–20
597. Carter, J. C. *The Sculpture of the Sanctuary of Athena Polias at Priene.* London, 1983
598. Childs, W. 'The authorship of the inscribed pillar of Xanthos', *Anat.*

Stud. 29 (1979) 97–102

599. Childs, W. 'Lycian relations with Persians and Greeks in the fifth and fourth centuries reexamined', *Anat. Stud.* 31 (1981) 55–80

600. Childs, W. and Demargne, P. *Fouilles de Xanthos* VIII: *Le monument des Néréides. Le décor sculpté.* Paris, 1989

601. Cook, J. M. 'The topography of Klazomenai', *ArchEph* (1953/4) II, 149–57

602. Cook, J. M. 'The palai-names', *Historia* 4 (1955) 39–45

603. Cook, J. M. 'The reliefs of "Sesostris" in Ionia', *Türk Arkeoloji Dergisi* 6.2 (1956) 59–65

604. Cook, J. M. 'Old Smyrna 1948–51', *BSA* 53/4 (1958/9) 1–34

605. Cook, J. M. 'Pliny on Icarian shores', *CQ* 9 (1959) 116–25

606. Cook, J. M. 'On Stephanus Byzantius' text of Strabo', *JHS* 79 (1959) 19–26

607. Cook, J. M. 'Greek archaeology in Western Asia Minor', *Archaeological Reports for 1959–60*, 27–57

608. Cook, J. M. 'Cnidian peraea and Spartan coins', *JHS* 81 (1961) 56–72

609. Cook, J. M. 'Some sites of the Milesian territory', *BSA* 56 (1961) 90–101

610. Cook, J. M. 'The problem of classical Ionia', *PCPhS* 187, n.s. 7 (1961) 9–18

611. Cook, J. M. *The Greeks in Ionia and the East.* London, 1962

612. Cook, J. M. review of F 698, *AJA* 75 (1971) 445–6

613. Cook, J. M. *The Troad: an Archaeological and Topographical Study.* Oxford, 1973

614. Cook, J. M. 'Cities in and around the Troad', *BSA* 83 (1988) 7–19

615. Cook, J. M. and Blackman, D. J. 'Archaeology in Western Asia Minor 1965–70', *Archaeological Reports for 1970–1*, 33–62

616. Coupel, P. and Demargne, P. *Fouilles de Xanthos* III: *Le monument des Néréides.* Paris, 1969

617. Cousin, G. and Diehl, C. 'Inscriptions d'Halicarnasse', *BCH* 14 (1890) 90–121

618. Crampa, J. *Labraunda Swedish Excavations and Researches* III.1. *The Greek Inscriptions Part I: Nos. 1–12.* Lund, 1969

619. Crampa, J. *Labraunda Swedish Excavations and Researches* III.2. *The Greek Inscriptions Part II: Nos. 13–133.* Lund, 1972

620. Cremer, M. 'Zwei neue graeco-persische Stelen', *Epigraphica Anatolica* 3 (1984) 87–100

621. Demand, N. 'The relocation of Priene reconsidered', *Phoenix* 40 (1986) 35–40

622. Demand, N. 'Did Knidos really move?' *ClAnt* 8 (1989) 224–37

623. Demand, N. *Urban Relocation in Archaic and Classical Greece: Flight and Consolidation.* Norman, OK, 1990

624. Demargne, P. 'Recherches en Lycie d'après des publications nouvelles', *Rev. Arch.* (1979) 291–6

625. Dentzer, J. M. 'Reliefs au "banquet" dans l'Asie mineure du Ve siècle av. J.-C.', *Rev. Arch.* (1969) 195–224

626. Ehrhardt, N. 'Milet und seine Kolonien: Vergleichende Untersuchung

der kultischen und politischen Einrichtungen'. Diss. Frankfurt, 1983

627. Engelmann, H. and Merkelbach, R. *Inschriften griechischer Städte aus Kleinasien*, 1: *Die Inschriften von Erythrai und Klazomenai 1 (Nr. 1–200)*. Bonn, 1972

628. Fleischer, R. 'Reisennotizen aus Kilikien', *Arch. Anz.* (1984) 85–104

629. Fontenrose, J. *Didyma: Apollo's Oracle, Cult, and Companions*. Berkeley–Los Angeles–London, 1988

630. Fraser, P. M. *Rhodian Funerary Monuments*. Oxford, 1977

631. Graf, F. *Nordionische Kulte*. Rome, 1985

632. Grainger, J. *The Cities of Seleucid Syria*. Oxford, 1990

632A. Gunter, A. C. 'Looking at Hecatomnid patronage from Labraunda', *REA* 87 (1985) 113–24

633. Gwatkin, W. E. *Cappadocia as a Roman Procuratorial Province* (University of Missouri Studies 5). Columbia, MO, 1930

634. Habicht, C. 'Die herrschende Gesellschaft in den hellenistischen Monarchien', *Vierteljahrschrift für Soziologie und Wirtschaftsgeschichte* 14 (1958) 1–16

635. Habicht, C. 'New evidence on the province of Asia', *JRS* 65 (1975) 64–91

636. Hanfmann, G. *Sardis from Prehistoric to Roman Times*. Cambridge, MA, and London, 1983

637. Hanfmann, G. and Ehrhardt, K. P. 'Pedimental sculpture from Sardis', in Simpson, W. K. and Davies, W. M. (eds.), *Studies in Egypt, the Aegean and the Sudan: Essays in Honor of Dows Dunham on the Occasion of his 90th Birthday*, 82–90. Boston, MA, 1981

638. Hanfmann, G. and Ramage, N. *Sculpture from Sardis*. Cambridge, MA, 1978

639. Hellström, P. *Labraunda Swedish Excavations and Researches 2.1. Pottery of Classical and Later Date*. Lund, 1965

640. Hellström, P. and Thieme, T. 'The androns at Labraunda: a preliminary account of their architecture', *Medelhausmuseet Bulletin* 16 (1981) 58–74

641. Hellström, P. and Thieme, T. *Labraunda Swedish Excavations and Researches 1.3. The Temple of Zeus at Labraunda*. Stockholm, 1982

642. Hermary, A. 'Un nouveau relief "gréco-perse" en Cilicie', *Rev. Arch.* (1984) 289–300

643. Herrmann, P. *Tituli Asiae Minoris* 5, 1 and 2. Vienna, 1981 and 1989

644. Hornblower, S. *Mausolus*. Oxford, 1982

645. Hornblower, S. 'Thucydides, the Panionian festival, and the Ephesia', *Historia* 31 (1982) 241–5

646. Hornblower, S. Review of F 661, *CR* 38 (1988) 175–7

647. Hornblower, S. 'A reaction to Gunter's look at Hecatomnid patronage from Labraunda', *REA* 92 (1990) 137–9

648. Hunt, D. W. 'Feudal survivals in Ionia', *JHS* 67 (1947) 68–76

649. Jacobs, B. *Griechische und persiche Elemente in der Grabkunst Lykiens*. Göteborg, 1987 = *SIMA* 78

650. Jameson, S. 'Lykia', *RE* Supp. 13 (1973) 265–308

651. Jeppesen, K. *Labraunda Swedish Excavations and Researches 1.1. The Propylaea*. Lund, 1955

652. Jeppesen, K. *Paradeigmata. Three Mid-fourth-century Works of Hellenic Architecture Reconsidered* (Jutland Archaeological Society Publications 4). Aarhus, 1958

653. Jeppesen, K. 'Paradeigmata: Nachträge', *Acta Arch.* 32 (1961) 218–30

654. Jeppesen, K. 'Explorations at Halikarnassus', *Acta Arch.* 38 (1967) 29–58

655. Jeppesen, K. 'Nisi absoluto jam': observations on the building[s] of the Mausoleum at Halikarnassus', *Mélanges Mansel*, 735–48. Ankara, 1974

656. Jeppesen, K. 'Mausolaet i Halikarnassos', *Naturens Verdens* (1976) 41–50

657. Jeppesen, K. 'Neue Ergebnisse zur Wiederherstellung des Maussolleions von Halikarnassos', *Ist. Mitt.* 26 (1976) 47–91

658. Jeppesen, K. 'Zur Gründung und Baugeschichte des Maussolleions von Halikarnassos', *Ist. Mitt.* 27/8 (1977/8) 169–211

659. Jeppesen, K. 'Zu den Proportionen des Maussolleions von Halikarnass', *Bauplanung und Bautheorie der Antike: Diskussionen zur archäologischen Bauforschung* 4 (1984) 167–74

660. Jeppesen, K., Højlund, F. and Aaris-Sørensen, K. *The Maussolleion at Halikarnassos: Reports of the Danish Archaeological Expedition to Bodrum* I, *The Sacrificial Deposit.* Copenhagen, 1981

661. Jeppesen, K. and Luttrell, A. *The Maussolleion at Halikarnassos: Reports of the Danish Archaeological Expedition to Bodrum* II, *The written sources and their archaeological background.* Aarhus, 1986

662. Jones, A. H. M. *The Cities of the Eastern Roman Provinces.* 2nd edn. Oxford, 1971

663. Judeich, W. *Kleinasiatische Studien.* Marburg, 1892

664. Jully, J. J. *Labraunda Swedish Excavations and Researches 2.3. Archaic Pottery.* Istanbul, 1981

665. Kinns, P. 'The coinage of Miletus', *Num. Chron.* 146 (1986) 235–60

666. Kinns, P. 'Ionia: the pattern of coinage during the last century of the Persian period', *REA* 91 (1989) 183–93

667. Kleiner, G., Hommel, P. and Müller-Wiener, W. *Panionion und Melie* (*JDAI* Ergänzungsheft 23). 1967

668. Kobylina, M. M. *Milet.* Moscow, 1965

669. Koenigs, W. 'Milet 1978–1979; 3: Bauglieder aus Milet II', *Ist. Mitt.* 10 (1980) 56–91

670. Krumbholz, P. *De Asiae minoris satrapis persicis.* Diss. Leipzig, 1883

671. Kuhrt, A. and Sherwin-White, S. *Hellenism in the East: The Interaction of Greek and non-Greek Civilizations from Syria to Central Asia after Alexander.* London, 1987

672. Sherwin-White, S., and Kuhrt, A. *From Samarkhand to Sardis.* London, 1993

673. Leaf, W. 'The commerce of Sinope', *JHS* 36 (1916) 1–15

674. Linders, T. and Hellstrøm, P. (eds.) *Architecture and Society in Hecatomnid Caria. Proceedings of the Uppsala Symposium 1987. Boreas* (Acta Universitatis Upsaliensis, Uppsala Studies in Ancient Mediterranean and Near Eastern Civilizations 17). Uppsala, 1989

675. Littmann, E. *Sardis. Publications of the American Society for the Excavation of*

Sardis 6: Lydian inscriptions. Leyden, 1916
676. Magie, D. *Roman Rule in Asia Minor.* 2 vols. Princeton, 1950
677. Marchese, R. *The Historical Geography of Northern Caria* (BAR 536). Oxford, 1989
678. Metzger, H. 'Sur deux groupes de reliefs gréco-perses d'Asie mineure', *Ant. Class.* 40 (1971) 505–25
679. Metzger, H. 'Ekphora, convoi funèbre, cortège de dignitaire en Grèce et à la périphérie du monde grec', *Rev. Arch.* (1975) 209–20
680. Mildenberg, L. 'Mithropata und Perikles', *Atti II Congresso Internazionale di Numismatica* (1965) 48–55
681. Mitchell, S. 'Archaeology in Asia Minor, 1979–84', *Archaeological Reports for 1984–85*, 70–105
682. Mitchell, S. 'Archaeology in Asia Minor, 1985–89', *Archaeological Reports for 1989–90*, 83–131
683. Mitchell, S. 'The hellenization of Pisidia', *Mediterranean Archaeology* 4 (1991) 119–45
684. Mitchell, S. and McNicoll, A. W. 'Archaeology in Western and Southern Asia Minor, 1971–8', *Archaeological Reports for 1978–79*, 59–90
685. Mørkholm, O. 'The classification of Lycian coins before Alexander the Great', *Jahr. Num. u. Geldgeschichte* (1964) 65–76
686. Müller-Wiener, W. (ed.) *Milet 1899–1980* (*Ist. Mitt.* Beiheft 31). 1986
687. Murray, O. 'Ο ΑΡΧΑΙΟΣ ΔΑΣΜΟΣ', *Historia* 15 (1966) 142–56
688. Osborne, M. 'Orontes', *Historia* 22 (1973) 515–51
689. Osborne, M. 'The satrapy of Mysia', *Grazer Beiträge* 3 (1975) 291–309
689A. Pareti, L. 'Per la storia di alcune dinastie greche dell'Asia minore', in *Studi minori di storia antica* II, 179–91. Rome, 1961
690. Parke, H. W. *The Oracles of Apollo in Asia Minor.* London–Sydney–Dover, NH, 1985
691. Parke, H. W. 'The temple of Apollo at Didyma: the building and its function', *JHS* 106 (1986) 121–31
692. Pembroke, S. 'The last of the matriarchs: a study in the inscriptions of Lycia', *Journ. Econ. and Soc. Hist. Orient* 8 (1965) 217–47
693. Petit, T. 'A propos des "satrapies" ionienne et carienne', *BCH* 112 (1988) 307–22
694. Pugliese Carratelli, G. 'Greek inscriptions of the Middle East', *East and West* 16 (1966) 31–6
695. Pugliese Carratelli, G. 'Nuovo supplemento epigrafico di Iaso', *ASAA* 47–8 (n.s. 31–2) (1969–70) [1972], 371–405
696. Pugliese Carratelli, G. 'Cari in Iasos', *Atti Acc. Naz. Lincei. Rend. Mor.* 40 (1985) 149–55
697. Pugliese Carratelli, G. 'Ancora su Iasos e i Cari', *Atti Acc. Naz. Lincei. Rend. Mor.* 42 (1987) 289–92
698. Radt, W. *Siedlungen und Bauten auf der Halbinsel von Halikarnassos* (*Ist. Mitt.* Beiheft 3). Tübingen, 1970
699. Radt, W. 'Eine gräko-persische Grabstele im Museum Bergama', *Ist. Mitt.* 33 (1983) 53–68
700. Ramage, N. 'A Lydian funerary banquet', *Anat. Stud.* 19 (1979) 91–5
701. Ramsay, W. M. *Cities and Bishoprics of Phrygia.* 2 vols. Oxford, 1895–7

702. Robert, J. and L. *La Carie 2* (all published). Paris, 1954
703. Robert, J. and L. *Fouilles d'Amyzon en Carie*. Paris, 1983
704. Robert, L. 'Rapport sommaire sur un premier voyage en Carie', *AJA* 89 (1935) 331–40
705. Robert, L. *Etudes anatoliennes*. Paris, 1937
706. Robert, L. *Le sanctuaire de Sinuri près de Mylasa 1. Les inscriptions grecques*. Paris, 1945
706A. Robert, L. *Villes d'Asie mineure*. 2nd edn. Paris, 1962
707. Robert, L. *Noms indigènes dans l'Asie mineure gréco-romaine 1*. (all published). Paris, 1963
708. Robert, L. *Nouvelles inscriptions de Sardes 1*. Paris, 1964
709. Robert, L. *Documents d'Asie mineure méridionale*. Paris–Geneva, 1966
710. Robert, L. in J. des Gagniers *et al. Laodicée du Lycos: le nymphée* 247–389, 'Les inscriptions'. Quebec–Paris, 1969
711. Robert, L. *A travers l'Asie Mineure (BEFRA* 239). Athens, 1980
712. Robert, L. *Documents d'Asie mineure*. Paris, 1987
713. Robert, L. and J. *Claros 1: décrets hellénistiques*. Paris, 1989
714. Robinson, D. M. 'Ancient Sinope', *AJP* 27 (1906) 125–53 and 245–79
715. Rostovtzeff, M. 'Notes on the economic policy of the Pergamene kings', *Anatolian Studies Presented to Sir W. M. Ramsay*, 359–90. Manchester, 1923
716. Säflund, M.-L. *Labraunda Swedish Excavations and Researches 2.2. Stamped Amphora Handles*. Istanbul, 1980
717. Sahin, S. *The Political and Religious Structure in the Territory of Stratonicea in Caria*. Ankara, 1976
718. Schmidt-Doumas, B. *Der lykische Sarkophag aus Sidon (Ist. Mitt.* Beiheft 30). 1985
719. Sekunda, N. 'Achaemenid colonization in Lydia', *REA* 87 (1985) 7–29
720. Sherwin-White, A. N. *Roman Foreign Policy in the East*. London, 1984
721. Six, J. 'Monnaies grecques, inédites et incertaines; IX Les dynastes de Teuthranie' *Num. Chron.* (1890) 185–259 at 188–98
722. Stylianou, P. 'Thucydides, the Panionian festival, and the Ephesia (III 104), again', *Historia* 32 (1983) 245–9
723. Treuber, O. *Geschichte der Lykier*. Stuttgart, 1887
724. Tuchelt, K. 'Die Perserzerstörung von Branchidai-Didyma und ihre Folgen – archäologisch betrachtet', *Arch. Anz.* (1988) 427–38
725. Varinluoglu, E. 'Inscriptions from Erythrai', *ZPE* 44 (1981) 45–50
726. Varinluoglu, E., Bresson, A., Brun, P., Debord, P. and Descat, R. 'Une inscription de Pladasa en Carie', *REA* 92 (1990) 59–78
727. Walbank, F. W. Review of F 671 (Kuhrt and Sherwin-White (1987)), *LCM* 13 (1988) 108–12
728. Waywell, G. B. *The Free-Standing Sculptures of the Mausoleum at Halicarnassus*. London, 1978
729. Westholm, A. *Labraunda Swedish Excavations and Researches 1.2. The architecture of the Hieron*. Lund, 1963
730. Wörrle, M. 'Inschriften von Herakleia am Latmos I', *Chiron* 18 (1988) 421–76
731. Wörrle, M. 'Inschriften von Herakleia am Latmos II', *Chiron* 20 (1990)

19–58

732.   Wörrle, M. 'Epigraphische Forschungen zur Geschichte Lykiens IV:
       Drei griechische Inschriften aus Limyra', *Chiron* 21 (1991) 201–39
733.   Woudhuizen, F. C. 'The recently discovered Greek-Sidetan bilingue
       from Seleucia', *Talanta* 20–1 (1988–9) 87–108
734.   Zahle, J. 'Politics and economy in Lycia in the Persian period', *REA* 91
       (1989) 169–82
735.   Zgusta, L. *Kleinasiatische Personennamen*. Prague, 1964
736.   Zgusta, L. *Kleinasiatische Ortsnamen*. Heidelberg, 1984

G. THE WEST

I. CARTHAGE

1.   Asheri, D. 'Carthaginians and Greeks', in *CAH* IV² (1988) ch. 16
2.   Astruc, M. *La necrópolis de Villaricos*. Madrid, 1951
3.   Astruc, M. 'Traditions funéraires de Carthage', *Cahiers de Byrsa* 6 (1957)
      29–58
4.   *Atti del Primo Congresso Internazionale di Studi Fenici e Punici* (Rome, 5–10
      Nov 1979) I–III. Rome, 1983
5.   Bacigalupo Pareo, E. 'I supremi magistrati a Cartagine', in *Contributi di
      Storia Antica in onore di Albino Garzetti*, 61–87. Genoa, 1976
6.   Barreca, F. *La Sardegna fenicia e punica*. Sassari, 1974
7.   Beloch, J. 'Die Könige von Karthago', *Klio* 7 (1907) 19–26
8.   Bénichou-Safar, H. 'Carte des nécropoles puniques de Carthage',
      Karthago 17 (1976) 5–35
9.   Bénichou-Safar, H. *Les tombes puniques de Carthage*. Paris, 1982
10.   *Carthage, sa naissance, sa grandeur*. *Archéologie vivante*, special number, I, no.
      8, Dec. 1968 – Feb. 1969
11.   Ciasca, A. *et al. Mozia*, I–IX. Rome, 1964–78
12.   Cintas, P. 'Le sanctuaire punique de Sousse', *Revue africaine* 40 (1947) 1–
      85
13.   Cintas, P. 'Deux campagnes de fouilles à Utique', *Karthago* 2 (1951) 1–88
14.   Cintas, P. *Contribution à l'étude de l'expansion carthaginoise au Maroc*. Paris,
      1954
15.   Cintas, P. 'Nouvelles recherches à Utique', *Karthago* 5 (1954) 89–155
16.   Cutroni-Tusa, A. 'Recenti soluzioni e nuovi problemi sulla monetazione
      punica della Sicilia', *Studi di Numismatica Punica* (Suppl. di *R. Stud. Fen.*
      11 (1983) 37–42)
17.   Di Vita, A. 'Les Phéniciens de l'Occident d'après les découvertes
      archéologiques de Tripolitaine', in Ward, A. (ed.), *The Role of the
      Phoenicians in the Interaction of Mediterranean Civilisations*, 77–112. Beirut,
      1968
18.   Dussaud, R. 'Précisions épigraphiques touchant les sacrifices puniques
      d'enfants', *CRAI* (1946) 371–87
19.   Duval, R. 'L'enceinte de Carthage', *CRAI* (1951) 53–9
20.   Falsone, G. 'Nouvelles données sur Melqart', in *Carthage; VI Colloque*,
      Groupe de contacts universitaires d'Etudes phéniciennes et puniques de

l'Université de Leuven. Brussels, 1986

21. Falsone, G. 'La Statua marmorea di Mozia', *Studi e Materiali* (Istituto di Archeologia, Università di Palermo) 8 (1988) 9–28

22. Fantar, M. *Eschatologie phénicienne punique*. Tunis, 1970

23. Fantar, M. *Kerkouane, cité punique du Cap Bon* I, II. Tunis, 1984, 1985

24. Garcia y Bellido, A. 'La colonización cartaginesa desde sus comienzos hasta la conquista cartaginesa, La colonias púnicas, El arte púnico en España', in Menéndez Pidal, R. (ed.) *Historia de España* II, 337–492. Madrid, 1952

25. Gauckler, P. *Nécropoles puniques*. 2 vols. Paris, 1915

26. Gauthier, P. 'Grecs et Phéniciens en Sicile pendant la période archaique', *Rev. Hist.* 224 (1960) 257–74

27. Grottanelli, C. 'Encore un regard sur les bûchers d'Amilcar et d'Elissa', in G 4, 437–42

28. Gsell, S. *Histoire ancienne de l'afrique du nord*. Paris, 1920–8

29. Guzzo Amadasi, M. G. *et al. Monte Sirai*, I–IV. Rome, 1964–7

30. Hans, L.-M. *Karthago und Sizilien* (Historische Texte und Studien 7). Hildesheim–Zurich–New York, 1983

31. Heuss, A. 'Die Gestaltung des römischen und des karthagischen Staates bis zum Pyrrhos-Krieg', in G 89, 83–138

32. Heuss, A. 'Der erste Punische Krieg und das Problem des römischen Imperialismus. Zur politischen Beurteilung des Krieges', *Hist. Zeitschr.* 169 (1949) 457–513

33. Hoffmann, W. 'Karthagos Kampf um die Vorherrschaft im Mittelmeer', *ANRW* I.1 (1972) 341–63

34. Humphrey, J. H. *Excavations at Carthage conducted by the University of Michigan* I–VII. Tunis, 1976–82

35. Hurst, H. 'Excavations at Carthage', *Antiquaries Journal* 55 (1975) 11–40; 56 (1976) 177–97; 57 (1977) 232–61; 59 (1979) 99–149

36. Hurst, H. 'The war harbour of Carthage', in G 4, 603–10

37. Huss, W. 'Vier Sufeten in Karthago?', *Le Muséon* 90 (1977) 427–33

38. Huss, W. 'Die Stellung des rb im karthaginischen Staat', *ZDMG* 129 (1979) 217–32

39. Huss, W. *Geschichte der Karthager* (Handbuch der Altertumswissenschaft, iii.8). Munich, 1985

40. Isserlin, B. S. J. and du Plat Taylor, J. *Motya, a Phoenician and Carthaginian City in Sicilia*, I. Leiden, 1974

41. Lancel, S. 'Nouvelles fouilles de la Mission archéologique française à Carthage sur la colline de Byrsa: campagne de 1974–1975', *CRAI* (1976) 60–78

42. Lancel, S. *Byrsa* I, II. Rome, 1979, 1982

43. Lindemann, H. *Untersuchungen zur Verfassungsgeschichte Karthagos bis auf Aristoteles*. Diss. Jena, 1933

44. Lipinski, E. 'Sacrifices d'enfants à Carthage et dans le monde sémitique oriental', in Lipinski, E. (ed.) *Studia Phoenicia* VI, 151–85. Leuven, 1988

45. Lo Cascio, E. 'La leggenda ṣyṣ delle monete siculo-puniche', *PP* 30 (1975) 153–61

46. Luria, S. 'Zum Problem der griechisch-karthagischen Beziehungen',

Act. Ant. Hung. 12 (1964) 53–75

47. Masson, O. 'Le "roi" carthaginois Iomolkos dans les inscriptions de Délos', *Studia Semitica* 29 (1979) 53–8
48. Maurin, L. 'Himilcon le Magonide. Crises et mutations à Carthage au début du IVᵉ siècle av. J.-C.', *Semitica* 12 (1962) 5–43
49. Meritt, B. D. 'Athens and Carthage', in *Athenian Studies* (*HSCP* Suppl. vol. 1, 247–53. Studies presented to W. S. Ferguson). Cambridge, MA, 1940
50. Morel, J.-P. 'Kerkouane, ville punique du cap Bon. Remarques archéologiques et historiques', *MEFRA* 81 (1969) 473–518
51. Moscati, S. *Fenici e Cartaginesi in Sardegna.* Milan, 1968
52. Moscati, S. *The World of the Phoenicians.* London, 1968
53. Moscati, S. *I Fenici e Cartagine.* Turin, 1972
54. Moscati, S. 'L'origine dell'idolo a botiglia', *R. Stud. Fen.* 3 (1975) 7–9
55. Moscati, S. *Il mondo punico.* UTET, 1980
56. Moscati, S. *Tra Tiro e Cadice* (*Studia Punica* 5). Rome, 1989
57. Moscati, S. and Uberti, M. L. *Scavi a Mozia: le stele.* Rome, 1981
58. Niemeyer, H. G. (ed.) *Phönizier im Westen* (Madrider Beiträge 8) 1982
59. Niemeyer, H. G. 'Die Phönizier und die Mittelmeerwelt im Zeitalter Homers', *JRGZM* 31 (1984) 3–94
60. Niemeyer, H. G. 'A la recherche de la Carthage antique; premiers résultats des fouilles de l'Université de Hambourg en 1986 et 1987', *Centre d'Etudes et de documentation, Carthage* 10 (1989) 20–2
61. Pesce, G. *Sardegna Punica.* Cagliari, 1961
62. Picard, C. *Carthage.* Paris, 1951
63. Picard, C. 'Les représentations de sacrifice *molk* sur les ex-voto de Carthage', *Karthago* 17 (1976) 67–138; 18 (1978) 5–116
64. Picard, C. 'Demeter et Kore à Carthage', *KOKALOS* 28/29 (1982/3) 187–94
65. Picard, C. 'Les navigations de Carthage vers l'Ouest', in G 58, 167–74
66. Picard, C. G. *Sacra Punica* (*Karthago* 13, 1967)
67. Picard, G. *Religions de l'Afrique antique.* Paris, 1954
68. Picard, G. *Le monde de Carthage.* Paris, 1956
69. Picard, G. 'Les sufètes de Carthage dans Tite-Live et Cornelius Nepos', *REL* 41 (1964) 269–81
70. Picard, G. 'Institutions politiques: de la fondation de Carthage à la révolution barcide', in G 10, 149–53
71. Picard, G. 'Les rapports entre gouvernants et gouvernés à Carthage', *Rec. Soc. Bodin* 23, 133ff. Brussels, 1968
72. Picard, G.-Ch. *La Révolution démocratique à Carthage*, in Coll. Latomus 62, 113–30. Brussels, 1968
73. Picard, G. Ch. 'I Cartaginesi in Sicilia all'epoca dei due Dionisi', *KOKALOS* 28/9 (1982/3) 271–7
74. Picard, G. Ch. 'Le Périple d'Hannon', in G 58, 174–80
75. Picard, G.-Ch. and Picard, C. *Vie et mort de Carthage.* Paris, 1970
76. Pritchard, J. B. 'The Tanit inscription from Sarepta', in G 58, 83–94
77. Quillard, B. *Bijoux carthaginois.* Louvain, 1979, 1987
78. Rakob, F. 'Die Ausgrabungen in Karthago', in *150 Jahre Feier, DAIR*,

121–32. Berlin, 1982

79. Seston, W. 'Des "Portes" de Thugga à la "Constitution" de Carthage', *Rev. Hist.* 237 (1967) 277–94

80. Sznycer, M. 'Mythes et dieux de la religion phénicienne', *Archeologia* 20 (1968) 27–33

81. Sznycer, M. 'L' "Assemblée du peuple" dans les cités puniques d'après les témoignages épigraphiques', *Semitica* 25 (1975) 47–68

82. Sznycer, M. 'L'expansion phénico-punique dans la Méditerranée occidentale. Problèmes et méthodes', in *Actes du IIe Congrès d'Etude des cultures de la Méditerranée occidentale (Malte, juin 1976)*, I, 35–48. Algiers, 1976

83. Sznycer, M. 'Carthage et la civilisation punique', in Nicolet, C. (ed.), *Rome et la conquête du monde méditerranéen (Nouvelle Clio* 8bis, 545–93; 473– 81, bibliography) 1978

84. Sznycer, M. 'L'emploi des termes "phénicien", "punique", "néopunique". Problèmes de méthodologie', *Transactions of the Second Congress on Hamito-Semitic Linguistics*, 261–8. Florence, 1978

85. Tarradell, M. *Marruecos punico.* Tétouan, 1959

86. Treu, M. 'Athen und Karthago in der Thukydideischen Darstellung', *Historia* 3 (1954/5) 41–59

87. Tusa, V. 'Il Giovane di Mozia', in J1, 1–11

88. Vives y Escudero, A. *Estudio de Arqueología cartaginesa. La necropóli de Ibiza.* Madrid, 1917

89. Vogt, J. (ed.) *Rom und Karthago.* Leipzig, 1943

90. Warmington, B. H. *Carthage.* Harmondsworth, 1964. (The first edn, London, 1960, has the same text, but no references)

91. Whittaker, C. R. 'Carthaginian imperialism in the fifth and fourth centuries B.C.', in A 22, 59–90

II. ITALY AND SICILY

91A. Aalders, G. J. D. 'The authenticity of the Eighth Platonic Epistle reconsidered', *Mnemosyne* 22 (1969) 233–57

92. Adamesteanu, D. 'Osservazioni sulla battaglia di Gela del 405 a.C.', *KOKALOS* 2 (1956) 142–57

93. Adamesteanu, D. *La Basilicata antica: storia e monumenti.* Cava dei Tirreni, 1974

94. Adamesteanu, D. 'Topografia e viabilità', in G 267, 173–206

95. Adamesteanu, D. 'Urbanizzazione in Magna Grecia', in *L'adriatico tra Mediterraneo e penisola balcanica nell' antichità.* Atti del congresso dell' Assoc. internaz. di studi del Sud-Est europeo, Lecce 1973, 155–64. Taranto, 1983

96. Adamesteanu, D. '"Poleis" italiote e comunità indigene', in G 269, 115– 34

97. Adamesteanu, D. 'Greeks and natives in Basilicata', in Descoeudres, J.- P. (ed.), *Greek Colonists and Native Populations*, 143–50. Oxford, 1990

98. Adamesteanu, D. and Lejeune, M. 'Il santuario lucano di Macchia di Rossano di Vaglio', *Mem. Linc.* ser. 8, 16 (1971) 39–83

99. Ampolo, C. 'Tributi e decime dei Siracusani', *Opus* 3 (1984) 31–6
100. Anello, P. *Dionisio il vecchio* I: *Politica adriatica e tirrenica*. Palermo, 1980
101. Anello, P. 'Il trattato del 405/4 a.c. e la formazione della "eparchia" punica di Sicilia', *KOKALOS* 32 (1986) 115–80
102. Arias, P. 'Rapporti e contrasti dalla fine del VI s.a.C. al dominio romano', in G 105, 231–57
103. Asheri, D. 'La popolazione di Imera nel V secolo a. C.', *Riv. di Filol.* 101 (1973) 437–65
104. Asheri, D. 'La diaspora e il ritorno dei Messeni', in Gabba, E. (ed.), *Tria Corda. Scritti in onore di Arnaldo Momigliano*, 27–42. Como, 1983
105. *Atti 3 Convegno, 1963: Metropoli e colonie di Magna Grecia*. Naples, 1964
106. *Atti 10 Convegno, 1970: Taranto nella civiltà della Magna Grecia*. Naples, 1971
107. *Atti 11 Convegno, 1971: Le genti non greche della Magna Grecia*. Naples, 1972
108. *Atti 15 Convegno, 1975: La Magna Grecia in età romana*. Naples, 1976
109. *Atti 16 Convegno, 1976: Locri Epizefirii*. Naples, 1977
110. *Atti 21 Convegno, 1981: Megale Hellas: nome e immagine*. Taranto, 1982 [1983]
111. *Atti 23 Convegno, 1983: Crotone*. Taranto, 1984 [1986]
112. *Atti 25 Convegno, 1985: Neapolis*. Taranto, 1986 [1988]
113. *Attività archeologica in Basilicata*. Matera, 1980
114. Baldassare, I. 'Osservazioni sull'urbanistica di Neapolis in età romana', in G 112, 221–31
115. Barreca, F. 'Tindari colonia dionigiana', *Rend. Linc.* VIII.XII (1957) 125–30
116. Beaumont, R. L. 'Greek influence in the Adriatic Sea before the fourth century B.C.', *JHS* 56 (1936) 159–204
117. Berve, H. *Dion* (Abh. Ak. Mainz 10). Wiesbaden, 1956
118. Blois, L. de. 'Dionysius II, Dion and Timoleon', *Mededelingen van het Nederlands Instituut te Rome* 40 (1978) 113–49
118A. Blois, L. de. 'Some notes on Plato's Seventh Epistle', *Mnemosyne* 32 (1979) 268–73
119. Borraro, P. (ed.) *Antiche civiltà lucane*. Galatina, 1975 (= *Collana di Cultura Lucana II*)
120. Bottini, A. 'La panoplia lucana del museo provinciale di Potenza', *MEFRA* 101 (1989) 699–715
121. Bottini, A. and Guzzo, P. G. 'Gli italioti fino alla conquista romana', *PCIA* 8 (Rome, 1986) 253–342
122. Bottini, A. and Guzzo, P. G. 'I popoli italici', *PCIA* 8 (Rome, 1986) 343–90
123. Braccesi, L. *L'avventura di Cleonimo a Venezia prima di Venezia*. Padua, 1990
124. Braccesi, L. 'Ancora sulla colonizzazione siracusana in Adriatico (Dionigi, Diomede e i Galli)' in G 131, 57–64
125. Brauer, G. C., Jr. *Taras, its History and Coinage*. New Rochelle, NY, 1986
126. Briquel, D. 'Le problème des Dauniens', *MEFRA* 86 (1974) 7–40
127. Bury, J. B. 'The Italian wars of Dionysius and his later wars with Carthage', in *CAH* VI[1] (1927) 127–30

128. Carter, J. C. *The Sculpture of Taras*. Philadelphia, 1975
129. Carter, J. 'Ricerca archeologica nella chora Metapontina – la campagna del 1985', in G 112, 477–91
130. Càssola, F. 'Problemi di storia neapolitana', in G 112, 37–82
131. Cassio, A. C. and Musti, D. (eds.) *Tra Sicilia e Magna Grecia. Aspetti di interazione culturale nel IV sec. a. Cr.* Pisa, 1991 (= *Atti Conv. 1987 = AION* 11 (1989) [1991])
132. Castellana, G. 'La Neapolis della chora Acragantina e la colonizzazione Dionisiana di Sicilia', *PP* 39 (1984) 375–83
133. Catalano, R. *La Lucania antica, profilo storico IV–II sec. a.c.* Salerno, 1979
134. Caven, B. *Dionysius I: Warlord of Sicily*. New Haven–London, 1990
135. Cerchiai, L. 'Il processo di strutturazione del politico: i Campani', *AION* 9 (1987) 41–53
136. Chisesi, F. 'Entella, il Crimiso e la Battaglia di Timoleone', *Rend. Linc.* ser. 6, vol. 5 (1929) 255–84
137. Christien, J. 'Mercenaires et partis politiques à Syracuse de 357 à 354', *REA* 77 (1975) 63–73
138. Ciaceri, E. *Storia della Magna Grecia*, II–III. Milan–Rome, 1927–32
139. *La civiltà dei Dauni nel quadro del mondo italico. Atti del XIII Conv. di Studi Etruschi ed Italici 1980*. Florence, 1984
140. Clemente, G. 'Introduzione alla storia della Puglia romana', in Marangio, Cesare (ed.) *La Puglia in età repubblicana*, 11–20. Galatina, 1988
141. Coarelli, F. and Torelli, M. *Sicilia* (Guide archeologiche Laterza). Rome–Bari, 1984
142. Colonna, G. 'Un "trofeo" di Novio Fannio, comandante sannita', in *Studi di antichità in onore di Guglielmo Maetzke* 229–42. Rome, 1984
143. Consolo Langher, S. 'Gli *Ἡρακλειῶται ἐκ Κεφαλοιδίου*', *KOKALOS* 7 (1961) 166–98
144. Consolo Langher, S. *Contributo alla storia della antica monetà bronzea in Sicilia*. Milan, 1964
145. Cornell, T. 'The conquest of Italy', in *CAH* VII².2 (1990) ch. 8
146. Costabile, F. 'Archontes e basileus a Locri Epizefiri', *PP* 35 (1980) 104–22
147. D'Agostino, B. 'Il mondo periferico della Magna Grecia', in *PCIA* 2 (Rome, 1974) 171–271
148. D'Agostino, B. '*Voluptas e Virtus*: il mito politico della "Ingenuità italica"', *AION* 3 (1981) 117–27
149. *La Daunia antica. Dalla preistoria all'altomedioevo* (Exhibition catalogue). 1984
150. De Franciscis, A. *Stato e società in Locri Epizefiri (L'archivio dell'Olimpieion locrese)*. Naples, 1972
151. De La Genière, J. 'Epire et Basilicate. A propos de la couronne d'Armento', *MEFRA* 101 (1989) 691–8
152. De Sensi Sestito, G. 'Il santuario del Lacinio nella lega achea ed italiota', *Misc. di studi storici* 2 (Cosenza, 1982) 13–33
153. De Sensi Sestito, G. *La Calabria in età arcaica e classica. Storia, economica, società*. Rome, 1984

154. De Sensi Sestito, G. 'Taranto post-architea nel giudizio di Timeo. Nota a
       Str. VI 3, 4 (280)', in *XI Miscellanea Greca e Romana*, 85–113. Rome, 1987
155. De Sensi Sestito, G. 'La Calabria in età arcaica e classica', in *Storia di
       Calabria* I, 227–303. Rome–Reggio, 1988
156. De Waele, J. A. 'La popolazione di Acragas antica', in *Φιλίας χάριν,
       Miscellanea in honore di Eugenio Manni* II, 747–60. Rome, 1979
157. Delatte, A. *Essai sur la politique pythagoricienne*. Paris, 1922
158. Di Vita, A. 'Le fortificazioni di Selinunte classica', *ASAA* 62 (1984
       [1988]) 69–79
159. Di Vita, A. 'Selinunte fra il 650 ed il 409. Un modello urbanistico
       coloniale', *ASAA* 62 (1984 [1988]) 7–68
160. Dunbabin, T. J. *The Western Greeks*. Oxford, 1948
161. Evans, A. *The 'Horsemen' of Tarentum*. London, 1889
162. Fabricius, K. *Das antike Syrakus* (*Klio* Beih. 28, 1932)
163. Felletti Maj, B. M. *La tradizione italica nell'arte romana*. Rome, 1977
164. Finley, M. I. *Ancient Sicily*. Revd edn. London, 1979 (first edn *A History
       of Sicily to the Arab Conquest*. London, 1968)
165. Fiorentini, G. 'Santuari punici a Monte Adranone di Sambuca di Sicilia',
       in *Φιλίας χάριν, Miscellanea in honore di Eugenio Manni* III, 905–16. Rome,
       1979
166. Fontana, M. J. 'Alcune considerazioni su Ermocrate Siracusano', in
       Scritti sul mondo antico in memoria di Fulvio Grosso, 152–65. Rome, 1981
167. Forti, L. and Stazio, Attilio. 'Vita quotidiana dei Greci d'Italia', in G 267,
       643–716
168. Fracchia, H., Gualtieri, M. and De Polignac, F. 'Il territorio di
       Roccagloriosa in Lucania', *MEFRA* 95 (1983) 345–80
169. Fracchia, H. and Gualtieri, M. 'The social context of cult-practices in
       pre-Roman Lucania', *AJA* 93 (1989) 217–32
170. Fraschetti, A. 'La "barbarizzazione" di Poseidonia', *AION* 3 (1981) 97–
       115
171. Frederiksen, M. W. 'Campanian cavalry: a question of origins', *Dial. di
       Arch.* 2 (1968) 3–31
172. Frederiksen, M. 'Archaeology in South Italy and Sicily 1973–6', *Arch.
       Rep.* 23 (1977) 43–76
173. Frederiksen, M. W. *Campania*, ed. N. Purcell. London, 1984
174. Freeman, E. A. *History of Sicily* (vol. IV completed by A. Evans). Oxford,
       1891–4
175. Fritz, K. von. *Pythagorean Politics in Southern Italy*. New York, 1942
176. Fuks, A. 'Redistribution of land and houses in Syracuse in 356 B.C. and
       its ideological aspects', *CQ* n.s. 18 (1968) 207–23 (= C 23, 213–29)
177. Gabba, E. and Vallet, G. *La Sicilia antica*. Naples, 1980
178. Gandolfo, L. 'Emissioni puniche di Sicilia a leggenda *ṣyṣ*', *Sicilia
       Archeologica* 17 (54–5, 1984) 75–87
179. Giangiulio, M. *Ricerche su Crotone arcaica*. Pisa, 1989
180. Giannelli, G. *La Magna Grecia da Pitagora a Pirro*. Milan, 1928
181. Gigante, M. 'La cultura a Taranto', in G 106, 67–131
182. Gitti, A. 'Ricerche sulla vita di Filisto, Adria e il luogo dell'esilio', *Mem.
       Linc.* ser. 8a, 4.4 (1952) 225–73

183. Gitti, A. 'Sulla colonizzazione greca nell'alto e medio Adriatico', *PdP* 7 (1952) 161–91
184. Giuffrida, M. 'Leontini, Catane e Nasso dalla II spedizione ateniese al 403', in Φιλίας χάριν, *Miscellanea in honore di Eugenio Manni*, III, 1137–56. Rome, 1979
185. *Gli ori di Taranto in età ellenistica* (Exhibition catalogue). Milan, 1984
186. Greco, E. 'Ricerche sulla chora poseidoniate: il "paesaggio agrario" dalla fondazione della città alla fine del IV sec. a.C.', *Dial. di Arch.* 2 (1979) 7–26
187. Greco, E. *Magna Grecia.* Rome–Bari, 1980
188. Greco, E. 'L'impianto urbano di Neapolis greca – aspetti e problemi', in G 112, 187–219
189. Greco, E. and Schnapp, A. 'Moio della Civitella et le territorie de Velia', *MEFRA* 95 (1983) 381–415
190. Grosso, F. 'Ermocrate di Siracusa', *KOKALOS* 12 (1966) 102–43
191. Guzzo, P. G. 'Archeologia e territorio nella sibaritide', in *Studi di antichità in onore di Guglielmo Maetzke* 309–15. Rome, 1984
192. Guzzo, P. G. *I Brettii. Storia e archeologia della Calabria preromana.* Milan, 1989
193. Guzzo, P. G. and Luppino, S. 'Per l'archeologia dei Brezi; due tombe fra Thurii e Crotone', *MEFRA* 92 (1980) 821–914
194. Hackforth, R. 'Southern Italy', in *CAH* VI¹ (1927) 299–301
195. Hinrichs, F. T. 'Hermokrates bei Thukydides', *Hermes* 109 (1981) 46–59
196. Hoffman, W. 'Der Kampf zwischen Rom und Tarent im Urteil der antike Überlieferung', *Hermes* 71 (1936) 11–24
197. Holm, A. *Geschichte Siziliens im Altertum* I–II. Leipzig, 1870–98
198. Höricht, L. A. Scatozza. *Le terracotte figurate di Cuma.* Rome, 1987
199. Hüttl, W. *Verfassungsgeschichte von Syrakus.* Prague, 1929
200. Jenkins, G. K. *Coins of Greek Sicily.* London, 1966
201. Jenkins, G. K. 'Coins of Punic Sicily', *Schweiz. Num. Rundschau* 50 (1971) 25–78, 53 (1974) 23–41, 56 (1977) 5–65, 57 (1978) 5–68
202. Jenkins, G. K. *The Coinage of Gela.* London, 1972
203. Jenkins, G. K. 'The coinages of Enna, Galaria, Piakos, Imachara, Kephaloidion and Longane', in *Le emissioni dei centri siculi fino all'epocha di Timoleonte e i loro rapporti con la monetazione delle colonie greche di Sicilia* (suppl. to *AIIN* 20 (1975)) 77–103
204. Johannowsky, W. 'Nuove tombe dipinte campane', in G 107, 375–82
205. Johannowsky, W. 'Pontecagnano', *Stud. Etr.* 49 (1981) 513
206. Knoepfler, D. 'La Sicile occidentale entre Carthage et Rome à la lumière des nouvelles inscriptions grecques d'Entella', *Annales de l'Université de Neuchâtel, 1985/1986* (1987) 4–27
207. La Regina, A. 'Appunti su entità etniche e strutture istituzionali nel Sannio antico', *AION* 3 (1981) 129–37
208. Lamboley, J.-L. 'Tarente et les Messapians: à propos de Strabon 6, 3, 4 (C281)', *MEFRA* 95 (1983) 523–33
209. Landi, A. *Dialetti e interazione sociale in Magna Grecia*, Naples, 1979
210. Lawrence, A. W. 'Archimedes and the design of Euryalus Fort', *JHS* 66 (1946) 99–107

211. Lazzeroni, R. 'Contatti di lingue e culture nell'Italia antica. Modelli egemoni e modelli subordinati nelle iscrizioni osche in grafia greca', *AION (Ling.)* 5 (1983) 171ff

212. Lepore, E. 'Per la storia economico-sociale di Neapolis', *PP* 7 (1952) 300–32

213. Lepore, E. 'La tradizione antica sui lucani e le origine dell'entità regionale', in G 119, 43–58

214. Lepore, E. 'Società indigena e influenza esterne con particolare riguardo all'influenze greca', in G 139, 317–24

215. Lepore, E. 'La tradizione antica sul mondo osco e la formazione storica delle entità regionali in Italia meridionale', in Campanile, E. (ed.) *Lingua e cultura degli Oschi*, 59ff. Pisa, 1985

216. Lipinsky, A. 'La corona votiva aurea da Armento', in G 119, 59–98

217. Littman, R. 'The plague at Syracuse in 396 B.C.', *Mnemosyne* 37 (1984) 110–16

218. Lo Porto, F. 'Topografia antica di Taranto', in G 106, 343–83

219. Lombardo, M. 'La Magna Grecia dalla fine del V secolo a.C. alla conquista romana', in G 269, 55–88

220. Macaluso, R. 'Monete a leggenda KAINON', in Φιλίας χάριν, *Miscellanea in honore di Eugenio Manni* IV, 1363–74, Rome, 1979

221. Maddoli, G. F. 'Megale Hellas; genesi di un concetto e realtà storico-politiche', in G 110, 9–33

222. Mambella, R. 'Su di un iscrizione vascolare', *Stud. Etr.* 52 (1986) 171–81

223. Manni, E. 'Alessandro il Molosso e la sua spedizione in Italia', *Studi Salentine* 14 (1962) 344–52

224. Manni, E. 'Sulla costituzione siracusana nel tempo di Timoleonte', in *Sodalitas. Scritti . . . A. Guarino* (Naples, 1985) I, 11–19

225. Manni, E. *et al.* 'I Cartaginesi in Sicilia all'epocha dei due Dionisi', *KOKALOS* 28–9 (1982–3) 127–277

226. Mazzei, M. 'Apri preromana e romana. I dati archeologici: analisi e proposte di interpretazione', *Taras* 6–7 (1984) 37–40

227. Mazzei, M. 'Nota su un gruppo di vasi policromi . . . da Arpi', *AION* 9 (1987) [1988] 167–88

228. Meister, K. 'Agathocles', in *CAH* VII².1 (1984) 384–411

229. Mele, A. 'I pitagorici ed Archita', in *Storia della società italiana* I, 272–84. Milan, 1981

230. Mele, A. 'Il pitagorismo e le popolazioni anelleniche di Italia', *AION* 3 (1981) 61–96

231. Mele, A. 'La Megale Hellas pitagorica: aspetti politici, economici e sociali', in G 110, 33–79

232. Mele, A. 'Crotone e la sua storia', in G 111, 9–87

233. Meloni, P. 'La contesa fra Taranto e Turi', *Rend. Linc.* 11–12 (1950) 591–3

234. Minar, E. L. *Early Pythagorean Politics*. Baltimore, 1942

235. Moretti, L. 'Problemi di storia tarantina', in G 106, 21–65

236. Musti, D. 'Problemi della storia di Locri Epizefirii', in G 109, 23–145

237. Musti, D. 'Il processo di formazione e diffusione delle tradizioni greche sui Daunii e su Diomede', in G 139, 93–111

238. Musti, D. 'La nozione storica di Sanniti nelle fonti greche e romane', in G 285, 73ff

239. Musti, D. *Strabone e la Magna Grecia*. Padua, 1988

240. Musti, D. 'Pitagorismo, storiografia e politica tra Magna Grecia e Sicilia', in G 131, 13–56

241. Mustilli, D. 'Civiltà della Magna Grecia', in G 105, 5–47

242. Nenci, G. 'Il problema storico di Cavallino', in Pancrazzi, O. (ed.) *Cavallino*, 9–50 (=Università di Lecce, Collana dell'Istituto di Archeologia e storia antica 2). 1979

243. Nenci, G. 'I rapporti fra la Daunia e il noto della Puglia fino alla romanizzazione', in G 139, 201–11

244. Niese, B. 'Dionysios' in *RE* 5A (1905) cols. 882–904

245. Nissen, H. *Italische Landeskunde*. 2 vols. Berlin, 1883–1902

246. Orlandini, P. 'La rinascità della Sicilia nell'età di Timoleonte alla luce della nuove scoperte archeologiche', *KOKALOS* 4 (1958) 24–30

247. Orth, W. 'Der Syrakusaner Herakleides als Politiker', *Historia* 28 (1979) 51–64

248. Pais, E. 'La spedizione di Alessandro il Molosse in Italia', in *Ricerche storiche e geografiche sull'Italia antica*, 135–98. Turin, 1908

249. Pareti, L. *Studi Siciliani ed Italioti*. Florence, 1914

250. Parlangeli, O. *Le iscrizione messapiche del Museo Provinciale Castromediano di Lecce*. 1970

250A. Parlangeli, O. and Santoro, C. 'I Messapi' in Prosdocimi, A. L. (ed.), *Lingue e dialetti* (Popoli e civiltà dell'Italia antica 6), 917–47. Rome, 1978

251. Pedley, J. G. *Paestum*. London, 1990

252. Penney, J. H. W. 'The languages of Italy', in *CAH* IV² (1988) ch. 15

253. Pisani, V. 'Ricognizioni osche e messapiche', in G 107, 107–24

254. Poccetti, P. 'Nomi di lingua e nomi di popolo nell'Italia antica tra etnografia, glossografia e retorica', *AION (Ling.)* 6 (1984) 160ff

255. Poccetti, P. *Per un identità culturale dei Brettii*. Naples, 1988

256. Poccetti, P. 'Le popolazioni anelleniche d'Italia tra Sicilia e Magna Grecia nel IV sec. a. Cr.', in G 131, 97–135

257. Pontrandolfo Greco, A. 'Segni di trasformazione sociale a Poseidonia tra la fine del V e gli inizi del III sec. a.C.', *Dial. di Arch.* 2 (1979) 27–50

258. Pontrandolfo Greco, A. *I Lucani. Etnografia e archeologia di una regione antica*. Milan, 1982

259. Pontrandolfo Greco, A. and Rouveret, A. 'Ideologia funeraria e società a Poseidonia nel IV sec a.C.', in *La mort, les morts dans les sociétés anciennes*, 299–31. Cambridge, 1982

260. Prosdocimi, A. 'Il conflitto delle lingue: per una applicazione della sociolinguistica al mondo antico', in G 108, 139–221

261. Prosdocimi, A. 'Sui grecismi nel Osco' in *Scritti in onore di Giuliano Bonfante*, 801–66. Brescia, 1976

262. Pugliese Carratelli, G. 'Per la storia dei culti di Taranto', in G 106, 133–46

263. Pugliese Carratelli, G. 'Samniti, Lucani, Brettii e Italioti dal secolo IV a.c.', in G 107, 37–54 (with preceding bibliography)

264. Pugliese Carratelli, G. 'Un nuovo testo orfico', *PP* 29 (1974) 108–26

265. Pugliese Carratelli, G. 'Ancora sulla lamina orfica di Hipponion', *PP* 31

(1976) 458–66
266. Pugliese Carratelli, G. 'Storia civile' in G 267, 5–104
267. Pugliese Carratelli, G. (ed.) *Megale Hellas, storia e civiltà della Magna Grecia.* Milan, 1983
268. Pugliese Carratelli, G. (ed.) *Sikanie. Storia e civiltà della Sicilia greca.* Milan, 1985
269. Pugliese Carratelli, G. (ed.) *Magna Grecia, lo sviluppo politico, sociale ed economico.* Milan, 1987
270. Quilici, L., Quilici Gigli, S. and Pala, C. *Carta archeologica della piana di Sibari* (= *Atti e Mem. Soc. Mag. Gr.* IX–X (1968–9)) 91–155. Rome, 1969
271. Raccuia, C. 'Messana, Rhegion e Dionisio I del 404 al 398', *Riv. stor. ant.* 11 (1981) 15–32
272. Rallo, A. 'L'abitato di Selinunte: il quartiere punico e la sua necropoli', *KOKALOS* 28–9 (1982–3) 169–77
273. Rallo, A. 'Nuovi aspetti dell'urbanistica selinuntina', *ASAA* 62 (1984 (1988)) 81–96
274. Ridgway, D. 'Archaeology in South Italy 1977–82', *AR* 28 (1982) 63–83
275. Ridgway, D. 'Archaeology in Sardinia and South Italy 1983–8', *AR* 35 (1989) 130–47
276. Rouveret, A. *Guerres et sociétés en Italie, 5me–4me siècle av. J.-C.* Paris, 1986
277. Sabbatini, C. 'Aspetti della politica di Dionisio in Italia: note sul testo diodoreo', *Riv. stor. ant.* 16 (1986) [1988] 31–48
278. Sabbatini, C. 'Diodoro, Turi, gli Italioti e la battaglia di Laos', *Riv. stor. ant.* 17–18 (1987–8) [1989] 7–37
279. Salmon, E. T. *Samnium and the Samnites.* Cambridge, 1967
280. Salmon, E. T. *The Making of Roman Italy.* London, 1982
281. Salmon, E. T. 'The Iron Age: The peoples of Italy', in *CAH* IV² (1988) ch. 14
282. Sanders, L. J. 'Dionysius I of Syracuse and the validity of the hostile tradition', *SCI* 5 (1979/80) 64–84
283. Sanders, L. J. *Dionysius I of Syracuse and Greek Tyranny.* London–New York–Sydney, 1987
284. *Sannio: Pentri e Frentani dal VI al I sec. a.C.* (Exhibition catalogue). 1980
285. *Sannio: Pentri e Frentani dal VI al I sec. a.C., Atti Convegno 1980.* Matrice, 1984
286. Santoro, C. 'Il dunastes dei Messapi Arta e la spedizione degli Ateniesi in Sicilia', in *Studi di storia pugliese in onore di G. Chiarelli*, 31–60. 1972
287. Santoro, C. 'La situazione storico-linguistica della Peucezia preromana alla luce di nuovi documenti', in Santoro, C. and Marangio, C. (eds.) *Studi storico-linguistici in onore di Francesco Ribezzo*, 219–330. Mesague, 1978
288. Sartori, F. 'Sulla δυναστεία di Dionisio il Vecchio nell'opera Diodorea', *Critica Storica* 5 (1966) 3–66
289. Seibert, J. 'Die Bevölkerungs Fluktuation in den Griechenstädten Siziliens', *AncSoc* 13–14 (1982–3) 33–65
290. Small, A. *Monte Irsi* (= BAR Suppl. 20). Oxford, 1977
291. Sordi, M. *I rapporti romano-ceriti e le origini della civitas sine suffragio.* Rome, 1960

292. Sordi, M. *Timoleonte*. Palermo, 1961
293. Sordi, M. *Roma e i Sanniti nel IV sec. a.C.* Bologna, 1969 (reviewed by Pinsent, J., *JRS* 61 (1971) 271–2)
294. Sordi, M. 'Dionigi I e Platone' in Φιλίας χάριν, *Miscellanea in honore di Eugenio Manni* VI, 2013–22. Rome, 1979
295. Sordi, M. 'I rapporti fra Dionigi I e Cartagine fra la pace del 405/4 e quella del 392/1', *Aevum* 54 (1980) 22–34
296. Sordi, M. 'Il IV e III secolo da Dionigi I a Timoleone', in G 175, II 1, 207–88
297. Sordi, M. 'Ermocrate di Siracusa, demagogo e tiranno mancato', in *Scritti sul mondo antico in memoria di Fulvio Grosso*, 595–600. Rome, 1981
298. Sordi, M. *La Sicilia dal 368/7 al 337/6*. Rome, 1983
299. Sprute, J. 'Dions syrakusanische Politik und die politischen Ideale Platons', *Hermes* 100 (1972) 294–313
300. Stazio, A. 'Moneta e scambi', in G 267, 105–72
301. Stroheker, K. F. 'Platon und Dionysios', *Hist. Zeitschr.* 179 (1952) 225–59
302. Stroheker, K. F. *Dionysios I: Gestalt und Geschichte des Tyrannen von Syrakus*. Wiesbaden, 1958
303. Tagliamonte, G. 'Alcune considerazioni sull'istituto italico della vereiia', *PP* 44 (1989) 361–76
304. Talbert, R. J. A. *Timoleon and the Revival of Greek Sicily 344–317 B.C.* Cambridge, 1974
305. Thesleff, H. 'Okellos, Archytas and Plato', *Eranos* 60 (1962) 5ff
306. Torelli, M. 'Contributo dell'archeologia alla storia sociale: l'Etruria e l'Apulia', *Dial. di Arch.* 4–5 (1970–1) 439ff
307. Torelli, M. *Elogia Tarquiniensia*. Florence, 1975
308. Torelli, M. 'Aspetti storico-archeologici della romanizzazione della Daunia', in G 139, 325–40
309. Toynbee, A. *Hannibal's Legacy*. London, 1965
310. Tréziny, H. 'Main d'oeuvre indigène et hellénisation: le problème des fortifications lucaniennes', in *Architecture et société de l'archaisme grec à la fin de la république romaine*, 105–118 (= *Coll. Ec. Fr. Rome* 66). Paris, 1983
311. Tusa, V. 'L'attività della Soprintendenza archeologico della Sicilia occidentale nel quadrennio maggio 1980–aprile 1984', *KOKALOS* 30–1 (1984–5) 539–610
312. Tusa, V. 'The Punics in Sicily', in F 304, 186–205
313. Tusa Cutroni, A. 'La monetazione di Siracusa sotto Dionisio I', in Φιλίας χάριν, *Miscellanea in honore di Eugenio Manni*, II, 629–48. Rome, 1979
314. Tusa Cutroni, A. 'Rapporti tra greci e punici in Sicilia attraverso l'evidenza numismatica', in G 4, 135–43
315. Tusa Cutroni, A. 'Recenti soluzioni e nuovi problemi sulla monetazione punica della Sicilia', *R. Stud. Fen.* 11.2 (1983) 37–42
316. Uguzzoni, A. and Ghinatti, F. *Le tavole greche di Eraclea*. Rome, 1968
317. Vattuone, R. 'Atene ed i Siculi nel 415 a.c. Nota a Thuc. VI.88', *Riv. Stor. ant.* 9 (1979) 1–9
318. Vattuone, R. 'Linee della politica di Agatocle in Magna Grecia', *Riv. stor. ant.* 17–18 (1987–8) [1989] 55–72

319.   Vetter, E. *Handbuch der italischen Dialekte*. Heidelberg, 1953
320.   Voit, L. 'Zur Dion-Vita', *Historia* 3 (1954–55) 171–92
321.   Westlake, H. D. *Timoleon and his Relations with Tyrants*. Manchester, 1952
322.   Westlake, H. D. 'Hermocrates the Syracusan', *Bulletin of the John Rylands Library* 41 (1958–9) 239–68 (= A 62, 174–202)
323.   Westlake, H. D. 'Friends and successors of Dion', *Historia* 32 (1983) 161–72
324.   Whitaker, J. A. S. *Motya*. London, 1921
325.   Woodhead, A. G. 'The "Adriatic Empire" of Dionysius I of Syracuse', *Klio* 52 (1970) 503–12
326.   Wuilleumier, P. *Tarente des origines à la conquête romaine*. Paris, 1939; repr. 1968

H. GREEK CULTURE AND SCIENCE

I. PHILOSOPHY, RHETORIC AND RELIGION

1.   Barnes, J., Schofield, M. and Sorabji, R. (eds.) *Articles on Aristotle*. 4 vols. 1: *Science*, 2: *Ethics and Politics*, 3: *Metaphysics*, 4: *Psychology and Aesthetics*. London, 1975–79
2.   Baynes, N. H. 'Isocrates', in *id., Byzantine Studies and Other Essays*, 144–67. London, 1955
3.   Berti, E. *La filosofia di primo Aristotele*. Padova, 1962
4.   Bignone, E. *L'Aristotele perduto e la formazione filosofica di Epicuro*. Florence, 1936
5.   Blass, F. *Die attische Beredsamkeit*. 2nd edn. 3 vols in 4. Leipzig, 1887–98
6.   Bowen, A. C. and Goldstein, B. R. 'Meton of Athens and astronomy in the late fifth century B.C.' in Leichty, E. and others (eds.), *A Scientific Humanist, Studies in Memory of Abraham Sachs* (Occasional Publications of the S. N. Kramer Fund 9), 39–81. Philadelphia, 1988
7.   Bremmer, J. (ed.) *Interpretations of Greek Mythology*. London–Sydney, 1987
8.   Bringmann, K. *Studien zu den politischen Ideen des Isokrates* (Hypomnemata 14). Göttingen, 1965
9.   Brink, K. O. 'Peripatos', *RE* Suppl. 7 (1940) cols. 899–949
10.   Bulmer-Thomas, I. 'Theaetetus', in *Dictionary of Scientific Biography*, XIII, 301–7. New York, 1976
11.   Cartledge, P. A. 'Yes, Spartan kings were heroized', *LCM* 13.3 (1988) 43–4
12.   Cherniss, H. *Aristotle's Criticism of Plato and the Academy*. Baltimore, 1944
13.   Cherniss, H. *The Riddle of the Early Academy*. Berkeley–Los Angeles, 1945
14.   Cherniss, H. 'The relation of the Timaeus to Plato's later dialogues', *AJP* 78 (1957) 225–66
15.   Cherniss, H. 'Timaeus 38A8–B5', *JHS* 77 (1957) 18–23
16.   Chroust, A.-H. 'What prompted Aristotle to address the Protrepticus to Themison of Cyprus?' *Hermes* 94 (1966) 202–7

17. Chroust, A.-H. 'Aristotle returns to Athens in the year 335/4 B.C.', *Laval Théologique et Philosophique* 23 (1967) 244–54
18. Chroust, A.-H. 'Plato's Academy: the first organized school of political science in antiquity', *Review of Politics* 29 (1967) 25–40
19. Chroust, A.-H. 'Speusippus succeeds Plato in the scholarchate of the Academy', *REG* 84 (1971) 170–6
20. Chroust, A.-H. *Aristotle: New Light on His Life and on Some of His Lost Works.* Notre Dame–London, 1973
21. Connors, R. J. 'Greek rhetoric and the transition from orality', *Philosophy and Rhetoric* 19 (1986) 38–65
22. Cornford, F. M. *Plato's Theory of Knowledge.* London, 1935
23. Cornford, F. M. *Plato's Cosmology.* London, 1937
24. Cornford, F. M. *Plato and Parmenides.* London, 1939
25. Decleva Caizzi, F. 'Antistene', *Studi Urbinati* n.s.B. 1–2 (1964), 48–99
26. Decleva Caizzi, F. *Antisthenis Fragmenta.* Varese–Milan, 1966
27. Decleva Caizzi, F. *Pirrone: Testimonianze.* Naples, 1981
28. Dihle, A. 'Das Satyrspiel "Sisyphos"', *Hermes* 105 (1977) 28–42
29. Dobesch, G. *Der panhellenische Gedanke im 4. Jh. v. Chr. und der 'Philippos' des Isokrates.* Vienna, 1968
30. Dodds, E. R. *The Greeks and the Irrational.* Berkeley–Los Angeles, 1951
31. Döring, K. *Die Megariker. Kommentierte Sammlung der Testimonien.* Amsterdam, 1972
32. Dover, K. J. *Greek Popular Morality in the Time of Plato and Aristotle.* Oxford, 1974
33. Düring, I. 'Notes on the history of the transmission of Aristotle's writings', *Göteborgs Högskolas Årsskrift* 56 (1950) 37–70
34. Düring, I. (ed.) *Chion of Heraclea.* Göteborg, 1951
35. Düring, I. 'Aristotle the scholar', *Arctos.* Acta Philologica Fennica, n.s. 1 (1954) 61–77
36. Düring, I. *Aristotle in the Ancient Biographical Tradition.* Göteborg, 1957
36A. Düring, I. *Aristotle's Protrepticus: An Attempt at Reconstruction.* Göteborg, 1961
37. Düring, I. *Aristoteles: Darstellung und Interpretation seines Denkens.* Heidelberg, 1966
38. Edelstein, L. *Plato's Seventh Letter.* Leiden, 1966
39. Eucken, C. *Isokrates. Seine Positionen in der Auseinandersetzung mit den zeitgenössischen Philosophen.* Berlin–New York, 1983
40. Fontenrose, J. *The Delphic Oracle.* Berkeley, 1978
41. Fowler, D. H. *The Mathematics of Plato's Academy. A New Reconstruction.* Oxford, 1987
42. von Fritz, K. 'Philippos (42) von Opus', *RE* 19 (1938) coll. 2351–66
43. von Fritz, K. *Platon in Sizilien und das Problem der Philosophenherrschaft.* Berlin, 1968
44. Fuks, A. 'Plato and the social question: the problem of poverty and riches in the *Republic*', *AncSoc* 8 (1977) 49–83 (= c 23, 80–114)
45. Fuks, A. 'Plato and the social question: the problem of poverty and riches in the *Laws*', *AncSoc* 10 (1979) 33–78 (= c 23, 126–71)

46. Gaiser, K. *Platons ungeschriebene Lehre. Studien zur systematischen und geschichtlichen Begründung der Wissenschaften in der platonischen Schule.* Stuttgart, 1963

47. Gaiser, K. 'Die Elegie des Aristoteles an Eudemos', *Mus. Helv.* 23 (1966) 84–106

48. Gaiser, K. 'Plato's enigmatic lecture "On the Good"', *Phronesis* 25 (1980) 5–37

49. Gaiser, K. *Theophrast in Assos. Zur Entwicklung der Naturwissenschaft zwischen Akademie und Peripatos* (Abh. Heidelb. Akad. d. Wiss. Philos.– hist. Kl. 3). Heidelberg, 1985

50. Gaiser, K. *Philodems Academica. Die Berichte über Platon und die Alte Akademie in zwei herkulanensischen Papyri* (Supplementum Platonicum I). Stuttgart–Bad Cannstatt, 1988

51. Gehrke, H.-J. 'Die klassische Polisgesellschaft in der Perspektive griechischer Philosophen', *Saeculum* 36 (1985) 133–50

52. Giannantoni, G. *Socraticorum Reliquiae.* 4 vols. Naples, 1983–5

53. Gottschalk, H. B. 'Notes on the wills of the Peripatetic scholarchs', *Hermes* 100 (1972) 314–42

54. Gottschalk, H. B. *Heraclides of Pontus.* Oxford, 1980

55. Günther, W. *Das Orakel von Didyma in hellenistischer Zeit* (*Ist. Mitt.* Beih. 4). Tübingen, 1971

56. Guthrie, W. K. C. *A History of Greek Philosophy.* 6 vols. Cambridge, 1962–81

57. Habicht, C. *Hellenistic Athens and Her Philosophers* (David Magie Lecture 1988). Princeton, 1988

58. Harding, P. 'The purpose of Isokrates' *Archidamos* and *On the Peace*', *CSCA* 6 (1973) 137–49

59. Howland, R. L. 'The attack on Isocrates in the *Phaedrus*', *CQ* 31 (1937) 151–9

60. Huxley, G. L. 'Studies in the Greek astronomers', *GRBS* 4 (1963) 83–96

61. Huxley, G. L. 'Eudoxus of Cnidus', in *Dictionary of Scientific Biography*, IV (1971) 465–7

62. Huxley, G. L. *On Aristotle and Greek Society.* Belfast, 1979

63. Isnardi Parente, M. *Speusippo: Frammenti.* Naples, 1980

64. Isnardi Parente, M. *Senocrate–Ermodoro: Frammenti.* Naples, 1982

65. Jaeger, W. 'Aristotle's verses in praise of Plato', *CQ* 21 (1927) 13–17

66. Jaeger, W. *Paideia: the Ideals of Greek Culture*, trans. G. Highet. Oxford, I⁴ 1954, II and III 1943–4

67. Jaeger, W. *Aristotle: Fundamentals of the History of His Development.* Trans. by R. Robinson. 2nd edn. Oxford, 1948

68. Johnson, R. 'A note on the number of Isocrates' pupils', *AJP* 78 (1957) 296–300

69. Kahn, C. H. 'Did Plato write Socratic dialogues?', *CQ* n.s. 31 (1981) 305–20

70. Kahn, C. H. 'On the relative date of the Gorgias and the Protagoras', *Oxford Studies in Ancient Philosophy* 6 (1988) 69–102

71. Kapp, E. 'The Theory of Ideas in Plato's earlier dialogues', *Ausgewählte Schriften*, 55–150. Berlin, 1968

72. Kessler, J. *Isokrates und die panhellenische Idee.* Paderborn, 1911
73. Krämer, H. J. *Arete bei Platon und Aristoteles. Zum Wesen und zur Geschichte der platonischen Ontologie* (Abh. Heidelb. Akad. d. Wiss., Philos.–hist. Kl. 959. 6). Heidelberg, 1959
74. Lasserre, F. *Die Fragmente des Eudoxos von Knidos.* Berlin, 1966
75. Lasserre, F. *De Léodamas de Thasos à Philippe d'Oponte.* Naples, 1987
76. Lynch, J. P. *Aristotle's School. A Study of a Greek Educational Institution.* Berkeley–Los Angeles–London, 1972
77. Mannebach, E. *Aristippi et Cyrenaicorum Fragmenta.* Leiden–Cologne, 1961
78. Marrou, H. I. *A History of Education in Antiquity.* Trans. by G. Lamb. London–New York, 1956
79. Mejer, J. *Diogenes Laertius and his Hellenistic Background.* (*Hermes* Einzelschrift 40). Wiesbaden, 1978
80. Mekler, S. (ed.) *Academicorum Philosophorum Index Herculanensis.* Berlin, 1902; repr. 1958
81. Merlan, P. 'The successor of Speusippus', *TAPA* 79 (1946) 103–11
82. Merlan, P. 'The life of Eudoxus', *Studies in Epicurus and Aristotle.* Wiesbaden, 1960
83. Mikkola, E. *Isokrates. Seine Anschauungen im Lichte seiner Schriften* (Annales Academiae Scientiarum Fennicae. Ser. B. vol. 89). Helsinki, 1954
84. Moraux, P. *Les listes anciennes des ouvrages d'Aristote.* Louvain, 1951
85. Morrow, G. R. *Plato's Epistles.* Revised edn. Indianapolis, 1962
86. Mulvany, C. M. 'Notes on the legend of Aristotle', *CQ* 20 (1926) 155–68
87. Neugebauer, O. *A History of Ancient Mathematical Astronomy* (Studies in the History of Mathematics and Physical Sciences 1). Berlin–Heidelberg–New York, 1975
88. Newman, W. L. *The Politics of Aristotle.* 4 vols. Oxford, 1887
89. Owen, G. E. L. 'The place of the Timaeus in Plato's dialogues', *CQ* n.s. 3 (1953) 79–95
90. Parke, H. W. and Wormell, D. E. W. *The Delphic Oracle,* I–II. Oxford, 1956
91. Parker, R. C. T. *Miasma.* Oxford, 1983
92. Parker, R. 'Were Spartan kings heroized?', *LCM* 13.1 (1988) 9–10
93. Patzer, A. *Bibliographica Socratica. Die wissenschaftliche Literatur über Sokrates von den Anfängen bis auf die neueste Zeit in systematisch-chronologischer Anordnung.* Freiburg–Munich, 1985
94. Pickard-Cambridge, A. W., rev. Gould, J. P. A. and Lewis, D. M. *The Dramatic Festivals of Athens.* Oxford, 1968 (Reprinted with additions, 1988)
95. Plezia, M. *Aristoteles: Privatorum Scriptorum Fragmenta.* Leipzig, 1977
96. Regenbogen, O. 'Theophrastos', *RE* Suppl. 7 (1940) cols. 1354–562
97. Rice, D. G. and Stambaugh, J. E. *Sources for the Study of Greek Religion.* Williamstown, 1979
98. Riginos, A. S. *Platonica: The Anecdotes concerning the Life and Writings of Plato.* Leiden, 1976
99. Rist, J. M. *The Mind of Aristotle.* Toronto, 1989

100. Ross, W. D. (ed.) *The Works of Aristotle Translated into English*, XII: *Select Fragments*. Oxford, 1952

101. Rossetti, L. '"Socratica" in Fedone di Elide', *Studi Urbinati* 47 (1973) 364–81

102. Russell, D. *Greek Declamation*. Oxford, 1983

103. Sarton, G. *A History of Science: Ancient Science through the Golden Age of Greece*. Cambridge, MA, 1952

104. Seck, F. (ed.) *Isokrates* (Wege der Forschung 351). Darmstadt, 1976

105. Seck, F. 'Die Komposition des "Panegyrikos"', in H 104, 353–70

106. von Straten, F. T. 'Did the Greeks kneel before their gods?', *Bulletin Antieke Beschaving* 49 (1974) 159–89

107. Szlezák, T. A. *Platon und die Schriftlichkeit der Philosophie: Interpretationen zu den frühen und mittleren Dialogen*. Berlin, 1985

108. Tarán, L. *Academica: Plato, Philip of Opus, and the Pseudo-Platonic Epinomis*. Philadelphia, 1972

109. Tarán, L. *Speusippus of Athens*. Leiden, 1981

110. Thesleff, H. *Studies in Platonic Chronology*. (Commentationes Humanarum Litterarum 70). Helsinki, 1982

111. van Groningen, B. A. *Aristote. Le Second Livre de l'Economique*. Leiden, 1933

112. Vlastos, G. (ed.) *The Philosophy of Socrates*. New York, 1971

113. de Vries, G. J. *A Commentary on the Phaedrus of Plato*. Amsterdam, 1969

114. Walzer, R. 'Fragmenta graeca in litteris arabicis', *Journal of the Royal Asiatic Society* (1939) 414–22

115. Wehrli, F. *Aristoxenos*. Basel, 1945

115A. Wehrli, F. *Die Schule des Aristoteles*. 10 vols. Basel, 1944–59 (2nd edn 1967–9)

116. West, M. L. *Early Greek Philosophy and the Orient*. Oxford, 1971

117. Westerink, L. G. (ed.) *Anonymous Prolegomena to Platonic Philosophy*. Amsterdam, 1962

118. Whitehead, D. 'Aristotle the Metic', *PCPhS* 201 (1975) 94–9

119. Whitehead, D. 'Xenocrates the Metic', *Rh. Mus.* 124 (1981) 235–8

120. Wilamowitz, U. *Platon*. Berlin, 1920

121. Wilcox, S. 'The scope of early rhetorical instruction', *HSCP* 53 (1942) 121–55

122. Wilcox, S. 'Isocrates' fellow-rhetoricians', *AJP* 66 (1945) 171–86

123. Wörle, A, *Die Politische Tätigkeit der Schüler Platons*. Darmstadt, 1981

124. Wormell, D. E. W. 'The literary tradition concerning Hermias of Atarneus', *YCS* 5 (1935) 57–92

II. MEDICINE

125. Artelt, W. *Studien zur Geschichte der Begriffe 'Heilmittel' und 'Gift'*. Leipzig, 1937

126. Baader, G. and Winau, R. (eds.) *Die hippokratischen Epidemien* (Sudhoffs Archiv Beiheft 27). Stuttgart, 1989

127. Bourgey, L. *Observation et expérience chez les médecins de la collection hippocratique*. Paris, 1953

128. Bourgey, L. and Jouanna, J. (eds.) *La collection hippocratique et son rôle dans l'histoire de la médecine*. Leiden, 1975

129. Breasted, J. H. *The Edwin Smith Surgical Papyrus*. 2 vols. Chicago, 1930

130. Cambiano, G. 'Dialettica, medicina, retorica nel "Fedro" platonico', *Rivista di Filosofia* 57 (1966) 284–305

131. Cambiano, G. 'Patologia e metafora politica: Alcmeone, Platone, *Corpus Hippocraticum*', *Elenchos* 3 (1982) 219–36

132. Campese, S., Manuli, P. and Sissa, G. *Madre materia*. Turin, 1983

133. Cohn-Haft, L. *The Public Physicians of Ancient Greece* (Smith College Studies in History 42). Northampton, MA, 1956

134. Deichgräber, K. *Die Epidemien und das Corpus Hippocraticum* (Abh. d. Preuss. Akad. d. Wiss., Jahrgang 1933, 3, phil.-hist. kl.). Berlin, 1933

135. Deichgräber, K. 'Die ärztliche Standesethik des hippokratischen Eides', *Quellen und Studien zur Geschichte der Naturwissenschaften und der Medizin* 3, 2 (1933) 79–99

136. Deichgräber, K. *Hippokrates, Über Entstehung und Aufbau des menschlichen Körpers* (Περὶ σαρκῶν). Leipzig, 1935

137. Deichgräber, K. *Pseudhippokrates Über die Nahrung* (Abh. Ak. Mainz, Jahrgang 1973, 3). Wiesbaden, 1973

138. Delatte, A. *Herbarius: Recherches sur le cérémonial usité chez les anciens pour la cueillette des simples et des plantes magiques* (Académie Royale de Belgique, Mémoires de la Classe des Lettres, 2nd ser. 54, 4, 3rd edn). Brussels, 1961

139. Di Benedetto, V. 'Cos e Cnido', in *Hippocratica* (ed. M. D. Grmek), 97–111. Paris, 1980

140. Di Benedetto, V. *Il medico e la malattia*. Turin, 1986

141. Diepgen, P. *Die Frauenheilkunde der alten Welt*. Munich, 1937

142. Diller, H. *Wanderarzt und Aitiologe* (*Philologus* Suppl. Bd. 26, 3). Leipzig, 1934

143. Diller, H. 'Ausdrucksformen des methodischen Bewusstseins in den hippokratischen Epidemien' (*Archiv für Begriffsgeschichte* 9 (1964) 133–50), in H 145, 106–23

144. Diller, H. 'Eine stoisch-pneumatische Schrift im Corpus Hippocraticum' (*Sudhoffs Archiv für Geschichte der Medizin und der Naturwissenschaften* 29 (1936–7) 178–95), in H 145, 17–30

145. Diller, H. *Kleine Schriften zur antiken Medizin*. Berlin, 1973

146. Ducatillon, J. *Polémiques dans la collection hippocratique*. Lille, 1977

147. Duminil, M.-P. *Le sang, les vaisseaux, le coeur dans la collection hippocratique*. Paris, 1983

148. Ebbell, B. *The Papyrus Ebers*. Copenhagen–London, 1937

149. Edelstein, E. J. and Edelstein, L. *Asclepius*. 2 vols. Baltimore, 1945

150. Edelstein, L. *ΠΕΡΙ ΑΕΡΩΝ und die Sammlung der hippokratischen Schriften* (Problemata 4). Berlin, 1931

151. Edelstein, L. 'Greek medicine in its relation to religion and magic', *Bulletin of the Institute of the History of Medicine* 5 (1937) 201–46 in H 152, 205–46

152. Edelstein, L. *Ancient Medicine* (eds. O. and C. L. Temkin). Baltimore, 1967

153. Edelstein, L. 'The genuine works of Hippocrates' (*Bulletin of the Institute

of the History of Medicine 7 (1939) 236–48), in H 152, 133–44

154. Edelstein, L. 'The history of anatomy in antiquity' (originally 'Die Geschichte der Sektion in der Antike', *Quellen und Studien zur Geschichte der Naturwissenschaften und der Medizin* 3, 2 (1932–3) 100–56), in H 152, 247–301

155. Festugière, A. J. *Hippocrate, L'Ancienne médecine* (Etudes et Commentaires 4). Paris, 1948

156. Goltz, D. *Studien zur altorientalischen und griechischen Heilkunde, Therapie, Arzneibereitung, Rezeptstruktur* (*Sudhoffs Archiv* Beiheft 16). Wiesbaden, 1974

157. Gomperz, T. *Die Apologie der Heilkunst*. 2nd edn. Leipzig, 1910

158. Gourevitch, D. *Le Triangle hippocratique dans le monde gréco-romaine: le malade, sa maladie et son médecin*. Paris, 1984

159. Grapow, H. *Grundriss der Medizin der alten Ägypter*, 9 vols. Berlin, 1954–73

160. Grensemann, H. *Die hippokratische Schrift 'Über die heilige Krankheit'* (Ars Medica Abt. 2, 1). Berlin, 1968

161. Grensemann, H. *Knidische Medizin*, I (Ars Medica Abt. 2, 4, 1). Berlin, 1975

162. Grensemann, H. *Hippokratische Gynäkologie*. Wiesbaden, 1982

163. Grensemann, H. *Knidische Medizin*, II (*Hermes* Suppl. Bd. 51). Stuttgart, 1987

164. Grmek, M. D. (ed.) *Hippocratica* (Actes du Colloque Hippocratique de Paris). Paris, 1980

165. Grmek, M. D. *Diseases in the Ancient Greek World* (transl. of *Les Maladies à l'aube de la civilisation occidentale*, Paris, 1983). Baltimore, 1989

166. Hanson, A. E. 'Hippocrates: *Diseases of Women* I', *Signs* I, 2 (1975) 567–84

167. Hanson, A. E. 'Diseases of women in the Epidemics', in H 126, 38–51

168. Hanson, A. E. 'The medical writer's woman', in Halperin, D. M., Winkler, J. J. and Zeitlin, F. I. (eds.), *Before Sexuality*, 309–38. Princeton, 1990

169. Harig, G. 'Bemerkungen zum Verhältnis der griechischen zur altorientalischen Medizin', in H 180, 77–94

170. Harig, G. 'Anfänge der theoretischen Pharmakologie im Corpus Hippocraticum', in H 164, 223–45

171. Harig, G. and Kollesch, J. 'Neue Tendenzen in der Forschung zur Geschichte der antiken Medizin', *Philologus* 121 (1977) 114–36

172. Harig, G. and Kollesch, J. 'Der hippokratische Eid. Zur Entstehung der antiken Deontologie', *Philologus* 122 (1978) 157–76

173. Harris, C. R. S. *The Heart and the Vascular System in Ancient Greek Medicine from Alcmaeon to Galen*. Oxford, 1973

174. Heidel, W. A. *Hippocratic Medicine: its Spirit and Method*. New York, 1941

175. Herter, H. 'The problematic mention of Hippocrates in Plato's *Phaedrus*', *Illinois Classical Studies* I (1976) 22–42

176. Herzog, R. *Die Wunderheilungen von Epidauros* (*Philologus* Suppl. Bd. 22, 3). Leipzig, 1931

177. Joly, R. *Recherches sur le traité pseudo-hippocratique Du Régime*

(Bibliothèque de la faculté de philosophie et lettres de l'Université de Liège 156). Paris, 1960

178. Joly, R. *Le niveau de la science hippocratique*. Paris, 1966
179. Joly, R. 'Remarques sur le "De Alimento" pseudo-hippocratique', in Bingen, J., Cambier, G. and Nachtergael, G. (eds.), *Le monde grec. Hommages à Claire Préaux*, 271–6. Brussels, 1975
180. Joly, R. (ed.) *Corpus Hippocraticum* (Actes du Colloque hippocratique de Mons, Editions Universitaires de Mons, Série Sciences Humaines 4). Mons, 1977
181. Joly, R. 'Un peu d'épistémologie historique pour hippocratisants', in H 164, 285–97
182. Joly, R. 'Hippocrates and the School of Cos', in Ruse, M. (ed.), *Nature Animated*, 29–47. Dordrecht, 1983
183. Joly, R. 'Platon, Phèdre et Hippocrate: vingt ans après', in H 202, 407–21
184. Jones, W. H. S. *Philosophy and Medicine in Ancient Greece* (Suppl. to the Bulletin of History of Medicine, 8). Baltimore, 1946
185. Jones, W. H. S. *The Medical Writings of Anonymus Londinensis*. Cambridge, 1947
186. Jouanna, J. *Hippocrate: pour une archéologie de l'école de Cnide*. Paris, 1974
187. Jouanna, J. 'La *Collection Hippocratique* et Platon (*Phèdre*, 269c–272a)', *REG* 90 (1977) 15–28
188. King, H. 'Bound to bleed: Artemis and Greek women', in Cameron, A. and Kuhrt, A., (eds.), *Images of Women in Antiquity*, 109–27. London, 1983
189. King, H. 'The daughter of Leonides: reading the Hippocratic corpus', in Cameron, A. (ed.), *History as Text*, 11–32. London, 1989
190. Knutzen, G. H. *Technologie in den hippokratischen Schriften Περὶ διαίτης ὀξέων, περὶ ἀγμῶν, περὶ ἄρθρων ἐμβολῆς* (Abh. Ak. Mainz 1963, 14). Wiesbaden, 1964
191. Koelbing, H. M. *Arzt und Patient in der antiken Welt*. Zurich–Munich, 1977
192. Kollesch, J. 'Ärztliche Ausbildung in der Antike', *Klio* 61 (1979) 507–13
193. Kudlien, F. *Der Beginn des medizinischen Denkens bei den Griechen*. Zurich–Stuttgart, 1967
194. Kudlien, F. 'Early Greek primitive medicine', *Clio Medica* 3 (1968) 305–36
195. Kudlien, F. 'Antike Anatomie und menschlicher Leichnam', *Hermes* 97 (1969) 78–94
196. Kudlien, F. 'Dialektik und Medizin in der Antike', *Medizinhistorisches Journal* 9 (1974) 187–200
197. Kudlien, F. 'Bemerkungen zu W. D. Smith's These über die knidische Ärzteschule', in H 180, 95–103
198. Kühn, J.-H. *System- und Methodenprobleme im Corpus Hippocraticum* (*Hermes* Einzelschriften 11). Wiesbaden, 1956
199. Laín Entralgo, P. *The Therapy of the Word in Classical Antiquity* (transl. of *La curación por la palabra en la Antigüedad clásica*, Madrid, 1958). New Haven–London, 1970

200. Lanata, G. *Medicina Magica e Religione Popolare in Grecia*. Rome, 1967
201. Langholf, V. *Medical Theories in Hippocrates. Early Texts and the 'Epidemics'* (Untersuchungen zur antiken Literatur und Geschichte 34). Berlin, 1990
202. Lasserre, F. and Mudry, P. (eds.) *Formes de pensée dans la collection hippocratique* (Actes du IVᵉ Colloque International Hippocratique, Lausanne, 1981). Geneva, 1983
203. Lefebure, G. *Essai sur la médecine Egyptienne de l'époque pharaonique*. Paris, 1956
204. Lefkowitz, M. *Heroines and Hysterics*. London, 1981
205. Lesky, E. *Die Zeugungs- und Vererbungslehren der Antike und ihr Nachwirken* (Abh. Ak. Mainz 1950, 19). Wiesbaden, 1951
206. Lichtenthaeler, C. *La médecine hippocratique. 1 Méthode expérimentale et méthode hippocratique*. Lausanne, 1948
207. Lloyd, G. E. R. (ed.) *Hippocratic Writings*. London, 1978
208. Lloyd, G. E. R. *Magic, Reason and Experience*. Cambridge, 1979
209. Lloyd, G. E. R. *Science, Folklore and Ideology*. Cambridge, 1983
210. Lloyd, G. E. R. *The Revolutions of Wisdom*. Berkeley–Los Angeles–London, 1987
211. Lloyd, G. E. R. *Methods and Problems in Greek Science*. Cambridge, 1991
212. Longrigg, J. 'Philosophy and medicine, some early interactions', *HSCP* 67 (1963) 147–75
213. Lonie, I. M. 'The paradoxical text "On the Heart"', *Medical History* 17 (1973) 1–15 and 136–53
214. Lonie, I. M. 'Cos versus Cnidus and the historians', *History of Science* 16 (1978) 42–75 and 77–92
215. Lonie, I. M. *The Hippocratic Treatises 'On Generation' 'On the Nature of the Child' 'Diseases iv'* (Ars Medica Abt. 2, 7). Berlin, 1981
216. Lonie, I. M. 'Literacy and the development of Hippocratic medicine', in H 202, 145–61
217. Mansfeld, J. *The Pseudo-Hippocratic Tract ΠΕΡΙ ΈΒΔΟΜΑΔΩΝ ch. 1–11 and Greek Philosophy*. Assen, 1971
218. Mansfeld, J. 'Alcmaeon: "Physikos" or Physician', in Mansfeld, J. and de Rijk, L. M. (eds.), *Kephalaion*, 26–38. Assen, 1975
219. Mansfeld, J. 'Plato and the method of Hippocrates', *GRBS* 21 (1980) 341–62
220. Mansfeld, J. 'The historical Hippocrates and the origins of scientific medicine', in Ruse, M. (ed.), *Nature Animated*, 49–76. Dordrecht, 1983
221. Manuli, P. 'Fisiologia e patologia del femminile negli scritti ippocratici dell'antica ginecologia greca', in H 164, 393–408
222. Manuli, P. 'Elogio della castità', *Memoria* 3 (1982) 39–49
223. Manuli, P. 'Medico e malattia', in Vegetti, M. (ed.), *Il sapere degli antichi*, 229–45. Turin, 1985
224. Manuli, P. and Vegetti, M. *Cuore, sangue e cervello*. Milan, 1977
225. Michler, M. 'Das Problem der westgriechischen Heilkunde', *Sudhoffs Archiv für Geschichte der Medizin und der Naturwissenschaften* 46 (1962) 137–52
226. Michler, M. 'Die praktische Bedeutung des normativen Physis-Begriffes

in der hippokratischen Schrift De fracturis-De articulis', *Hermes* 60 (1962) 385–401

227. Miller, H. W. '*Dynamis* and *Physis* in *On Ancient Medicine*', *TAPA* 83 (1952) 184–97

228. Miller, H. W. 'The concept of the divine in *De Morbo Sacro*', *TAPA* 84 (1953) 1–15

229. Moulinier, L. *Le pur et l'impur dans la pensée des Grecs d'Homère à Aristote* (Etudes et Commentaires 12). Paris, 1952

230. Müller, C. W. 'Die Heilung "durch das Gleiche" in den hippokratischen Schriften *De morbo sacro* und *De locis in homine*', *Sudhoffs Archiv für Geschichte der Medizin und der Naturwissenschaften* 49 (1965) 225–49

231. Nickel, D. 'Ärztliche Ethik und Schwangerschaftsunterbrechung bei den Hippokratikern', *Schriftenreihe für Geschichte der Naturwissenschaften, Technik und Medizin* 9, 1 (1972) 73–80

232. Nutton, V. 'The seeds of disease: an explanation of contagion and infection from the Greeks to the Renaissance', *Medical History* 27 (1983) 1–34

233. Oppenheim, A. L. 'Mesopotamian medicine', *Bulletin of the History of Medicine* 36 (1962) 97–108

234. Phillips, E. D. *Greek Medicine*. London, 1973

235. Pigeaud, J. M. *Folie et cures de la folie chez les médecins de l'antiquité gréco-romaine*. Paris, 1987

236. Plamböck, G. *Dynamis im Corpus Hippocraticum* (Abh. Ak. Mainz 1964, 2). Wiesbaden, 1964

237. Pohlenz, M. *Hippokrates und die Begründung der wissenschaftlichen Medizin.* Berlin, 1938

237A Potter, P. *Hippocrates* Vols v, vi. Cambridge/London, Loeb edn, 1988

238. Potter, P., Maloney, G. and Desautels, J. (eds.) *La maladie et les maladies dans la collection hippocratique*. Quebec, 1990

239. Roscher, W. H. *Die hippokratische Schrift von der Siebenzahl in ihrer vierfachen Überlieferung* (Studien zur Geschichte und Kultur des Altertums 6). Paderborn, 1913

240. Rousselle, A. 'Images médicales du corps en Grèce: Observation féminine et idéologie masculine', *Annales ESC* 35 (1980) 1089–115

241. Saunders, J. B. de C. M. *The Transitions from Ancient Egyptian to Greek Medicine*. Lawrence, Kansas, 1963

242. Scarborough, J. 'Theophrastus on herbals and herbal remedies', *Journal of the History of Biology* 11 (1978) 353–85

243. Scarborough, J. 'Theoretical assumptions in Hippocratic pharmacology', in H 202, 307–25

244. Schumacher, J. *Antike Medizin*. 2nd edn. Berlin, 1963

245. Senn, G. 'Über Herkunft und Stil der Beschreibungen von Experimenten im Corpus Hippocraticum', *Sudhoffs Archiv für Geschichte der Medizin* 22 (1929) 217–89

246. Senn, G. *Die Entwicklung der biologischen Forschungsmethode in der Antike und ihre grundsätzliche Förderung durch Theophrast von Eresos* (Veröffentlichungen der schweizerischen Gesellschaft für Geschichte

der Medizin und der Naturwissenschaften 8). Aarau, 1933

247. Simon, B. *Mind and Madness in Ancient Greece*. Ithaca, NY, 1978
248. Sissa, G. 'Maidenhood without maidenhead: the female body in Ancient Greece', in Halperin, D. M., Winkler, J. J. and Zeitlin, F. I. (eds.), *Before Sexuality*, 339–64. Princeton, 1990
249. Smith, W. D. 'Galen on Coans versus Cnidians', *Bulletin of the History of Medicine* 47 (1973) 569–85
250. Smith, W. D. *The Hippocratic Tradition*. Ithaca, 1979
251. Stannard, J. 'Hippocratic pharmacology', *Bulletin of the History of Medicine* 35 (1961) 497–518
252. Steuer, R. O. and Saunders, J. B. de C. M. *Ancient Egyptian and Cnidian Medicine*. Berkeley, 1959
253. Temkin, O. *Hippocrates in a World of Pagans and Christians*. Baltimore, 1991
254. Thivel, A. 'Le "divin" dans la *collection hippocratique*', in H 128, 57–76
255. Thivel, A. *Cnide et Cos: essai sur les doctrines médicales dans la collection hippocratique (Publications de la Faculté des Lettres de Nice 21)*. Paris, 1981
256. Trapp, H. *Die hippokratische Schrift DE NATURA MULIEBRI. Ausgabe und textkritischer Kommentar*. Hamburg, 1967
257. Vegetti, M. 'La medicina in Platone, IV Il Fedro', *Rivista critica di storia della filosofia* 24 (1969) 3–22
258. Vegetti, M. 'Nascita dello scienzato', *Belfagor* 28 (1973) 641–63
259. Vegetti, M. *Il Coltello e lo Stilo*. Milan, 1979
260. Weinreich, O. *Antike Heilungswunder* (Religionsgeschichtliche Versuche und Vorarbeiten 8, 1). Giessen, 1909
261. Wellmann, M. *Die Fragmente der sikelischen Ärzte Akron, Philistion und des Diokles von Karystos*. Berlin, 1901
262. Wilson, J. A. 'Medicine in Ancient Egypt', *Bulletin of the History of Medicine* 36 (1962) 114–23
263. Wittern, R. *Die hippokratische Schrift De morbis I*. Hildesheim, 1974

I. SOCIAL AND ECONOMIC HISTORY

1. Adamesteanu, D. 'Le suddivisioni di terra nel Metapontino', in I 35, 49–61
2. Andreyev, V. N. 'Some aspects of agrarian conditions in Attica in the fifth to third centuries B.C.', *Eirene* 12 (1974) 5–46
3. Audring, G. 'Über den Gutsverwalter (*epitropos*) in der attischen Landwirtschaft des 5. und des 4. Jhs.v.u.Z.', *Klio* 55 (1973) 109–16
4. Austin, M. M. 'Hellenistic kings, war and the economy', *CQ* n.s. 36 (1986) 450–66
5. Austin, M. M. 'Greek trade, industry, and labor', in Grant, M. and Kitzinger, R. I. (eds.), *Civilization of the Ancient Mediterranean. Greece and Rome*, 723–51. New York, 1988
6. *The Black Sea Pilot*. 11th edn. London (published by the Hydrographer of the Navy), 1969

7. Blackman, D. J. 'Ancient harbours in the Mediterranean', *International Journal of Nautical Archaeology* 11 (1982) 79–104, 185–211

8. Boardman, J. 'Delphinion in Chios', *BSA* 51 (1956) 41–54

9. Boardman, J. 'Excavations at Pindakas in Chios', *BSA* 53–4 (1958) 295–309

10. Bogaert, R. *Banques et banquiers dans les cités grecques*, Leiden, 1968

11. Bogaert, R. 'La banque à Athènes au IVe siècle avant J.C. Etat de la question', *Mus. Helv.* 43 (1986) 19–49

12. Boyd, T. J. and Jameson, M. H. 'Urban and rural land division in ancient Greece', *Hesp.* 50 (1981) 327–42

13. Bradford, J. *Ancient Landscapes*. London, 1957

14. Bravo, B. 'Le commerce des céréales chez les Grecs de l'époque archaïque', in I 58, 17–29

15. Bray, F. *Science and Civilisation in China*, VI. 2: *Agriculture*. Cambridge, 1984

16. Bresson, A. 'Aristote et le commerce extérieur', *REA* 89 (1987) 217–38

17. Brun, P. *Eisphora Syntaxis Stratiotika. Recherches sur les finances militaires d'Athènes au IVe siècle av. J.C.* Paris, 1983

18. Brunt, P. A. Review of I 143 in *JHS* 86 (1966) 245–7

19. Cambiano, G. 'Aristotle and the anonymous opponents of slavery', in I 39, 22–41

20. Camp, John Mc. K. 'Drought and famine in the 4th century B.C.', *Hesp.* Supplement XX (1982) 9–17

21. Carter, J. C. 'A classical landscape. Rural archaeology at Metapontum', *Archaeology* 33 (1980) 23–32

22. Cartledge, P. 'Rebels and Sambos in classical Greece: a comparative view', in A 14, 16–46

23. Casson, L. *Travel in the Ancient World*. London, 1974

24. Casson, L. *Ships and Seamanship in the Ancient World*. 2nd edn. Princeton, 1986

25. Cohen, E. E. 'Commercial lending by Athenian banks: cliometric fallacies and forensic methodology', *Cl. Phil.* 85 (1990) 177–90

26. Conophagos, C. E. *Le Laurion antique et la technique grecque de la production de l'argent*. Athens, 1980

27. Cooper, A. Burford. 'The family farm', *CJ* 73 (1977–8) 161–75

28. Crawford, D. J. 'Food: tradition and change in Hellenistic Egypt', *World Archaeology* 11 (1979) 136–46

29. Crosby, M. 'The leases of the Laureion mines', *Hesp.* 19 (1950) 189–312

30. Crosby, M. 'More fragments of mining leases from the Athenian agora', *Hesp.* 26 (1957) 1–23

31. Dover, K. J. *Greek Homosexuality*. London, 1978

32. Ehrenberg, V. *The People of Aristophanes*. 2nd edn. Oxford, 1951

33. Eyben, E. 'Family planning in Graeco-Roman antiquity', *AncSoc* 11–12 (1980–81) 5–82

34. Figueira, T. J. '*Sitopolai* and *sitophylakes* in Lysias' "Against the Graindealers": governmental intervention in the Athenian economy', *Phoenix* 40 (1986) 149–71

35. Finley, M. I. (ed.), *Problèmes de la terre en Grèce ancienne*. Paris–The Hague, 1973
36. Finley, M. I. *The Ancient Economy*. Berkeley–Los Angeles, 1973; 2nd edn. London, 1985
37. Finley, M. I. *Ancient Slavery and Modern Ideology*. London, 1980
38. Finley, M. I. *Economy and Society in Ancient Greece*. London, 1981
39. Finley, M. I. (ed.) *Classical Slavery*. London, 1987
40. Forbes, H. A. '"We have a little of everything": the ecological basis of some agricultural practices in Methana, Troizenia', in Dimen, M. and Friedl, E. (eds.), *Regional Variations in Modern Greece and Cyprus* (Annals of the New York Academy of Science 268), 236–50. 1976
41. Forbes, H. A. and Foxhall, L. 'The "thrice-ploughed field". Cultivation techniques in ancient and modern Greece', *Expedition* 19 (1976) 5–11
42. Forbes, H. A. and Foxhall, L. 'The queen of all trees', *Expedition* 21 (1978) 37–47
43. Foxhall, L. and Forbes, H. A. 'Σιτομετρεία: the role of grain as a staple food in classical antiquity', *Chiron* 12 (1982) 41–90
44. Frayn, J. M. *Subsistence Farming in Roman Italy*. London, 1979
45. Fuks, A. 'Isocrates and the social-economic revolution in Greece', *AncSoc* 3 (1972) 17–44 (= C 23, 52–79)
46. Fuks, A. 'Patterns and types of social-economic revolution in Greece from the fourth to the second century B.C.', *AncSoc* 5 (1974) 51–81 (= C 23, 9–39)
47. Gallant, T. W. 'Agricultural systems, land tenure, and the reforms of Solon', *BSA* 77 (1982) 111–24
48. Garlan, Y. 'Le travail libre en Grèce ancienne', in Garnsey, P. (ed.), *Non-slave Labour in the Greco-Roman World* (*PCPhS*, Suppl. vol. 6), 6–22. Cambridge, 1980
49. Garlan, Y. 'Greek amphorae and trade', in I 57, 27–35
50. Garlan, Y. 'War, piracy and slavery in the Greek world', in I 39, 7–21
51. Garlan, Y. *Slavery in Ancient Greece*. Ithaca–London, 1988
52. Garlan, Y. *Guerre et économie en Grèce ancienne*. Paris, 1989
53. Garland, R. *The Piraeus from the Fifth to the First Century B.C.* London–Ithaca, 1987
54. Garnsey, P. 'Grain for Athens', in A 14, 62–75
55. Garnsey, P. *Famine and Food Supply in the Graeco–Roman World. Responses to Risk and Crisis*. Cambridge 1988
56. Garnsey, P., Gallant, T. W. and Rathbone, D. 'Thessaly and the grain supply of Rome during the second century B.C.', *JRS* 74 (1984) 30–44
57. Garnsey, P., Hopkins, K. and Whittaker, C. R. (eds.) *Trade in the Ancient Economy*. London, 1983
58. Garnsey, P. and Whittaker, C. R. (eds.) *Trade and Famine in Classical Antiquity* (*PCPhS*, Suppl. vol. 8). Cambridge, 1983
59. Gauthier, P. 'De Lysias à Aristote (*Ath. Pol.* 51.4): le commerce du grain à Athènes et les fonctions des sitophylaques', *Revue Historique de droit français et étranger* 59 (1981) 5–28
60. Georgi, L. 'Pollination ecology of the date palm and fig tree: Herodotus I

193, 4–5', *Cl. Phil.* 77 (1982) 224–8
61. Georgoudis, S. 'Quelques problèmes de la transhumance dans la Grèce ancienne', *REG* 87 (1974) 155–85
62. Gernet, L. 'L'approvisionnement d'Athènes en blé aux Ve et IVe siècles', in Bloch, G., *Mélanges d'histoire ancienne*, 269–391. Paris, 1909
63. Giamfrotta, P. and Pomey, P. *Archeologia subacquea.* Milan, 1981
64. Golden, M. 'Demography and the exposure of girls at Athens', *Phoenix* 35 (1981) 316–31
65. Gow, A. S. F. 'The ancient plough', *JHS* 34 (1914) 249–75
66. Graham, A. J. 'The date of the Greek penetration of the Black Sea', *BICS* 5 (1958) 25–42
67. Guiraud, P. *La propriété foncière en Grèce jusqu'à la conquête romaine.* Paris, 1893
68. Halstead, P. 'Traditional and ancient rural economy in Mediterranean Europe: plus ça change?', *JHS* 107 (1987) 77–87
69. Hands, A. R. *Charities and Social Aid in Greece and Rome.* London, 1968
70. Hansen, M. V. 'Athenian maritime trade in the 4th century B.C.: operation and finance', *Class. et Med.* 35 (1984) 71–92
71. Harvey, F. D. 'The maritime loan in Eupolis' Marikas (P. Oxy. 2741)', *ZPE* 23 (1976) 231–3
72. Heichelheim, F. M. 'Sitos' in *RE* Suppl. 6 (1935) cols. 819–92
73. Heitland, W. *Agricola.* Oxford, 1921
74. Hodge, A. T. 'Massalia, meteorology and navigation', *AncW* 7 (1983) 67–88
75. Hodkinson, S. 'Animal husbandry in the Greek polis', in Whittaker, C. R. (ed.), *Pastoral Economies*, 35–74. Cambridge, 1988
76. Hopper, R. J. 'The Attic silver mines in the fourth century B.C.', *BSA* 47 (1953) 200–54
77. Hopper, R. J. 'The Laurion mines: a reconsideration', *BSA* 63 (1968) 293–326
78. Humphreys, S. C. 'The nothoi of Kynosarges', *JHS* 94 (1974) 88–95
79. Humphreys, S. *Anthropology and the Greeks.* London, 1978
80. Humphreys, S. C. *The Family, Women and Death.* London, 1983
81. Jameson, M. H. 'Agriculture and slavery in classical times', *CJ* 73 (1977–8) 122–45
82. Jameson, M. H. 'Famine in the Greek world', in I 58, 6–16
83. Jardé, A. *Les céréales dans l'antiquité grecque.* Paris, 1925
84. Jasny, N. 'Competition among grains in classical antiquity', *AHR* 47 (1941–2) 751–7
85. Jasny, N. *Wheats of Classical Antiquity.* Baltimore, 1944
86. Jones, A. H. M. 'Taxation in antiquity', in *id., The Roman Economy. Studies in Ancient Economic and Administrative History*, 151–86. Oxford, 1974
87. Jones, J. E. 'The Laurion silver mines: a review of recent researches and results', *G&R* 29 (1982) 169–83
88. Jones, J. E., Graham, A. J. and Sackett, L. H. 'The Dema house in Attica', *BSA* 57 (1962) 75–114
89. Jones, J. E., Graham, A. J. and Sackett, L. H. 'An Attic country house

below the cave of Pan at Vari', *BSA* 68 (1973) 355–452

90. Kent, J. H. 'The temple estates of Delos, Rheneia and Mykonos', *Hesp.* 17 (1948) 243–338

91. Kuenzi, E. *Epidosis. Sammlung Freiwilliger Beiträge zu Zeiten der Not in Athen*. Berne, 1923

92. Labaree, B. 'How the Greeks sailed into the Black Sea', *AJA* 61 (1957) 29–33

93. Langdon, M. K. and Watrous, L. V. 'The farm of Timesios: rock-cut inscriptions in south Attica', *Hesp.* 46 (1977) 162–77

94. Lauffer, S. 'Prosopographische Bemerkungen zu den attischen Grubenpachtlisten', *Historia* 6 (1957) 287–305

95. Lauffer, S. *Die Bergwerkssklaven von Laureion*, 2 vols. 2nd edn. Wiesbaden, 1975

96. Lefkowitz, M. and Fant, M. B. *Women's Life in Greece and Rome: A Sourcebook in Translation*. London, 1982

97. Le Gras, A. *General Examination of the Mediterranean Sea*, trans. by R. H. Wyman (United States Hydrographic Office, Pub. No. 25). Washington, DC, 1870

98. Lepore, E. 'Problemi dell'organizzazione della *chora* coloniale', in 1 35, 15–48

99. Lotze, D. *ΜΕΤΑΞΥ ΕΛΕΥΘΕΡΩΝ ΚΑΙ ΔΟΥΛΩΝ*. Berlin, 1959

100. McKechnie, P. *Outsiders in the Greek Cities of the Fourth Century* B.C. London, 1989

101. Meiggs, R. *Trees and Timber in the Ancient Mediterranean World*. Oxford, 1982

102. Michell, H. *Economics of Ancient Greece*. 2nd edn. Cambridge, 1957

103. Migeotte, L. 'Souscriptions athéniennes de la période classique', *Historia* 32 (1983) 129–48

104. Migeotte, L. *L'Emprunt public dans les cités grecques*. Paris, 1984

105. Miles, D. (ed.) *The Romano-British Countryside*. Oxford, 1982

106. Millett, P. 'Notes on a Greek text relating to credit transactions', *PCPhS* n.s. 26 (1980) 67–9

107. Millett, P. *Lending and Borrowing in Ancient Athens*. Cambridge, 1990

108. Moritz, L. A. *Grain Mills and Flour in Classical Antiquity*. Oxford, 1958

109. Mossé, C. 'Le rôle des esclaves dans les troubles politiques du monde grec à la fin de l'époque classique', *Cahiers d'histoire* 6 (1961) 353–60

110. Mossé, C. 'Le statut des paysans en Attique au IVᵉ siècle', in 1 35, 179–86

111. Murray, W. 'Do modern winds equal ancient winds?' *Mediterranean Historical Review* 2 (1987) 139–67

112. Nenci, G. 'Il problema della concorrenza fra manodopera libera e servile nella Grecia classica', *ASNP* ser. III, 8 (1978) 1287–300

113. Nixon, L. and Price, S. 'The size and resources of Greek cities' in c 52, 137–70

114. Osborne, R. 'Buildings and residences on the land in Classical and Hellenistic Greece: the contribution of epigraphy', *BSA* 80 (1985) 119–28

115. Osborne, R. *Classical Landscape with Figures: The Ancient Greek City and its*

Countryside. London, 1987
116. Patterson, C. B. 'Those Athenian bastards', *ClAnt* 40 (1990) 40–73
117. Pečirka, J. 'Homestead farms in Classical and Hellenistic Hellas', in I 35, 113–47
118. Pembroke, S. 'Women in charge: the functions of alternatives in early Greek tradition and the ancient idea of matriarchy', *JWI* 30 (1967) 1–35
119. Perlman, S. 'The Ten Thousand. A chapter in the military, social and economic history of the fourth century', *Riv. stor. ant.* 6–7 (1976–7) 241–84
120. Pflaum, H. *Essai sur le cursus publicus sous le haut-empire romain* (*Mém. Ac. Inscr. B.L.* 14). Paris, 1940
121. Pippidi, D. M. 'La main d'oeuvre dans les colonies grecques', in I 35, 63–82
122. Pomeroy, S. B. *Goddesses, Whores, Wives and Slaves*. New York, 1975
123. Pritchett, W. K. 'The Attic stelai, part II', *Hesp.* 25 (1956) 178–328
124. Rackham, O. 'Observations on the historical ecology of Boeotia', *BSA* 78 (1983) 291–351
125. Reed, C. M. 'Maritime traders in the Greek world of the Archaic and Classical periods'. Unpub. D.Phil. thesis, Oxford, 1981
126. Renfrew, C. and Wagstaff, M. *An Island Polity: the Archaeology of Exploitation in Melos*. Cambridge, 1982
127. Rhodes, P. J. 'Problems in Athenian *eisphora* and liturgies', *AJAH* 7 (1982) 1–19
128. Rich, J. W. and Wallace-Hadrill, A. (eds.) *City and Country in the Ancient World*. London, 1990
129. Richter, W. *Die Landwirtschaft im homerischen Zeitalter*. Göttingen, 1968
130. Rickman, G. *The Corn Supply of Ancient Rome*. Oxford, 1980
131. Riepl, W. *Das Nachrichtenwesen des Altertums*. Berlin, 1913
132. Robert, L. '*ΛΙΜΕΝΕΣ*', *Hellenica* 11–12 (1960) 263–6
133. Ruschenbusch, E. 'Zur Wirtschafts- und Sozialstruktur der Normalpolis', *ASNP* ser. III. 13 (1983) 171–94
134. *Sailing Directions (Planning Guide) for the Mediterranean* (Defense Mapping Agency, Hydrographic/Topographic Center, Pub. 130). 2nd edn. Washington, DC, 1975
135. de Ste Croix, G. E. M. 'Demosthenes' *timema* and the Athenian *eisphora* in the fourth century B.C.', *Class. et Med.* 14 (1953) 30–70
136. de Ste Croix, G. E. M. 'The estate of Phaenippus', in A 3, 109–14
137. de Ste Croix, G. E. M. Review of I 143, *CR* n.s. 16 (1966) 90–3
138. de Ste Croix, G. E. M. 'Ancient Greek and Roman maritime loans', in Edey, H. and Yamey, B. S. (eds.), *Debts, Credits, Finance and Profits*, 41–59. London, 1974
139. Schmiedt, G. *Antichi porti d'Italia*. Florence, 1975
140. Semple, E. C. *The Geography of the Mediterranean Region: Its Relation to Ancient History*. New York–London, 1931
141. Shurgoya, I. G. 'On the question of Bosporan–Egyptian rivalry in the grain trade of the eastern Mediterranean in the Early Hellenistic period', *KSIA* 138 (1975) 51. (In Russian)

142. Sutherland, C. H. V. 'Corn and coin – a note on Greek commercial monopolies', *AJP* 64 (1942) 129–47
143. Thomsen, R. *Eisphora: A Study of Direct Taxation in Ancient Athens.* Copenhagen, 1964
144. Vélissaropoulos, J. *Les Nauclères grecs.* Geneva–Paris, 1980
145. Veyne, P. *Bread and Circuses. Historical Sociology and Political Pluralism.* London, 1990. (Engl. trs. of *Le pain et le cirque.* Paris, 1976)
146. Vidal-Naquet, P. *The Black Hunter.* Baltimore–London, 1986. (Engl. trs. of *Le chasseur noir.* Paris, 1981)
147. Watson, A. *Agricultural Innovation in the Early Islamic World.* Cambridge, 1983
148. White, K. D. *Roman Farming.* London, 1970
149. Will, Ed. 'La Grèce archaïque', in *Deuxième conférence internationale d'histoire économique, Aix en Provence 1962.* 1. *Trade and politics in the ancient world.* Paris, 1965, repr. New York, 1979
150. Wood, E. M. 'Agricultural slavery in Classical Athens', *AJAH* 8 (1983) 1–47
151. Young, J. H. 'Studies in south Attica: country estates at Sounion', *Hesp.* 25 (1956) 122–46

J. ART AND ARCHITECTURE

1. *Archaische und Klassische Griechische Plastik* (H. Kyrieleis, ed., Akten des Internationalen Kolloquiums 1985). Mainz, 1986
2. Arias, P. E. *Skopas.* Rome, 1952
3. Arnold, D. *Die Polykletnachfolge: Untersuchungen zur Kunst von Argos und Sikyon zwischen Polyklet und Lysipp (JDAI*, Ergänzungsheft xxv). Berlin, 1969
4. Ashmole, B. *Architect and Sculptor in Classical Greece.* London–New York, 1972
5. Berve, H. and Gruben, G. *Greek Temples, Theaters, and Shrines.* New York–London, 1962
6. Boardman, J. *Athenian Red Figure Vases: the Classical Period.* London, 1990
7. Brown, B. R. *Anticlassicism in Greek Sculpture of the Fourth Century B.C.* New York, 1973
8. Bruno, V. *Form and Color in Greek Painting.* New York, 1977
9. Burford, A. *Greek Temple Builders at Epidaurus.* Liverpool, 1969
10. Burn, L. *The Meidias Painter.* Oxford, 1987
11. Crome, J. F. *Die Skulpturen des Asklepios-tempels von Epidauros.* Berlin, 1951
12. Dentzer, J. M. *Le motif du banquet couché dans le Proche-Orient et le monde grec du VII au IV siècle avant. J.-C.* (*BEFAR* 246) Paris, 1982
13. Diepolder, H. *Die Attischen Grabreliefs des 5. und 4. Jahrhunderts v. Chr.* Berlin, 1931
14. Dinsmoor, W. B. *The Architecture of Ancient Greece.* London, 1950

15. Dohrn, T. *Attische Plastik vom Tode des Phidias bis zum Wirken der grossen Meister des 4. Jahrhunderts v. Chr.* Krefeld, 1957

16. Dugas, C., Berchmans, J. and Clemmensen, M. *Le sanctuaire d'Aléa Athéna à Tégée au IVe siècle.* Paris, 1924

17. Gruben, G. *Die Tempel der Griechen.* Munich, 1966

18. Hill, B. H., Lands, L. T. and Williams, C. K. *The Temple of Zeus at Nemea.* Princeton, 1967

19. Homann-Wedeking, E. 'Samos 1964', *Arch. Anz.* (1965) 428–46

20. Johnson, F. P. *Lysippos.* Durham, NC, 1927

21. Laurenzi, L. *Ritratti Greci.* Florence, 1941

22. Lawrence, A. W. *Greek Architecture.* Revised edn by R. A. Tomlinson. Harmondsworth, 1983

23. Norman, N. 'The temple of Athena Alea at Tegea', *AJA* 88 (1984) 169–94

24. Overbeck, J. *Die antiken Schriftquellen zur Geschichte der bildenden Künste bei den Griechen.* Leipzig, 1868

25. Palagia, O. *Euphranor* (Monumenta Graeca et Romana 3). Leiden, 1980

26. Picard, C. *Manuel d'archéologie grecque. La sculpture. Période classique – IVe siècle.* Paris, 1948–63

27. Pollitt, J. J. *Art and Experience in Classical Greece.* Cambridge, 1972

28. Pollitt, J. J. *The Ancient View of Greek Art.* London–New Haven, 1974

29. Pollitt, J. J. *Art in the Hellenistic Age.* Cambridge, 1986

30. Pollitt, J. J. *The Art of Ancient Greece.* Cambridge, 1990

31. Richter, G. M. A. *The Portraits of the Greeks.* London, 1965. Revised by R. R. R. Smith. Oxford, 1984

32. Richter, G. M. A. *The Sculpture and Sculptors of the Greeks,* 4th edn. London–New Haven, 1970

33. Rizzo, G. E. *Prassitele.* Milan–Rome, 1932

34. Robert, F. *Thymélè.* Paris, 1939

35. Robertson, M. *A History of Greek Art.* Cambridge, 1975

35A. Robertson, M. *The Art of Vase Painting in Classical Athens.* Cambridge, 1992

36. Robinson, D. M. *et al. Excavations at Olynthus* (Johns Hopkins Studies in Archaeology). Baltimore, 1930–52

37. Roux, G. *Architecture de l'Argolide aux IVe et IIIe siècle avant J.C.* Paris, 1961

38. Rumpf, A. *Malerei und Zeichnung* (Handbuch der Archäologie 4.1). Munich, 1953

39. Rumpf, A. 'Zum Alexander Mosaik', *Ath. Mitt.* 77 (1962) 229–41

40. Schefold, K. *Kertscher Vasen.* Berlin, 1930

41. Schefold, K. *Untersuchungen zu den Kertscher Vasen.* Berlin, 1934

42. Schefold, K. *Die Bildnisse der antiken Dichter, Redner, und Denker.* Basel, 1943

43. Schefold, K. *Der Alexander-Sarkophag.* Berlin, 1968

44. Schlörb, B. *Timotheus* (JDAI, Ergänzungsheft 22). Berlin, 1965

45. Sjöqvist, E. *Lysippus* (Lectures in memory of Louise Taft Semple, 2nd ser.). Cincinnati, 1966

46.   Smith, R. R. R. *Hellenistic Royal Portraits*. Oxford, 1988
47.   Stewart, A. F. *Skopas of Paros*. Park Ridge, NJ, 1977
48.   Stewart, A. *Greek Sculpture: an Exploration*. New Haven, 1990
49.   Stuart Jones, H. *Select Passages from Ancient Writers Illustrative of the History of Greek Sculpture*. London, 1895
50.   Süsserott, H. K. *Griechische Plastik des IV. Jahrhunderts v. Chr*. Frankfurt, 1938
51.   Trendall, A. D. *Red Figure Vases of South Italy and Sicily*. London, 1989
52.   Waywell, G. *The Free-Standing Sculptures of the Mausoleum at Halicarnassus in the British Museum*. London, 1978

K. WARFARE

1.   Adcock, F. E. *The Greek and Macedonian Art of War*. Berkeley–Los Angeles, 1957
2.   Anderson, J. K. *Ancient Greek Horsemanship*. Berkeley–Los Angeles, 1961
3.   Anderson, J. K. *Military Theory and Practice in the Age of Xenophon*. Berkeley–Los Angeles, 1970
4.   Anderson, J. K. 'New evidence on the origin of the spur', *Ant. Kunst* 21 (1978) 46–8
5.   Andrewes, A. 'The hoplite *Katalogos*', in Shrimpton, G. S. and McCargar, D. J. *Classical Contributions. Studies . . . M. F. McGregor*, 1–3. Locust Valley, 1981
6.   Andronicos, M. 'Sarissa', *BCH* 94 (1970) 91–107
7.   Aymard, A. 'Mercenariat et histoire grecque', in A 2, 487–98
8.   Best, J. G. P. *Thracian Peltasts and their Influence on Greek Warfare* (Studies of the Dutch Archaeological and Historical Society, 1). Groningen, 1969
9.   Bosworth, A. B. '*ΑΣΘΕΤΑΙΡΟΙ*', *CQ* n.s. 23 (1973) 245–52
10.   Bugh, G. R. *The Horsemen of Athens*. Princeton, 1988
11.   Devine, A. M. '*ΕΜΒΟΛΟΝ*: a study in tactical terminology', *Phoenix* 37 (1983) 201–17
12.   Ducrey, P. *Guerre et guerriers dans la Grèce antique*. Fribourg, 1985
13.   Frost, F. 'The dubious origins of the "Marathon"', *AJAH* 4 (1979) 159–63
14.   Fuller, J. F. C. *The Generalship of Alexander the Great*. London, 1958
15.   Garlan, Y. *La Guerre dans l'antiquité*. Paris, 1972
16.   Garlan, Y. 'La défense du territoire à l'époque classique', in I 34, 149–60
17.   Garlan, Y. *Recherches de poliorcétique grecque*. Paris, 1974
18.   Garlan, Y. *War in the Ancient World: a Social History*. London, 1975
19.   Garlan, Y. "Il militare", dans l'*Uomo greco* (ed. J.-P. Vernant; Rome, 1991)
20.   Griffith, G. T. *The Mercenaries of the Hellenistic World*. London, 1935
21.   Guilmartin, J. F. *Gunpowder and Galleys*. Cambridge, 1974
22.   Hammond, N. G. L. 'A note on "pursuit" in Arrian', *CQ* n.s. 28 (1978) 136–40

23. Hammond, N. G. L. 'Training in the use of a sarissa and its effect in battle', *Antichthon* 14 (1980) 53–63
24. Hanson, V. D. *Warfare and Agriculture in Classical Greece*. Pisa, 1983
25. Hanson, V. D. *The Western Way of War, Infantry Battle in Classical Greece*. New York–Oxford, 1989
26. Hauben, H. 'The command structure in Alexander's Mediterranean fleets', *AncSoc* 3 (1972) 55–65
27. Jordan, B. *The Athenian Navy in the Classical Period. A Study of Athenian Naval Administration and Military Organization in the Fifth and Fourth Centuries B.C.* (University of California Publications in Classical Studies, 13). Berkeley–Los Angeles, 1975
28. Kroll, J. H. 'An archive of the Athenian cavalry', *Hesp.* 46 (1977) 83–140
29. Kromayer, J., and Veith, G. *Antike Schlachtfelder in Griechenland*. 4 vols. in 5. Berlin, 1903–31
30. Kromayer, J. and Veith, G. *Heerwesen und Kriegführung der Griechen und Römer* (= Handbuch der Altertumswissenschaft iv. 3. 2). Munich, 1928
31. Kunze, E. 'Ein Rammbock', *V. Bericht Olympia* (1956) 75–8
32. Lavelle, B. '*Epikouroi* in Thucydides', *AJP* 110 (1989) 36–9
33. Lawrence, A. W. *Greek Aims in Fortification*. Oxford, 1979
34. Lazenby, J. F. *The Spartan Army*. Warminster, 1985
35. Lendle, O. *Schildkröten* (Palingenesia 10). Wiesbaden, 1975
36. Lendle, O. 'Antike Kriegsmaschinen', *Gymnasium* 88 (1981) 330–56
37. Lendle, O. *Texte und Untersuchungen zum technischen Bereich der antiken Poliorketik* (Palingenesia 19). Wiesbaden, 1983
38. Lengauer, W. *Greek Commanders in the 5th and 4th Centuries B.C. Politics and Ideology: a Study of Militarism*. Warsaw, 1979
39. Leriche, P. and Tréziny, H. (eds.) *La fortification dans l'histoire du monde grec*. Paris, 1986
40. Lévêque, P. and Vidal-Naquet, P. 'Epaminondas pythagoricien ou le problème tactique de la droite et de la gauche', *Historia* 9 (1960) 294–308
41. Lonis, R. *Guerre et religion en Grèce à l'époque classique*. Paris, 1979
42. Marinovic, L. P. *Le mercenariat grec au IV⁰ siècle avant notre ère et la crise de la polis*. Moscow, 1975; French transl. Paris, 1988
43. Markle, M. M. III. 'The Macedonian sarissa, spear and related armour', *AJA* 81 (1977) 323–39
44. Markle, M. M. III. 'The use of the sarissa by Philip and Alexander of Macedon', *AJA* 82 (1978) 483–97
45. Marsden, E. W. *Greek and Roman Artillery. I. Historical Development. II. Technical Treatises*. Oxford, 1969–71
46. Marsden, E. W. 'Macedonian military machinery and its designers under Philip and Alexander', *Anc. Mac.* 2 (Thessaloniki) (1977) 211–23
47. Milns, R. D. 'Asthippoi again', *CR* n.s. 31 (1981) 347–54
48. Morrison, J. S. and Williams, R. T. *Greek Oared Ships, 900–322 B.C.* Cambridge, 1968
49. Ober, J. *Fortress Attica*. Leiden, 1985
50. Parke, H. W. *Greek Mercenary Soldiers*. Oxford, 1933
51. Pritchett, W. K. *The Greek State at War*. Berkeley–London, I, 1971; II,

1974; III, 1979; IV, 1986; V, 1991

52. Rodgers, W. L. *Greek and Roman Naval Warfare.* Annapolis, 1937
53. Roy, J. 'The mercenaries of Cyrus', *Historia* 16 (1967) 287–323
54. Seibt, G. F. *Griechische Söldner im Achaimenidenreich.* Bonn, 1977
55. Snodgrass, A. M. *Arms and Armour of the Greeks.* London, 1967
56. Taillardat, J. 'La trière athénienne et la guerre sur mer aux Ve et IVe siècles', in J.-P. Vernant (ed.), *Problèmes de la guerre en Grèce ancienne*, 183–205. Paris–The Hague, 1968
57. Tarn, W. W. *Hellenistic Military and Naval Developments.* Cambridge, 1930
58. Welwei, K. W. *Unfreie im antiken Kriegsdienst.* 2 vols. Wiesbaden, 1974–7
59. Whitehead, D. 'Who equipped mercenary troops in classical Greece?' *Historia* 40 (1991) 105–13
60. Winter, F. E. *Greek Fortifications.* Toronto, 1971

INDEX

Aegina *1 Cd, 2 Cb*, 173, 563, 858; in
  Corinthian War 98, 115–16, 559, 560, 884
Aegospotami *5 Bb*; battle of 33, 67, 79, 516–17
Aegytis *2 Bb*, 194
Aelian 694
Aeneas of Stymphalus (Arcadian general,
  perhaps identical with Aeneas Tacticus) 198
Aeneas Tacticus 8, 530, 533, 540, 679–80, 684
Aeniania *18 Bc*, 101, 188–9, 779
Aenus *1 Eb, 17 Cb*, 454, 456, 464, 773
Aeropus, sons of 794
Aeschines (orator) 19, 231, 573, 574, 578, 723;
  embassies 577, 753, 755, 758, 760, 763, 768,
  778, 782; impeachment 574, 575, 579, 757,
  760, 894; trial 578, 768–9, 894; trial of
  Ctesiphon 575–6
Aeschylus (tragic poet) 307, 308
Aesimus (Athenian politician) 98
Aetolia *1 Bc, 2 Aa*; in Corinthian War 112;
  alliance with Thebes 188–9; Molossian
  evacuation to 428, 432; alliance with
  Macedon 770, 779; on Alexander's
  accession 584, 848; and Exiles' Decree 856;
  alliance with Athens 858–9, 900; in
  hellenistic era 590
    Aetolian League 584–5, 590, 847; tribal
    society 584, 590, 679
Afsin (Abbasid general) 57
Agaetes, king of Scythians 484
Agapetus (Byzantine political philosopher)
  327
Agarus, king of Scythians 502
Agathinus (Corinthian naval commander) 105
Agathocles, tyrant of Syracuse 375, 379, 390,
  392–3, 399, 717, 718, 901
Agathon (Macedonian commander in
  Babylon) 862
Agathyrsi 499
Agesilaus (Antigonus' envoy) 334
Agesilaus (brother of Agis III of Sparta) 853
Agesilaus, king of Sparta: accession 42–3, 882;
  expedition to Asia, *see under* Sparta;
  boeotarchs prevent sacrifice at Aulis 44, 68,
  69, 97–8; recall to Greece 72, 101–2, 882; in
  Corinthian War 102–3, 109, 110, 111–12;
  wars against Thebes 160, 161, 162, 165,
  167–8, 172, 181, 184, 884; and Satraps'
  Revolt 85, 87, 200; in Hellespont 191;
  Egyptian expedition 191, 200, 341, 349;
  death 888
    guest-friendships 69, 72, 82, 85; Isocrates
    approaches 600n36; and Mantinea 156, 189–
    90; sources on 4, 6, 10, 12
Agesipolis, king of Sparta 102, 112, 156, 157,
  161, 553, 884
Aghurmi, sanctuary of Ammon at 811
Agighiol burial 461, 463

Agis, king of Paeonians 732
Agis II, king of Sparta 25, 26, 32, 41, 42, 882
Agis III, king of Sparta 557, 815, 852–5, 898
Agnone tablet 399n72
Agonippus (oligarch of Eresus) 847
Agrianians 440, 447, 687, 796, 813, 814, 835
agriculture 661–77; buildings 669, 671; climate
  and 661, 665, 668, 677; crops 662–70, 675,
  (*see also individual crops*); development 675;
  estate management 673–4; fertilizers 663–4,
  666, 667; garden plots 663, 667–8; irrigation
  665, 667; land 662–4, 670, (marginal) 661,
  675; landowners 671, 672, 673–4; landscape
  661, 670–2; lawsuits 661, 670; leasing of
  land 673–4, (*see also* lease inscriptions); and
  religion 546, 661, 668, 675, 676; sources 8,
  662; specialization 663, 663n7, 676, 677;
  techniques and theories 674–7; trade 677,
  719, (*see also under individual commodities*);
  traditional basis 661, 674, 675; war damage
  559, 666; workforce 401, 667, 672–4; *see also*
  livestock, *individual crops, and under individual
  states and areas*
Agrigentum, *see* Acragas
Agyrium *3 Cb*, 121, 715
Agyrrhius (Athenian naval commander) 115,
  163, 570n17
Ahiqar, Proverbs of 290
Ahura-Mazda, cult of 49
Aï Khanum *20 Lc, 21 Db*, 64, 867
Aianteion, Hellespont 81
Aisne, river *12 Cb*, 415
Alalia, battle of 365, 368
Alcaeus (lyric poet) 479
Alcetas (Spartan commander) 173
Alcetas, king of Molossi 147–8, 174, 177
Alcibiades (Athenian politician) 35, 42, 65, 69,
  139–40, 882; associates 34, 40; in
  Peloponnesian War 39, 493, 516
Alcidas (Spartan naval commander) 177
Alcimachus son of Agathocles (Macedonian
  noble) 782, 801, 852, 869, 898
Alcimenes (Corinthian politician) 106
Alcinus (Macedonian naval commander) 776
Alcomenae, Macedon 726
Aleuadae, *see under* Larissa
Alexander I, king of Macedon 194–5, 430,
  452, 723, 725
Alexander II, king of Macedon 727
Alexander III (The Great), king of Macedon
  791–881, 898, 900; birth 734, 738, 786, 890;
  education 734, 771, 786; command in
  Thrace 469; in war against Athens 777, 782,
  786, 896; accession 790, 791–7, 898; rule
  and eastern expedition, *see under* Macedon;
  death 579, 631, 842, 844–5, 875, 900;
  Successors' treatment of body 845, 881;

helmet, Celtic 415, *416*
Heloris (Syracusan in Rhegium) 145, 146, 151
helots 4, 7, 28, 43, 74; status 539–40, 589, 673; see also *neodamodeis*
Heman (singer in Temple at Jerusalem) 295
hemerodromoi (runners) 513
Henet 343
Hephaestion (Macedonian general) 771, 820, 852; in east 331, 820, 826, 827, 833, 839, 840; death 842, 843, 900; cult 842, 844, 862, 874–5
Heraclea on Latmus *5 Bd*, 224
Heraclea in Lucania *11 Db*, 387, 388, 662n5, 671
Heraclea Lyncestis *16 Ba*, 733
Heraclea Minoa *3 Bb*, 699, 720
Heraclea Pontica *4 Da*, *20 Db*; and Athens 489, 492, 500; and Bosporan kingdom 222, 489, 498, 500; colony at Chersonesus 489, 498; and Exiles' Decree 855; Mariandyni 673; trade 222, 475, 500, 504; tyranny 222, 498, 541, 580, 613n97
Heraclea Sintica 469
Heraclea Trachinia *18 Bc*, *19 Bb*, 31, 32, 97, 101, 185, 188–9
Heracles 304, 398, 482, 727, 808; Lysippus' colossal statue 660; Macedonian connexions 727, 808, 810, 827, 872
Heraclides (Syracusan politician) 694, 695, 697, 698–9, 700–2, 703, 704
Heraclides of Aenus (Cotys' assassin) 464, 613
Heraclides of Argos (mariner) 844
Heraclides of Cyme (historian) 47, 56
Heraclides of Pontus (philosopher) 21, 608, 609, 611, 889
Heraclides of Samos (Athenian metic) 851
Heraclitus (husband of Scythian Dedmotis) 505
Heraea *2 Ab*, 190
Heraeum (Heraion Teichos) 110, 468, 746, 890
Herbita *3 Ca*, 140
Herippidas (Spartan naval commander) 109–10
Hermae, mutilation of 39, 577
Hermes; Praxiteles' statue at Olympia 652
Hermias, tyrant of Atarneus 80, 94–5, 220, 224; and Aristotle 220, 620, 621–2, 623, 631, 770, 774; and Macedon 94–5, 220, 621, 770–1; Persians execute 94–5, 621, 774, 894
Hermisium 476
Hermocrates (Syracusan statesman) 125, 133, 133, 134; campaigns 124, 126, 127, 130, 883
Hermodorus of Syracuse (mathematician) 613
Hermolaus son of Sopolis (conspirator) 825
Hermonassa 476, 484, 486, *487*, 507
Hermopolis Magna *9 Bc*, 340–1, 343, 354, 355
Hermopolis Parva *9 Ba*, 354

Hermotimus of Colophon (mathematician) 614
hero cults 29, 654, 842, 844, 862, 871–5
hero portraits of rulers 659, 660
Herodes Atticus (sophist) 31–2
Herodas the Syracusan 67
Herodotus (historian) 46, 55
Hesiod (poet) 514
Hestiaea *1 Cc*, 170, 172–3
hetaireiai (political associations) 577–8
Heuneburg *12 Db*, 409
Hezekiah, king of Judah 293
Hicetas (mercenary general) 708, 709–10, 711, 712, 713, 721; Timoleon defeats 714, 715, 897
Hierax (Spartan naval commander) 115
Hieron, tyrant of Syracuse 136
Hieron Oros 468
Hieron of Soli (Macedonian admiral) 332, 843
Hieronymus of Cardia (historian) 479, 855, 881
Himarrë 443
Himera *3 Bb*, *10 Db*, *11 Bd*, 130, 142; 5th cent. battle of 366–7, 390; destruction (409) 129, 135, 366, 369, 373, 883
Himeraeus (Athenian politician) 630
Himilco, king of Carthage 132, 367; campaigns 131, 134, 142, 143–4, 368, 373, 883; penance and suicide 144, 366–7, 373, 376, 883
Hipparchus (Eretrian politician) 772
Hipparinus, tyrant of Syracuse 133, 136, 151, 708, 891
Hippias of Elis (sophist) 592–3
Hippocrates (physician) 634–5, 642
Hippocratic Corpus 634–7, 639, 640–1, 642, 643, 644, 645
Hippodamus of Miletus (architect) 679
Hippon (Syracusan democrat) 700
Hippon, tyrant of Messene 714, 715, 716
Hipponax (philosopher) 479
Hipponicus (mercenary general) 772
Hipponium *11 Dc*, 147, 149, 386, 387, 391, 393; succeeded by Veipo and Vibo 396n55, 399n69; Orphic tablet 399n72
Hirschlanden *12 Db*, 407
Histiaeus, tyrant of Miletus 489
histiokopoi (merchant galleys) 517
Histria *15 Ac*, *20 Cb*, 471, 473, 474
hoards, coin and metal: Borovo *461*; Cyzicene staters in 501; Duchcov 414; Egyptian, Greek coins in 352n71; Rhizon 439; Rogozen 461–2, *463*; Tell el-Mashkuta 352n71; Votonosi 434
Hochdorf burial *12 Db*, 407, *408*, 410
Hochwald-Nahe region 413
Hohenasperg hillfort 412
Hohmichele *12 Db*, 407

Pnytagoras, king of Salamis 316, 329, 330, 331, 333, 335
Podanemus (Spartan naval commander) 105
poetry 136–7, 231, 597; see also individual poets
Pogradec 428, 440
Polemarchus (Athenian metic) 35n52
Polemo of Ilium 480
Polemon of Athens (philosopher) 611
police, secret 53, 300, 301–2, 320
polis 563–4, 565–91, 648; alternatives to 563, 579–89, 880–1; as ideal 558, 581, 589–90; continuity 589–91, 648, 867; machinery of government 565–72; political life 16, 24, 39, 573–9; schools and 632, 648; size 536; see also citizenship
politicians, new 570, 573, 574–6, 576–7
Pollis (Spartan naval commander) 105, 173
Polyaenus (writer on stratagems) 84
Polybiades (Spartan general) 161, 162, 884
Polybius (historian) 11, 18, 363, 707
Polyclitus (sculptor) 655
Polyclitus the Younger (architect) 654
Polycrates, tyrant of Samos 524
Polydamas of Pharsalus 54, 175
Polydorus (brother of Jason of Pherae) 189
Polyeuctus (sculptor) 654
Polyidus (military engineer) 689, 690, 691, 692, 775
Polyperchon (Macedonian nobleman) 855
Polyphron (brother of Jason of Pherae) 189
Polyxenus (Syracusan noble) 143, 149, 151–2
Polyxenus (philosopher) 614
Pompeii; Alexander mosaic 688, 807n25
Pompeius Trogus, Justin's epitome of 18, 84, 120, 363–4, 480, 694, 723, 762
Pontecagnano 11 Cb, 402n78
Pontius Herennus, C. 399
population 535–7; Asia Minor 222, 225; Athens 33, 536, 566–7; floating, of exiles and mercenaries 15, 169, 533–4, 535, 591, 676, 678; Macedon 735; movement, (Alexander's) 809, 824, 866–8, (Assyrian and Babylonian) 286–7, (Philip II's) 733, 762, 894, (Roman) 402, (in Sicily) 124, 125, 131–2, 134, 385, 387, 400, 563–4, 719, (see also cleruchies; colonies)
Porthmieus 476, 487
Porthmus 2 Da, 772
portraiture 355, 459, 654–6, 659, 660, 874
ports 524–5
Porus (Indian prince) 23 Eb, 829, 831, 832, 863, 864
Posidonia, see Paestum
Posidonius (military engineer) 690
Potentino 402n78
Potidaea 1 Cb, 16 Ca, 158, 159, 161, 201, 426, 737; Macedon takes 737, 738, 890

pottery: Alexandrian 504; Attic 304, 305, 326, 335, 413, (black-figure) 217, 410, 456, 508, (red-figure) 217, 415, 456, 482, 508, 647–8, 652, 891; Celtic 407, 417, 419; Cypriot local 305; Italic 399–400, 415, 891, 901; Phocaean 409, 410; Phoenician red-varnished 364; pithoi 669; pseudo-Ionian native 410–11; Scythian 471; Thracian 475; see also vase-painting
poverty 534, 537, 551
Praeneste bowl 365
Praxippus, king of Lapethus 310, 334
Praxitas (Spartan polemarch) 106
Praxiteles (sculptor) 651–2, 656, 891
Presocratic philosophers 642, 644
Prespa, L. 13 Bb, 16 Ba, 422
Priene 1 Ed, 5 Bd, 61–2, 225, 228, 692, 869–70
prisoners of war 557, 750, 797, 867, 868
Proaemus (Rhium garrison commander) 110
Proclus (philosopher) 613–14
Prodicus of Ceos (sophist) 592, 593, 595
proeisphora (liturgy) 548
Promalanges (secret police of Salamis) 300
Pronnoi 174
property 533, 581; see also antidosis; confiscation; wealth
prophecy 267–8, 269, 292, 295–6
Prophthasia, see Phrada
Prosopitis, battle of 320
Protagoras of Abdera (sophist) 592, 593, 596
Proteas (Greek naval commander) 849
Protesilaus, shrine of, at Elaeus 798
Prothous (Spartan politician) 182, 553, 554
Protogenes (painter) 656, 657
proverbs 620
Proverbs, book of 294
Proverbs of Ahiqar 290
Proxenus (Athenian general) 753, 896
Proxenus (brother of Hermocrates of Syracuse) 130
Proxenus of Atarneus (Aristotle's guardian) 616, 617, 620
proxeny 69, 852
Prytanis, king of Bosporus 495, 497, 501–2
Psalms, book of 295
Psammetichus (possibly rival of Amyrtaeus) 347n48
Psammuthis, king of Egypt 340, 353, 354, 356–7, 358
psephismata (decrees) 567–8, 572, 574, 575
Psessi 476, 496
Psoa 502
Ptolemy I, king of Egypt 20, 771, 860, 862, 881; and Cyprus 333, 334–5; and Alexander's body 845, 881
Ptolemy II Philadelphus, king of Egypt 504
Ptolemy, regent of Macedon, see Macedon

II, Dion and Timoleon, *see under* Syracuse;
Carthaginian war (344) 379, 708, 709, 711–
12, 713–14, 879, 895, (peace) 714, 715, 718,
897; eradication of tyrants 563–4, 710, 712–
13, 714–16, 720, 721, 895, 897; Timoleon's
settlement 563–4, 712, 716–20, 895
  agriculture 719; Carthaginian influence
364, 378; citizenship 537; coinage 130, 142,
153, 231–2, 378, 719; corn 522, 558, 665;
economy 124–5, 719–20; ethnicity 124–5,
153, 673, (*see also* Sicans; Sicels); Greek *koine*
439; mercenary settlements 136, 141, 144,
153, 395, 534, 708, 719; Phoenician
influence 364; population movements 124,
125, 385, 387, 563–4, 716–17; shipping
lanes 514, 522–3; society 124–5; sources on
9, 13, 22, 120–4, 390, 693–5, 706–7; and
south Italy 386, 398, 439; tyrant families
587, 713n17; *see also individual cities and
peoples*
Sicyon *1 Cc, 2 Bb*; in Corinthian War 102, 103,
106, 109; in Spartan alliance 168, 184; *stasis*
176, 189; joins anti-Spartan alliance 191;
Euphron's tyranny 192, 193, 197, 198, 530,
541, 556, 580n58, 886, 888; alliances 204,
205, 206; and Sacred War 741; art 657, 660
Side *4 Dc, 5 Dd*, 84–5, 232
Sidon *8 Bc, 20 Ed*, 319, 321, 322; Persian vassal
264, 297, 319–20, 330; alliance with Athens
87–8; Tennes' revolt 91, 92, 239, 323, 329,
894; under Evagoras II 330; under
Alexander 330–1, 808, 861, 866; Antigonus
in 334
  coinage 321, 322, 328, 330, 866; palace
and park 324–5, 329; sarcophagi 321, 326,
335, (Alexander) 219, 326; temples 325;
wealth 92, 322, 335
Sidus *2 Cb*, 106, 111
siege warfare 679–80, 682–6, 689–92;
defensive measures 683–4, 691–2, 802;
engines 682, 683–4, 689–90, *691*, 692, 801,
809, (*see also* catapults); light-armed troops
681; mole 809; ramps 682, 690, 827;
treachery 680, 686, 689; *see also*
fortifications; mining; *and under* Carthage;
Macedon; Phoenicia; Syracuse
Sigeum *1 Ec*, 488
Silanion (sculptor) 655, 657
Sillyum *5 Dd*, 803
silver objects: Athenian processional hydriae
37n62; Bosporan 508, *509*, 510; of Jewish
Temple 263; Sidonian 92; Tell el-Maskhuta
bowl 279n38; Thracian 456, *461*, 462–3, 475
silver resources 127, 352, 543; *see also* Laurium
and under Illyrians; Thrace
Simeon the Righteous, High Priest of Judah
286

Simmias of Syracuse (philosopher) 624
Simus' attempted tyranny in Larissa 763–4
Simyra 321
Sin, cult of 250, 278
Sind 834, 863–4, 868
Sindi 476, 481, 486, *494*, 496, 497, 506
Sindos *13 Cb*, 427
Sinope *4 Fa*, 221, 475, 492–3, 500, 502, 504;
foundation legend 482–3; 5th cent. 489,
491, 492; Datames' revolt 85; Cappadocia/
Pontus attacks 504
Sintii *14 Bb*, 449
Sinuri 62, 229, 230
Siphnos *1 Dd, 20 Bc*, 104, 548, 804, 853
Sippar *6 Bc*, 241, 244, 247n49, 249
Sirach, book of 285
Siraci 501
Sirai, Mt *10 Cb*, 364
Sisicottus, hyparch of Aornus 826, 863
Sisimithres, ruler of Nautaca 825
Sisines (Persian emissary) 803
Sisygambis, queen of Persia 808
Sitalces (king) *see under* Odrysian kingdom
Sitalces (Macedonian general) 838, 864
sitophylakes 562
situlae, Celtic bronze 409, 413
Siwah Oasis *8 Bc-Cc, 9 Aa, 20 Ce*; oracle of
Ammon 346n46, 810–11, 844, 845, 872, 874
Skapte Hyle silver mine 452
skytalismos ('cudgelling', by extreme Argive
democrats) 189
slaves: agricultural 401, 672–3; Black Sea trade
504; debate on 532; at Laurium 545; League
of Corinth treaty on 528, 531, 784; metics
sold as 611; military enlistment 538, 796;
prisoners of war sold as 557, 750, 797, 868;
runaways, in wartime 532; and *stasis* 531–2;
see also under individual states
Sliven 475
Slovenia, Celts in 408–9
Smerdis (Gaumata), king of Persia 265
smugglers 525
Smyrna *4 Bb, 5 Bc*, 225
Sochi 805, 806
Social War 15, 56, 528, 736–9, 741, 890; effect
on Athens 465, 533, 544, 546, 547, 550, 551,
561; Persian role 58, 88, 89
society and economy 527–64; *see also individual
aspects*
Socrates 14, 35n53, 39–40, 883; philosophy
593–4, 596n19, 603, 605, 633
Socratic school 594, 595, 596
Sogdiana *20 Lc-Mc, 21 Db*, 812, 821, 868n59;
Alexander's conquest 64, 823–5, 863, 898;
Alexander's settlement 688, 863, 867
Sogdianus, king of Persia 237
Soli, Cilicia *4 Fc*, 312, 806